International and Cultural Psychology

Series Editor

Anthony Marsella, *University of Hawaii, Honolulu, Hawaii*

For further volumes:
http://www.springer.com/series/6089

Dan Landis • Rosita D. Albert
Editors

Handbook of Ethnic Conflict

International Perspectives

An International Academy
for Intercultural Research Book

Springer

Editors
Dan Landis
Department of Psychology
University of Hawaii
Hilo, HI, USA
danl@hawaii.edu

Rosita D. Albert
Department of Communication Studies
University of Minnesota
Minneapolis, MN, USA
alber001@umn.edu

ISSN 1574-0455
ISBN 978-1-4614-0447-7 e-ISBN 978-1-4614-0448-4
DOI 10.1007/978-1-4614-0448-4
Springer New York Dordrecht Heidelberg London

Library of Congress Control Number: 2011937572

Printed on acid-free paper

Springer is part of Springer Science+Business Media (www.springer.com)

For Rae, what can I say? 51 years ago they said it would not last!

And, to the late Ross Stagner and Charlie Solley, extraordinary scholars, teachers, friends and the persons who set me off on the journey of a lifetime. I hope they are pleased with what I have become.

Dan Landis

To the memory of my parents, Ella and Bernardo Daskal, whose life experiences and values imbued me with a profound desire to work for the amelioration of ethnic conflicts and the improvement of intercultural relations.

To my husband, Stuart Albert, for his love, companionship, and support

and

To Herbert H. Kelman, a wonderful mentor and role model, for his inspiring, life-long work towards the resolution of the Israeli–Palestinian conflict.

Rosita D. Albert

Foreword

There is a common saying that nothing in life is certain except death and taxes. As depressing as this outlook may be, it fails to include one, even more disquieting, foible of human existence: ethnic/cultural conflict. I recently became aware of this point when my family decided to plan a once-in-a-lifetime trip around the world. Each time we identified a "must visit" paradise, someone spoiled the party by pointing out, "We cannot visit there because group X and Y are engaged in violent conflict, and it is not safe." As one location after another was deleted from our list, the universality of violent ethnic conflict became painfully clear.

Although not its intention, the chapters in this book serve to emphasize this sad note on human relations. One, but only one, of the points that becomes clear in the chapters is how widespread ethnic conflict is. The chapters take us to all points of the world: Europe, Asia, Africa, South America, North/Central America, and New Zealand. The journey of conflict takes us through large, highly populated countries (China, Turkey, India) and small, less populated regions (New Zealand, Cyprus, Israel). And we are guided to well developed countries (France, Netherlands, Israel, Spain) and less developed areas (Congo, Uganda, Kurdish regions). The scope of ethnic conflict becomes more mind numbing when we realize that many regions where conflict thrives are not included (N. Ireland, many countries in Africa, Australia, United States, Russia). Indeed, it is difficult to identify a country or region that has not or presently is not dealing with destructive conflict between ethnic, cultural, or religious groups.

Pervasiveness, however, is only one of the characteristics of ethnic conflict. The chapters vividly tell the tale of the persistence of intergroup conflict and violence. Ethnic conflict is not a New Age phenomenon or passing fad. The conflicts of today have roots deep in the history of the regions. History is often used to "justify" violence and it serves as the basis for each group to claim the position as a "victim." Indeed, it is difficult to find a violent confrontation where each side does not label the other as the aggressor. I have spent several years working with a "peace camp" that brought youth from troubled regions (Middle East, Balkans, Cyprus) to a bucolic camp in the heart of the Maine woods. Although the names and faces of the campers changed from summer to summer, their discussions of the violent conflict in their region was always the same. When the focus of facilitation groups was the Middle East, the Arab and Jewish campers resorted to reciting history;

beginning with great detail of the confrontations over the last 60 years but then going back over 4,000 years. Each side claimed that it was the first inhabitant of the land, and, hence, the rightful owner of it. History is of great importance, not only to track the conflict, but also to understand how each side justifies its actions. This critical component in conflict is very clearly described in the chapters of this book. Each chapter traces the conflict in the region back in time, sometime hundreds of years. The historical context allows the reader to not only understand the conditions that gave rise to the conflict, but also to understand why each side believes that it has been victimized by the other.

Given the critical role of history in intergroup conflict, it is disappointing that research in Social Psychology generally ignores this factor in research and theory. Group history is typically treated as a confounding variable, something to be eliminated as completely as possible. For this reason, research designs often involve forming de facto groups without a history or expectation of a future. The clear message in the present chapters is that this approach is fraught with peril and bound to present an incomplete understanding of intergroup conflict.

The persistence of ethnic conflict is not only evident in the fact that its roots often extend backward hundreds, even thousands, of years. The pattern of conflict often involves violent outbreaks followed by years of relative quiet and "peace," only to give rise to another period of violent confrontation. This maddening pattern is evident in the Balkans where violence characterized the relationship between Serbs and Croats (and several other ethnic groups) in the period prior to and through World War II. Under the firm dictatorial hand of Tito, the groups lived together in peace for nearly a half-century. Intermarriage was common and sharing of power occurred. Yugoslavia enjoyed economic prosperity and played a unique role in world politics. However, the region erupted with some of the most terrible genocide since Hitler. Neighbors who had lived side-by-side for decades suddenly became bitter enemies. The intensity and viciousness of the slaughter shocked the world. The aftermath resulted in several, rather ethnically homogeneous, small countries being formed. It would be comforting to consider the sad situation of Yugoslavia as an exception, but unfortunately it is not. The eruption of tribal violence in Uganda, the inflamed racial tensions that are ignited by publicized incidents of police brutality in the United States, and sporadic violence in Turkey that involves both Kurds and Armenians gives testimony that ethnic violence is often a crouching tiger that lurks just below the surface of apparent harmony and peace. The clear message is that we should not be lulled into thinking that relatively calm relations between groups are an end state that signals harmony and a lack of tension. Indeed, I have argued that periods of peace are the best time for groups to work on conflict management.

If the pervasiveness and persistence of ethnic conflict were not sufficiently disturbing to get one's attention, we should consider two additional factors that will have profound implications for ethnic relations in the future. First, the world's population is growing at an alarming rate. There were one billion people in the world in 1800. The population on our planet doubled to two billion by 1930, within a period of 130 years. By 2030 (a 100 year period), there will be over eight billion humans on our planet. For my personal standpoint, the most startling figure is that the world's population grew by four billion people during the time when I started high school to the date I retired! The greatest increases are occurring in the least developed regions, such as Africa, South and Southeast Asia, and Latin America (the focus of half the chapters in this book). One consequence of this rapid growth is that we are living closer together, and group conflicts involve increasingly more people. More people also mean that there are more possible points of friction. A second consequence arises from the disproportional growth. Greatest increase in regions with the least opportunities for jobs, education, and standards of living has given rise massive immigration and shifts in populations. This immigration has created dramatic change in the social landscape of many countries. New groups are added to many regions and existing groups that were once only small minorities have experienced significant growth. The impact of immigration is discussed in chapters on Spain, France, and the Netherlands. Similar stories could be written about the United States, Germany, Italy, Switzerland, Australia, and the Scandinavian countries. (It is interesting to note the immigration patterns of today reverse the trend toward colonization that characterized the eighteenth and nineteenth century [see Munusamy (2012); Ward and Liu (2012); Mealy and Austad (2012); Bhawuk (2012); Martin (2012)]. In these cases, contact between new groups resulted from powerful, well-supported invaders taking control of new lands.)

Host countries are now faced with dealing not only with greater numbers, but also with greater diversity of languages, cultural/religious practices, and social relationships. Communities must adapt to this diversity, but underneath the surface is an increasing fear that groups who once enjoyed unchallenged power may become minorities in their own land. Indeed, the social identities of some countries are being challenged. I recall a recent conversation I had with a French friend who lamented, "What will we French do when the average Frenchman is a Muslim of Arab descent?" Population changes have not only increased the size of groups involved in conflict, but also the number of domains of conflict (economic, social, cultural, religious, identity, etc.). And the fire that keeps the pot of conflict close to a boiling point is fear; fear that the new and/or growing group is a threat to the position, identity, and livelihood of members of the dominant group. And herein lies the "political" side of the ethnopolitical conflict that is the focus of this volume. In many of the regions discussed in the chapters, leaders have seized on the fear generated by ethnic diversity. They have fanned the fires of this fear and focused it to blame "the other side" for problems in the region. The fear enables these leaders to consolidate political power, and it becomes the energy source for violent confrontations. Leaders who seek to rally supporters to fight the growing threat often exploit this fear. The appeal is cloaked in the clothing of "tradition." They (the outsiders) are a threat to traditional lifestyle and traditional values. The responses often include erecting barriers/quotas to keep immigrants out and/or passing laws that prohibit immigrant groups from wearing traditional clothing [see Kamiejski et al. (2012)], engaging in cultural rituals [see Oudenhoven (2012)], or speaking native language. Some countries, like

Spain, have hoped to enjoy the fruits of immigrant labor, but ensure that the immigrants will eventually return home, by forbidding immigrants to bring their families [see Aneas et al. (2012)]. But this ill-conceived effort has backfired because the "temporary" immigrants have established new families with members of the host group. The full impact of massive immigration is yet to be seen because the world is still in the middle of this phenomenon. However, many of the chapters in this book offer an insightful glimpse into the conflicts that are developing because of immigration.

If the root of ethnic conflicts were a virus, we would describe the situation as an epidemic. The conflict is widespread, persistent, and often deadly. If the human race is to survive this epidemic, it is critical that we develop a deep understanding of its causes, and develop effective means of reducing its destructiveness. For this reason, the present volume is extremely timely. By focusing on conflicts in different regions, it allows the reader to make comparisons between the conditions that have spawned violent confrontations in many regions of the globe. And through its descriptions of these conflicts, it also enables the reader to predict where new conflicts will arise. The authors also draw on existing theories and research to demonstrate and illuminate commonalities between conflicts in different regions.

It is easy to fall into a debilitating depression when one contemplates the message of a global epidemic of conflict and violence. However, humans have mobilized in the past to develop effective responses to other epidemics. Whether it is bubonic plague or polio, responses to previous global epidemics have taken two forms. One is treatment aimed at healing the infected, and the other has been prevention aimed at eliminating the causes and/or inoculating the population from succumbing to the disease.

On the treatment side of the equation, there has been considerable research and theory. The earliest view was the contact hypothesis (Allport, 1954). This hypothesis was based on the research showing that conflict often resulted in autistic hostility in which the sides retreated into their own groups and anger and hostility were allowed to fester. The contact hypothesis argued that contact between the various sides to conflict was necessary to start the healing process and reduce conflict. However, numerous investigators (Brewer & Campbell, 1976) pointed out that contact between the sides often provided the fertile ground for conflict and violence, and numerous studies demonstrated that contact alone did not reduce hostility. Several caveats to the contact hypothesis were introduced. One was that contact was beneficial only when it occurred between equals (Amir, 1969). A second position was that only contact that resulted in cooperative effort between the groups to achieve a common goal would enhance positive relationships between the groups (Sherif, Harvey, White, Hood, & Sherif, 1961). And my own research found that achieving the common goal, not simply working toward it, was a necessary ingredient (Worchel et al., 1978).

For nearly two decades, I have been involved with programs that, mostly inadvertently, applied the contact hypothesis to approaches designed to reduce hostility between groups. These efforts, generally known as peace camps/programs, bring participants from groups in protracted conflict (Arab/Israeli Jew, Irish Catholic/Protestant, Indian/Pakistani, Serb/Croat) together to discuss their situation and interact together on projects with common goals. Participants in the programs meet on neutral ground (e.g. a summer camp in Maine, a barge on Irish rivers) where neither side is on its home court. The participants often engage in enjoyable activities (e.g. art projects, sports, drama productions) and have the opportunity to discuss their perceptions of the conflict. The programs last from several hours to several weeks. The participants often live together and are in close contact throughout the program.

The question that always arises with regards to these programs is. "Do they work?" Anyone who has been involved with these programs or has visited them can only marvel at the apparent impact. The hate and fear that characterizes intergroup relations in the beginning seems to melt like ice in the summer Texas sun. During the course of the program, members from the different groups laugh, sing, and play together, and friendships form across group boundaries. The last day of the program is often accompanied by a flood of tears as participants recognize that they will not see each other again. Responses to questionnaires that my colleagues and I administered before and after several programs show that attraction crosses group boundaries, fear and blaming the outgroup for the conflict is reduced, and similarities between the groups are emphasized. These data not only offer reason for hope, but they also give support to the theories suggesting that under certain circumstances, contact between the opposing sides can reduce conflict and hostility.

However, before breaking out the champagne and declaring victory over intergroup conflict, other data present a more sobering picture. In addition to examining the short-term impact of peace programs, we also wanted to determine the longevity of the effects. Many of the initial participants in our study were contacted 3–5 years after being involved in peace programs. The results of their responses indicated that many of the positive effects did not stand the test of time. Specifically, the enhanced attraction for the outgroup and the reduction in placing blame on the outgroup disappeared. Both anger toward the outgroup and despair that the conflict "would ever" be resolved mimicked the responses from individuals who had not taken part in the programs. The bloom seemed to wear off the rose over time, with two important exceptions. Participants tended to view the outgroup as more heterogeneous than nonparticipants, both in the short run and long-term. Investigators (Quattrone & Jones, 1980) found that individuals tend to view the outgroup as homogeneous, while seeing their own group as heterogeneous. This pattern facilitates placing blame on the outgroup based on the actions of a few ("They are all the same"). Further, it can reduce motivation to expand interaction with members of the outgroup: "Met one, know them all." A second persistent result was that participation in the programs raised self-esteem and self-efficacy. As one participant reported, "I did the thing I feared most, lived with the enemy; I can now do anything I want." These results are potentially very important for efforts aimed at dealing with intergroup conflict and hostility. Although they do not reduce or alter the conflict, they suggest that the programs can be of value for preparing individuals on each side to work on developing better relations. Recognizing that there is diversity of attitudes and actions in the outgroup enables individuals to place blame for violence on those involved rather than on the whole group. And increasing feelings of self-efficacy empowers to take action to deal with the conflict rather than sink into states of learned helplessness and inaction. It is, however, important that peace programs take the additional step of showing what actions can be taken to address problems in the region.

In addition to the fleeting nature of the impact of peace programs, there are several other questions that must be examined. The research on autistic hostility that I mentioned earlier shows the strong tendency for people in conflict to withdraw and cease interaction: good fences (high walls) make for comfortable coexistence in cases of conflict. Groups that are engaged in conflict and feel animosity towards each other do not want to interact with each other: why should I interact with someone I hate? Under these circumstances, how does one go about enticing members of the various sides to attend peace programs? Indeed, many of the peace programs have been criticized for involving participants who already have positive, or at least neutral views, of the other side and who are not themselves centrally involved in the conflict. The criticism of "preaching to the choir" is a valid question, but it must be recognized that efforts to manage intergroup conflict may have to begin by focusing on those who are willing to take the initial steps. A second issue is the disjointed nature of peace programs. I was amazed to find relatively little communication or coordination between the literally hundreds of peace programs that focus on the Middle East. The programs often exist in relative isolation from each other, developing their own approaches, and scratching out their own funding. Waging a war involves developing an overall strategy, coordinating efforts, and communication. Waging peace seems to be lack these characteristics. Finally, one can question the general perspective that guides many approaches to "conflict resolution." Conflict tends to be viewed as a circumscribed "problem" that can be "resolved." However, a vitally important message that is emphasized in all of the chapters in this book is that ethnic conflict, but not necessarily interethnic violence, is part of the human condition. Ethnic conflicts have long histories and they are likely to persist. The challenge is to find constructive approaches to conflict that can benefit societies and eliminate violent responses, not "resolve" the conflict itself. Indeed, several investigators (Deutsch, 1973; Worchel, 1999) have pointed out that conflict has potential benefits for both the group and intergroup relations. Conflict can increase group cohesiveness; it can identify problems that need attention; it can create both energy and the need to focus on specific issues. Therefore, intergroup conflict is not necessarily evil, and it will be resistant to resolution. Violent responses, on the other hand, have destructive implications for both sides, and, hence, may be more amenable to change.

Related to this general perspective on conflict is the often implicit view that protracted intergroup conflict can somehow be "cured" or fixed if the "right" treatment can be applied. We have become an impatient breed, captured by our search for quick fixes. Our mechanic should be able to diagnose and repair a cranky engine in a few hours. A few sessions with a therapist should "fix" problems in our marriage; if it does not, it is time for a divorce and a new relationship. Illness should be quickly cured with a pill or surgery; even our excess fat should be eliminated with a 7-day diet. Wars should be conducted on a short time table with a clearly identified ending point. This approach is often evident in peace programs and other approaches in resolving ethnic conflict. There is often the implicit assumption that a few days or weeks in a program will bring about dramatic and lasting improvements in the relationship between the different groups. In many cases, there is little effort to nurture relationships that have developed through the initial contact. Unfortunately, this approach ignores the fact that ethnic conflict is deep-seated and permeates all domains of a society. It has developed over years, often centuries, and efforts to reduce the hostility must be persistent, widespread, and inclusive. John Wallach, the founder of Seeds of Peace camp, recognized that the camp can plant the seeds for peace, but there must be carefully planned follow-up if the seeds are to grow. Too often, there is little attention given to the follow-up.

Although peace programs can play a role in reducing hatred and violence, the role has significant limitations. Numerous other approaches have been employed. Doob (1970), Kelman (Kelman & Cohen, 1986), and others have employed workshops that bring together leaders from the various groups to find solutions to common problems. These efforts focus on leaders of the groups and have the advantage that they may influence large policy stands. But these efforts, too, are generally of limited duration and confined to small groups. Efforts at reconciliation have been developed, and the dramatic effects of Nelson Mandela's Truth and Reconciliation programs in South Africa have given great hope to this approach. In general, reconciliation involves members of one group admitting their transgressions and asking forgiveness from the victimized individuals/group. When possible restitution is made healing is achieved when the victims are able to give some degree of forgiveness. Despite the successes of some efforts at reconciliation, there are several factors that limit its effectiveness. First, it requires that one side be willing to admit wrongdoing. In many, if not most, interethnic conflicts both parties feel that their actions were justified and can point to the basis for their position. Even wanton violence and first strikes can be justified as being preemptive and based on the actions of the other party. Second, the acts of wrongdoing were often committed many generations earlier. What responsibility do present residents of Hawaii have for illegal confiscation of lands that occurred 100 years ago? Are present day Australians responsible for the slaughter of Aborigines in the nineteenth and twentieth centuries? A third issue concerns compensation. How can one compensate for acts of genocide? In the case of illegally obtained land, how does one deal with present occupants of land that was legally purchased, but was illegally confiscated several generations ago? Finally, the 800-pound gorilla in the room concerns exactly who should be considered a member of the various ethnic groups. Since many of the interethnic conflicts trace origins many years in the past, intermarriage has occurred over generations. An individual may be 1/16th ethnic group x. Does this individual have the right (legally and/or ethically) to claim restitution awarded to that ethnic group? And should his/her compensation be the same as someone whose family tree is more deeply rooted in the ethnic group? These, and other issues, have led some investigators to claim that reconciliation is of limited use in many interethnic conflicts. For example, the authors of the chapter on Yugoslavia argue for an approach, "social reconstruction," that is more focused on rebuilding a society on the conditions that exist in the present.

Dr. Landis is the 2012 recipient of the American Psychological Association's Award for Distinguished Contributions to the International Advancement of Psychology.

The chapters in this volume demonstrate that efforts to reduce violent interethnic conflict have met with some success, but the conflicts generally persist. Interethnic hatred is deeply seated in the individual psyche and the history of the group. Terrible stories of genocide, rape, and stolen lands cannot be erased, even if they can be forgiven to some degree. There is, however, another approach that can be taken to deal with interethnic violence. This approach focuses on prevention. Theories of Social Psychology have identified numerous conditions that are likely to ignite violence and discrimination between groups. The frustration–aggression hypothesis (Dollard et al, 1939) identified frustration as a condition likely to result in aggression, direct or displaced. Frustration can result from many sources such as economic or social crisis and competition for limited resources. Social Identity Theory (Tajfel & Turner, 1986) argues that the simple existence of groups sets the stage for discrimination. The discrimination will be more intense as specific group identities are made salient and group existence is threatened. These theories forewarn of situations and locations where ethnic conflict is likely to explode into violence. For example, immigration that brings new groups, and hence new competition, into a region is likely to increase tension and set the stage for eventual violence.

However, before the violence erupts and taints the relationship between the groups, steps can be taken to preempt the violence. Several years ago, a sheriff in a small Montana town recognized growing resentment by some against the few Jewish families. Fearing that this resentment would become violent during the Christmas season when religious identity was salient, the sheriff convinced nearly all the residents in the town to put a menorah in the windows of their homes with a sign "Not in our town." Violence was averted and tensions were abated. There are several other examples of more widespread prevention programs. One example is taking place in a small Massachusetts town. Several members of the community realized that the social environment of their town was changing due to an influx of Muslim residents. The Muslims added to the religious diversity of the region that already included Protestants, Catholics, and Jews, and several incidents within the high school indicated that the situation was potentially explosive. Representatives from all sectors of the community (education, religious, business, government) met and developed a program aimed at creating religious tolerance in the town. The program focused (and was guided by) on high school age youth and involved such activities as discussion groups, having participants attend religious services of the various religions in the area, travel to the Middle East to become acquainted with the roots of many religions, and visiting the homes of people from other religions. The program enjoyed the support of community leaders and allowed participants to develop activities that they felt would enhance religious tolerance. This latter fostered a sense of ownership, not only of the program but also in creating an atmosphere of tolerance in the community. Data that I have collected on the program suggests that it has had a profound and lasting effect on the attitudes of participants, and has motivated many of them to develop similar programs in colleges they later attend. Indeed, it may be easier to avoid interethnic violence than to stop it once it has erupted.

The chapters in this volume vividly demonstrate the tragic results of interethnic violence. They emphasize that no corner of the world and no ethnic is immune to this violence. In many cases, the seeds of this violence were planted centuries ago. Although the roots may be deep, these chapters remind us that interethnic violence and discrimination are alive and well in today's societies. Despite dramatic advances in medicine, travel, and communication, hatred of our neighbor because of his religious beliefs, skin color, or cultural practices persist. Although we would be foolish to ignore the concern raised by the chapters, there is also a very positive threat that runs through the volume. Whether the focus is New Zealand or Croatia, Malaysia or France, societies are focusing on building interethnic harmony. Faced with growing diversity and economic challenge, success at incorporating diverse groups has been achieved in many regions. Obviously more must be done to manage ethnic conflicts so that they do not disintegrate into violence. The psychological theories and research discussed in these chapters point out directions for these efforts. But to be successful, these efforts must be coordinated, consistent, and persistent.

This volume is unique in that it allows the reader to compare and contrast conflicts and approaches to conflict management throughout the world. By presenting a global picture, it sets the stage for developing coordinated responses across national boundaries. For the geographically challenged reader, the chapters also present maps to locate the region of focus. The volume presents approaches that have been taken to address interethnic violence, and it identifies approaches that can be taken in future efforts to deal with this issue. Above all, the chapters offer a message of urgency; increased efforts to improve interethnic relationships must be employed now, or the tragedies of the past will be repeated with greater intensity and destructiveness.

Stephen Worchel

References

Allport, G. W. (1954). *The nature of prejudice*. Cambridge, MA: Addison-Wesley.

Aneas, A., Garreta, J., & Molina, F. (2012) "Ethnocultural Conflict in Spain" Moroccans in Spain – So Near, Yet So Far: A Long History of Meeting While Not Meeting. In D. Landis & R. D. Albert (Eds.), *Handbook of ethnic conflict*. New York: Springer.

Amir, Y. (1969). The contact hypothesis in ethnic relations. *Psychological Bulletin, 71*, 319–341.

Bhawuk, D. P. S. (2012). India and the Culture of Peace: Beyond Ethnic, Religious, and Other Conflicts. In D. Landis & R. D. Albert (Eds.), *Handbook of ethnic conflict*. New York: Springer.

Brewer, M., & Campbell, D. (1976). *Ethnocentrism and intergroup attitudes: East African evidence*. New York: Halsted Press.

Deutsch, M. (1973). *The resolution of conflict*. New Haven: Yale University Press.

Dollard, J., Doob, A. Miller, N. Mowrer, O., & Sears, R. (1939). *Frustration and aggression*. New Haven: Yale University Press.

Doob, L. (Ed.). (1970). *Resolving conflict in Africa: The Fermeda workshop*. New Haven: Yale University Press.

Kamiejski, R., De Oliveira, P., & Guimond, S. (2012). Ethnic and Religious Conflicts in France. In D. Landis & R. D. Albert (Eds.), *Handbook of ethnic conflict*. New York: Springer.

Kelman, H., & Cohen, S. (1986). Resolution of international conflict: An interactional approach. In S. Worchel & W. Austin (Eds.), *Psychology of intergroup relations* (pp. 323–342). Chicago: Nelson Hall.

Martin, J. S. (2012). Mexico's Ethnic Conflict. In D. Landis & R. D. Albert (Eds.), *Handbook of ethnic conflict*. New York: Springer.

Mealy, M., & Austad, C. S. (2012). Sendero Luminoso (Shining Path) and the Conflict in Peru. In D. Landis & R. D. Albert (Eds.), *Handbook of ethnic conflict*. New York: Springer.

Munusamy, V. P. (2012). Ethnic Relations in Malaysia: The need for "Constant Repair" in the Spirit of Muhibbah. In D. Landis & R. D. Albert (Eds.), *Handbook of ethnic conflict*. New York: Springer.

Quattrone, G., & Jones, E. (1980). The perception on variability within in-groups and out-groups: implications for the law of small numbers. *Journal of Personality and Social Psychology, 38*, 141–150.

Sherif, M., Harvey, O., White, B., Hood, W., & Sherif, C. (1961). *Intergroup cooperation and competition: the Robber's Cave experiment*. Norman, OK: University Book Exchange.

Tajfel, H., & Turner, J. (1986). Social identity theory of intergroup relations. In S. Worchel & W. Austin (Eds.), *Psychology of intergroup relations* (pp. 7–24). Chicago: Nelson Hall.

van Oudenhoven, J. P. (2012). Frictions between Muslims and non-Muslims in the Netherlands. In D. Landis & R. D. Albert (Eds.), *Handbook of ethnic conflict*. New York: Springer.

Ward, C., & Liu, J. H. (2012). Ethno-cultural Conflict in *Aotearoa*/New Zealand: Balancing Indigenous Rights and Multicultural Responsibilities. In D. Landis & R. D. Albert (Eds.), *Handbook of ethnic conflict*. New York: Springer.

Worchel, S. (1999). *Written in blood: Ethnic identity and the struggle for human harmony*. New York: Worth.

Worchel, S., Axsom, D., Ferris, F., Samaha, C., & Schweitzer, S. (1978). Factors determining the effectiveness of intergroup cooperation on intergroup. *Journal of Conflict Resolution, 22*, 429–439.

Preface and Acknowledgements

This genesis of this book occurred at a dinner with Tony Marsella, the series editor, in Atlanta as the first author was returning from a conference in Germany, though in fact the idea had been perculating in both of the editors craniums for some years. The idea was to reach beyond Psychology to see what other disciplines would have to say about ethnocultural (it was later changed to the present title) conflict. This was to be done with series of chapters focused on particular conflicts in every part of the world. The gestation of the book took the better part of two years as potential authors were contacted and agreed to participate in the project. We did not rely only on psychologists but quite deliberately sought to include investigators from other disciplines. The authors came from many countries and cultures, and many brought an intercultural perspective to their writing. Some authors demurred due to political concerns, fearing repercussions would place their future careers in jeopardy. We also levied a constant format on the chapter authors which in some cases seemed anathema to the writers. But, we persevered, spurred on by Tony's faith in the project. For that faith, we owe him a sincere appreciation, for without his prodding, this project would have languished in file drawers in many different countries. So, to Tony, a loud and heartfelt Mahalo Nui Loa (Thank you very much in Hawaiian). Though not Jewish, he has been a true mensch (a person of integrity and honor) throughout the process.

There are many others who contributed significantly to this work. In Minneapolis we would like to acknowledge first and foremost the wonderful contributions, enthusiasm, and dedication of graduate student Susanne Gabrielsen, who worked tirelessly during all of 2010 on this project, and has been a marvelous junior colleague, as well as co-author of our concluding chapter. We also acknowledge the contributions of Claire Stienecker, Kelly Ramer and Jaturong Napadol, who, with Susanne read, discussed, and made important comments and suggestions on chapters as part of a seminar on Ethnopolitcal Conflict Worldwide. This book would not be as good without their spirited discussions, lively engagement, and great participation. We would also like to thank the following research assistants who were helpful in ways too numerous to list, and whose assistance in all tasks, large and small, was rendered with good humor and great willingness to learn and work at a level well beyond anything they had ever done before: Alex Meyers, Julian Swivala, Linnea Trandem, Keegan Freiburger, Josh Keily, and Whitney Taylor and Eric DeVoe.

In Hilo, there is Cheryl Jorgensen who took on the important and largely thankless task of reading every chapter and preparing the short summaries that appear in the front of the chapter. Her work is invaluable in providing the reader with a path into each of the chapters. Amy McWhinney provided much commentary on the early versions of several of the chapters and her work was included in those chapters.

We also acknowledge the important contributions of Sharon Panulla, Executive Editor, Psychology at Springer SBM Publications. Her support has made the present volume and the other volumes in the series possible.

Hilo, Hawaii, USA — Dan Landis
Minneapolis, Minnesota, USA — Rosita D. Albert

Contents

Editors

Dan Landis (Ph.D., General-theoretical Psychology, 1963, Wayne State University) holds several academic and consulting positions including Affiliate Professor of Psychology at the University of Hawaii (Hilo and Manoa campuses), Professor Emeritus of Psychology, Director Emeritus, Center for Applied Research and Evaluation, University of Mississippi, Emeritus Dean, College of Liberal Arts, University of Mississippi and President, D.K. Research and Consultation Group. He is past Chair of Psychology at Indiana University–Purdue University at Indianapolis and Founder of the Center for Social Development at the University City Science Center in Philadelphia. Dr. Landis is the author/coauthor of over 100 books, articles, technical reports, and presentations in areas such as, the measurement of equal opportunity climate in military and other organizations, racial discrimination, perception, statistics, sexual behavior and attitudes, and cross-cultural psychology and training. He is the founding and continuing editor of the International Journal of Intercultural Relations, the coeditor/author of Ethnic conflict (Sage, 1985), and the coeditor/author of Handbook of intercultural training, a three-volume work published by Pergamon Press in 1983. The second edition of the Handbook of Intercultural Training edited by Landis and Bhagat was published in 1996 and a third edition (edited by Landis, Janet Bennett, and Milton Bennett) was published in 2004. A Chinese version of the 3rd Handbook was published by Peking University Press in 2010. Dr. Landis is a Fellow of the American Psychological Association, the Society for the Psychological Study of Social Issues, and the American Psychological Society. He is the Founding President of the International Academy for Intercultural Research. In 1990, the Society for Intercultural Education, Training, and Research honored him with a special award for achievement. Dr. Landis is listed in Who's Who in America and other biographical compendiums. In 1987, Dr. Landis together with Dr. Mickey Dansby developed the Military Equal Opportunity Climate Survey (MEOCS) which is now in wide use throughout the U.S. Department of Defense. MEOCS has been adapted for use in civilian organizations, universities, and even foreign institutions. During 1994–1996, Dr. Landis was appointed the first Shirley J. Bach Visiting Professor at the Defense Equal Opportunity Management Institute. During his tenure, he conducted further studies of equal opportunity climate in the US Armed Forces as well as investigated racial disparities in the administration of military justice, both at the courts martial and Article 15 levels. In 2007, he was given a Lifetime Achievement Award by the International Academy for Intercultural Research.

Rosita D. Albert (Ph.D. in Social Psychology, University of Michigan) is an Associate Professor in Communication Studies at the University of Minnesota, where she leads the pioneering program in Intercultural Communication, the first program in the world to grant Ph.D.s in this area of specialization. She has taught at the University of Illinois, New York University, and Rutgers, and participated in the Program in Negotiation at Harvard. In 2006–2007, under the sponsorship of Herbert Kelman, the eminent scholar in Conflict Resolution, she was a Visiting Scholar in the Department of Psychology at Harvard University.

The daughter of European parents who fled from the Holocaust, she was raised in Brazil. In addition to speaking English and Portuguese, she speaks Spanish and French. She has lived in the USA, Brazil, and France, has travelled extensively in Europe, Latin America, and Asia, and has had long-term experience with a very wide range of cultures.

She has a Ph.D. in Social Psychology from the University of Michigan and has collaborated with the cross-cultural psychologist Harry Triandis. She has conducted extensive research on intercultural interactions between Latin Americans/Latinos and mainstream Americans. She has authored articles on the development and evaluation of the Intercultural Sensitizer, the most effective method for intercultural training.

She has also conducted intercultural research on Korean and African American conflict in the USA, the effectiveness of intercultural training, perceptions of negotiation among Koreans and American, the role of culture in Social Psychology, intercultural interactions in organizations, ethnic identification in response to threat, intercultural education, and the effect of computer mediated interactions on changes in attitudes towards those of another culture. She has recently published a chapter on what communication scholars and practitioners can contribute to the prevention and resolution of ethnic conflicts worldwide.

She has published in major venues in intercultural communication and intercultural training, such as the International Journal of Intercultural Relations (IJIR), two editions of the Handbook of Intercultural Training and the Handbook of Organizational Communication. Several of her articles have been widely cited and reprinted, and she was listed among the most cited authors in IJIR. She has presented her work at conferences and by invitation in Brazil, China, France, Israel, Japan, Korea, Mexico, New Zealand, Peru, Taiwan, and many other countries.

She is a Founding Fellow and a member of the Governing Board of the interdisciplinary International Academy for Intercultural Research (IAIR), which is comprised of seasoned researchers and practitioners in intercultural communication from the fields of Psychology, Communication, Management,

Anthropology, Education, and other fields. She is also the chair of the Membership Committee of IAIR. She has been recognized for "Significant Contributions" to IAIR. She is on the Advisory Board of the Center for Holocaust and Genocide Studies at the University of Minnesota.

Dr. Albert has worked at the United Nations and coled task forces to internationalize organizations. She has conducted workshops and served as a consultant for organizations such the World Bank, the National Association of Transplant Coordinators in the USA, 3-M, Booz Allen Hamilton, Deloite Minnesota, Minnesota Public Radio, and the University of Minnesota.

Contributors

Asssumpta Aneas (University of Barcelona) has a Ph.D. in Philosophy and Educational Science from the Universitat de Barcelona (UB). Her doctoral dissertation was the first research about the intercultural competencies in Spain. She is a lecturer at the Faculty of Pedagogy (Universitat de Barcelona, since 1997). She has been one of the first professors who have included the subject of Intercultural Competencies at the universitarian curriculum in Spain: Faculty of Pedagogy (UB), St Pol College of Tourism (UdG), Universitat Politécnica de Catalunya (UPC). Presently, Dr. Aneas is member of the IAIR and Sietar-Europe and IAIR and currently president of Sietar-España.

Harry Anastasiou is a professor of International Peace and Conflict Studies in the Conflict Resolution Graduate Program and International Studies Program at Portland State University. He holds a Ph.D. in International Peace Studies from the Union Institute and University, USA, a Doctorandus degree in Social Science and Philosophy from the Free University of Amsterdam, Holland, an MA degree in the Sociology of Technology from the University of Toronto, Canada, and a BA degree in Political Science and Philosophy from Geneva College, USA.

His academic endeavors have centered on International and Interethnic Peace and Conflict Studies, with contributions toward the development of theoretical and practical perspectives in conflict analysis, multidimensional peacebuilding, as well as in the design, facilitation, and implementation of interethnic and international conflict-resolution processes and initiatives.

For more than two decades, he has been playing a leading role in peace-building initiatives engaging Greek and Turkish citizens and policy leaders from Greece, Turkey, and ethnically divided Cyprus. He has designed and facilitated innumerable interethnic conflict-resolution workshops, policy developing think tanks, dialogue groups, and an array of peace-enhancing projects and programs in the Eastern Mediterranean. While living and working in Cyprus in the 1990s, Anastasiou was appointed Executive Director of the Institute of World Affairs Office of the Eastern Mediterranean and the Middle East, representing and working with the Institute of World Affairs headquarters in Washington DC.

Professor Anastasiou has lectured widely in the USA, Canada, and Europe, and has presented his research at various international conventions.

He has been an invited lecturer for The International Visitor Leadership Program, a U.S. Department of State professional development program fostering international mutual understanding. He has also been an invited frequent lecturer for the "Great Decisions" series of the World Affairs Council, and has been included in the organization's annual Recommended Speakers Book since 2007.

As an academic, Professor Anastasiou has published numerous peer reviewed books, book chapters, and journal articles on peace and conflict issues, including nationalism and ethnic conflict, peace building and the European Union, the Cyprus problem, Greek–Turkish relations, and conflict transformation. His most recent work focuses on American nationalism and peace-building challenges in US foreign policy. His recent publications include: The Broken Olive Branch: Nationalism, Ethnic Conflict and the Quest for Peace in Cyprus. Volumes I and II. Syracuse University Press, 2008; "Nationalism," (with B. J. Broome), in Roland L. Jackson II (Ed.) Encyclopedia of Identity. Sage, 2010;

"Encountering Nationalism: The Contribution of Peace Studies and Conflict Resolution" in Dennis J. D. Sandole, Sean Byrne, Ingrid Sandole-Staroste, Jessica Senehi (Eds.) Handbook of Conflict Analysis and Resolution. Routledge, 2008.

Dharm P.S. Bhawuk a Citizen of Nepal, is a professor of Management and Culture and Community Psychology, University of Hawaii at Manoa. He received his Ph.D. in Organizational Behavior and Human Resource Management from the University of Illinois at Urbana-Champaign under Professor Harry C. Triandis. His research interests include cross-cultural training, individualism and collectivism, intercultural sensitivity, diversity in the workplace, indigenous psychology and management, culture and quality, culture and entrepreneurship, and political behavior in the workplace. He has published more than 50 book chapters and papers. He is a coeditor of the book *Asian Contributions to Cross-Cultural Psychology* (1996), Sage Publishers.

Dinka Corkalo Biruski is an associate professor of Psychology at the Department of Psychology University of Zagreb. Since the war in Croatia, she has been involved in numerous domestic and international research and training projects dealing with psychosocial consequences of war experience. Her research interests are in the area of identity and intergroup relations, with emphasis on divided communities. She has been investigating issues of ethnic/national identity and nationalism, the role of social context in trauma recovery and reconciliation, and postwar social reconstruction processes in divided communities. In 2003/2004, Dr. Corkalo Biruski was a Fulbright Visiting Scholar at the University of Massachusetts at Amherst, where she was doing a research comparing the nature of patriotic and nationalistic identifications among American and Croatian students. In 2005, she received the annual National Scientific Award for her contribution to the understanding of social reconstruction processes in communities affected by the war trauma. Dr. Corkalo Biruski is the head of the Postgraduate Program in Psychology at the Department of Psychology, University of Zagreb.

Jordi Garreta holds a degree and doctorate in sociology from the Autonomous University of Barcelona and is currently teaching in the University of Lleida (in such subjects as educational sociology, sociology of migrations, and social research methods and techniques). He has carried out research on educational sociology and sociology of migrations. As well as presenting his work in congresses, he has published articles in national and international journals, including the Revue Européenne des Migrations Internationales (2000), Ville-École-Intégration (2000, 2010), Migrations-Société (2001, 2010), Revue des Sciences de l'Éducation (2001), International Journal of Migration Studies (2001), Revista Internacional de Sociología (1999, 2000), Revista Migraciones (2000), Revista de Educación (1998, 2000, 2004, 2008, 2010), Revista de Sociologia (1994, 1998, 2002, 2007), International Journal of Intercultural Relations (2006), Tempora (2006).

He is also the author of chapters in books among which are the two articles in the text Relations ethniques et éducation dans les sociétés divisées (Paris, Harmattan) edited by M. McAndrew and F. Gagnon (1999) and in Cultures, insertions et santé (Paris, L'Harmattan) edited by C. Sabatier and O. Douville. He was awarded the 2000 Prize for Research Projects by the Fundació Enciclopèdia Catalana and in 2002 he won one of the National Educational Research Prizes from the del Centre of Educational Research and Documentation (CIDE) of the Ministry of Education. He has also written the books: La integració en l'estructura social de les minories ètniques (Integration of Ethnic Minorities into the Social Structure) (1999; Lleida, Pagès), Diversidad cultural y educació en Quebec (Cultural Diversity and Education in Quebec) (2000; Lleida, Milenio), Els musulmans de Catalunya (The Muslims of Catalonia) (2001; Lleida, Pagès); El espejismo intercultural. La escuela de Cataluña ante la diversidad cultural (The Intercultural Mirage. The School in Catalonia and Cultural Diversity) (2003; Madrid, CIDE), La integración sociocultural de las minorías étnicas (The Socio-cultural Integration of Ethnic Minorities) (2003; Barcelona, Anthropos); La participación de las familias en la escuela. Las asociaciones de padres de alumnos (2007; Madrid: CEAPA and CIDE).

Finally it must be mentioned that he has carried out various research visits to the Centre d'Ethudes Ethniques at the University of Montreal (1996, 1998, 2000 and 2009) and the Ecole des Hautes Éthudes en Sciences Sociales in Paris (1997, 1998, 2007 and 2010).

Richard F. Bonnabeau is an associate professor at State University of New York Empire State College. He is currently serving as the Director for Academic Planning at the Center for International Programs. He holds a Ph.D from Indiana University in history and cultural anthropology. Dr. Bonnabeau was a Fulbright fellow. In 1994, Dr. Bonnabeau joined the International Programs division of his college and helped to establish programs in Greece, the Czech Republic, Albania, and Turkey. He has presented papers at a host of conferences, most recently at the Leadership and Management Conference in Zanzibar, July 2006. Dr. Bonnabeau coauthored a chapter for Jossey-Bass Publishers on the theme of lessons learned from innovative colleges, authored and coauthored seven study guides, and, in his capacity as college historian, is the author of a history of Empire State College.

Benjamin J. Broome is a professor in the Hugh Downs School of Human Communication at Arizona State University (ASU), where he teaches courses in intercultural communication, group facilitation, and conflict resolution. His research focuses on the third-party role in facilitating dialogue in intercultural conflicts. His publications have appeared in journals, such as International Negotiation, Systems Research and Behavioral Science, International Journal of Intercultural Relations, Human Communication Research, Management Communication Quarterly, Journal of Conflict Resolution, Journal of Social Psychology, International Journal of Conflict Management, Small Group Research, American Indian Quarterly, and Communication Education. He has been involved with peacebuilding efforts in Cyprus since 1994, working closely with groups of Greek Cypriots and Turkish Cypriots in conflict resolution, problem solving, and interactive design. In addition to his work in Cyprus, he has facilitated workshops with a number of government agencies, business organizations, professional associations, educational institutions, Native American Tribes, and community groups in the USA, Europe, and Mexico

Ayşe Betül Çelik received her Ph.D. in political science from the State University of New York at Binghamton in 2002 and is an Associate Professor at Sabanci University in Istanbul, Turkey. She teaches political science and conflict resolution. Her research areas include ethnicity, civil society, forced migration, reconciliation, and culture in conflict resolution. She has authored several articles and an edited book on Turkey's Kurdish Question, forced Kurdish migration and role of NGOs in conflict and post-conflict environments. She is also engaged in track-two initiatives in Kurdish Question in Turkey.

Neloufer de Mel is a professor of English at the Department of English, University of Colombo, Sri Lanka. She is the author of Militarizing Sri Lanka: Popular Culture, Memory and Narrative in the Armed Conflict (Sage, in press), Women and the Nation's Narrative: Gender and Nationalism in 20th Century Sri Lanka (Rowman and Littlefield, 2001) and coeditor of At the Cutting Edge: Essays in Honour of Kumari Jayawardena (Women Unlimited, 2007) and Writing an Inheritance: Women's Writing in Sri Lanka 1860–1948 (WERC, 2002). She is the recipient of many distinguished research awards including the John D. and Catherine T. MacArthur research and writing grant, a Fulbright Senior Research Fellowship at Yale University and a Ford Associate in Global Women's Studies Fellowship at the Five College Women's Studies Research Center, USA. Prof. de Mel has also been a visiting scholar at the Center for the Study of Gender and Sexuality at New York University, and the Women's Research Center at the University of Rutgers, given talks at various international universities, participated at a number of international conferences, and published book chapters and peer reviewed essays on gender, theatre and film studies.

Rana Eşkinat is an associate professor of Economics at Faculty of Law at Anadolu University, Turkey. She served as an Assistant Dean between 1993 and 2003 and currently serving as the Head of Economics and Finance Department at the Faculty of Law.

She had graduated from METU Faculty of Economics and Administration Sciences, Department of Economics, Turkey. She holds a Ph.D. in Economic Policy from Anadolu University.

She has published a book on Globalization. She is the coauthor of the books on World Economy and Industrial Organization. She has published research studies, and presented papers on globalization and Turkish economy, civil society organizations, and women in economics.

Susanne Gabrielsen is a doctoral student in Social Psychology at the University of Minnesota and a native of Norway. Her interests are volunteer behaviors and international helping relationships.

Serge Guimond is a professor of Social Psychology and Director of Research in the CNRS Laboratory of Social and Cognitive Psychology at Clermont-Ferrand, France. He has published numerous articles in scientific journals on the psychological, cultural, and political factors in intergroup conflicts. His previous publications include "Social comparison and Social Psychology: Understanding cognition, intergroup relations and culture" (2006) and "Social Psychology: A Multicultural perspective" (2010 in French).

Anat Guy (Ph.D., Hebrew University, 2009) is a lecturer at the School of Behavioral Science, College of Management – Academic Studies in Israel. Her interests include social policy, socialization, professionalism, attitudes forming, and personal values. She is the dean for Student Affairs at the School of Behavioral Science in the College of Management.

Wenshan Jia received the doctorate from University of Massachusetts at Amherst in 2000, and is Associate Professor, Department of Communication Studies, Chapman University, specializing in communication theory, intercultural communication and China Studies. A prolific author/editor of half a dozen books and dozens of journal articles/book chapters, he has received several major research awards such as the Early Career Award for his significant contribution to intercultural relations granted biannually by International Academy for Intercultural Research and Wang-Fradkin Professorship 2005–2007, the highest scholarly award to faculty members from Chapman University. Jia currently is the chair of Faculty Personnel Council of Chapman University and governor of All China Association for Intercultural Communication.

Laura R. Johnson is an associate professor of clinical psychology at the University of Mississippi. Dr. Johnson completed her B.A. at the University of Mississippi (with 1 year at Kenyatta University, Kenya), her Ph.D. at the University of Louisville and predoctoral internship at the University of Colorado Health Sciences Center (2003), where she specialized in refugee mental health. Dr. Johnson supervises clinical graduate students and teaches courses in multicultural psychology, intercultural communication, theories of psychotherapy, and human sexuality. She developed and teaches a study abroad course on environmental psychology in Tanzania and conducts workshops in cultural adjustment and intercultural communication for students of the Croft Institute of International Studies at the University of Mississippi. Her research interests include international psychology, youth civic engagement, intercultural attitudes, connection to nature, and evaluation of environmental education programs, including those in East Africa. Dr. Johnson is also active in research and program outreach in the university community, where her research focuses on international student adjustment and the multicultural climate of the university and her outreach programming focuses on the needs of international students and gay, lesbian, or bisexual students. Dr. Johnson was a Fulbright Scholar in Uganda (2000) and also received a National Geographic Conservation Trust grant (2007) to conduct collaborative, community-based intervention research with Ugandan youth involved in Wildlife Clubs of Uganda. Dr. Johnson has published book chapters and journal articles in the areas of cultural competence, diversity attitudes, and youth civic engagement. She has served in the US Peace Corps (1993–1995, Papua New Guinea) and on the American Psychological Association's Committee on International Relations in Psychology (CIRP) from 2008 to 2010. Most recently, Dr. Johnson received and Institute for International Education (IIE) grant through Project Go to conduct and evaluate intercultural training with Army ROTC that involves international students. In addition, she is involved in a large scale study to examine the psychosocial effects of the BP oil spill in the Gulf of Mexico, with particular attention to environmental attitudes and cultural factors.

Cheryl Jorgensen is a masters in Counseling Psychology student at the University of Hawaii at Hilo. She is also the Managing Editor of the International Journal of Intercultural Relations.

Rodolphe Kamiejski is a Ph.D. student in the CNRS laboratory of Social and Cognitive Psychology in Clermont-Ferrand. He is mainly interested in national models of integration and their implications for intergroup relations. He has conducted research investigating the effects of the French model of integration on intergroup attitudes and well-being from the perspective of both majority and minority group members. He is coauthor of a 2009 paper published in the European Journal of Social Psychology on the role of university exposure in decreasing antiegalitarianism.

Tony Karbo possesses over 25 years of experience teaching and 15 years of experience in workshop design and training in areas of peacebuilding, conflict resolution, conflict transformation, mediation negotiation, governance, and human security in nearly 20 African countries. He has engaged multiple stakeholders in peacebuilding processes, working with parliamentarians, senior civil servants, civil society organizations, and nongovernmental organizations. He currently serves as a senior program officer and an associate professor for the University for PEACE Africa Program in Addis Ababa.

He was previously a senior lecturer at the Institute of Peace, Leadership and Governance (IPLG) at the Africa University of Zimbabwe, where he coordinated the Peace and Conflict Unit and the Institute's training programs. He is an associate director and trainer for the South–North Center for Peacebuilding and Development. Dr. Karbo has also served as the Southern and Eastern Africa representative for the Institute of Multi-Track Diplomacy (IMTD). He holds a doctorate in conflict analysis and resolution from the Institute for Conflict Analysis and Resolution, George Mason University, Virginia, USA.

Grace M. Kibanja is the Deputy Director Institute of Psychology, Makerere University. Dr. Kibanja holds a Ph.D. in Social Psychology from Makerere University; an M.Sc. and an Honours degree both from Rhodes University, South Africa; and a B.Sc. degree from Makerere University. She teaches Introduction to Psychology, Social Psychology, Community Psychology, Psychology of Gender, and Conflict and Negotiation Management to the undergraduate students; and Advanced Research Methods, and Academic writing to graduate students. She supervises graduate students from within and outside the Institute of Psychology. She is currently board member of Multitech Business School and RICH (Right to Improved Child Health), an NGO; and external examiner for the Department of Educational Psychology, Mbarara University of Science and Technology. She is also a member of the Uganda employer of the year technical committee. This is a committee under the federation of Uganda Employer's Association. Dr. Kibanja is a DAAD scholar (since 2001) and also received a Carnegie Cooperation grant to conduct her doctoral research. She worked on a national project on "values and development in Uganda" sponsored by NIRP (Netherlands, Israel, development Research Programme) from 1995 until 2002. She is coauthor of the book entitled "Escaping from Behavioral Poverty in Uganda: The Role of Culture and Social Capital." Her research interests are in the areas of Ethnicity, Political Identity, Cultural Values, Gender, Negotiations, Social Capital, and Behavioral poverty.

James H. Liu was born in Taiwan as Liu Hou-fu. His parents emigrated to Taiwan following the civil war in China. They then emigrated to the United States where James grew up in a small town in the Midwest (Carbondale, Illinois). He obtained a Bachelor's Degree in Computer Science from the University of Illinois, and worked as an aerospace engineer for Hughes Aircraft in the mid-1980s. He received a Ph.D. in Social Psychology from UCLA in 1992, did a postdoc at Florida Atlantic University, and has been teaching at Victoria University of Wellington since 1994. His father, an eminent neo-Confucian philosopher, refers to himself and his discipline as a "gypsy spirit," and James shares this inclination. His decade plus in Wellington is the longest state of continuous residence in his life. He is an author of more than 80 articles and has edited volumes on New Zealand Identities: Departures and Destinations, Restorative Justice and Practices in New Zealand, Ages Ahead: Promoting intergenerational relationships, and Progress in Asian Social Psychology, Volumes 2 and 6. He is an associate professor of Psychology, and Deputy Director of the Centre for Applied Cross Cultural

Research (http://www.vuw.ac.nz/cacr/) at Victoria University of Wellington. He was Secretary General of the Asian Association of Social Psychology 2003–2007, Treasurer from 1999 to 2003, and is currently editor of the Asian Journal of Social Psychology. His research is in the cross-cultural psychology of intergroup relations and social identity, with a focus on social representations of history. A naturalized citizen of two countries, he describes himself as a Chinese–American–New Zealander.

Fidel Molina is a professor of Sociology, Faculty of Education and Faculty of Law and Economics, University of Lleida (Spain). He graduated both in Mediation and Conflicts Resolution and in Intercultural Education. He has published diverse books, articles and chapters of books about Sociology of Education (lifelong formation, Intercultural education, Youth and Socialization), Sociology of Leisure and Sport, Management and Formation of Human Resources. He has been the dean of the Faculty of Education (1998–2001 and 2001–2004). Currently, he is the member of the Association of Sociology of Education (ASE) of Spain, and member of the Experts Committee about Formation of Human Resources (Government of Catalonia). Also, he is the member of the Commission of Studies of Postgraduate in the European Higher Education of the University of Lleida. He is a coordinator of Master in Educational Research.

Jeanette S. Martin is a professor at the University of Mississippi, School of Business. She has served as associate editor of the Journal of Business Communication, is the recipient of national awards, and the author of dozens of articles, book chapters, and conference presentations on intercultural business communication, education, and management information systems. She is the coauthor of three books with Lillian Hunt Chaney.

Mayanja M. Kajumba is a psychologist and lecturer at the Makerere University Department of Mental Health and Community psychology. He holds a Bachelor of Science (Psychology) and Master of Science in Clinical Psychology from Makerere University. Mr. Mayanja was a German Academic Exchange (DAAD) Scholar, and is currently a J. W. Fulbright Fellow, pursuing a Ph.D. in Health Psychology and Neuroscience at the University of Texas, Arlington. Mr. Mayanja has been working in Makerere University since 2001, where he teaches neuropsychology, forensic psychology, introduction to clinical psychology, psychology in prisons, community psychology and psychology and gender. He has, for several years, supervised undergraduate research on various topics related to stress and the progression of terminal Illnesses (HIV/AIDS and cancer), the psychological impact of traumatic events such as war, rape, torture, and road traffic accidents, depression and suicide, family conflict, and the psychology of crime. His current research focuses on mind–body interactions and disease; the link between psychological stress and the onset and progression of cancer and the role of psychotherapeutic interventions in enhancing immune function and cancer survival. Mr. Mayanja also continues to research cultural differences in the interpretation of traumatic experience and vulnerability to posttraumatic stress disorder.

Marisa Mealy received her Ph.D. in Social Psychology from New Mexico State University. In 2006, she was appointed to a tenure track position at Central Connecticut State University. Her research focus is on cross-cultural psychology and intergroup relations, in particular, the use of theory to promote an understanding of cultures in Latin America and the United States. Other research interests include factors that influence the development and maintenance of prejudice and bias. She has lived and worked as an educator in South America.

Cristina Montiel is a professor at the Ateneo de Manila's Psychology Department, where she coordinates the Ph.D. in Social–Organizational Psychology program. Montiel serves as editorial board member of the Peace Psychology Book Series by Springer Publications, and was associate editor of Peace and Conflict: Journal of Peace Psychology. During the Marcos dictatorship, she chaired Lingap Bilanggo (Care for Prisoners), a social movement for the release of all Filipino political prisoners. Her international experiences cover academic visits to Xiamen University (China), National University of Malaysia, University of Hawaii, Ohio State University, Georgetown University, Whitman College, Technical University of Chemnitz (Germany), and The Australian National University. She has received the 1998 Outstanding Service Award from the Division of Peace Psychology of the American Psychological Association, the 1998 Distinguished Contribution Award from Psychologists for Social Responsibility, and was in the first group of senior research fellows of the Nippon Foundation's Asian Public Intellectuals program. Her recent publications include Toward a Psychology of Structural Peacebuilding (2001), Peace Psychology in Asia (2003), and Political Psychology of Nonviolent Democratic Transitions in Southeast Asia (2006). In 2007, Montiel received the Philippines' Republika Zonal Award for Most Outstanding Social Science Research for her work on Effects of Social Position on Societal Attributions of an Asymmetric Conflict.

Dahlia Moore a Social psychologist, is a professor and Head of Graduate Studies at the College of Management, Israel. Her research focuses on perceptions, attitudes, and feelings. Some of her studies focus on how Jews and Palestinians (within and outside Israel) perceive each other. These studies led to long-term collaborations with Palestinian researchers, a collaboration that produced a book and several joint papers. Many of these studies were supported by grants obtained through the Truman Research Institute for the Advancement of Peace in which Dahlia Moore was a research fellow. In her other studies, Moore focuses on working women and their strategies of combining family and careers. For 4 years, she acted as advisor to the Women's Status Committee of the Israeli parliament (the Knesset), and as the newsletter editor of the International Society of Justice Research (http://www.isjr.org/Newsletter.html).

Vijayan P. Munusamy is a senior research associate at the Center for Creative Leadership®-Asia. He started his career as a Mechanical Engineer in Malaysia and made his first "cultural crossing" after observing that many of the conflicts in the workplace and in society are due to cultural misunderstandings. Recognizing cultural education as a powerful tool to advance multicultural understanding, he founded a social enterprise to promote the sharing of children's stories from different cultures in Malaysia, Singapore, and Indonesia. The lessons he learned from this experience and the need to develop theoretical, methodological, and experiential expertise in cross-cultural issues led him to make his second "cultural crossing" toward becoming a Degree Fellow at the East–West Center, Hawaii and a Ph.D. student at The University of Hawaii. His recent publication includes a book chapter in "Teaching about Asian Pacific Islanders: Effective Activities, Strategies, and Assignments for Classrooms and Workshops" (AltaMira Press, 2006). An Asian Development Bank scholar and a recipient of The Wall Street Journal Student Achievement Award, he has been recognized numerous times for his achievement in academic, work, and community service.

Martha Mutisi is currently completing Ph.D. studies in the Institute for Conflict Analysis and Resolution (ICAR) at George Mason University, in Virginia. She is a native of Zimbabwe. Prior to her doctoral studies, Martha was a Lecturer in the Institute of Peace, Leadership and Governance (IPLG) at Africa University, located in Zimbabwe. She taught graduate courses in Peace and Conflict Studies, apart from coordinating a program on mainstreaming Peace and Leadership Education in Zimbabwean universities. Currently, Martha is a Senior Researcher with the African Centre for the Constructive Resolution of Disputes (ACCORD), which is based in Durban, South Africa. Ms. Martha Mutisi has regional experience in Africa, and has worked under different capacities as a researcher, social analyst, facilitator, educator, trainer, and program coordinator on critical issues at the intersections of peace, conflict, and development. She has experience working in areas of training, program design, management, evaluation as well as policy development and advising. Martha's research interests include, indigenous systems of conflict resolution, postconflict peacebuilding, democratization, development and gender, and she has published on these issues.

Pierre De Oliveira is a postdoctoral researcher in the CNRS laboratory of Social and Cognitive Psychology in Clermont-Ferrant, France. He is currently involved in a series international research projects on intergroup relations. His research on the role of social norms in moderating the effects of power on tendency to legitimize social inequality has been published in the International Review of Social Psychology.

Jan Pieter van Oudenhoven graduated from the University of Leiden in Social Psychology. He started his career in Latin America as a UNESCO associate expert in educational programmes for farmers. He is currently professor of cross-cultural psychology at the University of Groningen. His main research interests concern intergroup relations, immigration issues, international relations, and intercultural adaptation.

Rudy Buhay Rodil is an active Mindanao historian and peace advocate. In 1988 he was a commissioner of the Regional Consultative Commission in Muslim Mindanao which helped Congress draft the Organic Act for the Autonomous Region in Muslim Mindanao. As an acknowledged expert on the history of the Moro conflict, he was twice member of the GRP peace negotiating panel in the talks with the Moro National Liberation Front, 1993-96, and also vice chair of the GRP Panel in the talks with the Moro Islamic Liberation Front, Dec 2004 to 3 Sep 08. Having started his studies on Mindanao, especially on the Moro and Lumad affairs, in the summer of 1973, he has so far written four books, several monographs and 120 articles. As educator, he has taught in Sulu, Cotabato, Davao, Manila and Iligan. Now retired, he was professor of history in the last twenty-four years in Mindanao State University-Iligan Institute of Technology, Jun 1983 to Oct 2007. As peace advocate, he has so far participated as resource person in more than 659 forums, seminars and conferences related to the creation of a culture of peace in Mindanao.

Michael Salzman is a professor in Counselor Education and has published in the areas of cross-cultural psychology, cultural psychology, intercultural training, and counseling. His current project is to identify behaviors, viewed as respectful or disrespectful, by culturally diverse populations. A licensed psychologist, he has worked in cultural diversity, teaching in Brooklyn, counseling in the Navajo Nation, and serving as a clinician in a CMHC in South Tucson, AZ. He has worked with Alaska Natives coordinating a model rural mental health program and most recently with the Native Hawaiian Leadership Project and the Native Hawaiian Education Association. Dr. Salzman is interested in psychological functions of culture, consequences of traumatic cultural disruption, intercultural conflict, indigenous psychologies, movements of cultural recovery, and processes of psychological decolonization.

Kumudini Samuel is the director of the Women and Media Collective Sri Lanka and has been engaged with women's rights and human rights work from the early 1980s. Ms. Samuel was appointed to the Subcommittee on Gender Issues mandated to advice the plenary of the Sri Lankan Peace negotiations in 2002. Her writings have focused on gender, conflict, and peace building. She is also currently the South Asia Coordinator of the international women's network DAWN – Development Alternatives With Women for a New Era and the international representative on the Board of the World University Service, Canada.

Ulrike Schwegler Ph.D. (University of Chemnitz, Germany) is the director and cofounder of the Institute for Applied Trust Research in Stuttgart, Germany. Her business and research interests cover both "for-profit" and "not-for-profit" organizations in Europe, USA, Southeast Asia, the Middle East, and North Africa. Her activities link trust to peacebuilding processes in postconflict regions as well as strategic management processes. Dr. Schwegler worked for various NGOs in Indonesia for 7 years and is now a lecturer at FOM University of Applied Sciences in Stuttgart. She is a member in the

International Academy of Intercultural Research, and has published articles, book chapters, and books on trust-building processes in intercultural cooperation and on intercultural competence training.

L. Ripley Smith Ph.D. (University of Minnesota) is a professor of International Communication at Bethel University in St. Paul, MN, USA. He is a frequent speaker at national and international conferences on the subjects of intercultural social support networks, refugee resettlement, cross-cultural partnership development, and the role of trust in postconflict regions. His recent research has explored identity reconstruction among KaRen and Somali refugee populations and partnership criteria in German and American NGOs. A Fellow in the International Academy of Intercultural Research, he is the author of book chapters and journal articles appearing in Organizational Trust (Cambridge University Press). The International Journal of Intercultural Relations, the International and Intercultural Communication Annual, The International Journal of the Sociology of Language, the International Journal of Communication, The Proceedings of The Conference On The Discourse Of Environmental Advocacy, and the Arizona Communication Association Journal. Dr. Smith currently serves as the Chair of the board of directors for World Relief, MN, a nonprofit refugee resettlement agency.

Champika K. Soysa is an associate professor of Psychology and director of Women's Studies at Worcester State College, MA, USA. She studies ethnic identity and prejudice, as well as the psychological impact of war on women and children. More recently, she has investigated the impact of cumulative collective stressors such as war and natural disaster, following the tsunami of 2004 in Sri Lanka. Prof. Soysa was a Research Fellow at the Solomon Asch Center for Study of Ethnopolitical Conflict, University of Pennsylvania, in 1999. She has received research grants from the Asch Center and the American Institute for Sri Lankan Studies, amongst others. Prof. Soysa has presented her research at several international conferences and has contributed to book chapters in her field.

Colleen Ward is a professor of Psychology and Director, Centre for Cross-cultural Research at Victoria University, Wellington, New Zealand. At the most general level, she is interested in how culture affects human behaviour and experience and is particularly concerned with acculturation processes and measurements as well as the prediction of psychological and sociocultural adaptation of persons who make cross-cultural transitions. Ward also conducts research on cultural identity and intergroup processes, including the mutual perceptions of immigrants and members of a host society. These topics were recently examined during her tenure as the Royal Society of New Zealand's James Cook Fellow in Social Science (2005–2007).

Stephen Worchel is an Emeritus Professor of Psychology at University of Hawaii at Hilo, Emeritus Dean, College of Arts and Sciences at University of Hawaii at Hilo. Previous appointments have been at Texas A&M University, the University of Virginia, and the University of Maine. His is the author/editor of several books on ethnic conflict and race relations.

Güneş N. Zeytinoğlu is a professor of Management at Anadolu University, Turkey. She served as the Head of Business Department between 1997 and 2005 and is currently the dean of the Faculty of Economics and Administration Sciences at Anadolu University. She holds a Ph.D. in Management from Anadolu University. She serves as the Consulting Editor of Anadolu University Journal of Social Sciences. She has published books on Comparative Management, Newspaper Organizations and Management of Political Parties; has published research studies and presented papers on cross-cultural management, organizational culture, women in management, transformational leadership, strategic management and organizational teams.

Haiyang Zhang is a professor of Ethnology and Sociology, the Minzu University of China, Beijing, China. He is the director of The Ethnic Minority Studies Center of China (EMSCOC), as a National Social Sciences and Humanity Key Research Institute of the Ministry of Education on MUC Campus as well as Director, the Center of West China Development, and Director, the Institute of Taiwan Ethnic Studies. He has been Senior Fulbright Scholar, Department of Anthropology, Stanford University. He has published extensively on ethnic minorities in China both in terms of original research and translation. He is Deputy Secretary-General, Research Society of China's Ethnology and Anthropology, Member of Council, China Union of Anthropological and Ethnological Research Societies, Member of Council, Society of Ethnology in China, Member of Council, Ethnic Sociological Branch, Society of Sociology in China, as well as Member of Council, Society of Urban Anthropology in China.

Introduction: Models and Theories of Ethnic Conflict*

1

Dan Landis and Rosita D. Albert

Things fall apart; the centre cannot hold;
Mere anarchy is loosed upon the world,
The blood-dimmed tide is loosed

(William Butler Yeats, "The Second Coming," 1919)

Ethnic violence warrants our attention because it is appalling, not because it is ubiquitous

(Brubaker & Laitin, 1998)

Since 1955, according to research by Barbara Harff, nearly fifty ethnic and religious minorities have been targeted in forty-one episodes of genocide and mass political murder that killed at least thirteen million and as many as twenty million noncombatants.

(Gurr, 2007)

1 Introduction

Ethnic conflict and racial conflict are phrases often taken to describe the same phenomenon. However, when the usage of these terms in books over time is examined, a different picture emerges. Figure 1.1, taken from the Google search of words in books between 1800 and 2000, shows that neither phrase was in common use before 1900 when "racial conflict" began to appear. The other phrase did not make a significant appearance before 1960. "Racial conflict" peaked about 1970 and then declined. "Ethnic conflict," perhaps reflecting a disinclination to use the term "race" as a result of the civil rights fights of the 1960s, began a sharp positive acceleration which continues today. It is most likely true that while using the term "race" may brand the user with unfavorable attributions, "ethnic" carries no such baggage. But, it is also probably true that writers often still confuse the two and see "ethnic" as a more socially acceptable way of referring to "race." In this book, we make no such attribution and do not conflate "ethnic" with "race," if for no other reason than that the latter term has no precise scientific meaning and is, at best, a social construction. In this book, and in this chapter, we will look at different degrees of ethnic conflict. Some of these conflicts will be extremely violent, attaining the status of civil wars. Others will have little or no overt violence but contain serious negative effects on ethnic minority populations.

Two and a half decades ago, the first author of this chapter co-edited a book on ethnic conflict (Boucher, Landis, & Clark, 1987). In that book, we attempted to distil a set of "causes" from some 12 intra-national conflicts (Sri Lanka, Hong Kong, China, Malaysia, Basque, Puerto Rico, Native American, Philippines,

*An earlier version of this chapter was presented by the first author at the Defense Equal Opportunity Research Symposium, February 2009, held at the Defense Equal Opportunity Management Institute, Cocoa Beach, Florida. The views expressed here do not necessarily reflect those of the U.S. Department of Defense or any of its agencies. Any omissions or commissions are the sole responsibility of the authors. Comments on this chapter should be addressed to the first author at danl@hawaii.edu.

D. Landis (✉)
Department of Psychology, University of Hawaii, Hilo, HI, USA
e-mail: danl@hawaii.edu

R.D. Albert
Department of Communication Studies, University of Minnesota, Minneapolis, MN, USA
e-mail: alber001@umn.edu

D. Landis and R.D. Albert (eds.), *Handbook of Ethnic Conflict: International Perspectives*, International and Cultural Psychology, DOI 10.1007/978-1-4614-0448-4_1,

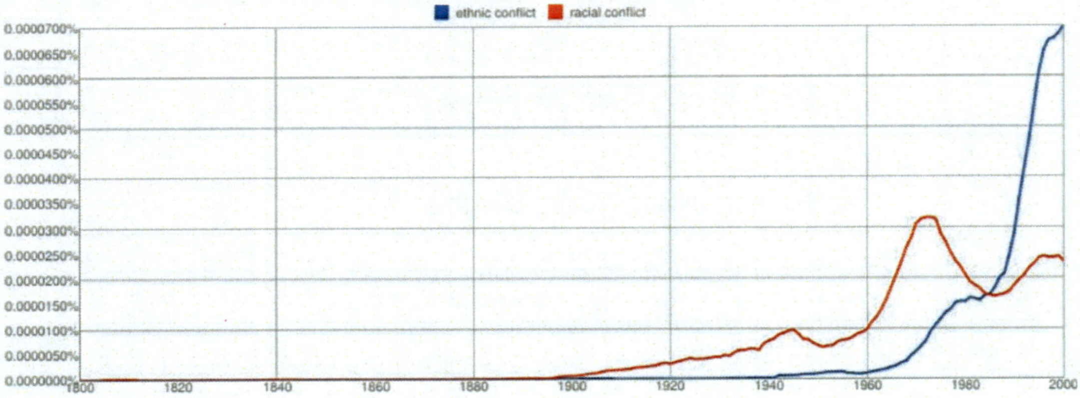

Fig. 1.1 Frequency of the appearance of the phrases "Ethnic Conflict" and "Racial Conflict" in the Google Books database: 1800–2000

New Zealand, and Hawaii). Other works, (e.g., Lee, McCauley, Moghaddam, & Worchel, 2004), cover many of the same conflicts, though from a somewhat restricted theoretical approach. In the 1987 work (Landis & Boucher, 1987), we extracted the following themes that seemed to encapsulate most of the studied conflicts:[1]

1. Perceived differences between groups, stereotypes, and ethnic identity
2. Land tenure and homeland issues, and immigrant versus native status
3. Involvement of outsiders
4. Disparate allocation of power and resources
5. Effects of language and language policy
6. Process of conflict resolution
7. Religion

Appealing and intuitively reasonable as these seven "causes" are, they do not form a theory of ethnopolitical conflict since they do not include propositions that could be subjected to empirical test (Mack & Synder, 1957). In the pages that follow, we will summarize the major theories that have been put forth to explain and predict ethnic conflict. These range from the individual to the community level and sometimes produce quite different empirical findings (Forbes, 2004). In general, theories can be arranged along two correlated dimensions:

1. Primordial versus instrumental (Blimes, 2006; Lake & Rothchild, 1998; Lee, Moghaddam, McCauley, & Worchel, 2004). In primordial theories, it is assumed that a fundamental characteristic of the human species, in this case ethnicity, is a need to categorize social stimuli. For conflict theorists, it is usually the ingroup versus the outgroup that forms the categorization. Conflict follows this tendency to value the ingroup positively and the outgroup negatively (Axelrod & Hammond, 2003). And since one of the salient characteristics dividing ingroups and outgroups is ethnicity, ethnic conflict can be the result. Indeed, some theorists (Kaznatcheev, 2010) suggest that ethnocentrism had survival value in an evolutionary sense. For instrumental theorists, no such primordial basis is assumed. Rather, ethnic conflict is seen as having other underlying causes, for example, competition for resources (Caselli & Coleman, 2010), and then the conflict becomes ethnically based due to other factors. The work of Campbell, Licklidder, Howell, and others are examples of instrumentally oriented theorists (Campbell, 1998; Howell, 1978; Licklidder, 1993).
2. A second division that is often used is Macro- versus Micro-focused theories (some authors add a "Meso" category midway between the other two: Landis, 2008; Pettigrew, 1997). However, it is useful for our purposes in this chapter to focus only on the extremes of the dimension. By micro, we mean theories that

[1] This list is somewhat smaller than that provided by Marsella. His list consisted of 20 "challenges," most of which can be subsumed under the seven that are listed here (Marsella, 2005).

have at their core (and their methodology) individual behavior and attitudes. Contact theory (Allport, 1954a; Pettigrew, 2008; Pettigrew & Troop, 2006) and its derivatives (Brewer, 1996; Gaertner & Dovidio, 2000) are relevant examples of micro-theories. We shall discuss contact theory in more detail below. At the other end are theories that focus on broad national and/or societal trends that are predicted to lead to conflict between ethnic groups (Brubaker & Laitin, 1998; Caselli & Coleman, 2010; Lim, Metzler, & Bar-Yam, 2007).

Micro-theories, at least those that appear in social psychology, tend to be primordial, whereas macro-theories often proposed by sociologists, political scientists, or economists tend to be instrumental. In practice, of course, the two dimensions are correlated. Nevertheless, conceptually the distinction may be useful.

2 Primordial Theories

2.1 Contact Theory[2]

It was a reasonable assumption that negative attitudes toward a group (prejudice) precede conflict. If that is so, then it is important to understand the conditions under which prejudice occurs and when it does not occur or is reduced. Though Allport (1954a) is generally credited with laying the theoretical groundwork for understanding this phenomenon, earlier scholars had certainly provided related analyses. For example, Stoufer and his colleagues had conducted a series of landmark studies on what results when African–American and Caucasians work together under combat conditions (Star, Williams, & Stoufer, 1949). Those studies clearly showed a decrease in prejudice. From these and similar studies, it was but a short step to formulate the "contact hypothesis:"

> Prejudice (unless deeply rooted in the character structure of the individual) may be reduced by equal-status contact between majority and minority groups in the pursuit of common goals. The effect is greatly enhanced if this contact is sanctioned by institutional supports (i.e., by law, custom, or local atmosphere), and provided it is of the sort that leads to the perception of common interests and common humanity between members of the two groups. (Allport, 1954a, p. 281)

Even more important, the military studies referred to above also put the lie to the belief that African–American soldiers were not effective fighters unless they were lead by Caucasians. And, they could certainly not be allowed to fight alongside of Whites lest they "infect those troops with their degraded ways."[3] It is quite clear that those studies were an important, but certainly not the only, factor that led President Truman to order the integration of the United States Armed Forces on July 26, 1948 (Dansby, Stewart, & Webb, 2001; Kauth & Landis, 1996; Moskos & Butler, 1996), an act of political courage in the middle of a presidential campaign that the common wisdom had already declared him the looser.

The contact conditions that Allport listed that were expected to lead to a reduction in prejudice did not include the emotional character of the encounter – whether it was pleasant or unpleasant. However, emotion was not ignored in the book; indeed an entire chapter was devoted to the topic of the role of anxiety and related negative affective states. In the same year that the *Nature of Prejudice* was published, Allport's history of social psychology also appeared (Allport, 1954b). In that essay, a good deal of attention was devoted to a discussion of the work on sympathy and empathy, and the role of these emotions in social

[2] There are many theories that derive from Allport's version of contact theory. It has been said about post-Freudians that because they stand on the shoulders of a giant and can see further, they think that the giant is of no use (Mullahy, 1952). The same is certainly true of Allport and the post-contact theorists.

[3] The negative attributions that were used to derogate African-Americans in the military are exactly the same ones that were trotted out against women and gays (Kauth & Landis, 1996; Thomas & Thomas, 1996), Women are now appearing in almost all military specialties (MOS) and will shortly be allowed to serve on submarines. As we write this chapter, the U.S. military's discrimination against gays in the guise of "Don't Ask, Don't Tell" has finally after seventeen years been repealed by the U.S. Congress.

behavior. Empathy was historically seen as the basis for attraction between individuals and, by extension, groups. So, in the framework of the Prejudice book, the contact conditions can be seen as ways to increase empathy across the ethnic divide. However, it may also be the case that contact, no matter how it meets the conditions, may actually increase anticipatory anxiety for a later contact. Thus, decreasing anxiety prior to contact may allow the requisite conditions to produce a decrease in prejudice and other negative attributions (Landis, Brislin, & Hulgus, 1985; Randolf, Landis, & Tzeng, 1977; Weldon, Carlston, Rissman, Slobodin, & Triandis, 1975). The two studies by Landis and colleagues used a Solomon four-group design so that the order of training and contact effects on anxiety and attributions could be assessed. A similar concern with the role of anxiety in inter-ethnic relations gave rise to the Integrated Threat Theory of Walter and Cookie Stephan (Stephan, Stephan, & Gudykunst, 1999). In a recent study, Gonzalez and colleagues included both intergroup anxiety and intergroup threat as mediators from contact, identity, and group distinctiveness to prejudice (Gonzalez, Sirlopu, & Kessler, 2010) in both Chilean and Peruvian respondents. In both cases, anxiety mediated the effect of contact on prejudice, but there were some significant differences between the two populations. Their model test did not allow them to assess order effects, which is a significant lacunae in the study.

The studies summarized above would seem to point to emotion (positive or negative) as underlying the effect of contact. Pettigrew (2008) suggests, drawing on the work of Zajonc (1968), that the underlying mechanism might be mere exposure which could either lower or raise anxiety and, therefore, lead to a reduction or increase in prejudice. One could wonder also of something like Piaget's Law of Relative Centrations (Piaget, 1961) in which each time the perceptual mechanism encounters an object (in this case, the "other"), the object grows larger and more powerful (and may be anxiety provoking) in cognition. As encounters continue, we could imagine that a phenomenon like semantic satiation (Lambert & Jakobovitz, 1960) reduces the anxiety as well as the perceived powerfulness of the other and eventually prejudice. The point here is that the underlying mechanism in the clearly occurring phenomenon of contact has yet to be fully articulated and experimentally determined.

In an extensive meta-analysis of over 700 independent samples from over 500 studies of contact effects across the world, Pettigrew and Troop reported that less than 5% found that contact increased prejudice (Pettigrew & Troop, 2006). Of course, in most of the cases, the affective component was not assessed prior to and after the contact situation; hence, the order effect could not be determined. Those authors, pointing to a number of studies on the effect of anxiety (Brown & Hewstone, 2005), place the occurrence of anxiety reduction after the contact, rather than before, as the studies of Landis and his colleagues have suggested. Pettigrew and Troop suggest (2006, p. 768) that the role of negative and maybe positive emotions will continue to be a fruitful area of research in determining the conditions under which contact impacts prejudice.

2.2 Macro-primordial Theory

Most of the studies of the impact of contact focus at the individual level even though the implication is often of group effects (Forbes, 2004). Such a change in level is difficult to navigate when the measures ultimately are of discrete persons. As Forbes has noted in the above referenced paper to assess the group or community effects, one has to gather data from communities that differ in theoretically interesting ways. The construct of ingroup/outgroup distinction and the notion that groups are more than simply an aggregate of individuals are old concepts in social psychology (Allport, 1954b, 1968). Despite the fact that the idea of a group mind has largely disappeared from modern discussions, it does have a more current version in the idea of the minimal group (Tajfel, 1970). In studies of such a group, the mere fact of being told that one is in a group sets up boundaries between one's "group" and other groups, much like high schools in the same city and with the same kinds of students developing intense rivalries and demonizing their opposite numbers (Gaertner & Insko, 2000). When competition is added into the mix, as demonstrated in the famous Robber's cave studies (Sherif, Harvey, White, Hood, & Sherif, 1961), the demonization of the rival groups intensifies. These studies were the foundation for the formulation of Realistic Conflict Theory (RCT). RCT held that by manipulating the situation from competition to cooperation, the level of prejudice can also be changed. When the competition (either real or perceived) is high, prejudice toward the outgroup is exacerbated due to a perceived threat to the ingroup. The question of the mechanism that produced the prejudice toward the outgroup still remained.

Social Identity Theory (Tajfel & Turner, 1979), SIT, posits that one's identity, be it national or ethnic or involving some other attribute, is a function of one's group membership. This identity is made ever more salient by focusing on the positive characteristics of the ingroup, which supposedly are not possessed by members of any other group (Gaertner & Insko, 2000). When ethnicity is part of the identity and when that identity is threatened in some way, then ethnocentrism is a result. However, a strong sense of ethnic identity may not lead to outgroup devaluation in young children (Marks, Szalacha, Lararre, Boyd, & Coll, 2007). It does appear that social identity forms quite early in childhood (Yee & Brown, 1992) and is, for most of these theorists, an essential part of development. For this reason, we place them in the primordial category. It is important to note that a strong ethnic identity does not necessarily lead to a negative evaluation of the outgroup (Phinney, Jacoby, & Silva, 2007); indeed, it may lead to a more positive view of that group.

Social Categorization Theory (SCT) is a variation of SIT and assumes that individuals break the social world into discrete categories. These categories result in the differences between persons in the ingroup being minimized and the boundaries between groups being emphasized. As boundaries between the social categories become less permeable, both cognitive and emotional aspects of the individual's makeup are affected (Brewer, 1996; Turner, Hogg, Oakes, Reicher, & Wetherell, 1987). Both SIT and SCT have brought the construct of identity into our understanding of how groups form and are maintained. As Worchel has noted (Worchel, 2004), these two theories, based on the seminal work of Tajfel (Tajfel & Turner, 1979), have resulted in a significant corpus of very clever (in the best sense of the term) research in the past 3 decades. They have also wetted researchers' and practitioners' appetite to find ways of increasing the permeability of group boundaries with the assumption that prejudice and conflict would be reduced if not eliminated. Techniques to do so include Brewer's Cross-Cutting Approach (Brewer, 1996), Gaertner and Dovidio's Common Ingroup Identity Model (Gaertner & Dovidio, 2000), Stephan's and Pedersen's use of empathy[4] (Pedersen & Pope, 2010; Stephan & Finlay, 1999), the use of a cognitive/attributional technique such as the Culture Sensitizer (Albert, 1983; Cushner & Landis, 1996; Landis, Day, McGrew, Thomas, & Miller, 1976; Triandis, Brislin, & Hui, 1988), Worchel's Seeds of Peace approach (Worchel, 2004), and Kelman's trust-building approach (Kelman, 2005). All of these approaches are attempts to increase the level of isomorphic attributions (Triandis, 1977), a modern version of the concern for the development of empathy which first appeared in Allport's historical essays in 1954 and 1968. A full description of these approaches is beyond the scope of this chapter, but they are interesting and potentially useful in reducing inter-ethnic conflict and should be consulted by activists and practitioners working to increase positive interaction between groups.

[4] There is a developing line of research that indicates that empathic responses across racial and cultural boundaries are moderated by activity in the anterior cingulated cortex and insula, an area thought to be involved in first person pain perception. This activity significantly decreases when viewing an ingroup member being subjected to painful stimuli. The result holds across both Chinese and Caucasian subjects. (Xu, Zuo, Wang, & Han, 2009). It will be interesting to see if these results hold when the in and out groups are not defined by either racial or cultural differences, but rather are work groups in competition or cooperation.

2.3 Instrumental Approaches

Most instrumental theories that are not fundamentally primordial tend to be macro in orientation and application. These theories usually, but not always, originate in sociology or political science and sometimes take the form of critiques of contact theory (Dixon, Durrheim, & Tredoux, 2005; Forbes, 2004; McGarry & O'Leary, 1995). Pettigrew (2008) has provided a cogent response to these critiques. Such macro-studies tend to use large multinational data sets such as the *Minorities at Risk* project (Minorities at Risk, 2009) and to analyze trends across nationalities and minority groups that differ in theoretically interesting ways. The MAR data set as of 2010 includes information on 283 conflicts; the 20 included in the present book form a very small part of those included in MAR. Of course, we did not select the conflicts in this book from the MAR data set, but we did try to cast as wide a net as possible and then do a detailed, in-depth, context-specific analysis of each conflict. We invited authors from a wide variety of countries and a variety of disciplines to write about ethnic conflicts in countries or regions that they knew well. Many of our contributors also brought to bear their expertise in intercultural relations, and we believe that this is a unique and important contribution of our volume to the understanding and amelioration of ethnic conflicts around the world.

It is worthwhile to see how a political scientist approaches the issue of ethnic conflict and for this we examine an early study by Gurr (1993). Gurr used the MAR data set and focused on analyzing the reasons behind the decision by minorities to rebel (Gurr, 1993). A notable feature of this study is the distinctions made among different types of minority groups: *Ethnoclasses* (usually groups descended from slaves or immigrants, e.g., African–Americans, other people of color in various other countries who often are relegated to caste-like status), *Ethnonationalists* (represented by many of the chapters in this book, e.g., Tamils in Sri Lanka), *Indigenous groups* (Maori of New Zealand, Native Hawaiians in Hawaii, and Kurds in Turkey and Iraq), *Communal Contenders* (heterogeneous alliances between contending groups, usually not ethnically based), and *Militant Sects* (e.g., Muslims within countries where the majority follows another religion or religious tradition as, for example, Turks in the Netherlands and Germany, Moroccans in Spain, and Sunnis in Iraq). Gurr suggests that aggregating an investigation across all of these groups runs the real risk of obscuring the actual reasons why a particular group rebels and engages in violence. In his study, the numbers in each group of conflicts range from a low of 39 (Militant Sects) to a high of 82 (Indigenous groups).

The disaggregation of minority groups in conflict by Gurr reveals an important cleavage in the study of ethnic conflict by political scientists and sociologists. That cleavage revolves around the centrality of ethnicity as a cause of conflict between groups, and the potential interaction between ethnicity and other group characteristics as predictive of conflict. It has also led to a brief kerfuffle in the pages of *Foreign Affairs* on whether ethnic conflict is inevitable (Habyariman, Humphreys, Posner, & Weinstein, 2008; Muller, 2008), and if so, is partition the rational and only answer? As many of the chapters in this Handbook demonstrate, ethnic conflicts, however they are defined, involve many complex and interrelated factors.

Gurr takes a large number of macro-variables (e.g., grievances about political rights and autonomy, contagion of protest from similar groups in the region in the 1980s, institutional democracy in 1986, etc.) and uses them to predict the level of communal protest and rebellion in the 1980s for each group (see Fig. 1.2).

If we consider just one group – ethnonationalists – Gurr reports an interesting pattern when predicting to actual rebellion. Grievances over political rights and mobilization to achieve those rights, but not grievances about political autonomy, are significant predictors of rebellion for this group. The only other predictor is a change in the scope of state power during the period 1960–1986, but not the mere occurrence of the level of state power in 1986. Other variables in the model failed to predict for this group. The R-squared for this equation is quite good (.46), giving some confidence in the reproducibility of the results. Notably absent from the equation are any variables that would lead us to

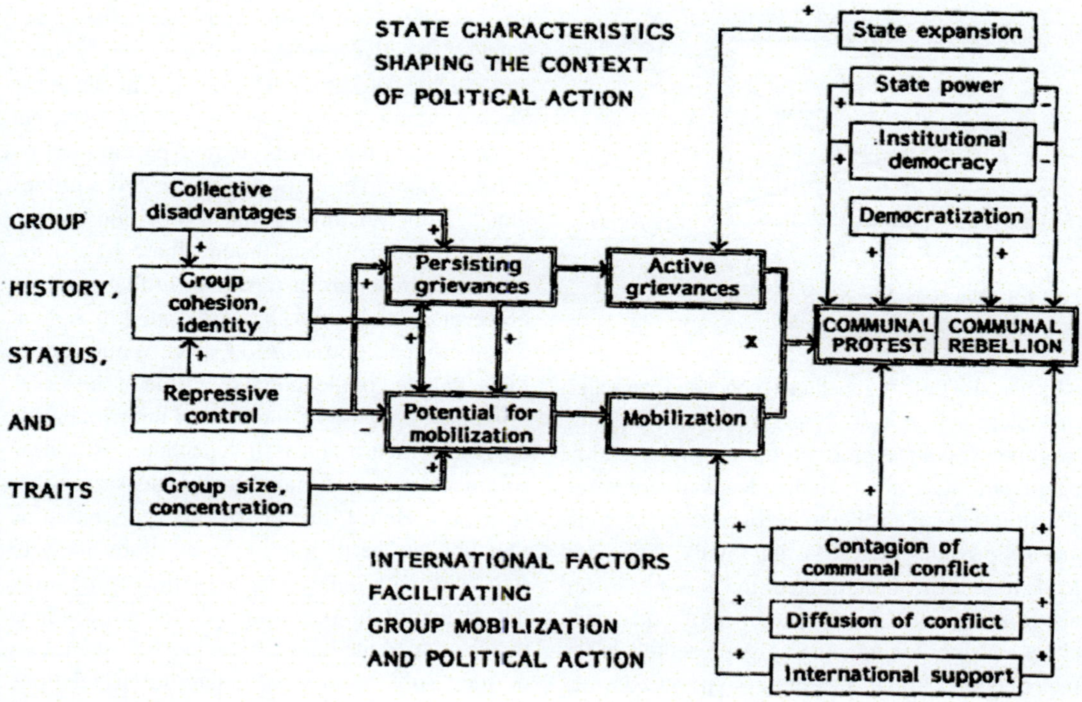

Fig. 1.2 Gurr's 1993 model

believe that one group is prejudiced toward the other one or has negative outgroup attitudes. To be sure, you might assume that such variables lie underneath the grievances over political rights, but it is hard to make such assumptions about an increase or decrease in the scope of state power over the 26 years indexed by the variable. These analyses certainly raise the issue of how important ethnicity is in communal conflict and whether it comes into play after the conflict has already started as a rationalization for mobilization.[5]

Gurr revisited some of the same issues in 1997 (Gurr & Moore, 1997) and he was, in fact, one of early users of the term "ethnopolitical." In this paper, the authors focused on rebellion, using the same 1980s data set as above, and attempted to make some predictions for the 1990s about which groups would enter into a period of armed rebellion. The model they tested had two main predictors: deprivation and resource mobilization. They defined the groups involved in ethnopolitical conflict as ones "…that define themselves by reference to some combination of common decent, shared historical experiences, and valued cultural traits who make claims on behalf of their collective interests against either a state or other groups" (Gurr & Moore, 1997. p. 1081).

The model Gurr and Moore propose has grievances ("widely shared dissatisfaction among group members about their cultural, political, and/or economic standing vis-a-vis dominant groups") leading to mobilization ("capacity of an organization that represents an ethnic group to get its members to support collective action"),

[5] At least one of the authors of this chapter (Albert) believes that the fact that power has often been allocated along ethnic lines makes the distinction important. The variables that Gurr used to predict rebellion (such as grievances over political rights) historically do not exist apart from ethnic divides. This interconnectedness is one reason why that an interdisciplinary approach is important to ethnopolitical conflict resolution. As we will see in most chapters of this Handbook, the failure to deal with historical grievances, economic disparities, and political and social structures that strongly and negatively impact ethnic minorities, often exacerbate and perpetuate ethnic conflict.

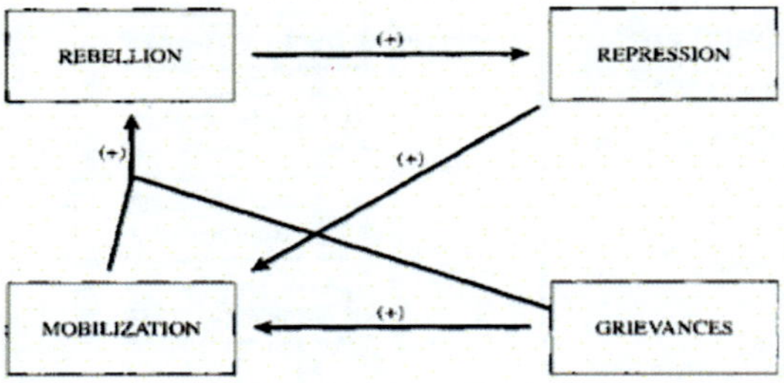

Fig. 1.3 The Gurr–Moore (2008) model of antecedents to rebellion

which in turn leads to rebellion ("concerted campaign of violent action used by organizations claiming to represent an ethnic group to make claims against the state"), which then leads to repression ("action that states take to enforce claims against an ethnic group" (p. 1081), and finally, repression leads to mobilization. Each of the variables listed above are derived from a number of other variables and the coding scheme is presented in the paper. For example, the repression variable has two factors: Severity of regime action (a six-item scale from "Conventional Policing" to "Geno/politicide") and outcome of last incident (a five-item scale ranging from +2 (regime win) to −2 (regime transformation)). Similar scales were used for the other three variables. Additional variables (democratic power, group coherence, political and economic discrimination, demographic distress, lost autonomy, past repression, and past repression success) which were predicted to form part of the original four variables were also included in the three-stage least squares analysis (Fig. 1.3).

The results of the analysis indicated that rebellion was predicted by mobilization and international rebellion, mobilization by group coherence and grievances, grievances by demographic distress and past repression, and repression by past repression success. In general, the model proposed by Gurr and Moore was mostly confirmed. The model is diagrammed in Fig. 1.2.

It is important to reiterate that the analysis was performed on data from the 1980s. To answer the "so what" question, the authors use the results to predict rebellion in the 1990s for the groups in the analysis. The predictive equations suggest that the groups that are most likely to engage in ethnopolitical rebellion and who have not engaged in active rebellion earlier are the Tibetans and Muslim Turkomen (Uighur) in China and the Shi'a in Saudi Arabia. The Uighur did rebel, but a decade later than the predictive period used by these authors. The only one of the three groups that has not yet moved into a rebellion are the Shi'a in Saudi Arabia, though there have been numerous incidents of terrorism in that country; however, most seem to be perpetrated by radical Sunni groups allied with Al Qaeda. While ethnicity is included in the model by virtue of the selection of the population, the level of the variables is decidedly macro and is independent, in a measurement sense, of individually measured phenomenon. Hence, models of this type, based as they are on "hard" data, may be more likely to find favor with policy makers. At the same time, the difficulty in resolving communal conflicts may be due to the failure to include consideration of the "soft" aspects of intercultural relations such as the development of trust, the importance of dialogue, and other aspects which are addressed in this Handbook.

Earlier we mentioned the controversy that erupted in 2008 over the inevitability of ethnic conflict (Habyariman et al., 2008; Muller, 2008). This is an important debate since it goes to the center of the rationale for the present Handbook and similar works. Conflicts that are ethnically based, however few there are, are so horrific in their specifics that Habyariman and his colleagues would argue that scholars develop a kind of tunnel vision and assume that all conflicts will inevitably become ethnic in character. Muller (2008) partially agrees but also disagrees. He agrees that most conflicts will become ethnic, but disagrees that ethnic conflicts are rare. The nub of his argument is historical in essence. Since the breakup of the Hapsburg and Romanov empires at the end of the First World War, there has been a rise of ethnonationalism, the idea that every ethnic group will desire and work toward a nation that is ethnically homogeneous. Muller points to the tensions that have arisen even in multiethnic states (such as France) as a result of immigration and the concomitant rise in right-wing political movements to limit immigration or even expel those that have already arrived. (Some might consider that the appearance of anti-immigrant rhetoric in the 2010 election in the USA is another reflection of the trend toward ethnonationalism.[6] But it bears noting that anti-immigrant rhetoric has flourished at several points in the history of the USA. Early on, Italians and Irish were socially denigrated, Japanese were interned during World War II, and there are many other examples in countries besides the USA). Muller then argues that the drive toward the goals of ethnonationalism will continue and that the only way to prevent the conflict from breaking out into civil war is partition. He writes:

> Partition may thus be the most humane lasting solution to such intense communal conflicts. It inevitably creates new flows of refugees, but at least it deals with the problem at issue. The challenge for the international community in such cases is to separate communities in the most humane manner possible by aiding in transport, assuring citizenship rights in the new homeland, and providing financial aid for resettlement and economic absorption. The bill for all of this will be huge, but it will rarely be greater than the material costs of interjecting and maintaining a foreign military presence large enough to pacify the rival ethnic combatants or the moral cost of doing nothing. (Muller, 2008, p. 35)

Habyariman et al. (2008) reply that Muller assumes that ethnic identity results in ingroup favoritism and outgroup derogation. The first has been consistently demonstrated by the SIT research; the latter is much more problematic. Recall that Allport did not assume that the outgroup would necessarily be seen as possessing only negative characteristics. Habyariman and colleagues note that in their own studies using a variety of intergroup games in Uganda in which the participants were of different ethnic groups, no evidence was found of the outgroup being viewed and treated negatively. Other writers (Bhavnani, 2006), e.g., have noted that even in the presence of behavioral norms toward negative treatment of the outgroup, not every member of a group will engage in violence against that outgroup. More to the point of Muller's argument, Habyariman et al. note that the work of Laitin and colleagues (Fearson & Laitin, 2003) found that ethnically based civil wars are extremely rare (only 3 of 127 conflicts studied). In any case, partition might well involve increased conflict as populations would not want to leave homes that they and their forebearers had occupied for generations. One can recall that the movement during the Indian Wars of the 1800s in the USA of populations onto reservations was only accomplished after many bloody encounters between the white and Native American groups. The aftereffects of those population transfers still resonate in the consciousness of Native Americans (Brown, 1970; Trimble, 1987).

The Fearson and Laitin (2003) study is important in that it empirically gets at a critical and central question: what is "the relationship between ethnic and religious diversity ….and the susceptibility of a country to civil war?" (Fearson and Laitin, 2003, p. 82). The essential result is that the primary determinants of civil war are income (as per capita income), population size, and whether the state was recently formed. Ethnic and religious fractionalizations have each failed to reach significance. If their results are reproducible, then what we often label as ethnic wars are really internal insurgencies that occur when the population is poor and the government is weak. In states where the reverse is true (i.e., states with high per capita income, and strong and administratively responsive governments) and where there is a high ethnic or religious fractionalization, civil war is unlikely. Of course, this does not mean that such wars might not occur; it is just that they are unlikely given the results of Fearson and Laitin.

It should be noted that the work of Laitin and colleagues described above refers specifically to civil wars. We chose, in this Handbook, to take a somewhat broader view and focus on ethnic conflicts that can present themselves in both violent and nonviolent manifestations. How ubiquitous are these conflicts and their relationship to civil war is at the very least an open question. In any

[6] An interesting development in American politics is the rise of proposals to repeal the Fourteenth Amendment to the Constitution. This amendment defines a citizen as one who was born in the United States. The "Fourteenthers" wish to remove from citizenship children born from parents who were in the country illegally at the time of their birth.

case, assigning causation to aspect or variable is problematic, as issues such as ethnicity, perceived history, economics, and political rights, among others, may intertwine in very complex ways. The reader is advised to keep such complex causation in mind while reading the chapters that follow.

The results in both the Gurr and the Fearson and Laitin studies focus only on main effects. Main effects, after all, are more understandable by policy makers who generally disdain "nuanced" recommendations. At the same time, some of the explanations of the results (Particularly in the Fearson and Laitin study, e.g., Fig. 1.2. on page 83) verge on interactions. where they graph income and ethnic group size against the probability of civil war. Blimes examined the interaction hypothesis in a 2006 paper (Blimes, 2006) using the same data set that was used in the Fearson and Laitin (2003) study. Whereas the earlier study had used probit analysis[7] which assumes direct influences, Blimes opted for a heteroskedastic probit analysis which is useful for examining interactions. The results indicated that both ethnic fractionalization and "largest ethnic group" were significant as moderators. Blimes concluded that "While there is no direct effect, ethnic cleavages increase the likelihood that other determinants will have an effect" (p. 542). Thus, he finds that as the level of ethnic fractionalization increases, all of the direct effects increase, with the largest enhancement occurring for the per capita income. Blimes' findings also suggest that it is at moderate levels of ethnic fractionalization that there are many more variables that predict civil war. He concludes:

> …Looking at the lack of significant variables at [high fractionalization levels], it seems that as a country becomes extremely fractured, any advantage in solving collective action problems provided by ethnicity may be offset by the difficulties of a highly fractured population….One explanation is that a very large number of ethnic groups act more like a large number of veto players, which can actually hamper collective action between groups that are too weak to oppose a central government alone. (p. 544)

[7] Probit analysis is a type of regression analysis which allows binominal rather than normal distributions in the variables.

So, with Blimes' study, ethnicity is brought back as a player in understanding the basis of violent conflict. But, it is to be understood as having an indirect and not a direct effect in leading to such conflicts. In other words, ethnicity may provide the fertile ground under which other seeds can flourish. Does this mean that separating ethnic groups (i.e., partition), as Muller would have it, is an optimum solution? Probably not, since these data also indicate, with Fearson, etc., that well-functioning democratic governments with relatively high per capita incomes act as a brake on the kinds of tensions that lead to conflict.

3 Acculturation and Ethnic Conflict

We have not discussed the possible contribution of the vast corpus of research on acculturation (Gudykunst, 1998; Kim, 2001, 2008; Sam & Berry, 2006; Triandis, 1972; Ward, Bochner, & Furnham, 2001). This was not an accidental omission, but a deliberate decision. It is difficult to articulate the theories of acculturation (e.g., Ward's, ABC theory in Ward et al. 2001) which deal primarily with immigrant populations of various origins with the realities of violent conflict, ethnically based or not. Most of the conflicting groups are not recent immigrants and often have lived within their nations for generations, and have histories as long as that of the other groups with which they are contending. There are, of course, exceptions: Muslims in France (Duprez, 2009), the Netherlands (see Chap. 19 in this Handbook and Buruma, 2007), Germany, Spain (see Chap. 17 in this Handbook), and elsewhere. However, in these cases, the conflicts are not the result of mobilization (a critical precondition for the breakout of civil war), but rather the acts of individuals or small groups. Indeed, it would seem that the theories of acculturation often come into play after civil conflict has occurred, and the minority population flees to safer ground and becomes once again a stranger in a strange land. So, it would be fallacious to assert that the reason that minority populations mobilize and engage in civil violence is that they have not been acculturated. But, by the same token, it would be reasonable to assert that the failure of the majority to recognize the aspirations (including the values) of the minority is one of the preludes to rebellion.

The second reason for not including acculturation is that while the extensive corpus does exist and has proven useful in certain circumstances, there is still considerable controversy over the theory and method for assessment of an individual's status (Berry, 2009; Rudmin, 2009; Schwartz, Unger, Zamboanga, & Szapoczik, 2010). These difficulties relate directly to determining the effectiveness of any program of acculturating immigrant or minority groups (Mendenhall et al., 2004).

4 Globalization and Ethnic Conflict

The term "globalization" has achieved the status of a buzzword (Li, 2000) with many writers including it in the belief that it will add some cachet to their work. A Google books search finds the word having almost a vertical usage curve from about 1985 until 2000, whereas, for example, "acculturation" is falling into disuse (except in the pages of some journals like *The International Journal of Intercultural Relations*)[8] over the same time period. We can assume that the usage curve has continued its upward trajectory in the past decade. Freidman's recent book, articulating the benefits of globalization using the metaphor of a "flat world," has only enhanced the term's popularity (Friedman, 2005). It was only natural that some writers would turn attention to an examination of globalization's impact on the probability of ethnic conflict (Dutceac, 2004; Landis, 2008; Stanton, St. Marie, & Naghshpour, 2007).

One of the problems for researchers trying to link globalization to ethnic conflict is the lack of a consensus on how to define it. The most common definition was provided by Stiglitz:

> Fundamentally, it is the closer integration of the countries and peoples of the world which has been brought about by the enormous reduction of costs of transportation and communications and the breaking down of artificial barriers to the flow of goods, services, capital, knowledge and (to a lesser extent) people across borders. (Stiglitz, 2002)

This definition seems to focus almost entirely on economic factors. These factors may be useful for economists but are less useful for other social scientists. Other writers have put forth more nuisanced definitions (Bornmann & Schoonraad, 2001; Stanton et al., 2007). Bornmann and Schoonraad (2001) distinguish between economic (cf. Stiglitz's definition quoted above), social, and cultural globalization. Stanton et al. propose another tripartite split: economic, social, and political. Whatever definition one accepts, it is clear that the basis of globalization for all writers is economic and refers to the "liberalization of barriers to the movement of goods and services across national borders" (Landis, 2008, p. 338).

Despite the laudable attempts to clarify the definition of globalization, consensus has yet to develop on either a model relating it to ethnic conflict or how to confirm that relationship using reliable and valid data. It is this consensus failure that leads to a decision not to include extensive discussions of globalization in this chapter. At the same time, there is an interesting attempt to move toward resolving both of the issues described above.

Stanton et al. (2007) used each of their three types of globalization (economic, social, and political) as independent variables. They posit that economic globalization will increase ethnic conflict; social globalization will reduce ethnic conflict; and, finally, political globalization will increase ethnic conflict. For data sources, they used two databases: the MAR data set that we have described earlier and the KOF index of globalization (Dreher, 2006). As others have done (see above), the dependent variable (ethnic conflict) was divided into protest and rebellion and operationalized following Gurr and others.

[8] Indeed, the International Academy for Intercultural Research (the sponsor of IJIR) had globalization as its theme for the 2007 meeting in Groningen, The Netherlands.

Economic globalization was indexed by variables such as actual capital flows and restrictions of capital flows. Social globalization was indexed by personal contacts (e.g., foreign telephone calls), information flows, and cultural proximity (e.g., number of McDonald's restaurants per 100,000 populations). Political globalization is indexed by such variables as number of foreign embassies in the country, membership in international organizations, and participation in the UN Security Council.

The results indicated that economic globalization had no effect on the level of ethnic protest or rebellion. Social globalization has no effect on protest, but does reduce rebellion and, finally, political globalization increases both protest and rebellion. The apparently paradoxical impact of political globalization is understandable from the standpoint of minorities who may see the results of increasing foreign embassies and other entanglements as leading to increased immigration and other policies favoring elites. In other words, the flattening of the political world may be perceived as bringing little good to ethnic minorities and thus, under the right circumstances, may lead to more protest and rebellion.

These results are certainly provocative given the widespread notion that economic globalization will decrease ethnic conflict. What these data and those of the other macro-theorists described in this chapter indicate is that researches need to take an explicitly interdisciplinary approach to understand and predict ethnic conflict.

5 Steps Toward a Synthesis

Both the micro- (e.g., contact theory and its descendants) and the macro- (e.g., economic and political theory) theorists have important, though incomplete, stories to tell and they need to be brought together to form models that are maximally descriptive and predictive. The case studies in this book should form the basis for such collaboration. The desire to link micro- and macro-data is, the well-known, yet seldom solved levels of analysis problem. However, given that the ability of either approach to predict when protest and/rebellion will break out is not all that great, the need for the linkage is imperative. We do live in the world where, despite the rosy scenarios of the supporters of globalization, ethnic conflict, which may be rare, is, as Brubaker and Laitin (1998) aver, horrendous in its execution. We simply do not know how to put societies on watch lists with any degree of confidence, even though various groups have attempted such a listing.

One approach to resolve the level of analysis issue is to take the most "psychological" appearing variable that appears in the various macro-analyses. A good candidate is "grievances." Individuals who belong to an ethnic group might form a grievance for many reasons, some of which might have to do with past behavior of majority or controlling groups that have blocked physical and psychological goals of ethnic groups over a period of time. We might also find that the minority members, if we were to ask them, would have negative emotional reactions to the majority members. For many of the societies in the MAR database, we might ask if any such data might exist. Such databases might be languishing is some scholar's file drawer awaiting time and funding to carry out a proper analyses. One such database, largely unanalyzed, is the Atlas of Affective Word Meaning (Heise, 1969; Osgood, 1969; Osgood, May, & Miron, 1975; Sewell & Heise, 2010; Tzeng & Landis, 1978) that, while at least 3 decades old, gives a reasonably reliable and valid index of some the emotional content of some 620 words in over 30 language groups. In any case, if we could link up micro-level data as antecedents to, e.g., "grievances," there might well be a significant increase in the level of predictability. A first step might be a general call for scholars to search their file cabinets for databases that might be useful. It is, at the very least, well worth trying to make the linkages.

6 Plan of this Book

The chapters in the book could have been organized in probably as many ways as there are ethnopolitical conflicts. We have chosen a geographical organization. We invite the reader to imagine that they are starting out from Hawaii and flying westward around the world, stopping off at some 19 countries, and investigating the origin, course, and resolution, if any, of each ethnic conflict. We start from Hawaii for no particular reason except that the first editor of this book is domiciled there. It is, of course, a bit more complicated than that. Hawaii is unique in the USA in that it was a fully functioning independent and internationally recognized country which was, most certainly, illegally annexed to the USA in 1898 (Liliuokalanii, 1960 (1898)). That annexation, and the overthrow of the legitimate government in 1893, as Michael Salzman (Chap. 2) clearly indicates, has reverberated down through the decades, producing conflict (though not violent) in almost every action of the state and federal governments where the descendents of the indigenous peoples are concerned (Dyke, 2008; Okamura, 2008; Osorio, 2002; Silva, 2005). The unique characteristic of Hawaii made it a natural starting point for our travel around the world of ethnoic conflict, though, of course, with a different aim than the James Fitzpatrick Travelogues of the 1930s and 1940s.

The perceptive reader will notice that there are no chapters dealing with conflicts in the USA and Canada. Such conflicts certainly exist (black vs white, Native Americans vs the USA; First Peoples vs the Canadian Government, and Francophones vs Francophobes in Canada to name a few). However, much has been written about those conflicts, even in the 1987 and 2004 books referred to earlier (Boucher et al., 1987; Lee et al., 2004), that we could safely move on to other conflicts about which much less is known, at least in the Western world.

There are many other conflicts not covered in this book and hence, we make no assertions that it contains a complete coverage of important or even interesting situations. We had hoped to have chapters on conflicts in the former Soviet Union, South Africa, Darfur, South Sudan, Tibet, and other regions. In some cases, authors who had originally committed to the project were forced to withdraw due to other obligations. In others, the identification of suitable contributors came too late for proper vetting and editing, and we had to forgo those contributions. Perhaps they will appear in a future edition.

So, we move from Hawaii to New Zealand, and then to the Philippines, Sri Lanka, and Malaysia, all places located around the Rim of the Pacific. In two of the cases (Hawaii and New Zealand), the indigenous peoples share common ancestry and to some extent language. China and India as the two most populous countries in the world with multiple ethnicities were strong candidates for inclusion in the book. From Asia, we jump across to the Eastern Mediterranean where the conflicts share a possibly trivial aspect of involving groups that differ in religion. In all of the cases, the conflicts have been violent and have seemed to be intractable and even involved countries either going to war or where there was, or is, the threat of such a conflagration.

Africa has been the setting for some of the most violent and genocidal conflicts in recent years. We provide descriptions of two of these: Uganda and the Democratic Republic of the Congo. There are many others, for example, Darfur; but these two conflicts are, unfortunately, emblematic of those that have bedeviled the sub-Sahara.

From Central Africa, we move to the Iberian Peninsula, then up the Atlantic to France, and finally to the Netherlands. All the three countries have experienced internal conflict arising from the immigration of Muslim populations (Moroccans in the case of Spain, Algerians for the French, and Turks for the Dutch).

The final two chapters focus on Latin America (Mexico and Peru). In both cases, there are minority indigenous populations that are, or have been, in conflict with the majority group.

In all of the chapters, the editors imposed a common format with a fixed set of section headings to facilitate the reader's transitions between conflicts. It is our hope that this format will allow both the reader and the editors to draw rational lessons from the conflicts that can inform policy. We feel that such a structure is often missing in edited books; those volumes often seem like a disconnected set of journal articles with little justification for their appearance between the same set of book covers. We hope that our aim has been realized.

7 A Final Word

We have not answered the question that lies at the heart of this book: Is ethnic conflict inevitable? Park certainly believed that it was (Park, 1950; Yang, Power, Takaku, & Posas, 2004), as do most of the primordialists (Allport, 1954a; Brewer, 1996; Gaertner & Dovidio, 2000). The instrumentalists, particularly those that probe at the macro-level, clearly do not think it is inevitable and have considerable difficulty even finding situations where such conflict exits. The chapters in this book would seem to demonstrate that such conflict is by no means an isolated phenomenon; but whether it is an inevitable result of being human has yet to be answered. It is our hope that this book will spur scholars of all stripes, including neuroscientists, to strive to find an answer. At the conclusion of his foreword to the Boucher et al. (1987) book, the late distinguished social psychologist Ross Stagner wrote about how important it is to find ways to eliminate ethnic conflict from the world. The comment bears repeating for it is no less prophetic today than it was in 1987:

> It is trite to say that any specific problem calls for more research if we are to evolve a mutually acceptable solution to a group conflict. However, the alarming possibilities for mutually assured destruction makes it urgent that we pursue the study of group conflict at all levels. It is, quite literally, a matter of life and death. (Stagner, 1987, pp. 15–16)

References

Albert, R. D. (1983). The intercultural sensitizer or culture assimilator: A cognitive approach. In D. Landis & R. Brislin (Eds.), *Handbook of intercultural training* (Vol. 2, pp. 186–217). Elmsford, NY: Pergamon.

Allport, G. W. (1954a). *The nature of prejudice*. Reading, MA: Addison-Wesley.

Allport, G. W. (1954b). The historical background of modern social psychology. In G. Lindzey (Ed.), *Handbook of social psychology* (Vol. I, pp. 5–56). Reading, MA: Addison-Wesley.

Allport, G. (1968). The historical background of modern social psychology. In G. Lindzey & E. Aronson (Eds.), *The handbook of social psychology* (2nd ed.). Reading, MA: Addison-Wesley.

Axelrod, R., & Hammond, R. A. (2003). *The evolution of ethnocentric behavior*. Paper presented at the Midwest Political Science Convention.

Berry, J. W. (2009). A critique of critical acculturation. *International Journal of Intercultural Relations, 33*, 361–371.

Bhavnani, R. (2006). Ethnic norms and interethnic violence: Accounting for mass participation in the Rwandan genocide. *Journal of Peace Research, 43*(6), 651–669.

Blimes, R. J. (2006). The indirect effect of ethnic heterogeneity on the likelihood of civil war onset. *Journal of Conflict Resolution, 50*(4), 536–547.

Bornmann, E., & Schoonraad, N. (2001). The many faces of globalization. *Mousaion, 19*(1), 83–114.

Boucher, J., Landis, D., & Clark, K. A. (1987). *Ethnic conflict: International perspectives*. Newbury Park, CA: Sage.

Brewer, M. B. (1996). When contact is not enough: Social identity and intergroup cooperation. *International Journal of Intercultural Relations, 20*, 291–303.

Brown, D. (1970). *Bury my heart at Wounded Knee: An Indian history of the American West*. New York, NY: Holt, Rinehart & Winston.

Brown, R., & Hewstone, M. (2005). An integrative theory of intergroup contact. *Advances in Experimental Social Psychology, 37*, 255–343.

Brubaker, R., & Laitin, D. D. (1998). Ethnic and nationalistic violence. *Annual Review of Sociology, 24*, 423–452.

Buruma, I. (2007). *Murder in Amsterdam: The death of Theo van Gogh and the Limits of tolerance*. London: Atlantic Books.

Campbell, D. (1998). *National deconstruction: Violence, identity, and justice in Bosnia*. Minneapolis, MN: University of Minnesota Press.

Caselli, F., & Coleman, W. J. (2010). *On the theory of ethnic conflict*. London: London School of Economics.

Cushner, K., & Landis, D. (1996). The intercultural sensitizer. In D. Landis & R. Bhagat (Eds.), *Handbook of intercultural training* (2nd ed., pp. 185–202). Thousand Oaks, CA: Sage.

Dansby, M. R., Stewart, J. B., & Webb, S. C. (Eds.). (2001). *Managing diversity in the military*. New Brunswik, NJ: Transaction Publishers.

Dixon, J. A., Durrheim, K., & Tredoux, C. (2005). Beyond the optimal strategy: A "reality check" for the contact hypothesis. *American Psychologist, 60*, 697–711.

Dreher, A. (2006). Index of Globilization (archived at www.globalization-index.org) (Publication. Retrieved January 1, 2011.

Duprez, D. (2009). Urban rioting as an indicator of crisis in the integration model for ethnic minority youth in

France. *Journal of Ethnic and Migration Studies, 35*(4), 753–770.

Dutceac, A. (2004). Globalization and ethnic conflict: Beyond the liberal-nationalist distinction. *The Global Review of Ethnopolitics, 3*(2), 20–39.

Dyke, J. M. V. (2008). *Who owns the crown lands of Hawai'i*. Honolulu, HI: University of Hawai'i Press.

Fearson, J. D., & Laitin, D. D. (2003). Ethnicity, insurgency, and civil war. *American Political Science Review, 97*(1), 73–90.

Forbes, H. D. (2004). Ethnic conflict and the contact hypothesis. In Y.-T. Lee, C. McCauley, F. Moghaddam, & S. Worchel (Eds.), *The psychology of ethnic and cultural conflict* (pp. 69–88). Westport, CT: Praeger.

Friedman, T. (2005). *The World is flat*. New York, NY: Farrar, Straus & Giroux.

Gaertner, S. L., & Dovidio, J. F. (2000). *Reducing intergroup bias: The common ingroup identity model*. Philadelphia, PA: Psychology Press.

Gaertner, L., & Insko, C. A. (2000). Intergroup discrimination in the Minimal Group Paradigm: Categorization, Reciprocation, or Fear. *Journal of Personality and Social Psychology, 79*(1), 79–94.

Gonzalez, R., Sirlopu, D., & Kessler, T. (2010). Prejudice among Peruvians and Chileasns as a function of identity, intergroup contact, acculturation preferences, and intergroup emotions. *Journal of Social Issues, 66*(4), 803–824.

Gudykunst, W. B. (1998). *Bridging differences: Effective intergroup communication*. Thousand Oaks, CA: Sage.

Gurr, T. R. (1993). Why minorities rebel: A global analysis of communal moblization and conflict since 1945. *International Political Science Review, 14*(2), 161–201.

Gurr, T. R., & Moore, W. H. (1997). Ethnopolitical rebellion: A cross-sectional analysis of the 1980s with risk assessment for the 1990s. *American Journal of Political Science, 41*(4), 1079–1103.

Gurr, T. R. (2007). Minorities, nationalists, and Islamists: Managing communal conflict in the twenty-first century. In C.A. Crocker, F. O. Hampton, & P. Aall (Eds.), Leashing the Dogs of War: Conflict Management in a Divided World. Washington, D.C.: United States Institute of Peace Press.

Habyariman, J., Humphreys, M., Posner, D., & Weinstein, J. (2008). Better institutions, not partition. *Foreign Affairs, 87*(4), 158–141.

Heise, D. (1969). Some methodological issues in semantic differential research. *Psychological Bulletin, 72*, 406–422.

Howell, J. (1978). Horn of Africa: Lessons from the Sudan conflict. *International Affairs, 54*(3), 421–436.

Kauth, M., & Landis, D. (1996). Applying lessons learning from minority integration in the military. In G. M. Herek, J. B. Jobe, & R. M. Carney (Eds.), *Out in force: Sexual orientation and the military* (pp. 86–105). Chicago, IL: University of Chicago Press.

Kaznatcheev, A. (2010). The cognitive cost of ethnocentrism. Paper presented at the The Cognitive Society, Portland, OR.

Kelman, H. C. (2005). Building trust among enemies: The central challenge for international conflict resolution. *International Journal of Intercultural Relations, 29*(6), 639–650.

Kim, Y. Y. (2001). *Becoming intercultural: An integrative theory of communication and cross-cultural adaptation*. Thousand Oaks, CA: Sage.

Kim, Y. Y. (2008). Intercultural personhood: Globalization and a way of being. *International Journal of Intercultural Relations, 32*, 359–368.

Lake, D. A., & Rothchild, D. (1998). *The international spread of ethnic conflict: Fear, diffusion, and escalation*. Princeton, NJ: Princeton University Press.

Lambert, W. E., & Jakobovitz, L. A. (1960). Verbal satiation and changes in the intensity of meaning. *Journal of Experimental Psychology, 60*(6), 376–383.

Landis, D. (2008). Globalization, migration into urban centers, and cross-cultural training. *International Journal of Intercultural Relations, 32*(4), 337–348.

Landis, D., & Boucher, J. (1987). Themes and models of conflict. In J. Bourcher, D. Landis, & K. A. Clark (Eds.), *Ethnic conflict: International perspectives* (pp. 18–32). Newbury Park, CA: Sage.

Landis, D., Brislin, E., & Hulgus, J. (1985). Attibutional training vs contact in acculturative learning: A laboratory study. *Journal of Applied Social Psychology, 15*(5), 466–383.

Landis, D., Day, H., McGrew, P., Thomas, J., & Miller, A. (1976). Can a Black "culture assimilator" increase racial understanding? *Journal of Social Issues, 32*, 169–183.

Lee, Y.-T., McCauley, C., Moghaddam, F., & Worchel, S. (Eds.). (2004). *The psychology of ethnic and cultural conflict*. Westport, CT: Praeger.

Lee, Y.-T., Moghaddam, F., McCauley, C., & Worchel, S. (2004). The global challenge of ethnic and cultural conflict. In Y.-T. Lee, C. McCauley, F. Moghaddam, & S. Worchel (Eds.), *The psychology of ethnic and cultural conflict* (pp. 3–20). Westport, CT: Praeger.

Li, V. (2000). What in a name? Questioning "globalization". *Cultural Critique, 45*, 1–39.

Licklidder, R. (1993). *Stop the killing: How civil wars end*. New York, NY: New York University Press.

Liliuokalanii. (1960(1898)). *Hawaii's Story*. Honolulu, HI: Mutual Publishing.

Lim, M., Metzler, R., & Bar-Yam, Y. (2007). Global pattern formation and ethnic/cultural violence. *Science, 317*, 1540–1544.

Mack, R. W., & Synder, R. C. (1957). The analysis of social conflict–toward an overview and synthesis. *Journal of Conflict Resolution, 1*, 212–248.

Marks, A., Szalacha, L., Lararre, M., Boyd, M., & Coll, C. G. (2007). Emerging ethnic identity and inter-ethnic group social preferences in middle childhood: Findings from the Children of Immigrants Development in Context (CIDS) study. *International Journal of Behavioral Development, 31*(4), 501–513.

Marsella, A. J. (2005). Culture and conflict: Understanding, negotiating, and reconciling conflicting constructions of reality. *International Journal of Intercultural Relations, 29*(6), 651–673.

McGarry, J., & O'Leary, B. (1995). *Explaining Northern Ireland*. Oxford: Blackwell.
Mendenhall, M., Shahl, G., Ehnert, I., Oddou, G., Osland, J., & Kuhlmann, T. (2004). Evaluation studies of cross-cultural training programs: A review of literature from 1988 to 2000. In D. Landis, J. Bennett, & M. Bennett (Eds.), *Handbook of intercultural training* (3rd ed., pp. 129–144). Thousand Oaks, CA: Sage.
Moskos, C. C., & Butler, J. S. (1996). *All that we can be: Black leadership and racial integration the army Way*. New York: Basic Books.
Mullahy, P. (1952). *Oedipus: Myth and complex*. New York, NY: Hermitage House.
Muller, J. Z. (2008). Us and them. *Foreign Affairs, 87*(2), 18–35.
Okamura, J. Y. (2008). *Ethnicity and inequality in Hawaii*. Philadelphia, PA: Temple University Press.
Osgood, C. (1969). On the whys and wherefores of E, P, and A. *Journal of Personality and Social Psychology, 12*(3), 194–199.
Osgood, C., May, W., & Miron, M. (1975). *Cross-cultural universals of affective word meaning*. Urbana, IL: University of Illinois Press.
Osorio, J. K. K. (2002). *Dismenbering lahui: A history of the Hawaiian nation to 1887*. Honolulu, HI: University of Hawaii Press.
Park, R. (1950). *Race and culture* (Vol. I). Glencoe,IL: Free Press.
Pedersen, P., & Pope, M. (2010). Inclusive cultural empathy for successful global leadership. *American Psychologist, 65*(8), 841–854.
Pettigrew, T. (1997). *How to think like a social scientist*. New York: Harper-Collins.
Pettigrew, T. (2008). Future directions for intergroup contact theory and research. *International Journal of Intercultural Relations, 32*, 187–199.
Pettigrew, T., & Troop, L. (2006). A metanalytic test of intergroup contact theory. *Journal of Personality and Social Psychology, 90*(3), 751–783.
Phinney, J. S., Jacoby, B., & Silva, C. (2007). Positive intergroup attitudes: The role of ethnic identity. *International Journal of Behavioral Development, 31*(5), 478–490.
Piaget, J. (1961). *Les Mecanismes Perceptifs*. Paris: Presses Universitaires de France.
Randolf, G., Landis, D., & Tzeng, O. C. S. (1977). The effects of time and practice upon culture assimilator training. *International Journal of Intercultural Relations, 1*(4), 105–119.
Rudmin, F. (2009). Constructs, measurements, and models of acculturation and acculturative stress. *International Journal of Intercultural Relations, 33*, 106–123.
Sam, D. L., & Berry, J. W. (Eds.). (2006). *The Cambridge handbook of acculturation psychology*. Cambridge, UK: Cambridge University Press.
Schwartz, S. J., Unger, J. B., Zamboanga, B. L., & Szapoczik, J. (2010). Rethinking the concept of acculturation: Implications for theory and research. *American Psychologist, 65*(4), 237–251.
Sewell, A., & Heise, D. (2010). Racial differences in sentiments: Exploring variant cultures. *International Journal of Intercultural Relations, 34*(4), 400–412.
Sherif, M., Harvey, O., White, B., Hood, W., & Sherif, C. (1961). *Intergroup conflict and cooperation: The Robber's cave experiment*. Norman, OK: University of Oklahoma Press.
Silva, N. K. (2005). *Aloha betrayed: Native Hawaiian resistence to American colonialism*. Durham, NC: Duke University Press.
Stanton, S. S., St.Marie, J. J., & Naghshpour, S. (2007). *The effects of globablization on ethnic conflict: A cross-sectional time-series analysis*. Paper presented at the Midwest Political Science Association.
Star, S. A., Williams, R. M., & Stoufer, S. A. (1949). Negro infantry platoons in white companies. In S. A. Stoufer, E. A. Suchman, L. C. DeVinney, S. A. Star, & R. A. Williams (Eds.), *Adustment during army life* (Vol. I). Princeton, NJ: Princeton University Press.
Stephan, W. G., & Finlay, K. (1999). The role of empathy in improving intergroup relations. *Journal of Social Issues, 55*(4), 729–743.
Stephan, W. G., Stephan, C. W., & Gudykunst, W. B. (1999). Anxiety in intergroup relations: A comparison of anxiety/uncertainty management theory and integrated threat theory. *International Journal of Intercultural Relations, 23*(4), 613–628.
Stiglitz, J. (2002). *Civilization and its discontents*. New York, NY: W.W. Norton.
Tajfel, H. (1970). Experiments in intergroup discrimination. *Scientific American, 233*, 96–102.
Tajfel, H., & Turner, J. C. (1979). An integrative theory of intergroup conflict. In W. G. Austin & S. Worchel (Eds.), *The social psychology of intergroup relations*. Monterey, CA: Sage.
Thomas, P. J., & Thomas, M. D. (1996). Integration of women in the military: Parallels to the progress of homosexuals? In G. M. Herek, J. B. Jobe, & R. M. Carney (Eds.), *Out in force: Sexual orientation and the military* (pp. 65–85). Chicago, IL: University of Chicago Press.
Triandis, H. C. (1972). *The analysis of subjective culture*. New York, NY: Wiley-Interscience.
Triandis, H. C. (1977). *Interpersonal behavior*. Monterey, CA: Brooks/Cole.
Triandis, H. C., Brislin, R., & Hui, C. (1988). Cross-cultural training across the individualism-collectivism divide. *International Journal of Intercultural Relations, 12*, 269–289.
Trimble, J. (1987). American Indians and interethnic conflict. In J. Boucher, D. Landis, & K. A. Clark (Eds.), *Ethnic conflict: International perspectives* (pp. 208–230). Newbury Park, CA: Sage.
Turner, J. C., Hogg, M., Oakes, P., Reicher, S., & Wetherell, M. (1987). *Rediscovering the social group: A self-categorization theory*. Oxford, UK: Basil Blackwell.
Tzeng, O., & Landis, D. (1978). Three mode multidimensional scaling with points of view solutions. *Multivariate Behavioral Research, 13*, 181–213.

Ward, C., Bochner, S., & Furnham, A. (2001). *The psychology of culture shock* (2nd ed.). Philadelphia, PA: Taylor & Francis.

Weldon, D. F., Carlston, D. E., Rissman, A. K., Slobodin, L., & Triandis, H. C. (1975). A laboratory test of effect of culture assimilator training. *Journal of Personality and Social Psychology, 32*, 300–310.

Worchel, S. (2004). Some unique characteristics of ethnic conflict and their implications for managing the conflict. In Y.-T. Lee, C. McCauley, F. Moghaddam, & S. Worchel (Eds.), *The psychology of ethnic and cultural conflict* (pp. 289–306). Westport, CT: Praeger.

Xu, X., Zuo, X., Wang, X., & Han, S. (2009). Do you feel my pain? Racial group membership modulates empathic neural responses. *Journal of Neuroscience, 29*(26), 8825–8829.

Yang, P. Q., Power, S., Takaku, A., & Posas, L. (2004). Immigration and ethnic conflict in comparative perspective. In Y. T. Lee, C. McCauley, F. Moghaddam, & S. Worchel (Eds.), *The psychology of ethnic and cultural conflict* (pp. 89–112). Westport, CT: Praeger.

Yee, M. D., & Brown, R. (1992). Self-evaluations and intergroup attitudes in children aged three to nine. *Child Development, 63*, 619–629.

Zajonc, R. (1968). Attitudinal Effects of mere exposure. Journal of Personality and Social Psychology: Monograph Supplement. V. 9, #2, Part2.

Part I

Conflict in the Pacific Rim

2 Ethnocultural Conflict and Cooperation in Hawai'i

Michael Salzman

Hawaii Chapter Summary

Salzman examines the development of ethnocultural tolerance in Hawaii as a potential model for the intentional creation of optimal intergroup contact. Various theoretical lenses are utilized to examine the progression from initial cultural conflict to relative harmony. Values inherent in Hawaiian culture are also explored as they have impacted the current cultural context.

Hawaii is recognized as unique in many respects including in its ecology, geography, and ethnic diversity. While Salzman points out that some cultural conflict is still present in Hawaii, cultural relations are largely reflective of the Hawaiian value of "Aloha Spirit" which is credited with affecting acceptance of the various cultures represented. The high rate of intermarriage in Hawaii is also discussed as it positively impacts cultural tolerance.

A historical overview of the colonization of Hawaii is provided and Terror Management Theory (TMT) applied to explore the mechanisms through which the loss of native culture creates a state in which conflict is imminent. The labor movement is presented as a catalyst which shifted Hawaii from conflict, through creation of a superordinate identity based on common goals. Salzman presents this shift as the beginning of "local" culture which is inclusive of individuals sharing common values and language.

Salzman concludes with a discussion of various theoretical models applicable to cultural contact. Factors that create conflict are examined along with those that enhance mutual appreciation. A potential solution to conflict styles of contact is provided which includes the intentional creation of specific conditions such as those exhibited in Hawaii. Hope for a future of people united in a common goal is proff.

Cheryl Jorgensen

M. Salzman (✉)
Department of Educational Psychology, University of Hawai'i at Manoa, Manoa, HI, USA
e-mail: msalzman@hawaii.edu

D. Landis and R.D. Albert (eds.), *Handbook of Ethnic Conflict: International Perspectives*, International and Cultural Psychology, DOI 10.1007/978-1-4614-0448-4_2,

1 Introduction

The fact of our increasing awareness of cultural and ethnic diversity does not provide any assurance that our multicultural future will be a just one based on respect, inclusion, and equality. The history of humankind is bloody with examples of culturally and racially diverse peoples slaughtering each other over differences large and small. History also provides evidence of moments and periods where intergroup relations were mutually beneficial, respectful, and nourishing. Humans possess these and other potentials. Demographics make clear that our future will be defined by how we address the promise and perils of diversity. The outcome of our efforts or our self-absorbed neglect will largely determine whether we shape a future nourished by justice, respect, and appreciation of human diversity, or one of intolerance, stratification, conflict, violence, and exploitation supported by racism. World history offers evidence of both potentials. The stakes are high (see Huntington, 1996).

Academics and popular opinion perceive ethnocultural relations in Hawai‘i as characterized by tolerance, equality, and harmony. The elevation of Hawai‘i as a multicultural model has emphasized Hawai‘i's tradition of tolerance and peaceful coexistence; harmonious ethnic relations and a high rate of intermarriage; equality of opportunity and status; and a shared local culture and identity (Okumura, 2008). Okumura questions the validity of the model while agreeing that the tradition of tolerance and peaceful coexistence is essentially valid because Hawai‘i's people do essentially endorse the norm of tolerance, respect, and appreciation of other ethnicities as a reflection of a strong Native Hawaiian inspired norm called the "Aloha Spirit." Okumura calls attention to a statewide survey in 1996, published in the Honolulu Advertiser, which found that 83% of its 800 respondents thought that the islanders from different ethnic groups "get along better than in other places" and 87% agreed that the aloha spirit is "important in how people live (cited in Pratt, 2000)." However, he strongly disputes the assertion that there is essential equality of opportunity and status among ethnic groups, and notes the "blatant racism of both Whites and non-Whites against Filipino Americans and Japanese Americans prior to World War II (p. 10)." He also criticizes the notion of Hawai‘i as a multicultural model based on the plantation experience as it ignores the historical experiences and contributions of Native Hawaiians "as the indigenous people whose lands were seized for the development of the plantation industry (p. 10)." However, as we shall see, these and other racisms and the stereotypes that supported them were overcome at a historical moment by an "interracial labor movement (Jung, 2006)" that allowed for the construction of a superordinate identity of workers whose interests were seen to be in contradiction to the concentration of capital (the Big Five) that dominated their lives. The "Big Five" (American Factors; C. Brewer & Company; Alexander & Baldwin; Castle & Cooke; and Theo Davies & Company) were agencies descended from the original missionary families that controlled the sugar industry and its related enterprises and dominated the economic and political life of the islands (Jung, 2006).

This chapter will apply relevant theory in an analysis of a Hawai‘i labor movement that united disparate ethnicities into a superordinate identity, which, while acknowledging and appreciating its diversity, transformed the politics of Hawai‘i from a conservative feudal and colonial past to what is arguably the most progressive state in the USA (the election of seemingly centrist Republican governor and some interisland variation not withstanding). The author, then, seeks to identify factors that contribute to both ethnocultural cooperation and conflict on this remote landmass in the middle of the Pacific – a place that is home to diverse peoples (e.g., Japanese-Americans, Native Hawaiians, Filipino-Americans, Caucasian-Americans, etc.) with diverse (and shared) worldviews as well as varied experiences with the political, economic, and cultural realities of Hawai‘i.

2 Current Status

2.1 The Ecological and Geographical Context

The Hawaiian archipelago is a string of islands and reefs, 3,300 km long, that forms a broad arc in the mid-Pacific. The archipelago begins in the east with the island of Hawaii and ends almost at the international date line with a small speck in the ocean called Kure Atoll. Only the easternmost 650 km of the state contains islands of any size, as well as almost all of the state's population. It is this portion that is usually considered as the actual "Hawai'i." The eight main islands of Hawaii – Oahu, Hawaii, Maui, Kauai, Lanai, Molokai, Niihau, and Kahoolawe – contain more than 99% of the state's land area and all but a handful of its people. The island of Hawaii, at 8,150 km^2, comprises nearly two-thirds of the state's total area, and is often referred to as simply the Big Island. The smallest of the eight, Kahoolawe, is 125 km^2 and is uninhabited.

The isolation of the Hawaiian islands, coupled with their generally temperate climate and great environmental variation, has created a plant and bird community of great diversity. There are several thousand plants native to Hawai'i that are not found naturally anywhere else; 66 uniquely Hawaiian land birds have also been identified. Interestingly, there were no land mammals on the islands until humans arrived. Hawai'i is near the middle of the Pacific Ocean. Honolulu, the state capital, is 3,850 km west of San Francisco, California, 6,500 km east of Tokyo, Japan, and roughly 7,300 km northeast of the Australian coast. This might be viewed as a case of extreme isolation, and until the last few centuries, this was probably true. But as countries around the Pacific Basin began to communicate more with one another and to use the ocean's resources, these islands became an important center of interaction. The Hawaiian chain is merely the visible portion of a series of massive volcanoes. The ocean floor in this area is 4,000–5,000 m below sea level. Hence, for a volcano to break the water's surface requires a mountain already approaching 5 km in height. Such is the ecological and geographical context within which the diverse populations of Hawai'i have lived and interacted (Figs. 2.1 and 2.2).

Fig. 2.1 A view of the Hawaiian Islands from space

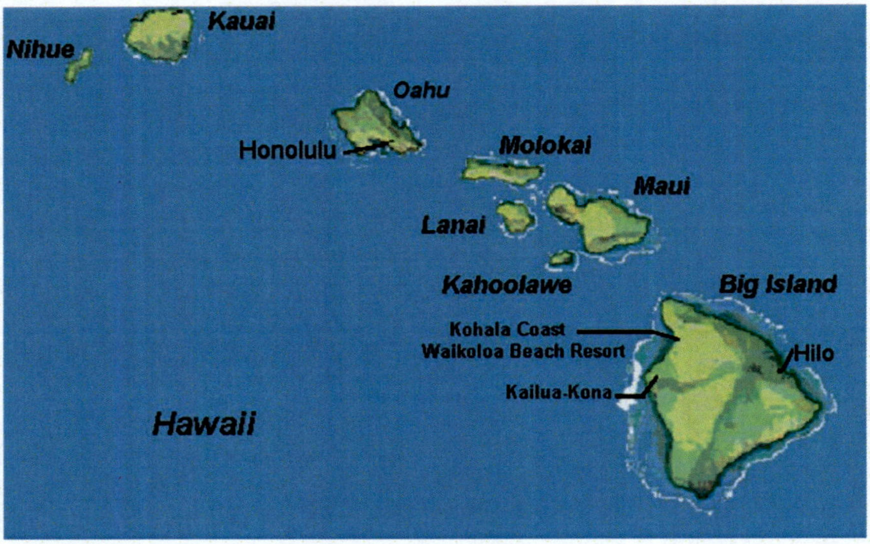

Fig. 2.2 Hawaiian islands

2.2 Ethnocultural Diversity in Hawai'i

Hawai'i is the most diverse state in the USA. It remains the state with the highest ethnic minority population in the nation according to the annual U.S. Census Bureau estimate (Honolulu Advertiser, May 1, 2008). According to the estimate, ethnic minorities account for 75% of Hawai'i's population. Asians make up 55%, and Native Hawaiians and Pacific Islanders are 21% of the state's population. In the context of this diversity, Hawai'i has been described as a model of ethnocultural harmony, a multicultural model for a diverse world to emulate.

The ethnic, racial, and cultural realities are complex and this complexity may contribute to values of tolerance and respect for diversity that most observers acknowledge. The high rate of intermarriage that has occurred throughout Hawai'i's history has produced a multicultural and mixed racial reality. Interracial and interethnic marriage was well established by the early nineteenth century between Hawaiian women and European and American men and, with some exceptions, there was limited social stigma attached to outmarrying. The prevalence of intermarriage increased progressively over the decades. Hawai'i's overall rate of intermarriage between 1983 and 1994 accounts for almost half of all marriages involving at least one Hawai'i state resident (Fu & Heaton, 1997). The state of Hawai'i has (U.S. Census Bureau, 2002) the highest percentage of people who reported being of two or more races in the 2000 census (21%), with the second highest state being Alaska with a multiracial population of only 5.4% of the population.

2.3 Race, Ethnicity, and Culture in Hawai'i

Race, ethnicity, and culture are related and often overlapping categories, but they are not identical. *Race* may be considered an arbitrary classification of modern humans based on shared physical characteristics typically encompassing peoples from a common geographic origin and often including multiple cultural and ethnic groups. *Ethnicity* refers to a common ancestry through which individuals have evolved shared values and customs over time. *Culture* may be thought of as a meaning system that addresses the essential existential questions of life as well as provides values to live by and a way to *be* (Becker, 1971). Although the term *interracial* and *interracialism* are used in this paper (consistent with Jung, 2006) to describe the accomplishment of and inclusive multiethnic labor movement, *interethnic* is probably more appropriate given Hawai'i's demographic landscape (i.e., Japanese and Chinese ethnicities are both classified racially as Asian).

Therefore, throughout this paper, ethnicity and culture will be emphasized over "race" as most salient in Hawai'i's diverse reality because "people of Hawai'i attribute greater social significance to the presumed cultural differences that distinguish groups from one another than to phenotypic differences such as skin color" (Okumura, 2008, p. 6).

There is no majority group in Hawai'i. The 2000 U.S. census, which allowed for people to identify with more that one racial category, has indicated the complexity and overlap of phenotypical characteristics. In the census of 2000, more than one-fifth (21.4%) of Hawai'i's residents identified with two or more races. This is unusual and is almost nine times higher than reported in the USA in general.

The largest ethnic group in Hawai'i as indicated by the census is White or "Haole." The literal meaning of the Hawaiian term "Haole" is foreigner. In popular usage, this term has been used to denote "Caucasian" and is experienced by some as pejorative. In the 2000 U.S. census, 39.3% reported being either White or White alone, or in any combination with other groups in a total Hawai'i population of 1,211,537. Those who reported being only White totaled 24.3%. Caucasians have been the largest percentage of the population since the 1960s following statehood. The second largest ethnic group is Japanese-Americans who total (alone or in combination) about one-fourth (24.5%) of the population. One-third of these reported mixed ancestry as a result of a great increase in the rate of "outmarriage" since 1970 among the *sansei* (third) and *yonsei* (fourth) generations. Japanese-Americans were the largest ethnic group in Hawai'i from 1900 to 1960s (e.g., 43% in 1920). Filipino-Americans, the largest immigrating group to Hawai'i, represent 22.8% (Filipino alone or in combination) of the population. This is a linguistically and culturally diverse group that is often differentiated by being "local" by virtue of being born in Hawai'i, or "immigrant" if they were not. It is likely that due to a relatively higher birth rate, Filipinos will emerge as the second largest ethnic group in Hawai'i by the 2010 census.

Native Hawaiians, the indigenous people of Hawai'i, are the fourth largest group comprising 19.8% (Hawaiian only or in combination) of the population of the state. The decimation of the Hawaiian population through contact with imported diseases and the impact of colonization are well documented and tragic. The population has been recovering from near extinction, although the percentage of "pure" Hawaiians has continued to decline to the point where some demographers predict that by 2044 there will be no "pure" Hawaiians left (Noyes, 2003). Before colonization and the introduction of imported diseases decimated the population of Native Hawaiians in the nineteenth century, they were obviously the most populous group on the islands. This potent underlying reality of ethnocultural relations in Hawai'i will be elaborated later in this chapter.

Chinese-Americans (alone or in any combination) constituted 14.1% of the state's population, with about one-third of that percentage claiming to be multiethnic or multiracial. In the 2000 census, Latinos/Hispanics (alone or in combination) constituted 7.2% of Hawai'i's population in 2000. Of this group, only Puerto Ricans, who arrived as plantation workers in 1900, have had a historical presence in Hawai'i. Koreans (alone or in any combination) constituted 3.4% of Hawai'i's population. They represent two communities. The first are the descendants of the 56,500 immigrants who arrived in 1905 to work on the sugar plantations, who were later joined by 1,000 "picture brides" between 1910 and 1920, and the second group are people who arrived after 1965. The immigration of other Asian groups such as (in descending order of population) Vietnamese Americans, Asian Indians, Laotian Americans, and Cambodian Americans reflects their much later immigration (Okumura, 2008). African–Americans (alone or in combination) represented 2.8% of the population, with most associated with the U.S. military.

Samoans are the next most populous Pacific Island group in Hawai'i (2.3%, Samoan only or in combination). There are increasing numbers of

"Micronesians" arriving in Hawai'i since 1990, particularly Marshallese and Chuukese who, like Samoans, can enter the USA without restriction.

Such is the multicultural and ethnic landscape of Hawai'i.

2.4 Causes of Ethnocultural Conflict

In the spring of 2007, three ethnicity-related incidents occurred in Hawai'i (Okumura, 2008). These highly publicized incidents may reveal tensions existing under the surface of a Hawai'i that has been described as a multicultural model characterized by ethnocultural tolerance, appreciation, and harmony.

In the first incident, a White male Iraq war veteran accidentally hit a parked car while entering a parking stall. A 16-year-old male joined by his 45-year-old father, both with a recognizable Hawaiian names, violently attacked the White male's car and occupants while yelling "fucking Haoles." The attack resulted in injury and unconsciousness of the White male and his wife.

In the second incident, a 34-year-old photography editor had a fatal encounter with a 21-year-old "local" male from Nanakuli (a Hawaiian community) on the leeward (west) coast who became angry at the photographer's picture-taking and delivered a lethal blow to the man's neck.

In the third incident, a popular Native Hawaiian radio host dismissed the comments of a White state senator by suggesting that his "blue eyes" and mainland origins denied the possibility of him being considered "local" and, therefore, excluded "Haoles" by using the original race-based meaning of "local."

Also in 2007, five South Kona men were accused of attacking two groups of mostly Caucasian campers at a beach in an alleged hate crime and were indicted on assault and terroristic threatening charges. The accused had recognizable Hawaiian names, and the indictment alleges that the men selected their victims because of hostility toward the actual or perceived race of the campers (Dayton, 2008). The campers reported that their assailants made comments such as "Any…haoles want to die?"

Okamura (2008) suggests that these encounters indicate "deep and persisting fissures in ethnic relations and the widening gap between the dominant and subjugated ethnic groups in Hawai'i society…and should be understood as constituting desperate expressions of protest against continuing conditions of institutionalized inequality directed to some of those considered responsible for maintaining that inequality" (p. 189). Although one should be cautious about overgeneralizing, these events may be considered in the light of the continuing displacement of Hawaiian people from their homes and land. The lack of affordable rentals and development policies designed to attract the affluent have exacerbated the homeless problem in such communities as the predominantly Hawaiian Waianae coast of Oahu. On October 15, 2006, the Honolulu Advertiser reported that the situation has spiraled into a full-scale social crisis: 16 miles of ramshackle tents packed with scores of bedraggled kids, women, men, dogs, and their remaining worldly possessions. Although Hawaiians represent approximately 20% of the population of Hawai'i, they are 30% of the sheltered homeless population (the largest group in homeless shelters) and 28% of the unsheltered homeless population (the second largest ethnic group) (Essoyan, 2010, p. 6).

In another case, as reported in the Honolulu Advertiser (January 13, 2008, pp. A1, A14), a potentially explosive situation was averted between a more established (Samoan) immigrant group and more recent immigrants from Micronesia. In the incident, a Samoan youth was stabbed in the heart by a Chuukese youth outside of a housing project in the working class community of Kalihi. The potential for revenge attacks was high but averted due to the Micronesian community employing an indigenous Samoan ritual of apology called *Ifoga* that involves the community of the attacker humbling themselves in ritual apology before the aggrieved. In this case, an offering was made and the apology was accepted. There was no revenge. The use of an indigenous Samoan ritual of apology by the Micronesian with the assistance of pastors from both communities was seen as instrumental in avoiding further conflict and bloodshed. It was an offering of profound apology and deep respect.

Ethnocultural conflict is a global and historic problem (Huntington, 1996). It is a big problem. The causes of ethnocultural conflict are multiple. Considering the vital psychological functions of culture (Salzman, 2001a, 2001b, 2003), we are challenged to study and consider how culturally diverse peoples can coexist in mutually enriching ways rather than killing each other in bloody conflicts based on such factors as alternative constructions of reality, competition for material or psychological resources, and efforts to manage anxiety through ingroup identification and outgroup demonization. Culture is a critical determinant and mediator of conflict in disputes between individuals, communities, and nations. Culture can be considered both as a source of conflict and as an essential means of its resolution. Marsella (2005) emphasized the role of culture in conflict and offers the following common cultural pathways to conflict and violence:

- Perception of danger to national or group survival, identity, and well being
- Perception of the "other" as evil, dangerous, or threatening
- Perception of situation as unjust, unequal, unfair, humiliating, or punishing
- Perception of self as self-righteous, moral, justified, and "good" by virtue of religion, history, and identity (e.g., "American Exceptionalism")

This chapter seeks to explore the multiple potentials of living in an ethnoculturally diverse reality.

What is the reality of ethnocultural relations in Hawai'i? What are the realities? Is the projection of Hawai'i as a multicultural model accurate, partially accurate, or false?

3 History of Struggle: Contact, Colonization, and Immigration

Prior to the overthrow of the Hawaiian monarchy in 1893 and the annexation of Hawai'i by the USA in 1898, Hawai'i was an internationally recognized sovereign nation. Missionaries arrived in Hawai'i following the introduction of killer diseases that began shortly after "contact" was made by Captain Cook in 1778. As the population of Native Hawaiians was being decimated by a series of epidemics, the "Kapu" system that governed life in Hawai'i collapsed as a ravaged and despondent population increasingly turned to Christianity as a religion that apparently immunized the settler population from the death and suffering visited upon the Native population (Daws, 1968). The consequences of contact and colonization for Native Hawaiian people will be described later in the chapter.

Pre-war (World War II) Hawai'i was described by Jung (2006) as an overseas U.S. colony, "beyond the nation-state but within the empire, with a small elite ruling over colonized natives and migrant laborer" (p. 61). He described a plantation system that was stratified in terms of race and ethnicity where Portuguese, Japanese, and Filipinos were subject to qualitatively different racisms based on notions of relative inferiority (e.g., Filipino) and national loyalty (Japanese). These and other groups had different status, living conditions, and stereotypes. It was a classic "divide-and-rule" system that benefited the owners and growers of the sugar, pineapple, and transport industries. The following historical time line roughly describes the process leading to the construction of current realities in Hawai'i (see Table 2.1).

4 Consequences

4.1 Consequences of Contact and Colonization

Salzman (2001a) used terror management theory (TMT) (see Greenberg, Solomon, & Pyszczynski, 1997) as a framework to conceptualize the effects of a traumatic disruption of a peoples' culture as occurred throughout the indigenous world. TMT strongly suggests that culture serves as a psychological defense against the terror inherent in human existence, and this chapter uses this theoretical lens to consider the context and effects of Western contact, trauma, and colonization on indigenous people of Hawai'i within the broader issue of ethnocultural relations.

Table 2.1 Historical time line

500–1000 ad	Estimated migration of the ancestors of Native Hawaiians from Marquesas Islands, Tahiti, and other south pacific islands
1100	Communal society and culture develops. Kapu system established
1778	Arrival of Captain James Cook. Population estimate 400,000–800,000 Native Hawaiians
1802	First Sugar Production starts on Lana'i
1804	Unknown epidemic diseases decimate Native population
1810	Kamehameha "the Great" unifies the Hawaiian Islands. The monarchy is established
1819	Death of Kamehameha and abolishment of Kapu System
1820	Protestant missionaries arrive
1823	First Chinese arrive to work on plantations
1826	Missionaries standardize the Hawaiian language
1838	Mumps epidemic
1848	Great Mahele dispossesses the Hawaiian people of their lands and allows foreigners to own land. Deadly measles epidemic
1852	Chinese migration. Second group
1853	Smallpox epidemic further decimates Hawaiian population
1868	Japanese migration
1878–1886	Portuguese migration
1885	Primary Japanese immigration begins
1887	Bayonet Treaty forced upon and signed by King Kalukaua. Kamehameha Schools are established. The USA acquires Pearl Harbor
1893	Overthrow of the Hawaiian monarchy. Native Hawaiian population estimate is 40,000
1895	"Republic of Hawaii" established by White businessman support by U.S. military. Opposed by President Cleveland, supported by President McKinley
1896	English becomes the official language of Hawai'i
1898	Annexation of Hawai'i to the USA
1900	Organic Act and Puerto Rican Migration: Provided for a government for the territory of Hawai'i, provided tariff protection for planters, outlawed penal labor contracts, forbidding indentured labor pivotal moment in Hawai'i's labor history. Okinawan migration begins, Chinese Exclusion Act
1903	Korean immigration begins
1905	Law is passed forbidding the use of Hawaiian language in schools
1906	Filipinos recruited to work on plantations
1907	Gentlemen's Agreement between the USA and Japan halted migration of Japanese labor. The sugar industry then turned to the Philippines, a U.S. Colony, for migrant labor. From 1907 to 1924, 57,675 Filipinos arrived in Hawai'i
1909	Major strike of Japanese workers
1911	Pearl Harbor opens as U.S. Naval Base
1920	Dual union (Japanese and Filipino unions) strike, initial interracial labor cooperation, workers defeated
1924	Strike by only Filipino workers
1927	First Waikiki hotel opens
1931	Massie case: five "local" men accused of kidnapping and raping a "Haole" woman. Mistrial and defendants freed. Husband kills one and "gets away with murder" of Hawaiian defendant. First articulation of "local" people and culture by identifying diverse "local" nonwhite defendants (as opposed to Haole/Military)
1936	Passenger airline service begins
1937	General Strike of Filipino sugar workers led by Vibora Luviminda was the last racial strike, a precursor to the interracial movement that followed. National Labor Relations Board (NLRB) arrives (Wagner Act enforced) and opens "space" for labor organizing
1941	Bombing of Pearl Harbor and WWII (note: 1941–1944 martial law suppresses union organizing and worker rights)
1945	ILWU organized plantation workers into first multiracial labor union

(continued)

Table 2.1 (continued)

1951	Post WWII Samoan immigration
1959	Statehood and Admissions Act
1970s	Reconstruction of "local" identity. Possible to be local Haole, local Japanese, etc.
1970s	Hawaiian (cultural and political renaissance, the Kaho'olawe struggle, grass-roots movements, emergence of the sovereignty movement)
1976	Hokule'a sets sail furthering the Hawaiian renaissance
1978	Establishment of OHA and Hawaiian language is reinstated as an official language
1980s	Emergence of hula competitions
1983	'Aha Punana Leo (language recovery movement) is organized
1987	Language immersion classes established
1990s	Micronesian immigration
1993	100 years since overthrow. Hawaiians demonstrate at Iolani Palace to grieve the overthrow and push for sovereignty. U.S. government apologizes for its actions. President Clinton signs the apology bill acknowledging that Native Hawaiians never relinquished their claim over lands "ceded" to the State of Hawai'i
2000	Rice v Cayetano decision of U.S. Supreme Court giving non-Hawaiians same right to vote for trustees of the Office of Hawaiian Affairs, representing increasing legal challenges to Native Hawaiian assets
2008	The Hawai'i Supreme Court overturns the lower court's decision and orders the state administration not to sell any "ceded" lands until the claims of Native Hawaiians have been resolved by the Hawai'i legislature. The U.S. Supreme court agrees to the Lingle administration's request for an appeal
2009	In a unanimous opinion, the U.S. Supreme Court overturned the Hawai'i Supreme Court ruling deciding that the Apology Resolution did not provide a legal justification for Native Hawaiian claims over the "ceded" lands and is expected to send the case back to the state Supreme Court. Governor Lingle acknowledged that Native Hawaiians had a moral but not legal claim to these lands and that the State of Hawai'i had the right to develop or sell these lands for all the people of Hawai'i

Native Hawaiian contact with the West was traumatic as has been the case of indigenous people throughout the world (Salzman, 2001a). In this and other cases, intercultural contact proved disastrous to an indigenous people. Imported microbes overwhelmed the elaborate Native system of medicine. Contact with Europeans beginning with Captain Cook in 1778 challenged the power of the gods and the great chiefs as new diseases ravaged the population. Wave upon wave of epidemics struck the people. In 1804, the "ma'oku" claimed many lives and the horror of it was so great that it was remembered for generations even after other plagues had assailed the Hawaiians. This terrible foreign disease appeared first in Oahu and then spread swiftly among the people, decimating the population (Kuydendall, 1938). Old Hawaiian customs previously bonded together by ancient Polynesian beliefs, now fractured by the overthrow of the traditional religion, were collapsing at all levels. As a result of the void that appeared, self-esteem among the understandably bewildered Hawaiians plunged to a new low (Doughety, 1992).

Ancient and traditional Hawaiian culture provided the psychological sustenance that functioning cultures seem designed to do. It provided a coherent worldview that included and explained how the world was created, what personality characteristics are most valued, what is the hierarchy of power, and where does one fit into it (Becker, 1971). In short, it provided a system of meaning and standards of value that anxiety-prone, meaning-seeking human organisms require (Salzman, 2008). The complexities of traditional Hawaiian culture are beyond the scope of this chapter, but they include values supporting a complex interactive meaning system of body, mind, and spirit (see McCubbin & Marsella, 2009). The cultural worldview prescribed behaviors that support the values promoted by the culture and that made survival more probable in the ecological niche described previously. For the ancient Hawaiians, the world was infused with gods, spirit (*mana*), and meaning. All occasions were times for prayer. Prayer was a natural part of Hawaiian life because the gods were always present and they guarded, guided, warned, blessed, and punished. Supernatural spirits inhabited plants, animals, rocks, streams, breezes, and the endless sea (Pukui, Haertig, & Lee, 1972). It was a world infused with meaning.

The worldview was shattered and invalidated by the trauma of contact and its consequences. In terms of TMT, the cultural anxiety buffer (a coherent worldview and standards of value and behavior prescribed by that worldview) was discredited. Anxiety-buffering self-esteem was, therefore, becoming inaccessible, leaving the anxiety-prone humans to cope with these aversive conditions by whatever means that were accessible. Anxiety-related behaviors would be expected to increase under such conditions. Crabbe and Kaholokula (1998) describe the consequences of Captain Cook's arrival (contact) in Hawai'i and the subsequent American colonization of Hawai'i.

- Dramatic, sudden, and traumatic decrease in population of Hawaiians due to diseases (e.g., tuberculosis, syphilis, and smallpox) brought by contact with Europeans. Culture undermined by the effects of the epidemics and the apparent inability of the culture and its healers to stop the dying and suppressed by colonial educational and legal mandates and institutions.
- Native Hawaiians have the highest mortality rates in Hawai'i. The five major causes of death are heart disease, cancer, stroke, accidents, and diabetes. Hawaiians at risk for suicide, child abuse, substance abuse, school adjustment problems, and various mental illnesses.
- Although Native Hawaiians comprise only 20% of the State's population, they make up 40–50% of the prison population.
- A disproportionate number of Native Hawaiians are on public assistance and are incarcerated.

4.2 The Colonial Context

The underlying reality in Hawai'i remains the colonization, marginalization, and decimation of the population of Native Hawaiians. It is useful here to consider the situational context of colonization and its influence in defining the roles and relational dynamics in Hawai'i after contact. Memmi (1965), in his classic work *The Colonized and the Colonizer*, describes the psychological effects of colonialism on both the colonizer and the colonized in the case of the French colonization of Algeria. He saw that colonialism was harmful to both cultures. Memmi suggested that the colonial situation casts its actors in the roles of the colonizer and the colonized, and it is this situation that is definitive. For these roles to change, the situation must change. The reader is invited to consider the relevance of this analysis to the case of Hawai'i. Memmi described the colonial situation as one that is based on economic privilege, despite suggestion of more noble goals of religious conversion or civilization. Its key tools are racism and terror. Racism is ingrained in every colonial institution and establishes the "subhumanity" of the colonized, fostering poor self-concepts in the colonized as well. He goes on to describe the dilemma of the colonizer who sees the injustice of the situation ("the colonizer who refuses") and the colonizer who, while being aware of his illegitimate privilege, accepts his role as usurper relying on the conviction and presumption of his "superiority." The colonizer who refuses recognizes the colonial system as unjust and may withdraw from the conditions of privilege or remain to fight for change. Yet although he is benevolent, he is detached from the struggle of the colonized. This is a difficult position. The role of colonizer changes only when the situation changes. Let us consider the case of Hawai'i.

4.3 Processes of Colonization and Decolonization

There are a variety of Hawaiian voices that address the issue of sovereignty and decolonization. Laenui (2000), a Hawaiian sovereignty activist who advocates for complete independence for Hawai'i, developed a model describing the processes of colonization and decolonization. These processes are familiar to many Hawaiians, Native Americans, Alaska Natives, and others.

Laenui's model demonstrates how seeds of anger are embedded in the colonization process through trauma, loss, tragedy, and grief.

Step 1: *Denial and Withdrawal*
When a colonial people first come upon an indigenous people, the colonial strangers will immediately look upon the indigenous population as a people without a culture, with no moral values, and possessing nothing of any social value to merit kind comment. Thus, the colonial people deny the very existence of a culture of any merit among the indigenous people. Indigenous people themselves, especially those who develop a closer relationship with the newcomers (coerced or voluntary in order to escape pain and inferiority feelings), may become quickly converted and later lead in the criticism of indigenous societies and culture.

Step 2: *Destruction/Eradication*
The colonists take bolder action, physically destroying and attempting to eradicate all physical representations of the symbols of indigenous cultures. This may include the burning of their art, their tablets, their god images, and the destruction of their sacred sites. At times, the indigenous people themselves may participate in this destruction. Some may even lead in the destruction. Memmi (1965) described how the colonizer's rewriting of history to his glorification removes the colonized from history. The colonized child is not taught his own history, but the unknown settings of his colonizer's history. The colonized then becomes "divorced from reality" (p. 106).

Step 3: *Denigration/Belittlement/Insult*
As colonization takes a stronger hold, the new systems which are created within indigenous societies, such as churches, colonial style health systems, educational systems, and new legal institutions, will all join to denigrate, belittle, and insult any continuing practice of the indigenous culture. Churches will represent indigenous religious practices as devil worship and condemn the practitioners to physical torture or their souls to hell. Colonially trained medical practitioners will refer to the indigenous doctors as witches if their medicine is successful and as ignorant superstitious fools if their medicine fails. The new legal institutions will criminalize the traditional practices, fine the practitioners, and may declare illegal the possession of traditionally sacred or healing materials.

Step 4: *Surface Accommodation/Tokenism*
In this stage of colonization, whatever remnants of culture have survived the onslaught of the earlier steps are given surface accommodation. They are tolerated as an exhibition of the colonial regime's sense of leniency to the continuing ignorance of the natives. These practices are called folkloric and represented as colonials showing respect to the old folks and to tradition. They are given token regard (e.g., Waikiki Hula).

Step 5: *Transformation/Exploitation*
The traditional culture, which simply refuses to die or go away, is now transformed into the culture of the dominating colonial society. A Christian church may now use an indigenous person as a priest, permitting the priest to use the indigenous language to incorporate some indigenous terms and practices within the churches' framework of worship. The indigenous art that has survived may gain in popularity and now forms the basis for economic exploitation. Indigenous symbols in print may decorate modern dress. Indigenous musical instruments may be incorporated into modern music. To support indigenous causes within the general colonial structure may become the popular and political (politically correct) thing to do as the culture is further exploited (i.e., the marketing of aloha). Indigenous and nonindigenous peoples may commit this exploitation. All this time, external oppression is ubiquitous and all-powerful. Notions of inferiority are internalized and supported by colonial institutions.

4.4 Processes of Decolonization

The decolonization process involves the identification of the source of the oppression, the naming of it, the story of it, and the integration of that trauma into the larger narrative of a people's history. This process may generate anger and energy. The internalized oppressor (i.e., internalized negative self-evaluations) must be purged and anger is an essential part of the process. Poka Laenui (2000) in consultation with Virgilio Enriques suggested five distinct phases of a people's decolonization.

Step 1: Rediscovery and Recovery
This phase sets the foundation for the eventual decolonization of the society.

People who have undergone colonization are inevitably suffering from concepts of inferiority in relation to their historical, cultural, and social background. They live in a colonial society, which is a constant and overwhelming reminder of the superiority of the colonial society over that of the underlying indigenous one. In this phase, young people seek and listen again to elders, rediscover history, listen to the stories, and try to make sense of a painful present by recovering a suppressed history. This is when language is revived, culture is revived, and traditional spirituality may be revived. Many different causes may bring a person or a society to enter the stage of rediscovery and recovery (recovery of history, culture, and spirituality). It may be curiosity, accident, desperation, escape, coincidence, or fate.

Poka Laenui (2000) describes his experience as a volunteer member of the U.S. military, when he came across a book, found at a military base library in Hawai'i, written by Queen Lili'uokalani, that started his entry into this phase of decolonization. He described his curiosity that led him to read the words left by Hawai'i's Queen years before, telling of the conspiracy and overthrow of the Hawaiian nation. Once coming upon these words, he undertook his own study of a history of which he had previously been unaware. Laenui read and interviewed every source of information he could find on Hawai'i's history and Hawaiian cultural foundations.

The Hawaiian society has been in this phase (rediscovery and recovery) since the late 1960s, as greater sensitivity for racial identity and pride as well as the growth of distrust for the government of the USA developed. This phase of rediscovery of one's history and recovery of one's culture, language, identity, and spirituality, Laenui suggests, is fundamental to the movement for decolonization. It forms the basis for the further steps to follow. He warns of the danger that indigenous peoples may take on the colonizer's concept of the indigenous person and the elevation of form over substance of dealing with indigenous culture from the foreigner/colonial perspective.

Step 2: Mourning
A natural outgrowth of the first phase is the mourning. It is a time to lament victimization and loss. Anger is part of the mourning/grief process. This is an essential part of the healing process. The oppressor is named and identified. It is the beginning of the expunging of the internalized oppressor. There is great anger released in this phase.

Laenui describes his experience "As a young member of the U.S. military, plodding through the mounds of history and recovering from a loss of native identity I experienced great anger, wanting to blow-up the colonial system, take up arms to drive that very same military out of my native home. Others have expressed themselves in very similar ways, finding that they had been lied to for so many years while in the educational systems of Hawai'i. Their anger and frustration have ranged from flying chairs across a room to roaming streets wanting to beat Americans to contemplating para-military action" (p. 157).

The mourning phase can also accelerate the earlier stage of rediscovery and recovery. Anger provides energy. There are wounds that need to be expressed. Anger is expressed, to the discomfort of many good but uninformed non-Natives and the intentionally ignorant or the outright apologists for the historical injustice. It must be expressed. Recovery from trauma requires that the story be told (Herman, 1992). It is a painful story and the pain will be expressed.

Step 3: Dreaming
This phase is most crucial for decolonization. The panorama of possibilities is explored (i.e., models of sovereignty in the Hawaiian context) and the process of dreaming of the possibilities of a new social order begins. The colonized are able to explore their own cultures, aspirations, and possibilities. This phase must be allowed to run its course and not cut short prematurely. True decolonization is more than simple, replacing indigenous or previously colonized people into

the positions held by colonizers. It is a psychological transformation. This process has been and is occurring.

Step 4: *Commitment*
The combining of voices into a clear statement of direction follows a process of a consideration of possibilities. In Hawai'i, this will involve a consensus around the manifestation and the operationalization of self-determination and sovereignty.

Step 5: *Action*
After a consensus in the commitment phase, action is taken toward the manifestation of the vision.

Since the 1970s, a cultural and political renaissance has developed among Native Hawaiians that has had significant impact on current realities. The recovery of language, values, culture, and culture-based meanings and the development of a sovereignty movement have resulted in the construction of a Native Hawaiian identity that has, without doubt, resulted in greater pride and consciousness of being Hawaiian. Until the 1970s, feelings of inferiority and inadequacy were common among Native Hawaiians, including youths, because of the widespread denigrating stereotypes of them as being "dumb, lazy, violent and criminally inclined" (Okumura, 2008, p. 100). The Hawaiian cultural renaissance and sovereignty movement provided Native Hawaiians with the strength, awareness, and will to contest negative stereotypes and advance political goals and agendas by reclaiming their history, culture, and identity.

The cultural renaissance and Native Hawaiian sovereignty movements (Kanahele, 1982) are political and cultural expressions of recovery and decolonization. The fruits of these movements include a growing public school Hawaiian Language Immersion program (Slaughter, 1997) and traditional forms of therapy and healing such as Ho'oponopono (Shook, 1985).

Kanahele (1982) saw the process of recovering and the reconstruction of Hawaiian culture as a psychological renewal and a purging of feelings of alienation and inferiority as well as a reassertion of self-dignity. The revalidation of one's culture and its standards for being and living in the world serves to strengthen the essential anxiety-buffering function of the culture. The revival of hula, language study, music, and traditional forms of healing serves to reconstruct a world of meaning for people to act in and achieve anxiety-buffering self-esteem through the meeting of accessible standards of value defined by a worldview infused with a new belief. Kanahele notes similar cultural activism occurring throughout the Pacific Islands. As a result of these efforts to reaffirm and recover the cultural foundations of living and being, "Hawaiians regard themselves, generally speaking, a lot better and with a greater sense of identity, self-assurance, and pride" (p. 7). Self-assurance, pride, and confidence are conditions that make adaptive action more probable in a wide variety of contexts including those imposed by current conditions.

It is important to note that even following the signing of the apology bill (for the illegal overthrow of the Hawaiian monarchy) in 1993, Hawaiians are still struggling for their recognition as an indigenous people. The assault on Hawaiian assets continues under the infuriating guise of civil rights and race discrimination used by those seeking what are still significant assets (Van Dyke, 2008). Legal challenges to indigenous rights are currently threatening Hawaiian institutions such as the Kamehameha Schools and the Office of Hawaiian Affairs. As noted in the time line, in March of 2009, the U.S. Supreme Court, in a unanimous opinion, overturned a 2008 Hawai'i Supreme Court ruling and decided that the Apology Resolution did not provide a legal justification for Native Hawaiian claims over the "ceded" lands. Governor Lingle acknowledged that Native Hawaiians had a moral but not legal claim to these lands and that the State of Hawai'i had the right to develop or sell these lands for all the people of Hawai'i. The "ceded" lands (approximately 1.2 million acres) were lands under the control of the Hawaiian monarchy when it was overthrown in 1893. These lands include the sites of the University of Hawai'i and the Honolulu airport and are extremely valuable material resources. They are essential spiritual and psychological resources for the Hawaiian people.

4.5 The Plantation System

Prior to the Reciprocity Treaty of 1876 which offered tariff protection to the sugar industry, agencies (e.g., Castle & Cooke and Alexander & Baldwin) primarily acted as intermediaries between the plantations and external markets. This growing industry required considerable capital to nourish its growth and that capital was supplied by the agencies. The debts owed to the agencies by the plantations were converted into the ownership of plantation stocks by the agencies. By the time of annexation in 1898 (tariff protection made permanent), five of the top agencies (The Big Five) controlled 34 of 54 plantations. These agencies were controlled by four kama'aina (one who has lived in Hawai'i for a long time – derived from kama/child and aina/land) families descended from the missionaries who arrived in 1820. By 1930, the Big Five controlled 41 of 47 plantations and over 95% of sugar production (Jung, 2006). Wealth and power were increasingly concentrated in the hands of a few.

A commonly told aphorism in Hawai'i is "The missionaries came to Hawai'i to do good and did very well" (Jung, 2006, p. 16). They did very well indeed. This small number of interconnected "haole" families concentrated wealth and ownership through intermarriage, interlocking directorates, and family trust companies. They cooperated in opposing unionism and eventually dominated the sugar, pineapple, and transport industries. They controlled Hawai'i and imposed a plantation system based on a rigid racial and ethnic hierarchy that institutionalized inequality among workers. With Whites (*haoles*) almost exclusively in top managerial and professional positions, a consistent pattern emerged among the three main groups of workers, with Portuguese, Japanese, and Filipinos occupying positions in descending order of status and power. This inequality included differences in the quality of housing, job status, income, promotions, and working conditions. It should be noted that unequal status in the situation (plantation) contradicts the prejudice reduction condition indicated in *Intergroup Contact Theory* (Allport, 1954; Pettigrew, 1998).

This hierarchical pattern remained at least until the mid-1940s. Okumura (2008) contends that an ethnic hierarchy continues to exist today with Chinese-, White, and Japanese-Americans holding economic and political dominance, suggesting that equality of opportunity remains elusive in Hawai'i today. Okumura's argument is supported by his observation of a chronically underfunded public education system that is largely populated by Filipinos, Native Hawaiians, Samoans, and other Polynesians. In addition, Hawai'i has the highest percentage of K-12 private school enrollment in the USA at 16% or nearly 35,000 students. White, Chinese, and Japanese students constitute the majority of private school students (Okumura, 2008). Along with other factors, such as dramatic tuition hikes at the University of Hawai'i, Okumura concludes that inequality is institutionalized in Hawai'i. From 1995 to 2005, the percentage of Filipino-American students at the flagship Manoa campus declined from 11.0 to 9.3%; the percentage of Native Hawaiian students declined from 10.2 to 9.3%; and the percentage of Caucasian students increased from 13.6 to 22.3%. Across all campuses, the percentage of Filipino-American students declined from 14.9 to 12.7%; the percentage of Native Hawaiian students increased from 12.7 to 13.8%; and the percentage of Caucasian students increased from 19.3 to 21.3%. Thus, the question arises whether the system of status stratification established in the plantation system has really changed.

4.6 The Construction of an "Interracial Labor Movement"

From disparate ethnicities, status, languages, races, and cultures, a superordinate "interracial" labor movement and identity coalesced in the 1940s into a working class movement that transformed the conservative, feudal political realities of Hawai'i into what many be considered to be the most progressive state in the USA. The prewar period that was characterized by profound and entrenched racial divisions was displaced by a protracted period of durable "interracialism" that continues to this day (Jung, 2006). Jung contends that the construction of this "we" did not negate or deny race (and ethnicity) but "rearticulated" it by constructing a schema and worldview that saw worker's struggle for racial and class justice as "coincident and mutually reinforcing" (p. 9). Factors that may have contributed to this historical development and how this process may be understood psychologically will be considered in the light of relevant theory.

Native Hawaiian and migrant workers mainly from China, Portugal, Japan, and the Philippines were recruited to work in Hawaii's sugar plantations in overlapping succession from the middle of the nineteenth century. By the end of the nineteenth century, Hawai'i had become a colony of the USA ruled by a cohesive oligarchy of *haole* capitalists (the Big Five) who possessed and wielded an enormous concentration of wealth and power (Cooper & Daws, 1985) throughout the first half of the twentieth century. As agricultural laborers, the workers endured low wages and terrible working and living conditions on the plantations where they were stratified by race and ethnicity. As indicated, different groups had access to different conditions based on race and ethnicity. These differences in working and living conditions were supported by stereotypical perceptions of relative inferiority to the elite and powerful, and the degree of perceived national loyalty and suitability for inclusion and citizenship. This policy was later redefined by a militant labor movement organized by the International Longshoremen's and Warehousemen's Union (ILWU) as a classic divide-and-conquer tactics that supported the interests of the oligarchy (the Big Five).

Laborers did protest and strike prior to WWII but did not do so interracially and across ethnicities. There was a "Great Strike" of Japanese workers in 1909, a Filipino worker strike in 1924, and a dual union (Japanese and Filipino) strike in 1920 that were met with organized and obdurate opposition from the capital. The collaboration of Japanese and Filipino workers was a collaboration of two ethnically based unions, not an integrated interracial movement. The crushing defeat of the 1920 collaboration caused Japanese workers to withdraw from the labor movement for two decades. The cause for the defeat was attributed to a weak coalition between the unions due to *unequal status in the plantation system* and the resulting stereotypical perceptions of each group toward the other. This attempt at collaboration had an unsuccessful outcome.

Environmental and contextual factors influencing plantation labor changed in the 1930s with the passage of the Wagner Act and the arrival of the National Labor Relations Board (NLRB), which facilitated organizing unions and subjected employers to sanctions for the most blatant anti-union actions. There was *authoritative* support, then, for organizing and the development of a labor movement across race and ethnicity. The NLRB changed the environment significantly throughout 1937 as the ILWU aggressively organized interracially and offered a class analysis to contradict the use of racial propaganda (i.e., Japanese workers were loyal to Japan) and other divide-and-conquer tactics such as favoritism based on race. The ILWU organized and armed workers with the "divide-and-conquer" *cognitive schema* to recognize such tactics as such. Perhaps most importantly, by connecting the isolated plantation workers to a larger progressive, militant working class movement, the organizers offered *a superordinate identity that did not deny race or ethnicity but subsumed it under a larger identity and common purpose.*

The 1937 struggles set the stage for the formation of the interracial movement that would transform Hawai'i. This development was suppressed by martial law imposed on Hawai'i during WWII. Martial law froze wages, made work mandatory, "loaned" workers to the military, and mandated severe conditions of work. The overall effect of martial law was to stifle unions and labor organizing and to foment discontent among workers, making them more susceptible to the analysis and organizing efforts of the ILWU. After the martial law was lifted, worker discontent boiled over (Jung, 2006). The ILWU was successful in constructing an ideology (worldview) that would unite the workers interracially *against* employers and ultimately the Big Five by offering an interpretive schema that created a common interracial identity without denying ethnic identity or racial histories. The ILWU practiced interracialism by promoting a diverse leadership, holding meetings in multiple languages, insisting on equal opportunity with present employees, and thereby creating *equal status contact in the situation*. In 1946, the interracial labor movement struck the sugar industry and won. They had a *successful outcome*. This movement was reaffirmed by successful outcomes in 1947, 1948, 1949, and 1951. There was, then, a succession of positive and successful outcomes from this intergroup cooperation based on equal status in service of a superordinate goal. A *local culture* was nourished by this historical process.

4.7 The Development of "Local Culture"

The use of the term "local" has been traced to the infamous Massie Case (1931) to categorize collectively people from Hawaii in contrast to the White military accusers of Hawaiian and mixed race working class youths accused of kidnapping and raping Thalia Massie. The criteria for being "local" seems to be cultural rather than racial, involving adherence to certain values (e.g., *aloha*) including a respect and appreciation of cultural diversity. It represents an appreciation of and commitment to the land, cultures, and peoples of Hawai'i. "Local" identity has been maintained as an expression of resistance and opposition to outside domination. The plantation experience and labor movement undoubtedly facilitated the development of "local" identity, where different ethnocultural groups developed a common language that enabled people from many places (e.g., the USA, Japan, the Philippines, Samoa, and Korea) to communicate with each other. This was passed on to subsequent generations to become a unique language that is, today, English based, but consists of seven diverse languages employed in the construction of a unique, common system of communication known as pidgin and Hawaiian Creole.

"Local" culture, then, may represent the development of a superordinate identity that may be seen as supplementing but not supplanting original ethnicities. For example, the affirmation of a local identity for the entire Japanese-American community is apparent in a statement prominently displayed on a wall in the Historical Gallery of the Japanese Cultural Center of Hawai'i, which states "We are no longer only Japanese-American, we are local. We have learned from others. We have absorbed their values and traditions while we have preserved our own. We are proud of our mixed heritage-our local Hawaiian way of life" (Okumura, 2008, p. 134). The appreciation of and familiarity with the different peoples and cultures of Hawai'i are then a major dimension of "local" identity.

5 Relevant Theoretical Perspectives and Conceptualizations

This section utilizes varied theoretical lenses that psychology has provided to consider how culturally diverse peoples can coexist in mutually enriching ways rather than killing each other in bloody conflicts based on factors such as alternative constructions of reality, competition for material or psychological resources, and efforts to manage anxiety through ingroup identification and outgroup demonization.

5.1 The Minimal Group Paradigm and Social Identity Theory

The Minimal Group Paradigm is a term used in social psychology experiments (e.g., Sherif, Harvey, White, Hood, & Sherif, 1954; Tajfel, 1970) where people are randomly assigned to groups. These studies have shown that simply being randomly assigned to be a member of a group is enough to change behavior. A phenomenon occurs where group members will begin to associate superiority to their group over and above other outgroups. Ingroup members associate their self-esteem through positive social comparisons with other groups where their group is seen as superior.

Results from Tajfel's (1970) experiments in intergroup discrimination indicate the following:

- People have strong tendencies to divide the social world into "us" and "them."
- Individuals seek to enhance their self-esteem by identifying with specific social groups.
- Self-esteem is enhanced only to the extent that the persons involved perceive these groups as somehow superior to other competing groups. So each group tries to see itself as different from and better than the other groups (rivals).
- The self-esteem motive "wins out" over a tendency toward fairness.
- Only when individuals feel secure in their own group or cultural identity can they be generous and tolerant to other groups (Hornsey & Hogg, 2000), that is, secure about its own group's superiority and goodness.
- Under certain conditions, when an individual feels that the distinctiveness (superiority) of their own group or culture is somehow threatened, they will react negatively to other groups, and moreover, these reactions will be intensified by perceived similarities between their own and other groups because similarity threatens the distinctiveness in one's own group (self-esteem threat?). But when the individual does not feel that the distinctiveness of one's group is threatened or challenged, similarities (under no threat) have the opposite effect and tend to produce positive reactions to others.
- For prejudice reduction, efforts to reduce prejudice between groups by breaking down the distinction between "us" and "them" can succeed, but only if doing so does not threaten each group's unique identity and/or sense of superiority. Our tendency to divide the social world into opposing categories seems to serve important self-esteem boosting functions for humans.

The Robber's Cave experiment (Sherif et al., 1954) is one of social psychology's most cited studies dealing with differentiation, showing how easily opposing ingroups and group hostilities can form. At the same time, it is one of the best examples of conflict resolution brought about by finding superordinate needs that transcend intergroup conflict. An essential condition of the reduction of conflict between groups was found to be the development of superordinate needs that transcend intergroup conflict. This condition was established in the development of the interracial/interethnic labor movement described earlier. Despite attempts by employers to exacerbate intergroup tensions through racial propaganda, favoritism, and ethnic stratification (unequal status), the labor organizers of the ILWU were able to formulate a superordinate identity (being an important part of a transformative labor movement) and goal of improving working conditions and achieving a sense of dignity. In the face of united and ferocious opposition from the Big Five employers, the distinctions among workers of varying races and ethnicities may have diminished as their common, new, superordinate identity coalesced. It is extremely significant that their intergroup cooperation was seen as successful after WWII, whereas racially and ethnically separate efforts (i.e., of Japanese workers and Filipino workers) failed. Positive outcomes reinforced interdependence and helped construct a durable interracial and interethnic movement.

5.2 Intergroup Contact Theory

Allport identified four conditions for optimal intergroup contact and prejudice reduction. They are as follows:

1. Equal status contact in the situation (implying equal power in the situation)
2. Common (superordinate goals)
3. Intergroup Cooperation in achieving common goals
4. Support of authority and cultural or societal norms for positive intergroup contact
5. Friendship potential (added later) – intimate not superficial contact

Allport (1954) and Pettigrew (1998) emphasized the condition of *equal status contact in the situation*, implying equal power in the situation. We are challenged to construct such situations as inequality pervade social, political, and economic life to greater or lesser degrees throughout the world whether between individuals, groups, or nations. A colonial situation was imposed on Hawai'i. Notions of inferiority and superiority are embedded in and supported by the colonial situation (Fanon, 1968; Memmi, 1965).

Another essential condition for prejudice reduction and positive intergroup contact is *the support of authority and cultural or societal norms for positive intergroup contact*. It is significant that there is a strong cultural norm that is informed by the core Native Hawaiian value of "Aloha" referred to as the "Aloha Spirit." This essential condition is broadly endorsed throughout the islands. It is a cultural norm that prescribes particular behaviors in evidence on the crowded freeways and in large and small expressions. People at least pay lip service to this value and are generally reluctant to behave in ways that contradict it. "Aloha" (literally meaning sacred breath) includes a spirit of generosity, welcome, kindness, and broad tolerance of differences among people. Aloha is often exchanged by individuals sharing "sacred breath" upon meeting.

A significant impediment to the development of positive relations between people from different ethnocultural identifications is the human tendency and capacity to stereotype. Okumura (2008) places great importance on the role of ethnic stereotyping in maintaining the social stratification and ethnic inequality that have existed and continue to exist in Hawai'i. What is their nature and what is their function?

5.3 The Functionality of Stereotypes

Stereotypes are closely associated with prejudice and discrimination. They pervade people's views of their social worlds. Stereotypes are usually simple, over-generalized assertions about what "they" are like. "They" are denied their individuality by having applied to them a set of beliefs about their character and propensities of behavior (Snyder & Miene, 1994). By denying "their" individuality, we are ultimately denying their humanity. We see only a category. Dehumanization lies at the root of the indignities and even atrocities that humans impose on fellow humans. What needs are met and psychological functions served by the stereotypes that afflict our social perception and interpersonal behavior? Snyder and Miene describe three orientations associated with three particular functions served by stereotypes.

The *cognitive orientation* assumes that humans are limited in the amount of incoming information they can process, and form stereotypes as one way to reduce the cognitive burden of dealing with a complex world. In this orientation, stereotypes serve the function of *cognitive economy* by reducing incoming data to a manageable level so as to imbue our worlds with a sense of predictability.

The *psychodynamic orientation* sees stereotypes as providing a variety of ego-defensive functions. They include the derogation of others (particularly those seen as competitors for scarce resources) and the building of self-esteem by engaging in downward social comparison. Stereotypes, therefore, are subjectively useful for making people feel better about themselves and less threatened by other groups of people. Therefore, in functional terms, stereotypes serve the function of ego defense and protection.

The *sociocultural orientation* suggests that stereotypes serve the social function of fitting in and achieving a sense of belonging which has long been recognized as a human need (e.g., Maslow, 1987). Sherif and Sherif (1953) saw such stereotypes as functionally related to becoming a group member, thereby serving a social function.

These three types of functions serve real human needs and humans are motivated to satisfy their needs as they are perceived (i.e., the need for a predictable world, the need for self-esteem, and the need to belong). Given their ubiquity and nature, stereotypes must be considered a source of error with potentially serious consequences that call for strategies to minimize their negative impact on human and intergroup relations. Pettigrew (1998) described the following as the optimal sequence of contact between groups as first, *decategorization*: seeing similarity with the "other" – seeing the "other" as an individual and interaction as an interpersonal not intergroup event; second, *salient categorization*: other's group made salient so the "other" is seen as representative of their group in some essential way; and third, *re-categorization* into a larger category such as "working class" or "human race" that is inclusive ("we-world") of all interactants. In this case, a person's individuality, culture, and universal humanity are acknowledged and the full humanity of the person is acknowledged so no dehumanization occurs, as dehumanization is a prerequisite for discrimination, demonization, and atrocity. This formulation does not "deracialize" but acknowledges differences while including them in a larger formulation. An example of this process may be the development of "local culture" in Hawai'i.

5.4 Terror Management Theory

TMT (see Greenberg et al., 1997) considers the relationship among existential terror, culture, and self-esteem. There have been over 300 studies in 14 countries of TMT hypotheses that have suggested the following:

- Culture is a psychological defense, cooperatively constructed and maintained to manage the terror inherent in human existence.
- Culture makes self-esteem possible. Self-esteem is a cultural construction. Self-esteem (however constructed across cultures) serves as an anxiety buffer. Self-esteem is constructed by having faith in a cultural worldview and seeing oneself as living up to its standards.
- Cultural conflicts are fueled by numerous factors and conditions and maybe particularly vicious due to the psychological stakes involved (competing constructions of reality and immortality strivings).
- TMT experiments have found that when people are made aware of their mortality, they bolster and affirm their cultural worldviews, and exhibit a strong tendency to like those who support their worldviews, while distancing, derogating, and even demonizing those who do not support their cultural worldviews, suggesting that culture (and/or religion) offers either literal or symbolic immortality. This may be one reason that wars are so difficulty to stop once blood flows (mortality salience).

In his exploration of the relationship between culture and conflict, Marsella (2005) suggested that "reality" is a cultural construction and differences in constructions of reality on issues of vital existential importance may introduce unacceptable levels of uncertainty and doubt. This point is consistent with TMT essential assertions, although TMT specifies awareness of mortality as the core existential threat. The heroic transcendence of mortality, either literally or symbolically, is a powerful human motive.

The relevance of TMT to intergroup relations and the realities of Hawai'i are most apparent in regard to the trauma (physical, cultural, and psychological) experience of the Native Hawaiian people and their efforts to recover their culture and the meanings embedded in it. Humans are motivated to address and satisfy their needs. The need for meaning is a human need. The tragic results of contact with the West and the attendant decimation of the Hawaiian population led to a collapse of faith in a culture and spirituality that had previously sustained the people. Religious conversion followed. If people's or a person's faith in a cultural worldview is shattered, it no longer matters if its standards are achieved because they seem meaningless and humans require a world of meaning. Self-esteem can only be achieved in a world of meaning. Culture infuses the world with meaning. The cultural trauma (Salzman, 2001a) suffered by Hawaiian and other indigenous peoples impairs the construction of a coherent cultural anxiety buffer needed to manage the terror inherent in human existence. One is then left with anxiety and must deal with it in any way seen as available. There are many destructive forms of anxiety management. Alternatively, the traumatized people may adopt the culture and worldview of the colonizers who seemed to escape the devastation of the diseases. However, simply adopting and having faith in the colonizer's culture and religion do not effectively construct the anxiety buffer. One must see oneself as achieving its standards. In a racist colonial system, the achievement of the colonizer's cultural standard is unlikely due to the racist barriers constructed by the colonial system. It may also be true that the new, foreign system just does not resonate deep enough to attract the faith required to construct the buffer.

An important empirical finding in the TMT literature is that when individuals are made aware of their mortality (mortality salience), they bolster and affirm their cultural worldviews and exhibit a strong tendency to like those who support their worldviews while distancing, derogating, and even demonizing those who do not support their cultural worldviews, suggesting that culture (and/or religion) offers either literal or symbolic immortality. Once blood flows in an intergroup conflict, mortality salience effects are activated and conflict is exacerbated as each group demonizes and dehumanizes the "evil" other, while seeing one's own group as "good." These effects are consistent with Marsella's (2005) common cultural pathways to conflict and violence. Hawai'i has not experienced explosive racial or cultural riots or conflicts as have been seen in other places. Therefore, it seems that mortality salience effects have not been activated to the extent where groups demonize each other beyond discrimination, supporting stereotypes. Perhaps this fact supports the relative tolerance and harmony among ethnocultural groups in Hawai'i. The Hawaiian cultural value of *Aloha* may explain the peaceful nature of the sovereignty movement. Hawaiian sovereignty leader, Bumpy Kanahele, for example, has emphasized militant, uncompromising struggle for total independence but with *Aloha First* indicating a nonviolent, tolerant, and generous approach to independence.

5.5 Integrated Threat Theory (Stephan & Stephan, 1996)

Stephan and Stephan (1996) hypothesized that prejudice toward ethnic groups may be associated with any or all of four different perceived threats. They are realistic threats, symbolic threats, intergroup anxiety, and negative stereotypes (see Smith, Bond, & Kagitcibasi, 2006, p. 231). All four threats are potentially activated when groups come in contact. Realistic threats may include a competition for scarce resources. In such a case, conflict is likely but may be transformed through the development of a superordinate goal of expanding the resources (i.e., jobs and food) through equal status collaboration and cooperation. Symbolic threats are central to TMT, which proposes that under conditions of existential threat, we tend to (in the words of Barack Obama) adhere to our cultural symbols (i.e., guns, flags, and faith) and, as evidenced by the American reaction to France after 9/11, derogate those who do not support our position. Intergroup anxiety is a threat and our responses to anxiety may only exacerbate the issue, producing conflict. As Cushner and Brislin (1996) have noted, anxiety is a primary theme in intercultural interactions. Stereotype threat is problematic because it essentially denies the full humanity of the stereotyped as it impairs adaptive behaviors.

5.6 Realistic Conflict Theory

Realistic Conflict Theory developed by Sherif (1966) argues that intergroup conflict arises as a result of conflict of interests between groups. For example, when two groups want to achieve the same goal but cannot have it, hostility is produced between them. The theory accounts for intergroup conflict, negative prejudices, and stereotypes as a result of actual competition between groups for desired resources. Sherif found support for his theory in one of his most famous experiments, "The Robber's Cave" that was previously cited. The recent court decisions related to the claims over the valuable and essential "ceded" lands represent a clear conflict of interest between the State of Hawai'i and the Native Hawaiian people. In addition to their material, spiritual, and psychological value, this conflict over land is a conflict over an extremely scarce resource.

5.7 "Kita", "Kami," and the "We-World"

Can there be a "we" without a "they?" Can there be an "us" without a "them?" Can there be an inclusive "we" that satisfies the physical and psychological needs that motivate the construction, maintenance, and defense of our social identities and cultural worldviews? Hassan (2004) suggests that we can indeed strive toward the construction of such a "we-world." He identifies two words used in Indonesia that connote different constructions of "we." The words are "kita" and "kami." "Kita" is an inclusive "we" and there is no "they" or "them." It is a shared world. It is a mode where every constituent part is free to develop and maintain their individual identities ("kami"). "Kami" affirms its shared identity by excluding others outside its boundaries. It is a "we" that maintains the demarcation separating those who belong and those who do not. It affirms the ingroup and excludes the outgroup. Hassan suggests that many "kami's" can be part of an inclusive "kita," that there is a constant oscillation between "kita" and "kami," and that cultural diversity is not by itself a hindrance for the sharing of a "we-world." Cultural diversity implies cultural freedom that provides alternative ways of living and most importantly, it allows us to inject meaning into our existence and meaning is a core existential concern (Frankl, 1984; Yalom, 1980).

In cultural and other intergroup interactions, the "kami" worlds may develop into the inclusive "kita" world through the development of common goals and interests. We can assist the process by developing ongoing ethnocultural encounters aimed at promising reciprocal understanding, tolerance, and respect based on the context of equal status in the situation. We can construct superordinate goals that require intergroup cooperation to achieve them, that are based on unifying universal values or virtues that may motivate the construction of a "we-world," that enable for the possibility of all to meet their essential material and psychological needs. "Kita" language does not preclude "kami" realities, but while acknowledging these culturally and historically diverse realities, this language defines overarching and inclusive common interests. It is an inclusive "we" that does not require the construction of a "them" or "other."

5.8 Dehumanization as a Perquisite for Discrimination and Atrocity

Zimbardo (2007) has long been concerned with the processes through which ordinary "normal people" can be transformed into indifferent or even enthusiastic perpetrators of "evil" or atrocity. He suggests that processes of dehumanization confuse the mind into thinking that other people are less than human. In American history, we see that the genocidal policies toward Native Americans and the enslavement of African people were justified by the belief that these peoples were less than human. The U.S. constitution enshrined this belief in its description of African slaves as only 3/5th human. The description of Native Americans as vicious savages devoid of "God" justified murderous and assimilationist policies that reduced any dissonance arising from such brutal treatment used by the good and god-fearing settlers of the "new land."

The consequences of dehumanization may range from the inconvenient to the catastrophic. As described by Zimbardo (2007), once certain groups are stigmatized as evil, morally inferior, and not fully human, the persecution of these groups becomes more psychologically acceptable. Restraints against aggression and violence begin to disappear. Not surprisingly, dehumanization increases the likelihood of violence and may cause a conflict to escalate out of control. Once violence breaks out, it may seem even more acceptable for people to do things that they would have regarded as morally unthinkable before. The processes of dehumanization must be understood and disrupted if exploitation, derogation, atrocity, and even annihilation are to be prevented. How and under what circumstances do we dehumanize our fellow humans? How can this process be disrupted?

6 Discussion

6.1 Possible Resolutions

This chapter has examined the complex ethnocultural realities and history that have produced what many consider to be a model of intergroup tolerance in this remote land mass in the middle of the Pacific. The history of contact, colonization, processes decolonization, the plantation economy, and intergroup cooperation through the attainment of a superordinate identity have been reviewed and analyzed in the light of psychological theory and research. In this light, how might the positive potentials of ethnoculturally diverse people be maximized and the negative potentials ameliorated and managed?

Allport (1954), Pettigrew (1998), and intergroup contact theory suggest a solution. They have identified conditions for optimal intergroup contact. These conditions of equal status contact, common (superordinate) goals, intergroup cooperation in achieving common goals, support of authority and cultural or societal norms for positive intergroup contact, and the potential for developing friendships through intimate not superficial contact may be intentionally constructed in our schools and communities. These known conditions provide a potential roadmap to a multicultural destiny characterized by an appreciation of diversity, mutual respect, and shared interests. By promoting equality and mutual respect, we work toward the development of the "equal status" contact. By identifying common interests, we suggest superordinate goals and promote cooperation as a mode to achieve them.

Gaertiner and Dovido (2000) used the principles of Allport and Pettigrew (i.e., re-categorization) to demonstrate methods by which both explicit and implicit stereotypes could be reduced. They investigated conditions for optimal intergroup contact in which two groups were encouraged to recategorize their boundaries in the direction of sharing a common group identity (e.g., "we're different groups, but all on the same team"). As predicted, they found that this intervention led to reduced intergroup bias and prejudice. These authors emphasize that a strong advantage of this kind of dual-identity procedure is that it does not require minority groups to forsake their own unique group identity when they adopt a broader, superordinate identity. This is an essential point because only when individuals feel secure in their own group or cultural identity can they be generous and tolerant to other groups (Hornsey & Hogg, 2000).

This approach is consistent with the insights offered by the Social Identity Theory (Tajfel, 1970, 1978) concerning the people's tendencies to derive and enhance self-esteem by identifying with specific social groups and to divide the social world into "us" and "them." These findings correspond to the "we-world" proposed by Hassan (2004), where a superordinate identity ("Kita") is constructed without a "them," while including and acknowledging multiple distinct "Kamis" underneath the common identity whose distinctiveness is not threatened by the inclusive "we" or "Kita."

Perspectives and empirical findings from TMT (Greenberg et al., 1997) suggest that culture serves as a psychological defense against the terror inherent in human existence. This is consistent with Becker's (1971) proposition that cultural differences are threatening because they provide a living example that life can go on heroically within a value framework totally alien to one's own. TMT research has shown a powerful tendency for people, when they are reminded of their mortality, to seek to derogate, distance, or actually harm "others" who do not support their world view. One may reasonably conclude that reminding "others" of their mortality through threat and saber-rattling is an ill-advised foreign policy if one seeks a more peaceful world. One recent study, appropriately entitled "Mortality Salience, martyrdom and military might: The Great Satan vs. the Axis of Evil" found that under conditions of mortality salience, Iranian and American samples each attributed "evil" to the other and supported extreme action (suicide bombing and massive military counterattack regardless of collateral damage), whereas diplomatic resolution was supported when mortality salience inductions were not employed. The implications are clear: when blood flows and war begins, the demonization and the dehumanization of the "other" result and the ensuing conflict becomes extremely difficult to stop.

How can one make peace with "evil"? War must be prevented. The use of indigenous mechanisms for conflict resolution such as the Samoan practice of Ifoga cited previously diffused a potentially bloody revenge scenario that threatened the relative peace between these communities. Such conflict resolution and mutual respect-enhancing mechanisms may be further identified and employed to prevent blood from being spilled and TMT defenses from being activated.

Consistent with the principles described by Hassan, Allport, and Tajfel, we can promote institutional and grass-roots (inclusive) community-building ("we" building) activities and programs that celebrate diversity within our common humanity. We can work to identify issues of common, overarching interests and available mechanisms to pursue those interests and build the "we-world" that is united against common problems while reducing perceptions of threat to vital interests.

There is no doubt that there are real conflicts of interests and realistic threats such as the continued assault on Native Hawaiian assets such as the successful attempt by the State of Hawai'i to claim title to the "ceded lands." The struggle for land remains central to the health and well-being of Native Hawaiian people. Fanon (1968) wrote that for a colonized people, land is the most essential value in that it will bring not only material sustenance but also dignity. Historical injustices must be acknowledged and to the degree possible corrected if ethnocultural harmony is to be truly realized. The recent actions of Governor Linda Lingle enabling the State of Hawai'i to claim title to the "ceded lands" suggest that the crime acknowledged in the aforementioned "apology" resolution is not purely history. The reader is invited to consider if the crime continues.

We can prevent dehumanization, which is the prerequisite for discrimination and atrocity. The psychological process of dehumanization might be mitigated or reversed through humanization efforts, and ethnic and racial insults and stereotypes can be disputed at the family dinner table and the streets of our cities. We can intentionally work toward the development of an empathic understanding of the historical experiences of "others" and the corresponding narratives that are communicated across generations. The high rate of intermarriage in Hawai'i has contributed to the relative intergroup harmony in the islands. It is difficult to "otherize" one's own family or parts of oneself. Intermarriage and mixing make it hard to think in terms of "us" and "them" while nourishing the sense of connection and "we-ness." In this sense, the once ubiquitous phrase "make love not war" comes to mind.

We can support and operationalize cultural norms that support intergroup understanding and appreciation. We can work for justice and practice respect.

Utilize culture-specific conflict resolution practice such as Ifoga, Ho'oponopono, and Aloha.

7 Summary and Conclusions

As we seek to apply psychological knowledge to the problems that afflict humankind, we can only use what we know and seek to know more because the problems remain and they are pressing. The stakes are high.

References

Allport, G. W. (1954). *The nature of Prejudice*. Reading, MA: Addison-Wesley.

Becker, E. (1971). *The birth and death of meaning* (2nd ed.). New York: Free Press.

Cataluna, L. (2008, January 13). Forgiveness shared at teen's funeral. *Honolulu Advertiser*, pp. A1, A14.

Cooper, G., & Daws, G. (1985). *Land and power in Hawaii*. Honolulu: University of Hawaii Press.

Crabbe, K. M. & Kaholokula, J. K. (1998). The effects of western contact and acculturation among Kanaka Maoli: Acculturative Factors and depression among Native Hawaiians. *Presentation to the World Indigenous Peoples Conference on Education*. Hilo, Hawaii.

Cushner, K., & Brislin, R. (1996). *Intercultural interactions: A practical guide* (2nd ed.). Thousand Oaks, CA: SAGE Publications.

Daws, G. (1968). *Shoal of time: A history of the Hawaiian islands*. New York: Macmillan.

Dayton, K. (2008, May 20). 5 men indicted in Kona 'hate crime.' *Honolulu Advertiser*, pp. A1–A2.

Doughety, M. (1992). *To steal a kingdom*. HI: Island Style Press.

Essoyan, S. (2010, February 15). In plain sight. *Honolulu Star Bulletin*, pp. 5–9.

Fanon, F. (1968). *The wretched of the earth*. New York: Grove Press.
Frankl, V. (1984). *Man's search for meaning: An introduction to logotherapy*. New York: Touchstone Books.
Fu, X., & Heaton, T. B. (1997). *Interracial marriage in Hawaii*. Lewiston, NY: Edwin Mellen Press.
Gaertiner, S. L., & Dovido, J. F. (2000). *Reducing intergroup bias: The common ingroup identity model*. Philadelphia, PA: Psychology Press.
Greenberg, J., Solomon, S., & Pyszczynski, T. (1997). Terror management theory of self esteem and cultural world views: Empirical assessments and conceptual refinements. In M. P. Zanna (Ed.), *Advances in experimental social psychology* (pp. 61–139). San Diego, CA: Academic Press.
Hassan, F. (2004). Cultural diversity and the prospect of peacebuilding through sharing a we-world. In B. N. Setiadi, A. Supratiknya, W. J. Lonner & Y. H. Poortinga (Eds.), *Ongoing Themes in Psychology and Culture. Selected Papers from the Sixteenth International Congress of the International Association for Cross-Cultural Psychology*. International Association for Cross-Cultural Psychology.
Herman, J. (1992). *Trauma and recovery*. New York: BasicBooks.
Hornsey, M. J., & Hogg, M. A. (2000). Intergroup similarity and subgroup relations: Some implications for assimilation. *Personality and Social Psychology Bulletin, 26*(8), 948–958.
Huntington, S. P. (1996). *The clash of civilizations: Remaking of world order*. New York: Touchstone.
Jung, M.-K. (2006). *Reworking Race: The making of Hawaii's interracial labor movement*. New York: Columbia University Press.
Kanahele, G. S. (1982). *Hawaiian renaissance*. Honolulu, HI: Project WAIAHA.
Kuydendall, R. S. (1938). *The Hawaiian kingdom 1*. Honolulu, HI: University of Hawaii Press.
Laenui, P. (2000). Processes of decolonization. In M. Battiste (Ed.), *Reclaiming indigenous voice and vision* (pp. 150–160). Vancouver, BC: University of British Columbia Press.
Marsella, A. J. (2005). Culture and conflict. Understanding, negotiating, and reconciling conflicting constructions of reality. *International Journal of Intercultural Relations, 29*, 651–673.
Memmi, A. (1965). *The colonizer and the colonized*. Boston, MA: Beacon.
Maslow, A. (1987). *Motivation and personality*. New York: Harper & Row.
McCubbin, L. D., & Marsella, A. (2009). Native Hawaiians and psychology: The cultural and historical context of indigenous ways of knowing. *Cultural Diversity and Ethnic Minority Psychology, 15*(4), 374–387.
Noyes, M. (2003). *And then there were none*. Honolulu, HI: Bess Press.
Okumura, J. Y. (2008). *Ethnicity and inequality in Hawaii*. Philadelphia, PA: Temple University Press.
Pettigrew, T. F. (1998). Intergroup contact theory. *Annual Review of Psychology, 49*, 65–85.
Pratt, R. C. (2000). *Hawai'i politics and government: An American state in a pacific world* (p. 244). Lincoln: University of Nebraska Press.
Pukui, M. K., Haertig, E. W. & Lee, C. A. (1972). *Nana i ke kumu (Look to the Source),* Vol II. Honolulu, HI: Queen Lili'uokalani Children's Center.
Salzman, M. (2001a). Cultural trauma and recovery: Perspectives from terror management theory. *Trauma, Violence & Abuse: A Review Journal, 2*(2), 172–191.
Salzman, M. (2001b). Globalization, culture & anxiety. *Journal of Social Distress and the Homeless, 10*(4), 337–352.
Salzman, M. (2003). Existential anxiety, religious fundamentalism, the "clash of civilizations" and terror management theory. *Cross Cultural Psychology Bulletin, 37*(3), 10–16.
Salzman, M. B. (2008). Globalization, religious fundamentalism and the need for meaning. *International Journal of Intercultural Relations, 32*(4), 318–327.
Sherif, M. (1966). *In common predicament: Social psychology of intergroup conflict and cooperation*. Boston: Houghton-Mifflin.
Sherif, M., Harvey, O. J., White, B. J., Hood, W. R., & Sherif, C. W. (1954). *Experimental study of positive and negative intergroup attitudes between experimentally produced groups. Robber's Cave Study*. Norman: University of Oklahoma Press.
Sherif, M., & Sherif, C. (1953). *Groups in harmony and tension*. N.Y.: Harper.
Shook, V. E. (1985). *Ho'oponopono: Contemporary uses of a Hawaiian problem-solving process*. Honolulu, HI: East-West Center.
Slaughter, H. B. (1997). Indigenous language immersion in Hawaii. In R. K. Johnson & M. Swain (Eds.), *Immersion education: International perspective* (pp. 105–129). London: Cambridge.
Smith, P. B., Bond, M. H., & Kagitcibasi, C. (2006). *Understanding social psychology across cultures: Living and working in a changing world*. London: Sage.
Snyder, M., & Miene, P. (1994). On the functions of stereotypes and prejudice. In M. P. Zanna & J. M. Olson (Eds.), *The psychology of prejudice* (pp. 33–53). Hillsdale, NJ: Lawrence Erlbaum Associates.
Stephan, W. G., & Stephan, C. W. (1996). *Intergroup relations*. Boulder, Colorado: Westview Press.
Tajfel, H. (1970). Experiments in intergroup discrimination. *Scientific American, 223*, 96–102.
Tajfel, H. (1978). Social categorization, social identity, and social comparison. In H. Tajfel (Ed.), *Differentiation between social groups*. London: Academic.
Census Bureau, U. S. (2002). *Census 2000 special reports: Demographic trends in the 20th century*. Washington, DC: U.S. Government Printing Office.
Van Dyke, J. M. (2008). *Who owns the crown lands of Hawaiÿi?* Honolulu: University of Hawaii Press.
Yalom, I. (1980). *Existential psychotherapy*. New York: Basic Books.
Zimbardo, P. (2007). *The Lucifer effect: Understanding how good people turn evil*. New York: Random House.

3 Ethno-Cultural Conflict in *Aotearoa*/ New Zealand: Balancing Indigenous Rights and Multicultural Responsibilities

Colleen Ward and James H. Liu

New Zealand Chapter Summary

Ward and Liu present the historical origins of interethnic relations in New Zealand between the Maori and *Pakeha* and the development of bicultural relations. Further discussion delineates the immigration of several different ethnic groups into New Zealand over the past century, creating a more complex demographic. Existent ideals of the general population reveal signs of tolerance and harmony between ethnic groups. Improvements for the future that will provide the greatest benefit for all New Zealanders are suggested.

Description of colonization reveals initial conflicts over land which was originally guaranteed to remain with the original owners. Recognition of Maori displacement and forced assimilation into cities reveals an early loss of indigenous culture. Protest movements are presented as engendering revival of culture and revision of the initial treaty to include tribal self-management, equality for all, cooperation, and redress.

Historical review of the government responses to arrivals of various immigrant groups demonstrates discrimination and European preference. Ward and Liu explain that while these policies have changed, discrimination is still present in many areas. The authors express the view that relative deprivation and relative advantage have increased negative attitudes between groups. Discussion of recent research reveals the prevalence of multicultural ideology in New Zealand today and factors associated with positive attitudes are described. Research is also cited which reflects a preference for integration, but unwillingness to accommodate other cultural practices.

C. Ward (✉)
Center for Applied Cross-cultural Research, Victoria University of Wellington, Wellington, New Zealand
e-mail: Colleen.ward@vuw.ac.nz

J.H. Liu
Center for Applied Cross-cultural Research, Victoria University of Wellington, Wellington, New Zealand
e-mail: James.Liu@vuw.ac.nz

D. Landis and R.D. Albert (eds.), *Handbook of Ethnic Conflict: International Perspectives*, International and Cultural Psychology, DOI 10.1007/978-1-4614-0448-4_3,

In exploring means to improve ethnic relations, the authors identify the blending of biculturalism and multiculturalism as necessary given the special circumstances in New Zealand. Recent government initiatives are noted to have provided services to help equalize immigrants, particularly the recently proposed Multi-cultural cultural Act which provides recognition of Maori status, cultural maintenance, and participation for all groups.

Cheryl Jorgensen

Ethnic conflict is not prevalent in New Zealand. There are isolated instances of race hate crime, but no significant conflict between ethnic groups as a whole. The main challenges relate to achieving racial equality, full recognition of indigenous rights, and acceptance of cultural diversity. Joris de Bres, Race Relations Commissioner of New Zealand (personal communication), in response to a request for a comment on current race relations in the country.

This chapter examines ethnic relations in *Aotearoa*/New Zealand.[1] It commences with an historical overview of ethnic relations, with particular emphasis on the British colonization of Maori, the indigenous peoples of *Aotearoa*. It reviews the historical basis for New Zealand as a bicultural nation and relations between Maori and *Pakeha* (New Zealanders of European descent) and describes the early immigrants, including the nineteenth and early twentieth century Chinese and Indian settlers and the post-World War II immigrants from Europe and the Pacific. The chapter then discusses the significant 1986 and 1991 changes in immigration policies that redefined New Zealand as a modern multicultural society.

Although conflict between ethnic groups is not common in New Zealand, two recent incidents that have had significant implications for ethnic relations in the country are described and discussed. The chapter then goes on to review contemporary research on ethnic relations in New Zealand, with particular attention given to achieving racial equality, full recognition of indigenous rights, and acceptance of cultural diversity. Finally, the chapter concludes with recommendations for enhancing ethnic relations in a bicultural and multicultural New Zealand.

[1] *Aotearoa* (the land of the long white cloud) is the Maori name for New Zealand. We use the terms *Aotearoa*, New Zealand and *Aotearoa*/New Zealand interchangeably as they are used within the country.

1 Ethnic Relations: History and Current Status

1.1 Colonization: Early Maori and *Pakeha* Relations

New Zealand was one of the last land masses on earth to be permanently settled by human beings. Maori people first arrived by *waka* (large ocean-going canoes) during several waves of migration from Polynesia about 800–1,000 years ago. The Polynesians who arrived lost touch with their Pacific origins, developed an autonomous culture suited to the temperate climate of the land, and shifted over the centuries from hunting and gathering to horticulture (Davidson, 1984). A social structure involving *whanau* (extended, intergenerational families), *hapu* (subtribes capable of controlling an area), and *iwi* (tribes, sometimes under a paramount chief) emerged (Walker, 1990).

The Dutch explorer Abel Tasman did not find welcome when he tried to make landfall in *Aotearoa* in 1642; the point of first contact between Maori and Europeans was named "Murderers Bay" (now called Golden Bay) by Tasman in memory of the four men he lost in a violent maritime encounter (King, 2003). Later concerted attempts at European settlement did not begin until James Cook "rediscovered" New Zealand on behalf of the British Empire in 1769. The first Europeans to settle in New Zealand were whalers, traders, and missionaries, and the initial exchanges across cultures were largely peaceful. However, intertribal warfare (unbalanced by the introduction of firearms) and European diseases took a toll on Maori, so that by 1840, the precontact population estimated at 100,000–110,000 was reduced to around 70,000 (King, 2003; Walker, 1990). Maori still outnumbered Europeans by more than 30–1, but with increasing British settlement and the indigenous culture reeling from warfare and disease, the door was open for a formal recognition of the relationship between Maori people and the British Crown.

In 1835, the British Resident James Busby, who symbolized the official British presence in New Zealand, convened a meeting of 34 chiefs from the Northern end of New Zealand to sign a declaration of confederation and independence. The tribes agreed to meet once a year to make laws for the preservation of peace and the regulation of trade. This declaration carried little weight, and Busby concluded that it was impossible to create a central authority composed of fractious and independent chiefs. So in 1840, British Consul William Hobson convened another meeting with Busby's assistance and instructions from London to arrange a peaceful transfer of sovereignty from Maori to the British Crown. The signing of the Treaty of Waitangi/*Te Tiriti o Waitangi* between Maori and the Crown is now regarded as the foundation of contemporary New Zealand sovereignty (Orange, 2004) and is commemorated as a national holiday and as the most important event in the nation's history (Liu, Wilson, McClure, & Higgins, 1999). As New Zealand operates according to British Common Law, it does not have a formal constitution, rather it relies upon a set of customs, legal precedents, and traditions, among which are included the Principles of the Treaty of Waitangi.

The Treaty was eventually signed by over 500 high-ranking Maori from many (but not all) tribes on both the North and South Islands and used by the British to declare sovereignty over New Zealand and block French colonization of the islands. It has three clauses. In English, the first clause cedes sovereignty of the land from Maori chieftains to the British Crown. The second clause guarantees Maori full and undisturbed possession of their lands and treasured possessions, while allowing the Crown to purchase land. The third clause offers the protection of the Crown to Maori and confers upon them rights and privileges of British subjects. The Maori version of the Treaty differs somewhat in that the first clause merely cedes governorship of the land to the Crown, a nebulous concept to Maori, and the second clause guarantees Maori full and undisturbed *tino rangatiratanga* over their lands and possessions; however, *tino rangatiratanga* in Maori (sovereignty or self-determination) is closer to the English language notion of sovereignty than the word *kawanatanga* (governorship), which was used by the translators of the Treaty in the first clause (see Walker, 1990).[2] This was the version understood by Maori signatories, who hoped that the British might be able to control or mediate intertribal warfare that had been ferocious after the uneven introduction of firearms among tribes.

Even before the signing of the Treaty, there were tensions around the appropriation of land from Maori by Europeans, and soon after the Treaty was signed, warfare between Maori and the British Empire erupted, continuing on and off for 40 years (Belich, 1986). While Maori resistance was fierce and effective, it could not withstand the force of the British Empire over time. By the end of this period, the Treaty had been thoroughly abrogated by continual violations by the government and the settlers it protected, the best land had largely been alienated from its original owners (by legal and extralegal means), and sovereignty was well and truly in the hands of the British authorities (see Orange, 2004). In 1877, Judge Prendergast declared the Treaty a "simple nullity" in a court of law, and subsequently theories of social Darwinism were invoked to declare Maori a "dying race" as a consequence of "fatal impact" with a superior civilization.

Indeed, the 1896 census showed a tally of less than 40,000 Maori. By the early twentieth century, European-educated Maori leaders like Apirana Ngata and Maui Pomare recognized the value of European science and health care and were able to stem the tide of mortality with vaccines. Unfortunately, they could not stem the tide of land alienation, as the small farms became economically unviable and as their impoverished people sold land to gain a foothold in the mainstream economy. Consequently, for the first three quarters of the twentieth century, assimilation appeared to be the only viable path toward survival, as Maori migrated en masse to the cities in search of economic opportunities and entered into alien educational systems and institutions that only acknowledged European ways of thinking. The Hunn report of 1961 is a particularly well-known document expounding the virtues of assimilation for Maori. The "benevolent" paternalism expressed in the report is characteristic of dominant culture myths of the time that New Zealand had the "best race relations in the world." An alternative reading of the situation was that Maori had been thoroughly colonized and rendered economically marginal by the British and subsequent settler governments. By the second half of the twentieth century, there was a marked Maori presence on all negative indicators of social well-being, including levels of incarceration (Liu, 2007).

1.2 Maori Renaissance and Contemporary Ethnic Relations

Maori might well have disappeared as a separate cultural group had not a Maori cultural renaissance begun in the late 1960s come to bear fruit in the 1970s. This cultural renaissance was given impetus by the famous 1975 *hikoi* (protest march) against land alienation, which involved tens of thousands of people and a march in the North Island from Cape Reinga at its northern tip to Wellington at the southern coast (Walker, 1990). Awareness of the living consequences and legacy of colonization was growing in *Aotearoa*. At the same time, the Parliament signed the Treaty of Waitangi Act, which established a tribunal that could judge the validity of Maori tribes' claims of redress for unjust land alienation and other government misdeeds (see Smith, 1999, p. 168). In 1995, the government set up a $1 billion fund (roughly $US 750 million) to cover Maori Treaty claims against the Crown. Several large successful claims have since been settled, in effect incorporating certain tribes as fiscal entities carrying financial assets; however, many other claims remain to be addressed.

Additional activities in the recent political arena include the establishment of *Te Puni Kokiri* (Ministry of Maori Development) in 1992 to provide advice on policy affecting Maori well-being.

[2] It is likely that the different versions of the Treaty are due to inefficiency rather than design as there were multiple drafts in English, only one of which was given to the missionary Henry Williams to translate; however, according to Ross (1972) that text does not appear to have survived. Today, as New Zealand is party to the Vienna Convention Law on Treaties (1969) and is guided by the rule of "contra proferentem" from international law, the Maori text should be treated as the prime reference in cases of ambiguity or where questions arise as to which text should prevail (Waitangi Tribunal, 1983).

In 2004, the Maori Party was formed, partially due to dissatisfaction with the government's handling of potential Maori claims to the country's foreshore and seabed (see Case Study 1 that follows). By 2005, there were 21 Maori (17.4%) Members of Parliament.[3] In addition, the interpretation of the Treaty of Waitangi has evolved to one of a bicultural partnership. Many public institutions now have charter statements "honoring the principles of the Treaty of Waitangi." The government's statement of these principles is as follows: *kawanatanga* (governorship by the Crown), *rangatiratanga* (tribal self-management), equality for all citizens, reasonable cooperation between Crown and *iwi*/tribes, and redress of past injustices.

On the cultural side, *kohanga reo* (Maori preschool language nests) and *kura kaupapa* (Maori language primary schools) were created by educators and activists to stem the tide of language loss. The massive urbanization of Maori in the twentieth century had the unintended consequence that by 1980, only about one in five Maori were native language speakers of *te reo* (the Maori language or literally "the language"). In 1975, *Nga Tamatoa* (Young Warriors) petitioned the Parliament to promote *te reo*. The first Maori immersion language teaching began in 1982, and Maori was recognized as an official language of New Zealand in 1987.

Despite these advances, the negative impacts of colonization are still evident, and there is a range of unresolved issues in Maori–*Pakeha* relations (see Smith, 1999). In 2000, Tariana Turia, then the Associate Minister of Maori Affairs and now the co-leader of the Maori Party, controversially declared that Maori suffer from Post-Colonial Traumatic Stress Disorder in her address to the New Zealand Psychological Society. The 2007 police anti-terror raids on members of the *Tuhoe* tribe precipitated a march on Parliament and drew comments from Pita Sharples, the co-leader of the Maori party, who described the incident as setting Maori–*Pakeha* relations back 100 years. In addition, there is sustained debate over the evolving nature of the Treaty, its relationship to statutory law, the principle of partnership, and the relationship between Maori and the Crown (Byrnes, 2005; Orange, 2004; Smith, 1999).

1.3 Immigration Policy and Practices in Postcolonial New Zealand

In addition to solidifying relations between Maori and British settlers in the colonial era, it has been suggested that the Treaty of Waitangi also articulated the country's first immigration policy (e.g., Walker, 1995). This is, of course, a matter of some debate, as the English version preamble cites British settlement and the anticipation of emigration from Europe and Australia as the major factors underlying treaty negotiations, whereas the Maori version highlights the establishment of a government that secures tribal *rangatiratanga*. Ranginui Walker (1995), a prominent Maori scholar, has argued that the Treaty only permitted entry of settlers from the regions named in its preamble and that admission of immigrants from other areas should be a matter for consultation with the descendents of the Crown's treaty partners. Despite the historical basis for Maori involvement in the development of immigration policy, however, successive governments have largely ignored Maori concerns and have traditionally relied upon practices that favored European settlers, particularly those of British, Irish, and Protestant Anglo-Celtic origins. Indeed, at the end of World War II, New Zealand had one of the world's most ethnically homogeneous societies of European settlement (Brooking & Rabel, 1995).

This is not to suggest that "white only" preferences prohibited immigration from other regions, but because of these preferences, early Asian and more recent Pacific immigrants were systematically subjected to discriminatory policies and

[3] New Zealand has 70 general and 7 overlapping Maori electorates to ensure Maori representation in Parliament. Persons of Maori descent may choose registration on either the general or Maori electoral roll to exercise their right to vote in a Mixed Member Proportional (MMP) voting system. Consequently, current Maori representation arises from a combination of seven Maori seats, elected Members of Parliament and those who come to Parliament on a party list as a result of proportional party votes under New Zealand's electoral system.

practices (Ip & Pang, 2005). The Chinese were the first of these immigrant groups, attracted to New Zealand by the gold rush of the 1860s. Between 1870 and 1881, approximately 6,000 Chinese entered New Zealand, at which point immigration restrictions were imposed with the introduction of the Chinese Immigrants Act (Pearson, 1990). This, in conjunction with the 1888 and 1896 amendments, increasingly limited Chinese immigration. This legislation also introduced and raised poll taxes on new immigrants (Beaglehole, 2007).[4] The limitations on Chinese immigration reflected the national sentiments of the era where Chinese were vilified as being "promiscuous and immoral, unhealthy, materialistic and greedy" (Pearson, 1990, p. 75). In truth, anti-Chinese sentiments were underpinned by both perceptions of economic threat and cultural and racial prejudice. By 1908, the Chinese were denied access to naturalization and permanent settlement, and it was not until 1951 that these rights were restored. Although most of the original Chinese immigrants did not intend to make New Zealand a permanent home, many did remain, and today their descendents have comfortably assimilated into New Zealand society while retaining their integrity as a cultural group (Moughan, 2010).

South Asians, particularly Punjabis and Gujuratis, began to enter New Zealand in the late nineteenth century as part of a wider emigration flow spawned by British imperialism and the commercialization of agriculture (Leckie, 1995). As British subjects, they were free to settle in New Zealand until the Immigration Restriction Act of 1899, which prohibited entry for those who were not of British or Irish parentage. The act remained in place for 20 years and was then amended to allow access for the family members of Indians already resident in the country. In addition to the restrictive immigration policies, the early Indian settlers were forced to contend with the White New Zealand League of the 1920s, which promoted xenophobia and fear of "Asian invasion." Social and economic discrimination against Asians continued for at least the next three decades, along with wide support for a "white New Zealand" policy (Beaglehole, 2007; Leckie, 1995).

Gradual changes were introduced to New Zealand's immigration policies after World War II, when it became obvious that labor needs could not be met through natural population growth. Preference remained for immigrants of European descent. Immigrants arrived not only from Great Britain and Australia, but also from Germany, Scandinavia, France, Italy, Switzerland, Greece, and Dalmatia (a historical region that now lies primarily in Croatia), often via assisted passages to New Zealand. In addition, New Zealand accepted approximately 5,000 refugees and displaced persons from Europe after the war. Consequently, the 1960s still yielded a population that was overwhelmingly European in origin (Beaglehole, 2007).

A review of immigration policy in 1974 resulted in major changes, officially basing permanent entry on skills and qualifications; however, in practice, traditional source countries continued to be favored (Beaglehole, 2007). Severe labor shortages of the 1960s and 1970s prompted a dramatic increase in Pacific immigration, which, despite the special historical and political position that New Zealand occupied in the region, had been relatively small until that time. Employment opportunities attracted citizens of the Cook Islands, Niue, and Tokelau who held citizenship due to New Zealand's previous colonial control over these territories. Samoans, the largest Pacific group in New Zealand, were subjected to a quota system, although this was not strictly enforced during the economic expansion of the 1960s and early 1970s. Tongans and Fijians also entered New Zealand during this period, primarily on temporary permits. The 1976 census reported over 65,000 residents of Pacific Island origin or descent, an increase from just over 3,000 who were resident 25 years earlier (Pearson, 1990). However, as the labor market cooled, so did the enthusiasm for Pacific immigration. The mid-1970s were known for the infamous "dawn raids" to identify and deport Pacific Island over-stayers (de Bres & Campbell, 1976), for tightening immigration regulations and introducing more formalized temporary work permits (Ongley, 1991). The dawn raids

[4] The poll tax was paid by each Chinese immigrant to be granted entry to New Zealand. The tax was used primarily as a means of deterring immigration.

were recognized as racist attacks on Samoans and Tongans at the time and remain bitter memories for older Pacific people today (Anae, 1997).

1.4 Recent Immigration Trends

It was not until the 1986 and 1991 changes in immigration policy that New Zealand entered a new era of immigration and the country saw a large influx of settlers, many from nontraditional sources (New Zealand Immigration Service, 1991). The proportion of overseas-born residents in New Zealand prior to these changes increased from 14.4 to 22.9% in the most recent census, and New Zealand now ranks fourth in the Organization for Economic Co-operation and Development for the percentage of overseas-born population (Ministry of Social Development, 2008; Zodgekar, 2005). Immigrants from the United Kingdom and Ireland, who previously supplied over half of New Zealand's immigrants, dropped to 29%, while Asian migration rapidly increased and now makes up 29% of the country's immigrants. Although China, India, and South Africa are the largest contributors to New Zealand's new immigrants, Pacific people also make up a significant proportion of the overseas-born population (Ministry of Social Development, 2008, 2010) (Table 3.1).

As New Zealand attracts approximately 40,000 immigrants per annum (about 1% of the total population), these new settlers have made a significant impact on the country's ethnic composition. Chinese have experienced the largest percentage growth among all ethnic groups over the last ten years due largely to immigration from the People's Republic of China, and at present the Asian population (9.2%) has exceeded the Pacific population (6.9%) for the first time. Among the Asian communities, Chinese, Indians, and Koreans compose the largest groups. For Pacific peoples, Samoans, Cook Island Maori, and Tongans are the most prevalent. Against the backdrop of immigration, Maori compose 14.6% of the population, and New Zealanders of European descent make up 67.6% (Statistics New Zealand, 2007a).[5] Due to differential fertility rates and immigration, projections indicate that the numbers of all "minority" ethnic groups in New Zealand will substantially increase between 2001 and 2021: Maori (by 29%), Pacific peoples (by 59%), and Asians (by 145%; Ministry of Social Development, 2008).

Table 3.1 Birthplaces of the overseas-born population (2006 census)

Birthplace	Number	Percent
Australia	62,742	7.1
Pacific Islands	135,852	15.4
UK and Ireland	251,688	28.6
North-west Europe	44,103	5.0
Southern Eastern Europe	23,964	2.7
North Africa and Middle East	16,533	1.9
South-east Asia	58,266	6.6
North-east Asia	135,168	15.4
Southern and Central Asia	57,699	6.6
The Americas	34,383	3.9
Sub-Saharan Africa	59,118	6.7
Total (specified)	879,516	100.0

In addition to targeted immigration, New Zealand accepts up to 750 mandated refugees each year under the 1951 United Nations Convention. Beyond this quota, New Zealand admits 200–300 asylum seekers and family members sponsored by refugees under a family reunification policy so that in total approximately 1,500 refugees are resettled in the country each year (Beaglehole, 2007; New Zealand Immigration Service, 2002). In the late 1970s through the early 1990s, New Zealand accepted a significant number of refugees from South-east Asia, particularly Cambodia, Laos, and Vietnam. In the 1980s, a flow of refugees from the Middle East entered New Zealand, particularly Bahais from Iran and Assyrians from Iraq. The largest refugee groups in more recent times have come from Somalia, Zimbabwe, Bosnia, and Afghanistan (Beaglehole, 2007).

With increasing immigration and a more diverse refugee population, there have also been significant changes in New Zealand's religious composition. Although non-Christian religions make up only a very small proportion of the religious spectrum (less than 6%), they are rapidly

[5] The New Zealand census permits identification with more than one ethnic group so that the total percentage may exceed 100%. In addition, the drop in the New Zealand European population from 80 to 67% between the 2001 and 2006 censuses was largely due to changes in the census ethnic categories, which in 2006 included New Zealander (now classified as other).

growing. Between 1991 and 2006, the Jewish population doubled, the Hindu population tripled, the Buddhist population quadrupled, and the Muslim population increased sixfold. Ethnic, cultural, linguistic, and religious diversity is a reality now and will only increase in the future.

Pearson (1990) noted that New Zealand has often been applauded for its good ethnic relations in the international arena; however, the changes to policies pertaining to immigration and refugee resettlement introduced for the country to remain internationally competitive in a global labor market and to meet its humanitarian obligations have not gone unchallenged. Through the 1990s and early 2000s, opposition politician and former leader of the New Zealand First party, Winston Peters, known for his anti-immigration rhetoric, was quick to play on New Zealanders' fears, highlighting the threat of immigration in both economic and cultural terms (Liu & Mills, 2006). The status of Maori in particular was to be threatened in his anti-immigration tirades by "… a flood of migrants – many of whom will directly compete with Maori in terms of jobs, housing and access to health service." But the general public also bore the brunt of his doomsday prophesizing as he argued that "there is the need to keep a tight lid on immigration if we are to avoid New Zealand's identity, values and heritage being swamped" (Peters, 2002). Indeed, Peters envisioned the rising tide of immigration as calling the society to war. "New Zealand First believes our heritage is worth fighting for. I urge you to join us in the battle" (Peters, 2002). In response, the New Zealand Federation of Ethnic Councils issued statements condemning the New Zealand First rhetoric, and a local poll found that 76% believed that Winston Peters' comments hurt New Zealand (Ward & Lin, 2005).

More recently, the then leader of the opposition party Don Brash tackled the issue of immigration by calling for new settlers to endorse the "bedrock values" of New Zealand society. In his 2006 speech, he noted the following:

> We can ask and expect people to fit in, but the reality is that many migrants to New Zealand in recent times, and indeed to the West more generally, have come from cultures that don't share the bedrock values that New Zealanders take for granted….We cannot be indifferent to whether migrants are likely to share our bedrock values. We can't just hope it'll work out fine….Put another way, we should not welcome those who want to live in New Zealand but reject core aspects of New Zealand culture (Brash, 2006).

Brash's statements were widely taken to refer to New Zealand's Muslim immigrants and evoked widespread accusations of racism and xenophobia. When subsequently interviewed in the popular press, Brash was reluctant to single out any group for exclusion, but he did make reference to bombings in the United Kingdom and "British-born people plotting mayhem against other British citizens," and suggested that had the Netherlands and France "screened immigrants for core values, they might not have nearly the problems that they have now" (Ansley, 2006). It is noteworthy that Brash was previously known for his "Orewa speech" in which he attacked biculturalism for being backward – rather than forward-looking and for being a source of unjustifiable categorical privileges for Maori. This type of discourse is consistent with the international literature on majority group resistance to affirmative action (e.g., van Dijk, 1993; Gamson & Modigliani, 1987).

In summary, to understand contemporary ethnic relations *Aotearoa*, it is necessary to consider the historical impacts of colonization, early Maori–*Pakeh*a relations, and the more recent Maori renaissance. Although the Treaty of Waitangi is viewed as broadly defining the status of Maori and *Pakeha* and as laying the basis for a bicultural nation (Liu, 2005; Liu et al., 1999), it is also recognized as an evolving contract (Byrnes, 2005). The notion of an equal partnership between Maori and *Pakeha* is a relatively recent extension of the Treaty interpretation; it contrasts markedly with the pre-1960s policies and practices of assimilation. Despite bicultural ideals and a Maori cultural renaissance, there is still a range of unsettled Maori grievances that must be addressed in the context of contemporary race relations.

Beyond these core bicultural issues, New Zealanders are facing the consequences of changes in immigration policies over the last two decades that have resulted de facto in a multicultural society. Indeed, New Zealand today is characterized by greater cultural diversity than Australia, the

United Kingdom, France, Germany, the Netherlands, and Scandinavian countries (Berry et al., 2006). Challenges arise in adjusting to these rapid social changes and finding the right balance among honoring the Treaty, respecting indigenous rights, and accommodating the increasingly diverse multicultural and multi-linguistic population.

2 Ethnic Conflict: Causes and Consequences

In this section, two cases in 2004 reflecting different aspects of ethnic tensions, conflict, and hostility are presented and discussed: the controversy over Maori claims to the New Zealand foreshore and seabed, and the desecration of Jewish graves in Wellington, the national capital. We draw on these recent events to elucidate some of the causes and consequences of ethnic conflict.

Case One: Maori Claims to the Foreshore and Seabed

In June 2003, the New Zealand Court of Appeal ruled that the Maori Land Court had jurisdiction to investigate customary title to the seabed and foreshore (the land, water, and air space between the high tide mark and the outer limits of the territorial sea) for Maori tribes. Furore arose from the majority population, driven by fears that access to beaches and waterways might be restricted. The Labor government released draft proposals for consultation involving *hui* (meetings with Maori tribes) and meetings with the general public, eventually receiving over 4,000 written submissions. Through a highly contested political process, the government eventually passed into legislation in 2004 an act detailing with rights of access and navigation, replacing the jurisdiction of the Maori Land Court, and vesting ownership of the public seabed and foreshore with the Crown. While the government debated and legislated, tens of thousands of Maori and supporters across the nation participated in a *hikoi* (protest march) against the extinguishing of customary title. Member of Parliament and Junior Minister Tariana Turia resigned from the governing Labor Party and established the Maori Party as a consequence of the rift.

The controversy over whether Maori were entitled to seek customary title over the seabed and foreshore of New Zealand's coastline is a classic illustration of turbulent politics between Maori and *Pakeha.* Customary title is recognized by British Common Law and international law, and the New Zealand Court of Appeal merely ruled that Maori had the right to seek (but not necessarily acquire) title over seabed and foreshore areas when they could demonstrate continual occupancy and use. Public discourse around this issue rarely rose above fear-mongering about loss of access to beaches, and dominant discourses portrayed the issue as a zero-sum game between Maori as the privileged party and non-Maori as the threatened group fighting for equality (Kirkwood, Liu, & Weatherall, 2005). The legal status of customary ownership never entered much into debate. It was portrayed as something that had to be legislated against for the benefit of the majority.

The discourses and practices of this controversy very clearly illustrate the opposition of *Pakeha* to categorical preferences in favor of Maori, even when backed by international law (see Sibley & Liu, 2004). The symbolic inclusion accorded to Maori when resources are not at stake quickly evaporated, extinguishing customary title under the guise of maintaining "free and fair access" to the seabed and foreshore for *all* New Zealanders.[6] The issue that 25–30% of the seabed and foreshore were already in private hands of capitalists never entered into debate (see Liu and Mills, 2006 for analysis of the "invisible hand" of capitalism).

The issue has had long-term implications for the political landscape of New Zealand. More than seventy years of alliance between Maori people and the Labor Party was shattered, and the Maori Party went on to secure five of the seven

[6] Similar issues have arisen in Hawaii involving not only land, but also access to education provided by private Kamehameha schools established to educate children of Hawaiian ancestry. See Chap. 2.

Maori seats in Parliament in the 2008 election. The Maori Party has since entered into a coalition government with the conservative National Party. The strategic alliance between a right-leaning, business-favoring National Party and a left-leaning, lower-income-oriented Maori Party is a marriage of convenience that has had important ramifications for political discourse. Such an alliance signals a new era where the small Maori Party can influence policy by making a strategic alliance with one of the two major political parties in the current proportional party representation electoral system (e.g., a repeal of the aforementioned Foreshore and Seabed Act). It also removes "Maori bashing" for electoral votes (accusing Maori of unjustified special privileges or living high off the public purse), which has been a regular staple for right wing political parties for decades (Liu & Mills, 2006). This new political configuration promises original solutions to the "New Zealand dilemma" (Sibley, Liu, Duckitt, & Khan, 2008) of the historical legacy of colonization, which has left Maori in a disadvantaged position relative to New Zealanders of European descent.[7]

Case Two: The Desecration of Jewish Graves

On 6th August, 2004, the desecration of over 90 Jewish graves occurred in Makara Cemetery in Wellington. This was widely assumed to be linked to an international incident in the previous month where two Mossad (Israeli) agents were sentenced to prison for their illegal attempts to obtain New Zealand passports. New Zealand strongly protested the actions to Israel, but Israel refused to acknowledge or respond to the protest. The desecration of graves, regarded as an attack on the local Jewish community, prompted strong reactions against racism and xenophobia across the country.

Spoonley (1993) argued that anti-Semitism was not transplanted from Europe to New Zealand, partly because of the small size of the community and their ethnic "invisibility." Certainly, the desecrations precipitated a range of supportive responses. Wellington's mayor condemned the actions and ensured that the damaged graves were promptly restored by the city council. Residents of Auckland (New Zealand's largest city) showed support with a Youth against Hatred rally. The Australasian Union of Jewish Students issued a statement condemning anti-Semitism and all forms of discrimination, and presented a petition with over 1,000 signatures to Chris Carter, the Minister of Ethnic Affairs. New Zealand's Parliament unanimously condemned anti-Semitism and all forms of racial hatred, persecution, and discrimination, and a Diversity Forum attended by community representatives was held on the forecourt of the Parliament (Levine & Gezentsvey, 2005–2006).

This subsequently led to annual Diversity Forums organized by the Human Rights Commission and the launch of New Zealand's Diversity Action Programme (DAP). By the end of 2007, the DAP grew to more than 250 organizations that undertake practical initiatives (e.g., cultural festivals, public forums, media displays, and sports events) to foster harmonious relationships among diverse peoples, going far beyond the initial impetus of fighting anti-Semitism. These organizations include ethnic, cultural, and religious groups; ethnic councils; businesses; media; district, city, and regional councils; government departments and agencies; research centers; educational institutions; health and social service providers; community service agencies; museums and galleries; and advocacy groups. In 2008, a national statement on race relations was presented by Prime Minister Helen Clark and Race Relations Commissioner Joris de Bres at the annual Diversity Forum. In the end, a hate crime that shocked the country prompted New

[7]The New Zealand Dilemma is the symbolic inclusion but resource-based (or economic) exclusion/marginalization of Maori as a consequence of the nation's wrestling with the historical legacies of colonization. While there are creative elements to this configuration that provide indigenous people with a place in the national consciousness of a settler nation, it falls short of Maori aspirations and expectations for the Treaty of Waitangi, and hence remains a dilemma just as the legacy of slavery is the American dilemma remarked on by Myrdal (1944).

Zealanders to reaffirm their values of respect and multicultural tolerance and to initiate constructive strategies to promote harmonious relationships across ethnic and religious groups.

3 Reducing Ethnic Conflict: Possible Solutions

3.1 Challenges and Aspirations

This section is organized around the challenges that *Aotearoa*/New Zealand faces in ethnic relations: achieving racial equality, the recognition of indigenous rights, and the acceptance of cultural diversity.

Achieving racial equality. Diminishing social inequality and eliminating discrimination form the basis of achieving racial equality.

Social inequality. Data from the 2001 and 2006 censuses show that there are significant differences in economic, educational, and health indicators amongst New Zealand's major ethnic groups. Comparative analyses reveal that Maori and Pacific people are particularly disadvantaged. There are also inequalities between native and overseas-born New Zealanders, particularly in terms of labor force participation and income. All of these issues must be addressed to achieve social equality in New Zealand.

Objective indicators of socioeconomic status and physical and mental health point to significant Maori disadvantage. Maori are more likely than the general population to leave school without a formal qualification, and they are underrepresented at the higher levels of education (Statistics New Zealand, 2007b). Sixty-nine percent of Maori are employed, most often in sales and service occupations; however, the Maori unemployment rate is higher and their median income and home ownership levels are significantly lower than that of their European counterparts (Statistics New Zealand, 2007b). They are also more likely to live in New Zealand's most socioeconomically deprived areas (Ministry of Health, 2006a). Maori are overrepresented in the prison population (Liu, 2007) and in mental health facilities as nonvoluntary patients; they are also more likely to be both victims and perpetrators of domestic violence (Fergusson, 2003). The morbidity and mortality figures are worse for Maori than non-Maori, and Maori life expectancy is on average eight years less than that of non-Maori (Ministry of Health, 2006a). Colonization, deprivation, and institutional racism have been implicated in these negative social, economic, and health outcomes (e.g., Quince, 2007). Although the 1999 Labor Party's "Closing the Gaps" program did result in improvements for Maori, there was little evidence that disparities significantly narrowed.

Social and economic indicators have been improving for Pacific peoples, but they are still markedly disadvantaged compared to the New Zealand population as a whole. Sixty percent of the Pacific population is New Zealand-born. Although about two-thirds of Pacific people over the age of 15 have some formal educational qualifications, fewer have post-school qualifications than the New Zealand adult population as a whole (Statistics New Zealand, 2007c). Sixty-five percent of the Pacific population is in the labor force, but their unemployment rate is significantly higher than the national average (Statistics New Zealand, 2007c). Median income and home ownership rates are lower for Pacific peoples than New Zealand Europeans (Statistics New Zealand, 2007c). The Ministry of Health (2007) reported that 27% of Pacific peoples meet the criteria for living in severe hardship compared to 8% of the total population and that this is a major contributor to their poor health outcomes, which include a lower life expectancy and a relatively high youth suicide rate. The Pacific population is overrepresented among violent offenders and has higher rates of criminal conviction than the general population; they are also more likely to be victims of violent offenses than New Zealand Europeans (Statistics New Zealand, 2002a).

Socioeconomic indicators for Asian New Zealanders present a more complex picture. The majority of the country's Asian population is overseas-born: Chinese (74%), Indians (73%), Japanese and Koreans (91%), and South-east

Asians (81%), and for the most part, new immigrants do not fare as well as their local-born peers (Office of Ethnic Affairs, 2005). This is illustrated by employment rate differentials between native (83.4%) and overseas-born (65.1%) Chinese, and large discrepancies in their median incomes (Statistics New Zealand, 2002b). On the whole, Asians have a higher level of education than other New Zealanders and are twice as likely to have a tertiary degree. Nevertheless, their labor force participation is less than the general population (Office of Ethnic Affairs, 2005). While Asians report the lowest median income of New Zealand's ethnic groups (Statistics New Zealand, 2007d), their health outcomes compare favorably to that of the New Zealand population (Ministry of Health, 2006b).

Immigrant groups from Anglo-Celtic countries fare particularly well in New Zealand and those from the United Kingdom, the United States, and Australia have higher median incomes than the native-born population (Ministry of Social Development, 2008). The same is true for those from South Africa and Zimbabwe. In contrast, peoples of Middle Eastern, Latin American, and African origin report a lower-than-average median income. These trends are consistent with the large variations in unemployment rates based on immigrants' regions of origin. Census data indicate that immigrants from the United Kingdom and Ireland (4.2%) and from North-west Europe (5.1%) have the lowest rates of unemployment, followed by those from the Americas (7.4%) and sub-Saharan Africa (7.9%). Immigrants from North Africa and the Middle East (23.8%) have the highest unemployment rates. Residents from Asia (North-east, 16.5%; South and Central, 13.9%; and South-east, 11%) and the Pacific Islands (13.5%) occupy an intermediate position (Statistics New Zealand, 2002b).

Both employment outcomes and income levels for refugees are poor. In 2006, the employment rates for prime working age migrants from "refugee" countries (Iran, Iraq, Somalia, Sudan, Ethiopia, Myanmar, Cambodia, Vietnam, Laos, and Balkan countries) were 26% below the rate for the New Zealand-born population (Ministry of Social Development, 2008). In the New Zealand Immigration Service's (2002) study of 209 refugees, only 15% reported that they were working for pay, and 88% indicated that a government benefit was their main source of income. Poverty, illiteracy, educational disadvantage, lack of employment opportunities, low levels of civic participation, and personal debt have all been cited as negative factors that lead to the social exclusion of refugee communities in New Zealand (Chile, 2002).

In summary, objective socioeconomic indicators reveal relative disadvantage for Maori, Pacific, and non-European immigrant and refugee groups. These inequalities have the potential to exert a negative influence on ethnic relations in New Zealand. First, relative deprivation has been implicated in the dynamics of intergroup hostility and prejudice (Mummendey, Kessler, Klink, & Mielke, 1999). Research from the United States, South Africa, Germany, Great Britain, France, and the Netherlands has shown that relative deprivation is a robust predictor of prejudice (Dambrun, Taylor, McDonald, Crush, & Méot, 2006; Pettigrew, 2002; Pettigrew & Meertens, 1995). Relative deprivation has also been posited to play an influential role in the militant political attitudes and collective protest movements of ethnic groups (Guimond & Dubé-Simard, 1983). Second, economic inequality is known to undermine social trust, an important component of social cohesion in ethnically and culturally diverse societies (Phan, 2008). Similarly, socioeconomic disadvantage is linked to greater perceptions of threat and more negative out-group attitudes (Ward & Leong, 2006). Third, relative advantage, studied under the rubric of relative gratification, has also been shown to have negative effects on out-group attitudes. Research in France demonstrated that relative gratification is linked to increased in-group bias, prejudice against out-groups, and willingness to support restrictive immigration policies (Guimond & Dambrun, 2002). A recent extension of this research to South Africans' attitudes to African and Western immigrants likewise supported the negative consequences of relative gratification (Dambrun et al., 2006). All of this converges to suggest that inequalities may lead to negative reactions to disadvantaged groups by

New Zealand Europeans and recent immigrants of European descent, hostility toward the majority group by disadvantaged minorities, and animosity between new immigrants and Maori, particularly if the former are unable to understand and appreciate the historical bases of indigenous rights.

Discrimination. What is the extent of ethnic discrimination in New Zealand? It depends on whom and how you ask. Researchers have suggested that discrimination is often underreported due to the psychological and social advantages of doing so (Finch, Kolody, & Vega, 2000). In addition, perceived discrimination is more likely to be recognized on the group, compared to the individual, level (Verkuyten, 2002). Consequently, the incidence and prevalence of discrimination may frequently be underestimated.

Harris et al. (2006) employed stratified random sampling in their survey of 12,500 New Zealanders about lifetime prevalence of racial discrimination. The areas of discrimination included ethnically motivated physical and verbal abuse and unfair treatment in work, housing, and health domains. Using weighted analyses to produce estimates representative of the New Zealand population, the researchers found that Maori reported the greatest experience of discrimination (34%), followed by Asian (28%) and Pacific (25%) peoples. The incidence of discrimination for Maori was more than twice as high than that for Europeans, and Maori were also ten times more likely than Europeans to experience multiple forms of discrimination. The most common form of discrimination for all ethnic groups was verbal abuse; however, in terms of unfair treatment, there was a tendency for Maori to report more discrimination in connection with housing and for Asians to report more employment-related discrimination.

The prevalence of verbal abuse has also been highlighted in smaller scale qualitative studies with various ethnic communities. Chang, Morris, and Vokes (2006) found that almost all of the participants in their study of Korean families experienced harassment and that the verbal abuse of "go back to where you came from" was very common. Guerin, Guerin, Diiriye, and Abdi (2004) likewise reported that Somali women were often victims of this type of verbal abuse. Although there has been little systematic research on discrimination among refugee communities, Chile (2002) noted that most black African refugees experience prejudice and discrimination.

Viewed from a different perspective, the Human Rights Commission received 407 complaints and enquiries on race-related grounds in 2008, out of a total of 1,518 complaints and enquiries about unlawful discrimination (Human Rights Commission, 2009). After disability, race was the most commonly cited grounds for discrimination and composed 14% of the total complaints. Other grounds included ethnic or national origin (10.5%), racial harassment (3%), racial disharmony (1.5%), and color (0.4%). The most common race-related complaints were in connection with obtaining or retaining employment, although bullying in the workplace was also noted. In addition to work-related discrimination, the provision of goods and services, denial of accommodation, and discrimination in educational settings were also reported.

Focus group research by Butcher, Spoonley, and Trlin (2006) with Asian and South African immigrants converges with these findings with employment and access to goods and services, particularly education and housing, frequently being cited as domains of discrimination. In addition, Muslim and Middle Eastern immigrants and refugees reported that the experience of discrimination related directly to the perceived threat of terrorism. The theme of terrorist-based discrimination toward Arab immigrants was also picked up in Stuart, Ward, Jose, and Narayanan's (2010) study of recently arrived African, Middle Eastern, and Asian families. Moreover, Jasperse and Ward (2009) found that Muslim women from the Middle East reported more discrimination than those from Asia, even after controlling for visibility arising from *hijab* (modest Islamic dress). It appears, then, that anti-Islamic feelings as an outcome of 9/11 make Muslims, especially visible Muslims, highly vulnerable to prejudice and discrimination.

Workplace discrimination has received considerable attention, particularly given that the admission of new immigrants is based on the

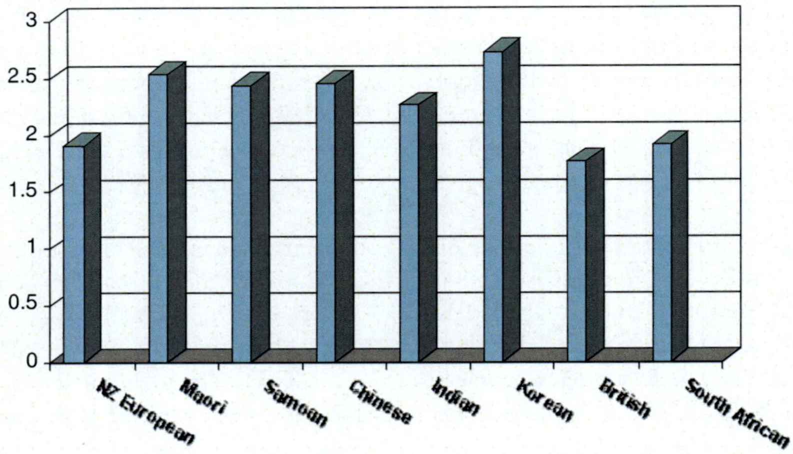

Fig. 3.1 Perceived discrimination across ethnic youth in New Zealand. Note. The measurement scale ranges from 1 to 5, with 5 representing greater perceived discrimination

country's skills shortages. New Zealand Immigration Service's (2004) report on the experiences of immigrants noted that seeking employment was the most commonly cited context for discrimination. Barriers to immigrant employment have been discussed in relation to issues pertaining to language proficiency and the discounting of overseas qualifications, as well as the unreceptive attitudes of employers (Henderson, Trlin, & Watts, 2001; Watts & Trlin, 1999, 2000). However, bias and discrimination have also been implicated (Podsiadlowski & Ward, 2010). Field research has shown that native-born New Zealanders of European descent are more likely to be pursued by recruitment agencies for further contact after the receipt of an unsolicited resume than Chinese immigrant candidates, despite equivalent educational qualifications and occupational experience and the same standard of written English (Ward & Masgoret, 2007). Further studies have demonstrated that both immigrant status and country of origin influence probable selection, with native-borns preferred to immigrants and those originating from Australia, Great Britain, and South Africa preferred to those from China and India (Coates & Carr, 2005; Wilson, Gahlout, Liu, & Mouly, 2005). In addition, simulated short-listing experiments with practicing managers found that Asian candidates increased the likelihood of being short-listed by anglicizing their names (Wilson et al., 2005).

Ward's (2009) research with immigrant and ethnic youth demonstrated that perceived discrimination is more a function of color than immigrant status. Figure 3.1 presents the levels of perceived discrimination in New Zealand European and Maori youth compared to that in first-generation British and South African immigrant peers, and first and later generations of Chinese, Indian, Korean, and Samoan adolescents, while controlling for the influence of age, gender, and length of residence in the country. The findings revealed that the level of perceived discrimination did not differ among the white groups (New Zealand European, British, and white South African) and that it was significantly less than the level reported by the Maori, Asian, and Pacific groups.

New Zealanders recognize that the playing field is not level. In a UMR survey reported by the Human Rights Commission (2010), 75% of respondents believed that Asians in New Zealand are subjected to some or a great deal of discrimination – more than any other identified group. There were similar expectations for new immigrants (63%) and refugees (61%).

Discrimination has negative consequences for individuals, groups, and society as a whole. On a personal level, discrimination has been linked to increased stress, negative self- and group-esteem, impaired health, and antisocial behaviors (Ward, Bochner, & Furnham, 2001). On the group level, perceived discrimination is associated with more negative intergroup attitudes (Liebkind, Jasinskaja-Lahti, & Teräsaho, 2007). It is also linked to separatist tendencies and a decreased willingness for integration (Barry & Grilo, 2003; Robinson, 2005). Indeed, there is strong evidence for reciprocal relationships amongst ethno-cultural groups in plural societies. Berry (2006) reported that in two national surveys undertaken with 12 groups in Canada, significant positive correlations were found between mutual intergroup perceptions. In Berry's (2006, p. 726) words, " If one group likes another group, the other tends to reciprocate that positive affect; and if one group dislikes another, this negative view tends to be reciprocated as well."

The recognition of indigenous rights: Symbolic biculturalism, liberal democracy, and national identity. The national identity of contemporary New Zealanders is influenced by the bicultural history of interaction between Maori and non-Maori in profound ways. For instance, New Zealand university undergraduates implicitly associate Maori (brown) faces just as closely to symbols of New Zealand national identity as they do European (white) faces (Sibley & Liu, 2007). This is in marked contrast to citizens of ostensibly similar Anglo-settler societies like the United States (Devos & Banaji, 2005) and Australia (Sibley & Barlow, 2009), where whites explicitly claim racial equality, but implicitly associate American or Australian symbols with the faces of white people more than with Blacks or Asians (in the case of America) or Aborigines (Australia). These implicit associations reflect the frequency with which representations and practices pertaining to the whole of New Zealand are made culturally distinct by pairing them with symbols of Maori people and culture, like the *haka* (expressive dance and narrative song), carvings, the singing of the national anthem in English and Maori, official ceremonies of welcome, and the entire layout of the national museum *Te Papa Tongarewa*.

The respect for this symbolic biculturalism, or what Sibley and Liu (2004) refer to as biculturalism in principle, is widely practiced and shared across many sectors of New Zealand society. It is relatively uncontroversial because symbolic biculturalism provides a "positive distinctiveness" that allows all New Zealanders to affirm their unique national identity (Liu, 2005). What is contested, on the contrary, is resource-based biculturalism, where the symbolic inclusion is translated into some form of practice whereby ethnicity becomes part of the equation for the distribution of resources.

Resource-based biculturalism is countered by widely promulgated societal discourses that deny the relevance of historical injustices to the current situation of Maori or relegate the dynamics of redress to "special privileges." In the first instance, Sibley et al. (2008) identified a highly coherent ideology of "historical negation" (declaring the past as irrelevant to the present and future) that powerfully mediates the effects of prejudicial orientations on opposition to social policy to rectify Maori disadvantage. In other words, although Maori are symbolically included in the New Zealand national identity, their claims for redress of historical injustice and their calls for a greater share of national resources are either denied or accepted with great reluctance by negating the relevance of history to the present (Sibley et al., 2008).

In addition to "historical negation," discourses of "special privileges" position Maori claims for redress of past injustices in opposition to widely held liberal democratic notions of fairness, equality, and individual deservingness (Kirkwood et al. 2005). This sets up a tension between the historical basis of biculturalism and the fundamental principles of a contemporary liberal democracy; it also undermines policies designed to rectify disadvantages. The future of these policies ultimately comes to rest on their capacity to shelter under the accommodation given to symbolic biculturalism, while endeavoring to educate people about the realities of the history of colonization and its current impacts on Maori.

These dynamics are consistent with sociologist Tracey McIntosh's (2005) scheme of three identity positions for Maori as fixed, forced, and fluid. Fixed identity is anchored by traditional notions of *whakapapa*, or genealogy, fluency in *te reo*, and ability to function on a *marae* (specifically a Maori meeting house, but more broadly understood as a symbolic location for the practice of Maori culture) or in other Maori institutions. This identity is unashamedly essentialized and often adopted by elite Maori who call upon the symbolic inclusion of Maori within the national identity to forge a powerful position for themselves in many sectors of society, particularly in the government provision of services. Forced identity, by contrast, is forged under conditions of deprivation, often upon urban Maori who have no choice but to be positioned by negative stereotypes, frequently without the benefits of actual fluency in Maori culture. Finally, the fluid identity is a hybrid constructed out of urban fusions of contemporary popular culture, including music, art, and humor.

The Maori cultural renaissance has had significant implications for the identity of non-Maori as well. Led by eminent historians such as Michael King (2003) and James Belich (1996), New Zealanders have begun to construct a story of themselves as a people through the lenses of a bicultural narrative of interactions between Maori and non-Maori. Perhaps as many as a quarter of New Zealanders of European descent self-identify as *Pakeha*, which is a self-designation that acknowledges a relationship with Maori as a part of one's own group identity (Liu, 2005). Alternatively, many white New Zealanders prefer to call themselves New Zealand Europeans (in recognition of their cultural origins) or prefer to claim the national identity and refer to themselves as "kiwis" or "just New Zealanders." Regardless of the subjective identity position adopted, all these identities either affirm or deny the relationship with Maori as part of their definition of self. Despite shortcomings in redressing injustices and achieving full recognition of indigenous rights, in New Zealand, Maori are a part of the national culture in a way that is not found for indigenous peoples in many other parts of the world. By way of example, Maori words have found their way into common discourse (as shown in this chapter), the *Aotearoa*/New Zealand national anthem is sung first in *te reo* and then in English, *powhiri* are often held to welcome guests at government functions, and the *haka* is performed at international sporting events.

Accepting cultural diversity. Beyond the recognition and acceptance of indigenous rights, New Zealand has a pressing need to resolve challenges linked to the country's increasing cultural diversity. The late Michael King was optimistic about the challenge:

> Most New Zealanders, whatever their cultural backgrounds, are good-hearted, practical, commonsensical and tolerant. Those qualities are part of the national cultural capital that has in the past saved the country from the worst excesses of chauvinism and racism seen in other parts of the world. (King, 2003, p. 520)

Recent research has largely borne out his contention. Ward and Masgoret's (2008) national survey of over 2,000 households found that New Zealanders strongly endorsed a multicultural ideology. Eight-nine percent of survey respondents agreed that it is a good thing for a society to be made up of different races, religions, and cultures, and this was significantly higher than the proportion of agreement found in comparable national polls in Australia (85%; Dunn, 2003) and 15 European Union countries (36–75%; Eurobarometer, 2000). In addition, 80% endorsed the statement that it is important to accept a wide variety of cultures in New Zealand. The researchers also found that perceptions of threat were low to moderate with one in four agreeing that immigration increases the level of crime and one in five maintaining that allowing immigrant cultures to thrive means the New Zealand culture is weakened. Although some studies suggest that New Zealanders believe that there are too many immigrants in the country (Spoonley, Gendall, & Trlin, 2007), Ward and Masgoret's (2008) research shows that when informed about the actual number of immigrants, the majority agree that the number is "about right."

Ward and Masgoret (2006, 2008) also examined the predictors of positive attitudes toward immigrants and immigration policy. More positive attitudes were found in those who were overseas-born, could speak languages other than English and Maori, and had higher levels of education. Synthesizing aspects of Integrated Threat Theory (Stephan & Stephan, 2000; Stephan, Ybarra, & Bachman, 1999), the Instrumental Model of Group Conflict (Esses, Jackson, & Armstrong, 1998), the contact hypothesis (Allport, 1954; Pettigrew & Tropp, 2000), and the multicultural hypothesis (Berry, 2006; Berry, Kalin, & Taylor, 1977), the researchers proposed and found support for a model where a strong multicultural ideology and more frequent intergroup contact led to perceptions of diminished threat and then on to more positive attitudes toward immigrants. Positive attitudes toward immigrants, in turn, predicted more support for current immigration policies regarding the number and diverse national origins of immigrants admitted to New Zealand.

Not all national surveys have produced such positive results. Spoonley et al. (2007) suggested that anti-immigrant sentiments in New Zealand peaked in the mid-1990s when the numbers were at their highest and that attitudes have since become more moderate. Their 2007 postal survey of 1,118 respondents sampled from the New Zealand electoral rolls found that although a majority (60%) agreed that the diversity that immigration brings to New Zealand is a good thing, almost half (47%) believed that the recent arrival of many Asian immigrants is changing New Zealand in undesirable ways. Despite these negative perceptions of Asian immigrants, just over half agreed that the government should develop policies to support multiculturalism in New Zealand. Spoonley et al. observed that the perceived positive aspects of immigration were pitted against concerns about its social and economic costs, and concluded that overall, the survey results could be interpreted as reflecting "racial intolerance or (at best) fragile racial tolerance" (p.29), at least with respect to non-English-speaking immigrants.

Both the Ward and Masgoret (2008) and the Spoonley et al. (2007) national surveys provided evidence that there is a hierarchy of desirable immigrants in New Zealand. Ward and Masgoret reported that settlers from Australia were viewed more positively than all other groups. The preference for Australians was followed by preferences for British, South African, and Indian immigrants, with each of these differing significantly from the others. There were no significant differences in perceptions of Indians and Chinese or between Chinese and Samoans, but new settlers from Somalia were viewed less favorably than all other groups. It is important to note, however, that the least favorable perceptions of immigrants in this study were not explicitly negative (mean = 51.4 on a scale of 100). With specific reference to the economic contributions of immigrants, Spoonley et al. found that 55% of their respondents believed that British immigrants were good for the country's economy and that half agreed this was the case for other Europeans, South Africans, and Chinese; however, just 30% endorsed this view of Indian immigrants and only 12% for Pacific peoples. Overall, the studies converge to demonstrate a preference for immigrants of European descent.

A smaller scale survey of 300 New Zealanders randomly sampled from the electoral rolls by Stuart, Ward, and Adam (2010) examined perceptions of both ethnic and religious immigrant groups in the country. The findings indicated a preference for immigrants with a Christian background and revealed slightly negative perceptions of those who are Muslim. The research also found slightly negative perceptions of immigrants from predominantly Muslim countries such as Pakistan, Indonesia, and Malaysia, and even more negative perceptions of those from Somalia, Iran, and Afghanistan, countries that are associated with New Zealand's major refugee populations.

Because of both historical and socio-political factors, a major issue relating to the acceptance of cultural diversity is the relationship between Maori and the country's new settlers. On this count, research findings are clear. Maori hold more negative attitudes to immigrants in general; they perceive them as being a greater source of economic competition and a more significant cultural threat (Leong & Ward, 2011). They are also more likely to endorse the exclusion of further immigrants to *Aotearoa*/New Zealand (Masgoret & Ward, 2005; Spoonley et al., 2007). There is little doubt that there is a widespread perception among many Maori that new immigrants are undermining their rightful place in New Zealand society.

Some of the most extensive research on this issue has been undertaken on the relationship between Maori and Chinese immigrants. Ip (2003) has noted the "overwhelmingly negative" Maori views of recent Chinese immigrants, including unfavorable stereotyping and perceptions of both realistic economic and symbolic cultural threat. This has also been borne out in Leong and Ward's (2003) research where 44% of Maori agreed that recent Chinese migrants are displacing New Zealand workers from their jobs, compared to 17% of non-Maori. Maori were also more likely to agree that Chinese culture threatens to overwhelm New Zealand culture (61% vs. 24%), while non-Maori were twice as willing to acknowledge that New Zealand society has benefited from attracting Chinese migrants.

It is not only the status of Maori as the indigenous people of *Aotearoa*/New Zealand and the lack of consultation about immigration policies and procedures that underpin their antipathy toward immigrants, but also their position of vulnerability in the wider New Zealand society that contribute to these reactions. Indeed, the consequences of immigration have been described in terms of its "beneficiaries" (largely the immigrants themselves) and the "losers" (mainly Maori) in some thoughtful analyses of immigration policy and the political economy in New Zealand, including analyses by Maori scholars (e.g., Walker, 1995). But perceptions of negative consequences arising from immigration are not limited to Maori. A major challenge to harmonious ethnic relations in New Zealand, then, is to ensure mutual acceptance and respect among all ethnic groups, rather than merely focusing attention on the relationship between the majority and the indigenous and ethnic minorities.

Beyond mutual intergroup perceptions, social opinion about how new immigrants should manage issues of cultural maintenance and participation in society is an important component of intergroup relations. The strong endorsement of a multicultural ideology would suggest that New Zealanders favor integration; that is, the belief that new settlers should not only maintain their culture and traditions but also adopt the aspects of New Zealand culture and participate in the wider society. Research has supported this contention. Eighty-two percent of respondents in Ward and Masgoret's (2008) national survey supported integration, compared to only 21% and 28% who endorsed assimilation (giving up traditional culture for the sake of adopting New Zealand culture) and separation (retaining traditional culture, but not mixing it with New Zealand culture), respectively. The strong endorsement of integration converges with immigrant preferences. Both adolescent and adult immigrants from the Asian region express a strong preference for integration, and only a small minority agree with the principles of assimilation and separation (Ward, 2009). Although these findings point to positive developments on the road to multiculturalism, in reality the social and political situation is not as optimistic. The majority of New Zealand Europeans readily agree with the principle that immigrants should retain their own culture while also adopting New Zealand culture, but when asked about their willingness to accommodate cultural maintenance in a broader sense, the responses shift markedly. Only 10% agree that New Zealanders should transform aspects of their culture in order to integrate immigrant cultures (Stuart & Ward, 2009). Achieving integration is not a simple process, and research again suggests that there is a substantial gap between lofty principles and accommodating practices. In addition to the gap between principles and practices, managing potentially competing pressures of biculturalism and multiculturalism presents a major challenge. This critical issue is discussed in the following section.

4 Enhancing Ethnic Relations: A View to the Future

Critical examination of the principles and practices that impact on ethnic relations in *Aotearoa*/New Zealand is the first step in framing a vision that might guide future developments. In undertaking such a task, it is important to acknowledge that despite the limitations of current research, which is largely confined to New Zealand European's relationships with either *tangata whenua* (indigenous people) or nonindigenous ethnic minorities, mutual perceptions and relations among all ethnic groups must be considered. That being said, the two core issues that must be tackled are (1) the relationship between biculturalism and multiculturalism and (2) the construction of a New Zealand national identity.

Academics, politicians, journalists, and "ordinary New Zealanders" have commented in various forms and fashions on the opposition and incompatibility of biculturalism and multiculturalism. From one perspective, multiculturalism is seen as valuing and supporting diversity and casting all cultures as equal. This poses problems for Maori, who are reluctant to see themselves as merely one minority culture among many. From an opposing perspective, biculturalism is portrayed as acknowledging and incorporating only two cultures – those based on Maori and British heritage – thereby marginalizing newer Asian, Pacific, and other immigrants in multiethnic *Aotearoa*/New Zealand. Not everyone, however, sees the two "isms" as conflicting (Thomas, 2004). Indeed, recent research indicated that support for biculturalism and multiculturalism is positively correlated for *Pakeha* youth and unrelated in their Maori, Chinese, and Pacific peers. There was no evidence that the two are seen as conflicting or mutually exclusive by any of these ethnic groups (Ward & Lin, 2005).

Much of the debate about biculturalism *versus* multiculturalism arises because of lack of consensus about what the terms actually mean. Drawing on work by Berry (1984, 2000), we suggest that multiculturalism is achieved when all cultures can be largely maintained and are respected, and when members of each culture can participate fully in the wider, plural society. There are two important aspects of this definition. First, multiculturalism involves both cultural maintenance and participation; second, multiculturalism is viewed as a process leading to an end point, acknowledging that, in reality, movement toward multiculturalism is a more viable phenomenon than reaching the final destination. This conceptualization of multiculturalism is one that transcends national boundaries and could readily be used in diverse ethnic and cultural contexts.

Biculturalism is another matter. The nature of biculturalism in *Aotearoa* is undoubtedly country specific. Indeed, the term has quite a different meaning in contemporary psychological theory and research in other countries (e.g., Haritatos & Benet-Martínez, 2002). The notion of biculturalism in New Zealand arises from the special status of Maori as *tangata whenua* and the Treaty of Waitangi signed between Maori and the Crown. While acknowledging that the Treaty is an evolving contract and its interpretation has altered over time, its fundamental principles include *kawanatanga*, *rangatiratanga*, equality for all citizens, reasonable cooperation between the Crown and *iwi*, and redress of past injustices. Consistent with the principles of multiculturalism, *rangatiratanga* ensures protection of Maori language and culture, and "equality for all citizens" addresses the issues of inclusion and participation in the wider society. But biculturalism provides additional rights for Maori, including a large degree of autonomy in control of "things Maori" and redress of past injustices. In addition, as the interpretation of the Treaty evolves into one of a bicultural partnership, there is an expectation that "things Maori" have a significant place in defining the national identity that elements from non-indigenous minority cultures would not have. In short, the Treaty principles are in keeping with the key features of multiculturalism, but they also endow Maori with additional rights and responsibilities. However, as long as intergroup relations between Maori and *Pakeha* reflect the symbolic inclusion of Maori culture, but resource-based marginalization and the historical negation of Maori grievances continue, the full recognition of indigenous rights cannot be achieved.

Research suggests that New Zealanders accept both biculturalism and multiculturalism in principle; however, there are limits to the extent to which New Zealanders of European descent are prepared to relinquish privilege to meet bicultural and multicultural ideals. *Pakeha* endorse the symbolic representation of biculturalism and acknowledge Treaty grievances, but are largely unprepared to support initiatives that are perceived to provide categorical privileges for Maori in terms of material resources, in order to address past injustices or achieve social equality (Liu, 2005). Similarly, New Zealanders overwhelmingly believe that it is a good thing for the country to be made up of different races, religions, and cultures, but are significantly less willing to make concrete changes that accommodate multiculturalism (Stuart & Ward, 2009). Competition over valuable and limited resources may partially account for these trends; however, it is also commonplace to argue that concessions on the basis of ethnicity, whether on the basis of special historical status as in the case of Maori or on the basis of relative need for new immigrants, violate the principles of a liberal democracy (Liu, 2005; Ward & Masgoret, 2006).

Despite ambivalent public attitudes about resources and social change, there is a range of government-supported initiatives that facilitate the achievement of objectives common to both biculturalism and multiculturalism, specifically cultural maintenance and participation. *Kohanga reo* and *kura kauapapa* are well resourced, as it is widely accepted that to function as Treaty partners, Maori must be able to practice their language and culture. Resourcing equal participation for Maori, however, has been more controversial as demonstrated by the rapid demise of the "Closing the Gaps" policy, which included both greater responsiveness to Maori from mainstream government departments and Maori capacity-building (Humpage & Fleras, 2001). For newer immigrants, issues of inclusion and participation are seen by policy makers as more pressing than cultural maintenance. Consequently, in addition to English as a second language, training opportunities for refugees, and language- and employment-focused programs for immigrants (Roach & Roskvist, 2007), the Office of Ethnic Affairs provides a national Language Line, interpreting services in 39 languages. It will be interesting to see how cultural maintenance issues for recent immigrants are addressed in the future as their communities become better established in New Zealand.

What about issues of biculturalism and multiculturalism seen from the perspectives of Maori and new settlers? There have been recent positive moves that bring these groups together in a shared understanding of the principles of biculturalism and multiculturalism. Recently, the New Zealand Federation of Ethnic Councils has begun to lobby the government for a Multicultural Act, premised on the recognition of the special status of Maori, the Treaty of Waitangi and Maori aspirations, and guaranteeing cultural maintenance and participation for all ethnic groups. At the same time, Tariana Turia (2008), co-leader of the Maori party, addressed the ethnic councils, highlighting Maori values such as *manaakitanga* that would ensure that all people who make New Zealand their homes are treated with fairness and dignity, and *kaitiakitanga* that underpins the growth and development of Maori, Pacific, and other ethnic groups and cultures in New Zealand. We believe that acceptance of both bicultural and multicultural principles is a prerequisite for strong and healthy ethnic relations in *Aotearoa/*New Zealand. Although turning these principles into practices remains a significant challenge, the five principles of the Treaty of Waitangi and their intersection with the core components of multiculturalism provide an appropriate framework for such a task.

The second major avenue to the enhancement of positive ethnic relations in New Zealand is the achievement of a superordinate national identity. This permits hyphenated identities, such as Chinese New Zealander or Samoan Kiwi, as well as inclusiveness for all ethnic groups under the encompassing category of New Zealander. Research has shown that immigrant and ethnic groups are already adopting these labels (Ward & Lin, 2005), but the implications for Maori and New Zealanders of European descent are less clear. Although survey research indicates that the former have both strong ethnic and national identities (Ward & Lin, 2005), popular discourse suggests that Maori identity is not simply an ethnic identity nested within the national identity. The *tino rangatiratanga* movement further suggests that there are aspirations among some parts of Maoridom for Maori identity to function as a national identity. Moreover, while there is a range of aspirations in this self-determination movement, among more activist elements *tino rangatiratanga* denotes sovereignty (see Walker, 1990), and there would certainly be a few *iwi* that would have an agenda to become a sovereign nation, or at least a nation within a nation.

Empirical research on this issue is lacking, but research based on the Common In-group Identity Model indicates that when national identity is used as an inclusive superordinate category, which permits the retention of ethno-cultural heritage, intergroup relations are enhanced and a more tolerant society evolves (Gaertner, Dovidio, Anastasio, Bachman, & Rust, 1993; Gaertner, Dovidio, & Bachman, 1996).

A challenge for New Zealand, however, is defining what, precisely, is national identity. As discussed in the 2010 Ministry of Social Development's Social Report:

> Defining national identity is not a simple matter. New Zealand is a diverse nation, made up of many cultural groups, with many different customs and traditions. While people may describe themselves

> as a New Zealander, how they define their New Zealander-ness may vary from person to person. For example, they might see a New Zealand identity in aspects of New Zealand history, in New Zealand achievements in sporting, artistic or other endeavors, through a sense of national characteristics or traits, or through national symbols or icons. Maori culture may form one aspect of national identity, since it is unique to New Zealand and forms part of our identity in the outside world. (p.1)

While we are also unable to articulate a clear definition of New Zealand national identity, the Social Report captures two important elements. First, Maori culture makes a unique contribution to New Zealand identity, and second, New Zealand is a diverse nation. Reflecting the reality of both biculturalism and multiculturalism, this forms a good starting point.

5 Summary and Conclusions

In summary, this chapter traced New Zealand's colonial history and described early Maori–*Pakeha* relations as well as the more recent Maori renaissance. Emphasis was placed on the significance of the Treaty of Waitangi/*Te Tiriti o Waitangi* as providing the foundation for a bicultural *Aotearoa*. At the same time, a shift in immigration trends was described, and the implications of the "changing face" of New Zealand for ethnic relations were discussed. Three broad strategies for reducing ethnic conflict were identified: eliminating social inequality, recognizing indigenous rights, and increasing acceptance of cultural diversity.

Beyond these generic objectives, *Aotearoa*/New Zealand faces the unique challenge of balancing the respect for indigenous rights with multicultural responsibilities in a culturally diverse society. The challenge does not lie in an incompatibility of bicultural and multicultural principles; indeed, biculturalism and multiculturalism share two core components of cultural maintenance and equal participation. Rather, this entails pragmatic social change that (1) supplements symbolic biculturalism with the practice of resource-based biculturalism for Maori and (2) goes beyond multicultural tolerance to reasonable accommodation for and social inclusion of other ethnic groups in in *Aotearoa*/New Zealand.

Glossary of Maori Terms

Hapu	Subdivision of iwi, a subtribe determined by genealogical descent
Hikoi	Protest march
Hui	A meeting, often on a marae
Iwi	Tribe, sometimes under a paramount chief
Kaitiakitanga	Guardianship of the environment, ensuring balance between nature and communities
Kawanatanga	Governorship
Kohanga reo	Preschool Maori language centers, also called Maori language nests
Kura kaupapa	Maori language primary schools
Manaakitanga	Looking after people and nurturing positive relationships, Maori hospitality
Marae	Maori meeting house
Nga Tamatoa	The Warriors, a Maori activist group
Pakeha	Non-Maori persons, typically used to refer to people of European descent
Te Papa Tongarewa	Container of treasures, *Aotearoa*/New Zealand's national museum
Te Puni Kokiri	Ministry of Maori Development
Te reo	The Maori language
Te Tiriti o Waitangi	Treaty of Waitangi
Tino rangatiratanga	Self-determination, also translated as sovereignty, sometimes used to refer to Maori independence
Waka	Large canoe
Whanau	Extended family

References

Allport, G. (1954). *The nature of prejudice*. Reading, MA: Addison-Wesley.

Anae, M. (1997). Towards a New Zealand-born Samoan identity. *Pacific Health Dialog, 4*, 128–137.

Ansley, B. (2006). So who do we keep out? *New Zealand Listener, 205*. Retrieved May 1, 2009, from http://www.listener.co.nz/issue/3460/features/6926/so_who_do_we_keep_out.htm.

Barry, D. T., & Grilo, C. M. (2003). Cultural, self-esteem and demographic correlates of perception of personal and group discrimination among East Asian immigrants. *American Journal of Ortho-Psychiatry, 73*, 223–229.

Beaglehole, A. (2007). Immigration regulation. *Te Ara-The Encyclopedia of New Zealand.* Retrieved May 3, 2009, *from* http://www.TeAra.govt.nz/NewZealanders/NewZealandPeoples/ImmigrationRegulation/en.

Belich, J. (1986). *The New Zealand wars and the Victorian interpretation of racial conflict*. Auckland, NZ: Penguin.

Belich, J. (1996). *Making peoples: A history of the New Zealanders*. Auckland, NZ: Allen Lane/Penguin.

Berry, J. W. (1984). Multicultural policy in Canada: A social psychological analysis. *Canadian Journal of Behavioral Science, 16*, 353–370.

Berry, J. W. (2000). Socio-psychological costs and benefits of multiculturalism: A view from Canada. In J. W. Dacyl & C. Westin (Eds.), *Governance and cultural diversity* (pp. 297–354). Stockholm: UNESCO & CIEFO, Stockholm University.

Berry, J. W. (2006). Mutual attitudes among immigrants and ethno-cultural groups in plural societies. *International Journal of Intercultural Relations, 30*, 719–734.

Berry, J. W., Kalin, R., & Taylor, D. (1977). *Multiculturalism and ethnic attitudes in Canada*. Ottawa: Ministry of Supply and Services.

Berry, J. W., Westin, C., Virta, E., Vedder, P., Rooney, R., & Sang, D. (2006). Design of the study: Selecting societies of settlement and immigrant groups. In J. W. Berry, J. S. Phinney, D. L. Sam, & P. Vedder (Eds.), *Immigrant youth in cultural transition: Acculturation, identity and adaptation across national contexts* (pp. 15–47). Mahwah, NJ: Lawrence Erlbaum Associates.

Brash, D. (2006). *Address to the National Conference of the New Zealand Association for Migration and Investment*. Auckland, New Zealand. Retrieved May 3, 2009, from http://www.nzherald.co.nz/opinion/news/article.cfm?c_id=466&objectid=10393450.

Brooking, T., & Rabel, R. (1995). Neither British nor Polynesia: A brief history of New Zealand's other immigrants. In S. Greif (Ed.), *Immigration and national identity in New Zealand* (pp. 23–49). Palmerston North, NZ: Dunmore Press.

Butcher, A., Spoonley, P., & Trlin, A. (2006). *Being accepted: The experience of social exclusion and discrimination by migrants and refugees in New Zealand. Occasional paper no. 13, New Settlers Programme.* Palmerston North, NZ: Massey University.

Byrnes, G. (2005). Nation and identity in the Waitangi Tribunal reports. In J. H. Liu, T. McCreanor, T. McIntosh, & T. Teaiwa (Eds.), *New Zealand identities: Departures and destinations* (pp. 88–103). Wellington, NZ: Victoria University Press.

Chang, S., Morris, C., & Vokes, R. (2006). *Korean migrant families in Christchurch* (Blue Skies Report no. 11/06). Wellington, NZ: Families Commission.

Chile, L. (2002). The imported underclass: Poverty and social exclusion of black African refugees in Aotearoa New Zealand. *Asia Pacific Viewpoint, 43*, 355–366.

Coates, K., & Carr, S. (2005). Skilled immigrants and selection bias: A theory-based field study from New Zealand. *International Journal of Intercultural Relations, 29*, 577–599.

Dambrun, M., Taylor, D., McDonald, D. A., Crush, J., & Méot, A. (2006). The relative deprivation-gratification continuum and attitudes of South Africans toward immigrants: A test of the V-curve hypothesis. *Journal of Personality and Social Psychology, 91*, 1034–1044.

Davidson, J. (1984). *The prehistory of New Zealand.* Auckland, NZ: Longman Paul.

de Bres, J., & Campbell, R. (1976). *The over-stayers: Illegal migration from the Pacific to New Zealand.* Auckland, NZ: Auckland Resources Center for World Development.

Devos, T., & Banaji, M. R. (2005). American = White? *Journal of Personality and Social Psychology, 88*, 447–466.

Dunn, K. (2003, April). *Attitudes toward immigrants and immigration: An Australian perspective*. Paper presented at New Directions, New Settlers, New challenges: Building and enhancing Communities Symposium, Wellington, New Zealand.

Esses, V. M., Jackson, L. M., & Armstrong, T. L. (1998). Intergroup competition and attitudes toward immigrants and immigration. *Journal of Social Issues, 54*, 699–724.

Eurobarometer. (2000). *Attitudes toward minority groups in the European Union: A special analysis of the Eurobarometer 2000 opinion poll on behalf of the European Monitoring Center on Racism and Xenophobia*. Eurobarometer Opinion Poll. Retrieved September 1, 2003, from http://europa.eu.int/comm/public_opinion/index_en.htm.

Fergusson, D. (2003). Ethnicity and interpersonal violence in a New Zealand birth cohort. In D. F. Hawkins (Ed.), *Violent crime: Assessing race and ethnic differences* (pp. 138–153). Cambridge: Cambridge University Press.

Finch, B. K., Kolody, B., & Vega, W. A. (2000). Perceived discrimination and depression among Mexican-American adults in California. *Journal of Health and Social Behavior, 41*, 295–313.

Gaertner, S., Dovidio, J., Anastasio, P., Bachman, B., & Rust, M. (1993). The common in-group identity model: Recategorization and the reduction of intergroup bias. In W. Stroebe & M. Hewstone (Eds.),

European review of social psychology (Vol. 4, pp. 1–26). Chichester, UK: Wiley.

Gaertner, S., Dovidio, J., & Bachman, B. A. (1996). Revisiting the contact hypothesis: The induction of a common in-group identity. *International Journal of Intercultural Relations, 20*, 271–290.

Gamson, W. A., & Modigliani, A. (1987). The changing culture of affirmative action. In R. G. Braungart & M. M. Braungart (Eds.), *Research in political sociology* (Vol. 3, pp. 137–177). Greenwich, CT: JAI.

Guerin, B., Guerin, P., Diiriye, R. O., & Abdi, A. (2004). Living in a close community: The everyday life of Somali refugees. *Network: Journal of the Australian College Community Psychology, 16*, 7–17.

Guimond, S., & Dambrun, M. (2002). When prosperity breeds intergroup hostility: The effects of relative deprivation and relative gratification on prejudice. *Personality and Social Psychology Bulletin, 28*, 900–912.

Guimond, S., & Dubé-Simard, L. (1983). Relative deprivation theory and the Quebec nationalist movement: The cognition-emotion distinction and the personal-group deprivation issue. *Journal of Personality and Social Psychology, 44*, 526–535.

Haritatos, J., & Benet-Martínez, V. (2002). Bicultural identities: The interface of cultural, personality and socio-cognitive processes. *Journal of Research in Personality, 36*, 598–606.

Harris, R., Tobias, M., Jeffreys, M., Waldegrave, K., Karlsen, S., & Nazroo, J. (2006). Racism and health: The relationship between experience of racial discrimination and health in New Zealand. *Social Science and Medicine, 63*, 1428–1441.

Henderson, A., Trlin, A., & Watts, N. (2001). Squandered skills? The employment problems of skilled Chinese immigrants in New Zealand. In R. Starrs (Ed.), *Asian nationalisms in an age of globalization* (pp. 106–123). Richmond, UK: Curzon Press.

Human Rights Commission. (2009). *Tui Tui Tuituia: Race relations in 2008*. Wellington, NZ: Human Rights Commission.

Human Rights Commission. (2010). *Tui Tui Tuituia: Race relations in 2009*. Wellington, NZ: Human Rights Commission.

Humpage, L., & Fleras, A. (2001). Intersecting discourses: Closing the gaps, social justice and the Treaty of Waitangi. *Social Policy Journal of New Zealand, 16*, 37–54.

Hunn, J. K. (1961). *Report on department of Maori affairs*. Wellington, NZ: Government Printer.

Ip, M. (2003). Maori-Chinese encounters: Indigine-immigrant interaction in New Zealand. *Asian Studies Review, 27*, 227–252.

Ip, M., & Pang, D. (2005). New Zealand Chinese identity: Sojourners, model minority and multiple identities. In J. H. Liu, T. McCreanor, T. McIntosh, & T. Teaiwa (Eds.), *New Zealand identities: Departures and destinations* (pp. 174–190). Wellington, NZ: Victoria University Press.

Jasperse, M., & Ward, C. (2009, August). *Persevere in adversity: Perceived religious discrimination, religious visibility and Islamic identity as predictors of psychological adaptation in Muslim women*. Paper presented at the Sixth Biennial Conference of the International Academy of Intercultural Research, Honolulu, HW.

King, M. (2003). *The Penguin history of New Zealand*. Auckland, NZ: Penguin Books.

Kirkwood, S., Liu, J. H., & Weatherall, A. (2005). Challenging the standard story of indigenous rights in Aotearoa/New Zealand. *Journal of Community and Applied Social Psychology, 15*, 1–13.

Leckie, J. (1995). South Asians: Old and new migrations. In S. Greif (Ed.), *Immigration and national identity in New Zealand* (pp. 133–160). Palmerston North, NZ: Dunmore Press.

Leong, C.-H., & Ward, C. (2003, April). *New Zealanders' attitudes toward Chinese migrants*. Paper presented at New Directions, New Settlers, New Challenges: Building and Enhancing Communities Symposium, Wellington, New Zealand.

Leong, C.-H., & Ward, C. (2011). Intergroup perceptions and attitudes toward immigrants in a culturally plural society. *Applied Psychology: An International Review, 60*, 46–65.

Levine, H., & Gezentsvey, M. (2005–2006). The Wellington cemetery desecrations of 2004 – Their impact on local Jews. *Journal of New Zealand Studies, 4–5*, 91–109.

Liebkind, K., Jasinskaja-Lahti, I., & Teräsaho, M. (2007). Ingroup vitality and intergroup attitudes in a linguistic minority. *Scandinavian Journal of Psychology, 48*, 409–418.

Liu, J. H. (2005). History and identity: A system of checks and balances for Aotearoa/New Zealand. In J. H. Liu, T. McCreanor, T. McIntosh, & T. Teaiwa (Eds.), *New Zealand identities: Departures and destinations* (pp. 69–87). Wellington, NZ: Victoria University Press.

Liu, J. H. (2007). Social and historical contexts for restorative and retributive justice: Te Ao Po- Te Ao Marama (worlds of darkness and light). In G. Maxwell & J. H. Liu (Eds.), *Restorative justice and practices in New Zealand: Towards a restorative society* (pp. 29–39). Wellington, NZ: Institute of Policy Studies.

Liu, J. H., & Mills, D. (2006). Modern racism and market fundamentalism: The discourses of plausible deniability and their multiple functions. *Journal of Community and Applied Social Psychology, 16*, 83–99.

Liu, J. H., Wilson, M. S., McClure, J., & Higgins, T. R. (1999). Social identity and the perception of history: Cultural representations of Aotearoa/New Zealand. *European Journal of Social Psychology, 29*, 1021–1047.

Masgoret, A.-M., & Ward, C. (2005, May). Attitudes toward immigrants and immigration in New Zealand. Fourth Biennial Conference of the International Academy of Intercultural Research, Kent, OH.

McIntosh, T. (2005). Maori identities: Fixed, fluid, forced. In J. H. Liu, T. McCreanor, T. McIntosh, & T. Teaiwa (Eds.), *New Zealand identities: Departures and destinations* (pp. 38–51). Wellington, NZ: Victoria University Press.

Ministry of Health. (2006a). *Tatau kahukura- Maori health chart book (2006)*. Wellington, NZ: Ministry of Health.

Ministry of Health. (2006b). *Asian health chart book (2006)*. Wellington, NZ: Ministry of Health.

Ministry of Health (2007). Pacific health. Retrieved April 30, 2009, from http://www.moh.govt.nz/moh.nsf/indexmh/pacifichealth-health-factors.

Ministry of Social Development. (2008). *Diverse communities: Exploring the refugee and migrant experience in New Zealand*. Wellington, NZ: Ministry of Social Development.

Ministry of Social Development. (2010). *The Social report*. Retrieved November 1, 2010, from http://www.socialreport.msd.govt.nz/documents/cultural-identity-social-report-2010.pd.

Moughan, A. (2010). *Identity and leadership in the long-term New Zealand Chinese community*. Unpublished Honors thesis, Victoria University of Wellington.

Mummendy, A., Kessler, T., Klink, A., & Mielke, R. (1999). Strategies to cope with negative social identity. *Journal of Personality and Social Psychology, 76*, 229–245.

Myrdal, G. (1944). *An American dilemma: The Negro problem and modern democracy*. New York: Harper & Row.

New Zealand Immigration Service. (1991). *New Zealand's immigration policy*. Wellington: New Zealand Immigration Service.

New Zealand Immigration Service. (2002). *Refugee voices- Interim report: A journey towards resettlement*. Wellington, NZ: Department of Labor.

New Zealand Immigration Service. (2004). *Migrants' experiences of New Zealand: Pilot survey report*. Wellington, NZ: Department of Labor.

Office of Ethnic Affairs. (2005). *New Zealand ethnic profile series (2001 census)*. Wellington, NZ: New Zealand.

Ongley, P. (1991). Pacific Islands' migration and the New Zealand labor market. In P. Spoonley, D. Pearson, & C. Macpherson (Eds.), *Nga take: Ethnic relations and racism in Aotearoa/New Zealand* (pp. 17–36). Palmerston North, NZ: Dunmore Press.

Orange, C. (2004). *An illustrated history of the Treaty of Waitangi*. Wellington, NZ: Bridget Williams Books.

Pearson, D. (1990). *A deferred dream: The origins of ethnic conflict in New Zealand*. Wellington, NZ: Allen & Unwin.

Peters, W. (2002, November). *Address to public meeting at Erinlea Lounge, Fahy's Motor Inn, Tauranga*. Retrieved February 12, 2005, from http://www.nzfirst.org.nz/content/display_item.php?t=1&i=808.

Pettigrew, T. F. (2002). Summing up: Relative deprivation as a key social psychological construct. In I. Walker & H. Smith (Eds.), *Relative deprivation: Specification, development, and integration* (pp. 351–373). New York: Cambridge University Press.

Pettigrew, T. F., & Meertens, R. W. (1995). Subtle and blatant prejudice in Western Europe. *European Journal of Social Psychology, 25*, 57–75.

Pettigrew, T. F., & Tropp, L. (2000). Does intergroup contact reduce prejudice: Recent meta-analytic findings. In S. Oskamp (Ed.), *Reducing prejudice and discrimination* (pp. 93–114). Mahwah, NJ: Lawrence Elrbaum.

Phan, M. B. (2008). We're all in this together: Context, contacts and social trust in Canada. *Analyses of Social Issues and Public Policy, 8*, 23–51.

Podsiadlowski, A., & Ward, C. (2010). Global mobility and bias in the workplace. In S. Carr (Ed.), *The psychology of mobility in a global era* (pp. 279–300). New York: Springer.

Quince, K. (2007). Maori and the criminal justice system in New Zealand. In J. Tolmie & W. Brookbanks (Eds.), *The criminal justice system in New Zealand* (pp. 333–359). Wellington, NZ: LexisNexis Butterworths.

Roach, K., & Roskvist, A. (2007). ESOL provision for adult immigrants and refugees in New Zealand: Policy, practice and research. *Prospect, 22*, 44–63.

Robinson, L. (2005). South Asians in Britain: Acculturation, identity and perceived discrimination. *Psychology and Developing Societies, 17*, 181–194.

Ross, R. (1972). Te Tiriti of Waitangi – texts and translations. *New Zealand Journal of History, 6*, 129–157.

Sibley, C. G., & Barlow, F. K. (2009). The ubiquity of Whiteness in majority group national imagination: Australian = White, but New Zealander does not. *Australian Journal of Psychology, 61*, 119–127.

Sibley, C. G., & Liu, J. H. (2004). Attitudes towards biculturalism in New Zealand: Social dominance and Pakeha attitudes towards the general principles and resource-specific aspects of bicultural policy. *New Zealand Journal of Psychology, 33*, 88–99.

Sibley, C. G., & Liu, J. H. (2007). New Zealand = bicultural? Implicit and explicit associations between ethnicity and nationhood in the New Zealand context. *European Journal of Social Psychology, 37*, 1222–1243.

Sibley, C. G., Liu, J. H., Duckitt, J., & Khan, S. S. (2008). Social representations of history and the legitimation of social inequality: The form and function of historical negation. *European Journal of Social Psychology, 38*, 542–565.

Smith, L. T. (1999). *Decolonising methodologies*. Dunedin: University of Otago Press.

Spoonley, P. (1993). *Racism and ethnicity* (2nd ed.). Melbourne, AU: Oxford University Press.

Spoonley, P., Gendall, P., & Trlin, A. (2007). *Welcome to our world: Attitudes of New Zealanders to immigrants and immigration*. Occasional paper no. 14. New Settlers Programme. Palmerston North, NZ: Massey University.

Statistics New Zealand. (2002a). *Pacific progress: A report on the economic status of Pacific peoples in New Zealand*. Wellington, NZ: Statistics New Zealand.

Statistics New Zealand. (2002b). *2001 Census: People born overseas*. Wellington, NZ: Information and Publishing Services, Statistics New Zealand.

Statistics New Zealand. (2007a). *Quick stats about culture and identity: 2006 Census on population and dwellings*. Retrieved from April 20, 2009, http://www.stats.govt.nz/census/2006-census-data/quickstats-about-culture-identity/quickstats-about-culture-and-identity.htm.

Statistics New Zealand. (2007b). *Quick stats about Maori: 2006 Census on population and dwellings*. Retrieved from April 20, 2009, http://www.stats.govt.nz/census/2006-census-data/quickstats-about-maori/2006-census-quickstats-about-maori-revised.htm.

Statistics New Zealand. (2007c). *Quick stats about Pacific peoples: 2006 Census on population and dwellings*. Retrieved April 20, 2009, http://www.stats.govt.nz/census/2006-census-data/quickstats-about-culture-identity/quickstats-about-culture-and-identity.htm?page=para016Master.

Statistics New Zealand. (2007d). *Quick stats about incomes: 2006 Census on population and dwellings*. Retrieved April 20, 2009, from http://www.stats.govt.nz/census/2006-census-data/quickstats-about-incomes/quickstats-about-incomes.htm?page=para014Master.

Stephan, W. G., & Stephan, C. W. (2000). An integrated threat theory of prejudice. In S. Oskamp (Ed.), *Reducing prejudice and discrimination* (pp. 23–46). Hillsdale, NJ: Erlbaum.

Stephan, W. G., Ybarra, P., & Bachman, G. (1999). Prejudice toward immigrants: An integrated threat theory. *Journal of Applied Social Psychology, 29*, 2221–2237.

Stuart, J., & Ward, C. (2009, November). *On being Muslim in New Zealand*. Presentation to the Office of Ethnic Affairs, Wellington, New Zealand

Stuart, J., Ward, C., & Adam, Z. (2010). Current issues in the development and acculturation of Muslim youth. *Bulletin of the International Society for the Study of Behavioral Development, 2*, 9–13.

Stuart, J., Ward, C., Jose, P., & Narayanan, P. (2010). Working with and for communities: A collaborative study of harmony and conflict in well-functioning, acculturating families. *International Journal of Intercultural Relations, 34*, 114–126.

Thomas, B. (2004). (The) nation-state matters: Comparing multiculturalism(s) in an age of globalization. In D. L. Li (Ed.), *Globalization and the humanities* (pp. 135–157). Hong Kong: Hong Kong University Press.

Turia, T. (2008). *Speech to the New Zealand Federation of Ethnic Councils AGM*. June 28, 2008. Retrieved May 3, 2009, from http://www.infonews.co.nz/news.cfm?l=1&t=0&id=23216.

Van Dijk, T. (1993). *Elite discourses and racism*. London: Sage.

Verkuyten, M. (2002). Perception of ethnic discrimination by minority and majority early adolescents in the Netherlands. *International Journal of Psychology, 3*, 321–332.

Waitangi Tribunal (1983). *Report of the Waitangi Tribunal on the Motunui–Waitara Claim*. Retrieved November 1, 2010, from http://www.waitangi-tribunal.govt.nz/reports/viewchapter.asp?reportID=0ff26c03-f956-40fa-adb0-61ea0843f885&chapter=1.

Walker, R. (1990). *Ka whawhai tonu matou (Struggle without end)*. Auckland, NZ: Penguin.

Walker, R. (1995). Immigration policy and the political economy of New Zealand. In S. Greif (Ed.), *Immigration and national identity in New Zealand* (pp. 282–302). Palmerston North, NZ: Dunmore Press.

Ward, C. (2009). Acculturation and social cohesion: Emerging issues for Asian immigrants in New Zealand. In C.-H. Leong & J. W. Berry (Eds.), *Intercultural relations in Asia: Migration and work effectiveness* (pp. 3–24). Singapore: World Scientific.

Ward, C., Bochner, S., & Furnham, A. (2001). *The psychology of culture shock*. London, UK: Routledge.

Ward, C., & Leong, C.-H. (2006). Intercultural relations in plural societies: Theory, research and applications. In D. Sam & J. W. Berry (Eds.), *Cambridge handbook of acculturation psychology* (pp. 484–503). Cambridge, UK: Cambridge University Press.

Ward, C., & Lin, E.-Y. (2005). Identity, acculturation and national identity. In J. H. Liu, T. McCreanor, T. McIntosh, & T. Teaiwa (Eds.), *New Zealand identities: Departures and destinations* (pp. 155–173). Wellington, NZ: Victoria University Press.

Ward, C., & Masgoret, A.-M. (2006). An integrated model of attitudes toward immigrants. *International Journal of Intercultural Relations, 30*, 671–682.

Ward, C., & Masgoret, A.-M. (2007). Immigrant entry into the workforce: A research note from New Zealand. *International Journal of Intercultural Relations, 31*, 525–530.

Ward, C., & Masgoret, A.-M. (2008). Attitudes toward immigrants, immigration and multiculturalism in New Zealand. *International Migration Review, 42*, 227–248.

Watts, N., & Trlin, A. (1999). Cultural resources of immigrants and international business in New Zealand. *New Zealand Population Review, 25*, 119–132.

Watts, N., & Trlin, A. (2000). Diversity as a productive resource: Employment of immigrants from non-English-speaking backgrounds in New Zealand. *Social Policy Journal of New Zealand, 15*, 87–101.

Wilson, M. G., Gahlout, P., Liu, L., & Mouly, S. (2005). A rose by any other name: The effect of ethnicity and name on access to employment. *University of Auckland Business Review, 7*, 64–72.

Zodgekar, A. (2005). The changing face of New Zealand's population and national identity. In J. H. Liu, T. McCreanor, T. McIntosh, & T. Teaiwa (Eds.), *New Zealand identities: Departures and destinations* (pp. 140–154). Wellington, NZ: Victoria University Press.

The Moro Struggle and the Challenge to Peace Building in Mindanao, Southern Philippines*

4

Cristina J. Montiel, Rudy B. Rodil, and Judith M. de Guzman

Philippines Chapter Summary

Montiel, Rodil, and Guzman describe the islands of Mindanao in the Southern Philippines and analyze the ethnic conflicts between two of the three primary groups which make up most of the population; the indigenous Muslim minority (Moro) and the Christian migrant majority. Peace movements at the individual, group, and government level are discussed along with suggestions for interventions at each level.

Historical review reveals the presence of self-sustaining tribal communities with animistic beliefs, followed by the arrival of Muslim missionaries introducing monotheism. Spanish colonization is credited with the addition of Christian religion and the beginnings of deeply rooted animosity created through many years of war. Additional tensions are postulated to result from inclusion of Moro sultanates in the American takeover, which were not previously part of the Philippine state under Spain. American colonial rule is also credited with contributing to the internal conflicts through labeling of groups, changing land ownership laws, and homestead movements which displaced indigenous people. Further under American governance, the authors describe a process of marginalization through mandatory English education and increasing Filipino presence in bureaucracy. These events are presented as setting the stage for the violent conflict between the Moro and Filipino which followed.

*GRP–MILF stands for the Government of the Republic of the Philippines–Moro Islamic Liberation Front Peace Panel for Negotiation.

C.J. Montiel (✉) • J.M. de Guzman
Department of Psychology, Ateneo de Manila University, Manila, Philippines
e-mail: cmontiel@ateneo.edu

R.B. Rodil
Mindanao Historian and Former Vice-Chair of the GRP-MILF Peace Panel,
e-mail: ompong42@yahoo.com

D. Landis and R.D. Albert (eds.), *Handbook of Ethnic Conflict: International Perspectives*, International and Cultural Psychology, DOI 10.1007/978-1-4614-0448-4_4,

The authors delineate several ongoing steps toward peace such as dialogues, peace seminars, training, peace education, and community peace zones. The need for elimination of poverty, injustice, underdevelopment, and corruption in conjunction with promotion of cultural sensitivity is also recognized. The authors call for peacebuilding to include psychological healing and creation of a sense of active nonviolence. The importance of a national movement with peace policies in government, economic awareness, and linkage between levels of peace movements is also noted. Montiel, Rodil, and Guzman emphasize the need to deal with land ownership issues and create some form of self-determination for the Moro people. The authors express the view that creation of a federally structured government may resolve many of these issues.

Cheryl Jorgensen

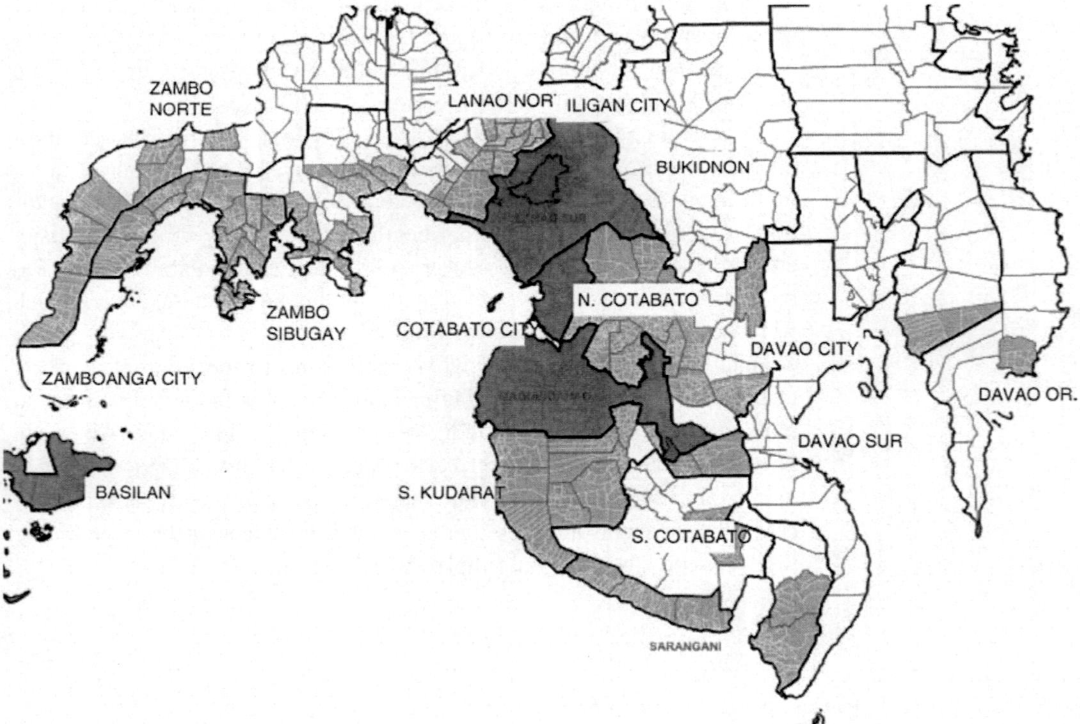

The dark-shaded territories are part of the current Autonomous Region in Muslim Mindanao

1 Introduction: The Land and Peoples of Mindanao, Philippines

Composed of more than 7,100 islands, the Philippines is home to some 90 million inhabitants. The Philippine archipelago is generally divided into three major island groupings, namely, Luzon, Visayas, and Mindanao. Of interest to this discussion is the major island grouping of Mindanao, which is located in the southernmost part of the country. Mindanao is home to a varied mix of people belonging to different ethnolinguistic and religious groups. Blessed with abundant land, water, mineral, and forest resources, the region is considered the source of much of the country's needs. For instance, almost 59% of the country's fish supply is obtained from the waters of Mindanao (Kamlian, 1999). Huge amounts of mineral deposits can also be found in the region. The forests of Mindanao used to serve as an important source of timber for wood products from the early 1960s, until these resources became depleted through massive commercial logging operations.

Over the last three decades, the population of Mindanao has been commonly categorized into three major groupings – Lumad, Moros or Muslims, and Christians (also called Settlers or Migrants). Lumad is a Cebuano Bisayan term which means "indigenous." This was adopted by the Indigenous Peoples themselves because whenever Lumad tribes come together for regional assemblies, Cebuano, the language of Cebu in the Visayas in central Philippines, is their lingua franca. Both Muslim and Lumad used to be lumped together as National Cultural Minorities in Mindanao. The Lumad are composed of 30 or more tribes and subtribes of the Indigenous Peoples. Consisting of approximately 10% of the region's population, they have been traditional inhabitants of the greater part of mainland Mindanao, except in Lanao del Sur, Basilan, Sulu, and Tawi-Tawi, which continue to be the domain of the Moros until today. Starting in 1997, the Lumad also began to refer to themselves as Indigenous Peoples, in consonance with the practice of international assemblies like the United Nations, but more particularly, in line with the passage of the Indigenous Peoples Rights Act of 1997 by the Philippine Congress. As a consequence of the resettlement program of the government, both colonial and Philippine, their population has not only been reduced to approximately 10% of the region's population, but they have also become the majority in only 11 municipalities in Mindanao.

Comprising around 20% of the population of Mindanao, the Moros or Bangsamoros, a recently adopted name that is becoming more popular with them, are distributed into 13 ethnolinguistic groups, the greater bulk of whom are traditional inhabitants of Central and Western Mindanao. They are indigenous to Mindanao and became Muslim when Arab traders–missionaries came to the region, married into the local population, and spread Islam starting as early as the fourteenth century, in Tawi-Tawi in the late fourteenth century, and in Central Mindanao in the early sixteenth century. They are now the majority in the five provinces of Maguindanao and Lanao del Sur in Central Mindanao; Basilan, Sulu, and Tawi-Tawi in Western Mindanao; and also in 15 other municipalities in adjacent provinces (National Statistics Office, 2000).

The term Moro was originally used by Spaniards for Muslims who occupied the Iberian Peninsula for nearly 800 years, from 711 to 1492. When the Spanish colonizers discovered there were Muslims in the Philippines, they also called them Moros. For many years, the Muslims of Mindanao resented this designation, because it came from Spaniards who waged war on them throughout most of the colonizer's 333 years' stay in the Philippines. Spaniards called Mindanao Muslims "*Moro piratas*" because the latter's retaliatory attacks on Christian communities in Spanish-controlled territories had caused so much havoc on colonial interest. We note, however, that Spaniards did not describe their own attacks on Muslims as piracy. It was only in the early 1970s that the name Moro became a badge of honor among Mindanao Muslims, after this label, along with Bangsamoro, was claimed by the Moro National Liberation Front (MNLF) as the collective identity of Muslims in Mindanao.

The third major category of people includes the largely Christian migrants and their descendants who came from Luzon and Visayas. At present, they constitute the majority population in Mindanao, comprising approximately 70% of the population in this region (Census of the Philippines, 2000). Through the resettlement programs of the US colonial government and the new Philippine state, the Christian migrants started to come to Mindanao in droves in 1913. In less than 60 years, these newcomers and their descendants became the majority in most of the provinces in Mindanao. Also included here are the indigenous inhabitants, largely of northern and eastern Mindanao, who were converted into Christianity by the Spanish missionaries. They numbered nearly 200,000 in the 1890s.

In the Philippines, it is in Mindanao that the country has experienced the longest and the most intense political conflicts with both ethnic and religious undertones. In this chapter, we provide an overview of the Moro struggle in Mindanao – its history, causes, and consequences, as well as the peace-building initiatives in the region, along with suggestions for possible resolutions to the conflict.

2 History of the Moro Struggle

A quick review of the history of Mindanao, spanning more than four centuries, will help us comprehend the Moro struggle and its major components, namely, the deep-seated prejudices between Muslims and Christians, the marginalization of the Muslim and Lumad communities covering all major aspects of life, the struggle for self-determination fought by the Muslims, and the Lumad assertion of their own right to self-governance. Part of the story is the long drawn out peace process that is slowly unfolding and creating new relationships among the peoples of Mindanao.

2.1 Pre-Islamic and Islamic Mindanao

We start our review from pre-Islamic Mindanao. We assume for lack of hard data that at this time, the various communities in Mindanao existed as autonomous *barangays* or small-clan communities that lived off the land and their natural environment. Travel by sea enabled them to practice limited trade and allowed them cultural interaction. They had their own indigenous faith traditions, a form of animism that revolved around belief in the spirits of the natural world known as *diwata*.

Brought by Arab missionaries–traders who subsequently married into the local population, Islam revolutionized the communities in Mindanao. A grave marker with Arabic scripts, indicating the year 1380 AD, is the earliest sign of Islamic presence in the province of Tawi-Tawi, in the archipelago of Sulu. There were stories of the early presence of Muslim missionaries in Maguindanao, but Shariff Kabungsuan, one of the earliest Muslim missionaries in Mindanao, is estimated to have arrived at the shores of Maguindanao in the early part of the sixteenth century. Carrying with it the belief in one God and his Prophet Muhammad and the concepts of political structures that developed in the Middle East from the seventh century, Islam facilitated the shift from an animistic faith tradition to a monotheistic belief system among the recipient communities in the islands. With the new belief also came new laws, ethical standards, political structures, and technologies, such as the Arabic system of speaking and writing. Islam provided the impetus for the establishment of sultanates. Sulu gave birth to the first sultanate in 1450; the Maguindanao sultanate came into existence from the unity of two Maguindanaon principalities in 1619 (Majul, 1973; Saleeby, 1963). Islam also spread as far as Manila, Mindoro, and other parts of Luzon and the Visayas, but this development was cut short by the arrival of another major social force, Spanish colonialism and Christianity.

Under the auspices of the sultanate system, the Muslim communities were able to accumulate wealth through intensified commercial activities. More importantly perhaps, the sultanates also fostered political, religious, and ideological organization and cohesiveness, thus enabling the Muslim communities to advance ahead of the other inhabitants in the islands. In essence, the Islamization process enabled the

Muslim communities to form their own collective identity and to develop a sense of community from which they drew their strength to resist foreign threats to their way of life (Majul, 1973).

2.2 Spanish Colonization

Though the colonization process was initiated by Ferdinand Magellan in 1521, Spanish occupation of the Philippine Islands formally started in 1565. Within approximately 50 years, the newcomers – employing the cross, the sword, and new technology of warfare like canons as their key weapons of conquest – controlled Luzon, Visayas, and northern and eastern Mindanao. But even during the first 50 years, Spain already set its eyes on subjugating the Muslims of the two sultanates. What followed were wars that lasted throughout the Spanish colonial presence – 333 years of war, punctuated by occasional peace. To the Spaniards, the wars with the Muslims, now called Moros, were "*guerras piraticas*," or wars against *Moro* pirates. To the Muslims, these were wars of self-defense to protect their political territories and those of their allies. The Spaniards conscripted and utilized thousands of Filipino Christian warriors to fight the Muslims; in return, the Muslims hit Spanish-controlled Filipino communities. The fighting between Christians and Muslims thus resulted in deep-seated mutual animosities, distrust, and dislike, which have since been carried over from generation to generation and are still felt to this day.

Although the Muslims of Mindanao remained uncolonized in the face of Spanish aggression, they suffered tremendously from the incessant hostilities. As a result of more than 333 years of intermittent Moro–Spanish Wars, the Muslims experienced deteriorating standards of living, poverty, and internal discord. Due to the loss in human and natural resources brought about by the wars, the sultanates were unable to promote the growth of the agricultural potential of their lands (Majul, 1973). Furthermore, the power of sultanates deteriorated due to incessant trade blockades and military aggressions from Spanish colonizers and other colonial powers within the Southeast Asian region, along with in-fighting among the Muslim ruling elite (Dery, 1997; Majul, 1973).

Parallel to the Muslim efforts to halt Spanish colonization, the Lumad also resisted missionary attempts to dominate them. Historical records spoke of several Lumad acts of resistance against missionary friars who ventured out to Christianize them. These small acts of opposition clearly expressed Lumad dislike for foreign interference or subjugation (Rodil, 2003; Schreurs, 1989).

One can sum up the contribution of the Spanish colonization to the development of the conflict in the Mindanao region along three dimensions. First, the colonization of the Luzon and Visayan regions of the Philippines, including northern and eastern Mindanao, led to the formation of a socioreligious collectivity called Christian, which may in turn have led to the development of the Filipino identity. Second, the Spanish divide-and-rule strategy created and sustained feelings of hatred and mistrust between the *Moros* and the Christianized Filipinos (Rodil, 2003). Third, Spanish colonial aggression weakened the Muslim sultanates economically and politically, thereby allowing for the easy conquest of the *Moros* and the occupation of their territory by another colonial aggressor, the USA (Majul, 1973; Rodil, 2003).

2.3 American Conquest, Amalgamation, and Marginalization

The American colonizers took over the Philippines from the Spaniards initially through the Treaty of Paris on December 1898 for the price of $20 million, and subsequently through armed conquest by separately defeating Filipino and *Moro* resistance. The treaty was the political settlement between the two colonial powers after the USA defeated Spain in the Spanish–American war (Gowing, 1977; Tan, 2002). It is important to stress at this point that at the time of the Treaty, the so-called subjects of the treaty were de facto states – the Philippines declared its independence from the Spanish colonizers 6 months earlier; in

Mindanao and the Sulu Archipelago, the Sulu and Maguindanao sultanates and the Pat a Pongampong ko Ranao were never colonized by the Spaniards; the Lumad, too, avoided contact with Spain and thus remained free – they were not owned by Spain at the time of the agreement. To this detail in history is traced one of the root causes of the Moro struggle: The Moros were attached to the Philippine state without their plebiscitary consent. The (Christian) Filipinos were never asked either. The agreement was purely a political settlement between two colonial powers. However, any question about the legitimacy of the Paris transaction turned moot and academic after the American victory in war over the Filipinos and Moros as well as over the rest of the inhabitants. They all became subjects of US colonialism.

Three aspects of US colonial rule contributed significantly to the Moro struggle: (1) labeling and classification of the population, (2) discriminatory provisions of public land laws, and (3) the resettlement programs. In the census of 1903, the peoples of the Philippine islands were classified into two broad categories – Christian and non-Christian, which were used interchangeably with civilized and uncivilized, respectively (Rodil, 1994). The Christians were those converted to Christianity during the Spanish colonial period; the non-Christians were the Moros and the Wild Tribes. These labels were not only utilized in important laws that dealt with the distribution and ownership of land, but these same tags also served to justify the creation of special transitory political structures, for instance, like the Moro Province for the Moros, which consisted of the five provincial districts of Davao, Cotabato, Lanao, Zamboanga, and Sulu; and Agusan, which consisted of the present provinces of Bukidnon, Agusan del Norte, and Agusan del Sur for the Lumad. The special tag was meant to facilitate their amalgamation into the mainstream Filipino community. Formed in 1903, these were abolished and upgraded after 10 years. It is important to contrast these political categories with Christian-dominated Mindanao provinces like Surigao and Misamis, which were designated as regular provinces, as all Christian-dominated provinces in the entire Philippine Islands were classified (Rodil, 1994).

The US colonial government not only refused to acknowledge the legitimacy of the traditional communal system of land ownership, land use, and distribution, but also introduced and institutionalized the Torrens system of private land ownership, including land classification, registration, and titling to private entities. One of its early laws on land declared null and void all land grants made by the traditional leaders of non-Christian tribes without the consent of the government. This was followed by public land laws which not only mandated the registration and titling of lands to private persons and corporations, a practice that was alien to the Muslim and Lumad peoples, but also pursued a land distribution scheme that was patently discriminatory against the local inhabitants. Three versions of public land laws were implemented in 1903, 1919, and 1936, the latter being an amendment of the previous one. Table 4.1 shows that individual Christian homesteaders were allowed to own up to 24 ha of land, while non-Christians could only have 10 ha at most, which was even reduced to 4 ha in 1936; the corporations were allowed 1,024 ha throughout (Rodil, 1994).

The American colonial government also opened up vast territories of the Philippines to resettlement, including the Cagayan Valley, Mindoro, Palawan, and Mindanao. Made to believe that they were moving into and occupying public lands, settlers from the northern and central regions of the Philippines were transported with government assistance to these areas or traveled on their own at their own expense. In Mindanao, the large-scale movement of settlers, also called homesteaders or homeseekers, from

Table 4.1 Land provisions under public land law and resettlement

	Number of hectares allowed for ownership		
Year	Christians homesteaders	Non-Christians (Moros and wild tribes)	Corporations
1903	16 ha	(no provision)	1,024 ha
1919	24 ha	10 ha	1,024 ha
1936	16 ha	4 ha	1,024 ha

Luzon and the Visayas started in 1913. By 1970, less than 60 years later, the original local population was brought down to 30%, while the new migrants increased to 70%. This was how the Muslims and the Lumad communities were displaced, dispossessed, and marginalized in their own ancestral lands. Ironically, the process was government initiated, largely legal, and in accordance with law and state policy (Rodil, 1994).

Two significant aspects of marginalization must be stressed here: governance and compulsory education. The evolution of political structures for non-Christians from special to regular status also indicates a form of marginalization. Within the framework of special provinces, for instance, structures like tribal wards were formed to facilitate assimilation. At first glance, they may seem like an American recognition of tribal culture and processes, which they admittedly were. But on closer examination, they must also be seen as transition mechanisms meant to hasten integration. They were in effect ultimately designed to sideline, others would prefer to use the word mainstream, indigenous culture and political systems, particularly those involving the two sultanates of Sulu and Maguindanao.

An added dimension of mainstreaming through governance was the Filipinization of the bureaucracy. By way of preparation for eventual independence, the Jones Law was passed by the US Congress in 1916. Its initial effect on governance was the rapid departure of American personnel from the bureaucracy and their takeover by Filipinos. Its impact on Mindanao, specifically on Moroland, as the Moro Province came to be known, was the increasing appearance of Filipino faces in the bureaucracy. The Moros reacted to this with their demand for the "*Moroization*" of the government within their territories. As an official US government mission was dispatched to the Philippines in the mid-1920s to investigate the preparedness of the people for independence, Moro leaders responded with manifestoes expressing their unwillingness to be part of the Filipino independence and to be governed by Filipinos, and instead declared their preference to remain under the tutelage of America (Rodil, 2003). However, these protests did not prosper. The participation of some of the Moro leaders in the Constitutional Convention of 1935 "constitutionalized" or sealed the integration process; the Moros and the Lumad communities were Filipinos and were now part of the forthcoming Republic of the Philippines.

Very early in the colonization process, the American colonial government also introduced compulsory education throughout the Philippine Islands as part of its military strategy. English was the medium of instruction. Public education had the effect of marginalizing local culture. It was designed to produce and it did produce a new generation of Filipinos, Moros, and Lumad, English-speaking and Westernized. Its impact on Mindanao was that hundreds of Filipino teachers were dispatched to the region to help transform the local people into loyal Filipino citizens. Not surprisingly, there were also instances of rebellion from among the Lumad and Moro populations owing to the unwanted imposition of the compulsory public education program, often misconstrued by Muslims as a systematic attempt to Christianize them (Rodil, 1994).

2.4 The New Philippine State: Marginalization Continues

What the American colonial government started, the independent Philippine government continued. As the new Philippine state was formed, the entire machinery of a unitary system of government was put in full force. The land distribution policy and the discriminatory public land laws remained in effect; the resettlement programs also intensified. Compulsory public education remained a tool of cultural integration. In local governance, more and more Moro leaders were absorbed into positions of power, both national and local. The political units that were earlier tagged as special were finally allowed by law in the mid-1950s to elect their local officials. At the start, Moro and Lumad leaders easily won in their traditional territories. But as a consequence of migration, as the arrival of more and more settlers led to numerical dominance, it became more difficult for Moro and Lumad leaders to win in their own towns. As a result, tension and resentment began to build up.

A quick look at the various censuses (1903, 1918, 1939, 1948, 1960, and 1970) will reveal that the weight of population balance tilted in favor of the newcomers after the Second World War and rapidly so until 1970. Nowhere is this most graphically illustrated than in the case of what used to be known as the empire province of Cotabato (now subdivided into the five provinces of Cotabato, South Cotabato, Maguindanao, Sultan Kudarat, and Sarangani). The territory of Maguindanao was traditionally the heart of the Maguindanao Sultanate and is presently also the area with the heaviest concentration of Moro Islamic Liberation Front (MILF) rebels, along with the adjacent Lanao provinces. The shifts in population patterns revealed in the censuses of 1918, 1939, 1948, and 1970 tell it all – the story of displacement and marginalization.

The Maguindanao population, one of the 13 Islamized groups mentioned earlier, in the Cotabato region dipped from 59.51% in 1918, to 54.52% in 1939, and then plunged to 27.75% in 1970; the Lumad slipped from 25.04% in 1918, to 24.84% in 1939, and then fell straight down to 6.68% in 1970. The settlers, on the contrary, shot up exponentially from 2.7% in 1918, to 24.04% in 1939, to 67.19% in 1970 (Rodil, 1994).

The fighting between Moros and Christians in Central Mindanao can be read as the eruption of the tension brought about by this story of displacement and marginalization. The hostilities could be likened to a prairie fire, raging and burning everything along its path, indiscriminate and lethal. More than 1,000 people died in the year-long event, which the media referred to as the Mindanao Crisis of 1971–1972. It became the catalyst that quickened the process toward war in Moroland.

2.5 The Moro Struggle

The Moro struggle took the form of a series of violent and nonviolent incidents. We have noted earlier that in the mid-1920s up to the mid-1930, several Moro leaders expressed, in response to the American team investigating the preparedness of Filipinos for independence, that they did not wish to be a part of Philippine independence; instead, they preferred to remain under the USA. In the 1956 congressional investigation on the nature of the Moro Problem, various complaints were documented, ranging from failure of governance to loss of land, from loss of identity to Moro resistance against integration. This investigation led to the establishment of the Commission on National Integration where those earlier tagged as non-Christians were now formally renamed National Cultural Minorities (Rodil, 1994). In 1961, the congressional representative of the province of Sulu filed a bill to declare the independence of Sulu from the Republic of the Philippines.

In February and March 1968, 26 Muslim trainees from Sulu were massacred by their military trainers, allegedly for mutiny, in the island of Corregidor; other versions said they were merely petitioning for the payment of their allowance which was already delayed by more than a month. This came to be known also as the infamous Jabidah massacre. Jabidah being the code name of the military training that took place in that island. This incident ignited a series of angry rallies from Muslim and non-Muslim activists in both Manila and Mindanao, as well as from opposition politicians and Muslim politicians, one of whom founded the Muslim Independent Movement (MIM) in the summer of 1968. The Jabidah massacre is believed to have fueled the formation of the MNLF. The MIM publicly declared its intention to establish an Islamic State in the predominantly Muslim areas of Mindanao and Sulu (Gowing, 1979). To open itself to non-Muslim interested parties, it modified its name to Mindanao Independence Movement. As a countermove, Ilonggo settler-politicians, hailing originally from the Island of Panay in the Visayas, and now political leaders in the Cotabato Valley area, formed a paramilitary group which later came to be known as *Ilaga* (rat).

During this time, there were all sorts of political rumors about secret military trainings of Muslim youths in Mindanao and abroad. The year 1971 exploded with a climate of violence among the civilian population, Muslims versus Christians in Central Mindanao, particularly in the provinces of Cotabato and Lanao. Christians were associated with *Ilagas* in both provinces. The Muslims in the Cotabato area were associated with the *Blackshirts*, the Muslim provincial security forces who were known for wearing black uniforms, while the Muslims in the Lanao area were associated with the *Barracudas*, another paramilitary group. From January to December 1971, not a single day passed without a violent incident. Several massacres were perpetrated against Muslim communities. One of these was the Tacub Massacre where a group of unarmed Muslim voters were machine-gunned by government troops at a military checkpoint and mutilated by civilian bystanders in Lanao del Norte (Gowing, 1979; Rodil, 1994). Another example was the Manili Massacre, in which Muslim men, women, and children who were gathered for a peace conference were slaughtered inside a mosque in the town of Carmen, Cotabato (Rodil, 1994).

Finally, in 1972, President Ferdinand Marcos declared martial law, allegedly for two reasons: (1) the Communist Party of the Philippines-New People's Army-led rebellion nationwide, and (2) the Muslim uprising in Mindanao. In late 1972, Moro rebels, who now called themselves Bangsamoro, organized as the Moro National Liberation Front (MNLF). They declared their war of national liberation and their intention to establish the Bangsamoro Republic in the region that they claimed as their ancestral homeland, in the islands of Mindanao, Sulu, and Palawan. Thus, from 1972 until 1976, war raged in Mindanao. It is estimated that between 100,000 and 120,000 people were killed during the war – 50% MNLF, 30% military, and 20% civilians (Rodil, 2000, 2003).

3 The Different Meanings of the Moro Conflict

In analyzing the Moro conflict, an important aspect that needs to be accounted for involves the divergences in the meanings of the conflict as a function of group membership and position. To further elaborate, we utilize data from existing research on the conflict.

Using data gathered through interviews with Muslims and Christians in Mindanao, Nuñez (1997) found that members of each group exhibited different perceptions of the causes of the Moro conflict. Muslim respondents cited the government's lack of fairness toward the Muslims as the main cause, while Christian respondents believed that the Mindanao conflict is rooted in the Muslims' desire to control and dominate Mindanao. Similarly, intergroup differences regarding attributions of the Moro conflict were also discovered (Montiel & Macapagal, 2006). Muslim respondents attributed the Moro conflict to structural factors such as the displacement and dispossession of the Bangsamoros as well as to the loss of their rights to self-determination. Conversely, Christian respondents attributed the Moro conflict to individual factors such as social and cultural discrimination and corruption of moral mind and fiber. In addition, this research showed that the meanings of the Mindanao conflict can vary as a function of the perceiver's group position, with the low-power Muslim group attributing conflict to structural causes and the high-power Christian group attributing conflict to subjective or person-based origins.

In other researches which emphasized the multiplicity of meanings assigned to the Moro conflict, Inzon (2007) found that the representations of Mindanao leaders in the history of conflict in Mindanao clustered around four main discourses: (1) land possession and dispossession, (2) political resistance and politicization of conflict, (3) armed struggle and nonviolent resistance, and (4) a peaceful past vis-à-vis the present conflict. Within each discourse, Christian, Lumad, and Muslim leaders assigned different meanings and took on different positions regarding the Moro conflict. For example, the history of the Moro conflict based on land possession and dispossession was represented by the Christians according to legal ownership of the land, by the Muslims in terms of historical territorial claims on the land, and by the Lumad in terms of tribal claims on the land. What is striking in this research is how

Mindanao leaders from different social categories represented the history of the conflict in Mindanao in different and contrasting ways.

These researches demonstrate how the Mindanao conflict can have diverse meanings as a function of group membership. This insight into the multiplicity of social meanings of the Mindanao conflict challenges us to understand the dynamism and contentiousness of the issues at hand.

4 Peace-Building Initiatives at the People's Level

Parallel to the history of conflict and war runs a history of peace building in the Southern Philippine region. From the ashes of war arose a vibrant peace movement that involved the different sectors in society – nongovernment organizations (NGOs), people's organizations, communities, academic institutions, and religious sectors. From the darkness and suffering experienced by the people in Mindanao came a resounding call for peace as evidenced in the various conflict-resolution and peace-building activities undertaken by these sectors. We discuss illustrations of these peace-building activities in the following section.

4.1 Nongovernment Organizations and People's Organizations for Peace

The pioneers in Mindanao peace building may have been the private NGOs that initiated Muslim–Christian dialog in the early 1980s. This was the joint effort of the Dansalan Research Center and the Prelature of Marawi. Soon after, the National Council of Churches in the Philippines' Program Aimed at Christian Education about Muslims (PACEM) and the Mindanao Sulu Pastoral Council (MSPC) came up with *Duyog Ramadhan* (Accompanying Ramadhan), which aimed to foster solidarity among people from different religions and cultures, particularly during the holy month of Ramadhan. In 1996, with the positive prospects of a peace agreement between the government and the MNLF, several NGOs organized the *Kalinaw Mindanaw* (Peace Mindanaw) peace movement, with assistance from the Office of Presidential Adviser on the Peace Process (OPAPP) and the Catholic Relief Services. Kalinaw Mindanaw conducted a series of culture of peace seminars and trainers' training all over Mindanao and Sulu.

More participants came after the signing of the Government of the Republic of the Philippines (GRP)–MNLF final peace agreement in 1996. From a modest exposure in 1997, the United Nations Development Programme (UNDP) has not only expanded its operations several fold, but it has also partnered with the Philippine government to set up Action for Conflict Transformation (ACT) for Peace Programme, operating all over Mindanao, Sulu, and Palawan, and supporting various private initiatives from communities to academic institutions. Several foreign donors have thrown in substantial funds for their operations. Among them are the USA, Canada, Australia, Japan, the European Union, England, Germany, and New Zealand.

Two NGOs, Balay Mindanaw in Cagayan de Oro City and the Institute of Autonomy and Governance in Cotabato City, should also be cited for launching peace education for military officers and noncommissioned officers as well as Philippine Marines and Philippine National Police officials. With the support of the Konrad Adenauer Stiftung Foundation and the Australian Government's Overseas Aid Program (AusAid), they have conducted peace education since 2006. As a result, hundreds of officers have already undergone this training. Similarly, the Davao-based Mindanao Peace Institute, although international in character and participation and offered only during the summer months, also admits a limited number of military officers, as part of its effort to create a climate of peace on a global scale.

4.2 Communities for Peace: Peace Zones

In Central Mindanao, peace zones stand out in local peace building not only because they rose out from the midst of war, but especially also because the decisions to create zones of peace were made by the community residents themselves. A peace zone is a community that was previously affected by armed conflict, but is now designated by its residents as an area where illegal and violent acts are not allowed and where conflict is resolved in a peaceful manner (LaRousse, 2001; Rodil, 2000). The establishment of a peace zone is carried out through negotiations with government and other armed groups, as supported by representatives from different sectors. Furthermore, the institution of a peace zone necessitates the following requirements: the designation of a specific territory; the formulation of rules, regulations, and conditions for peace zone residents; and the formation of a group of leaders with particular duties and responsibilities (Coronel-Ferrer, 1994).

Located in Sultan Gumander, Lanao del Sur, in Mindanao, the Maladeg Peace Zone provides us with an interesting illustration of peace building at the grassroots level. Inside the Maladeg Peace Zone, armed conflict, gambling, illegal drug use, and other crimes are prohibited. There is a Council of Leaders that facilitates the formulation, dissemination, and implementation of the rules and regulations of the zone. There are also committees assigned to resolve conflicts in a peaceful manner, and also to guard against any outburst of conflict in the zone. Furthermore, the Maladeg Peace Zone represents a space where the values, beliefs, and traditions of different groups are duly respected. For instance, both Muslims and Christians are provided with their own spaces where they can practice their own customs and traditions. This is undertaken through the clustering of Muslims on one side of the community and the banding of Christians on another side of the community. While both Christians and Muslims have lived near each other in peace before, certain cultural differences, such as the use of alcoholic beverages and the raising of hogs among Christians, have made it necessary for Muslims and Christians to have their respective spaces for the peaceful practice of their own religions (Rodil, 2000).

Today there are more than 50 communities that are self-sustaining spaces of peace in the Central Mindanao region. These peace zones stand as a testimony to the power of community peace building.

4.3 Peace Building Through Academic Institutions

Several schools, both within and outside Mindanao, are also active in the peace movement. In particular, these schools are involved in research and training on peace, development, and the cultural heritage of Mindanao, as well as in social action programs or extension services for Christian, Muslim, and Lumad communities.

The Notre Dame University of Cotabato City has pioneered in institutionalizing a peace program in its curriculum, at both undergraduate and graduate levels. This university also has a Peace Center, which holds peace training for participants from local government units, NGOs, church lay leaders, and youth leaders, using courses and modules on peace and development that the center has developed (LaRousse, 2001; Rodil, 2000). Lately, there is news that the Catholic Educational Association of the Philippines (CEAP) plans to produce history and social studies textbooks at primary, intermediate, secondary, and collegiate levels that reflect the history of the Lumad, the Moros, and the Christian settlers in Mindanao. The Mindanao State University (MSU) System has established its own Institute of Peace and Development in Mindanao (IPDM) anchored on each of its 11 major campuses in Mindanao and Sulu. The intention is to transform the entire MSU System into a peace university, a goal that was implied in its own charter. Recently, it has integrated peace education in its Civic Welfare Training Service (CWTS) program, the alternative program for the Reserve Officers Training Corps (ROTC), and is in the process of integrating peace education in its subject offerings for all degree and diploma programs. Thirty-two heads of state colleges and universities in Mindanao also recently came together for a peace summit in Penang, Malaysia, and committed themselves to integrate peace in their respective programs, partly in support of Executive Order 570 which mandates the integration of peace education at all levels of the educational system.

4.4 Interfaith Dialog and Peace Building

From the original Bishops–Ulama Forum formed in 1996, composed of Catholic and Protestant bishops from Christian churches in Mindanao and Muslim ulamas from the Ulama League of the Philippines, this group has now transformed itself into the Bishops–Ulama Conference (BUC), with a commitment to involve itself in peace-building and community development projects. This assembly emphasizes the activation of the faith dimension in the search for peace. From its modest beginnings in 1996, the BUC has inspired its members to put up their own interfaith local organizations in Davao, Cotabato, and Zamboanga. As a leading element in interreligious dialog in Mindanao, the BUC plays an important role in promoting mutual respect and tolerance among Christians, Muslims, and Lumad through discussion groups, training workshops, and celebration activities such as the Mindanao Week of Peace.

Although the Dansalan Research Center–Prelature of Marawi in Lanao del Sur has ceased operating as an institution that offered summer courses on Islam and Mindanao, the Silsilah Dialogue Movement, which specializes in interfaith education and dialog, has created its own momentum from its base in Zamboanga City (Rodil, 2000). Similarly, the Franciscan Mission in Mindanao has also undertaken its own Franciscan dialog program in Kidapawan City in Cotabato for the last 10 years. This program, which integrates theory and community exposure on interfaith and intercultural dialog, is designed for Franciscan priests, brothers, nuns, seminarians, and lay workers.

4.5 Women and Peace in Mindanao

At this point, allow us to mention that the picture is not complete without the "woman factor." An organization called Mindanao Commission on Women has committed woman power to the peace and development of Mindanao. Combining the energies of Mindanao women leaders for a few years now, the organization has created an ever-expanding ripple in the people's search for peace.

4.6 Poverty in Moroland: Prospects for Peace and Self-Reliance

There is the nagging feeling that things will not be right until a decisive way out of the pervasive state of poverty in the Autonomous Region in Muslim Mindanao (ARMM) has been properly addressed. ARMM is undeniably poor, the poorest region in the country. Since its inception in 1989, nearly 100% of its operating budget has been drawn from the Central Government. Its capacity to generate its own funds for governance, least of all for development, has remained unactivated. So, its desire to be politically autonomous is undermined by its own incapacity to finance its own affairs. Indeed, the interface between regional poverty and Manila-centered governance remains a major part of the Moro problem. Certainly, the dual problems of local poverty and political autonomy should be integral to a peace settlement.

5 Suggestions for Peace Building Among Peoples in Mindanao

Based on the history of peace building and on the prospects of peace and self-reliance in Mindanao, we now provide suggestions on how we can further build peace in Mindanao. We note two important characteristics of peace building. First, we argue that peace building is multidimensional. As multidimensional, peace building refers not only to the eradication of armed hostilities between conflicting groups, but also to the creation and maintenance of economic, political, and cultural systems that can be deemed as socially just and empowering. Thus, we look at peace building in consonance with measures undertaken to eliminate the factors that contribute to conflict such as poverty, social injustice, underdevelopment, and corruption, as well as programs that promote cultural sensitivity to dispel negative attitudes and stereotypes about particular ethnic groups.

Second, we also argue that peace building is multilayered. This means that there exists varying levels of peace building in the Moro conflict in Mindanao. We propose three levels of peace building in the Mindanao conflict – microlevel, mesolevel, and macrolevel (Montiel & Christie, 2008).

At the microlevel, we find the person of the individual peace-builder as an integral component to the peace building in Mindanao. Next to the individual, peace initiatives undertaken by groups, collectivities, and movements comprise the mesolevel of peace building. The largest and most inclusive level of peace building pertains to the macrolevel, which includes state, antistate, and global actors. These three levels can be understood as involving different actors, each in constant interaction with the actors in the other levels. Figure 4.1 summarizes the three levels of peace building in Muslim Mindanao.

5.1 Peace Building at the Microlevel: The Individual

With regard to the individual person, peace building in Muslim Mindanao involves two types of initiatives. First, the healing of traumas and internal conflicts among people exposed to violence and duress represents an important component of peace building. In particular, this healing process involves debriefing and psychological interventions for victims of the war in Mindanao. Second, the cultivation of active nonviolence in the interior life and subjective disposition of people in situations of conflict and violence also play a significant role in the process of building peace in Mindanao.

These two processes are reflected in the Self-transformation Seminars conducted by teachers from the MSU – Iligan Institute of Technology (Rodil, 2000). In these seminars, participants engage in activities focused on processing internal and interpersonal conflicts, in view of laying the groundwork for the development of skills in conflict resolution and conflict transformation. In particular, starting from the late 1990s, Self-transformation Seminars, which were initially offered as a 3-day module on character building and inner peace, became the latest component in peace education seminars given initially to officers and non-commissioned officers of the First Infantry (Tabak) Division, the Fourth Infantry

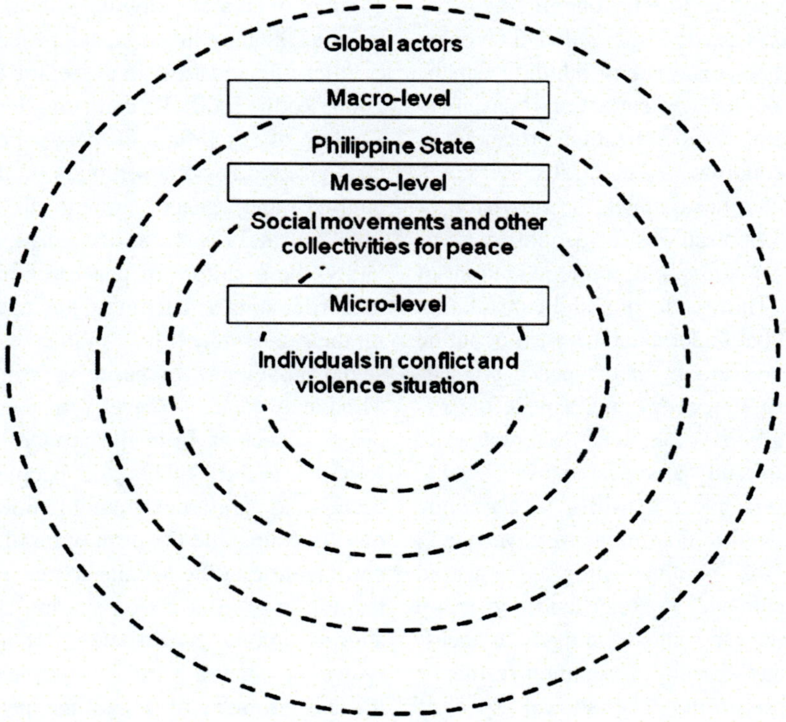

Fig. 4.1 Levels of peace building in Mindanao, Southern Philippines

Division, the Sixth Infantry Division, the Tenth Infantry Division, the Philippine Marines deployed in Basilan-Sulu-Tawi-Tawi-Palawan area, and the officials of the Philippine National Police covered in the Eastern and Western Mindanao Commands. Thus, aside from addressing internal conflicts and traumas brought about by the experience of war, the fostering of nonadversarial and nonviolent attitudes and values in individuals also serves as an important foundation for other peace-building initiatives at the different levels.

5.2 Peace Building at the Mesolevel: The Social Movements

At the level involving social movements and other collectivities for peace, the challenge of building and strengthening a national movement dedicated toward the achievement of peace in Muslim Mindanao is most apparent. By a national peace movement, we mean a well-informed and empowered citizenry among Christians, Muslims, and Lumad, not only in Mindanao but also in other parts of the country, most especially in Manila, where political and economic decision-making processes are concentrated. This process of national peace-constituency building can be undertaken through conscientization (consciousness raising) and democratization processes in the political, economic, and cultural spheres.

Politically, this necessitates the provision of capacities and opportunities for people's participation in the creation and implementation of peace policies. Thus, education and consultation processes can be undertaken to ensure public interest and involvement in the peace process. With regard to the economic aspect of this process, we identify the need to create and reinforce beliefs and value systems that enable people to become more sensitive to economic inequities that lead to conditions of poverty and deprivation. This involves programs geared toward propagating ideas about land ownership and development, especially of indigenous ancestral domains, and sharing of common resources and social responsibility. The cultural aspect of building a national peace constituency involves the raising of cultural awareness and the promotion of respect and tolerance toward peoples with different histories, religions, and cultures. The importance of this aspect lies in its contribution toward correcting prejudices and disconfirming negative stereotypes and attitudes toward people from different religious and ethnic groups.

Social movements and other collectivities for peace play an important role in this level of peace building, as they facilitate these consciousness-raising and democratization processes for the general public. In particular, we encourage social movements and other collectivities for peace such as NGOs, POs, schools, and parishes to organize public seminars, fora, dialogs, and mobilizations in response to issues on peace, development, and social justice. Furthermore, social movements and other collectivities for peace are seen to serve as a link between the individual and the structural levels, facilitating an active exchange between the grassroots and the state and global institutions.

Kalinaw Mindanaw represents one example of a social movement for peace in Mindanao. *Kalinaw Mindanaw* is an extensive movement composed of NGOs, POs, schools, parishes, communities, and individuals involved in peace building, peace education, and peace advocacy in conflict-affected areas in the region (Evangelista, 2003; Rodil, 2000). Its main aim lies in the propagation of a culture of peace in the region, through modules and seminars on the history of conflict and peace among the Christians, Muslims, and *Lumad* in Mindanao. More importantly, these culture of peace seminars envision its participants as becoming key agents of peace in their everyday life. Another example of a social movement for peace in Mindanao is the Mindanao Peace Weavers, a convergence of peace advocates from the academic sector, the religious sector, NGOs and people's organizations, and grassroots communities. Its main objectives include the promotion of civil society participation in the Mindanao peace process, the institution of information-sharing and concerted actions among civil society groups regarding issues on Muslim Mindanao peace and conflict, the development of a national peace constituency, and the advancement of a common peace agenda (Mindanao Peaceweavers, n.d).

In addition, the media sector plays a significant role in this process, as the task of mainstreaming discourses on peace in Mindanao falls within their domain. On the one hand, the media is challenged to exercise cultural sensitivity in its conduct of reporting about the Muslim and Lumad peoples in Mindanao. On the other hand, this role also involves reporting on the conditions of the conflict in Muslim Mindanao, providing constant updates on the peace process and echoing calls for peace and development in the region.

We emphasize that political, economic, and cultural considerations about peace in Mindanao should engage and face the issue of land and territorial ownership in Mindanao. Many peace activities, especially among Christians, do not tackle the issue of land ownership. But land is the primary language of peace propositioned by Muslim peace panels like the MILF.

5.3 Peace Building at the Macrolevel: History of Peace Talks Between the Philippine Government and the Moro Liberation Fronts

At the macrolevel, peace building involves state, antistate, and other global entities, such as foreign countries and international organizations involved in the Moro conflict. This section discusses in detail the history of peace talks between the Philippine government and two Moro liberation movements: the MNLF and the MILF.

The reason why both government and MNLF consented to bring themselves to the negotiating table remains unclear to this day. Nevertheless, the two parties decided to enter into peace negotiations through the facilitation of the Organization of the Islamic Conference (OIC). The process started in January 1975 and in December 1976, the two parties signed the Tripoli Agreement in Libya, the document that established the autonomous region for Muslims in Southern Philippines covering 13 provinces. Paragraph 16 of this accord provided further that the entire agreement should be implemented through constitutional processes. It took 20 years before the two could agree on the implementation of the agreement, or on the exact meaning of constitutional processes as stated in Paragraph 16. On September 2, 1996, after four rounds of talks in Jakarta, Indonesia, both the Philippine government and the MNLF signed the Final Peace Agreement on the Final Implementation of the Tripoli Agreement. To this day, however, 14 years after this signing, the MNLF is still complaining that several provisions of the Final Peace Agreement remain to be implemented. As of this writing, the two parties have had a number of tripartite meetings, involving the Philippine Government, the MNLF, and the OIC, to thresh out precisely how to complete the implementation of the agreement.

Meanwhile, several commanders of the MNLF have separated themselves from their organization in the late 1970s and formed themselves into the MILF in 1984. Believing that the Bangsamoro struggle for self-determination had been compromised, the MILF leadership refused to accept the terms of the 1996 GRP–MNLF Final Peace Agreement and decided to resume the struggle. This particular group has been engaged in both war and peaceful negotiation with the Philippine government since 1997. Despite several major wars in 1997, 2000, 2003, and 2008–2009, both sides have reached major accomplishments in the negotiating table, among them, the general cessation of hostilities which form the basis for the current joint cease-fire mechanism, the Tripoli Agreement on Peace in 2001 which set the three-point agenda technically called Security Aspect, Rehabilitation and Development Aspect, and Ancestral Domain Aspect. As of this writing, only the third, Ancestral Domain, remains to be threshed out. At this point, the most crucial item to be defined is what form of political self-determination for the Bangsamoro will be arrived at, somewhere between the present autonomy and independence.

An agreement was already reached in July 2008 when the GRP and the MILF initialed the Memorandum of Agreement on Ancestral Domain (MOA-AD) and scheduled the signing on August 5, 2008. However, opposition politicians brought the matter to the Supreme Court, which in turn issued an order to abort the signing and nearly 3 months later declared the document unconstitutional. Even before the Court could issue its ruling, Malacañang disbanded the government peace panel and issued a statement that the Philippine government would not sign the MOA-AD in its present form or in any other form, regardless of the Supreme Court decision. This was met with violent attacks on civilian communities in Central Mindanao allegedly led by three MILF commanders. The Philippine government reacted with a military campaign, although it publicly stated that this was not against the entire MILF organization, but only against the three commanders. In the next 10 months, the fighting displaced more than half a million inhabitants. A new government panel was formed, orders for cessation of hostilities were issued by both sides, and negotiation was resumed. But until the end of the term of President Gloria Macapagal-Arroyo in June 2010, the two parties could not reach any substantive agreement. What was signed on June 3, 2010, was technically called a *Declaration of Continuity.* Nevertheless, there is still some consolation that can be derived from this declaration, such as the revival of the joint cease-fire mechanism which assured real cessation of hostilities, the renewal of an expanded International Monitoring Team which was given new Terms of Reference, and the creation of an International Contact Group (Rodil, 2010b).

Recently, the present government of Philippine President Benigno Aquino III designated Mr. Marvic Leonen, a lawyer and dean of the Law School of the University of the Philippines, as chair of the new government peace negotiating panel. The MILF, which had earlier deactivated its panel, has just formed a new negotiating team. The good news is that peace talks between the Philippine Government and the MILF has resumed in Malaysia. This was even punctuated by a meeting in Japan between President Aquino and MILF Chairman Ebrahim Murad on August 4, 2011.

The public reaction to the MOA-AD varied and ranged from total acceptance to absolute rejection. Many Muslims, especially those in Central Mindanao (MILF territory), embraced the agreement. Other Muslims in Western Mindanao (MNLF territory) stood lukewarm. The Christian population, particularly in the locations that were listed within the ancestral domain claims of the Bangsamoro, was generally vehemently against the peace agreement. The Lumad communities were also generally opposed to this agreement, especially to the inclusion of their own ancestral domains within the claimed Moro ancestral domain (Rodil 2010a, 2010b, 2010c).

Angry Christian-led rallies were held simultaneously in Zamboanga City, Kidapawan City in the Cotabato province, and Iligan City. Note that these reactions surfaced even before the relevant official documents on the MOA-AD were released to the public, indicating that what were being expressed in these protests were previously stored and accumulated sentiments that were already in existence prior to the MOA-AD. These were expressions of opposition to imagined realities and fears rather than to the actual content of the document. Such vehement reactions were also exhibited in 1996, in reaction to the Southern Philippines Council for Peace and Development (SPCPD), the transitory mechanism that formed a part of the Final Peace Agreement with the MNLF. A similar manifestation also occurred in 1988–1989 over the issue of the name Muslim Mindanao (Rodil 2010a, 2010b, 2010c).

Organized Lumad groups held their own assemblies to express their collective sentiments in reaction to the MOA-AD. While they acknowledge the legitimacy of the Bangsamoro struggle for self-determination, the Lumad asserted that they are not Bangsamoro; they also have their own right to self-determination and are asserting their right to self-governance. Among the various Lumad groups, only the Teduray agree to their inclusion in the territory of the MOA-AD. Their situation is simple and beyond dispute. They are already physically located within the Bangsamoro ancestral domain, particularly in Maguindanao territory, deep within the ARMM, and cannot but be part of Bangsamoro ancestral domain. Nevertheless, they would like their being Teduray and their own ancestral domain to be recognized and respected as distinctly their own. This was allegedly contained in a pact which their ancestors, Mamalu and Tabunaway, agreed upon in the past. For both Teduray and Maguindanao, brothers Mamalu and Tabunaway were their ancestors. Thus, they would like to negotiate for an arrangement of an autonomy within an autonomy (Rodil 2010a, 2010b, 2010c).

Reducing the political choice to a bipolar decision by majority-voting about ancestral land in Mindanao may muffle the minority voices of Muslims and Lumad. Looking at the numbers angle, the Lumad population is only approximately 10% all over Mindanao; the Moro population is estimated at around 20%; and 70% is composed of Christian settlers and their descendants. As such, even if the first two are combined, they will not win in a referendum over the issue of ancestral domain. Yet the ancestral domain issue is seen by Muslims and Lumad as a natural historic right as fundamental as one's right to life.

A two-track forked solution may deal distinctively with Muslim and Lumad claims. On the one hand, there should be formal peace negotiations with the MILF, and at the same time, the implementation of the 1996 Final Peace Agreement with the MNLF should be pursued. In the process, the necessity of revising the constitution in order to find a permanent solution to the Moro conflict should be taken into consideration. On the other hand, the Philippine Government, particularly the National Commission on Indigenous Peoples (NCIP), must see to it that the processing of Lumad ancestral domain claims is completed at the shortest possible time, independently of the GRP–MILF peace process. This is the Lumad's guarantee that their domains will remain intact regardless of political restructuring. Active dialogs must be undertaken at the local level by local government units among the Lumad, Moro, and Christian settler populations to create a climate of mutual recognition of each other's concerns. They themselves will create the guarantee that they can live with each other in peace in their respective communities (Rodil 2010a, 2010b, 2010c).

5.4 Peace Building at the Macrolevel: Toward a Federal Political Structure; Antipoverty Socioeconomic Reforms

With regard to political reforms and restructuring, we propose transitioning from a unitary political system to a federal structure of government. A federal structure will provide us with mechanisms to the following conditions for peace in Mindanao: (1) the devolution of powers from Manila to the regions; (2) the creation of a more responsive system for addressing the economic, political, and cultural needs of the people; (3) the promotion of identity based on different histories, religions, and cultures; and (4) the strengthening of people's initiatives for self-rule and self-development. Thus, we argue for the possibility of addressing the economic, political, and cultural roots of the Moro conflict through the institution of a federal form of government.

Furthermore, we also set forth the following suggestions in exploring federalism for the Philippines. First, we need to review our previous attempts in instituting local autonomy and consider the triumphs and challenges that these experiences have brought about. What were the lessons learned from our experience with the ARMM? What were the roadblocks encountered by the MOA-AD? Second, we need to ensure that the calls for federalization emanate from an empowered Christian, Muslim, and Lumad constituency. The process of transitioning to a federal structure of government involves not only legislation concerning territorial claims and local government structure, but also community dialogs as a procedural requirement. The nature of this community dialogs will involve various types of discussion – workshops on intra- and intergroup levels, with Christians, Muslims, and Lumad carrying out grassroots discussions within their respective groups and between these three groups. At the heart of this transition process lies an empowered constituency claiming and advocating for their own autonomy. Thus, we need to make sure that capabilities and opportunities for cultural and political participation in the transition process are provided for the people in the regions. In this way, we hope to employ federalism as a potent tool for peace building in Muslim Mindanao.

On a related note, we also argue for socioeconomic reforms as an important step toward peace building. In addition to rehabilitation plans for areas destroyed by war, these socioeconomic reforms also include programs on agrarian reform, poverty alleviation, and environmental protection of forests and mineral deposits.

Table 4.2 Summary of peace-building suggestions for Mindanao across three layers

Level of peace building	Suggestions
Microlevel: Individuals in conflict and violence situations	Healing of traumas and internal conflicts Cultivation of active nonviolence in interior life and subjective disposition of individuals
Mesolevel: Social movements and other collectivities for peace	Conscientization and democratization processes in political, economic, and cultural spheres Peace conversations about land ownership in Mindanao
Macrolevel: State, antistate, and global actors	Political restructuring: Genuine federalism with community dialogs as a procedural requirement Socioeconomic reforms: Poverty-alleviation, development, and environmental protection Peace agreements between the Philippine government, Lumad, and Moro Fronts

Table 4.2 summarizes peace-building activities at these three levels. As mentioned earlier, peace building within the various layers is not static, but rather is engaged in continuous interaction with peace building in the other layers. Thus, our struggle for peace should move us to engage continuously in peace building across these different layers, in our hope of achieving a just, comprehensive, and lasting peace for the different peoples of Muslim Mindanao.

Acknowledgments We would like to acknowledge the partial support provided to Cristina J. Montiel, from an AusAID-ALA visiting research fellowship grant to the Centre for Dialogue at La Trobe University.

References

Coronel-Ferrer, M. (1994). *Peace-building and mediation in the Philippines*. Quezon City: Center for Integrative and Development Studies.

Dery, L. C. (1997). *The Kris in Philippine History: A study of the Impact of Moro Anti-colonial Resistance*, 1571–1896. Quezon City, Philippines: L. C. Dery.

Evangelista, A. R. (2003). Peace-building in Mindanao: A partnership between government and civil society. In A. Rasul (Ed.), *The road to peace and reconciliation: Muslim perspective on the Mindanao conflict* (pp. 49–65). Makati City: Asian Institute of Management Policy Center.

Gowing, P. G. (1977). *Mandate in Moroland: The American government of Muslim Filipinos, 1899–1920*. Quezon City: Philippine Center for Advanced Studies, UP System.

Gowing, P. G. (1979). *Muslim Filipinos: Heritage and horizon*. Quezon City: New Day Publishers.

Inzon, C. M. (2007). *A discursive construction of social representations of the history of conflict in Mindanao*. Unpublished doctoral dissertation, Ateneo de Manila University.

Kamlian, J. A. (1999). *Bangsamoro society and culture: A book of readings on peace and development in Southern Philippines*. Iligan City: Iligan Center for Peace Education and Research, Office of the Vice-Chancellor for Research and Extension, MSU-Iligan Institute of Technology.

LaRousse, W. (2001). *Walking together seeking peace: The local church of Mindanao Sulu journeying in dialogue with the Muslim community (1965–2000)*. Quezon City, Philippines: Claretian Publications.

Majul, C. A. (1973). *Muslims in the Philippines*. Quezon City: Published for the Asian Center by the University of the Philippines.

Mindanao Peaceweavers (n. d.). *About MPW*. Accessed September 8, 2010 from http://www.mindanaopeaceweavers.org/about-2/.

Montiel, C. J., & Christie, D. J. (2008). Conceptual frame for a psychology of nonviolent democratic transitions: Positioning across analytical layers. In F. M. Moghaddam, R. Harre, & N. Lee (Eds.), *Global conflict resolution through positioning analysis* (pp. 261–280). New York: Springer.

Montiel, C. J., & Macapagal, M. E. J. (2006). Effects of social position on societal attributions of an asymmetric conflict. *Journal of Peace Research, 43*(2), 219–227.

National Statistics Office (2000). *Household Population by Ethnicity, Region, Province, Municipality and Barangay: Mindanao, and Household Population by Religious Affiliation and Region: Mindanao*.

Nuñez, R. T. (1997). *Roots of conflict: Muslims, Christians and the Mindanao struggle*. Makati City, Philippines: Asian Institute of Management.

Rodil, B. R. (1994). *The minoritization of the indigenous communities of Mindanao and the Sulu archipelago*. Davao City, Philippines: Alternate Forum for Research in Mindanao.

Rodil, R. B. (2000). *KalinawMindanaw: The story of the GRP-MNLF Peace Process 1975–1996*. Davao City: Alternate Forum for Research in Mindanao.

Rodil, B. R. (2003). *A story of Mindanao and Sulu in question and answer*. Davao City: MINCODE.

Rodil, R. B. (2010a, April 4). Lakas ng loob makipag-isa. *Mindanews*.

Rodil, R. B. (2010b, March 19). Decolonize the Philippines, Adopt a New Constitution. *Mindanews.*

Rodil, R. B. (2010c, February). *Magpuyong malinawon sa yutang kabilin (Living in peace in their ancestral domain*). Presentation given at the University of the Philippines Academic Congress, Diliman, Quezon City, Philippines.

Saleeby, N. M. (1963). *History of Sulu*. Manila: Filipiniana Book Guild.

Schreurs, P. (1989). *Caraga Antigua, 1521–1910: The Hispanization and Christianization of Agusan, Surigao and East Davao.* Cebu City: San Carlos University.

Tan, S. K. (2002). *The Filipino-American War, 1899–1913.* Quezon City: University of the Philippines Press.

Part II

Conflict in South-East Asia

Ethnopolitical Conflict in Sri Lanka: Trajectories and Transformations

5

Neloufer de Mel, Kumudini Samuel, and Champika K. Soysa

Sri Lanka Chapter Summary

De Mel, Samuel, and Soysa explore the causes, consequences, and significant factors associated with the ongoing ethnic conflict in Sri Lanka between the Sinhalese, Tamil, and Muslim populations. Delineation of peace negotiations provides impetus for the implementation of suggested inclusions in policy.

Presentation of historical origins of ethnic tension focuses on the primacy given to Buddhism in the constitution as well as designation of Sinhala as the official language. Power struggles in the political arena are credited with amplifying cultural differences and lost opportunities for harmonious integration. Additional inequities are reflected in a lack of minority representation in administration and discriminatory practices in admission to higher education. The authors emphasize the resultant economic effects for minorities engendering increased tension between ethnic groups.

Attention is given to the role of women both as participants in combat, activists, and victims of violence. De Mel, Samuel, and Soysa discuss the predominantly male peace efforts, which focus on power and territory while addressing social issues minimally, and present their view that lasting peace requires inclusion of gender issues.

N. de Mel (✉)
Department of English, Faculty of Arts, University of Colombo, Colombo 7, Sri Lanka
e-mail: nelouferdemel@gmail.com

K. Samuel
Women and Media Collective, 56/1, Sarasavi Lane, Castle Street, Colombo 8, Sri Lanka
e-mail: kumudini.samuel@gmail.com

C.K. Soysa
Department of Psychology, Worcester State University, 486 Chandler Street, Worcester, MA 01602, USA
e-mail: csoysa@worcester.edu

D. Landis and R.D. Albert (eds.), *Handbook of Ethnic Conflict: International Perspectives*, International and Cultural Psychology, DOI 10.1007/978-1-4614-0448-4_5,

Review of failed past attempts to negotiate peace are recommended as a place to begin forming more effective methods. The psychological effects of war and the tsunami on the people of Sri Lanka provides stimulus for proposed changes in policy which the authors believe should include the differing experiences of individuals based on location, ethnicity, and religion. Local participation is seen as essential in establishing peace in Sri Lanka.

Cheryl Jorgensen

The ethnic war in Sri Lanka raged for more than 25 years, from 1983 until 2009. Some of the causes and circumstances that contributed to the conflict remain in the postwar context at this time. This essay will examine the policies and ruptures that contributed to the conflict, followed by a description of the changing status of the war. The humanitarian and economic costs of the war will be discussed as well. A timeline of peace initiatives and reasons for their failure will be presented together with highlights of the attempts at peace. The experience of women as peace makers is largely ignored in the literature on conflict resolution. This essay will explore challenges to peace building for women, and address the content of peace negotiations, participation in peace making, the Subcommittee on Gender Issues (SGI) in the Sri Lankan peace process, and the need to engender the peace process. We end with suggestions for policy makers, with a particular focus on the psychological impact of the war which was later layered with the psychological impact of the Asian Tsunami of 2004; the concerns of the Muslim minority, the second largest minority in Sri Lanka; and finally, economic and reconstruction planning.

1 Ethnic Relations in Sri Lanka: Policies and Ruptures as Potential Causes of Conflict

Ethnic enmity amongst the Sinhala, Tamil and Muslim communities worked as a significant catalyst in Sri Lanka's conflict, reflecting the struggle for political representation and group entitlements. Sri Lanka is a multiethnic society. At the last island wide census (Department of Census and Statistics, 1981), the Sinhalese whose origins are traced to migrations from Orissa and Bengal in Eastern India comprised 74% of the total population of Sri Lanka. The Tamils whose roots are in Tamil Nadu in Southern India were 18%. Of these Tamils, those who were brought to Sri Lanka by the British in the mid nineteenth century to work on the plantations and are known as "up-country Tamils" comprised 5.5%. The Muslims of Arab and Indo-Arab origin were 7%, and the Malays, descendants of Javanese mercenaries who accompanied the Dutch colonizers to Sri Lanka in the seventeenth century comprised 0.32%. The Burghers, descendants of the Portuguese and Dutch colonizers constituted 0.26%.

Of the Sinhalese, 90% are Buddhists and the rest are Christian. It is estimated that 90% of Tamils are Hindu (de Votta, 2004) and the rest are Christian. Tamil Buddhists are insignificant in number. Almost all Muslims adhere to Islam. At the 2001 Census the religious breakdown was as follows: 76.71% of Sri Lanka's population was Buddhist and 7.88% was Hindu. Followers of Islam were 8.49%, 6.06% were Catholics, and 0.81% belonged to other Christian denominations (Department of Census and Statistics, 2001).

Religion worked as an uneven catalyst of the war. Ethnographies of the Liberation Tigers of Tamil Eelam (LTTE) point to the presence of Hindu Saivite symbols and Bakthi traditions in its rituals, iconography, and performativities of martyrdom (Roberts, 1996, 2005). However, given its reliance on cadres drawn from both Hindu and Christian backgrounds, the LTTE did not overtly deploy a religious logic to its struggle. On the other hand, the rhetorical use of Buddhism in support of the war exerted a far greater influence in the Sinhala-dominated South (Abeysekera, 2002; Deegalle, 2006; Seneviratne, 1999). Buddhism is accorded primacy in the Sri Lankan constitution and is evoked at all State functions. It exerts an ambient presence in the daily lives of inhabitants of the South. The support of significant sections of the Buddhist clergy for the war and their resistance to constitutional reform that would confer on the Tamil and Muslim minorities living in the North and East of the country a greater role in self-government is a significant feature of the conflict. Buddhism is considered a nonviolent, pacifist philosophy and the militancy of Buddhist monks caught the attention of political commentators, anthropologists, and scholars of religion (Abeysekera, 2002). For the Buddhist monks, the war was a just one because it was an effort to protect Theravada Buddhism as practiced by the Sinhalese in Sri Lanka. Tamil nationalism and a separate Tamil state carved out from within the boundaries of Sri Lanka would have limited Buddhism's sphere of influence. This points to how, in conflict situations, when existing institutions (such as Buddhism in Sri Lanka) which enjoy primacy are sufficiently threatened, the stakes are raised and those vested in them attempt to reinforce them even by violent means (Sharma, 2009).

There were other significant roots to the ethnic tensions amongst the Sinhalese, Tamils and Muslims, and between the Sinhalese and Tamils in particular, which grew from the failures of early postcolonial power-sharing. State policies and ethnic outbidding in which successive Sinhala and Tamil politicians tried to out-do each other creating mistrust and missed opportunities for reconciliation were at the heart of these failures. These maneuvers heightened the differences between the Sinhalese and the Tamils rather than the considerable commonalities they share through acculturation as two groups domiciled in Sri Lanka since the second century BCE (Indrapala, 2007) and intermarriage, etc. Ethnic outbidding heightened the linguistic and cultural differences of the two: of Sinhalese and Tamils as two distinct linguistic groups (discussed later) and, following nineteenth century colonial racial theories which conflated language with race, the Sinhalese as Aryans, the Tamils as Dravidians. The establishment of Buddhism in the Anuradhapura kingdom (North-Central Province) in the third century BC, and the defeat of Tamil kings such as Elara, also paved the way for a distinct Sinhala-Buddhist identity which gained dominance, as opposed to a Tamil-Hindu one. Sinhala Buddhists, therefore, enjoy a majoritarian outlook over other ethnic groups in the country. These differences were both exploited and reinforced by State policies that served to undermine Tamil citizenship. The "up-country" or plantation Tamils were denied of citizenship altogether in 1948, a policy that was reversed following negotiations with India in 1964 (Jayasinghe, 2002). As for the Tamils of the North-East, amongst the policies which served to alienate them the most and place the country on the road to war were those related to language, colonization, education, territory, and economic development.

Regarding language in Sri Lanka, the majority of Sinhalese speak the Sinhala language, while Tamils speak the Tamil language. Muslims speak both Tamil and Sinhalese, and the Malays speak Malay, Sinhala and English. The Burghers, as descendants of the European colonizers, consider English their mother tongue although those who live in the East of Sri Lanka (where a significant number of Tamil speaking Tamils and Muslims live) are also fluent in Tamil. When the coastal areas of Sri Lanka (known then as Ceylon) came under British colonial rule in 1796, followed by the entire island from 1815 to 1948, English replaced Sinhala and Tamil as the language of administration, the law courts, and gradually, of education. A return to the use of native languages was, therefore, an important demand of the anticolonial struggle. de Votta (2004) notes that the *swabhasha* movement which sought to reclaim the native languages from their suppressions and neglect by the British colonizers was at first supported by both Sinhalese and Tamils. It began in the 1920s in Jaffna (Northern Province – see

Fig. 5.1 Map of Sri Lanka

Fig. 5.1) led by the Jaffna Youth Congress agitating for the use of native languages in administration (Wickramasinghe, 1995). However, the *swabhasha* movement failed to unite the Sinhalese and Tamils for long.

There were several reasons for the preceding failure. Because of American missionary education which provided Tamils with an English education, many Tamil men who could not get jobs in the North because of the lack of economic development and a rigid caste system which dominated Tamil society migrated to the capital Colombo (Western Province – see Fig. 5.1) in the "South" of the country to seek government jobs. By 1946, two years before independence from colonization, Tamils made up 33% of the civil service and 40% of the judiciary (de Votta, 2004). Anxiety at the "overrepresentation" of Tamils in these professions – also attributed as a divide and rule policy of the British who were seen to favor the Tamils by recruiting them to government jobs – propelled Sinhala politicians toward a linguistic ethnonationalism which would establish the supremacy of Sinhala as the language of administration, education, and legislature. This move, which mustered the support of large numbers of the Sinhala speaking electorate and adherents of the Buddhist revival, reached its apogee in 1956 when Solomon W.R.D. Bandaranaike swept to power as Prime Minister on the wave of Sinhala-Buddhist nationalism and the promise of "Sinhala-only, and in 24 h." It took longer than a day for the Official Language Act of 1956 to be proposed, and in the meantime, responding to Tamil pressure, Bandaranaike himself worked at a compromise that would secure some parity for the Tamil language with Sinhala. But the failure to do so and pressure from the Sinhala-only lobby led to the bill being presented in parliament on June 5, 1956.

The Official Language Act No. 33 of 1956 under which Sinhala became the "One Official Language" marks a watershed in Sri Lanka. In effect it barred Tamils from entering the administrative service. This separated Tamils of the North and East spatially and linguistically from the Sinhala speaking population of the South (Hettige, 2004). It also led to the emigration from the country of a significant number of English speaking Sri Lankan Burghers. The "Sinhala-only" Act was met with Tamil protests which included black flags, *satyagrahas* (nonviolent protest), shop closures, protest marches and political demands for both federalism and separatism. These protests set in place the first of successive rounds of anti-Tamil violence by Sinhala mobs which thereafter occurred in 1958, 1977, and 1983. In 1958, the violence led to the declaration of Sri Lanka's first postindependence period of Emergency Rule (Vittachchi, 1958; de Votta, 2004). As a response to the protests, the Sinhala-only bill was amended through the Tamil Language (Special Provisions) Act No. 28 of 1958 under which Tamil was permitted as a medium of instruction in schools, universities, public examinations, and for administrative purposes in the North and East. In 1965, Tamil was adopted as a language in judicial proceedings. It was not until the 1978 constitution that Tamil was granted the status of a national language and not until the 13th amendment to the Constitution in 1987 that it was conferred full parity with Sinhala as an official language. The implementation of this amendment, however, has lacked political will and resources. Many government departments continue to work in Sinhala. Tamils continue, therefore, to feel disadvantaged, particularly in a situation where important government information is available only in Sinhala. This contributed significantly to their "disaffection and sense of alienation from the State" (Gunawardana, 2006, p. 184).

Education was another source of alienation, and higher education policies implemented in the 1970s heightened Tamil grievance against the State. As Sahadevan and de Votta outline the issue (2006), entrance to universities which, until 1969 had been on merit was brought under a mechanism whereby Tamil students had to score up to 20 points higher than Sinhala students in certain subjects to gain university admission. This mechanism was "standardized" in 1974 when, responding to the growing demand for tertiary education of Southern youth who had been educated under the Sinhala-only language policy, the government allotted university places according to District quotas. Since Districts vary in their ethnic composition, the result of these maneuvers was the rapid decline of Tamil student enrolment in Sri Lankan universities, particularly in the departments of the sciences. From representing 48.3% in engineering, 48.9% in medicine, and 47.4% in agriculture in 1969, the ratio of Tamil students dropped in 1975 to 14.2%, 17.4% and 23.5% in each of these respective disciplines. Moreover, while the overall percentage of Tamil students in the sciences was 39.8% in 1969–1970, this ratio had dropped to 19% by 1975 (De Votta, 2004).

Given the value placed on higher education and the sciences in particular as a path to professions in the engineering, medical, financial services and academic professions, the discrimination Tamil students faced in being unable to enter universities to follow these subjects served as yet another index of prejudice on the part of the State which denied them the right to education and social mobility.

Territory marks another vector in the ethnopolitical tensions that led to the war, making the North and East of Sri Lanka the physical site, as well as the ideological heartland of the armed struggle. Tamils, who form the majority population of the North and East, consider these areas their traditional homeland. However, precisely because of Tamil dominance in the region, successive Sinhala governments put in place colonization schemes under which Sinhala farm-workers from the South were relocated to the North and East in a deliberate policy of demographic engineering that went against Tamil interests. de Votta (2004) notes that this colonization policy was in place even under the British colonial government from the mid 1930s. But it was intensified after independence in 1948. In a context in which resource allocation by the State for development projects in the North and East was minimal, Tamil resentment at this inequity was further strengthened by these postindependence colonization schemes which had financial and political support by the Sinhala-dominated government. By the 1960s these schemes had become so successful that the government was able to establish Amparai in the Eastern Province (see Fig. 5.1) as an area in which, while Muslims inhabited its coastal areas, 80% of its overall population was Sinhalese (de Votta, 2004).

The lack of economic development in the North-East, even when Sri Lanka adopted a liberalized economy in 1977, further marked the region as a place apart from the development taking place in the South and particularly the Western Province. In as much as the effects of the "open economy" and its structural adjustment policies led to an income disparity between the rich and poor and urban and rural areas that was felt throughout the country, the cleavage between the Sinhala South and the rest of the country proved to be another divisive feature (Kelegama, 1993). Many development projects inaugurated in the 1980s, from Export Processing Zones to *Gam Udawas* (village "reawakening" schemes that included road construction and the promotion of local industry) were located in the South. The Mahaweli river dam irrigation project under which the largest river in the country was dammed at various points to provide irrigation for agriculture was the largest public investment program during this period. However, it mainly benefited the Central and Uva provinces (see Fig. 5.1). The North-East was provided with only a few industrial projects (such as the paper, cement, and mineral sand factories) while the bulk of its economic production remained within the agricultural and fisheries sectors. But too little heed was paid to developing the necessary technology and infrastructure to provide these sectors better production facilities, transportation, and markets. Nor did the private sector invest in the North-East due to the deteriorating security situation in the region.

If current scholarship on civil war refutes linear causal explanations to argue that acute grievances alone (prevalent throughout the world) do not necessarily lead to armed violence (for not all societies have supported war), the task for us is to focus not only on the motives but also the opportunities that facilitated the outbreak of violence (Boix, 2008). The spatial context of the North and East of Sri Lanka provides an interesting example in this regard. Because a significant percentage of Tamils reside and work in Colombo (estimated at 24% of Colombo's population in 2001, and up to 45% of Tamils are thought to reside outside the North-East as of 2001; Roberts, 2007), the State's linguistic and educational policies confined Tamils who were not English educated or upper class to the North-East region. This paradoxically facilitated a concentration of Tamil youth in the region and provided a political opportunity by the mid 1970s for their radicalization at centers such as the University of Jaffna. By 1983–1984 approximately 30 militant Tamil groups including the LTTE, Eelam Peoples' Revolutionary Liberation Front (EPRLF), Eelam Revolutionary Organization (EROS), Tamil Eelam Revolutionary Organization (TELO),

People's Liberation Organization of Tamil Eelam (PLOTE), and the Eelam Peoples' Democratic Party (EPDP) had formed in the North and East (Roberts, 2006; Senaratne, 1997).

The LTTE was also successful at converting grievances into opportunities. It not only emphasized the discrimination suffered by Tamils in Sri Lanka and as the war evolved, memorialized martial histories of heroism and martyrdom (de Mel, 2007; Roberts, 1996, 2005) to elicit Tamil support for Eelam (Northern and Eastern Provinces together), but also established lucrative networks within the Sri Lankan Tamil diaspora on the European continent as well as Canada, Britain, Norway, Sweden and Australia. This diaspora that had begun with the anti-Tamil pogrom of July 1983 and grown throughout the war supported the LTTE by raising funds and lobbying international legislators on human rights abuses committed by the Sri Lanka government. Such transnational networks have considerably broadened our understanding of contemporary ethnonationalism. No longer restricted to the geographical borders of contested territories, these nationalisms become translocal, sustained by transnational information flows and transfers of capital. The LTTE's estimated income from this diaspora was ascertained at US $40–50 million per year by 2005 (Strategic Foresight Group [SGF], 2006) with which it bought arms, including Czech-built Zlin-Z143 light aircraft, on the international arms market, and funded its offices abroad.

If the "costs of choosing violence [shapes] the level and type of violence" (Boix, 2008, p. 207), the typology of the North-East and its linguistic identity provided other structural opportunities for how and why Tamil militant groups drew the Sri Lanka army into its own territory and why the North-East remained the primary theatre of the war even though LTTE suicide attacks and other smaller missions were carried out in the South. The jungle terrain, fences made of Palmyra branches, and urban alleyways of the North-East provided the ideal setting for guerilla warfare. Moreover, the widespread use of the Tamil language in the region, which neither the Sinhala speaking Sri Lanka army nor the Indian Peace Keeping Forces (IPKF) were very conversant with, gave Tamil militants an advantage. All these were benefits that the LTTE capitalized on to launch attacks on the Sri Lankan security forces, adopting guerilla tactics most suited to the ground from within a territory it was most familiar with. It took a considerable infusion of resources to the Sri Lanka military before it could make the gains it did by April 2009. However, the correlative of this decision to hold the war in the North-East was that while the costs of war have been felt by all Sri Lankans in diverse ways, it is the inhabitants of the North-East who have suffered the most by its violence.

2 Changing Status of Sri Lanka's War

The ethnic war in Sri Lanka, waged from July 1983 to May 2009 between the security forces of the Sri Lanka government and the LTTE was the longest running war in South Asia of its time. It was fought over the establishment of a separate Tamil State of Eelam in the North-East of the country and had four phases. Phase 1 began in 1983 following the ambush and killing of 13 Sri Lanka army soldiers by the LTTE in Jaffna, in the North of the country (see Fig. 5.1), and the subsequent pogrom against Tamil civilians by Sinhala mobs in the month now referred to as "Black July." It ended in 1987 with the arrival to the island of the IPKF. Phase 2 began in 1990 with the withdrawal of the IPKF from Sri Lanka and lasted until 1994 when the Sri Lanka military was pushed back by the LTTE at Pooneryn (North-West of Kilinochchi on Fig. 5.1) which also contributed to the electoral defeat of the ruling United National Party (UNP) government. Phase 3 waged as a "War for Peace" by the new People's Alliance government, began in April 1995 and continued until July 2001 when the LTTE attacked the Katunayake international airport near the capital city of Colombo (Western Province – see Fig. 5.1) which resulted in severe adverse economic repercussions for the country. From 2002 to 2004, a ceasefire was negotiated and peace talks facilitated by the Norwegian government were held. However, with the collapse of these talks, by August 2006, the fourth phase of the war began. It ended with the defeat of the LTTE in Mulaitivu (in the Northern Province – see Fig. 5.1) on May 19, 2009.

3 Humanitarian and Economic Consequences of the War

Protracted conflicts may begin with strong identitarian motives or convert people caught in the violence to the ideological cause(s) underpinning them, but they also draw on other economies as they evolve (Kalyvas, 2006). Intragroup rivalry, forced taxation, prestige, wealth, electoral advantage, and anticipated Statehood become other motivating factors which not only prolong conflicts but also reconstitute them in various ways. The Sri Lankan war was no different. As it progressed there was Intra-Tamil violence as the LTTE attacked rival Tamil militant groups in a bid to gain sole authority over the North and East. In turn, Tamil paramilitaries worked with the Sri Lankan security forces to hunt down the LTTE. At the same time, underworld criminals of Sinhala ethnicity were recruited by the LTTE to carry out attacks against high profile Sri Lankan military officers in the South. The war was, therefore, not a clear-cut Sinhala versus Tamil ethnic conflict (de Mel, 2007). However, the ethnic factor remained valid because it drew attention to the grievances that led to the armed struggle in the first place. It also served as the basis for the ethnic cleansing in October 1990 by the LTTE of Muslims who lived in Jaffna. These Muslims were chased from their homes with 48 h notice, an act through which Tamil dominance of the North was established. Ethnicity was also the grounds on which the LTTE staged its massacres of Sinhala villagers in the Eastern province. In 1984 Sinhala farmers who had settled under the previously mentioned colonization schemes at the Kent and Dollar farms were killed, followed by Sinhala villagers in Gonagala, a small Sinhala village in the Amparai district (Eastern Province – see Fig. 5.1) in September 1999. Currently, it is estimated that Sinhalese comprise under 3% of the population of the North and East (Reddy, 2009). Muslims enjoy a greater presence in the East, but Tamil-Muslim conflict in the region demanded a tripartite agreement (rejected by the LTTE at the last round of peace talks) under which areas in which Muslims enjoyed a majority would be noncontiguous units of autonomy (Uyangoda, 2007). Ethnicity and the devolution of power to the various ethnic groups in Sri Lanka remain, therefore, key factors in the conflict transformation process following the war.

The significant presence of LTTE women combatants and suicide bombers in Sri Lanka's war (as of August 1, 2006, 75, or 23.73% of the LTTE's suicide attacks were carried out by women (Gunawardena, 2006) drew attention to the complex roles women played in the armed conflict (De Mel, 2001, 2007) and the transformation of traditional Tamil women into dedicated frontline combatants elicited comment (Hoole, Somasunderam, Sritharan, & Thiranagama, 1998). But noncombatant Tamil and Muslims women living in the war zones also had to confront the military in particular ways. The weakness or absence of functioning State institutions in these areas paved the way for the Sri Lanka military, the LTTE, and paramilitaries to replace civilian State authorities in regulating security, transport, tax collection and food supply. Whether victim-survivors or aggressors in war, women responded to this militarized economy in various ways. With no alternative means of employment in the context of the breakdown of rural economies, mothers and wives accepted the military as the sole avenue of employment for their sons and husbands. Commensurate to this was the rise in the numbers of war widows and female-headed households. An estimated 89,000 women were widowed in the war (Bamunusinghe, 2010). Women were also vulnerable to gendered abuse/violence. Tamil women were subject to harassment at checkpoints and custodial violence during cordon and search operations and military police stations. Some of them were subject to rape by the Sri Lanka military, the most high profile case (prosecuted later at a Trial at Bar) being that of schoolgirl Krishanthy Kumaraswamy who was raped and murdered in 1996.

The war also affected children in various ways. Apart from disrupted education and psychosocial stress due to the war, they were the victims of landmines. The Sri Lanka Development Forum (as cited in SFG, 2006) reported that an estimated 1.8 million land mines were laid in the North-East targeting over 640 villages. Tamil children in the North-East were also the target of widespread recruitment as child soldiers by the LTTE. As of September 2007, it was believed that over 6,000 children had been enrolled as child soldiers since 2002 (Child Soldiers Global Report, 2008). During the last days of the war, this recruitment increased as the LTTE forcibly conscripted civilians including children to push back the advancing Sri Lankan army.

The economic cost of the war has been immense, deepened by the current global financial crisis. Reaping a "peace dividend" after the 2002–2004 ceasefire by registering a regional economic growth rate of 7% in 2004, and 2–3% above the national average in 2005–2007, when the last phase of the war began in 2006 the agriculture sector in the North-East recorded a decline of 10.3% (Daniel, 2009b; Wanasundera, 2006). Mined paddy fields and the overall security situation led to this decline in agricultural production. Similarly, naval blockades led to a drop in the region's fisheries sector. In the North, the catch of fish dropped from 56,000 metric tons in 2004 to 15,000 metric tons in 2007.

Damage to public infrastructure, particularly in the North-East, was also significant. Before the 2002 peace process it was estimated that 1,200 km of roads in the conflict areas were damaged, transport services severely disrupted or suspended altogether, and about 2,000 schools and 55 public health institutions (out of 400) were destroyed (SFG, 2006). This negative impact on public services was made worse by the tsunami which affected many areas already scarred by protracted war. During the war defense budgets also soared at the expense of investment in other sectors such as education and health. While defense expenditure peaked at 13% of total public expenditure in 2007, it was expected to come down to 10.3% in 2009. Yet this figure was higher than the estimated 2.8% of total public expenditure spent on education in the same year, or the 3.4% estimated for healthcare and nutrition (Sarvananthan, 2008). Despite the end of the war high defense spending has continued with an increase of 6% amounting to one-fifth of the total budget allocated for defense (Ferdinando, 2010).

The militarization of society is another cost of the war. At its most overt, in a militarized society the military has taken ascendancy over civilian institutions. But even if a military government is not in control, and a country's political leadership is democratically elected, a militarized society is one in which the military is valued over civilian institutions, mobility to and from certain areas is dependent on military approval, and military personnel are in charge of key governmental agencies, development and reconstruction projects, schools, provincial governments and rehabilitation centers, etc. All these features are to be seen in Sri Lanka. Therefore, the emphasis on security and a securitized approach to government/management has become part and parcel of its institutions today. Censorship, and the abduction and killing of journalists have also taken place in a militarized environment in which law and order, and accountable governance were suspended for military ends. During the war these conditions also prevailed in areas controlled by the LTTE. Even though the government of Sri Lanka continued to pay the wages of public servants in areas under LTTE control in the North and East, social control was the purview of the LTTE. Under its regime both combatants and civilians were severely disciplined if they failed to follow orders and at times summarily executed if suspected or found guilty of acting against the interests of the LTTE and its leadership.

Militarization is also understood as the process through which the *ideology* of militarism, which leads to aggressive, hypermasculinist, militant solutions to conflict and justifies violence and terror, is ushered into institutions and ways of thought (Chenoy, 2002; Enloe, 2000; de Mel, 2007). The manner in which militarism has seeped into everyday life in Sri Lanka is evident not only in the presence of military personnel at checkpoints and on public roads, but also in habitual aggression on roads, in commercial advertisements, TV soap operas, the increase of petty crime commensurate with the circulation of small arms, and the use of violence in dispute settlement. This signals both the presence of violence as a part of routine social relations and a high level of tolerance for violence as a means of solving conflicts including domestic disputes.

4 Timeline of Peace Initiatives Between the Sri Lankan State and Tamil Militants and Their Failures

(Agence France-Presse [AFP], 2009; Gooneratne, 2007; Ministry of Defence, Sri Lanka, 2007; Rupesinghe, 2006; Wijesinhe, 2008).

- 1984: The All Party Conference (APC) discussed a political solution to the ethnic conflict, lead by the UNP coalition government of President J. R. Jayawardene. These discussions continued across successive governments, Heads of State, and political parties, and remain an ongoing process.
- July 8, 1985: The first direct talks between the government lead by President Jayawardene and representatives of the TULF and several Tamil militant groups, in Thimpu, Bhutan. The government and the Tamil groups accused each other of intransigence, and the talks failed. Analysts have suggested that the talks failed because the Indian government was unable to influence the LTTE, marking a transition to their relative independence from Indian policy makers.
- July 29, 1987: President Jayawardene signs a peace accord with India. An IPKF (Indian Peace Keeping Force) is sent to Sri Lanka to end the conflict and disarm Tamil militants. Sri Lankan and Indian diplomats facilitated the process. The State offered amnesty to combatants. All Tamil militant groups except the LTTE accepted the amnesty (e.g., EPRLF, EPDP, PLOTE, and TELO). After an initial agreement to end hostilities, the LTTE soon became embroiled in war with the IPKF and the ceasefire ended. It is with this accord that the 13th Amendment to the constitution was devised, under which the government agreed to devolved greater power to Provincial Councils including the temporarily merged North-East Provinces (the area that constituted the contested separate Tamil state of Eelam). This Amendment remains controversial because the Sinhalese majority perceives it as one imposed by India and the Tamil minority feels that it does not provide enough decentralization of power. The Muslim minority is concerned about becoming a regional minority if the North and East Provinces are merged.
- 1990: The IPKF withdraws at the request of President Ranasinghe Premadasa of the UNP. By this time, the IPKF has lost 1,200 soldiers, killed by the LTTE. President Premadasa opens talks with the LTTE. During this time, Varadarajah Perumal, Chief of the Tamil militant group called the Eelam People's Revolutionary Liberation Front (EPRLF) moved a resolution which came to be widely regarded as a unilateral declaration of independence, on March 1, 1990. President Premadasa then dissolved the North-East Provincial Council, as desired by the LTTE. However, tensions between the Sri Lanka army and the government lead to skirmishes between the LTTE and the armed forces. These events escalated and the ceasefire broke down. Eventually, President Premadasa was killed by a LTTE suicide bomber on May 1, 1993.
- 1994: President Chandrika Bandaranaike Kumaratunge, leader of the Sri Lanka Freedom Party (SLFP) and the People's Alliance (PA) coalition government were elected on a peace platform, and opened peace talks with the LTTE. Following her election, however, the government failed to propose constitutional amendments that addressed Tamil and Muslim minority rights. On April 19, 1995, the LTTE attacked the Navy in Trincomalee, and the war resumed once more.
- The LTTE deployed a suicide bomber to assassinate President Kumaratunga in mid December, 1999. The President lost an eye and had shrapnel in her brain, but survived this attack. In December 1999–January 2000, President Kumaratunge invited Norway to broker peace between the LTTE and the State.

However, in the October 2000 elections, her party lost its parliamentary majority due in part to several military defeats, and could not gather the political strength to pursue a negotiated settlement to the ethnic conflict.

- In July 2001 the LTTE attacked the Katunayake International Airport, the only international airport in the country. The economic cost of this attack and the political stalemate that resulted from the inability to garner a sufficient majority in parliament lead to another general election in December 2001. Since there was no Presidential election at that time, President Kumaratunga retained her position. Ranil Wickramasinghe of the UNP became Prime Minister and initiated peace talks with the LTTE. In February 2002, peace talks were held in Norway and later, President Kumaratunge and Prime Minister Ranil Wickramasinghe's UNP government signed a permanent ceasefire agreement (CFA) with the LTTE. The Sri Lanka Monitoring Mission (SLMM) was formed to monitor the CFA. Unfortunately, this mission had no mechanism with which to enforce the ceasefire. Further, having a President from one political party and a Prime Minister from another was not conducive to peace negotiations.
- The Tsunami of 2004 devastated the coastal regions of the North, South, and East. A donor conference in May 2005 indicated that funding was contingent on a negotiated settlement of hostilities. President Kumaratunge developed a proposal called the Post-Tsunami Operational Management Structure (P-TOMS), delineating the distribution of international aid in conflict zones and outside. The P-TOMS indicated State recognition of the compound cost of the war and the natural disaster and the need to link these events in policies for reconstruction. The agreement was signed by the government and the LTTE. However, Sinhala nationalist political parties opposed the P-TOMS (as did several Muslims in the East), fearing that it would legitimize LTTE governance in the region. The Supreme Court ruled that the P-TOMS was unconstitutional. President Mahinda Rajapakse of the SLFP was elected President in November 2005, and formed a coalition government. Negotiations between President Rajapakse's government and the LTTE occurred in Geneva in 2006 and were attempted in Oslo and again in Geneva, that same year. Negotiations failed and CFA violations continued. LTTE leader Vellupillai Prabhakaran declared the CFA "defunct" in November 2006 and renewed his call for a separate State. The State withdrew from the CFA in January 2008.
- January 2008: The All Party Representative Committee (APRC) submitted its interim proposals for devolution within the scope of the 13th Amendment. Power-sharing proposals are currently being developed to form the basis of potential constitutional changes that would require a two-thirds majority in parliament, and for some clauses, a referendum as well.
- The final phase of the war between the Armed Forces of the Sri Lankan government and the LTTE occurred between January 2008 and May 2009. The Sri Lankan government focused on a military solution to the ethnic conflict, and defeated the LTTE on May 19, 2009. Thousands of primarily Tamil civilians in the Northern and Eastern Provinces were displaced from their homes during the last six months of the war and were restricted to camps for several months.
- The government of President Mahinda Rajapaksa has secured a military victory over the LTTE. At the general election in 2010, the SLFP won the majority of parliamentary seats. A political solution has yet to be developed to address the needs of the Tamil and Muslim minorities. The Sri Lanka government's response has been the establishment in May 2010 of the Lessons Learnt and Reconciliation Commission (LLRC), constituted by eight members drawn from the public and judicial services, and civil society. Given that the weakness of such commissions have been their implementation, the government instituted an intergovernmental agency (IGA) to implement the recommendations made by the LLRC based on the evidence recorded at its sittings. Amongst the issues that have emerged are the detention

of Tamils without charges, access to lands owned by Tamils in areas that became high security zones, reclamation of abandoned land, the lack of the use of Tamil in government information and documentation contravening the Official Languages Act, demilitarization, and demobilization of segments of the armed forces and Tamil militant groups who support the government. In order to reach the population most affected by the war, the LLRC has held sittings in Jaffna, Mannar, and Trincomalee districts (see Fig. 5.1).

4.1 Highlights of the Attempts at Peace

Throughout the war there have been several attempts at brokering a nonviolent political solution to the crisis by the key actors (Rupesinghe, 2006; Sahadevan & de Votta, 2006). In 1985, for example, talks between the Sri Lanka government and the LTTE were held in Thimpu, Bhutan. The 1987 Indo-Lanka Accord, under which the IPKF arrived in Sri Lanka, encompassed both a military and political goal: the disarming of the LTTE by the IPKF, and the merger of the North-East as a single province with devolved power, to be ratified at a later date through a referendum. Talks between President Ranasinghe Premadasa (later assassinated by the LTTE in May 1993) of the UNP and the LTTE were held during 1989–1990. On the agenda was the dissolution of the North-East provincial council governed by the EPRLF, a rival to the LTTE, and the withdrawal of the IPKF. Later, Chandrika Kumaratunga, leader of the People's Alliance party engaged the LTTE in talks in 1994 and procured a ceasefire in January 1995, but this was broken when the LTTE attacked Sri Lankan navy vessels on April 19, 1995 and an army camp in the East on April 22.

The most significant and lasting ceasefire and peace talks were held during 2002–2004 and began with a Memorandum of Understanding signed by the Sri Lanka government headed by Ranil Wickremesinghe of the UNP and the LTTE on February 22, 2002. Six rounds of talks facilitated by Norway were held, which included a donor conference at which aid was pledged for the reconstruction of the North and East. However, given the violations of the ceasefire committed by both sides, but predominantly by the LTTE which continued to amass weapons during the lull in the fighting, etc., and the reneging of the LTTE on its "Oslo Declaration" in which it indicated willingness to give up its goal of a separate State, the talks broke down. The rejection by factions of the Sinhala political leadership for an Interim Self Governing Authority also contributed to the impasse. By April 2006, this ceasefire was in tatters. On April 26, 2006, Sri Lanka air force jets attacked LTTE bases in Sampur, in the Trincomalee district in the North-East of the country. Any hopes of further political negotiations with the LTTE disappeared with increased LTTE attacks on Sri Lanka government targets. On January 2, 2008, President Mahinda Rajapaksa of the United Peoples' Front Alliance (UPFA) government officially informed the Norwegian government brokering the peace talks that his government was withdrawing from the CFA.

In the several rounds of peace talks, there were specific challenges to peace building from the point of view of women who, as noted earlier, experienced the war in various ways. For example, women's access to assets, employment and political representation in a postconflict society and the views of women active in the peace movement were not officially recognized and included on the agenda for discussion. These issues were tabled only with the formation of the SGI in 2002. The next section of our essay argues that gender forms a crucial category of analysis in peace building and focuses on the SGIs as a case study to offer critical insights toward a theory and practice of women and peace building.

5 Challenges to Peace Building and Peace Making for Women

As the Sri Lankan armed conflict intensified more women were recruited to the State military and the Tamil militant movement. By the mid 1980s the phenomenon of women in armed combat, whether in regular armies or militant national liberation struggles, was fairly commonplace internationally. However, the women suicide bombers of the LTTE were soon to capture the attention of the world through powerful media images of spectacular and deadly suicide missions. While their feats and their changed gender roles have been acknowledged, Tamil female guerrilla fighters have also excited much debate on the potential of armed struggle for women's emancipation.

The years of war also transformed the gendered roles of noncombatant women. Often marginalized and rarely acknowledged, these women used a multitude of strategies other than armed violence to survive the war. Commonly perceived merely as victims, women from Tamil, Muslim and Sinhala communities affected by the conflict were forced to defy or overcome traditional norms and barriers to ensure the survival of their families and communities. For example, they assumed de facto and de jure responsibility for the emotional as well as economic survival of their families; dealt with multiple displacements; engaged with political and military institutions on behalf of detained, tortured, raped, disappeared or executed loved ones; led movements demanding the protection of human rights; negotiated mutual coexistence with hostile neighbors, and campaigned for an end to the fighting.

Women's peace activism spans the entire period of the conflict. Notable in this period were the efforts of the Northern Mothers Front (1984), established to prevent the arrest and disappearance of young men in the Jaffna Peninsula, and Women for Peace (1984), a coalition of women from different class, ethnic, religious and regional backgrounds who came together to call for a political solution to the conflict. Other women's organizations engaged in peace work were the Women's Action Committee (1982), a broad-based group of women workers, media activists, academics and religious personnel, which campaigned for a negotiated solution to the ethnic conflict and dealt with conflict-related violations such as custodial rape, displacement and disappearances, and Mothers and Daughters of Lanka (1989), which campaigned on women's human rights concerns and peace. The Women's Coalition for Peace (1994) and the Sri Lanka Women's NGO Forum (1994) made up mostly of women academics and activists campaigned at the national level for legal and policy reform. The broad coalition Sri Lankan Women for Peace and Democracy (2004) attempted to prevent the abrogation of the CFA of 2002 and get both the government and the LTTE to resume negotiations. In addition, human rights groups such as the Home for Human Rights, the Forum for Human Dignity and the Centre for Human Rights and Development began to systematically follow-up and concentrate on the cases of sexual violence and torture against women in the 1990s, bringing both national and international attention to these violations. These groups focused essentially on legal assistance and legal redress, while others focused on meeting basic needs of survivors, providing counseling, etc., reflecting varying missions in response to violent conflict. The Home for Human Rights and the Forum for Human Dignity took many cases to court and also worked with women's groups on the problems of victims and their families and partnered with the peace campaigns of other women's groups in the North-East (Samuel, 2006).

In seeking solutions to conflict, it is imperative that the gendered nature of conflict and women's varied experiences of it be taken into account in the processes of conflict transition, peace building and peace making. Conversely, peace processes too, including the manner in which agreements are negotiated, who negotiates the agreements, and the content and focus of agreements, are inherently gendered (Bell, 2004). The negotiators are primarily men in positions of power, whether from State or non-State entities, and peace processes are often mediated or facilitated by men. High-level negotiations are identified as male domains, which means that they also employ discourses and practices that are closer to men's reality than to women's (Sørensen, 1998).

5.1 Content of Peace Negotiations

Peace negotiations are often based on the concept of a "peace deal" influenced by the "Realist" and behavioral assumptions of international relations.

Here, it is believed that the behavior of each political actor is governed by security dilemmas and their best strategy is to work toward a negotiated balance of power that guarantees each other's security needs. At the time of the 2002 peace negotiations, this was very much a reality in Sri Lanka.

Another assumption inherent in this leader-actor-centric approach is the belief that "peace is the absence of war" (Uyangoda, 2002, May, p. 1). As has happened in Sri Lanka, the parties concentrated on suspending hostilities (ceasefires) or pursuing military victory and did not address the root causes of the conflict. They did not rely on "building new relationships or addressing issues of identity, justice, and distribution of power so that peace would mean not only the absence of war, but also the presence of conditions that makes war unnecessary" (Uyangoda, 2002, May, p. 1).

The CFA brokered during Sri Lanka's aborted peace process of 2002–2004 and the subsequent proposals for an interim administration, one formulated by the government in July 2003 and the other formulated by the LTTE in November 2003, both dealt with interim devolved arrangements, concentrated on the main issues of territory, division of power, resources and defense. While these issues are of equal concern to women and men, the limiting of substantive negotiations to these questions alone suggests a "male" conception of the issues that needs to be addressed. While we are not promoting an essentialist argument that women are better peace makers, the history of contemporary peace making at the formal level suggests that male-dominated peace processes pay less attention to the deeper issues of systemic discrimination (gender/minorities); abusive use of power; respect for human rights and human dignity; inclusivity; democratic institutions and the improvement of physical, social and legal security. For instance research on peace agreements indicate that only 16% contain references to women (Bell & O'Rourke, 2007). Thus issues of discrimination, human rights, and gender justice are often considered secondary to the central issues of power and territory (Bell, 2004). It is in this context that the contested areas in the interim proposals of both the government of Sri Lanka and the LTTE centered on issues of territory, defense, police, power, and finance on the one hand, and single party political control without safeguards for plural representation on the other.

In processes of peace making, conventional notions of security also endorse a male-centered understanding of the world that privileges the power and status of men allowing "sovereign men" the "rational" choice of legitimating violence including in the control of women (Chenoy, 2002). This control is also exercised indirectly via cultural and ideological frames promoted by the State in the form of discriminatory laws, stereotyped representation of men and women in the media, and gender-biased religious and cultural practices such as restrictions to mobility and dress codes. Thus a "socially constructed masculine experience is validated as universal and imposed on women," preserving male privilege which is "perpetrated through social practices in the private and the public realms" (Chenoy, 2002, p. 45).

"National security" is also predicated on an assumption that identification with the nation-state overrides all other social and political identifications and concerns. It also assumes that identities are homogenous and stable with no contradictions. In Sri Lanka's peace process, when the negotiating parties – the government and the LTTE – agreed to set up a committee to deal with gender issues, the LTTE chose to nominate only Tamil women who were from their ranks rather than open up space for women, including Tamil women who lived in the conflict affected North-East to be part of the negotiating process who had different political, social and other identities. Therefore in times of conflict, even when such categories are being challenged, national interest is presumed to prevail. This assumption of a stable and homogenous national identity is challenged by feminists who emphasize multiple identities and the existence of collective identities, as opposed to a privileged single identity linked to citizenship of a nation/state (Chenoy, 2002).

Although security issues take center stage during the transition period from conflict to peace, the impacts of these issues on women are often ignored and women are often excluded from peace processes and discussions on postconflict transformation.

5.2 Participation in Peace Making

Feminist theorizing has served to provide a nuanced understanding of how conflict affects women differently from men, and how it affects women in different ways depending on their ethnic, religious, caste, class, regional and other identities and affiliations including political affiliations. Protracted conflict and long-term displacement also provide opportunities for greater personal and group autonomy and changes in identity, status and leadership for some women, despite the initial or continuing trauma of dislocation and dispossession (Manchanda, 2001; Thiruchandran, 1999; Zackariya & Ismail, 1998).

However, women affected by violent conflict continue to be perceived mainly as the archetype of marginalization, discrimination and disempowerment; their identity and autonomy are collapsed into the universal category of "victim." While normative frames bound by patriarchy contribute to such constructions, a range of human rights and humanitarian discourses and practices also tend to view women exclusively as victims and imbue their responses with a strong protectionist bias (Behera, 2006). For example, even U.N. Security Council Resolution 1325, which brings about a shift in global perception and a political framework for addressing issues of women, peacemaking, peacekeeping, and security in the context of conflict resolution, focuses on the "protection of women," instead of on the protection or enabling of women's rights in the context of conflict resolution and peace building (Strickland & Duvvury, 2003). In times of protracted conflict, women's initiatives for peace, often at the local level, mediated on a daily basis or even those that are mobilized at a national level, are almost without exception relegated to the "nonformal" process. They are largely unacknowledged, trivialized, or ignored (Samuel, 2003). Indeed, early literature on women and armed conflict was gender blind, and was as oblivious to women's participation in peace building and peace making as it was to women's complicity in violence (Behera, 2006) Women were instead positioned as victims of war in need of protection, particularly from sexual violence, while less attention was paid to women's everyday lived experience of conflict, displacement, shifting gender roles and agentive moments. The history of peace making is replete with women's struggles to enter and influence formal peace processes. In Ireland, women established an independent women's political party, the Northern Ireland Women's Coalition, just before the all party peace talks, thus enabling the presence of women at the negotiating table as a distinct political grouping in their own right (Bell, 2004). In a now famed, historic and inspiring move, women from Liberia, Sierra Leone and Guinea took the bold initiative to form the Mano River Women's Peace Network (MARWOPNET) and succeeded in persuading the leaders of the three Mano River region countries to meet and start a peace process (Femmes Africa Solidarité, 2002). In Liberia women were able to mount a serious lobby during the peace talks in Accra and Akomsombo in Ghana, presenting peace proposals and helping to move the process of negotiation forward. They continue their work monitoring the implementation of the Comprehensive Peace Agreement that resulted from the peace talks (Femmes Africa Solidarité, 2002). In the North-East of India, among the Naga, a group of Tribes who live in the states of Nagaland, parts of Manipur, Assam and Arunachal Pradesh, the "Naga Mothers" represent the mediatory force in the Naga struggle for self-determination and the Naga Mothers Association together with the Naga Council of Elders are now accepted as an integral part of the democratic mobilization for peace symbolizing changes in Naga society that now accept women in the public sphere after 50 years of struggle (Manchanda, 2001). In 2001 Muslim, Christian and Lumad women formed the Mindanao Commission on Women and created a "Women Working a Mindanao Agenda." In 2006 during the peace talks, this Commission facilitated the drawing up of recommendations and inputs for both the Mindanao government and the Moro Islamic Liberation Front (MILF) aimed at seeking a comprehensive peace agreement to address the root causes of the Moro Struggle (Government of the Philippines, 2006). Feminists there question the essentialist stereotyping of women merely as victims in times of conflict. They instead propose a notion of agency that

> attributes to the individual actor the capacity to process social experience and to devise ways of coping with life even under the most extreme forms of coercion. … for women as much as men, the experience of violent conflict and migration, as with social life, is not built upon a single discourse. As social actors, they form multiple ways of formulating their objectives, however restricted their resources (Moser & Clark, 2001, p. 5).

They thus created new spaces for political engagement that often defied the formal and the conventional and offered an emancipatory potential to peace building and peace making (Samuel, 2011).

5.3 The Sri Lankan Peace Process: Appointment of the Subcommittee on Gender Issues

None of the formal attempts at peace making in Sri Lanka prior to 2002 allowed space for women's participation except for the presence of Adele Balasingham, the wife of LTTE ideologue Anton Balasingham. Concerted advocacy by women's groups, however, strengthened by years of peace activism and engagement with campaigns for a negotiated political settlement to the conflict, enabled the establishment of a Subcommittee on Gender Issues SGI to "explore the effective inclusion of gender concerns in the peace process" during the 2002–2003 peace talks (Samuel, 2011). Facilitated by a senior Norwegian female Minister, Dr. Astrid Heiberg, the SGI was to identify issues of concern to women and bring them into the agenda of the peace process. The Committee was mandated to report directly to the plenary sessions of the peace talks and work closely with other Subcommittees to the peace process.

This mechanism was possibly the first of its kind set up within a formal peace process at a presubstantive stage of negotiations. It was also the first effort by the Sri Lankan government and the LTTE to recognize the involvement of women in peace building and peace making. In composition, the SGI included senior LTTE women leaders as well as nongovernmental/non-party feminist activists appointed by the government. Meeting just twice before the formal peace process was aborted, the SGI was able to make considerable gains in confidence building and consensus far in advance of the male led plenary negotiations at the peace table. Meeting in LTTE controlled territory instead of at overseas venues favored for the plenary talks, the face-to-face meetings between the women's delegations were important confidence-building measures. Visits to sites of rehabilitation and appreciation of efforts to deal with war-induced trauma helped break down latent antagonisms, and informal conversations ranging from marriage, caste and dowry systems to the emancipation of women brought the "personal" realm into the "political" one. This helped inform discussions on the changing social perceptions about women, and the need to transform discriminatory cultural practices against them, a topic of considerable interest to LTTE women militants. As divisions between the private and the public sphere were broken down, the female delegates were able to navigate the more difficult political terrain of formal discussion and consensus building (Samuel, 2011).

Importantly, the women also agreed on a conceptual frame around which to center their discussions and work, using gender as a category of analysis premised on the fact that women experience conflict differently from men and in particularly gendered ways. For instance, the stigma attached to rape or the ostracizing of widows or the marginalization of single women headed households. Inherent in this framing was also the understanding that gender is cross cut with other competing identities such as ethnicity, class, caste, religion, political affiliations and so on (Manchanda, 2002). The SGI was concerned that a limited focus on women would marginalize the work of the committee.

The first meeting of the SGI was considered to be "positive and constructive" (SGI, 2003). The delegation acknowledged the "widespread and profound suffering of women as a consequence of war, especially in the most affected areas" (SGI, 2003, p. 1). The SGI also decided to work closely with the other Subcommittees and other mechanisms associated with the peace process. It noted that their task was to "identify issues of concern to women that need to be addressed and bring those concerns into the agenda of the peace process" (SGI, 2003, p. 1). Further, the SGI decided to formulate Gender Guidelines for the Subcommittees and other mechanisms associated with the peace process. It also decided to engage directly with the Subcommittee on Immediate Humanitarian and Relief Needs (SIHRN) in the Accelerated Resettlement Programme for the Jaffna District (ARP-J) and the Fast-track Resettlement Programme for the Mannar District (FTRP-M), both districts in the conflict affected North and East of Sri Lanka (both in Tamil-dominated areas- see Fig. 5.1). At the substantive level, its discussions focused on the drafting of a Terms of Reference (TOR) for its work, and by the end of the first meeting the fundamental elements of a TOR were agreed upon.

At the second meeting of the SGI held on the 4th and 5th of April 2003, the Committee was able to finalize their TOR, which focused broadly on sustaining the peace process, resettlement, personal security and safety, infrastructure and services, livelihood and employment, political representation and decision making, and reconciliation. The TOR was to be presented by a delegation of the SGI to the plenary of the peace talks scheduled for later in April. However, this session of the plenary talks was postponed indefinitely with the LTTE's withdrawal from the formal process.

The government appointees on the SGI strove to inform and be informed by women's groups before they met formally as the SGI. Many of the areas of concern included in the SGI TOR were those put forward by women's groups throughout the periods of conflict and postceasefire. For example, the LTTE delegation brought to the forefront of the discussion the widespread war-induced suffering of the Tamil people, and its belief that conflict resolution had to deal fundamentally with reestablishing "normal life" in the affected areas. It wished to concentrate on meeting immediate needs such as resettlement, rehabilitation, dealing with the consequences of conflict such as trauma and the concerns of orphaned children, rebuilding of schools, and meeting the needs of students.

While both delegations agreed on what issues the SGI should work on, the manner of engaging with these issues was articulated differently. While a significant level of agreement was reached by the second meeting of the SGI in the drafting of the TOR, not all the issues were non-contentious. Some concerns placed on the table had to be postponed given their political sensitivity. Others needed compromise, and prudent judgment had to be exercised on both sides to determine which issues could not be solved immediately or in the short term, such as that of reconciliation, which had to be linked to the broader peace negotiations. However, issues related to women's immediate needs, and elements of legal reform on violence against women, political representation, land rights, policy on equal access to jobs and equal wages were areas on which the SGI could make common representation and were issues not addressed by the plenary of the peace process.

5.4 Engendering Peace Processes

The question remains whether current peace processes offer the potential to address gender insecurities and the concerns of political, economic, social, and personal insecurity for women. As much as war is a gendered activity, peace making too is inherently gendered. A fundamental lacuna in peace making at the formal level is the continued marginalization of women's agency and a gender perspective from the public discourse of peace. The absence of war or cessation of hostilities for the time being does not necessarily mean an end to violence. Nor does it, by itself, ensure the enjoyment of economic and social justice or guarantee inclusion, equality and nondiscrimination. As indicated above, peacemaking and peace keeping are integrally linked to security and a gendered focus on peace processes is an indispensable element of ensuring that the myriad of women's security concerns are addressed, met, and dealt with. It must also be acknowledged that questions of women/gender and peace/war are particular to each conflict in relation to time, place, race, ethnicity, class, religion and a range of other discrete circumstances. They are also related to different social constructs of gender, of masculinity and femininity (Bunch, 2004).

Reardon (1993) describes peace as the antithesis of exploitation, marginalization, and oppression – factors that deny human freedom and impede the fulfillment of security needs. Central to a feminist conceptualization of peace and human rights is the recognition of a continuum of violence against women. All forms of this violence, whether interpersonal, in the family, the community, or the State, are interrelated (Cockburn, 2001). Mainstreaming gender in peace processes, or more effectively, integrating gender into all aspects of a peace process needs to become a priority concern for the sustainability of peace and for the achievement of "positive" and "transformative peace" with inclusive democratic structures and processes, an active and egalitarian civil society and an open and accountable government.

6 Suggestions for Policy Makers Based on Empirical Data

The preceding sections of this chapter have addressed the confluence of events that have contributed to the ethnic war in Sri Lanka, the different phases of the war, the humanitarian and economic cost of this war, and suggestions for resolutions with a particular focus on the peace initiatives of women. The final part of this chapter will examine empirical data as a basis for making suggestions to policy makers regarding postconflict and posttsunami rehabilitation and reconstruction. The two disasters, war and the tsunami, are considered to have cumulative effects in the North and East of Sri Lanka. The lessons learned from posttsunami reconstruction initiatives demonstrated differences between the war-torn North and East and the South. These differences are examined with the hope that they might inform postwar rehabilitation and reconstruction. Since a complete review of policies is beyond the scope of this chapter, a sampler of issues will be considered.

The history of peace negotiations described earlier indicated that four different heads of State have engaged in peace negotiations with the LTTE over about 25 years, prior to the end of the war. Future efforts at developing peace policies may do well to explore the reasons for the failure of negotiations. One aspect that has been considered is the relative military efficacy of the State vs. the LTTE. A military victory is only one aspect, however, and winning the confidence of the constituents of the North and East in particular, as well as the rest of the country, is crucial. To this end, several points are worthy of consideration when developing policies for peace. First, the psychological cost of this protracted war must be taken into account when engaging in negotiations, because sustainable peace requires policies that address these needs in the rehabilitation and reconstruction process. Next, a recurring complaint is that Muslim perspectives are underrepresented at peace talks, despite the fact that Muslims comprise 7% of the population. The particular concerns of Muslims, therefore, require special attention. A viable policy for peace needs to include all major ethnic groups: Sinhalese, Tamils, and Muslims. Finally, decentralization of power from the central government to the Provincial Councils and local governments has been perceived as insufficient. The posttsunami relief and reconstruction process demonstrated the impediments posed by the current system. As postwar policy is developed and constitutional reform is proposed, these broad categories need to be addressed, if the goal is to achieve a lasting peace. While the country is currently in a postwar context, we have not yet achieved postconflict status, as the aspirations and concerns of ethnic minorities have yet to be sufficiently addressed. These three issues will be addressed below.

6.1 The Psychological Impact of War

The war has spilled over to the civilian population of all ethnic groups, Sinhalese, Tamils, Muslims, and others. Sri Lankans living in the war zone and the villages along its border have experienced horrors including: mortar shelling, cross-fire, attacks with machetes, aerial bombing, landmine explosions, arrest, detention, kidnapping, rape, torture, witnessing violence, bodily injuries, displacement, destruction of property, loss of income, and a host of other war-related threats to their physical and mental well-being. All actors in the war, the State, the Tamil militant groups, and the IPKF, have participated in some combination of these events. When calculating the cost of war, it is impossible to quantify human suffering. Interventions for conflict resolution must consider the experiences of war and their sequelae when developing policies for relief and reconstruction.

Regarding exposure to war, Somasundaram (2004) found that after 20 years of war in the Jaffna peninsula (see Fig. 5.1), among Tamils, 50% reported death of a friend/relative, 46% loss of property, 39% injury to friend/relative, 37% experienced bombing, shelling, or gunfire, and 26% witnessed violence as forms of direct stress. Further, this population experienced indirect stress as well, where 78% reported economic hardship, 70% displacement, 56% lack of food, and 45% unemployment. In their survey of displaced Tamils living in welfare centers run by the State in the Vavuniya area of the North-Central Province (see Fig. 5.1), de Jong et al. (2002) stated that 12% had been attacked, 18% arrested or kidnapped, 17% taken hostage or detained, 17% maltreated by police or army personnel, 11% were tortured, 60% had heard of rape cases, almost all had lost their homes and property, 97% had faced starvation, and 88% reported a constant feeling of being unsafe. In addition, 7% had lost a partner, 9% lost a child, 12% lost a parent, 18% lost a sibling, 10% had witnessed the death of their child or a child in their care, 48% had experienced separation from their families, and 24% said that a family member had attempted suicide. On the East coast in Batticaloa (see Fig. 5.1), Chase and Bush (2002) reported that among Tamil and Muslim schoolchildren, 41% had personally experienced conflict-related violence and 53% had family members killed or disappeared. Soysa (2005) found that Sinhalese children living in villages on the border of the war zone had experienced a range of war events including a direct attack on their village by Tamil militants, a war-related death in the family (as locally recruited security personnel called "home-guards," or in the military), heard gunfire, grenades, or mortar shelling, were displaced from their homes temporarily, and saw landmine explosions, although the frequency of these events was lower than those reported in the Northern and Eastern theaters of war. As the war progressed and escalated, greater proportions of the population of Sri Lanka have been exposed to events of war, both because of direct war exposure in the North and East, and because of retaliatory attacks by the LTTE inside and outside the war zone.

Somasundaram (2004) described the psychosocial sequelae of war in the Jaffna peninsula (see Fig. 5.1). He stated that at outpatient clinics, 80–90% of the Tamil population reported somatization which is the experience of psychological distress as physical symptoms, 70–80% said they had anxiety, 60–70% had posttraumatic stress disorder (PTSD), 50–60% reported depression, 40–50% experienced hostility, 40–50% complained of relationship problems, and 10–20% admitted to alcohol abuse. In the East, 95% of Tamil and Muslim schoolchildren had been exposed to extreme events, meeting the PTSD criterion of exposure to severe threat to oneself or others; 92% of these were war-related (Chase & Bush, 2002). The preceding authors stated that 20 and 39% of these children, respectively, reported severe and moderate levels of posttraumatic distress. Soysa (2003) studied Sinhalese children living in villages on the border of the war zone, called "border villages." Families living in these villages were subject to violent attacks by Tamil militants, and were sometimes caught in the cross-fire between the State armed forces and Tamil militants. The families living in these villages formed a human border along the boundaries of territory held by Tamil militants during the war. Based on the criteria set by Smith-Fawzi et al. (1997), Soysa found that 90% of Sinhalese children in an Eastern border village exposed to an intensive militant attack and 50% of Sinhalese children in a Northern border village exposed to moderate chronic war had posttraumatic symptom levels higher than the diagnostic cut-off point, thereby qualifying for the diagnosis. While there is contention about the interpretation of symptoms based on Western models of psychopathology, it is generally agreed that Sri Lankan children and adults have reported severe subjective distress.

Cumulative Psychological Impact of War and the Tsunami – Sri Lanka had the second highest number of deaths of all countries affected as a consequence of the tsunami on December 26, 2004. About 30,000 people were reported dead or missing (Neuner, Schauer, Catani, Ruf, & Elbert, 2006). The tsunami affected most of the coastline of Sri Lanka, including the North-East war zone. Adolescents living in the Northern war zone were born during the war and although they have had brief respites during ceasefires, they have never experienced life in peacetime. Based on the discussion in the previous section, we see that posttraumatic reactions are one of many possible psychological responses to extreme stress. Communities exposed to both war and the tsunami, therefore, were likely to experience even higher levels of distress.

Neuner et al. (2006) assessed posttraumatic responses 3–4 weeks posttsunami and 3 years into the ceasefire in Northern, Southern, and Western Sri Lanka. They set aside strict application of the time criterion, where PTSD is recognized only if symptoms have persisted for at least 4 weeks (American Psychiatric Association [APA], 2000). In their study, the Northern coastal sample was exposed to both war and the tsunami, while the Southern and Western samples were exposed to the tsunami alone. In the immediate aftermath of the tsunami, and in the context of the ceasefire, the majority of children in the preceding study reported a tsunami-related event as the worst event they experienced, across all three regions of the country. In these circumstances, Neuner et al. found that there was no significant difference in the rate of PTSD diagnosis between the Northern and Southern children, but both these groups of children reported higher rates of PTSD diagnosis compared to children in Western Sri Lanka. This is likely because tsunami exposure was less intense in the West of Sri Lanka. It could be argued that war-exposure plus tsunami-exposure contributed to the high levels of PTSD symptoms in the North, and that greater tsunami-exposure in the South contributed to their high levels of PTSD symptoms.

The situation was somewhat different one year posttsunami. In order to examine the impact of chronic war exposure alone in the war zone, posttraumatic symptom severity was assessed in Tamil adolescents living in an inland village (no tsunami-exposure) in the Northern war zone of Sri Lanka (Soysa & Jamunananthan, 2007). In addition, in the same study, posttraumatic symptom severity was examined in a proximal coastal village in the Northern war zone, in order to assess the cumulative impact of chronic war and the 2004 tsunami on Tamil adolescents. A similar study was performed in the South among Sinhalese adolescents exposed to the 2004 tsunami, but no direct exposure to war (Soysa, 2007). The results of the preceding studies revealed that posttraumatic symptom levels in Tamil adolescents in the Northern war zone were high, even four years into the ceasefire and one year posttsunami. Further, the severity of their symptoms was significantly higher than those of Sinhalese adolescents living in Southern Sri Lanka with no direct exposure to war, 1-year posttsunami. Within the Northern population, adolescents exposed to both the war and the tsunami reported even higher levels of posttraumatic symptomatology than those exposed to war alone, one year after the tsunami. Clearly, cumulative collective stress had a devastating psychological impact on adolescents, regardless of how their symptoms of distress are interpreted, one year after exposure to a second collective stressor. These results highlight the need to recognize the cumulative psychological impact of the war and the tsunami among Tamil children in the North. For children in the warzone, tsunami-related distress was layered on top of war-related distress, making them inseparable. Reconstruction processes must therefore acknowledge the impact of both the war and the tsunami when developing and implementing policies that might help the country to transition from a postwar to postconflict status.

6.2 Muslim Representation in Conflict Resolution

As stated previously, sustainable policies for peace must consider the special situation of Muslims. Throughout the history of the ethnic conflict in Sri Lanka, the primary focus has been on the Sinhalese majority and the Tamil minority, whether it is a description of the parties in conflict, peace negotiations, or proposals for devolution of power. Thus far, the Muslims of Sri Lanka have not been adequately represented in discussions about conflict resolution (International Crisis Group [ICG], 2006, 2007; Kelegama, 2004). Muslim political leaders represent multiple historical experiences and geographical realities of their constituents together with differing political perspectives, much like political leaders of Sinhalese and Tamil ethnicity. For example, Muslims living in conflict areas have different needs than those who are displaced, or those relatively untouched by war. A lasting peace can only happen with the participation of all political perspectives.

Sri Lankan Muslims are a sizeable minority at the national level, but their numbers in the East are of special significance. Based on the special enumeration conducted by the Department of Census and Statistics, Sri Lanka (2007), Sri Lankan Tamils represent about 40% of the Eastern Province, while Muslims constitute 38% and Sinhalese 21%. The Northern Province, on the other hand, is predominantly composed of Sri Lankan Tamils, because Muslims were forced to leave the area in 1990, and Sinhalese had left much earlier, after the onset of war. A point of contention when discussing decentralization amidst proposals for conflict resolution is whether the North and East should be governed as a single province or two separate provinces. If the East is subsumed under a single North-East Province, Muslims immediately become a minority in the area, whereas they would hold about equal representation in a provincial government if the East were to remain separate from the North. The issue of joint or separate governance of the North and East is, therefore, of paramount importance to Muslims. As described earlier, the 13th Amendment to the Sri Lankan Constitution addressed the merger of these provinces, causing concern to the Muslims in the East. Implementation or revision of this Amendment requires the participation of both ethnic minorities, Tamils and Muslims.

The victimization of the Muslim minority has taken various forms in the Sri Lankan ethnic conflict. In August 1990, militants identified as LTTE cadre killed more than 103 Muslim men and children at prayer in two mosques in Kattankudy (see Fig. 5.1), in the East (ICG, 2006, 2007). More recently, several Muslims celebrating a religious festival were killed by a suspected LTTE suicide bomber in Akuressa (in the Southern Province – see Fig. 5.1) in the South of Sri Lanka (Daily Mirror, March 10th, 2009). Apart from the 2006 LTTE order to leave their homes in Muttur (see Fig. 5.1) in the Trincomalee District, within 72 h, an event of great significance, as stated previously, was the expulsion of the Muslims from the North on October 30, 1990. In Jaffna alone (see Fig. 5.1), 28,000 Muslim men, women, and children were ordered by the LTTE to leave their homes with 2 h of notice (Jeyaraj, 2005). Jeyaraj has stated that Muslim civilians were permitted to take only one spare set of clothes and Rs. 150 (US$ 1.50) per person and that jewels and extra money were seized. He estimated that about 85,000 Muslims were expelled from the North by the LTTE in 1990, and that most of them are still displaced, primarily living in the West of Sri Lanka. Not surprisingly, Muslims have a considerable stake in proposals for conflict resolution, as they have been the victims of massacres, ethnic cleansing, and forced displacement at the hands of the LTTE (ICG, 2007).

6.3 The Economic Paradox, Reconstruction, and Planning

Sri Lanka's GDP growth has been estimated at 3.5% for 2009 (Central Bank, 2010), but is estimated to grow by 8.5% in 2011 (Central Bank, 2011). The reason that Sri Lanka has maintained its GDP growth despite the war is partially attributed to the fact that its main income was from sources that were largely unaffected by the armed conflict such as the garment industry, foreign employment remittances from the Middle-East, and agricultural exports (Deraniyagala, personal communication, March 23, 2009; Kelegama, 2004). While GDP growth has been maintained at a national level, however, local economies in the North and East have been, as noted earlier in this chapter, decimated by the war. Economic policies related to postconflict reconstruction will therefore have to focus on these areas. In fact, after the end of the Cease Fire Agreement in 2006, GDP growth in the North-East was high because of an influx of posttsunami reconstruction aid from abroad (Daniel, 2009a).

Although Nongovernmental organizations (NGOs) and the Private Sector contribute to relief and reconstruction efforts, vast amounts of local and international funding comes through the government, and therefore, regardless of the party in power, proactive policy planning, transparency, and accountability are of utmost importance. The Center for Policy Alternatives (CPA, 2006) evaluated the posttsunami relief and reconstruction process one year after the disaster, as a means of providing policy makers and stakeholders a document that could be used in the formulation of policies pertaining to rehabilitation, reconstruction, and development, in response to both the ethnic conflict and the tsunami. The basis of the proposals in this document was an examination of the status at that time, so that future plans could incorporate suggested changes. The CPA encouraged stakeholders to employ two overarching principles – conflict sensitivity in terms of doing no harm, as well as subsidiarity, where decision making occurs at the local level and the central government only participates in activities that cannot be implemented in an efficacious manner at the local level.

In its recommendations, the CPA (2006) critiqued centralized structures of government, where regulations were issued with minimal consultation and participation of local actors. Processes that foster inclusiveness and pluralism at the local level were suggested, to ensure that issues particular to each context are considered. In addition, it stated that national and regional mechanisms were set-up posttsunami, adding to preexisting structures. As a consequence, services were duplicated as was bureaucracy, hampering effective delivery of goods and services. Complementary structures rather than overlapping ones were recommended as more effective in the coordination of relief and reconstruction efforts. Access to information was lacking, as delays were inevitable when decision making had to travel from the center to local communities. Lack of transparency was highlighted as well, as accountability in disbursing funds in an equitable manner across ethnic groups, geographical regions, and conflict affected versus tsunami affected populations, was crucial in order to ensure that resources reached the intended beneficiaries. Overall, it was recommended that postconflict policy planning remedy these flaws in existing relief and reconstruction structures.

The Institute of Policy Studies (IPS) in Sri Lanka made a set of recommendations for policy makers as well, based on their particular assessment of posttsunami reconstruction of houses (Arunatilaka et al., 2006). These researchers found that although there were significant delays in the delivery of funds through the government at that time, the State was the main source of funds for the rebuilding process. This speaks to the importance of State funds in the reconstruction process. The authors reported that housebuilding completion was most efficient with funding from the private sector and foreign individuals (perhaps because of closer monitoring and a guarantee of funds), and worst when people relied on their own funding. In their study 2 years posttsunami, only 6% of surveyed relocated households had legal ownership of their homes, irrespective of donor source. An investigation of the factors that contributed to success would be useful, in order to replicate these measures in future policy planning.

Further, Arunatilaka et al. (2006) stated that most people living in relocated homes complained that access to services such as water, roads, preschools, and health clinics were limited, as was access to employment in the new location. This specific example of home-building reflected the overall problems of ignoring local input regarding service needs and employment opportunities, and a lack of coordination between donors and State regulations resulting in wasted resources. As described previously as an overall pattern, the researchers found a lack of access to information regarding credit. For example, although microcredit programs were available for tsunami-affected populations, only 15% of households in the East and South had applied for them, and only 10% of households in that area had received them. On the other hand, local funding sources such as rural banks (Samurdhi) were more accessible, and 80% of those who applied for loans received them. Once again, the need for local participation in decisions pertaining to the disbursement of resources was revealed. Providing support for the claim made previously that local administrators become overloaded when centralized agencies duplicate work, the authors found that aid distribution was impeded due to administrative overload at the local level.

In addition, Arunatilaka et al. (2006) stated that a higher proportion of households in the war-affected Eastern Province compared to the Southern Province (outside the war zone) reported that their livelihoods had not been restored to pretsunami levels. This reflects a lack of equity in implementing relief measures. Interestingly, of the preceding households, these researchers found that only 4% identified the war as an obstacle to income recovery. Participants in the preceding study said that the reconstruction process provided more employment opportunities than those provided by livelihood assistance programs in the rehabilitation process. This raises a concern that economic recovery could be short-term, unless livelihood assistance programs are fostered even amidst the reconstruction economic boom. Clearly, a lasting peace will require economic development policies that take account of local realities based on the differential experience of war and the tsunami among the Sinhalese, Tamils, and Muslims of Sri Lanka.

7 Conclusion

This chapter signaled the shifting phases of Sri Lanka's ethnic war and the confluence of language, educational, development and demographic policies that led to Tamil grievance, militancy and eventually armed struggle for a separate State of Tamil Eelam. It outlined some of the humanitarian and economic costs of the war and attempts at peace. It spoke in particular to the issues of women in conflict and peace building. Taking the SGI comprising women delegates nominated by the Sri Lankan government and the LTTE during the 2002–2004 peace process as a case study, it highlighted the processes by which the SGI was able to make common ground but also the conditions that circumscribed it.

The final part of this chapter examined empirical data relating to those who not only experienced psychological stress due to the war but also the devastating Asian tsunami of December 2004 which affected parts of Sri Lanka that had already been scarred by the armed conflict. It also marked the experiences of the Muslim community in the war, and argued for their greater inclusion – as with women survivors of war – in peace processes. The failures of the posttsunami reconstruction process were examined as well, as a means of suggesting new approaches to postconflict reconstruction. Its analysis was, therefore, toward a reformulation of peace processes and postwar reconstruction.

References

Abeysekera, A. (2002). *Colors of the robe: religion, identity and difference*. Columbia: University of South Carolina Press.

Agence France-Presse, AFP (2009, March 10). *Key dates in Sri Lanka's ethnic conflict*. Retrieved August 11, 2011, from http://www.reliefweb.int/rw/rwb.nsf/db900SID/ASAZ-7PZHWY?OpenDocument&RSS20=02-P.

American Psychiatric Association. (2000). *Diagnostic and statistical manual of mental disorders-text revision* (4th ed.). Washington, DC: Author.

Arunatilaka, N., Wickramasinghe, K., Jayawardena, P., Weerakoon, D., Steele, P., & Jayasuriya, S. (2006). *Post tsunami reconstruction and rehabilitation: Household views on progress and process*. Retrieved August 11, 2011, from http://www.ips.lk/other_reserach/tsunami_research/tsunami_research.html.

Bamunusinghe, M., (2010, September 30). Conflict leaves 89,000 widows. *Daily Mirror*, p. 1.

Behera, N. C. (2006). Introduction. In N. C. Behera (Ed.), *Gender, conflict and migration* (pp. 21–71). New Delhi: Sage Publications.

Bell, C. (2004). Women and the problems of peace agreements: Strategies for change. In R. Coomaraswamy &

D. Fonseka (Eds.), *Peace work – Women armed conflict and negotiation* (pp. 96–126). New Delhi: Women Unlimited.

Bell, C., & O'Rourke, C. (2007). The people's peace? Peace agreements, civil society, and participatory democracy. *International Political Science Review, 28*, 293–324.

Boix, C. (2008). Civil wars and guerilla warfare in the contemporary world: Towards a joint theory of motivations and opportunities. In S. N. Kalyvas, I. Shapiro, & T. Masoud (Eds.), *Order, conflict, and violence* (pp. 197–218). Cambridge: Cambridge University Press.

Bunch, C. (2004). Peace, human rights and women's peace activism: Feminist readings. In R. Coomaraswamy & D. Fonseka (Eds.), *Peace work – women armed conflict and negotiation* (pp. 28–53). New Delhi: Women Unlimited.

Center for Policy Alternatives. (2006). *Reflections on tsunami one year on: Lessons to be learnt*. Retrieved on August 11, 2011, from http://cpalanka.org/wp-content/uploads/2007/8/RADA_Discussion_Paper.pdf.

Central Bank. (2010, November 23, News Section). *The Island*. Retrieved August 11, 2011, http://www.island.lk/index.php?page_cat=article-details&page=article-details&code_title=11851.

Central Bank. (2011, January 5, Business section). *The Island*. Retrieved on August 11, 2011 http://www.island.lk/index.php?page_cat=article-details&page=article-details&code_title=15070.

Chase, R., & Bush, K. (2002). The mental health of war affected children: A community based rehabilitation and reconciliation programme in Sri Lanka's Eastern Province. Retrieved August 11, 2011, from http://www.aifo.it/english/resources/online/apdrj/selread102/chase.doc.

Chenoy, A. M. (2002). *Militarism and women in South Asia*. New Delhi: Kali for Women.

Child Soldiers Global Report. (2008). Retrieved August 11, 2011 from http://www.childsoldiersglobalreport.org/content/sri-lanka. Armed Groups: Liberation Tigers of Tamil Eelam (LTTE), paragraph 2.

Cockburn, C. (2001). The gendered dynamics of armed conflict and political violence. In C. O. Moser & F. C. Clark (Eds.), *Victims, perpetrators or actors? Gender, armed conflict and political violence* (pp. 178–201). London: Zed Books.

Daily Mirror. (2009, March 10). *Aftermath of Akuressa blast*. Retrieved August 11, 2011, from http://archives.dailymirror.lk/DM_BLOG/Sections/frmHome.aspx.

Daniel, D. (2009a). *Post CFA economic growth in North and East faster than country – Govt. Peace Secretariat*. The Permanent Mission of Sri Lanka to the United Nations Office at Geneva. Retrieved August 11, 2011 from the Sri Lanka Permanent Mission to the United Nations in Geneva, http://www.lankamission.org/content/view/1779/1/.

Daniel, D. (2009b, April 13). Post CFA North-East economies grew but with a worrying trend despite investments agriculture declined by 10.3 percent. *The Island*. Retrieved August 11, 2011, from http://www.island.lk/2009/04/13/business1.html.

de Jong, K., Mulhern, M., Ford, N., Simpson, I., Swan, A., & van der Kam, S. (2002). Psychological trauma of the civil war in Sri Lanka. *Lancet, 359*(9316), 1517–1518.

De Mel, N. (2001). *Women and the nation's narrative: Gender and nationalism in Twentieth Century Sri Lanka*. Colombo: Social Scientists Association.

De Mel, N. (2007). *Militarizing Sri Lanka: Popular culture, memory and narrative in the armed conflict*. Los Angeles: Sage.

De Votta, N. (2004). *Blow back: Linguistic nationalism, institutional decay, and ethnic conflict in Sri Lanka*. Stanford: Stanford University Press.

Deegalle, M. (Ed.), (2006). *Buddhism, conflict and violence in modern Sri Lanka*. New York: Routledge.

Department of Census and Statistics, Sri Lanka, (2007). *Population and housing statistics. Special enumeration, Trincomalee, Batticaloa, and Ampara Districts*. Retrieved August 11, 2011, from http://www.statistics.gov.lk/PopHouSat/index.asp.

Department of Census and Statistics, Sri Lanka. (1981). *Islandwide census*. Sri Lanka: Colombo.

Department of Census and Statistics, Sri Lanka. (2001). *Islandwide census*. Sri Lanka: Colombo.

Enloe, C. (2000). *Maneuvers: The international politics of militarizing women's lives*. Berkeley: University of California Press.

Femmes Africa Solidarité, (2002). Engendering the peace process in West Africa. Retrieved August 11, 2011, from http://www.peoplebuildingpeace.org/thestories/article.php?typ=theme&id=142&pid=32.

Ferdinando, S. (2010, August 12). Lanka rules out defence agreement with Pakistan – Gota explains why defence allocation was raised by 6 per cent. *The Island*, p. 1.

Gooneratne, J. (2007). *Negotiating with the Tigers*. Pannipitiya, Sri Lanka: Stanford Lake Press.

Gunawardana, R. A. (2006). Roots of the conflict and the peace process. In M. Deegalle (Ed.), *Buddhism, conflict and violence in modern Sri Lanka* (pp. 177–201). New York: Routledge.

Gunawardena, A. (2006). Female black Tigers: A different breed of cat? *Memorandum on female suicide terrorists*. Tel Aviv: Jafee Centre for Strategic Studies, University of Tel Aviv.

Hettige, S. (2004). Economic policy, changing opportunities for youth and the ethnic conflict in Sri Lanka. In D. Winslow & M. D. Woost (Eds.), *Economy, culture, and civil war in Sri Lanka* (pp. 115–130). Bloomington: Indiana University Press.

Hoole, R., Somasunderam, D., Sritharan, R., & Thiranagama, R. (1998). *The broken Palmyrah: The Tamil crisis in Sri Lanka – an inside account*. Clairmont: Sri Lankan Studies Institute.

Indrapala, K. (2007). *The evolution of an ethnic identity*. Colombo: Vijitha Yapa Press.

International Crisis Group (ICG) *Asia Report*, 124, (2006, November). *Sri Lanka: The failure of the peace process*. Retrieved August 11, 2011, from http://www.crisisgroup.org/en/regions/asia/south-asia/sri-lanka/124-sri-lanka-the-failure-of-the-peace-process.aspx.

International Crisis Group (ICG) *Asia Report*, 134, (2007, May). *Sri Lanka's Muslims: Caught in the crossfire*.

Retrieved August 11, 2011, from http://www.crisisgroup.org/en/regions/asia/south-asia/sri-lanka/134-sri-lankas-muslims-caught-in-the-crossfire.aspx.

Jayasinghe, W. T. (2002). *The Indo-Ceylon problem: The politics of immigrant labour*. Colombo: Stamford Lake.

Jeyaraj, D. B. (2005, October 30). *Fifteenth anniversary of Muslim expulsion from Jaffna*. Retrieved August 11, 2011, from http://www.thesundayleader.lk/archive/20051030/issues.htm.

Kalyvas, S. (2006). *The logic of violence in civil war*. Cambridge: Cambridge University Press.

Kelegama, S. (1993). Distribution of income and ownership of assets: Trends in Sri Lanka. *Pravada, 2*(8), 15–21.

Kelegama, S. (June 2004). *Economic dividend of the post-war period in Sri Lanka: Problems and prospects*. Paper presented at the UNU-WIDER conference on "Making Peace Work," Helsinki, Finland.

Manchanda, R. (2001). *Women, war and peace in South Asia: Beyond victimhood to agency*. New Delhi: Sage.

Manchanda, R. (2002). Ambivalent gains in South Asian conflicts. In S. Meintjes, A. Pillay, & M. Turshen (Eds.), *The aftermath: Women in post-conflict transformation* (pp. 99–121). London: Zed Books.

Mapsofworld.com. (2009). *Political map of Sri Lanka*. August 11, 2011, from http://www.mapsofworld.com/sri-lanka/sri-lanka-political-map.html.

Government of the Philippines (2006). *Mindanao women strengthen role in peace process*. Retrieved August 11, 2011, from http://reliefweb.int/node/200657.

Ministry of Defence, Sri Lanka (2007). *Peace attempts made by the government of Sri Lanka*. Retrieved August 11, 2011, from http://www.defence.lk/pps/peaceattempt.pdf.

Moser, C. O., & Clark, F. C. (2001). *Victims, perpetrators or actors? Gender, armed conflict and political violence*. London: Zed Books.

Neuner, F., Schauer, E., Catani, C., Ruf, M., & Elbert, T. (2006). Post-tsunami stress: A study of posttraumatic stress disorder in children living in three severely affected regions in Sri Lanka. *Journal of Traumatic Stress, 19*, 339–347.

Readon, B. (1993). *Women and peace: Feminist visions of global security*. Albany: State University of New York Press.

Reddy, M. B. (2009). Once the war is over, President Mahinda Rajapaksa must evolve a political solution acceptable to all parties to the conflict. Frontline, 26(4). Retrieved August 11, 2011, from http://www.hindu.com/fline/fl2604/stories/20090227260400800.htm.

Roberts, M. (1996). Filial devotion in Tamil culture and Tiger cult of martyrdom. *Contributions to Indian Sociology, 30*(2), 245–272.

Roberts, M. (2005). Saivite symbols, sacrifice, and Tamil Tiger rites. *Social Analysis, 49*(1), 67–93.

Roberts, M. (2006). The Tamil movement for Eelam. *International Sociological Association, 4*, 12–24.

Roberts, M. (2007). Blunders in Tigerland: Pape's 'muddles' on suicide bombers in Sri Lanka', *Heidelberg Papers in South Asian and Comparative Politics*. Working Paper No. 32. Heidelberg: South Asia Institute & Dept. of Political Science, University of Heidelberg.

Rupesinghe, K. (2006). *Negotiating peace in Sri Lanka: efforts, failures, and lessons*. Colombo: Foundation for Co-Existence.

Sahadevan, P., & de Votta, N. (2006). *Politics of conflict and peace in Sri Lanka*. New Delhi: Manak Publishers.

Samuel, K. (2003). Women's activism, motherhood and the state in the context of Sri Lanka's ethnic conflict. In W. Giles, M. De Alwis, E. Klein, & N. Silva (Eds.), *Feminists under fire: Exchanges across war zones*. Toronto: Between the Lines Press.

Samuel, K. (2006). *A hidden history: Women's activism for peace in Sri Lanka 1982–2002*. Colombo: Social Scientists' Association.

Samuel, K. (2011). Women in the Sri Lankan peace process included but unequal. In G. Oré Aguilar & F. Gómez Isa (Eds.), *Transitional Justice (Vol. 6). Rethinking transitions: Equality and social justice in societies emerging from conflict*. Mortsel, Belgium: Intersentia Publishers.

Sarvananthan, M. (2008). Budget 2009: Political war dividend or economic crisis deferred? Retrieved August 11, 2011, from http://www.pointpedro.org/images/AnnualBudgetReviews/budget%202009.pdf.

Senaratne, J. (1997). *Political violence in Sri Lanka 1977–1990: Riots, insurrections, counterinsurgencies, foreign Interventions*. Amsterdam: VU University Press.

Seneviratne, H. L. (1999). *The work of kings: The new Buddhism in Sri Lanka*. Chicago: Chicago University Press.

Sharma, V. (2009). *A Clausewitzian perspective on religion and conflict*. Paper presented at a seminar on Order, Violence and Conflict, Yale University.

Smith-Fawzi, M. C., Murphy, E., Pham, T., Lin, C., Poole, C., & Mollica, R. F. (1997). The validity of screening for post-traumatic stress disorder and major depression among Vietnamese former political prisoners. *Acta Psychiatrica Scandinavica, 95*, 87–93.

Somasundaram, D. (2004). Short- and long-term effects on the victims of terror in Sri Lanka. *Journal of Aggression, Maltreatment and Trauma, 9*(1–2), 215–228.

Sørensen, B. (1998). *Women and post-conflict reconstruction: Issues and sources*. Occasional Paper No.3. Geneva: UNRISD, PSIS.

Soysa, C. K. (2003, April). *Posttraumatic stress disorder symptomatology in Sri Lankan children exposed to war*. Poster presented at the biennial meeting of the Society for Research in Child Development, Tampa, FL.

Soysa, C. K. (2005, April). *Posttraumatic stress disorder and coping in Sri Lankan children exposed to war*. Poster presented at the biennial meeting of the Society for Research in Child Development, Atlanta, GA.

Soysa, C. K. (2007, March). *Tsunami 2004: PTSD symptom severity in Sri Lankan adolescents at 3 & 12 months post-disaster*. Poster presented at the biennial meeting of the Society for Research in Child Development, Boston, MA.

Soysa, C. K. & Jamunanantha, S. C. (2007, August). *One year post-tsunami: PTSD in two Sri Lankan ethnic groups*. Poster presented at the annual meeting of the American Psychological Association, San Francisco, CA.

Strategic Foresight Group. (2006). *Cost of conflict in Sri Lanka*. Mumbai: Strategic Foresight Group.

Strickland, R., & Duvvury, N. (2003). *Gender equity and peace building – from rhetoric to reality: Finding the way*. Washington: International Center for Research on Women.

Sub Committee on Gender Issues-SGI (2003, March 6). Press Release. Retrieved August 11, 2011, from http://www.peaceinsrilanka.org/negotiations/rng-051.

Thiruchandran, S. (1999). *The other victims of war emergence of female headed households in Eastern Sri Lanka* (Vol. II). New Delhi: Vikas.

Uyangoda, J. (2002 May). Peace process, the people and civil society. Retrieved August 11, 2011, from http://issues.lines-magazine.org/Art_May02/Uyang.htm.

Uyangoda, J. (2007). *Ethnic conflict in Sri Lanka: Changing dynamics*. Washington D.C: East West Center.

Vittachchi, T. (1958). *Emergency 1958: The story of the Ceylon race riots*. London: Andre Deutsch.

Wanasundera, L. (2006). *Rural women in Sri Lanka's post-conflict rural economy*. Colombo: Center for Women's Research (CENWOR) & Food and Agricultural Organization (FAO).

Wickramasinghe, N. (1995). *Ethnic politics in colonial Sri Lanka*. New Delhi: Vikas Publishers.

Wijesinhe, R. (2008). *The failure of successive peace processes with the LTTE – A historical overview*. The Permanent Mission of Sri Lanka to the United Nations Office at Geneva. Retrieved August 11, 2011, from http://www.lankamission.org/content/view/1083/40/.

Zackariya, F., & Ismail, Z. (1998). Early marriage and the cycle of violence in a displaced situation. In CENWOR (Ed.), *Confronting complexities: Gender perceptions and values*. Colombo: Centre for Women's Research.

Ethnic Relations in Malaysia: The Need for "Constant Repair" in the Spirit of Muhibbah*

6

Vijayan P. Munusamy

Malaysia Chapter Summary

Munusamy portrays a relatively peaceful Malaysia with a theme of unity underlying the nation's leadership since independence was achieved. Historical review reveals constant takeover attempts by different colonial powers which are attributed to Malaysia's unique and valuable qualities. Recognition of the change in demographic under British rule, due to importation of labor, is credited with influencing current interethnic relations. As the people of Malaysia began revolts for independence, the author elucidates the bases of historical and current tensions.

Unity is identified as the British prerequisite for independence initially achieved, but transient as political parties formed around ethnic identification. The lack of interethnic violence in Malaysia is viewed as engendering an inaccurate perception of success with regard to ethnic relations. Exploration of the various policies implemented in order to equalize distribution of wealth reveals limited success and causal factors are proffered. The author describes the most recent policy along with challenges that need to be addressed for successful implementation. Signs of protest and increasing tensions are presented providing stimulus for change.

Munusamy offers specific solutions to reach lasting harmony utilizing a holistic method, while recognizing the continuing effort required for resolution of multicultural issues. The fashion in which policies are executed and evaluated is also viewed as an important consideration for success. Discussion of factors associated with effective change informs the

*This chapter was based on author's dissertation Munusamy (2008), which won the Dissertation of the Year award from the Academy of Management (CMS), Rae and Dr. Dan Landis Outstanding Dissertation Award from the International Academy for Intercultural Research and the finalist Harry and Pola Triandis award from the International Association for Cross-Cultural Psychology.

V.P. Munusamy (✉)
Intercultural Leadership Centre, Asia
e-mail: vijayan.munusamy@iclc.asia

D. Landis and R.D. Albert (eds.), *Handbook of Ethnic Conflict: International Perspectives*, International and Cultural Psychology, DOI 10.1007/978-1-4614-0448-4_6,

methods that may function best in Malaysia. The author believes that a revival of the true spirit of tolerance would create a positive atmosphere in which interethnic relations may improve.

Cheryl Jorgensen

Blessed with all-year-round friendly tropical climate, showered by the lush rainforest with rich diversity of flora and fauna, the almost nonexistence of natural calamity, an abundance of various types of natural resources, and a location in strategic trading hub, Peninsular Malaysia and the lower region of Burma and Thailand were referred to as "Suvarnabhumi," a Sanskrit term for Golden Land (suvarna = golden color, bhumi = land) by ancient Indian traders as early as in the third century BC (Wheatley, 1955). In the twenty-first century, this Sanskrit term prominently denotes the name of a newly built international airport in Thailand (Suvarnabhumi Airport) to symbolize an aspiration of "a fertile land where inhabitants live peacefully as well as a business hub from which the economy thrives."[1] It is evident that in this century, "inhabitants living peacefully" characterizes what is a golden land and this is true for Malaysia, which is the focus of this chapter.

Though Malaysia has always been blessed with discovery of new "Suvarnas" (e.g., latex rubber, known as "white gold"; palm oil, known as "golden oil"; and petroleum, popularly known as "black gold"), (Sandhu & Wheatley, 1983), Malaysian leaders across generations have constantly advocated that much more work needs to be done to ensure that "inhabitants live peacefully." The distinguished late politician Tan Sri Mohd. Ghazali Shafie who had served four different Malaysian prime ministers aptly puts that "national unity must always be kept in constant repair (Ghazali Shafie, 1993, p.1)." Table 6.1, which shows quotes from speeches made by Malaysian prime ministers, also exemplifies this need well. National leaders have also worked hard to ensure peaceful coexistence by embedding messages of unity in national anthems and pledges, making economic and cultural policies and legislation with the aim of promoting peaceful coexistence, and safeguarding the interests of different cultural groups. Annual Merdeka (independence) celebrations since 1957 have also largely centered on the theme of unity in Malaysia (see Table 6.2 for examples of independence celebration themes).

It is clear that the constant reminder for peaceful coexistence in every aspect of daily life since independence affirms that the Malaysian journey toward peaceful coexistence has no final destination and needs "constant repair" to fully tap its multicultural demography for economic development, identity, culture, language, educational system, and political system (see Table 6.3). In the spirit of "constant repair," this chapter focuses on Malaysia's ethnic relations taking in account of its historical context, its current status and way forward.

1 Historical Context

Malaysian scholars have long argued that Malaysia's ethnic relations cannot be adequately explained without understanding Malaysian history (Abraham, 1997; Hashim, 1983; Kia Soong, 1987), and hence the context of pre-British colonization era, the British Colonization, and the Independence are discussed in relation to ethnic relations.

1.1 Pre-British Colonization Era

Archeological discoveries of stone tools in Kota Tampan, Perak, and human bones in Niah Caves, Sarawak, led historians to conclude that Malaysia has been inhabited at least since 40,000 BC (Hooker, 2003). Australo-Melanesians (African descent) or Proto-Malays were identified as the early settlers in Malaysia. This was followed by Austronesians (Chinese Descent or Mongoloid) or Deutero-Malays. Orang Asli in Peninsular Malaysia, Penan in Sarawak, and Rungus in Sabah who started settling in Malaysia 5,000 years ago have been argued to be the earliest

[1] http://bangkok.sawadee.com/airport/index.html.

Table 6.1 Examples of quotes from speeches made by Malaysian Prime Ministers

In 1964, the first Prime Minister Tengku Abdul Rahman stated that: "In this plural society of ours, racial harmony must always be our greatest concern….I will try my best to lead the people of our country towards the goal of unity in loyalty to Malaysia, and besides this common loyalty to promote greater understanding, goodwill and friendship between the various races" (The Strait Times, 21 Dec 1964, p. 1)
The second Prime Minister Tun Abdul Razak in 1965 put forward that: "We must all work towards the complete eradication of economic and social imbalances along with the other sources of friction between the races in Malaysia before a truly united Malaysia can be realized" (The Strait Times, 23 Aug 1965, p. 9)
In 1972, the third Prime Minister Tun Hussein Onn remarked that: "There were no justifiable reasons or excuses for continued agitation or criticism"…It is sadder still that it [Tengku Abdul Rahman College] has been been exploited to arouse racial feelings…Let us be far-sighted and reasonable in our attitude. Let us be magnanimous in what we say and do. It is up to us to make or break our country and our nation" (The Strait Times, 16 Sept 1972, p. 4)
Describing that disunity is a barrier for nation building, the fourth Prime Minister Tun Mahathir Mohamad stated in 1999: "I would like to call upon all races to maintain unity and moderation because these are the formulae for progress and development. I would like to also remind them that it is better to have a little of something than to have the whole of nothing. (New Strait Times, May 21, 1999, PM: Racial harmony essential to maintain progress, p. 2)
Datuk Seri Abdullah Badawi, the fifth Prime Minister, in 2006 commenting that race relations had deteriorated after the May 13 racial riot acknowledged: "It is not something I will ever forget. But after that, [relations] became better. These days, I know things are not good. It is still fragile. It is still brittle. (New Strait Times, December 7, 2006, "PM: We must unite or we will face a bleak future," p. 2)
Dato' Seri Najib Abdul Razak, current Prime Minister, calling for a shift from tolerance to acceptance, called attention to: "We have to work together by galvanizing all Malaysians, and work towards inculcating that conscience with a deep sense of understanding ….Accepting each other is the apex of celebrating each other's diversity. Once we have reached this final destination, we will think and act as one people, one nation with one dream." (Kaur, March 1, 2010, "Let's move from tolerance to acceptance, says Najib", p. 4, New Strait Times)

Table 6.2 Examples of independence celebration themes

Year	Theme (English)	Theme (Malay translation)
1970	Love and Unity	Muhibah dan Perpaduan
1974	Science and Technology as Tools of Unity	Sains dan Teknologi Alat Perpaduan
1977	United and Progressive	Bersatu Maju
1978	Culture is the Core of Unity	Kebudayaan Sendi Perpaduan
1979	United and Disciplined	Bersatu Berdisplin
1981	Discipline and Harmony	Berdisplin Berharmoni
1983	Together towards success	Bersama Ke Arah Kemajuan
1985	Nationalism is the core unity	Nasionalisme Teras Perpaduan
1987	Loyally United and Working Progressively	Setia Bersatu Berusaha Maju
1988	Unity	Bersatu
1989	Unity	Bersatu
1993	Together towards vision	Bersatu Menuju Wawasan
1999	Together towards the New Millennium	Bersatu ke Alaf Baru
2008	Unity is the core of Success	Perpaduan Teras Kejayaan
2009	One Malaysia	One Malaysia

Table 6.3 Information about Malaysia*

Population (million)	28.3
Ethnic Groups	Malays – 50.4% Chinese – 23.7% Indigenous – 11% Indian – 7.1% Others – 7.8%
Native % of total population (Bumiputera)	61% (Malays + Indigenous)
Modern origin of Nation/State	Independence from British Colonization (1957)
Political structure	Parliamentary Democracy with Constitutional Monarchy
GDP per capita (2010)	USD (14,700)

*https://www.cia.gov/library/publications/the-world-factbook/geos/my.html

present-day inhabitants. Currently, they together only account for less than 1% of the 28 million Malaysians as processes of urbanization and modernization, the Western concept of land rights, and new migrations have displaced many of these early settlers from their land.

Because of her many "Suvarnas" (golden attributes), Malaysia was vulnerable to many empires in South Asia. In the first century, northern states of Malaysia were ruled by the Hindu Kingdom of Langakasuka. In the second century, these states were ruled by the Funan Empire of South Indo-China. In the seventh century, most states within the modern Malaysia were ruled by SriVijaya Hindu Kingdom of East Sumatra. In the tenth century, Chola Kingdom conquered Kedah and Perak, northern states in Malaysia by defeating SriVijaya Kingdom and the Gangga Negara Empire. Because of the control of these empires, Malaysia was heavily influenced by Hindu and at a later stage by Buddhist cultures.

In the fourteenth century, the Javanese Empire of Majapahit defeated the SriVijaya Empire in Palembang and gained control of many states of Malaysia. Parameswara, a defeated prince of SriVijaya, fled from Palembang, and settled for a short period in Temasek (now Singapore) before being defeated again by the Siam Empire. He then settled in Melaka. Melaka under Parameswara grew into a bustling trading, political, and cultural hub. The timing of north-east and south-west monsoon wind was a natural catalyst that transformed Melaka to a "meeting" and a "mid-point" for Chinese and Indian traders. As India and China contributed three-fourths of World GDP until 1760 (Kennedy, 1988), it was not surprising that Melaka quickly became the most important port in the world in the fifteenth century (Elegant, 1999). A Portuguese writer during that time, Tom Pires (1515) declared that "whoever was the Lord of Melaka had his hand on the throat of Venice." It was also reported that more than 80 languages were spoken in Melaka and many diplomatic relations were formed during this time. Melaka was also established as a center for Islam in the Malay Archipelago. A small number of Chinese and Indians now known as Babas and Chettis also settled in Melaka during this time.

Around the same time (fifteenth century), Western colonial powers with more sophisticated war technologies began to colonize South Asian nations. Due to Melaka's strategic and bustling trading port, Melaka was constantly being fought over and conquered by many of the colonial powers – by the Portuguese in 1511, the Dutch in 1641, the British in 1795, the Dutch again in 1808, and the British again in 1819.

1.2 British Colonization

Colonization in Malaysia, however, was not limited to Melaka and was not limited to strategic consideration that led to wars. The colonization of Sarawak (a state in Borneo) is an example where British gained easy control because of internal fightings. In 1841, James Brooke from Britain was appointed as Rajah of Sarawak by the Brunei Sultanate because of his help in defeating the rebellions from the neighboring state, Sarawak. The Brooke dynasty continued ruling Sarawak for a century before they lost Sarawak to Japan in 1942. Infighting among the rulers also precipitated colonization by the British. Due to tin mining, Perak (a state in North Malaysia) became the envy of many Malay rulers and led to constant infighting among them. The ruler named Raja Abdullah requested British intervention and this led to the peace treaty in 1874 known as the "Pangkor Agreement" in which the British legitimized Raja Abdullah as the Sultan, and in exchange, Raja Abdullah gave the British a greater administrative control over Perak. Historians argue that this agreement set a precedent for British to gain the control of other states, resulting in the formation of the Federated Malay States in 1896. Another example where colonization was achieved without war was the colonization of Penang (an island state in the North Malaysia). In this case, the British was offered the control of Penang by Kedah (a state in the north) rulers in exchange for British military assistance. However, British withdrew their support later but never left Penang despite repeated requests for their departure.

During the British colonization, laborers were brought in large numbers from other British colonies to work in Malaysia's tin mines and rubber plantations. For the most part, laborers from China were recruited to work in tin mines and laborers from India (mainly Tamil speakers) to work on rubber plantations. The recruitment and placement strategy of laborers by British not only changed Malaysia's demographic landscape, but also contributed to shaping the political, economical [sic], and social landscape of Malaysia today. At one extended period, immigrant communities outnumbered the indigenous group (Abraham, 1997).

The rubber demand from the European countries and the boom in the automotive industry in America led rubber plantation estates to grow from 2,000 acres in 1898 to 2 million acres in 1920. Similar growth was also experienced in the tin mines, which led to the recruitment of more laborers from China and India. Abundant natural resources, steady and cheap labor supply, and favorable world economy and political climate helped Malaysia to become the biggest exporter of rubber and tin controlling almost 50% of the world production in the beginning of the nineteenth century. To further facilitate rubber and tin extraction, many infrastructure projects were completed around this time. For example, a total of 2,400 miles of road infrastructure between Prai and Seremban was completed by 1904 and by 1909, train services between Penang and Singapore were fully operational.

To meet the needs of the workforce, many educational institutions were also established. For example, the College of Medicine was established in 1910, the Raffles College for art and science education was established in 1928, and the Sultan Idris Training College for Malay Teachers started teacher training in 1922. Many missionary schools were also established during this time, but their role in strengthening British colonialism was limited (Abraham, 1997). The Malay College Kuala Kangsar was established in 1905 specifically to educate the Malay elite. To cater to the educational and cultural needs of the increasing Chinese and Indian laborers, many educational and social institutions were also established, mostly concentrated in the tin mine areas and rubber plantation estates. Record shows that Tamil medium education for the children of Indian laborers was available as early as the eighteenth century.[2]

During the First World War, Malaysia gained economically by continuing the production of tin and rubber for the Allies. However, Second World War affected Malaysia significantly in number of ways. First, the war contributed to the rise of Malay nationalism. Second, it contributed to the sentiment of anti-colonialism. It also led to the formation of the Malayan People's Anti-Japanese Rule (MPAJA), which had its origin in the Malayan Communist Party. Though Malayan Communist Party members were enemies of the British and some were jailed, they were released and trained by the British in Singapore to fight the Japanese force just before the Japanese gained control of Singapore. MPAJA members were largely Chinese and were often considered a threat to the Japanese. As a result, they faced harsher treatment than Malays and Indians during the Japanese occupation. The Sino-Japan war also contributed to this hostility. Soong (1987) described that "the most serious consequence of the Japanese occupation, and its most serious effects on communal relations, were the bloody riots after the war" (p. 22). After the Japanese surrendered in 1945 and British regained control, the MPAJA lost its influence. However, some MPAJA members formed the Malayan National Liberation Army (MNLA) as an opposition to the British. In order to stamp out MNLA, the British declared a state of emergency in 1948. The state of emergency fragmented MNLA and the emergency was lifted in 1960. A small number of MNLA members however, continued to operate at the Malaysian–Thailand border. Their operation ended when they signed a peace treaty with the Thai and Malaysian governments in 1989.

After the British regained their control in 1945, they immediately proposed the formation of Malayan Union as a way to rebuild Malaysia. The notion of Malayan Union, however, was a complete turn from their pre-war policies where they had recognized Malay privileges, the status of Malay rulers, and the status of immigrants. They instead proposed that all immigrants be given citizenship based on the "jus soli" (birthright citizenship) principles, equal rights be accorded to everyone, and the status of the rulers (Sultans) limited to the Malay culture and religion. The Malays strongly opposed the formation of Malayan Union, but the British went ahead with their plan in 1946. The Malay opposition to the Malayan Union resulted in Malays forming the United Malays National Organization (UMNO) in 1946 to unite all the Malays under one political unit. In the same year, Indians with a strong anti-British sentiment formed the Malaysian Indian Congress (MIC) to represent the Indian interests in the post-war period. Due to the strong opposition from UMNO and the lack of support from MIC, the Malayan Union was replaced with the Federation of Malaya. Unlike the Malayan Union, the Federation of Malaya gave recognition to the special position of Malays and established stricter citizenship rules for immigrants. While the Malayan Union and the anti-British sentiment were precursors for the formation of the UMNO and the MIC, the Chinese formed the Malayan Chinese Association (MCA) in 1949 mainly because of their opposition toward the Malayan Communist Party.

The establishment of political parties along ethnic lines has been attributed to the use of the "divide and rule" policy by the British. Though UMNO, MIC, and MCA were initiated and set up along the ethnic lines, attempts to form political units that were open to every ethnic group were made. Scholars argued that the notion of "Malayan nationalism" instead of Malay, Chinese, and

[2] http://mynadi.wordpress.com/tamil-schools/.

Indian nationalism, emerged after the Second World War period (Kheng, 2002). For example, the founder of the UMNO, Onn Jaafar, made an attempt to open UMNO membership to all races. However, this was not well received by the majority of UMNO members and as a result, Onn Jaafar left UMNO and formed a new multiracial party, Independence of Malaya Party (IMP), in 1951. It is interesting to note that while opening up the party memberships to all ethnic groups did not gain acceptance, the ethnic-based parties did come together for strategic political reasons. UMNO and MCA, for example, formed a coalition pact to avoid contesting the same seats in the 1952 and 1953 local council elections. Their strategy worked well and reduced the influence of Onn Jaafar's multiracial party. After disbanding IMP, Onn Jaafar formed the multiracial Parti Negara with a more pro-Malay bent as an attempt to oppose the UMNO/MCA coalition (Rabushka, 1973). UMNO and MCA, however, strengthened their coalition by forming the "Alliance" in 1954 and won 226 of 268 seats in that year's local council elections. Onn Jaafar's newly formed Parti Negara, however, failed again. In 1955, the MIC joined the Alliance, which resulted in the Alliance representing all three major ethnic groups in Peninsula Malaya. The "Alliance" strategy worked well again and they won 51 of 52 seats in the 1955 election. The other seat was won by the Pan Malayan Islamic Party, which was formed in 1951 by ulamas (Muslim scholars) who broke away from UMNO. Means (1970) noted the inner modus operandi of the Alliance as following:

> the committee never developed a genuine non-communal approach to the problems confronting Malaya, it did demonstrate that significant communal compromise was more likely to emerge from semi-secret and "off-the record" negotiations conducted by communal leaders (Means, 1970, p.124).

Learning from the conflict in Burma and following Burma's declaration of independence, the British announced that independence for Malaya would only be granted if all ethnic groups were united. This strengthened the solidarity of the "Alliance" and in 1956, Tunku Abdul Rahman, the leader for the Alliance led a group of Alliance members and representatives of the Malay rulers to broker the independence for Malaya. The independence was finally granted with the condition that an independent commission would be set up to draft the constitution for Malaya. This commission became known as the Reid Commission. Based on the commission's recommendations, Malaysia's new Federal Constitution came into force in 1957 and became the guiding document for Malaysia's governance.

1.3 Independence of Malaysia

Upon gaining independence in 1957, the country was known as the Federated States of Malaya. With the inclusion of Sabah, Sarawak, and Singapore in 1963, it became known as Federated States of Malaysia. Singapore, however, was expelled from Malaysia in 1965 over differences in ethnic policies. The Singapore leader, Lee Kuan Yew, objected to the policies of preferential treatment for Malays and advocated meritocracies. This, however, did not go well with Malay leaders in Malaysia.

Within the same time, political parties, which were largely ethnic based, were also having differences in their political approaches. UMNO was accused by Parti Islam SeMalaysia (PAS) of giving in to MCA's requests, and MCA was accused of giving in to UMNO requests by the Democratic Action Party (DAP). During this time, the DAP together with People's Progressive Party (PPP) also objected to the idea of having Malay as a sole national language. These tensions were compounded when the "Alliance" under the first Prime Minister Tengku Abdul Rahman suffered a major blow in the 1969 polls. While some argue that the victory celebration of the opposition parties had led to the 1969 racial riots, others argue that the riot had been engineered by the "ascendant state capitalist class" in the UMNO as a strategy to change the UMNO leadership (Kia Soong, 2007; Stenson, 1976). This riot led to a state of national emergency and suspension of Parliament until 1971. Economic gaps between Malays and non-Malays have been attributed as the root cause for the riot.

Following the1969 riot, policies such as the New Economic Policy, the National Culture Policy, and the Sedition Act were introduced to reduce polemic issues. Generally, the government under the premiership of Tun Abdul Razak took the approach of managing diversity with a mix of integrational and pluralistic strategies. Integration strategies were anchored in promoting national identity: one national language, one national culture, and one Malaysian race, while pluralistic strategies were anchored in maintaining the cultural freedom of the various ethnic groups. Slogans such as "Perpaduan" (unity) and "Muhibbah" (spirit of tolerance and harmony) were also often used. In 1970, to restore law and order, the "Rukunegara" pledge (see below) was introduced as a guiding principle for the country's nation-building (Hashim, 1983).

> Our Nation, Malaysia is dedicated to: Achieving a greater unity for all her people; maintaining a democratic way of life; creating a just society in which the wealth of the nation shall be equitably distributed; ensuring a liberal approach to her rich and diverse cultural tradition, and building a progressive society, which shall be oriented to modern science and technology.
> We, the people of Malaysia, pledge our united efforts to attain these ends, guided by these principles:
> - Belief in God
> - Loyalty to King and Country
> - Upholding the Constitution
> - Sovereignty of the Law, and
> - Good Behaviour and Morality

Tun Abdul Razak passed away suddenly in 1976 and Tun Hussein Onn became the third Prime Minister. His father, Jaafar Onn, had been the founder of the UMNO, as well as of the Independence of Malaya Party and of Parti Negara. Tun Hussein Onn became known as the "Father of Unity" for his contribution to ethnic relations. He promoted the concept of "Rukun Tetangga" (Neighbourhood Community Association) and launched the "Amanah Saham Nasional" (National Unit Trust Scheme) to rectify economic imbalances between different ethnic groups.

In 1981, Tun Mahathir Mohamad became Malaysia's fourth Prime Minister. His premiership was one of the longest in Asia, lasting 22 years. During his term, he served seven kings and had four different deputy prime ministers. He is credited for Malaysia's rapid economic growth and is known as the "Father of Modernization." His 1970 book "The Malay Dilemma," which put forward the need for affirmative action for Malays and was banned by the first Prime Minister, was put back on the bookshelf in 1981. Mahathir's

Table 6.4 Timeline of Malaysian History

Year	Event
~40000 BCE	First settlement of Natives
~200 BCE	Evidence of Indian influence
1000	Proto-Malays
1394–1511	Malay Sultanate of Melaka. Active trading with China, India, Arab, and Burma.
1445	Islam established as official religion
1511–1624	Portuguese colonization
1641–1824	Dutch Colonization
1786	Founding of Penang
1824–1941	British Colonization
1841	James Brooke made Raja of Sarawak
1841–1941	Brooke dynasty ruled Sarawak
1885	First train service between Taiping and Port Weld
1896	Federated Malay States
1900	Rubber plantation started
1904	2,400 miles road infrastructure and train service between Prai and Seremban
1906	Rubber boom – US automotive industry
1909	Treaty with Siam. Kelantan, Terengganu, Kedah, and Perlis came under British.
1909	Train service between Penang and Singapore
1910	Establishment of College of Medicine
1914	Treaty with Johor

(continued)

Table 6.4 (continued)

Year	Event
1914–1918	First World War – Malaysia continued to produce rubber and tin for the Allies.
1920	Malaria was under control
1923	Johor causeway
1928	Raffles College for art and science education
1941	Second World War – Japanese invasion
1945	Japanese surrendered and British gained control again
1948	Termination of Malayan Union
1951	Local election
1955	UMNO–MCA–MIC alliance won 51 of the 52 seats
1957	Independence
1961	Education Act – recognize vernacular primary schools but not secondary schools
1963	Formation of Malaysia
1965	Separation of Singapore
1966	Confrontation with Indonesia ended
1967	Formation of Association of Southeast Asian Nations (ASEAN)
1969	Coalition lost 2/3 majority; opposition victory parade did not go as a peaceful parade and contributed to racial riot
1971	NEP, National Cultural Policy, National Education Policy
1975	Industrial Coordination Act – State has power to implement equity policy
1979	Official rejection of Lion Dance – Tiger Dance
1981	Mahathir Mohamad became Prime Minister
1987	Operation Lalang (Political crackdown on opposition leaders and social activists)
1993	Power of royalty reduced
1997	Asian economic crisis
1998	Malaysia introduced capital control; Reformasi protest (movement initiated by Anwar Ibrahim and his supporters after he was sacked as Deputy Prime Minister)
1999	Suqui Demand
2001 – March	Localized ethnic clash between Malays and Indian
2003	Abdullah became Prime Minister with overwhelming majority
2006	HINDRAF protest
2008	Barisan Nasional lost four states in 2008 general election
2009	Najib Tun Razak became the sixth Prime Minister
2010	Introduction of New Economic Model policies, 1Malaysia

premiership saw major constitutional changes (e.g., reducing the power of monarchy), completion of large-scale national projects (e.g., Proton, North-South Highway, and Putrajaya), introduction of the "Look East Policy," and so forth. He also introduced Vision 2020, which outlined challenges that Malaysia must overcome to achieve a fully developed country by 2020 – economically, politically, socially, spiritually, psychologically, and culturally (Vision 2020).[3] Mahathir's term, however, was not a smooth one in regard to ethnic relations, as deteriorating signs of ethnic relations were evident with the Kampung Rawa and **Kampung Medan** ethnic conflict incidents.

As educational opportunities in public universities are limited and often a cause for ethnic tensions, Mahathir liberalized private university education that provided more opportunities for Malaysians regardless of race to pursue higher education. He also introduced the teaching of mathematics and science in English. Some argued that he provided economic solutions to cultural problems. Boo Teik (2004) described that

[3] Please see Malaysian: The Way Forward (Vision 2020) http://unpan1.un.org/intradoc/groups/public/documents/apcity/unpan003223.pdf.

> To the extent that ethnic differences and cultural grievances in Malaysia had always had an economic "essence" to them, the Mahathir regime in the 1990s seemed to have supplied economic solutions to cultural problems. The privatization of tertiary education, corporatization of public universities, and Mahathir's insistence on reviving the use of English on pragmatic grounds, combined to defuse interethnic squabbles over issues of language, tertiary educational quotas for students of different communities, and the Chinese independent schools (p.11).

In 2003, Mahathir was succeeded by Tun Abdullah Badawi. Abdullah took a different approach to economic development, placing more emphasis on agriculture and biotechnology. Though the Barisan Nasional (National Front Political Parties) under his leadership won 2004 general election with a high majority, the party suffered a major setback in 2008 election. For the first time, the party lost four out of 13 states and a federal territory. Ethnic relations further deteriorated but Abdullah was credited for allowing more openness in discussion of multicultural issues.

Dato' Seri Najib Abdul Razak succeeded Abdullah Badawi and became the sixth Prime Minister in 2009. His father, Tun Abdul Razak, was the second Prime Minister. Immediately after occupying the office, Najib introduced the 1Malaysia campaign, which stresses ethnic unity, transformation programs to improve economic growth, and the New Economic Model to address wealth inequalities. These initiatives are formulated to address the challenges of ethnic relations among others.

2 Current Status of Malaysia's Ethnic Relations

Malaysia has been hailed as one of the most successful decolonized countries in terms of managing ethnic relations (Goh & Holden, 2009). There was a lot of skepticism about whether Malaysia would survive after independence from the British in 1957. Skeptics were proven wrong. Not only has Malaysia survived, but it also became a model for other multicultural countries. It has enjoyed political stability, representative government, economic progress, rural modernization, increased literacy, and the rapid growth of the middle class (Goh, 1994). However, Malaysia's measure of success in managing ethnic relations has to a large extent been limited to the relative absence of violent racial conflict since the violent racial riot in 1969 (Poh Ping, 1999).

Although many initiatives have been undertaken to advance community building, the reality is that managing diversity has become more complex and challenging. Consider the following acknowledgment by the current Prime Minister Dato' Seri Najib Abdul Razak:

> Beyond the challenge of managing the Malaysian economy today, managing a diverse society that is growing sophisticated and mature by the day is the added challenge....How we manage a countries that is diverse in religion, culture and ethnicity is a challenge. Before this, the challenge may have been small but today, people are paying attention to matters such as conversion (of religion), marriage, deaths, divorce and issues arising from the use of the word Allah (Nik Anis, 2010).

Below, five important challenges that Malaysia currently faces are presented. This list is not an exhaustive one, but it does give a current snapshot of major ethno political challenges in Malaysia.

2.1 Narrowing the Economic Gap Among the Ethnic Groups

Traditionally, Malays have been involved in agriculture and Chinese have been involved in businesses. This has contributed to economic gaps as Malays as rural dwellers are relatively poor than other communities (Wicks, 1971). These gaps have been one of the major causes for ethnopolitical challenges in Malaysia, and the 1969 May 13 racial riot was attributed to the unequal distribution of national wealth among the ethnic groups. As an intervention, in 1971, the "New Economic Policy (NEP)" was introduced. The NEP formulated to achieve national unity had two major objectives:

1. To reduce absolute poverty irrespective of race through raising income levels and increasing employment opportunities for all Malaysians.

2. To restructure society to correct economic imbalances so as to reduce and eventually eliminate the identification of race with economic function.

Though the objectives of this policy do not identify Bumiputera (a Sanskrit term which can be translated as "son of the soil"; bumi = land, soil; putera = son) as sole beneficiaries, the implementation, however, has been primarily viewed as pro-Bumiputera policies (Jomo, 2004). Jomo (2004, p.15) described:

> On the one hand, many bumiputeras invoke indigenous or "native rights" and the need for "positive discrimination" and "affirmative action" to overcome historical disadvantage under colonialism. On the other hand, many non-bumiputeras protest "ethnic discrimination", "cultural oppression" and the official undermining of meritocracy.

When the NEP ended in 1990 and it was concluded that the policy did not achieve the desired outcome of 30% bumiputera economic equity in terms of corporate ownership, it was replaced by a similar policy – the National Development Policy (NDP) for the years from 1991 to 2000. However, there is wide disagreement on how ethnic economic equity is calculated. This has raised suspicion over the reliability and validity of the calculation put forward by the government. Some argued that bumiputera's corporate equity has actually exceeded the targeted 30% (Teck Ghee, 2006; Mauzy, 1995)[4] and as such policies promoting selective Malay entrepreneurs at the expense of other segments of the society should not be promoted as not to increase inter- and intra-ethnic cleavages. Others however, argued that these policies did not achieve both the narrowing of the economic gap and national unity. Statistics shows that though the overall incidence of poverty was reduced from 50% in 1970 to 3.6% in 2007, the gap between the urban and the rural population has been widening in the recent decade (NEM Report, 2010, p.57).[5]

A 2010 transformation roadmap report issued by the government acknowledged that these policies have also contributed to "a sense of deprivation, discrimination and even resentment felt by the non-Bumiputeras" (Government Transformation Programme, 2010, p. 76) and have contributed to a significant brain drain where these policies "have pushed many Malaysians, especially professionals, to work and reside overseas, in economically more advanced countries with attractive pull factors" (p. 76). These policies also created profession identities based on ethnic group where the majority of civil servants are Malays and entrepreneurs are Chinese, a situation that these policies were designed to reverse.

At the time this chapter was written, a New Economic Model with the goal of enabling all communities to benefit fully from the wealth of the country was launched. Among others, this new model aspires to reduce income disparity, create market friendly affirmative action, narrow regional differences, encourage reward on the basis of performance, and promote equal and fair access to opportunities (NEM Report, 2010). The government has finally recognized that "many of the policies and strategies [Malaysia] used to achieve the current state of development are now inadequate to take [Malaysia] to the next stage (NEM report, p.4) and acknowledged that the implementation of previous policies "has also increasingly and inadvertently raised the cost of doing business due to rent-seeking, patronage and often opaque government procurement" which "engendered pervasive corruption" (p. 7).

2.2 Overcoming Communal Politics Which Trump Nationalism

Ethnic-based political leaderships are inherently communal in their approach but "communalism itself does not adequately explain social conflict in Malaysia" (Singh, 2001, p. 43). For example, "Kenegaraan" (nationalism) was the uniting force in the pursuit of independence and "the divided communities agreed to come together for a Malayan identity in 1957" (Narayanasamy, 2006, para 3). The problem occurs when communal approaches trump national objectives, leading to narrow nationalism. Some have argued that in the post-independence period, some "who represented

[4] http://www.sun2surf.com/article.cfm?id=15779.

[5] Please see "New Economic Model For Malaysia: Part 1" available at http://www.neac.gov.my/sites/default/files/NEM%20for%20Malaysia%20-%20Part%20I.pdf.

the communities in the government conveniently forgot about national objectives and instead championed the rights of their own ethnic groups continuously" (Narayanasamy, 2006, para 3).

There are also many instances where leaders of political parties in their quest to champion their ethnic interest made remarks that are contentious and perceived as insensitive by other ethnic groups. This is even true in coalition parties where different ethnic political groups are represented. The late academic/politician Goh Cheng Teik summarized this behavior well in the passage below:

> Most leaders and members of communal parties such as UMNO, MCA, MIC, Parti Pesaka-Bumiputera Bersatu and PBDS are enlightened and forward-looking. …Unfortunately, they are prisoners of their own political environment… I am not saying that these politicians do not try to break out of the confines of their environment. They do. They make efforts to rise above race, to be broad-minded and big-hearted and to make decisions in the larger national interest. There is, unfortunately, a very definite limitation. When they participate in their respective internal party elections, they have to draw the line. They have to be communal! They cannot afford not to do so. The heart of a particular politician from a communal party may incline him to be rational and statesmanlike but his head tells him that if he wants to win his party election and safeguard his personal political future, he has to play it communal and emotional. Indeed, if his opponent campaigns communally, he has no choice but to follow suit (Teik, 1994, p.10).

There is a way out from narrow communal approaches and "political will and leadership to break the log-jam of resistance by vested interest groups and preparing the "rakyat" (citizen) to support deep seated changes in policy directions" (NEM Report, p.16) are needed.

2.3 Lessening the Climate of Fear and Its Consequences

There is a "climate of fear" that prevents the discussion of race-related issues among political and civil leaders. Unfortunately, this is even true for scholars and researchers, despite the fact that there is a clear role for the scholarly community in terms of providing intellectual leadership for dealing with multicultural issues (see NEM Report). Ethno-relations research in Malaysia has been identified as a contributor as early as in 1970 for anticipating needs (e.g., change of attitude), defining strategies (e.g., educational policy), evaluating the impact of policies (e.g., NEP), presenting findings in relation to policies (e.g., language policies) and studying receptivity to public policies (Glazer, Huntington, Nash, & Weiner, 1970). Because of this "climate of fear," there is only a handful of Malaysian scholars conducting research in the area of Malaysia's ethnic relations. The two statements below describe the dilemma for Malaysian scholars.

> Social science scholars are in a quandary as the prime minister's directive to halt public discussion on religion affects some of the core issues examined in the discipline. Prof Datuk Abdul Rahman Embong, president of the Malaysian Social Science Association (PSSM), lamented that certain developments of late are taking a toll on academic freedom. Of late, certain developments have been taking place which, to our mind, may have implications on the free flow of ideas and academic discourse on various complex issues facing our nation and in some ways, affect our core business as social science scholars, he said at the opening of the 5th International Malaysian Studies Conference at University Putra Malaysia (UPM) today. [In this situation], I must admit there is a degree of uncertainty among the academia, regarding what can and cannot be discussed openly, and how such discussion should be engaged [6]

> It is difficult to discuss and debate an issue today without risking being branded an ethnic chauvinist or as supposedly under the influence of parochial communal interest. However, the act of branding a discourse on a relevant issue such as the need for education reform is in itself a mischievous act of racism (Kay Peng, 2002, p.).

2.4 Reversing the Brain Drain of Skilled Malaysians

As the world is increasingly becoming global and competitive, a brain drain is unavoidable. However, the rate at which brain drain of skilled workers, especially non-Malay talents, is taking place in Malaysia is quite alarming – a prominent politician says it is a national disaster.[7] Former

[6] http://www.sun2surf.com/article.cfm?id=15037.

[7] http://blog.limkitsiang.com/2007/03/21/million-malaysian-brain-drain-a-national-disaster/.

Prime Minister Tun Mahathir Mohamad once put forward a radical solution that developed countries that hire Malaysians should consider paying compensatory fees in the same way that developed countries charge intellectual property fees (Rashid, 2007). His comment had its roots in the aggressive migration incentives introduced by the developed countries to attract skilled foreign professionals. Aggressive migration incentives coupled with prolonged economic policies that are not inclusive, many Malaysians have been seeking economic opportunities outside Malaysia, majority being non-Bumiputeras.

The impact of the increasing brain drain in Malaysia is also compounded by the fact that Malaysia's brain gain is also rapidly declining. Unofficially, some argue that over one million Malaysians are working abroad (Mokhtar, 2010). A report issued by the government shows that on average 550 people left Malaysia daily for job abroad between March 2008 and August 2009. In 2007, this number was 380 (Mokhtar, 2010). During the period of 2000–2008, foreign talent decreased by half from nearly 80,000 in 2000 to less than 40,000 in 2008 (Mokhtar, 2010).[8]

Low salaries, lack of postgraduate opportunities, and higher quality of life and work standards elsewhere are often cited as the reasons for the brain drain. Adding to this, Malaysia's education system "is [also] not producing the right talent needed for future growth" (New Economic Model Report, 2010, p.56). In a Johor Assembly meeting recently, the issue was raised that 15,000 Johor students are studying in Singapore, a significant potential brain gain for Singapore (Gasper & Camoens, 2009). It is unfortunate that for a country known as "Suvarnabhumi," Malaysia is currently not successful either in attracting foreign talent, or in retaining its own talent.

2.5 Overcoming Diminished Sensitivity and Respect for Other Ethnic Groups, and Finding Ways to Uphold Cultural Rights

Diversity of religion, ethnicity, and culture is what characterize a multicultural nation and every effort needs to be taken to protect, nurture and promote these characteristics. This is easier said than done, and Malaysian politicians in recent years are increasingly acknowledging that "there is diminishing sensitivity, respect and space for upholding the religious, ethnic and cultural rights and practices for non-Muslim Malaysians."[9] The definition of national culture in the "National Culture Policy" also has a strong bias toward the Malay culture; hence, it is strongly objected by other ethnic groups (Kia Soong, 1985). For example, a categorical objection was lodged when in 1979 a senior Malay minister asked the Chinese community to change the Lion Dance to a Tiger dance with the background of Malay music (Guan, 2000).

While Malaysia has generally maintained racial harmony after the May 13 incident and is often viewed as a model of a multicultural nation, racial tensions due to lack of sensitivity, respect, and space for upholding cultural rights have also risen in the last 10–12 years. These are smaller in scale than the May 13 incident. In 1998, a minor religious clash between Muslims and Hindus took place in Kampung Rawa, Penang, due to trivial issues relating to the noise level of prayer bells of a relocated Hindu temple. Four people were injured and nearly 200 rioters were arrested. In 1999, Suqui, the Malaysian Chinese Organizations Election Appeals committee representing more than 2000 Chinese organizations, demanded a list of actions to improve the well-being of the

[8] http://www.asiasentinel.com/index.php?option=com_content&task=view&id=2308&Itemid=199.

[9] http://www.dapmalaysia.org/english/2006/april06/lks/lks3854.htm.

Chinese. Among them was a reevaluation of New Economic Polices. However, their list was seen as a threat by the UMNO, which led Prime Minister Mahathir Mohamad to comment that "Suqui was not much different from communists" (Keng, 2002, p. 69). In 2000, the proposal of Vision schools heightened the tensions between Chinese activists and the government. The proposal outlined that three different curricula (Malay, Chinese, and Tamil), which are taught in separate building and physical locations, could be taught under one school and common facilities such as sport facilities and the canteen could be shared. The Dong Zhiao Zong (DZZ) (a joint group of the United Chinese School Committees" Association and the United Chinese School Teachers" Association), however, resisted this proposal until a clear guideline was drawn. The contention between the government and DZZ led the issue to become a very controversial one (Martinez, 2001).

In March 8, 2001, a localized ethnic clash between Malays and Indians took place in Kampung Medan, Kuala Lumpur, where six people died and more than 40 people were hospitalized.[10] In Aug 2006, the Hindu Actions Right Force (HINDRAF) filed a US$4 trillion class action suit at the Royal Courts of Justice in London. The suit was filed on the grounds that the UK government exploited Indians for 150 years and failed to protect the minority Indians' rights under the Malaysia's Constitution when independence was granted. To urge the UK government to appoint a Queen's Counsel, HINDRAF organized a march to the British High Commission in Kuala Lumpur on Nov 25, 2007. The 20,000 people march was regarded as the most surreal demonstrations ever in Malaysia (Kuppusamy, 2007) as it was the largest turnout for ethnic demonstration in the history of Malaysia's ethnic relations. Its leaders were arrested under the Internal Security Act on the grounds that they presented a threat to national security. This protest and the arrest are mentioned as one of the reasons for the devastating loss of the coalition ruling party in the March 2008 general election.

[10] http://www.indianmalaysian.com/memo_to_pm.htm.

3 Moving Forward: Suggestions for Amelioration and Prevention of Ethnic Conflicts in Malaysia

Malaysia should move beyond the absence of racial riots toward actively seeking solutions to achieve solid unity. Borrowing the concepts from the intercultural sensitivity literature (Bhawuk, Sakuda, & Munusamy, 2008), three steps are proposed of how the government can go about achieving this.

Step 1: Acknowledging the existence of multicultural issues.

The first step is for government leaders to acknowledge the existence of multicultural issues for the community. Using the perspective of community is important because sometimes what is important for the community may not be important for government leaders. Ignorance of the existence of multicultural issues is akin to denying the existence of different cultures.

Step 2: Accepting that multicultural issues can be complex.

The second step is that leaders need to accept that multicultural issues can be complex, requiring much time, focus, and energy. Leaders need to acknowledge that addressing multicultural issues is a long-term process that requires continuous effort. It involves thoughtful long-term planning and not ad-hoc solutions. Immediate interventions sometimes are necessary, but leaders need to look beyond immediate goals. In some cases, addressing multicultural issues involves changing institutional culture and correcting history, and these require substantial education, training, awareness, innovation, and learning from trial and error.

Step 3: Aiming to take appropriate actions to address multicultural issues.

The third step is that leaders need to aim to take proactive actions to address multicultural issues. Leaders need to be authentic in their actions and should demonstrate that they are willing and able to "walk the talk."

Multicultural issues are complex, hence any attempts by policy makers to ameliorate and prevent ethnic conflicts need to be based on holistic approaches – through formulating good multicultural policies, implementing those policies effectively, and rekindling the spirit of "Muhibbah" (spirit of tolerance and harmony). Metaphorically, holistic approaches necessitate the head (policies), hand (implementation), and heart (spirit) to work together. These three prerequisites for fostering good ethnic relations are discussed below.

3.1 Formulating Multicultural Policies

Multicultural policies, as any other policies, must have large reach or impact – from individual to organization to community and to nation. Since independence, Malaysia has formulated many education, language, economic, and religion policies that are intended to promote, protect, and safeguard ethnopolitical relations. However, these policies (e.g., National Economic Policy, National Cultural Policy, and Internal Security Act) while good can also have latent or unintended consequences for ethnopolitical relations – positively and negatively. Table 6.5 indicates of the intended and some unintended consequences of some policies.

Hence, it is important that the government evaluate multicultural policies from time to time taking into account both the majority and minority perspectives even if these policies are generally deemed to be successful. Successful policies are policies where intended outcomes are achieved without negative unintended consequences. A typology that may be useful to evaluate the quality of multicultural policies is described in Table 6.6.

3.2 Implementing Multicultural Policies

Even with good multicultural polices, their outcome can be disastrous if they are not implemented effectively, evaluated correctly, and revised accordingly. Negative unintended consequences of multicultural policies often result not because of poor policies, but rather because of ineffective implementation, inadequate evaluations, and ignorance of feedback. Hence, how policies are implemented, evaluated, and revised becomes salient for successful outcomes of multicultural policies. These responsibilities usually lie with leaders in government agencies or ministries tasked with the implementation of the policies. Their role is to transform the community through multicultural policies and their effective implementation. The implementation is extremely important.

In their study of change agents, Bhawuk, Mrazek, and Munusamy (2009) **identified** five characteristics of agents of successful transformations. These characteristics are relevant for successful implementations of multicultural policies.

Table 6.6 Quality of multicultural policies

Multiculturalism Outcome	Quality of policies
Manifest consequences – Yes Latent consequences – No	Good policies
Manifest consequences – Yes Latent consequences – Yes (+ve)	Great policies
Manifest consequences - Yes **Latent consequences – Yes (–ve)**	Fine tuning needed
Manifest consequences – No Latent consequences – Yes (+ve)	Reframing needed
Manifest consequences – No **Latent consequences – Yes (–ve)**	Bad policies
Manifest consequences – No Latent consequences – No	Useless

Table 6.5 Intended and unintended consequences of ethnic policies

	Intended consequences	Unintended consequences (negative)	Unintended consequences (positive)
National Economic Policy	Close economic gaps of different ethnic groups	Reduces national competitiveness Brain drain	Increases business interdependence among different ethnic groups
National Cultural Policy	Create a national identity	Reduces showcasing of Malaysia's rich diversity heritage	No clear consequence

As an illustration, one of the objectives of the proposed New Economic Model policy, reducing brain drain, is discussed in relation to these five characteristics.

First, Bhawuk et al. (2009) identified that change agents must be passionate facilitators embedded in the community. Here, it is apparent that change agents that are responsible for reducing the brain drain must be passionate about this issue. As change agents, besides interacting with individuals who have left and who have shown desire to leave, they must interact with other actors (e.g., immigration agencies, and educational agencies). Hence, it is important that the government assigns leaders who are passionate about reducing the brain drain and willing to work with the ecosystem to address these issues.

Second, change agents need to define the problem with individuals who have left the country or who are leaving the country. What contributes to brain drain? How can the brain drain be reversed? These are some of the questions that change agents need to get answers to and not simply assume they know.

Third, change agents need to use multiple methods and perspectives to measure policies implemented to reduce brain drains. Are these policies successful? What are the success measures?

Fourth, change agents need to ensure that implementations of policies to reduce the brain drain are conducted collaboratively with all actors in the ecosystem of talent (individuals, government agencies, businesses, etc.).

Finally, change agents must be flexible to change policies if needed "from problem definition to solution implementation, to accommodate a variety of opinions as well as the changing circumstances of the community involved" (Bhawuk et al. 2009, p. 44).

3.3 Rekindling the Spirit of Muhibbah

Muhibbah (spirit of tolerance and harmony) was a popular slogan in the 1970s. It is the spirit that had worked in the past to promote ethnopolitical relations even without the multicultural policies that exist today. It was a binding force for multiculturalism in Malaysia. Loosely translated, it means the spirit of tolerance and harmony. It is beyond the Muhibbah that we know today – Muhibbah festival open houses, Muhibbah dinners, Muhibbah durian parties, etc. Malaysia has lost the higher spirit of Muhibbah and hence the substitution for more multicultural policies, legislations, slogans, campaigns, and so forth. These substitutions are important as the demography has changed (from 6.3 million in 1957 to 28.9 million in 2010),[11] but the truth is all these will work only if the spirit of Muhibbah is rekindled. Why? Because, time-tested Muhibbah provides a safety net for authentic interactions, conflict resolution, difficult conversations, and intercultural dialogue. Formulation of good policies and effective implementation of those policies require authentic conversations, open dialogue and respectful debates or what a late academic politician Goh (1978) described "musyawarah" (a Malay term which translates as discussion or deliberation). "Muhibbah" is not something that can be promoted on an ad hoc basis; it has to be embedded in daily life with the understanding that this is a life-long journey. As the intercultural sensitivity literature points out, this embedding requires authentically acknowledging other cultures as ways of living, accepting them, aiming to learn them, and bridging differences that arise between one's own culture and other cultures (Bhawuk et al., 2008).

4 Summary

Malaysia aspires to be a fully developed country by 2020 – economically, politically, socially, spiritually, psychologically, and culturally. Peaceful ethnopolitical relations is a comparative advantage and is at the nexus of these developments, influencing them and being influenced by them. As other comparative advantages, ethnopolitical relations have to be nurtured and protected. The success of this nurturing and protection is not and cannot be simply the relative absence of

[11] http://www.epu.gov.my/html/themes/epu/images/common/pdf/eco_stat/pdf/1.2.5.pdf; Anand, 1983.

racial riots. Rather it is the presence of "inhabitants living peacefully." To achieve this, "constant repair" of multicultural policies in the spirit of Muhibbah must be fully embraced.

References

Abraham, C. E. R. (1997). *Divide and rule: the roots of race relations in Malaysia*. Kuala Lumpur: INSAN.

Anand, S. (1983). *Inequality and poverty in Malaysia – Measurement and decomposition* (p. 2). Oxford: Oxford University Press.

Bhawuk, D. P. S., Mrazek, S., & Munusamy, V. P. (2009). From social engineering to community transformation: Amul, Grameen Bank, and Mondragon as exemplar organizations. *Peace & Policy, 14*. Ethical Transformations for a Sustainable Future pp. 36–63

Bhawuk, D. P. S., Sakuda, K. H., & Munusamy, V. P. (2008). Intercultural Competence Development and Triple-Loop Cultural Learning: Toward a Theory of Intercultural Sensitivity. In S. Ang & L. Van Dyne (Eds.), *Handbook of Cultural Intelligence: Theory, measurement, and applications* (pp. 342–355). Armonk, NY: M.E. Sharpe.

Boo Teik, K. (2004). *Managing ethnic relations in post-crisis Malaysia and Indonesia: Lessons from the new economy policy*. United Nations Research Institute for Social Development.

Boon Keng, C. (2002). *Malaysia: The making of a Nation*. Malaysia: Institute of Southeast Asian Studies.

Elegant, S. (1999). A pyrrhic victory. *Far Eastern Economic Review, 162*, 45.

Gasper, D. T., & Camoens, A. (2009). *Johor Assembly: 15,000 Johor students study in Singapore*. Malaysia: The Star.

Glazer, N., Huntington, S., Nash, M., & Weiner, M. (1970, April 29). *Social Science Research for National Unity: A Confidential Report to the Government of Malaysia*.

Goh, C. T. (1978). *Integration in a plural society: The Chinese in Malaysia*. Malaysia: The Straits Echo Press.

Goh, C. T. (1994). *Malaysia: beyond communal politics*. Petaling Jaya, Malaysia: Pelanduk Publications.

Goh, D., & Holden, P. (2009). Introduction: Postcoloniality, race and multiculturalism. In D. Goh et al. (Eds.), *Race and multiculturalism in Malaysia and Singapore* (pp. 1–16). London: Routledge.

Government Transformation Programme – The Roadmap (2010). Malaysian Prime Minister's Office.

Guan, L. H. (2000). *Ethic Relations in Peninsular Malaysia: The cultural and economic dimensions*. Social and Cultural Issues (1). Institute of Southeast Asian Studies.

Hashim, H. W. (1983). *Race relations in Malaysia*. Kuala Lumpur: Heinemann Educational Books (Asia).

Hooker, V. M. (2003). *A short history of Malaysia: Linking east and west*. Crows Nest, NSW: Allen & Unwin.

Jomo, S. (2004). *The New Economic Policy and Interethnic Relations in Malaysia*. Identities, Conflict and Cohesion Paper Number 7, United Nations Research Institute for Social Development.

Kay Peng, K. (2002, October 10). *Politics without principle is what ails us* [Letter to the editor]. Malaysiakini.

Kennedy, P. (1988). *The rise and fall of the great powers: Economic change and military conflict from 1500 to 2000*. New York: Random House.

Kia Soong, K. (1985). National Culture and Democracy. Petaling Jaya: Kersani Penerbit – Penerbit Sdn. Bhd.

Kia Soong, K. (1987). *Polarization in Malaysia: The root causes*. Kuala Lumpur: Malaysian Chinese Research and Resource Center.

Kia Soong, K. (2007). *Declassified documents on the Malaysian riots of 1969 Malaysia*. Malaysia: Suaram Komunikasi.

Kuppusamy, B. (2007). *Facing Malaysia's racial issues*. Malaysia: TIME.

Martinez, P. (2001). Malaysia in 2000: A year of contradictions. *Asian Survey, 41*(1), A Survey of Asia in 2000 (Jan. – Feb., 2001), pp. 189–200.

Mauzy, D. K. (1995). The tentative life and quiet death of the NECC in Malaysia. In J. DiBernardi, G. Forth, & S. Niessen (Eds.), *Managing Change in Southeast Asia: Local Initiatives, Global Connections*. Montreal: University of Montreal.

Means, G. P. (1970). *Malaysian politics*. London: University of London Press.

Muhammad Ghazali bin Shafie & Institute of Strategic and International Studies (Malaysia). (1993). *National unity: key to the ultimate Malaysian society*. Kuala Lumpur: ISIS.

Munusamy, V. (2008). *Decoding the meaning of multiculturalism: An International Study of Malaysia, Singapore and Hawai'i*. Unpublished dissertation. University of Hawaii at Manoa.

Narayanasamy, K. (2006, June 12). *Education system reflects polarisation* [Letter to the editor]. Malaysiakini.

New Economic Model Report. (2010). Published by the National Economic Advisory Council, Malaysia.

Nik Anis, M. (2010). *PM: Managing a diverse nation is a major challenge*. Malaysia: The Star.

Pires, T. (1515). *The Suma oriental of Tome Pires: An account of the East, from the Red Sea to China*. Laurier Books Ltd.

Poh Ping, L. (1999). Stability in racially divided societies: The Malaysian case. In C. Young (Ed.), *The accommodation of cultural diversity: case-studies* (pp. 19–36). Basingstoke: Macmillan Press in association with UNRISD.

Rabushka, A. (1973). *Race and politics in urban Malaya*. Stanford, CA: Hoover Institution Press.

Rashid, R. (2007, Aug 10). *Dr Mahathir's radical solution for brain drain*. New Strait Times.

Sandhu, K. S., & Wheatley, P. (1983). *Melaka: The transformation of a Malay Capital C.1400–1980*. Kuala Lumpur: Oxford University Press.

Singh, H. (2001). Ethnic conflict in Malaysia revisited. *Commonwealth & Comparative Politics, 39*(1), 42–65.

Stenson, M. (1976). Class and race in West Malaysia. *Bulletin of Concerned Asian Scholars*, *8*(2), 45–54.

Teck Ghee (2006). Corporate Equity Distribution: Past Trends and Future Policy. Asian Strategy and Leadership Institute (This report has since been retracted by the institute).

Wheatley, P. (1955). The Golden Chersonese. Transactions and Papers. *Institute of British Geographers, 21*, 61–78.

Wicks, P. (1971). The New realism: Malaysia since 13 May, 1969. *The Australian Quarterly, 43*(4), 17–27.

India and the Culture of Peace: Beyond Ethnic, Religious, and Other Conflicts* 7

Dharm P.S. Bhawuk

India Chapter Summary

Bhawuk discusses the general state of peace existent in India and details the contributory cultural factors. Recognition of over two thousand represented ethnic groups, hundreds of languages, and diverse religions practiced reveals a unique continuing tradition of harmony. Proposed mechanisms of the conceptual framework termed General and Complete Peace are utilized to explain serenity in India and offer hope for engendering peaceful coexistence in other regions.

Exploration of cultural beliefs reveals significant importance placed on values of individual peace and care for others. Discussion of various spiritual texts provides additional insight into acceptance of contradiction and impermanence, which are viewed as contributing to inclusion. The value placed on dialog that permeates spiritual traditions provides evidence of understanding and appreciation of others. Further recognition of spiritual beliefs elucidates an unusual acceptance of various forms of religious

*Some of the ideas in this paper were presented at the International Association for Cross-Cultural Psychology conference in Bremen, Germany, July 2008. I appreciate the stories and insights shared by Dr. E. S. Srinivas, Dr. Vikramaditya Ekkirala, and Anand Chandrasekar, which helped me improve the paper. I am grateful to Susan Mrazek for working with me on peace research because preparing for our weekly meeting constantly inspires me to think about world peace. I am grateful to Acharya Satya Chaitanya for his comments and to Dan and Rosita for their support and guidance. This paper is dedicated to Mr. Khan, a taxi driver in Mumbai, who lives by the highest standards of peace and offers incense daily to Lord Venkateswara of Tirupati in his taxi and gets deeper in his own faith, Islam. I hope to be able to emulate him by chanting the name of Allah every day.

D.P.S. Bhawuk (✉)
Department of Management and Industrial Relations, Shidler College of Business, University of Hawai`i at Manoa, 2404 Maile Way, Honolulu, HI 96822, USA
e-mail: bhawuk@hawaii.edu

D. Landis and R.D. Albert (eds.), *Handbook of Ethnic Conflict: International Perspectives*, International and Cultural Psychology, DOI 10.1007/978-1-4614-0448-4_7,

practice as leading to the same God. In fact, the author points out that people from different religions may revere the same saints.

In describing current conflicts, Bhawuk notes the existence of the caste system which many credit with the existing conflicts; however, he iterates that this was historically functional in society. Delineation of study results implicates economic and political factors in local, minimally violent conflicts, although statistics are cited which show that these are escalating in specific regions. Religious conflicts are also explored, revealing the catalyst of conversion to Christianity as a major factor.

Bhawuk describes peace as a natural state, the absence of which begins at the individual and interpersonal levels. Results of a cited study provide insight into the need for compassion to reduce differences and promote humanitarian efforts.

Cheryl Jorgensen

sarve bhavantu sukhinaH sarve santu nirAmayA

sarve bhadrANi pazyantu mA kazciddukhbhAgbhavet

Om zAntiH! zAntiH! zAntiH!

(Let all be happy; let all be healthy; let all see positive; let no one be unhappy. Om Peace! Peace! Peace!)

Om dyauH zAntirantarikSaMzAntiH pRthavi zAntirApaH zAntirauSadayaH zAntiH vanaSpatayaH zAntiH vizve devAH zAntiH sarvaM zAntiH zAntireva zAnti sAmA zAnti redhiH. Om zAntiH! zAntiH! zAntiH!

(Om! Let there be peace in space; peace in horizon; peace on earth; peace in water; peace in medicinal plants; peace in vegetation; peace among all gods; peace in Brahman, the formless God; peace in everything; may peace give us peace. Om Peace! Peace! Peace!

A traditional Hindu service (pujA as well as sandhya) and the Aryasamaj *yajnas* started by Dayanand Sarasvati in the 1850s to reform Hinduism, which continues to this day, end with the above prayers, called the *zAntiH mantras*, or the prayers for peace. In the first one, people pray for happiness and health for everybody everywhere. They wish that all may see only auspicious events and that no one may be unhappy. In the second one, people pray for peace in the cosmos, sky (or horizon), earth, water, medicinal plants, vegetation, and the Brahman or the formless universal God. They pray for peace for all Gods. They pray for peace everywhere. They pray for ever-increasing peace. Thus, in the Indian culture, peace is an important part of daily life, and to emphasize its importance it is chanted or prayed for on every auspicious occasion.

In this chapter, India is presented as a culture of peace, peace that has existed for thousands of years in spite of the presence of many ugly conflicts and brutal wars recorded in its history. Stories of peace and peaceful practices that exist in the culture are presented to support this position. Following this, history of the absence of peace (or conflict) and their causes are presented. The objective here is neither to downplay conflict and violence nor to paint a biased positive image of India, its culture, or the society. The purpose is to shift the focus from conflict to peace, for peace exists constantly, and it is occasionally disturbed by conflicts. Peace is the way of life in India and most parts of the world for human beings, and conflict is an aberration. Peace is ubiquitous, and the few conflicts that have occurred are scattered over thousands of years of history. It is particularly important for cultural researchers to examine this shift and its merits for they are the ones who are going to present a template grounded in research to the global village to achieve peace and prosperity in the near and distant future.

Galtung (1964a) argued that peace studies as a discipline has to focus on the macro-level, and not on interpersonal and individual levels. This chapter takes a different position. Peace has to be examined at the individual and interpersonal levels, as much, and more so, than at the macro-level of communities and nation states. If a person is not at peace with himself or herself, he or she is likely to create conflict rather than bring peace between communities and nations. Gandhi, Mother Teresa, and other great peace builders were all at peace within and in their interpersonal interactions, and that is why they could bring peace to communities and nations. I remember having a brief conversation with a UN representative at a conference in August 2002. He had worked in the peace-building process in Serbia. I asked him how we should deal with people like Slobodan Milošević, the first President of Serbia. His knee-jerk response was – such people should be eliminated. This gentleman, and people like him, can never bring peace in the world, and at best can serve as poor diplomats who are already predisposed to violence and lack compassion.

Interpersonal peace also needs to be studied and attained for communities and nations to be in peace. Often, people brush aside interpersonal conflicts, and later these become fodder for building our subjective prejudices against the community that the individual we are in conflict with comes from. It is common to take an individual we do not like and to generalize this dislike to people like him or her. Thus, interpersonal peace needs to be understood and practiced, and conflict can be defined as the absence of individual and interpersonal peace, which manifests through multiple interactions, real and symbolic. In essence, this paper starts with peace and then discusses absence of peace, rather than starting from conflict and then studying peace as the absence of conflict, or what has been called negative peace. The culture of India can be examined as what cross-cultural psychologists call a naturally occurring experiment from the perspective of peace, and conflict as "absence of peace."

This chapter is organized differently for two reasons. First, a conscious effort is made to focus on peace rather than conflict, and so the chapter starts with an introduction to peace research and a discussion of Indian experience with peace and how India has maintained a culture of peace, and then various types of conflicts are discussed. Second, India faces multiple issues, and each has a different historical time frame, underlying variables and rationale. The issues with caste-related conflicts have a different historical background than Hindu–Muslim or other such conflicts. But they are also all related such that religion, caste, language, and ethnicity interact with each other. So issues are dealt with one by one. However, a historical framework is provided before discussing the various conflicts, which should guide the readers through the chapter.

1 A Wonder that Is India

According to the 2009 data by the International Monetary Fund and The World Bank, India is one of the largest economies in the world, and with its gross domestic product crossing 1 trillion (1.24 trillion in 2009), it is the tenth largest economy in the world, only behind the USA (14.12 trillion), Japan (5.07 trillion), China (4.99 trillion), Germany (3.34 trillion), France (2.66 trillion), the United Kingdom (2.18 trillion), Italy (2.12 trillion), Brazil (1.56 trillion), Spain (1.47 trillion), and Canada (1.37 trillion). India has the second largest population in the world, next to China, with its population reaching 1.2 billion people, and is expected to be the most populous country by the year 2050 (India Population, 2004). About one-fifth (17.31%) of the world population lives in India! Though it is one of the most ancient cultures, it has one of the most youthful populations with more than 50% of its population being younger than 25 years of age, and 65% below the age of 35 years. In just a decade, in 2020, Indian population will be 8 years younger than the Chinese population, and 19 years younger than the Japanese population (Basu, 2007).

Unlike the other Asian cultures that are relatively homogeneous, India has more than two thousand ethnic groups, second to only the entire continent of Africa. Indian languages represent all the four families of languages, including Indo-European (Spanish, English, Hindi, Portuguese, Bengali, Russian, German, Marathi, French, Italian, Punjabi, and Urdu, of which five languages are native to India, and English and Portuguese also have a long history of being present in India), Dravidian, Austro-Asiatic, and Tibeto-Burman (Lewis, 2009; Dinkar, 1956). India even claims to have a language isolate in the Nihali language spoken in Maharashtra in Buldana District. India is the home of 300–400 languages and 1,652 mother tongues, according to linguists. It is no surprise that it has 23 official languages, 87 languages of print media, and 104 languages in which there are radio broadcasts. In more than half of the districts, minority linguistic groups constitute more than 20% of the population (Mohanty, 2007).

According to the Indian census data from 2001, India is also one of the most diverse countries with respect to religion, and practitioners of most world religions can be found here. Hindus (80.5%) constitute the largest group with tremendous variability among rituals and much convergence in worldview and practice of spirituality. Sikhs (1.9%), Buddhists (0.8%), and Jains (0.4%) are all indigenous to India, and have traditionally lived harmoniously. For example, even when kings championed Buddhism in India, they did not use sword to convert people to their faith. On the contrary, they practiced ahimsa (or nonviolence) so much so that India, some Indians argue, became vulnerable to external aggression.[1]

Muslims (13.5%) constitute the second largest religious group in India, and based on the size of Muslim population, India is the third largest Muslim country (161 million) after Indonesia (203 million) and Pakistan (176 million), and has 10.2% of the world's Muslim population! There is both oral tradition and historical evidence that Islam has existed in India from the time of Prophet Mohammad,[2] and since Islam has been practiced in India for as long as it has been practiced elsewhere, it qualifies to be called an Indian religion. The second oldest mosque, Cheraman Perumal Juma Masjid (or Mosque), is claimed to be in Kodungallur, Kerala, and was established in 629 ad by the Prophet's disciple, Malik-Ibn-Dinar, where regular Jumu'ah prayers are offered on Fridays (the oldest being Saudi Arabia's Quba Mosque outside Medina).[3] Almost 45 % of the Muslims speak Urdu, but the rest speak the regional languages.

Christianity also has been in India for more than 2,000 years since the apostle St. Thomas came to India in ad 52. The oldest church named after him was erected in Kerala in ad 54 (Mundadan, 1989; Neil, 1984). Christians (2.3%) constitute a small percentage of the Indian population, but are quite an influential community because the missionaries emphasized education. Most of the prestigious schools (K to 12) in India are still run by the missionaries, which allows for a powerful social network among the alumni. Majority of Christians speak Malayalam (about one-third) and Tamil (about one-sixth), whereas the rest speak other regional languages. It is a misconception that they all speak English.

India is the largest democracy in the world, and there is some support that it might also have practiced some form of democracy during the Licchavi era a little before the time of Buddha (sixth century bce), making it the oldest democracy (Basham, 1954). India has the largest number of institutions of higher education in the world, double that of the USA! India produces the most number of modern cultural artifact, or films, in the world from what is now called Bollywood, about twice as many as Hollywood! As noted above, India is the most culturally diverse country in the world, only second to the continent of Africa! And one can still find snake charmers on the streets of India, while India is also one of the eight countries to have nuclear weapons (others being, the USA, Russia, UK, France, China, Pakistan, and North Korea)! Basham (1954) studied India from the antiquity up to 1200 ad and found the people, idea, and culture so fascinating that he called his book, "The Wonder that was India." Rizvi (1987) studied India from 1200 to 1700, and simply called his book, "The wonder that was India, Volume II." The cultural diversity that India maintains with peace, the innovations that it has maintained in spirituality for 5,000 years (Bhawuk, 2003), and the economic superpower that it was until 1760 (Kennedy, 1989) and is fast becoming suggest that India is still a wonder and will continue to be so in this new millennium. India is a wonder not only in cultural diversity but also in maintaining harmony among stark contradictions, which makes it a charming destination for intercultural researchers.

[1] Dinkar (1956) argued that internal conflict among kings, caste-based disagreement, and absence of a strong central level government were some of the causes for India's inability to protect itself from external aggression after the decline of Harshavardhan's monarchy (607 to 641 AD), which was the last strong central government that northern India saw. He also noted that for the most part people in the villages did not care about the kings and the shifting power between them. Life was quite peaceful for the most part for people in rural India, and hence there was no need for them to be concerned about the invaders, except for the occasional attack on the temples.

[2] A Muslim spiritual teacher who is respected as a Peer (or saint) and lives in Bhagalpur brought to my attention during my visit with him that Islam has existed in India from the time of the Prophet. See the following two blogs that provide some information about this claim. http://adhvaitha.blogspot.com/2009/01/oldest-mosque.html, http://www.pakspectator.com/second-oldest-mosque-in-the-world/

[3] There is another claimant for the second oldest mosque, the Al-Aqsa Mosque in Jerusalem, where the Prophet prayed.

2 Beyond Theories of Conflict

If we start with conflict, we will only find disagreement, clash, divergence, difference, argument, variance, quarrel, inconsistency, discord, contradiction, dispute, tension, controversy, fracas, competition, or aggression, battle, fight, war, struggle, encounter, skirmish, and weapons of mass destruction (WMD) – not concord, convergence, cooperation, or peace. It is transparent in the work of one of the most influential peace researcher of our time, Johan Galtung (1964a, 1964b, 1969, 1985). Though he started by defining negative and positive peace in the editorial as two states (Galtung, 1964a), a state of general and complete war (GCW) or a state of general and complete peace (GCP), he later defined even positive peace as the absence of structural violence and negative peace as absence of personal violence (Galtung, 1969, p. 183). Social justice or positive peace was merely a tortuous social construction of negative peace or absence of structural violence. Indeed, if we start from conflict, we will be unlikely to be able to define peace, or even be able to approach it intellectually.

It is my position that what Galtung (1964a) brilliantly proposed as GCP is possible through the mechanism of integration that he proposed. He posited that we are capable of empathy and solidarity and can become a part of a group where we cooperate on the basis of mutual exchange. This exchange can be rational or relational depending on one's culture (Bhawuk, 2001; Triandis, 1995), but does lead to some form of group identity. Through this mechanism of exchange, cooperation, and integration, it is possible to extend our identity beyond a small group to a larger society to the world. Gandhi suggested that a person be embedded in his or her village, then district, state, nation, and finally the universe, explaining the South Asian ethos of *udAra caritAnAm tU vasudhaiva kutumbakaM* (to the generous, the earth is his or her family). Extending one's identity beyond narrow boundaries is considered generous, and offers a way to achieve peace, or what Galtung called General and Complete Peace.

Galtung (1964a) also proposed another path to GCP, the path of control of violence, and prophetically drew our attention to the fact that humans are NOT capable of destroying others completely, which is evidenced in human history – "Man rarely uses all his means of destruction against all enemies all the time (Galtung, 1964a, p. 1)." He argued quite convincingly that even in World War II, no country went for mindless destruction, and so, though we were capable of much more destruction, we did not do it. This, he argues, is basic human nature that has stood the test of time over our long history, and can be cultivated to reduce the negative peace, i.e., war or social injustice. We clearly have made significant progress since Galtung wrote the editorial to the inaugural issue of *Journal of Peace Research*, but still have a long way to go considering the war waged by the USA and other Western nations in Iraq, which does divide us into west and east (Japan and the Philippines were the only two Asian nations supporting this war, and only the USA, UK, Australia, and Poland provided combat forces).

Galtung (1964a) also noted that GCW mirrored Hobbesian worldview where individuals were without any group identity and believed in the Darwinian principle of survival of the fittest in which "dog eats dog." Biological science has come to reject this Darwinian worldview, and it is now known that we do not live in a genetically determined world driven by competition, but rather in a world where genes respond to the environment, and just as cooperation is the way of the trillions of cells found in an individual human body, so it is for human beings at large (Lipton 2005; Lipton & Bhaerman, 2009). De Zutter (1995) captured this tension between individual and the collective in an interview to Chicago Reader –"In America, we have this strong bias toward individual action. You know, we idolize the John Wayne hero who comes in to correct things with both guns blazing. **But individual actions, individual dreams, are not sufficient. We must unite in collective action, build collective institutions and organizations** [emphasis added]." Obama's ideas of collective action and building collective institutions and organizations are consistent with the mechanism of integration that Galtung presented almost half a century ago.

There are many social science researchers, diplomats, and politicians who are still inspired by the Hobbesian worldview. Huntington is one of the oft-cited researchers representing this school of thought, and hypothesized that the primary source of conflict in the globalized world will be cultural differences rather than ideological or economic differences (1993). He went on to exaggerate cultural differences to "fault lines between civilizations" (p. 22), and insinuated these to be the future "battle lines" among nation states. He defined civilizations as "the highest cultural grouping of people and the broadest level of cultural identity people have short of that which distinguishes humans from other species (p. 24)," and argued that the seven major civilizations were Western (with two branches, namely, European and North American), Islamic (with three branches, namely, Arab, Turkic, and Malay), Latin American, Japanese ("Japan is a society and civilization unique to itself" p. 28), Confucian (spread over China, Taiwan, and Singapore), Hindu, and Slavic-Orthodox. He showed little respect to the African civilization, and thought that it could "possibly" be counted as the eighth civilization.

Huntington (1993) presented six reasons why these cultures will have conflict in the future. First, the differences between civilizations are real and basic. Second, people interact more frequently because of shrinking of the globe through internationalization. Third, the local identities of people are being diluted in favor of these civilization-based or cultural identities. Fourth, there is a growing trend for indigenous values to be strengthened as opposed to wholesale acceptance of Western values. Fifth, cultural values are more stable compared to economic and political values. And finally, regional economic blocs are emerging, reducing the economic influence of the West. He emphatically concluded that the civilizations that were most likely to clash with the Western civilization were Confucian and Islamic. His concern with the resurgence of indigenization against the "wholesale acceptance of Western values" is reminiscent of cultural colonialism, and particularly concerning that it comes from an established researcher at the Harvard University.

Huntington's recommendations are suggestive of not creating a peaceful world in the spirit of the United Nations or the Universal Declaration of Human Rights, but stimulating a us-versus-them thinking by asking the Western civilization to "promote cooperation and unity within its own civilization," "limit the expansion of the military strength of Confucian and Islamic states," "moderate the reduction of Western military capabilities and maintain military superiority in East and Southwest Asia," "**exploit** [emphasis added] differences and conflict among Confucian and Islamic states," and "strengthen international institutions that reflect and legitimate Western interests and values," among others (1993, pp. 48–49). All these recommendations reflect an ethnocentric mind-set rather than a global mind-set and go against the grain of globalization, which calls for a good faith business negotiation between nation states under the umbrella of World Trade Organization and other UN organizations. His recommendations reflect the fear of a generation that lived the cold war, and are rather Draconian and Machiavellian, which would tear the world apart if nurtured and implemented.

Sen (2008) criticized the clash of civilization theory (Huntington, 1996) as "the crudest" (p. 5) of cultural theories, since it utilizes religions as the primary criterion for categorizing civilizations (Christian, Islamic, Hindu, and Orthodox). He argued that Huntington's view of history was "oddly artificial" and a rather "imaginary history of the world" (p. 6) since these civilizations have had a long history of interaction with much positive exchange with each other in all areas of art, music, literature, mathematics, engineering, and science. These contacts have helped reduce prejudice and extend the humanness of people in all civilizations. Sen further argued that human beings have multiple identities that cannot be reduced to one single identity based on one's religion-based civilization. He called the clash of civilization approach not only a "huge oversimplification" but also an "impoverished approach to humanity (p. 6)" in which all levels and types of conflicts between people and groups were attributed to "animosity between distinct civilizations (p. 6)."

Sen's criticism seems justified on many counts. First, religion is a component of culture, which is not any more fundamental than language, time, and place that have been identified as the three major characteristics of cultures (Triandis, 1994). Second, diffusion of culture is a well-established fact in anthropology and cultural studies, and thus, despite the painful and ugly history of colonialism, interactions between peoples of different cultures have also been positive, and for hundreds of years, people of different cultures have been living peacefully with culturally different others. Third, the resurgence of indigenous psychologies has been a peaceful academic and social process (Berry, 2008; Bhawuk 2008), and the argument of clash seems exaggerated, to say the least. And finally, people have multiple identities even in homogenous cultures, let alone diverse cultures, and to assume that a single identity would emerge for a large populace, which would inevitably lead to conflict, also sounds alarmist in view of the knowledge of intercultural communication that exists among human civilizations (Kim, 2008; Kim & Bhawuk, 2008). The presence of thousands of years of peace in India presents evidence in support of what Sen has argued and refutes Huntington's worldview. Therefore, it may be relevant to examine the Indian approaches of peace creation, which is discussed next.

3 Creating Peace: Indian Approaches

Triandis, Kurowski, and Gelfand (1994) presented a model where history of conflict, cultural distance (religion, language, economics, politics, and so forth are each a source of distance), and lack of knowledge of the other culture (e.g., language competence) lead to a decrease in perceived similarity between people. The main thesis of this framework is that similarity leads to good feeling toward others, and when people are given the opportunity for contact with similar others, their interactions are rewarding, and more interactions result. More interactions in turn lead to intimacy (or small social distance), network overlap (i.e., common friends), sociotypes (i.e., accurate stereotypes), isomorphic attributions (i.e., people assign the same causes to the behavior of actors that the actors themselves assign to their own behavior), and finally, a sense of control. They also posited that in pluralistic societies when authorities approve contact, it rewards interactions and further fosters them. Ultimately, having a sense of control leads to little culture shock and to accommodation of people from another culture. However, the opposite would result if people perceive difference rather than similarity.

Following this model, and noting the numerous differences found in India would lead one to conclude that India can never have peace. There are regional differences in culture, food, religious practices, language, music, dance, art, literature, how people look, and so forth, and this is further complicated by ethnicity and ethnic, religious, and economic differences. The differences do not stop there and also cover ideological differences from communism to socialism to capitalism, and worldview differences from spiritual to the material.

However, the daily experience of peace and harmony that has characterized India for thousands of years of recorded history (Basham, 1954; Dinkar, 1956; Rizvi, 1987) contradicts the theory of difference, causing conflict that the model implicitly posits. Perhaps when people face so many differences, they stop caring for it, or they develop a worldview where all differences are to be denied to see the ultimate truth, and it is no surprise that *neti–neti*, "not this–not this," is a method used by spiritual pursuants to direct their journey inward. Perhaps this inward journey makes the outward differences less important; perhaps the internal peace experienced with this inward journey makes the outward conflict less relevant; perhaps that is why the most important desideratum of life is to experience this internal peace (*bhUmA* as noted in *Chandogya upaniSad*) and to live a life of *loksaMgraha* or service to humanity as noted in the *bhagavadgItA*

(Bhawuk, 2011). Such ideology and their historical deep roots going back thousands of years perhaps make India a culture of peace beyond the myriad of differences. It is also plausible that in the Indian culture, there has always been social approval for contact between people who are different within a social framework of *karma* (or social roles and actions) and *dharma* (or duty), allowing people of different castes and religions to live together in harmony, which would be consistent with the model of Triandis and colleagues. In this section, the methods of creating peace found in India are documented.

3.1 Synthesizing Opposites and Tentativeness

One of the cognitive tools used by Indians to create harmony and peace is the simultaneous acceptance of the opposites (Bhawuk, 2009, 2011). The Indian worldview is reflected in the *upaniSads*, which can be seen in the following verses.

> Those who worship *avidyA* (ignorance or rites) enter into blinding darkness; but those who are engaged in *vidyA* (knowledge or meditation) enter into greater darkness (9). They say that by *vidyA* a really different result is achieved, and they say that by *avidyA* a different result is achieved, thus have we heard the teaching of those wise people who explained that to us (10). He or she who knows these two, *vidyA* and *avidyA*, together, attains immortality through *vidyA*, by crossing over death through *avidyA* (11). (Gambhiranand, 1972, pp. 18–19).
>
> Those who worship the *asambhUti* (Unmanifested, *prakRti*, or non-becoming) enter into blinding darkness; but those who are devoted to the *sambhUti* (Manifested, becoming, Destruction, or *hiraNyagarbha*) enter into greater darkness (12). They spoke of a different result from the worship of the Manifested, and they spoke of a different result from the worship of the Unmanifested – thus we have heard the teachings of those wise people who explained that to us (13). He or she who knows these two – the Unmanifested (non-becoming) and Destruction (*hiraNyagarbha*) – together, attains immortality through the Unmanifested, by crossing death through Destruction (14). (Gambhiranand, 1972, pp. 20–22).

We can see that the Indian worldview is quite accepting of the opposites. In the ninth verse, *avidyA* and *vidyA* both are said to lead to darkness, and *vidyA*, the good knowledge, is said to be more damning than *avidyA*, the "bad" knowledge, which in itself is contradictory in that how can good be worse than bad? In the tenth verse, wise people are quoted to state that *avidyA* and *vidyA* serve different functions. And then in the eleventh verse, those who know both *avidyA* and *vidyA* conjointly are said to be wise, because they use one to pass over death, and the other to attain immortality. These ideas are explained further using the terms *sambhUti* (the manifested nature) and *asambhUti* (the unmanifested formless nature of *brahman*) in verses 12–14 quoted above, further capturing the idea that in the Indian worldview, opposite ideas are readily synthesized.

It should be noted that the Western logic system, which is the foundation of scientific thinking, is unable to accept "X" and "Not X" both as true. The Law of Contradiction, i.e., no proposition can be both true and false at the same time, and the Law of Excluded Middle, i.e., every proposition is either true or false, are taken as irrefutable axioms. If these fundamentals are contradicted, then the experience or fact itself is to be labeled as distortion or error (Mitroff & Kilman, 1978). In the *upaniSadic* literature, however, we find that people are very comfortable not only accepting but also practicing both "X" and "Not X" simultaneously, and X plus Not X does not become zero, instead it becomes, what could be labeled, infinity. Therefore, *vidyA* and *avidyA* or *sambhUti* and *asambhUti*, the opposite of each other, together lead to immortality.

This worldview that has survived thousands of years has led people in India to learn to partition the world in opposites, and then they are able to put them together into one whole, thus being able to accept two opposites simultaneously. People who have a worldview that can deal with such a system of logic and concepts are likely to be able to synthesize religious and cultural differences more comfortably. Dinkar (1956) calls the Indian culture a sAmAsik saMskriti, or a culture that is the result of synthesis between many cultures.

Another quality that the *upaniSads* teach could be termed tentativeness in everything, however serious the matter may be. In other words, people do not put their life on the line to defend a position; for everything is transitory, and even the ultimate truth is so slippery that one who thinks he or she has grasped it may completely miss it.

> I do not think, "I know *(brahman)* well enough." "Not that I do not know: I know and I do not know as well." He among us who understands that utterance, "not that I do not know: I know and I do not know as well," knows that *(brahman)* (2). It is known to him to whom it is unknown; he does not know to whom it is known. It is unknown to those who know well, and known to those who do not know (3). (*kenopaniSad*, Canto 2, Gambhiranand, 1972, p 59, 61).
>
> While sitting, It travels far away; while sleeping, It goes everywhere. Who but I can know that Deity who is both joyful and joyless (II, 21). This self cannot be known through much study, or through the intellect, or through much hearing. It can be known through the Self alone that the aspirant prays to; this Self of that seeker reveals Its true nature (II, 23). The discriminating man should merge the (organ of) speech into the mind; he should merge that (mind) into the intelligent self; he should merge the intelligent self into the Great Soul, he should merge the Great Soul into the peaceful Self (III, 13). (*kathopaniSad*, Canto 2–3, Gambhiranand, 1972, p 146, 148, 164).

Let us contrast this tentativeness with what Schopenhaur (1966) had to say about his philosophy that he presented in "*The world as will and representation*." He wrote in the preface to his first edition in 1818 – "But if he [the reader] has shared in the benefits of the *Vedas*, access to which, opened to us by the *upaniSads*, is in my view the greatest advantage which this still young century has to show over previous centuries, since I surmise that the influence of Sanskrit literature will penetrate no less deeply than did the revival of Greek literature in the fifteenth century; if, I say, the reader has also already received and assimilated the divine inspiration of ancient Indian wisdom, then he is best of all prepared to hear what I have to say to him. It will not speak to him, as to many others, in a strange and even hostile tongue; for, did it not sound too conceited, **I might assert that each of the individual and disconnected utterances that make up the *upaniSads* could be derived as a consequence from the thought I am to impart, although conversely my thought is by no means to be found in the** *upaniSads* (pp. xv to xvi) [emphasis added]."

Schopenhaur's confidence is what a wise person is to avoid when discussing truth and brahman, for such confidence leads the truth to slip out of one's hand as the *upaniSads* say – "He does not know to whom it is known. It is unknown to those who know well." If the truth is to be practiced rather than understood cognitively, and since it is so elusive, naturally people develop tentativeness toward everything, and thus conflict about any idea or object becomes silly, if not irrelevant. It seems that these cognitive and behavioral frameworks that the Indian population has received as their heritage have helped the culture to be peaceful over thousands of years despite external aggression. It is this mind-set that has allowed the Indian population to include all the migrants and their ideology, and create a mosaic called Indian culture that is diverse and inclusive.

Finally, it should be noted that the Indian worldview is not completely alien to the Western worldview, and is akin to what Mitroff and Kilman (1978) categorized as the "conceptual theorist," people who try to make a determination of the right versus the wrong schema by comparing two means-end schemas against each other, quite the opposite of the traditional scientific approach in which people select one single best explanation within a single means-end schema. It is no surprise that in India, people mock those who think they have "the solution" to any problem, and often people live with problems with equanimity, for what is a problem after all!

3.2 Dialog

vAde vAde jAyate tatva bodha is a well-known Sanskrit saying, which means that through dialog we understand the essence. Dialog is the Indian way of creating peace. This is reflected in the spiritual tradition in which two scholars would have a public *zAstrArtha* (zAstra means scriptures, and artha means meaning; zAstrArtha means interpreting the meaning of the scriptures), and it was customary for the one who was convinced by the other to become a disciple of that scholar. In other words, the two reach harmony and agree to one meaning or interpretation of the scripture. It is in this tradition that Buddha was able to convert all or most of India to his views, and nine centuries later, Shankaracharya was able to re-establish the Vedantic view by having dialogs with the Buddhist monks. Thus, dialogs go on, and people change their views when convinced by another person. Often times, those who know the classical texts, like the pundits of Varanasi or the Buddhist monks of later period, but have not experienced the truth are convinced by the enlightened ones like Buddha or Shankaracharya. And the world moves on. As the *upaniSads* say, "*yasyAmataM tasya mataM mataM yasya na veda saH; avijnAtaM vijAnatAM vijnAtamavijAnatAm*" (It is known to him to whom it is unknown; he does not know to whom it is known. It is known to those who know well, and known to those who do not know. Gambhiranand, 1972, p. 61). There are always dialogs, and never conflict or violence.

This tradition of dialog has helped India retain conflicting worldviews, and the tradition allows people to experience their own truth following whatever path they choose. It is no surprise that there are many schools of thought and philosophy in India, and they all coexist. India seems to favor a worldview of spirituality (Bhawuk, 2003, 2008, 2011). Moore (1967) distilled 17 themes from a thorough study and analyses of Indian philosophical thoughts, and concluded that the most important theme was spirituality – "a universal and primary concern for, and almost a preoccupation with, matters of spiritual significance" (Moore, 1967, p. 12). This was consistent with Sheldon's (1951) observation that in India, spirituality was the way of living in which merely knowing the truth was not valued but becoming one with the truth was the highest human goal. However, it still allows one of the most materialist worldview known as *cArvAka's* philosophy. This philosophy is also referred to as *lokAyat*, which is derived from *loka*, or the world, and is captured in a verse that is oft-quoted in India – *yAvajjivet sukhaM jivet; RNaM kRtvA ghRtaM pibet; bhasmIbhUtasya dehasya punarAgamanaM kutaH*. As long as you live, live happily; borrow money and have *ghee* (clarified butter), which symbolizes good food and other material goods of consumption; when the body is burnt upon death, from where does it come back, or it does not come back. In other words, the world is what we see, and life is about pain and happiness. Enjoy the world.

These ideas are also captured in verse 16.8 in the *bhagavadgItA*, which states, *asatyamapratiSThaM te jagadAhuranIzvaram; aparasparasambhUtaM kimanyatkAmahaitukam*. In this universe, there is no such thing as truth, no principles of *dharma* (the world is socially constructed, to borrow from Berger and Lukman (1966), without any absolute principle guiding it), and no *Isvar* or controller of the universe (i.e., there is no *brahman*). The world is created by the copulation of men and women who are driven by desires, and could not be for any other reason. Adi Shankar in his commentary attributes this to the *lokAyat* (*lokAyatikadRSTIH iyam*) worldview, which shows the acceptance of this materialistic worldview for thousands of years. However, it would be inaccurate to think that the *bhagavadgItA* recommends this lifestyle. It does not. In fact, it denounces this lifestyle at length in the next 12 verses (16.9–16.20) and finds this worldview destructive to the universe, as is apparent in the "Me–Me" culture found in many parts of the world. *bhagavadgItA* presents many paths (Bhawuk, 2011) and in principle, they seem to converge on a lifestyle that focuses on *niSkAma karma* (action without attachment to the fruits of one's endeavor) and one that is committed to *lokasaMgraha* or the welfare of the society (*bhagavadgItA* 3.20 and 3.25).

The tradition of dialog is well established not only in the 13 major *upaniSad*, but also in all the major spiritual texts of India. All texts are invariably a dialog between people, and it is no surprise that Sanskrit is the only language that has not only singular and plural but also *dvivacan* or verb conjugation for two. This tradition of dialog continues and is captured in the biography of Ramakrishna Paramahansa documented by his disciple Mahendra Nath Gupta (Gupta, 1984) and the dialogs of Raman Maharshi with his disciples in *Talks with Raman Maharshi: On realizing Abiding peace and Happiness* (2000). Similarly, talks with Nisargadatta Maharaj are captured in the book *I am That* (Nisargadatta, 1973); J Krishnamurti's dialogs are captured in many volumes including *Questioning Krishnamurti* (1996), *Dialogues with J. Krishnamurti* (Jayakar, 1995); and so forth. Reviewing these dialogs shows that there is never a loser and a winner in these debates. Pursuit of truth and knowledge is the only objective, and the dialog is followed by much reflection and practice by the spiritual pursuant. Indeed, the tradition of dialog seems to be the foundation of peace creation in India even to this day.

3.3 Stories Conducive to Peace

Peace is created in behavioral settings through action and then the stories of these actions in behavioral settings are narrated and perpetuated from generation to generation. A friend narrated a family story that exemplifies how peace is created in a community. A successful Indian Administrative Services (IAS) officer from Andhra Pradesh (a south-west state of India) was a spiritual leader for his community and was revered by people from his village and community, beyond his extended family or people of his own caste. His devotion of the *vedic* tradition was acquired from his father (Late Sri E. Ananthacharya) who was so committed to the *vedic* worldview that he did not believe in idol worshipping completely, and would often make fun of Tirupati Balaji, the deity of Tirupati Temple. Not to visit Tirupati and to even poke fun of Balaji are quite unusual and extreme for a Brahmin from Andhra, but such was his father's faith in the *Vedas* all his life. And though he visited Tirupati occasionally and had reverence for the deity, he too was an avid believer of the *vedic yajnas*.

When *vedic yajnas* were performed at this Brahmin's home or in his community under his leadership, a Muslim fakir or saint from a nearby village was always invited. The Muslim saint stayed outside, away from the *yajna* quarters, but remained for the duration of the yajna. At the completion of the *yajna*, all the children of the Brahmin were instructed to touch the feet of the Muslim saint to receive his blessings. Though in Islam touching the feet of another person is not accepted, the saint allowed them to touch his feet and blessed them. Such exemplary behaviors by spiritual leaders in the spirit of *mahAjano yena gataH sa panthAH* (the path to be followed is the one that great people have treaded) lead to a deep understanding of each other across ethnic and religious groups, and serves to create peace.

The brother of this same Brahmin spiritual leader (Late Sri E. Bharadwaja) was an iconoclast and an atheist, and once begrudgingly visited the shrine of Shirdi Sai Baba with his family. Shirdi Sai is a saint who is revered by both Hindus and Muslims even today. He sat next to the tomb of Shirdi Sai thinking about how the body of the saint must have decayed in the tomb, and had a general disparagement for the people who came there to visit a dead man's tomb. Next, he felt his body was being shaken by somebody, and he opened his eyes. As he opened his eyes, he realized that his relative was shaking his body. He learned that he was sitting by the tomb in a trans, unaware of anybody around him, for more than two hours. He did not say anything, but stopped criticizing Shirdi Sai. His life completely changed from this point onward. He became a devotee of Shirdi Sai and became a self-appointed messenger of the sage. He led a spiritual life, not desiring material things, and all his needs were met without his asking for or desiring things. When it came to his daughter's wedding, which is an expensive affair in India in general, and particularly in Andhra, a famous film star came forward and offered to meet all the wedding expenses. The wedding was carried out properly. This happened a few years after his departure from earth, and further strengthened the view of people in the community that Shirdi Sai does takes care of his devotees.

Sri E. Bharadwaja once prevailed on his father to visit Shirdi, and grudgingly his father obliged. When they got to the shrine, the father sat close to the idol of Shirdi Sai in the sanctum sanctorum, close enough to see the idol clearly. And then as he was looking at the bust of Shirdi Sai, the statue winked. He thought he was day dreaming, and rubbed his eyes and looked at the bust again. The statue winked again. He moved closer thinking that all the smoke from the incense was causing him to hallucinate or have a misperception. As he got closer and looked at the bust, it winked again. He tried it from many positions and the bust continued to wink. He gave up. When he got home to Hyderabad, one night he woke up and saw Shirdi Sai inside his room by the closed door. He taunted him, "I am not your devotee. I do not believe in you. So, please go and visit my son. He is your devotee." Shirdi Sai smiled at him and said, "But I like you." And then Shirdi Sai sprang in his lap and vanished within his body. He went back to sleep, not making a big deal out of this experience. The same experience happened again the next night, and a number of nights. Based on these personal experiences, he made concession to Shirdi Sai as a spiritual master. However, he never visited any temples and shrines, including Shirdi. He did not change his position, and continued to be a practitioner of *vedic yajnas*.

Sri E. Bharadwaja also prevailed on his brother who was an IAS officer and the spiritual leader of his community to visit Shirdi. His brother sat in the shrine and looked around. He found that the assembly was segregated into two groups, one for men and another for women. He looked at the bust and found that the bust was facing the women's group. He disparagingly thought, "There we go. Even the bust of God men are focused on women!" And the bust turned to him. He rubbed his eyes in disbelief, looked away, and then looked again at the bust. The sculpture of Shridi Sai was still looking at him, turned away from the women's congregation. He got up and changed his place and then looked at the bust again. Shirdi Sai was still looking at him. He gave up, and upon his return, stopped criticizing his brother or followers of Shirdi Sai. However, his faith in the practice of *vedic yajnas* remained unchanged for life.

People in this Brahmin family are deeply religious, but with a different approach to their faith. All of them respect Shirdi Sai but only some of them are "only Shirdi Sai" followers or devotees. They all take part in the family *yajnas*, which are still performed following the *vedic* tradition. However, none of the children are practitioners of *vedic yajnas* only like their grandfather or father. They are in different professions, academics, bankers, and so forth, and are not only tolerant but also accept other faiths. Spirituality seems to make this family deeply anchored in peace, and they propagate peace in their community, which comprises people of other religions.

Shirdi Sai is worshipped by Hindus and Muslims alike, and the Late Sri E. Bharadwaja's effort to take his message to Andhra Pradesh definitely helped create a large following for Shirdi Sai in his state. Three points should be noted. First, it is saints and fakirs like Shirdi Sai who have created a deep understanding between not only Hindus and Muslims but also among all communities of India, since people from all religious denominations revere them without any reservation. Second, it is people like this Brahmin follower of Shirdi Sai who continue to cultivate peace among all communities even today through their devotion and deep understanding of the commonality of humanity. Finally, it is stories like these that help create a general environment of peace among people of all faiths, for people are more likely to listen to these stories with interest since it is about somebody known to the story teller, rather than a distant story from the past.

3.4 Spirituality as Community Bridge

As was noted above, spirituality emerges as a dominant worldview in India not only for the majority Hindus but also for other religious groups. Spiritual leaders have emerged from all faiths who are able to bridge religious boundaries and have a following among people of all religions. Ramakrishna Paramhansa (February 18, 1836 – August 16, 1886) was a saint who lived at the Dakshinesvar temple by the Ganges near Calcutta. He was a mystic who did not travel much, but is known because of his disciple, Vivekanand, who founded the Ramakrishna Mission that serves needy people all over the world. He is known to have practiced various faiths and said, "I have practiced all religions, Hinduism, Islam, Christianity, and I have also followed the paths of the different Hindu sects… I have found that it is the same God toward whom all are directing their steps, though along different paths. You must try all beliefs and traverse all the different ways once" (Rolland, 1960, p. 79). Saints like Ramakrishna do help bridge people of India across the religious boundaries.

People go to saints and gurus irrespective of their beliefs vis-à-vis the belief of the saint. This has led to the creation of a unique spiritual culture, which is reflected in the hundreds of *dargahs* (or tombs) of Sufi saints that is visited not only by local members of the community but also by visitors from all over India, and the world. It should be noted that people do not go to the *dargahs* as tourists but with devotion, often with a wish. When the wish is fulfilled, which is often the case, people return to the *dargahs*, and the family stories further build the faith of other people. In Table 7.1, a list of how many *dargahs* are present in which state and city is presented. It is not a comprehensive list, but it does show that *dargahs* are found in most states of India, the highest number of them being in Karnataka (43), Uttar Pradesh (35), Andhra (33), Maharashtra (32), and Gujarat (22). In Mumbai alone, there are 44 listed *dargahs*, and thousands of people visit them everyday.

A recent news report on the Nagore *dargah* in Tamil Nadu captures the importance of these holy places and their contribution toward building community bridges. Hazrat Syed Shahul Hameed was the Sufi saint who lived in Nagore in the sixteenth century, in whose honor this *dargah* was built. The local people refer to the saint as "Nagore Andavar," and he was popularly called Meeran Sahib or Qadir Wali. The tomb was built about 500 years ago and is flanked by five minarets that can be seen from anywhere in the town. Mayilvaganan (2010) reported about the value of the *dargah* in creating religious harmony:

E. Karthikeyan, a Chennai businessman, never fails to make his annual trip to Nagore, a small, crowded pilgrim town in Nagapattinam district. Once in Nagore, Karthikeyan, accompanied by his family, drives straight to the Hazrat Syed Shahul Hameed dargah, popularly known as Nagore dargah, where he offers a heavily brocaded *chadar* (cotton sheet) to the Muslim saint's tomb. "The ritual of presenting the *chadar* started around the year 1900 when my great grandfather Palaniandi Pillai took his family for the Khanduri festival and presented a *chadar*," says Karthikeyan. Karthikeyan is one among the thousands of Hindus who visit the Nagore dargah during the annual Khanduri festival. Palaniandi Pillai, the great-grandfather of Karthikeyan, is supposed to have overcome a debt problem after praying at the saint's tomb. As a mark of gratitude, he built many of the gates at the *dargah* besides making liberal donations. Besides businessmen like him, the Naik rulers of Thanjavur and the Marathas during the later period have also patronized the *dargah*. The Maratha king of Thanjavur, Tulsi Maharaja, donated 4,000 acres of agricultural land for the maintenance of the *dargah*.

> Not just during Khanduri festival, Hindus visit the *dargah* throughout the year to get the blessings of the holy saint. Here, it is the soul of the person that matters and not the religion," says S Syed Kamil Sahib Qadiri, president of the Nagore *dargah*. Even Hindu devotees from Malaysia, Singapore, and Sri Lanka visit the *dargah* regularly, he said. "Where comes the question of religion when all are brethren? asks Syed Kamil Sahib Qadiri.

The spiritual saints create a unique bond among people of various religions, which is akin to having a superordinate goal of visiting the holy place that is equally shared by all. When visiting these places, people lose their intra-religious identities and become part of an intergroup community. The shared emotion of being devotees of the same saint and seeking his or her blessing in the same way help create what Shapiro (2010) calls a relational identity as opposed to social identity (Tajfel & Turner, 1986). This leads to positive feeling for what might have been an outgroup member before coming to the *dargah*. According to Relational Identity Theory (Shapiro, 2002, 2005), people cooperate with each other when their *autonomy* is respected or they are not dominated by the other group member, and when they experience *affiliation* through inclusion (as opposed to exclusion) and feeling of being welcomed (as opposed to treated with indifference or as unwelcomed).

When people go back from the *dargah*, they take positive feelings with them, and when their wish comes true, the positive feelings are further enhanced. Thus, the *dargahs* have probably served the people of India for hundreds of years to resolve identity-based differences emerging from innumerable invasions, and the positive emotions have nurtured relational identities and created social conditions that are impregnated with what Shapiro and Liu (2006) have called "a psychology of stable peace." Thus, the saints in their life and through the *dargahs* after their departure from earth create a unique culture of peace and harmony, which seems to be consistent with recent theoretical developments in intergroup conflict management.

3.5 Structuring Peace

3.5.1 Panchayat System

Panchayat system has existed in India for thousands of years. When a disagreement occurs in a village, five elders are selected to deliberate on the issue, and their decision is accepted by both parties. If one party is known to have erred, this party receives the punishment and pays fine or makes amend so that the grieving party's loss is ameliorated. If the dispute is such that both parties could be right from their own perspectives, the decision made by the panchayat often captures the middle ground so that both parties feel that the solution is fair. When the Allahabad High Court ruled in the *rAma janmabhUmi bAbri masjid* case and allotted one-third of the land to each of the three claimants, some observers said that it was a panchayat-like decision. Thus, there is a general cultural understanding of what a panchayat is and how it works, and people tend to use it in resolving differences in daily life using this principle. The voluntary panchayat system is different from the panchayat that is elected or where the most influential person of the village is chosen as the head of the panchayat. These later-day practices only work depending on the ethical standards and moral character of the panchayat members.

The panchayat system is much like the American jury system where common people deliberate and decide about the affair of other common people involved in a dispute. The difference being, wisdom reflected in age is an important criterion for selecting a *panch* (one of the five members). It can also be likened to the quality circles used in modern Japanese organizations where a group of selected people voluntarily work together to solve an organizational problem in their immediate work area.

One of the biggest advantages of this system is that the decision makers are from the community, are close to the ground, and are likely to have all the information, both hard and soft, objective and subjective. Second, everyone knows about biases that people have, and often the chosen five are different depending on who is involved in the dispute. It is not unusual to invite a respected person from the neighboring village if that is considered optimum. Thus, the decision makers are respected by the disputants, and both parties are willing to put their faith in the hands of these people. Finally, the panchayat is always guided by compassion for the disadvantaged. So, if the person who is at fault cannot afford to pay the fine, or compensate for the damages, nonfinancial solutions are often crafted.

3.5.2 Celebrating Differences

India is one of the few countries that celebrates religious diversity by granting national holidays to celebrate important festivals. Unlike most countries that only celebrate Christian, Muslim, or Buddhist holidays, India celebrates all of them. India has 17 national holidays. It includes 5 Hindu, 4 Muslim, 3 national days, 2 Christian (Christmas and Good Friday), 1 Buddhist, 1 Jain, and 1 Sikh holiday. The three national holidays (Republic Day, January 26th; Independence Day, August 15th; and Gandhi Jayanti, October 2nd) are nonreligious in nature. The other 14 holidays are chosen by the states depending on which festival people in that state popularly celebrate, and vary across them. For example, Pongal (January 15) is celebrated in Tamil Nadu, Andhra, and Karnataka; Rath Yatra (July 4) in Orissa; Ganesh Chaturthi (September 3) in Maharashtra; and

Guru Teg Bahadur's Martydrom day (November 24) in Punjab. The states have additional holidays beyond the 17 national holidays (See Tables 7.1 and 7.2 in Appendix 1). This does provide a structure for religious inclusion, which is missing in many other countries, and contributes to peace and understanding.

4 Absence of Peace in India

Researchers have looked at peace as the absence of war or structural violence. I would like to present it as the absence of peace, as noted earlier, and examine how despite thousands of years of culture of peace, India also sees an absence of peace across the country, for one reason or another, and much of it could be labeled ethnic conflict in the traditional sense. History of conflict (Triandis et al., 1994) can be traced in almost all the cases, but only if we shift history of peace to our blind spot. Otherwise, the conflicts can also be viewed as social attempts to address multiple issues facing this multicultural society. Absence of peace becomes a signal for people to resolve differences to go back to the peaceful state, which is natural.

If we use history as an analytical tool to examine peace and absence of peace, we would have to start with how the different ethnic groups came together in India, and how they interacted with each other. Dinkar (1956) analyzed the development of Indian culture over thousands of years and broke it into four phases or chapters, which is consistent with the generally accepted historical perspective that the roots of Indian culture as it stands today can be traced to at least 4,000 years (Basham, 1954; Rizvi, 1987). This continuity, which is not found in other ancient cultures such as Egypt, Mesopotamia, or Greece, is what led Basham to call his book, *The Wonder that was India* (1954). The first phase was the merger of Dravidian and Aryan populations into a community that came to be known as Hindus, maintaining numerous variations within itself that was noted in the introduction of the chapter earlier. Whether these two communities were originally from what is north and south India today, or they came from elsewhere, and who came first are less important than the fact that people of these two cultures learned from each other and created a synthetic shared culture, allowing as many differences as needed for people to function effectively in their ecological niche. This phase lasted anywhere from 7000 bce to 500 bce, to the time of Buddha.

The second phase was the religious reform presented by Buddha in 500 bce, which planted the seeds of change in the Indian culture. Despite many similarities between Hinduism and Buddhism in both philosophy and practice, Buddha's thoughts did question the status quo, adding a source of disharmony to the cultural mix. This phase lasted roughly from the time of Buddha until the arrival of the Muslim invaders from the middle-east in the thirteenth century (Basham, 1954; Dinkar, 1956; Rizvi, 1987). Considering that only 0.8% of the Indian population is Buddhist and that there are more Buddhists outside India than in India, it could be argued that India exported Buddhism, and within India it merged or morphed with Hinduism. Thus, this second phase could be viewed as less significant culturally than it is thought to be.

It is also likely that following Adi Shankar's successful restoration of *Advaita Vedanta,* which is as iconoclastic as Buddhism, as the crown jewel of *vedic dharma* in the ninth century ce, Buddhist philosophy lost its appeal to people of India. In other words, the internal reform of Hinduism that Adi Shankar brought about led to the integration of various schools of thoughts, making Buddhist revision secondary. Some modern scholars like the Late Raghunath Sharma have integrated Buddhism into the *sanAtan dharma* by proclaiming that Buddha indeed is Lord *viSNu*, and cogently argued that the teachings of Buddha are consistent with those of the *upaniSads* (athedaM viditamastu prekSAv-aTAM buddho hi bhagavAn viSUnH, Pandey, 2001, p. 39). Upadhyaya (1977) presents much evidence from the *purANas* to show how Buddha is accepted in Hinduism as the ninth incarnation of Vishnu.

The third phase was the 500-year rule in India by many dynasties of Muslim rulers and invaders including the Turks, Afghans, and Moguls, leading to cultural interaction between Hindus and Muslims. Many early invaders came to plunder the wealth of India, and the first ugly contact with foreigners occurred during this time when the invaders went beyond pillage to destruction and burning of temples and educational institutions. Eventually, this led to the emergence of the Moguls, and the majority Hindus learned to live in a Muslim-ruled community. But the transformation of India from a rural community to a mix of rural and urban society occurred in this phase, and this has important implications for the primarily urban ethnic conflict of today.

The fourth phase started when the English arrived in Surat in 1608 and received formal approval to do trade from Jehangir in 1613 (Rizvi, 1987) after visiting his court in Agra. This laid the foundation of the colonization of India by the British and eventually led to the British Raj (or rule by the British) starting in the eighteenth century. The 300-year experience with the British and the Europeans presented a new experience of intercultural interaction that was different in that the European culture was the most distant from the Indian culture. This period offered new ideas for social change. For example, the caste system had earlier been challenged by spiritual masters like Kabir and Nanak, but it got challenged again by other reformers like Dayanand Sarasvati, who founded the Arya Samaj. Besides these spiritual challengers of the caste system, which was quite acceptable to the Hindu population since even in *sanAtan dharma*, a *sannyAsi* or monk lives outside the social system and does not follow the social norms, there were also some social leaders who challenged the caste system, and some of them came from the upper caste, whereas others were non-Brahmins.

For example, in Maharashtra, the first reform movement *Paramahansa Mandali* (the Society of Supreme Being) was founded about a decade before the first revolution, and the second one, *Prarthana Samaj* (the Prayer Society), was founded about a decade after the revolution. These movements were followed by one that was led by a *Mali* or gardener's son in Pune, Jotirao Phule, who first started a school for girls of Shudra caste when he was barely 21 years of age. He later joined a missionary school as a teacher and published his play "*Trutiya Ratna*" or the Third Jewel (1855), and then two *powadas* (or poetry written in veer rasa or one that arouses heroism or gives adrenaline rush) in 1869, "*Chatrapati Shivaji Raje Bhonsle Yancha*" (1869) and "*Vidyakhathatil Bramhan Pantoji.*" He wrote *Gulamgiri* (or Slavery) in 1873, and founded the *Satyashodhak Samaj* (the Truth Seeking Society) in the same year. His criticism of the caste system came through his writings and it eventually took the form of a social movement (O'Hanlon, 1985).

These four (or three if we accept that the role of Buddhism was not that significant) phases offer interesting opportunity to learn about intercultural interactions. The Indian culture emerged from the assimilation of two different ethnic communities, the Dravidians and the Aryans, and then dealt with an internal reform presented by Buddhism. This was followed by invasions by people from the neighboring communities of Afghanistan, Iran, Turkey, and Mongolia, who also brought a new religion and a new worldview. And finally, the Indian culture faced interaction with people from overseas who were culturally the most distant, and were colonizers or a new breed of cultural invaders.

The conflict between Afghans, Turks, Persians, and Mongols over territory was no different from the conflict between the Hindu Kings, and power struggle between Muslim and Hindu rulers were often also about resource and not about religion. A major exception would be the discriminatory practice of *jizya* or poll tax that was imposed by the Muslim rulers over the Hindu population, which was lifted by Akbar in 1564, and later imposed by Aurangzeb again in 1659. The trauma of forced conversion from Hinduism to Islam and the fear of persecution were probably the worst cultural events of Indian history that happened in the third phase, which is quite recent considering that culture is superorganic (Kroeber, 1950) and lives beyond one human life. However, it should also be noted that personal relationships enriched Muslim and Hindu rulers and leaders, and many examples of this can be found in the history. For example, the seventh Sikh Guru Har Ray was a close friend of Dara Shukoh, the older brother of Aurangzeb, and his son Rama Ray was Aurangzeb's friend, though Aurangzeb is not well remembered for beheading Guru Teg Bahadur, the ninth Sikh Guru (Rizvi, 1987).

It is important to keep this brief template of Indian cultural history in mind to understand how peace continued to be negotiated in the rulers' courts over India's long history, and flourished among the vast rural population irrespective of who the rulers were, locally or in Delhi. All conflicts in India have a long history, and what may be religious conflict today could be traced to caste or class conflict of the past. It should also be noted that much of the conflict in India's recorded history was about personal gain, rather than ethnic conflict. For example, Aurangzeb executed his own brother Dara and his younger son Siphir Shukoh on the ground that he was a heretic for stating in his book *Majma'u `l-bahrayn* that Islam and Hinduism were twin brothers (Rizvi, 1987).

Modern day conflicts have their roots not only in history but also in recent social disparities, despite a modern constitution that ensures equal opportunity rights for all citizens by making a number of provisions, and has outlawed untouchability. Part III of the Indian Constitution enshrines fundamental rights. For example, article 14 ensures equality before the law and equal protection by the law; article 15 prohibits discrimination on the grounds of religion, race, caste, sex, and place of birth; article 21 guarantees protection of life and personal liberty through the legal system; article 25 provides the right to freely profess, practice, and propagate religion; article 26 grants right to manage religious institutions subject to public order, morality, and health; article 29 protects minorities' right to conserve their language, script, or culture; article 30 grants minorities a right to establish and administer educational institutions of their choice and the state must not discriminate against such institutions in granting aid; article 341 authorizes the President of India to specify "castes, races or tribes which shall for the purposes of this constitution be deemed to be Scheduled Castes"; and article 350A directs the State to provide facilities for instruction in the mother tongue at the primary stage of education.

The First Amendment to the Constitution passed in 1951 allowed the state to make special provision for advancement of socially and educationally backward classes of citizens of the Scheduled Castes and Scheduled Tribes. The government of India monitors the advancement of minorities and constitutes commissions (or committees) periodically to take stock of their state. For example, the Prime Minister of India formed a high level commission on March 9, 2005, to prepare a report on the social, economic, and educational status of Muslim community in India under the leadership of Justice Rajender Sachar.

The seven-member committee addressed the more general question of how different Socio-Religious Communities (SRCs) in India have fared in availing the development opportunities presented by the central and state governments, with a special issue on the Muslim population, and submitted its report on November 17, 2006, which constitutes the most recent report prepared for the central government of India. The committee advertised its intention to have public hearing sessions all over India using more than a hundred dailies all over the country, and visited 14 of the states, namely, Andhra Pradesh, Karnataka, Uttar Pradesh, Rajasthan, Jammu & Kashmir, Assam, West Bengal, Delhi, Kerala, Madhya Pradesh, Gujarat, Bihar, and Maharashtra. It had planned but could not visit Tamil Nadu, Jharkhand, and Lakshadweep. They collected data from central and state government agencies to supplement their public hearing data. The all-men committee immediately realized that it needed to pay special attention to listen to the voice of women, and so they spent much effort in organizing a one half-day meeting exclusively with women in all states, and a full-day meeting in New Delhi with women from all over India. They also invited women social activists to all the meetings they held all over the country (Sachar Committee Report, 2006).

In the meetings with people all over India, the issue that was brought to the attention of the committee most frequently was that of education, followed by others related to reservation, employment, and security. The committee noted three issues that Muslims and other SRCs face in India – identity crises, insecurity (e.g., lack of protection from law-enforcing agencies), and inequity (e.g., unequal access to education, employment, credit, infrastructure, and government programs, and participation in the political process), and submitted recommendations to address these concerns. The most pervasive of these is the one that deals with their identity. The Muslim population in India constantly faces a two-pronged discrimination from other communities resulting from their prejudice that Muslims are "antinational" and "appeased" by the government machinery. Many Muslim men are identifiable because of their beard and the *topi* (or cap) and are subjected to unreasonable security-related enquiries that other people do not have to go through. Similarly, Muslim women are visible because of their *burqua* or veil, and complain about mistreatment in the public space including the market, schools, public transportation, and hospitals. Muslim identity adversely affects access to property for rental or purchase and children's access to good schools (Sachar Report, 2006).

The fact that Muslims have served in the Indian Military and fought battles against Pakistan with valor and have been recognized for the same is neglected by the majority of the population. Of the 20 recipients of *Param Vir Charka*, the highest military honor given by the Indian military, 14 are Hindus, 3 are Sikhs, one is a Muslim (Company Qualrter-Master Havildar Abdul Hamid), one is a Parsi (Lieutenant Colonel Ardeshir Burzarji Tarapore), and one is a Christian (Lance Naik Albert Ekka). Other Muslims recognized for their valor include 3 *Kirti Chakra* and 23 (of the 1,082) *Shaurya Chakra* winners, among others. Despite these achievements, the media often paints the Muslims as "terrorists," which perpetuates the negative stereotype of Muslims being antinational. That the Muslim population is "appeased" or favored by the government and other institutions also does not hold up to scrutiny, since the Muslim population still constitutes of largely poor people employed in the informal sectors. Media does little to educate the public of these facts.

Muslims are not tied to the Hindu caste system; however, the committee noted that 0.8% of the Muslims did report affiliation to Scheduled Caste (SC) and an even smaller population categorized themselves as Scheduled Tribe (ST). Though this is a small category that the committee did not consider important as a category for their analysis, there may be some value in addressing the needs of these populations since their needs are much like that of other Dalits or Harijans. The committee noted that a number of parliamentary and assembly seats that are reserved for SC/ST people are in areas that are represented more by the Muslim population, and hence the Muslim population in these areas do not receive a fair representation in the political process. According to the 55th and 61st rounds of data collected by the National Sample Survey Organization (NSSO), the proportion of what is called Other Backward Class (OBC), which does not include SC/ST population, is about the same among Muslim and Hindu populations – about 41% of Muslims identified themselves as OBC in 2004–2005 compared to 32% in 1999–2000, whereas the number among the Hindus was 43% in 2004–2005 compared to 38% in 1999–2000. People recognized as belonging to SC/ST categories in 2004–2005 across India constitute about 31%.

One of the recommendations of Sachar committee was to enhance services related to all aspects of education, access to credit and government programs, and employment opportunities in both public and private sectors. The committee also stressed the need for efficacious delivery of all services related to education, health, and so forth through NGOs and other community initiatives like streamlining the waqf properties, which are Muslim endowments for religious or charitable purposes. Besides these specific measures and the need to collect data periodically regarding the state of the minorities and Muslims in India and to increase their participation in the political process, the committee also recommended that there was a need to enhance legal basis for providing equal opportunities by going beyond the National Human Rights Commission (NHRC) and the National Commission for Minorities (NCM) to the creation of an Equal Opportunity Commission

(EOC) similar to the UK Race Relations Act of 1976. The historical background and the information provided by the Sachar committee provide a useful backdrop for examining caste, religion, and regional conflicts in India.

4.1 Caste-Based Conflict

Caste is derived from *varNAzrama dharma*, and the four major *varNas* are *Brahmins*, *Kshatriyas*, *Vaishyas*, and *Shudras*, each with a traditionally dominant and prescribed job, to learn and teach, to protect and rule, to involve in agriculture and trade, and to do the cleaning jobs, respectively. The caste system as practiced in India today did not exist in the *vedic* times (Basham, 1954; Dinkar, 1956), and the only reference to caste in the *Rgveda* is to be found in the Purusha Sukta, which too is argued to be of a later origin based on its grammatical structure (Dinkar, 1956). Critics of caste system find fault in a verse in this prayer where it is said that the *Brahmins* constitute the head of the Divine Person, the *Kshatriyas* the arms, *Vaishyas* the trunk or torso, and the *Shudras* the feet. This classification has been viewed as derogatory to the Shudras. However, in the holistic Indian worldview, the human body parts are not arranged in any hierarchy as they can only function together. In another prayer in the *durgA saptazatI*, *brahmA*, the creator of the trinity (*viSNu* is the protector and *ziva* is the destructor), is said to be the feet of Goddess *durgA* (Bhawuk, 2011).

A modern definition of dominant caste was presented by Srinivas (1987), which included six characteristics, namely, ownership of many acres of agricultural land, large population size, seniority in local hierarchy, education, urban sources of income, and employment in the government. In the last 100 years, education has become Western and English based, but before that it was still in Sanskrit, Persian, or Arabic. The population has also become mobile now, but it was more local, with little migration over generations. Today, class has cut across the caste system, and economic power is not only in the hand of the upper castes, but also in the hands of many families that came from trade castes such as fishermen, carpenters, potters, and so forth. Thus, a mixture of caste and class structure (Mukherjee, 2000) can be found even in villages.

The traditional caste system in India is viewed as a source of conflict, despite its peaceful existence over thousands of years. Peaceful existence sounds questionable from today's perspective, perhaps even unconscionable that anybody can imagine that people can live peacefully under such a rigid hierarchical system. I am neither in support of the caste system, nor do I think that it should be perpetuated in any form. But to blame it for absence of peace may not be accurate. Indian villages have primarily been in peace for thousands of years, with people accepting and living within their caste-defined roles and boundaries. Even the lowest of caste has important social functions. For example, the Doams who live in villages in Bihar and are untouchables provide bamboo baskets and other products that are used by Brahmin families for auspicious occasions like the sacred thread ceremony and marriage. The Doams also provide fire for cremation, and without the fire coming from their home, the Brahmin's final rites and passage to the other world are considered incomplete. In spirit, though it might have been lost in practice, the caste system was guided by the basic principle of *dharma* – everybody did his or her *dharma* or duty as guided by their phase of life and caste. Thus, one pursued *mokSa* or liberation through the *varnAzrama dharma*, and the focus on the spiritual growth allowed the society to function peacefully in effect through, or despite, the caste system. What is important to note is that the Indian villages have remained in peace over the past 1,000 years despite Islamic and British influence, and the absence of peace could be as much due to the Western-style economic development as due to rapid social change.

Caste system has been blamed for most of India's social problems, and perhaps rightly so. However, India never saw a Marxist revolution, or anything like that, before Marx explicated his theory of conflict of social class. One reason could be because the castes were not drawn to exploit and dominate others, but for the functioning of the society, where everybody was guided by his or her *dharma*. The most privileged and the highest of the castes, the Brahmins, were supposed to involve in learning and teaching and were not to pursue material goods. For example, as late as 1950, a world-class Sanskrit scholar was known to have only two *dhotis* (to change one everyday) and two blankets (one to sleep on and one to use as a cover) in his possession (Indra Vidyavachaspati, 2007). This scholar earned a lot of wealth for his children, but his simple lifestyle did not change to the end. His son, an equally well-known scholar, toward the end of his life told his son that it really did not matter if he ate food cooked by a *chAndAl* (or an untouchable).

A learned Brahmin did rise above the caste system and devote himself or herself to the pursuit of knowledge. Thus, the Brahmins were at peace with themselves and also contributed to peace around them. It is instructive to quote a verse from the *manusmRti* (2–162), which describes how a Brahmin should act: *sammAnAd-brAmhaNo nityamudvijet viSAdiva; amRtasyeva AkANcheda avamAnasya sarvadA* – A Brahmin should be agitated when he or she receives honor as if he has been served poison; he or she should always desire insult like nectar. Clearly, if Brahmins were to follow this behavioral prescription, they would not only grow as kind and compassionate people, but also create harmony in the society. And to such Brahmins, *Manusmriti* bestows much privileges. Chanakya was a Brahmin who practiced such high standard and is known to have walked away from royal honor when his protégé, Chandragupta Maurya, became the king of Magadha, the most powerful kingdom in 4 bce (Dinkar, 1956).

It should not surprise serious scholars to find that Buddha, who is viewed as an iconoclast and a rebel Hindu thinker, spent the most number of verses in describing who a Brahmin is in his *dhammapAda* (Bhawuk, 2009). The *dhammapAda* has 26 chapters, most of them with 10–12 verses, except *yamakvaggo* (20 verses), *malavaggo* (21 verses), *bhikkhuvaggo* (23 verses), and *taNhAvaggo* (26 verses). The last chapter *bramhaNavaggo* has 41 verses and in 31 of them, Buddha says *tamahaM brUmi brAmhaNam* (or I call him a Brahmin), defining the qualities of a Brahmin. Rahula (1959) presented four of these and three are presented here to demonstrate how Buddha viewed a noble Brahmin of deeds, not by birth: "He for whom there exists neither this shore nor the other shore, nor both, he who is undistressed and unborn, him I call a Brahmin; he whose destiny neither the gods nor demigods nor men do know, he who has destroyed defilements and become worthy, him I call a Brahmin; he who knows former lives, who sees heaven and hell, who has reached the end of births and attained to super-knowledge, the sage, accomplished with all accomplishment, him I call a Brahmin" (Rahula, 1959, p. 136).

Gandhijee had no patience for untouchability and the social evil of the caste system. However, he did see some virtue in *varnAzrama dharma*, and in his interpretation, it provided the foundation of a cooperative village society in which people performed their own functions and thus were divided into castes for that reason, but all were equal irrespective of what they did for a living (Brown, 1969; Dalton 1967; Prabhu, 1962, 1964). It may be difficult to understand Gandhijee's perspective if we only look at it on a social plane, where he tested all his spiritual ideas and experiences. Gandhijee was dedicated to the *bhagavadgitA* and read parts of it every day, and even wrote his commentary on it (*Gita-Mata*, Gandhi, 1930). *bhagavadgitA* supports the idea of *varnAzrama dharma*, and so instead of rejecting the idea, it was more meaningful to him to interpret it in the modern context. For a *karmayogi* that Gandhijee was, rejecting *varnAzrama dharma* completely amounted to throwing the baby with the bathwater, or much of the useful lessons of the *bhagavadgitA* for the not-so-useful caste system.

The caste system also supported his basic idea of decentralization which can be found in Gandhijee's writing in *Harijan* from 1942, as cited by Hussain (1959, p. 36) – "The end to be sought is human happiness combined with full mental and moral growth. This end can be achieved under decentralization. Centralization as a system is inconsistent with the non-violent structure of society." It is plausible that Gandhijee accepted only the spirit of the caste system and attempted to bring about a slow cultural transformation, since it constituted such a basic component of the Indian social structure. It is prudent to bring about a slow change in the cultural value system to be effective, and practices do get dropped aside as new practices take root. Indeed, in the towns and cities, caste system is less pronounced today than in the villages in India. Thus, it made sense for Gandhijee to interpret the caste system for building a new society by retaining the good and discarding the unacceptable (e.g., untouchability).

Table 7.6 in Appendix 6 shows an interesting fact about the presence of caste system in India today. The Hindus are known to be laden by the caste system and even today there are 22% of them who identify themselves as belonging to Scheduled Caste, 9% of them to Scheduled Tribe, and 43% of them to OBC.[4] Seventy percent of Hindus identify themselves in these non-favorable social categories. What is intriguing is that despite converting to Buddhism, 90% of them identify themselves as belonging to Scheduled Castes and 7% to Scheduled Tribes. Clearly, dumping Hinduism has not helped these neo-Buddhists raise their self-esteem to simply deny such humiliating affiliation with the caste system. One may argue that it is in their best interest to affiliate with such castes for economic benefits, and hence the association. The simple observation to be made is that changing the name does not solve the problem. The problem is educational and economic disadvantage, and converting to another religion is not a solution.

Table 7.6 also shows that even the hardworking Sikhs have 31% of their members from scheduled caste and 22% in OBC, which is half the Sikh population. This is so much in contrast with the image of Sikhs as a hardworking, self-respecting, and proud community. Despite Guru Nanak's (1469–1539) effort to erase the caste system, half of the Sikhs still associate themselves with schedule caste and OBC. Jains and Zoroastrians are the only religious groups without any scheduled caste population, which clearly shows that these religions did not attempt to convert lower caste Hindus. Among Indian Christians, 9% belong to scheduled caste, 33% to scheduled tribes, and 25% to OBC. Thus, 57% of Indian Christians are still waiting for social change, though they have changed their religion. Thus, India offers an interesting case of how caste permeates even the casteless religious groups. This understanding should help us better understand caste conflict in India.

It is also illustrative to note how communities are formed in India across caste and class boundaries. Natrajan (2005) studied a *Kumbhkar Samaj* or community of potters in the state of Chhattisgarh (west of Orissa and east of Madhya Pradesh), using ethnographic approach to explore the dynamics of how caste and class interact in the creation of a community. This community cannot be viewed exclusively in caste or class terms. It is unlike a craft or trade association found in the West in function, yet is organized into local, state, and national levels like a trade federation. Across the nation, this community is only tied through caste association, and varies in languages spoken and food habits. Natrajan (2005) insightfully noted that in general, a lot of **class diversity** can be found among people of *upper castes*, whereas much more **caste diversity** can be found among the *lower classes* in India.

The incidences of crime against people of lower caste or scheduled caste are low, about 2.9% (national average). But some states have more of these crimes than other. For example, Uttar Pradesh had almost one-fourth and Madhya Pradesh had about one-fifth of the nation's crime in this category in 2008. To get a better understanding of ethnic conflict, we need to go beyond such averages and look into the details of caste-based conflicts. To this end, findings of a study done on communalism or ethnic conflicts in Tamil Nadu covering the period 1979–1991 (Ravichandran, 2001) are presented here. In this study, it was found that most conflicts were caste based and at the community level, but they all started with interpersonal interactions and had a history of interpersonal conflict,

[4] "Scheduled" in "Scheduled Caste/Scheduled Tribe" refers to the schedule of the constitution that includes certain communities as disadvantaged group of people, and provides affirmative action type of protection to them in education and employment.

with origin in conflict about resource sharing. The author created a data base from the Madurai edition of a Tamil daily newspaper, *Dinamani*, which has a reputation of being "sober" or noninflammatory. Newspapers avoid reporting the names of people involved in the conflict to avoid escalation of violence, since names would give away the caste of people. The author supported the primary data from this newspaper from other published sources as well as the Proceedings of the Tamil Nadu Legislative Assembly and Legislative Council. He collected information about 341 conflicts and analyzed them systematically. When needed, he visited the sites to obtain authentic information about the conflicts and damage caused by them (Ravichandran, 2001).

Caste conflicts constituted the biggest portion of the total (268 or 79%), and religious conflicts accounted for the rest (73 or 21%). Of these, most conflicts lasted only a day (275 or 80%), and a small portion of the conflicts lingered on for months (8 or 2%), weeks (16 or 5%), or a few days (42 or 12%). Most of these conflicts occurred in villages (256 or 75%), and next were small towns (71 or 21%), with cities accounting for the least number of them (14 or 4%). Since the population distribution between rural and urban areas in the state of Tamil Nadu is about 3:1, the proportion of conflict seems to be larger for villages than for towns and cities. This may indicate that there is some blurring of caste in the towns and cities, leading to the decrease in caste-based conflicts. Of the 341 conflicts, only one reached the state level, five reached the district level, two the subdistrict (called *tAluk*) level, and only 10 reached even the village level. In other words, most caste conflicts remain as local events. What is more important to note is that conflicts are resolved quickly (since most of them last only one day). Ravichandran (2001) attributed this to wisdom and self-restraint of the people in the community as well as quick intervention by the police and administration.

Of the 268 caste-based conflicts, almost three-fourths were between Harijans and other caste (195 or 73%), 61 or 23% among different castes, and only a few (8 or 3%) between Brahmins and non-Brahmins. Conflicts between fishermen and other people accounted for only 4 (or 1.5%) of the conflicts. Ravichandran (2001) attributed these conflicts to limited economic opportunities, interference by politician vying for votes of various caste groups, fear of losing social status experienced by upper caste people, refusal of following old social status quo or nonacceptance of the dominance of higher caste people by Harijans, and history of conflict between the communities. However, previous enmity accounted for the largest proportion (74 or 28%), highlighting the importance of interpersonal peace. Long-term rivalry and previous clash appeared to be long-term causes of conflict in many of the conflicts recorded in this study. Thus, if interpersonal differences are addressed in the community, then the community is less likely to see a major conflict involving many people divided on the basis of caste identities. Other reasons included disputes over celebration of festivals, business altercations, conflict related to public procession, dispute over place of worship, and so forth. Obstructing Harijans to enter a certain area, place of worship, or burial ground can still become a source of conflict, though only in a few cases (9 of 278).

Much of the violence is physical in nature, and people use stones and sticks to fight. There is a complete absence of sophisticated weapons in these conflicts. Cases in which property damage were reported accounted for 36% (123 of 341), and the ones that suffered the most damage included setting fire to houses, which occurred in 64 cases (Ravichandran, 2001). In the 341 conflicts that occurred over 12 years, 78 lives were lost. It appears that in these conflicts, people are more inclined to damage property rather than cause death, which indicates that the outgroup is not dehumanized or "othered" to the extreme that killing could be rationalized as not immoral.

Violent crimes create insecurity and fear, and affect public peace. They constitute about 11% of all crimes in India according to recent trends in crime, and crime rate is found to be lagging population growth (Crime Statistics, 2008). All large and populous states of India have more than ten thousand violent crimes according to crime statistics for 2008, except Gujarat (7,116), Haryana (5,671), Chhattisgarh (5,367), Jharkhand (8,686), and Assam (9,791).[5] However, rate of violent crimes (per one hundred thousand people) was the lowest in Gujarat (12.6), Punjab (13.6), Uttar Pradesh (14), and Andhra Pradesh (14.9), and the highest in Manipur (46), Kerala (33.1), Assam (32.2), Jammu and Kashmir (30.9), Arunachal Pradesh (29.3), Jharkhand (28.8), Pondicherry (27.5), Daman and Diu (27.5), Tripura (26.4), and Orissa (26.2). Other states are in the middle range of 15–25, namely, Bihar (24.7), Dadra and Nagar Haveli (24.5), Haryana (23.7), Delhi (23.1), Karnataka (22.8), Madhya Pradesh (22.5), Maharashtra (21.3), Meghalaya (19.5), West Bengal (18.7), Tamil Nadu (15.8), and Sikkim (15.3). So, if we use the findings of the study done by Ravichandran (2001) in Tamil Nadu presented above as a proxy for India, then caste-based conflict is likely to be the largest ethnic conflict in India, some states would have fewer than others.

It seems that these conflicts can be handled by the existing administrative system, and the situation could be further improved by having social organizations mediate the peace-building process in the daily interactions of people. Resource sharing in the community is likely to be more effective through a social process rather than through legislation, especially since all the necessary laws of equality among people of different castes are already in place. It is worthwhile to note here that Amul as a cooperative has done much to ameliorate the discriminatory effects of the caste system in Gujarat (Bhawuk, Mrazek, & Munusamy, 2009) without really addressing caste system directly. Other self-help groups in the rural areas near Lucknow, Uttar Pradesh, have been able to achieve similar outcomes by focusing on poverty alleviation and social change without addressing caste-related issues directly (Vidyarthi & Wilson, 2008). Thus, there is some support for the idea that caste-related conflict can be better addressed in the community locally than by the central or regional government.

4.2 Hindu and Muslim Conflict

Considering the history of Sufism in India, it is accurate to say that Hindus and Muslims have now lived in peace for hundreds of years. People flocking the *dargahs* today, and even during the times of riots in India, shows that there is sufficient understanding and tolerance between Hindus and Muslims to live peacefully with each other. Before we examine the absence of peace or conflict between these two communities, let us examine the long tradition of peace. Historically speaking, the spirit of religious syncretism characterized the ethos of precolonial India, which was blessed by Muslim and Hindu rulers alike (Rizvi, 1987).

For example, the Maratha ruler Mahaji Sindhia was a disciple of Mansur Shah, and his son, Daulat Rao Sindia, paid his tribute to Bala Qadir, the son of Mansur Shah (Bayly, 1985). The Sindhias and Holkars also gave generously to the Pirzadas of Sheikh Moin-ud-Din Chisti at Ajmer. Similarly, the nawabs of Awadha supported the holy places of Mathura and Ayodhya, and the nawab of Arcot in South India supported not only the shrine of Shahul Hamid Sahib in Nagore, but also the temples of Chidambaram and Tirupati. Tipu Sultan, who is known for attacking the temple in Srirangapatna in Karnataka to send a message to the Nayars, did have Brahmin administrators in his court, Hindu Beyadaru warriors in his force, and also supported the Tirupati temple (Hasan, 1971).

[5] In 2008, the eastern states had the least number of violent crimes: Sikkim, 91; Meghalaya, 497; Tripura, 931; Mizoram, 166; Manipur 1,213; Nagaland, 377; and Arunachal Pradesh, 363. Assam had, with 9, 691 incidents, had the highest number in the eastern region. Lakshadweep (18), Daman and Diu (52), Dadra & Nagar Haveli (65), Chandigarh (239), Pondicherry (297), and Goa (308) were other geographic areas with small number of incidences. States with incidences in the range of 1–5,000 included Jammu and Kashmir (3,864), Punjab (3,639), Uttarakhand (1,573), and Himachal Pradesh (1,284). Twelve states with more than ten thousands incidences of violent crimes during 2008 included Tamil Nadu (10,518), Kerala (11,363), Karnataka (13,128), Andhra Pradesh (12,275), Maharashtra (22,862), Orissa (10,478), West Bengal (16,504), Bihar (23,247), Uttar Pradesh (26,921), Madhya Pradesh (15,663), and Rajasthan (10,127). Total number of incidences all over India for 2008 was 228, 663 (Crime Statistics, 2008).

In precolonial India during 1700–1860, Hindu–Muslim conflicts were local outcomes of actions initiated by the rulers to make a general policy statement (Bayly, 1985). Temples and mosques were demolished by rulers, and that could start a reactionary conflict among people in that community. Some conflicts had origin in business communities competing for business privileges and others had landlords competing for land and control of power that came with it (Yang, 1980). Conflicts primarily occurred when the local governments were going through transition during the precolonial period, and it became worse when merchants and artisans became more mobile. Thus, it seems that politics rather than religious faith has been the cause of religious conflict in India. Some blame the British policy of divide and rule for this. Still others (Brass, 1974) argue that the relationship between groups of people is grounded in real or objective transactions, which acquire symbolic meaning over time, and thus we need to understand the interaction between the objective and subjective elements of culture to appreciate the source of intergroup conflicts. These objective and subjective elements that people construct are the building blocks of culture (Triandis, 1972).

The form of Hindu–Muslim conflicts changed after 1857, and their frequency increased significantly. The riot of 1893 in Basantpur is examined here to show how the dynamics between the two communities changed after the first independence movement of India in 1857. Yang (1979, 1980) and Freitag (1980) presented much of the information and background necessary to analyze this incident, and though I fully agree with his analysis that ethnic conflicts are complex and should not be analyzed by imposing dichotomous variables like religious (Hindu versus Muslim), economic (rich versus poor), or social (Harijan versus Brahmins or other higher castes) variables, I think he misses some important historical aspects that were at play in this incident. I also agree with him that identities are complex in themselves, and to view them as dichotomous is not useful (see also Sen, 2006).

After the first independence movement of 1857, the Hindus and Muslims learned to work together against the common aggressor, the British. However, the Hindus also realized that it was time for them to get their country and culture back from the Muslims and the British. The time was ripe for reclaiming India from the Muslim rulers who had been present in Orissa, Assam, and the southern states for about 300 years from 1570 to 1857, rather than 500 years, which was true for the other northern states. The period of 1890s saw many conflicts, and that can be viewed as the precursor of Indian freedom movement, starting with the formation of the Indian National Association in 1876 by Surendra Nath Bannerjee and Anandmohan Bose, which later morphed into the Indian National Congress in 1885 led by Dadabhai Naoroji and others in Mumbai (McLane, 1977).

In 1882, the Hindus started the *gaurakSini sabhA* or cow protection society, which quickly became the cow protection movement rapidly spreading all over northern India, starting in Punjab, where Arya Samaj was strong (Freitag, 1980; Pinney, 1997; Yang, 1980). A practical aspect of this movement was to create *gaushalas* or shelters for cows, much like the animal shelters found today in many parts of the world, which are run much like the Humane Society in the USA. The Hindu community made contributions to create and support these shelters. The champions of this cause were called *gau-swamis* (or masters of cow) who viewed cow protection as their *dharma* or calling and worked tirelessly, traveling to places to raise awareness of the cause. Yang (1980) considers cow protection as an antecedent of creating a Hindu identity, whereas I think this was a consequence of an already existing complex Hindu identity in which the cow occupied a significant space as *gau mata or* mother cow.

To outsiders, the association with an animal may seem like a small issue, a rather artificial and make-believe contraption of the Hindu identity. But cow not only occupies a central place in Indian rural economy and society, but also has well-established cultural moorings. Cow is the symbol of Laxmi, the goddess of wealth. A cow is given in *dAn* (or charity) to a Brahmin during the final rites when somebody dies, for it is said that one crosses the river *vaitaraNi* that separates the two worlds by holding the tail of a cow. Krishna was also called Gopal (or the protector of cow) or Govinda (the friend of cow), and in the *bhagavadgitA* (10.28), Krishna says, "I am *kAmadhenu* (the mythical cow that could give whatever one wished) among cows," thus merging himself with cow and providing it a central place in the life of all Hindus. The *Bhaja Govindam* written by Adi Shankar and the *Gita Govindam* by Jai Deva are famous devotional songs and pray to Govinda or Krishna. Mirabai's *bhajans* (spiritual songs) end with "*mere to giridhar gopAl dusaro na koi*" (or, I do not have anybody other than Gopal), implying a complete surrender to Krishna. The mountain that Krishna lifts to protect his clan from the wrath of Indra was called *govardhan*, or one that helps cows to multiply or grow in number. Cow is also associated with Lord Shiva who rides the bull called *Nandi*, and Nandi is worshipped in all Shiva temples including the one in Honolulu, USA, today. Cow is holy, and even its excrement is used for purification and has many uses in *Ayurveda*. Thus, cow permeates the Hindu life in a complex way and, therefore, is a natural part of his or her identity. This is true even today, and the sentiment must have been stronger in 1890s, 33 years after the first independence movement of 1857. This was captured in many pictures of cow that were created and circulated during the cow protection movement (Pinney, 1997).

As such issues always do, the cow protection movement divided the Muslim and Hindu communities. Muslims had started sacrificing cows instead of goats during Bakr-Id festival, and cow protection conflicted with this. This issue led the Hindus to boycott the Muslims in other activities in the villages. For example, the Muslims no longer could get their corn popped by the grain-parcher in the same pot in some villages and they were also barred from using the wells (Yang, 1980). These were practices that had kept the two communities together in peace in rural India for hundreds of years, which started to change. Hindus had also worked closely with the Muslims in preparing the *taziahs* during Muharram and always joined them in the procession of *taziahs*, but now they started boycotting them (Yang, 1980). And no effort was made by anybody from either side to resolve the differences. A middle path had to be found so that the Muslims could continue to have cow slaughtered away from the Hindu sight or locality. But the administrators only tried to enforce what they thought was right, rather than evolve a creative solution acceptable to both communities.

Over a period of 3 years starting with the creation of the *gaurakSini sabhA* in 1887, the cow protection movement had grown in strength as a popular people's movement. Hindus started protesting against Muslim traders taking cows through their villages to the nearby slaughter house. The police had to provide shelter to the cows to prevent the Hindus from taking them away from the Muslim trader. On September 6, 1893, this led a 2000 strong crowd to assemble on the weekly market day, a Wednesday, in Basantpur. This day was strategically chosen by the movement leaders for the protest because a large number of people naturally arrived in the local market for their shopping needs. It was easy to lead this crowd to the police headquarter, where they demanded that the cows that were being taken to the slaughter house by the Muslim trader be either sold to the Hindus or be freed.

Unable to resolve the issue, the police opened fire to disperse the crowd, and two people were killed. Several others were wounded. People scattered and withdrew but continued to shout slogans and swore to take future actions. Later riots started in many other parts of India, and it reached even Mumbai, and Rangoon in Burma. About 2000 people were killed in the riots (Freitag, 1980; Yang, 1980). In fact, the administration made things worse by requiring the Muslims to register for cow slaughter, which the Muslims thought was an approval to do so. Apparently, the intent of the policy was to help the administration decide if it would be appropriate to do the cow sacrifice in that locality. A court ruling also made things worse by supporting the legality of cow slaughter.

Therefore, the roots of communal riots are inherently embedded in the desire of the communities to make changes, and it is natural for some conflict of interest to emerge in a heterogeneous society (Melson & Wolpe, 1970). It should be noted that the communities tend to ignore the early signs of conflict (e.g., not allowing to go to the well, barring the use of the same pot for popping corn, or withdrawing help with *taziahs*), and also do not engage each other in the early phases of implementing social change (e.g., the creation of the *gaurakSini sabhA* to protect cow), which is inherently laden with conflicts.

We find similar patterns in Hindu–Muslim conflicts even today. For example, Ravichandran (2001) found that of the 73 religious conflicts, the ones between Hindus and Muslims accounted for 42 (or 58%) and the ones between Hindus and Christians accounted for 29 (or 40%). Muslims and Christians only had 2 conflicts (3%). Both Muslims and Christians constitute about 5% of the population of Tamil Nadu, but the proportion of conflicts with Muslims is much higher.

Varshney (2002) analyzed the pattern of Hindu–Muslim conflicts at the national and regional levels, and noted that during 1950 and 1995, there were 1,600 Hindu–Muslim conflicts in which 7,500 people were killed. Of these, only 45 of the death occurred in the rural area despite the population there being 65%, whereas in the urban area, despite population size being almost half (35%) of the rural area, 96% of the deaths happened. On further examination, he found that in the 8 large cities (Mumbai, Ahmedabad, Hyderabad, Meerut, Aligarh, Baroda, Delhi, and Calcutta), which account for 18% of India's urban population, 46% of the deaths occurred. Number of deaths in these cities varied widely – 1,137, 1,119, 312, 265, 160, 109, 93, and 63, respectively (Varshney, 2002), and it is quite surprising that this has no correlation with the population size or the proportion of Muslim population in the city. Furthermore, one might have expected more peace in Mumbai, the business capital of India, rather than in Delhi, the capital of India. He pointed out that 82% of India's urban population has not been prone to riots, supporting the idea presented at the outset of this paper that India is a peaceful country with a culture of peace.

There is general consensus among journalists and other researchers that politics is a major source of conflict between any two groups in India (Engineer, 1989; Varshney, 2002). Politicians are known to cultivate vote banks based on caste, religion, and other group identities. Politicians also are known to patronize goons, and even if this happens less often than otherwise, if Bollywood is used as a barometer of people's perception, then at least in perception, politicians are deeply entrenched into supporting and protecting goons for serving their personal political objectives. Varshney (2002) also blames the press for instigating violence among groups by publishing rumors rather than investigative reports, and suggested that Urdu and Hindi language newspapers and magazines have link with Muslim and Hindu criminals, respectively, who are also protected by politicians. Galtung and Ruge (1965) did present evidence that the structure of foreign news is biased such that media of each of the warring nations presents the other as irresponsible and callous. The same phenomenon is present between newspapers that support Hindus and Muslims in India.

Varshney (2002) compared three pairs of cities (Kozhikode–Aligarh, Lucknow–Hyderabad, and Ahmedabad–Surat) and argued that those cities that had civic societies that allowed interethnic dialog and had newspapers that made effort to find facts rather than fan rumors were less prone to Hindu–Muslim conflicts. Locating these cities geographically provides another perspective. Lucknow and Aligarh are only 230 miles apart, and both in Uttar Pradesh, yet Lucknow is more prone to riots than Aligarh. Similarly, Surat and Ahmedabad are only 160 miles apart, and both in Gujarat, but yet Ahmedabad is more prone to riots than Surat.

Varshney (2002) puts a lot of emphasis on integrated civic associations such as trade unions, businesses, and professional associations of engineers, doctors, and lawyers. He argued that such interethnic organizations are able to work effectively with government agencies, help monitor the situations as they evolve, and facilitate peace because they help resolve small clashes as they occur, not allowing them to grow out of proportion by clarifying rumors early on. Such organizations may need to be created, if not found in cities, and nurtured, if already existing, to diffuse differences and to bridge perceptions.

A comparison of some statistics from Kozhikode and Aligarh is worth taking a note of (Varshney, 2002). In Kozhikode, 83% of Hindus and Muslims eat together in social settings, 90% of their children play together, 84% of them visit each other, and when faced with a communal riot happening in another part of the country, they also are able to form peace communities at neighborhood and city level to investigate rumors and build solidarity. Aligarh experienced a Hindu–Muslim riot 19 times during the 35 years between 1950 and1994 (1950, 1954, 1956, 1961, 1966, 1969, 1971, 1972, 1977–1980 (every year), 1982, 1983, 1987, 1988, 1990, 1992, and 1994) for reasons as flimsy as dispute between a fruit seller and a customer, a road accident, random stabbing, arrest of two local journalists, or false rumors about patients killed in a hospital.

This city also hosts the Aligarh Muslim University, which is said to have laid the foundation for separation of India and the creation of Pakistan as an Islamic state in 1947. Such is the suspicion of each other and anybody who even wants to study Hindu–Muslim relations in this city that when Varshney started his research and his local assistant approached an agency for information, a journalist reported in a local newspaper that he was as an agent of CIA who was trying to learn how to instigate Hindu–Muslim conflict by learning the dynamics between these two communities in Aligarh (Varshney, 2002). With such a history of conflict between Hindus and Muslims, and such a heightened sense of distrust between each other, it is impressive that according to Varshney's data, 54% of Hindus and Muslims eat together in social settings, 42% of their children play together, and 60% of them visit each other. It is something that needs to be celebrated, its reasons need to be researched, and ways to build a harmonious society on this foundation needs to be acted upon. One could say Aligarh is a wonder!

4.3 Hindu and Christian Conflicts

Hindus are born in their religion, and though everybody can practice yoga, meditation, and many other practices of Hindu religion, there is not a ritual that can convert a person not born in a Hindu family to Hinduism. Christianity, on the contrary, believes in proselytizing, and historically, many Hindus have been converted to Christianity, especially the people of lower socio-economic class or tribal communities (see Table 7.6 in Appendix 6). It is often argued by Hindus that people convert to Christianity for the material goods, rather than because of a change in faith. This is reflected in the distribution of Christians in the Indian population – 9% are from scheduled caste, 33% from scheduled tribes, and 25% from OBC (Sachar Report, 2006). Thus, proselytizing continues to be a contentious issue between the two communities.

Ravichandran (2001) found that of the 73 incidents of religious conflicts in the state of Tamil Nadu, 29 (40%) of them were between Hindus and Christians, which constituted 8.5% of the total incidents. Though both Muslims and Christians constitute about 5% of the population of Tamil Nadu, the proportion of conflicts between Hindus and Muslims is much higher than those between Hindus and Christians (60% versus 40%). It should be noted that the Muslims and Christian communities have only had two conflicts (or 3%) in the 12-year period in the state of Tamil Nadu in this study (Ravichandran, 2001).

In almost half a century from 1950 to 1998, there were only 50 attacks against Christians in all of India. However, in 2000 alone, there were 100 clashes. In the following 5 years, three were almost 200 incidents of violence between Hindus and Christians every year, and the number crossed 1,000 in 2007.[6]

Hindu and Christians have been having conflict in Orissa for more than a decade, and perhaps the worst tragedy that has happened in recent memory was the burning alive of the

[6] This section draws from reports obtained from the Hindustan Times using LexisNexis.

Australian Christian missionary Graham Staines and his two sons, Philip (9) and Timothy (7), while they were sleeping in the jeep on January 22, 1999, in Manoharpur village in Keonjhar district about 150 miles from Bhubaneswar. Staines had served many years at the Mayurbhanj Leprosy Home at the district headquarter in Baripada. The offender Dara Singh is serving a life sentence for the murders.

In the Kandhmal area, 20% of the 650,000 tribal people have converted to Christianity, and Hindus are starting to convert some of them back to Hinduism. This competitive conversion of faith has seriously disturbed peace in Orissa, and it has gone from being the most peaceful for Christians to the worst. There were also some clashes between Hindus and Christians in December 2007, which started on the eve of Christmas. On August 23, 2008, a Hindu monk Swami Laxmanananda was murdered along with four of his associates. He was 90 years old and was actively involved in preventing proselytizing. This was followed by violence against Christians in the Kandhmal district of Orissa in the third week of August in which about 38 people died. In protest, around 30,000 Christian missionary-run schools were closed all over India on August 29, 2008.

The conflict has been going on between the Hindu population of Kandha tribals and the Pana Christians, who were Dalits before converting to Christianity. These two communities have been known to be in conflict even before the Pana had converted to Christianity. The Kandha tribals take pride in the fact that they fought against the British during the freedom movement. They have also been displaced because of economic development in the region, and have become a disadvantaged group that has not received any compensation and have lost their natural habitat, the forest (Rath, 2010). Though the issue seems to be only about religion, a closer examination shows that there are both social and economic factors at play. Despite other factors having an impact at the interactional level, at the value level, the major conflict between Hindus and Christians will continue to be proselytizing. Thus, the Hindus protest against conversion that the missionaries pursue, and the Dalits claim that they are better off converting since they gain in social class as Christians. To fend off the conversion, Hindu groups have become active, and this area in Orissa has drawn attention because of the conflicts that have occurred in the last 10 years. A new complication between Hindu and Christian conflict is the legislation of anti-conversion law in some states of India, which deprives one the freedom of faith but protects people against proselytizing.

4.4 Regional Conflicts

Most people in India carry a regional identity, which is either second to their being an Indian (e.g., proclaiming "I am an Indian"), but often this regional identity is more salient than being an Indian (Bhawuk, 2011). It makes perfect sense for people to have regional identities since the Indian states are organized according to linguistic groups, and every state has at least one major language and many other languages. As noted earlier, India is home of 300–400 languages and 1,652 mother tongues. It is no surprise that it has 23 official languages, 87 languages of print media, and 104 languages in which there are radio broadcasts. There were 81 languages used in primary education in 1970, which has declined to 41 in 1998. And in more than half of the districts, minority linguistic groups constitute more than 20% of the population (Mohanty, 2007). A person, therefore, is a Bengali, Tamil, Marathi, Gujarati, Oriya, Asami, Malayalee, Bihari, Punjabi, Sindhi, and so forth. In Uttar Pradesh, people are referred to as *Banarasi Babu*, *Avadh ke Nawab*, and so forth in daily conversation, which also alludes to regional identity. There are also derogatory terms for each of them, which are used by others when they cross their state border.

These regions are so large that they also have their own special food, clothing, music, art, and literature. Thus, each is a culture unto itself, and only a few 100 years ago, many of them also had a national identity. Thus, it makes sense for people to have a cultural identity embedded in the region. There are also similarities across these regions that make it possible for people to forge a national identity. Though some researchers argue that Indian identity was formed because of the British rule, people had an identity of being an Arya (as seen in Buddha's repeated use of the word Arya in his message to his disciples more than 2,500 years ago) or a resident of Bharatvarsha hundreds of years before the Muslim invasion began.

One of the most important consequences of regional identity is that it starts to influence the economic activities and political processes by controlling internal migration from one state to another. The protectionist policy where locals or natives are given preference in employment has been referred to as "sons of the soil" and has led to regional or ethnic conflicts (Weiner, 1978) in many parts of the world, and India is no exception. Historically, the protectionist policy can be traced to the idea of reservations, which was used by the British originally in the Morley-Minto reform of 1909 to reserve seats for Muslims in proportion to their populations in the Municipal and District Boards, the Provincial Councils, and the Imperial Legislature. Hindu leaders protested against this provision calling it undemocratic, and Muslim leaders supported it because it gave them proportional voice in the political process. This provision was later extended to include other minorities in 1919 (Weiner, 1978).

The reservation policy took another turn in 1938 when the chief secretary of Bihar, W. B. Brett, questioned if Bengalis should not be limited in the services in Bihar by issuing a memo titled "Percentage of members of different communities in Government Services," in which he suggested that Biharis should be preferred over Bengalis to ameliorate the discrepancy. The Working Committee of the Congress party asked Rajendra Prasad to look into it, and he recommended that Bengalis who had not made Bihar their home should be excluded from the services in Bihar, whereas those who had become residents of Bihar should be treated like natives or locals. This was already a practice in all other states except Punjab, and was referred to as the domicile rule. The guiding philosophy was to give preference to locals in service and education (Weiner, 1978). The precedence was already there, but now the Congress Party provided it legitimacy by giving it a formal approval. Thus, reservation became an Indian phenomenon for protecting both minorities and minorities.

Migration from one state to another creates competition, and often majority groups do not complain when migrant workers are doing the jobs that they themselves do not want to do. However, when the out-of-state workers start taking the professional jobs, a situation of zero-sum game emerges, and the natives start complaining as they lose positions to the migrant workers. If the majority group has the political power to change the conditions of employment, then the successful minority groups start feeling the pressure. This happened to the Indians in Burma, the Chinese in Malaysia, and the Tamils in Sri Lanka. Within India, it happened in Maharashtra between minority Tamils and majority Marathis and in Assam between majority Assamese and minority Bengalis (Weiner, 1978). Feeling the sons-of-the-soil pressure from Assam (Nag, 1990; Singh, 1990), Orissa, and Bihar, the Bengalis themselves started demanding preference in Calcutta and other cities where talented people from all over India contested for positions.

The sons-of-the-soil movement grew in the 1960s in Assam, Andhra, southern Bihar (now Jharkhand), and in Bombay and Bangalore. The state governments of Assam, Andhra, and Maharashtra imposed restrictions on employment, education, and housing. As population grew over the years, unemployment among educated people became a serious concern, and reservations for Scheduled Caste and Scheduled Tribe people in employment and education made competition acute for everybody. The extremely competitive economic environment gave justification to the protectionist movement of sons of the soil, and the regional identities collapsed into ethno-cultural identity further supported by linguistic divisions. There is some regional conflict in all states today, and each is couched in its own unique historical context. The creation of the new states of Jharkhand, Chhattisgarh, and Uttarakhand in 2000 demonstrates how these ethnic conflicts can also find peaceful expression in a democracy. There are many other communities like the Santals in Bengal (Chattopadhyaya, 1987) that are still struggling to find some resolution to their aspirations, and others are demanding more than statehood in Punjab (Sathananthan, 1983; Singh, 2000), Tamil Nadu (Palanithurai, 1993), and Nagaland (Kumar, 1995), among others.

5 Discussion

Peace, much like any other construct, is viewed in India at three levels: *manasA*, *vAcA*, and *karmaNA*, or in the mind, words, and deeds. Of course, the three levels are interconnected, and mind is the most subtle, and actions the most concrete. We have to start at all levels, and it is not sufficient to practice peace in our behaviors and words, but we must be at peace in our mind, too. The same is true for violence and conflict. Based on his personal lifelong experience and practice of *ahimsa* or nonviolence, Gandhi suggested that when violence is purged from our heart, then we can experience our natural human capacity of compassion. To do this, he practiced *ahimsa* or nonviolence all his life at all three levels of action, words, and thoughts. Perhaps this is one of the lessons that needs to be learned. It is important to study the absence of peace or conflict at all three levels, and we cannot stop at the level of behaviors or actions, for the seed of all actions lies in our thoughts, and their first expression is found in our words. Newspapers and other media reflect the state of our mind, and we need to work promptly on the absence of peace in our mind if we are ever to succeed in having lasting peace. The spiritual tradition of India does exactly this, as was discussed in the paper.

My experience in Mumbai in 2006 December is quite instructive of how people in India trust people of other religion or ethnic identity. To make sure that I was safe, my friend's wife arranged for a local taxi in Mumbai to take me to IIT Mumbai at Pawai. She asked a local shopkeeper for a reliable taxi driver, and he recommended one Mr. Khan. She happily handed me over to him and instructed him to take care of me and to also pick me up later at the end of the day. As I got in the taxi, I noticed Mr. Khan was offering incense to the deities on the dashboard of the car. After he was done with the prayer and we started our journey, I started a dialog with him. I asked him what about the deity. He replied, "It is Lord Tirupati." And then he realized that perhaps I was surprised that he as a Muslim was offering incense to Lord Tirupati. Without my asking, he volunteered, "Isn't God the same, sir, just different form." I was so moved by his sincerity that I chanted the name of Allah while I rode with him. It was a wonderful feeling of brotherhood. I was finally able to practice what Ramakrishna did (Bhawuk, 2003), to a much smaller degree, but I was delighted that I was able to cross religious boundaries in my heart and mind. Peace is not only a sublime thought but also a beautiful practice, and people in India live by this value and inspire others, even visitors, if they are open to it, to experience it and to adopt it.

One of the contributions of this chapter is to invite researchers to shift focus from conflict to peace, and to view peace as naturally occurring and absence of peace or conflict as an aberration. Unlike Galtung (1964a), who argued that peace studies as a field has to focus on the macro-level, and not on interpersonal and individual levels, this chapter has demonstrated that peace exists at the individual level, and its absence at the individual level leads to conflict at the interpersonal level. And the community and national level absence of peace, conflicts of various shades and wars, can be traced to the interaction of interpersonal conflict and other factors including identities of various types, resource issues, and a history of unresolved contradictions (Engineer, 1989; Melson & Wolpe, 1970; Ravichandran, 2001; Varshney, 2002; Yang, 1980). Thus, we need to turn to the individual, and the interpersonal interactions, and create peace there if we are to carve a peaceful society. Acceptance of contradictions, sharing stories of peace and creating new stories, creating a culture of dialog and debate, using spirituality as a community bridge, and creating social structures that support harmony and peace are some of the approaches that are grounded in the culture of India, and are worth cultivating in other parts of the world.

We have examples of how individuals who are at peace create peace around themselves, even when they are leading social change, which is mired in deep conflicts. Gandhi, Martin Luther King, Nelson Mandela, Malcolm X, Mother Teresa, and others who have led social change or revolutions were at peace at the core of their being, and that is why they were able to lead others to social change. In Gandhi's words, "man and his deed are two distinct things. Whereas a good deed should call forth approbation and a wicked deed disapprobation, the doer of the deed, whether good or wicked, always deserves respect or pity as the case may be. 'Hate the sin and not the sinner is a precept,' which, though easy enough to understand, is rarely practiced, and that is why the poison of hatred spreads in the world" (Gandhi, 1957, p. 276). Gandhi also said that the work of a person without ego is naturally for the good of others (Gandhi, 1930, p. 96). An egoless person is dedicated to the service of humanity and is at peace with himself or herself. Mother Teresa, with all her seemingly internal strife,[7] never for a moment vacillated from her service to humanity, and since she was at peace with herself, she engendered peace in others around her. Thus, a person who is not at peace himself or herself is likely to disturb peace rather than create it.

Interpersonal peace is as important since the evidence presented above shows that most conflicts start with interpersonal issues that are unresolved, and at some point gets compounded by other variables, often with issues related to resource, identity, and so forth. Philosophers like Scheler have argued that repressed interpersonal stress becomes what Nitche called *ressentiment* (Scheler, 1994) and leads to much long-term misunderstanding and conflict among communities (Bershady, 1992). Forgiveness and compassion are some of the known antidotes of ressentiment, and it is clear that the Indian culture has nurtured these values through spirituality over thousands of years. For example, *kSamA* (forgiveness), *Arjava* (simplicity), *dayA* (kindness), *toSa* (contentment), and *satya* (truth) are the five virtues that *aStAvakra* asks King *Janaka* to practice to be free from bondage (Hari Om, 2007).

Some of these practices have psychological explanation that is well grounded in theory. In an experimental study, Piff, Kraus, Côté, Cheng, and Keltner (2010) found that Socioeconomic Status (SES) is an important predictor of prosocial behavior, which would be critical to create peace and harmony between people of different social class. They found that people of lower social class who have less resource to their disposal are inclined to be significantly more generous, charitable, trusting, and helpful compared to the upper-class people. Through mediation analyses, they found that the participants in their study who were in the lower-class category demonstrated more prosocial behavior, showing their commitment to egalitarian values. These participants also showed more compassion. These findings are consistent with those of Bowen and Bok (1998) who found that minorities in the USA are more inclined to give back to the society compared to their White alums from Ivy League schools, who focused more on maximizing their own career. Together with the findings noted earlier about the low crime rate in Calcutta despite rampant poverty, it seems that India has a culture of tolerance and prosocial behavior, which results in tolerance for people of other groups.

What is more important to note is that compassion can be used to override the SES barriers.

[7] Where is my faith? Even deep down … there is nothing but emptiness and darkness … If there be God – please forgive me. When I try to raise my thoughts to Heaven, there is such convicting emptiness that those very thoughts return like sharp knives and hurt my very soul … How painful is this unknown pain – I have no Faith. Repulsed, empty, no faith, no love, no zeal, … What do I labor for? If there be no God, there can be no soul. If there be no soul then, Jesus, You also are not true. (Kolodiejchuk, 2007). Kolodiejchuk, who was her postulator or the official responsible for gathering the evidence for her sanctification as a saint, noted that some may interpret her personal thoughts as a lack of faith, but it was just the opposite. Christian saints like St. John of the Cross, St. Theresa of Jesus, and St. Ignatius Loyola have all noted this as the third phase preceding the final stage of union with God in which one feels dejected and has no connection with God, unlike the first two phases of purgation and illumination where grace is constantly experienced.

Piff et al. (2010) found that compassion moderated the prosocial behavior, and even the higher social class people in their sample when primed with compassion demonstrated significantly more prosocial behavior, and the statistically significant difference between the two classes disappeared in the presence of compassion. Spirituality, in general, and the *dargahs,* in particular, are likely to generate compassion among people, which is likely to generate communal understanding, harmony, and peace.

The government seems to be both a cause of conflict and a source of law and maintenance of law and order (Engineer, 1989; Ravichandran, 2001; Varshney, 2002). The government is a source of conflict, since it initiates changes that people are not likely to accept. When people do not identify themselves with the government, or when people are polarized about some issues, then legislation is not enough to effect a social change, and much social effort is needed to persuade people for the change. Varshney (2002) noted how civic societies can prevent riots, and stressed the need to create such civil organizations. This is consistent with the Gandhian view of decentralization in which the local communities take charge of their affairs rather than depending on a central government, which indeed becomes a source of violence. Only such civic organizations and local institutions can shape the behaviors of powerful elected leaders, or even correct them.

Buchanan (2000) reviewed scientific theories to analyze earthquakes, extinction of species, formation of snowflakes, and so forth and concluded that "...history matters, whether it is the science of earthquakes or extinctions, or the science of snowflakes, of science itself, or of human history" (p. 243). Buchanan offers credence to the idea presented above that we must study peace at the individual level and that individuals are the key to creating a peaceful world – "We know that history is made by individuals acting as individual, that the potential for both war and peace lives in every person..." (p. 242). Gandhi, King, Mother Teresa, Nelson Mandela, and others speak to this truth. We also know that geniuses interact with the *zeitgeist* and culture to shape cultural behaviors and to create new cultural behaviors (Bhawuk, 2003), presenting further theoretical support to the role of the individual in effecting peace.

Since "[h]istory is neither static nor changing randomly, but balanced precariously in some middle way between the two, and so always poised, like the sandpile, on the very edge of dramatic upheaval" (Buchanan, 2000, p. 239), and "since a record of unbroken sameness is not history, but the lack of it [is] (p, 238)," we should view absence of peace as an occasion to appreciate the ubiquity of peace, and a signal to work at individual, interpersonal, and community levels to create a new dynamics of peace. If the Indian experience of thousands of years is any indication, peace is the basic nature of human beings, and its absence for whatever reason is nature's only way to stimulate our creativity to resort it until another upheaval appears. Learning from nonequilibrium physics, as Buchanan recommends, I think we should take an active role in this process of peace creation through dialog, tentativeness in our worldview about what truth is, and connecting to our spiritual foundation as human beings. Writing about war and revolution, Leo Tolstoy said, "this is the nature of [human being], this is the law." I submit that peace is the nature of human being, and peace is the law.

A limitation of this paper must be noted. It is written by a Hindu, and, therefore, is likely to be biased, despite having Ramakrishna as my role model, who practiced all paths of Hinduism as well as Islam and Christianity; and chanting the name of Allah everyday in the same vein as the name of Rama, following Gandhi in my daily life. It is written by a Brahmin, and, therefore, is likely to be biased, despite my personal effort to practice what Manu recommended for Brahmins – a Brahmin should feel agitated by praise as if he has been given poison and should always welcome insult as nectar. It is written by an *Advaitn* who practices shedding identities, and identity is considered to be the source of conflict in much of the literature. It is written by an intercultural researcher who believes that world peace can be practiced in the time of peace by cultivating intercultural understanding and structures that support it. It is written by a romantic who sees peace as the nature of human being, and conflict as our desire to have permanent peace.

For what it is worth, after I wrote the paper, in an interfaith seminar, I was introduced to a book by the Dalai Lama (2010) where he too presents India as a culture of peace. I submit this as evidence offered by the universe, as Paulo Coelho (1993) would suggest, to see perennial peace in India despite the occasional conflict of various kinds found there today. I find peace in India. I find India peaceful. This should not make us complacent considering the ubiquity of disasters (Buchanan, 2000), but encourage us to work naturally (*sahaj* yoga) in peace in our daily living, in all our interactions, and to build habits and social structures to maintain interpersonal and communal peace. *Om zAntiH! zAntiH! zAntiH!*

Appendix 1

Table 7.1 National holidays. (Total: 17; 5 Hindu; 4 Muslim; 3 National; 2 Christian; 1 Buddhist; 1 Jain; 1 Sikh)

Jan 19 Muharram (Muslim)
Jan 26 Republic Day (National, nonreligious)
Mar 5 Maha Shivaratri (Hindu)
Mar 20 Milad-Un-Nabi (Prophet's Birthday) (Muslim)
Mar 21 Good Friday (Christian)
Mar 22 Holi (Hindu)
Apr 14 Ram Navami (Hindu)
Apr 18 Mahavir Jayanti (Jain)
May 20 Buddha Purnima (Buddhist)
Aug 15 Independence Day (National, nonreligious)
Oct 2 Gandhi Jayanti (National, nonreligious)
Oct 3 Ramzan (Id-ul-Fitar) (Muslim)
Oct 9 Dussehra (Hindu)
Oct 27 Diwali (Hindu)
Nov 13 Guru Nanak Jayanti (Sikh)
Dec 9 Bakr-Id (Idu'l Zuha) (Muslim)
Dec 25 Christmas (Christian)

Appendix 2

Table 7.2 List of restricted or optional holidays

New Year Day	1-Jan
Guru Gobind Singh's Birthday	5-Jan
Makara Samkranti (North India)	14-Jan
Makara Samkranti (Bengal)	15-Jan
Pongal	15-Jan
Basanta Panchami/Shree Panchami	11-Feb
Sivaji Jayanti	19-Feb
Guru Ravidas Birthday	21-Feb
Swami Dayanand Saraswati Jayanti	2-Mar
Holika Dahan	21-Mar
Easter (Sunday)	23-Mar
Chaitra Sukhladi/Gudi Padwa/Ugadi/Cheti Chand	7-Apr
Vaisakhi	13-Apr
Vishu	13-Apr
Mesadi	14-Apr
Vaisakhdi (Bengal)/Bahag Bihu (Assam)	14-Apr
Birthday of Rabindranath Tagore	7-May
Rath Yatra	4-Jul
Hazrat Ali's Birthday	17-Jul
Raksha Bandhan	16-Aug
Parsi New Year	19-Aug
Janmashtami	24-Aug
Ganesh Chaturthi	3-Sep
Onam	12-Sep
Jamat-Ul-Vida	26-Sep
Dussera (Maha Saptami)	6-Oct
Dussera (Maha Ashtami)	7-Oct
Dussera (Maha Navmi)	8-Oct
Maharshi Valmiki's Birthday	14-Oct
Deepavali (South)	27-Oct
Naraka Chaturdasi	27-Oct
Govardhan Puja	29-Oct
Bhai Duj	30-Oct
Guru Teg Bahadur's Martydrom day	24-Nov
Christmas Eve	24-Dec

Appendix 3

Table 7.3 State = Language = Culture

Jammu and Kashmir (Kashmiri, Dogri, Hindi, Punjabi)
Himanchal (Hindi, Punjabi, Kashmiri, Dogri)
Uttaranchal (Hindi, Urdu, Punjabi, Bengali, Nepali)
Punjab (Punjabi, Hindi)

(continued)

Table 7.3 (continued)

Haryana (Hindi, Punjabi, Urdu; Hariyanavi is the local language)
Uttar Pradesh (Hindi & Urdu, Punjabi; Bhojpuri, Avadhi, and so forth are local languages)
Rajasthan (Hindi, Punjabi, Urdu; Rajasthani is the local language)
Bihar (Hindi, Maithili, & Urdu; Bhojapuri, Magahi, Bajika, and so forth are other local languages)
West Bengal (Bengali, Hindi, Sabtakum Urdu, Nepali)
Assam (Assamese, Bengali, Hindi, Bodo, Nepali)
Arunachal (Bengali, Nepali, Hindi, Assamese)
Nagaland (Bengali, Hindi, Nepali; Nagamese is most common besides the 14 tribal languages; and English is the State's official language)
Manipur (Manipuri, Nepali, Bengali, Hindi)
Sikkim (Nepali, Hindi)
Mizoram (Bengali, Hindi, Nepali, Santali)
Tripura (Bengali, Hindi, Oriya, Manipuri)
Meghalaya (Bengali, Nepali, Hindi, Assamese)
Jharkhand (Hindi, Santali, Bengali, Oriya)
Madhya Pradesh (Hindi, Marathi, Urdu)
Gujarat (Gujarati, Hindi, Sindhi, Marathi, Urdu)
Maharashtra (Marathi, Hindi, Urdu, Gujarati, Telugu)
Chhattisgarh (Hindi, Oriya)
Orissa (Oriya, Hindi, Telugu, Santali, Urdu)
Andhra Pradesh (Telugu, Urdu, Hindi, Tamil)
Karnataka (Kannada, Urdu, Telugu, Marathi, Tamil, Hindi, Konkani, Malayalam)
Goa (Konkani, Marathi, Hindi, Urdu)
Tamil Nadu (Tamil, Telugu, Kannada, Urdu)
Kerala (Malayalam, Tamil)

Appendix 4

Table 7.4 Census of India, 1991. Statement 3: Distribution of 10, 000 persons by language. India, States, and Union Territories (Scheduled 22 languages and number of people by 10,000) (Sorted alphabetically and by size)

Assamese	128	Sanskrit	(N)
Bengal	812	Hindi	4,110
Bodo	13	Bengal	812
Dogri	22	Telugu	721
Gujarati	449	Marathi	701
Hindi	4,110	Tamil	592
Kannada	369	Urdu	502
Kashmiri	54	Gujarati	449
Konkani	24	Kannada	369
Maithili	119	Malayalam	322
Malayalam	322	Oriya	322
Manipuri	14	Punjabi	283
Marathi	701	Assamese	128
Nepali	28	Maithili	119
Oriya	322	Santali	63
Punjabi	283	Kashmiri	54
Sanskrit	(N)	Nepali	28
Santali	63	Sindhi	25
Sindhi	25	Konkani	24
Tamil	592	Dogri	22
Telugu	721	Manipuri	14
Urdu	502	Bodo	13

Appendix 5

Table 7.5 Number of famous Indian *dargahs* (Tombs of Sufi Saints) by State

Andhra Pradesh	33
Assam	2
Bihar	3
Chattisgarh	2
Gujarat	22
Haryana	6
Himachal Pradesh	1
Jammu Kashmir	6
Karnataka	43
Kerala	3
Madhya Pradesh	8
Maharashtra	32
Orissa	4
Pondicherry	1
Punjab	9
Rajasthan	13
Tamil Nadu	13
Union Territory	2
Uttaranchal	5
Uttar Pradesh	35
West Bengal	6
Total	249

Note: There are many more famous *dargahs* in India than the ones noted in the table above. For example, Bihar has more than three *dargahs* in Bhagalpur district alone. Mumbai alone has 44 *dargahs*, whereas in the table above, only two of the Mumbai *dargahs* have been counted. http://rahat.in/dargah/citiesasp.asp

Appendix 6

Table 7.6 Distribution of population of each religion by caste categories. *All India 2004–2005*

Religion/Caste	SCs	STs	OBCs	Others	All
Hindu	22.2	9.1	42.8	26.0	100
Muslim	0.8	0.5	39.2	59.5	100
Christians	9.0	32.8	24.8	33.3	100
Sikhs	30.7	0.9	22.4	46.1	100
Jains	0.0	2.6	3.0	94.3	100
Buddhists	89.5	7.4	0.4	2.7	100
Zoroastrians	0.0	15.9	13.7	70.4	100
Others	2.6	82.5	6.2	8.7	100
Total	19.7	8.5	41.1	30.8	100

Source: Sachar Report, Table 1.2, p. 7; Distribution obtained from merged sample of Schedule 1 and Schedule 10 of NSSO 61st Round Survey)

References

Basham, A. L. (1954). *The wonder that was India*. London: Sidgwick and Jackson.

Basu, K. (2007). India's demographic dividend. BBC News. Down loaded from http://news.bbc.co.uk/2/hi/south_asia/6911544.stm

Bayly, C. (1985). The pre-history of 'communalism'? Religious conflict in India, 1700–1860. *Modern Asian Studies, 19*(2), 177–203.

Berry, J. W. (2008). Globalization and acculturation. *International Journal of Intercultural Relations, 32*(4), 328–336.

Berger, P. L., & Luckman, T. (1966). *The social construction of reality: A treatise in the sociology of knowledge*. Garden City, New York: Anchor Books.

Bershady, H. J. (1992). *Max Scheler. On feeling, knowing, and valuing: Selected writings*. Chicago, IL: University of Chicago Press.

Bhawuk, D. P. S. (2001). Evolution of culture assimilators: Toward theory-based assimilators. *International Journal of Intercultural Relations, 25*(2), 141–163.

Bhawuk, D. P. S. (2003). Culture's influence on creativity: The case of Indian spirituality. *International Journal of Intercultural Relations, 27*(1), 1–22.

Bhawuk, D. P. S. (2008). Globalization and indigenous cultures: Homogenization or differentiation? *International Journal of Intercultural Relations, 32*(4), 305–317.

Bhawuk, D. P. S. (2009). *To be a Brahmin: The good, the bad, and the ugly*. Paper presented in the symposium on Intergroup Relations and Social Identity in Indian Culture at the 8th Biennial Conference of Asian Association of Social Psychology, New Delhi, December 11–14, 2009.

Bhawuk, D. P. S. (2011). *Spirituality and Indian Psychology: Lessons from the Bhagavad-Gita*. New York, NY: Springer.

Bhawuk, D. P. S., Mrazek, S., & Munusamy, V. P. (2009). From social engineering to community transformation: Amul, Grameen Bank, and Mondragon as exemplar organizations. *Peace and Policy: Ethical Transformations for a Sustainable Future, 14*, 36–63.

Bowen, W. G., & Bok, D. (1998). *The shape of the river: Long-term consequences of considering race in college and university admissions*. Princeton, NJ: Princeton University Press.

Brass, P. R. (1974). *Language, religion, and politics in North India*. London: Cambridge University Press.

Brown, J. M. (1969). The Mahatma and modern India. *Modern Asian Studies, 3*(4), 321–342.

Buchanan, M. (2000). *Ubiquity: Why catastrophes happen*. New York, NY: Three Rivers Press.

Chattopadhyaya, H. (1987). *Internal migration in India: A case study of Bengal*. Calcutta: K P Bagchi & Company.

Coelho, P. (1993). *The alchemist*. New York, NY: Harper Collins.

Crime Statistics (2008). *Crime Statistics in India*. National Crime Records Bureau, Ministry of Home Affairs, Government of India. Down loaded from http://ncrb.nic.in

Dalton, D. (1967). The Gandhian view of Caste, and caste after Gandhi. In P. Mason (Ed.), *India and Ceylon: Unity and diversity*. London: Oxford University Press.

De Zutter, H. (1995). What Makes Obama Run? An interview with Barack Obama in Chicago Reader. Downloaded on August 19, 2011 from http://www.chicagoreader.com/gyrobase/what-makes-obama-run/Content?oid=889221&mode=print.

Dinkar, R. S. (1956). *Sanskriti ke car adhyaya (The four chapters of civilization)*. Patna: Udayacal.

Engineer, A. A. (1989). *Communalism and communal violence in India: An analytical approach to Hindu-Muslim conflict*. Delhi: Ajanta Publications.

Freitag, S. B. (1980). Sacred symbol as mobilizing ideology: The North Indian search for a "Hindu" community. *Comparative Studies in Society and History, 22*(4), 597–625.

Galtung, J. (1964a). A structural theory of aggression. *Journal of Peace Research, 1*(2), 95–119.

Galtung, J. (1964b). An editorial. *Journal of Peace Research, 1*(1), 1–4.

Galtung, J. (1969). Violence, peace, and peace research. *Journal of Peace Research, 6*(3), 167–191.

Galtung, J. (1985). Twenty-five years of peace research. *Journal of Peace Research, 22*(2), 141–158.

Galtung, J., & Ruge, M. H. (1965). The structure of foreign news. *Journal of Peace Research, 2*(1), 64–91.

Gambhiranand, S. (1972). *Eight Upanishads (Volume 1)*. Calcutta: Advaita Ashrama.

Gandhi, M. K. (1930). *Gita-Mata*. New Delhi: Sasta Sahitya Mandal.

Gandhi, M. K. (1957). *An autobiography: The story of my experiments with truth*. Boston, MA: Beacon Press.

Gupta, M. (1984). *The gospel of Sri Ramakrishna*. New York, NY: RK Mission (Translated by Swami Nikhilananda).

Hari Om, K. (2007). *aStAvakra mahAgItA*. Delhi: Manoj Publications.

Hasan, M. (1971). *History of Tipu Sultan*. Calcutta: World Press.

Huntington, S. P. (Summer 1993). The clash of civilizations? *Foreign Affairs, 72*(3), 22–49.

Huntington, S. P. (1996). *The clash of civilizations and the remaking of world order*. New York, NY: Simon & Schuster.

Hussain, S. A. (1959). *The way of Gandhi and Nehru*. Bombay: Asia Publishing House.

India Population (2004). India population "to be biggest." BBC News. Downloaded from http://news.bbc.co.uk/2/hi/3575994.stm

Jayakar, P. (1995). *Fire in the mind: Dialogues with J. Krishnamurti*. New Delhi: Penguin Book.

Kennedy, P. (1988). *The Rise and Fall of the Great Powers: Economic Change and Military Conflict from 1500 to 2000*. New York, NY: Random House.

Kim, Y. Y. (2008). Intercultural personhood: Globalization and a way of being. *International Journal of Intercultural Relations, 32*(4), 359–368.

Kim, Y. Y., & Bhawuk, D. P. S. (2008). Globalization and diversity: Contributions from intercultural research. *International Journal of Intercultural Relations, 32*(4), 301–304.

Kolodiejchuk, B. (2007). *Mother Teresa: Come be my light*. New York: Doubleday.

Krishnamurti, J. (1996). *Questioning Krishnamurti: J. Krishnamurti in dialogue*. Chennai: Krishnamurti Foundation.

Kumar, B. B. (1995). *Tension and conflict in North-East India*. New Delhi: Cosmo Publications.

Lama, D. (2010). *Toward a true kinship of faiths: How the world's religions can come together*. New York, NY: Doubleday Religion.

Lewis, M. P. (Ed.). (2009). *Ethnologue: Languages of the World* (16th ed.). Dallas, TX: SIL International. Online version: http://www.ethnologue.com/.

Lipton, B. H. (2005). *The biology of belief: Unleashing the power of consciousness, matter, and miracles*. New York: Hay House.

Lipton, B. H., & Bhaerman, S. (2009). *Spontaneous evolution: Our positive future (and a way to get there from here)*. New York: Hay House.

Mayilvaganan, V. (September 30, 2010). Nagore dargah draws Hindus in droves. The *Times of India* (Chennai Edition). Downloaded on November 11, 2010, from http://timesofindia.indiatimes.com/city/chennai/Nagore-dargah-draws-Hindus-in-droves/articleshow/6654586.cms

McLane, J. R. (1977). *Indian nationalism and the early congress*. Princeton, NJ: Princeton University Press.

Melson, R., & Wolpe, H. (1970). Modernization and politics of communalism: A theoretical perspective. *American Political Science Review, 64*(4), 1112–1130.

Mitroff, I. I., & Kilman, R. H. (1978). *Methodological approaches to social science*. San Francisco, CA: Jossey-Bass.

Mohanty, A. K. (2007). *How are dominated and minority languages maintained? Study of collective action in two tribal cultures in India*. Invited paper presented at the University of Hawaii at Manoa on October 29, 2007.

Moore, C. A. (1967). Introduction: The comprehensive Indian mind. In C. A. Moore (Ed.), *The Indian mind: Essentials of Indian philosophy and culture* (pp. 1–18). Honolulu, HI: University of Hawaii press.

Mukherjee, R. (2000). Caste in itself, caste and class, or caste in class. *Journal of World Systems Research, 6*(2), 332–339.

Mundadan, A. M. (1989). *History of Christianity in India* (From the beginning up to the middle of the sixteenth century (up to 1542), Vol. I). Bangalore: Church History Association of India.

Nag, S. (1990). *Roots of ethnic conflict: Nationality question in North-East India*. New Delhi: Manohar.

Natrajan, B. (2005). Caste, class, and community in India: An ethnographic approach. *Ethnology, 44*(3), 227–241.

Neill, S. A. (1984). *A history of Christianity in India: The beginnings to AD 1707*. London, UK: Cambridge University Press.

Nisargadatta, M. (1973). *I am that*. Mumbai: Chetana (Translated from the Marathi tape recordings by Maurice Frydman; revised and edited by Sudhakar Dikshit).

O'Hanlon, R. (1985). *Caste, conflict, and ideology: Mahatma Jotirao Phule and low caste protest in nineteenth-century western India*. Cambridge: Cambridge University Press.

Palanithurai, G. (1993). *Management of ethnic conflict in India and Canada*. Delhi: Kanishka Publishers.

Pandey, N. N. (Ed.). (2001). *Dharmapadavyakhyanam of Srimad Raghunatha Sharma*. Varanasi: Sampurnanad Sanskirt University.

Piff, P. K., Kraus, M. W., Côté, S., Cheng, B. H., & Keltner, D. (2010). Having less, giving more: the influence of social class on prosocial behavior. *Journal of Personality and Social Psychology, 99*(5), 771–784.

Pinney, C. (1997). The nation (un)pictured? Chromolithography and 'popular' politics in India, 1878–1995. *Critical Inquiry, 23*, 834–867.

Prabhu, R. K. (Ed.). (1962). *Varnashramadharma by M. K. Gandhi*. Ahmedabad: Navajivan Publication.

Prabhu, R. K. (Ed.). (1964). *Caste must go and the sin of untouchability by M. K. Gandhi*. Ahmedabad: Navajivan Publication.

Raman, M. (2000). *Talks with Ramana Maharshi: On realizing abiding peace and happiness*. Carlsbad, CA: Inner Directions.

Rath, R. (2010 May–June). Kandha culture of kalahandi in Orissa. *Orissa Review*, pp. 76–82.

Ravichandran, T. (2001). *Communalism in Tamil Nadu and the way out*. Madurai: Gandhi Media Center.

Rizvi, S. A. A. (1987). *The wonder that was India Volume II: A survey of the history and culture of the Indian subcontinent from the coming of the Muslims to the British conquest 1200 1700*. London: Sidgwick & Jackson.

Rolland, R. (1960). *The life of Ramakrishna*. Mayavati, India: Advaita Ashram.

Sachar Committee Report (2006). *Social, Economic and Educational Status of the Muslim Community of India: A Report* (submitted by Prime Minister's High Level Committee, Cabinet Secretariat, Government of India, November, 2006). Downloaded from http://minorityaffairs.gov.in/newsite/sachar/sachar_comm.pdf

Sathananthan, S. M. (1983). *Hindu-Sikh conflict in Punjab: Causes and cure*. Bangalore: Sri Guru Singh Sabha.

Scheler, M. (1994). *Ressentiment*. Milwaukee, WI: Marquette University Press (Translated by Lewis B. Coser & William W. Holdheim).

Schopenhaur, A. (1966). The world as will and representation. Translated from the German by E. F. J. Payne. New York, NY: Dover Publications.

Sen, A. (2006). *Identity and violence: The illusion of destiny*. New York, NY: W. W. Norton & Company.

Sen, A. (2008). Violence, identity and poverty. *Journal of Peace Research, 45*(1), 5–15.

Shapiro, D. L. (2002). Negotiating emotions. *Conflict Resolution Quarterly, 20*, 67–82.

Shapiro, D. L. (2005). Enemies, allies, and emotions: The role of emotions in negotiation. In M. L. Moffitt & R. C. Bordone (Eds.), *The handbook of dispute resolution* (pp. 66–82). New York, NY: Jossey Bass.

Shapiro, D. L. (2010). Relational identity theory: A systematic approach for transforming the emotional dimension of conflict. *American Psychologist, 65*(7), 634–645.

Shapiro, D. L., & Liu, V. (2006). Psychology of a stable peace. In M. Fitzduff & C. E. Stout (Eds.), *The psychology of resolving global conflict: From war to peace* (pp. 307–329). Westport, CT: Praeger.

Sheldon, W. H. (1951). Main contrasts between Eastern and Western philosophy. In C. A. Moore (Ed.), *Essays in east-west philosophy* (pp. 288–297). Honolulu, HI: University of Hawaii Press.

Singh, M. (1990). *Assam: Politics of migration and quest for identity*. Jaipur: Anita Publications.

Singh, G. (2000). *Ethnic conflict in India: A case-study of Punjab*. Houndmills: Macmillan.

Srinivas, M. N. (1987). *The dominant caste and other essays*. Delhi: Oxford University Press.

Tajfel, H., & Turner, J. C. (1986). The social identity theory of intergroup behavior. In S. Worchel & W. G. Austin (Eds.), *Psychology of intergroup relations* (2nd ed., pp. 7–24). Chicago: Nelson-Hall.

Triandis, H. C. (1972). *The analysis of subjective culture*. New York: Wiley-Interscience.

Triandis, H. C. (1994). *Culture and social behavior*. New York, NY: McGraw-Hill.

Triandis, H. C. (1995). *Individualism and collectivism*. Boulder, CO: Westview.

Triandis, H.C., Kurowski, L.L., & Gelfand, M.J. (1994). Workplace diversity. In H.C. Triandis, M.D. Dunnette, & L.M. Hough (Eds.), *Handbook of industrial and organizational psychology (2nd ed.), vol. 4:* 767–827. Palo Alto, CA: Consulting Psychologists Press.

Upadhyaya, B. D. (1977). *Bharatiya dharma aur darshan (Indian dharma and philosophy)*. New Delhi: Chaukhambha Oriental.

Varshney, A. (2002). *Ethnic conflict and civil life: Hindus and Muslims in India*. New Haven, CT: Yale University Press.

Vidyarthi, V., & Wilson, P. A. (2008). *Development from within: Facilitating collective reflection for sustainable change*. Herndon, VA: Apex Foundation.

Vidyavachaspati, I. (2007). *Mere pita*. New Delhi: DK Printworld.

Weiner, M. (1978). *Sons of the soil: Migration and ethnic conflict in India*. Princeton, NJ: Princeton University Press.

Yang, A. A. (1979). The agrarian origins of crime: A study of riots in Saran District, India, 1866–1920. *Journal of Social History, 13*(4), 289–306.

Yang, A. A. (1980). Sacred symbol and sacred space in Rural India: Community mobilization in the "Anti-Cow Killing" riot of 1893. *Comparative Studies in Society and History, 22*(4), 576–596.

Part III

China

8 Ethno-Political Conflicts in China: Toward Building Interethnic Harmony

Wenshan Jia, Yueh-Ting Lee, and Haiyang Zhang

China Chapter Summary

Jia et al. discuss the historical treatment of ethnic minorities in China and examine governmental policies that have been implemented to create equality and autonomy. An analysis of both the positive and negative effects of these policies follows. The authors recognize that the current model requires change and offer suggestions to improve policy and enhance ethnic tolerance.

Detailed discussion regarding the current governmental policies describes a country providing for ethnic minorities through regional autonomy, protection of diversity, affirmative action in education, and political equality. Jia, Lee and Zhang, however, point out some existent realities. There is a noticeable lack of ethnic minorities in positions of political power. Economic disparity is escalating due to the designation of regional resources to the nation's GDP without benefit to the minority local residents. The Chinese government has increased education to ethnic minorities, but the manner in which it is provided suggests the presence of Han-Chinese ethnocentrism. The authors note that education providers are required to utilize standard national curriculum, and teaching most often occurs in the Mandarin Chinese language.

Evidence is presented reflecting intensifying ethnic conflict in the form of recent riots which targeted specific ethnic groups. Posited causes for this escalating conflict include resentment created by the programs the government has implemented in order to increase opportunities to ethnic minorities.

W. Jia (✉)
Department of Communication Studies, Chapman University, 209 Moulton Hall, One University Drive, Orange, CA 92866, USA
e-mail: jia@chapman.edu

Y.-T. Lee
Department of Psychology, University of Toledo, Ohio, USA
e-mail: YT.Lee@Utoledo.edu

H. Zhang
Minzu University of China, China
e-mail: hyz9988@gmail.com

D. Landis and R.D. Albert (eds.), *Handbook of Ethnic Conflict: International Perspectives*, International and Cultural Psychology, DOI 10.1007/978-1-4614-0448-4_8,

Suggestions for improving cultural relations are delineated and include increasing communication through dialog, education about minorities, and bilingual language fluency. Knowledge of multiculturalism is suggested as an important requirement for all individuals who work in the government ethnic affairs offices. The authors call for grass-roots, bottom-up movements similar to those in the USA. The need for dual identity labels is presented as a method through which to reinforce shared Chinese identity while recognizing ethnic diversity.

Cheryl Jorgensen

1 Introduction

Do in China as the Chinese do. China is a country with a territory of 9.6 million square kilometers, with Taiwan, Hong Kong, and Macao as its southeastern wing and Inner Mongolia, Xinjiang, and Tibet as its northwestern wing. The total population of China is over 1.3 billion. If we follow Edwin O. Reischauer and John King Fairbank (Reischauer & Fairbank, 1960) and regard it as a political entity and a complex civilization as big as Europe, we are not far from the fact. It is no wonder that most of the time, the core value of the Chinese culture or the big tradition represented by Confucianism along with Daoism and other beliefs emphasizes universal human nature and harmony of different peoples and cultures rather than individual group identity. It is also true that this big tradition contains Sino-centrism in its expansion and, at the time of crisis, it displays ethnocentrism or racial discrimination toward the outside threats, be it from outside the Central Plains or outside China as a whole (Dikotter, 1992).

Since the three regions on the southeastern wing of China are all islands by nature, all have colonial experiences resulting from European or Japanese expansion (often both), and thus all have separate political and administrative systems at the current moment, and their internal information is easier to access. This chapter focuses on the mainland, or the People's Republic of China (P.R. China).

During the past 3 decades of the economic reform, China has increasingly become a global power with increasing economic, political, and cultural influence. In retrospect, while most attention has been devoted to economic development, insufficient attention has been devoted to the issues of ethnic minorities in comparison with the first 3 decades since the founding of P.R. China in 1949. Through extensive research, the following problems have been identified as major concerns that warrant special attention from China's ethnic policy makers:

1. While it was in existence between China's Han-Chinese-centered east coast and the ethnic minority-populated China West in the past, just like the one between the city and the countryside, this economic disparity has escalated since the beginning of the economic reform in the late 1970s (Eide et al., 2008; Li et al., 2009; Ma, 2004; Wang, 2009; Xu, 2009).
2. The glass ceilings against the minority members' career mobility remaining to be shattered have been reinforced in one way or another.
3. The traditional ways of life and identities of the ethnic minorities, such as the Tibetans and the Uyghur, have been facing double pressures from Sinicization (i.e., Ma, 2004), a process of expanding the Han-Chinese influence, and Anglo–American globalization; Anglo–American globalization in turn has been increasingly embraced by the Han-Chinese-led Chinese Communist Party, the Chinese Central Government, and the Han-Chinese-dominated society (i.e., Eide et al., 2008; Sun, 2008).
4. The bidirectional geographic mobility of ethnic minorities into the eastern areas and the Han-Chinese migration into traditional western ethnic minority areas on a nationwide scale in search for jobs and a better life have made social, political, and organizational life in China multiethnic (Anonymous, 2006; Ge, 2009; Hao, 2009; Jin, 2007; Wang, 2009). However, a nationwide strategy for an effective management of interethnic relations at the

governmental, organizational and societal levels is still virtually absent (Wang, 2009).

Such problems have constituted major reasons for the intensified interethnic conflicts in recent years, particularly marked by the so-called March 14, 2008, Riots in Tibetan areas and the bloody July 5, 2009, Riots in Xinjiang. During the 2008 Riots, Tibetans used violence against Han-Chinese and Hui Muslims who were doing business in the localities. During the 2009 Riots, the Uyghur killed nearly 200 Han-Chinese and burned their vehicles and businesses in Urumuqi, the capital city of the Xinjiang Uyghur Autonomous Region, and invited an immediate revenge on the part of the Han-Chinese 2 days later. To end the conflicts, the Chinese police had to quell the two opposing sides, respectively.

The authors of this chapter are a US–China transnational team of researchers taking an ethnographic perspective on the interethnic conflicts in contemporary China. The purpose of this chapter is to contribute to China's effort to rebuild interethnic harmony and to inform the global audience about China's long march toward achieving this goal. This chapter presents a critical synthesis of literature in English, some fieldwork and original research resulted in the past few years, and some major pieces of indigenous Chinese literature (current scholarly sources in Chinese characters written by Chinese authors, many of whom are ethnic minorities themselves and have published Chinese government documents) which are not usually available to the international scholarly community. Based on the integration of the three types of sources, this chapter presents updated facts and figures about the status of interethnic relations, conflicts, their causes, and consequences as well as possible solutions in contemporary China.

2 History and Social Dynamics of Chinese Ethnicities

China has a long and rich history of diverse ecology, and multicultural and multiethnic interaction and integration. Archeological data can demonstrate this history as long as 10,000 years (Lin, 2001; Wang, 2000a). This chapter tentatively classifies it into three major periods: (1) the Neolithic (9000bce–3500bce); (2) the Ancient Historical (3500bce–1840cd), and (3) the Modern (1840–now). Since the discussion on the ethnicities of Neolithic China involves archeological elaboration and is beyond the scope and purpose of this chapter, we will focus on the last two periods.

2.1 The Ancient Imperial Time and Conflicts Between the Central Power and the Peripherals

According to the legend (see Bilik, Lee, Shi, & Phan, 2004; Lee & Li, 2010), the formation of ancient imperial Chinese central power started from a war between three major tribes: Emperors of Yan, Huang, and Chiyou, around 6,000 years ago. Emperor Huang (the Yellow Emperor) defeated the Yan and Chiyou in sequence, and the offspring of Chiyou escaped or was banished into the remote wildness of four cardinal directions called four seas and thus became four categories of barbarians (see Hsu, 1981; Wang, 2000a, 2000b; Wang & Song, 1998; Yuan, 1988). Since then, the central plain of China was formulated into a civilized political power called the Central Kingdom, and local states or tribes in four directions were regarded as barbarian but were incorporated into a nominally unified imperial system. Given the condition, it is no wonder that wars and natural disasters often made the peripheral barbarians resist or challenge the self-assumed civilized Central Kingdom.

According to a classic book *Shanhaijing,* or *Records of Ancient Mountains, Seas and Oceans* (Shang Hai Jing, c. 2200 b.c./1925; Xu, 1991), the ancient Central Kingdom (China) was surrounded by the Great Wilderness (*dahuang*), where half-man and half-animal barbarians lived. The people of the ethnic groups from the center of civilization confronted the barbaric people in the peripheral areas in the ethnic and cultural process of Zhongguo (China) or Sinicization as a Central Kingdom or in defense of their civilization. In other words, Chinese history is a history of the ethnic conflict between the Central Kingdom and the peripheral region. While many people may not fully understand the *Shanhaijing*, the book demonstrated diverse totems, lifestyles, and identities of ethnic groups outside the Central Kingdom over 4,000 years ago (Chinese Shanghaijing Scholarly Society, 1986; Xu, 1991). *Shanhaijing* recorded ethnographic diversity and various lifestyles of different tribes around the world.

Diverse cultural examples include the description of a tribe of one-eyed people (*Yimuguo*) and that of a country of three-headed barbarians (*Sanshouguo*). While *Shanhaijing* as a classic often raises an issue of validity, archeologists and historians in China often substantiate their arguments or interpretations with citations from this book (see Wang, 2000a, 2000b; Wang & Song, 1998; Yuan, 1988).

The earliest core area of the Chinese Central Kingdom is based on the middle and lower reaches of the Yellow River. Other peoples in the four directions (i.e., outside the Central Plain) were portrayed or stereotyped differently. The *Shanhaijing* has two implications. First, China as a country of cultural diversity in political unity has a long history of diverse ethnic cultures for the past 5,000 years in its written record. Second, China is a country that shows a constant internal cultural conflict between the center and the peripheral regions in its process of acculturation and integration.

As Bilik et al. (2004) verify, people in the east of central China were stereotyped as *Dong Yi*, including today's Koreans and Vietnamese; people in the south were stereotyped as *Nan Man*; people in the west were described as *Xi Rong*; and people in the north were described as *Bei Di*. These peripheral groups were all negatively stereotyped as barbarians in need of civilization. After thousands of years of war, trade, migration, and intermarriage, both the peripheral and central ethnic groups have shared much in common as a result of the interactions, despite the apparent ecological, linguistic, religious, and other cultural differences (Yuan, 1988).

It is only natural that both China and its ethnic groups constantly change their identities and status in a long process of interaction, and the cases of Korea and Vietnam are examples (Bilik et al., 2004). In various dynasties, different Chinese emperors in the Central Kingdom attempted to conquer Vietnam and the Korean Peninsula (which consists of North Korea and South Korea). In the biography of the Eastern Yi and Korean (chapter 55, volume 115, of the *Grand Historical Record* by Sima Qian, 100 b.c./1994), Korea was called the State of Yen and its ruler was designated by the emperor in the Qin and Han dynasties.

Sima Qian (100 b.c./1994) also wrote about Vietnam (Nan Yue, see vols. 113 and 116) as a part of the Han Dynasty. Mongolia, Xinjiang, and some Tibetan areas (called Qiang at the time) were also incorporated as parts of China in the Han Dynasty 2,000 years ago (Bilik et al., 2004). In the Tang Dynasty (ad618–917), the two empires of Tibet and the Central Dynasty interacted so frequently that they entered a marriage bond with an effect of political integration (Bilik et al., 2004).

In pre-modern China, political integration of the areas inhabited by peripheral-ethnic groups means the establishment of the shared administrative framework and a tributary system. Administration here means managing peripheral ethnic areas by a kind of local ethnic autonomy under the supervision of the central government. With the innovation of the Mongol Yuan Dynasty, it later evolved into a "Tusi" or local chiefdom system which was very much like the medieval hereditary feudalism. In China, it is an early practice of "one country, two systems" for it was different from the direct absolute system practiced in central China. The tributary system means that when conquered or defeated, the peripheral areas became integral parts of China and their local ethnic rulers were expected to pay annual tributes to the emperor of the Central Kingdom who was regarded as the common overlord of all under the heaven, and the emperor should confer title, gifts, and support in return. It is expected that when the Central Kingdom became weak politically or militarily, the peripheral ethnic rulers often refused to pay tributes and even attempted to grab the central throne or become independent for a while.

In short, communication, acculturation, political integration, and ethnic re-categorization in a celestial empire made ethnic mobility in pre-modern China easy and frequent. As Confucius put it, "human nature is pretty similar, but cultures or customs make a difference among humans" (Yang, 1965). In other words, "People are similar by nature, but through habituation become quite different from each other." People outside the Central Kingdom could become civilized after they had learned and followed "mainstream ways." The central Chinese people could also become outside "barbarians" if they lost their civilized ritual ways.

2.2 The Modern Transformation and Re-categorization of Ethnicity in China

The year 1840, when the Opium War took place, marked a modern beginning of history in China. It was not until after the Western notion of nation-state was introduced to China when the geographic boundary of China was seen more clearly. Since the 1840–1860 Opium Wars, China as a celestial empire has been continually exposed to unequal treaties, internal concessions, extraterritoriality, indemnity, and foreign control over maritime customs. At the same time, such foreign ideas as the important concept of nation-state were also introduced to China (see Bilik et al., 2004). The hundred years from 1840 to 1945 witnessed a series of bitter struggles between China and a number of foreign intruders and invaders including Britain, Japan, French, Spain, the Netherlands, USA, Germany, and Russia. During 1840–1910, wars, battles, and foreign interferences imposed on China by the nation-states from outside China viciously clipped China of its remote vassal states including Vietnam and Korea, and thus effectively strengthened the Chinese national identity.

The Qing Dynasty (1644–1911) headed by the Manchu emperors and Empress Dowager Cixi tried reluctantly to accommodate the modern foreign powers while trying to reform China into a constitutional monarchy. But the radical non-office-holding elites in China could wait no longer and a rushed revolution in 1911 shattered the Qing dynasty and ended the Celestial Empire which lasted from bc221–ad1911. The 1911 Revolution inaugurated a modern Republic of China (ROC). It also created an immediate frontier crisis during which the Outer Mongolia was lost and Tibet became especially difficult to control.

In the following 40 years, the Kuo Ming Tang (KMT) or the National Party leaders Dr. Sun Yat-Sen and President Jiang Kai-Shek sequentially from the top and the Communist Party of China (CPC) under Chairman Mao Zedong from the bottom jointly led Chinese people of various ethnicities in driving out foreign invaders from mainland China eventually. In the meanwhile, CPC and KMT as two antagonistic major modern parties bitterly competed for the supreme power in China. A civil war immediately following the anti-Japanese war broke out in 1945 and after 3 years, KMT, the nominal ROC, was driven onto Taiwan. Chairman Mao re-unified China except Taiwan, Hong Kong, and Macao in 1949 and proclaimed the birth of a new nation called the Peoples Republic of China (PRC).

In the 1950s, PRC staged an unprecedented ethnic identification for the sake of modern nation building by congregating the first National People's Congress. It mobilized linguists, historians, sociologists, anthropologists, and ethnic representatives in their joint efforts to re-categorize the over 400 applicant ethnic groups into 56, among which 55 were minority nationalities and the rest is the Han mainstream (Lee, Phan, & Shi, 2004).

3 Current Status

3.1 Current Chinese Discourse on Ethnic Relations in China

China is known as "diversity in unity" and variety in harmony (Fei, 1989, p. 1). While the Han-Chinese constitutes the mainstream, the ethnic minorities identify with the Chinese nation at a central level and their own ethnic culture at a regional ethnic level (Ma, 2004). In return, the central government recognizes ethnic diversity and authorizes ethnic/national regional autonomy by means of the National Constitution and the Ethnic-Regional Autonomous Law. Today, this diversity in unity is characterized by the so-called three dimensions of inseparability (Jin, 2007, p. 19), which means that

1. The mainstream Han-Chinese are inseparable from the ethnic minorities;
2. The ethnic minorities are inseparable from the mainstream Han-Chinese;
3. The ethnic minorities are inseparable from each other.

This kind of interdependence is believed to be true in the past, at present, and in the future. As discussed above, the inland Han-Chinese and the frontier ethnic (i.e., peripheral) minorities were in close contact under mutual influence. Contemporary China has witnessed two high tides of internal migration (Xu, 2009). The first was in the period of the planned economy from the early 1950s to the late 1970s; many Han-Chinese migrated to the ethnic regions either due to the famine or due to the national policy to support the economic development of the ethnic regions. In the meanwhile, many ethnic minorities migrated into the central plains for employment or for education. The second tide of migration started in 1978, when China began to adopt the reform and open door policy. It is also bidirectional: the migration of ethnically diverse migrants into the east, south, and central China in search for a better life either by employment or by marriage is accompanied by an influx of Han-Chinese into the western and frontier ethnic areas for a job opportunity or for the creation of natural resources-based businesses such as mining.

Due to mutual complementary nature of China's central plain and frontier ethnic areas in terms of geography, natural resources, cultural resources, and talent, China's further development depends on closer collaborations between the mainstream Han-Chinese and the ethnic minorities (Ge, 2009; Hao, 2009). Such interdependence between different ethnicities reflects "an interethnic view of me in you and you in me" (Hao, 2009, p. 455).

While the interethnic relationship is prescribed to be of equality, unity, mutual assistance, and cooperation, the market competition as a new trait of the relationship has come onto the stage since the early and middle 1990s (Jin, 2007). A more conscientious collaboration for co-prosperity and harmony is bound to be a shared mission of all ethnicities in China as a whole (Jin, 2007).

3.2 Spatial and Population Distribution of the Ethnic Minorities

Based on the 2005 nationwide census with 1% random sample in China, the total population of 55 officially recognized minority ethnic groups is 123.33 million, or 9.44% of the entire population of China. The 123 million is more than 1/3 of the entire US population and close to the entire population of Japan.

According to by Bilik et al. (2004), the 55 ethnic groups plus the mainstream Han-Chinese are the officially recognized collective members of the Chinese Nation, *Zhonghua Minzu.* It has the connotation of a huge Chinese family. The distribution of all Chinese population in groups is tabulated as follows (Census Office of the State Council, P.R. China, 2002 – see Table 8.1)

Table 8.1 The Chinese ethnic group

01	Han (1,137,386,112)
02	Mongol (5,813,947)
03	Hui (9,816,805)
04	Tibetan (5,416,021)
05	Uyghur (8,399,393)
06	Miao or Hmong (8,940,116)
07	Yi (7,762,272)
08	Zhuang (16,178,811)
09	Buyei (2,971,460)
10	Korean (1,923,842)
11	Manchu (10,682,262)
12	Dong (2,960,293)
13	Yao (2,637,421)
14	Bai (1,858,063)
15	Tujia (8,028,133)
16	Hani (1,439,673)
17	Kazak (1,250,458)
18	Dai (1,158,989)
19	Li (1,247,814)
20	Lisu (634,912)

(continued)

Table 8.1 (continued)

21	Wa (396,610)
22	She (709,592)
23	Gaoshan (4,461 within China/inland)
24	Lahu (453,705)
25	Shui (406,902)
26	Dongxiang (513,805)
27	Naxi (308,839)
28	Jingpo (132,143)
29	Kirgiz (160,823)
30	Tu (241,198)
31	Daur (132,394)
32	Mulao (207,352)
33	Qiang (306,072)
34	Blang (91,882)
35	Salar (104,503)
36	Maonan (107,166)
37	Gelao (579,357)
38	Xibe (188,824)
39	Achang (33,936)
40	Pumi (33,600)
41	Tajik (41,028)
42	Nu (28,759)
43	Uzbek (12,370)
44	Russ (15,609)
45	Eweki (30,505)
46	Deang (17,935)
47	Baonan (16,505)
48	Yugur (13,719)
49	Jing (22,517)
50	Tatar (4,890)
51	Derong (7,426)
52	Oroqen (8,196)
53	Hezhe (4,640)
54	Monba (8,923)
55	Lhoba (2,965)
56	Jino (20,899)

It is obvious that the largest ethnic minority groups in China in sequence are the Zhuang in Guangxi Zhuang Autonomous Region (in South China neighboring with Vietnam), the Manchu (in northeast China), the Hui (in diaspora, with a core in Ningxia Hui Autonomous Region and Gansu Province, Northwest China), the Mongols (in northern China), the Yi (in southwest China), the Miao (also known as the Hmong outside China, who are in central south China), the Tibetans (in west of China), and the Uyghur (in Xinjiang, northwest corner China). Refer to (http://www.chinamaps.org/china/china-population-map-large-2.html) for a map and check it especially against the topography of China.

It is remarkable to see that the ethnic population in China almost quadrupled while the Han-Chinese population more than doubled between 1950 and 2005. In 1950, the ethnic population was about 35.32 million, standing for 6.06% of the total nationwide population. The greater increase in the ethnic population is due to the ethnic exemption from the tight national family planning, which limits a Han-Chinese family to having one child in the past 30 years.

The ethnic population distribution in China is characterized by a broad interethnic mixture of smaller ethnic compact communities or clusters (Wang, 2009). While there are ethnic members, amounting to 1/3 of the total ethnic minority population in the mainstream Han-Chinese provinces and cities, there are more Han residents in most of the ethnic autonomous places. According to the fifth nationwide census in 2000, 11 of the 31 provinces/autonomous regions/cities have members of all the 56 ethnicities, and among over 2,800 counties/banners, nearly all have residents of two or more ethnicities. During the 10 years between 1990 and 2000, there was an increase of 10 regions/provinces/cities with 56 ethnicities and that rendered 17 of the 31, or over half of the provincial level units populated by members of at least 50 ethnic minorities. Of the 55 ethnic minorities, 29 have a nationwide presence on the provincial level. The newly added provincial-level units in central China that have over half a million ethnic minority residents are Henan (1.13 million), Shandong (0.62 million), Beijing (0.59 million), and Fujian Province (0.58 million). During the past 30 years, ethnic minorities have demonstrated a strong trend to migrate to metropolitan and coastal regions of southeast China where the economic development is more vibrant. The increase in ethnic minority population in the 1990s was 213.88% in Guangdong Province, 77.63% in Zhejiang, 55.75% in Jiangsu, and 41.20% in the City of Shanghai. The migration of minor ethnic groups with a relatively small population is more visible (see Bilik et al., 2004).

On the contrary, the degree of ethnic clustering (density) is still remarkable. In all, 73% of Mongols in China find their home in Inner Mongolia, and over 70% of Tibetans in China reside in Tibet and neighboring prefecture in western Sichuan Province. About 99% of Uyghur populate Xinjiang Uyghur Autonomous Region and 92% of the Zhuang population lives in the Guangxi Zhuang Autonomous Region. In short, autonomous administrative units on various levels are still the home of the bulk of ethnic minority populations.

The geographic distribution of the ethnic minorities is strongly associated with their livelihood and ecological resources (Wang, 2009). Most of them, i.e., 80.83 million, live in the higher, mountainous, and western part of China and claim 22.5% of the total local population and 65.5%, or 2/3, of China's ethnic minority population. In fact, 70% of the ethnic minority population lives in 10 border provinces/autonomous regions, indicating their extremely important role in national defense.

3.3 Political Status

According to the Press Office of the State Council of China (2005), ethnic regional autonomy or self-governance has been institutionalized since the first draft of China's Constitution in 1954. The Ethnic Regional Autonomous Law of China, drafted in 1984 and rectified in 2001, is the basic political constitution for the ethnic minority areas. By the end of 2003, 155 ethnic autonomous places had been established, consisting of 5 autonomous regions, 30 autonomous prefectures (*zhou*), and 120 autonomous counties. The ethnic autonomous places cover 6.15 million square kilometers and stand for about 64% of China's territory, and most are in the border areas.

Ethnic groups in the autonomous administrative units are granted rights to select their own ethnic leaders in their own communities. The people's congresses and the governments of the 155 autonomous places are headed by members of their own ethnicities as well. The National People's Congress has a disproportionately higher percentage of the ethnic minority representatives. The 10th National People's Congress (2003–2008), for example, consisted of 415 ethnic minority representatives, standing for 13.91% of the total body and is 5.5% higher than the percentage of the ethnic population. In all, 66% of the 10th People's Congress of Xinjiang Uyghur Autonomous Region's 550 representatives from 13 ethnicities are minorities, 6% higher than the average percentage in the total population of Xinjiang (Li et al., 2009, p. 198).

The people's congresses of the ethnic autonomous places enjoy the privilege of establishing their local legal adaptations consistent with their unique political, economic, and cultural traditions. By the end of 2003, 133 autonomous guidelines and 348 local ethnic exceptions had been passed. A total of 68 changes and modifications of civic laws such as marriage law, inheritance law, land law and prairie law, and so on had been approved to fit with the age-old traditions of the local ethnic minorities.

Members of major ethnic minorities have filled quite a few positions of national leadership such as vice-premier of the State Council, vice-chairman of the National People's Congress (NPC), and vice-chairman of the Chinese People's Political Consultative Conference (CPPCC) since the founding of PRC. Ulanhu from the Mongolian, Wei Guoqing from the Zhuang, Yang Jingren from the Hui, Tian Bao from the Titetan, and Seypidin from the Uyghur served as the Secretary of the Chinese Communist Party in Inner Mongolia, Guangxi, Ningxia, Tibet, and Xinjiang, respectively, in all the five autonomous regions of China before 1990s. Currently, Hui Liangyu, a member of the Hui ethnicity, is Vice-Premier of the State Council in charge of agriculture and ethnic work.

Ethnic autonomy has effectively protected the social stability, border security, ethnic minorities' equal rights, and enhanced economic productivity (Xu, 2009). However, since the 1990s, the provincial level Chinese Communist Party secretary's positions in ethnic autonomous regions have not been filled by ethnic minority members. The March 14th Riot in the Tibetan area in 2008 and the July 5th Riot in Xinjiang in 2009 have taken place against this background. A question arises if this model of ethnic autonomy has been implemented effectively in the recent decades of economic reform.

3.4 Economic Status

China's ethnic minority areas are rich in natural resources (Jin, 2007). For example, they house 75% of China's total prairie, 37.2% of China's forestry, 56.3% of China's total volume of timber, and 52.5% of China's irrigation resources, i.e., the strategic fresh water.

While there was an average annual economic growth of 8.7% in the ethnic minority areas between 1996 and 1999, the average growth in these areas was 10.1% between 2000 and 2004, which is almost on par with the central and east coastal areas. Among these areas, Xinjiang is worth special attention. It is reported that the net income of the peasants of Xinjiang per head is now 12.4 times more than that in 1977 (Li, 2009).

However, the economic disparity between the frontier ethnic minority areas and eastern and central China has escalated, especially since the beginning of China's economic liberalization at the end of 1970s. Today, the western ethnic minority areas in China have an annual GDP of 4,250 RMB per head, an equivalent of US$625, standing for a mere 60% of the national average and less than 47% per head in China's eastern coastal provinces and cities (Na, 2006; Wang, 2009). While the population in west China covers 23% of the national population, its total GDP is only 14% of the national GDP. This is further confirmed by the fact that while there are still 30 million people below the poverty line in China today, most of them are in central and western China. In fact, there are about 10 million ethnic minority members below the poverty line (Hao, 2009). Wang's statistics from China's poverty reduction office (Wang, 2009) are even more alarming. The ethnic minority population in absolute poverty by the end of 2004 was 47.7% of the total national population of absolute poverty. This may have been partly due to the Chinese Government's strategy of prioritizing the economic development of China's coastal regions over its inland regions (which include western China) since the end of the 1970s (Li et al., 2009; Na, 2006). To address this problem, the State Council has created the Plan of Affirmative Action for Minor Minority Groups to vitalize the economic development of the border areas and enrich the people's livelihood there (2005–2010). This aims to wipe out poverty among these ethnicities (Jin, 2007). Data are yet to be collected and analyzed to determine if this goal has been met.

3.5 Linguistic, Cultural, Religious, and Educational Status

The linguistic, ethnic cultural, and religious diversity has been increasingly respected and protected in contemporary China (Lee & Li, 2010; Li, 2009; Li & Lundberg, 2008; Ma, 2004; Press Office of State Council, P.R. China, 2006; Wang, 2009). More than 80 ethnic languages are still in use, and about ten written language systems have been artificially created for ten spoken ethnic languages, with little practical usage since 1957 (Ma, 2004).

According to Jin (2009), 53 of the 55 ethnic groups in China (except the Manchurian and the Hui who have their own languages but speak the Chinese language) speak their own languages. Of these ethnic minorities, 22 have 28 ethnic writings. Based on a survey conducted in 2000, over half of the total ethnic minority population, or about 68 million inhabitants, still speak their own language. Multilingualism or bilingualism is increasingly practiced in legal, government, and educational sectors in most ethnic areas, including Inner Mongolia, Xinjiang, and Tibet. The official documents and simultaneous interpretation at important occasions, such as annual plenary session of the central committee of the Chinese Communist Party, NPC, and the CPPCC, are also provided in major ethnic languages such as Mongolian, Tibetan, Uyghur, Kazak, Korean, Yi, and Zhuang. According to Wang (2009), some major ethnic languages such as Mongolian, Tibetan, Uyghur, Korean, and Yi have been computerized, and software versions of more ethnic languages are also coming up. Based on Ma's findings (2004), while more Han-Chinese learned ethnic languages during the first three decades since the founding of P.R. China, more ethnic minorities have studied the Mandarin during the second three decades. However, very few Han-Chinese today learn ethnic languages in the institutions of higher learning.

Since 1950s, the central government of China proclaims that over 100 million Chinese are believers of various religions; over half of them are ethnic minorities. Two of the five major religions in China are Tibetan Buddhism and Islam. Since freedom of religion is protected and respected by the Chinese Constitution (Press Office of State Council, P.R. China, 2006), by 2003, 1,700 Tibetan Buddhist temples had been refurbished with 46,000 resident monks in Tibet alone, while 3,788 mosques were in place with 26,000 resident imams in Xinjiang. In Ningxia Autonomous Region, there are 3,500 mosques with 5,100 imams. This is in contrast to that in the decades before the Economic Reform which began in 1978, especially during the Cultural Revolution (1966–1976) when temples and mosques were toppled and the religious believers were persecuted.

Ethnic cultural diversity has also been protected and promoted in China since 1978 (Press Office of State Council, P.R. China, 2006). Two of the ethnic cultural heritage sites – the Potala Palace in Tibet and the Lijiang Ancient City – have been inscribed into the world heritage list by United Nations Education, Science and Culture Organization (UNESCO). The Ancient Naxi Scripts have made the "List of World Memory Heritage Items." There are 157 ethnic minority hospitals, consisting of 55 Tibetan hospitals, 41 Mongolian hospitals, and 35 Uyghur hospitals. Seven nationwide competitions involving ethnic minority sports have been held. The most recent one was held in Ningxia Autonomous Region in 2003 and consisted of 14 ethnic minority sports contests and 125 kinds of ethnic minority sports.

During recent years, to resist the tendency of cultural homogenization and globalization, large-scale initiatives have been taken to protect and promote ethnic cultures. In 2003, a China Ethnic Cultures Protection Project of 18 years was initiated by China's Ministry of Culture and Ministry of Finance. In 2006, China's Eleventh Five-Year Plan for Cultural Development was issued which consists of special guidelines for the protection of ethnic minority cultures. Yunnan Province has included ethnic culture development as one of its three top strategies. Ms. Yang Liping, an internationally distinguished ethnic choreographer of the Bai from Yunnan Province, has become a spokeswoman for ethnic cultural diversity in Yunnan. Her *Impressions of Yunnan,* which the first author of this chapter watched during his field research, is put on the stage every night in the Hall of the People's Congress in Kunming, capital city of Yunnan Province. The show is created by Yang based on her insights into ethnic cultures of Yunnan. Inner Mongolia has also identified the development of regional nomadic cultures as its strategic goal. Guizhou Province branded itself as "the Land of Ethnic Arts" early in the beginning of the 1990s. Xinjiang, Ningxia, Tibet, and Qinghai have also taken similar measures. The Chinese Association for Promotion of Ethnic Minority Cultures and Arts, founded in 2003, has sponsored the First Western China Fair for Ethnic Minority Cultures and the First All China Ethnic Minority Cultures Fair. In 2009, The 16th Congress of International Union of Anthropology and Ethnology was held in Kunming, Yunnan, hosted by the Chinese Association for Anthropology and Ethnology. The conference theme was "Humanity, Development, and Cultural Diversity."

Educational opportunities for ethnic minorities have multiplied at various levels due to China's affirmative action programs, such as lowering the higher education admission scores for ethnic minorities. The rate of literacy in Mandarin has significantly increased among all ethnic minorities (Xu, 2009). For example, the literacy rate in Xinjiang in 1949 was 10%. Today, the middle school enrollment rate is 85%, with the goal of 95% in 2010. The high school enrollment rate is 60% of the age set. More than 80% K-12 educational facilities are expected to have Internet access by 2010 (Xu, 2009).

Tibet is also a case of educational improvement. According to Xu (2009), approximately 95%

of the total Tibetan people were denied the right to education before 1959. Tibet today enjoys a 70% elementary school enrollment rate. Also, 80% of the 21,000 members of the total teaching staff members in Tibet are Tibetan (Xu, 2009). The University of Tibet, Tibetan Ethnic College, and College of Tibetan Medicine have produced a total of 60,000 graduates in various disciplines such as Tibetan history and Tibetan medicine. The first author attended a Tibetan studies conference at the University of California at Irvine in Spring 2008, and even met a Tibetan monk who had been educated by one such institution in Tibet. He was studying for a Ph.D. in Public Health at the University of California at Los Angeles with a fund from the Chinese Government. This monk/student made a presentation on how to compile a trilingual Tibetan–Chinese–English dictionary of Tibetan medicine. During his field research in Fall 2009, the first author traveled to Deqen in the northwest tip of Yunnan, a Tibetan Autonomous Prefecture bordering with Tibet now called Shangri-la. He personally visited a Tibetan monastery that houses Tibetan medicine. This confirms what has been described by Xu (2009), i.e., efforts are being made to revive the Tibetan tradition now.

However, ethnic minorities do face an enormous challenge in language education, especially in underdeveloped ethnic areas. During the first three decades since the founding of P.R. China, ethnic minorities faced the challenge of linguistic education as they had to learn Mandarin Chinese as an interethnic language for the national unity or for employment at school, rendering it difficult to maintain their ethnic language education at school (i.e., Tournadre, 2003; Wang & Phillion, 2009). Since the beginning of the economic liberalization in China in late 1970s, as a result of globalization, ethnic minorities have increasingly found it imperative to learn English as a global language. As a result, the unfinished search for a bilingual education model is burdened with a search for a model for trilingual education (i.e., Adamson & Feng, 2009; Feng, February, 2005). Ethnic minority language education suffers due to the external imperatives to learn the mainstream Mandarin Chinese and to learn the global English. Finally, while there is an excess of ethnic civil officials, there is a severe shortage of ethnic engineers and managers in the ethnic areas (Wang, 2009). The demands for the skilled personnel from the Movement of West China Development initiated by the Chinese Government 10 years ago are far from being met.

3.6 Institutions for the Affairs of the Ethnic Minorities

There are altogether 15 institutions of higher learning for ethnic minorities in China (China State Council Information & Press Office, 2010). They are the Minzu (Ethnic/Nationality) University of China in Beijing; Southwest Ethnic University in Chengdu, Sichuan Province; Northwest Ethnic College in Lanzhou, capital city of Gansu Province; North China Ethnic University in Yinchuan, capital city of Ningxia Hui Autonomous Region; Dalian Ethnic College in Dalian, Liaoning Province; Inner Mongolia Ethnic Minority University in Tongliao, Inner Mongolia; Hubei Ethnic College in Enshi, Hubei; Guangxi Ethnic College in Nanning, capital city of Guangxi Zhuang Autonomous Region; Guizhou Ethnic College in Guiyang, capital city of Guizhou; Yunnan Ethnic College in Kunming, capital city of Yunnan Province; Tibet Ethnic College in Xianyang, Shaanxi Province; and Qinghai Ethnic College in Xining, capital city of Qinghai Province. Moreover, each autonomous region has a university with regional ethnic features. There are also quite a few ethnic minority vocational colleges such as Heilongjiang Ethnic Vocational College in Harbin, capital city of Heilongjiang Province; Hunan Ethnic Vocational College in Changsha, Hunan Province; and Ningxia Ethnic Vocational and Technological College in Yinchuan, capital city of Ningxia. There is also an ethnic minority cadres training institution called the Central Ethnic Cadres College specializing in training cadres of ethnic minority affairs.

There are eight ethnic cultural institutions, such as the China Ethnic Languages Translation

Center, the Ethnic Press, the Central Ethnic Song and Dance Troupe, the Ethnic China Journal, the Ethnic Pictorial Press, China Ethnic Minority Daily Press, Ethnic Cultural Palace, and China Ethnic Cultural Museum.

There are 21 national societies or associations for promoting ethnic studies and ethnic affairs action, divided into three categories. The first category comprises associations including China Association for National Unity and Progress, China Association for International Exchanges of Ethnic Scholars, China Society for Inter-national Cooperation & Promoting Ethnic Economy, China Association for Ethnic Middle Schools, China Association for Ethnic Medicines, and so on. The second category is scholarly societies such as China Anthropology/Ethnology Society, China Society for Ethnic Economics, China Society for Ethnic Bilingual Education, China Society for Ethnic Architecture, China Society for Ethnic Philosophies and Histories of Social Thought, Society for Promoting Research and Development of West China, China Society for Mongolian Philology, China Society for Korean Philology, and so on. The third category is institutions for social causes such as China Society for Protecting Ethnic Cultural Heritages, and China Society for Promoting Ethnic Cultures and Arts.

There are hundreds of institutions of ethnic minority studies around the country, of which the Ethnology and Anthropology Institute of China's Academy for Social Sciences is ranked number one. The Research Office of the Ethnic Committee of China's National People's Congress and the Ethnic Issues Research Center of the State Ethnic Affairs Commission also exert a direct impact on China's policy making toward ethnic minorities. There are similar research bodies at various levels of the government, especially at the autonomous regional/provincial/city levels. These research institutes are playing a more important and active role in advising on nationwide ethnic policy making. For example, initiated and sponsored by the Ethnic Minority Issues Research Center of the State Ethnic Affairs Commission, *Beijing-Oslo Recommendations on Protection for the Rights of Linguistic Minorities* (Eide et al., 2008) was presented to the Central Government and released to the public in Beijing in May 2008. So far as we are informed, a new effort is being made to hold a similar conference on ethnic cultural diversity between the Chinese scholarly community of ethnic affairs and a North American counterpart. In Fall 2009, a leading Canadian ethnic cultural psychologist, John Berry, conducted a lecture tour on the Canadian model of ethnic cultural diversity among ethnic universities in China. The first author personally met him while he was visiting the Minzu University of China in Beijing, China.

National bodies coordinating nationwide ethnic affairs include the State Ethnic Affairs Commission of the State Council, the Ethnic Minorities Committee of National People's Congress, and the Ethnic and Religious Committee of Chinese People's Political Consultative Commission. There are also similar bodies coordinating ethnic affairs at the ministerial, provincial, city and autonomous regional, and even prefectural and county levels. For example, the Chinese Ministry of Education is equipped with a Department of Ethnic Minority Education.

4 Causes of Conflicts Between the Han-Chinese and the Ethnic Minorities

Based on what is delineated above under "III Current Status," one is inclined to conclude that contemporary China's current state of ethnic affairs is in good condition. While this may be true comparatively and historically, the above also suggests that China's gigantic bureaucracy of ethnic affairs governance in all of the above six areas is state controlled and top-down. It is ineffectively and inadequately adapting to the changing times. In other words, it all looks good on static terms, but not in good usage. For example, ethnic education has been limited to ethnic institutions of higher learning only and to mostly ethnic minority students, though in reality ethnic education should be offered to all citizens regardless of one's ethnicity.

Political representation of ethnic minorities may also smack of tokenism. Given the above reasons as well as other ones, one should not be surprised about the intensification of interethnic conflicts during the past ten years. In fact, "III Current Status" documents some of the most recent efforts in some ethnic areas and regions to reduce such conflicts. Obviously, these efforts were too late or not forceful enough to prevent such conflicts as the March 14th Riots and the July 5th Riots from occurring.

The authors of this chapter identify four major causes for the intensification of conflicts between the Han-Chinese and the ethnic minorities during the past 10 years, despite the most recent efforts to address such conflicts by the Chinese Government at both the national, regional/provincial, city, and even county levels: (1) economic disparity; (2) political power deficit; (3) the unchecked social evolutionism or Han chauvinism; and (4) the outdated model of ethnic administration. Each of these four causes will be detailed below:

1. Despite the enormous improvement in the economic condition of ethnic minorities since 1949, especially since 1979, as documented above, the economic disparity between the eastern coastal mainstream and the western frontier ethnic areas has escalated, especially since the end of the 1970s when China began economic reform (Wang, 2009). On the one hand, the national strategy to prioritize the development of coastal areas in the first two decades of the reform pumped most resources there and invested significantly less on the ethnic minority areas. In the meanwhile, natural resources in the ethnic area have been opened up vigorously to serve national interest with little care of the local interest and ecological losses or stakes. "This is the biggest source of the (interethnic) conflict," according to Jin (2007, p. 214). Such disparity is also articulated by Ma (2004) who called the tendency "very worrisome" (p. 136). This explains why Hao Shiyuan (2009), Director of the Ethnology and Anthropology Institute, China Academy for Social Sciences, himself a Mongolian, advised China's top leadership face to face while he was lecturing China's Political Bureau: "To rid of poverty in ethnic minority areas should be the top priority of all the ethnic issues" (p. 455).

These scholarly observations are confirmed by the first author's findings through his field research in Inner Mongolia in the summer of 2008, a month before the Beijing Olympic Games began. A group of Inner-Mongolian informants in Hohhot said that most mines and other big businesses in ethnic autonomous regions such as Inner Mongolia, Xinjiang, and Tibet are owned by Han-Chinese businessmen from the east coastal provinces and cities. Taking the advantage of the first bucket of gold from the eastern coast such as Zhejiang and Jiangsu, these businessmen have been making a fortune out of these ethnic areas, but local ethnic residents have not seen themselves benefiting from such business developments. Again, according to these informants, some of these Han-Chinese entrepreneurs bribe the local officials to get their identity changed into an ethnic minority in order to tap the privileges allocated by the Central Government to ethnic minorities, including bearing two children per family (for the Han-Chinese, the one-child policy has been applied), lowering the scores for school and university admissions, tax exemptions, etc. In addition, employment opportunities for young and educated ethnic minorities are relatively scarce due to the cultural barriers between the businessmen and the local residents. As a result, some ethnic minority members feel discriminated or oppressed. These situations create resentment against the mainstream Han-Chinese among the ethnic minorities.

The local governments have put the basic livelihood of ethnic minorities and that of other subaltern social groups on the back burner to make room for economic, i.e., GDP, development, especially in the heydays of unbridled free market in the 1990s and early part of the first decade of the twenty-first century. For example, the native Yi minority members indigenous to the Stone Forest region of Yunnan were once asked to move out of the Stone Forest region with an offer of some compensation by the national Bureau of Tourism for making the Stone Forest a World Heritage Site. This is informed by a local Yi tour guide when the first author toured the Stone Forest. Since the development model has been primarily economic, emulating the free market economy and chasing after GDP, there was inadequate consideration of the uniqueness of the ethnic cultures and the special needs of the ethnic residents. It is understandable why the Hu Jintao–Wen Jiabao Administration today is calling for a more scientific model of development centering on meeting the needs of people or *yi ren wei ben,* and quality over speed in terms of *youhao youkuai* as a holistic and sustainable model (CCP Department of Publicity Theory Group, 2009).

2. The political dominance of the mainstream over the autonomous ethnic regions despite great improvements in the political status of China's ethnic minorities since the late 1990s. Currently, the CCP secretary positions of all the autonomous ethnic regions are filled by the mainstream Han-Chinese, and no ethnic minority members serve as the CPC Secretary of these autonomous regions. This is also true for all other top levels of the administrative units of the Central Government. For example, the Party boss of Inner Mongolia University, which the first author visited during his fieldwork in the summer of 2008, is a Han. In addition, the Department of Organization of CCP, which is in charge of evaluating and promoting high-ranking CPC officials and high-ranking government officials, has always been headed by a member of the mainstream cultural background. Last but not least, the CPC's 9-member Political Bureau standing committee does not have a single ethnic minority member or a woman, either. This makes it very much like the state of women and ethnic minorities of the USA before the 1970s. It is obvious that though Chinese ethnic minorities enjoy political equality in the law, a sustained effort should be made to implement nationwide diversity education about ethnic–cultural–religious (gender as well) equality and to implement the existing laws to ensure that such equality will be materialized.
3. The Han-Chinese ethnocentrism in the name of modernization has been on the rise since 1979 when China began to adopt the market economy policy. "There is a tendency to totally extend the institutions and ways from the mainstream Han areas to the ethnic areas with disregard to the specific situations of the ethnic regions and against the wishes of the ethnic minorities…," according to Ma (2004, p. 138). As a result, the case of disrespect (either real or perceived) for ethnic minorities' lifestyles and cultural norms occurs quite often (Wang, 2009). For example, some Muslim restaurants are not so Muslim and leave Muslim members' needs unmet or even have them offended. While most mainstream Hans are atheist and increasingly hedonist, most ethnic migrants are deeply religious and are finding themselves culturally and religiously alienated or marginalized. This is also true of ethnic minority education in the national education system. For example, all ethnic minority areas are obliged to adopt the same national curriculum, textbooks, and examinations, with little adaptation to the specific situation and special need of each and every ethnicity. There has also been a tendency to use Mandarin as the language of instruction in bilingual education due to the lack of consideration for ethnic cultural patterns.

This is no wonder. A perusal of hundreds of selected policy speeches on China's ethnic issues by the Chinese leaders since the founding of P.R. China (Jin, 2006a, 2006b) reveals this pattern: While the first generation of the Chinese leadership, such as Mao Zedong, Zhou Enlai, and Liu Shaoqi, was consistently and persistently vocal in anti-Han chauvinism, especially between 1949 and 1966, the discourse seems to have gradually died down in the subsequent generations of Chinese leadership. This has been especially so since the early 1990s, after the collapse of the former Soviet. In the first 15 years of the history of P.R. China, China's ethnic minority policy model can be best characterized as "diversity in unity and harmony," although partially thanks to the effect of class struggle discourse. It was fundamentally changed by the Cultural Revolution (1966–1976), and "class and conflict" dominated its second 15 years. During the most recent 30 years of the economic reform, with chasing a high GDP as the overriding goal, China's ethnic minority policy model seems to have become more and more assimilationist on the basis of the Han mainstream version of modernization. For example, Mao gave three speeches exclusively calling against Han chauvinism. On March 16, 1953, he wrote a short speech addressing all CCP members titled "Criticizing Han Chauvinism" (Jin, 2006, p. 488). It began by saying: "Interethnic relationship in some areas is very abnormal. This is intolerable to CCP. We must scathingly criticize Han chauvinism among many CCP members and CCP cadres" (Jin, 2006, p. 488). After only 3 days, Mao wrote again as a footnote to his previous speech: "Again the major danger is Han chauvinism, not ethnic chauvinism" (Jin, 2006, p. 489). On October 11, 1955, Mao wrote: "We must continue fighting against Han chauvinism…. There are still many instances of it, such as misrepresenting ethnic minorities, disrespecting their cultures, feeling a sense of superiority over them and looking down upon them economically, etc." (Jin, 2006, p. 531). Mao expressed his anti-Han chauvinism stance in many other occasions. Liu Shaoqi and Zhou Enlai, CCP's No. 2 and No. 3 leaders, echoed Mao with high frequency. However, in selected speeches on ethnic minority issues by more recent Chinese leaders, i.e., Deng Xiaoping, Jiang Zemin, and Hu Jintao, such vocal policy discourse is virtually absent.

4. The model of ethnic classification in China consistent with the planned economy is increasingly unfit for the open and mobile society of the market economy. The government policy of affirmative action in terms of food rations, childbirth, school admission standards, and crime leniency creates resentment of the mainstream society and enlarges the rifts between the two. The ethnic labels are also to blame for reinforcing the sense of ethnic identity while diminishing their sense of national citizenship. The everyday unreflective use of ethnic labels, such as the Mongols, the Han, the Tibetans, and the Huis, perpetuates and enlarges the divide between ethnicity and national citizenship, leaving different ethnic groups with a weak sense of connection and unity. Finally, the ethnic institutions of higher learning and its curriculum exert the same effect. Such curricula on ethnic studies are not usually offered in mainstream Chinese universities, either due to lack of such a vision or lack of faculties specializing in ethnic studies.

5 Consequences

As a combination of the above causes and possible instigation by outside pro-independence forces, two bloody interethnic conflicts occurred in 2008 and 2009. The first one is the March 14th Riot which occurred in Tibetan Areas represented by Lhasa (Xinhua Net, March 22, 2008). Some local Tibetans used violence against the Han and Hui businesspeople, their businesses on the streets of Lhasa, and some local government organs. They killed about 18 people and burned dozens of cars and shops. On July 5, 2009, a similar event occurred in Urmuqi, Xinjiang, on an even larger scale (Xian QQ.com, July 8, 2009). Hundreds of Uyghur youths killed 156 Han-Chinese and burned their businesses and vehicles, and the Uyghur suffered some backlash 2 days later. A total of 1080 persons were reportedly injured. As a result of these two bloody events, contemporary China has entered into one of the darkest eras of interethnic relationship in the history of P.R. China. This relationship is strained by a combination of interethnic resentment, misunderstanding, distrust, and even hatred built up over the past decades, and thus, they sound an alarm for deep reflection on the current ethnic policy model.

6 Possible Resolutions

Ethnic issues in current China are related to cultural and spiritual beliefs. Most of the ethnic groups in China, including the traditional mainstream Hans believed in either shamanism, Confucianism, Daoism, or Buddhism before the 1950s (Lee & Li, 2010). The Tibetan and Mongolian Chinese or their nearby areas believe in Tibetan Buddhism on top of Bonism or shamanism. The Uygur, Hui, and several other ethnic groups are Islamic. Dealing well with religious or spiritual beliefs will definitely help to deal with interethnic conflicts in China.

According to a recent report (Li, 2004), interethnic marriages between the Muslim, especially the Uyghur in Xinjiang, and mainstream Han-Chinese have become more difficult than before, partially due to the difference in beliefs. In fact, many Han people do not have any spiritual beliefs and there is a vacuum or hunger for spirituality (Lee, 2001).

The Chinese government needs a long-term strategy to harmonize ethnic relations by promoting a better mutual understanding about cultures and beliefs – i.e., humanistic values or beliefs among all ethnic minority groups in China, including the mainstream Han-Chinese (Lee & Li, 2010).

After the two tragic events, the Chinese Government has responded by doing the following: First, the criminals have been legally identified and punished; second, the leaderships of these two autonomous regions have been reshuffled; and third, large sums of funds as part of the stimulus money have been allocated to ethnic minority areas, especially Tibet and Xinjiang. For example, recently, the State Council of P.R. China has allocated 310 billion RMB (US$ 45.6 billion) to Tibet with the goal of boosting Tibet's GDP and catch up with the national average by 2020. In addition, provinces/cities of the east coast and central China have been asked by the Government to contribute to the development of Xinjiang and Tibet either in cash, goods, services, or personnel. However, the soft side of the disparity, such as political, social, ethnic/cultural/religious, and educational dimensions that could provide a more sustainable cure, still receives insufficient attention. Therefore, while applauding the proactive and forceful economic measures in addressing the conflicts, we give the following suggestions for amelioration and prevention of similar conflicts.

7 Suggestions

1. Create interethnic town-hall style dialogs in local interethnic communities to talk about how such conflicts came into being and how they could be ameliorated and prevented in the future. Solutions to such conflicts proposed by the grass roots could complement the solutions proposed by the political and intellectual elites. Such solutions are from within and tend to be organic. They are more likely to stay than solutions from top-down or from outside the local communities.
2. Create interethnic community mediation services to manage or resolve such interethnic conflicts. Both social and professional elites could be trained in interethnic knowledge and skills and recruited to identify and mediate interethnic conflicts before they escalate.
3. Create public media programs to teach about interethnic communication and develop skills in interethnic harmony. Real-life cases and real-life characters of successful interethnic communication and harmony cultivation in the workplace, in the community, and in private relationships could be highlighted in such programs. This could help reduce interethnic conflicts and cultivate interethnic harmony.

The above suggestions constitute a range of solutions in addressing a range of interethnic conflicts at different stages. While the first one aims to address the conflicts that have already broken out, the second one is intended to manage conflicts before they escalate, and the last one is designed to prevent interethnic conflicts from happening. Working together, they could make a significant contribution to the creation of interethnic harmony in China.

8 Suggestions for Policy Making Regarding Interethnic Relations

1. Many models of diversity management, such as the US model of bottom-up, initiated by grass-roots movements, including the Women's Movement/the Feminist Movement and the Civil Rights Movement, are good references. All educational institutions in China, not just ethnic education institutions, should research and teach about diversity, and civic institutions should create ways to create public consensus. It was based on the consensus reached by the different groups in the USA in the late 1960s that the Johnson Administration signed the Civil Rights into law. So, in a way, the US model of diversity is bottom-up, open ended, and legally ensured. The fact that a minority president has been elected President of the USA, and a female presidential candidate competed for the same office, demonstrates the effectiveness of this ever-improving model. In comparison, the Chinese Soviet model is still top-down and close ended. It remains virtually the same despite the dramatic changes the Chinese society has undergone during the past 30 years. We suggest that China should formulate her ethnic policies on the basis of the relevant laws. More room should be allowed for the civil society to emerge so that the model of diversity could be able to adapt to the new changes in a timely manner. Due to a heightened degree of interethnic mobility of the Chinese society at large during the past three decades, a new model of interethnic integration should come into play. This new model should aim to protect ethnic identity, cultivate interethnic identity, affirm national identity, and infuse a global identity into the other three.

   In a word, it is a four-layer (ethnic, interethnic, national, and global) identity model that is more inclusive, more cosmopolitan, and more forward-looking than the traditional model, which solely emphasizes ethnic identity. The new model should focus on the management of the interactions among multiple identities. The traditional model which focuses on control should retire.
2. Instead of relying solely on economic compensation to resolve interethnic conflicts, we suggest that more and better educational opportunities should be created to motivate and train ethnic minorities to succeed in all professions, especially in some key professions and industries such as law, economics, information technology, and cultural industries. Such new technological and professional elites of ethnic minority backgrounds should be given equal opportunity by law to compete with Han-Chinese, and should be encouraged to break the glass ceiling in politics and other key fields.
3. Make education about ethnic minorities and interethnic communication a part of the mandatory general education curriculum in all Chinese universities. This should be part of Chinese citizenship education for every adult member of all the 56 ethnic groups, including the Han-Chinese. All international studies, universities, colleges, departments, and programs in China should be strong in both internationally oriented intercultural studies and domestically oriented interethnic studies. The interethnic curriculum and international studies curriculum should be integrated as the two are increasingly interrelated.
4. All cadres (both Han-Chinese and ethnic minority members) whose jobs, positions, and assignments are closely related to ethnic affairs must be proficient in both bilingualism and multiculturalism in knowledge and leadership. This bilingual and multiethnic proficiency should be one of the basic criteria to evaluate all civil workers and government officials at all levels of the administration of each ethnic and interethnic area.
5. In the USA, before the Civil Rights Movement, terms such as the Italians, the Jews, the Blacks, and the Indians were used in the same way. However, since the Civil Rights Movement and the postmodern revolution, politically correct terms such as Native-Americans, Chinese-Americans, and African–Americans

have been introduced into education, law, and the public sphere. All racial/ethnic identities are equally recognized, respected, and all of them share in common American citizenship. China could learn from the USA in adopting dual-identity labels such as the *Hanzu zhongguoren* (the Han-Chinese), the *Zangzu zhongguoren* (the Tibetan-Chinese), and the *Urgur zhongguoren* (the Urgur-Chinese). Such a social linguistic practice should be legislated so that it will reinforce a strong sense of a shared Chinese citizenship among people of all ethnic backgrounds, while recognizing and respecting ethnic diversity.

By implementing the above five policy suggestions, hopefully, the deeply rooted sources of interethnic conflicts could be eliminated or significantly reduced so that ethnic minorities in China could be really on par with Han-Chinese economically and politically; the ethnic minority cultures could be really on par with Han-Chinese culture and modern Western culture, which the Han-Chinese have almost fully embraced. The vista for true interethnic harmony will emerge only on the basis of true interethnic equality economically, politically, and culturally.

9 Summary and Conclusion

Chinese ethnic relations are more complex and diverse than Western scholars might have thought. First, China has a long and rich culture with diverse ethnic groups. Second, the history of ethnic groups has been related to the conflict and struggle between inland China and peripheral ethnic minorities. Even today, this conflict or struggle has never ceased (Lee et al., 2004).

Third, ethnic minorities in contemporary China have been facing a double challenge of Sinicization and Westernization. On the one hand, ethnic minorities are economically and politically disadvantaged; on the other hand, they are culturally vulnerable and fragile. The harshness of their present economic and cultural condition has been historically unprecedented. One can imagine how severe their sense of identity crisis is. The strength, vitality, and potential for creativity and innovation to sustain ethnic cultural diversity remain far from being fully acknowledged and tapped in China. "The major reason for the continuation of Chinese civilization is that it integrates new blood, endlessly absorbs and radiates. This cultural renewal and ethnic integration go with the changing times and constitute a continuous and dynamic process" (Hao, 2009, p. 452). Hopefully, a mechanism will be created so that ethnic cultural diversity will be maintained and developed to keep Chinese civilization, Western civilization, and indeed human civilization going into the future. Perhaps, Fei (Summer 1989) and Ma's (2004) idea of ethnic/cultural diversity in political unity/harmony would offer a useful blueprint for constructing a politically harmonious China of ethnic diversity that we might call "the Middle Kingdom of the 21st century." To make it happen, we should give more room to truly allow a hundred flowers of ethnic diversity to blossom in order to live up to the expectations of Mao Zedong when he proclaimed in Yan'an, one of the revolutionary bases of CCP: "Letting a hundred flowers blossom and a hundred schools of thought contend is the policy for promoting the progress of the arts and the sciences and a flourishing culture in our land" (May, 1942).

Notes

1. Acknowledgment is made to Chapman University for a research grant and a sabbatical leave of one semester granted to Wenshan Jia for conducting field and library research as well as drafting most of the chapter. Acknowledgment also goes to the editors, my second and third authors, who all provided valuable suggestions for corrections and revisions. However, Wenshan Jia, including the second and third authors, is responsible for the ideas expressed in the chapter.
2. Wenshan Jia drafted the whole chapter except Part II, the first part of (2) under Part III, and the first part of Part VI (which are drafted by Yue-Ting Lee) and Part III (6) and the first part

of Part I (9) (which are drafted by Haiyang Zhang). Haiyang Zhang verified the facts and figures cited in the chapter.

References

Adamson, B., & Feng, A. (2009). A comparison of trilingual education policies for ethnic minorities in China. *Compare: A Journal of Comparative and International Education, 39*(3), 321–333.

Anonymous. (2006). Report on several important issues related to the ethnic work. By the Chinese Communist Party Central Committee Ministry of the United Front and China National Commission on Ethnic Affairs (01/23/1987). In B. Jin (Ed.), *Selections of China's key ethnic policy documents* (pp. 708–720). Beijing, China: The Minzu University of China Press. July 1921-May, 2005-Vol.1) (*Minzhu ganglin zhence wenxian xuanbian.*

Bilik, N., Lee, Y.-T., Phan, H. H., Lee, Y.-T., Phan, H. H., & Shi, K. (2004). The ethnic and cultural processes of Zhongguo (China) as a Central Kingdom. In Y.-T. Lee, C. McCauley, F. Moghaddam, & S. Worchel (Eds.), *The psychology of ethnic and cultural conflict* (pp. 193–215). Westport, CT: Praeger.

CCP Department of Publicity Theory Group. (2009). *The study guide on Hu Jintao's scientific development (Kexue fazhang guan xuexi duben)*. Retrieved on October 4, 2010, from http://www.faw.com.cn/kxfzg/jtbs/1236928304394.pdf.

Census Office in the State Department in China and Bureau of Chinese Population Statistics. (2002). *Census statistics Chinese 2000 population*. Beijing: Chinese Statistical Publishing House (国务院人口普查办公室、国家统计局人口和社会科技统计司：《中国2000年人口普查统计》，北京，中国统计出版社，2002.).

China State Council Information & Press Office. (2010, September 26). *Progress in China's human rights in 2009*. Retrieved on October 3, 2010, from http://news.xinhuanet.com/english2010/china/2010-09/26/c_13529921_7.htm.

Chinese Shanhaijing Scholarly Society. (1986). *New findings of Shanhaijing*. Chengdu: Sichuan Social Sciences Publishing House (in Chinese).

Dikotter, F. (1992). *The discourse of race in modern China*. London, UK: Hurst & Company.

Eide, A., et al. (2008). Beijing-Oslo recommendations on protection for the rights of linguistic minorities (*Beijing-Oslo Jianyishu*). In H. Li & M. Lundberg (Eds.), *Minority language use and cultural development-an international comparison of policy and law (Shaoshu minzu yuyanshiyong yu wenhua fazhan zhengce he falu de guoji bijiao)* (pp. 379–435). Beijing, China: The Minzu University of China Press.

Fei, X. (1989). The structure of the united entity of China's diverse ethnicities (*Zhonghua minzu de duoyuan yiti geju*). *Peking University Journal, 4*, 1–19.

Fei, X. (Summer 1989). The structure of unity in diversity among the Chinese ethnicities (*Zhonghua minzhu de duoyuan yiti gezhu*), a Tanner lecture. Chinese University of Hong Kong, Hong Kong, China.

Feng, A. (2005, February 11). *China's minority learn a difficult language lesson*. Retrieved on October 3, 2010, from http://www.guardian.co.uk/theguardian/2005/feb/11/guardianweekly.guardianweekly13.

Ge, J. (2009). The evolution of the land of China (*Zhongguo jiangyu d bianqian*). In The Editorial Group (Ed.), *Forty lectures on history and culture in Zhongnanhai-Issues Discussed between Famous Scholars and China's Top Leaders* (pp. 425–450). Beijing, China: The Editorial Group of the Book.

Hao, S. (2009). China's ethnicities and ethnic issues (Zhongguo de Minzu *yu minzuwenti*). In The Editorial Group (Ed.), *Forty lectures on history and culture in Zhongnanhai-Issues Discussed between Famous Scholars and China's Top Leaders* (pp. 451–467). Beijing, China: The Editorial Group of the Book.

Hsu, P. S. S. (1981). *Chinese discovery of America*. Hong Kong: Southeast Asian Research Institute.

Jin, B. (Ed.). (2006a). *Selections of China's key ethnic policy documents*. Beijing, China: The Minzu University of China Press (July 1921-May, 2005-Vol.1) (*Minzu ganglin zhence wenxian xuanbian*).

Jin, B. (Ed.). (2006b). *Selections of China's key ethnic policy documents*. Beijing, China: The Minzu University of China Press (July 1921-May, 2005-Vol.2) (*Minzu ganglin zhence wenxian xuanbian*).

Jin, B. (2007). *General introduction to interethnic relations theory (Minzuguanxi liluntonglun)*. Beijing, China: The Minzu University of China Press.

Jin, X. (2009). Major tasks facing the development of China's ethnic languages (*zhongguo minzu yuwen gongzuo mianling de zhuyao renwu*). In H. Li & M. Lundberg (Eds.), *Minority language use and cultural development-an international comparison of policy and law (Shaoshu minzu yuyanshiyong yuwenhua fazhan zhengce he falu de guoji bijiao)* (pp. 53–62). Beijing, China: The Minzu University of China Press.

Lee, Y. -T. (2001). The first capital needed for China in the 21st century's globalization: Rebuilding Chinese "Dao", "benevolent governance" and "socio-cultural and psychological beliefs. *Journal of Yuncheng University, 19*(1), 37–45 (in Chinese with an English abstract).

Lee,Y. T. (2010). Spiritual beliefs and ethnic relations in China: A cross-cultural and social psychological perspective. In Z. Zhu (Ed.), *The People's Republic of China today: Internal and external challenges*. World Scientific Publishing Company, 2010.

Lee, Y. -T., & Li, H. (2010). Spiritual beliefs and ethnic relations. In Z. Q. Zhu (Ed.), *The People's Republic of China: Internal and external challenges*. Hackensack, NJ: World Scientific Publishing Company, 2010.

Lee, Y. -T., McCauley, C., Moghaddam, F., & Worchel, S. (2004). *The psychology of ethnic and cultural conflict*. Westport, CT: Praeger.

Li, S. (2009). Xinjiang of China-its past and present. Urumqi, Xinjiang: Xinjiang People's Press.

Li, X. (2004). Analysis of the current interethnic marriage in China today. *Population Studies in China*, 3. Retrieved from http://www.usc.cuhk.edu.hk/wk_wzdetails.asp?id=5247.

Li, H., & Lundberg, M. (Eds.). (2008). *Minority language use and cultural development-an international comparison of policy and law (Shaoshu minzu yuyanshiyong yuwenhua fazhan zhengce he falu de guoji bijiao)*. Beijing, China: The Minzu University of China Press.

Li, S., et al. (2009). *The history and current status of China's Xingjiang (Zhongguo lishi yu xianzhuang)*. Urumuqi, Xinjiang: The Xinjiang People's Press.

Lin, H. (2001). *The history of Chinese Wu Nuo (Shamanism)*. Guangzhou, China: Flower City Press.

Ma, R. (2004). *Sociology of ethnicity: Sociological study of ethnic relations (Minzhu shehuixue-shehuixue de zhuqun guanxi yanjiu)*. Beijing, China: Peking University Press.

Ma, D. (2009). Research on the policies of Ancient China's frontiers (*Zhongguo lidai bianjiang zhengce yanjou)*. In The Editorial Group (Ed.), *Forty lectures on history and culture in Zhongnanhai-Issues Discussed between Famous Scholars and China's Top Leaders (Zhongnanhai lishi wenhua jiangzuo sishijiang)* (pp. 409–424). Beijing, China: The Editorial Group of the Book.

Mao, T. (1953, 16 March). Criticizing Han chauvinism (*Pi pan daminzu zhuyi*) (p. 488). In B. Jin (Ed., 2006), *Selections of China's key ethnic policy documents* (July 1921-May, 2005-Vol.2) (*Minzu ganglin zhence wenxian xuanbian*). Beijing, China: The Minzu University of China Press.

Mao, T. (1953, 19 March). A note on the report on the implementation of CCP's ethnic policy in Gansu (*dui zhongyang zhuanfa xibeizhu guanyu gansu lingxia jiancha minzu zhengce zhixin qinkuang baogao de fuzhu*) (p. 489). In B. Jin (Ed., 2006), Selections of China's key ethnic policy documents (July 1921-May, 2005-Vol.2) (*Minzu ganglin zhence wenxian xuanbian*). Beijing, China: The Minzu University of China Press.

Mao, T. (1955, 11 October). On criticizing Han chauvinism again (*zailun fandui da hanzu zhuyi* (p. 531). In B. Jin (Ed., 2006), *Selections of China's key ethnic policy documents* (July 1921-May, 2005-Vol.2) (*Minzu ganglin zhence wenxian xuanbian*). Beijing, China: The Minzu University of China Press.

Na, L. (2006). *The investigation of the interethnic issues from multiple perspectives (Duowei shijiaoxiade zhuji wenti tansuo)*. Beijing, China: The Ethnic Press.

Press Office of State Council, P. R. China. (2006). China's ethnic/regional self- governance (*zhongguo de minzu zizhi*). In B. Jin (Ed.), *Selections of China's key ethnic policy documents (July 1921–May, 2005-Vol.2) (Minzu ganglin zhence wenxian xuanbian)* (pp. 895–917). Beijing, China: The Minzu University of China Press.

Reischauer, E. O., & Fairbank, J. K. (1960). *East Asia: The great tradition*. Boston, MA: Houghton Mifflin Company.

Shan Hai Jing (Record of Mountains and Seas/Oceans) (c. 2200 B.C./1925) (in Chinese). 《山海经图说》 Shanghai, China: Jing Zhang Press.

Sima, Q. (100B.C./1994). *Shi Ji (The Grand Historical Record)*. Yin Chuan, China: Nin Xia People's Publishers (in Chinese).

Sun, H. (2008). Protecting China's minority languages on the edge of extinction. In H. Li & M. Lundberg (Eds.), *Minority language use and cultural development-an international comparison of policy and law (Shaoshu minzu yuyanshiyong yuwenhua fazhan zhengce he falu de guoji bijiao)* (pp. 109–115). Beijing, China: The Minzu University of China Press.

Tournadre, N. (2003). *The dynamics of Tibetan-Chinese bilingualism: The current situation and future prospects*. Retrieved on October 2, 2010, from http://chinaperspectives.revues.org/231.

Wang, D. Y. (2000a). *Chinese dragon culture*. Beijing: Chinese Society Press. (in Chinese) 《中 华 龙 种 文 化》.

Wang, D. Y. (2000b). *The times of San Huang Wu Di*. 《三皇五帝时代》 Beijing: Chinese Society Press.

Wang, X. (2009). *Ethnic process in the globalization*. Beijing, China: Social Sciences Academy Press (*Chuanqiouhua zhongde minzhuguocheng*).

Wang, Y., & Phillion, J. (2009). Minority language policy and practice in China: The need for multicultural education. *International Journal of Multicultural Education, 11*(1). Retrieved on October 3, 2010 from, http://ijme-journal.org/index.php/ijme/article/viewFile/138/312.

Wang, D. Y., & Song, B. Z. (1998). *Illustrations of American totems*. Beijing: People's Art Publishers. (in Chinese), 《图 说美洲图腾》.

Xian, QQ.COM. (2009, 8 July). *Urumuqi 7.5 Riots Left 156 dead and 1080 injured*. Retrieved on October 4, 2010, from http://xian.qq.com/a/20090708/000046.htm.

Xinhua Net. (2008, 22 March). *What really happened in Lhasa on March 4, 2008*. Retrieved on October 4, 2010, from http://news.xinhuanet.com/newscenter/2008- 03/22/content_7837535.htm.

Xu, X. Z. (1991). *The origin of the book Shan Hai Jing*. China: Wuhan Publishing House. (in Chinese) 《山海经探原》.

Xu, L. (Ed.). (2009). *The complete histories of China's Northwest minorities-the volume on their contemporary histories (Zhongguo xibei shaoshu minzu tongshi-dangdaijuan)*. Beijing, China: The Minzu Press.

Yang, B. J. (1965). *Lunyu (Confucian Aphorism) and its interpretation*. 《论语译注》 (扬伯峻编著) Beijing, China: Chinese Book Publishing Bureau (中华书局).

Yuan, K. (1988). *Chinese history of mythology*. Shanghai, China: Shanghai Literature Publishing House. in Chinese.

Zedong, M. (1942). *Talks at the Yan'an Forum on Art and Literature*. Ann Arbor, MI: Center for Chinese Studies. A Translation of the 1943 Text with Commentary by Bonnie S. McDougall.

Part IV

Eastern Mediterranean

The Israeli–Palestinian Conflict: The Sociohistorical Context and the Identities It Creates

9

Dahlia Moore and Anat Guy

Israel Chapter Summary

Moore and Guy discuss the ongoing Israeli–Palestinian conflict, which involves three main groups; Jewish–Israelis, who are the majority residents in Israel; Arab citizens of Israel; and the Palestinians, who are primarily refugees living in territories under the Palestinian Authority. History of this conflict is delineated along with detailed examination of various attitudes and values held by the different group members.

The origin of conflict is traced to the end of colonialism and creation of a home for Jewish people after World War I, which resulted in large-scale immigration of Jews into Palestine. Resulting rebellion by Palestinians eventually led to war for Israeli independence, from which the state of Israel was born. Historical review details the many years of conflict, including continued attempts at negotiations, involvement of the UN and other nations, influences of political leaders, and actions taken by both sides. Moore and Guy present the five core issues that both sides agree need to be resolved in order to reach peace.

The authors define the members of various collectivities and emphasize different perceptions of the conflict, associated causes, and potential solutions. Giddens' Theory of Structuration is utilized to explain how individuals within the sociohistorical context have affected the social systems in favor of the majority group. Social identity theory is applied to explain conflict behaviors as they relate to group identification. The authors further combine these two theories and present detailed descriptions of salient identities for each group under discussion. A recent study is presented which provides evidence of changing hierarchical structure of

D. Moore (✉) • A. Guy
Department of Behavioral Sciences,
College of Management Academic Studies,
7, Yitzhak Rabin Avenue, Rishon LeZion, 75190, Israel
e-mail: dmoore@colman.ac.il

D. Landis and R.D. Albert (eds.), *Handbook of Ethnic Conflict: International Perspectives*, International and Cultural Psychology, DOI 10.1007/978-1-4614-0448-4_9,

these identities and associated effects on attitudes toward conflict resolution. Moore and Guy present suggestions to promote peace through long-term use of the educational system as a means to change identifications from those associated with the conflict.

Cheryl Jorgensen

1 Introduction

The Israeli–Palestinian conflict, one of the most violent conflicts that threatens worldwide stability, is between two small, ancient national groups, fighting each other for the same tiny piece of land they seem unable to share (Israel is 20,770 km^2, and the occupied territories, ruled mostly by Palestinians, include 5,860 km^2 in the West Bank and 360 km^2 in the Gaza Strip (smaller than New Jersey, even when combined).

The conflict, which is part of the broader Arab–Israeli conflict, has escalated, as uncontrolled conflicts tend to do, so that presenting it as a territorial dispute is a misleading oversimplification. It includes economic, social, cultural, and power/dominance aspects that reach far beyond the borders of the disputed land. There is currently no other country in the world whose borders are contested, where two nationalities claim a legitimate right to the land (Jews – who base their claim on the rights accorded to them in the Bible and see it as the land of their forefathers, from which they were exiled in the past (with a small minority remaining in the country); and the Palestinians – who lived on this land after the Jews were exiled. When Jews began returning to Israel after World War II and the Holocaust, clashes between the two peoples intensified). Moreover, it is one of the conflicts in which many countries have allied themselves either with one side of the conflict or the other. Hence, the conflict reflects the opposing interests of many countries and diverse peoples.

Anyone who tries seriously to examine the contemporary Near East faces a considerable problem of balancing conceptions and divergent points of view, claims Edward Said (1995). Attempting to present an unbiased and impartial description of the chain of events that led to the increasing hostility among the people in the region often seems unmanageable. Indeed, many – on all sides of the conflict – may consider our account biased or unbalanced.

We focus on three groups that are involved in the conflict: Jewish–Israelis (the majority (about 80%) of all Israeli citizens),[1] Arab citizens of Israel (about 20% of Israelis),[2] and Palestinians (the refugees who live in the West Bank and Gaza Strip).[3] Following Giddens's (1979, 1984) conception of the interrelatedness of agents and the context in which they exist, the study examines how the conflict shaped the three collectivities and the social identities of members of these groups, and how the identities influenced the intensity of the conflict. The analysis may be relevant to different conflicts, in diverse areas around the world.

2 The Sociohistorical Context

The Israeli–Palestinian problem became an international issue toward the end of World War I with the disintegration of the Turkish Ottoman Empire.

[1]Though Jews all over the world may come to Israel and attain automatic citizenship upon entering the country, they are not part of the analyzed group in the current discussion.

[2]Although many today prefer the term "Palestinian citizens of Israel" when relating to Israel's non-Jewish citizens, many among the Arabs in Israel still do not refer to themselves as "Palestinian." We use the term "Arabs" when referring to the Israeli–Palestinian citizens and "Palestinian" when referring to the residents of the Palestinian authority in order to distinguish between the two categories.

[3]Many Palestinians live outside these areas, and they too are relevant to the conflict, but they are not part of the analyzed group in the current discussion.

Palestine was among the several former Ottoman Arab territories that were placed under the administration of Great Britain under the Mandates System adopted by the League of Nations. The Mandate had as a primary objective the implementation of the "Balfour Declaration" issued by the British Government in 1917, expressing support for "the establishment in Palestine of a national home for the Jewish people."

During the years of the Palestine Mandate, from 1922 to 1947, large-scale Jewish immigration from abroad, mainly from Eastern Europe, took place, the numbers increasing in the 1930s with the Nazi persecution of Jewish populations. Palestinian demands for independence and resistance to Jewish immigration led to a rebellion in 1936, followed by continuing terrorism and violence from both sides during and immediately after World War II. In 1947, Great Britain in frustration turned the problem over to the United Nations (Newman, 1991).

After World War II, both Jews and Palestinians began to prepare for a decisive confrontation to determine their dominance in the region. The UN proposed the partitioning of Palestine into two independent states, one Palestinian Arab and the other Jewish, with Jerusalem internationalized (Resolution 181 (II) of 1947). Despite Palestinian numerical superiority (1,300,000 to 600,000), the Jews were better prepared and proclaimed the independence of the State of Israel under David Ben-Gurion's leadership. The Palestinians were in disarray, and their principal spokesman – the Mufti of Jerusalem – refused to accept the UN's suggestion of partition, though the Jews agreed to it. He mobilized the Palestinian masses and instigated armed fighting. Failing to attain their goals, the Palestinians were defeated.

The independence of the State of Israel was declared on May 14, 1948. At once, five Arab armies (from Egypt, Jordan, Syria, Lebanon, and Iraq) joined the Palestinians and attacked the new state but were ultimately defeated. At the end of what is known as the first Arab–Israeli War, Israel's victory gave it more territory (about 77% of the territory of the hitherto Palestine, and the larger part of Jerusalem), while Jordan took the rest of Jerusalem and the West Bank, and Egypt the Gaza Strip (see Map 9.1).

Because of the war, about a million Palestinians fled or were expelled and became refugees. The refugees spread into neighboring countries where they have maintained their Palestinian identity in addition to the desire to return to their homeland (Khalidi, 1992; Masalha, 1992). With the establishment of the Palestine Liberation Organization (PLO) in 1964, they had a governing authority. In 1967, during the 6-Day War between Israel and the surrounding Arab nations, Israel gained control of the West Bank, the Gaza Strip, and other previously Arab-controlled areas, and Israel occupied the remaining territory of Palestine (the West Bank and the Gaza Strip) until then under Jordanian and Egyptian control, as well as the Egyptian Sinai Peninsula and the Syrian Golan Heights (see Map 9.2). The war brought about a second exodus of Palestinians, estimated at half a million. UN Security Council resolution 242 (1967) (see Time table in Appendix) of November 22, 1967, called on Israel to withdraw from territories it had occupied in the 1967 conflict. Israel did not comply.

Another war between Israel, Egypt, and Syria broke out in 1973, but the attempt to conquer back the lands taken by Israel failed. The following year, the U.N. General Assembly conferred on the PLO the status of observer in the Assembly.

In June 1982, Israel invaded Lebanon with the declared intention to eliminate the PLO. A ceasefire was arranged; PLO troops withdrew from Beirut and were transferred to neighboring countries. In September 1983, the International Conference on the Question of Palestine adopted inter alia the Geneva Declaration containing the following principles: (1) The need to oppose and reject the establishment of settlements in the occupied territory and actions taken by Israel to change the status of Jerusalem. (2) The right of all States in the region to existence within secure and internationally recognized boundaries, with justice and security for all the people. (3) The attainment of the legitimate, inalienable rights of the Palestinian people (Shikaki, 1999; Newman, 1991).

In December 1987, a mass uprising (the First *Intifada* ("uprising"), also referred to as the "Stones" *Intifada*) against the Israeli occupation began in the occupied Palestinian territory.

Map 9.1 Map of Israel with occupied territories

Map 9.2 Detailed map of Palestinian National Authority

The reasons for its beginning are the Palestinian poverty vis-à-vis Israeli wealth, with which Palestinians became acquainted because so many of them worked in Israel, and their growing desperation, the lack of progress in peace talks, and no change in their situation. *The response* of the Israeli Armed forces during the uprising resulted in mass injuries and heavy loss of life among the Palestinian population.

In 1988, King Hussein of Jordan ceded all territorial claims to the Israeli-controlled West Bank to the PLO. In November of the same year at a meeting of the Palestinian National Council in Algiers, Arafat announced the establishment of an independent Palestinian state with Jerusalem as its capital. The council also decided to utilize UN Resolutions 242 and 338, together with the right of the Palestinian people to self-determination, as the basis for an international peace conference.

In 1991, relations between the USA, pro-Western Arab states, and the PLO severely deteriorated, mainly because Arafat declared his support for Iraq during the Gulf War, according to *El Dabbagh* (ArabNet, 1996).[4] After that, in July 1991, the Syrian-backed Lebanese army

[4]ArabNet is owned by ArabNet Technology (ANT), part of the Saudi Research and Marketing Group, publisher of the leading newspapers and magazines in the Kingdom of Saudi Arabia including Asharq Al-Awsat.

forced the PLO to retreat from its positions in southern Lebanon.

A Peace Conference on the Middle East was convened in Madrid on October 30, 1991, with the aim of achieving a just, lasting, and comprehensive peace settlement through direct negotiations along two tracks: between Israel and the Arab States, and between Israel and the Palestinians, based on Security Council resolutions 242 (1967) and 338 (1973) (the "land for peace" formula).

In January 1993, Israel repealed its ban on contact with the PLO[5] and later in the year, on September 13, Arafat and the Israeli Prime Minister, Yitzhak Rabin, signed a peace accord in Washington, D.C. The plan stipulated Palestinian self-rule in Israeli-occupied areas, beginning with the Gaza Strip and Jericho.

In May 1994, Palestinian control and administration of these areas began. The subsequent implementation agreements led to several other positive developments, such as the partial withdrawal of Israeli forces from Palestinian cities, the elections to the Palestinian Council and the presidency of the Palestinian Authority, the partial release of prisoners, and the establishment of a functioning administration in the areas under Palestinian self-rule. Palestinian autonomy was limited to control of taxation, communication, policing, and travel documentation. Still, peace was not attained, and a second Intifada – Al Aqsa[6] Intifada – broke out in response to the failure of the Camp David Summit (July 25, 2000) and Ariel Sharon's visit to the Temple Mount in September 2000,[7] leading to suicide bombs, terrorism, and Israel's retaliation: reoccupation of Palestinian cities, curfews, capturing of individuals deemed dangerous, etc.

In December 2000, Clinton's peace initiative brought Ehud Barak, Israel's Prime Minister, and Yasir Arafat, the President of the Palestinian Authority, to Washington DC to sign a new agreement. The initiative included the following: (1) Israel recognition of an independent Palestinian state with territory on over 97% of the West Bank, Gaza Strip, and Jerusalem; (2) East Jerusalem as the capital of the new state (including the holy Al Aqsa area); (3) an international presence in place of the Israeli Army in the Jordan Valley; and (4) unlimited right of return for Palestinians to their new state. In return, Palestinians had to relinquish their desire to obtain the land Israel conquered in 1948, or the right of Palestinians to return to those lands. According to Dennis Ross (2002), one of the lead negotiators in the Middle East in the Bush and Clinton administrations, the agreement fell through because Arafat refused to commit himself and his people to it. "Instead, he pulled a classic Arafat: He did not say yes or no.... Arafat missed a historic opportunity when he turned down the Clinton proposal" (Ross, 2002, p. 19).[8]

There are, on the contrary, some serious doubts about the PLO's ability to enforce its rule in the areas the Israelis had relinquished. Arafat *can* control the militants in the area claimed, but he would not, claimed Ross (2002). "Arafat will only do so if they threaten his authority but that

[5]The ban was in effect ever since the PLO was created. Even initiating contact with anyone associated with the PLO was considered an act of treason, which may lead to imprisonment.

[6]"Al-Aqsa" is the name of the most important Muslim mosque in Israel, constructed in the eighth century on the area considered to be the holy site of the Jewish Temple Mount in Jerusalem.

[7]Sharon, who later became Prime Minister of Israel, was planned to visit the Jewish Temple Mount, not the Muslim Al-Aqsa Mosque. Because of the closeness of the two, the visit was construed a provocation.

[8]Having met and talked with Arafat, Dennis Ross seems to refer to Arafat's tendency to evade concrete and definite answers if he's not sure of their consequences. In the talks with Ehud Barak, then prime minister of Israel, the same was said about him by Israeli politicians and media representatives.

even then he will not 'completely shut the door' on either Hamas[9] or the Islamic Jihad movements" (Ross, 2002, pp. 22–24). Unfortunately, the anti-Arafat Palestinian splinter group, Hamas, instigated terrorist acts which led to clashes with Israeli security forces (Said, 1995).

During the past few years, there has been increasing concern at the stalemate in the peace negotiations. The General Assembly, particularly the Assembly's Tenth Emergency Special Session, was called upon to deal with the deteriorating situation in the occupied Palestinian territory. There has been increasing alarm at acts of violence against civilians, the position and actions of the Government of Israel with regard to Jerusalem, the expansion of settlements, land confiscation, and punitive collective measures, which were seriously undermining the peace efforts (Said, 1996; Tamari, 1993). The shift toward right-wing ideology in Israel in recent years brought Ariel Sharon to power (in 2004). The right-wing support has increased since then, as indicated by the 2009 elections, indicating that Israelis are not as ready to make concessions as in the past.

Violence continued into 2001 and 2002, and in 2002, Saudi Crown Prince Abdullah made a dramatic proposal to end the long Arab war against Israel in return for Israeli withdrawal from Palestinian territories, withdrawal in the Golan, and appropriate arrangements regarding Jerusalem and the refugees. This "Saudi initiative" was adopted by most of the Arab states at a meeting of the Arab League, and was later incorporated into the quartet roadmap plan.[10] On March, 12, 2002, the UN Security Council passed Resolution 1397, calling on the sides to stop the violence once again, mentioning the Saudi peace plan, and calling for the creation of a Palestinian state alongside Israel.

The Resolution was not heeded, and the cycle of Palestinian terrorism and Israeli reprisals continued. Yasser Arafat declared a cessation of violence several times, but this did not seem to affect the frequency or severity of suicide bombings. The Israelis, for their part, continued their policy of assassinating targeted individuals in the Palestinian areas.

After the explosion at the Park Hotel in the City of Netanya in which 27 people were killed and 140 were wounded during Passover dinner (March 2002), Israel launched a massive attack on Palestinian activist strongholds, intending to destroy their infrastructure and reoccupy Ramallah, Nablus, Jenin, Tulkarm, and other towns. In June, following another wave of Palestinian suicide attacks, Israeli forces essentially reoccupied all of the West Bank.

On March 20, 2003, US, British, and Australian forces invaded Iraq. The US forces entered Baghdad on April 9, and on May 1, President Bush declared the Iraq war over. The war produced an upheaval in the Middle East and especially

[9]The HAMAS ("Harakat Al-Muqawama Al-Islamia" in Arabic – Islamic Resistance Movement) is a radical Islamic fundamentalist organization, which became active in the early stages of the Intifada, operating primarily in the Gaza District and also in the West Bank, Israel, and Jordan. HAMAS was formed in late 1987 in opposition to the non-religious FATAH as an outgrowth of the Palestinian branch of the Muslim Brotherhood. Various elements of HAMAS have used both political and violent means, including terrorism, to pursue the goal of establishing an Islamic Palestinian state in place of Israel. HAMAS is loosely structured (with an unknown number of hardcore members, and assumed tens of thousands of supporters and sympathizers), with some elements working openly through mosques and social service institutions to recruit members, raise money, organize activities, and distribute propaganda. Militant elements of HAMAS, operating clandestinely, have advocated and used violence to advance their goals. HAMAS activists, especially those in the Izz el-Din al-Qassam Brigades, have conducted many attacks against Israeli civilian and military targets and suspected Palestinian collaborators. It also has engaged in peaceful political activity, such as running candidates in West Bank Chamber of Commerce elections (Pike, 1998).

[10]The "road map" is a plan to resolve the Israeli–Palestinian conflict proposed by the USA, the European Union, Russia, and the United Nations, leading to a two-state solution. The principles of the plan: In exchange for statehood, the road map requires the Palestinian Authority to make democratic reforms and abandon the use of violence. Israel, for its part, must support and accept the emergence of a reformed Palestinian government and end settlement activity in the Gaza Strip and West Bank (Roadmap For Peace in the Middle East: Israeli/Palestinian Reciprocal Action, Quartet Support, U.S. Department of State, Bureau of Public Affairs,16/7/2003.

affected the Palestinians as they supported Saddam Hussein and his regime (Saddan Hussein had trained Palestinian militants and provided payments for families of suicide bombers). Arab governments (including the Palestinians) declared their support for democracy, while still criticizing the occupation of Iraq, which generated resentment throughout the Arab world.

On April 29 and on June 4, 2004, a summit was held in Aqaba. Israeli Prime Minister Sharon and the newly elected Palestinian Prime Minister Mahmoud Abbas (Abu-Mazen) met US President George Bush, and together pledged to fulfill the conditions of the "roadmap to Peace".

The brief period of quiet was broken in the summer of 2003 by a series of suicide bombings in Israeli cities. In retaliation, Israel invaded Gaza as well as the Palestinian refugee camp in the city Jenin. A long period of relative decline in Palestinian attacks followed, but Israel continued to attack Palestinian targets, causing a considerable loss of civilian life. Sporadic suicide attacks by Hamas, Islamic Jihad, and the Fatah Al Aqsa brigades continued.

In December 2003, Israeli left-wing (opposition) political leaders and public figures (like Yossi Bailin and Amy Ayalon), and Palestinian leaders (like Yasser Abed Rabbo and Seri Nuseiba) announced an agreement on conditions for a final resolution of the Israeli–Palestinian conflict. The agreement, "the Geneva Accord" or "the Geneva initiative," proposed historic concessions by both sides. Israel would give up sovereignty in Arab portions of Jerusalem, all of the Gaza Strip, and most of the West Bank, while the Palestinians would agree to a limited right of Palestinian refugees to return to Israel and to renounce explicitly all other demands from Israel. Though it has no formal standing at present, the agreement received widespread publicity and the support of the USA. Both the Israeli and the Palestinian governments denounced the agreement and the people involved in it, as did extremists on both sides.

In contrast, Prime Minister Ariel Sharon adopted the concept of building a Security Barrier (also called "Security Fence" or "Apartheid Wall").[11] The Wall was supposed to follow the 1948 Cease-Fire Line (the "Green Line"), but in reality, the Wall often changed course and invaded Palestinian territory in order to include most of the Jewish settlements. It thus prevented territorial continuity for the Palestinians (see Map 9.2), leading to the creation of road blocks and the need to enter Israeli-held territories in order to move between neighboring Palestinian towns and villages (Bar-Siman-Tov, 2007).

The Israeli Labor Party proclaimed (during the 2003 elections) that if negotiations with the Palestinians fail, Israel would withdraw unilaterally from the Gaza strip and parts of the West Bank, and use the barrier to increase security (Waxman, 2008). Ariel Sharon and the Likud Party, one of the strongest political parties in Israel, damned this proposal as defeatist, but toward the end of 2003, Sharon himself announced after his election as prime minister that he was preparing a unilateral withdrawal plan. The idea met with intense opposition from fellow Likud members, settlers,[12] and the majority of right-wing Israelis.

On December 8, 2003, the UN General Assembly met for an Emergency session and adopted resolution ES-10/14, which asked the International Court of Justice (ICJ) at The Hague for an advisory opinion on the legality of the barrier. The ICJ began its hearings on February 24. Israel boycotted the hearings, but submitted a brief saying that the court should not rule on the matter. Similar proposals that the court should not rule on the matter because it was a political

[11] The Wall is being constructed by Israel not only as a separation barrier between Israel and the Palestinian territories, but also to protect the Jewish settlements from their Palestinian neighbors. In most areas, the barrier consists of fences, in others, the barrier is an 8-m concrete wall. Many checkpoints were created along the barrier where only Palestinians are stopped and searched by Israeli soldiers. In August 2008, the length of the barrier was over 800 km, and it is not yet finished.

[12] Settlers are Jews who live in the West Bank, on land conquered and occupied by Israel in the Six-Day War (1967), often on land belonging to Palestinians. Most of the settlers are religious.

question rather than a legal one were submitted by 30 other countries. These countries also did not attend the hearings. Still, the ICJ ruled that the barrier violates human rights and that Israel must dismantle it. Israel announced that it would not abide by the court decision, but it did plan changes in the route of the barrier to satisfy requirements of the Israeli High Court.

On March 22, 2004, after incessant suicide attacks in Israeli cities, Sheikh Ahmed Yassin, who was responsible for instigating the deaths of hundreds of people, and for efforts to sabotage the peace process, was assassinated by Israeli Defense Forces (IDF). The assassination drew protests from most of the world and vows of revenge from Hamas.

During the spring and summer of 2004, terror attacks within Israel diminished, despite numerous attempts. Israelis and Palestinians attributed the relative quiet to the partially constructed separation barrier and improved Israeli intelligence. The relative respite was broken on August 31, 2004, by Hamas's double suicide attack on buses in Beersheba, in response to the killing of their leaders (Sheikh Ahmed Yassin and Abed El Aziz Rantissi). The suicide Jihadists came from the area south of Hebron in the West Bank, where no fence had been built, and the attack accelerated construction of the barrier.

Palestinian Authority Chairman and long-time leader Yasser Arafat died in November 11, 2004, leaving an uncertain future. Some signs indicated that the death of Arafat had opened up new possibilities for peace, and for reform and democracy in the Palestinian authority: He was considered by many as one of the opponents to democracy for the Palestinian people, and among the most hostile toward Israel (Sayigh, 1997). Some (Rubenstein, 1995) even claim that because he created the PLO and headed it for many years, he could not conceive of a future without a war with Israel or conceding any land in a peace settlement.

On January 9, 2005, the first democratic election held in Palestine, Mahmoud Abbas was elected President of the Palestine National Authority, receiving about 61% of the vote. US President George W. Bush invited Abbas to Washington (after several years during which Palestinian leaders had not been welcome in the White House), and Israeli Prime Minister Ariel Sharon announced that he would call Abbas and plan a meeting.

Following his election, Palestinian President Mahmoud Abbas called on Palestinian factions to end the violence among them and negotiated a truce agreement known as Sharm El Sheikh Conference. In this conference, the *Intifada* was deemed to be officially over. However, the peace was soon shattered by a suicide bombing in Tel Aviv. Israel froze the planned handover of Palestinian towns to the Palestinian National Authority (PNA).

Shortly after the Sharm El Sheikh Conference, the Israeli parliament (the *Knesset*) approved the disengagement plan, which called for unilateral evacuation of 21 settlements in Gaza and 4 in the West Bank by the end of summer 2005. The disengagement was to be coordinated with the Palestinian Authority. The Palestinian president promised to help ensure quiet during the evacuation.

Israeli evacuation of Gaza settlements and West Bank settlements began on August 15 and was completed on August 24, 2005. Despite threats of civil war and demonstrations by right-wing Zionist groups, the evacuation was completed without major violence. As Israel withdrew, there were increasing omens of impending chaos. On September 11, the last Israeli soldiers left Gaza, and the settlements were officially handed over to the Palestinians. It has been under the Hamas rule ever since, and the rift between the Gaza Strip and the West Bank has been growing since.

The outcry against Sharon and the fierce opposition to the withdrawal from Gaza forced Sharon to leave the Likud Party (with about a third of the party members). He created and headed a new party – Kadima. Several members of the Labor party, led by Shimon Peres, joined Kadima, and the new party became the leading force in the Knesset. On January 4, 2006, Ariel Sharon suffered a massive stroke, leaving the leadership of Israel in the hands of Ehud Olmert. A few weeks later, on January 26, the Palestinians held their own elections and the radical Hamas movement won a victory over the Fatah and the majority (74 of the 133 seats) of the Palestine Legislative Assembly, and claimed that attacks on Israel would be stepped up.

In the 2006 elections, the Kadima party led by Ehud Olmert gained 29 (of 120) Knesset seats, more than any other party, while the right-wing Likud, formerly the governing party, got only 12 seats, and the Labor party 19 seats. Though change in Israeli public opinion seemed possible, the fact that Palestinians continued an almost daily barrage of rockets on Israeli towns within the green line (the international border defined after the 1948 war) prevented peace negotiations. At the same time, Israel continued arresting or killing terrorist leaders whom it claimed were planning attacks. In return, the Islamic Jihad and Hamas vowed revenge, and the vicious cycle continued.

About 1,000 rockets fell on the southern part of Israel up to June 2006. The rockets grew in size and range, their effect more psychological than physical, creating panic and stress among Israeli civilians. Israel responded with artillery fire into empty fields, attempting to respond with similar psychological warfare, and then took to attacking the launching sites. On June 25th, just as the PNA announced the conclusion of an agreement of a truce with Israel, Hamas attacked an Israeli army border outpost at Kerem Shalom, killing two soldiers and capturing a third – Gilad Shalit. Hamas offered to trade the soldier for a thousand Palestinian prisoners. Israel refused and began a siege of Gaza and later invaded in operation "Summer Rains" in an attempt to force Palestinians to return the soldier alive and stop the rockets. The Israeli invasion of Gaza lasted about 2 months, and although thousands of leaflets advising civilians to leave their homes were dropped on inhabited areas in the northern Gaza Strip region which Israel had identified as frequent launch sites for rockets, over 400 Palestinians were killed.

On the morning of July 12, Hezbollah terrorists crossed the northern border (from Lebanon) into Israel and attacked an Israeli army patrol, killing three and capturing two soldiers. At the same time, Hezbollah began a series of rocket and mortar attacks on northern Israel. Subsequently, Israel carried out massive but selective bombing and artillery shelling of Lebanon. Hezbollah responded by launching thousands of rockets on Haifa, Tiberias, Safed, and other towns deep in northern Israel.

After Israeli air-attacks proved ineffective at stopping Hezbollah rocket attacks, Israel launched a limited ground invasion of Lebanon. The desultory Israeli offensive was stepped up on August 11 when efforts to broker a cease-fire appeared to be at an impasse, and Israeli troops began advancing in force toward the Litani river, 30 km north of the Israel–Lebanon border. Both sides stopped the fighting on August 14, 2006. The aggressive invasion of an independent country and the war raised a storm of criticism in Israel, and the Israeli attack roused widespread resentment in the Arab world. During and after the Israeli offensive in Lebanon, Israeli military operations continued unabated in Gaza, as Palestinians continued to launch rockets on southern Israel even though Hamas insisted solemnly that it was keeping the truce. On November 26, the Palestinians and Israelis announced a new truce that was to apply only to the Gaza strip, but the truce was violated repeatedly by Palestinians in Gaza by barrages of rockets fired at Israeli towns.[13]

On December 23, 2006, Israeli Prime Minister Ehud Olmert met with Palestinian President Mahmoud Abbas and announced some concessions that would make life easier for the Palestinians (including release of tax funds frozen by Israel and removal of a number of checkpoints along the Wall). These moves were seen as attempts to support President Abbas in his rivalry with the Hamas-led government of Ismail Haniyeh.

In June 2007, serious fighting erupted among Palestinians after a Fatah activist launched a rocket-propelled grenade into the house of Ismail Haniyeh, Hamas leader in Gaza. Hamas forces

[13]The Hamas claimed that they could not control the dissident Islamic Jihad movement, which claimed that it would not adhere to the truce unless it was extended to the West Bank.

retaliated by attacking Fatah activists and Fatah-affiliated Palestinian police in Gaza. In response, Mahmoud Abbas, president of the Palestinian Authority, dismissed the Gaza-based unity government and announced that he would be forming a new government of independent technocrats. The Hamas officials in Gaza continued to claim that they were the legitimate government. Israel supported Abbas's actions, and has not acknowledged Hamas legitimacy or met with its leaders.

Hamas' popularity in Gaza declined sharply as living conditions worsened due to the Israeli and international blockade and as extremists attempted to suppress marks of Western culture. Violence escalated in the streets of Gaza and Hamas blamed it on Fatah. Large quantities of explosives and arms kept reaching the area from Egypt into Gaza for Hamas and Jihad fighters through lengthy, deeply dug tunnels. Egyptian security forces uncovered 60 tunnels after Israel protested Egyptian laxity in monitoring the border. Hamas and other militants fired an average of one rocket every 3 h on the Western Negev, while Israel conducted small-scale retaliatory raids and missile strikes on rocket-launching teams in Gaza, as well as nighttime raids to find wanted terrorists in the West Bank.

In November 2007, the USA organized a peace summit in Annapolis, Maryland. In addition to senior representatives from Israel and Palestine, Arab states including Syria attended as well as United Nations, Gulf Cooperation Council, European Union, Russian, and South African representatives. Israeli Prime Minister Ehud Olmert and Palestinian Chairman Mahmoud Abbas met several times, but a statement was agreed upon only at the last moment, after heavy pressure by the USA.

The conference recognized Mahmoud Abbas as leader of the Palestinians. Israel and the Palestinians agreed to renew negotiations for a permanent agreement, hoping to complete the process by the end of 2008, and both sides vowed to implement the roadmap, with the USA monitoring the progress.

During that time, Islamic Jihad and Popular Resistance Committee terrorists continued to launch rockets and mortar fire into the Israeli town of Sderot and other Western Negev targets, and also launched several on Ashdod. Israel continued to shoot at rocket-launching teams and leaders of the various groups in Gaza responsible for rocket fire, and killing civilians when Israeli missile fire went awry. Hamas eventually joined in the rocket fire as the situation escalated. A large-scale Israeli offensive began on February 2008 and continued for several days, killing over 100 Palestinians. Palestinian President Mahmoud Abbas suspended direct negotiations with Israel.

On November 9, a meeting of the quartet (Israel, the Palestinian Authority, Egypt, and the USA) was held in Sharm el-Sheikh to reaffirm support for Israeli–Palestinian negotiations in the framework of the Annapolis process and of the "roadmap." Both sides expressed support for the process. Hamas cancelled its attendance at a Palestinian reconciliation meeting that was to have been held in Egypt that week.

On December 24, Hamas bombarded Israel with over 60 rockets and mortar shells. On December 27, Israel began Operation "Oferet Yetzuka" (Operation Cast Lead). In a single Saturday morning, in the space of a few hours, Israeli Air Force destroyed arms caches, ammunition factories, smuggling tunnels, missile launching sites, and Hamas command and control centers in Gaza. Casualties according to the Palestinian Center for Human Rights (2009) reached 1,417 individuals, among them 313 children and 116 women. According to Israeli data (Lappin, 2009), 1,166 Palestinians were killed, 295 noncombatants died during the operation – 89 of them under the age of 16 years, and 49 of them women. Hamas intensified their efforts and launched Grad missiles that reached as far as Beersheba and Yavneh – about 45 km from Gaza. In response, Israel commenced a ground operation in Gaza. The major fighting ended on January 18, 2009, when a cease-fire was declared. Israel claimed a military victory, but the main issues that led to their attack remained unresolved: Hamas still rules Gaza, the kidnapped soldier Gilad Shalit was not found and recovered, and the constant flow of weapons through the tunnels continues.

On February 10, 2009, Israeli elections provided a marginal majority to the right-wing parties (the Likud, Israel Baiteinu, and Shas), strengthening the opposition to a two-state solution to the Israeli–Palestinian conflict. On June 4, 2009, US President Barack Obama gave a historic speech to the Muslim and Arab world, calling on Palestinians to renounce violence, calling on Arabs to recognize Israel's right to exist, reiterating US support for a two-state solution, and calling for an end to settlement construction. Israeli Prime Minister Netanyahu responded on June 14, by changing his total objection to a two-state solution to partial support. This support was conditional: Israel would support a two-state solution provided (1) its security is guaranteed, (2) Palestine would be a demilitarized zone, and (3) the Palestinian right of return would be to the Palestinian state, not to Israel. He also pledged that Israel would not build new settlements or confiscate land for settlements (though it would continue to build housing units for what he termed "natural growth").

3 The Israeli and Palestinian Conflict: Current Status

Both Israelis and Palestinians agree that five issues are at the core of the conflict today, leading to its continuation: (1) The status of *Jerusalem*. Will it be the capital of both States? (2) *Palestinian refugees*. Will they be allowed into Israel or only into the Palestinian State? (3) *Jewish settlements in the West Bank*. Should they remain? Should only some of them remain? Can land be offered in exchange for heavily populated areas? (4) *Israeli security*. Can it be guaranteed? What will guarantee Israelis feelings of safety and national security? (5) *The placement of borders*. Will territorial continuity for one state define lack of continuity for the other? This also raises the question of who controls the borders, and whether or not the new Palestinian State will be allowed weapons to defend its borders (Kimmerling, 2008; Winnick, 2009).

The debate over these issues is not only between Israelis and Palestinians, but it is also explicit within each of these societies: The Israelis, like the Palestinians, are a people deeply divided and with different perceptions of the conflict, its causes, and its possible solutions. The left–right distinction in Israel has been there since the very beginning of the state. Kimmerling (2008) argued that this distinction, in the Israeli context, reflects more than an economic ideology, as it does in Western societies, since it also reflects ethnic categorizations, social classes, religiosity, and education. Researchers found that in Israel, left-wing orientation is related to a more egalitarian view of society (Moore, 2003), to lower authoritarianism (Rubinstein, 1995), and to stronger liberal attitudes (Barnea & Schwartz, 1998) than right-wing orientation. Left-wing orientation is also strongly related to sustaining the peace process and supporting land concessions for peace. The Palestinian society is divided between Hamas and Fatah. Fatah, as the political branch of the PLO, has led the Palestinian first intifada during the late 1980s and the beginning of the 1990s. As support for the Fatah increased among Palestinians, a new political movement, Hamas, rose as an opposition in the late 1980s. This movement was based on a religious agenda, inspired by the Muslim Brothers' agenda in Egypt. Hamas had formulated its ideology in rivalry with the secular national Palestinian ideology of the PLO and Fatah, thus criticizing the PLO for portraying the conflict as one between Palestinian nationalism and Zionism, rather than a fight to expel the Jews completely from the area, understood from "throw them to the sea," as Yasser Arafat proclaimed when he first created the PLO and defined its goals. Hamas portrayed the Israeli–Palestinian conflict as a religious conflict between Muslims and Jews, and as part of a broader religious war waged between the Islamic world and the Western civilization (Litvak, 1998). During the last 20 years, the conflict between these two Palestinian movements escalated, especially after Hamas won the 2006 Palestinian election in the Gaza Strip. Since June 2007, internal

Palestinian fighting between Hamas and Fatah resulted in hundreds of deaths and many being wounded, and the gaining of complete control of Hamas over the Gaza Strip, while Fatah is in control in the West Bank.

Talks between Israelis and Palestinians have begun again in September 2010. However, public opinion reflected by both the Israeli and Palestinian mass media seems to indicate pessimism, disillusionment, and even apathy. After all the previous attempts to reach a peace agreement failed, trust among the opposing sides is hard to establish. Moreover, the prolonged conflict has influenced not only the intra- but also the intergroup processes, so that each collective created a different story to describe the common history. Or, as Kimmerling (1998) claimed in the title of his article: "Our nation, their disaster," "our" means Jews, "their" means Palestinians, and both refer to the same historical events. The next part of the chapter describes the different collectives, and how the historical context influenced the social orders in each collective.

3.1 Jewish–Israeli Collectivities

Israeli society is composed of a Jewish majority (of over 80%) and an Arab minority (of about 20%, divided into subgroups of Muslim and Christian Arabs, Druze, Bedouins, and Cherkessians). The two groups are segregated and differentiated in all respects: culturally, linguistically, geographically, and economically, and the relations between them are defined largely by the Arab–Israeli conflict.

Israel is both a Jewish and a democratic State. As a result, a conflict often arises between the two sets of laws: The Jewish-particularistic and the civic-universalistic one. The first not only favors its Jewish citizens, but also creates situations in which the democratic principles of the state are inapplicable to its Arab citizens (e.g., the Law of Return recognizes the right of every Jew to emigrate to Israel, but not the rights of Palestinians to return if they left Israel or were deported) before its independence (1948).

The Zionist ideology strove to integrate the two conflicting value premises: collective particularism of Jewish aspiration to an independent nation-state and universalism of current Westernized society. The two value systems represent two distinct, unavoidably clashing social orders: The *national* and the *civic* order (Eisenstadt, 1974). For Jews, the *national* social order connotes the religion-based Jewish primordial and particularistic value system that excludes from the boundaries of the collectivity all non-Jewish citizens, but includes all Jewish people in the Diaspora. The *civic* order includes all Jewish and non-Jewish citizens of the State. The inherently conflictual, precarious balance among these aspects often shifts, leading to the weakening of one or the other.[14]

Supporting the social orders means identification with their goals, normative value systems, and the collectives they create, thus translating the social order into a social identity. Although for most Jews in Israel national and civic social identities somewhat overlap (e.g., both identities maintain that Jews have a right to live as a free people in Israel), the two identities are inherently inconsistent, as they derive from irreconcilable social orders (Moore & Kimmerling, 1995).

Moreover, the Jewish society in Israel is deeply divided along ethnic and religiosity lines of demarcation. The main differentiation is between Jews of Asian–African origin [and their descendants ("Mizrachi")] who tend to be traditional or religious and Jews of Western origin ("Ashkenazi"), many of who are secular. These differences lead to different identity hierarchies, attitudes, and responses to the conflict (Moore & Aweiss, 2004).

[14] Kimmerling (1985) claims that the strengthening of the Jewish-particularistic (and religious) trends can be seen even earlier than that, in the centripetal movement of the national-religious strata toward the center of society. He shows that in 1974, Jewish identity was already stronger than the Israeli one among both the religious and the secular Jews (see also Auron, 1993; Avruch, 1981; Farrago, 1977).

3.2 Arab–Israeli Collectivities

Like the Jews in Israel, the Arab citizens of Israel are internally divided: Muslims, Christians, Bedouins and Druz, urban and rural residents, created a diverse society. In 1947, under British rule, before the war between Israel and the major Arab countries (including Egypt, Syria, Jordan, Lebanon, and Iraq), Arabs in Israel (then Palestine) were the majority of all citizens (over 1,300,000 people) and Jews were the minority (about 600,000 people) (Benziman & Manzur, 1992). That war reversed the proportions and created the refugee problem. About 640,000 Arabs either fled to diverse countries or were deported from the country altogether. Another 550,000 people either fled or were deported from their homes to live mostly in refugee camps close to the Israeli border, in territories conquered by neighboring Arab states (mainly in the West Bank conquered by Jordan (about 400,000 refugees) and in the Gaza Strip conquered by Egypt (about 150,000 refugees)). The rest, only 160,000 Arabs remained in Israel (Landau, 1993). Access to the land held sacred "al-ard al Muqddassa" (the Holy Land) by the Qur'an was barred for all Arabs in countries that were (and most still are) in conflict with Israel.

The result of that war was traumatic for the Arabs for several reasons. First, the Arabs in Israel together with the neighboring Arab armies were defeated. Second, about 90% of them became refugees. Third, the dispersal of Arab refugees strengthened the already existing kinship, economic, religious, and political ties between them and the people of Lebanon, Syria, Jordan, Iraq, Saudi Arabia, and Egypt. However, the Arabs who remained in Israel became a minority in the country where they used to be the majority, and most of their ties with the Arab world were severed (Farsoun & Zacharia, 1997; Shtendal, 1992).

In Israel's declaration of independence, the representatives of the National Council called the Arabs who were residents of the State of Israel to maintain the peace and partake in the building of the country on the basis of full and equal citizenship and rightful representation in its institutions. However, their rights and privileges were often revoked or denied (Rekhes, 1994).The most blatant violation of Arabs' rights was caused by the maintaining of military rule over all all-Arab towns and villages until the end of 1966. Military rule severely curtailed the Arabs' freedom of movement and freedom of speech. Suspected of conspiring with the enemy, or serving as "fifth column"[15] if an additional war broke out, military rule was portrayed to the Israeli public and to the world as an undemocratic yet unavoidable evil. Even the Ratner Commission, created in 1955 (7 years after Israel's independence), claimed that military rule should not be lifted in order to prevent Arabs who were uprooted from their homes, property, and villages from attempting to return to their lands. Those lands were reallocated and some of them were given to new immigrant Jews (in Ein Hod, Yoqneam, Nazareth, Beit Shemesh, and so forth). Military governance was canceled by the Knesset only on November 8, 1966.

In addition, three of the more discriminating laws are still implemented:

The Law of Return (1950), according to which any Jew can come to Israel and gain citizenship automatically. Non-Jews cannot gain citizenship even if their family members are already citizens. Moreover, unlike their Jewish counterparts, Arab citizens may lose their citizenship for diverse reason (for example, in May 20, 1999, a group of 140 Arab women who were citizens of Israel applied to Israel's high court demanding that their citizenship be restored. It was revoked because they married Palestinians and moved to areas in the Palestinian Authority (Haaretz, May 22, 1999). Needless to say, no Jewish woman had ever had her citizenship revoked if and when she married a non-Israeli.

The Law defining the status of the Zionist Jewish Agency (1961). The Jewish agency is responsible for planning new settlements and infrastructure development. The Arab settlements were left out of the arrangement as the Jewish agency serves only the Jewish population. Consequently, Arab settlements get no financial support from this

[15] A fifth column is a group of people who clandestinely undermine a larger group such as a nation from within, to help an external enemy.

institution, cannot obtain land, and some of them, at the end of the millennium, are still not connected to Israel's main power and water networks. The state itself devised the law that grants preferential national status to organizations that take care only of some of its citizens.

Fundamental Law: *The State's Land (1966)*. The law defines most of the land as owned by the state or the Keren Kayemet, whose codex forbids transferring land to non-Jewish hands. All lands owned by Keren Kayemet are supervised by the Land Authority, which is a national institution, and therefore, the state itself discriminates against its Arab citizens. Moreover, because of this law, a large number of Arab villages are not recognized as such by the state and are thus deprived of all basic services – water, electricity, schools, and so forth.

The continued implementation of these (and other) discriminatory laws, together with unequal sharing of the state's budget, reproduces inequality between the Jewish majority and the Arab minority in Israel, and created a deep sense of discrimination within the Arab community. Still, the majority of Arabs considered themselves Israelis. Until the first Intifada, most Arabs considered themselves both "Israeli" and "Arab." A minority (especially among those who had family members in refugee camps outside Israel) included an additional component in their identity and saw themselves as part of the Palestinian people as well. Since the Intifada, the balance has changed. Though no academic studies of the issue were conducted in Israel in recent years, the proportion of those who consider themselves "Palestinian" rather than "Arab"[16] seems to have changed: the actions of Arabs (e.g., demonstrations, participating in actions initiated by Palestinians against Israel, and the support of Arab members of the Israeli parliament for Palestinian issues) indicate that the proportions have changed and now most Arabs see themselves as part of the Palestinian people, in addition to being Israeli citizens (Shikaki, 1999; Shtendal, 1992). Unavoidably, the national (i.e., Israeli) and the civic (i.e., Palestinian) identities of these individuals clash. Moreover, considered "outsiders" by both Jewish–Israelis and Palestinians, they are constantly torn between the two identities.

3.2.1 Palestinian Collectivities

Data from the early 1990s indicate that about 30% of all Palestinians live in Gaza and the West Bank (whether under Israeli rule or under Palestinian Authority (PA) rule: 1,873,476 (18.6%) in the West Bank and Jerusalem, and 1,022,207 (10.8%) in Gaza).[17] There are different administrative apparatuses, educational systems, economies, and social structures in the two regions due to influences of Jordan (on refugees in the West Bank) and Egypt (on refugees in the Gaza Strip).

Living conditions in the two segments of the Palestinian Authority are different. For example, illiteracy among men in the West Bank is lower than that among men in the Gaza Strip (7.2% vs. 8.6%, respectively); fertility rates are lower in the West Bank than they are in the Gaza Strip (45% vs. 50%, respectively) (Palestinian Bureau of Statistics, 2001, 2007). Poverty among the Palestinians declined until the *El Aqsa Intifada* (that began in September 2000), but 20% of them were still under the poverty line in 1998 (in comparison with 23% and 24% in 1997 and 1996, respectively)[18] (Palestinian Bureau of Statistics, 2000). Since the Intifada, the rates of unemployment among Palestinians increased significantly (see Table 9.1) and wages declined (wages per hour seemed to have increased, but the rate of

[16]The term "Arab" connotes identification with a larger, more defuse category; "Palestinian" connotes identification with a specific group that considers itself "a people without a homeland" (Kimmerling & Moore, 1997).

[17]Another 10% live in Israel and the remaining 50% are dispersed in other countries and/or refugee camps mainly in Jordan, the United Arab Emirates, Tunisia, Algeria, Sudan, Syria, Iraq, Oman, Lebanon, Libya, Egypt, and Morocco.

[18]Poverty is more noticeable in the Gaza strip, where 33% of the households are below the poverty line (in comparison with 14.5% of the households in the West Bank). Poverty is more prevalent among bigger families, households headed by women, and households with the less educated heads.

Table 9.1 Employment rates of (a) Israelis (Jews and Arabs) and (b) Palestinians1995–2008a

a	Israelis					
	Israel (all population)			Arab		
	Percentage of unemployed of civilian labor force	Percentage of part time of civilian labor force	Percentage of civilian labor force of total population aged 15+ years	Percentage of unemployed of civilian labor force	Percentage of part time of civilian labor force	Percentage of civilian labor force of total population aged 15+ years
1995	6.9	24.7	54.1	6.0	9.6	82.1
1996	6.7	24.1	53.7	6.1	10.4	80.4
1997	7.7	24.0	53.5	7.2	9.6	79.4
1998	8.6	24.7	53.6	10.7	16.8	86.8
1999	8.9	24.2	53.8	11.4	15.4	69.0
2000	8.8	23.6	54.3	11.9	16.9	66.7
2001	9.3	24.9	54.4	10.6	13.8	71.8
2002	10.3	23.8	54.1	14.1	10.4	73.1
2003	10.7	24.7	54.5	11.5	18.5	66.4
2004	10.4	26.3	54.9	10.8	20.3	64.7
2005	9.0	26.8	55.2	11.3	20.7	64.7
2006	8.4	26.7	55.6	11.5	18.6	65.2
2007	7.3	27.1	56.3	8.5	20.3	67.2
2008	6.1	26.8	56.5	10.9	20.8	64.0

b	Palestinians					
	West Bank			Gaza strip		
	Unemployment	Underemployment	Employment	Unemployment	Underemployment	Employment
1995	13.9	20.8	65.3	29.4	22.0	48.6
1996	19.6	12.8	67.6	35.5	10.0	57.5
1997	17.3	11.6	71.1	26.8	4.4	68.8
1998	11.5	8.4	80.1	20.3	2.3	76.8
1999	9.5	7.0	83.5	16.9	1.9	81.2
2000	12.1	6.2	81.7	18.7	2.3	79.0
2001	21.5	4.7	73.8	34.2	1.9	63.9
2002	28.2	5.5	66.3	38.0	1.8	60.2
2003	23.8	7.5	68.7	29.2	3.6	67.2
2004	22.9	8.3	68.8	35.4	2.1	62.5
2005	20.3	8.5	71.2	30.3	2.3	67.4
2006	18.6	9.4	72.0	34.8	4.6	60.6
2007	17.7	9.5	72.8	29.7	4.7	65.6
2008	19.0	6.8	74.2	40.6	6.4	53.0

[a]Israeli Bureau of Statistics, 2008; Palestinian Bureau of Statistics, 2008

inflation is greater so that in actuality, each Shekel earned is worth less. See Table 9.2).

The society is thus dispersed and fragmented, its disintegration being the result of successive wars with the Israelis (most notably, the war of 1948 and the June 1967 war). The condition of exile, which has affected more than one half of the Palestinians, has stamped the collective consciousness, cultural trends, and the political behavior of Palestinians throughout the Middle East region and in the Diaspora (FAFO, 1993). In the Palestinian Diaspora, there are two kinds of Palestinian refugees, claim Farsoun and Zacharia (1997). The middle- and upper-class Palestinians, many of whom left the area just before the 1948 war, took refuge in Arab cities such as Amman, Beirut, and Cairo, and managed to reorganize their lives in exile. The sec-

Table 9.2 Employment and daily wage in the Palestinian territory by place of work and sector: 2000–2008

Indicators	2000	2001	2002	2003	2004	2005	2006	2007	2008
Percentage distribution of employed persons by sector									
Palestinian territory									
Public sector	19.4	23.0	23.6	2037	22.5	23.0	23.7	23.3	24.7
Private sector	61.0	63.2	66.1	69.6	68.8	67.1	66.7	67.3	63.8
Israel and settlements	19.6	13.8	10.3	9.7	8.7	9.9	9.6	9.4	11.5
West Bank									
Public sector	14.5	16.6	18.4	16.5	16.9	16.9	17.3	17.0	16.8
Private sector	63.1	65.4	68.3	71.0	71.5	69.3	69.7	69.9	67.5
Israel and settlements	22.4	18.0	13.3	12.5	11.6	13.8	13.0	13.1	15.7
Gaza strip									
Public sector	31.3	41.5	36.8	30.5	37.1	38.1	41.6	39.1	46.8
Private sector	55.8	56.6	60.7	66.2	61.8	61.5	58.4	60.9	53.2
Israel and settlements	12.9	1.9	2.5	3.3	1.1	0.4	–	–	–
Average daily wage in NIS for wage employees									
Palestinian territory									
Public sector	60.0	61.1	61.6	63.8	67.9	72.7	81.0	81.8	84.3
Private sector	66.4	66.9	68.4	65.9	66.4	66.2	68.9	69.0	76.1
Israel and settlements	110.4	107.2	117.3	125.1	126.7	126.9	131.6	131.2	139.7
West Bank									
Public sector	64.8	66.3	66.3	68.7	72.4	75.8	82.6	85.6	90.3
Private sector	73.1	71.8	75.0	75.4	72.8	72.5	75.0	74.5	82.9
Israel and settlements	108.7	108.8	118.9	127.2	126.8	126.7	131.5	131.2	139.7
Gaza strip									
Public sector	55.0	55.5	56.6	58.2	62.9	69.3	79.4	76.4	71.7
Private sector	49.1	51.4	52.0	47.5	51.5	51.7	52.7	53.2	50.7
Israel and settlements	117.1	62.3	96.7	106.6	122.4	–	–	–	–

Palestinian Bureau of Statistics, 2008

ond, far larger group of refugees is the mass of poor peasant Palestinians, most of whom became the refugee camp dwellers. Despite the fact that United Nation's resolution 194 in 1948 affirmed Palestinians' right to repatriation or compensation, and despite international pressure, Israel has refused to comply and no solution has been reached (Kimmerling & Migdal, 1994). Most of the exiled Palestinians were not absorbed by the communities and societies they reached. The well-off among them found it easier to live in the big cities, especially in the Arab world; the rest were forced to live in refugee camps without formal legal status in the countries in which they found themselves (Brand, 1988; Khalaf & Kongstad, 1973; Peretz, 1990). The segregation served to strengthen their social and cultural identities and enabled the development of solidarity and political consciousness among them.

Thus, despite cultural, linguistic, religious, and racial similarity, Palestinians formed a distinct minority group in the Arab countries they reached and the hosting countries refused to absorb them as full citizens[19] (Aruri & Farsoun, 1980). As such, they were treated differently by the legal and political systems in the host countries. Only in Jordan were they granted full citizenship. In Lebanon, they were and still are treated as foreigners in relation to work permits,[20] employment in the public sector, enrollment in universities, and participation in the political

[19] At the same time, Israel absorbed half a million Jewish refugees who fled from Arab countries, and accorded them full citizenship upon their arrival.

[20] When the number of Palestinians was estimated at 225,000 in 1969, only 1% held official work permits (Farsoun & Zacharia, 1997).

sphere (Abu-Habib, 1996; Sayigh, 1994). In the Gulf States, Palestinians have no rights of citizenship, residence, or work even if they were born there, and they were treated as foreign guest workers (Ghabra, 1987). Thus, the Arab world maintained their refugee status for over 60 years.

Moreover, violence against Palestinians can be seen in many of the host countries, especially in Jordan, Lebanon, and Kuwait.[21] In Israel, too, violence against Palestinians in the West Bank and the Gaza Strip was common, taking the shape of killings, injuries, deportations, sealing homes or demolishing them, and detaining hundreds without trial and without specifying for how long.

While war, dislocation, and occupation have joined the West Bank and Gaza to form a political entity, they also led to the fragmentation of Palestinian society. The fragmented reality has tangible meaning for Palestinians in these areas. First, Palestinians on either side of the "Green Line" continue to be linked by some degree of kinship and other ties. Second, the Palestinian Diaspora is a collectivity with functional ties with Palestinians in the West Bank and Gaza, tied to the community in the Palestinian Authority by shared consciousness and memories of Palestine as it was before the 1948 war (Taraki, 1997).

The social and economic trends suggest both a higher rate of social homogenization and a lower rate of social mobility than has been perceived in the less recent literature on Palestinians (prior to 1990s) (Heiberg & Øvensen, 1993). Loss of land and property enhanced the value of education as a resource that affects social mobility and emigration. The Israeli political control has also affected the social and economic trends and the daily life of Palestinians. Most importantly, perhaps, restrictions on movement and forcible changes in the housing situation of families shaped Palestinians' life experiences (Ugland & Tamari, 1993).

Since their mass dislocation in 1948, Palestinians have placed special emphasis on the value of education. Education is seen as a durable, but moveable asset that can be used in whatever circumstances a person eventually finds him- or herself in. Educational attainment among the Palestinians has improved remarkably over the past decades[22] (Heiberg, 1993). Men benefited more from the initial improvement in general educational levels. The gender gap in education did not significantly begin to narrow until some 25 years ago (i.e., mid-1970s).[23]

The difference in the literacy rates of men and women in the current Palestinian population is due mostly to high illiteracy rates among older women. Figures show that although male literacy rates over the past 30–40 years have doubled, women's literacy has grown eightfold in the same period. Palestinian women today add public, professional, and political roles to their more traditional ones (Palestinian Bureau of Statistics, 1996).

Thus, from a largely rural and traditional society, most of whose members were illiterate, the Palestinians were transformed into a more urbanized and literate one. This had a significant impact on improving standard of living in the West Bank, even though there are only limited opportunities to transform education to middle-class employment, especially for women. This may have a significant impact on their future expectations.

3.3 The Effects of the Occupation on the Sociohistorical Context

Structuration, the process that produces and reproduces societies and their cultures, is an ongoing process, but major events (whether man-made-like

[21] In Jordan during September 1970 (labled "Black September"). In Lebanon in 1950–1960 by the Lebanese army, in 1975–1982 by the Christian Maronite militia, and in 1985–1986 by Shi'a militias with Syrian support. In Kuwait after the Gulf War when Palestinians were collectively accused of collaborating with the Iraqis and were, therefore, expelled from the country without their property and valuables after many among them were tortured, maimed, and killed.

[22] The improvement is especially noticeable in the West Bank, but can be seen in Gaza too.

[23] The school system is not controlled by Israel – most of the schools are run by UNRWA. In the West bank, the Jordanian programs are taught, and in Gaza, the Egyptian ones. In schools controlled by the HAMAS, the programs are mostly religious.

wars or natural-like earthquakes) may change the course of the process and deflect it into a new one (Giddens, 1984). The 6-Day War in 1967 between Israel and its neighbors – Egypt, Jordan, Syria, and Lebanon – seems to have created such a shift in the structuration process. Israeli forces conquered lands that were part of Syria (the Golan Heights), Jordan (the West Bank), and Egypt (Sinai and the Gaza Strip), and maintained occupation forces in all these areas since then. To strengthen the hold over the occupied territories, Jewish civilians were allowed, even encouraged, to create settlements and towns in them.

Israel's occupation of these lands can be seen as one of the forces that not only changed the relations between Israel and the Palestinians, but also separated the two collective identities in Israel more clearly. Occupation of the Palestinians seems to have affected the normative systems which form the bases for the national and civic identities, and to tear Israeli society into two distinct blocks according to the social orders they support more strongly.

Many and diverse changes have occurred in the normative structure and the goals of Israeli society. Among the more noticeable and relevant to the present discussion are the change in perceptions of human rights and the reallocation of resources necessary to maintain the new objectives. The need to maintain the occupation is perceived as taking precedence over the rights and liberties of individuals. Consequently, the enforcement of norms stiffens, and there is less tolerance of dissent (e.g., arresting Jews, Arabs, and Palestinians and holding them in "administrative custody" without trial and without bringing charges against them if they are suspected of hostile actions). The military occupation also necessitates the reordering of priorities and reallocation of resources to maintain the changed norms (e.g., funds are allocated to develop settlements and to maintain forces to protect Jewish settlers).

For some Israelis, especially among the staunch supporters of the *national social order* (like the Settlers), the occupation and seeing Palestinians as the enemy seem to have led to dehumanizing them. This enables Israelis to distance themselves from the results of their actions and the consequences to the people they oppress, and leads to even greater violence and intolerance. For other Israelis, especially among the supporters of the *civic social order* (like members of the "Peace Now" Movement), the occupation is totally unacceptable and they demonstrate in the occupied territories against government policy (Moore & Aweiss, 2004).

A different type of normative change can be seen in the relationships between the Jewish majority and Arab minority in Israel. The stronger the link between Arabs in Israel and Palestinians in the West Bank, the easier it is for Israelis to consider Arabs in Israel a threat to national security. At the same time, most Israelis would agree that Arabs in Israel should be treated as equal citizens. The ambivalence toward the Arab citizens in Israel increases in proportion to the strength of their identification with their Palestinian families across the border (Moore & Aweiss, 2004).

Social psychological theories claim that conflict between two groups tends to strengthen group cohesion within each group (Islam & Hewstone, 1993; Tyler, Boeckmann, Smith, & Huo, 1997). Examination of both the Israeli and Palestinian societies shows that group cohesion is not always the consequence of conflict. The fragmentation of Israeli society has become more noticeable in recent years (e.g., the hostility between the ultraorthodox and the secular is constantly increasing), encumbering advancements in the peace process. Though less rapidly, and less intensely, cohesion in the Palestinian society seems also to be lessening: the centralist government no longer holds all segments and factions under a unified authority, and extremist movements and groups (like the Hamas, "Islamic Jihad," and "Izz a-din el-kassam") are pulling the Palestinian society apart.

However, the increased militancy of the Intifada in the new Millennium and the collapse of the hopes raised by the peace process that Clinton initiated seem to have led to a renewed cohesion of certain segments of the Jewish society and the greater parallel cohesion of Palestinian society, thus lessening intragroup differences while increasing intergroup differences.

4 Structuration and Social Identities

Identities are constructs that define social entities and are an essential part of the process of construction, maintenance, and change of the social order. Different theorists deal with the different aspects of social identity (Abrams & Hogg, 1999; Eisenstadt, 1974; Emmison & Western, 1990; Giddens, 1979; Sidanius, Pratto, & Bobo, 1996; Tajfel & Turner, 1986).

In the present analysis, we attempt to provide a comprehensive account of these multiple approaches and combine them in order to analyze the prevalent hierarchies of identity components among individuals, and the social orders they represent because we assume that the different hierarchies are related to values, attitudes, and demographic characteristics associated with the context of the Israel–Palestinian conflict. The examination of these issues is, therefore, context specific. Thus, to explore the structuration process of a conflict in a given sociohistorical context, one needs to examine the simultaneous influences of the agents' characteristics, their sociopolitical conflict, and their perceptions of that conflict.

Giddens' Theory of Structuration (Giddens, 1976, 1979, 1984, 1994) provides insights into the links between the individual and the social systems. At the core of this theory are individuals, known as agents of the social system, and the sociohistorical context within which they function.

The agents do not *create* systems or cultures but "reproduce or transform them, remaking what is already made in the continuity of *praxis*" (Giddens, 1984, p. 71). Agents are autonomous, skillful, and knowledgeable, although never fully aware of the consequences of their actions. Their actions are bound by the historical-situational context, compounded by existing power structures, which are not of the agents' choosing. However, agents are never fully culturally preprogrammed, and they are capable of offering "rational" explanations of the reasons and the motives of their actions (Swingewood, 1991; Thompson, 1989).

Giddens refers to social structures not as constants, but as the products of ongoing processes that structurate them. When the structuration process shifts, the patterns are transformed and new practices are shaped (Cohen, 1987). Thus, "structure is both a medium and outcome of the reproduction of practices" (Giddens, 1979, p. 4).

Although Giddens treats *all* individuals as social agents who reproduce social systems, some agents are less autonomous than others, bound by oppressive and nonegalitarian systems that limit their opportunity and ability to transform the social institutions in which they function (Moore, 1998). This is especially true for disadvantaged groups (Arabs and Palestinians) in situations of conflict with the advantaged ones (Jews) in any given society. In such contexts, the interests of the advantaged groups are better served than those of the disadvantaged ones who are also less able to change the situation. The process of structuration produces social identities that are located on different levels of a given social order, from small groups to large national or even transnational bodies (Giddens, 1994).

However, the term "agent" remains devoid of any significant social content and is no less metaphysical than any other traditional structuralist term. We turn to social identity theory (SIT) to complement that of Giddens' and to define the relationship between agents and social orders.

The social identities can become collective identities (i.e., identities that can *potentially* be held by all members of a certain society, like being "Jewish," or "Palestinian"). These identities reflect membership in broad social categories, as well as the goals, orientations, attitudes, and values of these categories. Such identities can also create "rules of the game" within the collectivity and can be a part of a hierarchy of individual identities, reflecting an actual, desired or imagined membership in collectivities and a person's location within them (Eisenstadt, 1974; Ellemers, Wilke, & van Knippenberg, 1993). In the case of Israel, for example, a collective identity like "being Jewish" connotes membership in the dominant group, identifying with the goals of that group and its culture; for Palestinians, collective identity like "being

Palestinian" connotes participation in the fight for a nation-state.

The collectivistic dimension dictates precedence of the collective needs over individual's needs. In collectivistic societies, all members are expected to join the collective effort and contribute to the attainment of its goals as much as they can, with whatever resources they have. Personal attainment of material resources such as wealth and power are accorded lower value and importance than the welfare of the collective and which are to be gained through the attainment of collective goals rather than individual actions (Lissak, 1969).

Prevalent collective identities seem especially typical of "societies in formation" (like Israel between the 1950s and the 1970s, and the Palestinian Authority today). The individual in such societies is seen as a "bearer of collective ideals whose commitment to these ideals makes him or her subordinate to their imperative....this called on the individual to sacrifice private interests and to place him or herself at the disposal of a movement that purported to serve collective goals and interests" (Horowitz & Lissak, 1978).

Choosing a collective identity means making it a part of the individual's hierarchy of identities and the embracing of the goals, attitudes, and values embedded in them (Kimmerling & Moore, 1997; Moore, 1996, 2000). In collective societies, social change is expressed and labeled by changes in collective identities, and fundamental internal struggles take place around the adoption of competing collective identities (Kimmerling & Moore, 1997).

Even in collectivistic societies, nonnationalistic social identities that emphasize alternative values and priorities may become salient for individuals (Lawler, 1992). Thus, for example, people's major loyalty may be to their immediate (nuclear) family[24] and that would increase the salience and centrality of the *family identity*; they may strive to maximize self-fulfillment through participation in the labor market and that would increase the salience and centrality of their *professional identity*; for others, ethnicity, religiosity, or locality may gain salience and centrality, and therefore *ethnic*, *religious*, or *local identity* will be placed higher on their hierarchy of identities.

As each identity represents a different set of values and diverse social orders, espousing one often means rejecting another. Some combinations of identities are possible even though they represent different values, but then people attenuate their adherence to each set of values by either adjusting the values or emphasizing each in different circumstances.

We assume that every social actor or "agent" (Giddens, 1976, 1984) has a relatively limited repertoire of social identities which are constructed by the individual's characteristics and his or her desire for membership in a specific collectivity and culture. As such, identities are a part of an ongoing sociopolitical struggle over alternative social identities and their contents in every collectivity and, thus, they reflect diverse social orders.

Moore and Kimmerling (1995) examined the existence of several strategic social identities, which when adopted by an agent from the larger repertoire determines large parts of the social order as carried, produced, and reproduced by that agent. They show, for example, that in societies in which national rights are unsettled, people will tend to define themselves in regional or nationalistic terms and emphasize this aspect of their social identity more than class, and in societies where religion is the major basis for social strife, people will define themselves in terms of the religious component of their social identity.

This incorporation of SIT extends and elaborates the sociological foundation of the theory to include sociopsychological assumptions. According to SIT (Tajfel, 1981; Tajfel & Turner, 1986; Turner, 1984), people tend to classify themselves and others into diverse social categories (such as national, religious, gender, and age groups) (Ashforth & Mael, 1989; Turner, 1985). The theory also focuses on the impact of group (or category) membership on people's distinction

[24]In the case of Arab society in Israel, we may consider loyalties to the extended family (the hamulla) in terms of a semi-individualistic orientation, because of the interchangeability of both types of families in this case.

between "us" and "them" or "ingroup" and "outgroup" (Tajfel & Turner, 1986).

Identification develops when an agent sees him- or herself as culturally and socially tied to the collectivity, its successes and failures, and privileges or lack of privileges (Kedourie, 1993). Many factors were cited as leading to group identification (Ashforth & Mael, 1989). The most relevant to our case is the distinctiveness of the group's values and practices in comparison with those of other groups that provides individuals with a sense of unique identities (De Cremer, 2001; Oakes & Turner, 1986); the group's prestige that may affect the individual's self-esteem (Chatman, Bell, & Staw, 1986; Walker, 1999); and the prominence of the out-group that strengthens the awareness of the in-group (Perkins, Nieva, & Lawler, 1983). Thus, when a hostile relationship exists between the in- and outgroups (as we often find in conflict situations), and the outgroup is clearly distinct (e.g., by skin color or dress code, as distinguished between Jews and Palestinians), the collective group identification intensifies the Jewish and Palestinian identities whenever members of the two collectives meet, as they can easily identify each other as belonging to their out-group).

Moreover, identification tends to strengthen social categorizations (especially when they are of a bipolar, either-or nature) that intensify conflicts among groups. According to Turner (1982), when an intense conflict exists between two subcultures, interactions among members of those collectivities will be more strongly influenced by their actual or imaginary membership, than when no conflict exists. Thus interactions between Jews and Palestinians tend to be strongly influenced by their collective identities. The stronger the identity, the less able they are to see the "other" as an individual; they all become stereotypic representatives of their respective groups.

In pluralistic societies in which diverse social categories coexist, each category tends to espouse a *relevant* ideology to justify the differentiation and to direct social action (Steel, Warner, Lovrich, & Pierce, 1992); the ideology espoused by the subordinate (or oppressed) group can be either a competing or a derivative ideology. Competing ideologies promote alternative views of the social order; derivative ideologies presuppose the existence of a dominant ideology and a distinct but contingent alternative. In the case of Jews in Israel, for example, the more general democratic/egalitarian ideologies in Western societies are less "relevant" for orthodox Jews, as their basic assumptions fail to address their religious needs of superiority over non-Jews and thus cannot replace religious values. For secular Jews, however, democracy is the core ideology. The democratic value system used to be the core ideology for the Arab citizens of Israel. However, shifting their views and becoming more "Palestinian" than "Israeli" has led to a decline in their support of democracy, as it fails to provide them with legitimation for their sociopolitical actions (which are, at times, against their state).

Such conflicts may appear between national, ethnic, racial, religious, and/or political groups who share the same resources. When the conflict that ensues is intractable (i.e., violent, durable, irreconcilable, and of zero-sum nature) (Azar, 1990; Goertz & Diehl, 1993), it tends to create a conflictive ethos (i.e., the value orientations, social identities, beliefs, attitudes, and feelings toward the out-group that is prevalent in a society (Bar-Tal, 2000). The ethos reflects, therefore, the way the group sees the conflict (in the Arab–Israeli context, for example, the historical views of Jews, Arabs, and Palestinians tend to be very different, with all sides unable to see the pain, the loss, and the heavy price the other side paid: Jews, right after the Holocaust, came to Israel to find a safe haven in a hostile world, but lost so many of the Holocaust survivors in the war for that safety; Palestinians fighting to protect their homeland, losing everything to become refugees). Once formed, it is one of the forces that maintain the conflict. It is expressed in beliefs about the justness of the goals of one's group, identification with this group, and delegitimization of the opponent.

By strengthening ingroup unity and outgroup delegitimization, the ethos hinders conflict resolution and/or reconciliation, and thus it prolongs the conflict and allows it to spread to additional domains (that were previously not conflictual) and to draw more individuals (that were not part of the conflict) into it (Bar-Tal, 1989). As societal conflicts tend to define all social relations between the groups involved, so does the conflictive ethos influence all aspects of societal and individual lives, even while it is reproduced by diverse social systems. It tends to become a part of the context that shapes the experiences of individual members of the groups in a society. The contexts, therefore, have different meanings for members of diverse social groups.

When an intense conflict exists between social groups, interactions among members of those groups will be more strongly influenced by their group membership than when no conflict exists (Islam & Hewstone, 1993). Often, individual members of these collectivities find it difficult to deal with each other as individuals and tend to treat all members of the outgroup uniformly (Moore, 1996, 2000).

We should remember, however, that a person belongs to several collectivities simultaneously and may identify with more than one of them. This often leads to complicated relationships among identity components that represent different social orders. The strain between social identities in each society is based on the specific diversifying issues prevalent in that society, but the consequences are the same: Agents' identities are organized into hierarchies according to their salience for the individual and reflect the social order the agent supports. In some societies, avoidance of strain within a hierarchy is impossible (e.g., Arabs in Israel may see themselves as both Palestinian and Israelis; Canadians may see themselves as both Quebecoise and Canadians; and Yugoslavs may see themselves as Slavs, Croats, or Moslems, and as belonging to a specific locality).

There is no a priori or theoretically based preference for placing any identity over all others. Priority is determined by the nature of the issue the agent deals with (Laclau & Mouffe, 1985), or according to the agenda in a particular society (Emmison & Western, 1990).[25] As the issues and agendas are reproduced in the structuration process, the salience of specific identities also changes. Moreover, according to Giddens (1994), norms and value orientations change in response to societal forces. The process of structuration constantly reproduces and changes both social institutions and the normative systems that legitimize them (see also Stone & Schaffner, 1988).

[25]But see Marshal et al., 1988. According to Marshal and his associates, class identity is the most important ingredient of social identity.

5 Hierarchical Organization of Identities: An Integrated Approach

Several researchers (Clark, Lipset, & Rempel, 1993; Emmison & Western, 1990) emphasize the pluralistic nature of social identity, claiming that salience is determined according to the issue the person deals with (Laclau & Mouffe, 1985), or according to the central debates in the particular society (Sanders, 1990, but see Hout, Brooks, & Manza, 1993; Marshal, Ross, Newby, & Vogler, 1988). Thus, in societies in which national rights are debated, people tend to define themselves in regional or nationalistic terms, and in societies where religion is the major basis for social strife, people define themselves in terms of the religious component of their social identity (Abrams & Emler, 1992; Devine, 1992; Tesser & Campbell, 1982).

Suggesting a hierarchical organization of identities, Stryker and Serpe (1994) provide a mechanism that emphasizes both the multiple parts and the singular whole that identities create. They posit that identity *salience* is the organizing mechanism underlying the hierarchical order. [Salience is defined as "A readiness to act out an identity as a consequence of the identity's properties as a cognitive structure or schema" (Stryker & Serpe, 1994, p. 17)]. Following Moore and Kimmerling (1995), we suggest that several hierarchies can exist concurrently in any society and that each hierarchy reflects a different social order and its values. In this respect, identities become codes for given social orders, capable of reflecting and reproducing social orders (Weigert, Teitge, & Teitge, 1990).

We also assume that some identity components are of a "more-or-less" structure (e.g., degree of religiosity) and others are constructed as bipolar "either-or" choices (e.g., gender).[26] But it is necessary to examine whether social identity components – like attitudes – are bipolar or dualistic in nature (that is, whether choosing a specific identity means the rejection of the alternative identity or an indifference to that alternative) and whether people can espouse identity components that are inherently conflictual. Still, as SIT posits, such hierarchies may include incongruous identities.

The centrality of political, religious, ethnic, and class identities in highly politicized and collectivistic societies, especially when the definitions of political, religious, ethnic, and class categories overlap, creates a tendency toward extremist "either-or" cleavages, which are reflected in distinct cultural systems within them (Lawler, 1992). Whether bipolar ("either-or") bases of identities lead to the escalation of social conflict or are the result of such conflicts, several of them may exist in any given society at the same time and each has the potential to split or divide a society. When several divisions overlap, the resultant split has the potential to motivate people much more than any single cleavage (McDonough, Barnes, & Pina, 1988). In Israel, overlapping cleavages include political ideologies, religion, ethnic origin, and socioeconomic cleavages. These components operate in tandem when sociopolitical issues are at stake, making the demographic lines of demarcation very clear. For example, Israel is "split" regarding the peace negotiations in the Middle East: the more religious Jews of Eastern origin[27] with lower education and lower socioeconomic status, tend to be Right-wing supporters and oppose territorial concessions. The secular Jews of Western origin with higher education and SES tend to be Left-wingers and support such concessions (Moore & Aweiss, 2004).

Sidanius and others (Sidanius, Levin, Rabinowitz, & Frederico, 1999; Sidanius & Petrocik, 2001; Sidanius et al. 1996) have elaborated SIT to form the *social dominance theory* according to which societies are organized as group-based hierarchies, with dominant groups enjoying disproportionate power, prestige, and privilege. Among the dominant groups, national and group identities are positively related, while among subordinate groups, they are often conflictual. These researchers also claim that communal (ethnic) identity will be stronger among subordinate groups and will be associated with less patriotism than among dominant groups (see also Lawler, 1992; Tropp & Wright, 1999).

Thus, these social splits both reflect and reproduce the hierarchies of identities. The contemporary Israeli–Arab–Palestinian context serves as an excellent example of a polity that is the subject of a long-standing struggle over its collective identity. The question now arises, "Which identity will be more central (or salient) for individuals with conflicting identities?"

6 Identities in the Israeli–Palestinian Context

6.1 Jewish Identities

Eisenstadt (1974) focused on the major components that constitute the Zionist identity, and the distinction between its particularist (Jewish religious) and universalist (Socialist, nationalist, and liberal) principles. "One of the salient features of political Zionism is that it purported to be not merely a 'nationalist' ideology, but strove to integrate two, in principle conflicting, value premises: the collective particularism of Jewish aspiration to an independent national state, and the universalism of modern Western civilization.... Both sets of premises... become fundamental components of the legitimation of the State of Israel. In political practice, however, they necessarily clashed" (Cohen, 1985, p. 322).

[26] Similar assumptions of linearity can be found in political attitudes' literature where many theorists present a linear and bipolar structure of attitudes, according to which sociopolitical attitudes are organized according to a single, transcending bipolar continuum (Moore and Aweiss, 2004).

[27] Shapiro (1985) claims that the ethnic cleavage "hides" a class differentiation with Westerners as the upper strata and Easterners as the lower strata to avoid class conflict.

The precarious balance among all these aspects, always problematic and inherently conflictual, has gradually changed, leading to the weakening of the socialist Zionist ideology because of demographic transformations, changes in the relative power of different social groups, and the relationship with the Arab world.[28] By the early 1970s, most of the Jews in Israel were immigrants from Islamic countries or their descendants, and they had not completely assimilated, as the Zionist establishment had hoped. Their estrangement from socialist values, which contradicted their more traditional ones, kept growing, as did their dissatisfaction with its institutions.

In the late 1970s, the majority of the Asian–African Jewish voters rejected the socialist Labor Party, in favor of right-wing and/or religious parties so that in the 1977 elections, the ideological-political situation changed drastically and the reign was transferred to the basically populistic capitalism[29] of the Likud Party and its coalition of right-wing and religious parties. This switch is viewed as a result of the Asian–African Jews' disillusionment with the existing sociopolitical system in which they occupied inferior social, political, and economic positions (Shapiro, 1985; Yishai, 1982). This coalition reflected the social changes that had taken place and legitimized the culture and value system of Asian–African ("Mizrahi") Jews (Kimmerling, 1983).

After gaining social legitimacy, Jews from Islamic countries reverted to the more traditional and religious values that the secular socialist ideology tried to force them to eschew as part of its attempt to create "the new Israeli man" (Horowitz & Lissak, 1989). The strengthening of religious tendencies could not be delegitimized because it translated the Zionist aspirations into religious ones, and fit with the nationalistic premises of the ruling right-wing (Arian & Shamir, 1983; Cohen, 1997). Kimmerling, (1985a) claims that the strengthening of the religious trends can be seen even earlier than that (e.g., in the centripetal movement of the national religious strata toward the center of society). He shows (based on Farrago, 1977) that in 1974, Jewish identity was already stronger than the Israeli one among both the religious and the secular Jews (Avruch, 1981; Herman, 1970). A continuous increase in the "valence" of Jewish identity and the decrease in the salience of Israeli identity were also found by Auron (1993).

The Arab–Israeli conflict has also contributed to the shift in power within Israel that has changed the Israeli identity structure. After the 1967 war, Israel expanded its borders, and the nationalist desire to keep and settle the occupied territories grew accordingly. However, the principles upon which the occupation is justified and rationalized undermine the Zionist-socialist premises. The gradual deterioration in the ability of the Labor government to reconcile the contradictions enabled the right-wing "Likud" Party to gain power. Its more pronounced religion-based nationalistic ideology provided legitimization for the continued occupation, in the eyes of Israelis and Jews around the world (Kimmerling, 1985). National resources were channeled to housing projects, road construction, and the massive settling of the territories that became the highest priority of the right-wing coalition. There are now about 400,000 Jews living in the occupied territories, and the proportion of religious people among them is higher than elsewhere in Israel (Israeli Bureau of Statistics, 2002).

These processes shifted the debate from the socioeconomic sphere (between socialist and capitalist ideologies) to the political sphere, focusing on the Israeli–Palestinian conflict and the future of the occupied territories. The shift may have important implications for social identities and the further strengthening of the bipolar structure. It may have also enhanced the centrality of the

[28]Kimmerling (1985) claims that the strengthening of Jewish-particularistic (and religious) trends can be seen even earlier than that, in the centripetal movement of the national-religious strata toward the center of society (see also Auron, 1993).

[29]We use the term "populistic" capitalism following Shapiro's (1985) definition: "Populism is composed of a distinct political ideology and a political structure. Populism is not an ideology of social change. It is designed for groups that feel deprived and cut off from the dominant culture....Populism is against the establishment, not against the state."

original Jewish nationalist identity over the universalistic Israeli one.

It seems, to a considerable degree, that Jewish and Israeli identities simultaneously contain both nationalist and civic ingredients. However, there are different measures in which a variety of identity configurations appear; some of them give priority or predominance to the nationalist component, while others favor the civic one (Kimmerling & Moore, 1997).

The precarious balance among these aspects has gradually changed, leading to the weakening of the civic collectivistic ideology in the 1990s and the strengthening of the nationalist component (Auron, 1993; Peres & Yuchtman-Yaar, 1992). Demographic transformations, changes in the relative power of different social groups, and relations with the Arab world contributed to the change. Moreover, Moore and Kimmerling (1995) show that the most salient identity among Jews in Israel is an individualistic (family) rather than a collectivistic identity, from which they conclude that Israeli society is moving away from the collectivistic goals set out by the two identities and the social orders they represent (see also Moore, 2000).

Though both the civic and nationalist identities are collectivistic and are not necessarily mutually exclusive, they represent fundamentally different orientations toward the social order (Kimmerling & Moore, 1997). "Jewish" is not only the more traditional basis for collectivistic identity, but also one of the major underpinnings for the meaning of "Israeli" (Eisenstadt, 1974).

Moore and Kimmerling's (1995) analysis of social identities shows several social orders corresponding to social identities:

The familial order: Looking at the correlates of this identity, they show that family identity, which is the highest ranked component, is more important for women than for men, and that it is usually the younger people who place it very high. It is salient among the traditional but not highly religious, among those who vote for parties that are in the center of the left-right continuum and oppose territorial annexation, and among those who believe that civil obedience is obligatory in all situations and at all times. More than others who do not consider the family to be an important component of their social identity, this group believes that the state should take care of its underprivileged social groups or classes (the elderly, battered wives, Arabs, and new immigrants).

Looking at this identity as a representation of social order reflects how and why society enables an identity that seems to be personal, specific, and noncollectivistic to become so central among the Jews in Israel. It may be said that this identity reflects, maintains, and reproduces central collectivistic values in the Jewish society in Israel such as the sanctity of marriage and social cohesion. And, indeed, it may be seen that in the Jewish society, family life is an essential, even cardinal, principle reflected in the very small proportion of unmarried persons, the even smaller proportion of individuals who live with others out of wedlock or the proportion of people who live with spouses of their own gender. The myriad of aspects of social life is arranged to suit families rather than single persons – from the structuring of day-care centers to familial evaluation of income tax, to the organization of vacation resorts, and the celebrating of holidays (most of which are religious) within families. The strong family ties are considered the basis for social stability and cohesion among both the orthodox and the less religious Jews. Espousing this identity and its characteristic attributes both reflects and reproduces a specific existing nonconflict-related social order. Thus, the more Israelis see this identity as their most salient identity, the less focused on the Arab–Israeli conflict they are likely to be.

The national-Jewish order: The agents of "Jewish" identity are highly attached to the country and will not consider emigration from it. They also strongly support territorial annexation. It is, therefore, hardly surprising that they are staunch supporters of right-wing and/or religious parties, and that many among them are very religious. More so than those who chose any of the other components of social identity. Their sociopolitical attitudes are in accord: they tend to be socially obedient and believe that the law should always be maintained, they do not organize or join protests, and they trust in the ability of the government and the armed forces to take care of their safety. The only social activity they are involved in (if any) is in the synagogues they belong to. They are also a distinct demographic group: they tend to be of Asian–African origin, less educated, with big families and low incomes, and many among them are unemployed.

The social order that this identity both represents and reproduces is the particularistic ethnocentric one. It entails defining who belongs to the collectivity, what is "loyalty," and what is "treason" regarding the national goal of survival. Being part of the collectivity is based on being Jewish (and agents of this social order feel that they have the right to define "who is a Jew"), and loyalty or treason is defined by adherence to religious laws and protecting the Jewish rule over the occupied territories. According to the social order that this identity represents, the collectivity boundaries are created by the equation: Nationality = Religion (hence, all non-Jews are excluded from the collectivity), and the physical boundaries are those of "larger Israel," which includes the biblical holy places that are in the occupied territories. This social identity and the social order it promotes are the strongest opposition to peace negotiations and to making concessions to Palestinians (they oppose land concessions in the West Bank, claiming that the whole area is part of the land the Bible promised Israel as their homeland, they oppose allowing Palestinians to return to Israel as a peace agreement will be reached, and so forth). As such, they are the strongest hindrance to peace. Their proportion may have grown in recent years (as the recent elections in Israel seem to indicate), but a study verifying this was not conducted.

The civic-Israeli order: Those with a strong Israeli identity tend to be left-wingers, who feel that they have influence and control over national processes, and they believe that the state should intervene in national security and economic processes (e.g., to help factories that are in financial difficulties, build new settlements, fight crime, and keep law and order). They are much more involved in their communities, at home, and in the schools. Demographically, their social profile is the complete antithesis to that of the "Jewish order" carriers: they are secular, Israeli born, or of Western origin (in which case they are old timers, not new immigrants). Most of them are older, employed, with midlevel incomes, and have small families. In addition, like those with a strong Jewish identity, the "Israelis" trust the ability of the government and the armed forces to protect them, and tend to be unresisting and obedient. Thus, they accept and maintain the basic definitions and rules of the Israeli society.

In addition to differences in characteristics, the democratic, secularist, and universalistic social order that this identity represents and reproduces is also different from the one that the Jewish identity represents. Like the agents who rank "Jewish" as their most important content of the carried order, those who rank "Israeli" as their most important component are strongly attached to the country.

However, although the consequent attachment is similar, it's bases and justifications are different. For the agents of the "Jewish order," the justification is primordial and religious, i.e., it is the "Land of the Bible" or the "Land of our forefathers;" for the agents of the "Israeli order," it is a shelter of refuge, granted to the Zionists by the United Nations in 1948. The boundaries of the collectivity that the Israeli identity defines includes *all* citizens of Israel (Jews and non-Jews alike), and the physical boundaries of the state are perceived – at least to some extent – as flexible in the context of peace negotiations.

The profession-based order: The social profile of those who ranked their profession highest seems somewhat alienated. Although they believe in their ability to influence national processes, they are not attached to their communities or to the country, and compose the group that considers emigrating from Israel more than all the other groups. Also, they do not trust the ability of the government and the armed forces to keep them safe, and their obedience is conditional (or – they do not believe that people should be obedient under any situation to authority).

Politically, those who ranked their profession highest are mostly left-wingers, according to Kimmerling and Moore (1997). If they are involved in any social activity, it is a "self-enhancing" type of activity (i.e., activity from which they or their families benefit directly). Their demographic profile is also different: they tend to be highly educated, Israeli born (or of Western origin), young men, mostly employed and with high income. They are also the least religious group, with many more holding active antireligious orientations.

As in other societies, this group of younger, highly educated secularists seem to be the harbinger of social and value changes (Inglehart, 1987). Their emphasis on personal attainment represents a divergence from the "traditional" collectivistic values (Moore & Aweiss, 2003). Similar to such orientations in advanced highly industrialized societies, the social order that this identity represents seems to entail weaker social control mechanisms and lower state intervention in daily life.

A similar hierarchical order of identities can be seen in Moore and Aweiss's (2004) sample of high school students as well (see Fig. 9.1 and Table 9.3). The two dimensions of the figure are complementary. The first – salience – shows which identities are salient and which are rejected (with 0="indifference"; high values=salience;

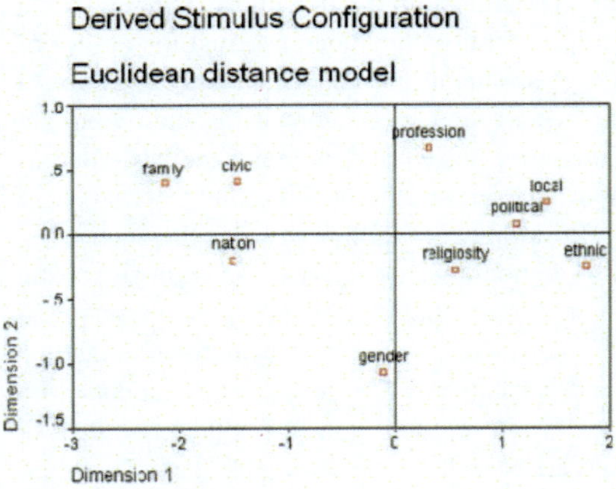

Fig. 9.1 Social identities of Jewish high school students. Stress=0.057 RSQ=0.983. RSQ values are the proportion of variance of the scaled data (disparities) in the partition (row, matrix, or entire data) which is accounted for by their corresponding distances. Stress values are Kruskal's stress formula 1

Table 9.3 Means and ranking of social identity components

	Students' sample						Adults' sample			
	Jews		Arabs		Palestinians		Jews		Arabs	
Variables	Rank	% in 1st or 2nd place	Rank	% in 1st or 2nd place	Rank	% in 1st or 2nd place	Rank	% in 1st or 2nd place	Rank	% in 1st or 2nd place
Social identity components:										
Being a student/ your occupation	6	20.4	2	51.7	3	32.6	2	35.8	1	34.9
Being Israeli/ Palestinian[a]	2	40.7	6	28.3	1	61.5	4	15.7	3	21.5
Your family	1	58.3	1	53.0	2	36.9	1	58.1	5	19.5
Being Jewish/ Arab[b]	3	41.4	3	46.1	4	25.5	6	14.2	2	32.2
Your place of residence	8	6.6	7	22.6	5	12.0	5	16.2	9	3.3
Your political attitudes (left-/right-wing)	7	11.4	9	18.1	9	6.1	9	14.8	8	4.7
Your ethnic origin/religion[c]	9	5.0	8	21.7	8	6.0	3	29.0	4	21.4
Your being religious or secular	5	16.8	5	29.7	7	8.9	7	15.6	6	15.5
Your being a man/a woman	4	30.8	4	45.0	6	10.5	8	16.8	7	14.8

[a]Israelis were asked about "Being Israeli" and Palestinians were asked about "being Palestinian"
[b]Jews were asked about "Being Jewish," and Arabs and Palestinians were asked about "being Arab"
[c]Jews were asked about "Being of Eastern or Western descent," and Arabs and Palestinians were asked about "being Muslim or Christian"

and low values = rejection of a specific identity), the second dimension – consensus – reflects the percentage of those who ranked a specific identity highly and those who ignored that identity (with 0 = "indifference"; high values = consensus; and low values = lack of consensus). The means in Table 9.3 indicate salience of each identity, while the percentages indicate the degree of societal consensus regarding its salience.

The most salient identity (i.e., with the highest mean) among Jews is the individualistic family identity[30] (58.3% placed it in the first or second place), followed by two collectivistic identities which are close to each other – the civic (Israeli) identity (ranked in the first or second place by 40.7%) and the national (Jewish) identity (ranked by 41.4%) – and by gender identity. In the adult Jewish sample, family is just as salient (ranked in the first or second place by 58.1%) and the two collective identities are less salient: The civic identity was ranked by 15.7% in the first or second place, and the national identity by only 14.2% (see Fig. 9.2).

This finding strengthens Kimmerling and Moore's (1997) conclusion regarding the weakening of collectivistic values in Israel: Most Jews nowadays are not willing to relinquish their personal goals in favor of collectivistic goals. Thus, family is both the most salient and most consensual. The national and civic identities, which compete for dominance, are almost as salient, but far less consensual. There is a high consensus regarding the lack of importance of ethnic, local, and political identities. This surprising and important finding seems to indicate that most Jewish–Israelis are less interested in the conflict than might have been assumed in view of its prolonged existence. By placing the family identity higher than all other possible identity components, most Israelis seem to be saying that they prefer to focus on their daily lives rather than on the Arab–Israeli conflict. If this interpretation is correct, there is a better chance of reaching an agreement between Israelis and Palestinians and gaining popular support for processes (e.g., peace talks) to resolve the conflict than politicians seem to assume.

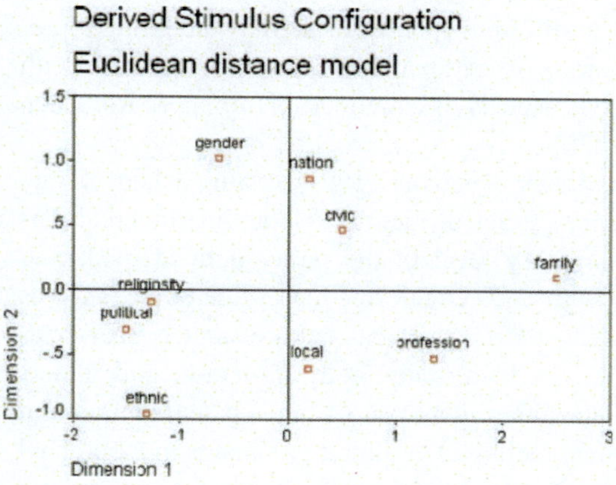

Fig. 9.2 Social identities of Jewish adults. Stress = 0.064 RSQ = 0.977. RSQ values are the proportion of variance of the scaled data (disparities) in the partition (row, matrix, or entire data) which is accounted for by their corresponding distances. Stress values are Kruskal's stress formula 1

6.2 The Arab Identities

Arabs remaining in Israel after the great exodus from the country in 1948 were subjected to attempts to shape them into an obedient and loyal minority (Morris, 1987; Pappe, 1992). This was attained by their physical, cultural, and political separation from their fellow Palestinians outside Israel's boundaries (Kimmerling & Migdal, 1994). Another powerful tool of the "Israelification" of the Palestinians was an attempt to create a new "Israeli–Arab" identity, on the part of the Israeli authorities, mostly by way of highly selected contents in school curricula (Mari, 1978).

At the first stage, the attempt to create a new minority quasiethnic (but not national) collectivity and identity was impressively successful, and the Arabs of Israel up until 1967 tended to adopt this "Israel–Arab" identity (Haidar, 1996; Peres & Yuval-Davis, 1969). However, after the "reunion" with the Palestinians of the occupied territories, the Arabs in Israel adopted a strategy whereby they compartmentalized their identity

[30] We consider family identity to be individualistic in nature because it has a different structure and different meanings for each individual.

into different spheres of activity, adopting a predominant nationalistic identity combined with civic aspects of Israeliness (Hofman & Rouhana, 1976).

Later, Rouhana (1991) distinguished among three circles of identity: (1) an instrumental participatory level in the polity defined by Israeli identity; (2) an intermediate value circle (such as style of life, political culture, and gender relations, which share both an Israeli and a new Palestinian identity); (3) a deep sentimental and loyal feeling of common fate that is monopolized by the Palestinian identity. In short, a new Israeli–Palestinian identity was created. Smooha (1992) adds to this what he called a trend of political radicalization among the Arab minority, accompanied by a new sense of political power, which leads several intellectuals to demand "cultural autonomy" for themselves (such as the creation of an Israeli–Palestinian university, which would enable Arabs to teach and study independently of oppressive Jewish hegemony).

Arab citizens of Israel also face two basic and competing social orders. However, the relationships between the two are more complex. The national social order connotes an ethnocentric and particularistic worldview, which is related to broader loyalties and implies affiliation with larger entities, especially the Pan-Arab world. The civic order represents a universalistic worldview, based on civic rights and obligations to the state. However, as Arabs are a minority in Israel with strong affiliation to others who are enemies of the state, they are often considered a potential "fifth column" within Israel and are excluded from national institutions (like the army), reviled by political parties that call for their "transfer" from Israel to other Arab countries, and so forth.

The fear that their representatives might divulge state secrets is also the main reason why Arab political parties were not included in any of the coalitions formed in Israel, not even in 1992 when they could have created the majority needed by the Left to form a government (Reiter & Aharoni, 1993). As a result, identification with the Israeli state is harder for Arab citizens than it is for Jewish ones and, unlike Jews, Arabs are often forced to choose between their national and civic identities (Hofman & Rouhana, 1976; Morris, 1987).

Moore and Kimmerling's (1995) analysis of social identities shows different social orders corresponding to social identities of Arabs in Israel:

Arab order: Among the Arab sample, those who ranked the Arab identity as their major identity tend to vote for Arab parties rather than for the bigger Israeli parties. They seem to reject the whole spectrum of the political system that is dominated by Jews. The lack of correspondence between this identity and territorial solution may be due to the fact that the majority of Arabs (about 90%) desire territorial concessions. Individuals in this category believe in their ability to influence political processes and are strongly attached to their communities and locales. The Arab identity is tied in with being Muslim so that Muslims – whether religious or not – place this identity higher than Christian Arabs. Their education is also higher, and they are active in the public sphere.

Palestinian order: Those who chose Palestinian as their most salient identity form a different social category. Even more than those who chose Arab as their major identity, they reject the Israeli political parties and favor Arab parties, are Muslim, and are highly religious. They, too, believe in their ability to influence political processes, but unlike those with a strong Arab identity, they actively participate in social and political protests and they do not believe that social obedience should always be maintained. Demographically, they tend to have big families, low incomes, and high levels of education. Taken together, these indicators seem to point to a more rebellious order, or to greater frustration with the existing system in which they occupy inferior socioeconomic positions. This group is the most politically active among the Arab citizens of Israel, with stronger ties to the Palestinians across the border. They are the leaders of the less extremist social orders (like those who ranked the Arab identity first) and are less flexible when solutions to the conflict are negotiated, strengthening Palestinian opposition to any kind of concession in the many attempts at peace negotiations between the two sides (Bregman & El-Tahri, 1998).

Arab–Israeli order: There are very few Arabs who chose Israeli as their major identity, but they too form a distinct group. First, more among them are Christian or Druze, and fewer are Muslims. Second, they tend to have smaller families and be more socially obedient. In addition, it seems that this group is less politically defined in comparison with those who define themselves as Palestinian or Arab: Their political attitudes are less clear-cut, and they do not feel that they have social or political influence, or external control over their environment. Unfortunately, this group is growing smaller. In the joint Israeli–Palestinian research, Moore and Aweiss (2004) hoped that this group could be a bridge between Arabs, Palestinians, and Jews. However, the dwindling number of Arabs who see themselves as Israeli first, and the lack of power bases in either Israeli or Palestinian societies make this option a rather improbable one.

The familial order: The carriers of the family identity among the Arab sample also form a distinct profile. This identity is politically distinct from both the "collectivistic" Arabic identities and the Jewish family identity. Those who rank it as their major identity component are less committed to living in Israel and show a greater willingness to emigrate. They are also willing to pay more for added private protection. Unlike the other groups, they are not demographically defined.

Kimmerling and Moore (1997) indicate that those who place their family highest believe that the best way to protect their family is leaving this area of conflict in search of other places in which they will have better opportunities. If being family oriented has the same meaning for Jews and Arabs, then the means to achieve family goals is the exact opposite for the two groups: For Jews, living in Israel maximizes life opportunities, whereas for Arabs, it is emigrating from Israel.

In Moore and Aweiss's study of high school students (2004), the ranking of family as most salient (53% have placed in the first or second rank) is followed by another individualistic identity: being a student (51.7%) (see Fig. 9.3). Only in the third place do we find a collectivistic identity:

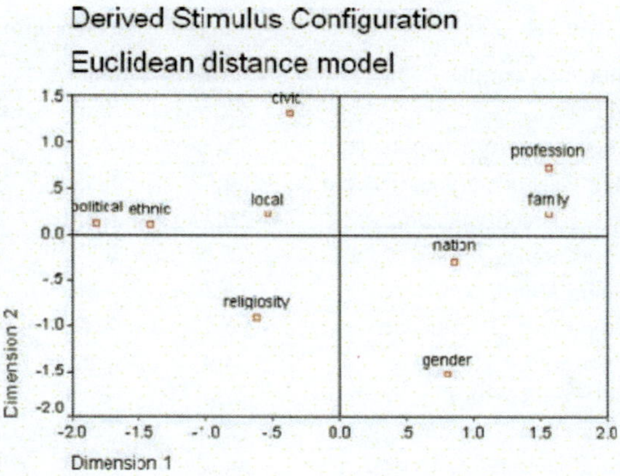

Fig. 9.3 Social identities of Arab students. Stress = 0.084 RSQ = 0.950. RSQ values are the proportion of variance of the scaled data (disparities) in the partition (row, matrix, or entire data) which is accounted for by their corresponding distances. Stress values are Kruskal's stress formula 1

the national (Arab) identity (ranked in the first place by 46.1%). Gender identity is in the fourth place. This seems to be an indication of their alienation from Israeli society as well as from the Arab world that has rejected their allegiance until recently. The differences between their hierarchy ranking of identities and those of Jews are highly significant (see Table 9.4).

Family and being a student are both salient and consensual, and there is indifference regarding the ethnic and political identities. The finding that shows that family identity is stronger among Jews than it is among Arabs (despite the fact that the Jewish family is much narrower than the Arabic extended family, the Hamulla) may suggest that the Arab society in Israel relies on the family to carry collectivistic values less than the Jewish society.

A different picture is seen in the adult Arab sample. Here, being a student (the equivalent of profession in adult samples) is the most salient identity, and nationality (being Arab) is the next in salience (ranked in the first or second place by 34.9% and 32.2%, respectively (see Fig. 9.4)). Being Israeli (civic identity) is ranked in the third place (i.e., 21.5% ranked it in the first or second place). Family is ranked only in the fifth place. This seems to support our claim that nationalism is strengthening among young Arabs and that

Table 9.4 Analysis of variance – comparing the three groups

Student's sample	Adults' sample						
Variables	Jews	Arabs	Palestinians		Jews	Arabs	
Social identity components:	Means			F-values*	Means		F-values
Being a student/your occupation	4.57	6.53	6.07	213.9	5.73	5.23	3.56 ns
Being Israeli/Palestinian[a]	6.53	5.05	7.17	228.1	4.87	4.63	.99 ns
Your family	7.14	6.77	6.20	53.6	6.53	4.39	55.87
Being Jewish/Arab[b]	6.27	6.46	5.77	25.2	4.41	5.50	19.97
Your place of residence	3.47	4.89	4.44	119.4	4.78	2.74	82.83
Your political attitudes (left-/right-wing)	4.07	4.27	3.18	63.6	3.94	2.95	17.36
Your ethnic origin/religion[c]	2.86	4.53	3.61	148.9	5.13	4.46	6.29
Your being religious or secular	4.69	5.18	4.16	46.6	4.38	4.09	1.34 ns
Your being a man/a woman	5.31	6.08	4.41	109.6	4.26	3.96	1.35 ns

***All F-values in the students' sample are significant** ($p \leq 0.0001$), but not in the adults' sample. F-values that are not significant are marked ns

[a]Israelis (both Jews and Arabs) were asked about being Israeli, and Palestinians were asked about being Palestinian

[b]Jews were asked about being Jewish, and Arabs and Palestinians were asked about being Arab

[c]For Jews, the distinction is Moroccan, Polish, and so forth. For Arabs and Palestinians, the distinction is Muslim, Christian, and Druze

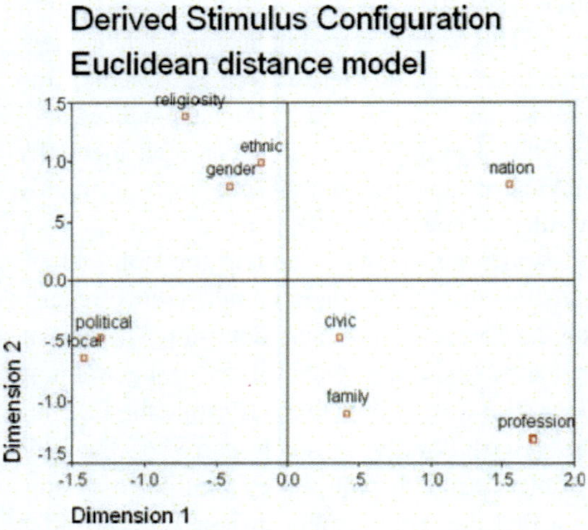

Fig. 9.4 Social identities of Arab adults. Stress = 0.084 RSQ = 0.950. RSQ values are the proportion of variance of the scaled data (disparities) in the partition (row, matrix, or entire data) which is accounted for by their corresponding distances. Stress values are Kruskal's stress formula 1

they are more alienated from Israeli society than the older Arabs.

These changes are influenced by changes in the historical conditions and situational contexts (like the peace negotiations between Israel and the Arabs, and the empowerment of the Palestinian authority) have had a multifaceted impact on how Arab agents are bound by the situational context. The changes have resulted in stronger and more centralized Jewish-dominated power structures but, at the same time, they have led to weaker identification of Arabs who are citizens of Israel with Israeli society, and stronger identification with their brothers and sisters who are not citizens. Their participation in the Al Aqsa Intifada (the September 2000 uprising) clearly indicates a shift in identifications so that more among them today consider themselves an underprivileged national (Palestinian) minority in Israel (Gabison & Abu Rea, 2000). Their refusal to participate in the elections in recent years (in contrast with their approximately 80% participation rate in previous elections) is an additional indication of their alienation.

6.3 Palestinian Identities

Experts seem to agree that a combination of factors is critical to an understanding of Palestinian society (i.e., those who are under Palestinian Authority control in the West Bank or the Hamas in the Gaza Strip) (e.g., Aruri, 1986; Heacok, 1990; McDowell, 1989; Tamari, 1993). First, it is a society under prolonged occupation. Second, a significant portion of the Palestinian residents in the area are displaced, refugees or recent returnees with the constant disruption of traditional social structures. Third, for several years, and until the signing of the Oslo Accords, this society has experienced low intensity warfare, the Intifada. Fourth, culturally, Palestinian society is an integral part of the Middle Eastern – Arab – society (Kimmerling & Migdal, 1994).

Consequently, a fragmented Palestinian identity exists in relation to the specific context in which the refugees found themselves, but a collective civic identity appeared only when those who were under Jordanian or Egyptian rule were united with each other after the Israeli occupation. Palestinian society in the West Bank and Gaza has emerged as a sociopolitical entity only recently, when the Israeli occupation of 1967 ended the isolation of the two regions that were under the rule of neighboring Arab states (Jordan and Egypt). According to Aruri and Farsoun (1980),Tamari (1993), Taraki (1997) and others, this integration of the two regions has meant that they have shared a common political reality by virtue of being under Israel occupation.

This shared destiny, according to Taraki (1997), has been the major impetus in forging a number of features held in common between the two regions, notably the experience of Israel military rule, resistance to that rule, and integration into the Israeli economic system. As a result of the Oslo Accords, the two regions constitute an administrative, political, and economic entity (World Bank, 1993). The impact of the affiliations on social identities was not examined in the past and is –as yet– unknown.

Examination of attitudes in the Palestinian society indicates that Palestinians seem to be moving in two directions simultaneously. On the one hand, this society is moving toward more liberal attitudes concerning the status of women in society, toward a greater degree of secularization and an enhanced emphasis on the value of democracy. On the other hand, spearheaded especially by disaffected sectors of the younger generation, Palestinian society also appears to be drifting toward a reinstatement of patriarchal values, a reinforcement of religiosity-defined social codes, and a drifting away from the acceptance of plurality (Heiberg, 1993; Tamari, 1993).

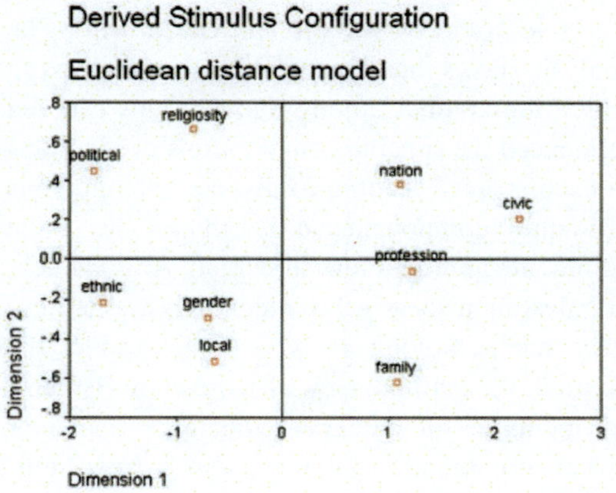

Fig. 9.5 Social identities of Palestinian students. Stress = 0.091 RSQ = 0.962. RSQ values are the proportion of variance of the scaled data (disparities) in the partition (row, matrix, or entire data) which is accounted for by their corresponding distances. Stress values are Kruskal's stress formula 1

In our sample of high school students, the most salient component among Palestinians is the civic (Palestinian) identity (placed in the first rank by more than 40%), followed by a much less salient family identity, being a student, and the national (Arab) identity (see Fig. 9.5). Thus, civic identity is both the most salient and most consensual, more so than in the case of Jews and Arabs. For them, too, local and ethnic identities are less salient. Palestinians seem to be emphasizing collectivism: The divided Palestinians, cut off from each other for many years, are rediscovering the common threads that bind them in their desire for an independent state.

That may also explain why the national (Arab) identity was placed only in the fourth place: Palestinians do not wish to be considered only as a part of the Arab world, but also as a people with a distinct civic identity.

7 Conclusions

This chapter examined the diverse social identities that are prevalent in the three distinct groups which are part of the Arab–Israeli conflict: Jewish–Israelis (the majority (about 80%) of all Israeli citizens), Arab citizens of Israel (about 20% of Israelis), and Palestinians (the refugees who live in the West Bank and Gaza Strip). The analysis shows that the sociohistorical context in which the conflict among these groups evolved influenced the specific combinations of identities in each society, leading to diverse combinations of identity components so that there is no single dominant identity in Jewish–Israeli, Arab–Israeli, or Palestinian society. Four identities are particularly salient among Jews in Israel today: the familial, the national (Jewish), the civic (Israeli), and being a student. These identities, and their diverse combinations, may be seen as representing the major hierarchical organization of identities and the major social orders in Israel.

Other identities (gender, religion, ethnic origin, politics, and locality) were chosen less often. This may be interpreted in several ways: First, the cleavages that these identities create are less central in Israeli society and are, therefore, eclipsed by the "major" identities. The second interpretation posits that the "neglected" identities are encompassed by the other, more general identities. Thus, the distinction between religious and secular or between Eastern and Western origins may be aspects of the national-Jewish and/or Israeli-civic identities. Thus, a person who chose one of these major collective identities has, by definition, taken into consideration one or more of the "minor" identities. A third viable interpretation is that less chosen identities remain unarticulated unless a specific context warrants them. In Stryker and Serpe's (1994) terms, these alternatives signify that the "neglected" identities are placed lower on the hierarchical schema of most members of the Israeli society.

Though all three interpretations seem plausible, the data seem to support the second one: Those who rank Jewish identity highest tend to be of a specific ethnic group (Asian–African origin), more religious, and Right-wingers; those who rank the Israeli identity highest tend to be of the other ethnic group (European–American origin), less religious, and Left-wingers.

The second group, that of Arab citizens of Israel, is forced into a different strategy. Most of them do not consider themselves equal citizens of the state, and many among them feel rejected by their Arab brethren as well, especially for acquiring citizenship of the enemy state. Unlike Jews in Israel, choosing either the civic (Israeli) or the national (Arab) identity seems to indicate taking sides in the Arab–Israeli conflict. Placing their national identity as most salient in their hierarchies seems to indicate emphasizing their ties to the Arab world and their Palestinian brothers and sisters. Choosing their civic identity as most salient seems to be a "rejection" of the Palestinians and their fight for an independent state. Analysis of their peace-related attitudes supports this interpretation: Those who consider themselves Arabs first tend to support the peace process most strongly, while those who consider themselves Israelis first support the peace process less than Arabs who placed other identities in the first rank (supporting the peace process is considered pro-Arab by most Israelis as it entails territorial concessions). Torn between conflicting loyalties, more of them place these identities lower in their hierarchy and choose instead family or being a student as the most salient identities.

Most of the third group – the Palestinians – emphasize their civic identity more than any other identity. Their desire for an independent state, which placed them in a prolonged Intifada ("uprising") with Israel, may be the reason for the consensual salience of this identity. This is similar to the heightened collectivistic identity that used to prevail in the Jewish Israeli society before and after Israel gained its independence. Much less emphasis is placed by Palestinians on their national identity. This may be the function of their unwillingness to be considered "unidentified Arabs," a definition that may make it easier for others (e.g., Israelis, the U.N.) to disperse and settle them among the other Arab nations. It may also be that because they were rejected by the Arab world for so long (in all Arab states except Jordan, Palestinians were not granted full citizenship and remained refugees), they have not developed identification with the Pan-Arab world.

Our findings suggest that identities are neither bipolar (i.e., espousing one identity means total negation of the identity at the other end of the continuum) nor dualistic (i.e., espousing one identity means indifference to the identity at the other end of the continuum). Instead, choosing two identities moderates the attitudes and beliefs associated with both identities and minimizes incongruity or contradiction between them. Consequently, choosing two identities that represent different social orders may moderate the extremism that may be embedded in each of them.

The contributions of our analyses are, therefore, threefold. Theoretically, our analysis combines nonempirical approaches with empirical ones to examine the former with tools provided by the latter. Empirically, it provides answers as to identity structures and their correlates using rather simple techniques of analyses, which may be replicated in many and diverse societies so that a comparative research among societies is facilitated. Contextually, it analyses and highlights what seems to be a major change in the identity structure of Jewish Israelis, Arab Israelis, and Palestinians. It seems that the shift from collectivistic identities (and the ideological orientations they represent) toward individualistic identities seen among Jewish Israelis has contributed to facilitating the peace process and the basic acceptance of territorial concessions. In contrast, the identities of Arabs and Palestinians seem to be influenced by the conflict in the opposite direction so that the growing salience of the collectivistic civic identity among Palestinians seems to reflect their fight for independence. Their resistance to compromise may stem, at least in part, from their central collectivistic identities, and the meetings of representatives of the two groups would reflect these differences. The shift in Arabs' identities strengthens the collectivistic trends among Palestinians as it supports the territorial trends of the latter.

Moreover, as can be seen for Israeli Jews, two salient individual identities tend to strengthen the drawing away from collectivistic values, emphasizing personal achievements, and the rejection of the demands to sacrifice private interests for "nation" or "society." No such "moderation" of collectivism can be seen among most Arabs and Palestinians.

Any conflict that may arise from adopting such identities affects the individual's everyday life and has behavioral implications. Because different identities dictate somewhat different issues and values, they may lead to ideological conflict.

Attempting to reconcile the conflicting demands created by two identities is possible when the differences are not too extreme or the person succeeds in moderating them. When the demands of two identities are irreconcilable and a blurring of the opposing issues does not occur, people rationalize and justify the strategies they use to deal with the contradictions.

Torn between inherently conflictual premises (i.e., the Jewish-national and the Israeli-civic identities), Jewish–Israelis may have developed a greater propensity or willingness to accept improbable combinations of identities and ideologies than people in societies with fewer political parties, or lower political involvement. No such compromises may be seen among Palestinians. For them, the salience of the national identity far exceeds that of all other identities, and necessitates no moderation. Arab Israelis, on the contrary, are torn between their national (Arab) and civic (Israeli) identities. Some of them choose a compromise that emphasizes their national identities, while others (a dwindling minority) choose to accord higher salience to their civic identity. However, conflicting premises exist in many societies even though the premises in conflict may vary. Therefore, the need to reconcile controversy in multiparty systems may lead to the same acceptance of cognitive imbalance found in Israel.

Consequently, when analyzing bipolar versus dualistic identity and attitude formations, especially in multiparty systems where political involvement is high, researchers must take into account an additional dimension – people's willingness and/or ability to accept and endure incongruous demands. These demands may be generated by diverse individual components or by political necessity.

The salience of collectivistic identities increased in the last years among members of all three groups. The intensified conflict strengthened the hatred toward outgroups, and the extremity of political attitudes (Moore & Aweiss, 2007).

8 Policy Suggestions

Peace talks between Palestinians and Israelis have been taking place intermittently for over three decades (see Appendix). Hope rises on both sides every time negotiations resume, only to be quenched by hostilities perpetrated by extremists on one side or the other, which usually lead to the cessation of talks and the withdrawal of both sides from willingness to compromise. The vicious circle continues with each side blaming the other for maintaining the conflict.

It seems logical to assume that reducing the salience of collective identities that are related to the conflict may lessen the intensity of involvement in the conflict, and create a willingness to find ways to attain a solution that will enable the opponents to live together. This, however, is very difficult to attain. People tend to protect their hierarchy of identities and resist changes. But as we have seen from the historical-political analysis, the intensity and salience of identities *do* change in response to sociopolitical events. Creating a political climate that is more supportive of peace negotiations and making concessions may increase the willingness of individuals to change their hierarchy of identities and to emphasize individualistic identities more than collectivistic ones. This may be attained by showing members of the diverse opposing groups what they may gain by such a shift, and by the weakening of the conflict. It may also lead individuals to move from an "either-or" view of identities to a more flexible, continuous view.

The education system may be used to bring about such a shift. However, this is a slow and lengthy process, and most political leaders prefer actions that yield more immediate results. Moreover, if leaders in democracies reflect the preferences of their electorate, the leaders in power may not be able to act against the desire of the majority who chose them. This type of change in the education system was tried once in Israel (2007–2008), when Professor Yuli Tamir (Labor Party) became minister of education, but the changes she introduced were cancelled when she resigned. The brevity of the experience precludes any significant conclusions as to its effectiveness.

A long-term program with full commitment is required to affect such a change through education, but the powers in both Israel and the Palestinian Authority are unwilling to implement them.

Appendix: Historical Time Table – The Arab–Israeli Conflict

1917	The "Balfour Declaration"
1920–1929	Palestine riots in Jerusalem, Jaffa, Hebron, and other cities
1922–1947	Jewish immigration from abroad
1936	Arab rebellion against the British Mandate; terrorizing the Jewish minority
1947	The U.N. proposed the partitioning of Palestine into two independent states (Resolution 181 (II))
May 1948	Declaration of independence of the state of Israel
May 1948	First Arab–Israeli War, First exodus of Palestinians
May 1964	The establishment of the Palestine Liberation Organization (PLO)
June 1967	Six-Day War, Second exodus of Palestinians
November 1967	UN resolution 242
October 1973	"Yom Kipour" War (October war)
March 1979	Peace agreement between Israel and Egypt
June 1982	Israel invaded Lebanon
September 1983	Geneva Declaration
December 1987	The "stones" *Intifada*

(continued)

November 1988	Council in Algeria – Arafat announced the establishment of an independent Palestinian state with Jerusalem as its capital
July 1989	First Palestinian suicide attack
February 1991	Arafat declared his support for Iraq during the Gulf War
October 1991	Madrid conference
January 1993	Israel repealed its ban contact with the PLO
September 1993	Peace accord in Washington – "Oslo declaration"
February 1994	Cave of the Patriarch attack by Baruch Goldstein
April 1994	Suicide bombing
May 1994	Palestinian control and administration over Gaza Strip and Jericho
October 1994	Suicide bombing in Tel Aviv
January 1995	A double suicide bombing
November 1995	Israeli Prime Minister Yitzhak Rabin assassinated by Yigal Amir
Winter 1996	Suicide bombings in Jerusalem and Tel Aviv
June 1996	Benjamin Netanyahu elected Prime Minister in Israel
September 1996	"Al Aqsa" tunnel riots
July 1996	Double suicide attack in the major market of Jerusalem
October 1998	Wye River Plantation summit
May 1999	Ehud Barak elected Prime Minister
March 2000	Peace negotiation between Israel and Syria
May 2000	The Israeli Army withdraws from southern Lebanon
September 2000	The second *Intifada* – "Al Aqsa Intifada"
October 2000	Public lynching of two Israelis in Ramallah
December 2000	Clinton's peace initiative – the Camp David Summit
January 2001	Taba summit
February 2001	Ariel Sharon elected Prime Minister
2001–2002	Palestinian suicide bombers massacre dozens in hotels, buses, restaurants, and streets throughout Israel: Tel Aviv, Jerusalem, Natanya, and Haifa are the main targets
September 2001	Terror attacks on World Trade Center in NYC
October 2001	Tourism Minister Rehavam Zeevi is assassinated
March 2002	"Saudi initiative"
March 2002	UN Security Council passed Resolution 1397
March 2002	Operation "Defensive Shield"
June 2002	Israeli forces reoccupied all of the West Bank
June 2002	Israel begins construction of the West Bank Fence
March 2003	US, British, and Australian forces invaded Iraq
Summer 2003	suicide bombings in Israeli cities
Summer 2003	Israel invaded Gaza as well as the Palestinian refugee camp in the city Jenin
December 2003	The UN General Assembly met for an Emergency session and adopted Resolution ES-10/14
Winter 2004	Suicide bombings in Israeli cities
March 2004	Sheikh Ahmed Yassin was assassinated by Israeli Defense Forces
April–June 2004	Aqaba summit
July 2004	International court of Justice (ICJ) rules that the Israeli security barrier violates international law and must be torn down
August 2004	Hamas's double suicide attack on buses in Beersheba
November 2004	Palestinian Authority President Yasser Arafat dies
January 2005	The first democratic election in Palestine. Mahmoud Abbas elected President of the Palestinian National Authority
February 2005	Sharm El Sheikh Conference
February 2005	Suicide attack in Tel Aviv
August 2005	Evacuation of Gaza settlements and West Bank settlements by Israel
January 2006	Ariel Sharon suffered a massive stroke

(continued)

January 2006	Palestinian election
March 2006	Israel election
Winter-spring 2006	Daily barrage of rockets on Israeli towns within the green line
June 2006	Gaza beach blast
June 2006	Hamas attacked an Israeli army border outpost (capturing Gilad Shalit)
July 2006	Hezbollah attacks on northern Israel; Israel retaliates
August 2006	Cease-fire
November 2006	Truce between Palestinian and Israelis
December 2006	Truce broken when barrages of rockets are fired at Israeli towns
December 2006	Concessions between Prime Minister Ehud Olmert and President Mahmoud Abbas
June 2007	Fighting among Palestinians
November 2007	Annapolis summit
November 2007	Terrorists launch rockets and mortar fire into the Israeli town of Sderot and other western Negev targets, and also launched several on Ashdod
February 2008	Israeli offensive on Gaza
November 2008	Sharm el Sheikh – meeting of the quartet
December 2008	Hamas bombarded Israel with over 60 rockets
December 2008 – January 2009	Operation "Oferet Yetzuka"
February 2009	Israeli elections
June 2009	President Barack Obama's historic speech to the Muslim and Arab world
June 2009	Israeli Prime Minister Netanyahu response speech
September 2010	Peace talks are resumed in Washington DC

References

Abrams, D., & Emler, N. (1992). Self-denial as a paradox of political and regional social identity: Findings from a study of 16- and 18-year olds. *European Journal of Social Psychology, 22*, 279–295.

Abrams, D., & Hogg, M. A. (1999). *Social identity and social cognition*. Oxford: Blackwell.

Abu-Habib, L. (1996). "Education and the Palestinian Refugees in Lebanon – A Lost Generation?" Refugee Participation Network 21, Accessed March 3, 2009 from http://www.fmreview.org/HTMLcontent/rpn218.htm.

Anderson, B. (1983). *Imagined societies: Reflections on the origins and spread of nationalism*. London: Verso.

Arian, A., & Shamir, M. (1983). The primarily political functions of the left-right continuum. *Comparative Politics, 15*, 139–158.

Aruri, N. (1986). *Occupation: Israel over Palestine*. Boston: Southern Press.

Aruri, N., & Farsoun, S. (1980). Palestinian communities and Arab host countries. In K. Nakhleh & E. Zureik (Eds.), *Sociology of the Palestinians*. New York: St. Martin's Press.

Ashforth, B. E., & Mael, F. A. (1989). Social identity theory and the organization. *Academy of Management Review, 14*, 20–39.

Auron, Y. (1993). *Jewish-Israeli identity*. Tel Aviv: Sifriat Poalim [Hebrew].

Avruch, K. (1981). *American immigrants in Israel: Social identities and change*. Chicago: Chicago University Press.

Azar, E. E. (1990). *The management of protracted social conflict*. Hampshire, UK: Dartmouth.

Barnea, M. F., & Schwartz, S. H. (1998). Values and voting. *Political Psychology, 19*(1), 17–40.

Bar-Siman-Tov, Y. (2007). *The Israeli–Palestinian conflict: From conflict resolution to conflict management*. New York: Palgrave-Macmillan.

Bar-Tal, D. (1989). Delegitimization: The extreme case of stereotyping and prejudice. In D. Bar-Tal, C. Graumann, A. W. Kruglanski, & W. Stroebe (Eds.), *Stereotyping and prejudice: Changing concepts* (pp. 169–188). New York: Springer.

Bar-Tal, D. (2000). From intractable conflict through conflict resolution to reconciliation: Psychological analysis. *Political Psychology, 21*, 351–365.

Benziman, U., & Manzur, A. (1992). *Sub-tenants*. Tel Aviv, Israel: Keter (Hebrew).

Bregman, A., & El-Tahri, J. (1998). *The sixty year war: Israel and the Arabs*. London: Penguin.

Brand, L. A. (1988). *Palestinians in the Arab World*. New York: Columbia University Press.

Chatman, J. A., Bell, N. E. and Staw, B. M. (1986). The managed thought: The role of self-justification and impression management in organizational setting. In J.H.P Sims & D.A. Gioia (Eds.), *The thinking organization: Dynamics of social cognition*. San Francisco, CA: Jossey-Bass: 191–214.

Clark, T. N., Lipset, S. M., & Rempel, M. (1993). The declining political significance of social class. *International Sociology, 8*, 293–316.
Cohen, E. (1985). Ethnicity and legitimation in contemporary Israel. In E. Krausz (Ed.), *Politics and society in Israel: Studies of Israeli society* (pp. 320–333). New Brunswick: Transaction.
Cohen, I. J. (1987). Structuration theory and social praxis. In A. Giddens & J. Turner (Eds.), *Social theory today* (pp. 273–308). Stanford: Stanford University Press.
Cohen, J. (1997). *Right-wing social movements in Israel, territories, the peace process, and the media*. Paper presented at the First Regional Conference on Social Movements, (ISA RC28) September, Tel Aviv, Israel.
Collins, R. (1981). On the microfoundations of macrosociology. *American Journal of Sociology, 86*, 984–1014.
De Cremer, D. (2001). Relations of self esteem concerns, group identification and self stereotyping to ingroup favoritism. *The Journal of Social Psychology, 141*, 389–405.
Devine, F. (1992). Social identities, class identity and political perspectives. *The Sociological Review, 40*, 229–252.
Eisenstadt, S. N. (1974). *Change and continuity in Israeli society*. New York: Humanities Press.
El Dabbagh, Y. (1996). *Palestine, history, Jewish-Arab conflict_files*. http://www.ArabNet.com
Ellemers, N., Wilke, H., & van Knippenberg, A. (1993). Effects of the legitimacy of low group or individual status on individual and collective identity enhancement strategies. *Journal of Personality and Social Psychology, 64*, 766–778.
Emmison, M., & Western, M. (1990). Social class and social identity: A comment on Marshal, et al. *Sociology, 24*, 241–253.
FAFO. (1993). Palestinian society in Gaza, West Bank and Arab Jerusalem: A survey of living conditions (Report 151). Oslo, Norway: Fagbevegelsens Senter for Forskning, Utredning og Dokumentasjon.
Farrago, U. (1977). *Stability and change in the Jewish identity of working youth in Israel: 1965–1974*. Jerusalem: Hebrew University, Levi Eshkol Institute for Economic, Social and Political Research [Hebrew].
Farsoun, S. K., & Zacharia, C. E. (1997). *Palestine and the Palestinians*. Boulder, CO: Westview.
Gabison, R., & Abu Rea, E. (2000). *The Jewish Arab rift in Israel*. Jerusalem: The Israeli Democratic Institute.
Gellner, E. (1989). *Nations and nationalism*. Oxford: Basil Blackwell.
Ghabra, S. N. (1987). *Palestinians in Kuwait: The family and the politics of survival*. Boulder: Westview Press.
Giddens, A. (1976). *New rules of sociological method: A positive critique of interpretative sociology*. New York: Basic Books.
Giddens, A. (1979). *Central problems in social theory: Action, structure, and contradiction in social analysis*. Los Angeles: University of California Press.
Giddens, A. (1984). *The constitution of society: Outline of a theory of structuration*. Berkeley: University of California Press.
Giddens, A. (1994). *Beyond left and right: The future of radical politics*. Stanford: Stanford University Press.
Goertzel, T. G. (1989). Authoritarianism and social change in the Soviet Union. *Journal of Social Psychology, 129*, 703–705.
Goertz, G., & Diehl, P. (1993). Enduring rivalries: Theoretical construct and empirical patterns. *International Studies Quarterly, 37*, 71–147.
Haidar, A. (1996). *The Arab population in the Israeli economy*. New York: St. Martins Press.
Heacok, R. (Ed.). (1990). *Intifada: Palestine at the crossroads*. New York: Praeger.
Heiberg, M. (1993). Opinions and attitudes. In M. Heiberg & G. Øvensen (Eds.), *Palestinian society* (pp. 249–282). Oslo: FAFO.
Heiberg, M., & Øvensen, G. (Eds.). (1993). *Palestinian society*. Oslo: FAFO.
Herman, S. N. (1970). *Israelis and Jews: The continuity of an identity*. New York: Random House.
Hofman, J., & Rouhana, N. (1976). Young Arabs in Israel: Some aspect of a conflicted social identity. *Journal of Social Psychology, 99*, 75–86.
Horowitz, D., & Lissak, M. (1978). Origins of the Israeli polity palestine under the Mandate. Chicago: University of Chicago Press.
Horowitz, D., & Lissak, M. (1989). *Troubles in Utopia*. Albany, NY: State University of New York Press.
Hout, M., Brooks, C., & Manza, J. (1993). The persistence of classes in post-industrial societies. *International Sociology, 8*, 259–277.
Inglehart, R. (1987). Value change in industrial societies. *American Political Science Review, 81*, 1289–1303.
Islam, M. R., & Hewstone, M. (1993). Dimensions of control as predictors of intergroup anxiety, perceived out-group variability, and out-group attitude: An interpretive approach. *Personality and Social Psychology Bulletin, 19*, 700–710.
Israeli Bureau of Statistics. (1995). *The statistical yearbook*. Israel: Jerusalem.
Israeli Bureau of Statistics. (1998). *The statistical yearbook*. Israel: Jerusalem.
Israeli Bureau of Statistics. (2002). *The statistical yearbook*. Israel: Jerusalem.
Israeli Bureau of Statistics. (2008). *The statistical yearbook*. Israel: Jerusalem.
Kedourie, E. (1993). *Nationalism*. Cambridge: Blackwell.
Khalidi, W. (1992). *Palestine reborn*. London: Tauris.
Khalaf, S., & Kongstad, P. (1973). *Hamra of Beirut: A case of rapid urbanization*. Leiden: E.J. Brill.
Kimmerling, B. (1983). *Zionism and territory: The socio-territorial dimensions of Zionist politics*. Berkeley, CA: University of California Press.
Kimmerling, B. (1985). Between the primordial and the civil definitions of the collective identity: *Eretz Israel* or the state of Israel? In E. Cohen, M. Lissak, & U. Almagor (Eds.), *Comparative social dynamics* (pp. 179–195). New York: Westview Press.
Kimmerling, B. (1993). State building, state autonomy, and the identity of society: The case of the Israeli state. *The Journal of Historical Sociology, 6*, 397–429.

Kimmerling, B. (1998). Our nation and their disaster. *Haaretz, June*, 5.

Kimmerling, B. (2008). *Clash of identities: Exploration in Israeli and Palestinian society*. New York: Columbia University Press.

Kimmerling, B., & Migdal, J. S. (1994). *Palestinians: The making of a people*. Cambridge: Harvard University Press.

Kimmerling, B., & Moore, D. (1997). Collective identity as agency and structuration of society: The Israeli case. *International Review of Sociology, 7*(1), 25–49.

Laclau, E., & Mouffe, C. (1985). *Hegemony and socialist strategy*. London: Verso.

Lambert, W. E., & Taylor, D. M. (1990). *Coping with cultural and racial diversity in urban America*. New York: Praeger.

Landau, Y. (1993). *The Arab minority in Israel 1967–1991: Political aspects*. Tel Aviv: Am Oved (Hebrew).

Lappin Y. (2009). *IDF releases Cast Lead casualty numbers. Jerusalem Post. March 28, 2009*. Archived from the original on February 22, 2010. Retrieved September 1, 2010. http://fr.jpost.com/servlet/Satellite?cid=1237727552054&pagename=JPArticle/ShowFull.

Lawler, E. J. (1992). Affective attachments to nested groups: A choice-process theory. *American Sociological Review, 57*, 327–339.

Lissak, M. (1969). Images of class and society in the Yeshuv and Israeli Society. In S. N. Eisenstadt, H. Adler, R. Bar-Yosef, & R. Kahana (Eds.), *The social structure of Israel*. Jerusalem: Academon Press (Hebrew).

Litvak, M. (1998). The Islamization of the Palestinian–Israeli conflict: The case of Hamas. *Middle Eastern Studies, 34*(1), 148–163.

Mari, S. K. (1978). *Arab education in Israel*. Syracuse: Syracuse University Press.

Markovsky, B. (1985). Toward a multilevel distributive justice theory. *American Sociological Review, 50*, 822–839.

Marshal, G., Ross, D., Newby, H., & Vogler, C. (1988). *Social class in Modern Britain*. London: Unwin Hyman.

Martin, J., Brickman, P., & Murray, A. (1984). Moral outrage and pragmatism: Explanations for collective action. *Journal of Experimental Social Psychology, 20*, 484–496.

Masalha, N. (1992). *Expulsion of the Palestinians: The concept of transfer in Zionist political thought, 1882–1948*. Washington, DC: Institute for Palestinian Studies.

McDonough, P., Barnes, S. H., & Pina, A. L. (1988). Social identity and mass politics in Spain. *Comparative Political Studies, 21*, 200–230.

McDowell, D. (1989). *Palestine and Israel: The uprising and beyond*. London: I.B. Tauris.

Moore, D. (1990). Discrimination and deprivation: The effects of social comparisons. *Social Justice Research, 4*, 45–64.

Moore, D. (1995). Attitude (In)congruence: Sociopolitical orientation and the gendered division of labor. *Sociological Imagination, 32*, 143–163.

Moore, D. (1996). The structure of postmaterialist attitudes among young and highly educated Israelis (1982–1992). *Contemporary Development Analysis, 1*, 62–90.

Moore, D. (1998). No longer complacent?: Why Israeli women did not rebel? *Journal for the Theory of Social Behavior, 28*, 169–192.

Moore, D. (2000). Intolerance of others among Palestinian and Jewish students in Israel. *Sociological Inquiry, 70*(3), 280–312.

Moore, D. (2003). Justice for self, group and nation: introduction. *Sociological Inquiry, 73*(2), 162–164.

Moore, D., & Aweiss, S. (2002). Hatred of 'Others' among Palestinian, Arab and Jewish students in Israel. *Journal of the Society for the Psychological Study of Social Issues, 2*(1), 151–173.

Moore, D., & Aweiss, S. (2003). Outcome expectations in prolonged conflicts, perceptions of sense of control and relative deprivation. *Sociological Inquiry, 73*(2), 190–212.

Moore, D., & Aweiss, S. (2004). *Bridges over troubled water: Political, economic and social attitudes (cross-cultural comparisons of Palestinians and Israelis)*. Westport: Greenwood Publishing Group.

Moore, D., & Aweiss, S. (2007). Strategies of constructing social identities in conflict-ridden areas: The case of young Jews, Arabs, and Palestinians. *Studies in Ethnicity and Nationalism, 7*(1), 2–27.

Moore, D., & Kimmerling, B. (1995). Individual strategies of adopting collective identities: The Israeli case. *International Sociology, 10*, 387–407.

Morris, B. (1987). *The birth of the Palestinian refugee problem 1947–1949*. New York: Cambridge University Press.

Newman, D. (1991). *Population, settlement and conflict: Israel and the West Bank*. Cambridge: Cambridge University Press.

Niemi, R. G., & Weisberg, H. F. (1984). *Controversies in voting behavior*. Washington, DC: CQ Press.

Oakes, P., & Turner, J. C. (1986). Distinctiveness and salience of social category membership: is there an automatic perceptual bias toward novelty? *European Journal of Social Psychology, 16*, 325–344.

Palestinian Bureau of Statistics (1996). The Demographic Survey in the West Bank and Gaza Strip: Preliminary Report, Ramallah, Palestinian Authority

Palestinian Bureau of Statistics (2000). http://www.new-paradigmfund.org/research/green-palestine-PCBS.pdf.

Palestinian Bureau of Statistics. (2008). *Poverty in Palestine* http://www.pcbs.gov.ps/DesktopDefault.aspx?tabID=3355&lang=en.

Palestinian Bureau of Statistics. (2001). *Summary of final results: Population, housing, and establishment census – 1997*. http://www.pcbs.org/english/phc_97/popu.htm.

Palestinian Bureau of Statistics. (2007). http://www.pcbs.gov.ps/DesktopDefault.aspx?tabID=3354&lang=en.

Palestinian Center for Human Rights. (2009). *The Dead in the course of the Israeli recent military offensive on the Gaza strip between 27 December 2008 and 18*

January. 2009-03-19. Retrieved September 1, 2010 http://www.pchrgaza.org/files/PressR/English/2008/list.pdf.

Pappe, I. (1992). *The making of the Arab–Israeli conflict, 1947–1951*. London: LB. Taurus.

Peres, Y., & Yuval-Davis, N. (1969). Some observations on the national identity of Israeli Arabs. *Human Relations, 22*, 219–233.

Peres, Y., & Yuchtman-Yaar, E. (1992). *Trends in Israeli democracy*. Boulder, CO: Lynne Rienner.

Peretz, D. (1990). *Intifada: The Palestinian uprising*. Boulder, Col.: Westview Press.

Perkins, D. N., Nieva, V. F., & Lawler, E. E. (1983). *Managing creation: The challenge of building a new organization*. New York: Wiley.

Pike, J. (1998). *Chemical weapons programs: History." federation of American scientists*. Available from http://www.fas.org/nuke/guide/iraq/cw/program.htm.

Reiter, Y., & Aharoni, R. (1993). *The political life of Arabs in Israel*. Beit Berl: The Institute for Israeli Arab Studies.

Rekhes, E. (1994). The Arab village in Israel – A reawakened national-political center. In R. Hochman (Ed.), *Jews and Arabs in Israel*. Jerusalem: The Hebrew University (Hebrew).

Ross, D. B. (2002). Yasir Arafat. *Foreign Policy, July–August*, 18–27.

Rouhana, N. N. (1991). *Palestinization among the Arabs in Israel: The accentuate identity*. Conference paper on Arab minority in Israel: Dilemmas of political orientations and social change. Tel Aviv: The Dayan Center, Tel Aviv University.

Rubenstein, D. (1995). *The mystery of Arafat*. New York: Steerforth Press.

Rubinstein, G. (1995). Authoritarianism in Israeli society. *Journal of Social Psychology, 135*, 237–249.

Said, E. (1995). *The politics of dispossession: The struggle for palestinian self-determination*. New York: Vintage.

Said, E. (1996). *Peace and its discontents*. New York: Vintage.

Sanders, P. (1990). *A nation of home owners*. London: Unwin Hyman.

Sayigh, R. (1994). *Too many enemies: The Palestinian experience in Lebanon*. London: Zed.

Sayigh, Y. (1997). *Armed struggle and the search for state, the Palestinian National Movement, 1949–1993*. Oxford: Oxford University Press.

Shapiro, Y. (1985). Political sociology in Israel: A critical view. In E. Krausz (Ed.), *Politics and society in Israel* (pp. 6–16). New Brunswick: Transaction Books.

Shikaki, H. (1999). Beyond democracy in Palestine: The peace process, national rehabilitation and elections. In A. Manna (Ed.), *The Palestinians in the twentieth century: An inside look* (pp. 63–104). Haifa: The Center for the Study of Arab Society in Israel (Hebrew).

Shtendal, U. (1992). *Israeli Arabs – Between the rock and the hard place*. Jerusalem: Academon, The Hebrew University.

Sidanius, J., Brewer, R. M., Banks, E., & Ekehammer, B. (1987). Ideological constraint, political interest and gender: A Swedish-American comparison. *European Journal of Political Research, 15*, 471–492.

Sidanius, J., & Duffy, G. (1988). The duality of attitude structure: A test of Kerlingers critical referents theory within samples of Swedish and American youths. *Political Psychology, 9*, 649–670.

Sidanius, J., Levin, S., Rabinowitz, J. L., & Frederico, C. M. (1999). Peering into the jaws of the beast: The integrative dynamics of social identity, symbolic racism, and social dominance. In D. A. Prentice & D. T. Miller (Eds.), *Cultural divides: Understanding and overcoming group conflict* (pp. 80–132). New York: Russell Sage.

Sidanius, J., & Petrocik, J. R. (2001). Communal and national identity in a multiethnic state: A comparison of three perspectives. In R. D. Ashmore, L. Jussim, & D. Wilder (Eds.), *Social identity, intergroup conflict, and conflict reduction* (Rutgers series on self and social identity, Vol. 3, (pp. 101–129)).

Sidanius, J., & Pratto, F. (1998). *Social dominance: An intergroup theory of social hierarchy and oppression*. New York: Cambridge University Press.

Sidanius, J., Pratto, F., & Bobo, L. (1996). Racism, conservatism, affirmative action, and intellectual sophistication: A matter of principled conservatism or group dominance? *Journal of Personality and Social Psychology, 70*, 476–490.

Smooha, S. (1992). *Arabs and Jews in Israel: Continuity in mutual intolerance*. Boulder: Westview Press.

Steel, B. S., Warner, R. L., Lovrich, N. P., & Pierce, J. C. (1992). The Inglehart-Flanagan debate over postmaterialist values: Some evidence from a Canadian-American case study. *Political Psychology, 13*, 61–77.

Stone, W. F., & Schaffner, P. E. (1988). *The psychology of politics*. New York: Springer Verlag.

Stryker, S., & Serpe, R. T. (1994). Identity salience and psychological centrality: Equivalent, overlapping or complementary concepts? *Social Psychology Quarterly, 57*, 16–35.

Swingewood, A. (1991). *A short history of sociological thought*. London: Macmillan.

Tajfel, H. (1978). The achievement of group identification. In H. Tajfel (Ed.), *Differentiation between social groups: Studies in the social psychology of intergroup behavior* (pp. 77–98). London: Academic Press.

Tajfel, H. (1981). *Human groups and social categories: Studies in social psychology*. Cambridge, England: Cambridge University Press.

Tajfel, H., & Turner, J. C. (1986). The social identity theory of intergroup behavior. In S. Worchel & W. G. Austin (Eds.), *Psychology of intergroup relations* (pp. 7–24). Chicago: Nelson-Hall.

Tamari, S. (1993). The transformation of Palestinian Society: Fragmentation and occupation. In: M. Heiberg & G. Øvensen (Eds.), *Palestinian society* (pp. 21–33). Oslo: FAFO.

Taraki, L. (1997). Palestinian women: A status report # 1. Ramallah, Womens Studies Program, Birzeit University.

Tesser, A., & Campbell, J. (1982). Self evaluation maintenance and the perception of friends and strangers. *Journal of Personality, 50*, 261–279.

Thompson, J. B. (1989). The theory of structuration. In D. Held & J. B. Thompson (Eds.), *Social theory of modern society: Anthony Giddens and his critics* (pp. 56–76). Cambridge: Cambridge University Press.

Tropp, L. R., & Wright, S. C. (1999). Ingroup identification and relative deprivation: An examination across multiple social comparisons. *European Journal of Social Psychology, 29*, 707–724.

Turner, J. C. (1982). Toward a cognitive definition of the social group. In H. Tajfel (Ed.), *Social identity and intergroup relations*. Paris: Maison des Sciences D\de L'Homme and Cambridge: Cambridge University Press.

Turner, J. C. (1984). Social identification and psychological group formation. In H. Tajfel (Ed.), *The social dimension: European developments in social psychology* (Vol. 2, pp. 518–538). Cambridge, England: Cambridge University Press.

Turner, J. C. (1985). Social categorization and the self-concept: Cognitive theory of group behavior. In E. E. Lawler (Ed.), *Advances in group processes* (pp. 77–122). Greenwich, CT: JAI Press.

Tyler, T. R., Boeckmann, R. J., Smith, H. J., & Huo, Y. J. (1997). *Social justice in a diverse society*. Boulder, CO: Westview Press.

Ugland, O., & Tamari, S. (1993). Aspects of social stratification. In M. Heiberg & G. Øvensen (Eds.), *Palestinian society* (pp. 221–247). Oslo: FAFO.

Wagner, U., Lampen, L., & Syllwaschy, J. (1986). Ingroup inferiority, social identity and outgroup devaluation in a modified minimal group study. *British Journal of Social Psychology., 25*, 15–23.

Walker, I. (1999). Effects of personal and group relative deprivation on personal and collective self-esteem. *Group Processes and Intergroup Relations, 2*(4), 365–380.

Waxman, D. (2008). From controversy to consensus: Cultural conflict and the Israeli debate over territorial withdrawal. *Israel Studies, 13*(2), 73–96.

Weigert, A. J., Teitge, J. S., & Teitge, D. W. (1990). *Society and identity: Toward a sociological psychology*. Cambridge: Cambridge University Press.

Winnick, A. (2009). The prospect of a two-state solution between the Israelis and Palestinians given the current situation in Gaza. In M. F. Salinas & H. Abu Rabi (Eds.), *Resolving the Israeli–Palestinian conflict: Perspectives on the peace process* (pp. 43–70). Amherst, NY: Cambria Press.

World, Bank. (1993). *Developing the occupied territories: An investment in peace* (Vol. 1, p. viii). Washington, D.C: World Bank.

Yishai, Y. (1982). Israels right-wing Jewish proletariat. *The Jewish Journal of Sociology, 24*, 87–97.

Ethnopolitical Conflict in Turkey: From the Denial of Kurds to Peaceful Co-existence?

10

Ayşe Betül Çelik

Kurdish Chapter Summary

In this chapter the author describes the Kurds as a heterogeneous minority group with shared cultural identity, yet differing religions and languages. This group is estimated to comprise 15–20% of the current population of Turkey. Conflict traces back to the Ottoman Empire, but takes a more ethnic character after the formation of the Turkish state, reaching a peak after 1984. The continuing conflicts, resolution attempts, and suggestions for a peaceful future are outlined.

Significant acts of rebellion over the last hundred years of conflict are delineated along with the underlying causal factors including nationalism, attempts to homogenize, and resettlement activities. The evolution of various legal and illegal groups which helped mobilize the Kurds in the struggle for equality and recognition are discussed. The author recognizes that while some progress was made through these efforts, there were also many negative outcomes such as human rights abuses, banning of Kurdish language in public, and forced migration.

The author notes that significant positive changes began to occur as Turkey prepared to harmonize with the EU.Emphasis is given to a continuing cycle of increased hope for the Kurds through state treaties and initiatives followed by lack of implementation which resulted in a persistent sense of mistrust. Discussion of a current state initiative granting specific rights to Kurds reflects many positive aspects, but the author points out the important issues that are notably absent.

A.B. Çelik (✉)
Faculty of Arts and Social Sciences, Sabanci University,
Orhanli Tuzla, Istanbul, Turkey
e-mail: bcelik@sabanciuniv.edu

D. Landis and R.D. Albert (eds.), *Handbook of Ethnic Conflict: International Perspectives*,
International and Cultural Psychology, DOI 10.1007/978-1-4614-0448-4_10,

Suggestions which the authors believe will assist in resolving this conflict are offered, including but not limited to the need to recognize and address the social tension between the Turks and Kurds. Studies are cited which reveal the existent misperceptions between these two groups. The authors call for each group to address the other in open dialogue, recognizing the pain, social polarization, and mistrust.

Cheryl Jorgensen

Map 1: Distribution of Kurds Across Turkey

The Kurdish Question is perhaps one of the most important issues with which Turkey has had to deal since the mid-1980s. Even though the roots of this problem can be traced back to the Ottoman Empire, the devastating consequences of the war between the PKK (*Partiya Karkerên Kurdistan* – Kurdistan Workers' Party) and the Turkish security forces that has taken place since 1984 in the southeast of Turkey and the fact that the demands of the ethnic Kurds have still not been effectively addressed by the Turkish state, places this issue at the core of Turkish politics. The war between the PKK and the Turkish army has resulted in **damaged infrastructure**, conflicts over land ownership between villagers and village guards,[1] and a legitimacy problem due to improper human rights practices during the *Olağanüstü Hal* regime

[1] Village Guards are locally recruited civilians armed and paid by the state to oppose the PKK. There are around 59,000 village guards on regular salaries, and 23,274 village guards are working on a voluntary basis (*Today's Zaman*, 2009). The national media have carried various stories in recent years about the criminal activities of village guards, such as the abduction of women, aggravated assault, and the formation of armed gangs (see Kurban, Çelik, & Yükseker, 2006).

(system of emergency rule).[2] It also created mistrust between the local state administrators and the local inhabitants, and produced internally displaced people (IDPs), who are still encountering problems returning to the conflict region. Conflict in the western cities of Turkey, on the other hand, has led to a degree of polarization among different groups and occasional discrimination against Kurds. Besides these bitter consequences, however, the last decade has also witnessed some improvements in the ways in which the governments have handled the conflict. From denial of the problem, they have moved to a position of seeking alternative solutions that can bring long-lasting peace to the country. This chapter will discuss the history of the conflict along various dimensions and analyze the recent peace-building efforts of the actors involved in the process.

1 Kurds: Stateless Nation of the Middle East

Many scholars and organizations refer to the Kurds as being one of the largest ethnic groups without a nation-state (Council of Europe, 2006; Izady 1992; MacDonald, 1993; McKeirnan, 1999). They make up an important percentage of the minority population in the countries where they live in the Middle East – namely, Turkey, Iran, Iraq, Syria, and Azerbaijan, and a considerable percentage in some Western countries such as Germany, Holland, and Sweden. There are no official statistics on the percentage of Kurds in Turkey. However, studies estimate that they make up 15–20% of the population of the country (Andrews, 1992; Gunter, 1997; McDowall, 1997).

The Kurds do not constitute a homogenous group; they follow various religions (Sunni, Alevi, and Yezidi) and speak a variety of languages (Zaza,[3] Kırmanji). That is why it is often hard to describe them. Kurds in Turkey can distinguish themselves from other groups by their language and culture. They speak two (Zaza and Kırmanji) of the many dialects of the Kurdish language, which belongs to the northwestern group of the Iranian branch of the Indo-European family. It is a close relative of Persian, which is in the southwestern group. Differentiating themselves on the basis of language sometimes can be problematic in the case of Kurds who never learned to speak Kurdish, either because their parents were afraid to teach them the language or because they were simply assimilated into Turkish culture. Most Kurds, therefore, define themselves on the basis of their parentage, place of origin, and/or self-identification. Geographically, there is no specific region where the population is exclusively made up of Kurds, although they constitute the majority in most parts of Eastern and Southeastern Anatolia (see blue and red areas on Map 1).

Another difficulty in talking about Kurds as a homogeneous group is their spatial diversity and dispersion in Iran, Iraq, Syria, and Azerbaijan. Although there is a Kurdish consciousness that binds them together, Kurds in these countries speak different dialects (the northern version, commonly called Kırmanji, is spoken in Turkey, Syria, and the northern part of the Kurdish-speaking areas of Iraq and Iran. The central version, commonly called Sorani, is spoken in western Iran and much of Iraqi Kurdistan. The Southern Kurdish dialects, and Hewrami or Auramani (Gorani) are spoken by few, especially in Iran.

[2] The OHAL regime was imposed in several cities of eastern and southeastern Anatolia in 1987. The governors of the cities under the OHAL regime acquired the right to pass regulations functioning like laws. Among several rights the governors enjoyed one can list the right to expel citizens from the region, restrict ownership and limit rights and liberties, and freedom of the press and of expression. Even though the regime had been lifted in the region by the end of 2002, albeit gradually, not only its legacy and tradition but also the mistrust it created between the locals and the public officers remain to a certain extent there.

[3] There are debates among scholars that Zaza is not a Kurdish dialect and that the Zazas are a different ethnic group. However, this debate is not supported by many research studies; therefore, most scholars still consider Zazas as part of Kurdish culture.

These are furthered divided into sub-dialects). Moreover, there are also differences in lifestyles among these groups because of being assimilated into or having lived together with different national groups in these countries.

Kurds have never existed as an independent political community,[4] and thus, have been under different rulers throughout their history, including the Sassanian Empire, the Safavid Empire, the Ottoman Empire, and the Turkish Republic, among others. In the early sixteenth century, Kurdish tribes fell under Ottoman rule as a result of the Safavid–Ottoman struggle (van Bruinessen, 1992; Entessar, 1992; McDowall, 1997). With respect to its relations with its subjects, the Ottoman Empire was different from nation-states: subjects were not classified according to their ethnic identities/origins but rather to their religions (Muslim vs. non-Muslim). Accordingly, Kurds, who had lived in the Ottoman domains since the sixteenth century, were recognized as part of the Muslim community, along with Arabs, Turks, Albanians, etc. The hostility between the religious and ethnic communities was aggravated in the late nineteenth century[5]; consequently, the roots of the "Kurdish question" should be contextualized within the transition from a multi-ethnic Empire to a nationalistic Turkish Republic in the first quarter of the twentieth century.

The first international recognition of the Kurds came with the Treaty of Sevres in 1920, which led to the partition of Ottoman lands by the Allied Powers after the First World War. The Treaty of Sevres recognized Kurds as an ethnically distinct people and a plan was drafted that included autonomy for Kurdish-populated areas. The treaty provided an independent, but non-unified, Kurdistan. However, the basic documents and international treaties (such as the Treaty of Lausanne in 1923), which shaped the legal foundations of the new Turkish state after the War of Independence, left no room for the official recognition of Kurds and other Muslim groups as distinct peoples. The Treaty of Lausanne recognized only non-Muslim groups (Greeks, Armenians, and Jews) as minorities. Even though it replaced the Sevres Treaty and formed a unified Turkey, the fears that the Allied Powers would divide the country continued and is still one of the major barriers for the resolution of the conflict. What is commonly known as *Sevres Paranoia*, fears that there are external powers who are trying to challenge the territorial integrity of the Turkish state and implement the provisions of the Sevres Treaty by establishing local autonomy for the predominantly Kurdish areas, still affects many Turkish citizens and policy-makers' perceptions on any ground-breaking policy on the issue.

2 Kurds in the Early Years of the Republic

During the first years of the Republic, there were several Kurdish uprisings. Of the 18 rebellions that broke out between 1924 and 1938, 17 were in Eastern Anatolia and 16 involved Kurds (Kirişçi & Winrow, 1997). Three of these deserve mention because the narratives of these rebellions have been passed from generation to generation through oral accounts, which were separate from, and opposed to, Turkish national identity, and were pivotal in constructing a separate Kurdish identity (Neyzi, 1999).

[4] The only exception is the short-lived Mahabad Republic in today's Iran in December 1945. The Republic ceased to exist when the Soviet forces and support, which helped the foundation of the Republic, were withdrawn in December 1946.

[5] Although Kurds lived under Ottoman rule without much challenge to its existence, there are several historical events that signify the emergence of Kurdish nationalist sentiments and of challenges to the Ottoman rule in the nineteenth century. The first significant sign of independence vis-à-vis Ottoman rule came from Bedr Khan, who established his authority over all Kurdish tribes, and refused to send tribal contingents when these were requisitioned in the Ottoman–Russian war of 1828–1829. The second Kurdish insurgency towards the Ottoman rule was a rebellion led by Şeyh Ubeydullah of Nehri, who sought to establish an independent state with the help of the British in 1880. Lastly, the Hamidiye Cavalries created by Abdulhamid II in 1891 strengthened the formation of Kurdish community as a distinct unit, by giving considerable power to Kurdish Hamidiye commanders, which posed a potential threat to the state (van Bruinessen, 1992; McDowall, 1997; Olson, 1989).

The first important Kurdish rebellion was led by Sheikh Said in 1925. This was the earliest large-scale Kurdish rebellion in the Republic. Although it was largely led by religious *şeyhs* (sheiks),[6] the Kurdish organization Azadi (Freedom),[7] which had the aim of establishing an independent Kurdistan (van Bruinessen, 1992), was instrumental in the unfolding of the rebellion. What is significant about the rebellion is that it "was a turning point in the history of the Kurds in that nationalism was the prime factor in its organization and development" (Olson, 1989, p. 154). Olson argues that although the rebellion was significant because of the nationalist elements it carried, it proved the weaknesses of the Kurdish mobilization. First of all, it lacked tribal connection with urban dwellers. Secondly, the rebellion failed because of existing tribal rivalries and Sunni–Alevi[8] differences among the Kurds (Olson, 1989). The rebellion followed systematic deportations and martial law in the East. It also led to the establishment of the Restoration of Order Law in 1926, which created Independence Tribunals to arrest the leaders of all opposing forces. The law was in effect for 2 years, and the two Independence Tribunals, one established in the east and one in Ankara, were successful in stifling all reaction and rebellion, and restoring "social harmony" (McDowall, 1997, p. 195). With the *Law on the Transfer of Certain People from the Eastern Regions to the Western Provinces* (Law No. 1907), which was passed by parliament on June 10, 1927, many Kurds were transferred to western provinces without an indication of where they were to be sent, and their land and other real estate were taken over by the treasury (Tekeli, 1994). The law was passed after the Ankara government realized that Kurdish recalcitrance had continued despite the suppression of the Sheikh Said Rebellion. The number of people transferred is unknown, but some argue that it was no fewer than 200,000 (Clerk as cited in McDowall, 1997).

From 1925 to 1927, Kurdish mobilization was largely suppressed. The second important Kurdish rebellion of the Turkish Republic came as an insurrection led by a former Ottoman army officer, Ihsan Nuri Pasha in the area of Ağrı (Ararat) in 1930. Frustrated by the Turkish state's homogenization project, whose foundation was based on the belief that all citizens are Turkish, combined with the government's emergency powers to administer the area, some Kurdish nationalist elites formed the Khoybun (Independence) group in 1927. The operational leader of the Bayt al Shabab mutiny, İhsan Nuri, assembled a small group of men trained in modern weapons, and moved his men to the Ararat region, where there were local tribes already in revolt. This time some Alevi tribes in Turkey and Kurdish tribes in Iran also joined the revolt. However, the Turkish army's superior weaponry, communications and logistics, and the lack of coordinated mobilization of Kurdish tribes led to the Turkish state's success in suppressing the rebellion (McDowall, 1997).

[6]According to Turkish official history, the Şeyh Said rebellion had a religious character, mainly because of the symbols used in the rebellion. It is argued that it was against the secular nature of the new republic, and the rebellion erupted because Atatürk, the president of the new republic, had abolished the Caliphate on March 3, 1924. There is still no agreement among the scholars working on Kurdish history whether the rebellion was a nationalist rebellion in essence. Van Bruinessen (1992) argues that prohibition of the use of Kurdish language in public places (*populism*), the exile of Kurdish landlords (*aghas*) and the expropriation of their land by the state (*abolition of feudalism*), and abolition of the Caliphate gave rise to grievances among Kurds, leading to the rebellion. Thus, the rebellion carries both national and religious elements. On the other hand, some argue that Kurdish intellectuals and military officers were at the heart of this movement, making it a nationalist rebellion. And, "the fact that the rebellion had a religious character was the result of Azadi's assessment of the strategy and tactics necessary for carrying out a successful revolution" (Olson, 1989).

[7]Azadi was a Kurdish nationalist party founded by Kurdish nationalists and officers from the Ottoman army in May 1923. Azadi was largely supported by Zaza-speaking tribes. It opposed the new government's policies of secularization (abolishment of the Caliphate) and the introduction of a modern education system based on Turkish (Kirişçi & Winrow, 1997).

[8]Alevism is a sect in Islam. There are significant differences in the beliefs and worshipping practiced by Sunnis and Alevis in Turkey, which has created a long-lasting animosity between the two. It is estimated that around 70% of the Kurds in Turkey are Sunni, and the remaining 30% consists of Alevis and Yezidis (Andrews, 1992).

The last important Kurdish rebellion dates back to the late 1930s. There were two important factors that laid the ground for the rebellion. The first came on June 21, 1934, when the Turkish parliament passed the Law on Resettlement (Law No. 2510), which regulated the settlement of immigrants and resettlement within the country. The law divided Turkey into three zones in accordance to adherence to "Turkishness": (1) localities where the population possessed non-Turkish elements and a concentration of population having Turkish culture was desired (as a result, immigrants from the former Ottoman provinces who had Turkish origins were settled in these localities); (2) regions reserved for people who were expected to assimilate into Turkish culture; and (3) regions to be totally evacuated (the inhabitants of these regions were to be settled in the first two zones) (McDowall, 1997; Tekeli, 1994). The law also aimed to break down the structure of potentially powerful tribes, and abrogated tribal property rights. Tekeli reports that 25,831 people from 5,074 households were transferred from 15 cities in the eastern and southeastern Anatolia to western Anatolia. However, many households which were transferred to other provinces in the 1930s returned to their homes in the 1940s when the obligation of the transferred people to stay where they were settled was lifted, as Turkey moved to a multiparty regime in 1947 (Tekeli, 1994).

The other factor which prepared the ground for the Dersim rebellion was the passing in December 1935 of a law by parliament that placed Dersim (renamed Tunceli after the rebellion) under military rule. In fact, Dersim was commonly known as the main problem area. The law also enabled the government to detain and deport the "potential threats" of the "notoriously defiant region." The inhabitants of Dersim resisted the imposition of direct government control, which initiated the Dersim rebellion led by Şeyh Seyyid Rıza in 1936. At the end of 1938, the rebellion was bloodily suppressed by the government. Seyyid Rıza was hanged and thousands were executed. Again the rebellion preceded deportations and population control. And the inhabitants and deported families of Tunceli had to wait for 1946 to be able to be free from the emergency powers and to return their homes.

3 Kurds in the Transition to the Multiparty Era

The suppression of the Dersim rebellion was so powerful that it left a bitter memory among the Kurds so great that it pushed back any possible Kurdish mobilization until the 1950s, when the single-party era came to an end. The strict state control following the rebellion in the Kurdish-populated regions made it almost impossible for the Kurds to mobilize against the Turkish state. From the late 1930s to the late 1950s, there was no significant Kurdish opposition to the Turkish regime.

It is the political environment of the 1960s which provided fertile ground for political mobilization. The immediate cause was the 1961 Constitution, considered to be the constitution providing the most explicit protection of freedom of association (Bianchi, 1984). The rights granted by the Constitution promoted the foundation of trade unions and student organizations, which would play an important role in the Turkish politics of the 1970s. However, it should be kept in mind that although the 1961 Constitution encouraged some freedoms in terms of organization and mobilization of the Kurds, and the publication of the first Kurdish journals at the beginning of the 1960s, the government imposed strict measures to control the Kurdish-populated regions. By Law No.1587, the National Unity Committee, which for a while took over the administration after the 1960 *coup d'état*, started to replace Kurdish place names with Turkish ones, claiming that names which hurt public opinion are not suitable for national culture, moral values, traditions, and customs (McDowall, 1997). Thus, the 1960s both created some liberties and led to greater restrictions on Kurdish rights.

Within this rather "democratic" environment, Kurds initiated legal mobilization in both associations and political parties. The establishment of the *Türkiye İşçi Partisi* (the Workers' Party of

Turkey – hereafter the WPT) in 1961 is a milestone in the legal Kurdish mobilization. The party gained support from the middle-class "progressives" in Istanbul, and overwhelmingly from Kurds and Alevis in the countryside (Samim, 1987). Even though the party was a pro-Soviet socialist party aiming to "transform the Turkish society through the creation of a mass workers' party" (Samim, 1987, p. 155), it also supported organizational activity in the late 1960s.

The perspective of the WPT in the western cities of Turkey such as Istanbul, Ankara, and Izmir was mainly based on class struggle against capitalist exploitation. On the other hand, in the cities of Eastern and Southeastern Anatolia, the WPT argued that in order to liberate people, the institutions of *şeyhlik,*[9] *ağalık,*[10] and feudalism should be abolished, land reform introduced, and human rights respected. These two different perspectives stemmed from institutional and structural differences between the east and the west of the country. However, the argument was about structurally changing the society by replacing the "exploitative" institutions. In this sense, party politicians did not pronounce "Kurdishness" as an ethnic right until the mid-1960s.

It was only in 1965 that the WPT's chairman, Mehmet Ali Aybar, "shifted his emphasis from 'class interest' to 'human freedom' in an attempt to broaden its appeal-especially to Kurds and Alevis" (Samim, 1987, p. 158). In 1966, at its Second Congress, the party experienced a break between those who supported the National Democratic Revolution (NDR) and the Socialist Revolution. In its monthly publication *Aydınlık, t*he NDR, led by Mihri Belli, published an article in November 1968, entitled "The National Reality," where it talked about the "Kurdish question" (*Sosyalizm ve Toplumsal Mücadeleler Ansiklopedisi – STMA*, 1988). Whereas the WPT continued its program along the lines of the Socialist Revolution, which argued that the revolution should take place under the leadership of the workers, the NDR criticized the party for being "pacifist and parliamentarist," and argued that a new struggle should take place. However, neither the NDR movement nor the WPT were able to get Kurdish youth, who realized the "Turkish" left organizations did not respond to their needs, to follow them. These young people later founded the first legal Kurdish organization of the Turkish Republic: *Devrimci Doğu Kültür Ocakları* (Eastern Revolutionary Cultural Hearths, hereafter the ERCH).

What is significant about the WPT in terms of Kurdish mobilization is that it was the first legal political party recognizing the existence of Kurds in Turkey. In its fourth Grand Assembly, on October 29, 1970, the WPT announced that

> There is a Kurdish people in the East of Turkey… The fascist authorities representing the ruling classes have subjected the Kurdish people to a policy of assimilation and intimidation, which has often become bloody repression (Chailand, 1993, p. 87; STMA, 1988, p. 2132).

One should note that although the party openly suggested an ethnic problem in Turkey, this analysis "was heavily laden with class and leftist terminology" (Barkey & Fuller, 1998, p. 15). The party argued that the most fundamental reason for the underdevelopment of the region and the suppression of the Kurds was the "economic and social policies of the dominant classes who were very much aware that the region was inhabited by Kurds" (Chailand, 1993, p. 87). Thus, the leftists of the era related the Kurdish question to the "colonization" of the region by the Turkish-dominant classes.

[9] *Şeyhlik* is a religious institution, and *şeyh* (sheikh) is a religious title given to the head of the Naksbandi order in Islam. Among the Kurds, şeyh was a very influential religious figure (Olson, 1989, p. 3). Although one can come across with influential Kurdish şeyhs who could "infuse religious phraseology full of millenarian and messianic symbols into … nationalist objectives" such as in the case of the uprising led by Şeyh Ubaydullah of Nehri who sought to establish an independent state with the help of the British in 1880 (van Bruinessen, 1992; McDowall, 1997; Olson, 1989), in the 1970s many Kurds argued that the existence of şeyhs, who mostly used their ties with the state to strengthen their own power, prevented the rise of Kurdish nationalism.

[10] *Ağalık* is an institution similar to landlordship. *Agas* (Aghas), in Kurdish-populated regions, were the leaders of Kurdish tribes, and they had a great amount of social, economic, and political power over the tribe members. In most cases ağas used their clientelistic ties with the state to exert their power over the population, which overshadowed the growth of Kurdish consciousness for decades. Also, the conflict between the tribal groupings led by ağas formed shifting patterns of alliance, preventing the rise of a united Kurdish mobilization (Barkey & Fuller, 1998).

According to the perspective presented by most of the members of the WPT, the "Eastern problem," as they put it, stemmed from the combined effects of colonization of the Eastern Anatolia, and its relative deprivation based on ethnic differences. Along with this argument came the belief that when the capitalist and imperialist forces are overthrown, Kurds will also be liberated. This ideology gained support, particularly among the Kurdish youth and intellectuals of the early 1960s.

The most significant event of the 1960s in terms of Kurdish consciousness is the *Doğu Mitingleri* (The Eastern Meetings). From August 1967 to August 1969, 12 meetings were held in several Eastern and Southeastern Anatolian cities, and in Ankara (*Devrimci Doğu Kültür Ocakları: Dava Dosyasi 1*, 1975). Although the meetings of the WPT in western cities of Turkey were rather unpopular, the Eastern Meetings gathered thousands of people. These meetings focused mostly on economic and social problems with an emphasis on the institutions of *ağalık* and *şeyhlik* (as sources of inequality) in the society, inequality between the regions, unequal income distribution and poverty. Although the meetings were largely organized by the WPT, the supporters of another pro-Kurdish party also joined and gave their support: the *Kurdistan Demokratik Partisi* (Democratic Party of Kurdistan – hereafter the DKP). This political organization, led by Sait Elçi, was an illegal party that had connections with the Iraqi Democratic Party of Kurdistan, led by Molla Mustafa Barzani. It was mostly supported by rich Kurdish peasants. Although the party provided support to the meetings, it could not mobilize many Kurds.

The discourse at the meetings combined the socialist rhetoric of relative deprivation with the demands for identity recognition. They emphasized the relative deprivation of "the East," and raised the issue that Easterners should get as great a share in national capital and resources as "Westerners." Some of the banners at the meetings emphasized this inequality between the regions: "If the West is the homeland, what is the East?" "The fate of the East is famine, unemployment, and degradation," "Where is democracy?" "We want protection of life," "Oil was our blood, you took that, too," "Inn for us, villas for them," "The Easterner has awakened. Now, he will look after his rights," "Rights are not given, but taken," and so on. What was important about the Eastern Meetings is that for the first time in the history of the Turkish Republic, a legal party was able to mobilize so many Kurds and ask for egalitarian income distribution between the regions. Although the word "Kurd" was not mentioned at the meetings, the problems of Easterners' were emphasized.

The formation of the Eastern Revolutionary Cultural Hearths in May 1969 stands as the first important legal step of the Kurdish mobilization in the history of Turkish Republic. However, note that even the title of the organization indicates that it brings together the people of the "East," and does not necessarily refer to the Kurds. "The founding objectives of the ERCHs were: (a) to encourage Kurdish university students to engage in cultural activities, and generate material solidarity among them, (b) to destroy all the racist-chauvinist ideologies of Turkey, and mobilize Kurds within the democratic and revolutionary institutions that struggle for the brotherhood and equality of nations" (STMA, 1988, p. 2119).

What is important to note about the ERCH is that it mobilized a significant number of Kurds, especially the youth. Barkey and Fuller (1998) argue that this young generation replaced the old one, "whose traditional ties limited its rebellious temptations," with "one raised with all the symbols of nation and state" (p. 15). The perspectives of the ERCH were reflected in the WPT so successfully that it led to the resolution regarding the existence of the Kurds in the eastern part of the country in the party's Fourth Grand Assembly in 1970. However, this resolution also paved the way for the banning of both the WPT and the ERCHs by the military memorandum of March 12, 1971.

The memorandum brought very strict restrictions on Kurdish rights. The court decision concerning the ban of the ERCHs argued that they were closed down because of high treason. The attorneys also claimed that

> Kurdish, rather than being a language, is a bunch of words (…) The Kurdish language does not actually belong to an existing or historical entity because it has been proven that Kurds come from Turkish descent (STMA, 1988, p. 2304).

With the establishment of the ERCHs, the Kurds learned to engage in political issues and to voice their demands through legal channels. However, because of the short-lived history of the ERCHs, and the banning of most of the leftist political parties and institutions in 1971, Kurdish mobilization found different paths in many illegal leftist organizations during the 1970s.

With the 1971 memorandum, most political parties as well as syndicates, associations, and trade unions were banned from the political scene and their leaders were put in prison. The members of the ERCHs were charged with training "militants who believed in Kurdism, to spread the argument that there is an independent Kurdish race, and to help establish an independent Kurdistan" (*Devrimci Doğu Kültür Ocakları: Dava Dosyası 1*, 1975, p. 25). The memorandum also restricted the rights of many associations granted by the 1961 Constitution. From 1971 to 1974 Kurdish mobilization was once again silenced. Many leaders were captured, and the state controlled a large segment of political life. The 1974 general amnesty granted by the coalition government formed after the transition period following the 1971 memorandum brought these leaders back into the political arena; however, this time, they mostly became part of illegal political groups.

During the mid-1970s, a highly politicized political system developed between extreme right and left groups. Within this environment, different illegal Kurdish groups emerged; while all were in the leftist camp, they had different political perspectives. McDowall (1997) argues that Kurdish nationalism was revived by "economic deprivation, social injustice and physical displacement as well as ideas of ethnic identity, all of which combined in the 1970s to create the conditions for revolt" (p. 402).

The 1970s are important for Kurdish mobilization since those years include the emergence of illegal Kurdish organizations, which are separate from similarly banned Turkish leftist groups, and more importantly, the emergence of the PKK as a political entity. Even though the discourse of these organizations was highly revolutionary, for the first time in Turkish Republican history, Kurdish nationalist demands were explicated, and Kurdish appeared in the names of these groups (e.g., *Yekitiya Proleterya Kurdistan – Kawa* (Kurdistan Proletarian Union), *Rızgari* (Kurdistan Independence Movement), etc.), after it was first used by an illegal political party *Türkiye Kürdistan Demokrat Partisi – TKDP* (Kurdistan Democrat Party of Turkey) in 1965.

Devrimci Demokratik Kültür Dernekleri (Revolutionary Democratic Cultural Associations – hereafter the RDCAs), which were founded in 1974 in Ankara and Istanbul, are worth mentioning in this regard. The RDCAs, in their monthly magazines, argued that they were following the paths of the ERCHs, which were banned by the "anti-democratic regime of the March 12th [1971]," and emerged when "there was a reawakening among the students after the relaxation of the regime's strict measures" (*Devrimci Demokrat Gençlik-DDG*, 1978, p. 8). These associations have largely been dominated by students, who were devoted to the defeat of "imperialism, colonialism, neo-colonialism and racism" (DDG, 1978, p. 9). They were successful in leading a great number of Kurds into the streets, and getting them involved in political life, through either conventional or unconventional participation. This resulted in the most successful Kurdish illegal mobilization ever: the PKK. Because of their active role in Kurdish mobilization, the functions of the RDCAs were under strict state control in the late-1970s, and they were eventually closed down by the 1980 military coup d'état. The September 12, 1980 coup d'état was a result of extreme ideological polarization of the society, coupled with the election laws, which prevented any single party from attaining a majority in the parliament, resulting in the inability of rapidly changing governments to respond to the increasing violence. It led to the arrest of hundreds of thousands and five hundred people receiving the death penalty. The military junta also imposed martial law and stripped many people of their political rights. Even though it returned the government to civilian hands within two years, the 1982 Constitution it prepared is still in effect and remains one of the important political barriers for the recognition of Kurds as a culturally distinct group.

4 Partiya Karkerên Kurdistan (PKK) and the "Kurdish Question"

Among all the Kurdish illegal organizations, perhaps the most important was the PKK, which was founded by Abdullah Öcalan and his friends in Ankara, during his university years at *Ankara Üniversitesi Siyasal Bilimler Fakültesi* (the Faculty of Political Science at Ankara University). Before the organization came into being in 1977, this group had prepared a document entitled "The Path of Kurdish Revolution," which argued that the Kurdish-populated regions of Turkey were colonies. They also argued that the colonization was enforced by Kurdish feudalists and bourgeoisie, who chose to collaborate with the Turkish ruling classes. According to Öcalan and his friends, this was why Kurds should lead a Marxist-Leninist revolution to create an independent Kurdistan. The document later became the program of the PKK (Kirişçi, 1998).

The emergence of the PKK as an armed force occurred in a period just after the military coup of September 12, 1980, which had silenced Kurdish mobilization, along with all sorts of non-Kurdish political mobilization. The 1980 coup d'état preceded a martial law regime and strict restrictions on the right to form associations. Within this environment, the regime paradoxically paved the way for the PKK's greater mobilization in the following years (Kutschera, 1994). The PKK launched its first open attack on the Turkish authorities with an armed assault on gendarme garrisons in 1984. Since then the conflict has taken many lives. There are no exact statistics on the number of causalities that the conflict has caused. However, most scholars and journalists estimate the number to be around 30,000–40,000.

From 1984 to the early 1990s, Turkey's "Kurdish question" started to attract increasing attention from both Turkish and international media and political circles. Yet, it is in the early 1990s that the issue acquired high priority as a consequence of escalating PKK attacks, on the one hand, and harsher state responses, on the other. When the conflict re-emerged with the PKK's separatist goals in the 1980s, it was perceived by many state officials as "terrorism," first, and an "underdevelopment," problem later on. It was common practice to refer to the Kurds as "Mountain Turks" in the 1980s. It took almost two decades for state officials to come to terms with the fact that Kurds do exist and this problem is also one that demands recognition of Kurds as a distinct group in Turkey.

The armed conflict peaked in the mid-1990s, when human rights abuses, torture, and disappearances were reported by NGOs in the region and state offices,[11] and the public use of Kurdish language was banned. Furthermore, around a million Kurd were forced to migrate (HÜNEE, 2006) to other cities either as a result of the evacuation of villages by the military, allowed by the 1987 emergency rule; or because of the PKK's pressure on villagers who did not support the PKK to abandon their villages; or due to the insecurity resulting from being caught between the PKK and Turkish security forces (Kirişçi, 1998).

The armed conflict started to de-escalate when the PKK leader Öcalan was captured by the Turkish National Intelligence Organization in Nairobi, Kenya, in February 1999. That year was also significant because of EU's acceptance of Turkey as a candidate to the Union. The negative peace that came with Öcalan's imprisonment and the PKK's decision of "inaction," which lasted until mid-2004, laid the fertile foundation for democratic reforms.

5 Post-1999: A New Era?

Between 1999 and 2004, the PKK declared a one-sided ceasefire, which it broke on June 1, 2004. However, this negative peace period was

[11] According to a report prepared by the Ministry of Justice on July 29, 2003, for example, the number of people taken into custody by the Diyarbakir State Security Courts and State Attorney in Diyarbakir, the biggest Kurdish city, during the OHAL regime was 48,697. According to the President of the Diyarbakir Bar Association, around 800 state officers have been expelled from the region and none of them have been able to file complaints against the state on the issue (interview, Diyarbakir, February 11th 2004). OHAL has also restricted many public activities. According to Tanrıkulu and Yavuz (2005), many art activities such as festivals, concerts, and public screening of movies have been restricted.

the signal that a new era was opening in Turkey's Kurdish Question. As part of harmonizing its laws with European norms in the process of adopting European Union (EU) Common Law, the Grand National Assembly of Turkey has accepted broadcasting in other mother tongues besides Turkish and has eased restrictions on languages other than Turkish, has abolished the death penalty, and has signed international treaties protecting the economic, social, cultural, and political rights of its citizens (see Çelik, 2005 for a detailed analysis of legal changes). Even though such changes were not made to deal with the issues underlying the Kurdish Question, they indirectly affected it. Such constitutional guarantees were provided reluctantly and slowly; yet they were crucial for leaving behind a period that had to a certain extent neglected the problems of the Kurds. Interviews conducted by the author with Kurds and Kurdish NGOs revealed that these steps were perceived by many Kurds as insincere attempts by the Turkish state that did not address the demands of Kurdish citizens. They were seen instead as an effort to prove to the EU that Turkey could democratize (Çelik & Rumelili, 2006).

In a speech delivered in Diyarbakır, the most important city for Kurds in Southeast Anatolia, on August 12, 2005, Prime Minister Erdoğan stated that "the Kurdish Question is everyone's problem, especially mine. Disregarding the mistakes made in the past is not an attribute of big states. The solution lies in providing more democracy, citizen rights and welfare" (*Radikal* 12/08/2005). Erdogan's speech, which stressed the existence of the Kurdish question and offered citizenship rather than "Turkish identity" as a supra-identity for both the Kurds and Turks, raised the hopes of Kurds for the democratic resolution of the issue for a short while. However, his emphases on the security of the state in his later speeches and the resort to military means since 2007 have diminished this hope. Such dissatisfaction and loss of hope on the side of the Kurds led to an escalation of violence. From mid-2004 to mid-2009, sporadic hostilities in the conflict-affected areas, as well as the spread of violence to the cities of western Turkey, hampered any attempt at bringing about peace. The conflict also became internationalized again[12] in late 2007 with the Turkish army's bombings of PKK camps within the territory of Northern Iraq. With the intensification of violence in the post-2004 period, the State's emphasis has been on the security and the territorial integrity of the country, whereas the main dissatisfaction of the different Kurdish groups has been with what can be summarized as the slow unwilling moves of the State in the EU integration process to grant more rights to the Kurds as a group.

6 Towards Resolving the Conflict?

Year 2009 marks another important turning point in the state's position towards the conflict. TRT-6, a TV channel owned by the Turkish state initiated broadcasting in Kurdish on January 1, 2009. While this was not the first case of Kurdish broadcasting, it was more significant than the earlier attempt in 2004. Following the signing of the National Program for the Adoption of the EU Common Law on March 8, 2001, the government initiated several reform packages. One of government's reform packages in 2004 included allowing the teaching of Kurdish (and other mother tongues and accents) in private courses and broadcasting in Kurdish; however, the state still retained the right to exercise strict control in such areas. For example, Kurdish TV programs could only be broadcasted on state television and were limited in content. The first private Kurdish courses opened their doors to students in April 2004 in the two Kurdish-populated cities in the regions affected by the conflict. In June 2004, the first Kurdish broadcast appeared on Turkish state

[12] The mass influx of Iraqi Kurds into Turkey in the early 1990s can be considered the initial internationalization of the Kurdish Question. World attention focused on the Kurds at the end of the Persian Gulf War in 1991 and continued throughout the 1990s as there were increasing levels of forced migration from the Kurdish-populated regions of eastern and southeastern Anatolia. Although this event was a spillover effect of what has happened in Iraq, the "Kurds" as a group subsequently became recognized in the international arena.

television. Even though this first attempt was seen as insincere and inadequate by many Kurds, it was the first step in overcoming the problems in making Kurdish language more public. Yet, it is the changes in 2009 that made the Kurdish broadcasting a reality in Turkey.

The positive developments continued throughout 2009, and for the first time in the history of the Republic, a government claimed to be initiating an extensive peace process to address the conflict. However, even though the project was commenced as the "Kurdish Initiative," meaning designed to address solely the Kurdish Question, it came to be referred to as the "Democratic Initiative," and, lastly, the "National Union and Brotherhood Project." These changes in names signify the government's confusion, and some desperation, in dealing with a complex and deep-rooted problem. Announced as the Kurdish Initiative by the Ministry of Interior in July 29, 2009, these attempts to resolve the conflict aimed at addressing several core problems. The proposal was believed to include greater cultural rights for Kurds (excluding teaching in Kurdish), some form of local autonomy, and incentives to demobilize and reintegrate the PKK fighters into the society. Such changes require first and foremost the changing of the 1982 Constitution, a byproduct of the 1980 coup d'état. Since it is regarded as undemocratic and opposed by many civil society groups and there is a need to comply with the EU's Copenhagen Standards,[13] several modifications have been made to it since 2001. The initiative of the ruling party, *Adalet ve Kalkınma Partisi* (Justice and Development Party, hereafter the AKP), aimed at "ending terrorism," and "advancing democracy"; however, while it has the will to address the conflict, it is still unclear as to what steps need to be taken. However, after mid-2010, with the increasing violence from both sides, even this will is being questioned by many Kurds.

After discussing the "initiative" in the National Assembly on November 13, 2009, the AKP published a report on what this new policy means. In its publication about the National Unity and Brotherhood Project (AKP, 2010) and in the prime minister's public speeches, the government claimed to address the following issues:

- Allowing the use of Kurdish in prisons. This was legalized by the government in the first week of November 2009.
- Reintegrating PKK members. The government aims to reintegrate PKK members who have not participated in any armed confrontation with the Turkish military. However, this objective does not have any concrete plan, and was not pronounced by the government in clear terms.
- Reintegrating the people in the Makhmour Refugee Camp, in cooperation with the Kurdish autonomous region administration in Northern Iraq: During the armed conflict in the 1990s, approximately 12,000 Kurds crossed the Turkish border into Iraq. Approximately 9,000 of these settled in the Makhmour Refugee Camp; 2,600 of them returned to Turkey in the following years (UNHCR, 2004). The return of the rest of the refugees was discussed extensively at the beginning of the initiative, but it was not mentioned in the AKP's 2010 publication. It might be due to the fact that people in the Makhmour Camp stated that they will not return to Turkey unless they believe that Turkey has fully been democratized and a general amnesty is granted to members of the PKK.
- Bringing prisons up to EU standards and closing the Diyarbakır Prison.[14]
- Rehabilitating minors involved in "terrorist acts." Especially following the violent uprisings in the funerals of several PKK members in Diyarbakır (April 2006) and increased clashes between the PKK and the Turkish army (since summer 2006), several minors in the big cities of the southeast Anatolia participated in

[13] According to the Copenhagen Criteria, all EU candidate states must meet several standards and criteria. Among them were political criteria indirectly affecting the issues related to the Kurdish Question. Of the political standards, respect for the principle of the rule of law and for minority rights serves as a crucial part of the basis of compliance.

[14] Diyarbakir is the most populous Kurdish city. Diyarbakir prison became a symbol of anti-1980 coup d'état because of human rights abuses that took place during the coup d'état and the military rule following it.

throwing stones at the Turkish security forces. These minors were sent to adult prisons after receiving long sentences in anti-terrorist courts. A bill on these minors passed by parliament on July 21, 2010. According to the new law, minors will no longer be tried at high criminal courts; those charged with violating the Law on Meeting and Demonstrations will not face prison terms if they do not use a weapon, a knife, or explosives against the security forces, and they will serve their sentence at institutes of education or doing community service.

- Allowing other channels besides the state-owned TRT to have continuous Kurdish broadcasting.
- Empowering the local administrations (decentralization). Such proposals have been discussed in public since the time of the eighth President Turgut Özal. However, up to now, there has been no concrete plan for carrying this out in a country with an historically strong unitary character. Moreover, the government has not pronounced plans for decentralization plans even though in June 2010, 99 pro-Kurdish *Barış ve Demokrasi Partisi* (Peace and Democracy Party, hereafter the BDP)[15] mayors in the southeast Anatolia declared that they would work toward establishing some sort of autonomy in their regions.
- Strengthening the right of freedom of expression. This mostly aims at removing Article 216 of the Turkish Criminal Code, which penalizes those "instigating a group of people having different social class, race, religion, sect or region to hatred or hostility against another group of people in a way that is dangerous for public security."
- Allowing the teaching of Kurdish language as an elective course in schools and teaching different languages and dialects in private institutions.
- Allowing the formation of Kurdish institutes and/or Kurdish Literature departments in universities.
- Allowing the use of the Kurdish language during election campaigns, which requires changing the election law. Another factor limiting representation of the Kurds in the Turkish National Assembly is the requirement that a political party receive 10% of the national vote to be eligible to enter parliament. Even though pro-Kurdish parties can obtain up to 65% of the local votes in the small cities of eastern Anatolia, they are not represented in parliament because they cannot reach this national bar. The government initiative does not address this problem, however.
- Easing the strict road and plateau controls in eastern and southeastern Anatolia to make life easier for the inhabitants. Put in effect, this can also increase the return of the Kurdish IDPs.
- Forming "Fight Against Discrimination Commissions," which would inspect the public and private sectors for possible discrimination cases. There will also be an independent civic Human Rights Commission to control human rights abuses throughout the country, including but not limited to human rights abuses of the village guards and security forces in the southeast.
- Renaming the places of former "locally-named" places. These include not only the villages that formerly had Kurdish names, but also those with other languages, such as Armenian, Arabic, and Circassian all around Turkey. According to a recent study (*Mynet*, 2009), the names of around 28,000 places have been changed since 1940 (*Hurriyet* November 13–14, 2009; AKP, 2010).

---

[15] Another important issue concerning Kurdish political representation is the formation of Kurdish political parties. According to the Articles 12 and 83 of the Law on Political Parties, put in effect in 2005, forming a political party based on ethnic, racial, and religious lines is unconstitutional (TBMM, 2005). Based on these articles, several pro-Kurdish political parties were banned. The BDP is the sixth party whose political ideology can be considered as pro-Kurdish. **The first pro-Kurdish party, HEP (Halkın Emek Partisi-**People's Labor Party), was founded in June 1990 by the Kurdish MPs who were expelled from the Social Democratic Party (SHP) after their participation in an International Conference held on the Kurdish Question in Paris. After HEP's closure by the Constitutional Court, the three consecutive pro-Kurdish parties, namely DEP (Demokrasi Partisi-Democracy Party), ÖZDEP (Özgürlük ve Demokrasi Partisi-Freedom and Democracy Party), and DEHAP (Demokratik Halk Partisi- Democractic Society Party) shared the same fate. After the inception of the Kurdish initiative the DTP was closed down by the Constitutional Court and its members, except for its two leaders, formed the new party, the BDP, at the end of 2009.

As seen by these issues and argued by Kemal Kirişçi (2008), it is easier to discuss the state's "redlines," reflecting its understanding of what not to include in this initiative: "transformation from a unitary state to a federal one," "territorial autonomy," or acceptance of Kurdish as an official language (p. 7). In its publication on the initiative, the government also claimed that amnesty for Öcalan or his re-trial is out of question (AKP, 2010).

The government's will to address the issues around the conflict was welcomed by the pro-Kurdish party of that time, the *Demokratik Toplum Partisi* (Democratic Society Party, hereafter the DTP) and the PKK even before the specific issues of the initiative were known. To show that they also support peace initiatives, the PKK sent to Turkey a "Peace Group" composed of some PKK members who had not joined in any armed confrontation with the Turkish army and some refugees from the Makhmour Camp in Northern Iraq. Even though this was an attempt on the part of the radical Kurds to "welcome peace," enthusiastic celebrations on the border between Iraq and Turkey by Kurds and the release of these returnees, despite Article 220 of the Turkish Criminal Code, which would have otherwise penalized them, elicited harsh reactions by the non-Kurds in the Turkish society. Since this welcoming by the state officers led to severe opposition to the AKP government, state officials later brought up cases against the members of the Peace Group, which resulted in the return of 20 out of 34 PKK members to Northern Iraq in July 2010. For many, this was a sign that the new positive era in Kurdish Question has ended once again.

Even though most Kurdish politicians, intellectuals, and ordinary Kurds appear to have been supporting these possible reforms, the PKK and some Kurdish members of parliament, in fact, had a different understanding of how peace should be achieved. According to an interview with higher-ranking PKK officers, they wanted the government to take Öcalan as the "addressee" of this negotiation process and Kurdish to be an official language along with Turkish (Çongar, 2008). After the contours of the initiative started to be discussed by the Turkish public, the PKK also released its requests. The "Peace Group," after its arrival in Turkey, made the letters from the PKK available to the journalists. These requests were: disclosing Öcalan's road map[16] to the people and along with possible negotiators, halting military operations, allowing freedom of the Kurdish language, developing democratic social organizations and political representation associated with Kurdish identity, abolishing the village guards system and bringing an end to the Turkish military's "special operations" in the region, and preparing a new democratic constitution. They requested that these be contingent upon a real democratization of Turkey and the Kurdish people's free will. They should be reached by dialogue and discussion and allowing Kurds to lead a free and equal life within the society on the basis of their Kurdish identity – under constitutional guarantees, as a part of the democratic nation of Turkey (*Radikal* 10/20/2009).

However, some of these demands (e.g., taking Öcalan as the addressee) can possibly lead to conflict escalation. Recent polls show that the "Kurdish initiative," even when it was not clear exactly what it meant, was supported by 48.1% of the population (36.4% did not support it and 15.5% had no opinion). However, a majority of the population is also afraid that the Kurds want a separate state (64.4%), and that Öcalan and the PKK do not represent the Kurds (50.1%) (SETA, 2009). Another study surveying only Kurds and Zazas[17] found that while the Kurds who had voted for DTP in the 2007 national elections were less willing to live together with Turks (62.9%) compared to those who voted for other parties

[16] The imprisoned PKK leader put forth his road map, that is, his understanding of how Kurdish Question should be addressed by the Turkish state, to the prison prosecutor on August 20, 2009. State representatives did not disclose the content of the letter. Öcalan also asked his lawyers to send the text to the European Court of Justice, which takes some time (*Bianet* 08/27/2009).

[17] Zazas are differentiated from Kırmanji-speaking Kurds based on the language they use. Whereas most Kurds speak Kırmanji, Zazas use Zazaki. There are debates among scholars as to whether Zazas are an ethnic group by themselves or a sub-group of Kurds. This study did not engage in these discussions, and regarded Zazas as part of the Kurdish culture.

(84.8%), overall, Kurds do not want a separate state. The same study also revealed that only around 19.77% of the population believes that Öcalan should be released (BILGESAM, 2009).[18]

However, as violence started to spiral once again in 2010 and the government was unable to come up with concrete plans for peace, the support for the initiative started to decrease. According to a study done by the A&G Research Institute, the support in June 2009 for resolving the Kurdish Question through non-violent means dropped drastically over the months to follow (from 69% in June to 46% in August and to 31% in November) (A&G as cited in *Taraf* 26/01/2010). Another study reached interesting conclusions concerning the performance of the government and how society sees the solution to the Kurdish Question. According to this study, compared to 2009, there was growing hope among Turkish citizens that the issue of "terrorism" could be resolved through peaceful means (increase from 52.3% in 2009 to 64.5% in 2010). However, in contrast, only 30.9% labeled government performance in "terrorism" as "good" and 30.1% saw government policies as the biggest reason for "terrorism" (Baybars Hawks, 2010). Besides these contradictions, it is also important to note how social science rhetoric on the issue is still confused in terminology: ""the initiative," "terrorism," "support for non-violent means," "support for peace" are all used to refer to the same phenomenon, which is in fact, complex, multi-layered, and deep-rooted.

Even though, the so-called Kurdish initiative was welcomed by the Kurds and most Turks [except for some ardent supporters of the opposition parties *Cumhuriyet Halk Partisi* (CHP) and *Milliyetçi Hareket Partisi* (MHP)], its popularity decreased as the government did not clarify its contents, all the while silencing the legal Kurdish voices. The recent operation against the elected Kurds in the southeast, in particular, led to increasing stone-throwing incidents by Kurdish children and PKK attacks on Turkish military bases. An indictment completed in June 2010 charged 150 people, including 11 BDP mayors from Southeast Anatolia, with membership in the illegal Kurdish Communities Union (KCK), the allegedly underground urban organization of the PKK (*Hürriyet*, 2010).

Besides all these shortcomings, however, the most important consequence of this recent initiative has been the positive atmosphere it created and the hope for a common future in the society. Yet, at the same time, many fear that if this chance of resolving the conflict is missed, social polarization of Kurds and Turks might result. Contrary to what many scholars and Turks argue, the Kurdish Question is not only a conflict between the state and the Kurdish separatists. As asserted by Çelik and Blum (2007), "it is possible to identify three fault lines along which the Kurdish conflict in Turkey plays out. At one level, the conflict is between the Turkish state and an ethnic minority. At another level, the conflict is between the Turkish state and an insurgent group, the PKK. At a third level, the conflict exists in the form of social tension between Turks and Kurds throughout Turkey, especially in the bigger cities in western Turkey" (p. 65). If not recognized by the policymakers, this last level is the least addressed and hardest to deal with. In fact, there have been studies addressing this possible social polarization. A KONDA study in June 2010 shows that even though many Turkish citizens support the legal reforms safeguarding Kurdish culture, they are not as liberal when it comes to welcoming different ethnicities into their close circles. Another striking finding is the dominance of Sevres Paranoia in the ordinary Turkish citizens' understanding of the issue. Almost three quarters of the people surveyed believed that Kurdish Question is the result of foreign countries' provocation and more than half (around 54.7%) believed that Kurds want a separate state (KONDA, 2010), even though other studies show the contrary (BİLGESAM, 2009).

With the government's new initiative, the tension that had been rising between the Kurds and Turks since the mid-2007 has started to give way to a

[18] However, these findings should be taken with a grain of salt since answering questions about demands for separation and Öcalan is still not easy especially in survey studies where the interviewer is not known to the respondent.

possible peaceful coexistence. As pointed out by a renowned Turkish journalist, Cengiz Çandar, at a meeting bringing together Kurds and Turks of different political ideologies for the first time, some 10 years ago, it was very difficult to see together an imprisoned Kurdish parliamentarian (Hatip Dicle), an ex-PKK member who had returned Turkey from abroad as a gesture of showing PKK's commitment to peace in 1999 and imprisoned afterwards (Seydi Fırat) and an ex-deputy secretary of the Turkish National Intelligence Organization (Cevat Öneş). However, it is hard to see such positive developments at the societal level since such long-lasting conflicts leave a legacy of mistrust and pain, which need time to heal. That is also why the initiative also attracted the reactions of the nationalists on each side, which assumed the form of violent urban unrest in several cities of Turkey in late 2009 and mid-2010.

7 Conclusion

From the foundation of the Turkish Republic to the mid-1980s, official Turkish discourse did not recognize the Kurds as an ethnic group in Turkey. When the "Kurdish Question" became publicized on Turkish political scenes through the PKK's activities, many state officials perceived the conflict as a "terrorist act," the aim of which was to carve out an independent Kurdistan within the territories of the Turkish state. The Turkish state refused to consider the PKK as the legitimate "other" in the conflict and treated its Kurdish population as part of its whole Turkish citizen population. That is why the "Kurdish Question" was mostly considered in terms of "terrorism" or, at best," a "southeast underdevelopment problem" by state officials and most of the rest of Turkish society.

The Kurdish Question, even though having unique historical reasons, shares some commonalities with other conflicts around the world. Most importantly, Kurdish and Turkish nationalisms have followed similar dominant ideologies and political movements. Kurdish nationalism in the 1960s and 1970s adopted a socialist discourse vis-à-vis the Turkish state's political and economic dominance. These reactions later took the form of asking for cultural rights and constitutional guarantees in the late 1990s and 2000s commensurate with the increasing globalization of human rights all around the world (Çelik, 2005). Turkish nationalism, on the other hand, perceived the Kurdish Question "mostly in terms of a fatal rivalry between the backward, premodern and tribal past and the prosperous present in the first half of the century," and

> "in terms of a tension between the peripheral economy and national market in the fifties and sixties. In the 1970s, the Kurdish unrest was believed to be a product of communist incitement. Despite this impurity in perception, one thing has remained nearly unchanged for Turkish nationalism: Kurds could become Turkish. In other words, Turkish nationalism of the republican era has principally perceived Kurds as future-Turks. (Yeğen, 2007, p. 119).

Today, for the first time in the history of the Turkish Republic, the Kurdish Question is being discussed along all of its dimensions, even though possible solutions might not necessarily address all issues. Yet, at the same time, this issue is also regarded as a "democratization problem," which can be tackled through legal reforms and constitutional changes by the government. Even though the conflict has historically pitted the state against an ethnic group, the long-lived war in the southeast and its spillover effects in the big cities have also led to a societal polarization in almost all cities in Turkey. The social polarization dimension of the conflict is the most neglected side of the issue. Presenting cases like the Kurdish Question as a problem of "terrorism" mostly legitimizes the acts of governments in other countries as well. However, long-lived violent conflicts leave a legacy of mistrust between the citizens and states but most importantly among different strata in the society. Whereas most Kurds feel a lack of justice, humiliation, and silencing, many Turks feel afraid (that "their land" will be taken away), angry (that "terrorism" took away their sons), and proud (to be a "Turk" for centuries). These feelings need to address "each other" and be opened up to dialogue. It is only when such conflicting claims as justice, recognition of and respect to identity, some sort of self-governance, re-constitution of trust towards the state and recognition of past mistakes on the part of the Kurds meet the demands of the Turks who ask for guarantees that Kurds will not partition the country and will use "Turkish citizenship" as an umbrella identity for peaceful co-existence. Undertaking this task, first and foremost, requires "communalization" of the pains that the war caused and producing a common language.[19]

It is essential to note that in the last 80 years, the Turkish state has moved from denial of the existence of Kurds to the recognition of cultural differences and a commitment to respect their culture. However, peaceful coexistence of people requires addressing social polarization and mistrust. There is a need for Turks, Kurds, and other groups in Turkey to come together and discuss what brings them under the same roof and whether their projection of future is commensurate. Even though, for the first time, Turkey's membership acceptance to the EU increased the hopes of many for peaceful existence in a democratic Turkey, the problems of mistrust, social polarization between Kurds and Turks, and nonrecognition of past mistakes still stand as barriers to such a shared future. Violent events between Kurds and Turks in the big cities of western Turkey following the discussions of the Kurdish Initiative can be presented as evidence of such problems. The violent events between the Turks and Kurds in the two towns in the north and south of the country in July 2010 worried all those who believed in the positive atmosphere that the Kurdish initiative has set. To address the multidimensional nature of the conflict, various strategies are needed. Whereas macro changes such as constitutional and legal reforms can guarantee the political, social, and legal rights of the Kurds and their culture, there is also a need for micro changes to address the long animosity between the Kurds, Turks, and the state. Track II workshops consisting of intergroup dialogues, joint projects, and other strategies can be designed to target specific problematic neighborhoods in the larger cities. The history of violence also creates the needs for programs, such as trauma healing, and individual skill-building that can be designed to support victims and perpetrators of violence, to encourage healing, to foster individual reconciliation and bridge between the state and the Kurdish citizens (Çelik and Blum, 2007). Social change towards peaceful co-existence is a long and a rough road, and there will always be spoilers and loss of hope on the journey to peace.

[19] One of the barriers of dialogue between the Kurds and the Turks is the conflicting language they use in describing their pains and referring to their history. The simplest example is that many Kurds call the deceased PKK militants "martyrs," whereas for Turks martyrs are the soldiers and security forces who die during the "fight against terrorism."

Appendix: Ethnopolitical Conflict in Turkey Timeline

1984 – Kurdistan Workers' Party (PKK) launches separatist guerrilla war in southeast Turkey.

1987 – Turkey applies for full European Economic Community (EEC) membership.

1990 – Turkey allows US-led coalition against Iraq to launch air strikes from Turkish bases.

1992 – 20,000 Turkish troops enter Kurdish safe havens in Iraq in anti-PKK operation.

1995 – Major military offensive launched against the Kurds in northern Iraq, involving some 35,000 Turkish troops.

1995 – Turkey enters European Union (EU) customs union.

October 1998 – Abdullah Öcalan, leader of the PKK, leaves his base in Syria after Turkey threatens to invade Syria.

February 1999 – PKK leader Abdullah Öcalan captured in Kenya.

July 1999 – Öcalan receives death sentence, later commuted to life imprisonment.

August 2002 – Turkish Parliament approves reforms aimed at securing EU membership. Death sentence to be abolished except in times of war and bans on Kurdish education, broadcasting to be lifted.

January 2004 – Turkey signs protocol banning death penalty in all circumstances, a move welcomed in EU circles

May 2004 – PKK says it plans to end a ceasefire because of what it calls annihilation operations against its forces.

June 2004 – State TV broadcasts first Kurdish-language programme. Four Kurdish MPs, including former MP Leyla Zana, freed from jail.

December 2004 – EU leaders agree to open talks in 2005 on Turkey's EU accession.

April 2006 – At least a dozen people are killed in clashes between Kurdish protesters and security forces in the south-east. Several people are killed in related unrest in Istanbul.

September 30, 2006 – PKK declares a unilateral ceasefire in operations against the military.

December 2007 – Turkey launches a series of air strikes on fighters from the Kurdish PKK movement inside Iraq.

October 2008 – Trial starts of 86 suspected members of a shadowy ultra-nationalist Ergenekon group, which is accused of plotting a series of attacks and provoking a military coup against the government. Terrorist activities peak with the PKK's, killing of 17 soldiers at the Aktütün military outpost.

January 2009 – The state-run Turkish Radio and Television Corporation (TRT) launches a Kurdish-language broadcast.

February 2009 – Protesters marking the 10th anniversary of the arrest of Abdullah Öcalan, the leader of the banned Kurdish PKK movement, clash with police in south-east Turkey.

Prominent Kurdish politician Ahmet Turk defies Turkish law by giving speech to parliament in his native Kurdish. State TV cuts live broadcast, as the language is banned in parliament.

July 29, 2009 – Interior Minister Beşir Atalay announces the government's Kurdish move, vowing to solve the problem through "more freedom and more democracy."

August 1, 2009 – The government holds its first workshop to hear suggestions on the move from important intellectuals, including columnists and academics.

August 20, 2009 – Öcalan delivers his own 160-page handwritten road map to resolve the Kurdish issue through his attorneys. It is confiscated by prison officials at İmralı Island where he is being held and Öcalan criticizes the AKP for its lack of sincerity.

October 19, 2009 – A 34-person "peace group," comprising eight PKK members and 26 residents of the Makhmour refugee camp in northern Iraq, heeds a call by Öcalan and surrenders at the Habur border gate between Turkey and Iraq. The welcoming ceremony held for the group and the members' release by judges at the border spark a huge public outcry.

December 7, 2009 – Seven Turkish soldiers die in a terrorist attack in the Reşadiye district of the central province of Tokat.

December 11, 2009 – The Constitutional Court closes the pro-Kurdish *Demokratik Toplum Partisi* (DTP).

May 31, 2010 – Six soldiers are killed in a PKK attack on a Turkish naval base in İskenderun, a district of the southern province of Hatay.

June 19–20, 2010 – Twelve soldiers are killed in PKK attacks in the southeastern province of Hakkari.

June 22, 2010 – Four soldiers and one teenage civilian are killed in a bomb attack on a military bus in Istanbul's Halkalı district. A PKK-affiliated group claims responsibility.

Adapted from BBC News Online (http://news.bbc.co.uk/2/hi/europe/1023189.stm), and Hurriyet Daily News (http://www.hurriyetdailynews.com/n.php?n=from-hope-to-misery-kurdish-move8217s-journey-2010-06-22) visited on 7 July, 2010.

References

AKP. (2010). *Soruları ve Cevaplarıyla Demokratik Açılım Süreci*. Ankara: Ak Parti Tanıtım ve Medya Başkanlığı.

Andrews, P. A. (1992). *Türkiye'de Etnik Gruplar (Ethnic Groups in Turkey)*. Istanbul: Ant Yayınları.

Barkey, H., & Fuller, G. E. (1998). *Turkey's Kurdish question*. New York: Rowman & Littlefield Publishers.

Bayrbars Hawks, B. (2010). *Türkiye'nin Gündemini Belirleme Araştırması*. Istanbul: Kadir Has Üniversitesi.

Bianchi, R. (1984). *Interest groups and political development in Turkey*. Princeton, NJ: Princeton University Press.

Bianet. (2009, 20 October). *Requests of the peace groups*. Available at http://bianet.org/english/english/117731-requests-of-the-peace-groups. Accessed 25 Nov 2009.

Bianet. (2009, 27 August). *Öcalan had handed 'road map' to prison management*. Available at http://bianet.org/bianet/english/116681-ocalan-has-handed-road-map-to-prison-management. Accessed 25 Nov 2009.

BİLGESAM. (2009). *Güneydoğu Sorununun Sosyolojik Analizi: Teknik Rapor*. Ankara.

Çağaptay, S. (2007). Can the PKK renounce violence. *Middle East Quarterly, 14*(1), 45–52.

Çelik, A. B. (2005). Transnationalization of human rights and its impact on internally displaced Kurds. *Human Rights Quarterly, 27*(3), 969–996.

Çelik, A. B. (2002). *Migrating onto identity: Kurdish mobilization through associations in Istanbul*. Unpublished PhD Thesis. Binghamton University, Binghamton.

Çelik, A. B., & Blum, A. (2007). Track II interventions and the Kurdish question in turkey: An analysis using a theories of change approach. *The International Journal of Peace Studies, 12*(2), 51–81.

Çelik, A. B., & Rumelili, B. (2006). Necessary but not sufficient: The role of EU in resolving Turkey's Kurdish question and Turkish–Greek conflicts. *European Foreign Affairs Review, 11*(2), 203–222.

Chailand, G. (1993). *A people without a country*. New York: Olive Branch Press.

Commission of the European Communities. (2007). *Turkey 2007 Progress Report*. Brussels.

Çongar, Y. 2008. "Bu Savaşın Galibi Yok." *Taraf*. February 3 2008, p.10.

Council of Europe. (2006).The cultural situation of the Kurds. Available at http://assembly.coe.int/Main.asp?link=/Documents/WorkingDocs/Doc06/EDOC11006.htm. Accessed 7 July 2008.

Devrimci Demokrat Gençlik (1978). No: 7–8.

Devrimci Doğu Kültür Ocakları: Dava Dosyası 1 (1975). Ankara: Komal.

Entessar, N. (1992). *Kurdish ethnonationalism*. Boulder: Lynne Rienner.

Gunter, M. M. (1997). *The Kurds and the future of Turkey*. New York: St. Martin's Press.

Human Rights Association (IHD). (2001). *Annual Report*. Unpublished paper.

HÜNEE. (2006). *Türkiye Göç ve Yerinden Olmuş Nüfus Araştırması*, Ankara: Hacettepe Üniversitesi. Available at http://www.hips.hacettepe.edu.tr/tgyona/TGYONA_rapor.pdf. Accessed 10 Feb 2008.

Hürriyet. (2010). Indictment against illegal Kurdish organization completed 8 June, 2010. Available at http://www.hurriyetdailynews.com/n.php?n=indicment-against-illegal-kurdish-organization-completed-2010-06-08. Accessed 19 July 2010.

Internet Haber. (2008). Available at http://www.internethaber.com/news_detail.php?id=128474. Accessed 18 Feb 2008.

Izady M. R. (1992). Kurds: A Concise Handbook. London: Taylor & Francis.

Kieser, H. (Ed.). (2006). *Turkey beyond nationalism: Towards post-nationalist identities*. London: I.B. Tauris.

Kirişçi, K. (1998). Turkey. In J. Hampton (Ed.), *Internally displaced people: A global survey* (pp. 197–200). London: Earthscan Publications.

Kirişçi, K. (2008). *Revisiting Turkey's Kurdish problem discussion paper Series- 2008/1*, EDAM, p. 5. Accessed online at http://www.edam.org.tr on 28 Feb 2008.

Kirişçi, K., & Winrow, G. (1997). *A translation of the Kurdish question and Turkey: An example of a trans-state ethnic conflict*. London: Frank Cass.

KONDA. (2010). *Siyasette ve Toplumda Kutuplaşma*. İstanbul: KONDA.

Kramer, H. (2000). *A changing Turkey: The challenge to Europe and the United States*. Washington, DC: Brookings Institute Press.

Kurban, D. & Çelik, A.B. & Yükseker, D. (2006). *Overcoming a Legacy of Mistrust: Towards Reconciliation Between the State and the Displaced*, Istanbul: TESEV and IDMC. Available at <http://www.internal-displacement.org>.

Kurban, D., Yükseker, D., Çelik, A. B., Ünalan, T., & Aker, A. T. (2007). *Confronting forced migration: Post-displacement restitution of citizenship rights in Turkey*. Istanbul: TESEV.

Kutschera, Chris (1994). "Mad Dreams of Independence: The Kurds of Turkey and the PKK", Middle East Report, July-August.

MacDonald, C. G. 1993. "The Kurds." In The Ethnic Dimension in International Relation, ed. B. Schechterman and M. Slann. Westport C.T. and London: Praeger.

McDowall, D. (1997). *A modern history of the Kurds*. London: I. B. Tauris.

McKiernan, K. (1999). Turkey's war on the Kurds. *Bulletin of the Atomic Scientists, 55*(2), 26–37.

Mynet. (2009). *Kaç Yerin İsmi Değişti?* Available at http://haber.mynet.com/detay/guncel/kac-yerin-ismi-degistirildi/465345. Accessed 6 July 2008.

Neyzi, L. (1999). "Gülümser's Story: Life History Narratives, Memory and Belonging in Turkey", *New Perspectives on Turkey* 20: 1–26.

Öcalan, A. (1999). *Statement by Abdullah Öcalan on his abduction from Kenya* on November 26, 1999. Available at http://www.hartford-hwp.com/archives/51/162.html. Accessed 13 Feb 2008.

Olson, R. (1989). *The emergence of Kurdish nationalism and the Sheikh said rebellion, 1880–1925*. Austin, TX: University of Texas Press.

Radikal. (2005). "Orhan Doğan: Öcalan Bir Gün Serbest Kalacak," 15 August, p. 6.

Radikal. (2007). *Kerkük'e karşı Diyarbakir'a karışırız*. Available at http://www.radikal.com.tr/haber.php?haberno=217846. Accessed 24 April 2008.

Radikal. (2008). *Kürt Sorunu Dizisi*. 3–7 March. Available at <http://www.radikal.com.tr>.

Sabah. **(2006). Plan Adım Adım. Available at** http://arsiv.sabah.com.tr/2006/09/29/gnd133.html. Accessed 13 Feb 2008.

Samim, A. (1987). The Left. In I. Schick & E. A. Tonak (Eds.), *Turkey in transition: New perspectives* (pp. 147–176). New York: Oxford University Press.

SETA. (2009). *Türkiye'nin Kürt Sorunu Algısı*. Ankara: SETA & Pollmark.

Sosyal Sorunları Araştırma ve Çözüm Derneği (SORAR). (2008). *SORAR 2007 PKK Workshop (Çalıştay) Raporu-PKK*. Available at http://www.sorar.org.tr/Raporlar/PKK_20071130.aspx. Accessed 13 Feb 2008.

STMA (Sosyalizm ve Toplumsal Mücadeleler Ansiklopedisi - Encylopedia of Socialism and Social Struggles). (1988). Vol.7. Istanbul: Iletisim Yayınları.

Tanrıkulu, S., & Yavuz, S. (2005). İnsan Hakları Açısından Olağanüstü Hal'in Bilânçosu. *Sosyal Bilimler Araştırma Dergisi, No:, 6*, 493–521.

Taraf. (2010). *Adil Gür: Türkle Kürdü 'din' birleştiriyor*. Available at http://www.taraf.com.tr/nese-duzel/makale-adil-gur-turkle-kurdu-din-birlestiriyor.htm. Accessed 20 July 2010.

TBMM (2005). Law on political parties. Available at http://www.tbmm.gov.tr/genser/kanun3.htm.

Tekeli, I. (1994). Involuntary Displacement and the Problem of Resettlement in Turkey from the Ottoman Empire to the Present. In S. Shami (Ed.), *Population Displacement and Resettlement: Development and Conflict in the Middle East* (pp.202-226). New York: Center for Migration Studies.

Today's Zaman. (2009). *Government to revise village guard system*, 24 September 2009. Available at http://www.todayszaman.com/tz-web/detaylar.do?load=detay&link=187841. Accessed 6 Aug 2010.

UNDP. (2007). *Reducing socio-economic differences in Southeast Anatolia*. Available at http://www.undp.org.tr/Gozlem2.aspx?WebSayfaNo=31. Accessed 9 July 2008.

United Nations High Commissioner for Refugees (UNHCR). (2004) *Briefing Paper on Voluntary Repatriation of Turkish Refugees from Northern Iraq*, 1 May.

van Bruinessen, M. (1992). *Agha, sheikh and the state*. London: Zed Books.

Yeğen, M. (2007). Turkish nationalism and the Kurdish question. *Ethnic and Racial Studies, 30*(1), 119–151.

Ethnopolitical Conflict in Turkey

11

Turkish Armenians: From Nationalism to Diaspora

Güneş N. Zeytinoğlu, Richard F. Bonnabeau, and Rana Eşkinat

Turkey/Armenians Chapter Summary

This chapter explores historical events which impacted the development of current cultural relations between the Turks and Armenians in the Republic of Turkey. Zeytinoğlu, Bonnabeau, and Eşkinat recognize that despite the available information there is no single cause or model which can be readily applied to this situation. Current sentiments of Turkish Armenians are discussed and areas through which reconciliation may finally be reached are suggested.

The authors note that under Ottoman rule, Turkey was culturally diverse and tolerant allowing freedom of religion, civil rights, privileges, and self-governance of relatively independent communities. Attention is given to the Armenian Christian minority who were perceived as inferior to the Muslims, yet generally viewed as the "loyal community." Exploration of a rising Armenian nationalism, external influences from surrounding nations, and government responses illuminates the process of a changing sentiment toward the Armenians.

Zeytinoğlu, Bonnabeau, and Eşkinat discuss years of revolution as the Armenians seek independence from the Empire and assistance from European powers. Significant law enacted during this time period resulted in the Armenian diaspora, which is credited with pivotal impact on current

G.N. Zeytinoğlu (✉)
Faculty of Administrative Science and Economics, Anadolu University, Eşkisehir, Turkey
e-mail: guneszeytinoglu@anadolu.edu.tr

R.F. Bonnabeau
Center for International Programs, State University of New York Empire State College, Saratoga Springs, New York, USA
e-mail: Richard.Bonnabeau@esc.edu

R. Eşkinat
Faculty of Law, Department of Economics, Anadolu University, Eşkisehir, Turkey
e-mail: reskinat@Anadolu.edu.tr

D. Landis and R.D. Albert (eds.), *Handbook of Ethnic Conflict: International Perspectives*, International and Cultural Psychology, DOI 10.1007/978-1-4614-0448-4_11,

cultural relations. The authors indicate reconciliation of disagreement regarding this dispersal, which some view as an attempt at genocide, has great potential to improve ethnic relations. Analysis of the successive Republic of Turkey reveals additional factors affecting cultural relations, particularly population exchange, relocation, and fusion of nationalism with Turkish cultural identity.

Interviews with Turkish Armenians are discussed along with preliminary conclusions revealing existent ethnic tensions. The authors offer additional suggestions for improving ethnic relations, particularly through resolution of the current crisis which resulted in the closing of the border between Turkey and Armenia. Open communication and government policy changes are recommended.

Cheryl Jorgensen

*ANATOLIA–1914

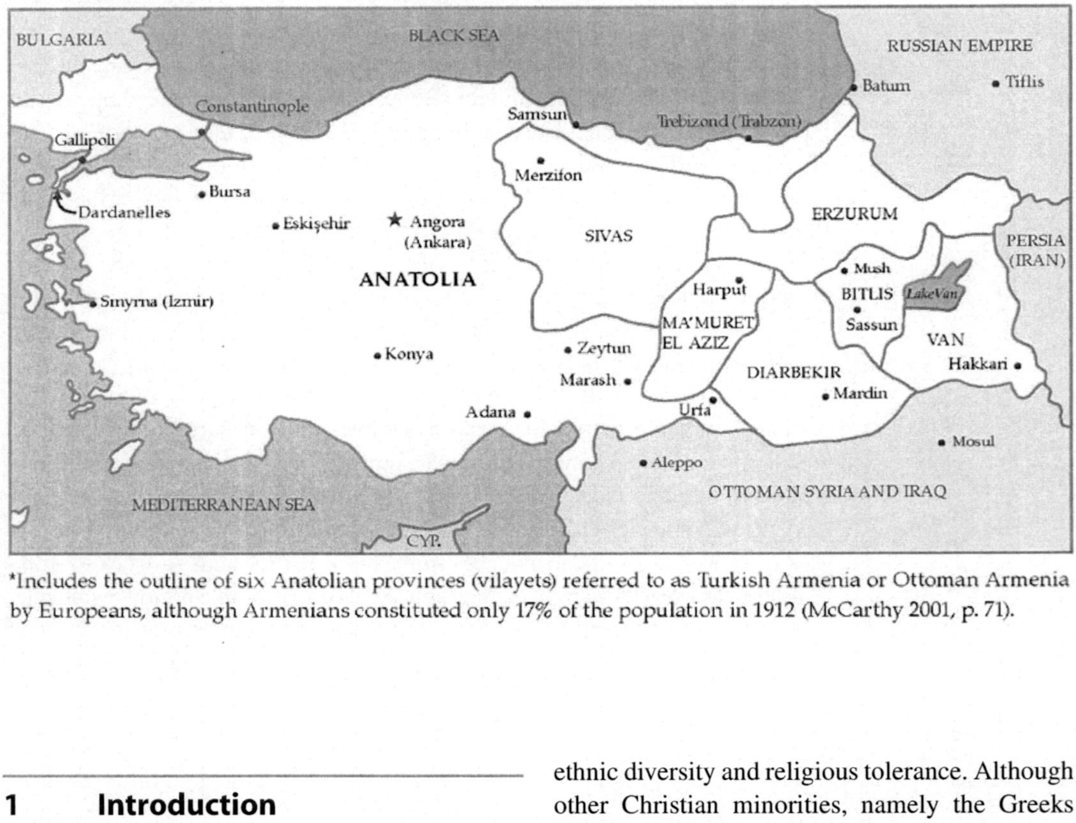

*Includes the outline of six Anatolian provinces (vilayets) referred to as Turkish Armenia or Ottoman Armenia by Europeans, although Armenians constituted only 17% of the population in 1912 (McCarthy 2001, p. 71).

1 Introduction

This chapter discusses how ethnicity informs the lives of Armenians in present-day Turkey. It is based on empirical research presented in the context of the long and complex history of Turkish and Armenian ethnic relations. It seeks to explain how severe inter-ethnic conflict between Muslims and Armenians suddenly arose in a society – the Ottoman Empire – that was remarkable for its ethnic diversity and religious tolerance. Although other Christian minorities, namely the Greeks and the Bulgarians, preceded the Armenians in rising up against the dynastic rule of the Ottomans earlier in the nineteenth century, their rebellions in that epoch of revolution have faded into history. The story of the Ottoman Armenians, beginning with the rise of the Armenian revolutionary movement in the 1880s and 1890s and ending with their tragic relocation on a massive scale from eastern Anatolia (Asia Minor) during World

War I to other parts of the Empire, has not lost its poignancy and has been kept alive by Armenians in diaspora.

This chapter should add to the understanding of a complex cultural phenomenon and offers insights about the transformational power of ideas, in this case nationalism, to suddenly, radically, and horribly alter human behavior. In this regard, the historical context should provide an appreciation for the complexity of causation and the magnitude of the conflict and its immediate consequences – the great suffering and loss of life for Armenians and Muslims alike. To this end, we draw upon a variety of sources, including the work of Armenian and Turkish scholars. Of special note in this account of ethnicity and conflict are the aggressive forays of the European Powers, especially Imperial Russia, in the waning decades of the Empire and their self-serving and destructive manipulation of nascent Armenian nationalism. The chapter further provides an overview of ethnic relations and policies as they unfold after the fall of the Ottoman Empire and the rise of the Republic of Turkey.

Given the limits of the chapter, we could not fully detail the historical context, which is both complex and controversial, but it should provide important insights with which to examine how present-day Turkish Armenians perceive their relationship to, and treatment by other Turkish citizens. This relationship is told in the voices of the people interviewed and points to the derivative and vital issues that stem from the legacy of history. The Turkish Armenian sense of belonging is compounded by this history, by the assassination of Turkish diplomats and officials in the 1970s and 1980s at the hands of Armenian terrorists, and by the continued campaign of Armenian Diaspora organizations to solicit warrants from the world community condemning Turkey for genocide and to memorialize the tragedy – efforts that have redoubled while Turkey seeks admission to the European Union. Our initial findings point to the need for further research to learn more about Turkish Armenians and the potential for reformulating existing policies.

Further, we discuss the efforts of Turkey and Armenia to establish diplomatic relations and re-open the border that was closed by Turkey in 1993 in support of Azerbaijan, a Turkic republic, at the height of the Nagorno-Karabahk conflict between Armenia and Azerbaijan. We review the rapprochement efforts by Armenia and Turkey over recent years, and at various levels of engagement that resulted in the signing of two protocols in the fall of 2009, and discuss the importance of the normalization of diplomatic relations for Turkish Armenians.

2 Current Status

2.1 Modern Turkey: At the Crossroad of Civilizations, Ethnicity, and Toleration

The Republic of Turkey, founded by Mustafa Kemal (Atatürk) and his revolutionary Republican People's Party in 1923, is confined now mostly to Anatolia and shares borders with Bulgaria, Greece, Syria, Iraq, Iran, Azerbaijan, Armenia, and Georgia. Anatolia has been at the crossroads of civilization for thousands of years. Akkadians, Assyrians, Hittites, Armenians, Greeks, Romans, Byzantines, Seljuk Turks, Crusaders, Mongols, and, subsequently, the Ottomans left their mark. In modern times, Turkey played a strategic role during the Cold War as a member of NATO and remains a bridge between Europe and the Middle East – between the Christian and Muslim worlds. Modern Turkey is a secular constitutional republic.

Though Turkey is an ethnically diverse nation, ethnic groups as a percentage of the population are no longer what they were during the reigns of Fatih Sultan Mehmet, the conqueror of Constantinople (1453), and subsequent Islamic rulers who continued adding new dominions in Southeastern Europe, Anatolia, other regions of the Middle East (Western Asia), including the Arabian Peninsula and North Africa, as well as major islands in the Aegean and Mediterranean seas. These conquests resulted in a multi-ethnic patchwork spread over three continents. The Ottoman toleration of the cultures of the people they conquered as well as their custom of providing shelter for refugees fleeing religious and political persecution preserved the multi-ethnic character of the Empire. This stands in striking contrast to the often inhumane measures employed by Christian nations such as *Reconquista* Spain to ensure the homogeneity of religious belief and practice. The enlightened policies of the Ottomans, grounded in Islamic law, gave Muslims, Christians – among them the Armenians – as well as Jews freedom of religion, civil rights, and privileges as members of their own religious communities (*millets*). These self-governing communities were abolished under the Republic of Turkey, when secular law replaced Islamic law.

2.1.1 World War I: Ethnicity and Nationalism

After the devastating Ottoman defeat at the hands of the Allies during World War I, General Mustafa Kemal (Atatürk) led a nationalist resistance movement, centered in Anatolia, against the Allied plan to partition what remained of the Empire to suit their appetites for large chunks of strategic land as well as to placate the territorial demands of Armenians, Greeks, Kurds, and others. The resistance movement, however, became a successful War of Independence. Atatürk overthrew Ottoman rule, forced the Allies to renegotiate the peace Treaty of Sevres (10 August 1920), and established the Republic of Turkey. Atatürk then went on to create a secular and ethnically Turkish nation.

The ethnic character of what was to become modern Turkey was radically altered by two decisions: First was the decision by the Ottoman government during World War I to order the expulsion of Armenians from eastern Anatolia. Following many years of revolutionary activity, Armenians were seen as a fifth column loyal to the invading Russian forces. Hundreds of thousands of Armenians were relocated to territories that eventually fell outside of the borders of what became the Republic of Turkey – an ex post facto deportation – and, as the fortunes of war changed, many thousands fled over the Russian border to Armenian settlements to what became the Republic of Armenia. The second decision was the enormous population exchange with Greece – Orthodox Greeks for Muslims – to eliminate any future threat of Greek nationalism. The convention on the population exchange (30 July 1923), signed by Turkey and Greece at Lausanne, Switzerland, was an attempt to bring order and closure to a process that began with the flight of Greek refugees from Anatolia during the War of Independence. These actions with the exception of a large minority population of Kurds in eastern and southeastern Anatolia resulted in a nation that was predominantly Turkish and overwhelmingly Muslim.

By the early years of the Republic, therefore, the multi-ethnic character of Turkey had been transformed dramatically. The large Christian populations of Anatolia were gone. Muslims went from being 80% of the population just before World War I to 98%. Turkey's population today is about 74 million. Of that number, approximately 90% are Turks, 6.76% Kurds, 1.08% Zazas, 1.08% Arabs, 0.41% Circassians, 0.27% Laz, and the remainder divided among Armenians, Jews, Greeks, and other ethnic groups (Önder, 2007, pp. 18, 46). In regard to the percentage of Kurds, Kongar (2007) estimates, on the other hand, a range of 10 to 15% (p. 527). The estimates of the Armenian population, according to various sources, range from 40,000 to 70,000. This is down dramatically from 1914, with estimates ranging for that year from 1,294,851 to 2,500,000 but probably 1,750,000 (Lewy, 2005, p. 235). Today, Turkey is over 99% Muslim.

2.1.2 The Treaty of Lausanne and Non-Muslim Ethnic Minorities

The existence of non-Muslim ethnic minorities in the Republic of Turkey has been an issue about defining who is a "Turk" (İçduygu, Toktaş, & Soner, 2008). The recognition of ethnic rights was affirmed by Turkey in the Treaty of Lausanne and witnessed by the other signatories – Great Britain, France, Italy, Japan, Greece, Romania and the Serb-Croat-Slovene State. Section III, Article 38, of the treaty placed minorities on an equal footing with other Turkish nationals: "The Turkish Government undertakes to assure full and complete protection of life and liberty to all inhabitants of Turkey without distinction of birth, nationality, language, race or religion" (The Treaty of Peace, 1923, 24 July). In regard to non-Muslim minorities, Article 40 states: "In particular, they shall have an equal right to establish, manage and control at their own expense, any charitable, religious and social institutions, any schools and other establishments for instruction and education, with the right to use their own language and to exercise their own religion freely therein" (The Treaty of Peace, 1923, 24 July).

The treaty did not include compensatory provisions for the Armenians and "marked the final Allied abandonment of the Armenian Question" (Hovannisian, 1999, p. 15). The status of Armenians and other ethnic minorities was placed under the supervision of the League of Nations. The Turkish Constitution of 1924 and subsequent constitutions asserted the equality of all Turkish citizens regardless of race and religion. The Constitution of 1982, which reflected more than a decade of political and ethnic turmoil as well as military interventions, "included a 'catch-all provision, Article 14, which restricted the freedoms of individuals and organizations and prohibited political struggle based upon class, sect, language or race'. It was a clear warning against Islamists, Marxists, and Kurdish nationalists"[1] (McDowall, 1996, p. 414).

Today, Turkish Armenians mostly reside in Istanbul. The terms "Western Armenian" and "Turkish Armenian" have been replaced by "Istanbul Armenians," the assumption being that Armenians in Turkey live almost exclusively in Istanbul (Mgrditchan, 2007, August 11, *Armenian weekly*). There are Turkish Armenians located in other regions of the country. The small village of Vakıflı, located near Antakya, an eastern Anatolian city, has been called "the last Armenian village" (Aslan, 2005, July, 25, *Aksiyon*). The existence of this village of 300 inhabitants was discovered through a visit to the region by military officials in 1996. This was followed by the restoration of an Armenian church.

[1] For information about the Kurdish–Turk conflict, see Chap. 10.

3 The History of the Struggle

3.1 The Ottoman Armenians: "The Loyal Community" and the Rise of Nationalism

Among the conquered Christian populations of the Ottoman Empire, the Armenians were the most admired and known as the *millet-i-sadika,* the "loyal community." They had an ancient attachment to the land that went back almost 3,000 years. By the sixth century bce they enter the historical record as a distinct people, eventually establishing a kingdom, stretching from the Caspian Sea region of present-day Azerbaijan to central Anatolia. Subsequently, the kingdom was assaulted and fragmented by conquering armies, namely Byzantines, Arabs, Seljuk Turks, Mongols, and the Ottoman Turks, though the Armenians succeeded in preserving their cultural identity, if not always their independence.

Key to their resilience was the early conversion to Christianity, dating back to the beginning of the fourth century with the founding of Armenian Apostolic Church. This was followed in the fifth century by the creation of the Armenian alphabet. The Armenians were subjugated by the Byzantines, heirs of the Eastern Roman Empire and culturally Greek. Following the defeat of the Byzantine Greeks and the Armenians by Seljuk Turks, who had originated in Central Asia and converted to Islam during their westward migration, the Armenians succeeded in establishing the short-lived Kingdom of Cilicia (1199–1375). Cilicia encompassed much of the southeastern half of Anatolia along the Mediterranean but subsequently conquered by the Mamluks, bringing to an end the last vestige of an independent Armenian state. "Armenians recall the following two hundred years as a dark age for their nation, the beginning of their great diaspora" (Jenkins, 2008, pp. 132–133). The subjugation of Cilicia was part of a larger process of the Islamic conquest of Anatolia, which was predominantly Christian and under Byzantine control. It began with the Seljuk Turks in the eleventh century, continued with the Ottoman Turks in the fourteenth century, and culminated in the fall of Constantinople (Istanbul) in the fifteenth century. But, as Panossian (2006) noted, "Even in adverse conditions, when they were living under the suzerainty of foreign powers, most Armenians maintained their separate cultural identity. This ancient identity was transformed into a modern national identity between the eighteenth and twentieth centuries" (Panossian, p. xii).

Under Ottoman rule, the Armenians became a community within an empire. Fatih Mehmet, whose ambition to conquer was boundless, devised a system of government, the *millet*, for the people he conquered. It minimized the Ottoman need to govern, maximized tax revenues, gained the support of non-Muslims, and allowed him to continue on a path of conquest. The *millet was a* "system of autonomous self-government under religious leaders, later extended to the Armenians, the Jews, and the other major non-Muslim minorities. . . .[who] were given more extensive power over their followers than had been the case in the Christian states that had previously dominated the area" (Shaw, 1976, Vol. I, p. 59).

Armenians as a religious community had their own courts of law, schools, churches, and charitable foundations. They were excluded from military service along with other non-Muslims, for which they paid a tax. Like the Jews who were forced from *Reconquista* Spain in the fifteenth century and fled from the Eastern European pogroms of the nineteenth, the Armenians for centuries had significant benefits being part of the Empire. Most tilled the soil and were virtually indistinguishable from their Muslim neighbors. Others flourished as shopkeepers, architects, craftsmen, bankers, medical doctors, and men of commerce. Some attained prominent positions in the bureaucracy of the Empire at a time when Muslims would not have been permitted to hold offices of public trust in Christian Europe. "Between 1856 and 1922, Armenians served at all levels of government… . The highest position in the Ottoman Empire was that of *vezir*, equal to that of marshall in the army. Dozens of Armenians rose to that level" (Öztuna, 2001, p. 49).

Armenians, however, had exchanged one dynasty for another – Byzantine for Ottoman masters. The grants of secular and religious rights were sufficient to sustain a covenant for hundreds of years but were held in place by the implicit threat of coercive force. As British Foreign Secretary Lord Salisbury observed in 1878, "the Government of the Ottoman dynasty is that of an ancient but still alien conqueror, resting more on actual power than upon the sympathies of common nationality" (Şimşir, 1989, p. 177). The Ottoman practice of ethnic tolerance for the Armenians and other Christians had thwarted assimilation and sowed the seeds for the Empire's eventual dismemberment. Armenian culture was made strong by its churches and schools, and their cohesiveness as a community was held together by the Patriarch, the Armenian religious, and secular leader. Armenians, although accorded respect as one of the "People of the Book," were considered inferior to Muslims – in spite of their education, professional accomplishments, and rising material prosperity arguing otherwise.

With time the preexisting cultural discontinuities grew and in the nineteenth century the covenant was shattered by Armenian nationalism – a convergence European ideological currents and Armenian ethnic identity that had survived centuries of "captivity." Armenians began to conceive of recreating in eastern Anatolia, part of their ancient kingdom, an autonomous existence – a sentiment that was buttressed by corrupt Ottoman officials as well as by oppressive Kurdish overlords exacting feudal taxes. But this faced a stark reality: Armenians were not a majority population. Even in eastern Anatolia, called Ottoman Armenia or Turkish Armenia by the European Powers, Armenians could not by force of numbers argue for the transformation of any one of the Ottoman provinces into a nation in its own right or even an autonomous state – not without the eradication or relocation of the Muslim majority of Kurds and Turks. According to McCarthy (2001), the highest concentration of Armenians, based on Ottoman statistics for 1912, did not exceed 32% (Bitlis) and oftentimes the Armenians had much smaller fractions of the populations in other provinces, even in eastern Anatolia, the Armenian heartland (p. 70).

Dadrian (1999) argued to the contrary, noting that the massive influx of Muslim war refugees from the Balkans and elsewhere – as many as two million – resulted in "tipping the delicate demographic balance in 'historical Armenia' in favor of the dominant Turks" (pp. 138–139); and in the last two decades of the nineteenth century Muslim majorities were assured through "gerrymandering" (pp. 141–144). But McCarthy (2001) asserts – while agreeing that the Armenian population in 1912 was a smaller percentage of the total than it was at the onset of the nineteenth century – that they "had not been a majority in any province of the Ottoman Empire since well before 1800" (p. 73).

3.1.1 Ethnic Conflict and the Dream of Independence

In 1876, the growing discontent of Armenians in eastern Anatolia caught the attention of British Ambassador Henry Elliot. He reported to Foreign Secretary Earl of Derby that "a MOVEMENT of discontent, which may become important, has been exhibited by the Armenians… . Their complaints refer chiefly to which they are subject by the tax-gatherers, and to the depredations which they suffer from the Koords [Kurds], against which the government afford them no protection," noting further that the Kurds were "equally oppressive to the *Turks*… . [and] daily getting greater" (Şimşir, 1989, p. 731). Less than 2 years later, British Ambassador Austen Layard reported "that Russia is already commencing her usual intrigues among Armenians of Asiatic Turkey. Russian agents are being sent into the provinces inhabited by them with the object of stirring up discontent against the rule and authority of the Porte [Ottoman government]" (Şimşir, 1989, p. 182). This discontent nurtured by Imperial Russia was eventually and dramatically compounded by the rise of Armenian revolutionary organizations in eastern Anatolia and elsewhere.

Discontent should be viewed in the context of the Tanzimat, the Ottoman reform movement (1839–1876). It aimed at modernizing the Empire, including the introduction of lay assemblies in the *millets* to counter the growing threat of nationalism among its ethnic populations. But a new generation of reformers, the Young Ottomans, founded in 1865, believed that the augmented secularization of the *millets* was not enough and even wanted them abolished. They worked toward creating a nationalist spirit based on Ottomanism – an identity to transcend ethnicity – and argued for constitutional and parliamentary government as the vehicle to achieve this end. "They believed that participating in a parliamentary system of government would nourish in non-Muslim as well as Muslim subjects a feeling of belonging to the same fatherland (vatan), weakening parochial interests and ending their desire to form separate national states" (Shaw & E. Shaw, 1977, Vol. II, p. 132). The Constitution of 1876 was the charter for this pathway but was struck a sudden blow when it was suspended by the autocratic Sultan Abdulhamid, thus alienating Armenians who had begun to enjoy representative government and the taste of equality under the law.

3.1.2 Cultural Discontinuity and Christian Missionary Schools

In addition, the nineteenth century witnessed the cultural boundaries between Armenians and Muslims becoming more pronounced. A proliferating network of missionary schools that was established mostly by American Protestants, and heavily attended by Armenians, magnified the existing cultural discontinuities. Edges of cultural divergence that had softened over the centuries became razor sharp boundaries. As British diplomat Sir Charles Eliot (1908) observed:

> The good position of the Armenians in Turkey had largely depended on the fact that they were thoroughly Oriental and devoid of that tincture of European culture common among Greeks and Slavs. But now this character was being destroyed: European education and European books were being introduced among them. Foreigners were talking of Armenia as they had once talked of Bulgaria [when Christians rebelled against Ottoman rule in 1876] (p. 401).

Through the missionary schools, Armenian students discovered their ancient past and traditions as well as the attendant symbols that promoted the distinctiveness of their history and culture. Eventually, student activism grew and became more difficult for school officials to contain as the curriculum quickened nationalistic fervor (Young, 2001, pp. 240–245). In time, cultural centers were established in Protestant and Catholic Armenian communities. They were key to an "Armenian national cultural revival" (Shaw & Shaw, 1977, Vol. II, p. 202). Sir Edwin Pears (1916), a British barrister who practiced in the consular courts of Istanbul and served as the president of the European bar, observed in his memoir, *Forty Years in Constantinople*, that "in a very real sense it may be said that the fomenters of political agitation in Armenia [eastern Anatolia], as in Bulgaria, were the schoolmasters and the missions, Catholic or Protestant" (p. 151). Wealthy Armenian parents who sent their children for further education to Western Europe exposed them to radical ideologies. Some students remained abroad to foment rebellion in Anatolia from afar and out of the reach of "The Red Sultan" – a popular sanguineous reference to Abdulhamid. Others returned to establish or join the growing ranks of revolutionary networks.

As the political disaffection increased and the cultural chasm widened, the perception of Armenians as the "loyal community" changed dramatically, especially after the Ottoman failure in the late 1870s to contain Russian aggression in the Caucasus. It was accompanied by a decided shifting of Armenian allegiance from the Sultan to the Czar. British diplomat Sir Charles Eliot (1908) observed, "The Turks thought that there was clearly an intention to break up what remained of the Ottoman Empire and found an Armenian kingdom" (p. 401). At the same time, a rising tide of Pan-Islamism intensified the cultural rift by accentuating the Sultan's role as caliph, and thus keeping "before the minds of Moslims the idea that the Sultan was the head of all Islam on one side, as opposed to all Christians on the other" (Eliot, 1908, p. 401). The nineteenth century further witnessed the rapid industrialization of England, Germany, and France and the relative economic decline of the Empire, pejoratively referred to as "The Sick Man of Europe." More and more, the Empire confronted increasing threats from its powerful Christian neighbors who coveted its vast and strategic territories, particularly from Russia, which pursued a program of the ethnic cleansing of Muslims in its conquest of Ottoman lands.

3.2 Rebellion in the Balkans: The Russo-Turkish War 1877–1878

The uprising of Christian Bulgarian rebels in 1876 against Ottoman rule greatly inspired Armenian nationalists. Ottoman forces in response to rebel atrocities against Muslims had brutally crushed the rebellion. Sensationalist reports flooded European printing presses with scant mention of Muslim victims. Former British Prime Minister Gladstone, recently defeated by Benjamin Disraeli, published his own pamphlet declaring his hatred for the Ottomans: "They were, upon the whole, from the first black day when they entered Europe, the one great anti-human specimen of humanity. Wherever they went, a broad line of blood marked the track behind them; and as far as their dominion reached, civilization disappeared from view" (Salt, 1993, p. 45).

Years later, Sidney Whitman (1914), a *New York Herald* correspondent who had been assigned to Turkey, excoriated the European press for the "the orgy of vilification let loose on Sultan Abdulhamid" as well as for the lack of professionalism in a "persistent campaign of misrepresentation which was carried out for years" (p. 60). Whitman especially condemned the behavior of questionable newspaper correspondents "who came up to the Palace with scarcely veiled intimation that it was to be a case of pay or slander" (pp. 230–231). The crazed atmosphere in Europe regarding Bulgarian Christians gave Czarist Russia which had territorial ambitions, very much the equal of the Ottoman Empire of centuries before, a convenient pretext to resort to arms.

The Russo-Turkish War featured an Armenian commander of a Russian army – augmented by Russian Armenians – invading Anatolia. The defeat of Ottoman forces was followed by the humiliating Treaty of San Stefano (3 March 1878). Negotiated a stone's throw from Constantinople

(Istanbul), it "created among Armenian intellectuals and clergy in Constantinople a belief in the irresistible Russian ascendance to power and in the ultimate doom of the Ottoman-Turkish State" (Şimşir, 1983, p. 7). In fact, Armenian Patriarch Nerses went to San Stefano to meet with Grand Duke Nicholas, commander-in-chief of the Russian forces, to pledge Armenian allegiance. The Patriarch presented a memorandum for Czar Alexander II, requesting that the conquered Ottoman lands be combined with Russia's Ararat province, which had a sizeable Armenian population "to create an Armenia under Russia" (Halaçoğlu, 2002, p. 18). Pasha Djemal (1922), a key member of the Young Turks and commander of the Turkish Fourth Army during World War I, noted in his memoir that the journey to San Stefano was also the Armenian passage from the most loyal nation to "a snake let loose by Russia" (p. 246).

The Treaty of San Stefano favored Russia so much, especially strategic gains in eastern Anatolia, that it threatened Great Britain's own interests. In league with Austria-Hungary, Great Britain forced Russia to accept less favorable terms at a congress of the European powers convened by German Chancellor Otto von Bismarck. The Treaty of Berlin signed that July was a setback for Armenian nationalists. Gone was the promise of Russian military occupation of eastern Anatolia to guarantee Armenian security and a degree of autonomy, though the treaty included what became a worthless provision (Article 61) assigning Armenian safety – protection from Kurds and Circassians – and the superintendence of various reforms to the European signatories. In the meantime, Abdulhamid's "cunning and shifty diplomacy" (Eversley & Chirol, 1924, p. 354) played one power against the other and succeeded in keeping Anatolia from becoming a European protectorate. The reforms were, thereby, delayed for years and at a time when Armenian loyalty was called into question for their conduct during a devastating and humiliating war. In fact, immediately after the withdrawal of Russian troops, "Kurds and Circassians pillaged Armenian villages in the border region, and thousands of Armenians took refuge in the Russian Caucasus. The massacres of 1894–1896 are unintelligible without taking note of this decisive change in the Turko-Armenian relationship" (Lewy, 2005, p. 7).

3.2.1 The Armenian Question

The treaty was a setback for Armenian aspirations, but Article 61 placed the welfare of Armenians in the forefront of the foreign policy objectives of Great Britain and other European powers. It gave them a ready excuse to have ethnic conflict as a reason to intervene in the internal affairs of the Empire to promote their own strategic interests. Armenians now – for the first time – had an internationally sanctioned vehicle with which to redress abuses, as well as a potential and promising pathway to autonomy, even independence, or so it seemed. Panossian (2006) observed: "This expectation that European (imperial) forces ought to – *and therefore will* – liberate Armenia(ns) from the Ottoman yoke had become an ingrained element in Armenian collective consciousness. …[and] was woven into national identity, becoming an inherent element of Armenians' liberation struggle in the nineteenth century" (p. 189).

Frederick Greene (1895), a missionary on the American Board of Van, a province located in eastern Anatolia, piteously observed how the Armenians had put their faith in Article 61 and what soon became hollow promises: "I have never been able to convince one of them that the course of England and the other powers has been anything but one of selfishness, jealousy, and dishonor as far as fulfillment of their treaty obligations is concerned" (p. 81).

3.3 The Rise of Revolutionary Parties

The failure of the Congress of Berlin to fully recognize Armenian demands spurred Armenian nationalists. Armenian revolutionary parties began to emerge in the 1880s. The Armenakan Party, established in 1885 and organized in the city of Van in eastern Anatolia, was the first to promote political goals through revolution. Two other parties, the Hunchaks and the Dashnaks, emerged shortly after, though with headquarters outside of the Empire. But soon branches spread to Istanbul and Anatolia. The Hunchaks (Hunchakian Revolutionary Party) was formed in Geneva, Switzerland, in 1887 by a handful of Russian Armenian students. They were steeped in Marxist ideology, formed a special division to carry out acts of terror, and aimed at creating an independent nation combining Turkish, Russian, and Persian Armenia. Its "immediate objective… was the political and national independence of Turkish Armenia" (Nalbandian, p. 108).

The Dashnaks (Dashnaktsuthiun or Armenian Revolutionary Federation) established in Tiflis in 1890, then part of the Russian Empire, merged a number of Armenian groups, mostly in Russia, into a single organization but failed ultimately to incorporate the Hunchaks. The Dashnaks developed a socialist platform that included the liberation of Turkish Armenia but not separation from the Empire, and supported terror as one of the "methods to be used by revolutionary bands" (Nalbandian, p. 168).

The Hunchaks, and especially the Dashnaks, became well-funded and powerful and spread rapidly to Constantinople and throughout Anatolia. While many Armenians freely supported these organizations, others were forced to do so through terror and other tactics.

McCarthy (1995) observed that the Armenian revolutionary parties "were a classic nineteenth-century response to the stirrings of nationalism. . . .[and] were similar to the successful revolutionary organizations of Greece and Bulgaria in their nationalistic ends and willingness to resort to mass violence or selective assassination whenever needed" (p. 118). Papazian (1934) in his book, *Patriotism Perverted*, condemning the nihilist terror tactics employed by the Dashnaks against their own people, observed: "Its doctrine was, that liberty is won by bloodshed only, and the more the Sultan is goaded into massacring the Armenian people, the stronger will become our claims for autonomy, and the greater will become the hope for European intervention" (p. 24).

3.3.1 Mounting Ethnic Tensions in Eastern Anatolia: The Sassun Rebellion

By the summer of 1894, eastern Anatolia was ripe for conflict. Armenian revolutionary groups had become more widespread and active, while the Ottoman perception of their threat to the Empire intensified:

> The change produced in Ottoman feeling was enormous….The loyal people…were as seditious as Greeks and Bulgarians; they had secret committees and revolutionary printing-presses; they were probably arming and conspiring to massacre good Muslims. Subsequent events can only be understood if we realize that the fears of Turks, however unfounded we may think them, were widespread and genuine (Eliot, 1908, pp. 399–400).

Sultan Abdulhamid added to the growing tension by creating the *Hamidieh* cavalry units to gain control over the Kurdish tribes in eastern Anatolia. Ottoman control of the region "had been virtually non-existent since the beginning of the war with Russia" (Duguid, 1973, May, p. 142). These rugged mountain men on horseback, recently the bane of Christians and Muslim Turks alike, confronted growing Armenian revolutionary activity. This proved to be a highly explosive mixture.

In August 1894, the growing tension between the Armenians and Muslims ignited in Sassun. It followed a period of the Hunchaks and others "exciting hostilities between the Kurds and the Armenians" (Nalbandian, 1963, pp. 120–121). The Armenians had been encouraged by Damadian, a revolutionary, and later by the Hunchak leader Murat (Hambardsum Poyadjian) not to pay the customary feudal tribute (*hafir*) for protection, essentially Kurds protecting Armenians from other Kurds, and for other services provided by their Kurdish overlords. Murat and his followers provoked the Kurds who in turn attacked the Armenians. The rebellion was finally crushed by *Hamidieh* cavalry with the help of the Ottoman army but "considered a great victory for their party as well as for the Armenian cause. . . . because the European Powers at last had recognized the crying need for reforms in Armenia" (Nalbandian, 1963, p. 122). "From the revolutionary point of view nothing could have provided stronger justification for European intervention than the scenes which took place in the . . . district, horribly reminiscent as they were of the 'Bulgarian atrocities' nearly 20 years before" (Salt, 1993, p. 123). However, a correspondent sent to Sassun by Reuters supported the Ottoman claim that the Armenians had been responsible for horrible outrages against Muslims, "in order that the infuriated Turks should shock the Christian world by the atrocity of the retaliation" (Salt, 1993, p. 123).

The events in Sassun brought about a wave of violence throughout Anatolia. "Believing that the Armenians were preparing for open rebellion and that the government sanctioned any actions to prevent such a rebellion, the Kurdish tribes, in most cases led by *Hamidieh* officers, began to harass and openly attack Armenian villages in most of the provinces" (Duguid, 1973, May, p. 149).

3.3.2 The European Press, Intervention, and Sultan Abdulhamid's Efforts at Appeasement

The reports in the European press of atrocities in Sassun and in other provinces resulted in renewed demands by the European Powers to implement the Treaty of Berlin's Article 61 reforms. For almost two decades, Abdulhamid had resisted reforms that called for separating Armenians, Turks, and Kurds. The reforms would augment the already considerable presence of Christians in local government, including in law enforcement and tax collection, and were sure to threaten Muslims. These renewed demands were of such a nature that the Sultan prophesized that "this business will end in blood" (Salt, 1993, p. 88).

While the Sultan pondered ways to appease the European Powers without triggering civil war, his hand was forced by a massive Hunchak demonstration in Istanbul on September 30, 1895. It resulted in widespread bloodshed, mostly Armenian, and "some at the hands of the many Kurdish porters there" (McDowall, 1996, p. 61). British diplomat Sir Mark Sykes (1915) observed that "the anarchists…threw bombs with the intention of provoking a massacre of their fellow-countrymen" (p. 417). The demonstrators called for the ethnic division of the eastern Anatolian *vilayets* (provinces) and the appointment of a European governor-general. These were among other demands that they shared with European embassies before the demonstration. About 2 weeks later, Abdulhamid issued but did not publish an *irade* (decree) designed to appease the European Powers while falling short of the original proposals. It referred to existing laws awaiting implementation rather than reforms (Salt, 1993, pp. 92–93).

Though a half measure, Abdulhamid's decree had actually mollified Great Britain, which had come to realize that military intervention was too costly a venture. The Hunchaks in turn declared victory. Turkish and Kurdish Muslims, however, were ready to pounce. "The reforms were seen as another example of European imperialism, one step on the road to Armenian independence" (Duguid, May 1973, p. 150). The chronic warnings of the Ottoman government that Armenian "independence would wreck the Empire and that Armenians were simply the tools of European imperialism" (Duguid, May 1973, p. 150) bred insecurities, fear, and ethnic hatred at a time when Muslims more and more questioned Abdulhamid's ability to safeguard their well-being. These threats and the insecurities resulted in the creation of secret organizations – Muslim correlatives of the Armenian revolutionary organizations – ready to take independent measures "to oppose by force the introduction of any reforms benefitting the Christians" (Duguid, May 1973, p. 150).

This was not merely just the reaction to alarms of the Sultan and his Sublime Porte. The chronic posturing by the European Powers, especially Russia, encouraged seditious Armenians to intensify the rhetoric of revolution and it worsened an already explosive situation. Further, the hundreds of thousands of Muslims from the Balkans had inundated Istanbul and Anatolia after the Russo-Turkish War. They brought with them nightmarish accounts of Russian Cossacks in collusion with Bulgarian rebels waging a campaign of terror. The systematic destruction of Muslim villages and butchery of the innocent were designed to rid the land of Muslims and Jews and prepare the way for settlement by Christians. Terrorism worked. The flight of Muslims to Ottoman safe-havens continued the suffering and the loss of life. Approximately 260,000 died from cold, starvation, disease, and slaughter; and "perhaps a million Bulgarian Muslims were driven from their homes, many of whom were Circassians and Tartars previously exiled from Russia" (McCarthy, 1995, pp. 88–91). The Russo-Turkish War was an unmitigated disaster for the Ottoman Empire, and, eventually for the Ottoman Armenians. Armenian revolutionaries took false hope in and acted upon the example of Bulgarian Christians who had been liberated by Russian arms.

3.3.3 Sultan Abdulhamid's reforms: The Muslim Ethnic Backlash

When Sultan Abdulhamid failed to release the full text of the Armenian reforms, Turkish and Kurdish Muslims feared for the worst – that Armenians had been granted autonomy – which ignited a new wave of violence. Şimşir (1990) noted that this was at a time when "the Armenian revolutionaries were doing their best to procure the intervention of the Powers by provoking all kinds of incidents throughout Anatolia, and in all of these incidents the aggressors were Armenians" (p. xi). The orchestrated nature of the violence gave the appearance of having been coordinated from Istanbul, though Lewy (2005) concluded that "the evidence for the personal responsibility of Abdul Hamid is weak" (p. 27), observing that some local officials actually prevented bloodshed while others invented plots to crush and receive rewards for massacring innocent Armenians. Hepworth (1898), although not excusing the Muslims for the massacres, blamed the Armenian revolutionaries – whom he denounced as criminals and fire-eaters – aimed at stirring up rebellion to trigger European intervention and causing a "prairie-fire" (p. 152) of persecution. In speaking of the massacres in his memoir, Djemal (1922) noted that "a very large number of Kurds and Turks were killed by the Armenians and the two sides vied with each other in thinking out every possible form of torture" (p. 247).

3.4 The First World War: The Prospect for Armenian Independence

The First World War presented what would become the last opportunity for the revolutionaries to secure European intervention. For more than a decade before the war, one of the Young Turk groups, the Committee of Union and Progress (CUP), a liberal faction of dissident Ottoman officers and others, as well as the Dashnaks recognized that they shared some common interests – the removal of Abdulhamid and the restoration of the Constitution of 1876. In two conferences held in Paris, one in 1902 and the other in 1907, CUP members as well as Dashnaks and other Armenian delegates closed ranks. Factions formed, however, among CUP representatives regarding the creation of an autonomous Armenian state. "The Armenians thought that through the implementation of this programme, they would first obtain autonomous status which would gradually lead to total independence" (Halaçoğlu, 2002, p. 31). In 1908, CUP revolted, forcing the Sultan to restore the constitution. The following year, CUP defeated a counter-revolution by loyalist troops and those opposed to the pro-Western and the radically secularist agenda of the Young Turks. Abdulhamid abdicated in favor of his brother, Mehmed V, an accomplished poet whose many years of seclusion made him ill-prepared for statecraft.

The success of CUP, which had Armenian support, ushered in a time of good feeling and expressions of "liberty, equality, and fraternity" but it was short-lived. In response to recent Ottoman military defeats in the Balkans and mounting Kurdish unrest in eastern Anatolia, the Armenian leaders from the Dashnaks and the Church as well as other Armenian leaders returned to the old agenda of seeking external intervention to settle the Armenian Question. A Russian draft of a plan that echoed Article 61, opposed by Germany and Austria-Hungary but supported by England and France, further destabilized the region with a rumor about the creation of a Christian state. Eventually, the European Powers accepted a compromise, though as Lewy (2005) noted, it was probably a factor in CUP's decision "to sign the secret military alliance with Germany on August 2, 1914" (p. 39) and fixed in the minds of the Young Turks the threat of Russia and the Armenians to its grip on eastern Anatolia. "The Armenians had regarded the reform agreement as a kind of down-payment on the eventual complete liberation from Turkish rule. They did not realize that the Turks would do anything in their power, no matter how ruthless, in order to prevent the loss of what they regarded as the heartland of Turkish Anatolia" (Lewy, 2005, pp. 37–39).

On October 28, 1914, Turkish battleships attacked three Russian cities on the Black Sea. CUP had joined the side of Germany and Austria-Hungary, the Central Powers, in the War to End All Wars against Russia, Great Britain, and France. In eastern Anatolia, Armenian rebels and volunteers allied themselves with the advancing Russian forces and thousands of Russian Armenian soldiers. The number of Muslims fleeing from them, according to official estimates of an Ottoman commission, was more than 850,000 but may well have exceeded a million by the summer of 1916. "Armenian units were especially feared and apparently were a major factor in the flight of the Muslim population. The great suffering of these refugees has often been ignored by Western authors" (Lewy, 2005, p. 120).

3.4.1 The Armenian Diaspora: The Allied advance and the Special Law of May 27, 1915

At the same time that Russian forces were rapidly advancing into Anatolia, another threat struck at the very heart of the Empire. On April 25, 1915, British and French forces landed at strategic locations, including Gallipoli, along the Dardanelles – within striking distance of Istanbul. The survival of Istanbul hung in the balance between the invading European armies and its Ottoman defenders. According to Halaçoğlu (2002), Armenian revolutionary activities were evident throughout eastern Anatolia. The revolutionaries had distributed detailed instructions on how to support the Allies. These included desertion from the Ottoman army, the killing of all Muslims residing near the Russian border – from 2-year-old children and up – and to "accuse the Moslems of all the atrocities committed by the Armenians and publish them in and outside the Ottoman Empire as widely as possible" (pp. 60–61).

In this time of desperation, which McCarthy (1995) describes as a civil war stemming from "Armenian plans to take eastern cities" (pp. 186–187) once the war started, CUP decided on a remedy for the survival of the Empire that became a prescription for disaster for the Armenian people. It was the Special Law of May 27, 1915, drafted by Interior Minister Talat Pasha and approved by the Ottoman cabinet, to remove Armenians from regions determined to be of strategic value and militarily vulnerable, though the area was enlarged as the perception of danger grew. Removing the Armenian populations of Van, Bitlis, and Erzurum, virtually in their entirety, was viewed as necessary because "It would be impossible to determine which of the Armenians would remain loyal and which would follow the appeals of their leaders" (Shaw & E. Shaw, 1977, Vol. II, p. 315). Notably, Armenians in nonstrategic areas of the Empire were not relocated. Istanbul and other cities with heavy Armenian populations were left out of the initial relocation order. Minister Talat's thinking about relocation may have been more than a temporary measure to cut off vital support to Armenian rebels and Russian forces. He was quoted as having said at a cabinet meeting that "We have to create a Turkish block, free of foreign elements, which in the future will never again give the European big powers the opportunity to interfere in the internal affairs of Turkey" (Lewy, 2005, p. 158). It would be a permanent solution to years of revolutionary activity throughout eastern Anatolia and a quintessential declaration of burgeoning Turkish nationalism as well as a foreshadowing of what was to come after the fall of the Empire and the rise of the Republic.

4 Causes

4.1 Cultural Pluralism and the Rise of Nationalism

The long chain, or rather web of causality, resulting in severe inter-ethnic conflict and the tragedy of the Armenian relocation is difficult to disaggregate. The Ottoman Empire was a multi-ethnic society of Muslims, Christians, Jews, and others. There were clear demarcations separating one group or *millet* from the other, promoting cultural distinctiveness and divergence, though there were rivalries and concomitant outbreaks of violence, even among different sects of Christians. The Ottomans had skillfully minimized the challenges to the sultanate by isolating one group from another, but they could not isolate the Empire from the tidal forces of modernization churning in Europe, including powerful currents of nationalism that swept over its borders in the nineteenth century. And as Toynbee and Kirkwood (1927) observed, "a separate communal life. . . eventually developed into a longing for an independent national life and gave every opportunity for foreign "nationalisms" to grow up in the midst of the Ottoman peoples" (p. 144). The Islamic regime of the Ottomans, held together for centuries by the connective tissue of cultural pluralism and the domination of one ethnic group, could not contain the forces of nationalism. The Austro-Hungarian Empire, another dynastic and multi-ethnic political entity succumbed to the convergent forces of ethnicity and nationalism. Even the Russian Empire of the Romanov dynasty, the Ottoman nemesis, was undone by the supranationalism of Marx and its Leninist postscript.

4.1.1 The Christian Missions and Seismic Cultural Changes

Further, in the latter half of the nineteenth century, the cultural divide between Muslims and Armenians had widened dramatically. The national awakening of the Turkish Armenians, which included a patriotic and emotional reconnection to their past as an independent people, and the celebration of their culture promoted by the proliferation of cultural centers and Christian mission schools, had a significant role in shifting the Armenian cultural locus from an Ottoman to a Western identity. This was accentuated as well by the expanding economic ascendancy of the Armenians that gave them greater material prosperity than their Muslim neighbors and by the Ottoman rebuff of Christianity – driven by a Pan-Islamism movement that grew in concert with the perceived Christian menace. These seismic cultural changes coupled with the intervention of the European Powers in the internal affairs of the Empire prepared the way for the clash of cultures on the killing fields of eastern Anatolia.

4.1.2 The rise of Armenian Revolutionary Parties: Divided Support

The rise of Armenian revolutionary parties should be seen in the context of powerful forces transforming the Empire. Clearly, the efforts, overt and covert, by the revolutionaries to free Armenians at horrific cost from Ottoman domination drove a wedge between the Muslims and the Armenians. The respect the former had for the latter – the "loyal nation" – evolved over centuries and had been earned. But the establishment of Armenian revolutionary headquarters in Western Europe and Imperial Russia – a malevolent power eating away at its borders – as well as the networks of revolutionaries in Istanbul and especially in eastern Anatolia, as well as the eruption of ethnic violence between 1894 to 1896 had resulted in "intense hatred between the three nations [Armenians, Turks, and Kurds]" (Djemal, 1922, p. 246). In eastern Anatolia, the predatory behavior of the Kurdish tribes in exacting feudal tributes from the Armenians as well as the corrupt behavior of Ottoman officials offered grounds for the revolutionaries to carry out a plan to recreate an autonomous or independent Armenia – abuses that Turkish Muslims shared with their Armenian neighbors. But the terror tactics employed by the revolutionaries to incite retaliatory Muslim atrocities to bring about the intervention of the European Powers was an enormous folly of self-deceit that caused great harm to the Armenian people and Muslims alike. As McCarthy (1995) noted, "In broad outline, their plan was to emulate the successful Bulgarian uprising of 1876 – instigate local Armenians to attack Muslims (or do the job themselves), thereby provoking massacres of Armenians, with a resulting European intervention in favor of an Armenian state" (p. 118).

What is not known is to what extent the Armenian people as a whole supported the actions of the revolutionaries. The Armenians were not a homogeneous group. They ranged from peasants to pashas. There were sharp differences in education, occupation, income, and even religion. Although most were Gregorian, members of the Armenian Apostolic Church, the number of Protestants and Catholics was increasing, and eventually each group had its own *millet*. Armenians were spread about the Empire, although mostly concentrated in eastern Anatolia, which had a decided Muslim majority of Turks and Kurds. Therefore, despite a crescendo of Armenians voicing dissatisfaction for Ottoman rule, which was so evident during the Armenian national awakening of the nineteenth century, Armenians cannot be viewed in the context of a homogeneous collectivity. To borrow applicable phrasing from Brubaker (2004), they were not speaking in a "unitary voice," nor pursing a "unitary action."

This is evident in the checkered support that Armenians gave the revolutionary parties. The strident radical rhetoric of socialism that so impassioned young revolutionaries was not always embraced by the "conservative-minded and mature leaders of the older generation" (Nalbandian, 1963, p. 183). "Although the older intelligentsia had been instrumental in propagating the new nationalism and played an important role in the literary and educational enlightenment of the youth, they did not readily join the parties or give direction to them" (Nalbandian, 1963, p. 183). Other Armenians, especially the more prosperous, despite the desire for reforms were not willing to pursue a revolutionary path that would risk their lives and fortunes. Therefore, a "considerable number of Armenians stood in the way of the revolutionists because of special motives and attitudes – from disapproval of the methods of the parties (as more destructive and dangerous than salutary), from a desire to preserve the status quo, or from a mere lack of concern" (Nalbandian, 1963, pp. 183–184).

Regardless of the cause of violent ethnic conflict, the growing threat to Armenian welfare likely transformed provocateurs of revolution into liberators, resulting in the growing and widespread support of the revolutionaries. McCarthy's (1995) assertion that by "May 1915, eastern Anatolia was in the midst of a civil war" – even before the Ottoman relocation order – points in that direction (p. 187). As Eriksen (2002) noted, "Ethnic identity becomes crucially important the moment it is perceived as being under threat" (p. 76). What we do know is that the Russian invasion of eastern Anatolia at the onset of World War I and the support by the Armenian revolutionary organizations for the Russians had disastrous consequences for the Armenians of eastern Anatolia.

Other than the rise of Armenian revolutionary parties, particularly the Hunchaks and the Dashnaks, we do not find a convincing explanation or a ready model (e.g., differential modernization) to explain what happened. Their terror tactics had the express purpose of provoking massacres and foreign intervention. They created a growing and violent polarization between Muslims and Armenians that once had been limited to sporadic and isolated outbreaks in the early 1800s that accelerated after the Russo-Turkish War (1877–1878) and culminated in the ethnic armageddon of intercommunal warfare in eastern Anatolia. But instead of an autonomous state or independent nation in eastern Anatolia, they created a condition in which the CUP leaders succumbed to the tragic logic of removing Ottoman Armenians from their ancestral homeland as a wartime exigency. In so doing, the architects of this decision, the Committee on Union and Progress, would change the cultural landscape of an entire region and, as it turned out, forever.

5 Consequences

There are both short- and long-term consequences stemming from the ethnopolitical conflict. The short-term consequence resulted in the massive, wrenching, and harrowing relocation from eastern Anatolia. The long-term consequences, which continue to ripple through the fabric of Turkish society, relate to the status of Armenians in present-day Turkey. Although Armenians are Turkish citizens, most of the interviewees expressed the sense of not being welcome in the very land in which they have such an historic attachment.

5.1 The Armenian Exodus from Eastern Anatolia and the Tragedy of 1915

Hundreds of thousands of Armenians were forcibly removed from Anatolia to the southern provinces of the Empire, often in poorly guarded convoys, which Panossian (2006) refers to as "death marches that were at the core of the genocidal process" (p. 232). Estimates of exact numbers vary greatly as does the number of those who perished. Death-toll estimates range widely, from 56,000 to 2,070,037, with Turkish scholars generally representing the lowest range and Armenian scholars the highest. Lewy (2005), using prewar population statistics, estimates that 642,612 or 37% of the Armenian population perished – a figure which is much lower than those generally proposed by Armenian scholars, though deeply tragic (p. 240).

The Armenians endured extreme physical hardships and were subjected to devastating diseases – cholera, typhus, dysentery, malaria – made much more virulent by overcrowded and unsanitary detention camps, severe food shortages and extremes of weather. In addition, those Armenians traveling on foot through Kurdish territories faced the added dangers of predation and slaughter. Armenians who journeyed from Cilicia and the western provinces that were free of Kurdish settlements, and especially those who had access to railroad transport, experienced less of the physical burdens and hazards faced by the others and consequently had less loss of life (Lewy, 2005, pp. 251–252). They still had to face epidemics and severe food shortages brought about by naval blockades and falling agricultural production as men and draft animals were directed to the war effort.

In terms of the accusations of genocidal intent of the relocation, Lewy (2005) noted that it "ignores the huge loss of life among Turkish civilians, soldiers, and prisoners-of-war due to sheer incompetence, neglect, starvation, and disease. All of these groups also experienced a huge death toll that surely cannot be explained in terms of a Young Turk plan of annihilation" (pp. 250–252). CUP, for example, had allowed many thousands of its own soldiers die from hunger and the lack of adequate provisioning. In one instance, a winter maneuver against Russian forces by an Ottoman General Enver Pasha in the Caucasus mountains resulted in some 80,000 soldiers dying from cold and hunger and "without fighting" (Aya, 2008, p. 399). This was more than 10% of the Armenian loses estimated by Lewy.

Dadrian (2002, Feb.) argued, based upon Imperial German and Imperial Austro-Hungary archives and other sources, CUP's intention to exterminate the Armenian people. World War I presented such an opportunity. "Put in more concrete terms, the wartime anti-Armenian measures are viewed as a major governmental effort to resolve during the war both the protracted Turko-Armenian conflict and the Armenian reform issue that underlay and fueled that conflict and that, for the Ottomans, was highly provocative" (p. 60). His analysis represents one extreme in the spectrum of those scholars who argue for genocide. At the other extreme are Turkish scholars and others who reject assertions of a state-planned, oft-stated, first genocide of the twentieth century. These two opposing extremes, however, may have the potential to attract productive dialog and possible resolution which is gathering momentum as Turkey and the Republic of Armenia are in the process of normalizing diplomatic relations.

5.1.1 The Muslim Tragedy

Muslims endured great loses as well. In the eastern provinces of Bitlis, Erzurum, and Van, the primary battlegrounds of the war in Anatolia, it is estimated that minimally 40% of the Muslim population perished. The Muslim losses were so staggering that the "death rate is well beyond that of most of the great disasters in world history, such as the Thirty Years' War and the Black

Death" (McCarthy, 1995, p. 230). During this tumultuous period of massacres, counter-massacres, clash of armies, famine and fierce epidemics there were "some 2.5 million Anatolian Muslim lives lost" (Zurcher, 2004, p. 163).

5.2 Ethnicity and the Ascent of Mustafa Kemal (Atatürk)

Ethnic conflict did not end with the relocation of Armenians and the defeat of the Ottomans at the hands of the Allies. As we have seen, the humiliating Treaty of Sevres energized a nationalist resistance movement spearheaded by General Mustafa Kemal (Atatürk). He had distinguished himself at Gallipoli[2] and turned the nationalist movement into a war of independence. The Kemalists waged two separate – ethnically charged – military campaigns to save Anatolia from further dismemberment. One campaign was in the east against the Republic of Armenia that had become an independent nation in the wake of the Bolshevik Revolution and wanted to annex eastern Anatolia. The other was in the west against the Greek army that sought to restore the long-lost territories of the Byzantine Empire. The armies of the Allies had been demobilized and the Greeks made themselves available to serve as an army of occupation but soon became an army of conquest fighting the Kemalists who would not recognize the Treaty of Sevres. By the summer of 1920, the Greek army had control of western and northwestern Anatolia as well as Thrace. "Only intense Entente [Allied] pressure prevented them from occupying Istanbul itself" (Zurcher, 2004, pp. 152–153), the former capital of the Byzantine Empire lost to the Ottomans in 1453.

Under Atatürk, the Turkish nationalists had a remarkable number of successes: They waged a successful military campaign against Armenia; negotiated a treaty with the Bolsheviks, funneling gold and military supplies instrumental in defeating the Greek forces; negotiated a treaty ending the French occupation of Cilicia toppled the Sultan's government, ending over 600 years of Ottoman rule; renegotiated the Treaty of Sevres in Lausanne, Switzerland, in 1923; and created the Republic of Turkey.

The massive population exchange of Greeks for Muslims, negotiated and signed in Lausanne (30 January 1923) by the governments of Turkey and Greece – combined with the Armenian relocation in 1915 – radically altered the ethnic landscape of Turkey. The convention, in recognition of a process that began during World War I and the Turkish War of Independence, provided for the exchange of approximately 900,000 Turkish Greeks for a much smaller number of Muslims from Greece (Zurcher, 2004, p. 164). The distinction of ethnicity was more legal than cultural. Though religion had remained after hundreds of years of assimilation, for many the mother tongue had been long lost; and now these cultural casualties of war were sent to homelands whose language and the lay of the land were decidedly foreign.

As Lewis (2002) noted, "A Western observer, accustomed to a different system of social and national classification, might even conclude that this was no repatriation at all, but two deportations into exile – of Christian Turks to Greece, and of Muslim Greeks to Turkey" (p. 355). These actions, further, were the consequence and culmination of the rise of Turkish nationalism under CUP, whose zeal for reform entered a phase of Turkification as nationalists got more control over its agenda. In its waning years, then, the Ottoman Empire succumbed to the siren call of Turkish nationalism that ultimately through Atatürk destroyed the Ottoman sultanate. As president, he recognized the importance of a homogeneous ethnicity to Turkey's stability as a republic and promoted policies that fused nationalism with a Turkish cultural identity. Turkishness became an ethnic ideology.

5.2.1 Ethnicity and Turkishness

By 1923, the Republic of Turkey had lost much of its multi-ethnic character, especially in Anatolia. The Armenian and Greek communities

[2] The beachhead at Gallipoli turned into an unmitigated disaster for the British (mainly Australian and New Zealand) forces.

had all but vanished. The original Armenian population had been drastically reduced. Many thousands had followed retreating Russian troops across the eastern Anatolian border to settle in what eventually became an Armenian republic of the Soviet Union. Those Armenians who survived the harrowing journey of ill-protected convoys to other parts of the Empire remained in territories that were taken from Turkey as trophies of war or eventually immigrated to Europe, the United States, and other countries. The remaining Greek population was radically reduced by the repatriation to Greece. Muslims, mostly ethnic Turks, the rest Kurds, and Muslims from other ethnic groups, including Arabs, constituted approximately 98% of the population, having been just 80% of the population before the war. There were also "many smaller groups" (Zurcher, 2004, p. 164) of linguistically distinct Muslims and Christians as well as Spanish-speaking Jews.

With the sultanate abolished and the caliphate days numbered, it was left to the Republic to define ethnic relations. As the Republic's first president, Atatürk forced the decoupling of Islam from government and *şeriat* law from the lives of its citizenry. Gone were the tolerant Ottoman policies that for centuries grouped non-Muslims and Muslims into communities defined by religion rather than blood. As a republic, Turkey saw itself as a modern nation state. Citizen of the republic replaced subject of the sultan, and nation replaced *millet*. The disparate religious communities held together by the linchpin of the sultanate that had made it possible for individuals, regardless of religion, to reach great heights in government service suddenly vanished. Nationalism and secularism had replaced Islamic dynasticism.

The drive toward secularism began with the Ottoman Committee for Union and Progress. CUP had pursued by fiat a "rapid program of secularizing schools and the judicial system" (Kamrava, 2004, p. 27). The new republic blew more wind into the storm of secularism that had been unleashed by the Young Turks. In striking contrast to the multi-ethnic bureaucracy of the Ottoman Empire, "the number of non-Muslims in the civil service dwindled rapidly" (Lewis, 2002, pp. 356–357). In fact, Turkish citizens from religious minorities either lost their employment or were "denied positions in various sectors of the economy" (Kirişci, 2000, July, p. 2). As Lewis (2002) observed, "there were signs that, despite secularism and nationalism, the older idea that Muslim equals Turk and non-Muslim equals non-Turk persisted" (p. 357).

The Treaty of Lausanne minority rights guarantees, including those of religious foundations, and beginning with the Civil Code of 1926, "were pruned off with various exceptions, restrictions and conditions imposed through a series of laws, acts and practices" (Kurban & Hatemi, 2009, p. 7). In June 1934, Law No. 2510 was promulgated, empowering the central government to redistribute the population through the relocation of nonethnic Turks into regions that would promote their assimilation. "All villages or urban quarters where Turkish was not the mother tongue were to be dissolved, and their inhabitants distributed in predominantly mother-tongue-Turkish-speaking areas" (McDowall, 1996, p. 207). The law was aimed at assimilating the Kurds but the task of applying it to a population of three million resulted in it being implemented on a small and, ultimately, ineffectual scale (McDowall, 1996, p. 207). Also, in the 1930s, "it became evident that pushing or directly forcing the few non-Muslims left in Turkey to abandon the country was an explicit state policy" (Kurban & Hatemi, 2009, p. 7).

Further, in addition to the population exchanges during the early years of the Republic, Atatürk promoted the immigration of Muslims from the Balkans – including non-Turkish speaking Muslims – while discouraging non-Muslims and non-Sunni Muslims as well as Muslims from other regions who were less likely to assimilate, that is, assume a national identity as ethnic Turks. "The immigration practice developed in such a manner that non-Turkish speaking ethnic groups from the Balkans such as Albanians, Bosnians, Pomaks and Tartars as well as Turkish speaking Romas were included, while Turkish speaking Christian Gagauz Turks, Azeris, and Kurds were excluded" (Kirişci, July 2000, p. 14). This continued after World War II, and by 1995 more than 1.6 million immigrants came to Turkey with

Bulgaria and Yugoslavia accounting for the largest percentage (Kirişci, July 2000, p. 8).

Further, Atatürk and his Republican People's Party pursued ethnically based policies in rebuilding Turkey's war-ravaged economy. It continued a process that began with the Young Turks during World War I that aimed at placing the control of the economy in the hands of Turkish Muslims. His first acts were convening a national economic congress in 1923 that promoted private enterprise and the "development of indigenous entrepreneurs" (Buğra, 1994, p. 98) and instructing his delegates in Lausanne to kill the Capitulations – special privileges and immunities granted by a succession of sultans to Europeans and Ottoman Christians that drove Muslims out of commerce and eventually exposed the economy to the onslaught of European industrial goods.

These actions point to the legacy of the threat of non-Turkish ethnicity to the nation state as it played out in the devastating nineteenth century uprisings in the Balkans and Anatolia and in the failed attempts in the early twentieth century by the armies of Greece and Armenia to defeat the independence movement.

6 Turkish Armenians in Their Own Voices

This section examines the present-day consequences of the ethnic conflict that ended with the Armenian Diaspora of almost a century ago. To this day, the historic and tragic conflict between Muslims and Armenians remains a matter of controversy, one that has at times politicized scholarship and one that remains a vibrant issue in the forum of international politics. The history of this relationship should provide a context with which to anchor the interviews conducted with Armenians in Turkey.

Because the aim of the historical section of the chapter was to investigate the whys and wherefores of the conflict, the information generated through the qualitative methodology of semi-structured interviews should be illuminating. To recruit individuals to interview from the Armenian community in Turkey, e-mails were sent to various Internet mail-list groups. The e-mails generated word-of-mouth communication that publicized the invitation beyond expectations. Despite the high number of the members of the Turkish Armenian community who learned about the project and the invitation, the rate of positive responses for participation was much less than expected. We concluded that the low response rate was explained by the potentially political nature of the inquiry. Consequently, the data from the 11 interviews, of which seven were conducted face-to-face in Istanbul and four by e-mail, constitute the most recent information from primary sources. It should be emphasized that those Turkish Armenians who were interviewed were very much willing to participate in the study.

After a brief description of each participant, the authors present and discuss the empirical material that reflects the thoughts and sentiments of the participants, ranging from positive to negative and from neutral to strongly ethnocentric. The sample is a small one and therefore cannot be generalized to the entire Armenian community in Turkey but the voices of the participants add valuable insights for developing a comprehensive view of what it means to be an Armenian in today's Turkey and signals the need to conduct more research.

6.1 Profile of the Participants

Although some participants permitted us to do so, their identities have been omitted.

P1: He is in his 40s. He has a graduate degree. In addition to being employed in the advertising sector, he teaches at one of the public universities in Istanbul. His income varies. He is divorced, and he and his former wife, a Turkish Armenian, have no children.

P2: She is in her 40s and is a finance director for a private company. Her income is approximately 11,100 Turkish Lira (TL) per month (USD at 1.20) at the time of the interviews. She has an undergraduate degree and is married to a Turkish Armenian. They have one child.

P3: He is in his 40s and is employed as a sales representative for his own company, earning approximately 10,000 TL income per month. He has a high school degree. He is married with two children. His wife is a Turkish Muslim.

P4: He is in his 50s and is employed in the textile and food sectors. He declined to provide income information. He has an undergraduate degree. His spouse is of Greek descent and is a Turkish citizen. They have one child.

P5: He is in his 40s and is self-employed, earning approximately 3,000 TL per month. He has a high school degree and is married to a Turkish Armenian. They have two children.

P6: She is in her 30s and works as a supervisor of service representatives. She reported her monthly income as in the medium range. She has an undergraduate degree and is preparing to marry a Turkish Armenian.

P7: She is in her 60s and is a lawyer. Her income affords her, as she notes, a comfortable lifestyle. She is divorced. Her former husband is a Turkish Armenian. They have two daughters.

P8: He is in his 30s and works for a computer company. His monthly income is 2,500 TL. He has an undergraduate degree and is married to a Turkish Armenian. They have one child.

P9: She's in her 30s and is employed in the importing business. She declined to give income information. She has an undergraduate degree and is married to a Turkish Armenian. They have one child.

P10: He is in his 40s. He did not provide information about his profession and income. He has an undergraduate degree and is married to a Turkish Armenian. They have no children.

P11: She's in her late 90s and enjoys good physical and mental health. She never married because of the chaos of her childhood and the struggle of her family to earn a living.

6.2 Analysis of the Empirical Research

In this part of the chapter, the empirical material generated from participant responses is analyzed in categories designed in terms of disaffection and conflict.

6.2.1 Perceptions About the Ethnic Status of Armenians in Turkish Society

For any ethnic minority in a country, how they perceive themselves may be seen as strong indicators of their social status. In this regard, the interviewees were asked questions related to how they describe and perceive themselves in Turkish society.

P11 was born in Merzifon, a city in the Black Sea region of Turkey. She migrated to Istanbul when she was 24 years of age. She then lived in Canada and the United States for a while and eventually returned to Turkey. She explained the reason for her return as follows: "I was born in Turkey, and I love Turkey." The other participants were born and live permanently in Istanbul.

The answers to the question about considering oneself a Turk, an Armenian or Turkish Armenian varied, although most referred to themselves as being Turkish Armenians.

While **P3** stated that he has not thought about it before, **P2** was enthusiastic about emphasizing that she is an Armenian and that she does not agree with the term "Armenian origin."

P7, believed by the authors to be a prominent figure in the Turkish Armenian community, described her status from a different perspective: "I am a Turk being faithful to the Constitution and the laws of the Republic of Turkey, but actually I am an Armenian."

P10's reaction is notable: "I consider myself an Armenian living in Turkey and having Turkish [legal] identity. This means that I am not a Turk. The status of a citizen designated as a minority in Turkey after the Lausanne Treaty is complicated.... A Turkish Armenian can only work in the private sector or may become a university teacher. The Armenians cannot work in the Ministry of Finance, the Ministry of Foreign Affairs, the military, etc. Therefore, we are first Armenian, and then Turkish."

Participants and their families have deep connections with Turkey's past. Their parents migrated to Istanbul from different cities. Participants made frequent reference to their families having lived in Anatolia for generations.

P7 tells with sadness about her family's history going back to Sivas, a small city in central Anatolia. The family still has properties in Sivas that provide income.

P2 strongly emphasizes that the roots of Armenian people in Anatolia go back thousands of years, noting that her father is from Sivas whereas her mother is from Sinop, a city in the Black Sea region.

P3 tells about his ancestors having resided in Kayseri, a city in central Anatolia, since the beginning of 1800s and that his grandfather used to work as a controller for Istanbul's Terkos reservoir.

Participants usually consider Armenians living in Turkey as a minority group. Some accept the minority status as a consequence of a legal category as noted by **P7**, and, as **P10** emphasized, a status defined by the Treaty of Lausanne. **P2** explains their status as "a group that can be placed into a stadium with a capacity of 80,000 people." **P3** uses an emotionally compelling logic that "without a majority there is no minority" and **P6** adds the term "*cemaat*" (a religious community) and underscores the religiosity of her family. She and her mother attend Sunday services at one of the Armenian churches in Istanbul.

The social relations among the Armenian community are commonly thought to be based on strong familial bonds. Most of the participants married other Armenian citizens. **P7** mentions that her daughter was criticized by the community for marrying a Turkish Muslim.

Participants associated the term "minority" to such cultural differences as language and the religion. Some of the participants perceived the term "minority" negatively. **P7** does not want to be called a member of a "minority group" and challenges the sub-identity of a minority label. **P5** rejects the term minority for Turkish Armenians and asks: "Can we be named as a minority in the land where we have been living for centuries?"

6.2.2 Relationships to and Perspectives Related to Diaspora Armenians

Participants were asked about their opinions and their relationships to Armenians living in other countries. The answers reflect different reactions that cannot be carried to a unifying conclusion. There are responses **(P1, P4, P9, and P10)** that can be described as being more emotional as stressed by **P8** in the following statement: "We and they are the pieces of a whole. We were all born [figuratively] in this land and then were flung all over the world"; and by **P5:** "At the end, all of us are Armenians and our homeland is also the land of Turkey."

Other responses indicated that not all Turkish Armenians have strong bonds with the Armenians living beyond the borders of Turkey or the methods employed to defend their arguments. When asked if they perceive themselves being part of the Diaspora Armenians, some responded as **P3**: "I don't, because I don't know them, and it is against my principles to move with a crowd." **P2** expresses her feelings clearly: "No, this is our homeland and the Armenians who live abroad lost their ethnic identity. An Armenian who lives in the United States is more American than an Armenian. The Armenian Diaspora has been divided and some seek their own benefit. Some ignore us and blame us for staying in Turkey and for speaking Turkish." **P7** observed, "Five years ago we went to Paris to attend a conference.…The Armenians who are born outside of Turkey [and Armenia] do not learn Armenian. Our culture is diminishing."

6.2.3 Perceptions About the Social and Economic Status of Turkish Armenians

For most ethnic groups their culture as exemplified by language, religion, music, literature, customs, and traditions remains in a delicate balance between establishing ways that preserve their identity such as media, schools, churches, other organizations, and, at the same time, avoiding isolation while remaining part of the political, social, and economic fabric of a nation.

Participants were asked to evaluate the economic conditions of Turkish Armenians in general, the nature of religious freedom in the country, and the social linkages among members of the Turkish Armenian community.

Participants mostly agree that economic conditions of the Armenians in Turkey are the same as for other Turkish citizens and that they are equally affected by the global financial crisis. It is well known in Turkey that Armenians, including other non-Muslims, are skilled in jewelry design, handicrafts, and the trade business, especially the older generation as observed by participants **P1** and **P4**. These traditional occupations are losing ground in Turkey as elsewhere in the developing world. **P4** observes further that the new generation is more educated and more qualified to pursue other livelihoods. **P6** points to the advantages of being a non-Muslim in the advertising sector. Turkish Armenian Patriarch II Mesrob states that the Turkish Armenians should preserve their own language, religion, and culture despite the difficulties they face (Research Institute on Armenian Studies, 2003).

Participants mostly state that they are involved in a social network among Turkish Armenians, although they do not agree on the strength of their bonds. Some participants believe that religion plays a central role in participating in Armenian community activities while some **(P2, P8)** note that the Armenians are not religious.

P3 describes Armenians as being individualistic rather than collectivistic, referring to the competition in business activities. **P7** emphasizes that they cannot unite easily to become one single voice.

As with other ethnic groups in Turkey, Armenians have their schools, churches, newspapers, cultural and business organizations. They have welfare trusts and opportunities to use and print the Armenian language (Yağmur, 2001, p. 420).

6.2.4 Turkish Armenian Perceptions About How They Are Perceived and Treated

The relationship of a minority with the dominant group in a country, either as integration or assimilation, is a critical factor for their tranquility and welfare. Although it is not as easy to clearly determine where the integration ends and the assimilation begins, Somersan (2004) stressed that social scientists see the integration process as a relatively positive solution for different ethnic groups to live together in a nation (p. 92). Participants were asked about their perceptions of how they have been treated, which is important to a sense of belonging. The answers mostly reflect anxiety among the participants, and this may be generally so for Turkish Armenians.

An incident that **P11** recounted happened approximately 40 years ago and is illustrative of the sense of not feeling fully integrated in society: "I was seated in a tram. A woman approached me and told me to get up and give her my seat, claiming that this is her homeland. Though feeling humiliated, I resisted saying that this is also my homeland."

P4 exclaimed that other Turkish people perceive Armenians as potential criminals or as far removed from being Turkish as an alien from another planet. **P9** also made a comment about being perceived as a foreigner in her own land. She noted, however, that negative perceptions diminish as the level of education increases.

"The others" is an expression used by **P1.** He believes that it is a common definition made by the Turkish Muslims for Armenians. It bespeaks an ethnocultural boundary separating Armenians from other Turks. He adds: "For 99% of them, we are 'the others' and we should be gotten rid of." He adds that the Turkish educational policies have been misleading the people about the Armenians.

P10 describes broadly how he understands the Turkish perception of Armenians. He begins with the word "bizarre." He continues to explain the perceptions by groups:

> The first group, the majority, is unaware of Turkish Armenians. For business reasons, I have several acquaintances and friends throughout Turkey, mainly medical doctors and health-sector businessmen. The first reaction of this group is a surprise because my name is different. They ask me where I am from; if I was born in Turkey; if I went to and completed my military duty; if I have a Turkish ID; or if I am a foreigner living in Turkey. This is the result of a typical education in Turkey.

> I may call it a-historical education that makes others oblivious to Turkey's past. Turkish people in this group, with or without knowledge, may even reject our common history and deny what happened in the past and even the existence of Armenians in the Ottoman days. The expectation of this group from us is simply to accept the official view of the Turkish State. . . .One other group of Turkish people, a small percentage, who are familiar with us and know who we are. The reactions of the individuals in this group are different. Another group has full knowledge of our history. . . .The deportation procedure was a necessity in their thinking, a defensive and simple measure to eliminate local collaborators. The last group is a minority who believe that the historical events have several facets to be discussed and can be expected to be empathetic.

P8 openly states that relationships even with the closest Turkish friends are shallow because of the image other Turks have of Armenians. **P2** strictly states that the majority of the Turkish citizens do not know what an Armenian is. She expresses her feelings by emphasizing that the word "Armenian" is used pejoratively by other Turks as illustrated by the following: "Even the Armenians don't do what you did!" This statement shares company with sayings that go back to Ottoman times (Astourian, 1999, p. 30).

P7 summarizes the status of Armenians as being perceived negatively by the majority. She believes that Turkish Armenians are reluctant to speak Armenian in public. She stresses that she has not witnessed any discrimination against Armenians in her business network. Also, she notes that "landlords prefer non-Muslims for renting their properties."

P6 emphasizes that there is no religious or cultural pressure on the Turkish Armenian community in Turkey. **P5** believes that in general, save a few radical groups, that there is no general ill-will toward Armenians, whereas **P9**, as noted before, connects the perception of Armenians to the level of education.

P3 expresses more positive feelings about the Turkish attitudes toward Armenian citizens. He is disheartened by the Armenian citizens who camouflage their names, although he himself has never found it necessary. He does not agree with statements that other Turkish citizens are opposed to Armenians or other non-Muslims living in the country. An incident that he had experienced reflects Turkish attitudes of tolerance:

> I was away in Samsun [a city in the Black Sea region and most likely a conservative community in those days] for business reasons at the age of 16 or so. I stopped by a restaurant at dinner time. The waiter asked me if I wanted to order my meal or wait. I ordered my meal telling him that I was alone and not waiting for someone. As I started eating, I noticed angry looks coming my way. I was told that it was Ramadan and it was not yet time to break the fast [after sunset]. With a low voice I told them that I was not a Muslim. As the people at the restaurant heard what I said, I received smiles with good appetite wishes.

6.2.5 Opinions About Feeling Secure in Turkey

As a derivative question, participants were asked if they felt secure living in Turkey and if they had considered living in another country, were it a possibility.

Some of the participants (**P3, P5, and P9**) were unable to clearly describe their feelings about the question of security and living in another country. **P3** explains the situation as "I feel secure/insecure. . . . I don't regret returning to Istanbul after living in Zurich for six years." **P5** tells that he and his family considered living in another country, which is in practicality quite difficult.

P8 emphasizes that his fear increases at definite times. He has made attempts to live in another country, although he has been unable to do so. **P2** is clear about her feelings, stating that she never felt secure and has been trying to find a way to start a new life in another country. **P1** feels the insecurity more intensely based on his childhood experiences of being abused as a non-Muslim, and especially after the recent assassination of Hrant Dink, a well-known journalist and a Turkish citizen of Armenian descent, who was killed by a young fanatic nationalist in 2007. The assassination was condemned by the Turkish government and by thousands of protesting Turkish Muslims. In their sympathy for Dink's family and the Turkish-Armenian community and in their outrage for this senseless act of violence, the Turkish-Muslim protesters declared in solidarity that they were Armenians.

6.3 Preliminary Conclusions from the Interviews

The opinions of the participants signal a social and political dissonance between Turkish and Turkish Armenian citizens. The participants, notwithstanding the public outpouring of expressions of good will toward the Armenian community evoked by the assassination of Hrant Dink, mostly believe that there is a negative attitude toward Armenian citizens that affects their quality of life and sense of wellbeing. This creates the need for a close-knit community as reflected in Armenians marrying other Armenians and enrolling their children in Armenian schools. It is understandable that the majority of the participants feel insecure. They express this sentiment as a result of the political discussions going on in the world about genocide; the Diaspora campaign's narrative of condemnation against the Turkish government; the reaction of Turkish citizens to the treatment of Turkey in the court of world opinion; and – still lingering – the memory of the assassinations in the 1970s and 1980s of Turkish officials and diplomats at the hands of Armenian terrorists.

Also, the analysis highlights different perceptions among the Turkish-Armenians regarding their relationship to other Turkish citizens and to the Turkish government. As mentioned at the beginning of this section of the chapter, more findings could be generated from additional qualitative and also quantitative studies. These could provide Turkish policymakers more information to evaluate and possibly reformulate existing policies as they govern ethnic relations.

7 Suggestions

The present relationship between Turks and Turkish Armenians cannot be reduced to a single cause or a simple explanation. It is at once multidimensional and controversial. It is deeply historical and cultural. It is circumscribed by the current relations between the republics of Armenia and Turkey and by the aggressive campaign of Armenian Diaspora organizations. It is a story that begins in nineteenth century Anatolia and continues with the tragedies of World War I for both Armenians and Muslim Turks alike. The question remains: When will it end? When will the dialog begin? When will two peoples find closure on the tragic decision made in the spring of 1915?

7.1 Diplomatic and Bilateral Relations with the Republic of Armenia

Clearly, improving the situation of Armenians in Turkey will rest to a large extent on first normalizing diplomatic and bilateral relations between the two republics and then working out a resolution on the issue of genocide. Progress has been compounded by the Nagorno-Karabakh crisis between Armenia and Azerbaijan. In 1988, while Nagorno-Karabakh – a region of Azerbaijan – was still part of the Soviet Union, a conflict between ethnic Armenians and Muslim Azeries broke out. The situation escalated after the collapse of the Soviet Union, which in 1991 brought the newly independent republics of petroleum-rich Azerbaijan, a Turkic republic, and neighboring landlocked Armenia into an armed conflict that ultimately favored Armenian forces and ended in a ceasefire. In 1993, at the height of the conflict, Turkey in support of Azerbaijan closed its border with Armenia. Today, a large area of Azerbaijan remains under Armenian control, including Nagorno-Karabakh. International negotiations conducted by the United Nations and the Organization for Security Cooperation in Europe as well as other mediators have yet to settle the crisis.

Mutual rapprochement efforts of both Armenia and Turkey in recent years resulted in a promising breakthrough. On August 31, 2009, both nations had announced their intention to establish diplomatic and bilateral relations. This was followed on October 10 by the signing of two protocols in Zurich, Switzerland, though U.S. Secretary of State Hillary Rodham Clinton, after a last minute disagreement between the Armenian and Turkish representatives, saved the signing from being scuttled. The second protocol includes a roundabout reference to addressing the issue of genocide and directs the foreign ministries of both countries to initiate "a dialogue on the historical dimension with the aim to restore mutual confidence between the two nations, including an impartial and scientific examination of the historical records and archives to define existing problems and formulate recommendations" (Protocols, August 31, 2009, p. 2).

Reactions to the signing were mixed, ranging from pledges of support to "waves of dissent. . . as well as the organized and spontaneous protests throughout the diaspora and in Armenia" (Manjikian, 2009, October 28, *The Armenian Weekly*). In Yerevan, the Dashnaks "led the largest anti-government rally since February 2008. . ." (Armenia-Turkey protocols, *Forgotten Diaries.org*., October 12, 2009). Some words of support came from Armenian expatriate groups in the United States. The Western and Eastern Dioceses of the Armenian Church, the Armenian General Benevolent Union, the Knights of Vartan, and the Armenian Assembly of America indicated that "they would back the agreement" (Landler & Arsu, 2009, October 11, *The New York Times*, pp. 6, 14.).

The ratification of the protocols was delayed and remains so. The border between the two republics, therefore, stays closed. For Turkey and Armenia, their respective differences on the conduct of the Nagorno-Karabahk negotiations and the renewed outcries regarding accusations of genocide and claims on Turkish territory have stirred powerful nationalist sentiments. Levon Zurabian of the Armenian National Congress was quoted as saying, "The U.S., the European Union and Russia made promises to Armenia, but betrayed us. The protocols are a political fiasco from the Armenian point of view "(Ziflioğlu, 2010, October 10, *Hürriyet Daily News & Economic Review*). In regard to the issue of genocide, Turkish Parliamentary Foreign Affairs Committee Chairman, Murat Mercan, was quoted as saying that Armenia's Constitutional Court "ruled out three vital articles [of the protocols] since the country's constitution demands land from eastern Anatolia and Turkish recognition of its genocide claims" (Sarıışık, 2010, March 27, *Hürriyet Daily News & Economic Review*). In a *Wall Street Journal* op-ed Armenian Foreign Minister Edward Nalbandian criticized Turkey for linking "the Armenian-Turkish normalization process to the settlement of the Nagorno-Karabakh conflict" (Nalbandian slams Ankara in WSJ op-ed. 2010, October 12, *The Armenian Weekly*).

The momentum toward normalization and the signing of the protocols reflected years of effort, at many levels of engagement, by both republics. In this regard, the Turkish Economic and Social Studies Foundation (2006) emphasized the need to establish linkages through academic institutions, business organizations, media, civil society organizations, and individuals of good will. The Foundation urged that all parties should discuss the Nagorno-Karabahk conflict openly and without any fear but with respect for each others rights. Kongar (2006) underscored the importance of involving representatives from the Armenian government, the patriarchs of the Armenian Church in Turkey and Armenia as well as Armenian foundations and Armenian civil society organizations and their Turkish counterparts (p. 122).

One of the first of many examples was the 2002 gathering of Turkish and Armenian journalists in Ankara that was followed by another meeting in Yerevan, the capital of Armenia. The *Hürriyet Daily News & Economic Review* captured the significance of these meetings as "Baby steps toward rapprochement" (2002, August 4). In October 2008, Turkish and Armenian historians and social scientists gathered in Yerevan to discuss the relationship between the two countries as recounted in the *Hürriyet Daily News & Economic Review* article entitled, "Academics grasp mantle of peace" (2008, October 30).

There were many other steps of a substantive and symbolic nature, including high-level meetings of Armenian and Turkish ministers, that excited optimism about the future and, undoubtedly, resulted in the fruits of these efforts being jointly announced by the two republics on August 31, followed by the signing of the protocols on October 10, 2009. And in spite of the current chorus of discontent, Turkey's decision to reopen an Armenian Church in Van for religious services and to educate the children of undocumented workers from Armenia, are promising reminders of the scores of efforts that moved the rapprochement forward. In referring to this decision, Murat Mercan was quoted as saying that "Both worship and education are basic human rights" (Sarıışık, 2010, March 27, *Hürriyet Daily News and Economic Review*). Though Turkey had closed its border in 1993, it eventually permitted chartered flights between the two countries to be resumed. This enabled the flow of Armenians seeking work in Turkey to continue. Tens of thousands of Armenian nationals are employed in Turkey.

7.1.1 The Importance of Diplomatic and Bilateral Relations for Turkish Armenians

Achieving normalization of relations between Armenia and Turkey, though currently mired in discord, would have a positive outcome for Turkish Armenians. **P10** expresses his opinions highlighting majority–minority relations:

> "What do we want? The priority of Turkish Armenians is to feel secure in all aspects. We want to be a part of the Turkish society without assimilation but full integration. We do not want discrimination against Turkish Armenians. We want to have freedom of thought. We do not want to be treated in a totalitarian way. . . .Negative treatment of minorities is practiced by the Turkish people because we are just guests to them, living and making money, exploiting the resources of the country, and viewed as potential betrayers, looking forward to stabbing them in the back. . . .This does not mean that all Turkish citizens think the same way."

P5 asks to focus on the feeling of security as well as minority rights, including education. He states that although he does not define himself as a minority person, the law does. **P4** emphasizes the necessity for the Turkish government to neutralize the negative image of Turkish Armenians, while **P1**'s demand is not having Turkish Armenians being the subject of the world politics. **P2** discusses the issue from a different perspective: "We are equal to [other] Turkish citizens according to the laws but it is not always the case in practice. We see the new regulation for minority foundations as a step forward [as **P7** also states] and we find the EU [membership] adaptation process as very important." **P8** suggests that the relations based on the past should be reconstructed within the present circumstances. **P9** looks forward to the reencountering of Turks and the people of the Republic of Armenia and believes that the opening of the border between the two countries would be an important first step to improve the relationship between the two governments.

P11, an elderly Armenian woman currently residing in a nursing home, advises: "We cannot blame Turkey for whatever happened in the Ottoman period."

7.2 Turkish Armenians and Policy Recommendations

As we have seen, there is perception on the part of most of the interviewees they have been marginalized. There are policy actions that the government can take to improve the status of Turkish-Armenians. The government could consider enacting measures in public and private education, and at all levels, aimed at further efforts to promote ethnic tolerance. Also, the government can work to ensure that hiring practices in the private and public sector employment do not discriminate against Turkish Armenians. Notably, the enjoyment of religious and cultural independence is emphasized by the participants as positive aspects for the Armenian community in Turkey. This point could be considered by the Turkish government as an important avenue to promote positive ethnic relations.

Some significant steps that should have a positive impact on Turkish minority relations have been taken already. Turkey's European Union membership process and the requisite legal adjustments in revamping the rights of non-Muslim foundations, for example, will improve relations and also benefit Turkey's international standing. The Law of Foundations (Law No. 5737) restored some of the rights of non-Muslim religious and charitable foundations that were first articulated as "fundamental laws" in the Treaty of Lausanne (Kurban & Hatemi, 2009, p. 27).

When the impasse in establishing diplomatic and bilateral relations is finally broken, there will be significant challenges ahead. A study launched by the Turkish Economic and Social Studies Foundation indicated a troublesome gap in the knowledge that the people of both countries have of each other (2005). Kentel (2006) noted the alienation existing between Turks and Armenians and concludes that the people of Turkey and the Republic of Armenia "do not know each other" (p. 64). The normalization of relations would increase the political, social, and cultural interactions and could very well lead to a final resolution of the complex issue of genocide and close the most troubled chapter in the history of the relations between the two republics. Both Prime Minister Recep Erdoğan and President Abdullah Gül – the latter in his April 6, 2009 press conference with President Barack Obama – expressed Turkey's desire to wrest this issue from the adjudication of politicians and placed into the hands of a joint commission of scholars to examine the historical evidence – a goal of the second protocol. Turkey's pledge to abide by the outcome should command the world's attention and go a long way to quell the polemical rhetoric of division.

8 Summary

The centuries of accommodation to the social hierarchy imposed by the sultanate and the mutual and beneficial interdependencies that existed between the Armenians and the Ottoman Turks could not withstand the forces of nationalism. Armenian citizenship in an "imagined community" that defined nationhood by blood and culture became a transformational ideal and a driving force as the nineteenth century advanced. The autocratic behavior of Sultan Abdulhamid, especially suspending the Constitution of 1876, overwhelmed the enfeebled case for his dynastic legitimacy, and made revolution to some an attractive alternative in the absence of parliamentary government. The Empire had been held together by a passive and inertial acceptance of Ottoman rule but its dynastic grip became progressively weakened by military setbacks and the economic servitude of the Capitulations that depleted the Ottoman treasury. Revolutionary organizations emerged which worked from within and outside the Empire. Their nihilistic gospel that justified employing terror against Muslim Turks and Kurds in order to trigger European intervention shattered the social covenant and ended centuries of stability. Ultimately, the widening cultural divide – the ethnic boundary – between Armenians and Muslims quickly transformed trust into fear, and admiration into hatred. The cultural divide and disassociation became so great that the removal of Armenians from eastern Anatolia at the onset of World War I had an overwhelming force of logic – a course of action that Imperial Russia took against its own ethnic populations of as many as 1.5 million Jews and Germans as well as Muslims prior to CUP's decision (Shaw, 2008, Vol. II, pp. 1005–1006).

Present-day Turkish Armenians have inherited the residual ill-will that survived that fateful decision and the preceding decades of revolutionary foment. The great momentum toward re-opening the border between the two countries and establishing diplomatic relations, though suddenly halted, still presents a vital pathway to heal the divisions that exist between Turkey and Armenia, between Muslim Turks and Turkish Armenians. Resolving the issue of genocide need not depend on Armenia and Turkey to establish an officially sanctioned body of scholars. But whatever the agency, whatever the vehicle that brings about a direct and impartial investigation and dialog, no successful resolution will emerge in the absence of ignoring the enormity of the suffering and loss of life endured by the Ottoman Muslims of Anatolia. Ultimately and inherently, the axis of dialog rests on a compass that points in two directions.

The people of these two nations should value a history that has many shared elements of language, music, theatre, architecture, and more in the forum of human achievement (Göyünç, 2001).

Appendix: Timeline

1453 – The Conquest of Constantinople: The massive forces of Ottoman Sultan Mehmet II breached the towering walls of Constantinople, bringing a death blow to the Eastern Roman (Byzantine) Empire. The conquest shocked Christian Europe.

1821–1830 – Greek War of Independence: Greece, after hundreds of years of Ottoman rule, secured its independence through the intervention of Great Britain, Russia, and France.

1839–1876 – Tanzimat: A reform movement to modernize the Ottoman Empire, the Tanzimat, meaning reorganization in Turkish, was mainly a response to the growing threat of the European Powers as well as to the rise of nationalism among its subject populations.

1877–1878 – The Russo-Turkish War: A rebellion by Christian Bulgarians in 1876, which followed the Greek pattern of massacring Muslims and Jews, eventually resulted in Imperial Russia declaring war and defeating the Ottoman Empire.

1878 – The Armenian Question: England and other European Powers overturned Russia's victory and dashed Armenian hopes of eastern Anatolia becoming a Russian protectorate. Article 61 of the Treaty of Berlin, however, promised reforms as well as some guarantees to protect Armenians – a large Christian population in eastern Anatolia (Asia Minor) – from Muslim Kurds and Circassians. Notably, the article gave the European Powers a vehicle to intervene in the internal affairs of the Empire, which became known as "The Sick Man of Europe."

1880–1890s – The Rise of Armenian Revolutionary Parties: The Armenians took false hope in Article 61, believing that the European Powers would intervene and liberate what was referred to as Ottoman or Turkish Armenia to establish an autonomous or independent state. Three Armenian parties, which reflected growing nationalistic fervor, emerged during this period. One originated in Tiflis, Russia; a second in Geneva, Switzerland; and a third in Van, a city in eastern Anatolia. The parties held firm to the strategy of employing terrorism to provoke Ottoman massacres and triggering intervention.

1894–1896 Massacres: In 1894, mounting tensions between Armenians and Muslims, occasioned by the rise of the revolutionary parties, ignited in the eastern Anatolian province of Sassun and spread through Anatolia.

1909 – Abdication of Sultan Abdulhamid: In 1908, the Committee of Union and Progress (CUP), a liberal and reformist faction of Young Turk officers, forced the autocratic Abdulhamid to restore the Constitution of 1876. The following year Abdulhamid abdicated after CUP defeated a counter-revolution by loyalists and those opposed to the secular agenda of the Young Turks.

1914–1918 – World War I: The Ottoman Empire signed a secret treaty of alliance with Germany in August of 1914. In October of that year Turkish battleships attacked three Russian coastal cities on the Black Sea. Russia declared war, which was followed by declarations of war against the Empire by Russia's allies, Great Britain and France.

1915 – Special Law of May 27: As a measure to cut off Armenian support to advancing Russian forces and their Ottoman and Russian Armenian auxiliaries, CUP forcibly removed the Armenian populations of the Anatolian provinces of Van, Bitlis, and Erzurum to nonstrategic locations of the Empire. The Armenian exodus resulted in great suffering and loss of life.

1923 – The Treaty of Lausanne: The Treaty of Lausanne overturned the very unpopular Treaty of Sevres (1920), imposed by the victorious Allies. The treaty, which called for a devastating partition of the Ottoman Empire, spurred a nationalist movement under the leadership of General Mustafa Kemal (Atatürk) and became the War for Independence. Eventually, the nationalists succeeded in negotiating a new treaty and recognition of the Republic of Turkey by the signatories.

1934 – Law No. 2510 (The Law on Settlement): The law authorized the Turkish government to redistribute the population through the relocation of nonethnic Turks into regions that would permit their assimilation.

1942 – The Wealth Levy: During World War II, profiteering by businesses alienated the radical wing of the Republican People's Party (established by Atatürk as the People's Party in 1922) and resulted in legislation that ultimately harmed the private sector and particularly Muslim business partnerships with non-Muslims.

2008 – Law No. 5737 (The New Law on Foundations): Turkey's candidacy for European membership and the requisite legal accommodations led to the revamping of non-Muslim minority rights regarding guarantees stipulated by the Treaty of Lausanne.

2009 – The Signing of Protocols by the Republics of Turkey and Armenia: On August 31, 2009, the two republics announced their intention to establish diplomatic and bilateral relations. The announcement was followed by the signing of protocols on October 10, 2009 but final approval has been stalled.

References

Academics grasp mantle of peace. (2008, October 30). *Hürriyet Daily News & Economic Review*. Retrieved from http://www.hurriyet.com.tr/english/home/.

Anderson, B. (1991). *Imagined communities: Reflections on the origin and spread of nationalism (revised edition)*. London: Verso.

Armenian Studies Institute. (2009, February 20). *Turkey steps up talks with Armenia as April looms (Bulletin Archive)*. Armenian Studies Institute: Retrieved from http//www.eraren.org/index.php?Lisan=tr&pageGBultenDetay&bultenNo=15421.

Armenia-Turkey protocols. (2009, October 12). *Forgotten Diaries.Org*. Retrieved from http://forgottendiaries-caucasus.blogspot.com/2009/10/armenia-turkey-protocols.html..

Aslan, A. Y. (2005, July 25). Son Ermeni köyü: Vakıflı [The last Armenian village: Vakıflı]. *Aksiyon*. Retrieved from http://www.aksiyon.com.tr.

Astourian, S. H. (1999). Modern Turkish identity and the Armenian genocide: From prejudice to racist nationalism. In R. G. Hovannisian (Ed.), *Remembrance and denial: The case of the Armenian Genocide* (pp. 23–49). Wayne, MI: Wayne State University Press.

Ataöv, T. (Ed.). (2001). *The Armenians in the late Ottoman period*. Ankara: Turkish Historical Society for the Council of Culture. Arts and Publications of the Grand Assembly of Turkey.

Aya, Ş. (2008). *The genocide of truth (No. 25)*. Istanbul: Istanbul Commerce University Publications.

Baby steps towards rapprochement. (2002, August 04). *Hürriyet Daily News & Economic Review*. Retrieved from http://www.hurriyetdailynews.com.tr.

Boucher, J., Landis, D., & Clark, K. (Eds.). (1987). *Ethnic conflict: International perspectives*. Newbury Park, CA: Sage Publications.

Brubaker, R. (2004). *Ethnicity without groups*. Cambridge, MA: Harvard University Press.

Buğra, A. (1994). *State and business in modern Turkey: A comparative study*. New York: State University of New York Press.

Dadrian, V. N. (1999). *Warrant for genocide: Key elements of Turko-Armenian conflict*. New Brunswick, NJ: Transaction Publishers.

Dadrian, V. N. (2002). The Armenian question and the wartime fate of the Armenians as documented by the officials of the Ottoman Empire's World War I Allies: Germany, Austria-Hungary. *International Journal of Middle East Studies, 34*(1), 59–85.

Davison, R. H. (1948). The Armenian crisis, 1912–1914. *The American Historical Review, 53*(3), 481–505.

Djemal Pasha, A. (1922). *Memories of a Turkish statesman,1913-1919*. New York: George H. Doran Company.

Duguid, S. (1973). The politics of unity: Hamidian policy in eastern Anatolia. *Middle Eastern Studies, 9*(2), 139–156.

Dumont, P. (1984). The origins of Kemalist ideology. In J. Landau (Ed.), *Ataturk and the modernization of Turkey* (pp. 25–44). Boulder, CO: Westview Press.

Earle, M. E. (1925). The new constitution of Turkey. *Political Science Quarterly, 40*(1), 73–100.

Eliot, C. (1908). *Turkey in Europe*. London: Edward Arnold. New Edition.

Eriksen, T. H. (2002). *Ethnicity and nationalism* (2nd ed.). London, England: Pluto Press.

Eversley, G., & Chirol, V. (1924). *The Turkish empire from 1288 to 1914 by Lord Eversley and 1914 to 1924 by Sir Valentine Chirol*. London: T. Fisher Urwin Ltd.

Extra, G., & Gortner, D. (Eds.). (2001). *The other languages of Europe*. Buffalo, NY: Multilingual Matters.

Fenton, S. (2003). *Ethnicity*. Cambridge, MA: Polity Press.

Göyünç, N. (2001). Turkish-Armenian cultural relations. In T. Ataöv (Ed.), *The Armenians in the late Ottoman period* (pp. 23–42). Ankara: Turkish Historical Society.

Greene, F. D. (1895). *The Armenian crisis in Turkey: The massacre of 1894, its antecedents and significance*. New York: G.P. Putnam's Sons.

Halaçoğlu, Y. (2002). *Facts on the relocation of Armenians (1914-1918)*. Ankara: Turkish Historical Society.

Hepworth, G. H. (1898). *Through Armenia on horseback*. New York: E.P. Dutton & Company.

Hoffmann, T. (2002). *Armenians in Turkey today*. Bruxelles, Belgium: The EU Office of Armenian Associations of Europe.

Hovannisian, R. G. (Ed.). (1999). *Remembrance and denial: The case of the Armenian genocide*. Wayne, MI: Wayne State University Press.

İçduygu, A., Toktaş, Ş., & Soner, A. B. (2008). The politics of population in a nation building process: Emigration of non-Muslims from Turkey. *Ethnic and Racial Studies, 31*(2), 358–389.

Institute of Atatürk's Principles and Revolution History. (1984). *Armenians in the Ottoman Empire and modern Turkey (1912–1926)*. İstanbul: Boğaziçi University Publications.

Intute. (2006–2007). *Turkey: Population and demographics*. Retrieved from http://www.intute.ac.uk/cgi.

Jenkins, P. (2008). *The lost history of Christianity: The thousand-year golden age of the Church in the Middle East, Africa, and Asia – and how it died*. USA: Harper Collins Publishers.

Jung, D., & Piccoli, W. (2004). *Yol ayrımında Türkiye [Turkey at the cross-roads]*. İstanbul: Kitap Publications.

Kamrava, M. (2004). *The modern Middle East: A political history since the First World War*. Berkeley, CA: University of California Press.

Karpat, K. H. (2004). *Studies on Turkish politics and society: Selected articles and essays*. Leiden: Brill.

Kentel, F. (2006). Turkiye ve Ermenistan toplumları: Turkluk, Ermenilik, ve onyargılar [Turkish and Armenian societies: Being a Turk, an Armenian and the prejudice] (pp. 62–85). In *Ermeni sorunu tartisilirken [Discussing the Armenian Issue]*. İstanbul: Heinric Böll Stiftung Society.

Keyder, Ç. (1987). *State and class in Turkey: A study in capitalist development*. London: Verso.

Kirişci, K. (July 2000). Disaggregating Turkish citizenship and immigration practices. *Middle Eastern Studies, 36*(3), 1–22.

Kongar, E. (2006). *Tarihimizle yüzleşmek [Facing our history]*. İstanbul: Remzi Publications.

Kongar, E. (2007). *21. Yüzyılda Türkiye [Turkey in the 21st century]*. İstanbul: Remzi Publications.

Kurban, D., & Hatemi, K. (2009). *The story of an alien(ation): Real estate ownership problems of non-Muslim foundations and communities in Turkey*. İstanbul: TESEV Publications.

Landau, J. (Ed.). (1984). *Ataturk and the modernization of Turkey*. Boulder, CO: Westview Press.

Lander, M., & Arsu, S. (2009, October 11). Long-bitter Turkey and Armenia sign pact to normalize relations. *The New York Times*, pp. 6, 14.

Lewis, B. (2002). *The emergence of modern Turkey* (3rd ed.). New York: Oxford University Press.

Lewy, G. (2005). *The Armenian massacres in Ottoman Turkey: A disputed genocide*. Salt Lake City, UT: The University of Utah Press.

Manjikian, L. (2009, October 28). Manjikian: A post-protocol reaction: What defines the Diaspora? *The Armenian Weekly*. Retrieved from http://www.armenianweekly.com.

McCarthy, J. (1995). *Death and exile: The ethnic cleansing of Ottoman Muslims, 1821–1922*. Princeton, NJ: Darwin Press.

McCarthy, J. (2001). The populations of the Ottoman Armenians. In T. Ataöv (Ed.), *The Armenians in the late Ottoman period* (pp. 65–85). Ankara: Turkish Historical Society for the Council of Culture. Arts and Publications of the Grand Assembly of Turkey.

McDowall, D. (1996). *A modern history of the Kurds*. London: I.B. Tauris & Company.

Mgrditchan, K. (August 11, 2007). İstanbul-Armenians or Turkish-Armenians? *The Armenian Weekly, 73*(32). Retrieved from http://www.armenianweekly.com.

Nalbandian, L. (1963). *The Armenian revolutionary movement: The development of Armenian political parties through the nineteenth century*. Berkeley, CA: University of California Press.

Nalbandian slams Ankara in WSJ op-ed. (2010, October 11) *The Armenian Weekly*. Retrieved from http://www.armenianweekly.com.

Öke, M. K. (2001). *The Armenian question*. Ankara: Turkish Historical Society.

Önder, A. T. (2007). *Türkiye'nin etnik yapısı [Ethnic structure in Turkey]*. Ankara: Fark Yayınları.

Ortaylı, İ. (2008). *Tarihimiz ve biz [Our history and us]*. Istanbul: Timas Publications.

Öztuna, Y. (2001). The political milieu of the Armenian question. In T. Ataöv (Ed.), *The Armenians in the late Ottoman period* (pp. 43–64). Ankara: Turkish Historical Society for the Council of Culture. Arts and Publications of the Grand Assembly of Turkey.

Panossian, R. (2006). *The Armenians: From kings and priests to merchants and commissars*. New York: Columbia University Press.

Papazian, K. S. (1934). *Patriotism perverted: A discussion of the deeds and misdeeds of the Armenian Revolutionary Federation, the so-called Dashnagtzoutune*. Boston, MA: Baikar Press.

Pears, E. (1916). *Forty years in Constantinople: The recollections of Sir Edwin Pears, 1873-1915*. New York: Appleton and Company.

Protocols to guide relations between Armenia & Turkey. (August 31, 2009). Retrieved from http://www.keghart.com/node/604.

Salt, J. (1993). *Imperialism, evangelism and the Ottoman Armenians, 1878–1896*. London: Frank Cass.

Saray, M. (2003). *The principles of Turkish administration and their impact on the lives of non-Muslim peoples: The Armenians as a case study*. Ankara: Atatürk Research Center.

Sarıışık, D. (Turkey, 2010, March 27). Armenia at political deadlock on protocols. *Hürryiet Daily News & Economic Review*. Retrieved from http://hurriyetdailynews.com on October 10, 2010

Shaw, S. (1976). *History of the Ottoman Empire and modern Turkey: Vol. 1: Empire of the Gazis: The Rise and Decline of the Ottoman Empire, 1280–1808*. London: Cambridge University Press.

Shaw, S. J. (2008). *The Ottoman Empire in World War I: Triumph and tragedy: November 1914-July 1916* (Vol. II). Ankara: Turkish Historical Society.

Shaw, S. J., & Shaw, E. K. (1977). *History of the Ottoman Empire and modern Turkey: Vol. II: Reform, revolution, and republic: The rise of modern Turkey, 1808–1975*. London: Cambridge University Press.

Şimşir, B. N. (1983). *The genesis of the Armenian question*. Ankara: Turkish Historical Society.

Şimşir, B. N. (Ed.). (1989). *British documents on Ottoman Armenians (1856–1880)*. (2nd ed., Vol. I). Ankara: Turkish Historical Society.

Şimşir, B. N. (Ed.). (1990). *British documents on Ottoman Armenians (1895)* (Vol. IV). Turkish Historical Society: Ankara.

Somersan, S. (2004). *Sosyal Bilimlerde etnicite ve ırk (Ethnicity and race in Social Sciences)*. İstanbul: İstanbul Bilgi Universitesi.

Sonyel, S. R. (2000). *The Great War and the tragedy of Anatolia: Turks and Armenians in the maelstrom of major powers*. Ankara: Turkish Historical Society.

Sykes, M. (1915). *The Caliph's last heritage: A short history of the Turkish Empire*. London: Macmillan.

Toynbee, A. J., & Kirkwood, K. P. (1927). *Turkey*. New York: Charles Scribner's Sons.

Treaty of peace with Turkey signed at Lausanne, July 24, 1923. (1924). *The Treaties of Peace 1919–1923*. Vol. II. New York: Carnegie Endowment for International Peace. Retrieved from http://wwi.lib.byu.edu.

Turkish Economic and Social Studies Foundation [TESEV]. (2005). *Armenian and Turkish citizen's mutual perceptions and dialogue project*. İstanbul: TESEV.

Ürer, L. (2003). *Azınlıklar ve Lozan tartışmaları [Minorities and Lausanne discussions]*. İstanbul: Derin Yayınları.

Whitman, S. (1914). *Turkish memories*. New York: Chas. Scribner & Sons.

Yağmur, K. (2001). Turkish and other languages in Turkey. In G. Extra & D. Gorter (Eds.), *The other languages of Europe* (pp. 407–427). Buffalo, NY: Multilingual matters.

Young, P. J. (2001). *Knowledge, nation, and the curriculum: Ottoman Armenian education (1853-1915) (Unpublished doctoral dissertation)*. Ann Arbor, MI: University of Michigan.

Ziflioğlu, V. (2010, October 10). Armenia resentful one year after signing accord with Turkey. *Hürriyet Daily News & Economic Review*. Retrieved from http://www.hurriyetdailynews.com.

Zurcher, E. J. (2004). *Turkey: A modern history*. London: I.B.Tauris.

12 Communication Across the Divide in the Cyprus Conflict

Benjamin J. Broome and Harry Anastasiou

Cyprus Chapter Summary

Broome and Anastasiou provide details and insights into the causes and consequences of interethnic conflict in Cyprus by examining both historical and recent events. Attention is given to efforts over the years to bring about peaceful resolution. While results to negotiate a settlement have been not resulted in a successful agreement, encouragement may be found in the ongoing activities of civil-society groups that are actively working to promote contact and build understanding among people from across Cypriot society.

Analysis of the conflict's origins begins with a description of the movement by Greek Cypriots in the 1950s against British colonial rule. The authors describe how the biethnic republic created in 1960 quickly fell apart, with events in 1974 leading to a geographic division of the island along ethnic lines. The authors explore the conflicts that led to this division, and while there are many contributing factors, the role of extreme nationalism is given particular emphasis. A summary is provided of efforts by the international community to mediate the conflict, which today is in a protracted stalemate.

Exploring the multiple areas through which peace is being promoted, descriptions are provided of interactive problem-solving workshops, conflict resolution training, seminars to promote dialogue, cultural events, and a variety of collaborative projects. The perseverance of the bi-communal groups, which have continued to work towards peace despite many obstacles, provides a sense of hope for the future.

Broome and Anastasiou explore the contributions of peace-building activities at the personal, relational, and structural levels. The chapter concludes by discussing implications for ethnic conflicts, including the need to balance international and local input into peacebuilding, to anchor civil-society initiatives in societal institutions, and to actively develop links between official and unofficial efforts toward peace.

Cheryl Jorgensen

B.J. Broome (✉)
Hugh Downs School of Human Communication,
Arizona State University, Tempe, AZ, USA
e-mail: benjamin.broome@asu.edu

H. Anastasiou
International Peace and Conflict Studies,
Portland State University, Portland, Oregon, USA
e-mail: harrya@pdx.edu

D. Landis and R.D. Albert (eds.), *Handbook of Ethnic Conflict: International Perspectives*,
International and Cultural Psychology, DOI 10.1007/978-1-4614-0448-4_12,

1 Introduction

The island of Cyprus is located in the eastern Mediterranean, at the closest points only 40 miles south of Turkey and 60 miles west of Syria. The total population of the island is less than one million, consisting of approximately 650,000 Greek Cypriots, 150,000 Turkish Cypriots, and at least 100,000 non-Cypriots of various national origins residing on the island as guest workers or part-time residents. Blessed by a mild climate, pleasant scenery, beautiful beaches, and hundreds of archeological and cultural sites that reflect its Greek, Roman, Byzantine, Venetian, and Ottoman past, Cyprus is a popular tourist destination, receiving well over two million visitors each year. The island is known as the birthplace of Aphrodite, the mother goddess associated with love and beauty, and in ancient times her temple was a place of pilgrimage for residents throughout the eastern Mediterranean.

Because it is strategically located at the crossroads of Europe, Asia, and Africa, Cyprus has rarely been free of outsiders. Over the past 5,000 years it has been raided, settled, and occupied by Phoenicians, Assyrians, Arabs, Greeks, Normans, Franks, Genovese, Venetians, Ottomans, and the British. Cyprus became an independent republic in 1960, after 80 years as a British Colony. It was set up as a single, ethnically mixed, independent bi-communal state. Unfortunately, independence did little to resolve the deepening alienation between the Greek-Cypriot and Turkish-Cypriot communities, and after interethnic conflict in 1963 and full-scale war involving Greece and Turkey in 1974, Cyprus was divided into two ethnic zones. Although a ceasefire brought an end to military operations less than a month after the war began, little progress has been made in negotiations to end the conflict, and today the division remains, as does the heavy presence of troops on both sides.[1]

Although there has been minimal violence between the two communities since the ceasefire in 1974, diplomatic efforts aimed at bringing the Cyprus conflict to a successful resolution have so far failed to produce a final settlement. Factors such as historical memory (Hadjipavlou-Trigeorgis, 1998), regional hostilities (Bahcheli & Rizopoulos, 1996,1997), major power interference in internal affairs, and reluctance to change the status quo (Bölükbasi, 1998) have prevented political leaders of the two communities from reaching an agreement to end the stalemate.

Today the island of Aphrodite is ethnically and geographically divided by a United Nations (UN) patrolled buffer zone that runs the entire length of the island from west to east. In addition to this physical dividing line, the Greek-Cypriot and Turkish-Cypriot communities are also separated by differences in language, cultural heritage, religion, politics, view of the past, and vision of the future. Both sides have experienced disruption, displacement, loss of life, and other forms of suffering, leading to a sense of victimization in each community and a lack of trust between them. The conflict has affected nearly every aspect of people's lives, including the psychological state of residents, who carry a sense of injustice about the past and anxiety about the future. Cyprus remains a prime example of a protracted conflict (Azar, 1990).[2]

In this chapter, we will examine the Cyprus conflict from both political and civil-society perspectives. We will discuss the history of the struggle, including the events that led to the division and that have thus far prevented a solution to the conflict, and the civil-society peacebuilding efforts that have helped push the peace process forward. Based on our review of civil-society contributions, we will conclude with implications for ethnic conflicts in general.

2 History of Struggle

2.1 Birth of the Republic of Cyprus 1960

The 1950s saw the formation of the National Organization of Cypriot Fighters (EOKA) comprised of right-wing Greek-Cypriot nationalists who premised their agenda on the "Great Idea" a nineteenth-century concept that anachronistically envisioned the founding of the Republic of Greece as the start of a glorious reestablishment of Byzantine and classical Greek culture. Moreover, it envisioned "redeeming" all Greek people in the broader region by eventually incorporating them into the Greek state. In 1955, motivated by the Great Idea, EOKA commenced a 4-year insurgency against the British. Its major purpose was threefold: to free Cyprus from foreign rule, to cleanse the country of the "blemish" of communism, and to "Hellenize" the island by brining about *enosis*, that is, the union of Cyprus with Greece.

In response to the Greek struggle for *enosis*, the Turkish Cypriots began to advocate *taksim*, or division of Cyprus into two geographical areas, each controlled by one of the communities. Unable to subdue the Greek-Cypriot guerilla movement, Britain granted Cyprus independence, negotiating treaties with Greece and Turkey to establish Cyprus as a bi-ethnic state. The Treaty of Establishment founded the Republic of Cyprus, while the Treaty of Guarantee established Britain, Greece, and Turkey as guarantors of the Republic's independence, sovereignty, and territorial integrity.

The constitution set up a government with executive, legislative, and judicial branches, headed by a president, with guarantees for the Turkish-Cypriot minority. A Greek-Cypriot president and

[1] In 1996, the Secretary General of the UN, Boutros Ghali, reported that relative to population, Cyprus was one of the most militarized areas in the world.

[2] For overviews of the Cyprus conflict, see Anastasiou, 2008a; Attalides, 1979; Barkey & Gordon, 2002; Bryant, 2004; Calotychos, 1998; Hitchens, 1997; Joseph, 1997; Kizilyurek, 1993; Koumoulides, 1986; Markides, 1977; Mirbagheri, 1998; Papadakis, 2006; Richmond, 1998; Savvides, 2002; Stearns, 1992; Volkan, 1979; Yesilada & Sozen, 2002.

Turkish-Cypriot vice president were elected by their respective communities for 5-year terms of office. Greek and Turkish were designated as official languages, and the two communities were given the right to celebrate, respectively, Greek and Turkish national holidays. Two communal chambers, with representatives elected by each community, were created and given responsibility for religious, educational, and cultural matters. In addition, a unicameral House of Representatives was designed to legislate in matters that lay outside those reserved for separate communal chambers. Thirty-five of its members were Greek Cypriots and 15 were Turkish Cypriots. In addition, a Council of Ministers was established, composed of seven Greek Cypriots (appointed by the president) and three Turkish Cypriots (appointed by the vice president). Each executive had the right of veto over certain laws or decisions of the House of Representatives and the Council of Ministers.

The resolution that led to independence and the resulting constitution were an attempt to curb the three sources of the Cyprus conflict, namely, colonialism, *enosis*, and *taksim*. Thus, independence brought colonial rule to an end while crafting a constitution that forbade both *enosis* and *taksim*. While Greece and Turkey convinced their Cypriot ethnic counterparts to accept the settlement, the question was whether the long-cultivated belligerent nationalisms that gave rise to the agendas of *enosis* and *taksim* could be curbed.

However "imperfect," the 1960 settlement offered Cypriots a historic opportunity for a new beginning. Unfortunately, it also had a serious deficiency. While it offered a system of bi-ethnic governance for the new republic, it had no provisions for building and institutionalizing peace-enhancing interethnic relations at the civil-society level. In the absence of any short- and long-term mechanisms for embedding the peace in the broader fabric of Cypriot society, this lacuna left the settlement vulnerable to the ethnocentric nationalism that had fueled the conflict in the first case. Nationalists on both sides of the ethnic divide saw the newly founded Republic of Cyprus as a deviation and even as an obstacle to their original agendas of *enosis* and *taksim,* respectively. Hard-line nationalists, especially on the Greek-Cypriot side, even saw the establishment of the Republic as outright betrayal to what they deemed "the sacred cause" of enosis. It was under these conditions that the British ended colonial rule and Greek Cypriots and Turkish Cypriots entered a power-sharing arrangement in the governance of the Republic of Cyprus. In such circumstances, it was difficult to view the peace settlement as sustainable.

2.2 Postindependence Crisis 1960–1963: The Breakdown of Constitutional Order

Within three years after independence, Cyprus was faced with a constitutional crisis. The difficulties emerged from an array of issues ranging from disputes over positions in the civil service to excesses in the use of veto power, the boundaries demarcating Greek-Cypriot and Turkish-Cypriot municipalities, and taxation practices. Underneath each issue that led to the constitutional crisis and the decades-long political impasse that followed, however, lay the mono-ethnic concepts of statehood and nationhood that the respective Greek-Cypriot and Turkish-Cypriot nationalists instated into the politics of the island.

In 1963, the crisis mounted when the President of the Republic, Archbishop Makarios, put forward a 13-point proposal for constitutional revisions. Although the proposal was designed, in his view, to eliminate impediments to the functioning of the government, it effectively transferred more power to the Greek-Cypriot majority. The 13 points involved constitutional revisions, including doing away with the veto power by both the president and the vice president. This idea was certain to be rejected by the Turkish Cypriots, who depended on the veto as a way to protect their minority community. Unsurprisingly, the Turkish Cypriots saw this attempted change as a blatant attempt by the Greek-Cypriot majority to disenfranchise and overwhelm the Turkish-Cypriot minority.

Intending to set up their own purely Turkish-Cypriot administrative system within their enclaves, Turkish Cypriots subsequently withdrew from the government, leaving the Republic of Cyprus by default in the hands of the Greek Cypriots. The Turkish Cypriots interpreted their move as a protest against Greek-Cypriot intimidation and dominance over Turkish Cypriots, and as an assertion that the bi-ethnic state was unworkable – the implication being that only partition would work. The Greek Cypriots, on the other hand, saw the Turkish-Cypriot move as a rebellion against the government of the Republic of Cyprus and as a disruption of the public order. The Greek-Cypriot view was that the bi-ethnic power-sharing arrangement obstructed the Greek-Cypriot ethnic majority from running the country, which in their minds was an essentially a "Greek state."

Assisted by clandestine support from their "ethnic motherlands" (Greece and Turkey), Greek Cypriots and Turkish Cypriots had been stockpiling arms since independence. Citizens were trained and armed, and paramilitary militias were formed on both sides of the ethnic divide. The stage was thus fully set for confrontation, and as interethnic tensions mounted and a volatile political environment was created, the crisis easily tipped into violence. Greece and Turkey, in their role as guarantor powers, should have promoted conflict-preventive measures or facilitated reconciliation. Instead, they participated in the mounting polarization and the fighting by siding with their Cypriot ethnic counterparts.

In an attempt to disarm the Turkish-Cypriot militia, the Greek-Cypriot-controlled government launched attacks on Turkish-Cypriot strongholds in the major cities. Killings, destruction of property, and displacement of Turkish Cypriots ensued. In 1964, after the United Nations helped negotiate a ceasefire, UN peacekeepers arrived in Cyprus, established a buffer zone that divided the capitol city of Nicosia and took positions along the ceasefire lines in different parts of the country. The UN peacekeeping forces are still in Cyprus, making it the longest UN mission in the history of the organization.

The ethnocentric nationalism that motivated the leadership of each community, as well as the governments of Greece and Turkey, essentially precluded any interest or effort in building sustainable interethnic relations. If anything, each action taken by the two parties between independence in 1960 and 1963–1964 fundamentally led to further deterioration of interethnic relations in Cypriot society. Moreover, the violence did not stop in 1964 but continued in 1967–1968. The outcome of the 1967–1968 fighting overwhelmed the Turkish Cypriots. The military victories of the Greek side, however, were offset by international condemnation that eventually led to the withdrawal from Cyprus of a controversial Greek military division, which was secretly smuggled to Cyprus from Greece to back the Greek Cypriots against the Turkish Cypriots.

Throughout most of the 1960s, in response to the fighting, Turkish Cypriots moved to confined self-governed enclaves scattered throughout the island. Under dire socioeconomic conditions, and with some assistance from Turkey, these enclaves were protected by the Turkish-Cypriot militia, while being surrounded by UN peacekeepers and an outer ring of Greek-Cypriot and Greek troops. This stalemated condition was frequently dotted with abductions and incidents reflecting the tenuousness of the situation.

2.3 Civil Conflict and War 1967–1974

In 1967, within the broader context of the Cold War, the Greek military, with the consent of the US, launched a coup d'état that brought Greece under military rule in an attempt to preempt the left from a likely electoral victory. In Turkey, similar but more extreme trends were unfolding. By 1971, against the backdrop of an economic recession, political fractionalization, civil unrest, and violence by rival ideological groups, the high command of the Turkish armed forces launched a coup d'état placing Turkey under direct military rule. As had been the case in Greece, the Turkish action was taken to deter a communist threat. Throughout the 1960s, the involvement of Greece and Turkey in the interethnic conflict in Cyprus was spearheaded by right-wing, nationalist governments.

The Greek coup d'état of 1967 and the Turkish coup d'état of 1971 marked a radicalization of both the nationalism and anticommunism of the Greek and the Turkish governments. As a result, the impact that Greece and Turkey had on Cyprus inevitably escalated the psychological and political tension between the Cypriot ethnic communities, as well as the tension between the far right and the far left within each community. The national rulers of Greece and Turkey viewed communists and any left-wing group as a national threat and a defilement of ethnonational identity. At the time, having developed their own brand of nationalism, communists identified the far right as oppressors and proxies of the capitalist West. The adversarial and often deadly relationships between the far right and the far left in Greece, Turkey, and Cyprus was exacerbated by the fact that leading communists with direct ties to the Soviet Union had, in turn, become proxies for the Soviets, whose intention was to facture the NATO alliance in the eastern Mediterranean.

In this context, ideological politics within each of the Cypriot communities became increasingly contentious. While on the Turkish-Cypriot side the left wing was placated by the far right, on the Greek-Cypriot side events took a more sinister turn. In view of the overarching ethnonationalist conflict, President Archbishop Makarios attempted to unite the Greek-Cypriot side under the banner of national unity. While continuing as a right-wing nationalist, he became more tolerant toward the Greek-Cypriot left, accommodating them into the civil service and the police force. His gesture was a strategic attempt to transcend ideological politics in the interest of ethnocentric Hellenic nationalism. From the perspective of the adversarial mindset of the Cold War, however, the Greek-Cypriot far right and the Greek junta perceived the openness of Makarios toward the left as treasonous and an abomination to "proper" national values and identity. In the late 1960s and early 1970s, these two versions of nationalism within the Greek-Cypriot community deepened intra-Greek conflict. Toxic ideological rhetoric, political killings and repeated assassination attempts by the far right against Makarios marked the dangerously evolving political landscape of Cyprus, adding to the continuing interethnic conflict between Greeks and Turks. In the eyes of the far right, Makarios was perceived as selling out on two accounts: abandoning the "sacred" cause of *enosis* and turning towards communism – issues over which the far right was ready to assume extreme actions. By the early 1970s core members of the far right created EOKA B, a nationalist militant organization that saw itself as the continuation of the anticolonial EOKA of the 1950s whose aim was *enosis* at any cost.

As the Greek-Cypriot National Guard had been under the direction of junta-sympathizer Greek officers, Makarios started to lose control of his army. He thereupon created a loyal auxiliary force, which he attempted to arm with the help of the Greek-Cypriot left by purchasing weapons from Czechoslovakia. By this time the West had identified Makarios as "the Castro of the Mediterranean," and sought his demise. On July 15, 1974, the Cyprus-based and Athens-directed Greek officer core, in collaboration with EOKA B, launched a bloody coup that overthrew the Makarios government. In the midst of the unfolding intra-Greek conflict, Turkey launched an air, sea, and land military offensive in Cyprus on July 20, quickly gaining control of the northern third of the island.[3] Three days later, in the face of a national crisis and utter confusion, the Greek junta collapsed, opening the road to civilian rule in Greece under dire circumstances. Without the support of the Athens dictatorship, the coup regime ended in Cyprus, resulting in the restoration of the constitution 8 days after the coup. Makarios did not return to Cyprus until January of the following year, working first to secure international recognition of his administration as the legitimate government of the whole island of Cyprus.

While premising its action on its obligation as a guarantor of the Republic of Cyprus and as protector of Turkish Cypriots, Turkey's military advances across Cyprus in 1974 led to the loss of thousands of lives and massive displacement of the Greek-Cypriot population. The forced

[3] The Turkish military intervention in 1974 is referred to by the Greeks and the international community as an "invasion," while Turkey and the Turkish Cypriots refer to it as a "Peace Operation." In this chapter, we use the more neutral term "intervention."

division of the island and population exchange that ensued created a de facto partitioned Cyprus with a Turkish north and Greek south separated by a ceasefire line, which was turned into a UN-patrolled buffer zone. The United Nations passed resolutions calling for the withdrawal of all foreign troops, Greek and Turkish, and the restoration of the Republic of Cyprus. These resolutions failed to change the situation, and Cyprus entered an era of protracted stalemate that exists to this day.

2.4 Failed Efforts to Reach a Settlement (1974–2001)

After the de facto ethnic division of the island in 1974, the Cyprus conflict entered two-and-a-half decades of political and diplomatic stalemate. Today, after nearly half a century with the Cyprus problem on the agenda of the international community, approximately 1,000 UN troops remain stationed on the island. Although there were several years of intense diplomatic efforts, primarily under the auspices of the United Nations, nothing fundamentally changed as the parties to the conflict continued to hold their respective positions, with each side locked into its familiar ethnocentric nationalism. Nevertheless, there were top-level agreements reached in 1977 and 1979, stating that in principle the solution would be based on a bi-communal bi-zonal federation. Neither side, however, has acted on the top-level agreements or exhibited genuine commitment to a federal solution. In their interpretations of the agreements, the Greek-Cypriot side always gravitated toward a schema with a strong central state, reminiscent of the pre-1974 Republic, while the Turkish-Cypriot side steadily oriented itself toward confederation, the arrangement closest to partition of the island into separate entities.

The questions that dominated the UN efforts during this period, and that are still unresolved today, revolve around power sharing within the proposed federation: What responsibilities will lie with the two constituent states and which with the federal government? How will the president of the federation be elected? Additionally, the two sides disagree over territorial adjustments. Turkish Cypriots constitute less than 20% of the population, yet they control nearly 40% of the island. How much will this ratio be adjusted? Which areas in the north will be placed under Greek-Cypriot administration? Further, there are large disagreements about how to deal with property that each side lost in 1974. How will the original owners be compensated? Will the compensation be based on 1974 values or on present-day values? Each side takes a different view of the Turkish settlers that arrived in Cyprus after 1974. How many settlers should be required to leave Cyprus and return to Turkey? What about their children who were born in Cyprus? Finally, the two sides have very different views of security issues. Should the guarantor system be maintained? What level of military presence should be allowed on the island?

Although the two sides are divided by these and other issues, the failure to reach a settlement is also rooted in the different approaches to negotiations taken by Turkish Cypriots and Greek Cypriots. The Greek-Cypriot approach to a political settlement was built on the assumption that any new federal republic must be based on the 1960 Republic of Cyprus. From their view the original republic, under which they continued to operate, was the sole and exclusive legal state entity on the island. In their perspective, it was necessary to maintain a strict legal continuity from the present Republic to any form of a federal settlement. Only the Republic of Cyprus could legally evolve into a new system of governance for the island. As seen by the Turkish Cypriots, the Greek-Cypriot approach was disingenuous, particularly since many in the Greek-Cypriot community continued to advocate a unitary state as opposed to a bi-communal, bi-zonal federation. The Turkish Cypriots had always suspected that the Greek Cypriots were not committed to the idea of federation, but rather they were attempting to use talk about federation to achieve physical reunification of the island under a single state.

As a result, the Turkish Cypriots gravitated toward confederation (a loose joining of two semiautonomous zones under a weak central government), rather than federation (a stronger federal government) or secession, and at times even toward the annexation of northern Cyprus by Turkey. Even though this was not always explicitly stated, the Turkish Cypriots approached the negotiation process with a goal of finding opportunities to assert and demand legitimacy for their breakaway state. They presumed that formal recognition of the self-declared Turkish Republic of Northern Cyprus (TRNC) was a necessary precondition for serious negotiations toward a bi-zonal, bi-communal, federal Cyprus. This view placed confederation as the desirable outcome of a Cyprus settlement. As a primary premise for negotiations, the Turkish Cypriots argued that since federation implies the existence of at least two states, it was necessary to first recognize the existence of two preestablished state entities of equal legal status. As a breakaway state not recognized by the international community, the Turkish side presented the TRNC as a de facto phenomenon that had to be legitimized by the international community before genuine negotiations for a Cyprus settlement could take place. The Turkish Cypriots thus tacitly aimed at conferring formal recognition to an independent Turkish-Cypriot state – the administrative entity formed in 1974 by the Turkish military occupation of northern Cyprus, and unilaterally declared a state in 1983.

The United Nations brokered negotiations between the two leaders in Cyprus in the early 1980s, but these ultimately failed, with the Greek-Cypriot government insisting on the a priori withdrawal of Turkish troops, and the Turkish and Turkish-Cypriot nationalists demanding to secede from the Republic. The subsequent 1983 unilateral declaration of independence by the Turkish side solidified the division of Cyprus. Neither the Greek side nor the international community accepted the legitimacy of the breakaway state. An additional UN-led push for resolution of the Cyprus conflict came in the early 1990s, when the Secretary General Boutros Boutros-Ghali proposed what came to be known as "the Ghali set of ideas," which suggested territorial adjustments and constitutional aspects of a federal arrangement. This effort also ended in failure, with the Turkish Cypriots insisting on many Turkish Cypriots remaining in the Greek-Cypriot houses they occupied after 1974, and the Greek Cypriots insisting on the right of return to their properties. Several other attempts at negotiated settlements during this period met the same fate.

2.5 From Stalemate to Hope (2001–2003)

Significant changes began to occur around the turn of the millennium, as a series of historical and political factors converged to create favorable conditions for a possible final resolution of the Cyprus problem. In the late 1990s, the government of Greece made the decision to forgo Greece's traditional nationalist foreign policy of isolating Turkey, pursuing instead a policy of engaging Turkey both bilaterally and within the broader EU process. Subsequently, with Greece's consent, the European Union (EU) heads of state at the Helsinki Summit of December 1999, unanimously accepted Turkey's application for candidate status for future EU membership. As Cyprus was already on the road to EU accession (with a planned entry date of May 1, 2004), this marked an extraordinary development in that Greece, an EU member state, Cyprus, an EU acceding state, and Turkey an EU candidate state, were brought within the EU framework and process (Anastasiou, 2002; Gündüz, 2001; Jenkins, 2001; Keridis, 2001).

Within the broader EU framework, Greece and Turkey had already embarked on a historically unprecedented process of bilateral rapprochement and confidence building measures at both the formal, political, level and the informal, civil-society level. This was initiated and catalyzed by the exchange of mutual humanitarian gestures between Greeks and Turks during the devastating earthquakes that struck first Turkey and then Greece during the summer of 1999. The impact of the outpouring of humanitarian sentiments and assistance shown in the mass media reflected the first signs of a meltdown of the nationalist "enemy" stereotypes through which the peoples of the two countries traditionally perceived each other. Building on the goodwill that emerged from the tragedy of the earthquakes, the Greek foreign minister, George Papandreou, and his Turkish counterpart, Ismail Gem, exhibited constructive conflict transformative leadership by proceeding with a series of bilateral agreements around low-level political issues, launching a peace-enhancing process that took root both politically and institutionally, and was greatly expanded with further bilateral agreements that have followed.

This rapprochement process came to be known as "earthquake diplomacy," and was complemented and greatly empowered by Turkey's acceptance as a candidate for future EU membership, and the requirement for democratic reform and the peaceful resolution of conflicts that always accompanies countries that are formally placed on the path of EU accession. But Greek-Turkish rapprochement was also strengthened by numerous civil-society initiatives engendering contact, dialogue, and joint projects between the two societies which are both quite independent from formal, track-one politics. Citizen initiatives built further bridges between Greece and Turkey through exchanges and joint projects by Greek and Turkish artists, journalists, academics, municipalities, and others (Keridis, 2001).

Moreover, all of these first steps at moving Greek-Turkish relations beyond adversarial nationalism closely resembled what had been occurring in Cyprus between some members of the Greek-Cypriot and Turkish-Cypriot communities. As discussed in more detail below, the small, but exemplary, bi-communal citizen-based peace movement gradually gave rise to an unprecedented third voice, above and beyond the polarizing adversarial nationalisms that had always dominated political discourse on Cyprus. These citizen peacebuilders premised their postnationalist approach on acknowledging a history of mutual injury and suffering, and a vision of power sharing in a new and united bi-communal, bi-zonal, federal Cyprus within the EU (Anastasiou, 2008b; Broome, 2004; Hadjipavlou, 2004). Needless to say, all the above-mentioned efforts at changing Greek-Turkish relations in Cyprus and the region evolved under the critical scrutiny, protest, and the objections of hard-line nationalists from both Greece and Turkey, as well as from Cyprus.

In the context of these historically innovative rapprochement processes in Cyprus, Greece, and Turkey, within the catalytic and evolving common EU framework, the UN launched a historic proposal in November 11, 2002 entitled "Basis for the Comprehensive Settlement of the Cyprus Problem" – a proposal built on past and current negotiations between Greek-Cypriot and Turkish-Cypriot leaders. The announcement of what came to be known as the *Annan Plan* marked the most elaborate, sophisticated, and comprehensive proposal ever articulated for the solution of the Cyprus problem.

The Annan plan proposed the creation of the United Cyprus Republic, establishing a federation of two constituent states – the Greek Cypriot State and the Turkish Cypriot State – joined together by a federal government that was loosely based on the Swiss federal model. A Presidential Council, selected by parliament, would consist of four Greek Cypriots and two Turkish Cypriots (allocated according to population) as voting members, with two additional nonvoting Greek-Cypriot members and one additional nonvoting Turkish-Cypriot member. A president and vice president would be chosen by the Presidential Council from among its members, one from each community, and they would alternate their positions every 20 months during the council's 5-year term of office. A bicameral legislature would consist of an elected Senate with members divided equally between the two communities, and a Chamber of Deputies, divided in proportion to the two communities' populations.

The plan included a federal constitution, as well as constitutions for each constituent state. It even proposed a design for a United Cyprus Republic flag and a national anthem. Importantly, it provided for a Reconciliation Commission to resolve outstanding disputes from the past and to develop ways to promote intergroup communication. It established a limited right to return between the territories of the two communities, and it brought large phased reductions in troop numbers (although it would have allowed both Greece and Turkey to maintain a small military presence on the island).

The announcement of the Annan Plan mobilized the growing pro-solution forces among the

Turkish Cypriots. The Europeanization process, ongoing reforms initiated by the ruling Justice and Development Party of Turkey, and the gradual abandonment by the Turkish government of its traditional secessionist position on Cyprus, empowered moderates in the Turkish Cypriot community to become more proactive and assertive in the search for a final Cyprus settlement. Contrary to the wishes of the Turkish-Cypriot hard-line nationalist leadership of the Denktash administration, moderate Turkish Cypriots, mostly of the political left, attended a series of large peace rallies stretching from November 2002 to January 2004, which supported the UN peace efforts. Through the rallies, the majority of Turkish-Cypriots declared their support for negotiations and reconciliation with the Greek Cypriots and for joining the EU in a reunited federal Cyprus. The phenomenon marked a historical novelty in that it was the first time that the Turkish-Cypriot community asserted its political voice above and beyond Denktash's secessionist agenda. Equally important was the fact that the Turkish-Cypriot pro-peace movement abandoned the Turkish side's decades-long secessionist position with the consent of the Turkish government.

The UN-led Cyprus negotiations during the preceding years had started with Turkish-Cypriot leader Denktash and Greek-Cypriot leader Clerides. At the high point of negotiations following the launching of the Annan Plan, however, Greek Cypriots elected a new president, Tassos Papadopoulos, a hard-line nationalist. Papadopoulos, the leader of the Democratic Party, which had gained merely 14% of the votes in the election, came to power through a coalition government. This meant that two hard-line leaders were now tasked with continuing negotiations on the Annan Plan, with which neither was pleased.

2.6 Top-Level Negotiations at The Hague and the Aftermath (2003)

At The Hague, where UN Secretary General Kofi Annan had summoned the leaders to finalize negotiations, Denktash rejected the UN plan outright and thus objected to putting it to a referendum. Papadopoulos reluctantly accepted the idea of a referendum based on the plan, even though he later revealed that had Denktash consented to the plan and thus to a referendum, he would have rejected it.

The UN, and particularly the EU, held the Turkish side primarily responsible for the failure of the negotiations at The Hague. The EU also made clear to Turkey that this jeopardized its candidacy for future accession into the Union. The Turkish government was thereby under great pressure to alter the negative image derived from the Denktash-led initiative to reject the Annan Plan.

On April 23, 2003, shortly after the collapse of the Hague talks, an extraordinary event took place in Cyprus. With Turkey's consent and prodding, the Denktash administration decided on a partial lifting of restrictions on citizen movement across the great divide of the "Green Line" – the ethnically segregating boundary that had become fossilized over 29 years along the 1974 cease-fire line. The EU's condemnation of Denktash's rejectionism and the EU's warnings to Turkey required a gesture that could somehow restore Turkey's credibility. The opening of the checkpoint can be interpreted as a response to this requirement.

What followed was historically unparalleled. Greek Cypriots flooded the northern part of Cyprus to visit homes, villages, and cities they had abandoned since 1974, while Turkish Cypriots crossed to the Greek-Cypriot south to see "how the other side lives" and visit places that were once part of their own world, but from which they had been restricted in the 1960s and which they had altogether left behind since 1974. Although these visits were highly emotional and packed with ambiguous feelings about the past, the opportunity for Turkish Cypriots and Greek Cypriots to mix freely for the first time after more than three decades of separation did not lead to any violent incidents. On the contrary, the widespread sense of euphoria and anticipation for historic change contributed to the creation of a general climate conducive to peace. It demonstrated that the two communities, in spite of the many reservations, might be ready for a final peace agreement. The challenge now lay with the leadership.

2.7 The Resumption of Peace Talks and Historic Referenda (2004)

The UN and the EU saw the period between the failed Hague talks and the anticipated entry of Cyprus in the EU on May 1, 2004 as the next window of opportunity for a Cyprus settlement. From the outset, however, there were clear signs that neither Denktash nor Papadopoulos was aligned with the UN–EU perspective. Nevertheless, in view of the upcoming entry of Cyprus into the EU, the UN Secretary General Kofi Annan invited, yet again, the Greek-Cypriot and Turkish-Cypriot leaders to meet with him in New York on February 10, 2004, for the purpose of recommencing negotiations on the basis of his plan.

This time around, a new player had taken a place at the forefront of the negotiations. The newly elected Turkish-Cypriot prime minister, pro-peace advocate Mehmet Ali Talat, was a member of the negotiating delegation, thus balancing the hard-line stance of Denktash. Simultaneously, Turkey exerted enormous pressure on Denktash, who was widely blamed for the collapse of an earlier round of talks the previous March.

Against the backdrop of the remixing of the Greek-Cypriot and Turkish-Cypriot communities after the Green Line opening, and the regenerated momentum of UN and EU diplomatic activity, the Greek-Cypriot and Turkish-Cypriot leaders had agreed to Kofi Annan's proposals for rapid negotiations on the basis of the UN plan. These negotiations would lead to a finalized version, which would be put to simultaneous, but separate, referenda in the Greek-Cypriot and Turkish-Cypriot communities on April 24, 2004. Not coincidentally, this was just days before Cyprus was due to join the EU on May 1. Intense negotiations continued in Cyprus.

Following a stalemate, however, the Secretary General moved the top-level talks to Bürgenstock, Switzerland. Denktash, still the chief negotiator for the Turkish-Cypriot community, refused to attend. He preferred to start campaigning among the Turkish Cypriots to promote the rejection of the Annan Plan on the grounds that it treasonously undermined the interests and independence of the Turkish Cypriots. Even without Denktash's negative presence, Talat and Papadopoulos could not bring the UN plan to definitive closure, so, as agreed, Mr. Annan "filled in the blanks" of the few remaining parts of the plan on which the leaders could not reach agreement. Thus, the final and fifth version of the plan was ready for the referendum. Contrary to the perception and position of nationalist hard liners on both the Turkish-Cypriot and Greek-Cypriot side, the final version of the Annan Plan entailed considerable improvements, incorporating a number of creative ways to address nearly all of the concerns of both sides, as these were put forward during the Bürgenstock talks (UN Report, "United Nations Report of the Secretary-General on his mission of good offices in Cyprus. [Report # S/2004/437]." 2004, May 28).

The outcome of the referenda, at the eve of the island's entry into the EU, was a great disappointment to all who had worked and hoped for a final political settlement of the Cyprus problem. On the Turkish-Cypriot side, 64.9% of the electorate voted in favor of the Annan Plan, while 35.1% voted against it. On the Greek-Cypriot side, on the other hand, 75.8% of the electorate voted against the Annan Plan, while 24.2% voted in favor. The Turkish-Cypriot yes vote had been influenced by the active campaigning of Talat and other moderates, while the Greek-Cypriot no vote was in line with the active campaign against the plan by Papadopoulos. The historical irony in the outcome of the referenda was that the Turkish side, which for decades had positioned itself in favor of secession and recognition of the TRNC, voted in favor of reunification and the de facto abandonment of the TRNC, while the Greek side, which for decades had positioned itself in favor of the reunification of the island, voted against the settlement at the most opportune historical moment, thus perpetuating the de facto partition of Cyprus.

2.8 Renewed Stalemate Followed by Renewed Push for Solution (2004–Present)

The failure of the Annan plan was a shock to the Turkish Cypriots, the pro-peace Greek Cypriots, and the international community. For a period of several years, there were no new negotiations and little genuine expression of interest from the international community in pushing forward with additional talks. Cyprus had returned to the stalemate that existed prior to the Annan plan.

The situation improved in February 2008, with the election of Demitris Christofias to the presidency of the Republic of Cyprus. Christofias, leader of the left-wing party, had a good relationship with the Turkish-Cypriot leader, Talat, and the international community saw this as a good opportunity to revive talks aimed at a solution to the Cyprus problem. For the first time in the history of the Cyprus conflict, the two major ethnic communities were led by pro-peace leaders. Additionally, in 2009 the Greeks elected George Papandreou, who as foreign minister in the late 1990s had been a primary architect of Greek-Turkish rapprochement. He immediately lent his full support to the negotiations. At the same time, he conferred directly with Turkey about the Cyprus problem, and the Turkish Government, under the leadership of Recep Tayyip Erdogan, expressed its strong support for a solution. Alexander Downer, former foreign minister of Australia, was appointed by Secretary General Ban Ki-moon to serve as his Special Adviser on Cyprus, and he immediately helped the parties start full-fledged negotiations aimed at reaching a comprehensive settlement. Working groups and technical committees were created to cover the various issues that needed to be negotiated, and after preparing the ground, on September 3, 2008, the two leaders commenced top-level negotiations. The two leaders remained actively engaged in negotiations until the early months of 2010, when new elections in the north brought to power a less conciliatory leader. Nevertheless, at the present time the negotiations are continuing, picking up where they left off when Talat was replaced by Eroglu. At the time of this writing, there is a push to make substantial progress by the end of 2010. Experts are skeptical, however, that the main issues of property, governance, and security can be resolved before attention turns once again to elections, this time to the presidential elections due in the south in early 2012.

The challenge facing the leaders in Cyprus is to come up with a credible solution that can be accepted by each community. The current push for a settlement is the first effort since Cyprus joined the European Union, which desperately wants to rid itself of the anomaly of a divided state within its borders. Although most of the "pieces of the puzzle" seem to be in place for a viable settlement, there are many forces in both communities fighting against a solution. Despite the encouraging signs, there is not a great deal of optimism that the two sides can reach a deal. Nevertheless, there is widespread agreement that this may be the last effort to avert permanent division of the island.

3 Consequences of the Conflict

From its start in the early 1960s until it reached its most violent heights in 1974, the conflict that tore apart the Republic of Cyprus instated an array of complex and enduring consequences that still plague the country. While driven by its own ethnocentric nationalism that staged and initiated the conflict, each community has had its own historical experience of suffering and injustice, which became largely alien and even contradictory to that of the other. Each community thus developed its own historical narrative of blame and its own particular sense of justice that is relative to its own particular experience of injury (Anastasiou, 1996). The difference between the two narratives hinges on the fact that the traumas that each side experienced during the conflict refer to and derive from different events, incidents, and historical periods. These traumas gave rise to divergent perceptions and memory of historical reality, of justice and thus, of the nature of the resolution.

For the Turkish Cypriots, the painful memories are connected mainly with the period between 1963 and 1974. They refer to the constraining, underdeveloped life in their enclaves, their repeated defeats in the bloody conflicts with the Greek Cypriots and Greek troops, and the loss of human life that appeared staggering in the eyes of the Turkish Cypriots, as a numerical minority (Crawshaw, 1978; Denktash, 1988). The configuration of Turkish-Cypriot memory was further marked by missing persons (483 Turkish Cypriots compared with only 32 Greek Cypriots in 1964) and by the feeling that for years they were living under conditions of perpetual siege (Volkan, 1979). Between December 1963 and the summer of 1964, 25,000 Turkish Cypriots became refugees. Serious damage occurred to Turkish-Cypriot property in 44 villages and the Turkish-Cypriot sectors in the major cities. By the summer of 1964, in the name of the sovereignty of the Republic of Cyprus, the Greek Cypriots had advanced to take direct control of 97% of the Island's territory, subduing or restraining the Turkish Cypriots. Thus, the life and movement of Turkish Cypriots, totaling 18% of the population, became largely limited to scattered enclaves which together encompassed just 3% of the territory of Cyprus.

Further intercommunal violence in 1967–1968 added to the history of pain for the Turkish Cypriots. The former far right-wing EOKA leader, General Grivas, who at the time was serving as supreme commander of the Greek-Cypriot National Guard, initiated a concerted attack on the Turkish villages of Kofinou and Ayios Theodoros. The reason behind this attack was to prevent the Turkish Cypriots from forming another autonomous enclave and from obstructing the communication system that passed through their area. The Turkish Cypriots saw the creation of the enclave as a necessity for their security. Although on the military level the Greek Cypriots celebrated a victory, on the human level the UN Secretary-General reported that the incident had "caused heavy loss of life and had grave repercussions" (Crawshaw, 1978, pp. 376–377).

Beyond the losses incurred in the 1960s, approximately 500 additional Turkish-Cypriot names were added to the death toll during the 1974 crisis, which marked a defining historical turning point for the Turkish-Cypriot community at the time (Attalides, 1979). Furthermore, despite the tradeoff of safety, the mass exodus of Turkish Cypriots from southern to northern Cyprus added to the Turkish-Cypriot community's collective memory of displacement under crisis conditions (Oberling, 1982).

For the Greek Cypriots the collective historical memory and experience of injustice originated mainly from the more concentrated, but devastating, events of 1974, the Greek *coup d'état* and the Turkish military intervention (Hadjipavlou-Trigeorgis, 1987). The tragic memories referred to the unprecedented loss of human life, to the mass uprooting from their homes, to the loss of property, to the refugees, and to the missing persons. In the midst of the crisis, the UN Security Council adopted an emergency resolution calling for the cessation of hostilities, the withdrawal of all foreign military personnel, respect of the sovereignty of Cyprus by all states, and the start of negotiations between Greece and Turkey for the restoration of peace and the constitutional government (UN, 1974). This resolution, however, was in vain. Within days following the Turkish military intervention, nearly 200,000 Greek Cypriots (one-third of the total population) became refugees (Loizos, 1981). Casualties, many of them civilians, were estimated at approximately 3,000 people, while the missing reached over one-and-a-half thousand. Thousands of Greek Cypriots were taken to prisons in Turkey, and some of these prisoners were later exchanged for Turkish Cypriots who had been captured by Greek-Cypriot and Greek forces in the south. The fate of those Greek Cypriots who were left in Turkey remains, to this day, a dark mystery, haunting the memories of their families and of the Greek-Cypriot community (Attalides, 1979).

Because 34% of the island's territory fell under the control of the Turkish army, the Greek Cypriots incurred heavy economic losses. At the time, the overall impact on the economy resulted in the Greek Cypriots losing 70% of their lucrative resources; 87% of the hotels under construction; the Famagusta port, which handled 83% of the island's trading activities; 56% of the extracted ore; 41% of stockbreeding units; 48% of agricultural production; 46% of plantations; and 20% of forested areas. In addition, the Greek Cypriots lost 40% of all school buildings, while their cultural heritage suffered severe damage in the areas occupied by the Turkish army (Report of Planning Bureau, 1975).

One consequence of the island's division is the changing makeup of the population, especially in the north, where increasing numbers of individuals and families have emigrated from Turkey. The number of settlers from the Turkish mainland is estimated to have reached between 80,000 (Turkish estimate) and 150,000 (Greek estimate). If the latter number is accurate, the number of Turkish settlers approximates the total number of Turkish Cypriots living in Cyprus.

The wounds from the conflict and violence of the period 1963–1974 have become rooted in the body and soul of each community (Volkan, 1979). The shock of the 1974 events was devastating to the Greek-Cypriot community. Never in their history had they experienced destruction of such magnitude, condensed into such a short period of time. To this day the effects of the war constitute a perpetual, albeit hidden, tragedy that still lingers in the lives of Greek Cypriots. Similarly, for the Turkish Cypriots, even after the overwhelming military victory of Turkey in 1974, they have continued to hold strong anxieties about issues such as security (Crawshaw, 1978), and uncertainty about the future weighs heavily on the collective consciousness. Thus, a long-term consequence of the conflict is the deep-seeded historical legacy in the psychology of both Greek Cypriots and Turkish Cypriots.

4 Causes of the Conflict

Like many similar situations, the conflict in Cyprus was driven originally by extreme nationalist rhetoric, intolerance of cultural differences, abuse of minorities, and use of violence to subvert the political process (Anastasiou, 2002; Anderson, 1995). At the very historical moment that Cyprus became free from the weighty yoke of colonial rule, it succumbed to the forces of extreme nationalism and slipped into an era of protracted conflict that resulted in historical and political stagnation. Not until nearly four decades later, in 2003, were there signs of positive change. One can postulate that the Cyprus conflict revolved around the legacy of the British colonial period and the influence of nationalism.

Almost universally, colonial powers have incubated a counter militant nationalism within the societies they govern or have intensified and radicalized an already existing one. British rule in Cyprus was no exception. The formation of EOKA by right-wing Greek-Cypriot nationalists, which sought to "Hellenize" the island by bringing about enosis, effectively alienated not only the Turkish-Cypriot community but also the Greek-Cypriot left wing. Although the communists in Cyprus initially condemned the insurgency against the British as the work of fascists and criminals, they eventually endorsed it as part of a general liberation struggle against what they deemed as Western imperialism. In other words, they adopted their own brand of nationalism.

As British soldiers and installations were targeted by EOKA, the British colonial government responded with curfews, intimidation, arrests, imprisonments, torture, and hangings of convicted insurgents, a response which further fueled and polarized the situation. The British, moreover, accommodated the Turkish Cypriots minority as a counterweight to the Greek-Cypriot majority that backed the enosis movement. While remaining sheltered by, and in collusion with, the colonial government, the Turkish Cypriots resorted to a dual response: on the one hand challenging the British to declare the enosis movement as seditious, while on the other beginning to organize their own underground nationalist paramilitary group. In 1958, Cyprus saw the creation of the Turkish Resistance Organization (TMT) as a countervailing force to EOKA. But like EOKA, it too was founded as a far right-wing nationalist organization with an exclusivist ethnocentric agenda. The premise of EOKA's uncompromising claim for enosis was that as the Greek Cypriots were the majority, they had the right to determine the future status of the island. Inspired by the pan-Turkish nationalism of Turkey, TMT's counter approach was to divide the island along ethnic lines, thus creating their own Turkish majority within their own portion of the island. Thus, the mobilizing slogan of TMT was taksim, that is, partition.

Both agendas reflected an ethnocentric nationalism that erroneously interpreted democracy as a mono-ethnic polity. With the highly emotive and idealized notions of enosis and taksim, EOKA and TMT, respectively, configured the public political culture of their ethnic community around ethnocentric concepts of nationhood, statehood, and identity that were essentially not only irreconcilable, but also potentially and historically erosive of interethnic relations within the ethnically mixed Cypriot society. Unfortunately, the polarizing impact that the nationalisms of EOKA and TMT has had on the political evolution of Cyprus outlasted both of these organizations.

In nationalism, democracy is constricted and distorted into a merely intraethnic polity. As such, for the nationalist mind, democracy can never be an interethnic system of governance, let alone an international one (Anastasiou, 2008a). This was precisely the underlying reason why both Denktash and Papadopoulos had a fundamental difficulty in accepting the Annan Plan in 2004, as it was based in principle on interethnic democracy – the essence of a bi-zonal, bi-communal federation. Despite their long standing rivalry, Denktash and Papadopoulos shared a profound similarity in that they both operated from an ethnocentric nationalist approach to politics, democracy, and statehood (Anastasiou, 2008a).

5 Beyond the Political Stalemate: Civil-Society as the Voice for Peace[4]

Perhaps the most far-reaching consequence of the divisions created in 1963 and 1974 was the severing of communication links between Greek Cypriots and Turkish Cypriots. Although the society had never been well integrated, relations were sometimes close between neighbors before the confrontations in 1963, and despite the religious and linguistic differences there was significant cultural overlap in customs and way of life. Communication across the buffer zone, however, practically ceased with the establishment of two distinct ethnic zones and restrictions that prevented contact via face-to-face meetings, telephone conversations, or postal mail exchanges. As a result, previous neighborly contacts, working relationships, and friendships were lost and there was no mechanism for new relationships to develop. Without regular contact in everyday affairs, it became easy for politicians, educators, and religious leaders to build a negative image of the other community, placing blame entirely on the other side for the troubles that had led to the division of the island. Furthermore, while Turkish Cypriots gained more autonomy to build their own political and social institutions, Greek Cypriots were psychologically devastated by the war and its consequences. Thus, a deep divide developed between the two communities in perceptions of each other and in the events that led to the current division of the island.

This divide, however, began to be bridged in the early part of the 1990s when international diplomatic missions and individual third-party facilitators responded to requests of individuals from both communities to help them find ways to meet across the buffer zone. By the mid-1990s, several bi-communal groups had formed and began to meet regularly. The number of people involved in these bi-communal groups grew steadily, and in spite of difficulties securing all the relevant permissions, by late 1997 bi-communal groups were meeting almost every day of the week. At its height, approximately 2,000 individuals were taking part in bi-communal activities, many of them participating in groups that met weekly.

The growth of civil-society peace groups abruptly stopped at the end of 1997, when authorities in the north denied further permissions for Turkish Cypriots to cross the Turkish-controlled checkpoint to attend bi-communal meetings with Greek Cypriots in the buffer zone. In spite of this setback, many groups found a way to continue communication and contact. Some groups started meeting in the mixed village of Pyla, located along the buffer zone next to the British sovereign area. Occasionally, there were social gatherings allowed in the buffer zone, usually sponsored by the United Nations, political parties, or trade unions. In addition, several meetings took place outside Cyprus, where various European and US organizations brought together Turkish Cypriots

[4]Portions of this section are based on Broome (2005).

and Greek Cypriots for workshops, seminars, and other activities. Finally, many individuals maintained contact through the UN-operated telephone lines, and with the arrival of Internet Service Providers (ISPs), through electronic mail. It was not until 2003, when restrictions on crossing the buffer zone were partially lifted, that regular meetings of civil-society groups became possible again.

In spite of numerous setbacks, a fledging civil-society peace movement developed in the latter part of the 1990s, resulting from the actions of pioneering individuals and groups that went against the odds to reach out across the dividing line. With assistance from outside third parties, this group eventually grew into a larger peace-building community that overcame a number of challenges, including direct attempts to shut it down. In spite of significant difficulties, civil-society peacebuilding groups have made many contributions to improved relations on the island, and if a settlement is found to the political situation, the individuals involved in these groups will play a critical role in developing a working bi-communal society. Perhaps more importantly, their actions helped push along a reluctant peace process in the larger society. In this section, we will provide an overview of these peacebuilding activities.

5.1 Peacebuilding Activities in Cyprus

Activities aimed at bringing together Greek Cypriots and Turkish Cypriots have spanned a wide range of issues, from practical projects such as keeping the sewage system operating properly in the divided city of Nicosia, to artistic events such as bi-communal concerts, art exhibitions, and dance performances. Before restrictions on crossing the buffer zone were relaxed in 2003, any gathering of individuals living on different sides of the buffer zone required special permissions. The remainder of this section will describe activities in several key areas that served to catalyze the peace movement in the initial years of civil-society initiatives. We will examine social gatherings and exchanges, meetings of business leaders and professionals, intercommunal dialogue initiatives, and other activities that brought together individuals across the buffer zone (see Broome, 2005, for a more detailed description of these initiatives).

5.1.1 Social Gatherings and Exchanges

Various diplomatic missions, particularly the United Nations office in Cyprus, held a number of receptions and other events that brought together a large number of people from each community. For example, the UN annually held an open house on October 24th each year at which special activities were planned by the UN staff. These events often attracted large numbers of individuals from both communities, sometimes totaling more than two thousand. There were also several receptions and programs sponsored by individual embassies, often on the occasion of a particular country's important holiday or in honor of a special guest to the island.

In addition to receptions and informal gatherings, the United Nations, often working with other diplomatic missions, organized several music concerts in the middle and late 1990s. Several concerts in the buffer zone featured local groups, and in every case the individuals in attendance mixed easily, dancing and singing together. In June 1997, a UN-sponsored pop concert featuring mainland Greek and Turkish singers brought together thousands of young Greek and Turkish Cypriots in the buffer zone. The event was marred by protests in each community, but participants joined hands, gave each other flowers, and sang together "Give Peace a Chance." In addition to these one-time musical events, a bi-communal choir met together for several years to learn and practice songs from each community's tradition.

Special exhibitions featuring art, photography, or other works by individuals in both communities were also held. For example, in 1996 there was an exhibition sponsored by the European Union of political cartoons by both Greek Cypriots and Turkish Cypriots. The American Center sponsored an exhibition of photographs taken on both sides of the buffer zone. The Peace Centre in the Greek-Cypriot community organized a recitation of Turkish-Cypriot poetry. These exhibitions served as important symbols of peaceful co-existence.

Finally, several pilgrimages were organized in which Greek Cypriots and Turkish Cypriots were able to visit holy sites on the "other side" of the buffer zone. Greek Cypriots were allowed on several occasions to visit one of the most important Orthodox sites on the island, Apostolos Andreas monastery in the Karpas. As many as 1,300 pilgrims travelled in buses from Nicosia to the remote church, usually on the saint's feast day. In a corresponding gesture of goodwill, programs were organized to bring Turkish-Cypriot pilgrims to Hala Sultan Tekke in Larnaca, one of Islam's most venerable shrines. In none of these visits was there much, if any, contact of the pilgrims with the local population. Nevertheless, the pilgrimages served to reconnect those who made the visits with the important places on the island, helping to ease the pain brought about by lack of access.

Although the various social gatherings and exchanges were designed to offer opportunities primarily for casual exchanges, these receptions, concerts, exhibitions, and visits to religious sites were very important in promoting a better future for Cyprus. They allowed people to meet face to face, and they allowed people to see that despite the differences that divided the two communities, ordinary citizens faced many of the same everyday concerns – supporting their families, educating their children, working to build better neighborhoods, etc. Although such results are important, they are insufficient by themselves to significantly alter the overall situation. Possibilities for more sustainable change were offered by contacts between members of the professional and business sectors, described next.

5.1.2 Meetings of Professionals and Business Leaders

Bi-communal contact between professional groups and business leaders provided some of the most practical arenas for promoting rapprochement. Certainly, economic and collegial ties are key to building a stable basis for future cooperation. Unfortunately, it is precisely these contacts that have been the most difficult to initiate and sustain, particularly when both sides have refused to engage in activities they believe might grant legitimacy to the other's political institutions.

In spite of the barriers, there were several groups that took initiatives to meet together long before restrictions were relaxed in 2003. A few years after the division in 1974, the mayors of the divided city of Nicosia formed a team of experts with the goal of finding a way to complete the sewage system for Nicosia, the construction of which had been interrupted by the hostilities in 1974. The success of this effort led to the creation of a joint force to create a Nicosia Master Plan, a development blueprint dealing with all aspects of life in a city that both mayors hoped would soon be reunited under a single government. Architects, city planners, sociologists, and economists met regularly during the 1980s and into the 1990s in order to develop a scheme for developing business districts, housing areas, parks, and even traffic patterns.

In 1997, representatives of trade unions in both communities held two historic meetings, one on each side of the buffer zone. The unionists discussed many issues, holding an open debate on such topics as the merits of Cyprus's entry into the EU. Later that year, on the occasion of International Peace Day, Greek- and Turkish-Cypriot trade unions submitted a joint declaration to the United Nations office in Cyprus urging the international community and the island's leadership to "hear the voice of the majority of the people and work towards a fair solution which will bring peace to the island."

Several initiatives brought groups of business leaders together. A group of senior business leaders was first brought together at the Ledra Palace in 1995 by the US Ambassador. Eventually, Richard Holbrooke, appointed by former US President Clinton as special envoy to Cyprus, brought this group together with their Greek and Turkish counterparts for a series of meetings outside Greece. Around the same time, the Cyprus Fulbright Commission started a group of young business leaders, and this group continued meeting on a regular basis for over a year. Both groups explored opportunities for cooperative business ventures that could be initiated prior to a settlement and under a future federated Cyprus. The Cyprus Fulbright Commission also sponsored a series of management training courses for mid-level and senior-level managers, involving more than 250 Greek Cypriots and Turkish Cypriots in a total of seven courses, each lasting for two to three weeks. The managers who took part in these courses continued their contact with one another, eventually forming an ongoing bi-communal group and organizing exchange visits to each side of the buffer zone.

Finally, a number of professional groups started meeting, including lawyers, educators, journalists, accountants, environmentalists, medical professionals, mental health care workers, social work professionals, and others. Some of these groups met outside Cyprus for workshops or special training. For example, a group of educators met in Boston, and a group of senior-level newspaper editors attended journalistic training together in Washington, D.C. In most cases, however, the professional groups focused on special projects in Cyprus related to their areas of interest. For example, a group of lawyers from the two communities took as their main task to review the changes in law that had taken place in the two communities since 1974, when the legal system had been a unitary one, so that integration of the now separated systems could be accomplished more easily after a political settlement is reached. Another example is provided by a group of educators who worked over a period of 1 year to identify ways in which the other community is portrayed in history books and literature taught to children in the school systems, proposing ways to eliminate the "enemy image" from such materials.

It is difficult to judge the overall impact these projects have had on the larger society, particularly because restrictions on trade and professional activities across the Green Line have made it challenging, if not impossible, for any formal business relationships to develop. Nevertheless, by bringing together those who are critical to the economic well-being of society, relationships were established that can have a positive impact once a settlement is reached.

5.1.3 Intercommunal Dialogue Initiatives

The most sustained and intense efforts to promote bi-communal contacts during the formative years of peacebuilding activities came in the form of workshops, training programs, and seminars that promoted intercommunal dialogue. These took the form of problem-solving workshops, introductory and advanced conflict resolution skills training, interactive design processes, mediation training, and special seminars and study groups dealing with issues such as identity, property concerns, federation, and European Union issues. Many of these initiatives took place with the assistance of external third parties, often from academic institutions, and they utilized methods from the growing field of conflict resolution.

Although intercommunal dialogue workshops had their beginnings in Cyprus in 1966, when John Burton and his colleagues in London offered a five-day workshop in "controlled communication" that brought together high-level representatives from the two communities (Burton, 1969; Mitchell, 1981), only a few additional workshops were held during the subsequent 25 years. These consisted of an informal seminar held in Rome in 1973 involving political leaders of the two communities (Talbot, 1977), a locally organized workshop involving intellectuals in 1985 (Doob, 1987), problem-solving workshops in 1979 and 1984 conducted by Herb Kelman (Doob, 1976; Stoddard, 1986), a series of four workshops facilitated by Ron Fisher focusing on the educational system in the two communities (Fisher, 1992, 1997), and a local initiative in 1989 under the name "The Greek-Cypriot and Turkish-Cypriot Citizens' Movement for Democracy and Federation in Cyprus" (Hadjipavlou-Trigeorgis & Trigeoris, 1993).

These early workshops led to additional requests for assistance from third-party facilitators and trainers, setting the stage for larger efforts to offer conflict resolution skills training on a broader basis across Cypriot society. An intensive workshop that took place in 1993 with a group of ten Greek Cypriots and ten Turkish Cypriots in Oxford, England (Diamond & Fisher, 1995) was followed by three-week-long conflict resolution workshops in 1994. During 1995–1997 additional workshops were conducted in both Cyprus and in the United States, including an advanced "training of trainers" workshop, which allowed local Cypriots to offer introductory conflict resolution skills workshops to their fellow citizens, both in bi-communal and mono-communal settings.

Although they were few in number and spread over more than two decades, the problem-solving and conflict resolution workshops fostered a new form of communication in Cyprus, which was based on attempts to understand and build trust rather than on accusatory rhetoric and condemnation of the other. These workshops served an important purpose by allowing a core group of Cypriots to experience the growing academic field of conflict resolution. The conflict resolution training workshops not only played an important role in introducing a new set of skills into Cypriot society, but they also provided a "therapeutic" setting in which individuals could come to terms with some of the pain and suffering brought about by the communal separation. The training led to the formation of new relationships and encouraged more accurate perceptions of the other. Perhaps most importantly, the conflict resolution activities brought together the primary players who would soon form a stronger civil-society peace movement.

Complementing the problem-solving workshops and conflict resolution training, a series of interactive design workshops took place from 1994 to 1997, in which a core group of participants from the conflict resolution training came together for a series of sustained sessions focused on developing a strategy for peacebuilding in Cyprus. During a 9-month period from October 1994 through June 1995, a process referred to as Interactive Management (IM) was used to help a bi-communal group of 15 Greek Cypriots and 15 Turkish Cypriots develop a strategy for their peacebuilding efforts in Cyprus. During these weekly sessions, the group progressed through three stages of planning and design: (1) analysis of the current situation; (2) goal setting for the future; and (3) development of a collaborative action agenda. This group produced a systems analysis of the obstacles to peacebuilding efforts in Cyprus, created a "collective vision statement" for the future of peacebuilding activities in Cyprus, and developed a plan of activities that would guide their work over the following 2–3 years. The latter consisted of 15 projects, including workshops, presentations, training programs, and other events. After the staging of an event to which individuals were invited to sign up for these projects, approximately 150 individuals became involved in 12 bi-communal projects (Broome, 1997, 1998).

Additional interactive design workshops were conducted from 1995 through 1997 with groups of young business leaders, youth leaders, students, and women's groups. Unfortunately, the continued growth of the design workshops was interrupted by the ban on bi-communal activities at the end of 1997. Just prior to the closing of the checkpoints, however, a training program was conducted in which 18 Greek Cypriots and Turkish Cypriots received instruction in interactive design methodologies, preparing them to offer workshops to other groups in Cyprus.

The interactive design workshops helped carry the bi-communal movement into an "action stage," in which participants in previous problem-solving and conflict resolution workshops began to take leadership roles in designing and implementing projects that involved members of both communities. This was a crucial stage for the bi-communal work, because it marked the transition from a primarily training activity to greater activism and local initiative. The third-party role shifted from instructor, trainer, or facilitator to that of consultant, advisor, and equal partner in strategy development. The former roles have continued to be important, but the primary responsibility for most of the training and development of new initiatives began to fall on the shoulders of those who had participated in earlier workshops, training, and design and problem-solving sessions.

In a society where conflict permeates the system, these activities played a crucial role in providing a way to deal more effectively with differences. They helped many individuals in each community gain a better understanding of the issues as perceived by the other side, and they introduced new skills into the repertoire of each community. Significantly, they provided a "safe space" in which healing and reconciliation could take place, thus relieving some of the immense psychological burden that plagues the whole of Cyprus. Finally, they resulted in many bi-communal friendships and working relationships that could not have existed otherwise.

5.1.4 Additional Peacebuilding Activities

The social gatherings and exchanges, meetings of professionals and business leaders, and inter-communal dialogue seminars and workshops resulted in the creation of additional initiatives and led to the formation of several ongoing bi-communal groups. Most of these groups adopted a special focus, oriented toward a professional area (e.g., education), a particular sector of society (e.g., women), or a special task (e.g., developing links among peacebuilders in the eastern Mediterranean). Many of these groups met on a weekly or monthly basis, and most of them developed and implemented special projects. For example, one of the most influential of the ongoing groups, which called itself the "Trainers" group, initially worked together over a 9-month period in a series of interactive design sessions (see previous section), creating a collective vision statement and a collaborative action agenda for peacebuilding activities. The meeting described earlier, in which the project was presented to a group of potentially interested individuals, led to the formation of a number of ongoing groups and several special projects. They continued working together after their initial project was finished, forming a "coordinating group" for the various bi-communal activities in which they were involved, and meeting together for support and further training. After 1995, they expanded their group to include others trained in problem-solving approaches, conflict resolution skills, interactive design methodologies, and mediation skills. This ongoing bi-communal group forms the core around which the majority of bi-communal activities in Cyprus took place during the period 1994–1997, and it is their "offspring" who continued to organize many of the bi-communal activities that developed after 1997. They endured many difficulties together and formed a very strong group identity. They were also a primary resource for many third-party facilitators and trainers who worked in Cyprus, and they were regularly called upon to give advice to various international diplomatic personnel.

In addition to the projects initiated and guided by the Trainers group, a number of other groups emerged and promoted a variety of peacebuilding activities. While the number of such groups are too numerous to catalogue in this essay, a few examples include: a bi-communal educators group that conducted an in-depth study of the educational systems as they operate in Cyprus and their impact on people's perceptions of the conflict; a bi-communal women's group that made efforts to write a "women's history" of Cyprus, to examine why there are so few women in decision-making bodies in Cyprus, and to create a "Cyprus Link" based on the successful "Jerusalem Link" (see http://www.batshalom.org/) that has been existence for many years; a bi-communal student group, consisting of students studying at public and private universities, which met with each of the two community leaders, and later went together for a one-week seminar in Budapest; a regional peacebuilding group that met together for the first time in the Swiss village of Les Diablerets to develop links between individuals and groups that are involved in rapprochement activities in the eastern Mediterranean, resulting in several "four-way" projects involving individuals from Turkey, Greece, and the two communities of Cyprus; an initiative called Youth Encounters for Peace (YEP) that brought together numerous groups of young people, ages 16–19; a bi-communal magazine called *Hade* that was created to share stories about peacebuilding groups and events, and about the experiences of individuals who participated in these activities; training in mediation that was offered to hundreds of Cypriots, resulting in the creation of a Mediation Centre that offers specialized training to individuals and groups in both the private and public sector; an NGO Resource Centre that was established, providing a meeting space and resource library for a wide range of organizations.

While these are but a few examples of the plethora of bi-communal projects that have occurred in Cyprus, they give a sense of the variety and scope of civil-society initiatives that brought together thousands of individuals across the buffer zone. These activities helped energize ordinary Cypriots after two decades of impasse at the political level, reconnecting a broken link between communities. The opportunity to meet and develop relationships with members of the other community affected both the individuals who participated and the society at large. Additionally, these activities provided impetus toward renewed efforts at the political level to negotiate a settlement to end the division. In the next section, we will discuss further the impacts of peacebuilding activities in Cyprus.

5.2 Impact of Peacebuilding Activities

Despite the large number of civil-society peacebuilding activities in Cyprus, their growth did not occur in an unhindered manner. Resistance occurred in many forms, from denial of permission from authorities in the north for Turkish Cypriots to cross the checkpoint to the buffer zone, to the media portrayals (in both south and north) of rapprochement activities as unpatriotic. From the beginning, individuals and groups involved in bi-communal initiatives were condemned by both officials and ordinary citizens, and those involved were generally dismissed as irrelevant and naive. Yet in spite of the barriers they faced, many groups persisted in their attempts to promote dialogue, to bridge differences, and to work together on joint projects.

The impact of the peacebuilding activities is evident on many aspects of Cypriot society. From a practical view, their meetings provided one of the only passageways through the physical barrier of the buffer zone during the years before 2003. They allowed thousands of ordinary Cypriots to meet across the Green Line, keeping alive the possibility of a future united Cyprus. Without these activities, very little contact across community lines between ordinary citizens would have occurred between 1974 and 2003. Even with the partial lifting of restrictions in 2003, the intergroup dialogue activities continued to be an important mechanism for meaningful contact across the buffer zone. While thousands of individuals crossed to the other side after the Ledra Palace checkpoint was opened, most of the resulting contact between Turkish Cypriots and Greek Cypriots was limited to brief encounters. Organized dialogue activities allowed more meaningful communication to take place, and they led to a number of joint initiatives.

Beyond the opportunity for more contact, the influence of peacebuilding activities is not easy or straightforward to gauge. Broome and Jakobsson-Hatay (2006) have discussed the effects of intergroup dialogue on three levels: the *personal level, relational level,* and to a limited extent, the *structural level* of Cypriot society.

On the *personal level,* participation in intergroup dialogue initiatives was shown to have three primary impacts. First, they provided one of the few means for reducing the psychological burden that Cypriots experience from the trauma of past events, helping to heal the chasm created by the ethnic divisions of 1963 and 1974. While the pain from past events cannot be erased, engaging in dialogue with those on the other side of the conflict can help individuals deal with these traumas in a healthier manner. Second, engaging in meaningful dialogue can assist individuals in understanding the fears, needs, and concerns of the other community. The buffer zone created not only physical division but also psychological separation between the two communities, and after a long period without contact, the fears, hopes, and concerns of each community were lost to the other side. Intergroup dialogue opportunities provided a means to enhance each community's understanding of the other community, opening a window into the world of the other. Third, participating in dialogue events helped reduce feelings of insecurity about the future, which is a common theme in many discussions about the Cyprus conflict. Dialogue with members of the other community and the insights this brings enables participants to challenge simplistic or erroneous notions about the other side, in this way contributing to a more informed debate on options for the organization of intergroup relations in the future, including political frameworks.

On the *relational level,* the process of dialogue helped break the cycle of mutual blame and accusations that characterizes rhetoric across community lines in Cyprus. One of the few places where this cycle was broken is within some of the bi-communal dialogue groups. Although these groups had to deal with the same mistrust that characterizes the larger society, they managed to get past these difficulties, moving to a place where individuals can be more open in expressing their perceptions and where people listen respectfully to views that are different from their own. By coming together in dialogue, the individuals involved essentially created a forum in which issues affecting a future united Cyprus could be discussed productively, thus building potential for collaboration in a postsolution era. Participants from the intergroup dialogues, especially those with significant experience over the years, may be the individuals best situated to promote true partnerships on the island. They have the necessary contacts with the other community, and they are at least minimally sensitive to the concerns of the other community. In addition, they are also aware of some of the issues that might cause misunderstanding and conflict, and they possess at least some of the skills for dealing with it.

At the *structural level,* the impact of intergroup dialogue initiatives is likely to be less visible than on the personal and relational levels. This is due partly to the influence of larger political and social forces at work, and partly due to the longer term nature of change at the structural level. Although it is difficult to point to ways that the dialogue groups in Cyprus have influenced policymaking in explicit and measurable ways, we believe that the peacebuilding movement has had many subtle but important effects on the official peace process. For example, several of the participants in intergroup dialogue initiatives have moved into positions of political leadership in both communities. In fact, both of the current leaders at the negotiating table have participated in intergroup dialogue sessions. For these political leaders and community influentials, the opportunity they had to engage in meaningful dialogue with their counterparts probably contributed to their confidence in making proposals for cooperation that went beyond what had been official policy for decades. Additionally, we have seen ideas and proposals developed in the dialogue groups over the years find their way into documents produced during official negotiations. For example, the Annan Plan (United Nations, 2003) included many ideas that had received attention from several of the bi-communal study groups. Additionally, many members of the official working groups created in 2008 to prepare the way for full negotiations have participated in various bi-communal groups, and they have brought into their discussions some of the ideas originally examined in the dialogue groups of which they were a part. In a future united Cyprus, there will continue to be a need for citizen input into policy decisions, and dialogue groups can both generate ideas that will benefit a changing society and can serve as a safe environment to test the viability of new ideas.

Research has shown that contact alone is rarely sufficient for breaking down stereotypes, prejudices, and discriminating practices, and in some cases can actually lead to negative consequences.[5] Meaningful contact often requires a number of facilitating conditions, one of which is creating special forums where individuals can come together in a supportive climate that does not emphasize power differences and that provides opportunity for all individuals to voice opinions, try out ideas, and learn from each other. While the civil-society peacebuilding activities in Cyprus clearly promoted increased contact, they also helped promote *relational empathy*, in which participants create a "third culture" that transcends the views that are brought by individuals, bridging differences, synthesizing horizons, and creating a context for joint action (Broome, 2009). After more than 15 years of concentrated, concerted efforts at citizen peacebuilding, the Cyprus case offers many lessons that we believe could be useful for other ethnic conflicts. The next section will examine these lessons in more detail.

---

[5]For a review of the contact hypothesis, see Amir (1969), Brewer and Miller (1984), Byrne (2001), Forbes (1997), Hubbard (1999), and Pettigrew (2008).

6 Implications for Ethnic Conflicts

In ethnic conflicts, the initial escalation of violence often gives way to an impasse or stalemate. When a conflict reaches a stalemate, both sides realize that they cannot accomplish their goals, but neither side wants to back down or accept loss. Although they may realize that progress is missing, it is usually difficult for parties to step away from the status quo and make positive moves toward a settlement. Particularly in long-lasting conflicts, people on both sides have been socialized to a polarized view of the other and the overall situation. They do not trust the other side and have little or no desire for reconciliation. Certain parties in both sides develop a vested interest in perpetuating the conflict, particularly those who benefit economically (e.g., individuals who take advantage of properties abandoned during the war) and those political actors who use fear appeals to help gain or stay in power. Eventually, conflicts reach a fragile equilibrium, in which neither side is able to gain what it wants, yet both sides are dissatisfied with the situation in which they find themselves.

By the early 1990s, the situation in Cyprus had clearly reached a stalemate. Even though negotiations were taking place on a regular basis, with several UN initiatives to bring the two leaders together, the political will to compromise was insufficient for any forward movement toward settlement. After nearly 20 years of little progress at the official level, there seemed to be no satisfactory political outcome in sight. Responding to this discouraging scenario, a small group of individuals took steps toward building peace at the level of civil-society. These peacebuilders were motivated in part by the failure of their respective political leaders to negotiate a settlement. Tired of waiting for progress from their elected leaders, they decided to take steps from a different vantage point, that of civil-society.

In an odd way, perhaps the stalemate actually set the stage for the emergence of civil-society peacebuilding initiatives by creating a void that required action from somewhere. In the conflict resolution literature, scholars often use the concept of "ripeness" to describe the situation that exists when parties in a stalemate reach a point where they are ready to seriously pursue a settlement (see Pruitt, Rubin, & Kim, 1994; Rubin, Pruitt, & Kim, 1994; Zartman, 1985, 2001). Sometimes the moment is ripe for settlement because the parties "find themselves locked in a conflict from which they cannot escalate to victory and this deadlock is painful to both of them (although not necessarily in equal degree or for the same reasons), [and] they seek an alternative policy or Way Out" (Zartman, 2001, p. 8).

Although the notion of "ripeness" was originally intended to describe a point reached in official negotiations, perhaps it is appropriate to consider civil-society peacebuilding as a "Way Out" from a stalemate. Rarely can conflict situations become "unstuck" through official efforts alone. The general population needs to be prepared for the prospects of living together with the "enemy," and intercommunal dialogue in civil-society groups may provide one of the few ways to help people come to grips with the past and anticipate a future in partnership with the other side. Just as importantly, civil-society peace movements can push political leaders toward making serious moves in the direction of settlement, even when these leaders have not reached such a place themselves.

We argue that peacebuilding activities at the civil-society level can help break the stalemate of political deadlock in ethnic conflicts. In the remainder of this section, we will discuss several important aspects of peacebuilding that we experienced in Cyprus and that we believe have implications for ethnic conflicts in general. We will draw upon the lessons we have gained from working with civil-society groups in Cyprus, as well as from the literature on peacebuilding, particularly the work of John Paul Lederach (1997), a leading theorist on the topic of building peace in divided societies. Like us, Lederach relies heavily from his own experience in working with groups that are dedicated to sustainable reconciliation in ethnic conflict arenas.

6.1 Developing Links Between Unofficial and Official Tracks

The terms *Track I* and *Track II diplomacy* were coined by Joseph Montville, a former US State Department official to distinguish between traditional diplomatic activities and unofficial, informal activities between members of conflicting parties (Montville, 1987). Track I diplomacy is conducted between official representatives of the state (or representatives of entities functioning in a state-like capacity to represent their side in the conflict). It may include heads of state, state department or ministry of foreign affairs officials, and other governmental departments and ministries. Track I diplomacy is primarily a tool for reaching mutual agreements that bring an end to conflicts, or at least a stop to the violence. It usually involves a third party, such as the United Nations, to help bring about a signed agreement between the states or parties involved in the conflict.

Track II diplomacy, consisting of dialogue between nonofficials, attempts to address the causes of the conflict by bringing people together to examine perceptions, stereotypes, distrust, and other factors that underlie different positions. Such approaches provide an environment that is free from the pressures and restraints of official diplomacy. By creating a space for dialogue that is nonjudgmental and noncoercive, that takes place in a safe setting, the hope is that participants will feel free to share perceptions, fears and needs, and to explore ideas for resolution that go beyond official positions. Track II processes are designed to encourage mutual understanding of each party's perceptions and needs, the creation of new ideas for approaching the conflict, the adoption of a problem-solving orientation, and the development of relationships across conflict lines.

Conflict resolution theorists such as Fisher (1997) and Kelman (1995) have long made a case for the complementarity of Track I and Track II efforts. The civil-society peacebuilding work in Cyprus demonstrates how important it is for unofficial groups, or "Track II" actors (see Chigas, 2003), to develop effective communication links with official entities, or "Track I" actors (see Nan, 2003). Although citizen peace initiatives cannot substitute for official negotiations, the process of moving from conflict to resolution and, eventually, to a peace culture, requires contributions at the levels of both formal politics *and* civil-society.

The intersection of Track I and Track II efforts is reflected in the conceptual framework proposed by Lederach (1997). He identifies three levels of leadership in peacebuilding. At the top level, political and religious leaders focus primarily on high-level negotiations. At the grassroots level, leadership is made up of persons directly involved with the larger population that represents the base of society. Between these two levels, middle-range leaders in various sectors of society (education, business, health, etc.) are positioned so they have well-established connections with both officials and with the constituency that the top leaders represent. Lederach believed that the middle-range actors occupy a unique position in society, one that renders their work vital in the process of conflict transformation and sustainable peacebuilding in divided societies.

One of the primary ways that Track II peacebuilding can positively affect a stalemate is by allowing greater flexibility of thought and action in addressing and approaching the conflict. Since the influence of middle-range leadership is not necessarily linked to political or military power or the desire to attain it, they are not constrained by a constituency and the constant scrutiny of the public media. Rather, their effectiveness derives from ongoing relationships and networking in society. This gives them greater flexibility and a distinct advantage in innovation and creativity, something that is sorely needed in a stalemate.

In its initial stages, the leadership of the civil-society peace movement in Cyprus was drawn from the middle-range of Lederarch's framework. Its unique societal position and political vantage point allowed the peace movement to make numerous inroads into the grass roots of Cypriot society, while at the same time it also established solid relationships with top-level, political leaders in each community. In addition, the peacebuilders connected in a myriad of ways with representatives of the international diplomatic community in Cyprus: they became involved with think tanks of international organizations; they interacted with local and international leadership through frequent informal discussions; and they prodded several embassies to add bi-communal, civil-society peacebuilding to their agenda. Acting through subtle, often intentionally quiet ways, the bi-communal peacebuilders built strong connections with the top-level echelons of Cyprus politics.

Although it did not happen overnight, the bi-communal movement in Cyprus also brought interethnic rapprochement to the agenda of numerous political parties on both sides of the buffer zone. In one case, the central committee of one of the largest parties in the south established a rapprochement committee within its organizational structure to promote contact and dialogue across the Green Line. Furthermore, the bi-communal peace movement added a transformative new dimension to the Turkish Cypriot opposition parties. The involvement of several leaders of the Turkish Cypriot left led to the gradual assimilation of bi-communal culture, approaches, and strategies into the party's platform, bringing with it the language of interethnic rapprochement. The politics of peace in relation to the Greek Cypriots, along with the politics of democratization in relation to the EU, became the defining messages of the opposition.

It is noteworthy that many Turkish Cypriots and Greek Cypriots from both the right and the left, having been seasoned by interethnic contact, moved on to assume formal political positions, while others successfully ran for political office. Over the years, the work of the peacebuilding community gradually became not only visible in the eyes of both the Cypriot society and the international community, but also became an example of what needed to occur if Cyprus had hope for one day ending its division.

6.2 Balancing International and Local Input in Peacebuilding

In his work on conflict transformation in divided societies, Lederach (1997) identified three conditions for rendering effective the role of ordinary citizens in peacebuilding processes: identifying the peacebuilders, building links with likeminded individuals on the other side of the conflict, and gaining recognition by the international community. Although it may not have done so through a carefully crafted plan, the bi-communal peace movement in Cyprus was able to meet all three of these conditions. Early in the process, a core group of individuals in both communities adopted an identity as peacebuilders, expressing a desire to take steps to promote a culture of peace on the island. They found a way to develop linkages with their counterpart in the other community, and eventually their work was endorsed by the international community, receiving support from the United Nations, the United States, and the European Union.

During its emergent stages, the civil-society peace movement received the assistance of numerous international scholars and practitioners of conflict resolution. The core leaders of the peace movement received training in conflict resolution and peace building from some of the most notable international organizations, universities, and individual experts in the field (Wolleh, 2001). The international peace scholars and practitioners who made the most lasting contributions were those who approached their trainees not as recipients of conflict resolution skills and ideas, but rather as the local human resources for activating and sustaining the locally initiated peacebuilding process.

While drawing from the skills and theory brought by the international scholars, the movement gradually took on a life of it own. As it moved forward it generated autonomous initiatives and assumed responsibilities in generating strategies and implementing actions that eventually established the basis for the emergence of a broad, locally directed citizen peace movement. In effect, the innovative and time-sensitive work performed by the local, bi-communal peacebuilders, relevant to the unique setting of the Cyprus conflict, radically enhanced and extended the peacebuilding process well beyond the more technical academic training they originally received. The totality of their work, both bi-communally and mono-communally, provided the seeds and the means for steadily diffusing the behaviors and values that were counterproductive to a culture of peace among the Turkish-Cypriot and Greek-Cypriot communities. Working quietly but persistently across and within their respective ethnic communities, initiating a variety of activities and projects, the citizen peacebuilders became the local sociocultural resource for incubating, developing, and sustaining a citizen-based process of conflict transformation. The peacebuilding community transposed the academic and sometimes abstract training offered by non-Cypriots into a practical, meaningful, and effective process of conflict transformation over the long term.

As the peace movement grew in size and scope, it also became more effective in articulating and promoting a nonadversarial approach to addressing the Cyprus conflict. The spontaneity, energy, and dedication of the people involved led to heightened interest and momentum. The long-term commitment and tireless determination of the local peacebuilders allowed them to pursue a peace-enhancing vision and peace-seeking options for Cyprus against much opposition. The positive force and stamina of the local peacebuilders furnished the vision-laden, human infrastructure that rendered sustainable the civil-society peace process and made possible the ever deepening and ever widening peacebuilding venture, in spite of the prospect of stigmatization and ostracism, and, in some cases, life threats.

6.3 Building a Peace Culture and a Peace Constituency

In her book *Cultures of Peace*, Elise Boulding writes about how conflict, violence, and aggressive behavior have become ingrained in the very fabric of our society (Boulding, 2000). She discusses the "war-nurtured identity of Western civilization," in which history is presented as a chronicle of wars, battles, military conquests, and the rise and fall of empires. Boulding believes we must develop instead a *peace culture* that promotes mutual caring, emphasizes appreciation of difference, encourages stewardship and equitable sharing of the earth's resources, and offers mutual security that sustains the well-being of all. While such a description is considered by some to be utopian, it nevertheless provides a vision for the type of transformation toward which peacebuilders continually strive.

The idea of a peace culture in Cyprus was articulated well by Sevgul Uludag, a Turkish-Cypriot activist in the peacebuilding community. Speaking at a bi-communal gathering in the buffer zone during the mid-1990s, she said:

> We are not politicians. It is not our job to solve the Cyprus problem. But we are the creators of a new culture, which will help resolve our conflict in a peaceful manner. Our dream is to help build a country where everybody's needs are everybody's concern…. We are unique since we are the only group in Cyprus that has a shared vision. We are unique because we have analyzed the conflict and created options and projects together. We are unique because we have gone deep into dialogue about some of the hottest topics. And our culture of peace is based on tolerance, understanding, and sharing (Uludag, 1996, p. 11).

Both in the principles that they espoused and in the practices in which they engaged, the peacebuilding initiatives helped develop what was the first interethnic conceptualization of democracy in Cyprus. For the first time in the island's political history, the idea of democracy expanded beyond the ethnocentric and mono-ethnic constraints of nationalism. Never before had democracy been viewed as an interethnic concept with its own set of values, actions, and vision. More significantly, the civil-society peace movement brought into the public domain the idea that the sustainability of democracy within and between ethnic groups is directly related to the emergence of a shared culture of peace. Through its initiatives and persistence, the peace movement had affirmed Curle's (1971) argument that there exists a structural linkage between the building of peaceful relationships and the opening up of justice and democracy.

Developing a peace culture is essential to one of the essential elements of settling long-standing conflicts, that of a viable *peace constituency*. Lederach (1997) stressed the importance of a peace constituency as a vital sociocultural resource and catalyst of conflict transformation. Especially in divided societies, a peace constituency is an imperative dimension of the overall effort of resolving conflict, in both attaining and subsequently sustaining a final political settlement. The positive impact of a peace constituency was evident in the transformation of the Turkish-Cypriot political reality in 2003, and the negative impact of an insufficiently developed peace constituency was demonstrated in the failed referendum in the Greek-Cypriot side in 2004.

The larger society must be prepared for accepting compromises, and even the best-crafted settlement will fail unless people are willing to give it a chance to succeed. Without sufficient exposure to the other community and an understanding of the hopes, fears, and concerns of the other side, it is unrealistic to expect the general population to fully embrace the compromises that are necessary to end the conflict. In Cyprus, as the bi-communal peace movement gradually introduced its values and actions to the broader society, it helped create the first small but visible peace-supporting constituency, adding a small but critical voice within the nationalist cultures dominating the political public life of Cyprus.

6.4 Shifting Away from the Nationalist Mind

For those Greek Cypriots and Turkish Cypriots who were involved in the rapprochement process, there was a gradual but distinctive shift away from the stereotypical nationalist assumptions and perceptions that traditionally dominated the national political cultures of the Greek and Turkish people. As they searched for more constructive, sustainable, and effective ways of addressing the conflicts and differences that divided the two sides, they changed the manner in which they viewed their own ethnonational group in relation to the other side, as well as the manner in which they began to understand the nature of the protracted conflict. Their new mental framework, based on different premises for knowledge, led to more realistic views of the situation than those that existed within the nationalist cultures of the two communities.

Moving beyond the nationalist mindset, the peacebuilding community adopted an approach that resulted in more fruitful communication between the two communities. First, they came to understand that the causes of the conflict are not the absolute fault of the other side, but rather the outcome of a complex interplay of different political ideologies, events, and actions. All the players involved are implicated – Greek Cypriots and Turkish Cypriots, as well as Greece, Turkey, and the international actors. They came to see that the causes of the conflicts and issues that separate them are in fact blurred, ambiguous, overlapping, mutually reinforcing, and intertwined, rather than a simple matter of right and wrong.

Second, those in the peacebuilding groups learned that the pain and suffering of their own ethnonational group has a counterpart in the rival ethnonational group. No longer able to deny the pain and suffering experienced by their enemy, they came to openly acknowledge each other's pain and accept a measure of responsibility for their common tragedy. Historical grievances concerning violations of human rights were no longer viewed as the exclusive prerogative of one side in the protracted Cyprus conflict. Such a shift in thinking is a vital element in promoting mutual understanding and addressing the concerns, fears, and hopes of all parties to the conflict.

Third, it became clear to participants in bi-communal groups that the adversarial, nationalist mindset they have inherited cannot serve as a way to move forward. They realized that continuing to operate within the framework of ethnocentric nationalism would simply reproduce and amplify the conflict, leading to new deadlocks and more severe historical impasses. On the other hand, developing and nurturing a mindset guided by a dialogical, cooperative, and conciliatory mode of thinking and doing is more likely to yield positive results. Framing national interests in terms of cooperative approaches and mutual benefits, rather than in a win–lose framework, can lead to the development and institutionalization of sustainable, peace-enhancing processes and alternative, nonbelligerent, security systems.

While it might be expected that those involved in dialogue activities are able to make the type of shift described earlier, the larger questions are whether and to what extent these assumptions can make their way into the wider society with sufficient impact to make a difference, especially in terms of affecting policy decisions. Although it is impossible to separate societal changes from the complexities and contradictions of historical, social, and political events and processes, there are signs that the shift to a cooperative approach has growing in strength and clarity among increasing numbers of citizens, political leaders, business leaders, intellectuals, and journalists. These groups may be a minority when compared to the entire population of each society concerned, but they constitute significant opinion formers with effective inroads to the world of public media and politics. In this regard, they are beginning to function as vital catalysts of socio-political change, more attuned with the domestic and international challenges of the times. These changes carry the potential for new alternative approaches, strategies, and actions that shift away from those that had been traditionally assumed, propagated, and propagandized by nationalism.

6.5 Anchoring Civil-Society Initiatives in Societal Institutions

The success of civil-society peacebuilding over the long term depends partially on its acceptance as a legitimate approach to managing differences and the corresponding disputes that inevitably arise because of these differences. Unless dialogue can be embedded into the very fabric of society, its promise for reshaping the conflict dynamics may be largely unfulfilled. The fact that there have been no serious violence incidents in Cyprus during the past few years, even as tens of thousands of individuals crossed the buffer zone, demonstrates the existence of a general goodwill between the Greek Cypriots and Turkish Cypriots. Engaging in friendly interactions in situations of limited contact, however, is different from handling the everyday tensions and difficulties that are inevitable whenever people work together more closely. Fortunately, the dialogue activities that have occurred since the early 1990s provide a pool of experienced individuals in both communities who can lead an effort to embed dialogue into the structures and programs around which society functions.

The goal of sustaining a permanent process of peacebuilding is one that cannot be ignored as Cyprus tries to move away from a divided society and toward a united future. In order to be sustainable, peacebuilding needs to be concerned with the question of how their work and the practical measures they have taken can be *institutionally anchored* (Ropers, 2003). Without becoming embedded in the working fabric of society, the positive effects of civil-society initiatives can easily fade into the background, and the good work they have done will not result in long-term transformation of society away from a conflict-habituated system based on extreme nationalism.

The institutionalization of the civil-society peacebuilding can take very different forms, ranging from semigovernmental interethnic commissions and joint task forces to multiethnic NGOs. Some of these have already formed in Cyprus, but many of these entities see their primary purpose as helping reach a settlement. If peacemaking at the political level succeeds, however, the continuing challenge will be to engage citizen peacebuilders at the level of civil-society to create mechanisms for interethnic peacebuilding that will entrench the settlement in the institutions, cultures, and practices of the broader society. As is the case with Lederach's (1997) four principles of "truth," "mercy," "justice," and "peace," which he posits as directives for engaging belligerents in conflict transforming processes, peacebuilding is a long-term process and must become part of the evolution of society. One way for this to happen is to institutionalize peacebuilding initiatives in key centers of society and even in the government itself. Despite shortcomings and even objections, reconciliation processes such as those that took place in the aftermath of WWII in Europe, or in the Truth and Reconciliation Commissions in South Africa, have brought about a humanizing process of conflict transformation to these societies.

Going even further, we believe that the creation of a Ministry of Peace as an official part of the new governing structure in Cyprus will serve to institutionalize peacebuilding as a legitimate function within society as a whole. Such a high-level office dedicated to peacebuilding can go a long way to create and sustain peace constituencies and peace alliances, but perhaps even more importantly, a visible and officially mandated and supported institution can make a significant difference in *promoting a dialogue-based dispute culture*. This means that the characteristic elements of constructive dialogue will not be limited just to the positive effects that happen in a handful of intergroup projects, but will become a basic paradigm of political culture.

7 Summary and Conclusion

From its establishment as an independent and bi-communal republic in 1960 to its current membership in the European Union as an ethnically divided country, Cyprus has been an anomaly. When its 1960 constitution established a system in which each community participated separately in elections for president (Greek Cypriots) and vice president (Turkish Cypriots), as well as separate communal legislative chambers, conditions were set up for deadlock and eventual breakdown. Similarly, when the European Union admitted a divided Cyprus, it was unable to extend the *acquis communautaire*[6] to the northern portion of the island under Turkish control, again creating an unworkable situation. Yet at the same time, since the ceasefire was put in place in 1974 and the UN-patrolled buffer zone was extended across the entire length of the island, creating two ethnic zones, Cyprus has been nearly free of intercommunal physical violence.

The absence of violence, however, does not signal the presence of peace (Galtung, 2005), and the social, psychological, and economic scars of conflict are evident in nearly all aspects of life in Cyprus. The lack of a settlement to end the conflict is continuing to extract a heavy toll, including the failure of Cyprus to live up to its potential as an example of ethnic cooperation. In today's world, where ethnic conflicts seem to be the norm rather than the exception, Cyprus could provide a beacon of light. Instead, it remains part of the dark shadows of ethnopolitical conflict.

In contrast to the lack of progress that has characterized the political situation in Cyprus, there has been significant evolution in civil-society peacebuilding during the past two decades. In many ways, Cyprus provides a prime example of what Harold Saunders, a former US diplomat, calls *sustained dialogue* (Saunders, 1999). Participants have repeatedly "returned to the table" over extended periods of time to discuss issues, exchange perceptions and views, design projects, and strategize about how to move the peace process forward in Cyprus. In so doing, they have built the relationships that are necessary for conflict transformation both "within the room" and in the wider society. They overcame many challenges, but at the same time they have a long way to go before their work sufficiently permeates Cypriot society and allows it to move past nationalism and toward a sustainable peace culture.

Although civil-society intergroup dialogue initiatives have played an important role as a peacebuilding strategy in Cyprus, and they hold promise for helping Cyprus make the transition from a divided society to an integrated future, it is important to bear in mind that civil-society initiatives are not isolated from the conflict dynamics at large. Although we have argued that the peace movement was able to alter the dynamics positively in some cases, helping to move Cyprus out of stalemate, we recognize that they have also tended to reflect the dynamics. During times of crisis, the peacebuilders have never found it easy to continue with their work, either because of roadblocks erected by the situation or because of their own sense of discouragement. Sometimes the forces against a settlement or against peace in

[6]The entire body of European laws, including treaties, regulations, and directives passed by the European institutions, as well as judgments laid down by the Court of Justice, is known as the *acquis communautaire*, often shorted to the *acquis*. Candidate countries wishing to join the union must adopt, implement, and enforce all the acquis to be allowed to join the EU. The various "chapters" of the acquis can be found at http://ec.europa.eu/enlargement/enlargement_process/accession_process/how_does_a_country_join_the_eu/negotiations_croatia_turkey/index_en.htm

general seem too great to fight against. In these situations, some people drop out from the peace movement. In some cases they decide it is better to "lay low" until a crisis moved a little past the boiling point. But civil-society movements have their limitations, and their survival often depends, at least to some extent, on progress at other levels.

Even after a solution is negotiated and accepted by the people of Cyprus, challenges are certain to arise. The increased freedom of movement and reduced military presence that comes with a settlement could allow greater possibilities for unpleasant or even violent incidents to occur. These events, if they happen, will make dialogue even more necessary, but at the same time they will make such events much more difficult to organize. The ultimate aim is to help shape conflict dynamics in a positive manner, but at the same time the impact of dialogue activities on individuals and the larger society will be constrained and limited by the very dynamics they are trying to influence.

In the final analysis, ethnic conflicts require a political solution. Peacemaking at the political level, however, is only the beginning of the peacebuilding process. The primary challenge is to create or modify the institutions, cultures, and practices of the broader society so that peace will have a chance to succeed. Living and working together successfully after decades of separation requires a significant commitment to building bridges of communication, healing past wounds, and creating a future in which both communities can work together without significant discord or violence. In other words, the future of societies torn apart by ethnic conflict will depend on building a sustainable peace, and strong civil-society peacebuilding efforts will be necessary for realizing this difficult but vital goal.

References

Amir, Y. (1969). Contact hypothesis in ethnic relations. *Psychological Bulletin, 71*(5), 319–342.

Anastasiou, H. (1996). Conflict alienation and the hope for peace: The struggle for peace in militarized Cyprus. *The Cyprus Review, 8*(2), 79–96.

Anastasiou, H. (2002). Communication across conflict lines: The case of ethnically divided Cyprus. *Journal of Peace Research, 39*(5), 581–596.

Anastasiou, H. (2008a). *The broken olive branch: nationalism, ethnic conflict and the quest for peace in Cyprus* (The impasse of ethnonationalism, Vol. I). Syracuse, NY: Syracuse University Press.

Anastasiou, H. (2008b). *The broken olive branch: nationalism, ethnic conflict and the quest for peace in Cyprus* (Nationalism versus Europeanization, Vol. II). Syracuse, NY: Syracuse University Press.

Anderson, B. (1995). *Imagined communities. Reflection on the origin and spread of nationalism.* London: Verso.

Attalides, M. A. (1979). *Cyprus: Nationalism and international politics*. Edinburgh: Q Press.

Azar, E. E. (1990). *The management of protracted social conflict. Theory and cases*. Aldershot: Dartmouth.

Bahcheli, T., & Rizopoulos, N. X. (1996|1997). The Cyprus impasse: What next? *World Policy Journal, 13*(4), 27–39.

Barkey, H. J., & Gordon, P. H. (2002). Cyprus: The predictable crisis. *National Interest, 66*, 83–93.

Bölükbasi, S. (1998). The Cyprus dispute and the United Nations: Peaceful non-settlement between 1954 and 1996. *International Journal of Middle East Studies, 30*, 411–434.

Boulding, E. (2000). *Cultures of peace: The hidden side of history*. Syracuse, NY: Syracuse University Press.

Brewer, M. B., & Miller, N. (1984). Beyond the contact hypothesis: Theoretical perspectives on desegregation. In N. Miller & M. Brewer (Eds.), *Groups in contact. The psychology of desegregation* (pp. 281–302). Orlando, FL: Academic.

Broome, B. J. (1997). Designing a collective approach to peace: Interactive design and problem-solving workshops with Greek Cypriot and Turkish Cypriot communities in Cyprus. *International Negotiation, 2*(3), 381–407.

Broome, B. J. (1998). Overview of conflict resolution activities in Cyprus: Their contribution to the peace process. *Cyprus Review, 10*(1), 47–66.

Broome, B. J. (2004). Reaching across the dividing line: Building a collective vision for peace in Cyprus. *International Journal of Peace Research, 41*(2), 191–209.

Broome, B. J. (2005). *Building bridges across the green line: a guide to intercultural communication in Cyprus.* Nicosia: United Nations Development Program.

Broome, B. J. (2009). Building relational empathy through an interactive design process. In D. J. D. Sandole, S. Byrne, I. Staroste-Sandole, & J. Senihi (Eds.), *Handbook of conflict analysis and resolution* (pp. 184–200). New York: Routledge.

Broome, B. J., & Jakobsson-Hatay, A. S. (2006). Building peace in divided societies: The role of intergroup dialogue. In J. Oetzel & S. Ting-Toomey (Eds.), *Handbook of conflict communication* (pp. 627–662). Thousand Oaks, CA: Sage Publications.

Bryant, R. (2004). *Imagining the modern. The cultures of nationalism in Cyprus*. London: I.B. Tauris.

Burton, J. W. (1969). *Conflict and communication: The use of controlled communication in international relations*. London: Macmillan.

Byrne, S. (2001). Consociational and civic society approaches to peacebuilding in Northern Ireland. *Journal of Peace Research, 38*(3), 327–352.

Calotychos, V. (Ed.). (1998). *Cyprus and its people. Nation, identity, and experience in an unimaginable community, 1955–1997*. Boulder, CO: Westview Press.

Chigas, D. (2003). Track II (Citizen) diplomacy. In G. Burgess & H. Burgess (Eds.), *Beyond intractability*. Boulder, CO: Conflict Research Consortium, University of Colorado. Posted: May 2004 http://www.beyondintractability.org/essay/track2_diplomacy/.

Crawshaw, N. (1978). *The Cyprus revolt. An account of the struggle for union with Greece*. London: George Allen & Unwin.

Curle, A. (1971). *Making Peace*. London: Tavistock.

Denktash, R. R. (1988). *The Cyprus triangle*. London: K. Rustem and Brother. Revised Edition.

Diamond, L., & Fisher, R. J. (1995). Integrating conflict resolution training and consultation: A Cyprus example. *Negotiation Journal, 11*(3), 287–301.

Doob, L. W. (1976). A Cyprus workshop: Intervention methodology during a continuing crisis. *Journal of Social Psychology, 98*, 143–144.

Doob, L. W. (1987). Adieu to private intervention in political conflicts? *International Journal of Group Tensions, 17*(1–4), 15–27.

Fisher, R. J. (1992). *Peace building for Cyprus: Report on a conflict analysis workshop, June 1991*. Ottawa, ON: Canadian Institute for International Peace and Security.

Fisher, R. J. (1997). *Interactive conflict resolution*. Syracuse, NY: Syracuse University Press.

Forbes, H. D. (1997). *Ethnic conflict. Commerce, culture, and the contact hypothesis*. New Haven, CT: Yale University Press.

Galtung, J. (2005). Violence, peace, and peace research. In M. Evangelista (Ed.), *Peace studies: Critical concepts in political science* (Vol. I, pp. 21–52). New York: Routledge.

Gündüz, A. (2001). Greek-Turkish disputes: How to resolve them. In D. Keridis & D. Triantaphyllou (Eds.), *Greek-Turkish relations in the era of globalization* (pp. 81–101). Dulles, VA: Brassey's.

Hadjipavlou, M. (2004). The contribution of bicommunal contacts in building a civil society in Cyprus. In A. Eagly, R. Baron, & L. Hamilton (Eds.), *The social psychology of group identity and social conflict* (pp. 193–213). Washington, DC: American Psychological Association.

Hadjipavlou-Trigeorgis, M. (1987). *Identity conflict in divided societies: The case of Cyprus*. Unpublished doctoral dissertation, Boston University

Hadjipavlou-Trigeorgis, M. (1998). Different relationships to the land: Personal narratives, political implications and future possibilities in Cyprus. In V. Calotychos (Ed.), *Cyprus and its people. Nation, identity, and experience in an unimaginable community 1955–1997* (pp. 251–276). Boulder, CO: Westview Press.

Hadjipavlou-Trigeorgis, M., & Trigeoris, L. (1993). Cyprus: An evolutionary approach to conflict resolution. *The Journal of Conflict Resolution, 37*(2), 340–360.

Hitchens, C. (1997). *Hostage to history: Cyprus from the Ottomans to Kissinger*. New York: Noonday Press.

Hubbard, A. S. (1999). Cultural and status differences in intergroup conflict resolution: A Longitudinal study of a Middle East dialogue group in the United States. *Human Relations, 52*(3), 303–325.

Jenkins, G. (2001). Turkey's changing domestic politics. In D. Keridis & D. Triantaphyllou (Eds.), *Greek-Turkish relations in the era of globalization* (pp. 19–41). Dulles, VA: Brassey's.

Joseph, J. S. (1997). *Cyprus. Ethnic Conflict and International Politics. From Independence to the Threshold of the European Union*. London: Macmillan.

Kelman, H. C. (1995). Contributions of an unofficial conflict resolution effort to the Israeli-Palestinian breakthrough. *Negotiation Journal, 11*, 19–27.

Keridis, D. (2001). Domestic developments and foreign policy: Greek policy toward Turkey. In D. Keridis & D. Triantaphyllou (Eds.), *Greek-Turkish relations in the era of globalization* (pp. 2–18). Dulles, VA: Brassey's.

Kizilyurek, N. (1993). *Cyprus beyond the nation*. Nicosia: G. Kasoulides & Son.

Koumoulides, J. T. A. (Ed.). (1986). *Cyprus in transition: 1960–1985*. London: Trigraph.

Lederach, J. P. (1997). *Building peace: Sustainable reconciliation in divided societies*. Washington, DC: United States Institute of Peace.

Loizos, P. (1981). *The heart grown bitter: A chronicle of Cypriot war refugees*. London: Cambridge University Press.

Markides, K. C. (1977). *The rise and fall of the Cyprus Republic*. New Haven, CT: Yale University Press.

Mirbagheri, F. (1998). *Cyprus and international peacemaking*. New York: Routledge.

Mitchell, C. R. (1981). *Peacemaking and the consultant's role*. New York: Nichols Publishing Company.

Montville, J. V. (1987). The arrow and the olive branch: A case for track two diplomacy. In J. W. McDonald Jr. & D. B. Bendahmane (Eds.), *Conflict resolution: Track two diplomacy* (pp. 5–20). Washington, DC: Foreign Service Institute, Department of State.

Nan, S. A. (2003). Track I Diplomacy. In G. Burgess & H. Burgess (Eds.), *Beyond intractability*. Boulder, CO: Conflict Research Consortium, University of Colorado. Posted: June 2003 http://www.beyondintractability.org/essay/peace_processes/.

Oberling, P. (1982). *The road to Bellapais: The Turkish Cypriot exodus to Northern Cyprus*. New York: Columbia University Press.

Papadakis, Y. (2006). *Echoes from the dead zone: Across the Cyprus divide*. London: I.B. Tauris.

Pettigrew, T. F. (2008). Future directions for intergroup contact theory and research. *International Journal of Intercultural Relations, 32*, 187–199.

Pruitt, D. G., Rubin, J. Z., & Kim, S. H. (Eds.). (1994). *Stalemate and de-escalation* (3rd ed.). New York: McGraw Hill College Division.

Report of Planning Bureau. (1975). Nicosia, Republic of Cyprus.

Richmond, O. P. (1998). *Mediating in Cyprus. The Cypriot communities and the United Nations*. London: Frank Cass.

Ropers, N. (2003). From resolution to transformation: The role of dialogue projects. *Berghof Handbook for Conflict transformation* Retrieved May 10, 2005, from http://www.berghof-handbook.net

Rubin, J., Pruitt, D., & Kim, S. H. (1994). *Social conflict: Escalation, stalemate, and settlement* (2nd ed.). New York: McGraw-Hill.

Saunders, H. H. (1999). *A public peace process: Sustained dialogue to transform racial and ethnic conflicts*. New York: St. Martin's Press.

Savvides, P. K. (2002). *Cyprus at the gate of the European Union*. Athens: Hellenic Foundation for European and Foreign Policy.

Stearns, M. (1992). *Entangled allies: U.S. policy toward Greece, Turkey, and Cyprus*. New York: Council on Foreign Relations Press.

Stoddard, P. H. (1986). An experiment in track two diplomacy. In D. B. Bendahmane & J. W. McDonald (Eds.), *Perspective on negotiations* (pp. 139–143). Washington DC: Foreign Service Institute, United States Department of State.

Talbot, P. (1977). The Cyprus seminar. In M. Berman & J. E. Johnson (Eds.), *Unofficial diplomats*. New York: Columbia University Press.

United Nations. (1974, July 20). Security Council Resolution 353: Cyprus. Retrieved August 1, 2011, from http://www.un.org/documents/sc/res/1974/scres74.htm.

Uludag, S. (1996). We are the new culture. In *The multicultural carpet: Reflections on bi-communal work in Cyprus* (pp. 10–11). Nicosia: American Center.

United Nations. (2003). The Annan Plan for Cyprus. Retrieved from http://www.cyprus-un-plan.org

United Nations Report of the Secretary-General on his mission of good offices in Cyprus. [Report # S/2004/437]. (2004, May 28). Retrieved June 30, 2004, from http://www.un.int/cyprus/s4372004.htm

Volkan, V. D. (1979). *Cyprus – war and adaptation. A psychoanalytic history of two ethnic groups in conflict*. Charlottesville, VA: University Press of Virginia.

Wolleh, O. (2001). *Local peace constituencies in Cyprus: Citizen rapprochement by the bi-communal conflict resolution trainer group*. Berlin: Berghof Research Center For Conflict Management.

Yesilada, B., & Sozen, A. (2002). Negotiating a resolution to the Cyprus problem: Is potential EU membership a blessing or a curse? *International Negotiation Journal, 7*(2), 261–285.

Zartman, I. W. (1985). *Ripe for resolution*. New York: Oxford University Press.

Zartman, I. W. (2001). The timing of peace initiatives: Hurting stalemates and ripe moments. *The Global Review of Ethnopolitics, 1*(1), 8–18.

Part V

The Balkans

13 Lessons Learned from the Former Yugoslavia: The Case of Croatia*

Dinka Corkalo Biruski

Yugoslavia/Croatia Chapter Summary

Corkalo Biruski presents a socio-psychological model to explain the destruction of interethnic harmony in Croatia through analysis of the community of Vukovar. Research surveys in this city are analyzed to create a picture of prewar and postwar interethnic relations. Theories are applied to the processes of change and offered as a means to reestablish a cohesive society.

A brief historical context delineates the early years during which Yugoslavia was established under a proclamation of unity and brotherhood and then divided in fix independentstates. Decentralization of government within the republic is presented as the catalyst which eventually engendered independence for Croatia following a 4-year war.

Vukovar is presented as a flourishing multiethnic community prior to the war. Early signs of interethnic schism are recognized following the war but the most significant are noted to have occurred after the fall of Communism in Eastern Europe. Social Identity Theory (SIT) is applied to this sudden shift in an effort to consider cause. Biruski suggests several factors that led to the eventual loss of community through fear and silence.

The author presents an argument for using the term "social reconstruction" versus "reconciliation" when describing a return to functional society. Recognition of the initial unpleasantness of this process and the length

*The preparation of this manuscript was supported by the Ministry of Science, Education and Sports of the Republic of Croatia (grant no. 130-1301422-1418). This chapter is a revised and more elaborated version of my keynote lecture at the Tenth European Conference on Traumatic Stress in Opatija, Croatia, in 2007. I am indebted to the people of Vukovar; they taught me everything I know about the wisdom of survival.

D. Corkalo Biruski (✉)
Department of Psychology, Faculty of Humanities and Social Sciences, University of Zagreb, Croatia
e-mail: dinka.corkalo@ffzg.hr

D. Landis and R.D. Albert (eds.), *Handbook of Ethnic Conflict: International Perspectives*, International and Cultural Psychology, DOI 10.1007/978-1-4614-0448-4_13,

of time required are iterated. Description of a divided society provides evidence of a major obstacle on the path to improved interethnic attitudes. Corkalo Biruski offers a model to bring ethnic groups back together through healing of trauma at the individual level, rebuilding community and enacting norms of tolerance at the societal level.

Cheryl Jorgensen

Probably no war after the Second World War has received such extensive and "real-time" media coverage as did the wars in the Former Yugoslavia (Cigar, Magas, & Zanic, 1999). Starting from 1991, the international media continuously sent the world hundreds of stories and images of the destruction of Croatia, Bosnia and Herzegovina, Macedonia, and Kosovo. However, the media within these countries also played a key role in preparing, instigating, and maintaining the atmosphere of war, even before the wars actually started (see Thompson, 1995). Yet at the same time, politicians from the international community were far less interested in the Yugoslav wars. As one of the most prominent researchers of the former Yugoslavia has said, "Western powerful countries hesitated greatly to intervene in the conflict" (Ramet, 2009, p. 492). This hesitation changed over the course of time, and the international community finally ended the war(s) with the Dayton Peace Accords in 1995, after years of killing and the most horrible atrocities. For example, during the war in Croatia, 13,583 people were killed, more than 37,000 were wounded, and by the end of 1991 about 700,000 people were internally displaced or took refuge abroad (Perkovic & Puljiz, 2001). In Bosnia and Herzegovina, the numbers are even more dramatic. Ramet, 2009 reports that estimates of those killed in the war in Bosnia and Herzegovina range from 110,000 to 237,500 people, while 2.7 million people were displaced. A similar change in interest about the wars in the former Yugoslavia could also be noticed within the scholarly community, developing from early disengagement and a lack of thorough analysis of the causes and immediate consequences of the Yugoslav wars (Cigar et al., 1999) into a scientific industry that happened with historical distance. The most intriguing question on the war was: "How could it have happened?" Indeed, how was it possible that this complex state that had seemed so highly integrated for decades was ripped apart so violently and abruptly? How it was possible that such an amalgam of ethnic groups, nations, religions, and cultures brought about the phenomenon of *ethnic cleansing*, a term that was barely known before but which became the most descriptive expression of what happened (Cohen, 1999). The immediate answer given readily by many journalists and some scholars (see Kaplan, 1993) was that of "ancient hatred" being the backbone of the conflict (for a more elaborated deconstruction of this perspective, see Gagnon, 2004). A similar "emotion-based approach" in explaining the dissolution not only of Yugoslavia, but also of the equally complex cases of some other multiethnic Eastern-European states, was also offered in the scholarly literature (e.g., Petersen, 2002). Our approach here is far less ambitious and comes from a socio-psychological perspective. By using the example of the city of Vukovar, Croatia (see map in Fig. 13.1), a city that was highly integrated and one of the most developed communities in the country, I want to disentangle the complex dynamic of community separation, and emphasize the processes that led to the destruction of friendly neighborly relations, as a real and tragic consequence of the recent war having a huge impact on everyday life in this particular community and many others like it. By relating the findings in this specific community to more global processes that have been going on in the former Yugoslavia, we hope to provide an illustrative case for the analysis of this complex and multidimensional conflict.

Fig. 13.1 Map of the states on the territory of the former Yugoslavia

1 A Short History of Croatia 1918–1991

Croatia declared its independence in 1991, after having shared its political destiny within the state of Yugoslavia with five other larger ethnic groups (Slovenes, Serbs, Muslims,[1] Macedonians, and Montenegrins) for more than 70 years. The purpose of this chapter is not to provide a detailed political analysis of the dissolution of the former Yugoslavia; there are many other sources that do this successfully (Banac, 2001; Gagnon, 2004; Magas & Zanic, 1999; Ramet, 1996, 2009). Rather, in this chapter I will construct a sketch built around a few historical events by describing the context in which they happened. Nevertheless, these landmark events have not been chosen by chance; they will provide us with a macrolevel background for understanding the processes that happened at the communal, microlevel.

Yugoslavia was established in 1918 as a product of mutual agreement among the winners of

[1] In the former Yugoslavia, "Muslim" (*Musliman*) was not a religious designation but one of ethnicity and was used for Slavic Muslims who inhabited Bosnia and Herzegovina. In 1993, after Bosnia and Herzegovima gained its independence, Bosnian Muslims started using the term "Bosniak" (*Bošnjak*) as the name of their ethnicity.

the First World War. The Serbian dynasty took the leading role in the newly established state and fulfilled the political agenda of the Serbian political elite – to unite all the Serbs within the territory of one state (Banac, 2001). The two other large ethnic groups – the Croats and the Slovenes – entered the new state with the hope of preserving their political equality by sharing the power with the Serbs. However, by the beginning of World War II, the Kingdom of Yugoslavia was a highly centralized monarchy, with a Serbian king, dominated by the Serbian political elite, with the other political elites, especially the Croats, struggling for their share of the power. World War II was the worst time in the history of Yugoslavia. The Kingdom disappeared when the king fled to London after the invasion by Nazi Germany in April 1941, and the country was divided by the Nazis and their allies, with the territories (see Fig. 13.1) of Serbia, Slovenia, and Bosnia and Herzegovina being occupied mostly by German forces. In Croatia and parts of Bosnia and Herzegovina, the Nazis helped to establish the so-called Independent State of Croatia, ruled by a militant and extremely nationalist movement called the Ustashe.[2] Their politics of ethnic cleansing was directed at the destruction of others who were considered to be of "non-Aryan" race, and tens of thousands of people, mostly Serbs, Jews, and Gypsies were killed or sent to concentration camps in Croatia and elsewhere. The pogrom was especially harsh towards Serbs (Zerjavic, 1992), and their tremendous suffering under the Ustasha regime has remained the major historical grievance of Serbs in Croatia. At the same time the Serbian royalists in Serbia (the Chetniks),[3] whose clearly promoted goal was to accomplish an ethnically homogenous Serbian state and fulfill their dream of a "Greater Serbia," soon started to collaborate with the Fascists of Italy, Germany, and even with the Ustasha regime in Croatia. Their atrocities against Croatian and Muslim civilians were massive and manifold (see Ramet, 2009).

The most serious rebellion against the pro-Nazi regimes was the resistance movement of antifascists organized by the Communist party throughout the territory of Yugoslavia. As Ramet (2009) noted, there are three elements that were important for the success of the Partisan movement: (1) although it was organized as a guerilla movement, the Partisans had a joint central command led by a Croat, Josip Broz Tito, who would after the war become lifelong president and marshal of the new socialist Yugoslavia; (2) the movement fought whole-heartedly against nationalism and proclaimed the ideologically important slogan of "brotherhood and unity," calling for the unification of the belligerent ethnic groups and promising a new Yugoslavia as a "land of the free," and (3) the partisans did not hesitate to take up arms against the Fascists immediately after they had invaded the country. Similar arguments were also presented in Schopflin (1993). At the end of the war Tito's war efforts were acknowledged by the Western allies, and although there were serious attempts to bring the runaway king back to the power, Tito won in the 1945 national election (which was boycotted by the political opposition), which marked the beginning of his rule over the second, socialist Yugoslavia. His indisputable authority and governance lasted for 35 years, until his death in 1980.

Postwar Yugoslavia was a fairly prosperous country consisting of six republics (Bosnia and Herzegovina, Croatia, Macedonia, Montenegro, Slovenia, and Serbia) and two autonomous provinces (Kosovo and Vojvodina), each of which was an integral part of the Republic of Serbia (see map on Fig. 13.1). According to the 1981 census data (Petrovic, 1985), Yugoslavia had almost 22.5 million inhabitants, with Serbs being the largest ethnic group (36.6%), followed by Croats (19.7%), Muslims (8.9%), Slovenes (7.8%), Albanians concentrated mostly in Kosovo

[2] The term *Ustashe* (plural) could be roughly translated as "insurgents" or "rebels". However, it is used exclusively as the name of the pro-fascist movement in Croatia during WWII, i.e., the word is only used as a historically marked proper noun and thus can never be politically neutral in contemporary Croatian.

[3] The term *Chetnik* could be roughly translated as a member of a small military unit, called *četa*. However, this term, as it is the case with the term Ustasha, is used only when referring to members of an extremely nationalist Serbian military organization that was active during WWII.

(7.7%), Macedonians (6%), Yugoslavs (5.4%),[4] and Montenegrians (2.6%). The Yugoslav communist regime was far less harsh than in the countries behind the Iron Curtain.[5] The very fact that Tito strongly opposed the Soviet attempt to take political control over the country made the Yugoslav regime softer; however, it was still far from being open, democratic, and liberal. The major political taboo was the national question (Banac, 2001), and the system successfully suppressed nationalism among the various ethnic groups. Tito controlled ethnic tensions by balancing the power given to the Yugoslav republics until the 1970s. In 1974, constitutional decentralization gave more authority and political power to the republics and loosened federal control, allowing all the Yugoslav republics the possibility of declaring independence through elections. This very constitutional change enabled Slovenia and Croatia to declare their independence less than 20 years later. The constitutional changes provided a way for the republics – especially the two most prosperous, Slovenia and Croatia – to question their federal position and ask for decentralization and a fair distribution of power. At the same time, the Federal Army under the command of Marshal Tito was a bastion of federalism. The military was the strongest institution of the system, and while it included all ethnicities, it was disproportionately populated by Serbs and endorsed the politics of a firm hand. An unjust distribution of economic goods at the expense of those who produced them, growing nationalism, and the inability of the system to carry out necessary reforms – these were the major features of Yugoslav society when Tito died (for a thorough analysis of societal processes in Yugoslav society see Ramet, 1992, and especially Ramet, 2009, Chaps. 7–9). After Tito's death an endless chain of misfortunes marked out the last decade of the united political entity: a growing economic crisis with a high rate of unemployment, a loss of control and authority in the Communist party, the fading influence of the ideology of "brotherhood and unity," and growing nationalism that was particularly strong among the Serbian political elite but not without a response from other republics. The fall of the Berlin Wall, which marked a new era in world politics far beyond the Old Continent, caught Yugoslavia unprepared. With no legacy of dealing with conflict peacefully (Corkalo Biruski, 2002), the political elites barely handled the processes of dissolution, facing at the same time an upsurge of overwhelming Serbian nationalism led by Slobodan Milošević. After a series of unsuccessful attempts aimed at gaining more autonomy within the federal state, but also asking for democratization and the possibility of confederation, Slovenia and Croatia started the process of their independence. In 1990, both countries organized their first free democratic elections and in 1991 both declared their independence. A strong, armed intervention was carried out in Slovenia by the Yugoslav People's Army (JNA)[6] in June 1991. This intervention was halted in Slovenia in 10 days. For Croatia, however, it was the beginning of 4 years of war.

The first democratic Croatian parliamentary elections were won by Croatian Democratic Union (HDZ), a strong nationalist party led by Franjo Tudjman, who would become the first Croatian president. One may say that nothing is comparable with Milošević's manipulative nationalism and his ability to mobilize masses, playing

[4] The national designation "Yugoslav" was used in the former Yugoslavia for those who did not identify with any of ethnic groups. It was used very often by people from the mixed marriages. This category was allowed for the first time during the 1961 national census (Sekulic, Massey, & Hodson, 1994).

[5] The Iron Curtain is an expression that was used to symbolize the division of post-WWII Europe, separated along ideological, political, and economic lines. The states "behind the Iron Curtain" were under the influence of the Soviet Union and were joined in the military alliance of the Warsaw Pact (as opposed to NATO). Starting in 1948, Tito successfully confronted the influence of the Soviet Union and in 1961 helped to establish the Non-Aligned Movement as a middle road opposing the politics of the *cold war*.

[6] Although the JNA was a federal military force, the Serbs were overrepresented, compared to their share in the overall population of Yugoslavia. For example, in 1990 60% of all JNA officers were Serbs, and the percentage was even higher among the top ranks: 81% of colonels and 62% of generals were Serbs (Zunec, 1998b).

on historical fears, smoldering old threats and grievances, and reawakening fabricated national myths. However, one may also say that Milošević's politics fell on fertile ground when it came to the new Croatian political elite. The euphoria caused by the national liberation of the Croats was soon replaced by ethnic tensions, as parts of the Serb minority in Croatia, which populated mainly rural areas, strongly opposed the newly formed Croatian state, invoking past grievances from World War II and called for the JNA's involvement. The Croatian political elite managed the tensions badly, and the general public demanded a solution. Fear and deep unrest began to develop in communities that had been peaceful until then, and this was particularly true of multiethnic communities like the city of Vukovar, which will be described in the following sections. The social networks of friends, neighbors, and in-laws of different ethnic backgrounds began to fade, and ethnicity predominated in the shaping of new social relations. In the following months, sporadic interethnic incidents developed into more and more serious conflicts between insurgent Serb paramilitary forces and the Croatian police. Open war broke out in the spring of 1991 with clear Federal Army involvement and command. By the end of the same year, one-third of Croatia was under the control of Serb paramilitary forces and the Yugoslav Army, which openly supported the paramilitaries. At the same time, more than 275,000 people, mainly Croats, were displaced (Ajdukovic, 1993). The Croatian war for independence, known as the *Homeland War* in Croatian historiography and public discourse, ended in 1995 after two major military operations were carried out by the Croatian military forces – Operation Flash (May, 1995) and Operation Storm (August, 1995). In Operation Flash, Croatian forces regained control over Serb-controlled territory in western Slavonia, and in Operation Storm, they took back the remaining occupied territories in Croatia. However, the advancement of the Croatian Forces caused tens of thousands of Croatian Serbs to flee either to Serbia or Serb-controlled parts of Bosnia and Herzegovina, and their slow return to Croatia is an ongoing process.

1.1 Was the War Possible to Predict?

One question that is intriguing to ask (although one could never know the answer) is the following: Had the communist regimes of the Eastern Bloc not collapsed, would Yugoslavia have broken up at all? And a related question: Had the ideology of "brotherhood and unity" not been insisted upon by the state, would Yugoslavia have lasted for such a long time? It is reasonable to guess that Yugoslavia would have come to an end sooner or later (see Schopflin, 1993). The faded potency of the central government that lived out its last days with no inner strength to carry out necessary economic, social, and political reforms made it unable for the political system to survive. The political context in the neighboring countries and in the entire European region only made it possible for the final collapse to happen sooner. However, with the benefit of my early socialization but also my postwar research experience, I can assuredly say that ideology was not the most important thing that kept ordinary people together. What served as an efficient glue was a strong multiethnic interconnectedness in communal social networks (Ajdukovic & Corkalo Biruski, 2004; Corkalo Biruski et al., 2004; Hodson, Sekulic, & Massey, 1994). There is a vast body of data showing that the upcoming war was hard to predict, at least based on empirical surveys done in the former Yugoslavia. This claim is compellingly supported by Gagnon's (2004) review of data collected throughout the country in the years before the war started. There was a high percentage of people (as high as 80% in Bosnia and Herzegovina, where the bloodshed would be the worst) who declared good or positive interethnic relations in their community and a low percentage of those who perceived their ethnic group's rights as being threatened. These findings are also supported by an increase in ethnic heterogamy (i.e., "mixed marriages") in all the Yugoslav republics since 1950, when these data started to be registered (Petrovic, 1985).

In the next sections I will give a detailed description of the processes that preceded the outbreak of the war, as well as of postwar attempts to rebuild war-torn communities and restore social life, by following the example of a community that was an exemplar of a successful multiethnic community in prewar Croatia – the city of Vukovar. Today this city is a symbol of Croatian suffering in the 1991–1995 war, but also an example of the extremely slow and painful process of social recovery. I will describe this community based on a series of quantitative and qualitative studies that we have conducted in the city in the period of 2000–2008. In 2000 we conducted a survey on prewar and postwar interethnic relations on a representative sample of the adult citizens ($N=404$) of the city of Vukovar, both Croats ($N=199$) and Serbs ($N=205$), and repeated the study in 2002 and 2008. Detailed descriptions of the first two surveys can be found in Biro et al. (2004) and Corkalo Biruski and Ajdukovic (2009). Interethnic relations were also in the focus of our survey of Vukovar adolescents, their parents, and their teachers in 2001 (see Ajdukovic & Corkalo Biruski, 2008; Corkalo Biruski & Ajdukovic, 2007) and in 2007 (Corkalo Biruski & Ajdukovic, 2008a). In these surveys, 1,421 adolescents, 1,802 parents, and 201 teachers from both ethnic communities participated. This large corpus gave us comprehensive and detailed insight into the social dynamics in Vukovar's ethnically divided schools. Our quantitative findings were refined and deepened with qualitative methodology, included ethnographic study, a series of focus groups with relevant social actors (war victims, entrepreneurs, youth, and NGO representatives) (Corkalo Biruski et al., 2004), and in-depth interviews with Croats and Serbs in the community who broke off their friendships because of the war (Ajdukovic, 2004; Ajdukovic & Corkalo Biruski, 2004). The following analysis of the complexities of postwar processes in this particular community, which also considers prewar interethnic relations as remembered by the citizens of Vukovar themselves, will be supported by the above-mentioned studies. Not everything that happened in this particular community can be generalized to other, similar communities affected by the 1991–1995 war. However, this specific case does a good job of informing us, in a dramatic way, about the factors that caused the relatively rapid disappearance of the integrated social fabric of multiethnic communities in the former Yugoslavia. It also effectively informs us about the very slow pace of the processes of social reconstruction.

2 The City of Vukovar: A Story of the Collapse and Division of a Community

Before the war, the city of Vukovar was a prosperous, multiethnic community. According to data from the national census in 1991 (Croatian national census, 1991), there were about 44,600 inhabitants. Croats made up the largest group (47%), followed by Serbs (32%) and Yugoslavs (9.8%). There were also Ruthenians/Rusyns (about 2%), Hungarians (1.5%), Ukrainians (slightly more than 1%), and other groups. In total, more than 20 ethnic groups lived in Vukovar before the 1991 war. This mixture of people and cultures made this city a true multicultural community, and its inhabitants were proud of it (Corkalo Biruski et al., 2004). The first postwar census, in 2001, registered slightly more than 31,600 inhabitants (a population drop of 30% compared to 1991). Although the ethnic patchwork was still present, the demographic landscape had changed significantly: 57% of the population were Croats and 34% were Serbs. The census still recorded 19 different ethnic groups, the next largest being the Rusyns (1.8%), the Hungarians (1.2%), and the Ukrainians (less than 1%). However, their numbers were lower than they had been in the prewar period (Census of the Republic of Croatia, 2001).

Vukovar (see map in Fig. 13.1) is located in the eastern part of Croatia, on the Danube River, which forms the border with Serbia. Before the war, it was an economically advanced and prosperous community, with well-developed rubber and shoe factories that employed more than 20,000 people. High industrial production and advanced agriculture made the city one of the economic centers of the country and the harmony of multiethnic living made Vukovar a model for a highly functional multicultural community. In fact, the notion of multiculturalism was not widely used in the Former Yugoslavia. Instead, the ideologically appropriate term was "brotherhood and unity of nations and nationalities," but the meaning was similar; it advocated peaceful and harmonious living. However, in Yugoslav society, dialogue on ethnic issues was not encouraged. On the contrary, the ideology promoted "Yugoslavianism," as a way of managing ethnic issues, and the creation of a Yugoslav culture (Ramet, 1996). The Yugoslav political elite did not care about identities and diversity. Moreover, ethnic promotion was condemned as a sign of nationalism and was strongly discouraged. In spite of the purposeful efforts to promote it, the ideology of Yugoslavianism did not take deeper roots; Sekulic et al. (1994) reported that the highest proportion of Yugoslavs in the Former Yugoslavia lived in Bosnia, which was the most multiethnic republic. Yet even in Bosnia the percentage of those who identified themselves as Yugoslavs never rose above 14.4% in 1989. This percentage was much lower in Croatia (9%) and in Serbia (4.6%).

2.1 Community as It Used to Be

In the city of Vukovar, according to census in 1991 the percentage of Yugoslavs was only slightly higher than in the rest of the country (9.8%). No matter how prevalent Yugoslavianism was, the perception of Vukovar's citizens of their prewar existence was that they lived in harmony with each other and that ethnic origin was not a relevant characteristic in everyday social relations (Ajdukovic & Corkalo Biruski, 2004; Corkalo Biruski et al., 2004). In our survey studies in Vukovar, 84% of Croats and 97% of Serbs reported that they had had close friends in the other ethnic community before the war (Corkalo Biruski & Ajdukovic, 2009). Interethnic tolerance and respectful coexistence in Croatia were corroborated by other researchers (Sekulic, Hodson, & Massey, 2001). As these authors clearly showed, the level of tolerance in Croatia in the years before the war had not changed significantly; however, there was an increase in intolerance after the war. In sum, these data from Croatian representative samples, together with our data from Vukovar, strongly suggest that the widespread notion of "ancient hatreds"[7] as a cause of the war is not well-founded. Dense and intimate social networks in prewar communities are well described in the narratives of our qualitative research participants. A typical statement one would hear while talking with community members about their prewar life was: "We lived normally; we did not even know who was of what ethnic background. We would visit each other in our homes, and we celebrated each other's religious holidays together" (Corkalo Biruski et al., 2004, p.145).[8]

Having in mind this harmonious prewar existence, at least in the memories of our participants, the question of how such a rapid and disruptive breakdown of communal life could have

[7] An abrupt breakdown of the former Yugoslavia has been a puzzle for social scientists and some accounts like "ancient hatred theory" look in many ways like a manifestation of *retroactive pessimism*, as Tykocinski and her colleagues (Tykocinski, 2001; Tykocinski, Pick, & Kedmi, 2002) called a specific hindsight bias caused by a disappointing development of events. In order to cope with distressing state of disappointment people tend to re-evaluate their chances for a successful outcome. If they may comfort themselves by reassessing the unpleasant outcome as predetermined and basically inevitable, this coping strategy makes disappointment more bearable. So by presenting a story on the long-term hatred, and by saying "They really never had a chance", the proponents of "ancient hatred theory" offered no more than the hindsight. Moreover, they were not able to explain where this "hatred" disappeared for many decades of peaceful living.

[8] Although this statement may appear contradictory, it describes well the social reality of most multicultural communities in the former Yugoslavia. It is not claimed that people were not aware of each other's ethnic background; the point is that ethnicity (and even more so, religion) was not a particularly relevant social element for making friendships and a dense communal network (Ajdukovic & Corkalo Biruski, 2004). Religious holidays were not observed officially and publicly, as was the case in all socialist countries, and they were more a traditionally cherished opportunity for social gathering with family and friends than they were events built around religious and identity issues. The role of religion and church (Catholic, Orthodox, and Muslim) in state and public life in the former Yugoslavia is well described in Ramet (1996).

occurred becomes even more puzzling. So how could this have ever happened? The sense of suddenness is nicely elaborated in Brubaker's (1996) notion of "eventfulness," an effective description of a general and overwhelming ethnicization of everyday life that occurred after the collapse of the Communist regime in Eastern Europe. Indeed, when trying to explain what had happened in the community, our participants often expressed a feeling of suddenness, as if everything had happened over night (Corkalo Biruski et al., 2004). Indeed, when political elites started to shape their politics around ethnic issues, and "in the name of the nation," they also started to heat up the atmosphere in communities and opened a "Pandora's box" of evils that would destroy these very same communities, but not without their involvement. The old Communist ideology of "we-ness" ceased to exist; in fact, "we-ness" started to be shaped in a completely different way; it stopped being inclusive, and started to be built around differences.

A need for positive distinctiveness is well-recognized in the socio-psychological literature. SIT (Tajfel & Turner, 1986) is premised on the hypothesis that our social world is structured around categories, and by comparing the position of the group to which we belong with the positions of other groups, we also orient ourselves in our social environment. By defining who we are and who we are not, we define our social world and give meaning to it. SIT also suggests that a part of our self-esteem is derived from the groups we belong to: when social comparison favors our group, we feel good about ourselves, that is, our self-esteem rises. However, if we compare ourselves with others who are too similar to us, this comparison may threaten our group distinctiveness and consequently our social identity (Branscombe, Ellemers, Spears, & Doosje, 1999). This lack of differentiation could be unbearable and threat provoking, and may even instigate aggression and the dislike of others. The very same mechanism is manifested by the Freudian notion of the "narcissism of small differences," introduced in 1917 (Corkalo Biruski & Ajdukovic, 2009; cf. Ignatieff, 1998), as well as by Tajfel's notion of group distinctiveness. This was also noted by Jetten, Spears, and Manstead (1999). This phenomenon of *searching for difference* is well-illustrated by the processes of group differentiations that occurred on the eve of the war. The process of identity (re) building started on shared ground and fell apart in subsequent years.[9]

[9] Trying to explain the causes of war by citing the cultural differences between Croats, Serbs, and Muslims (and others) is just as much oversimplified reductionism as is trying to explain them by "ancient hatred". It is true that Yugoslav ethnic groups spoke different languages, and the officially endorsed variant of "Serbo-Croatian" was supposed to alleviate linguistic differences. Three major religions, Roman Catholicism, the Serbian Orthodox Church, and Islam, also influenced the culture in different areas and with different effects. For example, according to the results of a 1985 survey, 62.3% of youth from Catholic families declared they were religious, while the percentages were much lower for young people from Muslim (43.8%) and Orthodox (26.2%) families (as cited in Ramet, 1996). Political influences throughout history also shaped each former Yugoslav republic differently, with Slovenia and Croatia being more "westernized" under the ruling influence of the Habsburg Monarchy, Serbia being influenced by the Byzantine Empire, and Bosnian culture being heavily affected by the Ottoman Empire and Islam. Economic development also varied, with Slovenia and Croatia being relatively more developed and the southern regions being relatively poor (especially Kosovo and Macedonia). By listing all these differences that shaped the culture, one might think that the argument of a "cultural war" has been corroborated. Nevertheless, due to the fact that the ethnic mixture was so intense, with different ethnic groups being under the same influences and the same ethnic group being under different influences depending on the territory where they resided, one could easily find arguments that intraethnic differences were often more profound than the differences between ethnic groups (cf. Banac, 1996). In our research (Corkalo Biruski & Ajdukovic, 2009), we asked participants to name the major obstacles to the community's social reconstruction. Both Croats and Serbs perceived "cultural differences" as being only a small (Serbs) or moderate (Croats) obstacle. The small (although statistically significant) difference in perception between Croats and Serbs has grown even smaller in time, so that in 2008 we did not register any differences between how Croats and Serbs perceived their cultural differences as being the obstacle for more harmonious community life.

2.2 Fear, Silence, and Mistrust: The Road of Losing Community

In the discourse of our participants there is agreement that things started to change some time before the war.[10] Identity building was strongly based on the political agenda of nationalist elites, and the communities obediently followed their leaders, although not without surprise and amazement. For an analysis of the intergroup dynamics before the conflict, it is also important to emphasize that each side put the blame for identity changes on the others, without much consideration about the identity transformations that were going on within their own in-group. The most prominent changes happened in the use of language by Croats and Serbs, including the purification of language and the revival of words and expressions from the old literature,[11] the use of Cyrillic among Serbs, the use of symbols (flags, coats of arms, and religious symbols), the revival of old songs and old traditions, etc. As Lyons (cited in Roe, 2003) claims, by using the past and memories in a specific way, groups show their "continuity, collective self-esteem, distinctiveness, efficacy and cohesion" (p. 66). Parallel with this process of *symbolization of public space*, other processes also happened that additionally sharpened intergroup boundaries. Symbols that were connected with past conflicts were widely used (for example, military symbols from World War II, especially Ustasha and Chetnick insignia), expressing a threat to the other group (see Kaufman, 2001). As a result, people no longer felt safe in their own communities and began to see their own ethnic group as their only source of protection and security (Ajdukovic, 2004).

While remembering those days, our study participants often mentioned that the conflict was "imported," i.e., not instigated within the community. This kind of account could be heard on both sides. However, the community itself obviously did not have enough inner resources to resist the pressure of outside influences, and to adjust to community changes. General insecurity in the community, together with an inability to explain what was happening both in the community and in the wider social environment, the ethnicization of everyday life, and national homogenization produced two dominant reactions: *fear and silence* (Corkalo Biruski & Ajdukovic, 2009). Fear simply outgrew the level of individual emotion, and in situations in which people sense a constant threat and lack of safety, fear becomes a collectively prevalent emotion. In such situations some authors talk about the "collective orientation of fear" (Bar-Tal, 2001; Jarymowicz & Bar-Tal, 2006). As Ignatieff (1993) notes, fear has tremendous power in motivating human behavior. He claims that what he calls *systemic fear*, which "arises when a state begins to collapse" (p. 24), is worse than other forms of fear. Ignatieff sees the source of this fear in the collapse of "legitimate authority" and this is how he explains the ethnic tension that appeared in the aftermath of the collapse of the Communist regimes.[12] In my opinion, "systemic fear" is less than half of the story; the major source of fear here was a *loss of community* (cf. "loss of communality" used by Erikson, 1976). All of a sudden the old social network was not functional anymore; after years, and even decades, of harmonious living, people perceived they could not count on each other any more, and they had to think about who to turn to if needed. A series of illustrative examples of the breakdown of social networks in Vukovar was given in our study on interethnic friendships and the sense of betrayal among former friends (Ajdukovic & Corkalo Biruski, 2004). Our research clearly showed that the loss of trust was a key component of current

[10] There is a certain amount of disagreement in perceptions about when this period of community changes happened: for some participants it was about two years before the war, while others mentioned a period of only a few months before the war (Corkalo Biruski et al., 2004). However long it may have been, the strong sense of suddenly being "caught between ethnic sides" was a dominant view of the prewar atmosphere in Vukovar.

[11] For a more elaborated discussion on the complexities of the language issues on the territory of the former Yugoslavia see Greenberg (2004).

[12] In fact, Ignatieff stressed ethnic hatred much more than tension. We have disagreed with this interpretation elsewhere (Corkalo Biruski & Ajdukovic, 2009).

interethnic relations and that this loss was caused by a series of events that had been interpreted in utterly different ways, depending on the "ethnic angle" of observation. From the beginning till the end of the war, there was no single event that Croats and Serbs from Vukovar would interpret in the same way, a phenomenon we called "*an ethnization of memory*" (Corkalo Biruski et al., 2004, p. 157). Serbs in Vukovar would often mention the period about a year before the war, when the HDZ won a majority in the parliamentary elections and when many of them felt threatened by Croatian nationalists. Croats would never mention this period. Instead, they pointed out that the Serbs knew there would be war, and failed to warn their closest Croat friends to take safety measures and protect their families (Ajdukovic & Corkalo Biruski, 2004). A deep feeling of betrayal and loss of trust in people with whom the victims shared their lives before the war has been registered in other studies conducted in the Former Yugoslavia (Agger and Mimica, 1996). These and other data show, as Hewstone et al. (2008) pointed out that "Trust in any relationship is hard to gain and easy to lose … Across ethnic lines this may be even more so." (p. 76). The dramatic breakdown of social relations, especially in the critical moments that could have meant life or death for a betrayed person, caused many people to profoundly doubt their neighbors and former friends and ask, "How could we have trusted them?" (Ajdukovic & Corkalo Biruski, 2004, p. 287).

When they tried to deal with the fear and anxieties of the prewar period, people preferred not to share their emotions, opinions, and attitudes with their social surroundings. Too much was at stake: sometimes their family ties, more often their relationships with colleagues and friends with different ethnic backgrounds, and certainly their relationships with their in-groups. So, with the purpose of preserving an illusion of social stability and order in the community, people chose *silence* (Corkalo Biruski & Ajdukovic, 2009): people did not dare to talk with their neighbors and friends about what was happening in the community, and believed this was the way to preserve their relations with friends from the other ethnic group.[13] At the same time, they perceived that the people they felt close to had been changing. There was also a fear that talking with acquaintances and friends would make ethnic tensions even worse. In the words of one of our participants: "In 1990, 90% of Croats supported Croatian politics and 90% of Serbs supported Serbian politics." Political changes intensely changed the relations in the community as well: people watched different TV news programs and read different newspapers; they stuck to their ethnically exclusive accounts of disturbing events, and stopped seeing each other in any other way but as members of one or another group. Serious ethnic tension started in the Vukovar region in the spring of 1991, with a major incident in May in the nearby village of Borovo Selo, when 12 Croatian police officers were ambushed and killed by Serb paramilitaries. For many people in the city of Vukovar, particularly Croats, this incident was a significant point of no return. As one young participant stated: "What happened in Borovo Selo was really critical; it was an impetus for everything else. Before that, it looked as if nothing would happen, as if it would all blow over; but then it became obvious that something terrible would happen, we felt this in the air.

[13] In personally important relationships one can easily choose not to discuss issues of dispute in order to avoid a potential conflict and preserve the relationship, the phenomenon known as self-silencing (Jack & Dill, 1992). By choosing a kind of *collective self-silencing*, the people of Vukovar and many other multiethnic communities could indeed have believed they would succeed in protecting their interethnic communal ties. Even more, the strategy could serve as a way to protect people's sense of invulnerability and their belief in a just world (Janoff-Bulman, 1992): self-silencing was a form of a "prescribed" cautious behavior that was believed to protect good citizens and decent communities from terrible experiences that many communities were already experiencing. "It won't happen to us, because by not talking about emerging differences we protect our community" could have been the line of thinking of Vukovar citizens before the outbreak of the war. This line of thinking probably contributed to the belief we mentioned earlier that unrest was being imported from outside the community. However, these two elements could be a serious obstacle for social reconstruction: they imply a lack of taking the community's share of responsibility for the misfortunate development of events in the early 1990s.

Everybody felt this – a sort of tension, a kind of waiting."

From a psychological point of view, when people stopped talking about what was going on in the community, this was a critical moment when people let the space between them continue to grow. This silence prevented intimate exchanges, and former friends became *ethnic beings*. If they had talked, maybe they would have come up with ideas of how to make joint efforts to strengthen their mutual ties and preserve their social network, as a key element of support in hard times (Erikson, 1976). Instead of sharing those worries that were common to both ethnic groups, people chose the protection of their own group. The price of acting differently would have been too costly: everybody felt that there were two practically unreconcilable sides, and that the space between them had become wider and wider. Paradoxically, many people felt that if they did not talk about community unrest, then it would go away on its own accord. In-group social pressure together with insecurity, silence, and fear put the people in the community in a mode of passivity: they failed to act, and this inactivity allowed the community fabric to become even more fragile. The changes in solidarity – from loyalty to one's immediate social network that was not safe anymore to a more distant "imagined community" that seemed to promise security – made the social breakdown more likely (cf. Ajdukovic, 2004; Useem, 1998).

During the spring and summer of 1991, the conflict between the Croatian military, Serb paramilitaries, and the JNA became intensified. The non-Serb population in the neighboring villages was forced to leave their homes, and thousands of people were deported to the areas controlled by the Croatian authorities. In July 1991 Vukovar was under attack by heavy artillery and in August by aircraft. The siege of the city lasted for 3 months, and Serbian forces took over the city on 18 November 1991. The city underwent tremendous material destruction (62% of its houses were destroyed) as well as a massive loss of human life: 1,700 people were killed (almost 4% of the population), almost 4,000 were wounded (nearly 10% of the population), and 30,000 people were displaced (almost 24% of the whole population of displaced persons in Croatia in 1992) (Zunec, 1998a). The major war crime that happened in Vukovar after the siege was the execution of about 260 civilians, prisoners of war, and hospital patients at Ovcara, a location near Vukovar. A mass grave was discovered in 1993, and the remains were excavated in 1996. Under the supervision of the international community, especially the United Nations, the city of Vukovar and the neighboring region were peacefully reintegrated into the Republic of Croatia during the more than 2-year-long process of negotiation between the Croatian and Serbian sides. The whole process was completed at the end of 1997.

3 Rebuilding the Community

For individuals and communities who have experienced massive loss, personal injury and betrayal by their closest friends, and the violation of trust and social norms, it is a major challenge to restore their relations and communal life. Social psychology literature most often uses the term *reconciliation* for processes that happen after severe conflicts (Bar-Tal, 2000; Nadler, 2002; Nadler, Malloy, & Fisher, 2008; Nadler & Shnabel, 2008; Staub, 2005, 2006). Although this term is used widely, most scholars emphasize its gradualism, underlining the difficulties of dealing with an upsetting past, and warn that a history of violation of trust prevent people from rebuilding strong bonds with their former adversaries. The difficulty in reestablishing relations even with formerly close friends was well established in our Vukovar studies (Ajdukovic & Corkalo Biruski, 2004). Our qualitative data are corroborated with quantitative findings: in 2000, 71% of the Croats and 52% of the Serbs who were interviewed answered that their relations with former friends were damaged (Corkalo Biruski & Ajdukovic, 2009). In 2002 broken relations were still present for 64% of the Croats and 44% of the Serbs, and in 2008 the situation had not changed much: 63% of the Croats interviewed reported that their relations with former friends were still broken, as did 44% of the Serbs. The same slow pace of recovery also applies for other, less intimate interethnic relation: changes in social distance, attitudes towards other former Yugoslav republics, and general attitudes towards reconciliation (Ajdukovic, Corkalo Biruski, Jelic, & Penic, 2008).

Given that reconciliation is so hard to accomplish and so fragile and easily ruptured, why is reconciliation so deeply appreciated and why this is the ultimate goal to be achieved after a conflict? The significance of the process is well illustrated by the words of Bar-Tal (2000): "the coming years will witness a major effort to study and practice reconciliation" (p. 362). We would agree that postconflict processes of restoring social order deserve much more attention from the community of researchers and practitioners. However, we would take with reservation the idea that efforts to maintain peace and to repair social ties within and between communities implies reconciliation. All postconflict societies need to be healed, rebuilt, and helped to reestablish functional social relations that enable individuals and groups within those societies to fulfill their different needs (cf. Nadler & Shnabel, 2008). However, the task of reconciling an entire society is too demanding, if indeed it is possible at all. Nonetheless, it is possible to work on a more integrated society that incorporates a variety of identities and groups, where the identities of former adversaries are transformed and these members of the community are accepted as social partners (Kelman, 2008; Long & Brecke, 2003; Staub, 2006). Reconciliation is an outcome that requires individual decisions about its usefulness and emotional determination that wrong-doings can be put behind and, more importantly, forgiven. However, even before individual forgiveness occurs, new relations could be (re)built based on trust, expectations about positive relations, and interdependence. Precisely these elements – trust, positive expectations, and mutual interdependence – are preconditions for a functional society where it is possible to satisfy a diversity of needs and interests. In this sequence, reconciliation comes at the end of the process and is a desirable but not crucial condition for achieving a functional society.

3.1 Reconciliation or Social Reconstruction?

Instead of using the term *reconciliation* for those processes that take place in postconflict communities, we prefer to use the term *social reconstruction*, defined as "… a process within the community which brings its damaged social functioning to a normal level of interpersonal and group relations, and renews the social fabric of the affected community" (Ajdukovic, 2004, p. 128). Moreover, social reconstruction processes are not related only to those happening within the community; the processes *around* the community are also vital for its social repair (Corkalo Biruski & Ajdukovic, 2009).

There are several inner contradictions in the meaning of the word *reconciliation,* as well as in the process of reconciliation itself that suggest using this term in an intergroup context cautiously and wisely:

1. When thinking about reconciliation, most of us would imagine peace and social harmony, friendships that have been restored, and some form of amity that has been achieved. Indeed, all of these characteristics are very close to what linguistic analysis would say about the word reconciliation. This is equally applicable to the Croatian and the English languages. The first entry in the *Merriam-Webster dictionary* of the modern English language says that to *reconcile* (reconcile, n. d.) means to restore to friendship or harmony. Similarly, the first entry in the Croatian dictionary (Anic, 1998) states that to reconcile means to stop a fight or enmity, to make peace, and to make something consistent with something else. However, when we use the word *reconciliation*, we rarely think about an additional meaning that is written usually as the third or fourth definition in a dictionary – the word *reconciliation* also means to accept something unpleasant, to consent with something *reluctantly and unwillingly*. This is not only an exercise in semantics – this inner paradox of meaning illustrates the course of the process itself: the process of social repair starts with unwillingness, discomfort, and unpleasantness felt by all parties

involved, and there is a very long journey to something that comes to mind so easily when the word *reconciliation* is mentioned – peace, friendship, and social harmony.

2. The other inner contradiction of the concept of reconciliation is in what the social psychologist Henry Tajfel called the *interpersonal–intergroup continuum* (Tajfel, 1981). Human beings act in their social environment as individuals and as members of the groups they belong to. An interpersonal encounter is mostly determined by the specific individual and the personal characteristics of the people involved. An interaction between friends is a fairly good example of such social behavior. Contrary to this, an intergroup encounter is directed mostly by the group characteristics or the group membership of the people involved (Tajfel, 1981). For example, when interaction between people is determined by their belonging to different ethnic groups, this interaction could be placed on the intergroup extreme of the continuum.

   Why is this continuum so applicable to the process of reconciliation, and why do we consider it as presenting an inner contradiction? The intergroup extreme of Tajfel's continuum is inherently included in every intergroup conflict. However, an act of reconciliation is at its core an *intrapersonal experience*, a personal struggle of making a decision to put behind the wrong-doing that has been done and move on with no intent to get even or retaliate (cf. McCullough, Pargament, & Thoresen, 2000 and Noll, 2005 on forgiveness; Staub, Pearlman, & Gubin, 2005; Tam et al., 2008). What we try to accomplish by an act of reconciliation is to repair our relationship with a single and concrete person who did something wrong to us. At this point our social behavior is interpersonal.

   We cannot possibly have meaningful, personal relationships that deserve to be repaired via reconciliation with a great many people. Trying to extend the meaning and power of reconciliation to the intergroup end of the continuum contradicts the purpose of the process itself – if we do not have a relationship, there is nothing to be repaired. If people have suffered personal injuries and wounds, they cannot reconcile with just anybody from the other group. Since the injury is personal, the reconciliation should also be personal. However, there is a possibility for symbolically connecting personal injury and the act of reconciliation with the members of a group who were responsible for past wrongdoings. Nevertheless, this symbolic connection has two sides: if a victim receives an apology from a representative of an adversary group, he/she may feel that this symbolic gesture is enough to pardon and maybe even forgive the deeds that were done in the name of the group. However, there is another side of this coin: the symbolic connection of any member of the group with wrongdoings committed by only some members opens a potentially dangerous road to blaming everybody, i.e., to ascribing collective guilt.

3. The next contradiction of reconciliation is concerned with who is "entitled" to reconcile. When a single victim steps out from his/her victimhood and accepts the presence or company of a member of the adversary group, by this interpersonal exchange the victim starts an important social process with strong intergroup implications: the victim gives the approval to start to communicate with others, to rebuild relations with the other side. In traumatized communities it is possible, and in reality it often happens in this way, for this process of social repair to be started by persons who were not personally victimized. This fact of not being personally victimized is their personal advantage, since they can have enough inner emotional and cognitive resources to start to rebuild community relations. However, the fact that they were not victims personally makes them less influential within their own in-group, and their reconciliatory acts could be perceived as disloyalty to the group, even as a betrayal; hence they are less likely to be accepted by the wider community (see Staub, 2005 for a similar argument on forgiveness). This is one of the many reasons why it is of crucial importance for

community recovery to provide the care needed to the traumatized individuals and show community support. They have their own personal burden that needs to be worked through in order to enable them to heal as individuals and to continue to live their lives as productively as possible. When the suffering, pain, and losses of many individuals in the community are not properly addressed and worked through, the process of community healing and social repair can be blocked by weighing and measuring over and over again who suffered and who did not, and hence, who is entitled to direct the process of social repair. This fact came out very notably in our focus group research in Vukovar (Corkalo Biruski et al., 2004). When asked about the possibility for community reconciliation, the groups from the both sides emphasized the importance of improving the economy for the process of reconciliation. The participants believed that improving the economy would create an atmosphere in which the people would have jobs, thus becoming preoccupied with other issues rather than ethnic division, spending more time working than discussing the past. Even then people were tired of ruminating about the past; this was true of all participants, except for the group of Croat victims. They doubted the possibility of reconciliation after they had suffered so much. If there was such a possibility at all, then the main condition for starting the reconciliation process was telling the truth about the victims' missing family members and punishing the perpetrators (see Gibson, 2004 on relationship between truth and reconciliation). We have not followed up on the same group of people today, but the social and societal processes in the meantime have had some influence, and the victim groups are now more open for dialogue. It would not be entirely accurate to say that they still direct the pace and rhythm of the community's social recovery processes; however, they still do have the power to push them back a step or two. What we can learn from this example is that, from the victims' point of view, there are preconditions to be fulfilled in order for them to be able even to start thinking about having any kind of relations with the former belligerents. This is why the truth telling is understood as being the key element of social recovery (cf. Cairns, Tam, Hewstone, & Niens, 2005; Gobodo-Madikizela, 2008; Kelman, 2008; Staub, 2005).

However, no matter how painful the process of social recovery is, it should take place. To start building relations within communities affected by intracommunal violence is simply adaptive; otherwise, neither side in the community can function. The point is that this highly adaptive process has its own pace, and it is not a very fast one – it cannot be rushed, and it is directed, as Ajdukovic (2003) points out, by the majority of community members who determine what level of social functioning is acceptable at a certain point. The process of social repair is not linear either: the social networks could be well established in some aspects of social functioning, while being significantly weaker or even completely absent in other aspects. The most pertinent illustration of the fragmentation of the social world is the division of acceptable social relations in the private and the public sphere. For example, during an interview with a young Croat woman from Vukovar, she said, "I work with a Serb whom I respect very much, and this is the only Serb who has come into my home. The rules are clear: we work together, but Croats visit Croats in their homes, and Serbs visit Serbs …" (Corkalo Biruski et al., 2004, p. 152).

When the relationship is severely challenged or damaged, as many relationships are in times of collective violence, it may take more time and effort and a greater number of reconciliatory acts in order to achieve the ultimate goal – a harmonious relationship. The nature, intensity, and dynamic of the conflict in this community mirror accurately what happened on a larger scale in the wars fought in the former Yugoslavia. This conflict was massive and overwhelming, intentional and strategically planned, aimed to destroy people, material goods, and the communal social fabric in order to create a definite, irreversible, and enduring defeat. The intensity and magnitude of the conflict are key factors that determine the extent of the injury inflicted on the relationship, and by the same token, the key factors influencing the pace, time, and effort needed for repairing the relationship, and for the process of reconciliation. The relation between these two is simple: the more intensive the conflict, the more time and effort will be needed in order to reestablish trust (Lewicki & Wiethoff, 2000; Long & Brecke, 2003). The reasons for this are obvious: in a more intensive conflict there is a greater variety of ways to hurt the other. When the conflict is as intense as it was in Vukovar (and this city was not unique in the former Yugoslavia), the intensity and means of hurting people covers a wide range: the damage was done physically by destroying human lives and their entire environment; psychologically by inflicting fear, intimidation, and terror; and symbolically by destroying identity signs, flags, insignia, cemeteries, monuments, and places of worship. Furthermore, although fought in the present, the conflict was not situated only in the present time – by choosing objects of identity for destruction, the conflict was intended to eliminate the symbols of memory and history and in doing so prevented the possibility of foreseeing and planning for the future. This totality of destruction has made this conflict multidimensional in many ways, traumatic on the individual, communal, and societal levels, and difficult to resolve and reconcile (Corkalo Biruski & Ajdukovic, 2009).

The destruction of trust among community members caused a complete rupture of social relations, and a divided society has started to develop – i.e., a community (society) where there is a *one major line of division* (this boundary could be defined by ethnicity, culture, class, etc.) that penetrates into all aspects of social life and profoundly shapes the inner dynamic of the community. Here it is important to note that, though a wall of silence between members of different ethnic groups is a serious obstacle to social repair, at the beginning of the process it had a protective social function – it was a way to prevent further conflicts. At this point there is a challenge to estimate when it will be safe enough, psychologically and socially, for both parties to start to cross ethnic lines, to communicate and rebuild social relations, mutual trust, and an intercommunal network. When contacts in the community are first established, they are very fragile, dependent on social pressure, and accepted with uneasiness and anxiety. Unlike in the past, today's intergroup contacts in Vukovar are very few and superficial, with sharply divergent perception between groups about the frequency, closeness, and nature of these contacts: While Croats see their relations with Serbs as less friendly and less frequent, Serbs perceive their relations with Croats as more friendly and as happening more often (Corkalo Biruski & Ajdukovic, 2007, 2009).

The policy of division continues in the organization of the schooling system by ethnicity, so the children actually attend schools separately. The curricula are the same, but they are taught in different languages.[14] In our numerous field contacts, parents have expressed their worries because of the separate schooling of the children. They are concerned, among other things, about the quality of the children's intergroup relations in the future. These concerns about the quality of their children's social life are expressed by both Serbian and Croatian parents. Moreover, the division of the children in school is perceived as one of the major obstacles to the process of social

[14] It is important to emphasize that the separated school system is a consequence of the recent war; before the war, all the children attended the same classes and were taught in the same language. However, in 1997, minority education for Serbs became regulated by an agreement signed by the Croatian government and Serbian representatives, and supervised by the international community. Its purpose was to ensure the protection of Serbian minority rights, including education. Division in schools is present even today, and it takes a creative step forward to organize the schools in such a way that both minority rights and the possibility of children's integration are satisfied (see Corkalo Biruski & Ajdukovic, 2007). The language of teaching is the major stumbling block. Although the Croatian and Serbian languages are very similar, there are differences in vocabulary and the alphabets – Cyrillic in Serbian and Latin in Croatian. Nevertheless, in everyday encounters people can communicate to each other with no major misunderstandings due to language differences. I refer again to Greenberg's (2004) book on language issues in the former Yugoslavia.

reconstruction, and this goes equally for Croats and Serbs. When our participants evaluated a set of community characteristics and assessed them on a scale of 1–5 if they were obstacles for improvement of interethnic relations, the separation of children in school was perceived as being one of the major obstacles, with no differences in degree between Croats and Serbs. Furthermore, the assessments were higher in 2008 ($M_{Croats}=3.98$; $SD=1.33$; $M_{Serbs}=4.39$; $SD=0.98$) than in 2002 ($M_{Croats}=3.57$; $SD=1.53$; $M_{Serbs}=4.19$; $SD=0.98$), indicating higher concerns of adults for future intergroup relations in the community. The point is that the children and adolescents of the post-war generation have no experience of an integrated city – the ethnic division of the urban space is complete (Corkalo Biruski et al., 2004) and does not leave children many chances, if any, for socializing after school hours. The parents' worry about future relations in the community seems realistic, as shown by the data in our study. We measured attitudes towards school integration and interethnic attitudes in children, their parents, and school teachers in both ethnic communities at two points in time, in 2001 and 2007. The results showed a tendency for these attitudes to improve with time, especially for the majority (Croat) sample; however, these changes were very small (Ajdukovic & Corkalo Biruski, 2008; Corkalo Biruski & Ajdukovic, 2008a, 2008b). These results corroborate a very slow pace of social recovery in a war-torn community (Corkalo Biruski & Ajdukovic, in press). It seems that children are especially affected by the communal social divisions: although their interethnic attitudes and behavioral tendencies have improved, they are still more negative than the attitudes of the adults. We believe that these results reflect the social reality of children who, unlike their parents, have not experienced an integrated community: they have adopted the standards of community division along ethnic principles since the earliest age. Moreover, since they go to separate schools, and are not encouraged to socialize in their free time, they may carry out the same ethnicized standards into the future.

4 Lessons Learned

Is there any possibility for reconciliation between formerly belligerent sides? What is the major lesson we have learned from the Former Yugoslavia and the city of Vukovar, which we have analyzed as a paradigmatic example of the "Balkan tragedy"? What we certainly know is that it takes time for such a deep trauma to heal. The amount of injury is even worse because it was caused so often by closest neighbors, friends, or even relatives. A tragic similarity of all massive conflicts with a strong intercommunal component is that they redefine the memories of the past: they throw into doubt that our past relations with people were sincere and authentic; they challenge our friendships and sometimes even family ties (Corkalo Biruski & Ajdukovic, 2009). Our research in Vukovar illustrates paradigmatically how a community affected by massive violence responded to what happened during the war.

What happened in many parts of the former Yugoslavia was similar to what Staub (2006) called "intimate genocide." This additionally complicates the process of healing. Time is widely believed to help the process. Indeed, time is needed for reviewing the past, integrating it into the present and turn to a better future. It could not happen quickly and not as an immediate response to the conflict and the wounds (Deutsch, 2008). However, our Vukovar participants expressed doubt that time could result in the normalization of interethnic relations in their community. In 2000 almost 16% of Croats and 41% of Serbs believed time would do the work; in 2008 this was believed by the same percent of Croats, but by only 26% of Serbs (cf. Corkalo Biruski, & Ajdukovic, 2009). As professionals, we know that time can be both an ally and an enemy. If we let it happen, time can turn against our ultimate goal and trauma – it is not being worked on, recognized, and healed – can strike back like a boomerang as soon as social circumstances allow it to rise to the surface and to be fed by any ideological "-ism." The recent wars in the former Yugoslavia were a tragic testimony to this claim. However, with the help of appropriate interventions directed at individuals, groups, and communities, enabling the processes that happen over time, social reconstruction is possible. To make time an ally in a highly traumatized community means to have patience, dedication, and above all, an awareness that the processes of social recovery are gradual and long.

Psychologists also believe that the healing of trauma is the key precondition for the recovery of individuals and groups. This may be true; however, when it comes to social healing, our empirical data are scarce and not very convincing. For example, Sekulic et al. (2001) showed in a Croatian sample no increase in intolerance related to personal war experiences (except for personal material losses). Our earlier data (Biro et al., 2004) also showed that personal injury alone was not significant for predicting readiness for reconciliation. However, when combined with the negative experiences with a conflicting ethnic group, war-related trauma also becomes significant. Moreover, we also showed that traumatic experiences included personal losses and threats to one's own life or to the life of significant others (for example, a violent death of a close person, being a witness of violence or deaths, being wounded, etc.) were negative predictors of reconciliation, whereas widely experienced stressful events (like the loss of one's house and personal belongings, family separation, unemployment, etc.) were not predictive (Corkalo Biruski & Ajdukovic, 2009). Other research (Corkalo Biruski & Penic, submitted) has demonstrated that there was a significant relationship between war experiences and measures of nationalism and social distance towards the former enemy in both the Croatian and Serbian adult samples; nevertheless, this relationship was not only direct, but also mediated by "collective" variables of identification with one's own ethnic group and collective guilt assignment. Strabac and Ringdal (2008) also found only a weak effect of individual war experiences on prejudice, while, as the authors stated, the usual "social and psychological factors" (p. 790) like (male) gender, a lower level of urbanization, lower education, higher religiosity, belonging to a majority group, higher media exposure, etc. had much stronger effects. On the other hand, there is some supporting evidence about the relationship between trauma and measures of reconciliation. In their study in Rwanda, Staub et al. (2005) found a weak but significant negative correlation between trauma symptoms and orientation towards others (including a measure of readiness for reconciliation). In Northern Ireland Hewstone et al. (2004) also found a weak but significant negative correlation between personal victimization and forgiveness. It is obvious that the relationship of individual trauma and attitudes and behaviors towards the formerly belligerent group is far more complex than we have assumed to date (Corkalo Biruski & Penic, submitted; Strabac & Ringdal, 2008), so further research refinements are needed in order to disentangle this relationship. This does not mean that individual traumatic experiences are not important. It means only that their influences are probably not direct, but they play a role in a complex pattern of influences with other conflict- and postconflict-related variables.

We believe that complex processes in postconflict societies that bring opposite sides together must follow simultaneously a bottom-up and a top-down approach (cf. Corkalo Biruski, 2002; Corkalo Biruski, & Ajdukovic, 2009; Lederach, 1997; Staub, 2006). This means that reconstructive actions and efforts between individuals and families must be accompanied by actions and efforts at higher levels of influence, i.e., formal and informal community leaders, group representatives, community activists, and politicians. If the levels of influence are not connected and interwoven, attempts at a certain level will remain at that level, and cannot bring about real social change. Our model (Fig. 13.2) assumes the necessity of trauma healing at the individual level as a baseline for working in the community. Our experiences show that highly victimized groups could make the social reconstruction processes slow if the community waits for them to say whether it is ok or not to communicate with the other side. Indeed, group victimization (among Croats) is perceived as a major obstacle for establishing better relation between Croats and Serbs, even many years after the conflict ended (Corkalo Biruski & Ajdukovic, 2009).

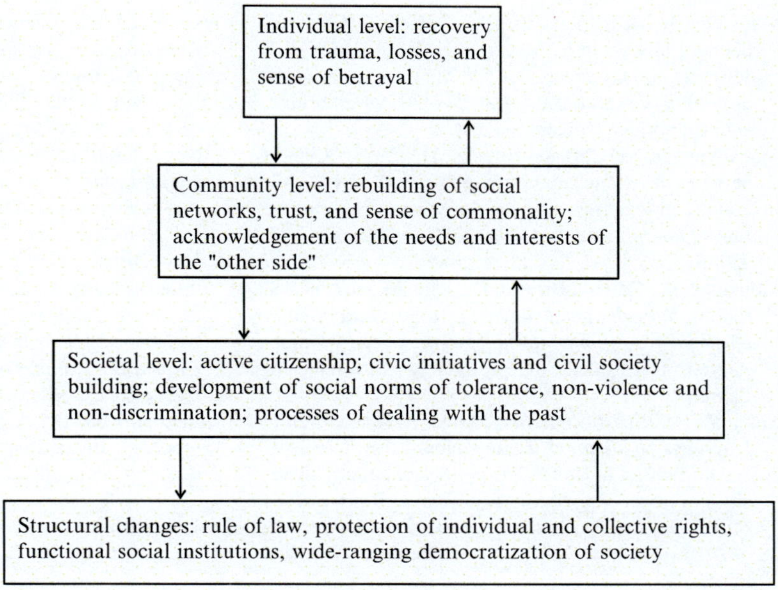

Fig. 13.2 Interconnectedness of four levels of social reconstruction after conflict (adapted from Corkalo Biruski & Ajdukovic, 2009)

The second level of recovery is the community level, where the renewal of basic assumptions for the development of social capital (Putnam, 2001) should happen: the establishment of intercommunity trust, social networking, and community/communality building. In an attempt to empower community groups to take a lead in community recovery, we developed a model for working with informal community leaders, people who had influence and a willingness to work for greater good of their community. In the form of two three day workshops we help them to understand the dynamic influence of loss and trauma on the community, we work with them on their skills for a constructive conflict resolution, and we help them to plan an appropriate social action aimed at instigating community change that was of interest to all the parties involved. This pilot project was designed to help rebuild connections between antagonized ethnic groups (Ajdukovic, Ajdukovic, & Corkalo Biruski, 2002).

Strengthening the community is a precondition for advancing to the next level – the level of society. The changes on this level imply further improvement in community building: the activation of civic initiatives, the development of the norms of tolerance, equality, and nonviolence. The changes on the top level – structural changes – give a normative framework for general social changes. Functional institutions, the rule of law, and the protection of individual and collective rights are fundamental principles for the development of a peaceful and stable society.

References

Agger, I., & Mimica, J. (1996). *Psychosocial assistance to victims of war in Bosnia-Herzegovina: An evaluation*. Brussels: European commission humanitarian aid office (ECHO).

Ajdukovic, D. (1993). Psihosocijalne okolnosti progonstva i izbjeglištva [Psychosocial circumstances of displacement and refuge]. In D. Ajdukovic (Ed.), *Psihološke dimenzije progonstva* (pp. 11–42). Zagreb: Alinea.

Ajdukovic, D. (2003). Socijalna rekonstrukcija zajednice [Community social reconstruction]. In D. Ajdukovic (Ed.), *Socijalna rekonstrukcija zajednice: psihološki procesi, rješavanje sukoba i socijalna akcija* (pp. 11–39). Zagreb: Društvo za psihološku pomoć.

Ajdukovic, D. (2004). Social contexts of traumatization and healing. *Medicine, Conflict and Survival, 20*, 120–135.

Ajdukovic, D., Ajdukovic, M., & Corkalo Biruski, D. (2002). *Community social reconstruction, conflict management and community mental health: Pilot project*. Zagreb, Croatia: Society for Psychological Assistance. Unpublished manuscript.

Ajdukovic, D., & Corkalo Biruski, D. (2004). Trust and betrayal in war. In E. Stover & H. Weinstein (Eds.), *My neighbor, my enemy: Justice and community in the aftermath of mass atrocity* (pp. 287–302). Cambridge, UK: Cambridge University Press.

Ajdukovic, D., & Corkalo Biruski, D. (2008). Caught between the ethnic sides: Inter-ethnic relations of children and parents in the post-war community. *International Journal of Behavioral Development, 32*, 337–347.

Ajdukovic, D., Corkalo Biruski, D., Jelic, M., & Penic, S. (2008). *Individual and community adjustment at times of social transition. Internal project documentation.* Zagreb: Department of Psychology, University of Zagreb.

Anic, V. (1998). *Rječnik hrvatskoga jezika [Croatian Language Dictionary]*. Zagreb: Novi Liber.

Banac, I. (1996). Foreword: The politics of cultural diversity in Former Yugoslavia. In S. Ramet (Ed.), *Balkan Babel. The disintegration of Yugoslavia from the death of Tito to ethnic war* (pp. xiii–xvii). Boulder: Westview Press.

Banac, I. (2001). *Raspad Jugoslavije: Eseji o nacionalizmu i nacionalnim sukobima. [Dissolution of Yugoslavia: Essays on nationalism and national conflicts]*. Zagreb: Durieux.

Bar-Tal, D. (2000). From intractable conflict through conflict resolution to reconciliation: Psychological analysis. *Political Psychology, 21*, 351–365.

Bar-Tal, D. (2001). Why does fear override hope in societies engulfed by intractable conflict, as it does in the Israeli society? *Political Psychology, 22*, 601–627.

Biro, M., Ajdukovic, D., Corkalo Biruski, D., Djipa, D., Milin, P., & Weinstein, H. (2004). Attitudes towards justice and social reconstruction in Bosnia and Herzegovina and Croatia. In E. Stover & H. Weinstein (Eds.), *My neighbor, my enemy: Justice and community in the aftermath of mass atrocity* (pp. 183–205). Cambridge, UK: Cambridge University Press.

Branscombe, N. R., Ellemers, N., Spears, R., & Doosje, B. (1999). The context and content of Social Identity Theory. In N. Ellemers, R. Spears, & B. Doosje (Eds.), *Social identity: Context, commitment, content* (pp. 35–58). Malden, MA: Blackwell.

Brubaker, R. (1996). *Nationalism reframed: Nationhood and the national question in the New Europe*. Cambridge, MA: Cambridge University Press.

Cairns, E., Tam, T., Hewstone, M., & Niens, U. (2005). Intergroup forgiveness and intergroup conflict: Northern Ireland, A case study. In E. L. Worthington Jr. (Ed.), *Handbook of forgiveness* (pp. 461–475). New York, NY: Routledge.

Census of the Republic of Croatia. (2001). Retrived from http://www.dzs.hr/Hrv/censuses/Census2001/Popis/H01_02_02/H01_02_02.html

Cigar, N., Magas, B., & Zanic, I. (1999). Foreword. In B. Magas & I. Zanic (Eds.), *Rat u Hrvatskoj i Bosni i Hercegovini 1991–1995 [War in Croatia and Bosnia & Herzegovina 1991–1995]* (pp. 7–17). Zagreb-Sarajevo: Jesenski i Turk.

Cohen, R. (1999). Ethnic cleansing. In R. Gutman & D. Rief (Eds.), *Crimes of war. What the public should know* (pp. 136–138). New York – London: W. Norton & Co.

Corkalo Biruski, D. (2002). Peace education in new democracies: A case of Croatia. In G. Salomon & B. Nevo (Eds.), *Peace education around the world: The concept, underlying principles, the practice and the research* (pp. 177–186). New Jersey, NJ: Lawrence Erlbaum Associates.

Corkalo Biruski, D., & Penic, S. (submitted). Facing trauma, facing the enemy: war trauma, in-group identification, collective guilt and outgroup attitudes in Croatian and Serbian samples. In D. Spini, D. Corkalo Biruski & G. Elcheroth (Eds.), War and community. Collective experiences in the former Yugoslavia.

Corkalo Biruski, D., & Ajdukovic, D. (2007). Separate schools – divided community: The role of school in post-war social reconstruction. *Review of Psychology, 14*, 93–108.

Corkalo Biruski, D., & Ajdukovic, D. (2008a). Stavovi učenika, roditelja i nastavnika prema školovanju: Što se promijenilo tijekom šest godina u Vukovaru? [Attitudes towards schooling among pupils, parents and teachers: What has changed over the six years in Vukovar?]. *Migracijske i etničke teme, 24*, 189–216.

Corkalo Biruski, D., & Ajdukovic, D. (2008b). Promjene međuetničke diskriminacije u djece i međuetnički stavovi i ponašanja njihovih roditelja. [Changes of children's discriminatory tendencies and parental intergroup attitudes and behaviors]. *Ljetopis socijalnog rada, 15*, 377–400.

Corkalo Biruski, D., & Ajdukovic, D. (2009). Od dekonstrukcije do rekonstrukcije traumatizirane zajednice: primjer Vukovara. [From deconstruction to reconstruction of a traumatized community: The example of Vukovar]. *Revija za socijalnu politiku, 16*, 1–24.

Corkalo Biruski, D., & Ajdukovic, D. (in press). Parallel worlds of divided community: Passing time does not make much difference. In O. Simic, Z. Volcic, & C. Philpot (Eds.), *Peace psychology in the Balkans: Mapping the pathways to peace* (Peace psychology book series). New York: Springer.

Corkalo Biruski, D., Ajdukovic, D., Weinstein, H., Stover, E., Djipa, D., & Biro, M. (2004). Neighbors again? Inter-community relations after ethnic violence. In E. Stover & H. Weinstein (Eds.), *My neighbor, my enemy: Justice and community in the aftermath of mass atrocity* (pp. 143–161). Cambridge, UK: Cambridge University Press.

Croatian national census (1991). Ethnic composition of population of Republic of Croatia according to location. Document 881, Zagreb: Croatian Bureau of Statistics.

Deutsch, M. (2008). Reconciliation after destructive intergroup conflict. In A. Nadler, T. E. Malloy, & J. Fisher (Eds.), *The social psychology of intergroup reconciliation* (pp. 471–485). New York, NY: Oxford University Press.

Erikson, K. T. (1976). Disaster at Buffalo Creek. Loss of communality at Buffalo Creek. *American Journal of Psychiatry, 133*, 302–305.

Gagnon, V. P., Jr. (2004). *The myth of ethnic war. Serbia and Croatia in the 1990s*. Ithaca and London: Cornell University Press.

Gibson, J. L. (2004). Does truth lead to reconciliation? Testing the causal assumptions of the South African Truth and Reconciliation Process. *American Journal of Political Science, 48*, 201–217.

Gobodo-Madikizela, P. (2008). Transforming trauma in the aftermath of gross human rights abuses: Making public spaces intimate through the South African Truth and Reconciliation Commission. In A. Nadler, T. E. Malloy, & J. D. Fisher (Eds.), *The social psychology of intergroup reconciliation* (pp. 57–75). Oxford: Oxford University Press.

Greenberg, R. D. (2004). *Language and identity in the Balkans*. New York, NY: Oxford University Press.

Hewstone, M., Cairnes, E., Voci, A., McLernon, F., Niens, U., & Noor, M. (2004). Intergroup forgiveness and guilt in Northern Ireland: Social psychological dimensions of "The troubles". In N. R. Branscombe & B. Doosje (Eds.), *Collective guilt: International perspectives* (pp. 193–215). New York, NY: Cambridge University Press.

Hewstone, M., Tausch, N., Voci, A., Kenworthy, J., Hughes, J., & Cairns, E. (2008). Why neighbors kill. Prior intergroup contact and killing of ethnic outgroup neighbors. In V. M. Esses & R. A. Vernon (Eds.), *Explaining the breakdown of ethnic relations: Why neighbors kill* (pp. 61–91). Malden, MA: Blackwell Publishing.

Hodson, R., Sekulic, D., & Massey, G. (1994). National tolerance in the Former Yugoslavia. *American Journal of Sociology, 99*, 1534–1558.

Ignatieff, M. (1993). *Blood and belonging. Journeys into the new nationalism*. New York, NY: Farrar, Straus and Giroux.

Ignatieff, M. (1998). *The warrior's honor. Ethnic war and the modern conscience*. New York, NY: Henry Holt and Company.

Jack, D. C., & Dill, D. (1992). The silencing the self scale: Schemas of intimacy associated with depression in women. *Psychology of Women Quarterly, 16*, 97–106.

Janoff-Bulman, R. (1992). *Shattered assumptions: Towards a new psychology of trauma*. New York: The free press.

Jarymowicz, M., & Bar-Tal, D. (2006). The dominance of fear over hope in the life of individuals and collectives. *European Journal of Social Psychology, 36*, 367–392.

Jetten, J., Spears, R., & Manstead, R. (1999). Group distinctiveness and intergroup discrimination. In N. Ellemers, R. Spears, & B. Doosje (Eds.), *Social identity: Context, commitment, content* (pp. 107–126). Malden, MA: Blackwell.

Kaplan, R. (1993). *Balkan ghosts: A journey through history*. London, UK: Papermac.

Kaufman, S. J. (2001). *Modern hatreds. The symbolic politics of ethnic war*. Ithaca, NY: Cornell University Press.

Kelman, H. C. (2008). Reconciliation from a socio-psychological perspective. In A. Nadler, T. E. Malloy, & J. D. Fisher (Eds.), *The social psychology of intergroup reconciliation* (pp. 3–32). Oxford: Oxford University Press.

Lederach, J. (1997). *Building peace. Sustainable reconciliation in divided societies*. Washington, DC: United States Institute of Peace Press.

Lewicki, R. J., & Wiethoff, C. (2000). Trust, trust development and trust repair. In M. Deutsch & P. T. Coleman (Eds.), *The handbook of conflict resolution: Theory and practice* (pp. 86–107). San Francisco, CA: Jossey-Bass Publishers.

Long, W. J., & Brecke, P. (2003). *War and reconciliation: Reason and emotion in conflict resolution*. Cambridge, MA: MIT Press.

Magas, B., & Zanic, I. (1999). *Rat u Hrvatskoj i Bosni i Hercegovini 1991–1995 [War in Croatia and Bosnia & Herzegovina 1991–1995]*. Zagreb-Sarajevo: Jesenski i Turk.

McCullough, M. E., Pargament, K. I., & Thoresen, C. E. (Eds.). (2000). *Forgiveness: Theory, research and practice*. New York, NY: The Guilford Press.

Nadler, A. (2002). Post-resolution processes: Instrumental and socio-emotional routes to reconciliation. In G. Salomon & B. Nevo (Eds.), *Peace education: The concept, principles, and practices around the world* (pp. 127–141). New Jersey, NJ: Lawrence Erlbaum Associates.

Nadler, A., Malloy, T. E., & Fisher, J. D. (Eds.). (2008). *The social psychology of intergroup reconciliation*. New York, NY: Oxford University Press.

Nadler, A., & Shnabel, N. (2008). Instrumental and socioemotional path to intergroup reconciliation and the needs-based model of socioemotional reconciliation. In A. Nadler, T. E. Malloy, & J. D. Fisher (Eds.), *The social psychology of intergroup reconciliation* (pp. 37–56). New York, NY: Oxford University Press.

Noll, J. G. (2005). Forgiveness in people experiencing trauma. In E. L. Worthington Jr. (Ed.), *Handbook of forgiveness* (pp. 363–375). New York, NY: Routledge.

Perkovic, M., & Puljiz, V. (2001). Ratne štete, izdaci za branitelje, žrtve i stradalnike rata u Republici Hrvatskoj. [War damages and the expenditure for the veterans and victims of the war in the Republic of Croatia]. *Revija za socijalnu politiku, 8*, 235–238.

Petersen, R. D. (2002). *Understanding ethnic violence. Fear, hatered, and resentment in twentieth-century Eastern Europe*. New York, NY: Cambridge University Press.

Petrovic, R. (1985). *Etnički meštoviti brakovi u Jugoslaviji. [Ethnically mixed marriages in Yugoslavia]*. Beograd: Institut za sociološka istraživanja Filozofskog fakulteta.

Putnam, R. (2001). *Bowling alone: The collapse and revival of American community*. New York, NY: Simon & Shuster.

Ramet, S. (1992). *Nationalism and federalism in Yugoslavia, 1962–1991*. Bloomington, IN: Indiana University Press.

Ramet, S. (1996). *Balkan Babel. The disintegration of Yugoslavia from the death of Tito to ethnic war*. Bouder, CO: Westview Press.

Ramet, S. (2009). *Tri Jugoslavije: Izgradnja države i izazov legitimacije 1918–2005. [The three Yugoslavias: State-building and legitimation, 1918–2005]*. Zagreb: Golden marketing.

Reconcile. (n. d.). *In Merriam-Webster Dictionary*. Retrieved from http://www.merriam-webster.com/dictionary/reconcile.

Roe, M. D. (2003). Cowlitz Indian ethnic identity, social memories and 150 years of conflict with the United States Government. In E. Cairns & M. D. Roe (Eds.), *The role of memory in ethnic conflict* (pp. 55–74). New York, NY: Palgrave Macmillan.

Schopflin, G. (1993). The rise and fall of Yugoslavia. In J. McGarry & B. O'Leary (Eds.), *The politics of ethnic conflict regulation* (pp. 172–203). London, UK and New York, NY: Routlage.

Sekulic, D., Hodson, R., & Massey, G. (2001). War and tolerance. *Revija za sociologiju, 32*, 157–174.

Sekulic, D., Massey, G., & Hodson, R. (1994). Who were the Yugoslavs? Failed source of a common identity in the former Yugoslavia. *American Sociological Review, 59*, 83–97.

Staub, E. (2005). Constructive rather than harmful forgiveness, reconciliation, and ways to promote them after genocide and mass killing. In E. L. Worthington Jr. (Ed.), *Handbook of forgiveness* (pp. 443–459). New York, NY: Routledge.

Staub, E. (2006). Reconciliation after genocide, mass killing or intractable conflict: Understanding the roots of violence, psychological recovery, and steps toward a general theory. *Political Psychology, 27*, 867–893.

Staub, E., Pearlman, L. A., & Gubin, A. (2005). Healing, reconciliation, forgiving and the prevention of violence after genocide or mass killing: An intervention and it's experimental evaluation in Rwanda. *Journal of Social and Clinical Psychology, 24*, 297–334.

Strabac, Z., & Ringdal, K. (2008). Individual and contextual influences of war on ethnic prejudice in Croatia. *The Sociological Quarterly, 49*, 769–796.

Tajfel, H. (1981). *Human groups and social categories. Studies in social psychology*. Cambridge, UK: Cambridge University Press.

Tajfel, H., & Turner, J. C. (1986). Theory of intergroup behavior. In S. Worchel & W. G. Austin (Eds.), *Psychology of intergroup relations* (pp. 7–24). Chicago, IL: Nelson-Hall Publishers.

Tam, T., Hewstone, M., Kenworthy, J. D., Cairns, E., Marinetti, C., Geddes, L., et al. (2008). Postconflict reconciliation: Intergroup forgiveness and implicit Biases in Northern Ireland. *Journal of Social Issues, 64*, 303–320.

Thompson, M. (1995). *Kovanje rata. Mediji u Srbiji, Hrvatskoj i Bosni i Hercegovini [Forging war. Media in Serbia, Croatia and Bosnia & Herzegovna]*. Zagreb: Hrvatski Helsinški.

Tykocinski, O. E. (2001). I never had a chance: Using hindsight tactics to mitigate disappointments. *Personality and Social Psychology Bulletin, 27*, 376–382.

Tykocinski, O. E., Pick, D., & Kedmi, D. (2002). Retroactive pessimism: A different kind of hindsight bias. *European Journal of Social Psychology, 32*, 577–588.

Useem, B. (1998). Breakdown theories of collective action. *Annual Review of Sociology, 24*, 215–238.

Zerjavic, V. (1992). *Opsesije i megalomanije oko Jasenovca i Bleiburga: gubici stanovništa Jugoslavije u drugom svjetskom ratu [Opsessions and megalomania around Jasenovac and Bleiburg: Losses of the population of Yugoslavia in WWII]*. Zagreb: Globus.

Zunec, O. (1998a). Rat u Hrvatskoj 1991–1995. 1. dio: Uzroci rata i operacije do Sarajevskog primirja The war in Croatia 1991–1995. Part one: The causes of the war and military operations till Sarajevo truce. *Polemos, 1*, 57–87.

Zunec, O. (1998b). *Rat i društvo. Ogledi iz sociologije vojske i rata (War and society. Essays on sociology of military and war)*. Zagreb: Jesenski i Turk – Hrvatsko sociološko društvo.

14 Ethno-political Conflict in Kosovo: Cultivating Trust in Serbian–Albanian Post-conflict Peace building

Ulrike Schwegler and L. Ripley Smith

Kosovo Chapter Summary

Schwegler and Smith explore the enduring conflict in Kosovo between the resident Albanians and Serbs. International interventions and peacekeeping attempts are examined along with reasons for unsatisfactory results. Kosovo's recent declaration for independence, which the authors posit may inhibit, if not prevent, further negotiations, provides impetus for renewed efforts. Examination of the historical and perpetual causes behind ethnic divisions informs the suggestions offered to reach stable reconciliation.

The joining of Kosovo and Serbia is recognized as exacerbating the complex array of contention between ethnic groups in the areas of land, language, religion, and politics. Description of the many years of struggle for control of Kosovo by different groups engenders insight into some specific obstacles to peaceful resolution in this region, including a pervasive sense of fear and victimization existent in both groups. The authors express the need to move beyond resolution and work to achieve reconciliation in order to obtain lasting peaceful relations.

Theories of social identity and categorization are applied and the authors suggest potential areas through which a development of trust may begin, which is viewed as a requisite for peace. Schwegler and Smith express optimism for the future through recognition of shared identities already present within individuals from these different ethnic groups. Types of trust are discussed and functional trust is identified as having potential in Kosovo, as it operates from the position of cooperation for mutual benefit. Specific policies are targeted for transformational change beginning at the local level

U. Schwegler (✉)
International Management, FOM University of Applied Science, Stuttgart, Germany
e-mail: ulrike.schwegler@ifavf.de; ulrike.schwegler@fom.de

L.R. Smith
Communication Studies,
Bethel University, Saint Paul, MN, USA
e-mail: r-smith@bethel.edu

D. Landis and R.D. Albert (eds.), *Handbook of Ethnic Conflict: International Perspectives*, International and Cultural Psychology, DOI 10.1007/978-1-4614-0448-4_14,

through focus on practical societal needs and creation of programs which bring individuals from different ethnic groups together around a shared identity. Areas in which government support may add to the foundation of trust are also suggested.

Cheryl Jorgensen

1 Introduction

Scholars agree that the United Nations Mission in Kosovo (UNMIK) has so far failed to reconcile the Kosovo Albanians and Kosovo Serbs and create, even in a preliminary form, any kind of nascent multiethnic state (Franks & Richmond, 2008). Kosovo's recent unilateral declaration of independence in February of 2008 appears to confirm that we have a long way to go toward any meaningful reconciliation. Furthermore, given the recent decision by the International Court of Justice to affirm the legality of that declaration, if pathways to successful cooperation are not identified soon, the prospect of negotiations could be paralyzed for the foreseeable future (Crisis-Group, 2010). The UN Secretary General's office suggested that events in Kosovo could take on "a momentum of their own, putting at serious risk the achievements and legacy of the United Nations in Kosovo. Moving forward with the process to determine Kosovo's future status should remain a high priority for the Security Council and for the international community" (Ban, 2008). As a result, scholars claim that the current situation is one of dual societies where the polarized communities have replicated parallel state institutions and whose ethnic networks are linked to and funded by their ethnic motherlands (Franks & Richmond, 2008). "The roots of the Kosovo conflict are largely perceived to lie in the struggle for power between ethnicities (Albanian and Serbs) represented by elites and states" (Franks & Richmond, 2008, p. 85), but fuelled by centuries old mythologies and ethnic identities (Anscombe, 2006).

The Serbian–Albanian ethnic conflict in Kosovo is "constructed on conflicting… historical narratives, national discourses and opposing identities… which create implacable enmities between the two communities rather than harmonious linkages" (Franks & Richmond, 2008, p. 85). Building peace in post-conflict regions is an extremely complex process that encompasses more than simply avoiding a relapse of conflict, disarmament, and restoration of order. Peace building is a time-intensive process that involves "transforming hostile and violent relationships into a peace system characterized by just and interdependent relationships… it is grounded on the premise that societies affected by violence are still comprised of individuals, groups, attitudes, and processes that promote peace" (Abiew & Keating, 1999, pp. 81–82). One of those processes, we shall argue, is developing functional trust that paves the way for reconciliation.

This chapter analyzes the current state of the conflict in Kosovo; in particular, we review the historical and social context of the opposing identities of the polarized ethnic communities in Kosovo. Next, we discuss the current state of the conflict and examine the conditions under which ethnic divisions can be addressed in order to reduce their salience. We then review research on post-conflict reconciliation, conflict resolution, and peace building with a focus on trust, which, the research literature suggests, is at the center of a sustainable peace-building process and at the heart of reconciliation (Kelman, 2008; Worthington & Drinkard, 2000). Against this background, we summarize key findings from our own recent research on trust in cross-cultural contexts and argue that trust is a highly relevant, but rarely examined, factor in the complex process of peace building and reconciliation. We argue that functional trust-building processes can be fostered by reducing the salience of ethnic differences and by supporting the development of alternative identities. Finally, we will discuss steps for trust building and reconciliation in post-conflict Kosovo and recommend policy initiatives that can facilitate and build on current interethnic cooperation.

2 History of Ethnic Conflict in Kosovo

Atrocities have lasting memories. It is difficult for the ethnic Albanians in the village of Raçak to forget a massacre of forty-five of their neighbors in January of 1999 (Crisis in Kosovo, 1999). These memories, whether lived or learned (Anscombe, 2006), have a tendency to work themselves into ethnic identities, identities that are partly constructed on past injustices and state-sponsored, ideological historiography (Cvijic, 2008). On the other side of the ethnic fault line, there is a long-held tradition among the Serbian people that the region of Kosovo is their ancestral homeland, or the "cradle of the Serbs' historical existence" (Greater Serbian Ideology, 1986). The history of separatism between these two Balkan ethnic groups is centuries long.

2.1 Origins of Separatism

Serbian identity narrative. According to Anscombe (2006), "Serbian nationalism draws its strength and passion from tales of Kosovo" (p. 761). Three primary events construct the Serb identity narrative (see Fig. 14.1). First, an identity of national resistance and perseverance was constructed by the story of Serb defeat at the hands of Sultan Murad I of the Ottoman Empire at Kosovo Polje (Blackbird's Field) near Pristina in 1389. The Serbian Nemanjic Dynasty had ruled Kosovo since the late twelfth century, most recently under King Lazar Hrebeljanovic. The story tells of King Lazar who, leading a multiethnic army, valiantly gives his life defending "Old Serbia" rather than lose his homeland. This battle marks the end of the Serbian state in the Serbian national identity narrative. Some scholars see this rhetorical moment as "the defining moment in Serbian national history" despite its questionable validity (Anscombe, 2006, p. 760). However, it is important to note that Kosovo was recognized as part of Serbia prior to being seized by the Ottoman Empire. Second, an identity of manifest destiny was constructed based on the narrative of the Serbian Orthodox Church's Patriarchate, relocated in 1346 to the city of Pec on the western edge of Kosovo. Many significant churches and monasteries were subsequently constructed across Kosovo. The Patriarchate also held fast to preserve "the Serbian identity [as well as their property interests] for the nation during the centuries of Ottoman rule" (see Fig. 14.1) (Anscombe, 2006, pp. 760–761). As a result of this narrative, many contemporary Serbians refer to Kosovo as Metohija, or the "monastic lands."

The first two narratives generate much of the historical precedent for Serbian sovereignty in the region and explain why Kosovo is viewed by most Serbs as Serbia's former "heartland" (Bandow, 2009). A final narrative, "The Great Migration of 1690," works in conjunction with the two previous narratives. This narrative describes an event in which "most" of the Serbians in Kosovo were forced to emigrate to Hungary only to be replaced with Albanian Muslims by the Ottoman Turks. The circumstances of the migration coincide with a brief invasion of Kosovo by the Habsburgs, who held Belgrade only 1 year before being driven back across the Danube by the Ottomans. As they withdrew, apparently thousands of Serbs, including church clergy, joined them (Anscombe, 2006). These "myths of Kosovo," suggests Anscombe (2006), form the foundation of Serbian nationalism and lie "at the root of the conflicts" (p. 761).

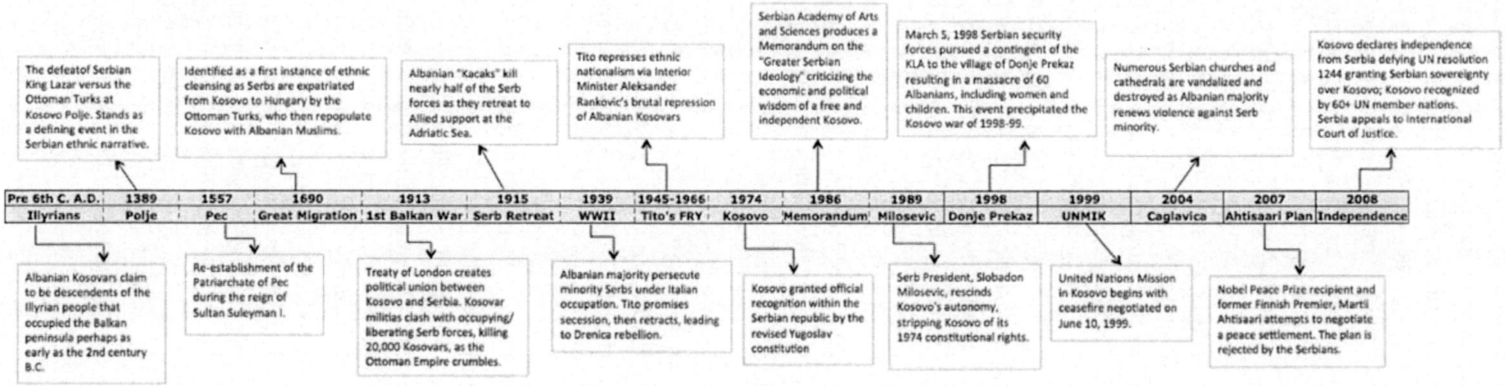

Fig. 14.1 Conflict event timeline

Kosovo Albanian identity narrative. For the Albanian Kosovar,[1] the identity claim can also be traced back to an ancient narrative connecting them to the Illyrian people who migrated to the Balkan Peninsula long before the Serbs ostensibly arrived in the sixth century ad (Rogel, 2003, p. 169). Unlike the Serbian identity narrative, complete with heroes and orthodoxy, the Albanian narrative is marked by invisibility. An unrecognized, stateless group, the Kosovars were continually victimized and subjected to assimilation tactics by imperial powers beginning with the Bulgarians and the Byzantine empire in the seventh century to the Ottoman empire and most recently Serbia. Absent a manifest destiny or uniting myth, their narrative is anchored in a sense of honor embodied in the moral code of the Kanun of Dukagjin, codified in the 1400s (Rogel, 2003). The Kanun (Canon) is a common legal and moral code that has historically united Ethnic Albanians in Kosovo in the absence of a common religious identification. It emphasizes personal honor, courage, and integrity in a set of traditional Albanian laws. A controversial tenth article (10.3) describes how to deal with murder and has been cited in recent years as the source of blood feuds that exacerbate ethnic tensions. The importance of honor can be seen in Kosovar reaction to events like the sensational, trumped up trials of prominent figures like the Albanian Journalist Azem Vllasi. Vllasi was arrested when Serbia jailed a number of Kosovo party leaders in November of 1988 and was later tried in a court surrounded by tanks (Rogel, 2003). Events like these are etched in the national consciousness as instances of dishonor and represent one more example of tension as a result of an economically dominant ethnic minority (Chua, 2004).

2.2 Alternating Oppression

These competing identity narratives have accompanied Serbian and Albanian tensions in Kosovo through the twentieth and twenty-first centuries. The details that make up each flashpoint are complex, involving land, language, religion, polity, and broken promises. From the very beginning of their modern relationship, Serbia appealed to historical precedent from the Middle Ages when, after regaining its independence from the Ottoman Turks in the first Balkan War (1912), it sought to formally acquire Kosovo. Serb statesmen looked at nation building as a means to greater wealth and influence in the late nineteenth and early twentieth centuries and began to design the Greater Serbia plan (Rogel, 2003). Part of that plan called for Serbia to include not only lands in which Serbians lived, but also lands in which they had previously lived. The ensuing Conference of London after the first Balkan War joined Kosovo, then inhabited largely by Albanian Muslims, with the Orthodox Christian Serbia. We consider that it is at this juncture that the modern era of Balkan tension began. For centuries, the national boundaries in Southeastern Europe were irrelevant given the hegemony of the Ottoman Empire. But with the swift stroke of a pen, on May 30, 1913, competing religious and linguistic groups were thrust into political union. The Albanian Kosovars had been closely allied with Albania during the Balkan War and preferred to become part of that newly freed country (Anscombe, 2006). Kosovar militias immediately clashed with occupying (liberating?) Serb forces. Some 20,000 Kosovars died as a result of the repression, and the first Kosovar diaspora began.

The Serb paramilitary forces, or the "Kamitadjis," mercenary units known for their brutality, committed numerous atrocities against Kosovar civilians. These "atrocity stories" remain in the psyches of Kosovars to this day, woven

[1] The label 'Kosovar' is most often used in the literature to refer to ethnic Albanians native to Kosovo, while the minority Serbian population is most often referred to simply as Serb, or Serbian, prejudicing their historical ethnic identity over their native nationality. However, some sources refer to each group respectively as Kosovo Serbian and Kosovo Albanian, or ethnic Serbian and ethnic Albanian. We employ all three labeling conventions depending on context in order to preserve the readability of the document.

into the ethnic identity narrative that shapes Kosovar self-understanding. However, the atrocities were not one-sided. Coincident with World War I, a second Kosovo War (1915–1918) took place when Serbia was invaded by the Central Powers (German, Austrian-Hungarian, Bulgarian, and Ottoman Empires). While the Serbian army was in retreat through the Dinaric Alps of Kosovo and Northern Albania, the Albanian guerrillas, or "Kaçaks," reciprocated the violence inflicted upon them only a few years earlier, cutting the Serbian force nearly in half as the Serb army made its way to allied support at the Adriatic Sea (Lee, 2008). At the end of the Great War and the defeat of the Ottoman Empire, a second political union further enmeshed Serbian and Kosovar destinies. Only this time, Kosovo was not accorded independent recognition, but rather was seen as part of Serbia. Serbia, Montenegro, Slovenia, Bosnia, and Croatia were united to form the new nation of Yugoslavia (formally becoming the Kingdom of Yugoslavia in 1929), but Serbia constituted the dominant presence in the government and military of the nascent nation. The new Yugoslavian army proceeded to occupy Kosovo in 1918 amidst ongoing resistance from the Kaçaks, leading to further atrocities at the hands of the now internationally recognized Yugoslavian army. Ethnic Albanians in Kosovo lost many of their rights and were encouraged by Belgrade to emigrate to the new nation of Turkey – many had their property annexed for Serbian colonists' purposes (Rogel, 2003). Massacres, burning villages, emigration of Serbians to Kosovo, and the banning of Albanian language instruction were perceived as tactics to assimilate Albanian Kosovars into a united Serbian republic.

During World War II, Kosovo was occupied by the Italians who stood by as the majority Albanians now persecuted the minority Serbs. Because the region was administered by the Albanian government, tens of thousands of Serbs were killed and at least one-hundred thousand forced to flee. The Albanian Prime Minister, Mustafa Kruja, made his position clear, "We should endeavor to ensure that the Serb population of Kosovo be – the area be cleansed of them and all Serbs who had been living there for centuries should be termed colonialists and sent to concentration camps in Albania. The Serb settlers should be killed" (Reuter & Clewing, 2000, p. 158). The Albanians likewise stood by as Tito's Partisan Communist, and largely Serbian, army waged a guerrilla war against the Axis powers. In order to finally gain ethnic Albanian support during World War II, Tito's National Liberation Movement promised some support for a unified Albanian state, including Kosovo. Albanian Kosovars only then joined in the resistance when Tito promised the right of secession upon liberation – a promise he reneged later, and which led to the Drenica rebellion of 1944–1945.

Tito effectively suppressed nationalism until his death in 1980, largely by Interior Minister Aleksander Rankovic's brutal repression of Albanian Kosovars from 1945 to 1966. The mid- to late 1960s brought a brief period of political reprieve for the Albanians who were granted provincial status, a separate constitution, and permission to establish a national university (Rogel, 2003). Tito sought to reign in Serbian nationalism in this latter period by giving ethnic Albanian's more influence in Kosovo; however, "the result was violence against the ethnic Serbian minority" (Bandow, 2009). It was not until 1974 that Kosovo was granted official recognition within the Serbian republic by the rewritten Yugoslav constitution, establishing a national bank, police force, and independent legislative assembly. The concessions granted in the new constitution were interpreted by some as restitution for years of repression (Anscombe, 2006). However, that constitutional recognition may have primed the pump for further agitation.

Serbian claims to Kosovo rest in part on an article in the 1974 Yugoslavian Constitution. The revised constitution organized semi-autonomous regions within a sovereign state founded on "cooperative federalism" (Staub, 2009, p. 55). The sticking point relates to the fact that Kosovo was recognized as a distinct region in the federation, and granted "full-fledged normative rights in the Yugoslav Constitution of 1974" (Staub, 2009, p. 55) along with Croatia, Serbia, Macedonia, Slovenia, Bosnia-Herzegovina, Montenegro, and Vojvodina. At the same time, Kosovo did not share the same republic status as the other seven-member states and was described as a "part of Serbia" (Staub, 2009, p. 56). On the basis of Kosovo's and the Yugoslavian Constitution, however, the region acted autonomously in most "national" and international respects. Perhaps because the region was mired in impoverished insignificance in the early 1960s, the Yugoslavian government granted increased autonomy by upgrading Kosovo's recognized status to that of a province, and after a state visit by Tito, the label "Metohija" was eliminated from the formal provincial name in 1968 (Rogel, 2003). Another likely factor was that during the early Cold War period, Kosovo's aspirations to unite with Albania had lost urgency due to Albania's bizarre relationships with Russia and China. Consequently, the years leading up to the 1974 constitution were seen as a series of setbacks and loss of control by Serbia, both with respect to Kosovo and with their role in greater Yugoslavia.

2.3 Escalation of Conflict

After Tito's death in 1980, it did not take long for tensions to flare once again. Influenced by the Polish Solidarity movement, Albanian students at the University of Pristina began protests in the capital city in the spring of 1981. What began as a demonstration for better cafeteria food escalated to bigger social and economic issues, ultimately calling for democracy and secession from Yugoslavia (Lee, 2008). In the years between Tito's death and Milosevic's rise to political prominence, nationalism trumped localism in Kosovo. Serbian media fanned nationalistic sentiment, evidenced by the large turnout for former Interior Minister Aleksander Rankovic's funeral, celebrating him as a champion of Serbian manifest destiny. In response to abuses of power by Serbia, key economic sectors within Kosovo were threatened by strikes and riots (e.g., the miner strike in Trepca, near Mitrovica). It was in the context of student riots in the early 1980s, increasing Serbian nationalism fostered by media events like the Paracin "massacre,"[2] and the Serbian Academy of Arts and Science's 1986 Memorandum laying out the "Greater Serbian Ideology"[3] that Slobodan Milosevic rose to power in Serbia in 1987 on a wave of nationalistic rhetoric (Rogel, 2003).

The modern flashpoint is traceable to the Serbian government of Slobodan Milosevic and his rescinding of Kosovo's autonomy on March 28, 1989, in response to Kosovo's desire for independence (Whitney, 1998). Declaring Serbia to be whole again, Milosevic's action came after a decade of repression in which hundreds of thousands of Kosovars were routinely arrested and interrogated. The political fallout from losing autonomy was that there was a voting majority for Milosevic in the Yugoslav assembly, giving him carte blanche for his legislative agenda within the Yugoslav republic. A referendum soon followed in 1991 in which Albanian Kosovars were removed from state jobs, Serbian curricula were instituted across the republic, Albanian language media were terminated (including the sole Albanian newspaper, the *Rilindja*), a national curfew was imposed, and the Kosovo legislative assembly was disbanded. Given the level of nationalization in the industrial sector, the loss of autonomy had far-reaching implications for the economy. The loss of representation and services precipitated strikes in education, mining and manufacturing, and retail – all met with swift action by Serbian police forces. The Albanian Kosovars

[2] The Paracin "massacre" was hardly a massacre at all – an Albanian military recruit went on a brief shooting spree in his barracks in 1987, killing four – only one of which was Serbian. While tragic, the Nationalist Serbian media used the episode as a chance to promote anti-Albanian sentiment by exaggerating the harm to Serbians and labeling the event a massacre.

[3] Over 200 intellectuals in Belgrade contributed to an ideological statement in which they "claimed that a 'long, fatal genocide' against Serbs was taking place in Kosovo and demanded an end to abuses suffered since the great migration" (Anscombe, 2006, p. 768).

increasingly lived in a virtual state, cut off from education, health care, and other essential state services. As a result, a policy of parallel structures was initiated by the Kosovo Albanians to provide essential civic services; "They organized schools and hospital care when Belgrade cut off these services for Albanians; moreover, they collected the taxes needed to pay for them. They formed their own trade unions and also established a new leadership, which directed the political affairs of the province" (Rogel, 2003, p. 173). As we shall see, this policy of parallel structures is now being employed by Kosovo Serbians as a sign of resistance against Kosovo independence.

In response to the Milosevic crackdown, the Democratic League of Kosovo, championed by writer Ibrahim Ragova, sponsored a passive resistance movement that culminated in a referendum calling for an independent Kosovo in September, 1991. Ninety-nine percent of Albanian Kosovars voted for independence in those elections. During the early to mid-1990s, wars in Croatia and Bosnia distracted the Serbian government, while a radical element grew in Kosovo that formed the Kosovo Liberation Army (KLA or UCK). The KLA was modeled after a similar militia from the nineteenth century that ended the Ottoman rule in the Balkans (Karpat, 2005) and was contrastingly described as insurgents or freedom fighters by the opposing sides. A series of KLA-coordinated attacks on Serbian security forces on April 22, 1996, quickly caught the attention of Belgrade. The ensuing Kosovo war of 1998–1999 waged by the KLA against Serbia was a brief, though tragic, conflict. On March 5, 1998, Serbian security forces pursued a contingent of the KLA to the village of Donje Prekaz, resulting in a massacre of 60 Albanians, including women and children. The attack drew international criticism from leaders of state. The KLA increased their activity during the summer of 1998, prompting Serbia to escalate military intervention in Kosovo, climaxing on September 28th with an attack on the village of Gornje Obrinje. The bloody image of a child's doll from a mutilated family coupled with streams of displaced persons seeking safety in the chilly countryside was more than the international community could stomach with the memory of Srebrenica so fresh.[4] The North American Treaty Organization (NATO) soon found itself in an uneasy coalition with the KLA (Fig. 14.2).[5]

A brief cease-fire between ethnic Albanian and Serbian forces ended with the Panda Bar Massacre, a brutal KLA attack on Serbian civilians in the city of Pec on December 15, 1998. The Račak massacre on January 15, 1999, was the culminating event of the long winter's war with the Serbian forces; 45 Albanians were mutilated, and this drew accusations of war crimes against the Milosevic regime (Rogel, 2003).[6] NATO joined the armed conflict after repeated diplomatic efforts were rebuffed by Belgrade, and commenced bombing on March 24, 1999 (Clinton, 1999). The NATO campaign lasted from March 24th to June 9th when a Military Technical Agreement was signed between NATO and Yugoslavia at Kumanovo establishing a cease-fire. Subsequently, NATO installed a peacekeeping force that eventually turned the operation over to the UNMIK. Participating NATO members included the USA, the United Kingdom, France, Germany, Belgium, Canada, Denmark, Hungary, Italy, Netherland, Norway, Portugal, Spain, and Turkey. The conflict "officially" ended on June 10, 1999, when NATO discontinued bombing exercises over Serbia. However, the end of official hostilities did not put an end to the human rights abuses, this time perpetrated by the Albanians against the Serbs who remained in Kosovo. During and

[4] During the Bosnian War over 8,000 men were massacred in Srebrenica July, 1995. The attacks were perpetrated by Serbian special forces under the command of general Ratko Mladic. These same special forces were accused of committing war crimes in Kosovo in 1999 (Frost, 2010).

[5] The KLA was an unofficial military group often associated with terroristic actions. Naturally NATO could not enter into a formal alliance with them. Furthermore, NATO lacked a UN resolution granting them permission to intervene in a non-NATO member nation's internal conflict.

[6] Though as with other atrocity stories, the veracity of the Racak massacre has been disputed (Nikolic-Ristanovic, 2008).

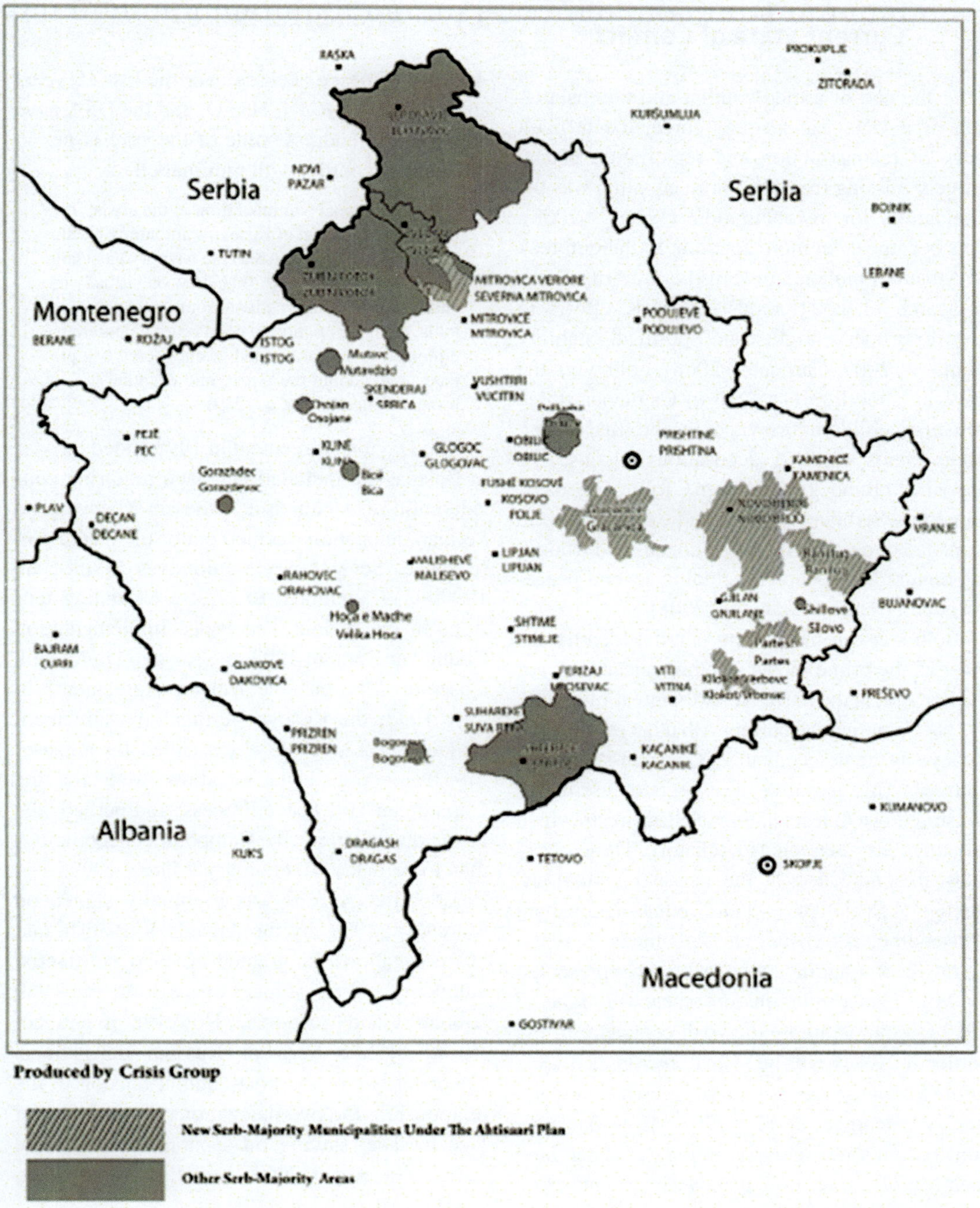

Fig. 14.2 Ethnic population distribution

immediately following the NATO campaign, it is estimated that more than 240,000 Serbians and people from other minority groups were driven from Kosovo (Carpenter, 2008). The tit-for-tat game continued, prompting the editor of Kosovo's leading newspaper, *Koha Ditore*, to call for all Kosovars to honor human rights in light of the cease-fire (Rogel, 2003).

3 Current State of Conflict

After the end of armed conflict and the installation of a UN peacekeeping force, the difficult work of reconstruction and repatriation began. Largely missing from the entire equation was the foundation for reconciliation (Waters, 2008). This became even more apparent in the outbreak of Albanian violence toward the minority Serbs in March of 2004 amidst UNMIK efforts to restore property rights and political stability (Bandow, 2009; Carpenter, 2008). Following the drive-by shooting of a Serb in Caglavica, three Albanian children drowned in the Ibar River. Both events sparked accusations against the opposing ethnic group. In the following days, numerous Serbian churches and cathedrals were damaged or destroyed, killing dozens and wounding hundreds of people, including several peacekeepers (Nikolic-Ristanovic, 2008).

Both sides in the present conflict identify the other as the prime mover in ethnic cleansing. For the Serbs, it is the narrative of the great migration of 1690, painting the current Albanian residents of Kosovo as the descendants of Ottoman-sponsored émigrés. This narrative is especially useful for constructing a first act of ethnic cleansing to which all others may be seen as retaliatory. These narratives are embedded in the national mythology, driving patriotism and ethno-nationalism (Anscombe, 2006). For the Albanians, it is the narrative of ongoing oppression as represented by Milosevic's inflammatory speech in June of 1989 to commemorate the sixth centenary of the battle of Kosovo Polje, "now recognized as a turning point on the road to Yugoslavia's destruction" (Anscombe, 2006, p. 763). Both narrative constructions are highly mythologized to heighten their usefulness for propaganda. Each contending ethnic group perceives the other as encroaching on sovereignty and independence while denying the same rights to the other. That same denial was extended to other minority groups like the Roma, Ashkali, and Egyptian populations that have suffered, almost in obscurity, during the ongoing tensions between the two dominant ethnic groups (Bloom, Hoxha, Sambunjak, & Sondorp, 2007; Crowe, 2008).

3.1 Attempts at Peace

A series of peace accords over the last 15 years sponsored by the UN, NATO, and the USA have attempted to address some of the core issues in the Kosovo conflict with minimal effect.

> The international administration of the crisis, from the virtual abolition of Kosovo's autonomy by Slobodan Milosevic in 1988 to the territory's declaration of independence in 2008, drew on virtually the entire arsenal of international conflict management tools, from negotiation to good offices, conference diplomacy, mediation and even coercive diplomacy – including the threat, and eventual use, of force. (Weller, 2008a, p. 1239)

The Dayton Agreement in 1995 ended the war in Bosnia, but included language requiring consideration of Albanian demands in Kosovo. The Serbian delegation stormed out of the meeting in response. Several peace initiatives in the late 1990s also attempted to diffuse escalating tensions in the region: The Peace Implementation Council at Bonn in 1997; the Kosovo Diplomatic Observer Mission [the Yeltsin Agreement] in May 1998; the Kosovo Verification Agreement on October 12, 1998, which called for a ceasefire from Yugoslavia to allow time for the Christopher Hill Peace Process; and perhaps the most notable failure, the Rambouillet negotiations that took place in February–March 1999. The Rambouillet Accord was eventually signed on March 18, 1999, by the Albanians, British, and US delegations. It granted Kosovo substantial autonomy and reinstituted many of the pre-1989 structures and freedoms.[7] However, it was not signed by the Serb or Russian delegations. Characteristic of the post-conflict tension in the relationship, the two delegations never even met face to face, staying on separate floors of the same hotel (Rogel, 2003). Less than a week later, NATO inserted itself in the conflict.

Following NATO's military intervention, what some call the first humanitarian war, UN Security Council Resolution 1244 was adopted on

[7] The Kosovo Albanian coalition was apprehensive about the agreement, but eventually agreed to sign when they received assurances from U.S. Secretary of State Madeline Albright that the U.S. would support an independence referendum within 3 years.

June 10, 1999. It authorized a civil and military UN presence, or peacekeeping mission, in Kosovo [UNMIK] and parts of the Federal Republic of Yugoslavia (F.R.Y). Under UNMIK, the region was split into five zones – a French zone in the north, including the Serbian-majority city Mitrovica; an Italian zone in the west; a German zone in the south (including Russian, Dutch, Australian, and Turkish battalions); a British zone in the central/northeast – including the capital city of Pristina; and an American zone in the southeast.

During the intervening 10 years of UNMIK, negotiations have ebbed and flowed between the two parties, with the clearest formulation of a plan forward coming in the form of the Ahtisaari Proposal (Waters, 2008; Weller, 2008a).

The 2007 Ahtisaari plan represents the most formal proposal for resolving the Kosovo situation. Nobel Peace Prize winner and former Finnish Premier, Martii Ahtisaari, was brought in as a UN Special Envoy to mediate a peace settlement. The Ahtisaari plan laid the groundwork for eventual separation of Kosovo from Serbia, recommending that "supervised independence would be the only viable solution for Kosovo" (Weller, 2008, p. 1223). The Serbian government was not satisfied with the Ahtisaari plan, however, and appealed to Russia for new negotiations from the ground up. Political gamesmanship ensued at various international meetings in the following months, including the G8 in Heiligendamm, in an effort to convince Russia to get on board with the UN Special Envoy's plan. The Contact Group (Italy, Belgium, the UK, Germany, France, and the USA were the formal international mediators that established the Guiding Principles for negotiation in 2005) even put forward a modified proposal that included additional time for negotiation rather than clear adoption of the Ahtisaari plan. The Serbian coalition responded positively to further negotiations and offered to relinquish some degree of sovereignty in certain areas; however, after 15 months of negotiations with the Ahtisaari talks, the Albanian Kosovar coalition was not inclined to modify its position. They were intent on independence at that point. As in the Rambouillet talks, the Serbian delegation protested a flawed process and the negotiations were considered an impasse. A multinational group of mediators explained in the final report "that it explored with the parties every realistic option for an agreement, but it was not possible to find a mutually acceptable outcome" (Background Note: Kosovo, 2009).

The most recent round of negotiations was commissioned by the Contact Group in 2007. Led by Ambassador Wolfgang Ischinger of Germany, a "Troika" of negotiators attempted to rekindle talks during 120 days (10 sessions) of negotiations in late 2007. The Serbian contingent was more active in putting forth concrete proposals during these sessions than they were during the Ahtisaari meetings; however, the Kosovo representatives were suspect (and short on trust) at this point and were more committed to the Ahtisaari proposal and independence. Serbia continued to feel that these negotiations, like the Ahtisaari plan, was a trap leading to the inevitable loss of sovereignty over Kosovo. The government in Pristina did eventually agree to a Troika proposal that focused on practical cooperation between the two sides with the assumption that Kosovo would eventually be an independent nation. The Serbian contingent, however, persisted in defining the status of Kosovo as a province with substantial autonomy while giving Serbia territorial sovereignty (controlling frontiers, customs, monetary policy, etc.). The Serbian government was resolute in characterizing Albanian Kosovars as a "national minority" (Weller, 2008, p. 1229) when it came to sovereignty.

In the end, the Troika commission submitted a ten-point plan (recommendation) that avoided a pronouncement on status, but rather advised the two parties to exercise state powers separately but cooperate in mutually advantageous areas (Weller, 2008). Serbia was chilly to the proposal in that it represented de facto independence for Kosovo.

Albanian Kosovars felt that they had little choice but to move toward independence after the Troika negotiations, declaring it on February 17, 2008. The decision was met with violent protests by Serbian opponents (Beary, 2008; Pancevski, 2008). At the time this chapter was written, only

69 voting countries in the UN are in favor of a divided Serbia. Belgrade appealed to the International Court of Justice (ICJ) for a decision on the matter of Kosovo's unilateral declaration of independence (Bandow, 2009). The ICJ partially upheld Kosovo's action in their July 22, 2010, opinion, asserting that it did not violate international law or UN Security Council resolution 1244 (Crisis-Group, 2010). International political perspectives continue to be divided along Cold War lines, with Russia viewing the declaration as a dangerous precedent with implications for Taiwan and, closer to home, South Ossetia (Harzl, 2008). The declaration also has potential implications for the Balkans. Macedonia has a large population of Albanians that has already sought increased autonomy in the region (Casule & Robinson, 2008). Likewise, Turkey and China are not apt to condone Kosovo's unilateral declaration as it may create a precedent for Cypriot and Kurdish situations in the former and Xinjiang in the latter (Karpat, 2005).

As Abiew and Keating (1999) describe,

> One of the problems that confronts any attempt to reconcile societies divided by years of bitter conflict is that the institutional and procedural devices for addressing social problems are often destroyed or so severely corrupted that they are effectively inoperable. They involve fundamental questions not only about what to reconstruct but also about how to do so in order not to recreate the unsustainable institutions and structures that originally contributed to the conflict. (p. 101)

Due to the severity of the conflict between these ethnic groups, some have called for establishing a Truth and Reconciliation Commission similar to that formed in South Africa (Bloom et al., 2007). But reconciliation commissions beg the question of end results. Does reconciliation hinge on democratic elections? Reformed justice systems? Civil service sectors and police forces? Or do these cosmetic changes merely "paper over" the underlying fault lines until the next eruption (Abiew & Keating, 1999, p. 102)? And as evidenced by the competing identity narratives, one of the primary divisions in Kosovo pertains to property rights, both private and corporate. The significance of property in this particular conflict has led some to suggest that the issue is critical in the reconciliation process (Carpenter, 2008). In fact, one scholar argues that the Montenegro model of a multiethnic democracy is unattainable in Kosovo and that finishing the European redistricting along ethnic lines will be the only solution for lasting tolerance and peace in the Balkans (Jost, 1999). Finally, what is the appropriate role for outside mediators in reconciliation? Some question the legitimate role of outsiders in the reconciliation process if we are to understand root causes and realize sustainable solutions (Donais, 2009; Pankhurst, 1999, 2000). Abiew and Keating (1999) identify the necessity of restoring civil society through restoring the relationships between ethnic groups, which is a much more difficult task than rebuilding economic and political infrastructure. It involves "promoting psychosocial healing and reconciliation" at the local level (p. 87).

We next turn our attention to what is needed in order to "make visible a multitude of truths" (Nikolic-Ristanovic, 2008, p. 102) about the past and a shared vision for the future; for "where peoples cannot yet agree about what transpired, or where no common national identity can be sculpted from competing collective memories, the time is not yet ripe for reconciliation" (Bradford, 2002, p. 151).

4 Post-conflict Reconciliation

First, it must be noted that despite common usage, "post-conflict" society is a misnomer. As the rate of violence recurrence in war-torn societies suggests, deep-seated conflicts remain long after the cease-fire is negotiated (Call, 2008; Donais, 2009). Reconciliation is certainly the ultimate goal for Kosovo. On 1 July 1999, the Organization for Security and Cooperation in Europe's (OSCE) Permanent Council decided that the OSCE mission would be "guided by the importance of bringing about mutual respect and reconciliation among all ethnic groups in Kosovo and of establishing a viable multi-ethnic society where the rights of each individual are fully and equally respected" (Simonsen, 2004, p. 294). The ambition of the OSCE mission, to reduce the salience

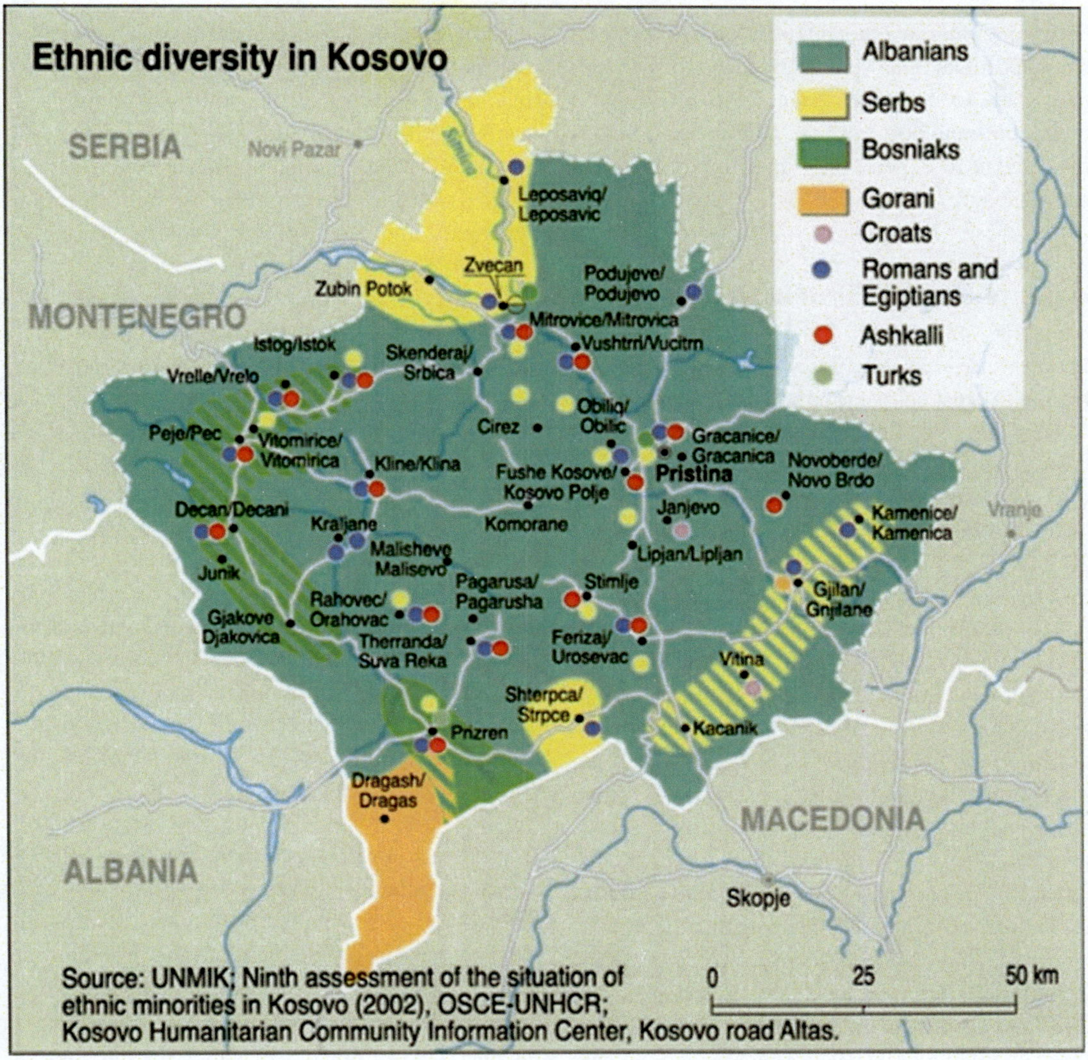

Fig. 14.3 Ethnic diversity in Kosovo

of ethnic identities, and stimulate new, integrative ones, has shaped the reconstruction efforts in postwar Kosovo. The difficulty lies in the fact that due to physical segregation and a high level of mistrust (see Fig. 14.3), Kosovo has a limited number of areas where shared interests and experiences may occur (Simonsen, 2004). In addition, in the 10 years since Belgrade ceded Kosovo to UN and NATO control, integration of the Serbs into Kosovo's political life has been one of the greatest challenges (Serb Integration in Kosovo: Taking the Plunge, 2009). The Serb policy toward post-declaration Kosovo has largely been intent on undermining independence. Belgrade has underwritten Serbian parallel civic structures, discouraged emigration, and subsidized salaries of municipal leaders (Serb Integration in Kosovo: Taking the Plunge, 2009).

The new emphasis on reconciliation, both in theoretical and in practical terms, can be explained by the change in the nature of warfare in the post-Cold War era (Kelman, 2008; Nadler & Shnabel, 2008; Ramsbotham, Woodhouse & Miall, 2005). Kelman (2008) notes that there has been an increase in the frequency and intensity of deep-rooted conflicts, "not across national borders, but between ethnic or other identity groups within a single political unit" (p. 15). Because former enemies have to live together in these situations in their common post-conflict neighborhood, it is insufficient to depend only upon diplomatic and strategic agreements.

4.1 Foundations of Reconciliation

For centuries-old enemies to coexist peacefully requires a great deal of time and significant healing of mind and soul. Thus, reconciliation goes beyond most concepts of conflict resolution, and implies that "the deep rooted sources of conflict are addressed and transformed" (Ramsbotham et al., 2005, p. 231). A change in attitudes and in behavior toward former enemies implies a change of heart (Curle, 1995). For Kosovo Albanians and Kosovo Serbs, to learn to live together is clearly challenging. Kelman (2008) explains that the essence of reconciliation is the "transformation of their relationship" and the changes in the ways former enemies "think about each other, feel about each other, and act toward one another" (p. 16). In other words, reconciliation can be described as a process "that reflects *identity changes* that each of the adversaries undergoes (Nadler & Shnabel, 2008, p. 40).

Reconciliation is also distinct from reparations. Reparation "is grounded in the common law of torts and in the international law principle that when an intentional wrong cannot be undone, justice requires compensation of victims for injuries and punishment of the wrongdoer" (Bradford, 2002, pp. 75–76). Due to the number of legal and political complexities involved in cases of ethnic injustice perpetrated by a sovereign state, Bradford suggests that reparations is not the most appropriate path to pursue. While it is possible to restore land and establish legal structures, it is more difficult to transform attitudes (Von Carlowitz, 2005). In fact, the manner in which reparations transpire may inhibit the legitimization of the nation and the reconciliation of interdependent and cohabiting ethnic groups. Reconciliation focuses on enduring features of justice and healing, rather than temporal political or property gains (Bradford, 2002). "Reconciliation, or 'restorativism,' is a non-punitive, eclectic paradigm that reorients redress from money toward healing, via demythification and exchange of apologies for forgiveness" (Bradford, 2002, pp. 134–135). In the case of Kosovo, the alternating historical violence exacted on the other group by both Kosovo Albanians and Kosovo Serbs makes it nearly impossible to sort out punitive reparations.

Finally, it is important that all parties are equally invested in the reconciliation process. According to Bradford (2002), remedies must be:

> jointly crafted to encourage the dominant group to recognize moral responsibility for past injuries, to reconstruct and repair, by affirmative measures, the dignity and position of the aggrieved group, and to usher in a 'new moral economy' in which repetition of the past is unthinkable. (pp. 135–136)

The path toward interethnic cooperation depends on conciliatory gestures. Kosovo-Albanians point toward recent reconstruction projects in Serb communities as an indicator of good will. They suggest as well that decentralization is "an essential step in creating a multiethnic community" (Malazogu, 2009, p. 18; Serb Integration in Kosovo: Taking the Plunge, 2009). According to Project on Ethnic Relations' (PER) sponsored dialogs, "Simply engaging locals in the process of reconciliation is not sufficient in Kosovo. Because of the depth of the problems in this small country, locals need to become the main stakeholders for community development… they need to become the owners of the integration process" (Malazogu, 2009, p. 24). The report goes on to conclude that the Albanian and Serb Kosovars "must first change the misperceptions each community has about the other" (p. 24). To understand the role of ethnic identities and to reach the objective of harmonious coexistence between antagonistic groups in Kosovo, it is important to understand the causes and consequences of social categorization processes.

4.2 Social Categorization

Reconciliation at the transformative level of bridging differences and restoring trust poses the most acute challenge after violent conflict (cf. Ramsbotham et al., 2005). Social categorization is a basic process that is fundamental to intergroup conflict, and has been referred to as a starting point to understand intergroup relations and promote reconciliation (Riek et al., 2008). Social categorization is the automatic tendency of categorizing objects and people into groups due to limitations in people's ability to process information and the enormous complexity of the social and psychological environment (Fiske & Taylor, 1991). Social psychology research has offered general theories to explain these processes (Allport, 1954; Brewer, 1999; Brown & Gaertner, 2001; Fiske, 2002; Fiske & Taylor, 1991; Pettigrew, 1998; Sherif, 1966; Tajfel & Turner, 1979; Turner, 1985). Social Identity Theory (Tajfel & Turner, 1979) and Social Categorization Theory (Turner, 1985) address these fundamental processes of social categorization and their consequences for intergroup relations. For Tajfel (1978), the social identity is "that part of an individual's self-concept which derives from his knowledge of his membership in a social group (or groups), together with the value and emotional significance attached to that membership" (p. 63). Hence, being a member of an esteemed group is important because the group provides a positive self-concept and positive identity. In addition, group identification meets two human needs: The need for belonging or inclusion that motivates adaptation with the ingroup – and the need for differentiation, that is satisfied by distinguishing the self from others (Brewer, 2001). In other words, belonging to an ingroup necessarily means that others do not. From this perspective, a key issue we need to address is how intergroup contact, specifically interethnic contact in Kosovo´s post-conflict period, could be structured to modify cognitive representations of group boundaries.

To highlight the need for group boundary modification, it is instructive to note that several of the intergroup contact situations in the Kosovo conflict-resolution process have not been ideal. In the case of the Rambouillet Accord negotiations, perceived ingroup/outgroup distinctions played a significant role in the failed talks. First, NATO's presence at the talks heightened the differentiation function of group identity for the Serbs and was a primary factor in their rejection of the proposal. Second, some of the conditions in the peace accord, like NATO peacetime presence in all republics of the former FYR, were very "outgroup" oriented and were even cited as unacceptable by former U.S. Secretary of State, Henry Kissenger. Numerous other characteristics of the Rambouillet meetings violated specific qualities of intergroup contact that have been shown to have an impact on intergroup relations (Allport, 1954; Amir, 1969; Pettigrew, 1998). To a large extent, the series of Kosovo peace negotiations, including Rambouillet, the Ahtisaari talks, and the Troika, have operated under that assumption that the more contact there is, the more scope there is for group boundary modification. However, Allport (1954) proposed that it is the nature of intergroup contact that leads to improved relations and reduced conflict (cf. Ramsbotham et al., 2005). Equal status between the groups, cooperative intergroup interaction, and supportive norms by authorities are critical prerequisites for improved intergroup relations. The nature of intergroup contact is of critical importance due to its influence on social categorization processes.

There are two prominent Social Identity Theory models that have been tested empirically in field and experimental settings: de-categorization and re-categorization (cf. Worchel & Coutant, 2008). According to Riek et al. (2008), each of these models provides recommendations "for how to structure cognitive representations of situations in which there is contact between the groups, the psychological processes that promote attitude change, and the mechanisms by which contact experiences are generalized to improve attitudes toward the out-group as a whole" (p. 260).

De-categorization aims to reduce or eliminate group distinction and viewing each person as an individual. The de-categorization perspective assumes that repeated contact with a variety of outgroup members should decrease the value of category stereotypes and change the overall perception about members of that group (Brewer & Miller, 1996). In line with this personalization perspective, "intergroup contact should be arranged to downplay categorical distinctions while creating opportunities to get to know out-group members as unique individuals, thus decreasing the biases arising from categorization" (Riek et al., 2008, p. 260). Repeated personalized contact with members from the other group facilitates perspective taking and the development of empathy (Riek et al., 2008). Again, in the case of the Rambouillet Accords, members of the two ethnic groups never met face to face during the negotiations (Franks & Richmond, 2008; Karpat, 2005).

A second model for reducing intergroup segregation is *re-categorization*. In contrast to the de-categorization model, re-categorization seeks to restructure group boundaries rather than dissolve them (Gaertner & Dovidio, 2000; Riek et al., 2008). The common Ingroup Identity Model (Gaertner & Dovidio, 2000; Sherif, Harvey, White, Hood, & Sherif, 1988) focuses on the mediating role of group representations via processes such as the well-known *autokinetic effect*. From this perspective, intergroup bias and conflict can be reduced by factors that transform people's representation of memberships from two groups to a more inclusive *superordinated* identity (Gaertner & Dovidio, 2000). "When recategorization interventions create or strengthen a common in-group identity, the cognitive and motivational processes that initially produced in-group favoritism are redirected to the former out-group members who now share the superordinate group identity" (Gaertner et al., 2002, p. 102). With a common ingroup identity, ideally, individuals may see themselves as belonging to the same group (e.g., village) rather than as belonging to two separate groups (e.g., ethnic groups). Hence, the process of re-categorization allows individuals from different groups to create (cognitively) one "supergroup" that incorporates the members of both groups (Gaertner & Dovidio, 2000). Both models, de-categorization (personalization) and re-categorization (common ingroup identity), explain the implications of category differentiation and help us to better understand the relevance of reducing or eliminating the salience of intergroup differentiation.

4.3 Challenges to Reconciliation Models

According to Worchel and Coutant (2008), there are several reasons why re-categorization and de-categorization may have limited value in dealing with conflict involving enduring groups such as ethnic groups. The salience of group identity, the severity of the conflict, the degree of concern for security, and the difficulty in initiating the forgiveness process all affect the applicability of social categorization approaches to complex situations.

A critical issue in Kosovo concerns *the nature and salience of group identity.* According to Worchel and Coutant (2008), re-categorization and de-categorization "may be effective in reducing conflict when change in real or perceived category membership is possible" (p. 431). But if group membership is permanent (e.g., ethnic groups), re-categorization and de-categorization may challenge coveted distinctions that legitimize identity narratives. These narratives are often the basis of conflicting groups' fear of one another. Especially in cases like Kosovo where armed conflict has deepened divisions between groups, ethnicity becomes an "all-dominant marker" (Simonsen, 2005, p. 297), and the idea of eliminating the importance of intergroup differentiation may be unpopular. The renewed violence in 2004, despite the UNMIK presence, is a good illustration of the durability of ethnic group categories. Most of the Albanian violence targeted *Metohija,* destroying many historical Serbian religious sites (Terdevci, 2004).

Another critical issue concerns *the severity of the conflict.* In many explanations for intergroup conflict, the role of history is not given sufficient weight (Worchel & Coutant, 2008, p. 426). In Kosovo, the causes of the conflict are related to religious heritage, property rights, constitutional clauses, and many other factors that are more often than not mythologized for propagandistic purposes. Milosevic's 1989 speech commemorating the battle of Kosovo Polje capitalized on such mythologized historical symbolism to drive nationalism. The multifaceted nature of the conflict combined with the deep connection to group identity may limit the opportunity for social category modification in Kosovo. Social categorization models designed to improve intergroup contact, and in the long run cultivate reconciliation, provide recommendations on how to structure cognitive representations of situations in which there is contact between conflicting groups. Either they aim to eliminate group distinctions (de-categorization) or they try to reshape group boundaries by building a common ingroup identity (re-categorization). Both approaches are valuable, but their utility is questionable in situations with a long history of interethnic conflict and low motivation to eliminate group distinctions.

A further critical issue pertains to *the concern for security*. Concern for group security is endemic to situations of ethnic conflict; "History demonstrates that the out-group is a threat to the security and existence of the in-group" (Worchel & Coutant, 2008, p. 427). In these situations, the dominant characteristic of ethnic conflict is fear (Bar-Tal, 2001), and even if contact might be beneficial for the sake of reconciliation, the question remains of how to motivate groups to engage in cooperative contact without focusing on the features of negative peace (Galtung, 1996; Nikolic-Ristanovic, 2008). Currently, the strong ethnic divisions between northern and southern Kosovo, with heavy concentrations of Serbs in Mitrovica and north of the Ibar River, create pockets of territorial fear. The situation has led some to suggest that the only solution in Kosovo is extending the European redistricting along ethnic divisions (Jost, 1999).

A fourth critical issue concerns *the apology-forgiveness cycle*. Worchel (1999) points out that it is difficult to identify a single example of a war in which one side admits that it was the aggressor. He points out in his discussion of groups involved in intractable conflict that in most cases, both sides are convinced that their group is the victim, "and endless debates revolve around which side has suffered the greatest wrong" (Worchel & Coutant, 2008, p. 434). Several paths toward reconciliation are available and have implications for the apology-forgiveness cycle. In order to consider the unique qualities of the Kosovo conflict, we will distinguish between a "realist" and a "psychological needs" approach to peace building (Nadler & Shnabel, 2008, p. 38). The *realist approach* assumes that competition over scarce and real resources causes conflict, and agreement on how to distribute them brings an end to the conflict (Nadler & Shnabel, 2008; Sherif, 1966). Such an agreement is seen as the result of a negotiation process between two rational actors "who put their differences on the table and seek an agreement on how to divide the resources" (Nadler & Shnabel, 2008, p. 38). In contrast to the realist approach, the *psychological needs perspective* refers to "causes that are rooted in the threat to parties' basic psychological needs" (Nadler & Shnabel, 2008, p. 38). During conflict, parties cause harm and pain to each other, and this results in threats to basic psychological needs for safety, self-respect, and dignity. These threats evoke and maintain emotion-filled identity narratives on both sides of the Kosovo ethnic conflict that trace back to the Ottoman Empire and continue to recent incidents in Mitrovica in July 2010 (Kosovo and Serbia After the ICJ Opinion, 2010; cf. history of ethnic conflict in Kosovo in this chapter). These recent incidents illustrate that violence remains a threat and contributes to the maintenance of the constructed identities.

From a psychological needs perspective, Nadler and Shnabel (2008) point to two different reconciliation approaches. *Instrumental reconciliation* is directed to the future, and not concerned with the past of a conflict. Instead, it refers to repetitive cooperation projects where adversaries gradually learn to cooperate with each other and to achieve goals that are important for both parties. *Socioemotional reconciliation,* however, seeks to overcome the "*emotional* barriers of victimhood and guilt through an *interaction* [emphasis in original] that involves an admission of past wrongdoings and subsequent forgiveness" and implies an apology-forgiveness cycle (Nadler & Shnabel, 2008, p. 41). The cycle acknowledges that "responsibilities to atone and forgive are reciprocal... peace requires justice, which requires the guilty to admit to, accept responsibility for, and repair unjust acts, while requiring the victims to grant forgiveness in exchange" (Bradford, 2002, p. 149). Nadler and Shnabel (2008) view this cycle as "consisting of a social exchange between perpetrator and victim in which each provides to the other psychological commodities that are needed to ameliorate the threats to their respective identities" (p. 42). Accordingly, the apology-forgiveness cycle, which is seen as lying at the heart of socioemotional reconciliation, "is expected to increase the parties' willingness to end the conflict" (Nadler & Shnabel, 2008, p. 42).

Thus, the challenge of reconciliation via the apology-forgiveness cycle would require that a group accepts the role of being the perpetrator. In the case of Kosovo's centuries-long conflict, both groups would have to accept the roles of perpetrator and victim.

As we can see, in cases of intense, historically embedded conflict with little foundation for an apology-forgiveness cycle, an approach is needed that addresses the limitations of Social Categorization Theory (Turner, 1985). In our view, it is more promising to reduce the salience of ethnic identity by promoting alternative identities that already exist. Therefore, we next outline the process of activating these alternative cultural identities as a means for developing a functional trust relationship.

Identity narratives are not so malleable as to be able to "reduce" or "abolish" ethnic identities. Instead, our approach is to change the salience of ethnic identity by strengthening alternative identities, which people already have. This approach relies on the *cultural mosaic model* by Chao and Moon (2005) and suggests that individuals, for the sake of alternative identity building, do not have to create new artificial identities – because multiple identities already exist in each of us. The cultural mosaic model conceptualizes this multifaceted identity using three primary categories. Demographic facets, or tiles, include physical attributes such as age, gender, race, and ethnicity. Geographic tiles include natural or human-made aspects, such as urban vs. rural identities or coastal versus inland-oriented identities, etc. Finally, associative tiles include the identities of high involvement, such as family, religion, or job, organization, or political affiliations. Each facet or tile represents participation in an aspect of culture at some level and to a certain degree – with its own artifacts and behaviors, beliefs, and values, and underlying assumptions that may influence the way a person thinks or acts. Actually, these tiles may complement each other, coexist, or clash – depending on the strength and implications of each cultural identity in a given situation.

Therefore, each person has to some extent, a hybrid identity. And given a specific context or situation, it is possible, consciously or subconsciously, to activate those identities accordingly. For enhancing cross-ethnic contact and relations, this model may serve as a heuristic guide for dealing with the relative salience of ethnic identity in interethnic relations.

In our next section, we introduce trust-building processes in order to open the space for examining the critical aspect of ethnic identity and how to modify the salience of ethnic identity.

5 Trust-Building Processes

Trust is increasingly seen as a core concept for peace-building processes and reconciliation in post-conflict areas (Bijlsma-Frankema & Klein Woolthuis, 2005; Mertens, 2000; Newton, 2001; Smith & Schwegler, 2010; Williams, 2001). "[A] peace process would have a better chance of success if parties to the conflict agree to focus on peace incentives and confidence and trust-building first" (Sukuma, 2007, p. 11). Hence, the absence of trust between the parties engaged in former conflicts makes it impossible for the involved parties to negotiate directly (Sukuma, 2007). This was evident at the Rambouillet conference in 1999, in which the Serbian delegation would not meet with the Albanian Kosovar delegation face to face (Rogel, 2003).

Scholars identify trust as a relevant precondition for various processes: "Trust is likely to be a key concept in conflict resolution and peace building" (Hewstone et al., 2008, p. 212). Nadler and Liviatan (2004) note that recent experimental research suggests that a high degree of trust in an adversary's apology for past wrongdoings can lead to a greater willingness to reconcile with the enemy group. In addition, Kelman (2008) emphasized that if interactions between groups within a society are to be cooperative and mindful of each group's sense of security and well-being, they must be based on mutual acceptance and mutual trust.

In other words, if trust can be established, it has a number of positive consequences. However, despite the large consensus about the relevance of trust within peace-building processes, there is a lack of clarity regarding the preconditions of trust as it relates to reconciliation.

Kelman (2008) distinguishes between conflict settlement, conflict resolution, and reconciliation. He conceptualizes conflict resolution as the process of building trustworthy relations and distinguishes it from the process of reconciliation. Other scholars see building trusting relations as central to reconciliation. For Worthington and Drinkard (2000), for instance, "the restoration of trust in an interpersonal relationship through mutual trustworthy behaviours" (p. 93) is central to the meaning of reconciliation (cf. Nadler & Shnabel, 2008). What is clear in the extant literature is that there exists a gap between the ascribed importance of trust, both as a precondition and as an output of reconciliation, and the conceptual and empirical understanding of trust-building processes between individuals and groups of former enemies in post-conflict contexts.

In the pages that follow, we want to provide an understanding of trust and its implications for reconciliation processes. Toward this end, we first define trust and then move to some key findings of empirical research conducted in a cross-cultural context (Schwegler, 2008; Smith & Schwegler, 2010). We distinguish between three types of trust and four steps of a prototypical process of trust building. Then, we discuss these key findings against the background of altering the salience of alternative identities. In the final section, we turn to practical considerations and conclude with some implications of our analysis for reconciliation, focusing particularly on trust-enhancing strategies after intense social conflicts.

5.1 Definition of Trust

Trust is said to be like a glue that holds relationships together (Lewicki & Wiethoff, 2000). Trust becomes relevant in the situations in which we are not able to control or monitor the behavior of others fully (Luhmann, 2000); this includes situations where well-developed institutional structures, complete contracts, and hierarchies are lacking (Bijlsma Frankena & Klein Woolthuis, 2005). In other words, the need for trust arises in situations where risk or vulnerability is present (Luhmann, 2000; Ring & Van de Ven, 1994). That is exactly the case in postwar Kosovo, where the situation is seen as "calm but tense" (senior KFOR personnel, in Franks & Richmond, 2008).

To date, there is no clear consensus about the meaning and definition of trust within the scientific discourse. Nevertheless, most scholars accept that a situation of trust requires some degree of uncertainty and some degree of interdependence. In accordance with these widely accepted preconditions of trust, Rousseau, Sitkin, Burt, and Camerer (1998) suggest the following definition: "Trust is a psychological state comprising the intention to accept vulnerability based upon positive expectations of the intentions or behavior of another" (p. 395). As a complex, multidimensional psychological state, trust includes cognitive, affective, and motivational components (Smith & Schwegler, 2010). Furthermore, conceptualized as a social orientation toward other people, trust entails relational aspects (Kramer, 1999).

5.2 Empirical Research

Despite a growing literature on interpersonal trust, researchers are only beginning to understand the process of trust development. This is especially true for trust-building processes across

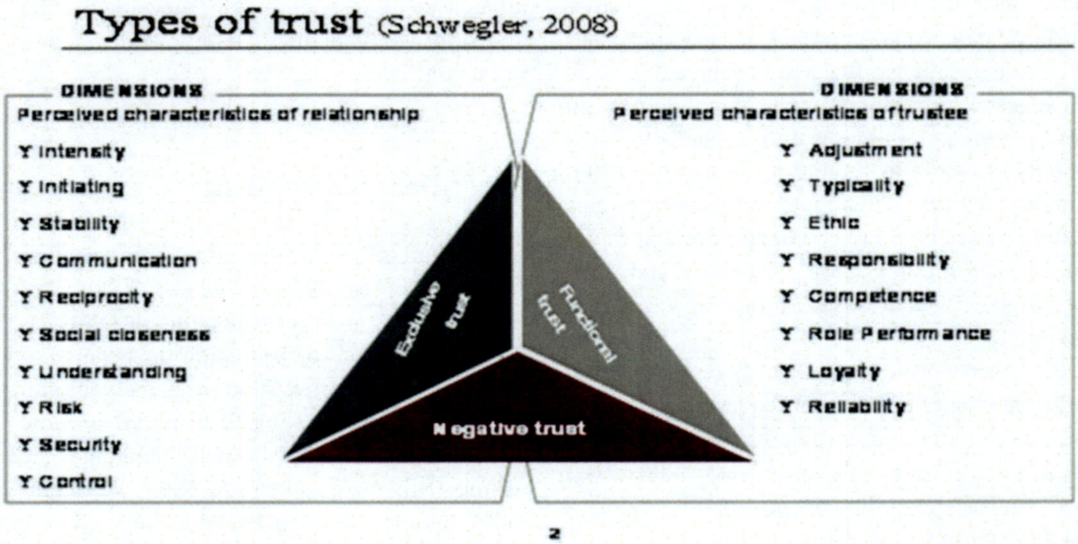

Fig. 14.4 Types of trust

different cultures and in the context of postwar peace-building processes. Therefore, at this stage, we will present key findings of research conducted in a cross-cultural context in order to draw relevant implications to the problem under discussion. The empirical research presented here is based on a theoretical approach of relational trust, where predisposition of a trustor, characteristics of a trustee, characteristics of a social context, and their interrelationships come into play.

5.3 Three Types of Trust

Schwegler (2008) examined cross-cultural cooperation between individualistic and collectivistic cultures as it related to subjective perceptions about trusting relationships. One of the key findings revealed that trust takes different forms based upon cultural frame of reference, that is, "trust is not equal." When people talk about trust and their trusting relationships, they have different concepts in mind. Talking about their trusting relationships with members from another group or culture, they refer not only to different levels and different qualities of trust, but also to different consequences of their trusting relationships.

By clustering and analyzing the empirical data, three different types of trust emerged: *exclusive trust, negative trust,* and *functional trus*t. The three types of trust are characterized by ten relationship dimensions and eight characteristics of the trustee. These various dimensions ultimately determine and characterize the nature, determinants, and consequences of the three distinct types of trust. The term "types" of trust is applied because trust is perceived fundamentally differently for each distinct type of trust (Fig. 14.4).

We will first examine *exclusive trust*. This type of trust is described as a highly emotional relationship, where people feel secure and comfortable, where the parties believe in and stand for the same ideas and values, and can be confident that the *Other* has the same desires and intentions. The label "exclusive" alludes to the sense that most respondents have very few exclusive trust relationships with members from the other group, meaning the foreign culture. In some respects, this type is similar to the identification-based trust conceptualized by Lewicki and Bunker (1996). Risk and control are not an issue in these relationships due to open and affirming communication. In addition, the interactants perceive the cooperation as highly effective, energizing, and rewarding. In post-conflict societies, this type of trust rarely occurs. In Kosovo, an indicator for exclusive trust among former opponents would be that Albanians and Serbs would be willing to invest in cooperation without any suspicion, and that both parties feel secure about the true goals of the other.

The second type of trust is *negative trust. Negative trust* is characterized by respondents having negative experiences with a large number of members from the foreign culture. Negative trust can, therefore, be described as a generalized negative attitude toward members of the other cultural group. Concretely, the findings show negative trust varying from "just having no trust" up to "extreme distrust" (Schwegler, 2008). Similar to exclusive trust, negative trust is also based on emotions, implying the feeling of high *in*security. The communication is guarded and characterized by misunderstandings. And since people perceive a high level of risk, they attempt to add permanent control mechanisms. Overall, cooperation is seen as exhausting. This type of trust is particularly evident in the multiple attempts at negotiating peace accords between Serbian and Albanian Kosovars.

Most respondents in Schwegler's (2008) research exhibited *functional trust* relationships to at least some of the members of the foreign culture. In comparison to the exclusive trust level, where people trust each other because they strongly believe in the honesty, sincerity, reliability, and trustworthiness of their partner, individuals at the functional trust level do not believe entirely in the trustworthiness of their partner but realize and accept the importance of extending some degree of what might be called "operational" trust. This type of trust is based primarily on rational thought. In other words, individuals do not necessarily enjoy, love, or respect each other, but they at least are fully aware that it is advantageous and perhaps more efficient to trust each other. Consequently, having a functional trust relationship means trusting another person at least to some extent and with regard to specific aspects of the relationship. In addition, it means that trusting another person leads to acting *as if* the other person was trustworthy, therefore, granting that person a certain amount of trust.

Granting functional trust on a political level would mean that both the Government of Serbia and the Government of Kosovo engage in talks as equal parties and recognize the affordances of cooperation. Procedurally, functional trust might entail identifying zones of possible agreement (ZOPAs) and restricting cooperation to those zones for the time being. Measures on a political and institutional level, like supporting each other in securing the rule of law in North Kosovo and establishing good neighborly relations by concluding trade, customs, and transport agreements (see Kosovo and Serbia After the ICJ Opinion, 2010), could serve as preconditions to building mutual confidence in the daily-based face-to-face communication of individuals.

In sum, exclusive trust underlies an unintentional trust-building process. People develop an exclusive trust relationship for various reasons: they identify shared goals and values over time; they have shared common experiences; and this developed mutual understanding enables parties to substitute for each other. And since this is unintentional, it cannot be enforced. Changing negative trust requires an enormous effort and this kind of trust can at best be modified into a functional trust relationship. Functional trust is the only type of trust based heavily on rational thinking, or a calculative approach (see Smith & Schwegler, 2010). Furthermore, it is the only type of trust that can be consciously initiated, developed, maintained, and improved. Consequently, it is the type of trust that can also be trained and cultivated.

5.4 Four Stages of Trust

Schwegler (2008) developed a model of the prototypical process of trust building within a cross-cultural context. Within cross-cultural situations, relationships may have to pass through four stages: confrontation, construction, constitution, and consolidation. At all steps of the process, the most crucial question is how individuals deal with

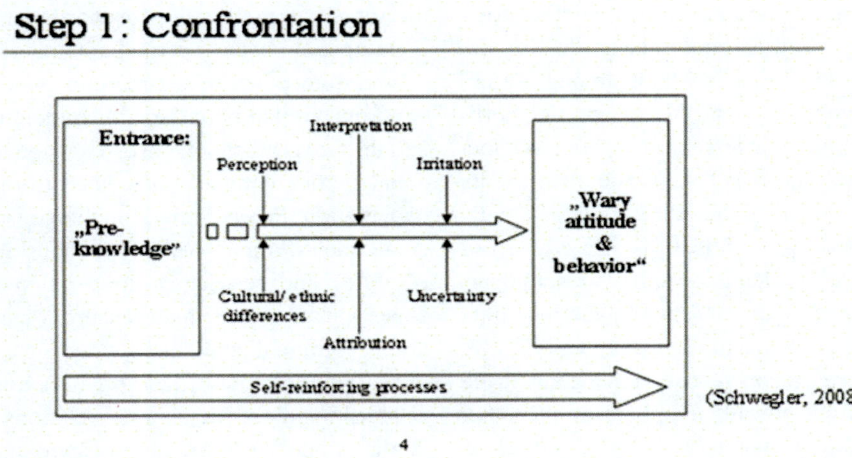

Fig. 14.5 Four stages of trust: Step one confrontation

perceived (both individually constructed and group-based) cultural differences (Fig. 14.5).

At the first stage, *confrontation*, individuals enter a new cultural context – or even meet with partners, colleagues, or any person from a different culture. The model assumes that people at this stage feel highly insecure when confronted with cultural differences. This insecurity can be due to the perceived unfamiliar behavior of others, or because the individual's own norms and values seem to be questioned, or simply because the individual does not to function well in the intercultural situation. While almost all – if not all – models of trust-building processes start at a neutral or zero point, this model, in contrast, assumes that when people enter an intercultural situation, they already have a relatively clear and fixed predisposition to the members of the other culture in their minds. People bring to interactions their ideas about this "generalized other" which influence the way they think, feel, and behave in concrete situations. At this stage, one assumption is in line with the social categorization theory discussed earlier: When individuals are viewed as representatives of a social group, interpersonal and intergroup interactions fuse so that the affect and beliefs associated with that social group influence interpersonal interactions with specific group members (cf. Fiske & Neuberg, 1990; Williams, 2001).

Accordingly, when meeting a person from another cultural background, individuals feel that they already "know" something about this person, even if they have never met before. This may be problematic, especially if these predispositions about the other have a negative bias. Such categorization processes are likely to influence trust development, because beliefs about trustworthiness are often associated with social group membership. For instance, people usually hold positive perceptions of fellow group members' trustworthiness. In contrast, people of one group often believe that members of the different group are less trustworthy than members of their own group (Williams, 2001, p. 377). This distrust mind-set was especially apparent during the Troika meetings in late 2007, when the Serbian representatives felt they were being trapped into the inevitability of Kosovo independence (Weller, 2008b) (Fig. 14.6).

The second stage of trust development, *construction*, reveals how people may react. Since the feeling of insecurity can lead to a restricted ability to act or behave competently, individuals have to choose a coping strategy in order to regain cognitive, emotional, and behavioral security. The research shows (Schwegler, 2008) that most respondents choose between two coping strategies: Either they try to reinforce perceived cultural or ethnic differences and go on, for example,

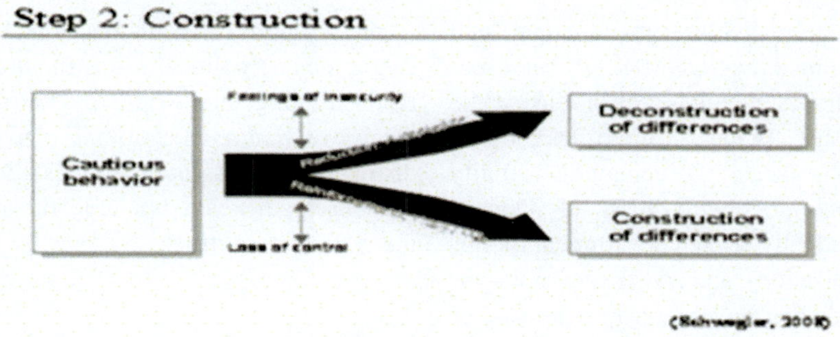

Fig. 14.6 Four stages of trust: Step two construction

to categorize people oppositionally into "them" and "us." Or they try to reduce the perceived cultural and ethnic differences by adapting to the new situation. In the latter case, they will open their minds to new thoughts, ideas, or social interaction in intercultural communication. Actually, both of these strategies will lead to more security. However, the adaptation coping strategy offers more positive, productive possibilities. Here, individuals search actively for common or shared meanings, and they look for areas of mutual benefit, or ZOPAs, to bridge the gap to the other person.

Stage three, *constitution*, describes the consequences for the development of trust. The *strategy of reinforcement* of perceived cultural and ethnic differences (us-them) appears to lead to negative trust in most relationships. If people believe in the "us-them" differentiation, they will likely hold on to their ideas about "the other" as not being trustworthy and are vigilant for signs confirming their expectations and beliefs. It creates a downward spiral that is difficult to break. These downward spirals involve self-fulfilling prophecies (Merton, 1948). The resulting dynamic can be problematic for both parties, confirming their assumption about the other as not trustworthy. The *strategy of adaptation*, however, not only avoids negative trust building, but may also lead to the formation of functional, if not exclusive, trust. It creates an upward spiral where individuals actively look for positive alternative explanations for the outgroup member's behavior (Heider, 1958).

The fourth stage of trust development, *consolidation*, explains how these dispositions are reinforced via a process of consolidation of the categorization processes, preferred strategies, and the distinct trust types that have emerged. At this level of the trust-building process, individuals stick to their dispositions about the other in general; they believe either in the trustworthiness or untrustworthiness of the other. Any modification of the established and relatively stable dispositions about the other requires an intervention by third parties and the willingness of both parties involved to modify predispositions.

6 From Distrust to Trust: Policy Recommendations for Reconciliation in Kosovo

The conflict situation in Kosovo has been described as "intractable." Two ethnic groups with charged identity narratives handed down and reinforced for generations (Nikolic-Ristanovic, 2008, p. 108). Significant ingroup–outgroup barriers exist that serve to legitimize hate and violence toward the *Other*; "Eight years after the end of the war, Kosovo's ethnic communities remain suspicious of each other and largely uncertain about the future" (Malazogu, 2009, p. 3). It is clear from the competing ethnic identity narratives and the generationally intrinsic negative trust in the Kosovo situation that fundamental changes must occur if peace is to be achieved. These changes will need to occur at the societal, institutional, community, and individual levels. Some would argue, and indeed have claimed, that UNMIK has been succeeding in their peace-building efforts using the dominant standards for measuring success: nonrecurrence of war (security), economic stability (often via economic liberalization, cf. Donais, 2009), democratically elected government (political institutionalization), and addressing root societal causes (reducing poverty, promoting rule of law, lowering unemployment, etc., cf. Call, 2008). However, it is certainly possible to pursue peace based on any of these standards without developing interethnic trust that leads to reconciliation. And the peace that we procure in the absence of trust will be very tenuous at best. At times, the way we go about rebuilding post-conflict political institutions and physical infrastructure often undermines the process of ethnic reconciliation. Whereas the process of peace building requires a "sincere and objective commitment from outsiders" (Abiew & Keating, 1999, p. 92), the process of ethnic reconciliation requires a sincere and objective commitment from the internal, affected parties.

Moving from conflict to peace via reconciliation in Kosovo will require a transformational process. It will need to be a process that "embraces economic, social, cultural, political, and humanitarian issues and goes beyond the absence of violence to include notions of sustainable development and social justice" (Abiew & Keating, 1999, p. 82). Clearly, ethnic identities are not easily reducible to such common denominators as economic relationships or party affiliations (Conces, 2002). In order to reconcile, groups must transition from reciprocal conflict to peaceful coexistence and mutual acceptance; in some rare cases, reconciliation can lead to reciprocal trust and support for attainment of material and social reinforcement (Malloy, 2008, p. 346). "Indeed, the trust that oils political institutions is often also an issue of trust across ethnic boundaries. And that, in turn, reflects on the issue of reducing the salience of ethnicity, creating small arenas where trust can be generated" (Simonsen, 2005, p. 312). Reconciliation entails the necessity of restoring civil society through rebuilding the relationships between ethnic groups, which is a much more difficult task than rebuilding economic and political infrastructure. It involves reconstructing ethnic identity narratives at the local level and re-categorizing ingroup/outgroup distinctions across communities. Each of these immensely difficult, but crucial, tasks requires the cultivation of trust.

6.1 Local Community Trust

Trust building and reconciliation are difficult to achieve as long as people perceive each other as representatives of the outgroup. It is our opinion that at present, building up a genuine interethnic trust in Kosovo is not achievable; "The resolution of even simple problems are too often dismissed [by the local communities] due to the high level of distrust between Serb and Albanian communities in Kosovo" (Malazogu, 2009, p. 16). Interethnic cooperation in Kosovo needs to begin at the local community level, focusing on pragmatic needs where step by step, a functional trust relationship across group boundaries can form (see Fig. 14.7). Given the need for utilities, commerce, transportation, education, and host of other daily necessities, individuals on the community level are most ready to invest in trusting cooperation (Serb Integration in Kosovo: Taking the Plunge, 2009). As trusting behaviors are enacted on the municipal level, an upward positive spiral will put pressure on the civic institutions and political structures to create an atmosphere of cooperation and put into place mechanisms that will facilitate continued peaceful interethnic relations. Unfortunately, local municipalities in Kosovo have a history of ethnic discrimination to overcome in the administration of utilities, education, and health services (Donais, 2009; Malazogu, 2009; Malgurski, 2009). We, therefore, recommend policy initiatives at the state level that provide opportunities for enacting functional trust on the societal level. Initiatives like programs already designed by the *Project on Ethnic Relations* (PER), Women for Women International – Kosova, Handikos, Kosova Organization for the Handicapped, and other like-minded programs (Malazogu, 2009).

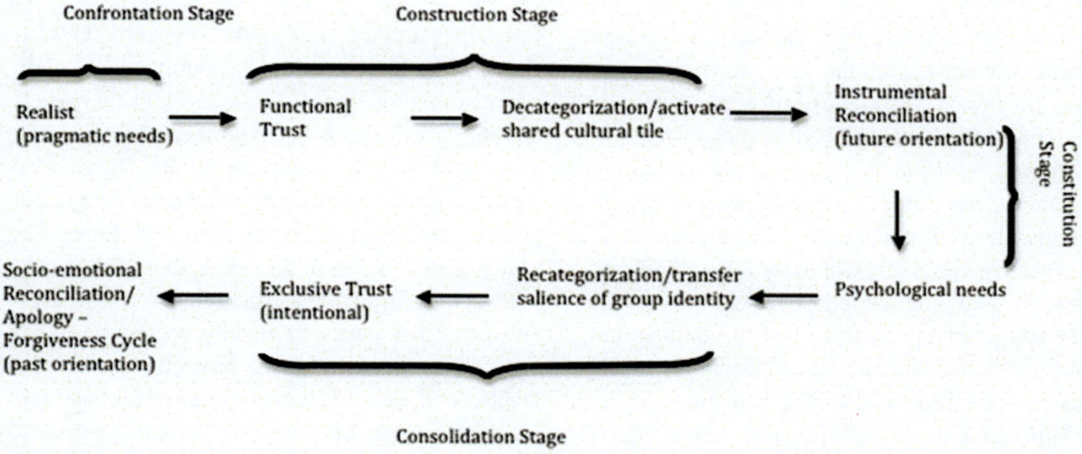

Fig. 14.7 Integrated trust-building process for post-conflict reconciliation

Programs that foster contact take place in everyday life, both at the individual and the group level, and may enable individuals to produce joint efforts with conciliatory outcomes. One peace-making gesture coming from Kosovo Albanians is sympathy with Kosovo Serbs who have to patronize the Belgrade regime while at the same time cooperating with the government in Pristina. According to PER dialogs, rhetoric alone will be insufficient to ameliorate old wounds; it will take stakeholder investments like these in municipalities and form relationships that demand mutual trust. The existence of common problems in infrastructure, utilities, agriculture, education, and health care present opportunities for cooperation and functional level trust; "recognizing that community needs will only be met once Albanian and Serb leaders work together on practical issues" is the key to establishing rapport and "future inter-ethnic integration" (Malazogu, 2009, p. 10).

The communication and activity at this early stage should focus on shared cultural tiles and de-emphasize contentious tiles. Local engagement should specifically refrain from addressing the divisive status issue and instead confine itself to ZOPAs where common identity tiles can be accessed. The approach to trust (functional-calculative to exclusive-intentionality) will depend on the individual's generation and degree of first-hand experience with ethnic violence (degree of negative trust). There are communities within Kosovo that have been somewhat removed from the violence and are more prepared to activate a shared cultural tile. These individuals could serve as *positive deviants* by acting in an unexpected manner toward the outgroup and could enact intentional trust based upon shared beliefs and values (Doney, Cannon, & Mullen, 1998; Dura & Singhal, 2009). Alternatively, segments of the younger (future) generations might resist dominant ethnic narratives and engage in socioemotional reconciliation immediately. In this case, the apology-forgiveness cycle will foster intentional trust as the basis for relationship and cooperation. Encouraging that cycle in the primary and secondary education system should be a primary objective. As argued above, it is our opinion that the current generation of Kosovars that experienced direct ethnic violence has no alternative but to build a rationally based, functional trust that calculates the rewards and costs of acting in a trusting manner.

According to our experience in Kosovo, in order to move from a *negative trust cycle* to a *positive trust cycle,* individuals must pass through the four stages of trust-building and social categorization (Schwegler, 2008). Thus, to get from negative trust to functional trust, alternative cultural identities must be encouraged. By strengthening one of these alternative identities, for instance, a demographic tile such as "feminine identity of being a woman," or one of the associative tiles such as "identity of being a teacher," individuals may recognize that they have a lot in common with another person (e.g., woman or teacher) even if this person belongs to a different ethnic group. If people are able to activate these alternative identities, which they already have, in dealing with other people who belong to a different ethnic group, salience for the demographic tile of "being Albanian" vs. "being Serb" may take a back seat in the long run. Interaction in controlled contact settings, such as enlightenment programs, problem-solving programs, contact programs, and skill-based programs (Stephan, 2008), may provide opportunities for initiating functional trust-building processes utilizing these shared cultural tiles. These programs will in turn not only facilitate the reconciliation process at least among a selected group of the parties involved in the former conflict, but may also have a potential benefit for the whole society.

Therefore, as the trust-building process allows and enables individuals to develop alternative ingroups over time, group-based categorization processes and differences may be "peeled away" and individuals will become able to recognize that which they share in common with "the other," that is, the others' humanness. "Instead of allowing shared commonalities to be overshadowed by differences… we need to dwell on the universal, that which unites us in the greater community of humanity" (Conces, 2002, p. 289).

6.2 SocioPolitical Level Trust

First, we recommend support from the governments in Belgrade and Pristina, as well as the international community, for interethnic dialog and interethnic cooperation. Specifically, this should entail facilitating decentralization and full participation of ethnic minorities in the election process and municipal government. These are primary targets for cultivating functional trust at the local level and should not be squandered. It is crucial that both governments advocate for common municipal structures. Second, the governments of Serbia and Kosovo should support an ongoing negotiation process at the state level where parties are able to engage as equal partners (Kosovo and Serbia After the ICJ Opinion, 2010). These talks may then consider models of shared or guided sovereignty in partnership with the European Union Commission in an atmosphere that eliminates administrative uncertainty at the local level (Karpat, 2005, para. 17). Finally, security must be a primary objective, for the protection of human rights, for the establishment of rule of law, and for the preservation of historical Serbian Orthodox Church sites (Ban, 2009; Kosovo and Serbia After the ICJ Opinion, 2010). As a conciliatory gesture, the Kosovo government should declare self-governing autonomous status for Serbian Orthodox Church sites as proposed in the Ahtisaari Plan, beginning with the 34 cultural heritage sites being reconstructed due to the damage from the March 2004 violence. "Every effort to establish a functional relationship will need to address the position of the Serbian Orthodox Church in Kosovo… Serb religious structures… form an integral part of the emotional attachment to Kosovo which has often influenced Serbian state policy" (Kosovo and Serbia After the ICJ Opinion, 2010, p. 18). As a return conciliatory gesture, we recommend that the Serbian government discontinue its support of parallel civic structures in northern Kosovo (north Mitrovica and north of the Ibar River) and encourage the Serbian inhabitants of the region to begin cooperating with the Kosovo government toward full structural integration.

As the International Crisis Report (2010) suggests, a comprehensive settlement between Serbia and Kosovo would have to encompass recognition/status, borders, minority Serb populations – especially in the north, and an agreement on religious sites. We do not believe that a comprehensive settlement is achievable under the current trust levels. We believe instead that the best way forward from the sociopolitical level is to facilitate and encourage an atmosphere of functional trust on the local level, to the degree possible, while the larger national and international issues are being negotiated.

7 Conclusion

In this chapter, we have examined the ethno-political conflict in Kosovo and offered a trust-building process for achieving a multiethnic state in what some have called an intractable situation. Given the recent decision by the International Court of Justice to affirm the legality of Kosovo's declaration of independence in July 2010, it is imperative that pathways to successful cooperation be identified and implemented (Crisis-Group, 2010). The UN Secretary General's office views Kosovo as stable, but tense, realizing that the current, precarious peace could take on "a momentum of [its] own, putting at serious risk the achievements and legacy of the United Nations in Kosovo" (Ban, 2008).

Reconciliation via functional trust building in post-conflict Kosovo is neither a very optimistic nor a utopian outcome. Nevertheless, the foundation of peace building in societies where ethnicity is a dominant marker is the cultivation of trusting, interdependent relationships. Interventions must address these ethnic divisions by reducing their salience if national healing is ever to be achieved.

References

Abiew, F. K., & Keating, T. (1999). Outside Agents and the Politics of Peacebuilding and Reconciliation. *International Journal, 55*(1), 80–106.

Allport, G. W. (1954). *The Nature of Prejudice*. Cambridge: Addision-Wesley.

Amir, Y. (1969). Contact Hypothesis in Ethnic Relations. *Psychological Bulletin, 71*, 319–342.

Anscombe, F. F. (2006). The Ottoman Empire in Recent International Politics-II: The Case of Kosovo. *The International History Review, 28*(4), 758–793.

Background Note: Kosovo (2009, 12/09). *Bureau of Public Affairs: Background Notes* Retrieved 1-18-2010, 2010, from http://geography.about.com/gi/o.htm?zi=1/XJ/Ya&zTi=1&sdn=geography&cdn=education&tm=819&f=00&tt=14&bt=0&bts=0&zu=http%3A//www.state.gov/r/pa/ei/bgn/100931.htm

Ban, K. (2008). *Report of the Secretary General on the United Nations Interim Administration Mission in Kosovo*. New York: United Nations.

Ban, K. (2009). *Report of the Secretary-General on the United Nations Interim Administration Mission in Kosovo*. New York: United Nations.

Bandow, D. (2009). US Policy toward Kosovo: Sowing the Wind in the Balkans, Reaping the Whirlwind in the Caucasus. *Mediterranean Quarterly, 20*(1), 15–30.

Bar-Tal, D. (2001). Why Does Fear Override Hope in Societies Engulfed by Intractable Conflicts, as it Does in the Israeli Society? *Political Psychology, 22*, 601–627.

Beary, B. (2008). Separatist Movements. *CQ Global Researcher, 2*(4), 85–114.

Bijlsma-Frankema, K., & Klein Woolthuis, R. (Eds.). (2005). *Trust Under Pressure. Empirical Investigations of Trust and Trust Building in Uncertain Circumstances*. Cheltenham, UK: Edward Elgar.

Bloom, J. D., Hoxha, I., Sambunjak, D., & Sondorp, E. (2007). Ethnic segregation in Kosovo's post-war health care system. *Eur J Public Health, 17*(5), 430–436.

Bradford, W. (2002). "With a Very Great Blame on Our Hearts": Reparations, Reconciliation, and an American Indian Plea for Peace with Justice. *American Indian Law Review, 27*(1), 1–175.

Brewer, M. B. (1999). The Psychology of Prejudice. Ingroup Love or Outgroup Hate? *Journal of Social Issues, 55*, 429–444.

Brewer, M. B. (2001). Intergroup Identification and Intergroup Conflict: When Does Ingroup love become Outgroup Hate? . In R. Ashmore, L. Jussim & D. Wilder (Eds.), *Social Identity, Intergroup Conflict, and Conflict Reduction* (pp. 2–41). New York: Oxford University Press.

Brown, R., & Gaertner, S. L. (Eds.). (2001). *Blackwell Handbook of Social Psychology* (Vol. 4). Oxford: Blackwell.

Call, C. T. (2008). Knowing Peace When You See It: Setting Standards for Peacebuilding Success. *Civil Wars, 10*(2), 173–194.

Carpenter, T. G. (2008). A New Era of Turbulence in the Balkans? *Mediterranean Quarterly, 19*(3), 6–22.

Casule, K., & Robinson, M. (2008, 12 March). Albanian Party Threatens to Bring Down Macedonian Government. *Reuters*.

Chao, G. T., & Moon, H. (2005). The Cultural Mosaic: A Metatheory for Understanding the Complexity of Culture. *Journal of Applied Psychology, 90*, 1128–1140.

Chua, A. (2004). *World On Fire*. New York: Anchor.

Clinton, W. J. (1999). Remarks Prior to a Briefing With the National Security Team and an Exchange With Reporters, *Weekly Compilation of Presidential Documents* (Vol. 35, pp. 519): Superintendent of Documents.

Conces, R. J. (2002). Unified Pluralism: Fostering Reconciliation and the Demise of Ethnic Nationalism. *Studies in East European Thought, 54*(4), 285–302.

Crisis in Kosovo (1999, January 20). *New York Times*.

Crisis-Group (2010). *Kosovo and Serbia After the ICJ Opinion* (No. 206). Brussels: International Crisis Group.

Crowe, D. M. (2008). The Roma in Post-Communist Eastern Europe: Questions of Ethnic Conflict and Ethnic Peace. *Nationalities Papers, 36*(3), 521–552.

Curle, A. (1995). *Another Way: Positive Response to Contemporary Conflict*. Oxford: John Carpenter.

Cvijic, S. (2008). Swinging the Pendulum: World War II History, Politics, National Identity and Difficulties of Reconciliation in Croatia and Serbia. *Nationalities Papers*, pp. 713–740. from 10.1080/00905990802230563 http://ezproxy.bethel.edu/login?url=http://search.ebscohost.com/login.aspx?direct=true&db=aph&AN=33826445&site=ehost-live&scope=site.

Donais, T. (2009). Empowerment or Imposition? Dilemmas of Local Ownership in Post-Conflict Peacebuilding Processes. *Peace & Change, 34*(1), 3–26.

Doney, P. M., Cannon, J. P., & Mullen, M. R. (1998). Understanding the influence of national culture on the development of trust. *Academy of Management Review, 23*(3), 601–620.

Dura, L., & Singhal, A. (2009). *Will Ramon Finish Sixth Grade? Positive Deviance for Student Retention in Rural Argentina.* . Boston: Tufts University.

Fiske, S. T. (2002). What We Know Now About Bias and Intergroup Conflict, the Problem of the Century. . *Current Directions in Psychological Science, 11*, 123–128.

Fiske, S. T., & Neuberg, S. L. (1990). A Continuum of Impression Formation, From Category-Based to Individuating Processes: Influences of Information and Motivation on Attention and Interpretation. In M. P. Zanna (Ed.), *Advances in experimental social psychology* (pp. 1–74). New York: Academic Press.

Fiske, S. T., & Taylor, S. E. (1991). *Social Cognition* (2nd ed.). New York: McGraw-Hill.

Franks, J., & Richmond, O. P. (2008). Coopting Liberal Peace-building: Untying the Gordian Knot in Kosovo. *Cooperation and Conflict 43*(81), 80–100.

Gaertner, S. L., & Dovidio, J. F. (2000). *Reducing Intergroup Bias: The Common Ingroup Identity Model.* Philadelphia: The Psychology Press.

Gaertner, S. L., Dovidio, J. F., Banker, B. S., Houlette, M., Johnson, K. M., & McGlynn, E. A. (2002). Reducing Intergroup Conflict: From Superordinate Goals to Decategorization, Recategorization, and Mutual Differentiation. *Group Dynamics: Theory, Research, and Practice, 4*(1), 98–114.

Galtung, J. (1996). *Peace by Peaceful Means: Peace and Conflict, Development and Civilisation.* Oslo: International Peace Research Institute.

Harzl, B. C. (2008). Conflicting Perceptions: Russia, the West and Kosovo. *Review of Central & East European Law, 33*(4), 491–518.

Heider, F. (1958). *The Psychology of Interpersonal Relations*. New York: Wiley.

Hewstone, M., Kenworthy, J. B., Cairns, E., Tausch, N., Hughes, J., Tam, T., et al. (2008). Stepping Stones to Reconciliation in Northern Ireland: Intergroup Contact, Forgiveness, and Trust. In A. Nadler, T. E. Malloy & J. D. Fisher (Eds.), *The Social Psychology of Intergroup Reconciliation* (pp. 199–226). Oxford: Oxford University Press.

ICG (2009). *Serb Integration in Kosovo: Taking the Plunge* (No. 200). Brussels: International Crisis Group.

Jost, K. (1999). Democracy in Eastern Europe. *CQ Researcher*, 865–888.

Karpat, C. (2005). Kosovo: A new state or a new bone of contention in the Balkans? *Global Challenges Research*. Retrieved 10.27.2010, 2010, from http://www.axisglobe.com/article.asp?article=495

Kelman, H. C. (2008). Reconciliation From a Social-Psychological Perspective. In A. Nadler, T. E. Malloy & J. D. Fisher (Eds.), *The Social Psychology of Intergroup Reconciliation* (pp. 15–36). Oxford: Oxford University Press.

Kosovo and Serbia After the ICJ Opinion (2010). (No. 206). Brussels: International Crisis Group.

Kramer, R. M. (1999). Trust and Distrust in Organizations. Emerging Perspectives, Enduring Questions. *Annual Reviews of Psychology, 50*, 569–598.

Lee, R. A. (2008, 02.17.08). The History Guy: Warfare and Conflict Between Kosovar Albanians and Serbs Since 1912. Retrieved January 12, 2009, from http://www.historyguy.com/kosovar_serb_warfare.html

Lewicki, R. J., & Bunker, B. B. (1996). Developing and Maintaining Trust in Work Relationships. In R. M. Kramer & T. R. Tyler (Eds.), *Trust in Organizations*. Thousand Oaks, CA: Sage.

Lewicki, R. J., & Wiethoff, C. (2000). Trust, Trust Development, And Trust Repair. In M. Deutsch & P. T. Coleman (Eds.), *The Handbook of Conflict Resolution: Theory and Practice* (pp. 86–197). San Francisco, CA: Jossey-Bass.

Luhmann, N. (2000). *Vertrauen. Ein Mechanismus der Reduktion Sozialer Komplexität*. UTB: Lucius & Lucius.

Malazogu, L. (2009). *Interethnic Dialogue and Reconciliation in Kosovo*. Princeton, NJ: Project on Ethnic Relations.

Malgurski, B. (2009). Should Kosovo Be Independent? (January 14, 2009), Web article

Malloy, T. E. (2008). Intergroup Relations and Reconciliation: Theoretical Analysis and Methodological Implications. In A. Nadler, T. E. Malloy & J. D. Fisher (Eds.), *The Social Psychology of Intergroup Reconciliation* (pp. 345–368). Oxford: Oxford University Press.

Mertens, R. (2000). Brick by brick, US troops build trust with Kosovars. *Christian Science Monitor, 92*(194), 7.

Merton, R. K. (1948). The self-fulfilling prophecy. *The Antioch Review, 8*, 193–210.

Nadler, A., & Liviatan, I. (2004). Integroup Reconciliation Process in Israel : Theoretical Analysis and Empirical Findings. In N. R. Branscompe & B. Doosje (Eds.), *Collective Guilt: International Perspectives* (pp. 216–235). Cambridge: University Press.

Nadler, A., & Shnabel, N. (2008). Instrumental and Socioemotional Paths to Intergroup Reconciliation and the Needs-Based Model of Socioemotional Reconciliation. In A. Nadler, T. E. Malloy & J. D. Fisher (Eds.), *The Social Psychology of Intergroup Reconciliation*. Oxford: Oxford University Press.

Newton, K. (2001). Trust, social capital, civil society, and democracy. *International Political Science Review, 22*(2), 201–214.

Nikolic-Ristanovic, V. (2008). Local conflicts and international interventions: Victimisation of civilians and possibilities for restorative global responses. *Contemporary Justice Review, 11*(2), 101–115.

Pancevski, B. (2008, 23 February 2008). Serbian Settlers Plan Partition of Kosovo. *Telegraph*.

Pankhurst, D. (1999). Issues of Justice and Reconciliation in Complex Political Emergencies: Conceptualising Reconciliation, Justice and Peace. *Third World Quarterly, 20*(1), 239–256.

Pankhurst, D. (2000). Unravelling reconciliation and justice? land and the potential for conflict in namibia. *Peace & Change, 25*(2), 239.

Pettigrew, T. F. (1998). Intergroup Contact Theory. *Annual Review of Psychology, 49*, 65–85.

Ramsbotham, O., Woodhouse, T., & Miall, H. (2005). *Contemporary Conflict Resolution* (2nd ed.). Cambridge: Polity Press.

Reuter, J., & Clewing, K. (Eds.). (2000). *Der Kosovo-Konflikt : Ursachen, Verlauf, Perspektiven* (Lizenzausg. der Bayerischen Landeszentrale fuÃàr politische Bildungsarbeit, MuÃànchen. ed.). Klagenfurt :: Wieser.

Riek, B. M., Gaertner, S. L., Dovidio, J. F., Brewer, M. B., Mania, E. W., & Lamoreaux, M. J. (2008). A Social Psycholgogical Approach to Postconflict Reconciliation. In A. Nadler, T. E. Malloy & J. D. Fisher (Eds.), *The Social Psychology of Intergroup Reconciliation* (pp. 255–274). Oxford: Oxford University Press.

Ring, P. S., & Van de Ven, A. H. (1994). Developmental Processes of Cooperative Interorganizational Relationships. *Academy of Management Review, 19*, 90–118.

Rogel, C. (2003). Kosovo: Where It All Began. *International Journal of Politics, Culture, and Society, 17*(1), 167–182.

Rousseau, D., Sitkin, S. B., Burt, R. S., & Camerer, C. (1998). Not so Different After All: A Cross-Discipline View of Trust. *Academy of Management Review, 23*, 393–404.

Schwegler, U. (2008). *Vertrauen zwischen Fremden: Die Genese von Vertrauen am Beispiel deutsch-indonesischer Kooperationen*. Frankfurt am Main: IKO-Verlag.

Serb Integration in Kosovo: Taking the Plunge (2009). (No. 200). Brussels: International Crisis Group.

Sherif, M. (1966). *In Common Predicament. Social Psychology of Intergroup Conflict and Cooperation*. Boston: Houghton-Mifflin.

Sherif, M., Harvey, O. J., White, B. J., Hood, W. R., & Sherif, C. W. (1988). *The Robbers Cave experiment: Intergroup conflict and cooperation*. Hanover, NH: Wesleyan University Press, University Press of New England.

Simonsen, S. G. (2004). Nationbuilding as Peacebuilding: Racing to Define the Kosovar. *International Peacekeeping, 0*(0), 289–311.

Simonsen, S. G. (2005). Addressing Ethnic Divisions in Post-Conflict Institution-Building: Lessons from Recent Cases. *Security Dialogue, 36*(3), 297–318.

Smith, L. R., & Schwegler, U. (2010). The Role of Trust in International Crisis Areas: A Comparison of German and US-American NGO Partnership Strategies. In M. Saunders, D. Skinner, G. Dietz, N. Gillespie & R. J. Lewicki (Eds.), *Organisational Trust: A Cultural Perspective* (pp. 281–310). Cambridge: Cambridge University Press.

Staub, C. (2009). 1991 The Acquired Rights of Kosovo. *New Presence: The Prague Journal of Central European Affairs, 12*(3), 55–58.

Stephan, W. G. (2008). The Road to Reconciliation. In A. Nadler, T. E. Malloy & J. D. Fisher (Eds.), *The Social Psychology of Intergroup Reconciliation* (pp. 369–394). Oxford: Oxford University Press.

Sukuma, R. (2007). *Managing Peace in Aceh: The Challenge of Post-Conflict Peace Building*. Paper presented at the The First International Conference of Aceh and Indian Ocean Studies.

Tajfel, H. (Ed.). (1978). *Differentiation Between Social Groups: Studies in the Social Psychology of Intergroup Relations*. London: Academic Press.

Tajfel, H., & Turner, J. C. (1979). An Integrative Theory of Intergroup Conflict. In W. G. Austin & S. Worchel (Eds.), *The Social Psychology of Intergroup Relations* (pp. 94–109). Monterey, CA: Brooks-Cole.

Terdevci, F. (2004). Uneasy Calm After the Storm. *Transitions Online*, N.PAG.

The Greater Serbian Ideology (1986). Retrieved 1-13-2010, 2010, from http://www.trepca.net/english/2006/serbian_memorandum_1986/serbia_memorandum_1986.html

Turner, J. C. (1985). Social Categorization and the Self-Concept: A social cognitive theory of group behavior. In E. J. Lawler (Ed.), *Advances in Group Processes* (pp. 77–121). Greenwich, CT: JAI Press.

Von Carlowitz, L. (2005). Resolution of property disputes in Bosnia and Kosovo: The contribution to peacebuilding. *International Peacekeeping (13533312), 12*(4), 547–561.

Waters, C. P. M. (2008). 'Kosovanizing' the Ombudsperson: Implications for Kosovo and Peacekeeping. *International Peacekeeping (13533312), 15*(5), 648–662.

Weller, M. (2008a). Kosovo's final status. *International Affairs, 84*(6), 1223–1243.

Weller, M. (2008b). The Vienna negotiations on the final status for Kosovo. *International Affairs, 84*(4), 659–681.

Whitney, C. R. (1998, June 25). France Urges Allies to Define Plan for Autonomy for Kosovo *The New York Times*.

Williams, M. (2001). In Whom We Trust: Group Membership as an Affective Context for Trust Development. *Academy of Management Review, 26*(3), 377–396.

Worchel, S. (1999). *Written in Blood: Ethnic Identity and the Search for Human Harmony*. New York: Worth Publishing.

Worchel, S., & Coutant, D. K. (2008). Between Conflict and Reconciliation: Toward a Theory of Peaceful Coexistence. In A. Nadler, T. E. Malloy & J. D. Fisher (Eds.), *The Social Psychology of Intergroup Reconciliation* (pp. 423–446). Oxford: Oxford University Press.

Worthington, E. L. J., & Drinkard, D. T. (2000). Promoting Reconciliation Through Psychoeducational and Therapeutic Interventions. *Journal of Marital and Family Therapy, 26*, 93–101.

Part VI

Central Africa

Ethnic Conflict in the Democratic Republic of Congo (DRC)

15

Tony Karbo and Martha Mutisi

Democratic Republic of Congo Chapter Summary

The Democratic Republic of Congo (DRC) is recognized as the second most ethnically diverse nation in the world. Karbo and Mutisi provide an account of the many years of ethnic conflict in this region including an analysis of origins and crucial events. Various probable causes and consequences are reviewed which provide impetus for the associated recommendations for obtaining peace.

Several factors are noted as contributing to the negative sentiments between ethnic groups in the DRC, including early political decisions regarding eligibility for citizenship of specific regions. The authors acknowledge the early existence of a shared culture between two of the groups involved in conflict and present perspectives that a mythology of ethnic difference has been created and perpetuated by colonizers, political powers, foreign interests, rebel groups and media.

Karbo and Mutisi provide some reasons for the continued conflict throughout several states, including and surrounding the DRC, such as the weakness of state government. Foreign and rebel control of mining operations are viewed as contributing to the poor economy, thus exacerbating government inability to provide adequate social services, and resources for redevelopment projects. The authors view the current sense of deprivation and loss of security as setting the stage for further violence and conflict behavior.

Descriptions of the dire conditions in which the citizens of the DRC live are presented and provide motivation to enact the recommended changes that the authors hope will finally end these conflicts. Proposed actions include international assistance to strengthen the government, create

T. Karbo (✉)
United Nations Mandated University for Peace
(UPEACE Africa Program), San Jose, Costa Rica
e-mail: tkarbo@upeace.org

M. Mutisi
Senior Researcher, African Centre for the Constructive
Resolution of Disputes (ACCORD), Durban, South Africa
e-mail: marthamutisi@yahoo.com

D. Landis and R.D. Albert (eds.), *Handbook of Ethnic Conflict: International Perspectives*, International and Cultural Psychology, DOI 10.1007/978-1-4614-0448-4_15,

security for citizens, address poverty, provide troops to cease current hostilities, and build a functional legal infrastructure. Internal steps towards conflict resolution are proffered, including peace conferences and challenge of the perpetuated ethnic mythology to engender civil society.

Cheryl Jorgensen

1 Introduction and Background

The Democratic Republic of Congo (DRC), formerly known as Zaire, is the third largest country in Africa (before the break up of Sudan), and has an estimated population of 70 million. Located in the center of the continent, with over 200 ethnic groups the DRC is one of the most ethnically diverse nations on earth, second only to India. Of over 200 distinct ethnic groups, (some estimate close to 500 ethnic groups), the majority are Bantu-speaking people. The four major ethnic groups in the DRC include the Mongo, Luba, and Kongo (all Bantu), and the Mangbetu-Azande (Hamitic), which together make up about 45% of the population.

DRC is endowed with extremely valuable natural resources, such as diamonds, coltan, (a mineral used in the manufacture of cell phones), tin, copper, and timber. Despite this abundance of natural resources and the potential for economic progress and national development, the DRC has unfortunately been the site of colonial domination, repressive dictatorships, and internal and regional conflict.

The Congolese population remains one of the poorest and most conflict ridden in the world. The fall of the Soviet Union ushered in a period of instability and unrest, in Africa, and elsewhere around the globe. This was due, in large measure, to the withdrawal of support for dictatorial regimes, including the dictatorship of Mobutu Sese Seko of Zaire (now DRC), who came to power through a 1965 coup d'etat. The one-party system, established after Mobutu's ascension to the throne, secured negative peace at the expense of severe human rights violations, political repression, and statewide corruption.

Following the 1994 genocide in Rwanda, a group of Hutu extremists migrated into eastern DRC. In October 1996, the Rwandan People's Army (RPA), entered into eastern DRC and in alliance with the rebel group "Alliance des Forces Democratiques pour la Liberation du Congo-Zaire (AFDL) commenced the insurgency that ultimately ousted Mobutu Sese Seko, who was viewed by Rwandan President Paul Kagame as supporting Hutu rebels. Of course, the AFDL had the sole objective of overthrowing Mobutu and assuming power in Kinshasa. Efforts to broker a peace agreement between Mobutu and the leader of AFDL, Laurent Kabila, failed and led to a situation which, in May 1997, forced Mobutu into exile, offering Kabila the opportunity to march unchallenged into Kinshasa. Laurent Kabila declared himself President of the Republic and renamed the country, Zaire, to Democratic Republic of Congo (DRC). Although the objective of the RPA had been achieved, RPA military units continued to operate in the country and assist DRC military efforts.

The DRC war has been described as Africa's First World War. A number of African and international actors were involved, making it a very complex conflict to resolve. It is estimated that as many as 9 African countries were directly involved in the fighting. Since August 1998, the war in the DRC has claimed about four million lives (Martin, 2009).

2 Understanding the History of Ethnic Conflicts in the DRC

Ethnicity is a notoriously complex and difficult concept. It is simultaneously imagined and real, a social construction and a powerful basis for mobilization. Ethnicity can be reflected through individual and community identity and frames of references, such as lineage, shared history, and common interests. Understanding the contemporary conflict and political crisis in DRC requires an exploration of the history of this society and an analysis of watershed events that created the country as it stands today. The process of historicizing and contextualizing the notion of Congolese identity allows scholars to understand the development and coagulation of ethnic tensions in the current DRC. Kevin Dunn (2003), for example, contends that the history of the Congo has been largely one of struggles over discursive narratives and representations of identity. The history of DRC is littered with violent events that have had extraordinary impact on the political manifestation of the country, and on relations between the various ethnic groups.

3 Pre-colonial Period

To understand events in contemporary DRC, it is helpful to explore how settlements by various ethnic groups occurred and the development of relationships between ethnic groups, even before the advent of the colonizers. First, the nature and extent of the violence in DRC are not only embedded in the history of the Great Lakes Region (GLR), but also reflected in the politicization of ethnic groups by the Mobutu regime. Whether or not people of Rwandan origin, or Banyarwanda (Hutu, Tutsi, and Twa), can claim Zairian/DRC citizenship has been on the basis of being native to Zaire as of August 1885, when the country came into existence as the Congo Free State (Nzongola-Ntalaja, 1999). Second, the conflict also emanates from the political decisions adopted by President Mobutu in 1972, in which he accorded citizenship to all natives of Rwanda and Burundi, who had settled in Zaire before 1950.

It must be remembered that Rwanda and Burundi were viable pre-colonial kingdoms that survived Western conquest and occupation (Nzongola-Ntalaja, 1999). Between 1959 and 1961, the Rwandan monarchy was completely destroyed. The Burundian monarchy was also destroyed between 1965 and 1968. Both the Tutsi and Hutu are a Bantu people who share a common Bantu culture and language. Both began emigrating into DRC at different times for different reasons. As in other parts of the world, the entire GLR constituted a commercial frontier for relatively powerful states like ancient Rwanda. There is historical evidence according to Nzongola-Ntalaja (1999), that in the eighteenth century, Rwandan agricultural colonies were established on the island of Lake Kivu. Lake Kivu now falls under the DRC, in the hills that were known as "Mulenge" between Bukavu and Uvira in the South Kivu province of DRC. Accordingly, inhabitants of this region call themselves "Banyamulenge." The legal distinction between the Banyamulenge and the other Congolese ethnic groups became academic after the Belgians took control of Rwanda and Burundi in 1929, as the League of Nations mandatory power, and in 1945, under the United Nations trusteeship authority (Nzongola-Ntalaja, 1999).

4 Colonization Period

Colonization in the DRC began with the advent of the Portuguese in the fifteenth century, followed by the Belgians. Edgerton (2002) underscores how DRC's wealth of natural resources was a pull factor for the French, the Arabs, the British, the Germans, and the Americans such that by the nineteenth century, all these external powers had interfered with the Congo in one way or the other. However, around 1885, the Belgians had managed to solidify their control of the Congo. Journalist/historian Hochschild (1998) documents the atrocities committed by King Leopold II during the nineteenth century, who not only plundered Congo's rubber, but also brutalized the Congoles people and wiped out approximately ten million people during the process. By 1960, the growing nationalist sentiments and agitation were too much for the Belgians. In May 1960, the *Mouvement Nationalist Congolaise* (MNC), led by Patrice Lumumba, won the first parliamentary elections; and the MNC elected its leader as Prime Minister. Joseph Kasavubu of the of the *Alliance des Bakongo* (ABAKO), party was elected president of the republic. Soon after the declaration of independence on June 30, 1960, under the leadership of Moise Tshombe, the provinces of Katanga launched secessionist struggles against the leadership of Kasavubu and Lumumba. The Belgians left Congo after 75 years of colonial rule, relinquishing the political rights to the people of Congo.

Three months after the declaration of independence, the alliance of Kasavubu and Lumumba fell apart, leading to the dismissal of Lumumba as Prime Minister. Lumumba refused to honor the president's dismissal, declaring it unconstitutional. The situation led to a serious leadership crisis, which Joseph Mobutu, Lumumba's new Chief of Staff of the Congolese Army, exploited through securing support within the army toward mutiny. Lumumba was assassinated in 1961 by Katangan forces assisted by Belgian troops. Several years later, in 1965, with the support of Western powers (principally the USA and Belgium), Mobutu overthrew Moise Tshombe, one of the several successive short-lived presidents in post-independent Congo, in a coup.

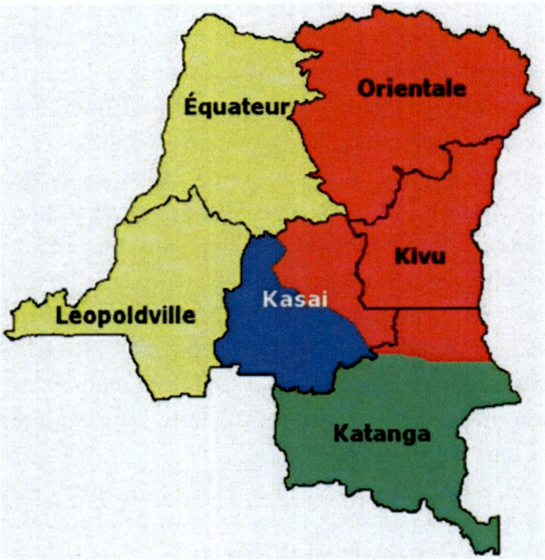

Fig. 15.1 Map of DRC provinces

5 Post-independence Period

Within a week of the power transfer, the army mutinied. Belgian officers and administrators fled the capital. Katanga, the wealthiest province, made several attempts to secede (see map of DRC). Sustained armed confrontation was, for the most part, limited to the secessionist zone of Katanga, where youth militia soon emerged to challenge the secession and the secession's links with Belgian and Katanga colonial establishment (Young, 2003). However, by the end of 1960, a rival central government was established in Kisangani, with its own armed detachments. A second separatist regime was proclaimed in the diamond-producing zones of south Kasai (Young). The deployment of a United Nations Peacekeeping Force of 20,000, managed to restore calm, although soon after its withdrawal, the state imploded, leading to the 1964–1965 Congo rebellion. The violence was perpetrated by small clusters of disaffected elites, who had no established political base and no political organizational experience (Fig. 15.1).

The Katangan secessionist movement dates from the colonial era. The movement, led by Moise Tshombe, was a major event in the course of the Congo crisis. The secession was supported by the Belgians and upheld by 6,000 Belgian troops.The southeastern state of Katanga holds some of the most valuable natural resources in the country. Business interests between the secessionist government and the Belgians intended the control and exploitation of gold, copper, and uranium. At independence, Katanga province accounted for 75% of Congo's mineral output, about 50% of total national resources, and roughly 20% of total government's budgetary expenditures (Young, 2003). Without Katanga, Congo would lose a major source of its mineral assets, and the revenue from their sale.

Katanga is also the home of the dominant ethnic groups of the Lunda, Baluba of Katanga, and Bayeke, who always claimed to be unfairly represented in the central government (Young, 2003). During the colonial era, Katanga province took an early lead in the development of an urban nonagricultural wage earning population that served as a basis for political mobilization based on ethnicity. Under the Congo Free State, Katanga had been administered by the privately owned *Comité Spécial du Katanga* until 1910, when its administration was transferred to a Vice Governor General (Meditz & Merrill, 1994; Léonce & Emitzet, 2003). In 1993, administrative reorganization brought Katanga in line with other provinces under the central colonial administration, despite strong resentment by Katanga's European residents. Because of the diversity and abundance of its natural riches, Katanga attracted a large number of Europeans and accounted for over 30% of the total non-African population in the Congo in 1955. However, only 7% of these (2,310 of 31,847) could be regarded as bona fide settlers, the rest consisted of temporarily employed civil servants, industrialists, technicians, and missionaries (Lemarchand, 1964).

As stated earlier, shortly after gaining independence, Mobutu Sese Seko (president from 1965 to 1997), with support from the USA and some European states (mainly Belgium and France), organized a coup that toppled the government of Kasavubu and Tshombe. The rationale for the US backing of Mobutu was that Mobutu was an ally of the USA in the fight against communism. In 1971, the country was renamed the Republic of Zaire.

Zaire's size and lack of infrastructure made it impossible to govern the country from Kinshasa. The center, therefore, over the years progressively lost control of the volatile eastern part of the country. Kivu, the most important eastern province in the country, became more integrated into the GLR than in Zaire. North Kivu and South Kivu both have large numbers of Banyarwanda populations. The relationship between *autochtones* tribes[1] and the (relative) newcomers has been poor (Prunier, 1995). The matter of citizenship had seemingly been settled by the 1972 law, which gave clear rights of citizenship to the Rwandophone populations of Kivu (Prunier). The law had been influenced by presidential adviser to Mobutu, Barthelemy Bisengimana, a Kinyarwanda-speaking Tutsi from Kivu, who was at the time probably the second most powerful man in Zaire (after Mobutu) (Prunier). Soon after Bisengimana fell out with President Mobutu, the law was redefined. The new law included new requirements for citizenship and essentially excluded the Kivu Banyarwanda. The new law demanded that in order to become a citizen, one must prove the presence of an ancestor on Zairian soil at the time of the 1885 Berlin Conference, when the Congo Free State was born.

Banyarwanda had migrated to Kivu various times. The so-called Bayabisha of North Kivu had lived in DRC for hundreds of years. The Banyamulenge of South Kivu had arrived in the mid-nineteenth century, fleeing from the feudal wars of King Rwabugiri. Then the *Mission d'Imigration des Banyarwanda* created in the 1920s had brought quite a number of people from Rwanda to work in the plantations and mines of what was then Belgian Congo. And finally, several thousand Tutsi had come between 1959 and 1963, fleeing the ethnic persecutions in Rwanda. Since they had intermarried over the years, it was extremely hard to tell who was a "native" and who was not (Prunier, 1995).

The new law was put into effect in 1981, although it did not have any immediate and direct political ramifications. Given the tensions between the Banyarwanda and their neighbors in North and South Kivu, the citizenship law became a major rally point for political support in the early 1990s.

By 1994, the Rwandan civil war had quickly spread to Eastern Zaire. In North Kivu, for example, the war evolved into a conflict between the *autochtones* and the Banyarwanda as a whole (Prunier, 1995). As the violence spread and the war progressed, it became a war between the *autochtones* tribes, the *Tutsi*, and the *Hutu*. By the summer of 1994, approximately 1.5 million Banyarwanda Hutu refugees had fled across the border into North Kivu. The local Hutu, both new arrivals from Rwanda and others who had lived here for years, experienced violence on several fronts, including fighting against the Bahunde and Banyanga militia. The new Hutus saw this as a great political opportunity and diligently sought to ally themselves with local Hutu in order to gain entry into Kivu society. The goal was to carve out for themselves a kind of "Hutuland" (Prunier, 1995). The creation of Hutuland could potentially be used as a base for the re-conquest of Rwanda or, if that failed, a new Rwanda outside the old one.

This new alliance was soon to be sealed in blood, which was given through the *rubanda nyamwishi* ideology that the hard-liners had

[1] Autochones ('native') is the name given to themselves by non-Banyarwanda tribes of Kivu in order to stress their supposed 'more genuine' rights to Ziirian citizenship and economic privileges.

carried with them from Rwanda, blood of the now outnumbered Bahunde and Banyanga, and the blood of the local Tutsi (Prunier, 1995). By late 1995 and early 1996, the violence had killed about 30,000 people, with over 12,000 Tutsi refugees fleeing into Rwanda, together with about 8,000 Bahunde and Banyanda.[2]

The chaotic situation in the eastern DRC, coupled with the total breakout of civil war in Rwanda, created opportunities for ADFL to oust president Mobutu and seize power in mid-May, 1997. According to a Human Rights Watch Report (1997), the rebellion was sparked by the government's move to strip the ethnic Tutsi Banyamulenge of their citizenship and drive them from the country. Even before the war erupted, the country was on the verge of disintegration. A failed Mobutu presidency, an unruly military, a collapsed economy, an unelected parliament, and the new trends in the discrimination and expulsions of Banyamulenge led to uprisings in the eastern parts of Zaire (Human Rights World Report for DRC, 1997). Because Rwanda was now led by a Tutsi-dominated government and because Mobutu had threatened to withdraw Tutsi Congolese citizenship, Rwanda's government seized the Banyamulenge uprising as an opportunity to disband the refugee border camps and destroy the *Interhamwe*. RPA troops took part in the rebel offensive, and the ADFL received military and diplomatic support from *Banyamulenge* and government troops from Rwanda, Uganda, and Burundi. This led to the overthrow of Mobutu, who fled the country when the Kabila-led ADFL marched into Kinshasa. The new president immediately changed the name of the country from Zaire to the Democratic Republic of Congo. Several months after he seized power, for fear of excessive influence and a possible orchestrated coup, he requested all foreign troops to withdraw from DRC territory. As a consequence, the Rwandan army retreated to the border DRC city of Goma, and established a new rebel group called the *Rassemblement Congolaise pours la Democratie* (RCD). The RCD was led by Tutsis who were determined to destabilize DRC. As a measure to counter Rwandan influence in the region, Uganda supported the establishment of a rival rebel movement called the Movement for the Liberation of Congo (MLC) led by Jean Pierre Bemba. Continued onslaughts on Kabila and his government by Rwanda, Uganda, and Burundi led to the intervention of forces from Angola, Namibia, and Zimbabwe under the auspices of the Southern African Development Community (SADC) allied forces. However, the military operations of Rwanda and Uganda, which started as counter-security threat measures, soon became distorted and dictated by economic interests. On July 10, 1999, DRC, along with allies Angola, Namibia, and Zimbabwe, signed the Lusaka Cease-fire Agreement with its belligerents, Rwanda and Uganda. By 1998, the two rebel movements had started what became known as Africa's Second World War.

In November 1999, the United Nations Security Council deployed the UN Mission in the Democratic Republic of Congo (MONUC) to oversee the cease-fire. Despite the UN intervention and a peace agreement brokered by the Zambian government, the conflict in the Congo erupted again and raged on, peaking at the assassination of President Laurent Kabila in May 2001. Laurent Kabila was quickly succeeded by his son Joseph Kabila. Once he had managed to consolidate his power, Joseph called for peace talks involving all parties to the conflict, including Rwanda and Uganda. A formal peace agreement between the three countries was signed in February 2001, and by April 2001, the MONUC was established, leading to the withdrawal of all foreign troops from the country. The conflict was reignited in January 2002 by ethnic clashes in the northeast, and both Uganda and Rwanda then halted their withdrawal and sent in more troops. Talks between Kabila and the rebel leaders led to the signing of a peace accord in which Kabila would share power with former rebels. By June 2003, all foreign armies except those of Rwanda

[2] Gerard Prinier (1995), quoted from UN Department of Humanitarian Affairs/Integrated Regional Information Network (IRIN), Situation Report on Masisi, North Kivu, Zaire, Nairobi, 26 February 1996; Human Rights Watch Africa/Federation Internationale des Ligues des Droits de l'Homme, Forces de fuir: la violence contre les Tutsi au Zaire, New York/Paris, July 1996; Doctors without Borders, USA, Ethnic War in Eastern Zaire, Masisi (1994–1996), New York, 7 November 1996.

YEAR	EVENT
1960 June	Congo becomes independent with Patrice Lumumba as prime minister and Joseph Kasavubu as president.
1960 July	Congolese army mutinies; Moise Tshombe declares Katanga independent; Belgian troops sent in ostensibly to protect Belgian citizens and mining interests; UN Security Council votes to send in troops to help establish order, but the troops are not allowed to intervene in internal affairs.
1960 September	Kasavubu dismisses Lumumba as prime minister.
1960 December	Lumumba arrested.
1961 February	Lumumba murdered, reportedly with US and Belgian complicity.
1961 August	UN troops begin disarming Katangese soldiers.
1963	Tshombe agrees to end Katanga's secession.
1964	President Kasavubu appoints Tshombe prime minister.
	Mobutu years
1965	Kasavubu and Tshombe ousted in a coup led by Joseph Mobutu.
1971	Joseph Mobutu renames the country Zaire and himself Mobutu Sese Seko; also Katanga becomes Shaba and the river Congo becomes the river Zaire.
1990	Mobutu agrees to end the ban on multiparty politics and appoints a transitional government, but retains substantial powers.
1993	Rival pro- and anti-Mobutu governments created.
1996-97	Tutsi rebels capture much of eastern Zaire while Mobutu is abroad for medical treatment.

Fig. 15.2 DRC events time line. Tony Karbo

had pulled out of Congo. Much of the conflict was focused on gaining control of substantial natural resources in the country.

An important stipulation in the 2001 peace agreement between different factions in the DRC was the removal of all foreign troops from the country. The removal of all foreign troops from DRC territory marked the beginning of the work of the MONUC (the United Nations Peacekeeping Force in DRC).

The 2002 massive violence was initiated by General Laurent Nkunda's Tutsi-dominated rebel group, which was fighting in North Kivu. Renewed tensions would be witnessed in 2003, and violence would soon erupt again such that in March 2005, the then UN Undersecretary General for Humanitarian Affairs Jan Egeland stated that conflict in the Eastern Congo was the greatest humanitarian disaster in the world, overtaking even the Darfur crisis in terms of death toll (Fig. 15.2)

6 Explanations (Causes) of the Conflict

6.1 Colonial Legacy and Imperialism

Like most conflicts in Africa, the DRC conflict is a replica of the colonial legacy. In the DRC, this can be traced back to the violent Belgian conquest in 1885. The end of colonialism was accompanied by a significant amount of woes for the continent, as first the Belgians left quite abruptly. After gaining independence, Africa inherited artificial borders that ended up aggregating different ethnic groups across borders. As if the border problem was not enough, the newly independent Congo was fragile, hence the overthrow of the first African Prime Minister Patrice Lumumba a few months after independence. A partial explanation of the conflict during the Mobutu era can be explained by US involvement for the stated reason of fighting communism. However, as Hartung and Moix (2000) note,

> U.S. policy toward Mobutu was rationalized on the grounds of fighting "communism" and Soviet influence in Africa, but the USA was clearly more concerned with securing its own interests in the region than helping foster a stable, secure, and peaceful future for the people of Central Africa. The USA prolonged the rule of Zairian dictator Mobutu Sese Seko by providing more than $300 million in weapons and $100 million in military training. Mobutu used his U.S.-supplied arsenal to repress his own people and plunder his nation's economy for three decades, until his brutal regime was overthrown by Laurent Kabila's forces in 1997.

As Guy Martin (2008) posits,

> Congo's predicament may best be explained in terms of its historical relationship with the West, based on political domination and economic exploitation and the pursuit by the West of a consistent and systematic policy of "balkanization" or "divide and rule."

6.2 Ethnicity and Distribution of Power

Historically, conflict in the DRC has always carried ethnic undertones. During the struggle against Belgian colonialism, Congolese ethnic groups argued about how they perceived an independent Congo, with some arguing for a more unified state, while others wanted to be independent. The tensions among various ethnic factions continued to present themselves, even after independence. Regions such as Katanga and South Kasai began to make declarations of independence, resulting in the creation of two rival national governments in different cities. The conflict in Kivu and in the Eastern parts of the DRC bears some ethnic undertones. This conflict is a replica of decades of interethnic rivalry and marginalization.

Some scholars have used the argument that ethnic identity fueled the conflict in the DRC, alongside other factors. According to Rotberg (2002a, 2002b), "The fear of "the other" that drives so much ethnic conflict may stimulate and fuel hostilities between ruling entities and subordinate and less-favored groups" (p. 86). Cheap labor was brought in from other regions, notably Kasai province, parts of Rwanda, and elsewhere to work in the mineral-rich Katanga. According to Donald Harowitz (1985), "the new mining towns of Elizabethville, Jadotville, Kolowezi and others, began filling with "strangers" from outside Katanga, predominantly Luba from Kasai, who were particularly receptive to European influences and social change …In both commercial and clerical jobs in Katanga towns, the Luba/Kasai were markedly more numerous than the Katangans" (Harowitz, 1985, 2005). Ten years before independence in 1960, the demographics of Katanga had been greatly altered with Lunda and other indigenous groups being greatly outnumbered by migrants from other regions. In several mining towns of Katanga, the Kasai Baluba, for example, outnumbered the Lunda by more than four to one. According to Harowitz, this fact was reflected in later election results.

As the nationalist sentiment developed, and as calls for independence grew louder, political organization in Congo, especially in Katanga, responded to the threats of Kasai Baluba domination in Katanga, by establishing a political party based on ethnicity. Thus, the Moise Tshombe party CONAKAT rightly described itself as a movement for "authentic Katangans" (Harowitz, 1985). Such a political organization was meant to draw the attention of Kasai Baluba; the real Katangans are

Lunda and Bayeke of southern Katanga. CONAKAT enjoyed a brief support from the Baluba of northern Katanga (a different group from the Kasai Baluba).

By this time, Northern Katanga seemed to be gaining increasing influence at the central government in Kinshasa, a situation which seemed to have pushed Moise Tshombe to call for secession barely 2 weeks after independence. Whereas the movement for secession was concentrated in the southern part of the province (an area concentrated by Lunda and Bayeke), and in the north, a separate movement developed among the Katanga Baluba (Harowitz, 1985).

The large number of different ethnic groups within and outside of the DRC does play a role in influencing conflict in DRC. Events in neighboring countries such as Rwanda and Burundi have, during key historical moments, impacted on the crises. As such, the First DRC War of 1996–1997 was intimately connected to ethnic tensions and violence in Rwanda, particularly the 1994 genocide, where according to different sources, anywhere from eight hundred thousand to a million Tutsis were massacred by Hutus, the majority ethnic group in Rwanda. After the genocide, approximately two million Hutus fearing reprisals from the Tutsis fled into eastern DRC. Baylis et al. (2007) argued that "The genocide in Rwanda was an indirect catalyst for the Congo Wars, as its events ultimately resulted in the creation of massive Hutu refugee camps that were central to subsequent events in the DRC."

Soon some sections of the Hutu refugees in the DRC began to regroup and re-strategize, subsequently launching attacks on Rwanda from the DRC. Historically, even the Mobutu government long had quietly supported the Hutus against the Tutsis and Banyamulenge. Baylis et al. (2007) comment that the move by Mobutu demonstrated how "…ethnic affiliations and alliances were far more important to all the parties involved than was citizenship" (Baylis et al. 2007). As such, the use of the Eastern parts of Congo as a training ground and launching sites for the Hutu *Interahamwe* is one of the reasons given by the current Rwandan government to justify its involvement and intervention in the DRC.

The deteriorating relationships between Laurent Kabila and his one-time allies Paul Kagame and Yoweri Museveni (presidents of Rwanda and Uganda, respectively) led to fresh Rwandan and Ugandan troops entering DRC. In early August 1997, Rwandan troops flew to Bas-Congo intent on ousting Kabila and replacing him with someone from the new RCD. This bold move by Rwandan was undermined by the entry of Angola, Namibia and Zimbabwe into the conflict. The initial reason for the entry of the three Southern Africa Development Cooperation (SADC) members was to assist Kabila under the common security framework of SADC. The intervention of SADC forces led to the withdrawal of Rwandan forces from eastern DRC, where literally, Rwanda had established a de-facto government of their own and controlled large portions of the region.

6.3 Economic Causes

Many scholars dismiss ethnicity as a factor in explaining conflicts in Africa. The greed and grievance thesis by Paul Collier (2000) and the theory of rationality by historian Lermachand (2009) argue that the ethnic differences among the people of Congo, are not the cause of the conflict, but that ethnicity has been used manipulatively by leaders and opportunistic individuals who seek to benefit from the immense resources the country was blessed with. Paul Collier's "Greed versus Grievance" thesis asserts that among the people who are most susceptible to the discourse of grievance are those who care most passionately about oppression, inequality, and injustice. Rebellion will attract as noncombatant supporters those who normally support protest movements. "The economic theory of conflict argues that these people have been taken in by accepting the discourse at face-value. As a proposition in social science this theory of conflict is a case of modern economics meeting old Marxism. As in Marx, the underlying cause of conflict is economic: in this case, the rebel organization is predatory upon certain parts of the economy. As in Marx, the "superstructure" is a set of beliefs which are false. The difference is simply that it is the *rebel* supporters who have the "false consciousness": they are gulled into believing the discourse which self-interested rebel leaders promote (Paul Collier, 2006).

According to Louise Watt (2010), "The conflict in eastern Congo is being fueled and funded by a tussle for mineral resources that end up in cell phones, laptops and other electronics." Reports from civil society organizations demonstrate how "elite networks" of key political, military, and business elites have benefitted from plundering the DRC's natural resources. Using this argument, Dearing (2009) charges that "Elites from the Ugandan People's Defense Force have succeeded in manipulating the ethnic conflict between the Hema and Lunda militias FNI, UPC, and PUSIC in Orientale and Ituri provinces, in order to maintain control over the gold-rich territory of eastern DRC."

Furthermore, the report by the United Nations Panel of Experts on Illegal Exploitation of Natural Resources and Other Forms of Wealth in the Democratic Republic of Congo (UN Panel of Experts) appointed by the UN Security Council concludes that apart from financing the conflict, the rich natural resource base in the DRC has also attracted foreign powers and multinational companies. The Panel of Experts singles out countries such as Rwanda and Zimbabwe as having benefitted directly from natural resource exploitation in the DRC. In addition, the ethnic conflict within the DRC is exacerbated by competition over control of local natural resources. According to Hentz (2004), "Zaire had always struggled with the mineral rich areas in its periphery: Shaba (Katanga), rich in copper; Eastern Zaire, gold, coltan, and agriculture; and East Kasai, industrial diamonds."

Indeed, the Eastern parts of the DRC are well endowed in gold, coltan, copper, cobalt, zinc, diamonds, oil, timber, coffee, palm oil, and tantalum. Tantalum is a rare, valuable, metallic element that is twice as dense as steel and highly resistant to heat and corrosion (Hayes & Burge, 2003). It can store and release an electrical charge, a property that has made it a vital material for capacitors in miniaturized and portable electronic equipment, including mobile phones (Hayes & Burge, 2003). In 2000, increased demand for new electronic products caused a tantalum supply shortfall, precipitating a rush of panic-buying and a massive price increase. In the DRC, this became like the gold rush into the World Heritage Site National Parks where coltan, a tantalum-bearing gravel ore, can be easily surface-mined with shovels and sieves. The mines are in rebel-held areas of the war-torn, impoverished DRC where internal warring factions are responsible for humanitarian atrocities, and neighboring countries have been accused of human rights abuses on an unprecedented scale as a cover for systematic exploitation of minerals (Hayes & Burge, 2003).

The prolonged violence and tensions seem to be spreading along areas rich in mineral resources; hence the human rights violations in these regions are directly linked with the extraction of these commodities. Such violence-ridden communities include parts of South Kivu province, North Kivu, Goma, Bukavu, Bunia, and Kisangani (see map). Responding to the August 2002 spurts of violence in Bunia, Ituri, the UN Secretary-General's Special Envoy to the DRC, Amos Namanga Ngongi, dismissed the primordial argument about ethnicity causing conflict. Instead, Namanga Ngongi asserted that "Everyone is convinced that this is not only an ethnic problem but also a political matter fuelled by economic interests." (Fig. 15.3)

In addition, the strategies of war and forms of rebel governance in the Eastern DRC do reflect a desire by various rebel factions to benefit from the conflict. Most often, the war is accompanied by looting and pillage of material resources to enable the fighters to finance the conflict. Most targeted resources include food aid, medical supplies, and money. In communities such as Ituri in the eastern DRC, foreign armed forces such as the Uganda Defence Forces and other armed political groups collect customs duties and other taxes to sustain their rule. For example, in August 2001, the rebel group RCD-Goma reported that it was raising approximately US$1.5 million a month, primarily through

Fig. 15.3 Map of DRC

direct and indirect taxes on businesses, and through customs duties at the borders with Rwanda, Uganda, and Burundi (Human Rights Watch, 2002). Similarly, UN Panel of Experts report (2001) revealed how the Ugandan army's economic strategy of "military commercialism" through exploitative taxation and unregulated import of Ugandan products largely benefits a few officers and business persons from Uganda and from the DRC, to the detriment of the eastern DRC economy. In addition, local populations have often been forcibly displaced to make way for mining activities by rebel groups or foreign armed forces. A report by Amnesty International (2003) indicates, how, for example, in 2001 RCD-Goma and Rwandese armed forces forced local people off a plantation in Kabati, Masisi territory, to make way for coltan mining (Amnesty International, 2003).

The economic aspects of the DRC conflict are manifested by pervasive poverty, massive unemployment, and ethnic tensions in eastern DRC. These situations are worsened by the presence of armed rebel groups backed by Rwanda and Uganda. A report by Global Witness (date) indicates that the government and the many rebel factions active in eastern DRC willingly exploited hundreds of thousands of adults and children in their prosecution of the war.

Furthermore, poverty among ordinary citizens in the DRC has tended to create situations of relative deprivation, a phenomenon that lures these populations into engaging in violent conflict behavior. Le Billon (2001) notes that

> as the wealth and power gap between the ruling and the ruled increases so does the frustration of marginalized groups seeing political change as the only avenue for satisfying their greed, aspirations, or expressing their grievances.

Dearing (2009) also recognizes the role of the international community in exacerbating the conflict and reinforcing the ethnic hostilities in the DRC.

> The competition for scarce resources by international concerns and multinational cooperations has also been a significant factor in the persistence of political instability and the continuation of the violent hostilities in the DRC.

By the international community, this chapter refers to countries and multinational corporations that are involved in the DRC. The United Nations and some scholars agree that the role of multinational corporations is extremely important in the DRC conflict. They point toward evidence of the unfettered access to DRC's natural resources by multinational companies and neighboring countries (Rwanda and Uganda) to the extent that the DRC government has lost any semblance of control over the resource extraction process. Although multinational cooperations do not necessarily sponsor and direct violence, it is widely believed that their complacency and indifference to the killings and suffering of war victims indirectly contributes to the protractedness of the violence.

6.3.1 State Fragility and State Failure

Strong states control their territory and provide public goods, while weak or collapsed states are unable to perform these functions. Failed states often have a decayed infrastructure because the government is unable to provide basic social services.

The chaos and instability in the DRC could also be explained by the impact of the state collapse on the emergence and coagulation of non-state armed actors in eastern DRC (Hentz, 2004; Kieh, 2007; Lermachand, 2003; Tefron et al., 2004; Rotberg, 2003). Zartman (1995) defines state collapse as "a situation where the structure, authority (legitimate power), law and political order have fallen apart and must be reconstituted in some form, old or new." The collapse of the state has become a contemporary development malaise and a challenge to sustainable peace, hence the following statement by Helman and Ratner (1993): "From Haiti in the Western Hemisphere to the remnants of Yugoslavia in Europe, from Somalia, Sudan, and Liberia in Africa to Cambodia in Southeast Asia, a disturbing new phenomenon is emerging: the failed nation-state, utterly incapable of sustaining itself as a member of the international community."

Using the example of Mobutu Rothberg (2002a, 2002b) posits that failed states prey on their own citizens by oppressing, extorting, and harassing the majority of their citizens while favoring a few political and military elite. Ultimately, the exploitation of citizens by rulers will invoke sentiments of resentment, hence the emergence of rebellion and insurgency. The failure of Mobutu's state in Zaire is one of the factors that precipitated the coup by Laurent Kabila.

The dwindling and withering presence of the state has led to a takeover by non-state actors, including religious institutions (Verhoeve, 2004; Ganguly, 2006). Such a situation confirms predictions by some analysts (Ganguly, 2006; Rotberg, 2002a, 2002b) that states that are in the process of collapse or have collapsed are highly susceptible to organized violent ethnic conflict. In addition to absent capacity of state governments to deliver public goods to its citizens, another defining characteristic of a collapsed or collapsing state is pervasive violence. In collapsing or collapsed states, government institutions are absent or nonfunctional in many or most parts of its territory, leading to and creating opportunities for insecurity and lawlessness. As such, citizens respond by looking for alternative means of security provision, usually relying on entities such as rebels, warlords, and local militia. As such, a failed state becomes susceptible to violent conflict and anarchy in some instances. Furthermore, Wright (2006) concurs with Rotberg, asserting that "when the state is unstable and cannot provide for its people, and when it cannot heed their grievances, citizens turn elsewhere for security, generally mobilizing along ethnic lines" (Watt, 2010)

This analysis explains why militias like FNI and FARDC are in control of North and South Kivu, respectively. The existence of multiple non-state actors competing for control and fighting over local resources has ostensibly led to more chaos in the DRC. As Rotberg (2002a, 2002b) explains, "failed states are tense, deeply conflicted, dangerous, and bitterly contested by warring factions."

Since attaining independence, the DRC's central state has never been able to project authority out to its periphery and to control its entire territory fully. Reno (2006) discusses how DRC has moved from Mobutu Sese Seko, being a paradigmatic example of an absolutist president who has engaged in state building to a status of a failed state. The weak government institutions, coupled with the state's inability to maintain successfully a monopoly on violence, expose the country to what Baylis et al. (2007) label "strategic entrepreneurs" or non-state actors such as rebels and warlords who go on to establish their own zones of control. In the presence of a power vacuum left by a weak, malfunctioning state, these non-state actors end up behaving in ways that challenge international norms (Yannis, 2003).

The developments in the DRC confirm Robert Dorff's (1996) assertion that in collapsed states," democratic institutions and processes can easily fall prey to the forces of uncertainty and fear, especially when there are indigenous actors ready, willing, and able to exploit human emotions for the sake of redirecting or killing democratic reforms (Dorff, 1996). The DRC case is a reflection of the experiences of many Third World states in the twenty-first century which are failing to provide human security and conditions for the rule of law. Since the demise of colonialism, the central state in the DRC has never fully controlled the entire country, and particularly regions such as Kivu. This explains the rise of many secessionist movements and rebel groups such as the Mai-Mai group from Bunyakiri in South Kivu, which vies to establish public authority and political legitimacy through breaking away. The failure of the central government to reach out to every citizen has subsequently led to the development of states within the state. Such rebel governance has resulted in the institutionalization of authoritarian and militarized forms of government. In addition, the absence of the state has led to pervasive human insecurity problems in the DRC. In *The Coming Anarchy*, David Kaplan (1994) warned that political unrest, environmental degradation, and corrupt governments, among other problems, are likely to draw a growing number of countries into anarchic violence. With a thoroughly weak center, DRC cannot provide the necessary elements required for the provision and promotion of human security. Even within Kinshasa, the capital city, the ability of the state to provide physical security and other human security needs is extremely limited.

6.4 The Great Lakes Regional Conflict Complex

A through and holistic analysis of the conflict in the DRC requires an understanding of the regionalization of the identity crisis in the GLR. The GLR of Central Africa comprises several countries, namely the DRC, the Republic of Congo, Burundi, Rwanda, and Uganda. The trans-border nature of the DRC conflict makes it intricately complex and protracted involving various identity groups in the region. No matter where the conflict emerges, conflicts in the Great Lakes tend to possess "mutually reinforcing linkages with each other throughout a broader region, making for more protracted and obdurate conflicts" (Center on International Cooperation, 2001).

Conflicts in the GLR have taken on an increasingly "regional" character. A conflict in one country has tended to become diffused and escalate, threatening regional security. When information regarding stereotypes about one ethnic community flows across one state into another, there is a high potential for conflict. Edmond Keller (2002), for example, states that new information about ethnic groups in one state whether true or not contains a high potential for conflict based on one or more forms of cultural pluralism. An ethnic group may potentially ally itself with transnational kin groups with the results being intentional or unintentional spill over, irredentism, or border conflicts. Keller goes on further to identify the roots of transnational ethnic conflicts, citing perceptions of ethnic groups that their security is in jeopardy at the hands of some other ethnic groups. When such a situation exists and the state is either unwilling or unable to mediate between groups or to provide them with assurances that they will be protected, groups that perceive a serious threat will at the very least be prepared for violent conflict, and may even go so far as to engage in a pre-emptive strike (Edmund Keller, 2002). Myths and memories of exploitation, discrimination, and violence perpetrated on one group by another drive the groups' further apart (Gurr, 1993, pp. 5–6; Keller, 2002). This was the case after 1994 when the Rwandan Patriotic Front (RPF) entered DRC in pursuit of Hutu extremists who were seen by Tutsis as posing a threat from their refugee camps in DRC. Tutsi ethnic entrepreneurs made certain that their compatriots recollected what happened at the hands of the Hutus during the 1994 genocide. These sentiments were used by RPF operatives in DRC to engage Hutus in DRC. This situation led to the escalation of violence started in 1997–1998 and only somewhat abated in 2001 after the signing of a ceasefire agreement and then in 2006.

Lake and Rothchild (1998) note that under conditions of extreme insecurity and ethnic distrust, the situation is ripe for a diffusion and/or escalation of ethnic conflict across borders. Fears are diffused within states and sometimes between them. When kin groups exist in neighboring states, ethnic conflict can either intentionally or unintentionally become transnationalized. Much depends on political opportunities as perceived by ethnic entrepreneurs (Keller, 2002).

Anthropologists and historians contend that the conflict in the Great Lakes can be explained by the political manipulation of ethnic mythology, specifically the ethnic or pseudo-racial distinctions between "Bantu" and "Nilotic" peoples (Malkki, 1995). Anthropologists and historians dismiss the notion of pure racial distinction between Hutu and Tutsi, arguing that these groups emerged as castes or social strata from within the same culture (Lemarchand, 1994; Maquet, 1961; Newbury, 1993).

In Rwanda, Burundi, and Eastern DRC, these Nilotic people were the Tutsis, while the short, stocky, and dark-skinned Hutus fitted the "Bantu" description. Colonialists came to believe and use the distinctive descriptions of these groups, asserting that the Bantu were "short, thickset, darker of skin, flatter of face, laborers, sons of toil," while the Nilotes were "regal, aquiline, tall and thin, lighter of skin, haughty," a process which anthropologist, Lisa Malkki (1995) refers to as "necrographic maps." Scholars further posit that the ethnic and quasi-racial differences were exacerbated by differential treatment of these groups by colonizers, who gave preferential treatment to the Tutsis, who were used as colonial intermediaries in the process of indirect rule. As a result of the differential treatment, during the colonial era the Tutsis were of elevated status, being pastoralists with lots of cattle and wealth, while the Bantu were mostly regarded as lowly peasants, who were oppressed and dispossessed. In contemporary Great Lakes conflicts, such mythology is given credence and "pervades all layers of society, affects many actions and dominates the thoughts of the average person in the street" (Goyyaerts, 2000) as well as interpretations by observers and scholars alike.[3] As such, despite its lack of substantive evidence, the Bantu/Nilotic distinction has become the central linchpin for ethnic mobilization and political organization, adding potency to a variety of the already existing conflicts in the Great Lakes. The lethal potency of ethnic mobilization has helped to animate tensions between ethnic groups in the DRC, Burundi, Rwanda, Sudan, and Uganda, among others.

According to Jackson (2007), ethnic mobilization and political organization based on ethnicity take on a regional character when ethnic stereotypes attached to one ethnic group in one area transmigrate into other countries, thereby filtering into the perceptions of others who may be disconnected to the original conflict and issues being fought for. Ultimately, due to the regionalization of the Bantu/Nilotic mythology in the GLR, the seemingly disparate conflicts are fused together to form a collective narrative of "mega-ethnic" cleavage between population blocs, thereby paving way to heighten highly localized conflicts.

In his etiology of the Great Lakes conflict, historian Lermachand illustrates the intricate con-

[3] Even journalists and scholars view the tensions as being between Bantus and Nilotes. Reacting to the 1994 Genocide, the New York Times deplored a "Rwandan Tribal war between Bantu and Nilotes." See The New York Times, April 10, 1994. Also See, "Tribal Lives, for better and for worse." Power, Jonathan. New York Times, May 25 2006.

nections between ethnicized politics, political exclusion, and refugee flows. Using case studies of Rwanda, Burundi, and the DRC, Lermachand discusses the linkages between the 1959 revolution in Rwanda, the 1972 mass slaughter of Hutu civilians in Burundi by a Tutsi-dominated army, and the 1994 genocide in Rwanda. Thus, events in Rwanda during the 1994 genocide have had lasting and unbounded effects in countries such as Burundi and the DRC. In addition, Rwanda's 1998 invasion of Eastern DRC has also increased anti-Tutsi perspectives and stereotypes, thereby reinforcing the Hutu–Tutsi fissure and the general Bantu–Nilotic divisions among other groups. For example, groups such as the Bashi in South Kivu and the Nande in North Kivu are groups regarded as "almost Rwandan" by many Kivu people (Jackson, 2001, 2007). However, anti-Bashi sentiments in Eastern DRC and their popular identification with "Rwandanness" or "foreignness" are notably exacerbated by the reality that the Bashi and Nande are of a more prominent and elevated status as powerful traders and intermediaries in the lucrative mineral business (Jackson, 2001; MacGaffey, 1991; Mukohya, 1991). Political elites and leaders have manipulated this Bantu/Nilotic mythology to mobilize support around their local grievances and interest.

In addition, the media have also played an instrumental role in deploying and dispensing the mythology for the purposes of mobilization. In Kivu, the hatred of Tutsis or those resembling them is passionately and virulently exemplified below by the written notice at a border post which was noted by researcher and scholar, Jackson (2007): "Attention Zaireans and Bantu people! The Tutsi assassins are out to exterminate us. For centuries, the ungrateful and unmerciful Tutsi have used their powers, daughters and corruption to subject the Bantu. But we know the Tutsi, that race of vipers, drinkers of untrue blood. We will never allow them to fulfill their dreams in Kivuland."[4]

Jackson (2007) observes how in Uganda, the Bantu–Nilotic mythology is also used to mobilize and galvanize opposition against the Museveni regime, wherein opposition argue that Uganda is a Tutsi colony, evoking the Nilotic origins of several of Museveni officials, arguing that they "disguise as Banyankole or Bakiga …" yet in essence they are "crypto-Tutsi." The attacks in Southwestern Uganda by the rebel group ADM, which had support from the late Zaire leader Mobutu, were influenced by the group's perceptions and conviction that Museveni is a "Rwandan."

In addition, the conflict in the DRC is also partially explained by the fluidity of the borders in the GLR. The DRC's borders are porous and its population diverse, and some of the Congolese major ethnic groups such as the Tutsi and Hutu also live in other countries such as Rwanda and Burundi. The DRC conflict is as much an internal crisis as it is a regional one. As such, during the 1998 conflict, Rwanda and Uganda supported different factions, each trying to protect its northwest frontier with the DRC.

6.5 Other Regional and International Dimensions

The conflict in the DRC was so burgeoned that it involved approximately a dozen African states, including Angola, Burundi, Central African Republic, Chad, Congo Brazzaville, Eritrea, Ethiopia, Libya, Namibia, Rwanda, South Africa, Uganda and Zimbabwe. According to Weiss,

> The was involved numerous African states in interlocking alliances which often appear to be motivated by only one principle: "the enemy of my enemy is my friend."

One major reason why the DRC conflict has continued to become protracted is because it has not received noteworthy attention from the important stakeholders in the international community. This is reflected in the level of commitment of the international community toward supporting peacekeeping and peacemaking processes in the DRC, including support of the MONUC. Until recently, the dispassionate interest in the DRC

[4]Notice at the Cyangugu/Bukavu border, 1994 – from Leslie Crawford, "Hutus see France as their Saviour," Financial Times, 27 June 1994, cited in African Rights, Death, Despair and Defiance, 1994:59.

could be partly explained by the notion that the DRC is not of prominent critical strategic national interest to key players in the international community such as the USA, Britain, China, Russia, and France, despite the country's abundant natural resources. Specifically, on the part of the USA, the skepticism of its involvement in Africa is based on a historical lesson which was learned bitterly when the USA intervened in Somalia in 1992. Despite these seemingly rational reasons for their cool involvement in the DRC, the failure to treat the DRC as a key international crisis has led to massive loss of lives as well as destruction of social, economic, and political capital. In recent times, however, DRC has seen a resurgence of interest from the international community including China and the USA, mainly due to its natural resources. The USA is looking to counter China's growing influence in Africa and where else could this be demonstrated than in DRC, where large deposits of oil, diamonds, coltan, and other natural resources are abundant.

7 Consequences: Possible Resolutions, Amelioration, and Prevention of Similar Conflicts

Efforts to end the DRC crises began to bear fruit in 2003 with the signing of the Lusaka Peace Agreement which led to the formation of a transitional government. Although this was the case, the crimes against humanity continued unabated, leading some members of SADC to take a leading role in trying to avert further catastrophes that would further escalate what others have dubbed "Africa's First and Second World Wars." One of the most serious consequences of DRC war was crimes committed by various factions against civilian populations. Crimes such as rape, sexual slavery, recruitment of child soldiers, and forced displacement have continued in the Eastern parts of the country in spite of numerous peace agreements that have been signed. Some estimates indicate that as many as four million people have been killed since 1998, with many more displaced, abducted, and tortured (International Rescue Committee, http://www.theirc.org).

In 2003, the Special Rapporteur of the United Nations Yakin Erturk referred to the situation in the DRC as the worst she had seen since taking up the office. A similar observation was made by the UN Special Advisor for the Prevention of Genocide Dr. Francis Deng. In a visit to the GLR between November and December 2004, Dr. Deng observed and concluded that massive violations of international human rights and international humanitarian law were being systematically committed by all groups based on ethnicity in the DRC.

A 2008 report by the International Rescue Committee estimates that nearly 5.5 million people have died in the DRC since the beginning of the armed conflict in 1998 (International Rescue Committee, http://www.theirc.org). Violent activities by several armed groups have continued unabated, causing insecurity, violence, and displacement in the east. These groups included the Rwandan Democratic Forces for the Liberation of Rwanda (*Forces démocratiques pour la libération du Rwanda* (FDLR), and the Ugandan Allied Democratic Forces and National Army for the Liberation of Uganda (ADF-NALU)). A small number of Ugandan Lord's Resistance Army troops were located in the remote Garamba Park area (United Nations, 2007). By late 2007, about 15,300 foreign fighters, primarily from the FDLR, had been repatriated.8 However, regional relations continued to be characterized by tension and mistrust. In 2004, Rwanda threatened three times to renew military operations in the DRC, citing the need to protect Congolese Tutsi and to counter the threat posed by the FDLR (United Nations). Hostilities continued in several areas, particularly Ituri, Katanga, and North and South Kivu provinces, where ethnic tensions were manipulated for political ends or control of economic resources in politically or militarily strategic areas. Tensions have since subsided after central government forces of the DRC, Rwanda, and Uganda participated in a joint military operation to wipe out rebel groups operating in the area in 2009.

According to the report, about 45,000 more Congolese – half of them children – die from hunger, preventable disease, and other consequences of violence and displacement every month. Over one million people have fled their homes within Congo as a result of the ongoing conflict. The report further states that Eastern Congo is perhaps the worst place in the world to be a woman. Used as a weapon of war, rape in Congo exists on a scale seen nowhere else in the world. Often successful in its intent to destroy and exterminate, rape as a weapon of war is causing the near total destruction of women, their families, and their communities (United Nations, 2007).

The 2008 Child Soldier Global Report estimates that 7,000 child soldiers remained in government forces and armed groups, including foreign-armed groups mostly found in the eastern provinces of Equateur, Ituri, Katanga, North and South Kivu, and Maniema (Child Soldier Global Report, 2008). Children were recruited from refugee camps in Rwanda, brought to North Kivu, and used as combatants, porters, guards, and sexual slaves. Children were recruited and used by all parties to the armed conflict for combat and support roles, and thousands of girls were used as sexual slaves. An estimated 30,000 children were awaiting demobilization from armed forces and other parties to the armed conflict at the end of 2003. National army unification and the national disarmament, demobilization, and reintegration (DDR) programs did not begin in earnest until 2005; some 30,000 children had been demobilized by mid-2007 (Child Soldier Global Report, 2008). Thousands of others, including many girls, were abandoned or left the armed forces without being officially demobilized.

However, some 7,000 child soldiers remained in armed groups and the Armed Forces of the DRC (*Forces armées de la République démocratique du Congo*, FARDC). Active recruitment continued in some areas in 2007, particularly in North Kivu (Child Soldier Global Report, 2008). Some 300–500 children, some as young as 13 years of age, were reportedly serving in newly formed "mixed" brigades in North Kivu in April 2007, and were deployed to fight against Mai-Mai and the FDLR (Child Soldier Global Report, 2008).

At the start of military operations against the FDLR militia in January 2009, more than 1,000 civilians were killed, 7,000 women and girls raped, and over 6,000 homes burned down in the eastern provinces of North and South Kivu. Nearly 900,000 people were forced to flee their homes and live in desperate conditions with host families, in forest areas, or in squalid displacement camps with limited access to food and medicine (International Rescue Committee, http://www.theirc.org.).

In an essay published in 2003 entitled "Covered in Blood," Human Rights Watch described the eastern city of Ituri as the "bloodiest corner of the Democratic Republic of Congo (DRC)" (Human Rights Watch, 2003). In spite of three previous peace agreements being signed, 2002 and 2003 have been described as the bloodiest years in the DRC war. According to Human Rights Watch, in early May 2003, hundreds of civilians were slaughtered in the town of Bunia and other parts of Ituri, with tens of thousands or more forced to flee. Based on the information gathered by its researchers and on other reports, Human Rights Watch estimates that at least 5,000 civilians died from direct violence in Ituri between July 2002 and March 2003. These victims are in addition to the 50,000 civilians that the United Nations estimates died there since 1999. These losses are just part of an estimated total of 3.3 million civilians dead throughout the Congo, a toll that makes this war more deadly to civilians than any other since World War II (Human Rights Watch, 2003).

7.1 Economic Consequences of the Conflict

As in all violent conflicts, the protracted conflict in the DRC has dramatically reduced the production capabilities of the government and drastically reduced the government's ability to collect much needed revenues for economic development. Consequently, the inability of the government to raise revenues through a functional tax system has led to a substantial increase in external debt. The dilapidated infrastructure and the political instability in the country have forced most business concerns to close shop and move to other places in the region, with Rwanda becoming a major beneficiary of such capital flight. Although DRC is one of the richest countries in Africa, it suffers from mass unemployment and lack of development. As a result of the protracted conflict in the DRC, the 2007 UNDP Human Development Report ranks DRC 168 of 177 countries surveyed in the Human Development Index. More than a decade of insecurity and violent conflict has led to the collapse of the economy, with the annual per capita income declining from $380 in 1985 to $120 in 2005.

8 Policy Recommendations for the DRC

Based on what is happening on the ground, the following are suggestions for policy:

8.1 Supporting State-building Efforts in the Great Lakes

Since state fragility and failure have been identified as one of the principal contributors to the conflict in the DRC, it is through interventions at the state level that significant change in the region can come about. Strengthening a weak nation-state is not only for the benefit of the DRC but is also urgently required to address the problem of security in the GLR. In addition, to address the plethora of post-conflict reconstruction challenges facing the DRC, it is important for the African Union, SADC, and the international community to assist the country to design a coherent state-building strategy so that a functioning state will be better able to support and promote any conflict resolution and peace-building efforts. State-building efforts in the DRC would encompass the strengthening of government, security sector reform, and infrastructural development in areas such as construction. A reformed government will also become more visible and accessible.

Corruption and politicization within the administrative apparatus undercut the state's capacity to collect revenues or use them. The DRC has one of Africa's weakest collection capacities, with revenues (excluding aid) amounting to just over 10% of GDP. Hundreds of millions of potential tax dollars are embezzled or lost. Hiring and promotions in the administration depend more on connections than competence. Corruption in the armed forces has been particularly detrimental. It has been relatively easy for higher authorities to embezzle their troops' salaries. The troops, who live in terrible conditions, in turn harass the local population.23 The army is itself a threat to civilians in the country, while the police are seen as a menace in many areas. Some steps have been taken to address the disease of corruption, particularly by local civil society groups, but much more needs to be done.

8.2 Economic Development Assistance and Poverty Reduction

In its 2001 report, UN Expert Panel on the Illegal Exploitation on Natural Resources and Other Forms of Wealth in the DRC concluded that progress toward peace in the DRC would not be sustainable unless the economic issues that contributed to armed conflict there were resolved. Similarly, this study recommends the improvement of livelihoods through economic development assistance in the DRC government and at local levels. This also requires first and foremost, the provision of humanitarian assistance to prevent the humanitarian catastrophe. In addition, the DRC government, together with business and civil society, should work together to address growing level of poverty in the country. It is pragmatic for the DRC to pursue a resource-aided and conflict-sensitive development paradigm. To do this, the country need not necessarily eliminate its trade in mining and other resources. What is required is the establishment of legal and alternative livelihoods for rebels and citizens who currently profit from the illicit resource extraction in the DRC. One way to do that would be through the localization of value-adding industries such as smelting and processing of minerals so that jobs are created in the DRC rather than be exported to developed countries.

First, addressing issues of war economies as a means to mitigate and prevent future conflicts requires in the simplest form a legal infrastructure that is centered on the protection of rights (human, contract, and property rights). To create such an infrastructure requires legal rules with accompanying institutions to enforce such rules. Second, it is important to bring to bear a robust governance system that is responsive to the needs and aspirations of citizens. Third, there needs to be a minimum standard of accountable leadership in the implementation of legal, policy, and institutional rules. This simply means that in its ideal form (an important qualification), the machinery consists of competent, ethical, and well-paid professional judges who administer rules that are well designed for the promotion of economic activities. The judges are insulated from interference by the legislative and executive branches of government. They are advised by competent, ethical, and well-paid lawyers (Posner, 1998). However, the varying contextual factors of different countries must be taken into consideration.

8.3 Addressing the Conflict Entrepreneurship in the DRC

Based on the UN Panel of Experts report 2001, the international community is compelled to help curb the illegal exploitation of DRC resources. Networks of illegal trade and fiscal transactions and beneficiaries of various forms of "rebel governance" including buyers of conflict diamonds and other minerals should be named, shamed, and prevented from conducting their transactions. Targeted sanctions should continue to be enforced on the elites and organizations that are benefiting from the illegal transactions and the conflict in general.

8.4 Resolving the Security Dilemma in Eastern DRC / Great Lakes

Since Rwanda's security dilemma in eastern Congo significantly informs the former's foreign policy toward the DRC, it is important to have this situation resolved. Uganda and Rwanda's governments have continually accused the UN and DRC troops of failing to control the rebel groups that occasionally launch attacks across their borders. Rwanda further argues that the presence of Hutu combatants in the Eastern DRC justifies its invasion of the DRC. As such, Rwanda and Uganda use this lack of security in Eastern Congo as justification for the invasion of Congo and subsequent interference in Congolese affairs and governance. Given such a background, the DRC government forces should be assisted to have the capacity to disarm the Hutu *Interahamwe* militias who are operating in the Eastern Congo. Thus, in addition to a more strengthened MONUC, the African Union could contribute troops to oversee the cessation of hostilities until such a time the DRC is able to provide security in this part of the country. After cease-fire, the Congolese army should also be trained and have its capacity for self-defense enhanced. A secure Eastern Congo would eliminate the chances of Rwanda and Uganda invading this part of the Great Lakes. The adoption of United Nations Resolution 1653 by the Security Council which acknowledges the regional dimensions of peace and security in the GLR of Africa is a significant step toward holistic analysis and comprehension of the conflict.[5] The peace process in the DRC has so far tended to be circular, fractured, and flawed. As such, it is important to revitalize this process by organizing a series of peace conferences for the Great Lakes as well as local level problem-solving workshops and dialogs with other local and regional players in the conflict.

9 Combating Sexual Violence and Human Rights Violations in the DRC

Since the United Nations has already developed a Comprehensive Strategy on Combating Sexual Violence in the DRC, it is important to see that this strategy is implemented at the national and

[5] The resolution was adopted in January 2006.

grass-roots levels. In line with the UNSC Resolution 1794 (2007), which requests MONUC "to pursue a comprehensive mission-wide strategy" for strengthening the "prevention, protection and response to sexual violence," stakeholders such as NGOs, CSOs, government, and regional bodies should be extensively involved in implementation, monitoring, and evaluation of this strategy.

9.1 Rewriting History

The DRC case aptly illustrates the case of a politically controlled process of memory-making that inhibits sustainable reconciliation. As such, academics and journalists must continue publicly to challenge and interrogate the Nilotic–Bantu mythology because giving it space will serve to reinforce and justify existing differences and race-based distinctions in the GLR. Scholars and journalists should play a helpful role by demystifying the much unsubstantiated Nilotic/Bantu hypothesis because "To reassert the salience of ethnic identity in conflict risks appearing to swing the pendulum back to primordialism" (Jackson, 2007).

9.1.1 Supporting De-ethnicized Civil Society in the Great Lakes

Although civil society is a well-recognized actor in peace building, sometimes the ethnic fractionalization of this entity can pose threats to ethnic healing. As such, it is important for the international community and development community to support de-ethnicized civil society, which will bridge the divide between various groups.

9.1.2 Media Reform for Peace

Since the media have been instrumental in spreading ethnic mythology, it is through media reform that ethnic stereotypes and hate language can be combated. Peace broadcasting and printing could be used to counter efforts of hate media.

9.1.3 Increasing United Nations and African Union Oversight

One factor that makes the DRC such a lethal war zone is that the UN peacekeeping Mission MONUC is largely ineffective in its operations because of inadequate resource endowment. An ill-equipped peacekeeping mission dulls the prospects of sustainable peace. As such, it is important for the United Nations to increase funding for MONUC and other United Nations agencies in the DRC so that they can effectively deliver their mandate. In addition, such bodies like the African Union should assist the United Nations and the DRC government to regulate the trade in natural resources and mining processes by providing guidelines and sanctions that would encourage diligence for observing the said guidelines. Entities that directly and indirectly contribute to human rights abuses in the DRC should also be made accountable so as to prevent further humanitarian catastrophes in this conflict.

10 Summary and Conclusions

As the conflict in the eastern DRC rages on, it appears that the long-term prospects for peace and democracy in the country are dim. The DRC remains an unstable and troubled nation requiring concerted efforts from within and without the country. The then United Nations Secretary-General Kofi Annan had stated in the year 2001, "One of the biggest challenges facing the Africa and the UN is the challenge of bringing peace and stability to DRC." Ten years later, the challenge continues to occupy centre stage as it did more than ten years ago. The country now has a democratically elected government, but insecurity continues to affect most parts of the east. Since the beginning of the conflict, in 1998, millions of people have been killed, unaccounted for, injured, and millions of others displaced. The conflict had shattered the economy and virtually destroyed infrastructure with decades of mismanagement and authoritarian and corrupt rule. Health and educational services too have been severely affected. The persistent conditions provide enough evidence that recovery from conflict in the DRC can take many years.

The problems associated with ethnicity and power distribution have an immediate impact on the humanitarian situation. Ultimately, the spirit of nation not ethnic groups must rule if positive steps are to be taken to turn the situation around. To avoid the return of the conflict, the reconstruction process has to accompany initiatives to contain violence. The DRC needs international assistance in order to recover from its insecurity and economic malaise and to ensure that the fruits of the development are distributed equitably.

References

Adelman, H., & Raof, G. C. (Eds.). (2004). *War and peace in Zaire/Congo: Analyzing and evaluating intervention: 1996–1997*. Trenton, NJ: Africa World Press.

Amnesty International. (2003). A Past the Hunts the Future; April 8, 2003 obtained from www.amnesty.org/en /library/info/POL/10/003/2003/en.

Baylis, J., et al. (2007). All against all: The conflict in the Congo. In J. Baylis et al. (Eds.), *Strategy in the contemporary World*. Oxford: Oxford University press.

Braathen, E., Boas, M., & Saether, G. (Eds.). (2001). *Ethnicity Kills: The politics of war, peace and ethnicity in SubSaharan Africa*. New York, NY: Zed Books.

Child Soldier Global Report. (2008). *Coalition to stop the use of child soldiers*. http://www.childsoldiersglobalreport.org.

Collier, P. (2006). *Economic causes of civil conflict and their implications for policy*. Oxford: Department of Economics, Oxford University.

Collier, P., & Hoeffler, A. (2000). Greed and grievance in Civil War. Policy Research Working Paper no. 2355, Washington, DC: The World Bank, 2001. In M. Berdal & D. M. Malone (Eds.), *Greed and grievance: Economic agendas in civil wars*. Boulder, CO: Lynne Rienner Publishers.

Collier, P., et al. (Eds.). (2003). *Breaking the conflict trap: Civil war and development policy*. Washington, DC: World Bank and Oxford University Press.

Cramer, C., & Goodhand, J. (2002). Try again, fail again, FAIL better? War, the state, and the 'post-conflict' challenge in Afghanistan. *Development and Change, 33*, 885–909.

De Boeck, F. (1996). Postcolonialism, power and identity: local and global perspectives from Zaire. In R. P. Werbner & T. O. Ranger (Eds.), *Postcolonial identities in Africa*. London: Zed Books.

Dearing, C. (2009). A global approach to regulating trade in conflict goods in the DRC. *International Affairs Review, 1(3)*, 5.

Doornbos, M. (2002). State collapse and fresh starts: Some critical reflections. *Development and Change, 33*, 797–815.

Dorff, R. H. (1996). Democratization and failed states: The challenge of ungovernability. *Parameters*, Summer, 17–31.

Duffield, M. (2001). *Global governance and the new wars. The merging of development and security*. London: Zed Books.

Dunn, K. (2003). *Imagining the Congo: The international relations of identity*. Hampshire: Palgrave Macmillan.

Edgerton, R. (2002). *The troubled heart of Africa: A history of the Congo*. New York, NY: St. Martin's Press.

Edmond J. KELLER, Polis / R.C.S.P. / C.P.S.R. Vol. 9, Numéro Spécial, 2002.

Ganguly, R. (2006). *State collapse and ethnic conflict: evidence from afghanistan and the democratic Republic of Congo*. Paper presented at the annual meeting of the International Studies Association, Town & Country Resort and Convention Center, San Diego, California, USA.

Gondola, D. (2002). *The history of Congo*. Westport, CT: Greenwood Press.

Goyyaerts, D. (Ed.). (2000). *Conflict and ethnicity in Central Africa. Institute for the Study of Languages and Cultures in Asia and Africa*. Tokyo: Tokyo University of Foreign Studies.

Gurr, T. R. (1993). Minorities at Risk, Washington, DC. USIP Press.

Harowitz, D. L. (1985). *Ethnic groups in Conflict*. Los Angeles, CA: University of California Press.

Hartung, W. D., & Moix B. (2000). *Deadly legacy: US arms to Africa and the Congo war*. Arms Trade Resource Center, World Policy Institute, January 2000.

Hayes, K., & Burge, R. (2003). *Coltan mining in the democratic republic of Congo: How tantalum-using industries can commit to the reconstruction of the DRC*. Cambridge: Fauna & Flora International.

Helman G., & Ratner, S. (1993). Foreign Policy Number 89, Winter 1992–1993, Washington DC.

Hentz, J. (2004). The obligation of empire: United States' grand strategy for a new century; Lexington, University Press of Kentucky.

Hochschild, A. (1998). *King Leopold's ghost: a story of greed, terror, and heroism in colonial Africa*. New York: Mariner Books.

Human Rights Watch. (2002). The war within the war: Sexual violence against women and girls in Eastern Congo. June 2002, http://www.hrw.org.

Human Rights Watch. (2003). Covered in Blood. July 2003, http://www.hrw.org.

International Rescue Committee. (2008). Mortality in the DRC: an Ongoing crisis. January 2008, http://www.theirc.org.

Jackson, R. (2001). The Global Covenant: Human Conduct in a World of States; London, Oxford University Press.

Jackson, R. H. (2007). Sovereignty: Evolution of an Idea; Cambridge, UK, Malden, MA, Polity Press.

Kaplan, R. (1994). The coming anarchy. How scarcity, crime, overpopulation, tribalism, and disease are rapidly destroying the social fabric of our planet. *The Atlantic Monthly February 1994.*

Keen, D. (1998). *The economic functions of violence in civil wars, Adelphi Paper No. 320*. Oxford: Oxford University Press for the Institute of Strategic Studies.

Kieh, G. K. (2007). *Beyond state failure and collapse: Making the state relevant in Africa*. Lanham, MD: Lexington Books.

Lake, D., & Donald, R. (1998). The International Spread of Ethnic Conflict: Fear, Diffusion and Escalation; New Jersey, Princeton University Press.

Le Billon, P. (2003). *Fueling war: Natural resources and armed conflicts*. Oxford: Oxford University Press.

Lemarchand, R. (1964). Political Awakening in the Belgian Congo, Chicago, Chicago University Press.

Lemarchand, R. (1994). Burundi: Ethnic Conflict and Genocide, Washington DC Woodrow Wilson Center.

Lemarchand, R. (1997). Patterns of state collapse and reconstruction in central Africa: Reflections on the Crises in the Great Lakes' African Studies Quartely, Obtained from: http://www.kcas.ufl.edu/africa/asq/legal.htm.

Léonce, N., & Emizet, K. (2003). *The economics of civil war: The case of the Democratic Republic of Congo*. Working Paper Series, Political Economy Research Institute, University of Massachusetts.

Lermachand, R. (2003). The Democratic Republic of the Congo: From failure to potential reconstruction. In R. Rotberg (Ed.), *State failure and state weakness in a time of terror*. Washington, DC: Brookings Institution Press.

Lermachand, R. (Ed.). (2009). *The dynamics of violence in Central Africa*. Philadelphia, PA: University of Pennsylvania Press.

MacGaffey, J. et al. (1991). The Real Economy of Zaire: The Contribution of Smuggling and other Unofficial Activities to National Wealth; Pittsburg, University of Pennsylvania Press.

Malkki, L. H. (1995). Purity and Exile: Violence, Memory, and National Cosmology among Hutu Refugees in Tanzania Chicago. The University of Chicago Press.

Maquet, J. J. (1961). The Premise of Inequality in Ruanda: A Study of Political Relations in a Central African Kingdom; London, Oxford University Press for the International African Institute.

Martin, G. (2009). Understanding African conflicts: Theoretical, historical, and contemporary perspectives. *African Studies Review, 52*, 149–154.

Mazrui, A. (1995). The blood of experience: The failed state and political collapse in Africa. *World Policy Journal, 12*, 28–34.

Meditz, S., & Tim, M. (1994). Zaire: A Country Study (4th. Edition); Volume 550, Issue 67, Pam Series; Washington DC, American University.

Migdal, J. S. (1998). *Strong societies and weak states. State relations and state capabilities in the third World*. Princeton, NJ: Princeton University Press.

Migdal, J. S. (2001). *State in society. Studying how states and societies transform and constitute one another*. Cambridge: Cambridge University Press.

Milliken, J., & Krause, K. (2002). State failure, state collapse, and state reconstruction: concepts, lessons and strategies. *Development and Change, 33*, 753–744.

Mukohya, V. (1991). in Janet MacGaffey et al. (1991). The Real Economy of Zaire: The Contribution of Smuggling and other Unofficial Activities to National Wealth; Pittsburg, University of Pennsylvania Press.

Newbury, C. (1993). The cohesion of oppression: Clientship and Ethnicity in Rwanda, 1860–1960; New York, Columbia University Press.

Nzongola-Ntalaja, G. (1998). *The current political and social situation in the Democratic Republic of the Congo*. Paper prepared for the Nordic Africa Institute, January 1998.

Nzongola-Ntalaja, G. (1999). Background to the crises: Crises in the Great Lakes Region. In I. Mandaza (Ed.), *Reflections on the crises in the Democratic Republic of Congo*. Harare: SAPES Books.

Nzongola-Ntalaja, G. (2002). *The Congo from Leopold to Kabila*. London: Zed Books.

Nzongola-Ntalaja, G. (2004). *From Zaire to the Democratic Republic of the Congo*. London: Zed Books.

Posner, R. A. (1998). Creating a legal framework for economic development. The World Bank Research Observer, *13*(1).

Prunier, G. (1995). *The Rwandan crisis: History of a genocide*. London: Hurst and Company.

Reno, W. (2002). The politics of insurgency in collapsing States. *Development and Change, 33*, 837–858.

Reno, W. (2003). *Sovereign predators and non-state armed group protectors?* Paper presented at the conference 'Curbing Human Rights Violations of Armed Groups.' UBC Centre of International Relations, 13–15 November 2003.

Rotberg, R. I. (2002a). Failed states in a World of terror. *Foreign Affairs, 8*, 127–140.

Rotberg, R. I. (2002b). The New nature of Nation-State Failure. *The Washington Quarterly,* Summer, 85–96.

Tefron, T., et al. (Ed.). (2004). *Reinventing order in the Congo: How people respond to state failure in Kinshasa*. London: Zed Books.

Turner, T. (2007). *The Congo wars: Conflict, myth and reality*. London: Zed Books.

United Nations. (2007). *Report of the Secretary-General on children and armed conflict in the Democratic Republic of the Congo*, UN Doc. S/2007/391, 28 June 2007.

Verhoeve, A. (2004). *Conflict and social transformation in Eastern DR Congo*. Brussels: Academic scientific.

Watt, L. (2010). *Mining for minerals fuels Congo conflict*. London: The Green Economics Institute.

Weiss, H. (2008). War and peace in the Democratic Republic of Congo. *Series Central Africa Issues* 22.

Wright. (2006). *Ethnic Conflict in the DRC*. An Electronic Briefing Paper. Center for International Political Studies 22.

Yannis, A. (2003). State Collapse and Its Implications for Peace building and Reconstruction in Jennifer Milliken (ed.) (2003); State Failure, Collapse and Reconstruction; Institute for Social Studies, Cornwall, Blackwell Publishing.

Young, C. (2003). Contextualizing Congo conflicts. In J. F. Clark (Ed.), *The African stakes of the Congo war*. Kampala: Fountain Publishers.

Zartman, W. (Ed.). (1995). *Collapsed States: The disintegration and restoration of legitimate authority*. Boulder, CO: Lynne Rienner.

16 Ethnocultural Conflict in Uganda: Politics Based on Ethnic Divisions Inflame Tensions Across the Country

Grace M. Kibanja, Mayanja M. Kajumba, and Laura R. Johnson

Uganda Chapter Summary

Kibanja, Kajumba, and Johnson describe the ethnocultural conflicts currently occurring in the various regions of Uganda whose population includes over 40 different ethnic groups. Broad reasons presented for these conflicts include competition for resources and positions of power which are traced back to colonial history when tribal divisions became more pronounced. The authors delineate the various conflicts for political power that have occurred since independence, and associated factors and consequences.

Social Identity Theory is applied to explore causes of increasing differentiation between groups. Ethnicity is presented as the socially constructed overarching identity to which individuals ascribe; however, beyond this tribal identification, three major religions are recognized as creating further divisions. The authors emphasize several dichotomous stereotypes which are increasing a sense of hatred between groups.

Cultural and structural theories are utilized to explain the contributing factors in the conflicts, specifically poor political leadership, kingdoms mobilizing in protest along ethnic lines, religious influence in politics, and competition for minimal resources. Attempts at resolution are analyzed in each of the major regions, and notable positive acts along with reasons for their failure are provided.

Benefits of ethnic identification are mentioned particularly with regard to mental health and social support, although risks are also noted. Kibanja, Kajumba, and Johnson suggest that optimal intercultural relations can be

L.R. Johnson (✉)
University of Mississippi, Oxford, MS, USA
e-mail: ljohnson@olemiss.edu

G.M. Kibanja
Makerere University, Kampala, Uganda
e-mail: gkibanja@muip.mak.ac.ug

M.M. Kajumba
Makerere University, School of Psychology,
P. O. Box 7062 Kampala, Uganda
e-mail: kajumba@muip.mak.ac.ug

D. Landis and R.D. Albert (eds.), *Handbook of Ethnic Conflict: International Perspectives*, International and Cultural Psychology, DOI 10.1007/978-1-4614-0448-4_16,

achieved by developing ethnic identity while sharing a common goal. Suggestions for change in specific areas are offered, and the need for research in order to achieve optimal results is noted. Obtaining counsel from community leaders and working within African values are presented as important steps toward creating group cohesion with appreciation of differences.

Cheryl Jorgensen

Uganda has struggled with ethnic conflict and political violence for decades. Even during the writing of this chapter, tensions between the central government and the Buganda Kingdom erupted into violence. In March 2010, the Kasubi Tombs, the Ugandan equivalent of the Egyptian pyramids and a UNESCO world heritage site, were burned to ashes. The government is being accused of involvement (Musoke, 2010). The following day, gunfire rocked Kasubi when protesters attempted to block President Yoweri Museveni's entry. At least three people were killed as the military used force to usher in Museveni to tour the destroyed royal tombs. Several others (close to 20 according to the Red Cross) were seriously injured and admitted to Mulago Hospital.

Pointing a finger at central government as a first suspect indicates the lack of trust and escalated conflict between the two parties. The government and Buganda Kingdom have been at loggerheads since the September 2009 riots, when the Baganda accused the government of blocking Kabaka Ronald Muwenda Mutebi (the King of Buganda) from visiting Bugerere county in Kayunga district, a part of his kingdom. At least 20 people died in riots linked with that incident. The burning of the Buganda cultural treasure at Kasubi, the government's response, and public reactions are indicative of the issues at the heart of this chapter. Ethnocultural conflict in Uganda has been, and remains, a tool used to obtain resources and protect positions. Ethnicities and their meaning are reified, accentuated, or otherwise manipulated by those in power to enhance divisions and to minimize shared values or common goals among different groups. This approach advantages the privileged and creates tensions between ethnic and religious groups. As we discuss in this chapter, when mistrust between groups is high, when parties feel threatened, and when resources are scarce, interethnic tensions and competition can easily break into violence.

The recurrence of ethnic conflict in Uganda is rooted in the colonial history of this country and is perpetuated today through differential power and resource inequities based on tribal divisions. Uganda has over 40 ethnic groups, and during the colonial era, these diverse groups were integrated into the Ugandan state. The colonialists used a divide-and-rule policy, hence "tribal identity" became an important element for political power and control. Tribalism was used as a basis for mobilization of the people for social and political purposes, and major political parties were founded on tribal and religious grounds. Since independence, regimes have closely identified with different tribes and each president favors particular ethnic groups. This continues to result in conflicts drawn upon ethnic lines. In this chapter, we discuss current conflicts, their history and development in Uganda, common causal themes, attempts made to resolve them, and consequences of ethnopolitical unrest. We also discuss approaches and provide specific suggestions for policy makers to advance intercultural relations and peace.

1 Current Status: Facts and Figures

Uganda has experienced decades of political unrest, including the 1964 Lost Counties dispute, the Obote-Kabaka 1966 crisis, the 1979 War that ousted Idi Amin, the war in Toro/Kasese, the war in Teso district under the Uganda Peoples' Army, the Allied Defense Forces (ADF) war on both sides of the Uganda–Congo border, the National Resistance Movement (NRM) – Luwero Triangle war, and the 23-year Lord's Resistance Army (LRA) war, which has devastated northern Uganda and spilled into the Democratic Republic of Congo (DRC), Sudan, and the Central African Republic. The war in the DRC (Africa's World War) has resulted in 90% of all conflict-related deaths since WWII, while the war with the LRA has killed tens of thousands of people, displaced close to two million, and led to the kidnapping of more than 60,000 children conscripted as soldiers (Horowitz, 2000). The Acholi and other tribes in northern Uganda continue to suffer from over 20 years of violence, despite attempts to negotiate a peace deal. Government involvement in the Hema–Lendu conflict on the DRC border has resulted in accusations of Uganda's involvement in ethnic cleansing. In the Kibale region, ethnic fighting between the Bakiga and Banyoro has been on the rise since the 1990s, and in 2003 resulted in two Banyoro children being beheaded (Green, 2007). As indicated by the Kasubi tombs incident, simmering tensions between the central government and the Buganda Kingdom have, since September 2009, been rising to the surface.

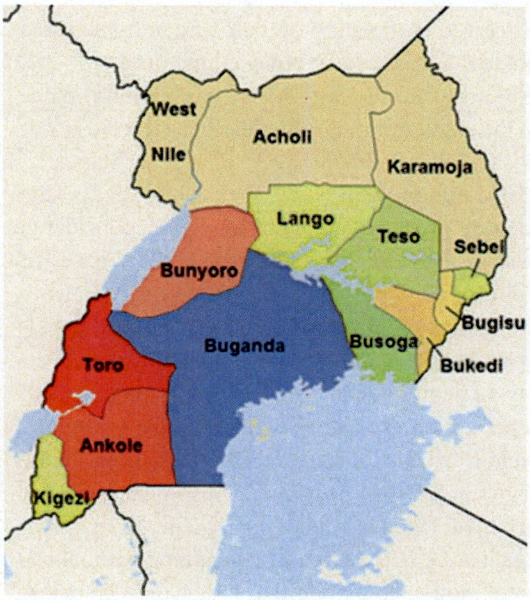

Fig. 16.1 Kingdoms in Uganda

The integration of the diverse ethnic groups into the Ugandan state has up to now been very challenging and characterized by pervasive conflicts over the role of the different ethnic groups in national politics. The conflicts, in part, reflect the way the state was constructed through manipulation of preexisting differences, administrative policies of divide and rule, and economic policies that further fractured the colonial entity (see Fig. 16.1 for a map illustrating some of the major regions and kingdoms involved in the conflicts). These policies undermined the faltering legitimacy of the state, impeded the emergence of a Ugandan nationalism, and generated ethnic, religious, and regional divisions that were to contribute in later years to instability and political violence. While the roots of fighting lie largely in struggles for resources and power, ethnic divisions fuel the struggles (Fairhead, 2000). The Ugandan government has been accused of aggravating ethnic tensions.

The divide-and-rule approach favoring some tribes over others has continued to be exploited by those in power, resulting in conflicts over resources and recognition based on ethnicity or religion. For example, the NRM government has supported the creation of Buluri and Bunyara "subkingdoms" in parts of Buganda. This has resulted in tensions between the Buganda Kingdom and the NRM government, characterized by riots, including one in September 2009 that left at least 20 people shot dead and five radio stations closed. The creation of these new subkingdoms is controversial, given the fact that the government has refused to embrace the restoration of Ankole and other kingdoms that were in existence for centuries before the abolition of monarchies in 1966 by Milton Obote. The NRM government restored Buganda, Toro, Bunyoro, and Busoga kingdoms, but Ankole, and the Rwenzoluru kingdoms were not restored for political reasons.

The Banyala and Baruli are in areas believed to have been conquered by Buganda from Bunyoro before the colonial era, and the creation of these subkingdoms is seen as an effort by government to exploit the Buganda–Bunyoro disagreements over these "lost counties." Buganda has persistently pushed for federal status, a demand the NRM government has rejected, and the creation of subkingdoms could be an effort to weaken the Buganda Kingdom and undermine its demand for federalism. Currently, Busoga Kingdom has two rival "kings" and there are allegations that the government has a hand in this conflict as well. Although the Bakiga have been in Bunyoro for decades, there are still ethnic disputes over land ownership, and the discovery of oil in the region has worsened these conflicts. There have been reports that the NRM has fueled these ethnic divisions and that the President recently directed the Bakiga not to run for political positions. This has widely been perceived as violation of their human rights and a polarization of people along ethnic lines.

The social identity theory has a central place in the study of intergroup relations (Horenczyk & Nisan, 1996; Kibanja, 1999; Roccas & Schwartz, 1993; Simon, Kulla, & Zobel, 1995), and social identity processes have for long been considered crucial to the social and psychological bases of political conflict (Kelman, 1999). Consistent with the theory, members of certain tribes have developed a sense of cohesion among them, and a feeling of legitimized hostility toward members of other ethnic groups. For example, the Langi and Acholi tribes were favored by the Milton Obote regime, and the post-Obote insurgences in the north of Uganda, including Joseph Kony's war against the NRM (central Ugandan government), were motivated by fear that they would be persecuted by the southern-dominated NRM government. In the recent past, riots have been characterized by violence toward members of certain ethnic groups believed to be benefiting from the current regime. For example, in 2007, Asian-Indian Ugandans were targeted when an Asian-owned company (the Mehta Group) was permitted to purchase government-owned forest land, the Mabira forest, for the purpose of sugar cane production. The nation's first environmental protest turned violent when a mob began throwing stones and chased several Asians, targeted for their ethnicity, into a mosque. At the end of the day, three deaths had resulted. Consistent with the relative deprivation theory, even tribes such as the Baganda that would be expected to appreciate the NRM government's decision to give them key political positions (including that of the Vice president, Prime Minister, and Speaker of Parliament) are disgruntled by the perception that their "share of the national cake" is less than it should be in relation to that of "other" tribes (Table 16.1).

1.1 Northern Uganda: Joseph Kony and the Lord's Resistance Army

The war between the Ugandan government and the LRA is one of Africa's longest running conflicts. The LRA led by Joseph Kony is a self-proclaimed Christian guerilla army that started its operations in 1986 and has mainly affected the districts of Gulu, Kitgum, Pader, Amuri, Lira, and Apac in Northern Uganda. Kony claims to be the spokesperson of the Christian Holy Spirit, which most Acholi believe can represent itself in manifestations. This war started as a political response to the current government and cattle theft by the government soldiers. The purpose of the LRA is to establish a theocratic state based on the biblical Ten Commandments and the Acholi tradition (Senabulya, 2009). Although the cause of the war had political inclination, the LRA later resorted to human rights violations such as abduction, murder, sexual abuse, and forcing children to serve in their army (see Fig. 16.2). It is estimated that the war led to the displacement of over two million people and abduction of an estimated 60,000–70,000 children and adults.

The government's response to the war and its related human rights abuses has mainly been by use of force rather than dialog. This strategy greatly affected people's attitudes toward the government and its willingness to end the war. After twenty years, the government and the LRA started peace talks in July 2006 in Juba, Southern Sudan. These continued for 2 years until 2008. Currently, security in northern Uganda has improved, leading to massive deployment of the local people from camps for internally displaced persons (IDPs) back to their homes. Rehabilitation of child soldiers has begun in some areas, but the physical and psychological wounds are deep and the threats to safety and security have not yet disappeared.

1.2 Western Uganda: Banyoro and Bakiga Conflict

Kibaale district is dominated by two major tribes: the native Banyoro and the Bakiga, who were resettled in the area in 1968. The area is also home to Basoga, Baganda, Banyankole, Bafumbira, Banyarwanda, Acholi, Bakonjo, Batoro, Bagisu, Alur, and the Masebetis from Kenya in small

Table 16.1 Overview of current conflicts

Area (Regions)	Groups involved	Description
West (Bunyoro, Kibaale)	Banyoro, Bakiga, and the central government	Tribe-based clashes and attacks related to election outcomes (2001, 2006) and subsequent NRM interventions. The Bakiga, considered non-native to the region, have won district and parliamentary elections, upsetting the Banyoro. Ethnic-based attacks and murders have occurred, targeting children.
North (Acholi, Gulu, Kitgum) with recent activity in the west, Sudan, and Central African Republic	Lord's Resistance Army (Acholi and Langi) and the central government	Since 1986, the Joseph Kony-led Christian rebel movement has wreaked havoc in the north; est. 60,000 children conscripted as child soldiers and over 2 million persons displaced, resulting in devastation in northern Ugandan; more recent attacks in Sudan, Central African Republic, and Congo (with 250 Congolese killed in a 2009 Christmas day massacre).
Central (Buganda, Kasubi, Kampala)	Baganda and the central government	NRM attempts to weaken Buganda Kingdom through ethnic manipulation and creation of "subkingdoms." Violence began in 2008 with the arrest of several Mengo (Buganda) ministers, followed by closure of the Buganda Kingdom radio station (CBS) in September 2009, and Kasubi tombs incident.
West and South West (border with DRC)	Allied Defense Forces (ADF), Interahamwe, Mai Mai, central government (UPDF soldiers), other countries (Burundi, DRC, Rwanda, Sudan)	Beginning in the 1990s, "spill over" from Africa's World War resulted in about 73,000 Uganda deaths, 100,00 being displaced, and 1, 000 children orphaned in the Bundibugyo district; UPDF officially withdrew from DRC in 2003, fighting among rebel factions remains a reality in the Ruwenzori Mountains, with recent UPDF maneuvers in the Ituri region. Rumors that the ADF is regrouping in the rainforest fuel Ugandan fears of renewed rebel massacres.

Fig. 16.2 Child soldiers were conscripted into the LRA, completely confounding universal and Ugandan notions of childhood (Permission to use photo from Invisible Children, Inc.)

scale. In 2002, a Mukiga (Fred Ruremera) and a Munyoro (Sebastian Ssekitolekko) contested for the District Chairman post and the former won by 56% majority vote. The Banyoro considered it unacceptable to have a Mukiga born in another district rule over them. They became violent by blocking roads with logs, setting fire to government offices, and killing people, which actions caused the displacement of over 200 Bakiga families (Green, 2009). This instigated the president to intervene in the crisis by nullifying Fred Ruremera's election (a Mukiga) and replacing him with George Namyaka (a native Munyoro). This was done because the Ugandan constitution gives the president powers to take over district leadership if it is deemed necessary. The conflict, however, did not come to an end. The Banyoro started grabbing the Bakiga's land and redistributing it to themselves (Green, 2009). In response, the Bakiga killed two children of the Banyoro, escalating the conflict. The Banyoro in turn mobbed up ready to massacre any Mukiga they could find but were not successful as the government anti-riot police got into the area and dispersed the mob. This conflict illustrates how the Banyoro in order to counteract their perceived threat by the settlers in their district mobilized themselves on the grounds of ethnic identity for collective actions against the outgroup. Perceived discrimination by members of a particular ethnic group (i.e., non-Banyoro in Kibaale not voting for a Munyoro candidate) increases ethnic identification (among the Banyoro), leading to negative attitudes to the outgroup or discriminating group (Jasinskaja-Lahti, Liebkind, & Solheim, 2009).

Research in social identity theory indicates that discrimination against the outgroup and favoritism toward the ingroup are greater when ingroup members consider that their status or well being can be enhanced by devaluing outgroups, and when ingroup members believe that outgroups threaten their status in some way (Nesdale & Scarlett, 2004, cited in Winstok, 2010). The Kibaale conflict is that result of the perceived threat by the Banyoro that the Bakiga are taking over leadership of the district to which they are mere settlers, denying the natives opportunity for key political involvement in their region.

1.3 The Central Region: Buganda Kingdom and the Central Government

Despite their favored status, a conflict between Buganda and central government has been brewing which rose to the surface during riots in September 2009. This day was marked by a widely spread riot that covered all the districts of Buganda, leading to deaths of many people and burning of public and private vehicles (and the Nateete police station). The riot was sparked off by the central government denying the Kabaka a visit to his subjects in Kayunga, one of the districts within the Buganda Kingdom. The peak of the day was the closure of five Radio stations, including the one for the Buganda Kingdom (CBS) and for the Catholics. Shortly after, the other radio stations were reopened except CBS which was accused of propagating hatred toward the government. The CBS was reopened on Saturday 23rd October 2010, two days before the incumbent president registered for presidential candidacy for the 2011 elections. He registered for presidential candidature with the electoral commission on Monday 25th October 2010.

In March 2010, the government was suspected of involvement in the Kasubi Tombs burning and subsequent unrest. The *Monitor* of Saturday March 20th 2010 stated that the current conflict between Buganda and central government is not too dissimilar from what flowed in the lead-up to the 1966 crisis where the Kabaka, the king of Buganda, was exiled (Butagira, 2010). Most people think that central government is taking rudimentary measures against Buganda (such as closure of CBS, amending the land bill, etc.), with the assumption that the government's status can be strengthened by weakening Buganda. However, the conflicts between the Buganda Kingdom and the central government have strengthened Buganda's ethnic loyalty as evidenced on Friday 26th March 2010 when thousands of Baganda and well-wishers turned up for prayers to close the 5-day mourning for the Kingdom over the burned traditional shrines. The attendance to this activity was overwhelming, leaving at least one person dead, 16 admitted to the national hospital, and over 100 receiving first aid due to suffocation (Figs. 16.3 and 16.4).

Fig. 16.3 Buganda cultural heritage site, the Muzibu Azaalampaga house at Kasubi Royal Tombs, being burned to the ground (permission to use from New Vision)

Fig. 16.4 Civilians take cover as government security forces take fire (permission to use from the Monitor)

Following from the social identity theory, the conflict between Buganda and central government has increased discrimination against the outgroup and favoritism toward the ingroup in Buganda. On the contrary, it has also increased discrimination against Buganda by the central government because it assumes that it can gain more control over the state when Buganda is devalued.

2 History and Development of Uganda's Ethnopolitical Conflicts

Knowing the history of Uganda is key to being able to understand the current conflicts fully (Marblestone, 2005). Most of Uganda's ethnopolitical conflicts have existed for decades and stem from the consequences of colonization and from the histories of the different ethnic groups. Like other developing countries, the Ugandan conflicts are both political and economic and, therefore, cannot be understood without taking into account the historical experiences, respective social networks, cultural factors, and the geographic/environmental context (Johnson, Kim, Johnson-Pynn, Schulenberg, Balagaye, & Lugumya 2011; Zeo, 2001). In this section, we begin with a general discussion of the ethnic identity in Uganda and then describe important historical events that shaped the ethnopolitical landscape and set the stage for Uganda's ongoing struggles.

2.1 Ethnicity and Identity in Uganda

In the African context, identities based on race, culture, language, and religion are often subsumed under ethnicity. Ethnicity encompasses all forms of identity that have at their root the notion of a common ancestor-race, as well as tribe or clan (Deng, 1996). Following from this perspective, ethnicity implies that "a group is in a large part, biologically self-perpetuating; shares fundamental values, realized in overt unity in cultural forms; makes up a field of communication and interaction; and has a membership that identifies itself, and is identified by others, as constituting a category distinguishable from other categories of the same order" (Deng, 1996, p. 47). All the above suggest that ethnicity may be looked at as a cultural phenomenon, a political phenomenon, a biological phenomena, a symbolic expression, a social organization, and a psychological process (Thompson, 1989).

How one defines his or her ethnic identity will vary depending on the culture, geography, religion, phenotypic features, nationality, language, tribe, clan, economic or class status, and/or kinship ties. Moreover, the salience of different aspects of one's identity, ethnic or otherwise, will vary based on histories, values, and experiences of oppression and discrimination (Aponte & Johnson, 2000). For example, amid the fervent anti-gay persecution occurring in Uganda now, we would anticipate that an individual's identity as being heterosexual or homosexual is taking on increased significance. Because Ugandan society is very heterogeneous, ethnic identification is not easily attributable on the basis of phenotypic features or place of origin. Ethnicity in Uganda is not simply a matter of being, for example, a Muganda or Munyoro; the differentiation in ethnic groups is attributable to several behavioral patterns such as language used, traditions, cultural values, dress, religion, and form of lifestyle subscribed to (Kibanja, 1999). Given the complex and multidimensional nature of identity in Uganda, it has historically been rather mutable and claimed by individuals rather than ascribed by others. Therefore, in this chapter, we consider ethnicity to be a largely socially constructed, ongoing and dynamic process with individual and group-based aspects and implications. Moreover, one's ethnicity is not a static quality but a process of personal, social, and cultural construction (Hayes & Mare, 1997).

2.2 Ethnicity in the Pre-colonial Period

Ideas about ethnicity, its construction, meaning, and function in Ugandan society have evolved over time. Uganda is considered an ethnically diverse society representing four major ethnolinguistic groups (Bantu, Nilotic, Hamitic, and Nilo-Hamitic) and about 44 different ethnic groups, or tribes (Fearon, 2003). Before Uganda existed as a country, it consisted of a great number of kingdoms and chieftains occupied by different rivaling ethnic groups (Collison, 1981; Segall, Doornbos, & Davis, 1976). The Baganda were the largest group and remain the most populous today, accounting for about 17% of the population. Other notable ethnic groups included the Banyoro, Batoro, Banyankole, Iteso, Basoga, Bakiga, Langi, Bagisu, Acholi, Lugbara, and the Karamojong. Although there is not a lot of written history of Uganda before British colonization, what has been documented reveals a pattern of cultural disputes between different ethnic groups in the region which contribute to the current problem (Marblestone, 2005).

Before colonialism, the different societies of the country adopted either a stateless or state-governed form of political organization (Kintu-Nyago, 1996). Stateless political organization involved centering political power around the clan system. This basically relied on generational lines, with power being executed through a council of elders, while their clan heads and chiefs were elected by their fellow elders (Mamdani, 1976). State-governed political organization, on the contrary, involved execution of power through an established monarch under a king. By then, the dominant state-governed societies were the Kingdoms of Buganda and Bunyoro, and the stateless ones included predominantly the societies in the now northern part of Uganda. Present-day Uganda was built on the Buganda Kingdom (Segall et al., 1976).

2.3 Colonialism Fuels Ethnic and Religious Divisions

Like many other African states, the boundaries that now shape the process of nation building in Uganda were drawn by the colonialists with little regard for the preexisting patterns of cultural and ethnic identity (Segall et al., 1976). In order to govern, colonial authorities frequently found it expedient to divide in order to rule. Ugandans divided up into a society of contradictory and mutually suspicious interests (President Yoweri Museveni; MISR, 1987, p. 20). In 1890, the British signed a treaty with Buganda establishing colonial rule, and in 1894, Britain declared a protectorate over Uganda. Although Uganda did not suffer from the same degree of colonialism as its neighboring countries, territories (and thus resources) were developed along ethnic lines, laying the foundation for future tensions and conflict.

Britain set up an indirect government which favored the Baganda and upset other tribes (Marblestone, 2005). Britain also granted special privileges to the Kabaka of Buganda in the Buganda Agreement of 1900, allowing a very high level of internal autonomy. Britain also favored Buganda vis-à-vis other polities of the protectorate, especially Bunyoro. Through their system of indirect rule, other kingdoms such as Toro and Ankole were also recognized, territorially defined, and allocated some autonomy. Life for many of the pastoralist peoples of the north and eastern Uganda was hardly changed by the advent of colonialism (Clark, 2002). This had the inevitability of producing inequalities, which in turn generated intense and disruptive conflicts between the different groups. The rivalry over access to opportunities gave rise to the formation of attitudes of superiority and inferiority complexes, stereotypes, and prejudices (President Yoweri Museveni; MISR, 1987 p. 20).

The British-made Buganda (the central area of the country) and, to some extent, areas in the east produce cash crops for export, while the northern region was a reservoir of cheap labor and for recruiting forces into the colonial army. Many northerners, such as the Acholi, were stereotyped as fierce warriors and forced to join the Ugandan army, which was seen as a position for uneducated people. The civil service was largely left in the hands of the Baganda and the army largely in the hands of the Acholi and other northern ethnic groups. This was further sustained by the administrative policy that relied on the Baganda as colonial agents in other parts of the country, and led to widespread anti-Buganda sentiments (Otunnu, 2002).

Another significant divide was along the lines of religious affiliation, which can be traced back to the arrival of Islam, Protestantism, and Catholicism in Buganda. These religious groups engaged in a ferocious competition for dominance, and the Protestant faction emerged victorious after the Imperial British East Africa Company intervened in their favor. Anglicans were to later dominate the top positions in the civil service, and this structural inequality was maintained after the colonial era. Consequently, religious beliefs and political party affiliations were to become entangled (Otunnu, 2002). By the end of the 1950s, two main nationalist political parties had emerged: the Uganda People's Congress (UPC), with a Protestant base, and the Democratic Party (DP), with a strong Catholic support (Clark, 2002).

2.4 Kingdoms Vie for Recognition During Independence

Anticolonialism grew slowly in Uganda in the 1950s, yet the formation of political parties had a poor start. Major dissenters were the Baganda Catholics, who had been marginalized since 1892 and were organized into the Democratic Party of Benedicto Kiwanuka, and the UPC, a coalition of non-Baganda groups, led by Milton Obote and determined not to be dictated to by the Baganda. Anticolonialism was complicated by the strong desire of the Baganda to maintain their separate political identity. By the 1960s, this country still had no political party which was comparable to those that existed in the neighboring countries (Kenya and Tanzania). Yet in actual sense, Uganda was economically better off and had more literacy than those mentioned (Low, 1962). The country had its first modern political party in 1952, the Uganda National Congress (UNC) founded by I.K. Musazi and Abu Mayanja. This party like the others that followed started with the aim of recovering Uganda's independence.

Uganda's independence was granted without any political struggle however, so political parties immediately redefined their aims and interests from obtaining independence to who would inherit the post-colonial Uganda (Hansen, 1977; Langlands, 1977). At the London Conference of 1960, the British decided to allow elections which would ensure Ugandan independence afterward. In 1961, with independence looming, the Kabaka Yekka ("Buganda King Only" – KY) party appeared to campaign for the preservation of Buganda's special status within Uganda. The British favored the KY party, and when the election results were in favor of the UPC party, the British announced a new plan for Uganda. The British government declared that Buganda would be allowed internal autonomy (a state within a state status) if they participated in the national government (Marblestone, 2005). Uganda achieved independence in 1962 under a Westminster-type constitution, with the added feature of a ceremonial presidency (the Kabaka of Buganda). In the elections of that year, the UPC, under Milton Obote, forged an alliance with the KY and won a solid majority of seats in the parliament. The peace between these two parties led to the Independence Constitution of 1962 and a separate Ugandan government.

As a result of the UPC and the Buganda monarchy party (Kabaka Yekka) alliance, the leader of the UPC, Milton Obote, was elected prime minister of Uganda in October 1962, and Kabaka Edward Mutesa II became the President and Head of State. The formal leader of Uganda was the Kabaka (King), but Obote made great attempts to seize power. Although he worked with the Kabaka Yekka in the beginning of his reign, in 1964 he began to attempt to consolidate his power (Marblestone, 2005). The alliance collapsed over a conflict over land (the "lost counties") between Bunyoro and Buganda.

The 1962 constitution reflected attempts to manage the various conflicting interests. With a complete lack of popular confidence in his rule, colonial governor Andrew Cohen was forced to agree to Buganda's demands for a continued privileged status (a state within the Ugandan state) in the new constitution. This compromise document provided for a federal status for Buganda and a semi-federal status for the other four kingdoms, and unitary relations between the districts and the central government. However, the constitutional arrangement did not satisfy all groups. In 1962, the "Rwenzururu" rebellion broke when the Bakonzo and Bamba took up arms against domination by the Toro Kingdom and fought for "recognition of the rights of minority ethnic groups in independent Uganda" (Stacey, 2003; Syahuka, 1983).

It did not take long before the spirit of compromise and institutional restraints on the use of power, which had reluctantly been adhered to, dissipated. In 1964, Obote made a deal with several DP ministers in which they would cross the floor to join the UPC if Obote could return the "lost counties" to Bunyoro. The Kabaka opposed the planned referendum and a civil war was avoided when the Kabaka backed down, allowing the referendum in which the populations of the "lost counties" overwhelmingly expressed a desire to return to the Bunyoro Kingdom.

2.5 Obote and Amin Regimes Poison Ethnic Relations

The UPC itself fell into disarray in 1966 after it was revealed that Obote and his associates, including Amin, were smuggling arms to a secessionist group in neighboring Congo in return for ivory and gold. Faced with nearly unanimous disapproval, Obote did not take the expected step of stepping down as prime minister, but instead had Amin and the army carry out what was in effect a coup d'état against his own government. After suspending the constitution, arresting dissident UPC ministers, and taking the powers of the presidency for his own, he announced the promulgation of a new constitution, abolishing the autonomy of the kingdoms guaranteed by the former federal system.

The national assembly was instructed to create a new republican constitution which would create a strong executive presidency and minimize the power of other leaders (Marblestone, 2005). When the Buganda legislature rejected the constitution, Obote declared a state of emergency in Buganda and sent the army under Amin to attack Kabaka Mutesa II's palace. The Battle of Mengo Hill resulted in the palace being overrun, with the Kabaka barely escaping into exile. The government occupied Buganda's palace following the flight of the Kabaka to England. Some Bantu-speaking groups perceived this struggle for legitimacy and power as a conflict between the Bantu south and the non-Bantu (Nilotic) north. Obote secured his position with the creation of the General Service Unit, a system of secret police staffed mostly with ethnic kin people from the Lango region.

In 1967, Obote introduced a new constitution which strengthened executive powers even more, and in 1969, he created a one-party state by banning all groups opposed to the UPC (Marblestone, 2005). This resulted in a crisis of legitimacy and heightened conflict in the ethnically fragile state. In December 1969, Obote narrowly escaped an assassination attempt, apparently carried out by Baganda monarchists.

These crises were compounded by a conflict between Obote and his army commander, General Idi Amin. In 1970, Obote escaped another assassination attempt after the attackers mistakenly targeted the car of the vice-president. Obote was suspicious of Amin but could not take direct action as he was totally reliant upon the army that Amin led to keep him in power. In response, Obote increased the recruitment of ethnic Acholi and Langi to counter the recruitment by Amin of soldiers from his home West Nile subregion. In October 1970, Obote put Amin under house arrest on charges of increasing military expenditure over budget, and continuing to support Sudan's Anyanya rebel group in the civil war against the government of Gaafar Nimeiry, after Obote had decided to switch his support to Nimeiry. Despite protestations by Amin that he remained loyal, Obote decided to rid himself of the perceived threat in January 1971. While leaving on a foreign trip, Obote ordered Langi military officers to arrest Amin and his close supporters. However, word of the plot was leaked to Amin before it could be carried out, prompting Amin to carry out a preemptive coup. The successful coup is often cited as an example of "action by the military," where the Ugandan Armed Forces acted against a government whose politics posed more of a threat to the military privileges (Lofchie, 1972).

Amin's rule was characterized by violence and it poisoned ethnic relations as the regime alienated one ethnic group after the other (African Contemporary Record, 5 (1972–1973); Hansen, 1977). Immediately after he came to power, Amin ordered Acholi and Langi soldiers, who constituted the backbone of the army, to surrender their arms. The overwhelming majority of them did so. However, many were subsequently killed. In July 1971, Langi and Acholi soldiers were massacred in the Jinja and Mbarara barracks (Lautze, 2007) and by early 1972, some 5,000 Acholi and Langi soldiers had disappeared (Kibanja, 1999). Amin's rule was welcomed by the Baganda, but tens of thousands of Obote supporters fled south into Tanzania. Tanzanian president Julius Nyerere would prove to be a strong opponent of the Amin government, an attitude mirrored by Kenya, South Africa, and the Organisation for African Unity, though

Israel, Great Britain, and the USA were quick to recognize the legitimacy of the Amin government. Also in 1972, the professional classes, including the 70,000 Indian Ugandans, were expelled.

The government extended its conflict with the Acholi and Langi by arresting, detaining, and killing highly educated and influential members of the ethnic groups. To protect the regime, which lacked political legitimacy in the country, Amin recruited new soldiers into the national army from West Nile. In addition, he appointed prominent Bantu to important positions in his government. The regime, however, largely maintained the dominance of southerners in the civil service and commerce, while the northerners largely controlled the government and army.

Amin was preoccupied with the dissident groups that Obote had gathered in exile in Tanzania. This prompted Amin to task the General Service Unit, now renamed the Special Research Bureau, and the Public Safety Unit with an intensified search for suspected subversives. Thousands of people disappeared. Amin also retaliated by further purging the army of Obote supporters, predominantly those from the Acholi and Langi ethnic groups (Boddy-Evans, 2003). The political environment became increasingly unstable and paranoia inducing as the regime continued, and Amin's circle of supporters grew smaller and smaller due to the "purges" and "disappearances."

In 1978, General Mustafa Adrisi, an Amin supporter, was injured in a suspicious automobile accident and units loyal to him, including the once-loyal Malire Mechanized Regiment, mutinied. Amin sent loyalist units to crush the uprising, causing some of the mutineers to flee south into Tanzania. Amin, seeking to deflect blame and rally the populace, then accused Tanzania's Nyerere of being the cause of the fighting and sent troops across the border to annex formally 700 miles of Tanzania known as the Kagera Salient. In response, Nyerere declared a state of war and mobilized the Tanzania People's Defense Force for a full-scale conflict. Within several weeks, the Tanzanian army was expanded from 40,000 to over 100,000 with the addition of police, prison guards, militia, and others. They were joined by the various anti-Amin forces, which in March 1979 coalesced into the Uganda National Liberation Front (UNLF). The UNLF was led by the political newcomer Yoweri Museveni, as well as several smaller anti-Amin groups.

The Tanzanian army, with the support of the UNLF, drove the Ugandan forces out of Tanzania and began an invasion of Uganda. In April 1979, the exiled rebels, who were overwhelmingly from Acholi and Langi, assisted by the Tanzanian army and Yoweri Museveni's Front for National Salvation (FRONASA), overthrew the Amin regime, marking the first time in the post-colonial era that an African nation successfully invaded another (Mutibwa, 1992). Amin then went into exile where he lived a luxurious life until his death in 1999.

After Idi Amin was overthrown, violence and disorder continued, and the successive regimes were confronted with the problems of reestablishing societal and political order (Decalo, 1990; Gertzel, 1980). Different groups positioned themselves for political control, and there was a series of interim governments between 1979 and 1980. The major political actors of the time, most of whom were political returnees whose claim to a role in national politics rested on their "roles" in the overthrow of Idi Amin, were deeply divided along political, ethnic, religious, military, and ideological lines (Gertzel, 1980). Yusuf Lule assumed power immediately after Amin was overthrown. However, ideological and ethnic conflicts within the UNLF and the national army led to the collapse of the Lule administration within three months. Godfrey Binaisa, a former minister in the UPC, took over.

2.6 The Rise of Museveni/The NRM and Ongoing Troubles

While the UNLF force that helped overthrow Amin numbered only 1,000, in 1979, Museveni and David Oyite-Ojok, a Langi, like Obote, began a massive recruitment of soldiers into what were their personal armies. When Binaisa attempted to stop this rapid military expansion, he was deposed by Museveni, Oyite-Ojok, and Muwanga in May 1980. After Muwanga's rise to power, the new administration organized general elections in December 1980. Obote returned to the country to stand in the elections held in December 1980. Obote was re-elected president with Muwanga as his vice-president, but widespread irregularities and political violence undermined the legitimacy of the elections. The main challenger, the DP, rejected Obote's victory. Museveni also rejected the results. Thereafter, a number of armed groups, including Lule's Uganda Freedom Fighters, Museveni's Popular Resistance Army (later they were to merge to form the NRM, and Uganda Freedom Movement/ Army (UFM/A), declared war against the Obote government. In Amin's home in the West Nile subregion, Brigadier Moses Ali's Uganda National Rescue Front (UNRF) and General Lumago's Former Uganda National Army (FUNA) also engaged the army and the UPC in bitter armed opposition (Otunnu, 2002).

The war polarized Uganda along the regional north–south divide and along ethnic lines. The NRM was a predominantly southern guerrilla army fighting against a northern dominated government army, the Uganda National Liberation Army (UNLA). There were also many rival armed groups such as Uganda Freedom Movement (UFM), Federal Democratic Army (Fedemo), UNRF, and FUNA, among others, vying for political control. The NRM insurgency was based largely in the anti-Obote strongholds of central and western Buganda and the former Kingdoms of Ankole and Bunyoro (Library of Congress Country Studies, December, 1990). Fighting was particularly intense in the Luwero triangle of Buganda, where the bitter memory of the counterinsurgency efforts of the UNLF's Langi and Acholi soldiers against the populace would prove an enduring legacy. The brutality of the counterinsurgency further inflamed anti-Obote sentiment in the occupied areas. Following the death of General Oyite Ojok in a helicopter crash at the end of 1983, the Acholi–Langi alliance began to fracture. On 27 January 1985, Acholi troops under Brigadier Bazilio Olara-Okello staged a successful coup and put fellow Acholi General Tito Okello Lutwa into the presidency as Obote once again fled into exile. Okello urged all political and insurgent groups to support the new government, but the large NRM group refused to join. Peace talks occurred between the government and the NRM, and after an Okello–Museveni peace agreement broke down, the NRM began a final offensive and entered Kampala in January 1986 as the Acholi troops fled north to their homeland. Yoweri Museveni declared the presidency on January 29, 1986.

With the capture of power, the newly established NRM government was greeted with optimism about resolving issues related to the struggle for political control and the roles of various ethnic groups. These issues remained unresolved, and within a few months, there was resurgence of violent conflict in northern Uganda between the NRM and former soldiers of the UNLA, which the NRM had defeated. Tension escalated into full-scale war when former soldiers of the UNLA who had re-organized under the banner of the Uganda People's Democratic Army (UPDA) attacked NRMA positions in Gulu and Kitgum districts in August 1986.

The conflict spread to the entire north and eastern Uganda. A number of armed groups emerged to challenge the NRM regime (Africa Contemporary Record, Vol. 19, 1986–1987). These included the UPDA, UPA/F, Ninth October Movement (NOM), Force Obote Back Again (FOBA), and NALU, which was active in western Uganda around the foothills of the Ruwenzori Mountains. The most resilient group has been the LRA, which has tormented northern Uganda since 1987. The NALU rebellion was led by Amon Bazira, a former minister in the deposed UPC government who was assassinated in 1993.

The outbreak of armed conflicts in northern and south-western Uganda presented the NRM with a dilemma of whether to adopt a military or democratic approach to resolve the conflict. The NRM criminalized its opponents to prevent them from gaining domestic and international support. It used military repression, co-optation, and patronage to respond to conflicts. When the conflict in northern Uganda had just started, President Yoweri Museveni (April 7, 1987) described it as a result of "rear-guard actions of the defeated, moribund, sectarian, and neo-colonial elements," and labeled his opponents as "the elements that have caused untold suffering to the people of Uganda, violated human rights, murdered people, destroyed the economy and violated the sovereignty of the people of Uganda. Fighting and annihilating these types of elements is a justified cause" (President Yoweri K. Museveni, October 9, 1987). In line with its views that political parties were "sectarian" and "divisive," in March 1986, 3 months after it came to power, the NRM regime directed political parties to suspend activities, holding meetings and rallies. The NRM pledged to establish a "broad-based" government. However, within the NRM, decision-making powers remained with an identifiable "core" committed to NRM's basic ideology. The NRM government also determined those to include and exclude, as well as the parameters of participation. Such an approach is not conducive for building national consensus and resolution of conflicts. Participation in politics was limited by the principle of "individual merit." People were expected to participate in politics in their individual capacities, but not as members of political organizations.

In 1988, the NRM government appointed a constitutional commission and mandated it "to consult the people and make proposals for a popular and lasting constitution based on national consensus" (Uganda Constitutional Commission Statute; Statute 5 of 1988). The president appointed the Chairman and members of the Commission without any democratic consultation, a step that is viewed as having deprived the country of an opportunity to build national consensus and establish a framework to accommodate divergent groups and interests.

The Commission recommended the suspension of political party activities for a 5-year period. This was approved, and the "Movement" or no-party system of governance and restoration of kingdoms/traditional leaders were entrenched in the constitution. To its credit, the Commission recommended that a democratically elected Constituent Assembly (CA) should debate the constitution. However, the NRM preempted discussion on the role of traditional rulers when it introduced constitutional amendments and restored traditional rulers and institutions (Oloka-Onyango, 1995). In restoring traditional institutions, the government acted opportunistically to win political support among the Baganda, after failing to intimidate Baganda monarchies and activists from dropping their demands for a federal system of government. It subordinated traditional rulers to NRM rule, by not spelling out powers of traditional institutions. It is the president who has the powers to sanction the creation or recognition of a cultural institution. The government has withheld recognition for the restoration of Ankole Kingdom, and the President has supported the creation of new kingdoms and chiefdoms where they never existed. Such was the case of Buruuli and Banyala "Kingdoms" in districts within Buganda whose creation was sanctioned, if not instigated by the government, to the chagrin of Buganda Kingdom. This has contributed to reduced support for the NRM and also increased animosity between the central government and the Buganda (Mengo) government (Table 16.2).

3 Causes of Ethnopolitical Conflicts in Uganda

The history above illuminates the unsettled nature of politics in Uganda. The formation of political parties in the country was from the start organized along tribal, religious, and regional lines (Hansen, 1977; Kasfir, 1976). The idea of a political party being a body of organized opinion along rationalistic, ideological lines does not have a convincing history in Uganda. Yet ingroup favoritism based on ethnicity is undoubtedly a motivating force for conflicts in modern Uganda. Social scientists argue that ethnopolitical conflicts can be explained by either the cultural or the structural paradigms. According to the structural paradigm, ethnopolitical conflicts are as a result of economic and political factors. Ethnicity is used to access economic or political gains

Table 16.2 Important actors and their roles in the conflict

Actor	Role
I.K. Musazi and Abu Mayanja	Founders of the first political party (UNC) in 1952
Benedicto Kiwanuka	Founder of the second political party (DP) in 1954
E. M. K. Mulira	Founder of Progressive Party (PP) in 1955
Dr. Milton Obote	In 1966 drove Mutesa II into exile in England, and appointed himself President. In 1969 declared Uganda a one-party state, with his party (UPC) as the only legal political party In 1970 put Amin under house arrest on charges of supporting Sudan's Anyanya rebel group
General Idi Amin	In January 1971, overthrew Obote in a military coup d'etat when he had gone to Singapore to attend the Commonwealth Heads of Government meeting. In 1971 he banned UPC, making Uganda a country with no political parties and thus no formal outlet for political activity and no established means for expressing opposition or disagreement
UNLF	In 1979 overthrew Idi Amin
Paul Muwanga	In 1980 organized general elections and Obote was elected president
Yoweri Museveni	In 1981 started guerilla war under the NRM/A In January 1986, captured power
Brigadier Bazilio Olara-Okello	In January 1985 staged a successful coup and Obote fled into exile. Appointed fellow Acholi General Tito Okello Lutwa president
General Tito Okello Lutwa	In 1985 held peace talks with NRA but Museveni did not cease fighting
UPDA	In August 1986, solders of former government organized under UPDA attached NRA positions in Gulu and Kitgum
LRA	In 1987 started rebel activities in northern Uganda

through manipulation of the powerless group. On the contrary, the cultural paradigm postulates that ethnopolitical conflicts are a social identity phenomena whereby the marginalized ethnic group in its effort to counteract the real or perceived threat resorts to group identity.

In the Ugandan sense, both paradigms hold water. The conflict between the Bakiga and the Banyoro in Kibaale district correspond with the cultural paradigm and that between the Buganda and the central government is illustrative of the structural paradigm, though, we would argue that there are elements of both paradigms in each and that the causes are, in fact, complex and interactive. There is no single theory that illustrates a widely acceptable approach to the causes and consequences of ethnopolitical conflicts (Imtiyaz & Stavis, 2008) because such conflicts are caused and manifested in varied ways depending on the conflicting parties and the history of the nation in question. In Uganda, several factors are responsible for contributing to ethnic conflicts.

1. *Favoritism and Lack of Dynamic Leadership Within Political Parties*. Political leadership structures in Uganda are not changing. Political parties are led by founder members as long as they are still alive (Kibanja, 1999). For example, UPC started as a non-Baganda faction led by Obote (a Nilotic). All the time Obote was in exile in Zambia, he was still the party leader. After his death, his wife became the party president until March 2010 when Otunu was elected new party president. DP started as a Baganda Catholic party by Benedicto Kiwanuka. Kiwanuka was killed by Amin, and after him, secession of the leadership of the party has been by the Baganda until March 2010 when Nobert Mao, an Acholi from Northern Uganda, was elected party president. NRM, although founded by members of differing ethnic groups, still has its founding leader as the party president.

Political parties are still tribal, regional, and religion based, and centralized (Mukyala-Makiika, 2000). This makes it rather hard for the people to have confidence in them because they are wrangled over issues of power and leadership. From Hayes and Mares's (1997) assertion that ethnicity is formed through a process of social identification, under historically specific conditions, it can be argued that the way political parties were formed in Uganda was in itself a process of ethnic identification. It may not necessarily be that political parties attract specific ethnic groups, but instead that ethnic groups influence party formation. In this way, it is argued that political parties exist on the basis of ethnic demands as opposed to ethnicity influencing existing parties (Kibanja, 1999). Moreover, successive governments have failed to address the issue of national identity, being preoccupied with maintaining their positions. Favoritism and the disintegration over ethnic lines have been and are likely to continue being the causes of ethnopolitical conflicts.

2. *Restoration of kingdoms.* When Museveni came to power in 1986, he promised to restore the kingdoms and this was received with approval by the masses (especially those from Buganda, Toro, Bunyoro, and Busoga Kingdoms). Shortly there after, the kingdoms were restored. These kingdoms have traditional kings but with no constitutional powers outside their kingdoms. These kings are only supposed to play cultural roles but not participate in politics, as determined by the president's interpretation of what is political and what is not (Omach, 2009). This has caused tension, especially in Buganda where a federal system of governance is cherished, to the disapproval of central government. Gurr's (2000) model presumes that ethnopolitical rebellion is more likely to develop within the groups that have the strongest, most cohesive identities; the greatest extent of grievances supplying the incentives to organize; the most elaborate networks and leadership capabilities, and a set of external political factors furnishing the opportunities to mobilize against the state (Saxton, 2005).

Gurr's (2000) model of ethnopolitical behavior argues that ethnopolitical action presupposes an identity group that shares valued cultural traits and some common grievances or aspirations. These sentiments and the interests provide the essential basis for mobilization and shape the kinds of claims made by group leaders, timing of action, and the choice of strategies of participation, protest, or rebellion depends largely on political opportunities external to the group, principally its relationship to the state and external actors (Saxton, 2005, p. 89). The riot of 10th September 2009 provides a clear example of this. The Buganda Kingdom has up to now maintained socializing its members into commitment to the group through cultural exploration (i.e., making efforts to expose them to history, talks, cultural events, etc.). This has strengthened members' ethnic identity.

3. *Politics and religion.* The churches in Uganda play a major role in the politics of the country. Competition between the British (Protestants) and French (Roman Catholic) during colonization rooted competition which has remained in the post-colonial period. Religion has been a major factor stimulating popular support for political parties in the country: influencing elections and sometimes public acceptance of government measures (Mujaju, 1974). During colonialism, there was simultaneous arrival of foreign missionaries of differing faiths in the country. Uganda became a British protectorate and thus welcomed the Protestant missionaries from Britain warmly. The Catholic missionaries came from France and the Moslem missionaries were mostly Arabic. Because France was a competing colonial power with the British, the coming of the Roman Catholic missionaries created suspicion and insecurity within the country. The relationship between the three dominant religious groups in the country was shaped by the colonialists. Protestant missionaries assumed close collaboration with the colonial rulers and thus obtained the power to spread faster in the country. In this way, the protestant religion was favored, and received special attention compared to the others. UPC was an Anglican-oriented (commonly known as Protestant) party backed by Britain, and DP, a Catholic-oriented party backed by France. These two were the major colonial powers in the partition of Africa which was achieved in pursuit of economic interests. By the

time political party formation started in Uganda, religious conflicts were already in existence and this shaped the formation of the parties. Members of a particular religion tended to think in terms of receiving power to enable them to spread their religion faster (Mudoola, 1996).

It may be argued that since each religious group wanted to spread, they all tried to struggle for political powers. UPC became Protestant dominated and DP Catholic dominated. The Kabaka was a Protestant. The prominent Moslem group in Uganda was led by Prince Badru Kakungulu, the uncle of the Kabaka. This implies that many of the prominent members of this Moslem group were closely associated with the Buganda Kingdom, thus a greater likelihood for Moslems to still crave for the kingdoms. Mudoola (1996) also elaborates on the good relationship that was there between Protestants and Moslems as opposed to one of the two with Catholics. Reflecting on the above, it is understandable that religious affiliation is ethnic based. This way, religion and politics were tied together. The way religion was brought to Uganda (wrapped around political colonial powers) may have shaped it to always be associated with political struggles (Kibanja, 1999). Given that religion is attached to ethnicity, which is the primary shaping force of party politics in Uganda, religion also influences ethnopolitical conflicts in this country.

4. *Competition for scarce resources.* Competition for political, economic, and natural resources causes interethnic conflicts, and the formation of ethnic social and political movements (Nagel, 1995). Indeed, while "tribalism" has long been implicated in ethnic conflicts on the African continent, more contemporary views identify poverty, dependence on natural resources, and ineffective governments at the roots of violent conflict (Elbadawi & Sambanis, 2000). In Uganda, dependence on natural resources is high, with 68% of the population engaged in subsistence farming (Population and Housing Census Report, 2002). Ugandans face contextual challenges, including poverty; high rates of communicable diseases, such as malaria, AIDs, TB, and diarrhea; malnutrition; illiteracy; and a lack of jobs. The needs for infrastructure development, education, health, and human services remain high. Moreover, like other sub-Saharan countries, Uganda is already suffering grave environmental effects related to climate change, including deforestation, loss of biodiversity, human–animal conflict, and poor soil. Melting ice caps in the Ruwenzori Mountains have changed cattle corridors and resulted in an increase in mosquito breeding and related illnesses in new areas of the country. The doubling of Uganda's human population over the last 20 years has resulted in a reduction in tropical forest quantity and quality, creating ecological islands surrounded by poor communities who depend on the forests for their livelihoods. Threats to forests, particularly in the Lake Victoria basin, are likely to intensify given the projected population of 50 million in the next 20 years (Baranga, 2004; Naughton-Treves & Chapman, 2002). Climate change threatens to frustrate poverty eradication programs, such as those stated in the United Nation's Millennium Development Goals (MDGs), and it is suggested that 5–10% of Uganda's gross domestic product will be spent adapting to negative consequences of climate change (Tenywa, 2007).

Rural to urban migration and rapid social cultural changes have also placed new demands to adapt education, employment, family structures, and daily life to keep pace in a rapidly modernizing environment. A shortage of resources, whether environmental, economic, political, or social, can engender competition which is frequently framed along ethnic lines (Horowitz, 2000; Johnson et al., 2011). For example, fighting in the west of Uganda along the border with the DRC is associated with oil and minerals (gold and diamonds), while fighting in the north is associated with water shortages and infertile soil. With high rates of poverty and a concomitant need for resources, an environment of competition is created in which social identities and social group membership become the basis for allocating or denying resources and services. Thus, scarce and inequitable distribution of resources contributes to the ethnopolitical nature of the violence in Uganda (Winstok, 2010) (Table 16.3).

Table 16.3 Theories used in the analysis of ethnopolitical conflicts

Theory	Assumption	Consequences
Social Identity Theory	Social identity emerges from social and cognitive processes of categorization and comparison An individual's membership to social groups makes an important contribution to his or her self-concept by providing a source of social identity	People categorize the social world into ingroups and outgroups which stand in power and status relations to one another
Ultimate Attribution Error	An extension of the fundamental attribution error, group members attribute negative outgroup behavior to dispositional causes and positive outgroup behavior to situational factors	This predisposes individuals to outgroup prejudice as outgroup members' negative actions are always used against them
Relative Deprivation Theory	During social comparison, group members who perceive unfavorable outcomes as both stable and illegitimate are said to be in a state of relative deprivation	Individuals may be deprived of some desirable thing relative to their own past, another person, or group of individuals
Gurr's Model of Ethnopolitical Behavior	Ethnopolitical conflict is more likely to develop within the groups that have the strongest, most cohesive identities; the greatest extent of grievances supplying the incentives to organize; and the most elaborate networks and leadership capabilities that give them the capacity to mobilize successfully.	Identity, grievances, and mobilization are responsible for ethnopolitical conflicts
Intercultural Communication Theory (e.g., Anxiety-Uncertainty Management)	States that in times of threat or uncertainty, such as communication in a diverse or cross-cultural context, individuals are more prone to engage in negative stereotyping.	Anxiety and uncertainty associated with intercultural contacts can result in assumptions and stereotypes. Stereotypes can reduce cognitive dissonance in otherwise "nice" or "good" individuals, which paves the way for them to violate personal values of fairness or compassion, paving the way for discrimination, oppression, violence, and other tactics.

4 Consequences and Implications

The multiple, interrelated causes of the ethnopolitical conflicts in Uganda combine with the various atrocities occurring during the wars to undermine a nation and a people in nearly all domains of life. Economic, environmental, political, social, cultural, and psychological effects of conflict are interconnected, and in an environment where about a third of the population lives in poverty (with far greater percentages in the Ruwenzori and in the north), the effects may be exponential. The same hunger that make youth vulnerable to join the rebel ranks and become a killer may be there to greet him upon release from rehabilitation (Cheney, 2007). Though the economic, political, and environmental consequences of ethnic conflict cannot be minimized, here we discuss consequences in terms of perpetuation of negative ethnic stereotypes, ongoing ethnic polarization, and psychosocial effects of the long running ethnic conflicts in the country – one which, many say, never had a chance to develop a sense of unity before ethnic politics fragmented the country.

4.1 Stereotypes and Negative Intercultural Attitudes

From the beginning of colonial rule to the present, the history of Uganda has been reconstructed in neat looking but deceptive stereotypes, which can be summed up as follows: aliens versus natives, centralized/developed/sophisticated versus primitive stateless societies, the oppressor and the oppressed, the developed south and the backward north, the rulers and subjects, and the monarchists/traditionalists and the republicans. Uganda's history has also been reconstructed in terms of the modernizers versus the luddites, and the self-serving elite and the long-suffering oppressed/exploited masses. Not only do stereotypes distort history through oversimplification, but they are also extremely dangerous breeding grounds for bigotry, fear, resentment, irrationality, animosity, hatred, and ethnic conflict. Stereotypes generate self-serving attitudes such as "we deserve more because we sacrificed more than others," "they are suffering because it is their own fault," "it is their problem since they are killing their own people," and "it is their government and we have nothing to do with it." In extreme cases, stereotypes have culminated in mass violence, the mass displacement of millions of fellow citizens, ethnic cleansing, and genocide (Gourevitch, 1998; Kasozi, 1999; MISR, 1987; Prunier, 1995).

Negative social stereotypes can enhance the risk of interethnic violence or be used to justify violence as individuals and groups engage in the "ultimate attribution error" (Mio, Barker-Hackett, & Tumambing, 2008), an extension of the fundamental attribution error, in which people tend to blame an individual's undesirable behavior on perceived negative attributes of the group. This has certainly been the case, with attitudes and actions in Uganda indicating that the problems in the north are an "Acholi problem." This is ironically similar to the Western racist mentality about tribal or ethnic conflict occurring in African states being an "African problem," as if previous colonization and current globalization have no role. Intercultural communication theory (e.g., Anxiety-Uncertainty Management, Gudykunst, 1995) states that in times of threat or uncertainty, such as communication in a diverse or cross-cultural context, individuals are more prone to engage in negative stereotyping. These stereotypes can reduce cognitive dissonance in otherwise "nice" or "good" individuals, which paves the way for them to violate personal values of fairness or compassion and to engage in discrimination, oppression, violence, and other tactics.

4.2 Ongoing Ethnic Polarization

Museveni (1992) in his book "what is Africa's problem?" states that in Uganda, religion is sometimes used to bring about divisions among the people, but argued that there is nothing like ethnicity in Uganda. Museveni asserts that ethnicity is not a problem in Uganda, but does agree that past leaders used it to divide people. Unfortunately, a lot of what is currently happening in Uganda (i.e., the creation of chiefdoms within Buganda) is a clear illustration that he is also following the foot steps of the past leaders by using ethnicity to divide and rule. Deng (1996) warned that "the politics of identity based on ethnicity will remain a feature of African politics in the foreseeable future because ethnicity is still recognized as a vital fact of life that politicians take into consideration as they organize their political parties, form their governing organizations, and enter into reciprocal relations with ethnic and sub regional representation" (p. 55).

Ten years ago, Mukyala-Makiika (2000) predicted that the decentralization system of governance promoted by Museveni could not bring unity to the Ugandan state that is dominated with philosophies of regionalism, religion, and ethnicity. That is exactly what is unfolding. The popularity that the Museveni government enjoyed in the 1990s is declining. Voting patterns in the national presidential elections show this decline over the years. In the 2001 presidential elections, the incumbent president won by 69% majority vote. This was a 6% decline compared to the 1996 results. In 2006, he won by 59% majority vote, a 16% decline compared to the 1996 results. Generally, the president started loosing popularity among the elite when he influenced the parliament to pass a bill that removed presidential limits. This was a signal that his leadership was turning dictatorial (Oloka-Onyango, 2006). The voting pattern also shows that the president is slowly losing popularity in Buganda, a region that was home for his guerilla war. For instance, in 2001, Museveni got 1,435,448 votes in Buganda against Besigye's 724,309; while in 2006, Museveni got 1,080,324 votes (a reduction of 355,124 votes from 2001) against Besigye's 729,446 votes (an increase of 5,137 votes from 2001) in Buganda.

Instead of taking a diplomatic move to resolve its conflict with the Buganda Kingdom, the central government is instead using other avenues that frustrate the Buganda (Nabudere, 2009) such as amendment of the land bill to the disadvantage of Buganda in order to force it to drop its demand for a federal system of government. Identity conflicts become severe when one of the conflicting parties insists that the other give up beliefs, values, interests, goals, or practices (Deng, 1996). The central government, being in a high status position, is key to the resolution of this conflict. This is expected because in a conflict, the highest intergroup bias is displayed by the high status group (Teichman, Bar-Tal, & Abdolrazeq, 2007) and, therefore, the same can be applied in the resolution of the conflict. Unfortunately, the central government has consistently used state machinery to suppress Buganda's request for a federal system instead of using amicable ways. Moreover, when facing situations of threat and fear, societies may tend toward shared collectivist perspectives that emphasize ingroup/outgroup perspectives and ethnocentric thinking (Triandis, 1995).

When differences between ethnic groups are used to discriminate between these groups, ethnic conflicts may arise (Horowitz, 2001). Ethnic conflicts including riots, expulsion, ethnic cleansing, civil war, segregation, and genocides result when parties see violence as the only means of resolving their grievances (Reljic, 2004). In Uganda, ethnopolitical conflicts escalate because of increased competition for the domination of the modern politics (as is the case for the Bakiga and Banyoro in Kibaale), and the power of the state is responsible for intensifying these conflicts through deliberate manipulation of ethnic identities (Imtiyaz & Stavis, 2008).

4.3 Psychological, Social, and Cultural Effects

The felt impact of the ethnopolitical conflicts on Uganda varies greatly depending on the region in which one lives and his or her personal experiences. For example, while the Kampala district and surroundings have remained relatively protected from violent conflict, the northern districts have been devastated from the ravages of twenty-three years of war and nearly twenty-three years of virtual neglect. Rates of disability (e.g., from maiming), posttraumatic stress, and other socioemotional problems, including depression, substance abuse, risky sexual behavior, conduct problems, and adjustment disorders, among others, are especially high in war zones. For example, one study found rates of depression of nearly 45% in the war-affected north (Vinck, Pham, Stover, & Weinstein, 2007) compared to already elevated rates of 14–22% in the rest of the country (Bolton, Wilks, & Ndogoni, 2004; Ovuga, Boardman, & Wasserman, 2005).

While it is clear that much suffering has resulted, it is important to point out that these particular concepts of mental disorders are derived from a different context and not necessarily applicable to Uganda (Johnson, Mayanja, Bangirana, & Kizito, 2009). Those coming from collectivist societies may view PTSD as more social in nature, calling for a social or community-based perspective and intervention (Johnson, & Sandhu, 2010). Cultural clashes in rehabilitation treatment approaches are also evident. For example, counselors at the World Vision Rehabilitation centers may base treatments on communication of feelings and experiences, which in their direct forms of expression are not the cultural norm for Acholi, who prefer not to discuss private emotions directly, but to suffer stoically (Cheney, 2007). Creative and expressive arts, however, are also used by programs and may offer more culturally congruent modes of expression (indirect, group oriented) for addressing mental health and other rehabilitation needs (Johnson, Bastien, & Hirschel, 2009).

In fact, social and cultural level consequences of ethnopolitical conflict are often not considered by non-government organizations (NGOs) which tend to operate from Western-based individualistic perspectives. Social and also cultural devastation in Acholiland demands attention in order for the region and its people to recover. In her powerful ethnography of children's lives and childhood identity in northern Uganda, anthropologist Kristin Cheney (2007) points out that the LRA war has completely upset both traditional and universal views of childhood through its conscription and indoctrination of child soldiers into the rebel movement. A generation of children, adolescents, and young adults who "have only known war" unwittingly became both the hunted and the hunters, vulnerable and threatening at the same time. Parents of resettled youth have reported that Acholi (and Ugandan) cultural values that emphasize parental obedience and respect have disappeared among many of these children (Cheney, 2007). Cheney suggests that traditional Acholi customs, such as fire side lessons, music, and dance, are needed to build family and community relations, not to recapture a culture per se, but to create new cultural products that are relevant in a society which must rebuild and redefine its very conception of childhood.

5 Attempted Conflict Resolution Approaches

Various conflict resolution approaches have been used to solve the ethnopolitical conflicts. Some of them led to conflict escalation, others caused no significant change, others have lead to temporary peace, and the impact of others is yet to be determined. The approaches include military war (force), dialog, arbitration, and use of law (court).

5.1 Resolution of the Kibaale conflicts

All strategies so far used in the resolution of the Kibaale ethnic conflict lack an integration of effective conflict resolution principles and, therefore, cannot lead to permanent peace and stability in the subregion. For instance, early efforts to suppress the conflict in 2002 involved the use of constitutional powers by the President. He nullified the 2002 Kibaale district chairman election results that had been won by a Mukiga and replaced him with a Munyolo. This did not solve the conflict; it instead escalated it, leading to several injuries and deaths (Green, 2009).

Another attempt has been the President's proposal to "ring-fence" all top elective positions in the Bunyoro region for indigenous Banyoro. He claimed that ring-fencing positions for specific groups is a constitutional provision and is already implemented for youth, women, and persons with disabilities who are representatives in parliament (Ssekika, 2009). Although this was positively received by the Banyoro, the Bakiga rejected the proposal on grounds that it denies them their inherent rights as stipulated in the 1995 Ugandan constitution.

Another alternative has been the President's proposal that the Bakiga should start speaking Runyoro if they want to stay in Bunyoro (Ssekika, 2009). In other words, the President is suggesting that the Bakiga adopt a social mobility strategy. This implies that the Banyoro's position in the conflict is legitimate, and there are no cognitive alternatives to the existing conflict other than the illegitimate group (Bakiga) accepting to adopt the characteristics of the legitimate group (Banyoro). Such a proposal cannot definitely be accepted by the Bakiga who have been in a process of social comparison with the Banyoro for over 40 years, and it is this comparison that has enhanced their sense of group identity and emotional significance for their place in society (Horenczyk & Nisan, 1996). According to social psychology, people strongly depend on social comparison for understanding reality and checking the veracity of their perceptions and opinions if they encounter conditions of uncertainty (Festinger, 1954 cited in Abrams, 1997). As a third party, the president is supposed to be neutral and impartial. When a third party starts directing the resolution, trust in him/her is lost.

In September 2009, the President set up a reconciliation committee of both the Banyoro and Bakiga to find an amicable resolution to the Kibaale conflict. Like the previous attempts, this committee did not bear any fruits because its composition, process of formation, and leadership did not involve grassroots participation. For instance, its chairperson does not come from Kibaale, yet lower level leaders in Kibaale still think that their conflict can amicably be solved without outsiders (Ssekika, 2009).

On 29th March 2010, the district council passed the resolution to create new administrative units (i.e., counties, constituencies, subcounties, and town councils) to create political space and reduce the ethnic conflicts between the Bakiga and Banyoro over political positions. Although this may reduce political pressure in the region, it will not lead to conflict resolution because the new administrative units were split according to tribes, which is likely to accentuate the tribal differences (Kasooba, 2010) forming grounds for other forms of conflict.

Because administrative units have been created on tribal lines, religious leaders under the Bunyoro interreligious council have, on the contrary, planned to carry out civic education for all intending political leaders for the 2011 elections (Tusiime, 2010). On face value, the name of the council is biased toward Banyoro, and one wonders whether the Bakiga intending political leaders will be embraced. It is, therefore, evident that up to date, an effective conflict resolution strategy is yet to be implemented in the Kibaale district.

5.2 Resolutions of the Buganda–Central Government Conflicts

Conflict resolution strategies started in 2004 when Mengo and the central government engaged in several meetings over the federal system of governance. This did not yield any positive outcomes because government ended up giving Mengo a regional tier system instead of federal and the later rejected it. There were also several talks and letters over the land bill. After the 10th September 2009 riot, and closure of CBS, several attempts have been made to resolve the differences between the groups but to no avail. On 30th September 2009, the Kabaka of Buganda and the President held talks at State House Entebbe. In December 2009, a cabinet committee was set up to look into the issue of CBS. This committee met CBS's proprietors in December 2009 for the first time, but the meeting did not yield positive results until October 2010 when the Head of the Communications Commission reopened the station without any conditions. The weekly observer newspaper of Monday 25th October 2010 noted that CBS was reopened due to the political pressure mounted on the president from different sources (Kiggundu, 2010). Meetings between the central government and Buganda did not lead to any resolutions because each side perceived itself as being important, and at every sitting, each of the sides gave the other conditions to consider before further negotiations. For instance, the president set a condition that for CBS to be reopened, it should not broadcast political programs but rather stick to cultural issues ("Saleh offers CBS lifeline," 2009), particular employees should be dismissed, and particular political figures mainly from the opposition should not be allowed to speak over the station. The Buganda kingdom rejected the condition.

On the contrary, when the President made efforts to rebuild good relations with Buganda kingdom after the burning of the Kasubi tombs, the kingdom also gave his government 12 conditions to consider before rebuilding relations. The kingdom's Lukiiko (council) claimed that for any relations to be rebuilt, government must first of all reopen CBS, return Buganda's expropriated property currently in the hands of government, pay the pending debts owed by central government, make a public apology for the deaths in Kasubi Tombs, stop tapping the Kabaka's phone, and return the Kabaka's cultural spear that he gave to the president while still in the bush; and the president should stop trespassing into private Buganda cultural sites, apologize for refusing the Kabaka to visit Bugerere, and relocate Buganda's districts that have been transferred to the central government (Museveni asattira, 2010).

The conditions given by either side are an indication that each side considers itself strong and in control of the conflict. In such a state, no meaningful resolutions can be reached. Effective resolutions will be realized when each party either realizes that it cannot win the conflict or suffers costs from the conflict.

5.3 Resolutions of the Northern Uganda War

Resolution of this conflict has had several key players such as the religious and traditional leaders, the international community, and civil society organizations that have all along been struggling to end this conflict through dialog. Attempts to end the war started in 1988 when NRM and UPDA signed a peace accord. Between 1993 and 1994, talks were held with Joseph Kony on behalf of government, but these did have any positive result because of the government's lack of respect and commitment to them (HURIPEC, 2003).

In 1997, the Acholi Religious Leader's Peace Initiative was formed. This is an organization of leaders from all religious sects in the region and its purpose is to advocate for peace in the region. This organization advocated for the comprehensive amnesty Act of 2000 which grants amnesty from prosecution to all former rebels who voluntarily come out. By 2004, over 5,000 former LRA rebels had applied for amnesty (Tim, 2006).

In 2002, about 50 organizations came together to form the Civil Society Organization for Peace in Northern Uganda (CSOPNU), which has played a major role in advocacy and fostering of reconciliation at all levels ((HURIPEC, 2003). In the same year (2002), the president set up a Presidential peace team for political and military affairs in northern Uganda. Although the team did not immediately become operational (HURIPEC, 2003), some of its members were later very instrumental in the 2006–2009 peace negotiations.

In July 2005, the International Criminal Court (ICC) issued arrest warrants against the five key LRA leaders (including Joseph Kony), charging them with crimes against humanity. Details of the warrants were sent to Uganda, Southern Sudan, and the DRC, which are the countries where LRA operate from. All along, the LRA leadership had been promising never to surrender unless they were granted immunity from persecution. So the ICC's orders to arrest them are an indication that the conflict may not be amicably solved through dialog (Senabulya, 2009). Contrary to the ICC's move, the people of northern Uganda insist that if Kony came back, they would forgive him. They prefer amnesty to ICC (Obore, 2009).

In July 2006, peace talks between LRA and the Uganda government began in Juba, Southern Sudan. These were mediated by the deputy president of Southern Sudan Dr. Riek Machar. When peace talks started, there was a cease-fire and displaced people slowly moved to satellite camps. As of now, most of them have gone back to their homes. Although peace talks went on for 2 years, a final peace agreement was not signed. The LRA set a condition that "the ICC lifts indictments issued against their leaders" for signing the final peace agreement.

Currently, the government is determined to pursue the LRA leader until he is captured (Okino, 2010). The government is accusing Joseph Kony of failing to sign the peace agreement after 2 years of negotiations. Most Ugandans emphasize that the NRM's insistence to use force rather than dialog is the major contributor to the prolonged war and instability in Northern Uganda (Obore, 2009). As the Ugandan army, with international support, advances in pursuit (even employing former LRA child soldiers in its efforts), Kony and his LRA have moved across the Western border where they continue to attack villages and abduct more children to fortify their ranks.

6 Suggestions for Policy Makers

As evidenced with past and current violence, much is at stake. The recurrence of ethnopolitical conflict in Uganda demands attention from policy makers, human rights organizations, educators, and scholars. What are the best routes to resolve current conflicts and also to prevent escalations of interethnic tension and develop harmonious and peaceful societies? Given that ethnicity has, at least in recent history, often played a divisive role, does it make sense to encourage the development of ethnic identity in Uganda? In particular, what are the psychological, social, and political implications for developing a strong tribal or religious identity? Should an agenda of national identity be advanced? What about the creation of the subkingdoms and other current issues facing the NRM government – is there an approach that would reduce interethnic tensions and conflicts? The answers are key to policy development, yet raise a number of unexamined issues regarding the conception, meaning, and function of ethnicity and ethnic identity across cultural, geographic, and historical contexts.

6.1 Is Ethnic Identity a Nice Thing to Have?

The function of ethnicity and ethnic identity for individuals and societies will vary based on its conceptualization (e.g., whether it is visible, such as based on phenotypic features or dress; ascribed versus chosen, relative mutability, etc.) and its meaning (e.g., positive or negative valence, privileged with power or resources versus denied access or rights). The relative salience and importance of ethnic identity (and other social identities) are related in part to the make up of the population (percentage of majority–minority and whether there is a dominant group), ethnic differences in terms of power and resources, and extent of social inequities, discrimination, and oppression (Aponte & Johnson, 2000). For example, racial identity is identified as more important or salient to African–Americans in the USA compared to their white counterparts, due to a history of (and current) oppression based on skin color. conversely, among the Shona, a dominant ethnic group in South Africa, ethnic identity appears to be less salient due to their majority status (Worrell, Conyers, Mpofu, & Vandiver, 2006).

Globally, intercultural contact is increasing and identities are evolving as individuals, groups, and societies undergo processes of acculturation and changing dynamics of majority–minority group status, group relations, cultural climates, and power differentials. Developmental, behavioral, and acculturation theories (e.g., Berry, 1997; Bronfenbrenner, 2004) indicate the importance of context in determining the most adaptive approach to a situation. So, in the Ugandan context, does cultivating ethnic identity carry the risk of contributing to divisiveness, intercultural tensions, and ethnopolitical violence in Uganda? Or might it be used as a tool in the formation of healthy and harmonious societies?

President Museveni has advocated an approach that moves beyond ethnic, tribal, and clan identities and ideology (Museveni, 1997), suggesting that Uganda will be fully evolved when only national, not tribal, identities exist. Despite lip service to cultural unity, Museveni has fueled ethnic divisions by recognizing and favoring particular tribal kingdoms. In U.S. psychology, culturally competent service models urge against such a "color-blind" or "culture-blind" approach as devaluing the important roles of culture, race, and ethnicity in human development and behavior (Helm, 1990; Johnson & Tucker, 2008). However, despite efforts by researchers, policy makers, and educators to promulgate the benefits of and need for cultural pluralism, the lay public, certain religious groups, and political bodies continue to push a nationalistic agenda which argues for the primacy of nationalism and devalues certain cultural identities (e.g., "English Only" laws and strict immigration policies in the USA).

In a multicultural context with current ethnic tensions, attempts to ignore ethnicity or suppress ethnic identification will likely backfire because of the historical and current importance of tribal and religious identity in certain situations (Pittinsky, 2010). Ten years after the genocide in Rwanda, the concept of "ethnicity" was essentially forbidden for fear it would cause intergroup tensions to resurface between the Hutu, Tutsi, and Twa groups, which, we should note, were reified into distinct groups by the Belgians (Hilker, 2009). Paul Rusesabagina (2006), in his compelling account about creating a relative safe haven for over 1200 people at the Hotel Mille Collines during the genocide, worries that silence on the topic is not the answer, "it frightens me to death that my countryman are not talking…that my country is packed with a lot of angry people not talking to each other. We could be witnessing the roots of a future holocaust" (2006, p. 195).

Moreover, as Wagari Maathai, Nobel Peace Prize nominee and founder of the Kenyan Green Belt Movement, has asserted, minimizing tribal identity in lieu of national identity will not occur when the nation states in Africa are so fragile (Maathai, 2008). Indeed, in Uganda, suppressing or denying ethnicity (while at the same time manipulating divisions) has done little to shift allegiances to a nation identity. Interestingly, in one study in which we asked young Ugandan adults to define their ethnicity, 53% provided a tribal category, followed by ethno-linguistic group, such as Bantu (37%). Only 5% described their identity as Ugandan, while 3% gave a pan-national identity (i.e., African) (Johnson et al., 2011). So, while it may not always feel like a "nice thing" to discuss ethnicity and its related cousins, racism and discrimination, these factors remain key to understanding the past, ameliorating current conflicts and preventing future escalations. In the years since segregation ended in the USA and apartheid was banished in South Africa, efforts toward racial reconciliation have finally come to terms with the notion that advances toward intercultural understanding and reconciliation, in fact, depend on discussions of ethnicity in previous and current struggles.

6.2 Positive Aspects of Cultural Identity and Diversity

Group identity has an impact on one's psychological well-being and health (Haslam, Jetten, Postmes & Haslam, 2009; Jasinskaja-Lahti et al., 2009). To deny tribal identity (or other types of social and cultural identity) is to deny people of their cultural heritage, social support, and positive health and psychosocial benefits that go along with that sense of identity. This view is consistent with theory and research from developmental and multicultural psychology, indicating that healthy attitudes toward diverse cultures and identification with one's ethnic heritage can function to promote mental health, protect against behavioral or emotional problems, and prompt civic engagement (Benson, Scales, & Mannes, 2003; Flanagan & Faison, 2001; Phinney, 1992; Scales, Benson, & Leffert, 2000).

In U.S. psychology, ethnic identity is considered a strength. Research indicates that ethnic identity is related to a number of protective mental health variables, such as feelings of belonging, support, and connection to the group, which may serve as protective factors among adults and youth (Aponte & Johnson, 2000; Johnson, Bastien, & Hirschel, 2009). There is a consensus among psychologists that developing a firm ethnic and cultural identity is something positive to be nurtured in young people. Research among U.S. youth demonstrates that adolescents with "achieved" ethnic identity show a higher awareness of diversity issues and have more positive regard toward members of different ethnic groups compared to those with a diffuse ethnic identity (Phinney, Jacoby, & Silva, 2007). Ethnic identity has also been associated with pro-social attitudes and self-esteem in U.S. youth (Smith, Walker, Fields, Brookins, & Seay, 1999). Beyond the benefits to individuals, some assert that ethnic diversity can contribute to, rather than impede, the stability of African nations, providing a means of resource exchange and sources of diverse knowledge, perspectives, and skills (Elbadawi & Sambanis, 2000; Maathai, 2008).

Efforts to cultivate ethnic identity may be viewed with suspicion and, given that ethnic and cultural labels have the potential to wreak havoc, discussions and educational efforts promoting cultural identity should recognize the complexity and multidimensionality of constructs such as ethnicity and culture. Identity must be understood as a collection of various personal and social identities and "subgroups" or "micronationalities" (Pittinsky, 2010; Maathai, 2008). Developing an appreciation of various ethnic, tribal, religious, national, and other identities is crucial to the development of just and peaceful societies. Understanding the dynamic and multidimensional interplay (intersectionality) of various social identities within each person (such as tribal, religious, age related, gender, economic status, disability, sexual orientation, and so on) can allow individuals more flexibility, fluidity, and potential support from various social groups. Moreover, maintaining one's sense of individuality and personhood may aid in the prevention of "groupthink" and the vulnerability to social pressures to act unjustly in the name of ethnic differences (Rusesabagina, 2006).

Policies should ideally flow from sound scientific evidence that is reliable and valid. Given the dearth of research on ethnopolitical conflict, ethnicity, and intercultural relations in Uganda, there is little evidence on which to create effective policy. One study by Habyarimana, Humphrey, Posner, and Weinstein (2008) used experimental games to examine ethnicity and intercultural attitudes. The authors found no evidence that people care more for the welfare of individuals from their ethnic groups than the welfare of those from other ethnic groups. However, other studies have illustrated that empathy to one's own cultural group arouses a different pattern of brain activation, indicating possible differences in the means of learning, activating, and/or expressing empathy toward various groups based on familiarity, among other things (Xu, Zuo, Wang, & Han, 2009). The meaning of the discrepant findings remains unclear, yet consideration of the multiplicity of identity and identity salience are likely at play, indicating the complexity of "ethnicity." As discussed above, individuals have multiple social identities, and the social identity salient as the dimension of comparison will determine ingroup favoritism or outgroup bias. For example, a similar study found differential brain activation when helping ingroup members, where ingroup bias was based on sports team rivalries (Hein, Silani, Preuschoff, Batson, & Singer, 2010). Given that participants in the (Habyarimana et al., 2008) study were put into pairs to complete a task, the study outcomes may have confounded ethnic identification with workgroup identification. Social identification with a workgroup has a positive long-term impact on individual's health, well-being, and morale because it is associated with support and appreciation (Haslam et al., 2009). Subjects may have perceived their partners as workgroup members regardless of ethnic identity. Shared identity has a positive impact on work and life satisfaction because it serves as basis for the receipt of effective support from ingroup members (Cohen & Wills, 1985 cited in Haslam et al., 2009).

At the same time, working toward a shared goal, and thus developing a common work identification, may be a promising pathway to develop healthy intercultural attitudes and behaviors (Johnson-Pynn & Johnson, 2005, 2010). For example, in a study of intercultural attitudes and ethnic identity among youth members of Wildlife Clubs of Uganda, a government funded youth conservation education program, youth reported that the program resulted in new awareness of diverse groups (Johnson-Pynn & Johnson, 2005, 2010). For example, youth stated "I learned how to associate with people of different ethnicities," and "I have got new friends who made me learn about ethnicity and backgrounds." Several mentioned attitude and behavior change afforded through the group; for example, one Ugandan youth stated that

> I have changed my behavior towards different ethnicities or tribes because the group consists of different tribal backgrounds.

Moreover, in a psychometric study with 224 Uganda WCU members, positive diversity attitudes were associated with the Multi Ethnic Identity Measure (Phinney, 1992) affirmation scale (Johnson et al., 2011), suggesting that developing one's own identity does not preclude positive intercultural attitudes.

6.3 Forging New Identities to Promote Intercultural Harmony

Uganda, like other nations across the globe, must come to terms with its diverse and changing multicultural makeup and make strategic efforts to advance intercultural relations and ethnopolitical cooperation. Challenged with extreme poverty, high demands for infrastructure development, health crises, and environmental degradation, the challenges facing governments and societies in sub-Saharan Africa are especially immense. Moreover, Uganda may be characterized as having a "youth bulge," with 45% of its population being under 25 years of age (CIA World Factbook, 2009). Nations with youth bulges are thought to be particularly influential in shaping their communities, and nations may propel them either toward peace and cohesion or toward ethnic division and violence (Fuller,

1995; Hart, Atkins, Markey, & Youniss, 2004). Developing a sense of national unity and commitment to intercultural harmony will, however, depend on government, social, and individual support for an equitable system of allocating power and distributing resources which does not pit tribes against one another or against the central government.

While some African leaders, including Museveni, have espoused a shift from community (i.e., tribal or clan identities) to national identity and loyalty to the nation-state, we argue that this approach is at best unproductive and ineffective in the Ugandan context, and, at worst, a strategy that escalates violent conflict and worsens ethnic divides (Pittinsky, 2010). Addressing intercultural attitudes and shaping new ethnic identities that are relevant and adaptable in today's Uganda and in the global community are essential (Maathai, 2008). Thus, we argue that ecologically valid programs to promote intercultural relations are needed, and further, that government and non-government (NGO) programs promoting youth, community, and women's development hold promise for forging healthy cultural identities and awareness. Strengths-based approaches to youth development help youth cultivate positive personal and cultural identities and emphasize positive intergroup attitudes (Benson, Scales, & Mannes, 2003; Johnson & Tucker, 2008). In the USA, positive youth development and service learning-based programs, in which learning is accomplished through hands-on service, have also reported gains in cultural identity, diversity attitudes (Myers-Lipton, 1996), and commitment to civic society (Limber & Kaufman, 2002). Although research is sparse, studies have indicated that 14–24-year-old Ugandan young people involved in youth service programs (i.e., Wildlife Clubs) report gains in attitudes toward other tribes as a result of contact and mutual activities (Johnson & Johnson-Pynn, 2007; Johnson et al., 2011; Johnson-Pynn & Johnson, 2005, 2010).

6.4 Specific Strategies

Ethnicity and identity are multifaceted, interrelated, and dynamic constructs that have important ramifications for ethnopolitical conflict and for intercultural harmony in Uganda. Efforts to improve interethnic and intercultural relations and to develop healthy ethnic identities should be undertaken through concerted efforts by government and NGOs and institutions in the education, health, social service, community development, and political sectors. There is a great need for research to inform policy in government relations, communications, education, and even at the community level and within tribes and clans. Intergroup bias and ethnic prejudice should be addressed before it escalates into further violence (Allport, 1958). Because ethnic prejudice is learned, social interventions can be effective in reducing negative attitudes or enhancing positive attitudes. Programs to improve intergroup dynamics may be most effective and garner community buy-in when based on an action research paradigm in which community and tribal stakeholders are involved in the development and evaluation of the intervention (e.g., Lewin, 1946).

- Government, NGOs, businesses, and villages must work toward ethical, equitable, and sustainable development, which includes achieving the United Nations MDGs.
- Where resource shortages remain, a new approach is needed that does not manipulate ethnic, religious, or other social group divisions to further benefit the privileged and powerful.
- Minority groups (ethnic, religious, persons with disabilities, sexual orientation minorities, etc.) need to have a voice and to have their rights protected and interests acknowledged. Social justice values should be cultivated and modeled by the government, educators, religious leaders, community elders, and families.
- Due to the historical and current role of ethnic identity in politics and social life, tribal, ethnic, and cultural identity can neither be ignored, nor should they be downplayed.
- A firm and well-developed cultural identity, based on tribe and other affiliations, may be seen as a protective factor or mental health asset that could be cultivated with traditional cultural education.
- Efforts to strengthen ethnic, religious, or cultural identity should be provided in tandem with efforts to cultivate positive intercultural

attitudes, exposure to diverse groups, and awareness for the benefits and value of having diverse groups and perspectives (i.e., valuing diversity and liking other groups).

- Because ethnicity has often been used in a negative way in Uganda to separate tribes and promote the agendas of various regimes, it is important to identify and cultivate new ways of understanding ethnicity and identity that do not intensify ethnocentric thinking and stereotypes.
- Recognizing the complex nature of individual and group identities and how they affect power and privilege may reduce simple, dichotomous, ingroup and outgroup thinking and behaviors, and increase awareness of social justice issues.
- Community and youth development programs, as well as schools, can incorporate intercultural learning and civic engagement in their programs.
- Collaborative working toward shared goals and building on traditional and newly produced cultural and religious values may be incorporated to strengthen the value of cultural diversity.
- Museveni and the current government should adopt a strategy of transformational leadership.

The strategies outlined are rooted in theory and research from community, behavioral, multicultural, cross-cultural, social, and developmental psychology. A multipronged strategy is consistent with our contemporary, multidimensional understanding of prejudice, discrimination, and racism (Dovido, 2000). A multidimensional approach is also consistent with the organizational perspective provided by Pittinsky's (2010) two-dimensional model of intergroup leadership. The model, developed to better understand leadership in the context of diversity, emphasizes the unique importance of two dimensions: 1) reducing negative intergroup bias, stereotypes, and ethnocentric thinking, and 2) increasing positive feelings and recognition of the value of other groups (a dimension that Pittinsky and colleagues have termed "allophilia") (2010, p.195; Pittinsky, Montoya, Tropp, & Chen, 2007). The model asserts that leaders in a diverse collective must work to unite individuals and subgroups, and also that leaders must understand that positive and negative intergroup attitudes are two different dimensions of intercultural relations, with different causes and outcomes.

Implications of the two-dimensional model are similar to those regarding the cultivation of ethnic identity. That is, a "both/and" approach, rather than an "either/or" approach is needed: encouraging unity and support for the collective good *AND* encouraging tribal/cultural identity, and reducing prejudice *AND* promoting liking, respect, and appreciation for "the other" tribes. These ideas provide a more complete approach to leadership of diverse groups and interests, and thus, one that may produce better results. The approach is consistent with bicultural models of cultural adjustment and also with traditional African values of interdependence, mutuality, caring, and concern for others' welfare (e.g., "I am because we are"). Opportunities and supports for two-dimensional intercultural education may be developed and offered through schools and youth and community programs. The government should support community, youth development, and rehabilitation programs, which are in desperate need of more funds, especially outside of Kampala.

Additionally, the current government needs an approach that unites, rather than escalates tensions between diverse groups with its hard-line use of force and its manipulation of ethnic divisions, such as the creation of the subkingdoms which fractionates the region. Instead, Museveni should adopt a leadership style that promotes collective caring and universal values (and yes, a national identity), while also modeling fair and equitable appropriation of resources for the good of all Ugandans, rather than to further fortress his own position. In a transformational approach, leaders such as Gandhi, Martin Luther King, Nelson Mandela, and Julius Nyerere have advanced social justice and diversity concerns by committing themselves to unity amid diversity and risking much in the process. This strategy works to bring groups together, as they rally in support of their leader (Pittinsky, 2010). While Museveni may have benefitted initially from similar sentiments and a Ugandan populace willing to rally support in desperate hopes of a change from the previous dictatorships, clearly, that faith and support evidenced in the late eighties and nineties have eroded. For Museveni and the

NRM, steps toward transformational leadership are needed. Museveni should promote positive relations among tribes and behave consistently by forming high-quality relations with each tribe (Pittinsky, 2010). A softer approach to leadership (Nye, 2008) relying on inspiration and consensus building must be more effective in creating a "collective we" than what is currently offered by the central government.

However, Museveni's position and leadership potential may not be salvageable after two decades of leadership and, since 2000, an increasingly autocratic and dictatorial style. Frustration is high and it appears that ethnic manipulations will only increase, resulting in more ethnic conflict. Additionally, a new cultural conflict has recently emerged in which sexual minorities (gay, lesbian, bisexual, and transgender individuals) are being targeted for "criminal behavior" as are those considered sympathizers, such as individuals who fail to report/identify gay people or who promote acceptance. Although the harsh criminalization law which included death penalty for repeat offenses (homosexual acts) did not pass parliament (only after threats from the international community of withdrawal of financial aid), anti-gay sentiment and prejudices are high in Uganda. Lists of gay and lesbian persons and their places of employment are being displayed, with print messages indicating a tacit permission to engage in violence, of which there are growing reports (Sharlett, 2010). This newfound "other" is somewhat convenient for the president because it allows a new approach to divide and rule, promulgating prejudice, discrimination, and oppression, and thus, furthering divisions and break down of power within the tribes, churches, and other social organizations. Museveni should avoid such drastic human rights violations and prevent further ethnopolitical bloodshed by changing course drastically.

7 Summary

In Uganda, political conflicts and violence have been framed along tribal and religious lines since before the formation of the Uganda state. A divide-and-rule policy adopted by the colonialists favored Buganda by giving it land that belonged to other kingdoms and putting the Baganda in administrative positions to run the public service sector entirely. They were the educated tribe and most colonial schools were in their kingdom. This laid the foundation of ethnicization of politics in the country as evidenced by the other regimes. The present-day government is employing the same tactics, not only to win elections but also to manage, dominate, and exploit the country's resources. Violent ethnic conflicts have remained in the periphery of the county (i.e., north and west) until more recently, as the simmering tensions between Buganda and the NRM have begun to affect the south and central areas of the country, including Kampala, the capital city. The threat of continued conflict and violence remains as the policies and actions that contribute to tensions and status quo in the current government have not changed. Accordingly, all attempts made to resolve these conflicts have instead escalated them or had no significant impact.

Ultimately, for peace to flourish in Uganda, intercultural attitudes will need the necessary ingredients (resources) that allow peace to take root. Massive efforts are needed to move Uganda along in meeting the MDGs to eradicate poverty, control infectious diseases, and improve education. Families and communities have been uprooted due to war, infertile soil, or lack of other basic resources, and the lure of jobs that are in actuality far too few in the urban centers. There is a need to promote sustainability among communities and also the equitable and socially just distribution of resources. A transformation in leadership is needed.

References

Abrams, D. (1997). Analyses of the complex reactions to the death of DIANA Princess of Wales. *The Psychologist, 10*(11), 500–508.

Allport, G. W. (1958). *The nature of prejudice (abridged).* Garden City, NY: Double Day.

Aponte, J. F., & Johnson, L. R. (2000). The impact of culture on intervention and treatment of ethnic populations. In J. F. Aponte & J. Wohl (Eds.), *Psychological intervention and cultural diversity* (2nd ed., pp. 18–39). Needham Heights, MA: Allyn & Bacon.

Baranga, D. (2004). Forest fragmentation and primates' survival status in non-reserved forests of the 'Kampala area', Uganda. *African Ecology, 42*, 70–77.

Benson, P. L., Scales, P. C., & Mannes, M. (2003). Developmental strengths and their sources: Implications for the study and practice of community building. In R. M. Lerner, F. Jacobs, & D. Wertlieb (Eds.), *Handbook of applied developmental science* (pp. 369–406). Thousand Oaks, CA: Sage.

Berry, J. W. (1997). Immigration, acculturation, and adaptation. *Applied Psychology: An International Review, 46*, 5–68.

Boddy-Evans, A. (2003). Biography: Idi Amin Dada. Despotic president of Uganda in the 1970s. About.com Guide.

Bolton, P., Wilks, C., & Ndogoni, L. (2004). Assessment of depression prevalence in rural Uganda using symptom and function criteria. *Social Psychiatry and Psychiatric Epidemiology, 39*(6), 442–447.

Bronfenbrenner, U. (2004). *Making Human Beings Human: Bioecological Perspectives on Human Development*. Thousand Oaks, CA: Sage Publications.

Butagira, T. (2010, March 20). What next for Buganda?. *Saturday Monitor*, pp. 3.

Cheney, K. (2007). *Pillars of the nation: Child citizens and Ugandan national development*. Chicago, IL: The University of Chicago Press.

CIA World Factbook. (2009). *The World factbook: Uganda* . Washington, DC: Central Intelligence Agency. https://www.cia.gov/library/publications/the-world-factbook/index.html

Clark, J. F. (2002). *Uganda: Self-determination conflict profile for foreign policy in focus website*. Available at http://www.selfdetermine.org/conflicts/uganda.html. (Posted January 2002).

Collison, R. L. (1981). *World bibliographical series* (Uganda, Vol. 11). Great Britain: Clio Press Ltd.

Decalo, S. (1990). *Coup and army rule in Africa: motivation and constraints*. New Haven, CT: Yale University Press.

Deng, F. M. (1996). Identity in Africa's internal conflicts. *American Behavioral Scientist, 40*, 46–65.

Dovido, J. F. (2000). On the nature of contemporary prejudice: The third wave. *Journal of Social Issues, 57*, 829–849.

Elbadawi, E., & Sambanis, N. (2000). Why are there so many civil wars in Africa? Understanding and preventing violent conflict. *African Economics, 9*, 244–269.

Fairhead, J. (2000). The conflict over natural and environmental resources. In E. W. Nafziger, F. Stewart, & R. Vayrynen (Eds.), *War, hunger and displacement: The origins of humanitarian emergencies* (pp. 147–178). New York: Oxford University Press.

Fearon, J. (2003). Ethnic and cultural diversity by country. *Journal of Economic Growth, 8*, 195–222.

Flanagan, C., & Faison, N. (2001). Youth civic development: Implications of research for social policy and programs. *Social Policy Report: A Publication of the Society for Research in Child Development, 15*, 3–15.

Fuller, G. (1995). The demographic backdrop to ethnic conflict: A geographic overview. In Central Intelligence Agency (Ed.), *The challenge of ethnic conflict to national and international order in the 1990s* (pp. 151–154). Washington, DC: Central Intelligence Agency.

Gertzel, C. (1980). Uganda after Amin: The continuing search for leadership and control. *African Affairs, 79*(317), 461–89.

Gourevitch, P. (1998). *We wish to inform you that tomorrow we will be killed with our families*. New York: Picador.

Green, E. D. (2007). Demography, diversity and nativism in contemporary Africa: Evidence from Uganda, in nations and nationalism. *Journal of the Association for the Study of Ethnicity and Nationalism, 13*, 717–736.

Green, E. D. (2009). *Demographic change and conflict in contemporary Africa*. Paper presented at a conference on Demography and security: The politics of popular change. Weatherhead Centre for International Affairs, Harvard University.

Gudykunst, W. B. (1995). Anxiety/uncertainty management (AUM) theory: Current status. In R. Wiseman (Ed.), *Intercultural communication theory* (pp. 8–58). Thousand Oaks, CA: Sage.

Gurr, T. R. (2000). *Peoples versus States: Minorities at risk in the New Century*. Washington, DC: United States Institute of Peace Press.

Habyarimana, J., Humphrey, M., Posner, D., & Weinstein, J. (2008). Is ethnic conflict inevitable? Parting ways over nationalism and separatism. *Foreign Affairs, 87*(4), 138–141.

Hansen, H. B. (1977). *Ethnicity and the military in Uganda*. Uppsala: Scandinavian Institute of African Studies.

Hart, D., Atkins, R., Markey, P., & Youniss, J. (2004). Youth bulges in communities: The effects of age structure on adolescent civic knowledge and civic participation. *Psychological Science, 15*, 591–597.

Haslam, S. A., Jetten, J., Postmes, T., & Haslam, C. (2009). Social Identity, health and well-being: An emerging agenda for applied psychology. *Applied Psychology: An International Review, 58*(1), 1–23.

Hayes, G., & Mare, G. (1997). *Ethnicity: Between the real and the imagined*. Unpublished Paper, Department of Psychology, University of Natal, Durban, South Africa.

Hein, G., Silani, G., Preuschoff, K., Batson, C., & Singer, T. (2010). Neural responses to ingroup and outgroup members' suffering predict individual differences in costly helping. *Neuron, 68*(1), 149–160.

Helms, J. E. (1990). *Black and White racial identity: Theory, research and practice*. New York: Greenwood.

Hilker, L. M. (2009). Everyday ethnicities: Identity and reconciliation among Rwandan youth. *Journal of Genocide Research, 11*, 81–100.

Horenczyk, G., & Nisan, M. (1996). The actualization balance of ethnic identity. *Journal of Personality and Social Psychology, 70*(4), 836–843.

Horowitz, D. L. (2000). *Ethnic groups in conflict* (2nd ed.). Berkeley, CA: University of California Press.

Horowitz, D. L. (2001). *The deadly ethnic riot*. Berkeley, CA: University of California Press.

HURIPEC. (2003). *The hidden war: the forgotten people. War in Acholiland and its ramifications for peace and security in Uganda*. Uganda, October 30, Retrieved August 14, 2010, from http:///www.huripec.ac.ug

Imtiyaz, A. R. M., & Stavis, B. (2008). Ethnopolitical conflicts in Srilanka. *Journal of Third World Studies, 25*(2), 135–139.

Jasinskaja-Lahti, I., Liebkind, K., & Solheim, E. (2009). To identify or not to identify? National disidentification as an alternative reaction to perceived ethnic discrimination. *Applied Psychology: An International Review, 58*(1), 105–128.

Johnson, L. R., Bastien, G., & Hirschel, M. (2009). Psychotherapy in a culturally diverse world. In S. Eshun & R. Gurung (Eds.), *Culture and mental health: Sociocultural influences, theory, and practice*. Hoboken, NJ: Wiley-Blackwell.

Johnson, L. R., & Johnson-Pynn, J. (2007). Cultivating compassion and youth action around the globe: A preliminary report on Jane Goodall's Roots and Shoots Program. *Journal of Youth Development: Bridging Research and Practice, 2*(2), #0702FA002. Available at http://www.nae4ha.org

Johnson, L. R., Kim, E. H., Pynn, J., Schulenberg, S., & Balagaye, H., & Lugumya, D. (2011) Ethnic identity, self-efficacy and intercultural attitudes in East African and U.S. youth. *Journal of Adolescent Research*. doi 10.1177/0743558411412955.

Johnson, L. R., & Sandhu, D. S. (2010). Treatment planning in a multicultural context. In M. Leach & J. Aten (Eds.), *Culture & the therapeutic process: A guide for mental health professionals*. Lawrence Erlbaum Associates: Hillsdale, NJ.

Johnson, L. R., Mayanja, K. M., Bangirana, P., & Kizito, S. (2009). Contrasting concepts of depression in Uganda: Implications for service delivery in a multicultural context. *Journal of Orthospsychiatry*, 79, 275–289.

Johnson-Pynn, J. S., & Johnson, L. R. (2005). Successes and challenges in East African conservation education. *Journal of Environmental Education, 36*, 25–39.

Johnson-Pynn, J. S., & Johnson, L. R. (2010). Exploring environmental education for East African youth: Do program contexts matter? *Children, Youth and Environments, 20*(1), 123–151. Retrieved March 1, 2010, from http://www.colorado.edu/journals/cye/

Kasfir, N. (1976). *The shrinking political arena: Participation and ethnicity in African politics, with a case study of Uganda*. Berkeley,CA: University of California Press Ltd.

Kasooba, I. (2010, April 01). Kibaale District to be split. *New Vision*. Retrieved from August 23, 2010, from http://www.newvision.co.ug

Kasozi, A. B. K. (1999). *The social origins of violence in Uganda*. Kampala: Fountain Publishers.

Kelman, H. (1999). The interdependence of Israeli and Palestinian national identities: The role of the other in existential conflicts. *Journal of Social Issues, 55*, 581–600.

Kibanja, G. M. (1999). *The relative influence of value priorities, ethnicity and worries in the determination of political party affiliation amongst Ugandan University Students*. Unpublished Masters thesis, Rhodes University, South Africa.

Kiggundu, E. (2010, October 25). Forces behind CBS reopening. *The Observer*, pp. 4

Kintu-Nyago, C. (1996). *Defining governance in Uganda in a changing world order: 1962 – 1994*. Unpublished Masters thesis, Rhodes University, South Africa.

Langlands, B. (1977). Students and politics in Uganda. *African Affairs, 76*, 3–20.

Lautze, S. (2007). *Research on Violent Institutions in Unstable Environments: The livelihoods systems of Ugandan army soldiers and their families in a war zone*. Hertford College, Oxford University. Retrieved 12 June 2007, from http:///www.livesandlivelihoods.com.

Legum, C. (Ed.). (1972–1973) *African contemporary record*, 5. Holmes & Meier Publishers

Lewin, K. (1946). Action research and minority problems. *Journal of Social Issues, 2*, 34–46.

Library of Congress Country Studies. (December, 1990). *Uganda: The Second Obote Regime: 1981–1985*. New York: Library of Congress.

Limber, S. P., & Kaufman, N. H. K. (2002). Civic participation in children and youth. In N. H. Kaufman & I. Rizzini (Eds.), *Globalization and children: Exploring potentials for enhancing opportunities in the lives of children and youth* (pp. 81–90). New York: Kluwer.

Lofchie, M. F. (1972). The Uganda coup – Class action by the military. *The Journal of Modern African Studies, 10*(1), 19–35.

Low, D. A. (1962). *Political parties in Uganda 1949–1962*. University of London: The Athlone Press.

Maathai, W. (2008). Tribal clashes, healing and reconciliation; how and when? Retrieved July 25, from http://www.greenbeltmovement.org

Mamdani, M. (1976). *Politics and class formation in Uganda*. London: Heinemann.

Marblestone, C. (2005) The History of Uganda. Prepared for web by Harold Marcuse on12/6/05; last updated: 12/14/05

Mio, J. S., Barker-Hackett, L., & Tumambing, J. (2008). *Multicultural psychology: Understanding our diverse communities*. San Francisco, CA: McGraw-Hill.

MISR. (1987). *Uganda: International seminar on internal conflict*. Kampala: Institute of Social Research, Makerere University.

Mudoola, D. M. (1996). *Religion, ethnicity, and politics in Uganda*. Kampala: Fountain Publishers.

Mujaju, A. B. (1974). *Youth action and political development*. Unpublished DPhil. Thesis, Columbia University, USA

Mukyala-Makiika, R. (2000). Traditional leaders in the decentralization process civil society, indigenous populist institutions and implications for political reforms in Uganda. In K. K. Prah & A. G. M. Ahmed (Eds.), *Africa in transformation: Political and economic transformation and socio-political responses in Africa* (pp. 63–82). Addis Ababa: OSSREA.

Museveni, Y. (1997). *Sowing the mustard seed: The struggle for freedom and democracy in Uganda. Oxford*. UK: Macmillan Education.

Museveni asattira. (2010, April 02). *Kamunye*, p. 2.

Museveni, Y. K. (7 April 1987) 'Speech on the opening of the national resistance council session at the national assembly', Kampala.

Museveni, Y. K. (MISR, 1987:20) *Stereotypes as sources of conflict in Uganda*. Justus NIL, gaju. Editorial Consultant/BMG Wordsmith, Kampala.

Museveni. Y. K. (October 9, 1987). Address to the Nation on the Anniversary of Uganda's Independence Day Celebrations.

Musoke, C. (2010, March 21). Kasubi rumours anger Museveni. *New Vision*. Retrieved August 27, 2010, from http://www.newvision.co.ug.

Mutibwa, P. (1992). *Uganda since independence: a story of unfulfilled hopes*. London: Christopher Hurst and company.

Myers-Lipton, S. J. (1996). Effect of service learning on college students' attitudes toward international understanding. *Journal of College Student Development, 37*, 659–668.

Nabudere, D. W. (2009, October 6). Ethnicity and conflict in Uganda: Is national consensus possible? *The Monitor.* Retrieved March 28, 2010, from http://www.monitor.co.ug

Nagel, J. (1995). Resource competition theories. *American Behavioral Scientist, 38*(3), 442–458.

Naughton-Treves, L., & Chapman, C. A. (2002). Fuel wood resources and forest regeneration on fallow land in Uganda. *Journal of Sustainable Forestry, 14*, 19–32.

Nye, J. (2008). *The powers to lead*. New York, NY: Oxford University Press.

Obore, D. (2009). *Attitudes and beliefs about peace building and restoration in Northern Uganda*. Unpublished Dissertation, Makerere University, Kampala, Uganda.

Okino, P. (2010, May 13). Hunt for Kony to continue – Kiyonga. *New Vision,* p. 8.

Oloka-Onyango, J. (1995). Constitutional transitions in Museveni's Uganda: New horizons or another false start? *Journal of African Law, 39*(2), 158.

Oloka-Onyango, J.(2006, August 1). Oloka responds to the president on term limits. *New Vision, 8–9.*

Omach, P. (2009). Democratization and conflict resolution in Uganda. *Les Cahiers d'Afrique de l'est, 41*, 1–20.

Otunnu, O. (2002). Northern Uganda: Causes and consequences of the war in Acholiland. Conciliation Resources (CR). http://www.c-r.org/our-work/accord/northern-uganda/causes-dynamics.php

Ovuga, E., Boardman, J., & Wasserman, D. (2005). The prevalence of depression in two districts of Uganda. *Social Psychiatry and Psychiatric Epidemiology, 40*(6), 439–435.

Phinney, J. (1992). The multigroup ethnic identity measure: A new scale for use with diverse groups. *Journal of Adolescent Research, 7*, 156–176.

Phinney, J., Jacoby, B., & Silva, C. (2007). Positive intergroup attitudes: The role of ethnic identity. *International Journal of Behavioral Development, 31*, 478–490.

Pittinsky, T. L., Montoya, R. M., Tropp, L. R., & Chen, A. (2007). How and when leader behavior affects intergroup liking: affect, approval, and allophilia. In B. Mannix, M. Neal, & C. Anderson (Eds.), *Research on managing groups and teams: Affect and groups* (pp. 125–144). Oxford, England: Elsevier.

Pittinsky, T. L. (2010). A two-dimensional model of intergroup leadership: The case of national leadership. *American Psychologist, 65*, 194–200.

Population and Housing Census Report. (2002). Uganda Bureau of Statistics.

Prunier, G. (1995). *The Rwanda crisis: History of genocide*. Kampala: Fountain Publishers.

Reljic, D. (2004). *The news media and the transformation of ethno political conflicts. Berghof Research Centre for Constructive Conflict Management*. http://www.berghof-handbook.net.

Roccas, S., & Schwartz, S. H. (1993). Effects of intergroup similarity on intergroup relations. *European Journal of Social Psychology, 23*, 581–595.

Rusesabagina, P. (2006). *An ordinary man*. New York, NY: Penguin Group. Saleh offers CBS lifeline. (2009, December 09). *The Observer.* Retrieved March 24, 2010, from http://www.observer.ug/new

Saxton, G. D. (2005). Repression, grievances, mobilization, and rebellion: a new test of Gurr's model of ethno political rebellion. *International Interactions, 31*, 87–116.

Scales, P. C., Benson, P. L., & Leffert, N. (2000). Contribution of developmental assets to the prediction of thriving among adolescents. *Applied Developmental Science, 4*, 27–46.

Segall, M. H., Doornbos, M., & Davis, C. (1976). *Political Identity: A case study from Uganda*. New York: Maxwell School of Citizen & Public Affairs.

Senabulya, R. (2009). *Peace building and resettlement in northern Uganda: A case of Gulu district*. Kampala, Uganda: Unpublished Dissertation, Makerere University.

Sharlet, J. (September, 2010). Straight man's burden: The American roots of Uganda's anti-gay persecutions. *Harper's Magazine*, 36–48.

Simon, B., Kulla, C., & Zobel, M. (1995). On being more than just a part of the whole: Regional identity and social distinctiveness. *European Journal of Social Psychology, 25*, 325–340.

Smith, E. P., Walker, K., Fields, L., Brookins, C. C., & Seay, R. (1999). Ethnic identity and its relationship to self-esteem, perceived efficacy and prosocial attitudes in early adolescence. *Journal of Adolescence, 22*, 867–880.

Ssekika, E. (2009, September, 07). Speake Runyoro, Museveni now orders Bafuruki.*The Observer.* Retrieved March 28, 2010, from http://www.monitor.co.ug

Stacey, T. (2003). *Tribe: The hidden history of the mountains of the moon*. London: Binder and Stacey International.

Syahuka, M. (1983). The origin and development of the Rwenzururu movement:1900–1962. *Mawazo, 5*(2), 60–75.

Teichman, Y., Bar-Tal, D., & Abdolrazeq, Y. (2007). Intergroup biases in conflict: Re-examination with Arab pre-adolescents and adolescents. *International Journal of Behavioral Development, 31*(5), 423–432.

Tenywa, G. (2007, April). Climate change hits Uganda. *New Vision,22(84)*.

Thompson, R. H. (1989). *Theories of ethnicity: A critical appraisal*. New York: Greenwood Press.

Tim, A. (2006). *Trial Justice: The International Criminal Court (ICC) and the Lord's Resistance Army (LRA)*. London: Zed Books.

Triandis, H. C. (1995). *Individualism and collectivism*. San Francisco, CA: Westview Press.

Tusiime, R. (2010, June, 17). Religious leaders move to stem violence in Kibaale district. *Monitor.* Retrieved August 21, 2010, from http://www.monitor.co.ug

Vinck, P., Pham, P. M., Stover, E., & Weinstein, H. M. (2007). Exposure to war crimes and implications for peace building in Northern Uganda. *JAMA, 298*(5), 543–554.

Winstok, Z. (2010). The effect of social and situational factors on the intended response to aggression among adolescents. *The Journal of Social Psychology, 150*(1), 57–76.

Worrell, F. C., Conyers, L. M., Mpofu, E., & Vandiver, B. J. (2006). Multigroup ethnic identity measure scores in a sample of adolescents from Zimbabwe. *Identity: An International Journal of Theory and Research, 6*, 35–59.

Xu, X., Zuo, X., Wang, X., & Han, S. (2009). Do you feel my pain? Racial group membership modulates empathic neural responses. *Journal of Neuroscience, 29*(26), 8525–8529.

Zeo, G. A. (2001). *Prevention and Intervention of Ethno political Conflict.* Paper presented at the Annual Meeting of the American Psychological Association (109th, San Francisco, CA, August 24–28).

Part VII

Europe

17 Ethnocultural Conflict in Spain: Moroccans in Spain – So Near, Yet So Far. A Long History of Meeting While Not Meeting

Assumpta Aneas, Jordi Garreta, and Fidel Molina

Spain Chapter Summary

Aneas, Bochaca, and Luque explore interethnic relations between the native Spaniards and the Moroccan immigrants, whose population has increased significantly over the last several years. Although there have been few overt conflicts, recognition of an underlying tension provides impetus for increasing efforts to improve intercultural harmony through suggested policy changes.

The recent increase in Moroccan migration to Spain is attributed to a move toward economic opportunity and prosperity. A need for recent immigrants to access housing and employment through social support networks is noted as a causal factor in the creation of primarily Moroccan communities. However, establishment of these growing communities may be negatively viewed by the native population as territorial takeover.

Cultural values of Moroccans and Spaniards are explored and found to be largely similar. Aneas, Bochaca, and Luque express the view that rejection of Arab influence on Spanish culture carries the potential to create conflict between these groups. Religious differences are explored and while pluralism is the official position of Spain, Islam is noted as less accepted in comparison with other religions in this largely Catholic society. Moroccans' strong identity as Muslim is presented as creating perceptions of resistance to integration by the host society. Recent studies of acculturation are explored as they reflect a precarious coexistence.

The authors discuss the political concerns of immigration that have recently gained attention, which include improving communication, managing

A. Áneas (✉)
Department of Methods of Research and Diagnosis in Education, Faculty of Education, University of Barcelona, Passeig de la Vall d'Hebron, 171, 08035 Barcelona, Spain
e-mail: aaneas@ub.edu

J.Garrreta • F. Molina
Department of Geography and Sociology, University of Lleida, Plaça Víctor Siurana, 1., 25003 Lleida, Spain
e-mail: jgarreta@geosoc.udl.cat; molina@geosoc.udl.cat

D. Landis and R.D. Albert (eds.), *Handbook of Ethnic Conflict: International Perspectives*, International and Cultural Psychology, DOI 10.1007/978-1-4614-0448-4_17,

conflict through understanding, and creating resources to assist with transition. They recognize the necessity for inclusion of all levels of public administration in order to meet these requirements effectively. The authors express the view that education in intercultural competence is needed for those working in administration, health centers, security, libraries, teaching, and journalism. Several suggestions for policy change are offered and specific strategies for the host society and the Moroccan community are offered.

Cheryl Jorgensen

This chapter will examine the complex set of relationships between Spain and Morocco, and between Spaniards and Moroccans. Moroccans are not recent arrivals to Spanish shores and have, in one form or another, long been present in Spain. Indeed Spanish culture is precisely as it is, due to the long-lasting influence of the Berber and Arab presence following their arrival in the Iberian Peninsula from North Africa almost 2,000 years ago. But after 1492, their Spanish presence was very low until late last century when a deluge of Moroccan immigrants increased it to become Spain's largest ethnic group. Despite the fact that this relationship has come and gone over the years, ever since the Catholic kings period in the sixteenth century, it has been characterized by more by tensions, prejudice, and the mutual lack of confidence between one group and the other. This chapter will examine the complex set of circumstances that form the historical core relationship between the Spaniards and the Moroccans.

Evidence behind this relationship can be found throughout Spanish culture. The Arabic language, which arrived in Spain via Morocco, has provided modern Spaniards with a host of words, concepts, and traditions, along with a long artistic and cultural heritage. Yet Morocco remains something of an enigma to most Spaniards. This mystery has not generated an entirely positive view of Moroccans. Spanish fables tend to present Moroccans in a negative light. The term *Moro* (Moor) refers to Moroccan people and is associated with distrust and fear. The nature of this historical relationship has become especially relevant at the present time given that many Moroccans are migrating to Spain in search of work. The process of living together in villages and neighborhoods scattered across Spain has not been easy for either party. Despite the fact that to date there has not been that many serious conflicts between the two communities, a latent tension, underpinned by a mutual distrust, continues to exist. The rise of Islamic Fundamentalism on a global level and the terrorist bombings in Madrid in March 2004, the received threats of terrorist attacks in September 2001, and the current economic crisis that has resulted in Spain having the highest EU unemployment rate have further strained the already insecure relationship between the two groups. These recent events serve to draw attention to just how fragile the present equilibrium between day-to-day communal life and long-term sociocultural relations between Spaniards and their North African neighbors actually is.

The aim of this chapter is to help the reader do the following:

- Learn more about the long and complex history of relations between Morocco and Spain, as well as the influence that this history has had on contemporary Spanish culture.
- Understand that modern Spain is a multicultural country which contains diverse social and cultural realities within its frontiers, including its new Muslim population, especially those that originate from Morocco. Spain's modern social reality varies considerably according to the territory or autonomous region under consideration.
- Gain some understanding of the most typical forms of interaction between Spaniards and Moroccans.
- Learn about the differing responses that have been offered from the various levels of Spanish public administration to address the tensions that exist between Spaniards and Moroccans.

1 Spain and Morocco: One Conflict Between FACTS AND Fantasies

In this first section, we will offer an overview of some of the most characteristic features of the dense web of relations that currently exist between the two communities under study. As we have already indicated, the relationship between Spain and Morocco is certainly complicated. There has not been any open or violent conflict between the two communities, but there is a latent relation of untruth that is always at risk to be exploited in open and violent conflict.

The historical dimension is important, but at the present time the sheer scale of recent immigration into Spain and the competition for access to social benefits, exacerbated by the crisis, give this topic special significance. Immigration, unemployment, and the presence of an Islamic Fundamentalist threat are severely testing the capacity of both parties to build a communal life based on respect and equality.

This new situation requires response, effort, resources, and commitment from all involved. Given the weight of the immigration issue, we will start with a brief summary of the general background to the most recent Moroccan population in Spain and how Moroccans became the largest migrant community in the country until few years ago. We will then go on to examine the socioeconomic and cultural profile of the Moroccan community, and the role of religion in both cultures. We will conclude with a summary of opinions which are to be found in both the academic community and the popular discourse of how one community relates to the other.

1.1 Moroccans in Spain

1.1.1 Who Are the Moroccans?

Morocco (Arabic: المغرب) is officially known as the Kingdom of Morocco (Arabic: المملكة المغربية) and is ruled by the present king Mohammed VI (Arabic: محمد السادس). The country lies on the north-west tip of Africa, with coastlines on both the Atlantic Ocean and the Mediterranean Sea. Although Morocco forms part of the African region known as the Maghreb, Morocco is itself a single geographical and cultural entity. It also has significant European influences given its geographical proximity to the continent and its history of French colonization (Fig. 17.1).

Moroccans receive a bilingual education (in Arabic and French) and Spanish is widely spoken in the North. Despite the unifying role of the Arabic language, many Moroccans are in fact Berbers and have their own language (Tamazight) and culture, a characteristic which gives them a special identity with the country. The monarchy, which claims direct descent from the Prophet Mohammed, and the tribal structure, which is noteworthy in the rural areas, continue to be important and distinctive characteristics of the country. Even though the education system has improved steadily since the country obtained independence in 1956, a significant proportion of the population is still functionally illiterate,[1] especially in the rural areas in the south and the interior. This evident educational and cultural divide separates the aristocracy and the social elite from the rest of the population.

1.1.2 Profile of Moroccans in Spain

The early migrants who came to Spain from the Maghreb were mainly young males with largely economic motivations, characteristics which for many years were the defining characteristics of many immigrants in Spain. This profile has changed somewhat as Moroccan migrants are no longer almost exclusively male due to a growing number of females. On the contrary, the increased rates of Moroccans born in Spain and the number of young children arriving via family unification mean that the age distribution of the Moroccan population has been steadily changing. The main reason for making the passage to Spain is still economic, but family reunification plays an increasingly important role, as are cases of political asylum, especially among those coming from the troubled region of the Western Sahara. The vast majority of the

[1] http://www.unicef.org/infobycountry/morocco_statistics.html. Retrieved 30 August 2011.

Fig. 17.1 Morocco map

Moroccans in Spain come from rural areas with high rates of illiteracy and low skills.

The principal ambition of most migrants is to improve their general life situation and prospects for themselves and their family. In most cases, the decision to emigrate is taken as a collective one by the family. Most take the decision because of the difficult economic and social conditions of their home country which make the idea of improvement a hard one to believe in. Therefore, they have a tendency to place considerable expectation and hope on a new "El Dorado" in Europe which friends, family, and acquaintances have all recommended to them. Social networks and the impact of the mass media idealize the route to Europe as the preferred pathway toward economic and social success. The reality becomes quite different to the ideal when, once they have arrived in Spain, they do not find what they were led to believe would be waiting for them, so they start the process of adapting their objectives (Garreta, 2003).

1.1.3 The Largest Migrant Community in Spain

The scale of recent immigration into the country is surely one of the most important catalysts for the multitude of social changes that have taken place in Spain during the last decade. In 1998, a mere 719,647 non-native Spanish people were officially reported as residing in Spain.[2] By 2010, this figure had risen to 4,744.169. That means an increase of more than 500% in a little less than 10 years. Of this total, some 729,672 came from

[2] For a fuller account of the migration phenomenon in Spain, see Izquierdo (2008) and http://extranjeros.mtin.es/es/InformacionEstadistica/. Retrieved 30 August 2011.

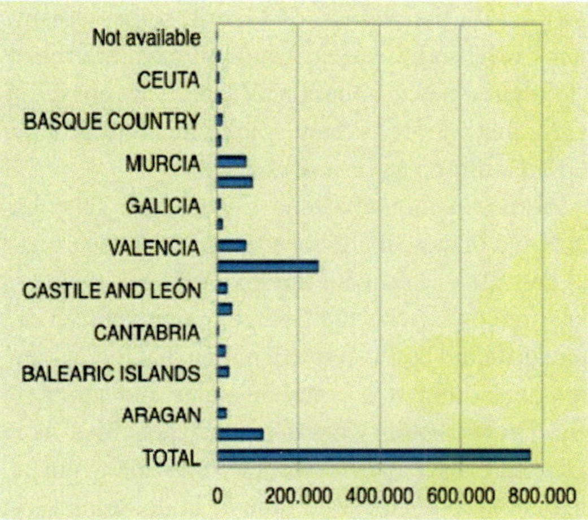

Fig. 17.2 Moroccans with municipal registration or residence permit by autonomous communities of residence as of 31-12-2009

Morocco (or 16.23% of the total non-Spanish population), making Moroccans the largest single migrant group in the country until 2009, when the population from Rumania grew to be ranked first. This increase has represented a big effort of adaptation to a new social and cultural environment from the host society (Figs. 17.2 and 17.3).

The uneven distribution of the Moroccan population is partly a result of the impact of network effects on the migration process, as well as the strategies that Moroccans use in order to find work. Most Moroccans enter the labor market informally during their initial period in Spain, using contacts that are borne out of trust and personal acquaintance. This in turn leads to migrants living and working where they find others in similar situations. As has already been indicated

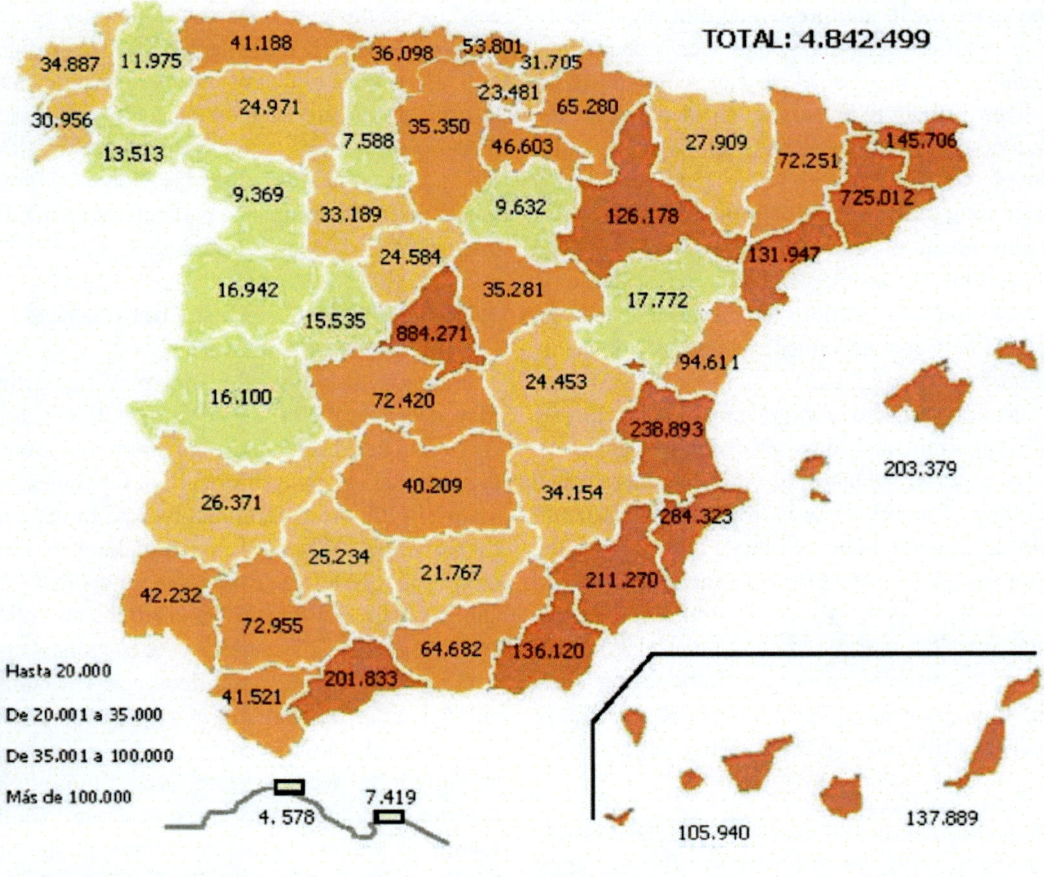

Fig. 17.3 Number of Foreigners with registration certificate or residence permit, by province 31/03/2010. Source: Ministry of Immigration

(Garreta, 2003), decisions on where to live are largely driven by personal relations (acquaintances, friends, and family), housing costs, and the communal shelter provided by a large local population with a similar origin culture. Depending on the prevailing circumstances at the time of migration, residential proximity may be seen as positive or negative (see Blanco, 2009; Fullaondo, 2009).

In most Spanish cities, towns, and neighborhoods where Moroccan communities exist, mistrust and concerns are raised from within the native communities which would prefer the distribution of Moroccan settlers to be more geographically disparate and contribute a lower percentage to the total local population. A high concentration of immigrants is perceived on a local level, by the host population, as an occupation of territory, which can devalue the value of homes, orchestrate a cultural transformation of the space itself, and present significant competition in educational and social access or medical grants. Within the Moroccan community, it proves difficult to preserve their identity and tradition, protect themselves from Western influences, achieve the economic goals set at the beginning of the migration project, and live in an environment of mutual mistrust. All of these related factors have developed into a scenario, in which the competition for resources and the debate between the values and laws are of fragile equilibrium.

Moroccans who immigrate to Spain are largely of rural origin, and some 40% of those who arrive work as unskilled laborers, with all the associated feelings of work insecurity (61% have been unemployed at some point or other), according to the Council of the Moroccan Community Abroad (CCME) in 2009.[3] Moroccan immigrants represent over 70% of the total non-Spanish labor force in the construction and agriculture sectors. It is the immigrant group least evident in the tertiary sector. Indeed, the fact that they live largely on the coast and in the vicinity of Madrid helps explain their work profile. The intention of most migrants is to regulate their situation as rapidly as possible by finding stable, urban employment (Cachón, 2007; Domingo & González, 1996).

Moroccan migrants tend to work on subcontracts and in more marginal activities, and the irregularities associated with the kind of work they do make relations with the Spanish population even more difficult. It is also worth noting that there is an important difference between males and females here. The men often work in external activities, like agriculture or building work, while the women remain indoors, either at home or in domestic service (Pumares, 1993). The usual reason for female Moroccan immigration is family reunification, although in recent years there have been a growing number of young Moroccan women arriving in Spain for domestic service or to work in light industries associated with agriculture and food processing, but this represents only a minority.

In general terms, the pattern of Moroccan migration also applies to that of other groups: they tend to occupy the hardest, most dangerous, and most precarious positions in the labor market (Cachón, 2004). This instability makes the Moroccan immigrants, like all immigrants, particularly vulnerable in times of crisis, like that of present.

1.1.4 How Can We Best Characterize Morocco Culturally?

Margaret (Omar) Nydell (1996, p. 19) describes Moroccans as "North Africans with a shared Arab culture whose beliefs are structured around the idea that (a) many, if not all, of the things that matter in life are determined by fate rather than by individual will and decision making (b) children should be loved, (c) wisdom grows with age, and (d) male and female personalities are inherently different". These beliefs are broadly shared with few regional or class differences. The beliefs and values of those living in societies that have been strongly influenced by Arabic culture are strongly influenced by Islam, even if those holding them are not themselves Muslims. Childrearing practices are nearly identical and the family structure is essentially the same. Arabic cultures are not as mobile as Western cultures

[3] http://www.elpais.com/articulo/espana/inmigrantes/marroquies/Espana/estan/integrados/resto/Europa/elpepuesp/20090716elpepunac_16/Tes. Retrieved 30 August 2011.

Basic Arab Values

- A person's dignity, honor and reputation are of paramount importance, and no effort should be spared to protect them, especially one's honor.
- Honor (and shame) is often viewed as collective, pertaining to the entire family group.
- It is important to behave at all times in a way that will create a good impression on others.
- Loyalty to one's family takes precedence over personal needs.
- Social class and family background are the major determining factors of personal status, followed by individual character and achievement.

Fig. 17.4 Basic Arab Values. Margaret (Omar) Nydell (1996)

Basic Arab Self-Perceptions

- Arabs are generous, humanitarian, polite and loyal (Melikian, 1981).
- Arabs have a rich cultural heritage, as is illustrated by their contributions to religion, philosophy, literature, medicine, architecture, art, mathematics and natural science (Omram 1980).
- Although there are many differences among Arab countries, the Arabs perceive themselves as being members of the Arab Nation (al-umma al-'arabiyya)
- The Arab people have been victimized and exploited by the West. As an example, the Gulf War, for them, is seen (in part) as a Western action to enforce Iraq's compliance regarding an internationally recognized border, in contrast to the absence of enforcement in the case of Israel.
- Indiscriminate imitation of Western culture, by weakening traditional family ties and religious values, is thought to have a corrupting influence on Arab society.
- Arabs are misunderstood and wrongly characterized by most Westerners. Many people in the West are basically anti-Arab and anti-Muslim.

Fig. 17.5 Basic Arab self-perceptions. Margaret (Omar) Nydell (1996)

and tend to be much more strongly influenced by tradition. Nydell has summarized the basic values, religious attitudes, and self-perceptions of those who live in an Arabic-influenced culture (see Figs. 17.4 and 17.5).

1.2 Spain as an Intercultural Entity?

1.2.1 Some Descriptive Data about Spain

Spain, or, as it is officially known, The Kingdom of Spain, is a sovereign state and member of the European Union. The head of state is a monarch, and the country is governed by a parliamentary democracy. The country, with its capital Madrid, occupies the majority of the Iberian Peninsula, the Balearic Islands (in the Mediterranean Sea), and the Canary Islands (in the Atlantic Ocean). Spanish territory also extends to a small strip of north-west Africa in the form of the two autonomous cities of Ceuta and Melilla and there are small sections of territory off the Moroccan coast. Spain is the fourth largest country in continental Europe following Russia, Ukraine, and France. Spain is the second most mountainous country in Europe after Switzerland. Spain has a population of almost 47 million inhabitants, according to the 2010 municipal register. The population is unevenly distributed over the landmass and is

Fig. 17.6 Spain's autonomous communities

largely concentrated along the coastline, in Madrid, and other main cities. Spain's political landscape is characterized by its 19 autonomous communities (Fig. 17.6).

A variety of people, religions, and cultures have left their mark on contemporary Spain. A good example of this diversity of origin is to be found in the languages spoken within Spain. Spanish is the official national language and is widely used across the whole national territory.[4] There are three other official languages: Catalan, Euskera, and Gallego. These are the official languages of the autonomous communities of Catalonia, the Basque Country, and Galicia, respectively. The regional extension of the use of these languages can be seen on the map (Fig. 17.7).

Other languages and dialects also exist, although none of these are officially recognized by the Constitution. One of these, the Caló language used by Spain's gypsies, is not territorial.

1.2.2 Some Ideas About the Culture of Spain

The debate as to whether there is a single Spanish culture or whether several different cultures interact to form modern Spain is a very complex one, and has produced extensive literary, historical, philosophical, sociological, and political literature. Given the complexity of the issue, we will attempt to offer a synopsis, based on the work of Aneas and Schubert (2006) and Almeida (2004). In the boxes below, we summarize the way Spanish people tend to see themselves and some of their basic values and beliefs (Figs. 17.8 and 17.9).

Now you can see that there are certain common elements between the values of both cultures. But the strong identification of Western and Arabic block countries and the minimizing

[4] The Spanish language is also known as Castellano, since it originated in one of the country's regions: Castilla.

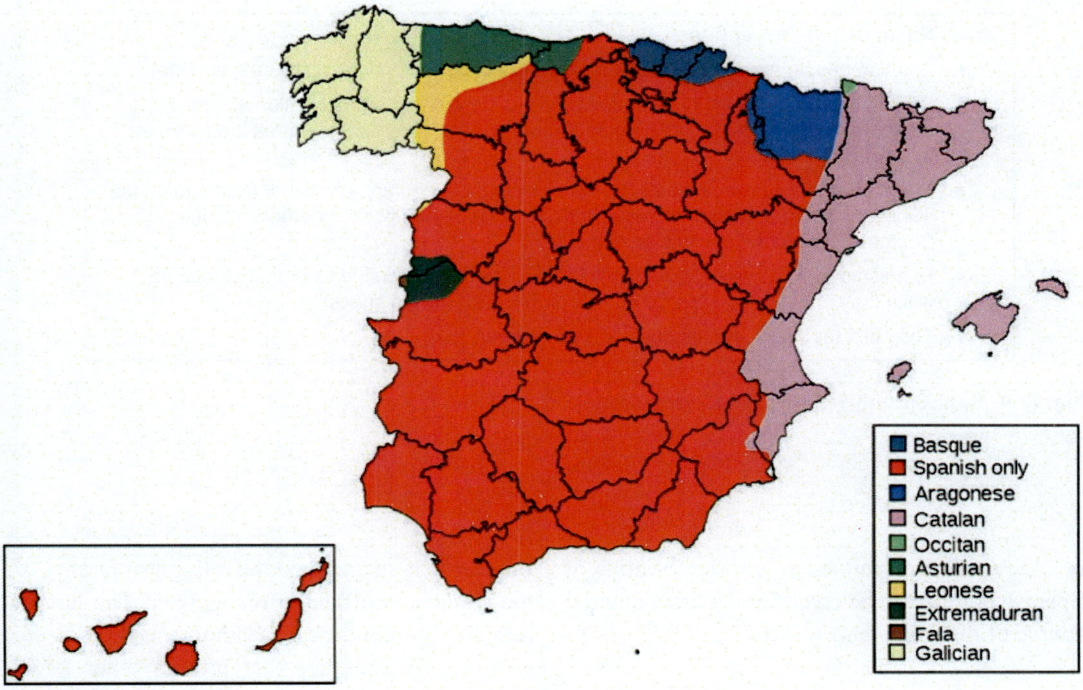

Fig. 17.7 The languages of Spain

Basic Spanish Values

- The family is the single most important factor which gives stability and security to the individual. In Spain the objective of building or forming part of a harmonious and stable family is a fundamental value which is shared by almost everyone, no matter their age, ideology, social status, etc. The Spanish family is diverse, and can be either extensive (grandparents, uncles, aunts, cousins, nephews and nieces) or nuclear (parents and children) and today the idea of family has moved towards offering legal protection to other family models, like the single parent, or families based around non-traditional sexual partnerships (gay and lesbian). The common characteristic of all of these is the willingness to form an affective nucleus to offer security, care and mutual affection to its members. This value is considered to be so important that even professional decisions are seldom if made without taking the consequences for the family into account.
- Social relationships are the fundamental base for personal and professional development within the Spanish culture.
- Living for the day, and enjoying life are present in Spanish culture both historically and in the modern world. Spanish people still publicly demonstrate only a rather distant interest in material and economic issues, preferring generally to appear to center attention on leisure activities and enjoying life.
- In Spain, people do not look towards the past. Almost no one now remembers the Imperial age, or the Civil War of 1936. People look to the future in order to try to safeguard the security they value so highly, but what really matters is the present. Once Spanish people feel themselves to be psychologically secure there is no urgency in planning for the future. Things can be done from one day to the next.
- To be accepted, positively valued and to feel part of a group is something which is very important for the Spanish individual, with reputation and personal prestige being among the foremost of their objectives.

Fig. 17.8 Basic Spanish values. Aneas and Schubert (2006)

Basic Spanish Self-Perceptions

- Spanish people normally consider themselves to be open, humanitarian, and happy.
- Spaniards from any part of the national territory are proud of their national heritage, both cultural and historic, although this should not be taken to mean that they care for it as they should.
- They feel satisfied with their life, freely accepting the country in which they live (although it is important to note that for some this country is Spain, while for others it is the Basque Country or Catalonia or Andalucia).
- Spanish people generally do not officially recognize Arab influences on their culture, while they are extremely proud of their Greek and Roman ancestry.
- They feel themselves to be completely European.

Fig. 17.9 Basic Spanish Self-perceptions. Aneas and Schubert (2006)

of Arab cultural influence on the origins of Spanish culture can be considered a first potential source of disagreement.

1.3 The Role of Religion in the Relationship Between Spaniards and Moroccans

A very important element in the analysis of relations between the two countries is the factor of religion. Historically, this has always been a substantial element in the identity of both countries and the complex relationship between them. There have also been important social and political consequences on religious identity, particularly following events such as the terrorist bombing in Madrid on 11 March 2004 and the rise of Islamic fundamentalism as a global phenomenon. These events have been critical in determining Spanish perceptions of the modern Muslim world and of their new Moroccan neighbors. About 99% of Moroccans are Sunni Muslims and normally practice the Maliki rite. If we want to understand Moroccan culture in Spain, we also need to understand the religious attitudes of the Moroccans and the Spaniards.

1.3.1 Spain's Attitudes Toward Religion

The 1978 Spanish Constitution describes Spain as a state where no religion has official status. Education is secular and the religious plurality of the country is officially recognized. The largest religious community is Catholic, but there are growing communities that profess other faiths (Islam, Protestant, Judaism, Hindu, Buddhism, Orthodox Christian, etc.). However, despite this apparent diversity, as Almeida (2004) emphasizes, the influence of Catholicism is still predominant, as has been repeatedly stressed in the literature. We believe that this Catholic predominance, which will be explained in more detail below, is an important factor in understanding the attitudes in relation to Moroccan religion, which is overwhelmingly Muslim.

Historically, authors have located the fundamental influence of the Catholic religion in what they perceive to be the Spanish character: "unpreoccupied with material interests and trusting in the ultimate pardon, with the full certainty that faith guarantees salvation in such a way that the sense of guilt is almost totally absent" (Almeida, 2004, p. 103). The real issue, however, is the extent to which such traditional traits are still present in and shared by the modern day Spanish population. As Aneas and Schubert (2006) describe "Despite the fact that a day to day presence in church is not considered important, most Spaniards still think of themselves as being Catholic. Many still celebrate their Saint days and identify with local religious traditions and festivals. Many of these religious rites are still celebrated with a passion that can often surprise outsiders. Therefore, the majority of modern Spaniards express and experience their religious faith in their own individual way, believing that it is the act of faith itself that matters over and above liturgical dogmas or ecclesiastical authorities."

In one sense, Spanish Catholicism has become a phenomenon which started in the past. Spain is now a global, democratic society. Eibl-Eibesfelt (1980, p. 79), who studied the complex issue of the survival or transformation of historic "values in rapidly changing societies, stressed that even if traditional values are transformed, there can be no doubt about their long-term survival capacity". On the contrary, Almeida (1993) carried out an analysis which found that despite the almost monopolizing position which Spain's Catholic faith enjoys, real religious feelings are quite fluid and adjust to fit in with the developing global mentality of the believer. If religion was historically able to serve as a structural element which oriented other areas of civic life (political, social, moral, etc.), the defining characteristic of our age would seem to be the reverse: religious feeling evolves from within an intimate relationship with the values, attitudes, and behaviors of the nonreligious world, and in the process becomes more secular.

Thus, Spanish society has accepted without conflict the presence of other religious beliefs and practices – except in the case of Islam. Building or extending a mosque is a frequent source of conflict in communities. Conflicts arise between the Spanish and their politicians when these buildings are allowed to consolidate the settings of a suspicious community. Further conflict occurs between religious authorities and politicians when the first do not respect regulations or recognize the authority of the latter; between the police and religious authorities when the first fears that these places of worship breed terrorism; and among the faithful who have their rights to practice their rituals and beliefs limited.

1.3.2 Islam in Spain (Moroccans and Their Relations with Islam)

As Nydell (1996) puts it, for a Muslim, religion permeates personal daily life in a way which non-Muslims may find hard to understand. In Muslim countries, Islam is habitually taught in the schools, the vernacular language is full of religious expressions, and people practice their religion openly, almost obtrusively, expressing it in a wide variety of different ways. Faith for a Muslim is more than just a religion, it is a complete way of life. Islam is politics, law, and social behavior.

There are, and have long been, Spanish Muslims, but the faith of these Spanish nationals has little connection in reality with the faith and rites of the Moroccan newcomers.[5] Non-Spanish Muslims had no formal religious recognition in Spain until the Law of Religious Freedom (44/1967 of 28 June 1967) which officially allowed existing cultural centers to convert themselves into the first registered Islamic Associations. From this inauspicious beginning, as the migrants have continued to arrive, modern Islamic presence in Spain has steadily grown. According to Moreras (1999), it is possible to distinguish some key stages of the new Muslim presence in Spain:

- From 1939 to 1966: the first modern Muslim chapel was built in Cordoba (Morabito de los Jardines de Colón), constructed by General Franco in gratitude to the Moroccan soldiers who fought for him during the Spanish Civil War.
- From 1967 to 1975: the first law guaranteeing religious freedom was passed. The first Muslim associations were created in the cities of Ceuta (1968), Melilla (1971) and in Madrid (1971). The first mosque of Spain's was built in Madrid this same year.[6]
- From 1975 to 1989: the first tensions among the Muslims Communities in Spain were

[5] In UCIDE (2008), it is reported that in 2007, Muslims represented some 2.5% of the resident population in Spain and of these, 30% are Spanish nationals and 70% were immigrants (50% Moroccans and 20% other nationalities).

[6] See also: López and Olmo (1995) and Garreta (2000a, 2000b, 2000c).

beginning to appear and the number of prayer centers started to increase throughout Spain.

- From 1989 to 1992: the consolidation of Islam in Spain occurred; the most important step was the creation of the Spanish Federation of Islamic Religious Organizations (FEERI) in 1989 with 15 federated associations. This growth caused conflict and division among the various Muslim communities.
- From 1992 to date: this period is characterized by the creation of the Islamic Commission. The increasing numbers of migrants, their geographic dispersion, and their settlement into communities all combine to create a growing number of places for meeting and prayer. At this stage, we find frequent splits and unifications between religious centers (Garreta, 2000a, 2000b, 2000c, 2001). Such schisms are normally the consequence of internal conflicts associated with the level of adherence to the precepts or "line" imposed by the local Imam[7] as a result of the economic strains involved in trying to maintain a center and the ease with which members of the community are able to rent or acquire another, etc.

The gradual establishment of Muslim communities across Spain has meant that there are now mosques and prayer centers in many Spanish cities. Most of those who attend these centers are Moroccan. The mosques and prayer centers carry out a number of functions in the Muslim community which sees them convert into important social arenas for all Muslims living in the catchment area. In addition, they offer a structural framework for the whole community in the consolidating process for the presence of Islam. For Muslim migrants, these religious centers offer spiritual support while at the same time reinforce their distinct identity with respect to the host population. They also ensure the continuity of religious practice.

Islam in this new context acquires three interrelated connotations which prior to the time of immigration were not seen as important (López and Olmo, 1995): ascriptive ethnic traits (Islam reveals itself as an ethnic trait), a distinctive ethnic trait (Islam as a distinctive element among immigrants, separating those who are Muslims from those who are not, as well as distinguishing the Muslim migrants from the Spanish population who are not Muslim), and a facultative trait (identification with Islam is a voluntary decision[8] and the practitioner decides whether to form part of the religion or not, and up to which point). For López and Olmo, Islam is important because it plays the role of a collective identity generator and helps to unite the ethnic group. In the specific case of Moroccans, Islam is present in the network of informal relations (both within and outside of prayer centers) but is absent from the network of formal relations that surround these structures and serve as a bridge to the Spanish society.

1.4 Historical Bias: As Seen by Both the Original Spanish Population and the Moroccan Migrants

1.4.1 Discourses Concerning Muslims from the Maghreb

In this new context, Muslim immigrants, especially Moroccan ones, tend to find themselves on the receiving end of many of the most negatively charged prejudices. Within the Spanish hierarchy of racism,[9] the most rejected communities are always and without fail either the Moroccans or the Gypsies. Even if immigration is now quite diverse, it is the Moroccan who is most closely identified with the stereotypical image of the immigrant, and this identification has only increased in recent years (Terrén, 2004).

[7] The Imam reinforces the maintenance of community values and attempt to ensure that communal rites and traditions are not lost.

[8] "We need to specify that we consider the formation of new identities to have a voluntary element, even if it is evidently conditioned both by the attributes which the individual originally possesses due to their background culture as well as by the context where the new identity is developed" (López & Olmo, 1995, p. 269).

[9] Order of level of rejection of the immigrant as classified by national origin. This order tends to be repeated in one study after another.

According to Terrén, the Moroccans have come to embody the social visibility of the migration phenomenon in Spain, and the reason for this situation is the presence of racial prejudice which leads one group to attain a stronger ideological representation than the rest. The persistence of this prejudice toward Moroccans has its roots in a negative image which comes from Spain's historical ties with North Africa. The image which circulates is basically the traditional one of the "moro" albeit "modernized" by the selection and filtering process that applies to the immigration process.

The level of racial prejudice is often measured in terms of the expressed preferences of Spanish citizens toward the reality of living with others, and such preferences are normally measured by studies carried out by the Spanish Government's Center for Sociological Investigation. It is clear from the surveys they have carried out that the closer the two communities live together, the greater the level of mutual distrust that is produced. Acceptance only becomes more prevalent through increased contact, whether this is at neighborhood association level, through citizen participation, or intermarriage.

In a 2007 study of attitudes toward racial or ethnic discrimination in Spain,[10] the Ministry of Labor and Social Affairs found that country of origin was an important factor and that some groups were better accepted than others. Among respondents who recognized any group of immigrants as inspiring confidence (only 36.7% of the total) 31.5% referred to South Americans and Latinos, and 12% to sub-Saharan Africans, while only 3.2% mentioned Moroccans, 0.7% Arabs, and 0.1% Muslims. Further details of these surveys that show the attitude of the Spanish are taken from the 40% of those interviewed in the study who found it perfectly acceptable that people "organize protests against the construction of a mosque in their neighborhood," and nearly 30% thought it reasonable that a student "should be excluded from school for wearing the Islamic headscarfs."

Another study from this Center for Sociological Investigation which examined "Discrimination and how it is perceived"[11] and which interviewed members of the majority population found that the groups for which there was least sympathy were Gypsies and Muslims (51.7 and 45.8%, respectively), immigrants in general (31%), homosexuals (24.8%), and young people (7.7%).

According to Balta (1990), the existence of stereotypes among the Spanish population and the orchestrated visibility of these which is promoted by some media lead to the isolation and community self-protection and a significant reduction in intercultural contact which reinforces the influence of precisely those fundamentalists who seek to promote this very isolation. In fact, many prayer centers now try to remain as unnoticed as possible (Garreta, 2001).

As Moreras (2003) suggests, what we have observed since the beginning of the twenty-first century is a steady shift in public opinion regarding the way people perceive immigrants and their religious affiliations. This is perceived as increasingly important as are the reactions against any religious symbol that suggests change in religious affiliation is permanent and correspondingly strong. From being a phenomenon which steadily became socially visible during the 1990s, the immigrant moved to the much more problematic situation of being seen as a direct threat to the traditional European social model.

1.4.2 The Expectations of Moroccan Muslims Regarding the Host Society

All immigrants have a project that they aim at, but their path and the extent to which this objective is modified or even aborted depend on the circumstances they find themselves in. Therefore, while we can refer to the general expectations of this immigrant population, its complexity means that this is no more than a partial snapshot.

As mentioned, immigration from North Africa mainly occurs for economic reasons and its

[10] Study published 15 September 2007 http://www.cis.es [Study 2731 del Ministerio de Trabajo y Asuntos Sociales].

[11] Study published 12 December 2007 http://www.cis.es [Study number 2745, Ministerio de Trabajo y Asuntos Sociales].

expectations focus on this aspect. Finding work and obtaining documentation (in order to legally remain in the job market) are the priorities for most immigrants,[12] even more so at this present time of economic crisis that is especially severe for them. We should bear in mind that the migratory project in general is a family project, and therefore, those who stay behind expect help from those who have traveled to Europe. Housing is another of the priorities and is governed by the need to save money to reunite the family at some point, so people are prepared to put up with overcrowded accommodation and renting homes in poor conditions.[13] However, the family cannot physically be reunited in these conditions, so when that moment comes, the quality of housing and having an adequate space not shared with other immigrants acquire more importance. Furthermore, the continuity of the immigrant's culture, language, and religion is of maximum importance, especially after the family arrives from the place of origin. This is when there is greatest interest in the creation of a prayer room if there is none, or, if one already exists, in reinforcing its role to maintain the social order from their origins and the commitment to their language, culture, and religion. A good number of these prayer rooms teach these important social aspects to the younger children. A study with Muslim families (Garreta et al., 2007) concludes that their concerns are mainly about the continuity of the language, culture, and religion, as well as the contents of school meals and respect for their clothing. The school, along with hospitals and clinics, is an institution that feels the impact of diverse cultures on the organization and most acutely. These institutions are immersed within the debate about limits imposed on these cultures in the public and private spheres. In fact, this is why intercultural mediation has developed in these organizations so that the strategies to follow in situations of cultural or religious disputes are defined more clearly.

From the above, we can conclude that in practice, the integration of immigrants is very often categorized under multiculturalist and interculturalist discourse, where some appear easier to "integrate" than others who are seen as non-integratable Muslims. This especially applies to the Moroccans, who are presented and perceived as the most resistant to and least interested in "integrating" themselves into the society that hosts them. Consequently, their cultural and religious manifestations are considered signs of social and cultural segregation.

2 History of the Conflict: A Millenary Relationship

In this section, we will attempt to examine some of the origins of the complex relationship that now exists between Spain and Morocco. It is important to notice that there is no critical detonator; no historical year zero. The relationship goes back over many centuries during which there have been periods of harmony and positive interaction as much as periods of heavy tension and at other times almost no contact. The points of tension have, however, changed over the centuries where they have moved from the political to the religious terrain.

From the third century BC to the fith century AD, Spain formed part of the Roman Empire. During the sixth century, the Visigoths, who came to Spain from Germany, settled in what had previously been Roman Spain. It was at this time that Catholicism consolidated and extended itself across Spain, since prior to this date it had been in competition with other strands of Christianity. In the final decades of the seventh century, the Visigoth Kingdom became fragmented, due to continuing rivalry between local nobles, and the situation deteriorated further in the eighth century. In 711, groups commanded by the Muslim leader Tarik arrived from the North of Africa (Arabs, Berbers, and Syrians) and defeated the Visigoth Don Rodrigo in the battle of Guadalete. The defeat at Guadalete signified the end of the

[12] We must also mention that there is a minority of people who come to Spain for studies and whose priority will, therefore, be to finish these (Garreta, 2000a, 2000b, 2000c; Moreras, 1999, 2003).

[13] See Garreta (2003).

Visigoth rule in Spain and the start of Arab domination in the Iberian Peninsula, which was to last eight centuries, until 1492.

The Arab conquest of Spain was rapid. The Hispano-Gothic cities offered little resistance, either reaching agreement before combat ensued or surrendering soon after it started. In less than 8 years, almost the whole of Spain had been conquered with the exception of a small strip of land in the North where early centers of resistance developed, later becoming incipient Christian kingdoms. Spain was conquered under the name of Al-Andalus.

Throughout almost 800 years of history, Al-Andalus was governed by a whole variety of political regimes which left a profound influence on its culture and social structure. The region passed from being ruled by Damascus to a series of independent Muslim kingdoms. But aside from the numerous internal power struggles that characterized the region, the history of Al-Andalus is best understood in terms of its changing relations with the Muslim powers of the Eastern cities and with the other two religious communities (Catholic and Jewish) that occupied the same territory and with whom they struggled against.

The Catholic Kings (Isabel I of Castille and Fernando of Aragon) brought to an end a period which is known in Spain under the generic name "The Reconquest." The new structure came into being as a result of internal tensions following the advancements of the various Christian kingdoms of León, Castille, Navarre, Aragon, and Catalonia. These kingdoms became stronger over the centuries, consolidating themselves through a series of political alliances and marriages into a common Catholic front which sought hegemony over the Muslim kingdoms of Al-Andalus and the Jewish population which was dispersed throughout the entire Iberian Peninsula. By 1492 Al-Andalus had been reduced to the Kingdom of Granada. The handing over of this city to the Catholic Kings by Granada's king (Abu Abd Allsh) meant the definitive disappearance of Al-Andalus and the start of absolute hegemony by the crown of Castille.

The lasting influence of Al-Andalus and its culture on Spain is undeniable. It is evident, for example, in the number of Arab words that are to be found in the Spanish vocabulary and other languages spoken across the peninsula. Words of Arab origin represent about 8% of the total vocabulary (around 4,000 words) (Cano, 1999, p. 53). According to Lapesa (1995, p. 133), they became, after Latin, the most important lexical source for modern Spanish, at least up to the sixteenth century. Words of Arabic origin are to be found in all areas of science and academia, institutions and customs, commercial and domestic activity, clothing, and leisure activities. Arabic influence is also extremely evident in place names, not only in the areas where the Muslim population previously had their settlements, but also, even if with less frequency, in the center and north-west of Spain. The notable artistic, literary and scientific legacy which the kingdom of Al-Andalus left to posterity was neglected and ignored in the New Spain of the Catholic Kings, but even so, Spain's Arab heritage continued in its music, architecture, gastronomy, and agricultural techniques and equipment.

Invasion, reconquest, and expulsion are terms that are widely used in historical narrative to describe the interaction between North Africa and Spain. These expressions are not used with anything like the same frequency to describe interactions with other nations that came to Spanish shores – the Greeks, the Romans, and the Germanic tribes – who all arrived, settled, and then disappeared, whether defeated by or absorbed into the local people. Despite this large presence and influence, the establishment of Al-Andalus in Spain and its lasting legacy have always been the source of debate and controversy. And history is today repeating itself in the form of controversy surrounding the latest wave of settlers from the Maghreb. The very fact of conquest has lead to some of the most extreme controversies in modern Spanish historiography Illustrated by the controversy between the positions of Américo Castro (1996, 2000) and Claudio Sanchez Albornoz (1943, 1975). The passion that this topic arouses is hardly surprising given that for centuries the Arab invasion represented a decisive interruption in what would otherwise have been the continuing development of an essentialist Spain. Furthermore, the settlement of a Moroccan population on Spanish territory was an evident eruption into what would otherwise have been the normal course of Spanish history, an eruption whose reality could only be explained by resorting to the idea of treason and treachery. Unsurprisingly, such traumatic events left an indelible mark on the collective subconscious of the Spanish people over the centuries that followed.

3 Complex and Fuzzy Causes

In this section, we will try to outline some of the factors that, in our judgment, enable us to understand why the relationship between the Spanish and Moroccan populations is as complex as it is.

We are aware of the presence of an infinite number of variables, actors, scenarios, etc., all of which can help explain the various levels of interaction and inter-relationship that have traditionally existed between the two communities. This complexity makes it impossible, in our opinion, to identify a set of definitive and unequivocal causal factors.

3.1 Spain's Cultural Diversity Faced with Moroccan Immigration: Paradoxes and Contradictions

The question as to when Spain could first be considered a cultural entity with a common identity has been the subject of great debate among historians. Some would look for origins in the prehistoric Spain, while others, like Américo Castro (1996), go as far as to suggest that it was the existence of Al-Andalus which provided the stimulus needed to create the necessary common identity. It is normally accepted that the period of the Catholic Kings in the fifteenth century was the critical moment in the founding history of modern Spain, since it was at this point that the process of bringing together the various separate kingdoms (Castille, Aragon, and Navarre) and the defeat of Granada led to the process of state construction. In this sense the history of Spain begins at a comparatively early date when compared with that of other European states like Germany or Italy.

Despite this, it is interesting to note that during Spain's entire history, some parts of the national territory (in particular, Catalonia and the Basque Country) were asserting their own historic identities based on structures whose origins go back to the Middle Ages (kingdoms and countdoms descending from the Visigoths and the Franks). The maintenance of their own language, the conservation of their own system of laws, a clear political attitude toward the throne (which was always occupied by Castille), and the existence of a distinct identity continue to characterize these regions today. It is also possible to say that the process of state formation was more a question for Castille, given its political hegemony, steadily imposing its own cultural vision on the entire country.

Since this time, there has been constant tension between unity and multiplicity, between the acceptance of diversity and the rejection of the evident reality that some parts of the Spanish territory were fundamentally different from the rest. The struggle between unity and diversity, on the one hand, and the quest for the uniformity that opposed the acceptance of difference, on the other, have led to the fear of a serious division in national unity to become one of the greatest preoccupations of the most fervent supporters of Spanish identity. The issue has dominated Spanish national thinking throughout Spanish history, and was one cause, among others, of the civil war that broke out in 1936. Even today, it is still an underlying cause of the present political conflict in the Basque Country, and the search for a solution has become a cornerstone of the internal politics of the modern Spanish state.

As has been stated, the issue of the recognition and acceptance of diversity in Spain is a complex one, and has been in existence over the centuries. Given this, it is only to be expected that something which was still a problem for the various groups brought together to form Spain today would be exacerbated once immigrants from other and more distant cultures started to arrive on Spain's shores. This is especially true in the case of Morocco given the uniqueness and historical significance of this relationship.

3.2 Cultural Differences

If we look in more detail at the above-mentioned cultural traits, we should be able to appreciate that there are in fact few substantial differences between the two cultures under examination. Both groups share similar values concerning the family, the value of social networks, and the importance of reputation and honor. According to the cultural taxonomy developed by Hofstede (1999), the differences are not excessive, given that both cultures occupy relatively centered positions on each of categories. It therefore seems at face value that there must be that some other component which plays the key role in this historically conflictive relationship.

It can be argued that the religious factor, from an identity dimension of each group's practice or values, has been articulated as the axis around which each group has built its own identity, primarily in opposition to the other. But the religious factor is not, by itself, the cause of the conflict because Spanish society normally accepts other Muslim groups from Asia or sub-Saharan Africa.

The influence of the past and their complex relationship and all the complex economic and social factors that accompany Moroccan immigration must be added to the culture factor.

3.3 Asymmetrical and Unequal Acculturation Contexts

Migrants, upon arrival, often find themselves in the midst of a complex network of legal relations and restrictions which make it hard for them to integrate and even harder to realize their expectations of justice and well-being (Izquierdo, 2003). Such asymmetrical conditions only increase the risk of social fragmentation (García-Ramírez et al., 2006).

The spiral of exclusion in which they are immersed only reinforces lifestyles which are conducted on the margins of mainstream society. The feelings of segregation create the psychosocial profile which reinforces only the fear and racist that are widely held by the native Spanish population (Hernández-Plaza, 2003).

From a transcultural perspective, there are a number of models which can help explain and understand how such experiences and outcomes are associated with given types of intercultural contact or psychological acculturation. Such approaches link the well-being of the immigrant population with its capabilities of culturally adapting into the host communities (Berry, 2005,1997; Birman, Trickett, & Vinokurov, 2002).

New theoretical approaches, like the psychology of liberation, understand immigration as an ecological transition that implies profound changes in interaction processes, social norms, and values. At the same time, this model explains the asymmetric relations between the reception population and the new arrivals on the basis of privileges and weaknesses, and the respective strengths and weaknesses that may be derived from them (Sonn & Fisher, 2005). From this perspective, the integration of the immigrant population involves the partial transfer of co-ownership of the new society to the new arrivals (Penninx, 2006). It also implies the acquisition of a degree of control, and the enjoyment of opportunities to take decisions together with effective participation in the relevant domains of social life, such as the labor market, as well as the enjoyment of cultural, educational, and political right, and access to health, housing, and essential social services (Sonn & Fisher, 2005). This shift, especially in times of crisis like that of present, can generate a lot of suspicion by the host society and requires a good social policy to avoid situations of imbalance manifesting (Aneas, 2009a, 2009b, 2009c).[14]

[14] For example, current regulations establish objective criteria such as number of children or declared income to access educational or social grants. Because many immigrant families have larger families and work on the black market, income is not declared. These families often have access to grants by obtaining the highest scores in valuations, while Spanish families with one of its members unemployed or on low incomes cannot access grants due to receiving lower valuations because they do declare income and have fewerchildren. This creates a huge upset in the host society.

According to García-Ramírez et al. (2006), intergroup power dynamics are a key factor associated with the feeling of well-being and sense of satisfaction that are achieved by the immigrant population, and this is especially true in the case of the host population. Empowerment involves having the material and psychosocial resources within a system of social relations which offer the opportunity and the ability of access to well-being (Nelson & Prilleltensky, 2002). To take an example, high levels of community participation through neighborhood interaction in informal activities (chatting with neighbors over topics of local interest, inviting neighbors into your home, etc.) and reduced tolerance of violence (not taking the denial of basic rights as a given, not being habitually exposed to verbal abuse and the threat of physical, social or psychological violence, etc.) are strongly related to improved levels of well-being and satisfaction (Farrell, Aubry, & Coulombe, 2004; Herney, Cartland, Ruchross, & Monahan, 2004).

Access to power is determined by social and historical circumstances (democracy, colonization, etc.), structural factors (social class, gender, ethnic group), and more personal circumstances (education, skills, etc.). Even if power is ideally oriented toward the acquisition of well-being, normally some groups exercise such power to obtain privileges in relation to others, and limit their possibilities of self-determination and well-being. Migrants in new European contexts often find themselves at a disadvantage when it comes to accessing material, cultural, and social resources, and see themselves as passive victims of external factors (cultural, ethnic, religious, social, etc.) which means they lack both the competence and the capacity to acquire them (Sonn & Fisher, 2005).

In many parts of Spain, the asymmetrical relations which are imposed on the newcomers by the host population (especially on the Moroccans) tend to generate a social dynamic characterized by fragmentation and acceptance of a limited capacity of response on the part of the new arrivals which only serves to expose them to even greater risk of social exclusion (García-Ramírez & Camacho, 2005; Hernández-Plaza, Pozo, & Alonso-Morillejo, 2004). Racist attitudes both justify and sustain this set of asymmetrical relations and reinforce the perception that Moroccans serve as a threat to community life (Van Dijk, 1996). The host population holds the Moroccans responsible for their own problems and difficulties, attributing the situation to their poverty and to their having an inferior culture combined with an absence of the personal characteristics that would enable them to improve their situation genuinely (Rebolloso, Hernández, & Cantón, 2001). In this way, the newcomers are kept at bay, while at the same time ethnocentric sociopolitical agendas are legitimized in a way which only serves to further reduce their expectations (Sonn & Fisher, 2005).

García-Ramírez et al. (2006) concludes that the presence of immigrants in a given town or district should not imply that they belong to the community which is physically formed by such boundaries. The psychological sense of community, and a feeling of belonging, companionship, and affiliation to a group all help change the way the level of well-being and conditions, which might otherwise be seen as oppressive, are perceived (McMillan & Chavis, 1986; Perkins, Florin, Rich, Wandersman, & Chavis, 1990). However, such feelings do not arise automatically and should not be assumed present. In multiethnic communities, exclusion from or oppressive relations with neighbors tend to be associated with low levels of satisfaction with the neighborhood, while inclusion has the opposite effect, in such a way that lower levels of satisfaction among one group is positively associated with lower levels of satisfaction for the other and for the community as a whole (Portes & Rumbaut, 1996). It is also evident that such low levels of communal satisfaction produce poor levels of adaptation, higher levels of social conflict, and higher levels of problematic activities such as drug consumption, vandalism, and school drop-outs (Portes & Rumbaut, 1996). The results from this earlier research are in complete harmony with those obtained in studies recently carried out in Spain, showing that when Moroccans live in marginal social contexts, they experience integration difficulties and low levels of neighborly satisfaction (Hernández-Plaza et al., 2004;

Martínez, García-Ramírez, Maya, Rodríguez, & Checa, 1996; Pérez Yruela & Rinken, 2005).

3.4 Attitudes Toward Acculturation

In anthropological discourse, the term "acculturation" has traditionally been considered to relate to "those phenomena which result when groups of individuals from different cultures come into continuous first-hand contact with each other, and subsequently, when there are changes in the original culture patterns of either or both groups" (Redfield, Linton, & Herskovits, 1936, p. 149).

Navas et al. (2004, 2005) have developed what is known as the Relative Acculturation Extended Model (RAEM). According to Navas, Rojas, García, and Pumares (2007, p. 70), RAEM postulates that there is no single or general acculturation attitude as may be inferred from some of the more traditional models (e.g., Berry, Kim, Power, Young, & Bujaki, 1989). In RAEM, the adaptive process is understood to be complex (contradictory options can be adopted and preferred at one and the same time) and relative, since the same strategies are generally not employed and neither are the same options usually preferred for interaction with persons from other cultures in different areas (e.g., in peripheral areas such as work versus private or core areas such as family relationships, religion, or values). Because of this, seven areas are distinguished in the model, from those nearest to the material world and peripheral elements (political, work, economics, etc.) to those farthest away, such as symbolic representation, ideology, or religion (religious beliefs and customs, and ways of thinking: principles and values), with intermediate areas (social and family relationships).

The above authors have conducted an extensive investigation into attitudes toward acculturation among groups in Andalucía, with findings which could well give an indication of that the situation is in the rest of Spain (Navas, García, Rojas, Pumares, & Cuadrado, 2006; Navas et al., 2007).

These results suggest that the differences in means between Magrhebian immigrants (MI) and the members of the majority population

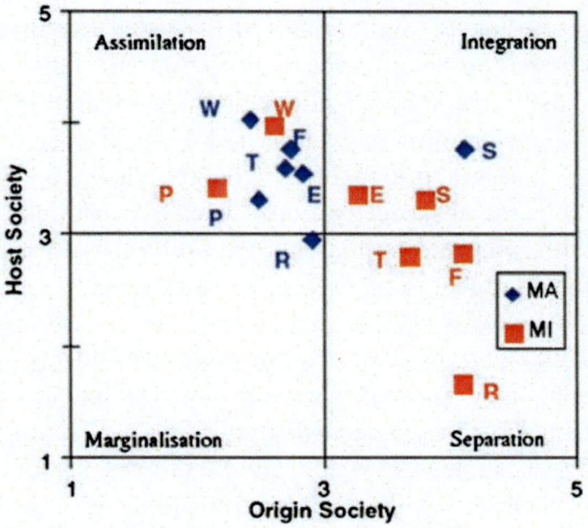

Fig. 17.10 Acculturation attitudes by domain (ideal plane). MA. and MI groups. *P* political system and government; *W* work; *E* economic; *S* social relations and friendship; *F* family relations; *R* religious beliefs and customs; *T* ways of thinking: principles and values (Navas et al., 2006, 2007)

(MA) are statistically significant for questions in all domains, except in those of labor or work (W) and the political system and government (P). Here, the differences only appeared in the first question (to maintain original customs). In these two domains, both groups prefer "assimilation," but the Magrhebians expressed a stronger desire to maintain the customs of their country of origin more in the first (work, W) and less in the second (political, P), in contrast to what the host population would like to see from them (or what they perceive they would like to see, in the case of the political domain).

These results can be seen in Fig. 17.10. In general, the Magrhebian immigrants prefer to maintain their original customs and not adopt Spanish customs ("separation") in their family relations (family domain, F), religious beliefs and customs (R), and ways of thinking (principles and values, T). However, the host population would prefer to see just the opposite response from this group in all those domains ("assimilation"), except for religion, in which there does not seem to be a clear option.

There is also a preference on the part of the Spanish population for "assimilation" in the economic domain (E) in which the immigrants prefer "integration." Finally, in the social domain (S), the option preference of both groups is the same ("integration"), although it is more intense among the host population (who would prefer the immigrants to maintain more friendships and adopt the host society more, which is in contrast with what the immigrants themselves want as they find themselves closer to "separation").

If studies such as that of Navas et al. (2006, 2007) give us a portrait of some the "ideals" held, they also offer us some insight into the respective strategies adopted by each group. These strategies, which are a complex set of behavioral postures in given situations, give an indication of the real level of acculturation that occurs when both groups interact, either through living or working together. One of the most interesting conclusions raised from their work is the difference found between the ideals and the actual strategies adopted, especially in the case of the host population. Another finding is that the strategies adopted by the Magrhebian population and the way these are perceived by the host population coincide in each area.

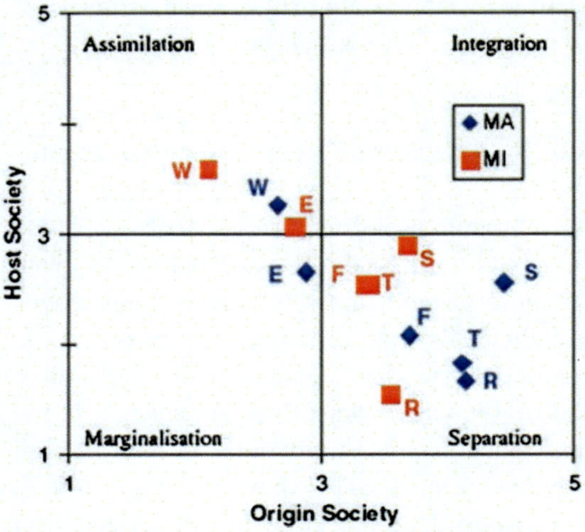

Fig. 17.11 Acculturation strategies by domain (real plane). MA and MI groups. *W* work; *E* economics; *S* social relations and friendship; *F* family relations; *R* religious beliefs and customs; *T* ways of thinking: principles and values (Navas et al., 2006, 2007)

That is, in the labor or work (W) domain, the immigrants say they are "assimilated" and the natives also perceive this "assimilation"; while in the social (S), family (F), religious beliefs and customs (R), and ways of thinking (principles and values, T) domains, the strategy identified by the immigrants was perceived by the host population to be one of "separation"; finally, in the economic (consumer habits and family economy, E) domain, the host population believe that Magrhebians live in a "marginalized" situation, while they themselves feel they are half way between this and "assimilation." This can be seen in Fig. 17.11, in the labor or work (W) domain, since "assimilation" is the adoption of Spanish customs rather than what the immigrants say they do. That is, the perception of "assimilation" by the host population is much less intense than the feeling of assimilation acceptance as expressed by the immigrants.

Such empirical results give us important clues as to the complex relations that currently exist between the Moroccan migrants and the Spanish hosts. In addition to the socioeconomic differences previously described, a significant part of the host population would prefer the Moroccans to assimilate along most of the dimensions where interaction occurs, while the Moroccans mainly prefer a gradual process in which they are prepared to assimilate in public domains while maintaining their own traditions in more intimate and personal ones. But in contrast to these ideal situations, what we actually have in practice are relationships that tend to reinforce the sense of distance and separation, relationships that are reflected in feelings of frustration in both communities concerning objectives that have been set and not achieved.

So why do these differences exist? We believe that the economic, social, and labor market situation of both communities has a negative impact on both groups (each perceiving the other as a threat, or as a competitor; see Garreta, 2003) and that the traditional cultural prejudices of both groups then weigh down on these current realities in a way which helps to explain the lack of mutual confidence which characterizes most of the interactions between the two communities.

In this section, we have seen that the relationship of Moroccans in Spain today is influenced by cultural factors, especially religious; socioeconomic factors and their own acculturation strategies of both groups are not inclined to true integration in all areas of daily life. This gives an idea of the fragile balance of coexistence between the two groups.

4 Consequences

In the section that follows, we will attempt to describe some of the consequences of the flawed interaction process described above, even if some of the factors included here could easily be incorporated in the previous section given that they are recursive. In any event, these consequences represent some of the key factors that awaken the greatest preoccupation among Spain's social and political leaders. As such, these are the factors which set the political agenda, as well as the differing socio-educational programs that have been created. In general, the debate is seen to revolve around the topics of marginalization, xenophobia, ethnic segmentation in the labor market, the issue of "second generations," the social isolation of the Moroccan woman, the construction of identity as Moroccans in Spain and Europe, and the growing influence of Muslim fundamentalism within the Moroccan community.

4.1 Xenophobia

According to the latest data from the BVA Institute (Institut BVA, 2009), Moroccan immigrants in Spain are less integrated than they are in other European countries, although curiously Moroccans in Spain express less feeling of rejection than they do in other countries (especially in comparison with the Netherlands and Italy). Of all, 64% of Moroccans living in Spain think that Spanish people have a high opinion of Morocco. On the contrary, 80% of those interviewed answered that they encounter discrimination in the labor market, and 67% of them said they experienced discrimination when looking for somewhere to live.

This type of marginalization and xenophobia is especially associated with the idea of "secondary racism" (Taguieff, 1987) – so called because it implies the combined presence of a number of elements (affective, discursive, and notional) framed within the context of primary racism based on arguments such as competition in the labor and housing markets, etc. Such marginalization and xenophobia are strongly associated with the kind of ethnocentrism which assumes that one's "own culture" is at or near the center of the entire cultural universe, and as such is more "natural," and more self-evident than other strange and "more exotic" cultures.

Raxen Report (VVAA, 2009) found strong evidence of such racist and xenophobic attitudes in Spanish schools, with Moroccans and Gypsies receiving the most hostile and negative responses. According to the latest study from the Spanish Center for Sociological Investigation (2009), some 37% of Spanish people reject the idea that Muslim girls should be permitted to wear a headscarf at school. At the same time, the majority of Spaniards do not identify immigration as one of the three principal problems facing Spain (July 2009), since these are considered to be unemployment (74%), the economic crisis (48%), and ETA terrorism (19%). Nonetheless, immigration was the fourth most important problem identified by respondents (18%). One year earlier (July 2008), the response to the same question was ten points higher (28%), while racism was only identified as the principal problem by 0.2% of the interviewees. If the question is presented in another way, "What is the problem which affects you most personally?", then immigration was identified by only 5% of those questioned, far behind the economic crisis which came first (41%), followed by unemployment (35%) and housing (11%).

Bennis (2005) singles out the role played by the Spanish media in influencing public opinion when they speak of a worrying "avalanche" of immigrants, especially those coming from Morocco, stressing their cultural and religious differences. In this sense, the growing presence of Moroccan migrants in large urban areas, with the impact this has on the ethnic and cultural makeup of the country, did not need long to provoke unease among large sections of Spanish society and to generate a debate about the "integratability" of the newcomers.

Bennis laments the fact that those who defend the cultural, religious, and linguistic uniformity of the country are simply expressing a preference for Latin Americans over Moroccans. From this point of view, the Spanish think that Latin Americans are easier to integrate since they have a shared language and religion (Aneas & Donoso, 2007). Bennis (2005) argues that this whole debate is misleading and has been fuelled by the Spanish media. It produces outbursts of rejection like those seen in Terrasa (Cataluña) in 1999 and Ejido (Andalucía) in 2000,[15] events which demonstrated the hostility on one part of the Spanish population to newly arrived Moroccans. Equally, the absence of similar public expressions of rejection during the first decade of the twenty-first century could be considered a reflection of the growing number of encounters, which tend to overcome the earlier divide.

4.2 Ethnical Divisions and Discrimination in the Labor Market

In Spain, there has been a growing segmentation in the workforce and the labor market between groups with different cultural backgrounds. In the case of Moroccans, work is largely centered in agriculture (both male and female), construction (male), and (on a much lower level) tourism and domestic service (both largely female). In this sense, it is neither hard to talk about the ethnic segmentation of the Spanish labor market, nor is it out of place to talk about marginalization. Most of the more recent immigrants work in situations of the greatest fragility on temporary contracts, or in the casual labor economy, and evidently they have been exposed most to the traumatic implosion in the Spanish labor market that has followed the onset of the current economic crisis.

The migratory model on which the Spanish labor market has been based is one of a reserve army of labor to fill positions of the lowest quality. In addition, as well as being of poor quality, the jobs migrants are actually offered may well be in the casual labor sector, without normal labor contracts and with little in the way of positive integration opportunities. Spanish society lacks coherent positive attitudes to immigration, and this means that immigrants constantly find themselves up against latent barriers of incomprehension and lack of trust (Tezanos & Tezanos, 2006, pp. 28–29).

On the contrary, it is also true that the growing "regularization" of those who were previously irregular migrants following the recent amnesties has meant that there has been some degree of improvement in the situation. This improvement is now being put at risk by the intensity of the crisis in Spain's labor market. In fact, according to Cachón (2007, p. 72), whole migrants arriving in Spain are not especially poorly educated. At the beginning of the last economical crisis, they also have higher work activity rates (between 20 and 25% higher than those of the native Spanish population which are around the 56% level). Other positive consequences of immigration that have been identified include the type of labor that migrants are increasingly able to offer, their geographical mobility, and their contributions to the Spanish social security system (Cachón, 2007, p. 73).

It is, therefore, possible to conclude that there are ethnic stratification processes at work in the Spanish economy, that an ethnic division of labor exists, and that the explanations offered for these observed differences are given in terms of the "cultural differences" between the respective populations rather than in terms of the structural characteristics of the labor market. As Cachón (2004, pp. 401–402) suggests, Moroccans are the ones who experience the most systematic discriminatory practices, on both the institutional and the structural level, leading them to be labeled "conflictive" or "difficult to work with" when compared with other workers, for example from Ecuador or sub-Saharan Africa (Aneas & Donoso, 2007; Aneas, 2009c) .

[15] Both cases were serious public disturbances in which there was an open confrontation between Moroccan and Spanish neighbors motivated by a trigger point that catalyzed around months of simmering tensions.

4.3 "Second Generations" Conflicts

The so-called second generations are torn between the conflicting demands of "super loyalty" and "super integration," between loyalty to the traditions of their parents and grandparents and assimilation to the youth culture they see in the host population. Some writers have described such young people as "children of the night" in order to draw attention to their intermediate situation, one which can provoke sharp internal conflicts in the individual and social groups – conflicts which, if not resolved in an adequate fashion, can degenerate into labor and social marginalization or violence.[16]

The very term "second generation" is itself a subject of some controversy, since it is a temporary and sequential concept which constantly draws attention to the status of the young person as "immigrant" or "child of an immigrant" (and, therefore, not a true member of the host society into which he or she is born). At the same time, their status is extended across generations. Second-generation immigrants tend to be defined as those who were born in the host country and whose mother or father (or both) is a foreigner who were not born there. Alternately, the group may include those born outside the host country but who came to live there on a permanent basis at an early age (normally defined as under 12 years of age). This latter group may also be known as "generation 1.5" (Portes, Aparicio, & Haller, 2009). More than "second generation," we could describe such young people as being "of migrant origin."

The position of these young people is, nonetheless, a mirror to the entire immigrant population and how it is accepted and included in the host society. In this sense, it offers the opportunity to understand the problem of social exclusion and lack of integration from a dynamic perspective. The inability to offer such young people the same sense of identity as that felt by their peers represents an important structural and institutional failure. If, in addition, belonging to such a group also brings with it difficult life circumstances, such as higher levels of unemployment, labor market uncertainty, and greater exposure to violence, the likelihood of longer term social conflicts is increased, as was witnessed in Paris[17] in 2005 (where the majority of the young people involved were aged between 14 and 20 years, and a significant proportion of them were unemployed North Africans and sub-Saharan Africans).

Episodes such as those seen in Paris in 2005 have not yet occurred in Spain, but their absence to date is scarcely a guarantee for the future. In fact, the recent Raxen Report (VVAA, 2009) produced by the "movement against intolerance" identified 350 cases of what it considered to be xenophobia. Racist and xenophobic incidents are increasing in Spain's schools, with Moroccans and Gypsies being the most frequent victims. It is also true, however, that in the study carried out by Portes, Aparicio, and Haller (2009) over half of the teenagers interviewed stated that they had never felt discriminated against, and only some 5% suggested that they had been subject to discrimination frequently. The second generation does not appear to experience a substantial feeling of rejection at this point and indeed continue to have some confidence in the possibilities of upward mobility. Such data are hardly conclusive, but it does allow a glimpse of circumstances which may offer a certain degree of hope regarding future possibilities.

[16] The treatment of juvenile gangs, like the "Latin Kings" or 'Ñetas,' has been a hot topic in cities like Madrid or Barcelona. The answers have varied from consideration as a group punishable – criminal treatment – to the consideration of legal youth organization – socio-treatment.

[17] The riots in France in 2005 began on Thursday October 27 near Paris but quickly spread to the rest of France and other European cities. The riots were marked by the burning of cars and violent clashes between hundreds of youths and French police. The incidents began after the death of two young Muslim men of African origin while fleeing the police in Clichy-sous-Bois, a poor community in a banlieue ("suburb") east of Paris, and were exacerbated by the statements of Interior Minister Nicolas Sarkozy, who called the initial protesters "scum." The riots have spread to other areas of France (Seine-et-Marne, Val-d'Oise, Lille, Rouen, Dijon, and Marseille) and also other countries (Belgium, Denmark, Germany, Greece, the Netherlands, and Switzerland). On the night of November 3, 500 cars were burned and several fires were set in Aulnay-sous-Bois, Neuilly-sur-Marne, Le Blanc-Mesnil, and Yvelines.

Regarding Moroccan youth, according to the most recent data from the BVA Institute (2009), some 66% of young Moroccans living in Europe do not study Arabic, 70% do not attend any form of Islamic religious instruction, and 71% do not participate in religious associations or in activities organized by mosques. This gives us a clear visualization of what we have been explaining about young Moroccans in Europe in general (Spain, Italy, France, Germany, the Netherlands, and Belgium).

It is also important to distinguish between those born in their parents' home country but came to Spain as part of a family reunification process and those born in Spain, since the socialization process is different in each case. In the case of young Moroccans, according to a study carried out by López and García (2006), the Internet offers a virtual environment which gives these young people access to possibilities of interaction they would like to enjoy in the real world. In cyberspace, they are neither foreigners, nor Moroccans nor Muslim – they are whoever they want to be. As the authors of the study say, here these young people move in a global space which unites them with other young people, and it is this common identity which facilitates their contact with other young people. "Beyond the normal stereotypes of young Moroccans with little enthusiasm for integration, it is notable how virtual relations are based on a framework of equality, and how, in an environment where identities are not pre-established, social relations tend to multiply" (López & García, 2006, p. 78).

In any event, we should also be aware of the existence of other possibilities in the range between the individual and the social, and one of these is the idea of "self-exclusion," a process where the experience of being excluded from the public domain in the host society is converted into an internal survival strategy, a way of playing from the interior against the exterior. Self-exclusion in the above sense can be either voluntary or imposed. In fact, inclusion and exclusion are not mutually exclusive processes, and can be complementary and interact as alternatives between one and the other.

4.4 To Be a Moroccan Woman in Spanish Society

Before proceeding to describe the profile of Moroccan women in Spain, we will briefly describe the role of women in Morocco, this way you can sense the challenges and potential conflicts that may arise in this transition.

The Moroccan Constitution which was introduced in the 1960s recognized the woman as a full citizen, even if this formal equality also coexisted with and was interpreted by the Mudawana (a family code based on custom[18] which recognizes the woman's dependence on the man). The female role in Moroccan society is defined in terms of the woman's relation with the male. Whether or not a woman is married is important, not only because of the social status associated with being a wife, but also on the socioeconomic level. Normally, the class status of the Moroccan woman is mediated by that of her husband. The separation between Moroccan men and women is not only spatial, but also quite pronounced, and this naturally influences the part they play in the broader society. The traditional normative framework for the Moroccan family sees the role of the man as that of ensuring material support for wife and children, while that of the woman is centered in the home, looking after the needs of the male partner and caring for the children. All the public activities of the family are the husband's responsibility.

Given that the majority of the North African population living in Spain, and especially those coming from Morocco are male, it becomes easier to identify the specific characteristics of the female migrants. Alcalde, García, Moreno, and Ramírez (2002) summarize the situation as follows: (a) A key group consists of the women who have come to Spain via a process of family reunification. Since they are married, they are economically and socially dependent on their husbands (and also legally, since it is normally the husband who has the work permit). These women tend to reproduce the social role they had in Morocco. (b) Another group consists of

[18] In the case of Islam, many customs are legitimized and turned into law.

divorced women. These often leave Morocco as a result of the social stigma that is still associated with divorce. They are normally looking for more independent and autonomous social roles. (c) There are also single women who come to Spain in the search for some kind of social emancipation. Normally, they use their own social networks in order to come to Spain[19] (for example, other women who have come before them).

As far as the relation between education and immigration goes, many of the Moroccan immigrants in Spain are functionally illiterate, and this is especially true in the case of women who have come as part of a family reunification process. The more educated part of the female Moroccan community in Spain tend to be Moroccan women belonging to the second generation (dating from the 1990s) as well as single women who have migrated more recently. The number of Moroccan women with some form of higher education qualification is growing, and among them are those who came to Spain to study and then decided to stay (Belardbi, 1993).

In terms of the kind of work Moroccan women find in Spain, jobs are often associated with domestic service (both in the home and out of it). Moroccan women are also found in the tourist industry (cleaning and cooking) and in the textile industry, especially in Catalonia. This kind of work is typical of the casual labor economy and this makes it much more difficult for the migrants to regularize their situation and consequently for Moroccan women to enter the normal labor market. In general, the types of employment found are fairly similar regardless of the prior educational status of the woman in Morocco, which suggests that the structural situation of most Moroccan women arriving in Spain is fairly similar, whatever their actual background in Morocco. In other words, there is a declassification of the newcomer, in the sense that the kind of work done has little direct connection with the social status of the individual in their home country. The characteristics of the Spanish labor market, therefore, do not favor social advancement for the Moroccan woman, enabling her to acquire a new and improved socially accepted gender role and become less dependent on her husband (Alcalde et al., 2002).

As we have said, the social relations of Moroccan migrant women after arriving in Spain basically depend on family and work. The level of dependency on a husband, the reasons for the migration, and whether or not the woman works are all closely related elements in the degree of social interaction experienced by the woman. On her arrival in Spain, the Moroccan woman needs to build a network of relations and contacts with other women which will give some degree of independent leisure life. The key factors here are the place of origin, and neighborhood and family ties, with the neighborhood being the most important factor among these. This is why residential pattern is such a critical dimension in terms of the social and cultural development of Moroccan women. The more a woman finds contact with other Moroccan women in the vicinity of her home, the more she is likely to have relationships with them, and the less likely she is to form close social ties with members of the majority host community. Married women tend to build social networks quickly ,and if the woman arrives in Spain as a wife via a process of family unification, and does not work, then typically her husband introduces her to a broader circle of social contacts which will normally have quite traditional characteristics. Dependence on the husband and the reconstruction of a traditional environment limit the field of action and the general sense of freedom of women, and act as a brake on her transition into the host society, at least at the beginning.

For those women who do not have a husband, the objective is to build a network of contacts which will enable her to optimize her resources in terms of her migratory objectives: information, work, housing, learning the language, and social relationships for leisure purposes. Among younger

[19] There are also networks which exist to facilitate illegal immigration, but this kind of network normally caters to people in more marginal situations. In any case, there is a considerable difference between the percentage of Moroccan men who arrived in Spain illegally (18.9%) and the percentage of women (1.9%).

Moroccans, the barriers between male and female are more fluid, since it becomes more difficult to maintain separate male and female spaces. The most frequent problem in establishing meaningful contact with the host population is the language and the difficulty of finding people with a similar social level and background.

According to Alcalde et al. (2002), it is possible to identify three acculturation strategies adopted by Moroccan women: (a) Women who remain within the confines of tradition and who follow what could be called the "enclave" strategy, which is normally characterized by the segregation of public and private spaces according to gender criteria. This strategy equally persists in the productive and reproductive areas, where the relational network normally consists of other immigrants from a similar background where a day-to-day and habitual separation exists between men and women.[20] (b) Women who begin to move away from the traditional model and start to develop what we could call transition strategies, where despite the continuing maintenance of the traditional role, elements of change begin to appear. In this model women begin to reproduce elements from the lifestyle of the other women they encounter, at the same time introducing new features, such as starting work and occupying new social spaces whilst maintaining the principle of separation. These women normally continue to restrict their contacts to members of their own social group. (c) Women who begin to alter their gender role and to develop strategies based on the idea of change. In this type of strategy, the idea of spatial segregation begins to disappear and there is normally a greater desire for autonomy and the express wish not to reproduce the life role models of the women around her. These women begin to occupy new social spaces in terms of reproductive activities and move away from the idea of segregation according to gender.

4.5 Identity of the Moroccans in Spain – Between Asserting the Past and Betting on the Future

The construction of identity is always a complex and conflictive process, which covers at one and the same time the most personal areas and most socialized parts of the cultural framework. In any event, identity is always part of a rather unstable equilibrium between the personal and group recognition which can not only facilitate access to a wider social group but also, on occasions, makes it more difficult to open communication with other groups. This is especially true if we think of our identity as unique and incompatible with others. Perhaps it is here that we can begin to glimpse a solution to this particular conflict in the idea of multiple identities so that via the acquisition of intercultural competences we can come to have more than one single, unitary identity.

In fact, the phenomenon whereby the social customs and practices of the migrant become even more "orthodox" than those in their country of origin is normally a result of a need for security of identity, a feeling of belonging, and to preserve one's roots (hence a feeling of radicalism which can arise). We also need to remember that on occasion, the consolidation of one's own identity is not a product of a socialization process, but rather the result of interaction processes with others who are different from us (Molina, 2002). Group cohesion is not to be especially sought in the specific identifiable aspects of the actual group, but rather in the differences the group seeks to establish with other similar groups. The major problem with immigration as far as identity goes is that it appears fragmented, between

[20] The level of traditionalism in the practices of some of these women can arouse social concern considering direct threat from the values of the host society. In this sense, the Spanish Senate passed a proposal in June 2010 to ban the Burka (the garment, that covers the entire body of the woman, who can only see out through a screen) and the "Niqab" (a veil over her face freeing only the eyes and a floor length tunic) in all public spaces, including streets. This motion urges the government to "make the legal and regulatory reforms necessary to prohibit their use in public spaces or at events when strictly religious clothing or accessories that cause the face to be completely covered are not required as this practice constitutes discrimination contrary to the dignity of people and damaging the real equality of men and women."

what has been learnt from parents and what has been experienced as part of the subject's own individual life.

Sabar (2002) explains that the immigrant's identity is in a process of continuous construction, between the sensation of "uprooting" and the impact of contact with a symbolic universe which is experienced as "alien." This is one of the reasons why recourse to an exaggerated loyalty to the traditional culture becomes an attractive option in some cases, since it appears to offer a nostalgic and secure return to cultural origins (Molina, 2008).

The construction and reconstruction of identity are processes that involve a constant change between loyalty and what is increasingly seen as obsolete tradition and a process of assimilation that abandons roots. This internal tension (which is both individual and collective) reaches its climax, as we will see, among members of the second generation.

In fact, the debate which has surrounded the issue of identity construction has to move from being a mere reflection on a resistance identity which leads to the creation of communes or communities. These communities serve to reinforce the frontiers of exclusion in order to work on reciprocal communication between such excluded and excluding identities, and the support for an identity project which produces subjects who are equipped to participate in a social transformation project.

4.6 The Islamization of the Moroccan Communities

Under conditions of cultural uprooting like those that are to be found in immigration processes, religious meeting places and cultural practices become important reference points for the new arrivals and a way of maintaining the legacy of their origin culture. In fact, immigration often involves changes in religious practice whether due to an unfavorable external context (absence of structures which make it possible) or the constant re-housing and moving that the migrant experiences before finding a permanent residence, leading to a systematic loosening of the normal frameworks of social control.[21] Many Muslims, for example, modify their religious practices during the migration period (alcohol consumption, eating pork, not praying five times a day, and neglecting observation of Ramadan). Collective practices are, however, reinforced by the presence of other Muslims and indeed even serve as the basis for social relationships (like the lamb festival which accompanies the end of Ramadan)[22] (Garreta, 2000a, 2001). Collective practices that disappear can reappear once a community is settled, whether it is a result of the influence of the new environment or even just to feel recognized as a Muslim by other Muslims. These practices may be followed with more rigor than previous. In such a situation, where the absence of strong social control has led to the steady abandonment of religious rites, the construction of mosques and the creation of prayer centers can be seen as counter-secular practices, with the Iman being cast in the role of promoter of religious order in circumstances where this would seem to have disappeared to some extent.

This collaboration and participation not only refers to the personal practices of individuals, and the need to help establish the center, but it can also attempt to bring those Muslims who have wandered in a more secular direction back to the fold. But it is important to be clear that abandoning certain practices is not the same thing as not being Muslim so that a steady return to the observation of rites and customs quickly means that the individual is once again considered to be a

[21] As well as continuing residence in a given place, family reunification and the arrival of children are key moments in the restoration of traditional patterns of religious observance.

[22] "Islam is a central cultural referent for adult Moroccan immigrants, even if its influence tends to weaken among young single people whose families are in Morocco. But even among the latter the abandonment of religious practices is never complete (for example, the majority still fast during Ramadan) nor does this loosening imply any overall questioning of Muslim beliefs. Such behavioural processes are to be more associated with personal insecurity, and in some cases abandonment, in favour of a more personalized systems of values" (Colectivo IOE, 1994, p. 265).

good Muslim. The counter-secularization initiatives which are taken by Imans through Islamic associations garner their strength from the proselytism of friends and acquaintances. In such situations, the Muslim identity itself becomes the focus of attention, with the consequence that inner belief becomes far more evident in the shape of an external identity.

Mosques and prayer centers are, in a non-Muslim context, meeting points for the relationships between the community and institutions of religious practice. Attitudes toward religion, the distance from the center and from other practicing Muslims, age, work, and life circumstances are normally considered to be the most important factors that influence the extent to which religious activity is maintained. In this sense, secularization is not simply a voluntary or a personal act, since there are a number of practical factors in day-to-day life that have an influence on the process.[23]

A considerable part of the responsibility for maintaining the faith in the new context falls on the parents, family reunification, and in particular the presence of children, all of which imply a higher priority in the continuity of religious traditions. It is also the case that both families and Imans have the view that mosques and schools play an important part in the process[24] (Garreta, 2001; Garreta et al., 2007). In fact, many Muslim families live in the expectation that it will gradually become more possible to have the school play a real part in the transmission process, with the Muslim religion becoming a real option at school, as has already happened to some extent in Madrid and Barcelona. But this desire on the part of the parents to maintain the continuity of religious practice can itself find conflict with the behavior and opinions of the second generation. The need to follow given rites, in particular in the case of female second-generation Muslims, can produce, and indeed is producing, intergenerational conflict.

5 Possible Solutions: Suggestions for the Improvement and the Avoidance of Conflict

In this section, we will outline some of the approaches currently being adopted by public and social actors to try and improve relations between the Moroccan community in Spain and the majority population. A wide variety of initiatives have now been taken, ranging from civil society initiatives (NGOs, associations, etc.) to political initiatives and academic research. Campaigns have been conducted in the streets, in schools, and among women, men, and young people. The effort has been substantial and extensive, and we will only try to offer a brief summary here.

5.1 Policies for Immigration

5.1.1 Political Discourse and Immigration

Spain is a parliamentary democracy in which there are three main levels of public administration. First, there is the national or state level, where legislative decisions are taken either in the Congress of Deputies or in the Senate, while executive responsibility rests with the central government. But the Spanish administrative system is also quite decentralized, so a great deal of responsibility now lies in the hands of the various autonomous communities which have their own legislative and executive powers. Finally, there is local authority level which is largely composed of municipalities and associations of municipalities.[25] Responsibility for immigration

[23] Some companies, for example, adapt their timetables to conform to the needs of prayer and even Ramadan, although this is not common.

[24] Consequently, all Moroccans can receive such religious education regardless of the geographical distances involved or the presence of an Islamic association in the neighborhood.

[25] These associations are called "Diputaciones provinciales."

questions is to some extent divided across all three levels, so all have a role to play and share responsibility for the ongoing development of relations between Moroccans and the native Spanish population.

After analyzing the legislation produced by all these entities on immigration, Zapata-Barrero (2008) has identified two premises which serve as the starting point for Spanish political discourse on immigration: (a) the idea of zero immigration is totally unrealistic, and (b) the phenomenon of immigration is unevenly experienced across the Spanish society.[26] Both facts justify discourse on immigration regarding restriction and state protection.

Spanish legislation referring specifically to the question of immigration has existed since 1985, but it is generally agreed that the question passed from being merely an administrative one to becoming a live issue on the social and political agenda (Zapata-Barrero, 2003) after 2000. This agenda has increasingly been set by the need to respond to the kinds of tension we have been examining in the earlier sections and the ways in which to manage these. In particular, an improvement in the level of communication and understanding between the two communities and the establishment of a social framework, which will help avoid and defuse potential points of future conflict, are now major priorities (Zapata-Barrero, 2008).

The two discourses mentioned above have different approaches to the idea of conflict and different reference populations. The objective in the first case is conflict management, and focuses on the negatively perceived changes in the wake of an increase in immigration. The migration process is inherently viewed as one which produces conflict between immigrants and Spanish citizens, and as a result is seen as a threat. The discourse is essentially directed toward native Spanish citizens (those who vote and have what is perceived to be a homogeneous cultural identity) who are always given priority over the non-citizen population (who do not vote and have a different cultural identity).

The second type of discourse aspires to equip citizens with the resources and instruments they need to manage the process of change that accompanies immigration, which is accepted as being irreversible. Immigration is seen in this view as a historic opportunity and a challenge that needs to be confronted, as yet one more of the transformations to which a society is subjected in an ever-more globalized world. As such the discourse is directed towards the whole population, without consideration of either their right to vote or their cultural identity.[27]

Zapata-Barrero (2008) summarizes three definitive traits of the political discourse on immigration in Spain. In the first, the process is directed toward the legislative framework as opposed to political processes in a more general sense. It is, essentially, a prescriptive discourse which seeks to identify the most appropriate legal framework through which to handle immigration. It normally concentrates on the issue of frontiers (and migrant access to the country) rather than coexistence, integration, and/or cultural adaptation.

In the second, the Spanish Constitution is a constant point of reference, used to legitimize both classes of discourse mentioned above. That is to say, the Constitution is used both as a basis to limit the range of possible action on the part of

[26] Since it largely affects those citizens who live in neighborhoods which are either on the fringes of large cities or in the center of them, and whose living standards tend to be well below the national average. A second group in close contact with Spain's migrants are residents in rural areas with an active agricultural sector. What this means is that areas which are already socially deprived are now confronted with an immigration process which itself becomes yet one more factor producing inequality. In addition the newcomers are seen as competitors in the labor and housing market and for social services like hospitals and schools. In rural areas the impact is often notable, since the large scale arrival of immigrants has often dramatically changed the earlier cultural equilibrium. Indeed it is not uncommon to find towns with populations of under 5,000 where over 40% of the residents are now immigrants. For example, in Guissona (Lérida) out of a total population of 5.683, 44% are migrants from outside the European Union.

[27] As an illustration, both these discourses can be found to be reflected in Spanish law, and especially in the laws relating to the right to association and to vote as well as the right to access of health and education systems.

the migrant and to defend the extension of his or her rights.

In the third place, due to the relative recency of the immigration phenomenon in Spain, there is as yet no clear political discourse that refers to identity, or even to the multicultural situation that has been produced by the arrival of the immigrants.

The components of the political discourse can, therefore, be summarized as follows. In the first place, the issue is treated as a question of state. Immigration is a fundamental source of controversy between the political parties with parliamentary representation. It is also a multilevel topic insofar as various levels of public administration are involved (central, autonomous community, and local) and as such requires integrated policies that cover a wide range of areas (housing, health, education, etc). The discourse implicitly assumes that immigration is a complex phenomenon which requires a basic consensus (institutional, parliamentary, political, and social). There is a shared consensus that to try and gain political advantage from immigration is undesirable and reproachable, since such politicization can easily lead to the consolidation of extremist organizations and discourses and raise the level of communal tension and xenophobia. Consequently, there is a shared desire to avoid "social alarm" and any kind of increased polarization.

The reference framework is the European Union and its policies, and this serves as a context which offers much needed legitimacy for innovations and policy changes which are inevitably seen as being controversial.

The other key idea is that the immigrant should not introduce cultural practices and forms of religious and social organizations which violate the principles of liberty and equality that underlie European institutions (Zapata-Barrero, 2005, 2008).

5.1.2 General Legislative Framework

As has been mentioned previously, the 1978 Spanish Constitution is the principal legal point of reference. The analysis of the Spanish Constitution, made by De Lucas (2001), distinguishes three groups of rights: A first group, the rights attached directly to the guarantee of human dignity, that is the right to life and physical integrity and morality, privacy, freedom of thought, individual freedom and effective judicial protection with respect to recognizing the full equalitybetween citizens and aliens.

A second group of rights, including meetings, demonstration, association, education, unions, and strike, belong to foreigners as long as they do not dispose of treaties and laws that exist between nations. The final group of rights cannot be recognized as such by foreigners, as they would be exclusive to the Spanish, among which would include political participation. Of these three groups or categories of rights, only the former regime would be universal. Invulnerable minimum rights belong to somebody as a person as such, not as a citizen, and would include the right of "indispensability of the guarantee of human dignity."

In addition, there is the Organic Law of 2000 (Ley Orgánica 4/2000, 11th January), which refers to the rights and responsibilities of foreigners in Spain, and their social integration. We summarize in the box below some of the key themes in both laws relating to the rights of non-European Union immigrants (Figs. 17.12–17.14)

The governing immigration legislation is not enough to build an intercultural society. A framework to regulate public participation is needed, as is the right to freedom of religion and worship as well as legislation to normalize coexistence out of respect for the values of the host society and in recognition of each group's rights to belong to their culture and the duty to contribute to society.

5.2 Immigration Plans

The Spanish state at national level has legal responsibility for the planning, coordination, and regulation of immigration. The management of immigration at state level is conducted by the

Spanish nationality

Spanish nationality may be obtained by birth, residence or consolidation.

Who has the right to Spanish citizenship by birth?

- Those born to a Spanish father or mother.
- Those born in Spain to non Spanish parents if at least one of these was also born in Spain.
- Those born in Spain to non Spanish parents if neither of these is able to provide the child with a valid nationality.
- Those born in Spain with no clear national affiliation.
- A child of non Spanish origin under the age of legal majority acquires, on adoption by parents of Spanish nationality, Spanish nationality.

How can Spanish nationality be obtained by residence?

Any non Spanish national who resides legally in Spain may, according to the given criteria of country of origin and length of stay.

Spanish nationality through consolidation

Any person may opt for Spanish nationality if they have previously used and possessed Spanish nationality during a period of ten years. In good faith, and basing themselves on an entry in the Civil Register, any person may opt for Spanish nationality if:

- They are or have been in or under the charge of a Spanish citizen.
- Their father or mother is/was Spanish and born in Spain.

Fig. 17.12 Access to Spanish nationality

Education

According to Spanish law, basic education between 6 and 16 years of age is both a right and a responsibility for all non Spanish children (even for those whose parents are in a legally irregular situation) and this education is regulated by norms which are equivalent to those applied to Spanish nationals, including grants and public assistance (art. 9).
Post basic education is, according to Spanish law, only available to those legally residing in Spain, as are the respective qualifications, grants and offers of public assistance.

Fig. 17.13 Access to education

Health

Non Spanish citizens, who are in Spain legally, have the right to health care under the same conditions as Spanish citizens. Such non Spanish citizens also have the right to urgent medical treatment following the onset of illness or accident regardless of cause, and to the continuation of such treatment for the duration of the problem.

Fig. 17.14 Access to health

Strategic Plan for Citizenship and Integration. Government of Spain

- Reception. Provision of the knowledge and skills necessary for the immigrant to function in the host society.
- Education. Promotion of measures against school segregation, host educational programs and teacher training.
- Employment. Promotion of entrepreneurialism, self-employment, social economy enterprises, measures against discrimination.
- Housing. Strengthen mediation programs and combat discrimination in the housing market to prevent sub-standards and overcrowding.
- Social Services. Adaptation to the diverse population and strengthen the training of professionals.
- Health. Adaptation of the system to the diverse population served, promotion of prevention programs and health education.
- Childhood and youth. Promote standardized access children and young people of immigrant origin to childhood and youth programs.
- Equal treatment. Comprehensive program of care to victims of discrimination.
- Women migrants. Gender mainstreaming in the design, development and evolution of policies and programs of integration.
- Participation. Extension of the right to vote and stand in municipal elections, through the conclusion of bilateral reciprocity.
- Awareness. Improvement to the public image of immigration.
- Co-development. Identification and promotion of development opportunities in immigrants' countries of origin.

Fig. 17.15 The integration plan for immigrants. Period 2007–2009. Budget 2,000 million Euros

Ministry of Labor and Immigration. This Ministry develops plans to be applied throughout all the whole territory in relation to the central exclusive powers. The first plan was implemented in 2007, a brief summary of its objectives is in Fig. 17.15:

In the case of autonomous communities, they develop their own plans, supplementary to the state plan, which embellish and adapt policies and resources according to each social and cultural reality.

The example of Catalonia,[28] the most populous Moroccan community in Spain, is paradigmatic.[29] Its first Plan of Immigration was created in 1993. Since then, there have been four plans that have deepened and expanded the resources and strategies for integrating immigrants into various areas of life (Fig. 17.16).

This general plan, at regional level, is defined by specific plans (Education, Health, Territorial

[28] For analysis of integration policy in Catalonia, see: Garreta (2009).

[29] According to the Generalitat de Catalunya, in 2009 this region had 7,367,423 inhabitants of which 15.9% were foreigners. The Moroccan community was the largest with 225,244 people. Retrieved from http://www20.gencat.cat/portal/site/bsf/menuitem.ce32baba3744d8fa172a63a7b0c0e1a0/?vgnextoid=80d8b5e22c5a4210VgnVCM1000008d0c1e0aRCRD&vgnextchannel=80d8b5e22c5a4210VgnVCM1000008d0c1e0aRCRD&vgnextfmt=default&newLang=ca_ES.

Catalonian Citizenship and Immigration Plan

The Plan sets out three main aims:

* Progress in the management of migration policies.
* Ensure access to public services on equal terms.
* Promote the integration of immigrants into a common public culture based on pluralism.

The basic principles are:

* Citizenship: Involves the extension of full citizenship to all persons who live in Catalonia under the Catalan administration's jurisdiction.

* Paradox: Immigration as a phenomenon with a global dimension, requiring public policies with a cross-sectioned perspective on integrated and multidimensional issues. Thus, the actions and programs envisaged in the Plan are characterized by attention incorporated by the diversity of the various Government departments involved in a strategic line and common criteria established by this Plan.

* Coordination: The authorities involved in the management of immigration policies through a stable co-operative . This avoids the possible duplication in actions and follows the same strategic line.

* Territoriality: Immigration is also a widespread phenomenon throughout Catalonia. To respond to the diverse needs of the country, the actions and programs envisaged in the Plan tailored to the different demographic, functional and organizational dimension and management capacity for each region.

* Multidimensionality: Foreign immigration is characterized by heterogeneity. That is why the actions envisaged in the Plan include the perspective of origin, gender and age.

* Equity: The plan is clearly committed to ensuring immigrants receive standard access to public services. Clearly, at certain times it is necessary to take specific actions and time for corrective measures to ensure disadvantaged people achieve the same level of access as the rest of the population. Policies focused on equity shares to facilitate the knowledge of the host society and language, as well as the labor market.

* Globalization: Because immigration has an impact on society as a whole, migration policies should be directed not only to immigrants but to all citizens.

Fig. 17.16 IV Catalonian immigration Plan. 2009–2012. Budget of 212.480.642,80€

Policy, Social Action, etc.) developed in several Catalonia Governmental Departments.

In Spain, the main differences between the various plans of autonomous communities and municipalities are actually the result of differences in the demographic, social, and economic impact of immigration in each of the regions and the ideology of those communities' governments.

The objective of all such plans is, however, to facilitate the development of harmonious communal life (in terms of the first type of political discourse mentioned above), through training and education, information, and a process of adapting existing resources and norms to the new and changing social reality. In this sense, it is possible to say that at the social and labor market level, the objectives of public policy have been quite clear. On the contrary, the issues associated with real cultural integration have scarcely been touched on. Depending of the political discourse of each community in relation to interculturalism, it is possible to find an added concept of diversity which masks an assimilatory model and an attempt to reconcile the distinct differences and needs of the new minority population within a pre-established framework or an effort to build an intercultural society.

Thus, the recency of the immigration phenomenon in Spain, its complexity, and the arrival of

Islamic terrorism have all combined in a way which means there has been little in the way of serious public debate about the kind of cultural immigration model that should be adopted.

5.3 Education for the Citizenship

Modern education is increasingly based on the notion of citizenship and the development of a complete citizen identity (Bartolomé & Cabrera, 2007; Folgueiras et al. 2008 and Vilà & Del Campo, 2009). This is why citizenship education has become such an important topic (whether at a formal or an informal level; whether through the family, the mass media, etc.) since, as Cortina (1997, p. 219) suggests, one learns to be a citizen not through law and punishment, but through experience and "trying it out". Such education in and for citizenship has to be an education for all, an education which is intercultural and anti-racist, one which singles out the values of solidarity, mutual tolerance, equality, and social inclusion. The fundamental rights of the individual, the constitution, and the system of democratically determined laws form the solid platform on which the status of citizens may be exercised. Schooling is normative, and it is not enough simply to recognize this; the education process itself needs to be founded on a consensual and universal basis which makes it evident that we are all at one and the same time both equal and different.

The response needs to be both a political and an educational one, which prioritizes the processes that lead to the genuine creation of a space for social debate in the classroom (Molina, 2002). It is necessary to promote respect for social and cultural differences, but such respect has to be critical and framed within a structure which recognizes individual rights and constitutional law.

As has been said above, the educational response in Spain is given at state level under the General Laws of Education and at regional level through the development of this general law tailored to each territory. The initiative with the greatest impact at state level, regarding the integration of immigrants, has been the creation of a compulsory subject on Education for Citizenship and Human Rights. This is taught in the last cycle of primary schools and in all secondary schools (Figs. 17.17 and 17.18).

In addition, each autonomous community develops its own plans to accommodate the new students, integrate families into the educational centers, and provide training programs for the youth, etc.

The Spanish educational system is trying to adapt and respond to the challenges presented by the new models of Citizenship Education and Intercultural Education.[30] Citizenship education should provide the tools required to learn to live in a world of cultural difference, with mutual respect and tolerance, and enable those who participate in it to communicate and collaborate with people from different cultures in the construction of a fairer and more harmonious world (VVAA, 2001).

5.4 Intercultural Competence

There is no doubt that living in such a complex and global world, where recognition, integration, and participation processes exist on a whole number of levels, implies and requires a special competence, one which permits the individual to work, relate to others, overcome prejudices, and resolve the conflicts which arise from the very existence of cultural differences. The key to all of this lies in the acquisition of intercultural competence[31] (Aneas, 2003 or Aneas et al., 2005). All person that live and work with people from others countries should have intercultural competencies. These competencies should be trained at the

[30] Intercultural education is analyzed in Garreta, (2000c, 2006).

[31] Intercultural competences consist of "The body of knowledge, skills and attitudes which when incorporated and applied enable the diagnosis of those personal needs and requirements which stem from working in a culturally diverse environment. Such competence enables the subject to negotiate, communicate and work in intercultural teams, and handle the many issues which may arise in such environments by the application of a process of intercultural self learning" Aneas (2003).

The contents of Primary Education.

Block 1: INDIVIDUAL AND SOCIAL RELATIONSHIPS

Proposes a model of relations based on the recognition of the dignity of all people, respect for others whilst keeping opinions and beliefs to themselves, diversity and rights of individuals.

From everyday situations, it addresses the equality of men and women in the family and the workplace.

A priority issue related to autonomy, always as an assumed responsibility.

Block 2: LIFE IN COMMUNITY

Is the coexistence of relations with the environment, civic values which underpin a democratic society: respect, tolerance, solidarity, justice, equality, mutual aid, cooperation and culture of peace.

Is how to deal with coexistence and conflict on group membership (family, school, friends, civilians) and the exercise of the rights and duties of each person within these groups, identifying the diversity that opposes discrimination and values participation within these channels.

Also, the recognition of cultural and religious diversity present in the surroundings, and assuming the equality of all women and men in rights and duties and critical respect for the customs and lifestyles other than their own, can provide elements to identify and reject situations of marginalization, discrimination and social injustice.

Block 3: LIVING IN SOCIETY

It proposes a broader society: the need and knowledge of rules and principles of social relations established by the Constitution.

Knowledge and valuation of public services and common goods.

The obligations of public authorities and citizens in their maintenance.

Some public services and common goods received specific treatment appropriate to the age of these students, in the case of civil protection, security, protection of peace and education.

Fig. 17.17 Subjects on education for citizenship and human rights. Primary education

school, the university or the companies. In relation to the migration phenomena, Intercultural competence is especially relevant in public administration, where services like health and education are offered directly to the public. The arrival of large numbers of migrants from different cultural backgrounds and different systems of education has only served to reinforce the need to have comprehensive intercultural education for those working in public administration (Aneas, 2009a).

The need for intercultural competence in areas of conflict resolution in the working environment has become a key issue for many involved in local and regional administration. Entering the labor market is a fundamental objective for the migrant and is key to the whole integration process ,since it takes the individual away from situations of exclusion and marginalization. And especially now, at a time of economic crisis, the importance of having a body of professionals who are equipped with the competences and strategies needed to optimize the resources the migrant possesses and facilitate their ability to exploit these to the full is greater than ever (Aneas 2008a).

The contents of Secondary Education

Develop and expand, in response to the increasing age of the students, all contents of the subject in primary education, adding some others, such as:

Block 1: FRIENDLY APPROACH TO DIVERSITY

Training in dialogue, debate and respectful approach to the personal and cultural diversity.

Block 2: RELATIONSHIPS AND PARTICIPATION

Try aspects of human relationships based on respect for personal dignity and equality of individual rights, the recognition of differences, rejection of discrimination and promotion of solidarity.

It addresses the participation and representation in school

Block 3: CITIZENS' RIGHTS AND RESPONSIBILITIES

Knowledge of the principles contained in international strategies.

Identification of situations of violation of human rights.

Action corresponding to the ordinary courts and international tribunals when situations of violation of human rights occur.

Block 4: THE DEMOCRATIC SOCIETIES OF THE CENTURY

Functioning of democratic states, particularly focusing on the Spanish political model. We analyze the role of various public services

Block 5: CITIZENSHIP IN A GLOBAL WORLD

It addresses some of the characteristics of modern society: inequality in its various forms, the process of globalization and interdependence, the main conflicts in the world today and the role of international organizations in their prevention and resolution.

Fig. 17.18 Subjects on education for citizenship and human rights. Secondary education

Most actions relating to the development of intercultural competence have been developed in Catalonia. The following describes some of them:

- More studies are needed to help identify the training needs of the professionals involved in order to optimize the programs of continuous education and training (Aneas 2003, 2009c). As an illustration, we would cite the program of intercultural diagnosis carried out by the Catalan Government's labor department (Cabrera et al., 2008; Donoso et al., 2009. The most relevant needs identified were related to an improved understanding of the legal framework surrounding immigration, knowledge of the key languages, and more intercultural competences. At the same time, initiatives have been taken to encourage greater intercultural appreciation at trade union level and within employers associations, both of which are seen as important bridges to ease the entry of the newcomers into the local labor market.
- Another important area is the health system, since all migrants are entitled to the access of health provision. The cultural factor in health care has been widely studied in many countries, although in Spain the topic is still in its infancy Aneas et al., 2010 and Armadans et al., 2009). Practically, all Spain's autonomous communities now have cultural intermediation services in their primary care centres. The emphasis on such services varies according to the specific needs and the experience of each community. In areas with less, or more recent, immigration, such services are normally limited to transla-

tion, providing information, and accompanying, and is normally carried out by volunteers and non-professionals. In other communities, like Catalonia, where immigration is a more extensive and longer-standing phenomenon, the service is far more sophisticated, there is a higher proportion of professional staff, and the level of prior training is relatively greater.

- Spain's security services have also started to make special provision for some level of intercultural communication. In Spain, there are a number of different bodies responsible for law enforcement, and each body has its own specific areas of activity. There are national bodies like the National Police and the Guardia Civil, but in some communities, notably Catalonia and the Basque Country, there are also local police forces. The Catalan Security School (responsibility of the Catalan Government) has collaborated closely with the UNESCO Center in Catalonia and the Center for Interreligious Dialogue for many years, as well as with the local university system in an attempt to introduce some element of intercultural competence into the police training school (which is responsible for all levels of activity within the Catalan Police Force). Since many communal conflicts have their origins in cultural misunderstandings where the police tends to play a key role as mediator in these conflicts, the issue of intercultural communication is naturally given some importance (Aneas, 2008b).
- The local Catalan public library system has also been steadily adapting itself to the needs of a more diverse population, and as a result, the administration in the city of Barcelona has organized a training course in intercultural competence for library staff. The issues raised not only extended to the question of opening hours, the organization of the inner space within the library, and the issue of the reading materials on offer, but also to cultural mediation among users.
- In the education system, there has naturally been a substantial expansion of intercultural training provision, directed largely at the teaching staff (Aneas, 2010). Such programs are directed toward helping the teacher carry out tutorial responsibilities, and to attend to family needs and demands, while at the same time focusing attention on the need to develop teaching strategies that are more in harmony with the diversity which now exists in the classroom. Such courses are normally financed out of the budgets of the autonomous communities that have offered them.
- There has also been an interesting initiative in intercultural journalism (Aneas & Santos, 2007) developed by the Catalan Broadcasting Corporation, which is the public authority in Catalonia. The Corporation, aware of the challenges presented by having over 1 million new immigrants arrive over the last decade, decided – in collaboration with the UNESCO Center in Catalonia and Barcelona University – to offer support to all staff involved with documentation, program production, and news services in their radio, TV, and Internet services. The objective was to make the staff interculturally aware and offer them competences which could help them develop intercultural approaches to program provision in terms of the treatment of images, personalities, news, and information in such a way as to avoid reinforcement of negative stereotypes.

It would be impossible to close this section without giving at least a mention to the need to continue to extend the availability and provision of intercultural education. In this sense, it is important to take note of the multitude of citizenship training programs that are being developed by NGOs, immigrant associations, and cultural organizations with the help and support of the public administration as well as private sources for finance. Intercultural education is also steadily moving forward in a number of universities in Catalonia – including the main public universities like the University of Barcelona and the University Polytechnic of Catalonia. The School of Catering and Tourism in Sant Pol (Girona University) has also introduced a module in intercultural competence into its bachelor's and master's degree (Aneas & Montané, 2009).

5.5 A Spanish Islamic Community?

Spain has shown a notable reluctance to recognize Islam and the Muslims living in Spain as its own. The attitudes that we have outlined here demonstrate how, for both historical and contemporary reasons, many Spaniards have a negative image of Muslims in general and Moroccans in particular. In addition, many Spanish citizens seem to identify Islam with immigration, and see Muslims as the most different of all the communities who have recently arrived in Spain. Hence the difficulty in accepting Islam as something truly Spanish, as one religion among all the others that are practiced by Spanish citizens. One typical example of this resistance is the response which is normally given to the proposal to install a mosque or prayer center in a given vicinity.

A country which has been so strongly identified with Catholicism and which is now steadily secularizing finds it difficult to accept a religious experience whose most visible images as presented in the media (often associated with fundamentalist groups or acts of terrorism) or seen in the street (different forms of dress, especially in the case of women) are considered to be so "foreign." The fact that they also seem reluctant to enter social relations, have gender practices which seem reprehensible, and show little apparent interest in integration only adds to the problem.

In addition, despite the formal legislative recognition which has been awarded to Islam which allows for a greater public presence for the religion (in schools, for example), such recognition is not followed through with as much enthusiasm as might have been anticipated. The lack of action is undoubtedly due to the resistance and fears that exist on both sides. The host population are wary of the social and cultural impact that a more public Islamic presence may bring in its wake, while the Moroccans remain unconvinced of the benefits that the improved recognition may bring.

As Martín Muñoz (2004) suggests, in Spain, cultural and religious demands from within the Muslim community are still in an incipient state and where these do exist, they still tend to come from within a minority group, especially from those who have converted to the religion, given that the principal preoccupations of the majority of the Muslim population are socioeconomic ones. On the contrary, in the areas where there is a large Muslim presence an autonomous religious leadership is now emerging, and this may well allow for a reshaping of the Muslim identity in Spain in the longer term. For Martín Muñoz, what is involved is a silent majority who found themselves without the necessary means of response to the accusation "incapable of integrating." So at this point, it is still impossible to speak of "Spanish Islam," it is more precise to continue to refer to "Muslims in Spain."

6 Conclusions and Suggestions for the Reconciliation

6.1 Recommendations for Policy Makers

It is not easy to lay down clear recommendations for a program capable of achieving real social integration and meaningful interculturality, since this requires both active participation and positive attitudes on the part of all involved. In addition, what is involved is not simply a matter of individual behavior and attitudes. It is essential Polity Makers and State Staff fulfill their responsibility to require all parties the responsibility and commitment to follow the rules and respect the values of the host society. And do not create discriminatory procedures that stress the balance in the access to state resources by the whole population. The problems are structural and institutional and requires a policy which is systematically applied over a broad perspective including daily life, education, the labor market, the political arena and the legislative framework, etc.

Still it is possible to identify some broad lines of approach, as well as some very specific proposals which can help achieve a greater degree of integration between populations and a higher level of mutual understanding and tolerance.

In the first place, as Cachón (2007, p. 74) argues, "the issues need to be addressed at state level between the two countries, since both have an interest in creating a successful migration outcome". Cachón uses the expression co-development.

Again, since the integration of immigrants should occur in conditions of equality, to cite Cachón (2009) again, a policy of integration of/with the immigrants should be based on the three great principles of equality, citizenship, and interculturality, as they are outlined in Spain's strategic plan for citizenship and integration, which should be seen as the principal instrument for developing structural responses and a pedagogic device to help raise the level of understanding of immigration as a phenomenon across Spanish society.

Education is one of the fundamental environments where intolerance can be effectively confronted, as was recognized by UNESCO in 1995.

The legal framework obviously needs to be based on anti-discrimination and, as Spain's "Movement Against Intolerance" proposes, inflammatory activities like demonstrations and concerts which serve to incite racism should be curtailed and prohibited. But in the main, the emphasis should be positive and constructive, with an explicit educational intent. The idea of multiple and flexible identities should be increasingly promoted, as should the idea of identity as a project that is open to change without necessarily implying the need to abandon a traditional core. For this reason, Sabar (2002) argues that the identity of the Moroccan in contemporary Europe should be seen as one of "another in the process of becoming" and not the "another in his otherness," which is in fact a stereotypical image created in the West by a society in need of an exotic caricature, or that of the "ex-colonial Moroccan" who serves as an endless source of cheap labor.

As Sánchez Rosell (2009) argues, one of the best ways to promote understanding and acceptance is the creation of common spaces which facilitate a mutual "getting to know of one another."[32]

As Pérez-Díaz et al. (2002) recommended, it is important to recognize the fluidity of public opinion composed by a majority who are reasonably open, at the same time by a minority who are often in closer proximity to the immigrants and often express serious reservations about the quality of communal life.

Knowledge and a recognition of the "other" as an equal is a necessity. The educational environment is the optimal arena to develop this knowledge. In this sense, the school has to be the starting point for any effective intercultural initiative. Educational processes are long and complex but in *the school for all,* everyone has the right to participate. Elements and structures which favor the development of respect for the other in harmony with equality of opportunity need to be identified and developed along with the feeling of belonging to a common culture and the right of access to non-marginal situations.

The European Committee for Migration has already sounded a warning, drawing attention to the importance of ensuring that immigrants enjoy the same level of well-being that their fellow citizens have come to expect (COM, 2007). In this way, we need to find the path toward identities which are compatible with both all our cultural heritages and the values of social justice,

[32] Amparo Sánchez Rosell, president of the Centro Cultural Islámico de Valencia: "The image people have of North African people is negative largely in relation to gender inequality, sexism and the passivity of the woman. This is the image we have been "feeding ourselves" on. This cultural baggage is no more than prejudice but it is generalized, and influences even those with an express interest in the culture of the Maghreb. These are stereotypes but they have become extremely 'internalized'" (Retrieved from http://www.elmagrebconojosdemujer.org (30/10/2010).

tolerance, and respect for human rights which have long formed part of our common identity as Europeans.

6.2 Suggestions

At this point, we will propose some suggestions and specific forward-looking reflections.

To build a new society:

According to Bartolomé et al. (2007) and Marin (2010), the goal would be to build a society that can:

- Overcome passivity
- Encourage the development of a participatory democratic culture
- Combat exclusion and promote social cohesion
- Facilitate coexistence in multicultural societies
- Combat alienating fundamentalist positions
- Exercise responsible behavior
- Prevent conflict and violence

In order to achieve this goal, it would be necessary to promote the following civic values among all citizens:

- Citizen participation
- Social responsibility
- The coming together of diversity and dialog
- The fight against exclusion
- Overcoming traditional prejudices and stereotypes
- The promotion of sustainable development and civic values

Integrate other new approaches that are:

- More open to accommodate differences
- Wider and go beyond the territory
- Complex and accepting of multiple identities

Next, we are going to present a series of suggestions for both sides in conflict.

- Strategies for Spain, the host society:
- Ensure that the Moroccan community, like other foreign groups, attain a legal status allowing them the full exercise of citizens – Integrate the contributions of intercultural files to the plans of social and cultural integration
- Develope the legislative framework for new social and cultural reality S. XXI
- Fight against anything which perpetuates or creates stereotypes, prejudices, and discriminatory behavior
- Give full recognition within the state of law, practices, social organization, and traditions of diverse cultures and communities nationwide

Strategies for the Moroccan community:

- Open to the host society, allowing each member of the community to build their own identity of Moroccans in Spain
- Fight against fundamentalist influences using the faith politically against their fellow citizens
- Recognize the values and rules of their society, and respect their laws and social rules

Suggestions for both communities:

- Create awareness that citizenship is a process of social construction
- Interact and share values and norms to promote coexistence
- Promote a collective identity
- Remember that citizenship not only depends on status recognition, but also requires a sense of belonging that is built in and through community participation
- Develop a critical sense of own culture so not to resign beliefs but be aware that they are fallible

6.3 Conclusions

Possibly the most ethno–cultural conflicts are like that of Spain and Morocco: a complex puzzle composed of common history, collective imagination, socioeconomic crisis, cultural differences, ethnic, religion, gender, age, and other external agents such as Islamic fundamentalism. That is, the complex relationship between Spain and Morocco is motivated not only by the history of the neighborhood, culture, religion, or immigration but also by the multiplication of all these factors among themselves.

Although this conflict has not erupted in violent incidents and social division, it has permeated and imbued with much mutual mistrust between the Spanish and Moroccans living in Spain. In addition to this distant relationship, if not almost nonexistent among many Spanish and Moroccans living in Spain, the consequences of conflict are identified in terms of social vulnerability, xenophobia, self-exclusion, discrimination, and fundamentalism.

The various state administrations (central, regional, and local) and the social agencies have raised social and educational legislative responses to mitigate this mutual lack of trust and move toward a society for responsible citizenship.

References

Alcalde, R., García, C., Moreno, R., & Ramírez, M. (2002). Las mujeres marroquíes en Cataluña: entre la transgresión y el cambio. *Revista Catalana de Sociologia, 18*, 27–44.

Almeida, J. (1993). *El problema de España en Américo Castro*. Córdoba: Publicaciones Universidad de Córdoba.

Almeida, J. (2004). Españoles en cuerpo y alma. *Cuenta y razón, 133*, 91–106.

Aneas, A. (2003). *Competencias Interculturales transversales: un modelo para la detección de necesidades formativas*. Barcelona: Universidad de Barcelona. Retrieved from http://www.tdx.cesca.es/TDX-1223104-122502/

Aneas, A. (2008a). Integration and identity issues. In N. Arthur & P. Pedersen (Eds.), *Case incidents in counseling for international transitions* (pp. 169–189). Alexandria: American Counseling Association.

Aneas, A. (2008b). Bases conceptuals per a una Policia Intercultural. In E. Masllorens (Ed.) *Seguretat, convivència i diversitat cultura.* (pp. 135–142) Barcelona: Publicacions UNESCO.

Aneas, A. (2009a). Aportes interculturales para las políticas públicas de inmigración. Orientaciones para una sociedad inclusiva. *Revista Abaco, 62*, 68–79.

Aneas, A. (2009b). Gestión de recursos humanos multiculturales: proyecto capital humano en organizaciones multiculturales.Formación intercultural. *Col·lecció OMADO (Objectes i materials docents) del Dipòsit Digital de la UB*. Retrieved from http://hdl.handle.net/2445/8843

Aneas, A. (2009c). Integración socio-laboral de las personas inmigrantes en la empresa de España. *Col·lecció OMADO (Objectes i materials docents) del Dipòsit Digital de la UB*. Retrieved from http://hdl.handle.net/2445/8822

Aneas, A. (2010). Competencia Intercultural: Competencia clave en las organizaciones actuales. In E. Soriano (Ed.) *Vivir entre culturas: una nueva sociedad* (pp. 10–28). Almería: Ediciones La Muralla.

Aneas, A., Armadans, I., & Fernández, R. (2010). Interculturalidad y salud en España. In P. Casanoves & N. Galera (Eds.), *Nuevos caminos para la Justicia* (pp. 175–186). Barcelona: Huygens Editorial.

Aneas, A., & De Santos, J. (2007). *Formación intercultural: Medios de comunicación*. Madrid: Fundación Atman.

Aneas, A. Montané, S (2009) Let's Go Work Together! Introducing Intercultural Competencies as a University Subject in Catalonia, Spain. International Journal of Learning.16 (10), 355–368.

Aneas, A., & Schubert, W. (2006). *Cultural detective in Spain*. Retrieved from http://www.culturaldetective.com/package.html#SPAI

Aneas, A., Simons, G., Lambert, J., & Myers, S. (2005). *Competencia Global. 50 actividades de formación para lograr el éxito en los negocios internacionales*. Madrid: Diaz de Santos.

Aneas, A. & Donoso, T. (2007). Estudio sobre los procesos de integración socio-laboral de los inmigrantes. *Revista Española de Orientación y Psicopedagogía, 19*(1), 51–60.

Armadans, I., Aneas, A., Soria, M. A., & Bosch, L. (2009). La mediación en el ámbito de la salud. *Medicine Clinical (Barc)., 133*(05), 187–92.

Balta, P. (1990). *Le grand Maghreb*. Paris: Éditions la Découverte.

Bartolomé, M. (2002). *Identidad y ciudadanía. Un reto a la educación intercultural*. Madrid: Narcea Ediciones.

Bartolomé, M. & Cabrera, F. (2007). *Construcción de una ciudadanía intercultural y responsable*. Madrid: Narcea Ediciones.

Bartolomé, M., Cabrera, F. & Sandín, M.P. (2007). Educación ciudadana en el currículo. In M. Bartolomé & F. Cabrera (Eds.), Construcción de una ciudadanía intercultural y responsable. Guía para el profesorado de Secundaria, pp.(53–75). Madrid: Narcea-MEC.

Belardbi, A. (1993). *Le salarie de madame*. Casablanca: Le Fennec.

Bennis, S. (2005). *Marruecos-España. El tratamiento de la inmigración por los medios de comunicación españoles y su repercusión sobre la percepción y la situación de los inmigrantes marroquíes*. Retreived from http://www.mundoarabe.org/inmigraci%C3%B3n_marruecos_espa%C3%B1a.htm.

Berry, J. W. (1997). Immigration, acculturation and adaptation. *Applied Psychology, 46*, 5–68.

Berry, J. W. (2005). Acculturation: Living successfully in two cultures. *International Journal of Intercultural Relations, 29*, 697–712.

Berry, J. W., Kim, U., Power, S., Young, M., & Bujaki, M. (1989). Acculturation attitudes in plural societies. *Applied Psychology, 38*, 185–206.

Birman, D., Trickett, E., & Vinokurov, A. (2002). Acculturation and adaptation of Soviet Jewish refugee adolescents: predictors of adjustment across life domains. *American Journal of Community Psychology, 30*(5), 585–608.

Blanco, C. (2009). Pautas de asentamiento residencial de los inmigrantes ¿exclusión social o estrategia étnica? In C. Blanco & I. Barrero (Eds.), *Pautas de asentamiento de la población inmigrante: implicaciones y retos socio-jurídicos* (pp. 27–61). Madrid: Dykinson.

Cabrera, F., Donoso, T., Aneas A., De Santos, J., Mas, J., & Curós, P. (2008). Diagnòstic de competències interculturals en l'administració pública. In Generalitat de

Catalunya Recerca i Immigració. Barcelona: Publicacions de la Generalitat de Catalunya.
Cachón, L. (2004). Marroquíes en el mercado de trabajo en España. In B. López & M Berriane (Eds) Atlas de la Inmigración marroquí en España. Madrid: UAM
Cachón, L. (2007). Diez notas sobre la inmigración en España. *Vanguardia Dossier, 22*, 68–75.
Cachón, L. (2009). *La "España inmigrante": marco discriminatorio, mercado de trabajo y políticas de integración*. Barcelona: Anthropos.
Cano, R. (1999). *El español a través de los tiempos*. Madrid: Arco.
Castro, A. (1996). *España en su historia. Cristianos, moros y judios*. Barcelona: Grijalbo Mondadori.
Castro, A. (2000) *Sobre el nombre y el quien de los españoles*. Madrid:Taurus.
CIS. (2009). *Estudio Sociopolítico de España*. Madrid: Centro de Investigaciones Sociológicas.
Colectivo, I. O. É. (1994). *Marroquins a Catalunya*. Barcelona: Institut d'Estudis Mediterranis.
COM. (2007).Communication from the Commission to the European Parliament, the Council, the European Economic and Social Committee and the Committee of the Regions - Towards a Common Immigration Policy. Retrieved from http://eur-lex.europa.eu/LexUriServ/LexUriServ.do?uri=CELEX:52007DC0780:EN:NOT.
Cortina, A. (1997). *Ciudadanos del mundo. Hacia una teoría de la ciudadanía*. Madrid: Alianza.
De Lucas, J. (2001). Sobre las garantías de los derechos de los inmigrantes. *Cuadernos Electrónicos de Filosofía del Derecho. 4-2001*. Retrieved from http://www.uv.es/CEFD/4/Delucas.html
Domingo, C., & González, V. (1996). La inmigración magrebí en España: actualidad y futuro. *Boletín de la AGE, 23*, 3–12.
Donoso, T., Cabrera, F., Aneas, A., De Santos, J., & Curós, P. (2009). Diagnóstico de competencias en la Administración Pública. *Revista de Investigación Educativa, 27*(1), 149–167.
Eibl-Eibesfeldt, I. (1980). *El hombre preprogramado*. Madrid: Alianza.
Farrell, S., Aubry, T., & Coulombe, D. (2004). The influence of neighborhood characteristics on sense of community, neighboring behaviour and well-being. *Journal of Community Psychology, 32*, 9–26.
Fullaondo, A. (2009). Inmigración y ciudad. El caso del área metropolitana de Barcelona. In C. Blanco & I. Barrero (Eds.), *Pautas de asentamiento de la población inmigrante: implicaciones y retos socio-jurídicos* (pp. 63–94). Madrid: Dykinson.
Folgueiras, P.; Massot, I.; Sabariego, M. (2008). La ciudadanía activa e intercultural en alumnado de la ESO. *Revista Electronica Interuniversitaria de Formación del Profesorado, 11*, 3–27.
García-Ramirez, M., & Camacho, C. (2005). Adaptation and satisfaction among Moroccans in Spain: The community context role. In *10th Biennial Conference of Society for Community* Psicología de la Liberación e Integración Comunitaria de Inmigrantes 23 *Research and Action: Community Psychology in Global Perspective*. University of Illinois at Urbana-Champaign.
García-Ramírez, M., Camacho, C., Hernández-Plaza, S., Albar M. J., Manzano, V., & Paloma, V. (2006). Psicología de la liberación en España y respuestas a la opresión en inmigrantes marroquíes. Identificando las Condiciones de Opresión en Marroquíes del Sur de España. *Conferencia Internacional de Psicología Comunitaria*. San Juan de Puerto Rico. Retrieved from http://www.institucional.us.es/ppici/documentos/puertorico.pdf.
Garreta, J. (2000a). Inmigrantes musulmanes en Cataluña. Los retos sociales, culturales y educativos de la diversidad religiosa. *Revista Internacional de Sociología, 25*, 151–176.
Garreta, J. (2000b). *Els musulmans a Catalunya*. Lleida: Pagès.
Garreta, J. (2000c). *El espejismo intercultural. La escuela de Cataluña ante la diversidad cultural*. Madrid: CIDE.
Garreta, J. (2001). The process of consolidation of the Islamic communities of Catalonia (Spain). *International Journal of Migration Studies, 144*, 787–809.
Garreta, J. (2003). *La integración sociocultural de las minorías étnicas: inmigrantes y gitanos*. Barcelona: Anthropos.
Garreta, J. (2006). Ethnic minorities in the Spanish and Catalan educational systems: From exclusion to intercultural education. *International Journal of Intercultural Relations, 30*(2), 261–279.
Garreta, J. (2009). *Sociedad multicultural e integración de los inmigrantes en Cataluña: discursos y prácticas*. Lleida: Universitat de Lleida.
Garreta, J. (2011). L'immigration et les politiques d'intégration en Catalogne: quelques enjeux. Migrations-Société, 23, 139–151.
Garreta, J., Samper, L., Mayoral, D., Llevot, N., Molina, F., Lapresta, C., et al. (2007). *La relació família d'origen immigrant i escola: l'Islam en els centres educatius de Catalunya*. Lleida: Universitat de Lleida.
Hernández-Plaza, S. (2003). *La otra cara de la inmigración: Necesidades y sistemas de apoyo social*. Almería: Servicio de Publicaciones de la Universidad de Almería.
Hernández-Plaza, S., Pozo, C., & Alonso-Morillejo, E. (2004). The role of informal social support in needs assessment: Proposal and application of a model to assess immigrants' needs in the south of Spain. *Journal of Community and Applied Social Psychology, 14*, 284–298.
Herney, D. B., Cartland, J., Ruchross, H., & Monahan, K. (2004). A return potential measure of setting norms for aggression. *American Journal of Community Psychology, 33*(3/4), 131–149.
Hofstede, G. (1999). *Culturas y organizaciones*. Madrid: Alianza Editorial.
Institut BVA. (2009). *Interviewe sur l'immigration marocaine en Europe*. Casablanca: CCME.
Izquierdo, A. (2003). *Inmigración: mercado de trabajo y protección en España*. Madrid: CES.

Izquierdo, A. (2008). Terremoto en los cimientos del modelo migratorio. In J. García & J. Laomba (Eds.), *La inmigración en la sociedad española* (pp. 75–91). Barcelona: Edicions Bellaterra.

Lapesa, R. (1995). *Historia de la lengua española*. Madrid: Gredos.

López, B., & García, P. (2006). Jóvenes y menores en la inmigración magrebí actual en España. *Anales de Historia Contemporánea, 22*, 57–78.

López, B., & Olmo, N. (1995). Islam e inmigración. In M. Abumalham (Ed.), *Comunidades islámicas en Europa* (pp. 257–276). Madrid: Trotta.

Marin, M.A. (2010). Educación para la ciudadanía. In Puig (Ed.), *Entre todos. Compartir la educación para la ciudadanía* (pp. 15–32). Barcelona: ICE-Horsori.

Martín Muñoz, G. (2004). Emigración e Islam. In G. Aubarell & R. Zapata (Eds.), *Inmigración y procesos de cambio* (pp. 351–374). Barcelona: Icaria.

Martínez, M. F., García-Ramírez, M., Maya, I., Rodríguez, S., & Checa, F. (1996). *La integración social de los inmigrantes africanos en Andalucía. Necesidades y recursos*. Sevilla: Junta de Andalucía.

McMillan, D. W., & Chavis, D. M. (1986). Sense of community: A definition and theory. *American Journal of Community Psychology, 14*(1), 6–23.

Molina, F. (2002). *Sociología de la Educación Intercultural*. Buenos Aires: Lumen.

Molina, F. (Ed.). (2008). *Alternativas en Educación Intercultural*. Lleida: De París.

Moreras, J. (1999). *Musulmanes en Barcelona*. Barcelona: CIDOB Edicions.

Moreras, J. (2003). Un Islam en Cataluña o un Islam Catalán. In M. Roque (Ed.), *El Islam plural* (pp. 335–351). Barcelona: Icaria.

Navas, M., García, M. C., Rojas, A. J., Pumares, P., & Cuadrado, I. (2006). Actitudes de aculturación y prejuicio: la perspectiva de autoctonos e inmigrantes. *Psicothema, 18*(2), 187–193.

Navas, M., García, M. C., Sánchez, J., Rojas, A. J., Pumares, P., & Fernández, J. S. (2005). Relative Acculturation Extended Model: New contributions with regard to the study of acculturation. *International Journal of Intercultural Relations, 29*, 21–37.

Navas, M., Pumares, P., Sánchez, J., García, M. C., Rojas, A. J., & Cuadrado, I. (2004). *Estrategias y actitudes de aculturación: la perspectiva de los inmigrantes y de los autóctonos en Almería*. Sevilla: Dirección General de Coordinación de Políticas Migratorias, Consejería de Gobernación de la Junta de Andalucía.

Navas, M., Rojas, A. J., García, M. C., & Pumares, P. (2007). Acculturation strategies and attitudes according to the Relative Acculturation Extended Model (RAEM): The perspectives of natives versus immigrants. *International Journal of Intercultural Relations, 31*(2007), 67–86.

Nelson, G., & Prilleltensky, I. (2002). *Doing psychology critically. Making a difference in diverse settings*. New York, EEUU: Palgrave Macmillan.

Nydell (Omar), M. (1996). *Understanding Arabs. A guide for Westerns*. London: Intercultural Press.

Penninx, R. (2006). Introduction. In R. Penninx, M. Berger, & K. Kraal (Eds.), *The dynamics of international migration and settlement in Europe* (pp. 7–17). Amsterdam: Amsterdam University Press.

Pérez Yruela, M., & Rinken, S. (2005). *La integración de los inmigrantes en la sociedad andaluza*. Sevilla: Consejo Superior de Investigaciones Científicas.

Pérez-Díaz, V., Aneas, B., & González, C. (2002). Barcelona: Fundación "la Caixa", Colección Estudios Sociales.

Perkins, D., Florin, P., Rich, R., Wandersman, A., & Chavis, D. (1990). Participation and the social and physical environment of residential blocks: Crime and community context. *American Journal of Community Psychology, 18*, 83–113.

Portes, A., Aparicio, R., & Haller, W. (2009). *La segunda generación en Madrid: un estudio longitudinal*. Madrid: Informe Fundación Spencer de Chicago.

Portes, A., & Rumbaut, R. G. (1996). *Inmigrant America: A portrait*. Berkeley, CA: University of California Press.

Pumares, P. (1993). *Problemática de la integración marroquí en España* (pp. 139–147). *Política y sociedad, 12*, 139–147.

Rebolloso, E., Hernández, S., & Cantón, P. (2001). El discurso social del prejuicio hacia los inmigrantes en la provincia de Almería. *Apuntes de Psicología, 19*(2), 207–234.

Redfield, R., Linton, R., & Herskovits, M. J. (1936). Memorandum on the study of acculturation. *American Anthropologist, 38*, 149–152.

Sabar, K. (2002). *La inmigración como proyecto de vida: búsqueda y recomposición de una identidad fragmentada*. Retrieved from http://ayp.unia.es

Sánchez-Albornoz, C. (1943) *España y el Islam*. Buenos Aires: Editorial Sudamericana.

Sánchez-Albornoz, C. (1975) España: un enigma histórico. Madrid: Fundación Universitaria Española.

Sánchez-Rosell, A. (2009). Acercamiento entre las dos culturas. Retrieved from http://www.levante-emv.com/secciones/noticia.jsp?pRef=2009060900_33_599404__Juntos-importante-cascara-dentro

Sonn, C. C., & Fisher, A. T. (2005). Immigration and adaptation: Confronting the challenges of cultural diversity. In G. Nelson & I. Prilleltensky (Eds.), *Critical Community psychology: In pursuit for wellness and liberation* (pp. 348–363). London: Palgrave Macmillan.

Taguieff, P. A. (1987). *La force du préjugé. Essai sur le racisme et ses doubles*. París: La Découverte.

Terrén, E. (2004). Opinión pública y visibilidad: las encuestas sobre racismo y xenofobia. In B. López García (Ed.), *Atlas de la inmigración marroquí en España* (pp. 439–441). Madrid: Observatorio de la Inmigración magrebí en España de la Universidad Autónoma de Madrid.

Tezanos, J. F., & Tezanos, S. (2006). La cuestión migratoria en España. *Tendencias en inmigración y exclusión social. Sistema, 190–191*, 9–39.

UCIDE. (2008). *Estudio demográfico de la población musulmana. Explotación estadística del censo de ciudadanos musulmanes en España referido a fecha 31/12/2007*. Observatorio Andalusí Retrieved from http://mx.geocities.com/hispanomuslime/estademograf.doc

Van Dijk, T. A. (1996). *Discourse, racism and ideology*. Tenerife: RCEI.

Vilà, R. & Del Campo, J. (2009). Desarrollo de la ciudadanía intercultural en Sant Quintí de Mediona a través de redes comunitarias. Revista de Investigación Educativa, 27(2), 427–450.

VVAA. (2001). *Inmigración y escuela. De la educación intercultural a la educación para la ciudadanía*. Madrid: Ministerio de Trabajo y Asuntos Sociales – FETE-UGT.

VVAA. (2009). *Informe Raxen. Racismo, Xenofobia, Antisemitismo, Islamofobia, Neofascismo, Homofobia y otras manifestaciones de Intolerancia a través de los hechos. Crisis Económica, Xenofobia y Neofascismo en España*. Retrieved from http://www.movimientocontralaintolerancia.com/html/raxen/raxen.asp

Zapata-Barrero, R. (2003). Spain. In J. Niessen & Y. Schibel (Eds.), *EU and US approaches to the management of immigration comparative perspectives* (pp. 459–89). Brussels: Migration Policy Group.

Zapata-Barrero, R. (2005). The Muslim community and Spanish tradition: Maurophobia as a fact and impartiality as a desideratum. In T. Modood, A. Traindafyllidou, & R. Zapata-Barrero (Eds.), *Multiculturalism, Muslims and citizenship: A European approach*. London: Routledge.

Zapata-Barrero, R. (2008). Política del discurso sobre la inmigración en España. In E. Zapata-Barrero, E. Gonzalez, & E. Sanchez (Eds.), *El discuso político en torno a la inmigración en España y en la UE*. Madrid: Documentos del Observatorio permanente de la inmigración, Ministerio de Trabajo e Inmigración. Retrieved from http://extranjeros.mtin.es/es/ObservatorioPermanenteInmigracion/Publicaciones/El_discurso_polxtico_en_torno_a_la_inmigracixn_en_Espaxa_y_en_la_UE.html.

18 Ethnic and Religious Conflicts in France*

Rodolphe Kamiejski, Pierre De Oliveira, and Serge Guimond

France Chapter Summary

This chapter presents a detailed analysis of current and historical interethnic relations in France. Kamiejski, De Oliveira, and Guimond apply several theories in exploration of the variables related to the development of the existent ethnic tensions in this region. Policy models are also evaluated and considered as means of engendering harmony in the future.

Discussion of the most recent and largest immigrant group to France, the Maghrebians, reveals several factors associated with increasing tensions including the large degree of assumed difference in values, religion, and culture. The authors recognize that France has set the stage for positive interethnic relations with its policy of a neutral state and equality of all citizens. However, evidence contrary to this policy is noted in recent political and media activities which, as the authors demonstrate through research, serve to reinforce differences and exacerbate ethnic tensions.

Emphasis is placed on several theories that explain attitudes toward immigrants and these are applied to the development of current ethnic tensions in France. Kamiejski, De Oliveira, and Guimond present five factors that they believe, and research has concluded, to be applicable: Threat, relative deprivation and gratification, SDO, national identity, and acculturation orientation. The Social Identity Model of Collective Action is applied to the recent riots in France that the authors attribute to social activism.

*This research was supported by Grant ANR-06-CONF-07.

R. Kamiejski (✉) • S. Guimond
Laboratoire de Psychologie Sociale et Cognitive,
CNRS UMR 6024, Clermont Université, Université
Blaise Pascal, Clermont-Ferrand, France
e-mail: Rodolphe.Kamiejski@etudiant.univ-bpclermont.fr;
serge.guimond@univ-bpclermont.fr

P. De Oliveira
Laboratoire SPMS – EA 4180,
Université de Bourgogne, Dijon, France
e-mail: Pierre.De_Oliveira@etudiant.univ-bpclermont.fr

D. Landis and R.D. Albert (eds.), *Handbook of Ethnic Conflict: International Perspectives*, International and Cultural Psychology, DOI 10.1007/978-1-4614-0448-4_18,

Kamiejski, De Oliveira, and Guimond conclude by offering suggestions to improve interethnic relations, such as the use of the contact hypothesis to reduce prejudice. Analysis of various forms of policy and the associated implications on interethnic relations is presented and a solution specific to the situation in France is offered.

Cheryl Jorgensen

1 Introduction

This chapter presents an analysis of intergroup conflict in contemporary France from a social–psychological perspective. More specifically, our focus will be on describing and understanding the tensions that exist between the dominant French majority and ethnic minorities, particularly French people of North African origin. Before we start, it is important to spell out briefly what we mean by conflict. First, conflict is often considered in a negative manner. However, it is important to keep in mind that conflict can also be associated with positive consequences. Progress, innovation, and social change can hardly happen without conflict (Moscovici, 1976). Thus, one may distinguish between constructive and destructive conflicts. Second, it is also useful to distinguish between manifest and latent social conflict. One can state that there is a conflict between two groups and what that means is simply that the interests of these two groups are in contradiction (Deutsch, 1973). In this sense, the attitudes and behaviors of members of the two groups may not necessarily reflect any actual hostility. Members of conflicting groups can enjoy each other and have a good time together. This reflects the fact that the concept of conflict as incompatibility of interests refers to a latent conflict, one that is not necessarily expressed in attitudes or behaviors. On the contrary, when we observe hostile intergroup attitudes and behaviors, when members of one group are actually fighting with members of another group, this is manifest social conflict. Our interest in this chapter will be with the explanation of hostile or negative intergroup attitudes and behaviors.

After describing the social and political context of contemporary ethnic relations in the first section, we will discuss how theories and research in social and cross-cultural psychology can provide an understanding of the manner in which the conflict is expressed in prejudice, discrimination, and collective action. In the final section, we will discuss possible ways to improve ethnic relations in France.

2 History and Current Status of Ethnic Relations

With a population of over 62 million people in 2005, representing 1% of the world population, France is nevertheless among the most economically powerful nations in the world. With 5 million immigrants in 2006, representing 8% of the French population (Héran, 2007; INSEE, 2006), France is one of the leading countries of immigration in Europe. Thus, the French population is extremely diverse. Figure 18.1 shows the regional distribution of immigrants in France with three regions having a relatively higher proportion of immigrants: Paris and its suburbs (region called *Ile de France*), the east with *Alsace,* and the south with *Provence-Alpe-Côte d'Azur*. One of the single largest immigrant group in France is made up of people coming from the former colonies of the Maghreb, particularly Algeria, Morocco, and Tunisia, representing 1.55 million people in 2006. The name "*Maghrébins*" in French, that can be translated as Maghrebian in English, is often used to refer to this population. Since 1974, immigrants from Portugal, Italy, and Spain, representing 1.17 million people in 2006, have been outnumbered by immigrants from the Maghreb region (for the history of immigration in France, see Noiriel, 2006; Weil, 2005).

The history of immigration in France suggests that there has always been periods during which relationships between French nationals

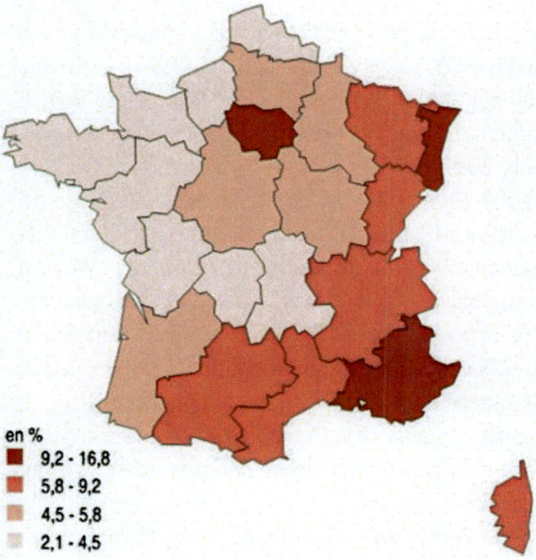

Fig. 18.1 Distribution of immigrants among the regions of France (INSEE-2005)

and immigrants were smooth and other periods, usually when economic conditions were difficult, during which things got bad (Noiriel, 2007). For example, at the beginning of the twentieth century, with the arrival of large numbers of Italian immigrants, well-documented incidents of intergroup violence, riots, or lynching occurred in the south of France with Italians as the main target. Nevertheless, it is only in the 1970s and 1980s that France "discovered" the problem of immigration. This problem was construed, initially at least, as the outcome of a change from an European immigration to an African and Muslim one. Moreover, whereas European immigrants were assumed to be integrated easily, the reverse assumption is made concerning Africans and Muslims. Thus, the basic concern for the French people at large can be summarized by the question: "Why don't they want to integrate themselves?"

Numerous laws and regulations have been proposed over time to deal with immigration. According to Noiriel (2007), the first major change in policy occurred in 1974 with the creation of the Secretary of State for immigration and the first attempt to definitely curb the number of immigrants who are allowed to get into the country. Since then, political and public discussions of immigration have more often than not focused on this question of how to limit the number of foreigners in France. Not surprisingly, national surveys conducted annually by the Human Rights Commission since 1990 (*Commisssion Nationale Consultative des Droits de l'Homme*, CNCDH) suggest that, overall, the French are suspicious about immigrants in general and about people with a North African background in particular. For example, in 2009, 47% of the population agreed that "there are too many immigrants in France," (CNCDH, 2009). However, the fact that Maghrebians, rather than Black Africans, are the main target of prejudice and discrimination in France is suggested by surveys revealing that 63% of the population agree that "there are too many Arabs in France" whereas only 38% agree that "there are too many Blacks in France" (Guimond, 2004).

Systematic social–psychological studies confirm these indications. Twenty years ago, Lambert, Moghaddam, Sorin, and Sorin (1990) questionned 40 middle-class and 40 working-class families from a mid-size city in the north of France about ethnic relations in France. Measuring acceptance of other ethnic groups using a social distance scale, they found that after the French, "Italians were the second most acceptable group, then Portuguese and Vietnamese, then African blacks, and clearly last, Maghrebian Arabs" (p. 402). Findings using other type of measures confirmed these results. Using data of the 1988 Euro-Barometer survey with large samples from France, West Germany, the UK, and the Netherlands, Pettigrew et al. (1998) also found that French feelings toward North Africans were especially negative. However, the cross-national comparison suggested that these negative feelings were not exceeding what can be found in other countries, such as the attitudes of Germans toward the Turks or those of the British toward West Indians.

In recent years, international events such as 9/11 have somewhat channeled these reactions and brought to focus a religious dimension with concerns being expressed about Islam.

2.1 French Muslims

The French population is approximately 90% Catholics, 4% Muslims, 2% Protestants, and 1% of Jewish faith (Atlaséco, 2002). Moreover, it is estimated that as much as 30% of the population is agnostic or atheist. Following the terrorist attacks in New York and Washington in 2001, researchers have suggested that attitudes toward Muslims in Europe have become more negative (Gonzales-Castro, Ubillos, & Ibanez, 2009). Terrorist violence perpetrated by various religious fundamentalists has occurred in Europe numerous times since, most notably in Madrid in 2004, in London in 2005, and in the Netherlands in 2004 with the murder of filmmaker Theo Van Gogh. The largest Muslim community in Europe, estimated at around 5 million people (ministère de l'intérieur, décembre 2009), is found in France. Thus, these international events have an important bearing on the relations between French people and ethnic minorities, especially those who are mainly of Muslim faith such as the Maghrebians. In this context, an influential series of surveys carried out in 2006 by the PEW research institute, based in Washington D.C., painted a relatively surprising picture.

One project called "Conflicting views in a divided world" provides the results of large surveys carried out in 15 countries on Muslim-Western relations (see http://pewglobal.org/2006/?cat=survey-reports). Of all the countries surveyed, the highest proportion of people who say that "there is no conflict between being a devout Muslim and living in a modern society" is in France, with 74%. In contrast, only a minority of Germans (26%), Spanish (36%), British (35%), or Americans (42%) subscribe to this view. On a host of other questions, attitudes toward Muslims appear to be more positive in France than in any other Western country. For example, among non-Muslim respondents, the highest proportion of people who associate Muslims with positive characteristics such as "honest" and "generous" is found in France (64 and 63%, respectively), whereas the figures are much lower in Germany (52 and 40), Great Britain (56 and 34), and Spain (43 and 29). One year later, the results of a survey published in the *Financial Times* and involving people from France, Italy, Spain, Germany, and the UK largely confirmed the PEW results (see Keppel, 2008). Whereas nearly 40% of the British think that Muslims are a threat to national security, only 20% of the French do so. Similarly, only 19% of the French would object if their child was to marry a Muslim. The same figure is 36% in Great Britain, 29% in Italy and 39% in Germany. We will come back to these results later on in this chapter. For now, one may note with Keppel (2008) that these converging results, obtained one year apart, by independent English-speaking institutions, quite clearly suggest that France may be more at ease with its Muslim population than is the case in other Western countries.

Nevertheless, to understand the French case, one needs to be open to contradictions, debates, and diversity of opinions and values. This is perhaps best summarized by noting that there are in France several major political parties, each with millions of followers, that span from the extreme-left, the left, the center, the right, and the extreme-right, not to forget a green party that has been on the rise in recent years. Furthermore, political orientations in France has a large bearing on intergroup attitudes, with people on the left being more tolerant of ethnic and cultural diversity than those on the right (see Guimond, De Oliveira, Kamiejski, & Sidanius, 2010; Lambert et al., 1990). Thus, if one can find, in France, evidence of positive views toward Muslims, there is also clear evidence, as we will demonstrate below, of various forms of social exclusion and systematic discrimination against North Africans and Muslims.

2.2 Discrimination: Basic Facts and Figures

French social scientists have done very little research on ethnic relations and immigration until recently (Schnapper, 2007). This is because since the French revolution, the traditional model of integration, called in public life the Republican model, emphasized the neutrality of the State and the equality of all citizens regardless of color, creed, or religion. As such, several basic concepts commonly used by English-speaking social scientists, such as ethnic or racial groups and minorities, were frowned upon in France. The idea is that using such categories is, in effect, making distinctions and discriminating against various individuals on the basis of their race or ethnicity. While this is still a topic of considerable debate and discussions, dramatic changes have occurred. Indeed, as we will highlight briefly here, a tremendous amount of work has been done in recent years on the topic of discrimination.

A powerful method to study discrimination called "testing," reminiscent of the famous study by LaPiere (1934), has been used in several recent studies (see Amadieu, 2004, 2006). This method involves setting up the conditions to observe cases of actual discrimination in various settings. For example, are people of North African origin discriminated against in their leisure by being prevented from entering night clubs? To find out, the method of testing would involve sending out in various night clubs, first some couples including North Africans and then, a few minutes later, some couples of Whites, with observers to record what happens. Invariably, this method led to observe discrimination with the North Africans not allowed to get in, while the Whites were accepted. This type of evidence is now accepted as proof of discrimination by the courts in France.

This method was also used to study job discrimination. Applications to various job offers were sent by systematically varying the age, sex, and ethnicity of the applicants. The results revealed that with identical experience, ability, and background, a white male with a French name had, in 2004, five times more chances to be selected for an interview than a similar applicant with an Arab name. Similarly, in order to rent an apartment, and with the same profile, a white French person received in 75% of the cases the opportunity to rent the apartment after a visit, whereas the same figure for a North African was 17% (HALDE, 2008). Finally, in their study of stop-and-search practices by the police in Paris, Jobard and Levy (2009) report that ethnic minorities are more likely to be subjected to arbitrary identity check than Whites. With some variations depending on the sites, Blacks were overall six times more likely than Whites to be stopped by the police. Arabs (of North African or Maghrebian origin) were overall 7.6 times more likely than Whites to be stopped by the police.

A major study of discrimination carried out in 2008 for Ined-Insee, among 22,000 people aged between 18 and 50 years, revealed that 26% of immigrants in France and 24% of their children have experienced discrimination over the last 5 years (Beauchemin, Hamel, Lesné, Simon, & équipe TeO, 2010). These figures are higher among adults of North African origin: 30% in the case of those from Algeria and 33% in the case of those from Morocco or Tunisia. The children of the latter groups are also reporting the highest level of discrimination: 39% for the children of people from Algeria and 37% for those with parents from Morocco or Tunisia.

2.3 Social and Economic Integration

One distinction that can help understand some paradoxical findings regarding ethnic minorities in France is that on the cultural side, ethnic minorities and immigrants can be relatively well integrated in the society. However, on the social and economic side, this is much less the case (see Schnapper, 2007; Weil, 2008). In other words, although there are some exceptions, the vast majority of immigrants in France quickly adopt the language, customs, and cultural practices of the French majority (Tribalat, 1995). Nevertheless, their social and economic position lags behind. Schnapper (2007) has discussed the results of several comparative studies showing that relative to Germany or the UK, members of immigrant groups in France have more difficulties to find a good job and to climb the social ladder. Thus, she noted that "Overall, the unemployment rate is of 10% for the French population at large, but it is of 20% for young people aged between 16 and 24 years old and of more than 40% when their parents are immigrants" (Schnapper, 2007, p. 109). Such a mixture between, on the one hand, a strong cultural integration, that is, acquiring the French language and customs, and on the other, a weak social and economic integration, that is, not being recognized as French and not being able to participate in the economic life, can be quite explosive.

2.4 November 2005: Is France Burning?

The most important recent manifestations of an underlying state of ethnic tensions in France occurred in November 2005. These events made headlines news internationally with descriptions that more often than not overstated the case. Fox news in the USA, for example, spoke about a state of "civil war in France." When these events did not directly involve any single death, this is close to being ludicrous. It is also consistent with the claim that Fox news can be regarded as one of the least impartial "news" outlet. Nevertheless, these events were major ones and deserve to be considered carefully.

On the basis of a number of publications and reports, it is possible to summarize how the events unfolded (see Jobard, 2008; Lapeyronnie, 2006; Mucchielini & Aït-Omar, 2007). On October 27, 2005, in Clichy-sous-bois near Paris, three young men on their way back from a football game ran away from the police. Hiding in a dangerous electrical station, two of them were electrocuted and died. One of them, Bouna Traoré, was 15 years old, the other, Zyed Benna, was 17. Both were of African origin. Then, according to Jobard (2008): "For three nights, in the town and two of its neighboring cities, unrest developed, with 30 cars set alight on each night" (p. 1289). However, what made these events the most significant ones in France since the student revolt in May 1968 is that while they were at first, strictly limited to three cities, they slowly started to spread to the neighboring cities and then all over France, and lasted for approximately three full weeks. There were numerous clashes with the police, burning of cars, destructions of property, many schools and public buildings being damaged. The highest peaks occurred during the night between November 7 and 8 in which close to 300 cities all over France were involved and 1,500 cars were burned (Lapeyronnie, 2006). On the 7th, the Prime Minister declared a state of emergency. After some 20-day period of unrest, 10,000 cars had disappeared in flames and 250 public buildings had been damaged for a total cost of 250 million Euros according to insurance companies. Yet, there was hardly any use of firearms and no casualties were reported besides the severe injury suffered by a disabled woman trapped in a bus on fire.

These events are mainly referred to as "riots" or "urban violence" by social scientists in France, and their precise social and political meaning is the topic of ongoing debates. Several things became clear however. First, this was not in any way an attack by young Muslims on the Western world as some media suggested. This was not a movement driven by Islamic militancy. Although some religious leaders tried to influence the course of events, all the evidence showed that they did not have more than a very slim impact at best (see Keppel, 2008). Second, it also became clear that these were not simply a bunch of juvenile delinquents acting out. Yet, this was the analysis being offered at first by the head of the national police and various officials who stated that among the arrested perpetrators, the large majority of them or 80% were young offenders well-known by the police. In other words, the participants in the riots were assumed to be largely anomic individuals involved in the past in small criminal activities and acts of delinquency. This turned out to be completely false. All the evidence coming from the court cases, with a relatively high rate of discharge, and various research reports later on suggested that only a minority of the rioters were known by the police or had a criminal record (Jobard, 2008). Thus, these events qualify rather as an instance of collective action, a relatively spontaneous social movement seeking to protest against a state of affairs. As such, we will come back to them later on to examine the extent to which social–psychological theories of collective action can allow us to make sense of them.

2.5 A Law Banning the Islamic Veil

Up until recently, Islam was not very much politicized in France. Questions and debates around the "Muslim headscarf" as a public issue (see Sala Pala & Simon, 2008, for more details) started in 1989 when the director of a secondary school near Paris decided to exclude three young girls because he considered that their Muslim Headscarf undermined the secular nature of public schools in France. This highly valued principle of "secularism" (or *Laïcité* in French) goes back to the law of 1905 instituting a separation of the Churches and the State in France. It implies that the State and its agents should be neutral with regard to religious matters. After a number of "headscarf affairs" such as this one, that were considered on a case-by-case basis, and after various rulings by the Conseil d'Etat, the highest French administrative court, the climate became such that some kind of permanent solution had to be found. In 2003, the President, Jacques Chirac, decided to set up a committee of experts and intellectuals, known as the "Stasi Commission," to make recommendations on the implementation of the principle of secularism in the Republic. In its final report, the Stasi Commission took a radical stance as it proposed the adoption of a law forbidding conspicuous religious signs in public schools. This decision was supported by all members of the Commission, except one: Jean Baubérot. Head of the department of history and sociology of secularism at the Ecole Pratique des Hautes Etudes in Paris, Bauberot maintained his opposition to such a law that did not seem to him an effective way to deal with the issues. Nevertheless, the law banning conspicuous religious signs in public schools became effective on March 15, 2004.

In principle, this law concerned all religious signs. In practice, it is clear that it was targeting the Muslim headscarf. It is difficult to pinpoint the precise reasons that led the Stasi Commission to reach such a decision. The general climate at the time, making salient the need to fight against religious fundamentalism, and the "call for help" of young girls and women facing the domination of certain "Islamist groups" relayed by various associations no doubt played an important role. As such, it is surprising to learn that the Commission devoted in fact very little time to the hearing of these young girls themselves.

One year later, in 2005, a report by the general inspector of education and former member of the Stasi Commission provided a positive assessment of the application of the law. However, many associations and committees, such as the Committee against Islamophobia in France, disagreed strongly. A research report of the European Monitoring Center on Racism and Xenophobia (EUMC) published in 2006 gave credit to some negative impact. This qualitative study, giving the opportunity to Muslims in Europe to express themselves, revealed that "In France, respondents [Muslims] believe that the ban [of the headscarf] in public education has contributed to the development of a negative climate for Muslims" (p. 51). In other words, Muslims in France felt singled out and stigmatized by this law. Indeed, a paradoxical implication of the law is that pupils refusing to remove their headscarf were simply excluded completely from public schools. As Laborde (2010) recently pointed out, this implication seems to be in contradiction with the stated purpose of the law. The schools being the place where one learn how to be independent and autonomous, shouldn't one make sure instead that those young girls who are assumed to be the most vulnerable to manipulation and domination can benefit from them?

Since the end of 2008, the economic and financial crises confronting the USA and Europe raised a number of important concerns. As one French humorist suggested, what is the best means of dealing with this economic crisis according to the French government? Simple, let us ban the burqa and niqab! As odd as it may seem, this is indeed one of the main topic of political discussion since 2009. It is not clear how many women in France wear this black cloth (the burqa) covering the whole body and entire face, leaving only the eyes visible. Nevertheless, despite the fact that they are extremely few in numbers, the National Assembly in France has now approved (July 2010) a proposal for a law banning the complete covering of one's face in public.

2.6 The French Media and the Danish Cartoons

Another event occurring outside of France that had a large impact on intergroup relations in France is the strong Muslim protest that was generated by the publication of cartoons of Mahomet (Mohammed) in a Danish newspaper on September 2005. Several months later, in February 2006, a satiric newspaper in France called "Charlie Hebdo" published a special edition about the affair of the Mahomet cartoons in which the 12 Danish cartoons were themselves reproduced. The newspaper justified this action by stating that "Charlie Hebdo attempts to analyse the controversy and its consequences. The aim is to show that freedom of expression must be stronger than intimidation." Heated debates and arguments ensued in all of the news media (for more details, see Sala Pala & Simon, 2008). Many Muslim organizations in France saw this as a clear "provocation." Eventually, Charlie Hebdo was attacked in court, on the count that it was racist and injurious toward a group of individuals who belong to a religion. The trial ended on March 22, 2007. The director of publication, Philippe Val, was acquitted. The court considered that despite the shocking and hurting nature of the publication, the whole Muslim community was not targeted, and the context of the publication did not indicate the intention to offend the Muslims directly and groundlessly as a whole. Thus, for the courts, the limits of freedom of expression were not exceeded.

These types of events can obviously have a strong impact on public opinions and on the social representation of a whole community. However, it is very difficult to know what kind of impact. Thanks to an ingenious study by Guimelli, Lo Monaco, and Deschamps (2010), we know a bit more about this particular case. The results of their research are clear: The effect of this trial was to increase the expression of negative attitudes toward Muslims in France. These negative attitudes were probably there before the trial, but people did not feel it was proper to report them. After the trial, the French participants were more likely to agree even with such explicit statements as "The religion that Muslims practice can be conducive to terrorism." As Guimelli et al. (2010) suggest, the justice system in a country is a legitimate authority. As such, its decisions can legitimize the expression of certain (negative) attitudes that people would otherwise try to hide.

3 Causes of Ethnic Tensions in France

In the previous sections, we have documented various forms of ethnic exclusionism on the part of the dominant group in France, that is, various aspects of prejudice and discrimination directed mainly at immigrants of North African origin. Moreover, we have described the riots of November 2005 that remain up to this day the most significant collective action that may be related to an underlying intergroup conflict. In this section, we consider in some detail the relevant social–psychological theories and research in order to identify potential causes of these hostile intergroup attitudes and behaviors. We start by considering the perspective of the dominant group and explore the role of some of the main social-psychological factors in prejudice and discrimination. Then, moving to the perspective of the subordinate group, we consider theories of collective action and attempt to identify the motivational factors that can explain the participation in these riots.

3.1 Perspective of the Dominant Group

Many different theoretical perspectives have been proposed in social psychology in order to explain prejudice and discrimination. Below, we discuss the role of five distinct factors that can be important in order to explain attitudes toward immigrants: threat, relative deprivation and gratification, social dominance orientation (SDO), national identity, and acculturation orientations.

3.2 Integrated Threat Theory

Research suggests that when people are afraid or feel psychologically threatened by others, they will develop negative attitudes toward them. Many studies have shown that this can be directly related to prejudice against immigrants (Esses, Jackson, & Amstrong, 1998; Stephan, Renfro, Esses, Stephan, & Martin, 2005). In proposing Integrated Threat Theory, Stephan and Stephan (1996, 2000) have argued that one can distinguish between different types of threat such as realistic threat, symbolic threat, and anxiety-related threat.

The concept of realistic threat refers to cases where an outgroup is perceived as a threat for economic, political, or physical reasons. As such, this concept can be linked to Realistic Group Conflict Theory (Bobo, 1988; Levine & Campbell, 1972; Sherif & Sherif, 1969), which argues that intergroup competition for scarce resources generates the perception of the outgroup as a threat and, as such, represents the main source of hostile intergroup attitudes and behaviors. Correlational and experimental evidence has confirmed the link between feelings of realistic threat and prejudice toward immigrants in various settings (Bizman & Yinon, 2001; Esses et al., 1998; Esses, Dovidio, Jackson, & Amstrong, 2001; Stephan et al., 2002). Indeed, when people assert that "immigrants are stealing our jobs," they are likely to have negative attitudes toward these immigrants, confirming this principle.

In a major European study involving interviews with large random samples of participants from 17 European states including France, Coenders, Lubbers, and Scheepers (2004) found support for the hypothesis that ethnic competition relates to ethnic exclusionism. For example, at the individual level, the results showed, as predicted, that those social categories who hold positions similar to those of ethnic outgroups, and thus are more likely to be in competition with them, do actually express higher levels of ethnic exclusionism. Similarly, at the contextual level, the higher the level of unemployment in a country in the year preceding data collection, the more widespread was the hostility toward immigrants. Thus, it seems likely that realistic threat is one of the factor explaining negative attitudes toward immigrants in France. Nevertheless, this does not explain why there can be more prejudice and discrimination toward members of a particular ethnic group. Symbolic threat may be involved here. Symbolic threat arises from the perceived differences in beliefs, norms, and values. Thus, to the extent that Maghrebians are perceived by the French as being more different than Italians, for example, in terms of their beliefs, norms, and values, one could predict more negative attitudes toward Maghrebians. Indeed, the study by Velasco, Gonzalez, Verkuyten, Weesie, and Poppe (2008) showed a significant relation between feelings of symbolic threat and prejudice toward Muslims in the Netherlands. Similarly, with data from several European countries, McLaren (2003) found that the more people feel that their traditional way of life is threatened by the religious practices of certain ethnic groups, the more they support sending back immigrants to their home countries.

3.2.1 Relative Deprivation (RD) and Relative Gratification (RG)

Somewhat related to the concept of threat is the notion of relative deprivation (RD) that can be defined, following Crosby (1976), as the feeling that one has been unjustly deprived of (something of value) X. The main components of a general model of RD/RG are presented in Fig. 18.2 (see Guimond & Tougas, 1999; Martin, 1981). At any given time, there is an "objective" pattern of distribution of resources in a society with some people receiving a lot and others receiving much less. In contrast to the Realistic Group Conflict Theory, RD theory suggests that there is often no direct correspondence between this objective economic situation and the subjective feelings of deprivation and gratification that people experience. Rather, the feelings of being deprived or gratified depend on the social comparison that people engage in (see Guimond, 2006). Thus, the director of a large company earning a big income may nevertheless be dissatisfied because he or she compares himself or herself with the director of another similarly large company who earns much more. Conversely, somebody who is poor and living on the street may be relatively happy because this person does not expect more out of life and compares himself or herself with other similarly deprived individuals. The social comparison component then is a critical intervening variable between an objective pattern of inequality and the subjective reactions of individuals. Furthermore, RD theory suggests that the individual's attitudes and behaviors will depend on these subjective feelings of deprivation and gratification rather than on the objective pattern of inequality.

Considerable evidence supports the hypothesis that RD can explain intergroup attitudes and behaviors. However, not all types of RD are equally important in this respect. Following Runciman (1966), research has repeatedly shown that it is critical to distinguish between personal RD and group or collective RD. Personal RD refers to feelings of injustice or dissatisfaction that an individual experiences because his or her own personal situation compares unfavorably with others (see Tougas & Beaton, 2008). Collective RD refers to feelings of injustice or dissatisfaction that an individual experiences because he or she belongs to a group that compares unfavorably with another group (see Guimond & Dubé-Simard, 1983; Tougas & Beaton, 2002). Personal RD is best suited to explain individualistic or interpersonal phenomena, such as attempts at social mobility (Hafer & Olson, 1993). Group RD is best suited to explain intergroup phenomena, such as attempts at social change, a topic to which we will return in discussing theories of collective action.

Prejudice, by definition, is an intergroup phenomena (Brown, 2010). It refers to a negative attitude or an unfavorable evaluation of another individual *because this individual is a member of an outgroup*. Saying openly that you dislike Andy because he is stupid is a negative evaluation, but it is not prejudice. Saying openly that you dislike Andy because he is Jewish is prejudice or antisemitism. Thus, the type of RD that should be most relevant to explain prejudice is group RD. Both correlational (Dambrun & Guimond, 2001) and experimental (Guimond & Dambrun, 2002) studies have confirmed the hypothesis that prejudice against North Africans in France arises out of feelings of group RD, not out of personal RD. Extensive research by Pettigrew and colleagues in Germany, France, the Netherlands, and the UK has provided strong evidence that group RD predicts prejudice toward immigrants in Europe (see Pettigrew, Christ, Meertens, & van Dick, 2008; Pettigrew & Meertens, 1995; Pettigrew et al., 1998).

What about RG? As Fig. 18.2 indicates, the opposite of RD is RG, feelings of being better-off compared to others. Although RD theorists have often noted this distinction between RD and RG, little interests have been shown for RG. Thus, Pettigrew et al. (2008) do not even mention the concept of RG. Yet, recent research carried out in France has shown that RG may be even more important than RD to explain prejudice. How can that be the case? Logically, if RD increases prejudice, then its opposite, RG, should decrease prejudice. However, logic is often of little use in understanding people's behavior.

To understand the potential importance of RG in explaining prejudice, one needs to consider what is the *social function of prejudice*. Presumably, people have prejudice because it serves a certain purpose. Most theorists who have considered this issue have concluded that prejudice essentially serves to justify economic and

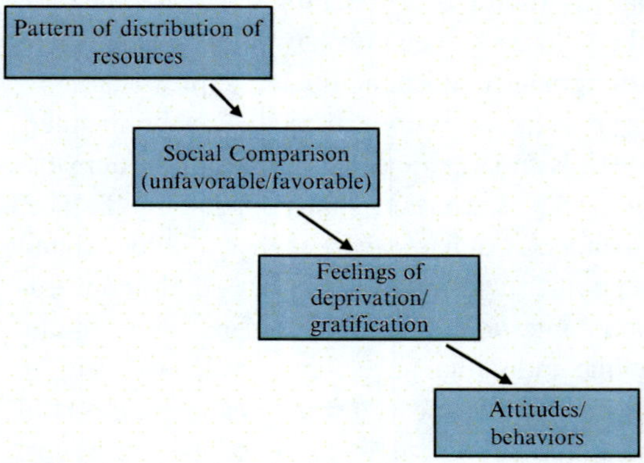

Fig. 18.2 General model of relative deprivation/gratification

social privileges (see Guimond, 2000; Jost & Banaji, 1994; Sidanius & Pratto, 1999; Tajfel, 1981). Thus, Guimond and Dambrun (2002) argued that studying the effects of RG on intergroup attitudes may represent a paradigm to study the social function of prejudice. If prejudice serves to justify economic inequality, then placing individuals in a relatively privileged or gratified position ought to increase their level of prejudice (in order to justify such privileged position relative to others). This hypothesis received strong support in the first two experiments ever designed to test the effect of RG on prejudice (see Guimond & Dambrun, 2002). Relative to a control condition, first-year university students placed in a situation where their job prospects were much better than others displayed greater feelings of satisfaction, confirming the effectiveness of the manipulation of RG, and more prejudice against Maghrebians in France as well as more ethnocentrism generally. In the second experiment, two scales of more extreme manifestations of prejudice were included as dependent variables to test the limit of this effect. For example, there were questions on the approval of a policy designed to send back to their countries all Africans and North Africans, including those born in France. The effects of RG were highly significant even on these two scales of extreme manifestations of prejudice, whereas the effects of RD were not. As such, it was no surprise to find out in another study that RG was also related to a positive evaluation of the most well-known political party of the extreme-right in France, the "Front National" (see Dambrun, Maisonneuve, Duarte, & Guimond, 2002).

Subsequent research showed that RG is related to ethnic prejudice even when prejudice is measured at the implicit level, using a lexical decision task that prevents participants from controlling their response (see Dambrun & Guimond, 2004). In addition, it was found that RG can be a powerful factor in various intergroup contexts (see Dambrun, Guimond, & Taylor, 2006; Dambrun, Taylor, McDonald, Crush, & Méot, 2006; Guimond, Dif, & Aupy, 2002; Postmes & Smith, 2009). For example, using data from the South African Migration Project, based on a large representative sample, Dambrun, Taylor et al. (2006) showed that both feelings of RD *and* feelings of RG are statistically significant predictors of prejudice against immigrants in South Africa. These results support what is known as the V-curve hypothesis (see Dambrun, Taylor, et al., 2006). The role of RG in intergroup relations also appears to be quite consistent with one of the most recent theories of intergroup relations in social psychology, Social Dominance Theory (Sidanius & Pratto, 1999).

3.2.2 Social Dominance Orientation

In studies using measures of a wide variety of psychological constructs, Social Dominance Orientation (SDO) is often found to be one of the most important variables to predict prejudice (see Altemeyer, 1998; Duckitt, 2001). SDO is a new psychological construct that was proposed as part of Social Dominance Theory, a multilevel integrative perspective on intergroup conflict which assumes that group-based hierarchies are a central and universal feature of all complex societies (see Pratto, Sidanius, & Levin, 2006; Sidanius & Pratto, 1999). As such, the theory conceptualizes prejudice as a hierarchy-enhancing legitimizing myth, a set of beliefs and attitudes that justify intergroup inequality. Consequently, it argues that the psychological tendency to support hierarchical systems and group-based inequality, namely SDO, is a primary source of prejudice. Research has shown that SDO is predictive of various kinds of prejudice and outgroup hostility in many different countries (Altemeyer, 1998; Bourhis, Barrette, El-Geledi, & Schmidt, 2009; Pettigrew et al., 2008; Pratto, Sidanius, & Levin, 2006; Sidanius & Pratto, 1999).

Research in France has confirmed that SDO is related to negative attitudes toward North Africans (De Oliveira, Dambrun, & Guimond, 2008; Duarte, Dambrun, & Guimond, 2004). However, a critical issue is the question of causality. Most studies using the SDO scale are of a correlational nature. As such, it is possible that SDO is a consequence rather than a cause of prejudice. Guimond, Dambrun, Michinov, and Duarte (2003) examined this question in a series of four studies. They developed three central hypotheses on the basis of a group socialization model.

First, they argued that contrary to a personality model of prejudice (e.g., Altemeyer, 1998), SDO is not a personality trait but a set of beliefs that varies as a function of the position in the social structure and the socialization process related to such a position. Those who are socialized into a dominant position in the social hierarchy are expected to acquire higher levels of SDO compared to those socialized in a less dominant position. This was confirmed in a field setting by showing that the number of years of university training in law, arguably a power profession preparing for a dominant social position, is related to an increase in SDO, whereas the number of years of university training in psychology, a field that is clearly nondominant in France, is related to a decrease in SDO (see Guimond et al., 2003, Study 2).

Second, it was argued, partly on the basis of results such as the effect of RG noted above, that those having higher status and power (i.e., dominants), because of their greater need to justify their privileged position in the social hierarchy, should display higher levels of prejudice than others. Finally, it was proposed that SDO may function as the mediating mechanism, explaining why the position held in the social hierarchy can have an impact on prejudice. This group socialization model was supported in two field studies and two experimental studies. The two field studies capitalized on preexisting differences in power and dominance between university students in different academic major, as noted above, and contrasted students in law (high power and dominance) to those in psychology (nondominant). As predicted, upper-level law students in France, well socialized into a dominant position, displayed significantly higher levels of prejudice toward Maghrebians compared to upper-level psychology students. Moreover, in two independent studies, this effect was explained by the higher level of SDO of law students compared to psychology students. In other words, the effect of the dominant social position (Law vs. Psychology) on prejudice disappeared when SDO was taken into account. The reverse model, suggesting that law students have higher levels of SDO because they are more prejudiced was not supported. Law students scored higher on SDO regardless of their level of prejudice. Thus, these results are consistent with the claim that SDO is indeed a mediating mechanism that generates prejudice. Nevertheless, being correlational in nature, they are not sufficient to conclude definitely about the status of SDO as a mediator.

As Baron and Kenny (1986) proposed, to identify a mediator, it is necessary to show first the causal impact of the independent variable (dominant social position) on the mediator (SDO) and on the dependent variable (prejudice). Thus, in two distinct experiments (see Guimond et al., 2003), first-year university students were randomly allocated to a dominant social position or a nondominant social position. For example, in Study 3, students were invited to participate in a study of "Leadership and behavior in business organizations". They were first asked to complete a "scientific inventory" assessing their leadership potential. Bogus feedback led half the students, at random, to believe that with a score above average, they had a high leadership potential and they were very well suited to occupy a position of high responsibility. Students in the control condition learned that they had an average score. After various other tasks, the experiment came to an end. The experimenter then asked the students if they were willing to fill out a very short questionnaire for another study totally independent from the previous one. All participants agreed. The questionnaire contained the measures of SDO and prejudice.

The results showed a significant effect of the experimental manipulation on prejudice. Compared to those in the control condition, students in the dominant social position displayed significantly higher level of prejudice toward the low-status Maghrebians in France. There was also a significant effect of condition on SDO, and SDO mediated the effect of condition on prejudice. Thus, the results of the field studies described above were successfully reproduced in the laboratory where all the relevant variables were carefully controlled. This was especially important here. The results of the field studies could still be explained by a personality model. SDO, as a personality trait, would explain why law students have more prejudice and why they have chosen the field of law. Their dominant personality is the basic cause. This personality model is shown to be incorrect by the experimental studies showing that a simple allocation to a dominant social position has a causal effect on SDO.

This series of studies allows us to go beyond the evidence suggesting that SDO is correlated with prejudice. We have identified a mechanism that specifies the role of SDO in explaining the effect of the position occupied in a social hierarchy on prejudice. When people find themselves near the top of the social hierarchy (dominant social position), they come to believe that inequality is not that bad (SDO increases), and supporting group-based inequality lead to higher levels of prejudice against low-status outgroups. However, this research deals with prejudiced attitudes, not discriminatory behaviors. Discrimination is more difficult to study from a methodological standpoint. Thus, in another study, a new computer-based method designed to study discrimination was introduced (see Michinov, Dambrun, Guimond, & Méot, 2005).

Very briefly, participants are told that the aim of the research is to study behavior and decision making within a working environment. They are asked to assume that they are a part of an office with six other employees. The figure of each of these employees (i.e., drawings of white and dark-skinned people), each identified by a first name, is presented on the computer screen. Some employees are males, others are females. Some are European (light skin), others are North African (dark skin). The first name was used to reinforce the ethnicity of each of these coworkers. Beneath these six representations was a white empty box representing the participants. Each participant was instructed to put his or her initials inside the box.

Participants are told that they will have to take various decisions in order to make sure that the office is running as best as possible. In the crucial task, they are presented with an organizational structure with four levels and eight distinct positions hierarchically structured. At the top is the label group leader. Using the computer mouse, participants are requested to place themselves and the six employees in the structure, one position remaining empty. Participants are unaware of the fact that the computer records their every move: where they place each target in the hierarchy, but also the time they take to place each target and in what order. Given that participants know nothing about these coworkers except their sex and ethnicity, placing North African targets lower in the social hierarchy is an instance of discriminatory behavior: behaving in an unfavorable manner toward an individual solely because that individual belongs to an outgroup.

In the last part of the study, participants were asked to fill out a questionnaire including measures of anti-immigrant prejudice and the SDO scale. If placing the North African targets last, or placing them lower in the hierarchy, is an instance of discrimination, one would expect that SDO would correlate with such behavior. The results confirmed this expectation (see Michinov et al., 2005). For example, participants scoring high on SDO tended to place fewer North African targets at the top of the hierarchical structure than would be expected by chance, and more of these targets at lower levels. Similarly, our measure of prejudice was significantly related to the behavior of the participants. Furthermore, there was evidence that the effect of SDO on the assignment of the targets in the structure was partially mediated by prejudice. Thus, consistent with Social Dominance Theory, these results suggest that SDO is one of the significant psychological factors that can explain not only prejudice but also the discrimination to which Maghrebian Arabs are often confronted in France.

3.2.3 National Identity

The concept of social identity, in general, and that of national identity, in particular, is important to understand how members of the majority in a country react to the arrival and integration of immigrants. As social identity theory (Tajfel & Turner, 1979, 1986) suggests, prejudice, and more specifically ingroup bias, is largely a matter of social categorization and social identity. To be unfavorable toward an outgroup implies that one categorize the environment in terms of ingroup and outgroup. Decades of laboratory research have shown that people will discriminate against an outgroup in order to establish a positive social identity (see Bettencourt, Charlton, Dorr, & Hume, 2001). Thus, the more people define their nation as their ingroup, the more they can be expected to define immigrants as an outgroup, and thus display ethnocentrism and ingroup favoritism.

As such, organizing a nation-wide debate on national identity in France, as if one wants to distinguish between the "real" French and the others, may not be the best idea to foster positive intergroup relations. In fact, one would expect such a debate to stir up prejudice and ethnocentrism, especially given the fact that historically, the theme of national identity has been raised in France mainly by the extreme-right (Noiriel, 2007). Under the leadership of President Nicolas Sarkozy, who was elected in 2007 by appealing to the extreme-right wing supporters (see Mayer, 2007), the government in France did exactly this in October 2009. Through every news media possible, including the Internet, the minister of immigration announced that a large public debate was going to be held on the topic of "national identity" and invited all the population to take part in this debate. Practically, all social scientists in France were stunned, and a large number demanded that this debate be stopped. The socialist opposition, and the green party, also did not approve of this debate. In fact, many members of the government tried to distance themselves from such an initiative. Nevertheless, it was too late. In a very short while, negative comments about people who live in France but are not "pure enough" entered this public debate that turned out to be a total stigmatization of ethnic and religious minorities in France. National identity is obviously a sensitive matter that can quickly be transformed into ethnocentrism and prejudice in the hands of the layperson. Indeed, in a recent cross-national study, involving participants from France, the UK, Canada, and Germany, we found that national identity is predictive of ingroup bias in all four countries, even when other important predictors such as SDO are taken into account (Guimond, et al., 2011).

3.2.4 Acculturation Orientations

Research on acculturation in cross-cultural psychology has greatly improved our understanding of cross-cultural relationships and ethnic conflicts (Berry, 2005; Kosic, Mannetti, & Lackland, 2005; Ward & Masgoret, 2006; Zick, Wagner, van Dick, & Petzel, 2001). Prejudice toward ethnic minorities and immigrants can be related to the acculturation expectancies and the national policy that the dominant group endorses (Berry, Kalin, & Taylor, 1977).

Research in various Western countries has shown that immigrants tend to favor integration over assimilation as an acculturation orientation (Barrette, Bourhis, Personnaz, & Personnaz, 2004; Berry, Kim, Power, Young, & Bujaki, 1989; Guimond, 2010; Lambert & Taylor, 1988). In other words, most immigrants wish to adopt the language and customs that are normative in the host culture but at the same time do not want to abandon completely their cultural characteristics of origin. On the contrary, national surveys have also shown that the dominant group in these societies often prefer assimilation over integration (Dovidio, Gaertner, & Saguy, 2007; Van Oudenhoven, Prins, & Buung, 1998; Wolsko, Park, & Judd, 2006). Such a discrepancy between the acculturation orientation of minorities and majorities is held by the Interactive Acculturation Model of Bourhis and colleagues (see Bourhis, Moise, Perreault, & Schmidt, 1997) to be a condition that increases the probability of intergroup conflict. Indeed, it makes sense to suggest that people who disagree about the kind of relationships that they want to have together may not be on the road to perfect harmony. However, recent research suggests that things may be a bit more complicated than that.

The Interactive Acculturation Model predicts that harmonious intergroup relations are most likely when dominant group members and immigrant group members agree on acculturation.

Thus, if both groups want assimilation, Bourhis et al. (1997) predicts harmony. Recent research indicate, however, that conflict is more likely to occur. According to Thomsen, Green, and Sidanius (2008), assimilation may be threatening to members of the dominant group because it blurs existing status boundaries between groups and, thus, raises serious question about the viability of the existing hierarchical system. To examine this possibility, they primed half of their participants at random with the case of an immigrant who wants to assimilate completely into the dominant culture (adopting host culture and giving up home culture). The other half read about an immigrant favoring separation (holding home culture and forgoing host culture). The dependent variable was a scale measuring the intention to take part in the persecution of immigrants (e.g., "I would help hunt down members of immigrants organizations and turn them over to the police," cf. Thomsen et al., 2008, p. 1458). They predicted, and found, that people who score high on the SDO scale would be the most threatened by assimilation and, thus, would react the most aggressively against immigrants in the assimilation condition compared to the separation condition. The results confirmed this prediction both in the USA (Study 1) and in Switzerland (Study 2). A more recent study carried out in France confirmed and extended these findings by contrasting an assimilation condition to an integration (multiculturalism) condition (see Guimond et al., 2010).

Indeed, in the original study of Thomsen et al. (2008), the two conditions differ on both the home culture component and the host culture component. Thus, it is not possible to know which component of acculturation is actually threatening for the dominants. In the latter study by Guimond et al. (2010), the two experimental conditions differ only on the home culture component that is valued in the multiculturalism condition and relinquished in the assimilation condition. Thus, the critical component of acculturation that is threatening to those who have high SDO is the loss of the home culture that is implied by assimilation. In sum, it appears that in France, as in other countries, violence on the part of the dominant group against ethnic minorities and immigrants may be more likely to occur, not less, if immigrants appear to lose completely their culture of origin.

3.2.5 Perspective of Ethnic and Religious Minorities

Understanding ethnic and religious conflict requires an understanding of the motivation of both the dominant majority and the ethnic and religious minorities. Space precludes an elaborate discussion of this topic. Nevertheless, to complement our preceding analysis of the behavior of dominant group members, we will briefly consider in this section the extent to which existing theories in social psychology can help us understand the riots that occurred in France 5 years ago.

As mentioned above, these riots can be seen as an instance of collective action on the part of ethnic minorities in France, a major protest reaction in an ongoing social and political struggle. The first thing to note is that although the riots of November 2005 in France were important, they are not by any means unique. To the contrary, as Lapeyronnie (2006) notes: "The behavioral repertoire of the rioters and the sequence of events obviously situate the riots of November 2005 in continuity with a long series of riots that have occurred in France over the last 25 years" (p. 5, our translation). Indeed, the riots of November 2005 can be distinguished from other ones by the fact that they spread all over France. Beyond that, the sequence of events leading to the riots of November 2005, to earlier ones or to more recent ones, is remarkably similar:

1. Everything usually start after some incidents with the police, involving the death of a member of the community
2. This generates an intense emotion and
3. Some sorts of protest reaction occur, with clashes between young people and the police, the burning of cars, and the destruction of public buildings

Can research on the determinants of collective action in social psychology help us make any sense of these events? Let us consider the Social Identity Model of Collective Action

(SIMCA) proposed by van Zomeren, Postmes, and Spears (2008) as one of the most recent integration of existing research in this area. On the basis of their meta-analytic review of the evidence, they argue that three main factors contribute independently to explain collective action: Injustice, identity, and efficacy.

The role of injustice comes from research on relative deprivation discussed above, and more recently, from studies related to intergroup emotions (see Yzerbyt, Dumont, Mathieu, Gordijn, & Wigboldus, 2006). Briefly, this work suggests that a major cause of collective action is an intense feeling of collective injustice or group-based anger. In contrast, more cognitive forms of group RD, such as perceiving that the ingroup is deprived relative to the outgroup, or more individualistic emotions, such as feelings of resentment and anger arising from unfavorable inter-individual comparisons, do not directly relate to collective action (see Dubé & Guimond, 1986; Grant, 2008). This seems to be quite consistent with the nature of the events that usually trigger the riots. In November 2005, as in many other riots of smaller scale that have occurred in France, and in fact in many other countries (see Lapeyronnie, 2006), the police is connected to the death of a young person or a community member. Given that the police in France often target ethnic minorities rather than Whites, as discussed above in relation with the work of Jobard and Levy (2009), the death of a young person as a result of police actions comes as a striking confirmation of suspicion of racism and generates an intense emotion of moral indignation or injustice, a feeling of collective relative deprivation.

Contrary to a number of analyses that were made in France, the riots of 2005 were not simply the product of absolute deprivation, poverty, and unemployment. Indeed, the rioters were not generally unemployed (Lapeyronnie, 2006). Rather, they were triggered by events related to police action that were experienced as fundamentally wrong and morally unjust.

Two important points should be noted here. First, this relation with police malpractices is far from unique to the French context. To the contrary, ethnic and racial riots that have occurred repeatedly in various countries such as the USA or the UK also share this feature (see Dubé & Guimond, 1986; Lapeyronnie, 2006;). For example, in reviewing extensive research on variables related to the participation in "guetto riots" during the 1960s in the USA, Mc Phail (1971) notes: "The category of independent variables yielding the highest proportion of moderate and high associations – 'Experience and Opinions about Discrimination' – involves associations between respondents' opinions about (*not their personal experiences of*) police malpractices toward Blacks" (p. 1065, emphasis added).

Second, the implications of this analysis are that police malpractices, often leading to death, is far from exceptional. This is consistent with the Social Dominance Theory (Sidanius & Pratto, 1999), the only theory in social psychology to argue that such police malpractices are not aberrations or some kind of abnormality of the system. Rather, they represent an integral part of a system of social dominance in which agents at the service of the dominant group work to keep members of the subordinate groups in their place, even by violent means if necessary.

One final element related to this first factor proposed by SIMCA should be mentioned. Many observers have noted that during the months preceding the riots, the public statements of Nicolas Sarkozy, then minister of Internal Affairs, probably played no small part in instigating the riots and perhaps also in accounting for the fact that they spread all over France. As Mucchielli and Aït-Omar (2007) report, the minister repeatedly referred to the fact that he was going to "flush" this "bunch of trash (*racailles*)" out of France, that he was going to "clean up the place" with"Kärcher." Interviews with rioters revealed that many of them felt humiliated by such comments and wanted to respond to the minister (see Mucchielli & Aït-Omar, 2007).

Coming back to SIMCA, the second factor proposed to explain collective action is social identity, directly derived from research related to social identity theory. Collective action is behavior on behalf of the group. Consequently, it can occur when an individual defines himself or herself as a group member (social identity) rather than as a unique individual (personal identity). Lapeyronnie's analysis of what the rioters said about their motivation does indeed reveals the role of social identity or a collective "we." For example, one rioter says: "The police insults us on the street…," he doesn't say the police has insulted me. Lapeyronnie (2006) suggests that "Racism, harassment and pressures by the police contribute to the creation of a kind of collective 'we' on the basis of a shared experience and in opposition to 'them' the police" (p. 11). Thus, the riots of November 2005 in France do seem to be consistent also with the role of this second factor.

Finally, SIMCA proposes that perceived group efficacy is a third major cause of collective action. It is defined as "a sense of control, influence, strength, and effectiveness to change a group-related problem" (van Zomeren et al., 2008, p. 513). In short, collective action occurs when people think that their action will succeed in changing things. We have seen little evidence or comments about the riots in France that can be related to this factor. Mucchielli and Aït-Omar (2007) report that revenge against the police came up repeatedly in interviews with various participants. Perhaps this can be related to the role of efficacy in that revenge has the goal to get even with others by punishing or hurting them. As such, efficacy may be inherent to an act of revenge. Nevertheless, further research would be needed on this issue.

In sum, there is evidence suggesting that in the riots of 2005 in France, two of the major causes of collective action identified in social psychology were clearly present: collective RD or a feeling of collective injustice, and social identity. We did not find direct evidence of group efficacy, but this is not to suggest that this factor did not play a role. Compared to doing nothing, taking part in collective action of this sort certainly indicates the presence of a strong motivation.

4 Toward More Harmonious Intergroup Relations: Some Suggestions

In this final section, we consider the question of how to manage the relations between various ethno-cultural groups in France so that these relations can be the most beneficial to all. What are the policies that could help foster harmonious intergroup relations? To answer this question, we turn to research on the contact hypothesis.

4.1 Reducing Prejudice and Discrimination: The Role of Intergroup Contact

In France as in many other countries, people who display prejudice against immigrants usually have very little contact with immigrants (see Guimond, 2010). This is consistent with the "contact hypothesis" (Allport, 1954), the idea that greater intergroup contact can dispel ignorance and suspiciousness and generate more positive intergroup attitudes. Many different methods have been proposed in social psychology in order to reduce prejudice and discrimination (see Paluk & Green, 2009). However, none has attracted as much attention and generated as much research and applications than the contact hypothesis. In fact, during the last 25 years, three distinct and highly influential models of intergroup contact have guided these efforts: the Common Ingroup Identity Model (Gaertner & Dovidio, 2000) based on the principle of recategorization, the Personalization Model (Brewer & Miller, 1984) based on the principle of decategorization, and the Mutual Intergroup Differentiation Model (Hewstone & Brown, 1986). The aim of these models is to specify the theoretical conditions under which intergroup contact will result in positive intergroup relations and reduced prejudice. Thus, they can serve as a basis to formulate policy. Indeed, as shown below, there are striking similarities between some of the central propositions of these theoretical models and well-known national policies that have been pursued in various countries as a way to manage relations between host society members and immigrants. More specifically, we will argue that the Common Ingroup Identity Model is similar to an assimilation policy whereas the Mutual Intergroup Differentiation Model is similar to a multiculturalism policy and the Personalization Model is similar to a republican/color-blind policy.

Assimilation/melting pot. As noted by Jones (2002), the Common Ingroup Identity Model is highly similar to an assimilation policy that represents one of the oldest and most pervasive political philosophies guiding cross-cultural relations. According to such a policy, ethnic and cultural minorities in general and immigrants in particular should adopt the language, customs, and values of the dominant group and leave behind their own cultural characteristics. Much like the proposals made within the Common Ingroup Identity Model, the idea of a "melting pot" implies that immigrants in France should all adopt the French way of life and become "French" as quickly as possible. This is the policy that seems to underlie the actions of the French government in recent years. As we have seen, the results are not pleasing. We have noted above that contrary to the Interactive Acculturation Model, there is evidence that such an assimilation policy may in fact be conducive to ethnic violence on the part of certain members of the dominant groups (see Guimond et al., 2010; Thomsen et al., 2008). Thus, research offers little support for the effectiveness of assimilation as the basis of a policy in the area of immigration and integration.

Multiculturalism. Hewstone and Brown (1986) have proposed, within the Mutual Intergroup Differentiation Model, that social categorization into distinct groups should remain salient during contact so that positive attitudes toward a given member of a group can be generalized to other members of that group. This theoretical model corresponds to the policy that is usually contrasted with assimilation, that is, the policy of multiculturalism. Indeed, a policy of multiculturalism, by definition, seeks to recognize and promote cultural diversity as a positive national feature (Berry, 2006; Berry, Kalin, & Taylor, 1977; Verkuyten, 2005). As such, it implies that categorization into relatively distinct cultural or ethnic groups becomes the rule rather than the exception (see Park & Judd, 2005).

First introduced in 1971 in Canada where it became national policy, multiculturalism has been pursued ever since by every Canadian government, whatever their political orientation. Many other countries have subsequently adopted similar policies, most notably Australia and Sweden (see Berry et al., 1977; Bertossi, 2007; Bloemraad, Korteweg, & Yurdakul, 2008; Guimond, 1999). Both correlational and experimental research have confirmed that multiculturalism reduces prejudice and improves intergroup relations (see Berry & Kalin, 1995; De Oliveira, Dambrun, & Guimond, 2008; Park & Judd, 2005; Richeson & Nussbaum, 2004; Verkuyten, 2005). Consistent with these findings, a recent series of research by Er-rafiy and Brauer (2010) has shown that stressing the existence of diversity within the group of Maghrebians in France is highly effective to reduce prejudice and discrimination against members of this group. Thus, research suggests that ideas contained in the Mutual Intergroup Differentiation Model and in multiculturalism offer a sound basis for the development of policy. However, the national context needs to be taken into account, and efforts to dispel misunderstanding about what multiculturalism means are necessary. In various countries that have adopted some form of multiculturalism, besides Canada, heated debates around the policy have occurred. Much of these debates rest on some fundamental misunderstanding concerning what multiculturalism is all about (see Guimond, 2010). Nevertheless, these debates indicate that the particular history and traditions of a given country need to be taken into account in developing a policy.

Republican/Color-blind model. In contrast to the Common Ingroup Identity Model, which argues for recategorization into a common group, the Personalization Model of Brewer and Miller (1984) suggests that it is best if people come into contact as individuals rather than as members of distinct groups. The principle of decategorization on which this theoretical model of intergroup contact is based is the heart of a third major national policy that can be referred to as the Republican/Color-blind policy.

As a policy, this model of integration is often considered to be similar to, and interchangeable with, an assimilation policy (e.g., Plaut, Thomas, & Goren, 2009). However, there are fundamental distinctions between the two. The Republican/Color-blind model suggests essentially that racial or ethnic membership should not matter; that regardless of their race, ethnicity, or religion, people are all basically the same; and that as such, one should not categorize people along ethnic, racial, or religious lines (Richeson & Nussbaum, 2004). In other words, this policy rests on the principle of decategorization advocated by Brewer and Miller (1984) in their Personalization Model. The main reason why this model should not be confused with an assimilation policy is that the Republican/Color-blind model is fundamentally egalitarian. It implies that "everyone should be treated equally" (Markus, 2008, p. 657). This is very different from an assimilation policy that is fundamentally inegalitarian in nature. Research has confirmed that endorsing a color-blind ideology is correlated with positive attitudes toward multiculturalism and negative attitudes toward assimilation (see Levin, et al., 2011; Ryan, Hunt, Weibe, Peterson, & Casas, 2007).

Although color blindness has been widely discussed in relation to the US national context (see Markus, 2008), this model shares some basic features with the traditional model of integration in France (Brouard & Tiberj, 2005; Schnapper, 2004, 2007; Weil, 2005, 2008). As noted earlier, the French republican model does have some unique features, such as the principle of secularism. Nevertheless, it shares with color blindness the fact of resting on the principle of decategorization. For example, in summarizing this French model of integration, Bertossi (2007) notes: "Built on elements of the ideology introduced during the French Revolution, French citizenship is perceived as refusing any form of distinction on ethno-racial lines in the public sphere" (p. 2). Similarly, Felouzis (2006) states: "The French State, currently, does not recognize any group membership whatsoever based on religious, cultural or other grounds, it only sees 'free and equal' citizens" (p. 318, our translation). Thus, this color-blind approach has deep roots in national policies in France. However, the French government of Nicolas Sarkozy has somewhat forgotten about this tradition in favor of a more assimilationist model, if not, starting at the end of July 2010, a policy of exclusion.

Several recent studies were carried out in France in order to examine the impact of the Republican model of integration on intergroup attitudes. The results revealed, something that we did not totally expect, that the idea of "republican citizenship," stressing the equality of all citizens regardless of color or religion, is a dimension of the Republican/color-blind model that is highly effective in reducing prejudice and improving intergroup relations in France (see Kamiejski, Guimond, De Oliveira, Er-Rafiy, & Brauer, 2011). Furthermore, members of the French majority and people of Maghrebian origin in France both endorse this principle of "republican citizenship" very strongly, even more strongly than multiculturalism that is also evaluated favorably. Thus, although more research is needed on this topic, these positive results lead us to advocate the development of a policy that connects with this republican tradition and its attachment to equality, and blends it with modern ideas about diversity. If the values of equality and diversity become the social norms in France, being reflected in all the social and economic policies that the government develops, and young people are socialized into a system that values equality and diversity, we would predict a clear improvement in relations among different ethnic and religious groups in the years to come.

5 Summary

In this chapter, we have presented an overview of recent sociopolitical events in France in the relations between the dominant French majority and ethnic and religious minorities. We have described evidence of prejudice, discrimination, and collective action. We have then examined, from the perspective of the dominant group and from the perspective of the minorities, the extent to which theories and research in social psychology can help us understand and explain conflict-enhancing relations between members of different cultural or ethnic groups. Although this is a challenging exercise and we have considered only a selection of potentially relevant variables, we believe that we have demonstrated the relevance of existing theories and research. If this is indeed the case, then societies that take into account the knowledge produced by social scientists across the world ought to increase their chance of living a peaceful and productive life in which conflict is more likely to lead to constructive social change.

References

Allport, G. (1954). *The nature of prejudice*. Cambridge, MA: Perseus Books.

Altemeyer, B. (1998). The other authoritarian personality. In M. P. Zanna (Ed.), *Advances in experimental social psychology* (Vol. 30, pp. 47–92). New York: Academic.

Amadieu, J.-F. (2004). *Enquête « Testing » sur CV [« Testing » with CV]*. Paris: l'Observatoire des discriminations.

Amadieu, J.-F. (2006). *Baromètre Adia [Adia Barometer]*. Paris: l'Observatoire des discriminations.

Atlaséco. (2002). *Atlas économique mondial 2003 [World economic Atlas]*. Paris: Le Nouvel Observateur.

Baron, R. M., & Kenny, D. A. (1986). The moderator–mediator variable distinction in social psychological research: Conceptual, strategic, and statistical considerations. *Journal of Personality and Social Psychology, 51*(6), 1173–1182.

Barrette, G., Bourhis, R. Y., Personnaz, M., & Personnaz, B. (2004). Acculturation orientations of French and North African undergraduates in Paris. *International Journal of Intercultural Relations, 28*, 415–438.

Beauchemin, C., Hamel, C., Lesné, M., Simon, P., & équipe TeO, (2010). Les discriminations : une question de minorités visibles [Discrimination : An issue of visible minorities]. *Population & Sociétés*, n° 466.

Berry, J. W. (2005). Acculturation: Living successfully in two cultures. *International Journal of Intercultural Relations, 29*, 697–712.

Berry, J. W. (2006). Mutual attitudes among immigrants and ethnocultural groups in Canada. *International Journal of Intercultural Relations, 30*, 719–734.

Berry, J. W., & Kalin, R. (1995). Multicultural and ethnic attitudes in Canada: Overview of the 1991 survey. *Canadian Journal of Behavioural Science, 27*, 301–320.

Berry, J. W., Kalin, R., & Taylor, D. (1977). *Multiculturalism and ethnic attitudes in Canada*. Ottawa: Supply Services.

Berry, J. W., Kim, U., Power, S., Young, S., & Bujaki, M. (1989). Acculturation attitudes in plural societies. *Applied Psychology: An International Review, 38*, 185–206.

Bertossi, C. (2007). *French and British models of integration – Public philosophies, policies and state institutions*. Working paper No. 46, University of Oxford, ESRC Center on Migration, Policy and Society.

Bettencourt, B. A., Charlton, K., Dorr, N., & Hume, D. L. (2001). Status differences and in-group bias: A meta-analytic examination of the effects of status stability, status legitimacy, and group permeability. *Psychological Bulletin, 127*(4), 520–542.

Bizman, A., & Yinon, Y. (2001). Intergroup and interpersonal threats as determinants of prejudice: The moderating role of in-group identification. *Basic and Applied Social Psychology, 23*, 191–196.

Bloemraad, I., Korteweg, A., & Yurdakul, G. (2008). Citizenship and immigration: Multiculturalism, assimilation, and challenges to the Nation-State. *Annual Review of Sociology, 34*, 153–179.

Bobo, L. (1988). Group conflict, prejudice, and the paradox of contemporary racial attitudes. In P. A. Katz & D. A. Taylor (Eds.), *Eliminating racism: Profiles in controversy* (pp. 85–114). NewYork: Plenum.

Bourhis, R. Y., Barrette, G., El-Geledi, S., & Schmidt, R. (2009). Acculturation orientations and social relations between immigrant and host community members in California. *Journal of Cross-Cultural Psychology, 40*(3), 443–467.

Bourhis, R. Y., Moise, L. C., Perreault, S., & Senécal, S. (1997). Towards an interactive acculturation model: A social psychological approach. *International Journal of Psychology, 32*, 369–386.

Brewer, M. B., & Miller, N. (1984). Beyond the contact hypothesis: Theoretical perspectives on desegregation. In N. Miller & M. Brewer (Eds.), *Groups in contact: The psychology of desegregation*. New York: Academic.

Brouard, S., & Tiberj, V. (2005). *Français comme les autres? [French, like all the others?]*. Paris: Presses de Sciences Po.

Brown, R. (2010). *Prejudice: Its social psychology*. Cambridge, MA: Wiley-Blackwell.

Coenders, M., Lubbers, M., & Scheepers, P. (2004). *Majorities' attitudes toward minorities in European Union member States*. Report 2 for the European Monitoring Centre on Racism and Xenophobia.

Commission nationale consultative des droits de l'homme (2009). La lutte contre le racisme, l'antisémitisme et la xénophobie [The fight against racism, antisemitism and xenophobia]. Rapport annuel. La Documentation Française.

Crosby, F. (1976). A model of egoistical relative deprivation. *Psychological Review, 83*(2), 85–113.

Dambrun, M., & Guimond, S. (2001). La théorie de la privation relative et l'hostilité envers les Nord-Africains.

[Relative deprivation theory and hostility toward North Africans]. *Revue Internationale de Psychologie Sociale, 14*, 57–89.

Dambrun, M., & Guimond, S. (2004). Implicit and explicit measures of prejudice and stereotyping: Do they assess the same underlying knowledge structure? *European Journal of Social Psychology, 34*(6), 663–676.

Dambrun, M., Guimond, S., & Taylor, D. M. (2006). The counter-intuitive effects of Relative Gratification on intergroup attitudes: Ecological validity, moderators and mediators. In S. Guimond (Ed.), *Social comparison and Social Psychology: Understanding cognition, intergroup relations and culture* (pp. 206–227). Cambridge: Cambridge University Press.

Dambrun, M., Maisonneuve, C., Duarte, S., & Guimond, S. (2002). Modélisation de quelques déterminants psychosociaux de l'attitude envers l'extrême droite. [Sociopsychological determinants of the attitude toward right-wing political groups]. *Cahiers Internationaux de Psychologie Sociale, 55*, 49–63.

Dambrun, M., Taylor, D. M., McDonald, D. A., Crush, J., & Méot, A. (2006). The relative deprivation-gratification continuum and the attitudes of South Africans towards immigrants: A test of the V-curve hypothesis. *Journal of Personality and Social Psychology, 91*, 1032–1044.

De Oliveira, P., Dambrun, M., & Guimond, S. (2008). L'effet de la dominance sociale sur les idéologies de légitimation: le rôle modérateur de l'environnement normatif. [The effect of social dominance on legitimizing ideologies: the normative environment as a moderator]. *Revue Internationale de Psychologie Sociale/International Review of Social Psychology, 21*, 115–150.

Deutsch, M. (1973). *The resolution of conflict: Constructive and destructive processes*. New Haven, CT: Yale University Press.

Dovidio, J. F., Gaertner, S. L., & Saguy, T. (2007). Another view of «we»: Majority and minority group perspectives on a common ingroup identity. In W. Stroebe & M. Hewstone (Eds.), *European review of social psychology* ((pp, Vol. 18, pp. 296–330). New York: Psychology Press.

Duarte, S., Dambrun, M., & Guimond, S. (2004). La dominance sociale et les « mythes légitimisateurs »: validation française de l'échelle d'orientation à la dominance. [Social dominance and letgitimizing myths: Validity of a French version of the scale of social dominance orientation]. *Revue internationale de psychologie sociale, 17*, 97–126.

Dubé, L., & Guimond, S. (1986). Relative deprivation and social protest. In J. M. Olson, C. P. Herman, & M. P. Zanna (Eds.), *Relative deprivation and social comparison: The Ontario symposium* (pp. 201–216). Hillsdale, NJ: Lawrence Erlbaum.

Duckitt, J. (2001). A cognitive-motivational theory of ideology and prejudice. In M. P. Zanna (Ed.), *Advances in experimental social psychology* (Vol. 33, pp. 41–113). San Diego: Academic.

Er-rafiy, A., & Brauer, M. (2010). L'effet bénéfique de l'augmentation de la variabilité perçue sur le niveau de préjugés et la discrimination. [The positive effect of increasing perceived variablity on prejudice and discrimination]. *L'Année Psychologique, 110*, 103–125.

Esses, V. M., Dovidio, J. F., Jackson, L. M., & Armstrong, T. L. (2001). The immigration dilemma: The role of perceived group competition, ethnic prejudice, and national identity. *Journal of Social Issues, 57*, 389–412.

Esses, V. M., Jackson, L. M., & Armstrong, T. L. (1998). Intergroup competition and attitudes toward immigrants and immigration: An instrumental model of group conflict. *Journal of Social Issues, 54*, 699–724.

European Monitoring Center on Racism and Xénophobia (EUMC). (2006). *Perceptions of discrimination and islamophobia. Voices from members of Muslim communitiesin the european union.* Retrieved from http://Eumc.europa.eu

Felouzis, G. (2006). Ethnicité et ségrégation dans les écoles françaises. [Ethnicity and segregation in French schools]. In J. Polard, A.-G. Gagnon, & B. Gagnon (Eds.), *Diversité et identités au Québec et dans les régions d'Europe* (pp. 305–318). Québec: Presses de l'Université Laval.

Gaertner, S. L., & Dovidio, J. F. (2000). *Reducing intergroup bias: The common ingroup identity model.* Philadelphia, PA: Psychology press.

Gonzales-Castro, J. L., Ubillos, S., & Ibanez, J. (2009). Predictive factors of ethnic prejudice toward immigrants in a representative subsample of Spanish young people. *Journal of Applied Social Psychology, 39*(7), 1690–1717.

Grant, P. R. (2008). The protest intentions of skilled immigrants with credentialing problems: A test of a model integrating relative deprivation theory with social identity theory. *British Journal of Social Psychology, 47*, 687–705.

Guimelli, C., Lo Monaco, G., & Deschamps, J.-C. (2010). The lawsuit against «Charlie Hebdo» and its effect on the social representations of the Muslim community. *International Review of Social Psychology, 23*(3), 5–36.

Guimond, S. (1999). Le multiculturalisme comme politique de gestion de la diversité culturelle. [Multiculturalism as a policy to manage cultural diversity]. In W. Dans, N. Doise, D. W. Doise, N. Dubois, & J. L. Beauvois (Eds.), *La psychologie sociale (Tome 4): La construction sociale de la personne* (pp. 173–181). Grenoble: Presses Universitaires de Grenoble.

Guimond, S. (2000). Group socialization and prejudice: The social transmission of intergroup attitudes and beliefs. *European Journal of Social Psychology, 30*(3), 335–354.

Guimond, S. (2004). Lutter contre le racisme et le sexisme en milieu scolaire. [Fighting against racism and sexism in schools]. In D. M.-C. Toczek & D. Martinot (Eds.), *Le défi éducatif: Des situations pour réussir* (pp. 169–195). Paris: Armand Colin.

Guimond, S. (Ed.). (2006). *Social comparison and Social Psychology: Understanding cognition, intergroup relations and culture*. Cambridge, England: Cambridge University Press.

Guimond, S. (2010). *Psychologie sociale: perspective multiculturelle. [Social psychology: A Multicultural perspective]*. Wavre, Belgium: Editions Mardaga.

Guimond, S., Crisp, R. J., De Oliveira, P., Kamiejski, R., Kteily, N., Kuepper, B., Lalonde, R. N., Levin, S., Pratto, F., Tougas, F., Sidanius, J., & Zick, A. (2011). Integration policy and prejudice: testing universal theories and culture-specific models of intergroup relations across four Western Nations. Unpublished manuscript, Laboratoire de Psychologie Sociale et Cognitive, Université Blaise Pascal, Clermont-Ferrand.

Guimond, S., & Dambrun, M. (2002). When prosperity breeds intergroup hostility: The effects of relative deprivation and relative gratification on prejudice. *Personality and Social Psychology Bulletin, 28*, 900–912.

Guimond, S., Dambrun, M., Michinov, N., & Duarte, S. (2003). Does social dominance generate prejudice? Integrating individual and contextual determinants of intergroup cognitions. *Journal of Personality and Social Psychology, 84*, 697–721.

Guimond, S., De Oliveira, P., Kamiejski, R., & Sidanius, J. (2010). The trouble with assimilation: Social dominance and the emergence of hostility against immigrants. *International Journal of Intercultural Relations*. doi:10.1016 /j.ijintrel.2010.01.002.

Guimond, S., Dif, S., & Aupy, A. (2002). Social identity, relative group status and intergroup attitudes: When favorable outcomes change intergroup relations… for the worse. *European Journal of Social Psychology, 32*(6), 739–760.

Guimond, S., & Dubé-Simard, L. (1983). Relative deprivation theory and the Quebec nationalist movement: The cognition emotion distinction and the personal-group deprivation issue. *Journal of Personality and Social Psychology, 44*, 526–535.

Guimond, S., & Tougas, F. (1999). Sentiments d'injustice et actions collectives: La privation relative. [Feelings of injustice and collective actions: Relative deprivation]. In R. Y. Bourhis & J.-P. Leyens (Eds.), *Stéréotypes, discrimination et relations intergroupes [Stereotypes, discrimination, and intergroup relations]*. Liège, France: Mardaga.

Hafer, C. L., & Olson, J. M. (1993). Beliefs in a just world, discontent, and assertive actions by working women. *Personality and Social Psychology Bulletin, 19*(1), 30–38.

Haute Autorité de Lutte contre les Discriminations et pour l''Égalité. (2008). *Rapport annuel 2008*. [High autority for the fight against discrimination and for equality-Annual Report] Paris: le Collège de la Haute Autorité de Lutte contre les Discriminations et pour l'Égalité.

Héran, F. (2007). *Le temps des immigrés. [The time of immigrants]*. Paris: Seuil.

Hewstone, M., & Brown, R. J. (Eds.). (1986). *Contact and conflict in intergroup encounters*. Oxford: Basil Blackwell.

Institut national de la statistique et des études économiques. (2006). Catherine Borrel, *INSEE Première n° 1098, août 2006*. [National Institute of statistics and economic studies] Retrieved from http://www.insee.fr/fr/themes/document.asp?ref_id=ip1098&reg_id=0#inter6

Institut national de la statistique et des études économiques. (2006). Les immigrés selon leur pays de naissance. *INSEE*. [National Institute of statistics and economic studies] Retrieved from http://www.insee.fr/fr/themes/tableau.asp?reg_id=0&ref_id=NATTEF02158

Jobard, F. (2008). The 2005 French urban unrests. Data-based interpretations. *Sociology Compass, 2*(4), 1287–1302.

Jobard, F., & Lévy, R. (2009). *Police et minorités visibles: les contrôles d'identité à Paris. [Profiling minorities: A study of stop-and-search practices in Paris]*. New-York: Open Society Institute.

Jones, M. (2002). *Social psychology of prejudice*. Upper Saddle River, NJ: Pearson Education.

Jost, J. T., & Banaji, M. R. (1994). The role of stereotyping in system-justification and the production of false consciousness. *British Journal of Social Psychology, 33*(1), 1–27.

Kamiejski, R., Guimond, S., De Oliveira, P., Er-Rafiy, A., & Brauer, M. (2010). *Le modèle républicain d'intégration: Implications pour la psychologie des relations entre groupes.* [The republican model of integration : Implications for the psychology of intergroup relations] Manuscript submitted for publication.

Keppel, G. (2008). *Terreur et martyr. Relever le défi de civilisation. [Terror and martyrdom: Taking up the challenge of civilization]*. Paris: Flammarion.

Kosic, A., Mannetti, L., & Lackland, S. (2005). The role of majority attitudes towards out-group in the perception of the acculturation strategies of immigrants. *International Journal of Intercultural Relations, 29*, 273–288.

Laborde, C. (2010). *Français, encore un effort pour être républicain! [French people, last chance to be republican]*. Paris: Seuil.

Lambert, W. E., Moghaddam, F. M., Sorin, J., & Sorin, S. (1990). Assimilation vs multiculturalism: views from a community in France. *Sociological Forum, 5*, 387–411.

Lambert, W. E., & Taylor, D. M. (1988). Assimilation versus multiculturalism: The views of urban Americans. *Sociological Forum, 3*, 72–88.

Lapeyronnie, D. (2006). Révolte primitive dans les banlieues françaises Essai sur les émeutes de l'automne 2005. [Primitive revolt in the French suburbs : analysis of the autumn 2005 riots] *Déviance et Société, 4 (Vol 30)*.

LaPiere, R. T. (1934). Attitudes versus actions. *Social Forces, 13*, 230–237.

Levin, S., Matthews, M., Guimond, S., Sidanius, J. Pratto, F., Kteily, N., Pitpitan, E., & Dover, T. (2011). Assimilation, multiculturalism, and colorblindness: Mediated and moderated relationships between social dominance orientation and prejudice. *Journal of Experimental Social Psychology*. doi:10.1016/j.jesp.2011.06.019.

Levine, R. A., & Campbell, D. T. (1972). *Ethnocentrism: Theories of conflict, ethnic attitudes, and group behavior*. New York: Wiley.

Markus, H. R. (2008). Pride, prejudice, and ambivalence: Toward a unified theory of race and ethnicity. *American Psychologist, 63*, 651–670.

Martin, J. (1981). Relative deprivation: A theory of distributive injustice for an era of shrinking resources. *Research in organizational behavior, 3*, 53–107.

Mayer, N. (2007). Comment Nicolas Sarkozy a rétréci l'électorat Le Pen. [How Nicolas Sarkozy did shrink the extreme-right electorate of Le Pen]. *Revue Française de Sciences Politiques, 57*, 429–445.

Mc Phail, C. (1971). Civil disorder participation: A critical examination of recent research. *American Sociological Review, 36*(6), 1058–1073.

McLaren, L. M. (2003). Anti-immigrant prejudice in Europe: Contact, threat perception, and preferences for exclusion of migrants. *Social Forces, 81*, 909–936.

Michinov, N., Dambrun, M., Guimond, S., & Méot, A. (2005). Social dominance orientation, prejudice, and discrimination: A new computer-based method for studying discriminatory behaviors. *Behavior Research Methods, 37*(1), 91–98.

Moscovici, S. (1976). *Social influence and social change*. London: Academic.

Mucchielini, L., & Aït-Omar, A. (2007). Les émeutes de l'automne 2005 dans les banlieues françaises du point de vue des émeutiers. [The riots of autumn 2005 in the French suburbs from the point of view of the rioters]. *Revue Internationale de Psychosociologie, 30*(2), 137–156.

Noiriel, G. (2006). *Le creuset français: Histoire de l'immigration XIXe-XXe siècle [The French melting pot: history of immigration XIXth–XXth century]*. Paris: La Découverte.

Noiriel, G. (2007). *Immigration, antisémitisme et racisme en France (XIXe-XXe siècle) – Discours publics, humiliations privées. [Immigration, antisemitism and racism in France (XIXth-XXth century) – Public discourse, private humiliations]*. Paris: Fayard.

Paluck, E. L., & Green, D. P. (2009). Prejudice reduction: What works? A review and assessment of research and practice. *Annual Review of Psychology, 60*, 339–367.

Park, B., & Judd, C. M. (2005). Rethinking the link between categorization and prejudice within the social cognition perspective. *Personality and Social Psychology Review, 9*, 108–130.

Pettigrew, T. F., Christ, O., Meertens, R. W., & van Dick, R. (2008). Relative deprivation and intergroup prejudice. *Journal of Social Issues, 64*, 385–401.

Pettigrew, T. F., Jackson, J., Ben Brika, J., Lemain, G., Meertens, R. W., Wagner, U., et al. (1998). Outgroup prejudice in Western Europe. *European Review of Social Psychology, 8*, 241–273.

Pettigrew, T. F., & Meertens, R. W. (1995). Subtle and blatant prejudice in Western Europe. *European Journal of Social Psychology, 25*, 57–75.

Plaut, V. C., Thomas, K. M., & Goren, M. J. (2009). Is multiculturalism or color blindness better for minorities? *Psychological Science, 20*, 444–446.

Postmes, T., & Smith, L. G. E. (2009). Why do the privileged resort to oppression? A look at some intragroup factors. *Journal of Social Issues, 65*, 769–790.

Pratto, F., Sidanius, J., & Levin, S. (2006). Social dominance theory and the dynamics of intergroup relations: Taking stock and looking forward. *European Review of Social Psychology, 17*, 271–320.

Richeson, J. A., & Nussbaum, R. J. (2004). The impact of multiculturalism versus color-blindness on racial bias. *Journal of Experimental Social Psychology, 40*, 417–423.

Runciman, W. G. (1966). *Relative deprivation and social justice*. London: Routledge Kegan Paul.

Ryan, C. S., Hunt, J. S., Weibe, J. A., Peterson, C. R., & Casas, J. F. (2007). Multicultural and colorblind ideology, stereotypes, and ethnocentrism among Black and White Americans. *Group Processes and Intergroup Relations, 10*, 617–637.

Sala Pala, V., & Simon, P. (2008). *Public and political debates on multicultural crises in France*. Report on national and European level cases, EMILIE.

Schnapper, D. (2004). La République face aux communautarismes. [The republic and communautarism]. *Etudes 2004/2 Tome, 400*, 177–188.

Schnapper, D. (2007). *Qu'est ce que l'intégration? [What is integration?]*. Paris: Gallimard, Folio actuel.

Sherif, M., & Sherif, C. W. (1969). Ingroup and intergroup relations: Experimental analysis. In M. Sherif & C. W. Sherif (Eds.), *Social psychology* (pp. 221–266). New York: Harper & Row.

Sidanius, J., & Pratto, F. (1999). *Social dominance: An intergroup theory of social hierarchy and oppression*. New York: Cambridge University Press.

Stephan, W. G., Boniecki, K. A., Ybarra, O., Bettencourt, A., Ervin, K. S., Jackson, L. A., et al. (2002). The role of threats in the racial attitudes of Blacks and Whites. *Personality and Social Psychology Bulletin, 28*, 1242–1254.

Stephan, W. G., Renfro, C. L., Esses, V. M., Stephan, C. W., & Martin, T. (2005). The effects of feeling threatened on attitudes toward immigrants. *International Journal of Intercultural Relations, 29*, 1–19.

Stephan, W. G., & Stephan, C. W. (1996). Predicting prejudice. *International Journal of Intercultural Relations, 20*, 409–426.

Stephan, W. G., & Stephan, C. W. (2000). Anintegrated theory of prejudice. In S. Oskamp (Ed.), *Reducing prejudice and discrimination: The Claremont Symposium on applied social psychology* (pp. 23–45). Mahwah, NJ: Lawrence Erlbaum Associates, Inc.

Tajfel, H. (1981). *Human groups and social categories*. Cambridge: Cambridge University Press.

Tajfel, H., & Turner, J. C. (1979). An integrative theory of intergroup conflict. In W. G. Austin & S. Worchel (Eds.), *The social psychology of intergroup relations*. Monterey, CA: Brooks/Cole.

Tajfel, H., & Turner, J. C. (1986). The social identity theory of intergroup behaviour. In S. Worchel & W. G. Austin (Eds.), *Psychology of intergroup relations* (pp. 7–24). Chicago, IL: Nelson-Hall.

Thomsen, L., Green, E. G. T., & Sidanius, J. (2008). We will hunt them down: How social dominance orientation and right-wing authoritarianism fuel ethnic persecution of immigrants in fundamentally different ways. *Journal of Experimental Social Psychology, 44*, 1455–1464.

Tougas, F., & Beaton, A. M. (2002). Persobal and group relative deprivation: Connecting the "I" to the "We". In I. Walker & H. J. Smith (Eds.), *Relative deprivation: Specification, development, and integration* (pp. 119–135). Cambridge, England: Cambridge University Press.

Tougas, F., & Beaton, A. M. (2008). Personal relative deprivation: A look at the grievous consequences of grievance. *Social and Personality Psychology Compass, 2*, 1753–1766.

Tribalat, M. (1995). *Faire France: une grande enquête sur les immigrés et leurs enfants. [Doing France: A study of immigrants and their children]*. Paris: La Découverte.

van Oudenhoven, J. P., Prins, K. S., & Buunk, B. P. (1998). Attitudes of minority and majority members towards adaptation of immigrants. *European Journal of Social Psychology, 28*(6), 995–1013.

van Zomeren, M., Postmes, T., & Spears, R. (2008). Toward an integrative social identity model of collective action: A quantitative research synthesis of three socio-psychological perspectives. *Psychological Bulletin, 134*(4), 504–535.

Velasco Gonzalez, K., Verkuyten, M., Weesie, J., & Poppe, E. (2008). Prejudice towards Muslims in the Netherlands: Testing integrated threat theory. *British Journal of Social Psychology, 47*, 667–685.

Verkuyten, M. (2005). Ethnic group identification and group evaluation among minority and majority groups: testing the multiculturalism hypothesis. *Journal of Personality and Social Psychology, 88*, 121–138.

Ward, C., & Masgoret, A. M. (2006). An integrative model of attitudes toward immigrants. *International Journal of Intercultural Relations, 30*, 671–682.

Weil, P. (2005). *La république et sa diversité [The republic and its diversity]*. Paris: Seuil.

Weil, P. (2008). *Liberté, Égalité, Discriminations. L'« identité nationale » au regard de l'histoire, [Liberty, equality and discrimination: National identity in history]*. Paris: Grasset.

Wolsko, C., Park, B., & Judd, C. (2006). Considering the tower of babel: Correlates of assimilation and multiculturalism among ethnic minority and majority groups in the United States. *Social Justice Research, 19*, 277–306.

Yzerbyt, V., Dumont, M., Mathieu, B., Gordijn, E., & Wigboldus, D. (2006). Social comparison and group-based emotions. In S. Guimond (Ed.), *Social comparison and Social Psychology: Understanding cognition, intergroup relations and culture* (pp. 174–205). Cambridge, England: Cambridge University Press.

Zick, A., Wagner, U., van Dick, R., & Petzel, T. (2001). Acculturation and prejudice in Germany: Majority and minority perspectives. *Journal of Social Issues, 57*, 541–557.

Frictions Between Muslims and Non-Muslims in the Netherlands

19

Jan Pieter van Oudenhoven

Netherlands Chapter Summary

Van Oudenhoven describes the current population demographics in the Netherlands, with specific attention to the increasing number of Muslims who have entered the country, largely from Turkey and Morocco. Cultural differences are examined and similarities identified in an effort to provide suggestions for more harmonious relations.

Polarization is presented as the means by which the Dutch historically and currently manage relations among different groups. The author recognizes that although past conflicts have been largely avoided, the degree of cultural difference between Muslims and the Dutch creates a more challenging situation such that earlier methods to resolve inconsonance are not effective. The sense of threat which followed the incidents of 9/11 is interpreted to have exacerbated negative attitudes toward Islamic immigrants.

Application of the similarity-attraction hypothesis is utilized to explain the existent ethnic hierarchy in the Netherlands, which places Islamic groups in the lowest level. Suggestions are offered to increase attraction by encouraging contact, inclusion in a superordinate group, and educating individuals to mediate differences. Van Oudenhoven also identifies the use of mutual virtues as a means to enhance integration.

The presence of religious freedom, equality, and freedom of expression in the Netherlands is surmised to create optimal conditions for positive intergroup relations. The author submits evidence that some positive changes have already occurred in politics, art, employment, higher education, and a new form of Dutch Islam which exhibits an integration of cultures.

Cheryl Jorgensen

J.P. van Oudenhoven (✉)
University of Groningen, Groningen, the Netherlands
e-mail: j.p.l.m.van.oudenhoven@rug.nl

D. Landis and R.D. Albert (eds.), *Handbook of Ethnic Conflict: International Perspectives*, International and Cultural Psychology, DOI 10.1007/978-1-4614-0448-4_19,

1 Current Status of Muslims Versus Non-Muslims in the Netherlands

The Netherlands has known for centuries a tradition of immigrants: French Huguenots, German peddlers, German Jews, Dutch Indonesians and Surinamese, and Spanish and Italian guest workers. They have all been relatively well adopted into the Dutch society. Problems were solved or conflicts could be avoided, because cultural differences were relatively limited. For the first time, however, Dutch society is confronted with a group of immigrants and their offspring – from Islamic countries – who do not seem to be integrated that easily into Dutch society. This is not too surprising because Islamic cultures are essentially different from Dutch culture on some essential issues. It is a fundamental psychological law that people tend to like others who hold similar or related points of view. Similarity of ideas facilitates social interaction and reinforces the conviction that one's ideas are right and valid. When values differ largely, common approaches of conflict resolution, such as encouraging contact or stressing commonality in opinions, do not work anymore. This may be the case between Muslims and non-Muslims in the Netherlands. When there exist large differences in values, it may yet be fruitful to have open debates in the media and in the political arena about those differences, provided the debaters stay within rules as they are written down in the constitution.

Currently, there is a polarization taking place between Muslims and non-Muslims which has been fueled by a number of events. These events have sharpened the contrasts between Muslims and non-Muslims in the Netherlands. As a consequence, the media daily report about Muslim issues. Google pages in Dutch count 3,220,000 hits for "moslims" (Muslims) against 600,000 for "christenen" (Christians). References to "Muslims" will grow faster since a new party called Freedom Party, which has made Muslim immigration its main issue, has become the third largest party in the most recent parliament elections. It won 24 of 150 seats in the parliament. The main events are as follows:

1. The strong increase in immigration from Islamic countries during the last 40 years. After World War II, a couple of hundreds of Muslims lived in the Netherlands. Nowadays, over a million of first- and second-generation immigrants originate from Islamic countries. The largest groups are Turks and Moroccans. These groups share a culture that differs strongly from the Dutch culture.
2. The terrorist attacks in New York, Madrid, and London, and the wars in Iraq and Afghanistan.
3. A series of incidents in the Netherlands culminating in the dramatic murder of the Dutch filmmaker Theo van Gogh by a Moroccan Muslim fundamentalist.
4. Many young Muslims suffer from an identity crisis as a consequence of strong discrepancies between the culture of the current Dutch society and the culture of their parents.

1. Polarization is attended by distortion of perceptions. An example of such a distortion is that the Statistics Netherlands (Centraal Bureau voor de Statistiek) estimated the number of Muslims in the Netherlands until recently as more than a million. Apparently, Statistics Netherlands took it for granted that every immigrant from an Islamic country would effectively be a Muslim. In the meantime, Statistics Netherlands has adjusted its estimation of the number of Muslims to 850,000 (CBS, 2009). More conservative estimations, based on numbers of mosque visitors, suggest that there are approximately 200,000 actively practicing Muslims in the Netherlands (Blank & Leemhuis, 2008). The much higher estimations of Statistics Netherlands must probably be attributed to the criterion they used. They asked whether the individual considered himself or herself as a believer. In Islamic societies, unbelief is a serious crime. Non-Muslims may be converted to Islam, but a Muslim may never give up his religion. In view of the enormous pressure regarding not to give up one's religion and the factual exclusion if such a thing happens, it is understandable that in the polls of Statistics Netherlands, such a large number alleged to be a

Table 19.1 Numbers of Muslims as part of the Dutch population

	% Muslims	Estimated number
Native Dutch	0.1	13,000
Western immigrants	3	39,000
Non-Western immigrants		
Turks	87	329,000
Moroccans	92	314,000
Surinamese	10	34,000
Afghans	84	32,000
Iraqis	63	31,000
Somalis	95	21,000
Pakistanis	100	19,000
Iranians	43	13,000
Other groups	11	62,000
Total	6	907,000

Table 19.2 European countries with the highest numbers of Muslims

Countries	Estimated numbers	% Muslims
Russia	16,482,000	11.7
Germany	4,026,000	5
France	3,554,000	6
Albania	2,554,000	79.9
Kosovo	1,999,000	89.6
United Kingdom	1,647,000	2.7
Bosnia-Herzegovina	1,522,000	40
The Netherlands	946,000	5.7
Bulgaria	920,000	12.2
Macedonia	680,000	33.3
Remaining Europe	3,814,000	1.1
Total Europe	38,112,000	5.2

Muslim, even though many of them do not practice. A report of Statistics Netherlands about "religion at the start of the 21st century" (Centraal Bureau voor de Statistiek, 2009) estimates that the percentage of Muslims who visit the mosque at least once a month has dropped in the last couple of years from 47 to 35%. This percentage is comparable to that of Catholics and Protestants. For Muslims, just as other religious groups in the Netherlands, religion has become a private matter. Because somehow all immigrants from Islamic countries share an Islamic cultural background, even though a number of them may not be practicing or not be religious at all, it is useful to also have an idea of the total group of individuals from Islamic cultures. The most numerous groups of such immigrants (first and second generation) originate from Turkey, Morocco, Afghanistan, Somalia, Pakistan, Iraq, Iran, and Indonesia. All these groups together represent almost 8% of the Dutch population of 16.7 million inhabitants. Of them, the two most important groups are the Turkish and Moroccan who together form a group of 720,000. It remains a matter of estimation how many of them are real Muslims. In Table 19.1, recent data are presented about the percentages of Muslims in each of the largest immigrant groups in the Netherlands. The data are estimates on the basis of the population in 2009 by Forum, an institute for multicultural issues (Forum Factbook Moslims, 2010). The overall majority of the Dutch Muslims are Sunnis; a small minority consists of Shiites.

In Table 19.2, we see the distribution of Muslims in Europe (The Pew Forum on Religion & Public Life, 2009). The highest percentages of Muslims are found in countries or regions that in the past belonged to the Ottoman Empire: Kosovo, Albania, Macedonia, Bulgaria, and southern parts of Russia. After Bulgaria and France, the Netherlands has the highest percentage of Muslims within the European Union. In Europe, Muslims account for over 5% of the population. In the USA, in contrast, less than 1% of the population is Muslim (CIA Factbook, 2010).

In general, the socioeconomic position of immigrants from Islamic countries in the Netherlands is less favorable than that of the native Dutch. Among immigrants from Islamic countries, there is more school desertion, lower participation in higher education, more unemployment, lower income, and higher participation in criminal activities than among the native Dutch. The good thing is that these discrepancies apply less to the second generation of immigrants and to females.

2. The terrorist attacks in New York, Madrid, and London, and the wars in Iraq and Afghanistan have shaken the world. For the first time since Pearl Harbor, the USA experienced a serious attack by a foreign group in its own territory. And a

large part of the Western world, which had adopted immigrants from Islamic countries, felt equally threatened by small groups of terrorists who claimed to be Muslims.

3. Until the end of the 1990s, the threat of radical Islamism was still remote in the Netherlands (Veldhuis & Bakker, 2009). In May 2001, a Moroccan imam, Khalid al-Moumni, in the city of Rotterdam was interviewed on television about the growing discrimination against homosexuals by Moroccan youth. In his answer, Khalid al-Moumni said that homosexuality was a pandemic disease all over the world that posed a threat to Muslim youth. The interview led to broad public indignation. A news agency found out that Khalid al-Moumni was a Muslim fundamentalist ousted by the Moroccan government. This incident led to debates in the Parliament that called for closing Islamist mosques and possibly expelling radical imams. A further sad moment for Muslim versus non-Muslim relations was the series of attacks on the USA and the elated reactions to those attacks by a group of young – Moroccan – Muslims who openly expressed their satisfaction with the attacks (Veldhuis & Bakker, 2009).

The most dramatic and symbolic event was the murder of the filmmaker Theo van Gogh. He produced a provocative short film *Submission*, based on a script by Hirsi Ali, a former Somalian Dutch politician, fiercely criticizing Islam. In the film, verses from the Koran were projected onto the body of a naked woman wearing only a veil. Following the showing of the film *Submission*, both Hirsi Ali and Theo van Gogh received death threats. On November 2, 2004, Mohamed Bouyeri, a former student who was brought up in the Netherlands, assassinated Theo van Gogh in a most dramatic way. In a letter stabbed with a knife into Van Gogh's back, Bouyeri expressed his disgust against the Dutch society and Western societies in general and their policies. Soon after the murder of Van Gogh, it became clear that Bouyeri was a central person in an important terrorist network.

4. Muslim youngsters in the Netherlands, particularly of the second generation, are confronted with a postmodern predominantly secular society, with a low power distance between students and their teachers and toward other authorities, and with a high tolerance toward expression of sexual preferences. This is in large contrast with the culture their parents left when they immigrated to the Netherlands. As a consequence, they feel alienated in the Netherlands and often try to find an identity that fits them better in their own *Ummah* (the Muslim community). These feelings of an insecure identity and of alienation are not only typical for Muslims in the Netherlands, but may also be shared by young Muslims in most Western countries (Malik, 2007).

2 History of Relations Between Muslims and Dutch

Through the ages, the Netherlands has experienced polarization between groups. Polarization is the process of exaggerating contrasts between groups accompanied by a distortion of common points of view. In the Netherlands, this most frequently took place between Protestants and Roman Catholics. The dramatic start of it was the iconoclasm in 1566, which indirectly prompted the 80 years' war of independence of the more dominantly protestant Dutch provinces against the Catholic Spanish rulers. More than four centuries were needed in order to reconcile the Protestants and Catholics in the Netherlands. Its final accomplishment took place by the merger of a Catholic, a Lutheran, and a Calvinist party into one big Christian political party. Nowadays a new polarization is evolving, this time between Muslims and non-Muslims. Again religion plays the crucial role. Historically, there had never been a particular sensitivity from the Dutch side toward the Muslim world. The Dutch never had a significant role in the crusades. On the contrary, there had even been intensive and positive economic and diplomatic relations with the Ottoman Empire for centuries. It started in the early seventeenth century and lasted until the collapse of the Ottoman Empire in 1923. The current polarization between Muslims and non-Muslims is a very recent phenomenon largely created by a number

Table 19.3 A history of racist violence in the Netherlands after World War II (Witte, 2010)

Period	Main target groups	Main forms of violence
1950–1970	Dutch–Indonesians	Fights between youngsters
	Guest workers (first from Italy/Spain, later Turkey/Morocco)	Fights between groups and individuals
	Dutch Jews	Offensive graffiti and threats
1970–1980	Turkish, Moroccan, and Surinamese Dutch	Violence against residents in neighborhoods, restaurant owners, and individuals
	Moluccans (Dutch–Indonesians)	Fights between groups (of youngsters)
1980–1990	Individuals with an immigrant background	Violence against individuals
End of the 1980s	Asylum seekers, especially Tamils	Violence against individuals and groups
1990–2000	Individuals with an immigrant background	Violence against individuals
	Asylum seekers and refugees	Violent threats against refugee centers
	Muslims	Arsonism and offensive graffiti on mosques
2000–2010	Muslims	Violence against individuals
		Destruction, arsonism, and related acts of aggression to mosques
	Dutch Jews	Violence threat and intimidation, often by groups of Muslims

of factors mentioned above, which have intensely affected Dutch society in the last decade.

One special factor is the strong increase in the number of immigrants since World War II. In a recent book with the ironic title "Al eeuwenlang een gastvrij volk" ("A hospitable nation for centuries"), Witte (2010) describes racist incidents and acts of discrimination that took place in the Netherlands between 1950 and 2010 (see Table 19.3). Not until the last 2 decades, however, actions against Muslims were registered. The first groups of Turks and Moroccans had arrived earlier, but were seen as temporary guest workers and did not express their religion publicly. These actions may be seen as a threat to the social cohesion of a society. In Table 19.3, we see the pattern of violent actions over the last 60 years and the shift in target groups. It is clear from the data that with the exception of some incidental actions of anti-Semitism, there have always been incidents against new groups of immigrants from less rich countries. Nevertheless, Witte depicts a too gloomy picture of the last 60 years. It is not until the last decade that a substantial proportion of the Dutch population has become more outspoken against immigrants and Muslims in particular. Moreover, the majority of the people would be reluctant to consider themselves as anti-immigrant.

3 Origins of Problems

It is not a surprise that there exists some friction between Muslims and native Dutch. First, hardly any Muslims lived in the Netherlands until the late 1960s, whereas 40 years later, 8% of the population originates from an Islamic culture. In addition to this, the largest groups among them, from Turkey and Morocco, differ from mainstream Dutch, not only with respect to religion but also with respect to other essential characteristics such as language, socioeconomic status, level of education, and other aspects of culture than religion. In fact, the first waves of immigrants were low-educated guest workers – often illiterate – with large families – who came from remote rural areas with a strongly collectivistic culture. They came to the Netherlands, an individualistic country that had just experienced a cultural revolution regarding relations to authorities, male–female relations, and views on sexuality and religion. Apparently, discrepancies are not limited to the contrast of Muslims and non-Muslims. Nevertheless, there are crucial differences regarding women rights between Muslims and native Dutch. According to Islamic jurisprudence, women have fewer rights than men, and although Sharia law is not valid in the Netherlands, it is still influential in Muslim communities. Remarkably, scarcely any frictions between Dutch Muslims from Suriname and Indonesia (two former Dutch colonies) and native Dutch are observed, although a large percentage of them are Muslims. This must probably be attributed to the greater cultural congeniality and longer experience of living together between native Dutch and Surinamese or Indonesian Dutch. In the next section, I will present some empirical data with respect to the mutual appreciation between Dutch citizens from Islamic countries and native Dutch.

In a study with an anthropological approach, approximately 1,500 psychology students each interviewed an immigrant in the Netherlands (Van Oudenhoven, 2009). The immigrant could be of any non-Dutch cultural origin. The main task for the students was to let the interviewees tell what their most important and salient experiences were with the Dutch. More than 10% of the interviewees were from Islamic countries. The results of interviews of five large immigrant groups from Islamic countries are presented in Table 19.3. There is a remarkable overlap in experiences among the five groups. They all find Dutch women more independent than women from their home countries. Some – more women than men – appreciate that; others – more men than women – despise it. In several domains of society, the respondents from Islamic countries mention the experience of individualism in the Netherlands: the interviewees observe a reduced hospitality in the Netherlands, loose family ties, and a relatively low or absent respect to parents, teachers, and authorities. Most are shocked – and a minority is thrilled – by the relative lack of taboos with respect to the use of drugs, sexual freedom, and the acceptance of homosexuality. Other aspects that widen the cultural gap are the difficulty of the Dutch language, the often-experienced unfriendly and prejudiced attitude, the distance in contact, and the less important role of religion in the Dutch society (Table 19.4).

In June 2009, Turkey's largest newspaper published the results of a survey among 1715 Turks in relatively secular Turkey (Today's Zaman, 2009). The results also very clearly show that there exists a value gap between Dutch and Islamic cultures: Seventy-two percent said they wouldn't want to have neighbors who consumed alcohol and 62% wouldn't like irreligious people as neighbors. Eighty-one percent told the European Union's ultimate goal was to spread Christianity in the world. A total of 71% indicated that the head of the family should be the man, and 88% said that the most important things a woman wants in life are a husband and children. Fifty-eight percent believed that a woman should always obey her husband, and an equal percentage said that a woman walking on a beach in a swimsuit committed a sin.

In 1987, Hagendoorn and Habra published a stuy of ethnic prejudice in the Netherlands, which showed an ethnic hierarchy that has not changed ever since. European groups were placed on top, followed by groups from former colonies and with Islamic groups at the bottom. Verkuyten, Hagendoorn, and Masson (1995) observed that the scheme of preferences of the Dutch corresponded inversely to the rank ordering of the ethnic groups in terms of collectivism; immigrants from individualistic cultures were appreciated most and those from collectivistic countries least. The similarity-attraction hypothesis can explain this hierarchy. According to the similarity-attraction hypothesis, similarity leads to attraction (Byrne, 1971). The hypothesis states that when one perceives another to be similar to oneself on various characteristics (for instance, attitudes and cultural values), this other will be positively evaluated. In other words, we like people and groups who we think are like our selves and our own group. The similarity-attraction hypothesis offers an easy explanation for why people do not appreciate cultural differences or dissimilar cultures. Similarity may reduce insecurity in interpersonal and intergroup relations. Therefore, cultural similarity may be rewarding because it suggests that

Table 19.4 Most frequently mentioned cultural differences by immigrants from five Islamic countries in the Netherlands

Most frequently mentioned themes	Less traditional male–female role patterns	Less close family ties	Less hospitable	Little respect for the elderly and authorities	Individualism	Less taboos (sex, drugs, and homosexuality)	Prejudice and discrimination	Dutch difficult language	Aloof/distant	Religion less important
Countries (N)										
Iraq (27)	18	17	11	5	12	12	6	12	8	10
Iran (32)	19	14	11	11	4	10	9	14	10	15
Morocco (26)	5	12	6	6	7	5	12	11	5	13
Turkey (44)	25	24	18	20	13	13	11	18	15	19
Indonesia (30)	9	14	19	17	6	9	7	12	8	7
Total (159)	76	81	65	59	42	49	45	67	46	64
Total (%)	48	51	41	37	26	31	28	42	30	40

our beliefs and values are correct. As a consequence, interactions between individuals and groups occur more smoothly.

Clear support for the similarity-attraction hypothesis was found in a large survey (Van Oudenhoven, Judd, & Hewstone, 2000) of Dutch-speaking citizens ($N=2{,}389$) of the Netherlands, who were asked to indicate their liking for individuals who varied in their ethnicity, religion, and employment. Respondents were given the following scenario: *Suppose you got some new neighbors. You have a brief introductory chat with the man and the woman. You don't know whether they are married, but you do know that they are Dutch (Turkish), that the man was employed (unemployed), and that they were Muslims (that they did not practice their religion, but did celebrate Christmas, Easter, and "Sinterklaas"* (**St Nicholas**). Each respondent was thus told that the couple was either Dutch or Turkish, that the man was either employed or unemployed, and that they were either Muslims or did not practice their religion but celebrated Christmas, Easter, and "Sinterklaas", which is the modal "religious" attitude of mainstream Dutch. After reading the scenario, respondents were asked to indicate their liking of the couple and to what degree they found the couple to be similar to them. The results of this study showed that outgroup membership on each different social category contributed additively to less liking of the target and to less perceived similarity. As long as the target did not share all characteristics of the ingroup, he or she was liked considerably less than the target who shared all characteristics of the ingroup. Respondents indeed felt most attracted to the employed Dutch "Christian" neighbor who was assumed to be most similar to himself or herself, and felt least attracted to the unemployed Turkish Muslim neighbor who was assumed to be most dissimilar to themselves. Religion, nationality, and employment status, all three categories, had roughly equal effects on perceived similarity and sympathy scores.

The similarity-attraction hypothesis is further supported by a number of survey studies on attitudes toward immigrants in which acceptance of immigrants appeared to depend on their cultural distance from the host society. Somehow, this is a reassuring thought. People all around the world appear to have a preference for individuals who are like themselves. There are several ways to deal with the "dissimilarity-non-attraction" problem, from fostering contact so that one comes to discover that differences are not that great, to interventions to enhance the inclusiveness of several cultural groups within one superordinate group, to training people to deal with cultural differences. Cultural dissimilarity becomes problematic, however, if cultural differences become associated with threat and reinforced by salience and distinctiveness of the outgroup. And this is what happened after 9/11 and the series of attacks afterward. The increasing numbers of Muslim immigrants further enhanced the feelings of threat. Do we see any evidence for an increase in prejudice in the Netherlands after 9/11 toward immigrants from Islamic countries? Yes, we do.

In two representative Dutch polls in 1996 ($N=2{,}389$) and 2002 ($N=2{,}023$), respectively, respondents were asked to mention which groups they found least friendly. In 1996, only 6.2% of the respondents mentioned Moroccans and Turks as least friendly, which rose to 15% in 2002 (Van Oudenhoven, 2002). Simultaneously, the endorsement of the statement that immigrants should assimilate to Dutch culture rose from 75 to 85%.

Another large-scale study (Entzinger, 2007) took place in the city of Rotterdam, one of most culturally diverse cities in the Netherlands, where almost 15% of the city's inhabitants are from Turkish or Moroccan background. Comparisons were made between 1999 and 2006. The results show that Turkish and Moroccan (18–30 years old) youth integrate more and more, which means that they participate increasingly in Dutch society, and that they remained unchangingly positive of ethnic Dutch. However, in contrast, native Dutch youths see immigrants, especially Moroccan youths, more often in a negative light. Nationalism markedly increased among ethnic Dutch youth. In 1999, 10% said they were willing to defend Dutch identity if it was being crushed. In 2006, the percentage tripled. Immigrants may try to integrate as much as they want, but they still stay "that immigrant." Ethnic Dutch youth want their immigrant colleagues to adapt more to Dutch society. Preferably they want them to assimilate. Just like ethnic Dutch youth, immigrant youth in Rotterdam emphasize their own – Muslim – identity since the attacks of 9/11 and the murder of Van Gogh. Especially Moroccan youth are becoming more intense believers. In 1999, 40% of Moroccan youth strictly followed the rules of Islam; 7 years later that grew to 60%. Meanwhile, Turkish and Moroccan youth integrate more and more. Although their educational level is still lower than that of their ethnic Dutch colleagues, they are in the process of catching up. They are more often members of a sports club, and thanks to complementary newspapers, they are better informed about the news. To summarize, Turkish and Moroccan youth in the Netherlands have not only become more Dutch than before, but also more Muslim.

This conclusion with respect to Muslim identification is in line with the results of a dissertation in which Ketner (2008) found that Moroccan youth identified primarily as true Muslims, next as Dutch, and then as Moroccans. Interestingly, they viewed to be Muslim is an individual choice, "something between me and God," as many of them told the interviewer. They may drink beer, or not find it necessary for females to cover the hair, and many girls claim equal rights. Apparently, a Dutch Islam is gradually developing.

Similar tendencies are being found in Great Britain where young Muslims are drifting away from their parents' views of Islam (Ansari 2009; Pauly, 2004). They develop a new way of expressing Islam, which is more in line with the European context.

3.1 Comparison of Attitudes Toward Muslims in Eight European Countries

Apparently, relations between Muslims and non-Muslims are far from optimal and appear to in sharp contrast with a – rapidly vanishing – positive stereotype of the Dutch as tolerant people. Must we conclude that the Dutch belong to the most intolerant people in Europe, or are they more or less representative of what Europeans in general think?

An answer to this question is given by two German researchers who published the results of a survey on "Attitudes towards the Islam and Muslims in Europe" (Zick, Küpper, & Hövermann, 2011). A sample of 1,000 respondents came from Germany, Great Britain, France, Italy, the Netherlands, Portugal, Poland, and Hungary. Below, the relevant questions are shown together with the percentages of respondents in the Netherlands versus all European respondents:

The Muslim culture fits well into the Netherlands.	38.7 versus 31.3%
There are too many Muslims in the Netherlands.	41.6 versus 44.2%
Islam is a religion of tolerance.	46.6 versus 54.4%
Muslims in the Netherlands are too demanding.	51.8 versus 55.4%
Muslims' attitudes toward women contradict our values.	78.2 versus 78.2%
Women should take their roles as wife and mother more seriously.	36.4 versus 60.2%
There is nothing immoral about homosexuality.	83.5 versus 57.4%

The data show that the Dutch in general are slightly less negative about Muslims than the other seven European samples. With respect to other issues, gender roles, and attitudes toward homosexuality, however, the Dutch are much more liberal than any other European group. Apparently, the Dutch still seem to be relatively tolerant, but to a lesser extent with respect to Muslims.

4 Consequences and Possible Resolutions

4.1 Between Pessimism and Hope

Immigrants from Islamic backgrounds have lived next to ethnic Dutch for decades in the Netherlands. Many of them have gradually been influenced by Dutch belief systems. The last 10 years, however, several native Dutch, e.g., the politician Pim Fortuyn who was murdered; Rita Verdonk, a former minister of integration; Geert Wilders, the founder of an anti-Muslim political party; and the film maker Theo van Gogh who was murdered, have uttered outspoken statements against Muslim presence in the Netherlands. More generally, discontent with the conduct of Islamic groups –and particularly of Moroccan youth – is expressed without any political correctness. In spite of that directness – or maybe because of these outspoken points of view – a growing understanding has been established between Muslims and non-Muslims, and the socioeconomic position of Islamic Dutch has considerably improved. Some of these favorable developments are as follows:

- Politics: A large and growing number of city council members and members of parliament are from Turkish or Moroccan origin. Rotterdam, the second largest city in the Netherlands, has a mayor who was born in Morocco, and the last government included one vice-minister who was born in Turkey.
- Arts: Many successful participants in cabaret, journalism, and pop music come from predominantly Islamic cultures. Naema Tahir, from Pakistani background, is a successful writer who writes openly about sexual feelings (see picture); and Kader Abdolah, one of the most renowned writers, is a refugee from Iran. A version of the Koran written by Kader Abdolah is a bestseller, and sells even better among native Dutch than among Dutch Muslims.
- Employment: Percentages of unemployment, although still higher among immigrants from Islamic countries than among native Dutch, are much lower than a decade ago. Turkish and Moroccans are starting to occupy higher positions. Turkish and Moroccan parents realize that education is the main path to social mobility. Their children are much more fluent in Dutch than the parents, and they increasingly participate in higher education. Particularly, the number of Islamic women who participate in higher education has risen considerably. For instance, whereas in 1995 only 14% of the 18–20 years old Moroccan women entered higher education, in 2007 this percentage had risen to 47%, and for Turkish women of the same age, the percentage from 12 to 43% (Forum Factbook, 2010).
- Demography: Interestingly, the average age at which women of non-Western descent have their first baby has increased considerably. Second-generation Turkish and Moroccan women have their first baby almost at the same age as the native Dutch women. The number of children they have has also sharply decreased. These demographic patterns facilitate female participation in higher education.
- Responses of Muslims to criticism of Islam: In 2008, the radical politician Geert Wilders released his anti-Islam movie "Fitna." People anticipated strong protest, violent demonstrations, and aggressive reactions within the country. Contrary to these expectations, there were only a few insignificant incidents. Young representatives from the Muslim community explicitly distanced themselves from radical and violent action by Muslims in answer to the film. Likewise, orthodox Muslims made strong pleas to react in a dignified way to "Fitna" (Veldhuis & Bakker, 2009).
- In a study in four big cities in Belgium and the Netherlands (Antwerp, Brussels, Liege, and Rotterdam), Moroccans had a stronger identification with their own culture in the Dutch-speaking cities of Antwerp and Rotterdam, but at the same time were more inclined to be in contact with the native population and more satisfied with life than Moroccans in the French-speaking cities (Van Oudenhoven & Lubbers, 2007). In the French-speaking cities, there were more Moroccans who assimilated, but a larger group did not have any substantial contact at all, although Moroccans are more familiar with French than with Dutch.

5 Virtues in Contemporary Dutch Society

Religion apparently plays a dominant role in the public debate on immigration. In view of that dominant role, religion may also play a key role to improve relations between relevant religious and nonreligious groups. Unfortunately, little is known about the effect of religion on the integration of Muslims. Integration refers to participation in Dutch society while simultaneously keeping one's own cultural identity. When thinking of integration, moral aspects such as tolerance, respect, and solidarity come to one's mind. A crucial question is, "to what extent moral principles, because of their possible influence on social cohesion, differ or concur between the various religious and nonreligious groups in the Netherlands?" Virtue was chosen as a concept that is concrete enough to investigate moral principles. In fact, we have investigated the relation between Muslim virtues and those of Catholics, Protestants, and nonreligious people (Van Oudenhoven, Pomp, & Sluis, 2008).

Research on virtues is a specific approach of describing and analyzing polarization or convergence within a society. Virtues are morally good personal characteristics that everyone can either possess or learn, and about which – in principle – people can agree within a society. They prescribe how the individual should behave. Many virtues refer to concrete interactions between ordinary people, in contrast to the debate in the media and politics, which pass over their heads. This is why virtues can become guiding principles when advancing integration.

An approach was made to compile a list of contemporary virtues in the Netherlands by interviews and surveys. We started by extensively interviewing 36 local spiritual leaders. This study yielded 15 crucial virtues that summarized all the morally good characteristics that were spontaneously mentioned by them. Next, 83 teachers filled out a questionnaire. Spiritual leaders and teachers have in common that both have a moral mandate. Subsequently, the questionnaire was administered to 217 municipal council members. These political opinion leaders form an interesting group because they are in direct contact with community members and often implicitly express moral statements. Finally, 283 pupils with a mean age of 15 years also participated in this study. Pupils were chosen because they, more than the other groups, tend to have contemporary views on virtues, and do not have any special moral mission.

The first question was whether virtues still played a role in general. There is no doubt about this: spiritual leaders, teachers, municipal council members, and adolescents answered without any hesitation the question of what virtues are important to them, regardless of whether they were religious or nonreligious.

In addition, we asked all respondents with exception of the spiritual leaders to put in order the 15 virtues in blocks of three virtues from the most important to the least important. Because the three groups strongly agreed in their judgment of the degree of importance of the 15 virtues, the adolescents were grouped together with the teachers and council members (see Fig. 19.1). Virtues that were rated as the most important are rather social virtues: respect, reliability, justice, and love. One may conclude that a shift has taken place from introvert virtues, such as faith, hope, and temperance, toward virtues of a more social character, such as respect, love, and helpfulness.

The crucial question of the study was how different religious groups thought about the virtues. The term virtue is strongly associated with religion; this is why we expected considerable discrepancies between the different groups, particularly between Muslims and non-Muslims. However, this hardly appears to be the case; there even appears to be a similar pattern between the groups (see Fig. 19.2).

On the whole, Muslims do not differ from the other groups in their interpretation of the virtues. They do, however, attach greater importance to faith, and to some extent to wisdom. Higher scores on faith for Muslims may be due to the way we selected them, because the Muslim teachers and students were approached via their Islamic schools. The ratings by the Islamic council members did not show such a high rating of faith, which suggests that situational factors may be of influence here. There seems to be more convergence than polarization in the appreciation of virtues in the Dutch community. A four-nation study in which virtues were compared across nations (Van Oudenhoven et al., 2010) shows that Muslims

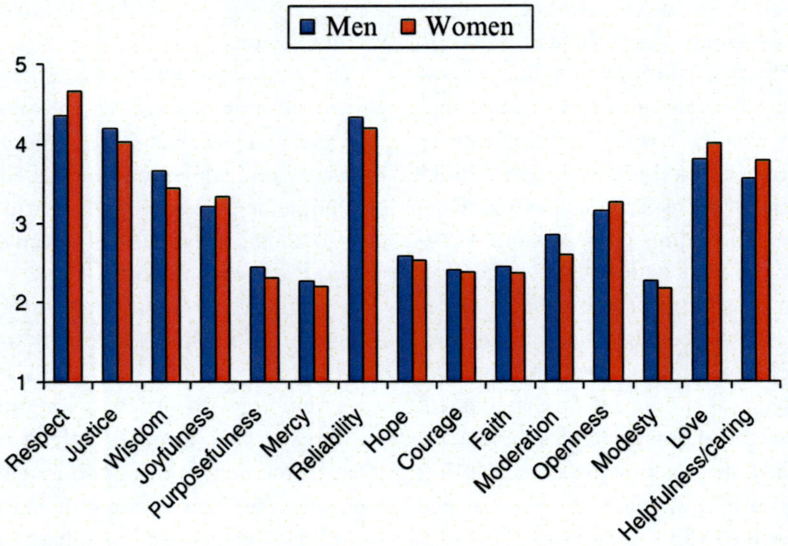

Fig. 19.1 Men and women concerning virtues (1 = least important; 5 = most important).

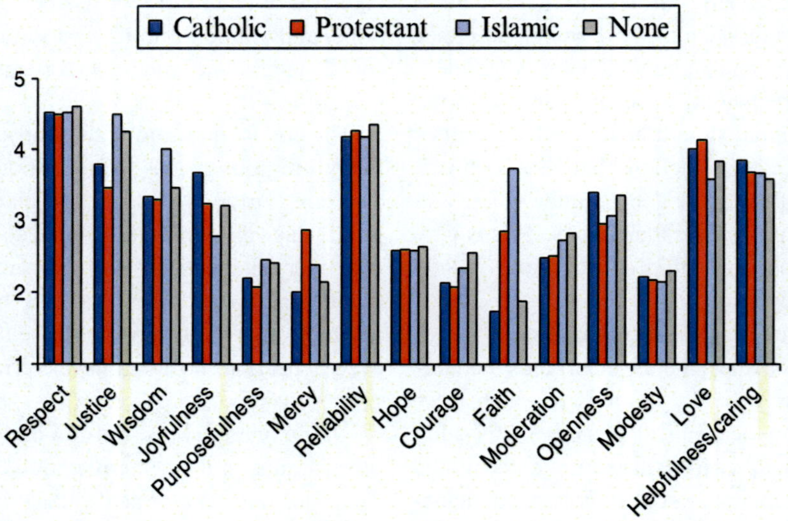

Fig. 19.2 Importance of virtues across three religions (1 = least important; 5 = most important)

from Malaysia and the Netherlands strongly differ from each other in the importance they attribute to the above-mentioned set of 15 virtues. Dutch Muslims are more similar to Dutch Protestants than to their Malaysian fellow Muslims.

Men and women appear to have the same concepts of virtues in general (See Fig. 19.2). The data of men almost appear to replicate those of the women. However, there are some slight differences. Men score a bit higher on more control-oriented virtues such as justice, wisdom, and moderation, while women score a bit higher on the more social virtues such as respect, love, and caring. This is in line with the general stereotype that

Table 19.5 The most morally influential role models according to pupils (1 = Never influenced by them; 5 = Always influenced by them)

Influential role models	Nonreligious (*N*=117)	Protestants (*N*=45)	Catholics (*N*=37)	Muslims (*N*=68)	Total (*N*=267)
Parents	3.67	3.80	3.86	4.15	3.84
Friends	3.18	3.16	3.27	3.05	3.16
Brothers and sisters	2.64	2.53	2.67	3.18	2.76
God/Allah	1.21	2.69	1.47	4.54	2.45
Teachers	2.03	2.04	2.14	2.55	2.17
Preacher/Priest/Imam	1.07	1.91	1.19	3.32	1.77
Celebrities (for example, singers)	1.44	1.34	1.46	1.50	1.44

women have innate "warmth" and that men are more "rational." In this context, it is interesting that Phalet and Hagendoorn (2003) stated that "… especially the higher educated second generation Muslim women are the pioneers of an inclusive Islam in the making." By an inclusive Islam the authors meant an Islam that adapts to the Dutch society.

6 Suggestions

We may thus conclude that virtues have an important role as a moral framework for the way of thinking of different groups of people. Important "modern" virtues like respect and love have a strong social character. Moreover, there is a large degree of concurrence with regard to the relative importance of the virtues for these different groups. This makes virtues attractive as a trigger for programs concerning the promotion of integration or social cohesion. The virtues can count on a broad acceptance because they appear to be shared by all groups. All groups labeled respect as the most important virtue.

Furthermore, this was not only seen as a crucial virtue, but also as the best concrete way to improve the relation between different ethnic groups. Several groups indeed suggested similar actions to enhance respect, for example, open communication, and listening and gathering more knowledge about each other. Future research should focus on shared concrete ways to put the relevant virtues into practice.

6.1 Who Are Moral Anchors?

In the same study, an additional question was who influenced adolescents most when they were in doubt of what is good or bad. The results of the influence of different categories of role models were unambiguous (Table 19.5). First, there is a clear order in the degree of moral influence. In general, this hierarchy goes from parents, friends, brothers and sisters, God or Allah, teachers, and spiritual leaders to celebrities, although a different rank order was found in the moral influence of God/Allah and spiritual leaders for the religious groups. Whereas the moral influence of spiritual leaders for the majority of the adolescents is quite small, and for Catholic and nonreligious adolescents even negligible, the influence is eminent on Islamic teens. Furthermore, the moral influence of brothers, sisters, and teachers is greater for Islamic adolescents than for the other three groups. This is to be expected in view of the collectivistic character of Islamic societies. The results show that people who interact daily with the adolescents, the family and friends, have the highest impact on them. The influence of celebrities and singers can be seen as marginal. Girls indicate to be influenced by others to a greater extent than boys.

The most remarkable finding is the strong moral impact of parents on adolescents. It is greater than that of friends, which is surprising for this age group, if we take into account that in general in adolescence the influence of friends tends to increase greatly.

Another study of child rearing in which nonreligious, Calvinistic, Hindu, Jewish, and Muslim families in the Netherlands were compared, also clearly showed that Muslim parents, both mothers and fathers, score highest of the five groups on parental support, control, and family relations (Mousavi Thorshezi, 2009). Muslim families apparently have imported what Kagitcibasi (1996) called the *family model of interdependence* as opposed to the *family model of independence*, which is more characteristic of Western urban societies with individualist values.

In accordance with the results of this study, it is recommended that integration programs that focus on parents be developed. In the political arena, spiritual leaders are seen as influential figures in the moral sphere. However, only Islamic teens seem to take them seriously. Another finding of the study was that spiritual leaders recommended mainly introverted suggestions for the promotion of virtues, such as, for instance, meditation and prayer. It does not seem plausible that these actions lend themselves for programs focused on integration. Furthermore, women are underrepresented in the group of spiritual leaders, while women promote more pro-social virtues, and may increasingly become important role models.

7 Summary and Conclusions

The Netherlands is used to vivid and ferocious debates between Muslims and non-Muslims concerning Muslims. This debate is most prominently on the Internet, in the Media, and in the political arena. In contrast to these debates, there are lots of interactions between Muslims and non-Muslims at school, at work, on the street, and in the neighborhoods where Muslims and non-Muslims are in direct contact with one another. In these environments, debates are also taking place, but at the same time efforts are made to get along with each other.

Examination of the importance of virtues among different groups shows a general, shared set of moral ideas. It is reassuring to see that teachers, pupils, and local politicians with different spiritual beliefs share the same moral principles. Apparently, there is convergence of viewpoints among people who are in direct contact, while there still is polarization of viewpoints on the national level. Inglehart and Baker (2000) found convergence of moral principles between religious communities in several countries. According to the authors, religious traditions that shaped a national culture in the course of history, through national institutions such as, for example, laws, schools, churches, and municipalities, maintain their influence on the society as a whole, including on newcomers. The German and Dutch Catholics who were shaped by the dominant Protestant institution in their country were presented by Inglehart and Baker as an example of such a religious influence. The above-mentioned study in which virtues were compared across nations (Van Oudenhoven et al., 2010) showed that Dutch Muslims are more similar to Dutch Protestants than to Malaysian Muslims.

We may conclude that a Dutch Islam may be emerging; this is called the "polder Islam." In Amsterdam, for example, there is a "polder mosque" where preachings are given in Dutch, men and women may share the same space, and non-Muslims are welcome. The Netherlands has a good constitution, which guarantees freedom of religion, equality of men and women, and freedom of expression. These principles offer precious conditions for constructive relations between Muslims and non-Muslims in the Netherlands.

References

Ansari, H. (2009). *The infidel within: Muslims in Britain since 1800*. London: Hurst & Company.

Blank, A., & Leemhuis, F. (2008). Nederlandse islam [Dutch Islam]. In J. P. van Oudenhoven, A. Blank, F. Leemhuis, M. Pomp, & A. F. Sluis (Eds.), *Nederland deugt [Virtuous Netherlands]* (pp. 49–93). Assen: Van Gorcum.

Byrne, D. (1971). *The attraction paradigm*. New York: Academic.

Centraal Bureau voor de Statistiek. (2009). *Religie aan het begin van de 21e eeuw.* [Religion at the start of the 21st century]. CBS(http:www.cbs.nl.).

CIA. (2010) *The United States World Factbook*. https://www.cia.gov/library/publications/the-world-factbook/geos/us.html

Entziger, H. (2007). Rising demands and growing frustrations. Mutual perception and value change in multiethnic Rotterdam since '9/11' (2007). In E. Poppe & M. Verkuyten (Eds.), *Culture and conflict* (pp. 83–215). Amsterdam: Aksant.

Factbook. (2010). *De positie van moslims in Nederland: feiten en cijfers*. Utrecht: Forum.

Hagedoorn, L., & Habra, J. (1987). Social distance towards Holland's minorities: Discrimination against and among ethnic outgroups. *Ethnic and Racial Studies, 10*, 120–133.

Inglehart, R., & Baker, W. E. (2000). Modernization, cultural change, and the persistence of traditional values. *American Sociological Review, 65*, 19–51.

Kagitcibasi, C. (1996). *Family and human development across cultures: A review from the other side*. Mahwah, NJ: Erlbaum Associates.

Ketner, S. (2008). *Marokkaanse wortels, Nederlandse grond.* [Moroccan roots, Dutch soil]. Unpublished doctoral dissertation. University of Groningen, the Netherlands.

Malik, S. (2007). My brother the bomber. *Prospect Magazine, 31*, 5.

Mousavi Thorshezi. (2009). *Gepraktiseerde religie thuis en sociale limieten.* [Practised religions at home, and social limits]. Unpublished doctoral dissertation. University of Groningen, the Netherlands.

Pauly, R. J. (2004). *Islam in Europe: Integration or marginalization? Islam in Europe*. London: Ashgate Publishing.

Pew Forum on Religion & Public Life. (2009). Mapping the global Muslim population.

Phalet, K., & Hagendoorn, L. (2003). *Identity, culture and politics in plural societies: The case of Muslim minorities in the Netherlands*. Utrecht: Ercomer.

Van Oudenhoven, J. P., Judd, C. M., & Hewstone, M. (2000). Additive and interactive models of crossed-categorisation in correlated social categories. *Group Processes and Intergroup Relations, 3*, 285–295.

Van Oudenhoven, J. P. (2002). *Nederlanders over andere volkeren [Dutch about other nations]*. Hilversum: Stichting Teleac/NOT.

Van Oudenhoven, J. P. (2009). *Op zoek naar de Nederlandse identiteit [In quest for the Dutch identity]*. Bussum: Coutinho.

Van Oudenhoven, J. P., & Lubbers, H. (2007). Marokkanen in Antwerpen en Rotterdam redelijk gelukkig. [Moroccans in Antwerp and Rotterdam relatively happy]. *Kennislink, 24/01/2007*.

Van Oudenhoven, J. P., Pomp, M., & Sluis, A. F. (2008). Een empirische deugdenanalyse [An empirical analysis of virtues]. In J. P. van Oudenhoven, A. Blank, F. Leemhuis, M. Pomp, & A. F. Sluis (Eds.), *Nederland deugt* (pp. 1–48). Assen: Van Gorcum.

Van Oudenhoven, J.P. et al. (2010). *Virtues across nations*. Paper submitted for publication.

Veldhuis, T., & Bakker, E. (2009). *Muslims in the Netherlands: Tensions and violent conflict.* MICROCON Policy Working Paper 6, Brighton: MICROCON.

Verkuyten, M., Hagendoorn, L., & Masson, K. (1995). The ethnic hierarchy among majority and minority youth in the Netherlands. *Journal of Applied Social Psychology, 26*, 1104–1118.

Witte, R. (2010). *Al eeuwenlang een gastvrij volk [For centuries a hospitable nation]*. Amsterdam: Aksant.

Zick, A., Küpper, B, & Hövermann, A. (2011). *Intolerance, Prejudice, and Discrimination. A European Report*. Berlin: Fridrich Ebert Stiftung.

Part VIII

Latin America

Mexico's Ethnic Conflict

20

Jeanette S. Martin

Mexico Chapter Summary

In this chapter, Martin describes the social and political movements that have impacted ethnic minorities in Mexico. Detailed history is presented as it provides insight into the current identity of ethnic minorities and associated treatment by the government. Suggestions for improvement through government policy are offered.

The actions and effects of the Zapatista Movement are examined as an influential force through which different groups of minority Indians came together to work toward equal inclusion in power, politics, and economics while still being appreciated as culturally different. This movement is emphasized as it provided several positive changes for Indian minorities, including the government permitting education in native languages and building more schools in Indian communities. Martin notes that ethnic pride among local Indians has increased as a result of the government rejection of proposed legislation to promote equality and diversity.

The author explains the government efforts to reduce ethnic tension through application of the term Mestizo to all people as an attempt to ignore cultural differences. Historical origins and meanings of "Mestizo" are explored as Martin describes this term from the Indian perspective as a representation of colonial domination and rejection of indigenous knowledge and culture. This is noted as indicative of the ongoing struggle for Indian identity in Mexico.

Martin suggests several things the government of Mexico can do in order to improve ethnic relations, which include recognizing indigenous

J.S. Martin (✉)
School of Business Administration,
University of Mississippi, P.O. Box 1848
University, MS 38677-1848, USA
e-mail: jmartin@bus.olemiss.edu

D. Landis and R.D. Albert (eds.), *Handbook of Ethnic Conflict: International Perspectives*, International and Cultural Psychology, DOI 10.1007/978-1-4614-0448-4_20,

people as both Indian and Mexican, providing better schools in order for Indians to be competitive economically, and equality of political representation. It is noted that the government is currently working with the people to enact change.

1 Introduction

This chapter will review the history and current events surrounding the indigenous Indians, mestizos, and Castilianos. As these ethnopolitical conflicts have survived over 400 years in some areas of Mexico, it is interesting to study how the conflicts started and where there is still conflict today. As with most ethnic conflicts, there is not a neat, simple way to correct them. Many different ideas have been used throughout the history of these ethnic conflicts to "make things right." This has involved divergent approaches from denying there is a problem, to trying to rename everyone and "make everyone equal."

Mexico has tried to deal with the differences of the indigenous people from the main culture by getting the indigenous to assimilate into the larger national culture. This, of course, would mean that eventually the Indian identities would be lost. Because of the Zapatista Movement, the government is now in the process of fostering acculturation, wherein the Indians participate in the economic world of the country, but socially continue to be themselves (Schmidt-Diaz de Leon, 2001).

"Ethnic or racial strife is an expression of class conflict whenever different ethnic groups are unequally ranked and where it is possible to identify subordinate and superordinate ethnic groups who have unequal access to power" (Schyrer, 1990, p. 17). In Mexico, there are ethnic differences between the other Mexicans and the Indians, with the Indians feeling subordinate to the superordinate Mexican ethnic group, and historically, the Indians have had unequal access to power.

It will be helpful to start with some definitions. Mestizo has changed meanings over the years. Originally mestizo was anyone of mixed ethnicities. Mestizo has always been a term the Mexican government has used; most people in Mexico throughout history would not refer to themselves as a Mestizo. Mexico is now trying a movement where everyone is referred to as a mestizo, changing the meaning of the word yet again. Mulattos were people of mixed African and white European ethnicities. Creole were people of mixed Spanish or French and African ethnicities, generally these people had a separate language. Crillo is an American born Spaniard. A Spaniard is a person born in Spain.

What makes the conflict in Mexico particularly interesting is that modern day media attention has finally enabled Indians to bring their situation and desires to the world and not just the Mexican government. When this happened, it created a situation where the Mexican government was being watched and given advice by the world. Therefore, what started as a military action in Chiapas became a rhetorical situation.

2 Current Status

First, we will look at the Zapatista Movement since it is the most current ethnic movement within Mexico; then, we will put everything into an historical context.

2.1 Zapatista Movement

The Zapatista Movement is interesting because it is the first ethnic movement that had a very short militaristic period followed by trying to solve the problems through rhetoric. We will follow the movement historically through its triumphs and its problems. Zapatista and EZLN (Army of National Liberation) are used interchangeably. Also, Indians and indigenous are used interchangeably depending upon the source of information. Since many different Indian groups throughout the country have been involved in the struggles, most of the literature does not differentiate by individual groups, but uses the terms Indian or indigenous.

2.1.1 The Beginning of the Movement

The Maya Indians capturing municipalities in Chiapas on January 1, 1994, and the Zapatista Army of National Liberation (EZLN) are examples of how the Indians felt disenfranchised from the rest of the Mexican nation. The Zapatistas were able to bring a number of Indian tribes together due to common practices they all saw as discriminatory. The rebels wanted to modify three regulations: the changes in agrarian reform in Article 27 which ignored Indians, the declining economic status of the rural Indian communities, and the exclusion of the Indians from the political process (Camp, 2007). At this point, the Mayas were landless, and wanted recognition, rights, dignity, justice, and inclusion in the political processes of Mexico. They were disenfranchised from what they saw as their land. The Mayas' Zapatista movement was fueled by their lost identities and silenced political voice. The Zapatista movement was successful because it appealed to both the nonindigenous and the indigenous segments of society, and to the ideals of democracy and the Mesoamerican culture. Currently, more indigenous people live in Mexico City than in the rural areas as they once did (Levi, 2002). At the time of the rebellion, the Movement had 80,000 followers. The Las Canadas region, which was the center of the Zapatista Movement, consisted of 214,000 people in 780 settlements; 83% spoke indigenous languages, one-quarter were connected to electricity, and less than half had access to run-ning water (Jarque, 2000).

The government's Campaign Plan Chiapas 1994 objective was to reach and maintain peace, destroy the EZLN's combativeness, isolate them from the civilian population, and gain the support of the civilian population. The government offered lots of aid to displace the Zapatistas. At that time, the government was defining what it meant to be indigenous without letting the indigenous people define their identity (Stahler-Sholk, 2007). During this time period, the World Bank was also pushing for policies that would give the indigenous the capacity to develop on their own, free of the national government (CIEPAC, 2003).

A consequence of this uprising has lead to the Zapatistas trying to support the cultural diversity that exists among the indigenous peoples of Mexico. After all, the Zapatistas were an amalgamation of Indians with similar repressive political histories and religious practices who joined forces to confront the elite, governmental structures of Mexico. While there was respect for the differences between the Indian ethnic groups at the cultural level, this was not the case at the political level of the Mexican government. The government used the Indian lands to build hydroelectric dams, to build ranches, to do logging, and to do oil exploration without compensation or consideration of the Indians in the area. The Zapatistas social movement has been called the world's "first post-modern revolution" (see Carrigan, 2001; Nash, 1997). The Zapatistas were subordinate and responsible to the Indian people. Rather than overthrow the government or secede from the country, the Zapatistas wanted from transform the power and politics of Mexico. Because the majority of Mexicans agreed with them, they were successful in bringing political change to Mexico (Levi, 2002).

2.1.2 The "Others" Part of the Movement

In July 2005, the Zapatistas announced their Other Campaign. When the government talks broke down the Zapatistas went into a period of silence. In opposition to President Fox stating that the Zapatistas were a thing of the past, the campaign broke the strategic silence (Weissert, 2005). The Zapatistas enlarged their campaign to all "others" and stated that they would not have contact with the State party system, that autonomy could not be achieved through the Liberal State, and that the Zapatistas were part of a global war for indigenous life (EZLN, 2005).

The Zapatistas wrote about how the Indians were treated as "others" within Mexico's political structure. The writings brought out the plight of the Indians and how the government was challenging their identity, community, and democracy with its movement for modernity (Popke, 2004). In trying to break the modern obsession with legal codes and rights, the Zapatistas were trying to bring political realism to the situation (Marcos, 2001). The Zapatista movement looked at the long history of violence and exploitation of the indigenous/Indian population and looked for concrete changes, not just philosophical changes, in Mexico's political and legal infrastructure. The Zapatistas used discourse to challenge the ethical ideals of Mexico by using ethical subjectivity that transcended cultural differences and borders, and then they argued for political changes in the future (Popke, 2004). The main importance of the Zapatista and EZLN movement was that it transformed a regional struggle into a country struggle, which (some would argue) affected global civil society and the development of social and cultural agency, recognizing a different form of ethics and politics (Couch, 2001; Stahler-Sholk, 2001).

The Zapatistas took the concept of the Economic Man, who is only interested in wealth, and turned it upside down. Many people in the world, including the Zapatistas, are concerned with their cultural heritage, and are not willing to sell that heritage for more economic items (Esteva & Prakash, 1998). The Zapatistas have decided that "autonomy for them means the community arguing, discussing, planning, and deciding how we want to live, how we want to share the wealth" (Weinberg, 2000, p. 143). The Zapatistas did not want to submit to the governmental universalities that controlled the rest of the Mexican people (Subcomandante Marcos, 2003). While the liberal establishment is multiculturalist, the Zapatistas have allegiance to their way of life (Subcomandante Marcos, 1994). While liberal theorists would say that they promote human rights and multicultural tolerance, those who are affected have come to realize the theorists' actual agenda of political disempowerment (Speed, 2005). One person's universal rights are another person's prison (Deleuze & Guattari, 1994). Those who espouse the liberal establish-ment see others as good if the others accept the way of life, otherwise the others are seen as different (Badiou, 2002). Marcos asks two questions, "What continually makes something different? And what prevents that which is different from being allowed to differ?" (Evans, 2008, p. 516).

> We are "other" and different... we are fighting in order to continue being "other" and different... And what we are – far from wanting to impose its being in the "other" or different – seeks its own space, and, at the same time, a space of meeting... hat is why Power has its armies and police, to force those who are "other" and different to be the same and identical. But the "other" and different are not looking for everyone to be like they are... The "everyone doing his own thing" is both an affirmation of difference, and it is a respect for other difference. When we say we are fighting for respect for those who are also "other" and different, who are not like ourselves. (Subcomandante Marcos, 1999, August).

History has shown that the left wants to subsume minorities into their hegemonic designs – making everyone the same; and those who do not comply have been deemed problems of society. In the Americas, the Indian has always been seen as out of step with the general society and outside of progress (Hayden, 2002). The Zapatistas do not want to take power; rather, they want the power to listen to the people and govern accordingly. Currently, they do not see a government that serves the people. but a government that controls the people (Vodovnik, 2004). The Zapatistas do not view their ideas as eternal, nor are they trying to impose a certain way of life upon anyone. Instead, the movement aims toward defending a way of life, and making those in political power realize that there is no absolute truth in governing (Subcomandante Marcos, 2003).

2.1.3 The Masks' Meaning

The writings gave the Indians a face and made them ethical subjects who the Mexican Government had to consider. The masks they wore symbolized the anonymity of the Indian peoples and critiqued the Mexican nation. Part of the movement was to recover the face of the Indians as subjects and citizens. Their hope was that once they had a name, they would be given back their faces. They wanted the nation to acknowledge that it is not made up of equals but of others. The people in power, including armies and police, had the ability to force the "others" to be identical to the mainstream. The movement was asking for openness and inclusivity (Marcos, 2001).

In 1995, when a Subcomandante was unmasked, demonstrators took to the streets in support of the Zapatista Movement (Taussig, 1999) and the Zapatistas once more stated for what stated what they were fighting for. The EZLN was fighting for a new way of "being a political subject, a 'nation without nationality': 'dignity is that nation without nationality, that rainbow that is also a bridge, that murmur of the heart no matter what blood lives it, that rebel irreverence that mocks borders, customs and wars" (The Zapatistas, 1998, p. 13).

2.1.4 The Government Reaction

In December 1997, 45 Indians were assassinated when a peace and justice effort of the local Catholic Church took place. The victims included 1 baby, 14 children, and 21 women – four of whom were pregnant. The governor and Mexico's interior minister were forced to resign. Bishops have asked that peace talks mediated by the Bishop be resumed. Two of the bishops were also ambushed by paramilitary gunmen. Even one of the bishops who was sent to pacify opponents of the diocese's justice work was transformed and joined in on denouncing the human rights violations and the persecution of the Indians and the church (Chiapas, 1998).

Indian autonomy struggles were occurring in many areas of Mexico, despite the fact that the news headlines were focused on the Chiapas region. Many of the Indian groups were in fact the poorest and the most exploited people in Mexico.

When President Vincente Fox took office, he remarked that he would end the Zapatista conflict in 15 minutes. At that point in time, the struggle had been going on for 6 years. Fox ordered the military to withdraw, and congress took up the Congressional Chiapas Peace and Reconciliation Commission Bill (U.S. Department of State, 2001). However, the bill that was passed on April 28, 2001 was radically different and the movement felt betrayed. The bill eliminated Indian autonomy at the national level but granted it at the local level, and the national government still maintained control over natural resources. Also, the demilitarization was not complete (CIEPAC, 2001). Unfortunately, the reaction of the Zapatistas was to cease dialog with the Fox administration for the entire 6 years that Fox was in office (EZLN, 2001).

What came of this struggle? As a writer stated in December 2003, 10 years after the initial uprising, "the rebels had barely been heard from since the spring of 2001 when the Mexican Congress had mutilated the Indian Rights law for which the Indians had battled so doggedly...they insisted there would be no celebration that year to mark the rebellion. What was there to celebrate anyway?" (Ross, 2003, p. 12). But come January 1, 2004, they did gather 20,000 strong people from all five Zapatista regions. After the initial insurrection, the government and EZLN negotiated. A landmark agreement titled the San Andres Accords on Indian Rights and Culture gave the indigenous Indians control over local governance, bilingual education, Indian justice, natural resources, and collective agrarian policies; however, President Zedillo vetoed the agreement under the pretense that it would allow Mexico's Indians to secede from the nation (Ross, 2003). The Indians have spent 8 years battling to implement a law, yet their delegations have been denied such a law three times. Support has increased nationally; one result being that Mexico's self-reported Indian population has doubled from 10 to 20 million in the last 10 years because of mestizos taking pride in their Indian blood. Although it was not approved, many of the Indians adopted the Indian Rights law as their own (Ross, 2003).

2.1.5 The Achievements

The Zapatistas have made achievements in the last 10 years. They have developed an autonomous system that has 2,222 villages that have a population of near 100,000 Zapatistas (Ross, 2006). The communities have improved their local infrastructures, organized their political affairs, and started Good Government Councils to govern the municipalities and five regional caracoles (Ross, 2005). The Councils administer health, education, community justice, food, commerce, and information. The Councils have also refused to accept any Mexican State aid. The

Zapatistas saw this refusal as a weapon of resistance (Subcomandante Marcos, 1999, October). Although lacking government aid can be difficult, the Zapatistas do not want to sell out to the current political climate in Mexico. Instead, the Zapatistas want the climate to change to incorporate their people. The Zapatistas want respect, not a handout (Zapatista Commission, 2005). The Zapatistas have created reciprocal solidarities based on their mutual connections that invoke a "reconfiguration between the local, the national, and the global" (Olsen, 2004, p. 255). The Zapatistas are developing new ways of looking at Liberal providers and beneficiary global relations of power. In particular, they are pushing against conditions that are imposed and accepted by indigenous groups in order for those groups to be considered good citizens. They are using poverty conditions and indigenous ways of thinking, and projecting alternative methods for political and cultural expression (Warren & Jackson, 2002).

While there were challenges when many of the indigenous people left the EZLN, the remaining members realized the fruition of programs such as community schools, a health system, and production collectives (Barmeyer, 2008).

One of the Movement's successes was the government building more schools, allowing the Indians to teach their children in their native language, and allowing books that taught the history of the Indian people. Originally, the Mexican government felt it could only be nationally strong if all the people were united with a common set of values and feelings. This meant having a history book that was common to all. The Movement has helped the government realize that a nation can still have unity without everyone being culturally alike. The government now produces indigenous free textbooks in 56 indigenous languages; the government also produces national textbooks in Spanish focused on the national ideals. Many of the Movement's members received what they wanted – schools, textbooks in their language, their history being taught, and ways to participate in the economics and politics of Mexico. When many of the Indians began receiving government aid, they no longer needed the Zapatista Movement (Schmidt-Diaz de Leon, 2001).

2.1.6 The Challenges

Although the Zapatistas were unanimous within the first few years of the uprising, this changed with time. While in 1996 the Zapatistas were one, by 2000 there was political division among the core of EZLN's communities. At the same time, schools were operating again, and there were production collectives, an independent health system, and stronger cohesion among the remaining Zapatistas. Many of the people within the group split. While the EZLN was telling supporters to resist acceptance of the "alms" that the government was providing, some were happy with the ability to participate in the economic and social capital that the state provided. After the initial insurrection in 1994, one of the governmental "alms" included a better education system. This was a threat to the guerilla part of the movement, which at that time was gaining support across the globe. The Zapatistas were increasingly relying on external support from around the globe. The request by the EZLN was not well received in all indigenous communities. Many of the Indian people who had lived in the mountains during the insurrection felt that the EZLN had not kept its promises and left the organization. Hardships for the people included the suspension of school, the increase in prices of basic goods, and the lack of monthly PROCAMPO government monies. The indigenous people no longer saw a need to make additional sacrifices because they could not see a future in the struggle. Education was one of the areas that was important to the indigenous people. The state, of course, had more money to build educational alternatives than the Zapatista Movement did. Basically, the forms of capital that were available satisfied some of the Zapatista's original followers and did not satisfy others (Barmeyer, 2008).

One of the dividing issues was the exploitation of rare woods on communal lands. Many members wanted funds split with the EZLN command and helped the government get the rare trees they wanted. The government took advantage of the situation and provided a new school and gave them PROGRESA stipends, development aid, and the PROCAMPO monies again. When other families saw this, they too decided to leave the EZLN. In San Emiliano, this resulted in two-thirds of the village leaving the EZLN and becoming involved with the government (Barmeyer, 2008).

The remaining Zapatistas started their own schools, health system, and collectives. However, this education often consisted of only preschool, primary school, and lower secondary school. Many of the people who left the Movement did so because they did not feel the Zapatista Movement provided the necessities they needed, and the government had improved in what they were giving (Barmeyer, 2008). The state education system for the indigenous people was bilingual and aimed to include 164,696 indigenous 6–14-year olds. The goal of the state was to help the indigenous people become part of the contemporary Mexican nation economically, politically, socially, and culturally (Comité, 1997). Programs included in the schools were a breakfast project, preventive health care, and additional food. The state and the Zapatistas were in competition for the same individuals; however, the state had more money to work with (Jarque, 2000). While many of these government programs were not in the interests of the indigenous people, the indigenous people who broke away ignored the fact that the government was stripping their lands (Rus, 1994).

A major difference in the two education systems is in the area of history. The Zapatistas wrote their own history because the national history book was not accurate. While government schools prepared children to leave the village, the Zapatista schools enabled the children to stay in their villages and acquire knowledge to make them better farmers. However, the Zapatista schools did not have sufficient supplies, or teachers who would stay for extended periods of time (Barmeyer, 2008).

2.2 Mestizos All

By the middle of the twentieth century, the Mexican government realized that it needed to reach out to the Indian population. With the passage of Article 4 of the Federal Constitution, it was recognized that the "Mexican nation has a pluricultural composition, fundamentally sustained by the presence sustained by the presence of indigenous peoples" (Levi, 2002, p. 33). This happened before the Chiapas incident.

The Mexican government is calling all Mexicans mestizos. It is currently believed that more than 90% of the population is mestizo; that is, they are currently defined as a mixture of the indigenous Indians with the European, and/or African slaves (Historia y Civismo, 1982; Nolasco, 1988). Of course, there are supporters of a "cosmic race" in Mexico (Vasconcelos, 1925), and there are those who argue that there is no validity to the claim of a national mestizo culture or an ethnically dominant group (Knight, 1986). Because cultural integration and conflict between the multiple cultural layers of a country are constants in many nations, including Mexico, the concept of a national culture is always being redefined. While nations want an identity, what that identity should be is not always agreeable for all residents of the country. An identity has many times come at the expense of nondominant ethnic groups (Gutiérrez, 1998).

In Mexico, examples abound of literary texts that are written in native languages and discuss the values, traditions, and culture of indigenous people (King, 1991; Watanabe, 1995). These cultural and linguistic revivals show that the connection to ethnicity is still active in Mexico. Two items help to promote the continuation of indigenous languages: the limited access to education in the national language, and the ethnic self-interest of promoting the indigenous languages. Part of the problem is that the different indigenous groups are each a minority and are not in any way joined together in their endeavors to keep the indigenous cultures separate from the Mexican national culture. Another problem for particular indigenous groups is they are not domiciled in one country, but in as many as five different Latin American countries. This fact leaves many of the indigenous groups' people without a nation-state of their own (Gutiérrez, 1998).

2.3 Mestizo Problems

The mestizo unification movement helped to separate Mexico from Spain. Using cultural artifacts such as the national emblem of the Eagle with a snake in its talon sitting on a cactus, helped to unify the people and draw people of all ethnic backgrounds into one unified group. Using past ethnicity in developing nationalism is proposed by some researchers as a way to determine ethnic ties and to share an ethnic past (Armstrong, 1982; Smith, 1986). Other researchers feel that accepting elements of the past in the form of culture and language does not help to explain modern nationalism; they feel that internal cohesion and a standard language of communication through the educational system develop nationalism (Gellner, 1983). The mestizo story is definitely one of using the past to embrace a modern nationalism.

But does the mestizo story accurately portray the mestizo population? Is it true that the colonial mestizo population was produced through the intermixing of the Europeans, Indians, and Africans; or through immigration and assimilation? But are these intermarriages broader than just the three original groups? In the twentieth century, mestizo symbolized the desired features of what it meant to be Mexican, including speaking the Spanish language and adopting Western values such as urbanization and industrialization (Gutiérrez, 1995). Many educational movements since the 1920s were undertaken in the Indian communities with the idea of acculturating the Indians by making them more like the mainstream mestizos (Aguirre, 1979).

Currently, the Indians are campaigning through the bureaucracies for cultural rehabilitation and management of their own ethnic affairs (Gutiérrez, 1998). The minority Indians have gained some cultural strength because of their accessibility to the media, the reformulation of article 4 of the Mexican constitution that protects and recognizes the Indian people, the international efforts to protect the Indians, and the UNU's International Year for the World's Indigenous Peoples. The Indian communities in Mexico definitely do not see themselves as mestizos (Gutiérrez, 1998).

While mestizo has integrated the ethnic diversity that exists in Mexico, it has not successfully included the Indians in the integration. Instead, the mestizo movement has left the Indians feeling culturally and racially inferior, with feelings of having their culture appropriated (Gutiérrez, 1998). The struggle has valued the Indian population at points and devalued the Indian population at other points in history.

Currently, most Mexicans will identify two cultural groups (rather than racial groups) in Mexico: Mestizo and Indian. Mestizo means anyone who has adopted the Mexican Hispanic culture (the meaning has changed from the original meaning). Indians may choose to call themselves mestizo when they acknowledge having dominant Hispanic societal cultural values. An Indian is someone who identifies him or herself as an Indian, uses the indigenous language on a daily basis, is involved in Indian village communal affairs, participates in the religious ceremonies of the Indians, and lives in harmony with the environment rather than trying to control it. The problem is many non-Indians do not like using the term mestizo to identify themselves.

While the Indians live throughout Mexico, there are areas that are predominately indigenous, as shown in Fig. 20.1.

In 1990, 7.5% of the Mexican population (5.3 million people) spoke an indigenous language. The different states in Mexico have from less than 5% to a high of 44% of their population that speaks an indigenous language (Country Studies, 2008). In some areas of the country, where there are high concentrations of Indians, it is easier for them to separate culturally from the mainstream.

3 History of Struggle

Before the Zapatista's emergence, Mexico's 56 indigenous groups with forty different languages were virtually invisible to the outside world. It is not possible to discuss the Zapatista Movement without understanding the long history between the Indians and the government. Until the Zapatista Movement, the plight of the indigenous peoples of Mexico was not part of the national conscience.

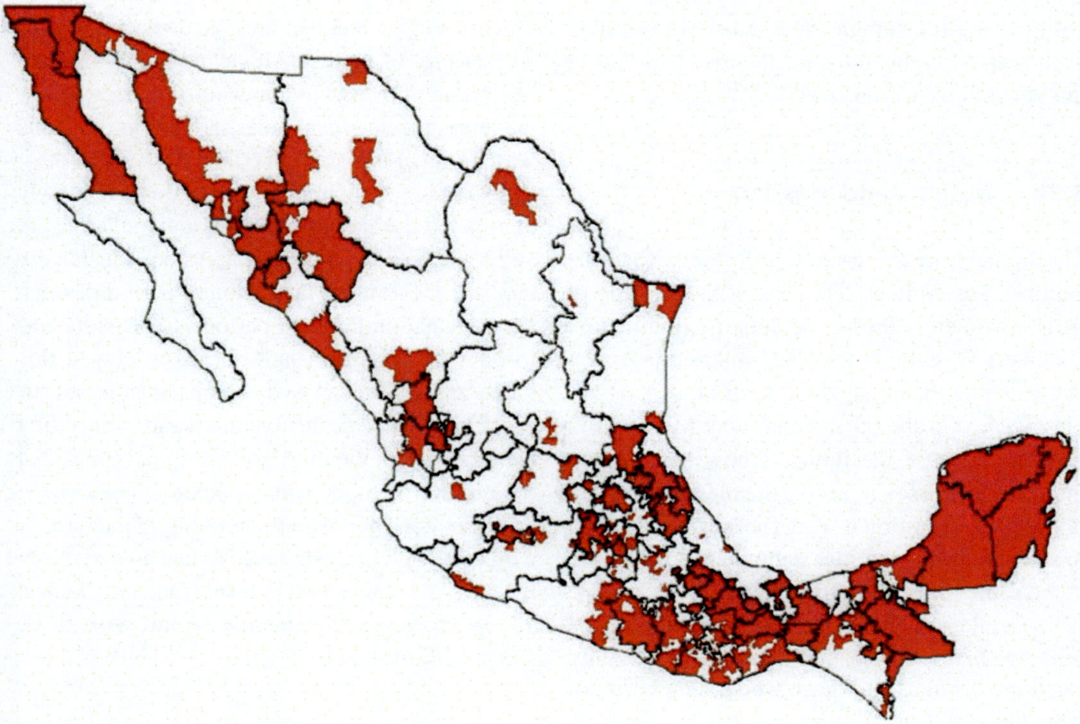

Fig. 20.1 Indigenous Indian regions in Mexico (2002)

3.1 Ethnicity

Ethnicity is defined as an ethnic quality or affiliation and includes language. The term "ethnic" refers to a community that shares physical and mental traits through common heredity and cultural tradition. Race is an anthropological term used to describe a group of people with distinct physical characteristics.

The history of Mexico is a history of many different Indian groups, African slaves, Castilians (Spanish), and of mestizos who emerged as a result of the mixing of various peoples. By 1650, Mexico had approximately 160,000 mestizos. The mestizos outnumbered the Spanish, survived better than the Indians, and bred faster than the Spanish (Fehrenbach, 1973). Mexican nationalism made its appearance as a political movement from 1810 to 1821, and then as a project to build nationalism in the nineteenth and twentieth centuries. The movements assumed all along that Indians should and wanted to be assimilated into the mainstream culture, and that the Indians would let this happen without objection (Friedlander, 1975). Research on Indian intellectuals found that the Indians rejected the shared ethnic and biological origin as included in the term mestizo, felt there is permanent conflict and tension between the Indians and the mestizos, and felt that their culture was being destroyed (Gutiérrez, 1998).

Because many of the initial Spaniards came without wives, they took mistresses or wives from the Indians. Many of the African slaves brought to Mexico to work in the mines were men, and they also took Indian women for their wives. While the Spaniards (peninsulares) and criollos (American-born Spaniards) always saw themselves as superior to everyone else, they were eventually displaced by the mestizos, or those of mixed blood. During the Mexican Revolution (1910–1920) the mestizos took political control from the Spaniards. Many Indian groups also fought alongside the mestizos during this revolution (Camp, 2007).

3.2 Indians and Mestizo

The Indians see the mestizo differently than the national government. They see it as the rape of their women during colonial domination (Lafaye,1985); this is why the Indians reject mestizo as being the amalgamation of all of the peoples of Mexico and the nationality of Mexicans in general. Because the Indians know their origin, they have no reason to accept the mestizo national origins. The question is, can a nation survive with localized ethnic identities and a national identity at the same time (Gutiérrez, 1998)?

It is interesting that most Mexicans will not refer to themselves as mestizo, except for educated intellectuals and those who are members of large cities. The term mestizo has taken on many meanings over the 400 years of its existence. Early on, mestizos were considered illegitimate, but by the 1792 census, that was no longer possible, because 90% of the mestizos were married in the church. At this time, the distinction between creole and mestizos also became indistinguishable. In Oaxaca, the mestizos were incorporated into the urban stratification and status system of the area by the white elites. By the close of the eighteenth century, economics and ethnicity were used to determine rank within the society. However, psychologically, the white elite had trouble giving up ethnicity as a social marker (Chance, 1979).

By the beginning of the nineteenth century, mestizo and creole were merged into one group, mestizo. During the seventeenth to the nineteenth centuries, mestizos had a very flexible social identity, rather than a shared cultural background – they were not a homogeneous ethnic group. Also, many mestizos who were economically successful or made "good" marriages were no longer considered mestizos. The Revolution of 1910 is seen by some as the war to legitimize the mestizos who had strong feelings for nationalism. The ideology of the Revolution of "Power to the People" brought the mestizos to the center of the process. Others feel that mestizo does not work as a descriptor of modern Mexican society until the beginning of the twentieth century. In fact, today, the terms mexicano and mestizo are synonymous with political nationalism (Chance, 1979).

Census classifications in Mexico have slowly eliminated the classes of whites and mulattoes. In 1822, the racial classification system was legally abolished. From the late colonial period through the early nation-building periods, to be white was to have power, and many mestizos played this game and did not classify themselves as mestizos. The mestizo of the twentieth and twenty-first centuries is not the mestizo of colonial times, but the culture of modern day Mexico. The current Mexican does not want to be Indian, Spaniard, or a mixture, and the term mestizo has no direct ethnic or racial connection to history today (Chance, 1979). However, the Indians do not wish to be considered mestizo.

3.3 Indian Languages

There are currently 56 different Indian groups which make up 28.2% of the towns in Mexico (Instituto Nacional Indigenista, 1993). The language identifies the indigenous group as shown in Fig. 20.2. These are the groups of people who are being labeled as Indian or indigenous.

Part of the problem is that there are many independent groups with different languages. Mexican history included different Indian groups fighting each other before the Spaniards took control of Mexico. The Indian groups never had a strong coalition with each other, but were acting independently for the most part until the Zapatista Movement.

3.4 Ethnicity

Since the education that the Indian children received in school (before the Zapatista Movement) stated they were mestizo, this makes it difficult for Indians, as individual pueblos or as a whole, to pass their culture and history to the next generation.

Classification of Indigenous Languages of Mexico					
Family	**Groups**			**Language**	**Territory**
Uto-Aztecan languages This is the family of Amerindian languages most prevalent in Mexican territory. It is that which has the largest number of speakers.	**Southern Uto-Aztecan**	**Tepimano**		Papago	Sonora
				Pima	Sonora, Chihuahua
				Tepehuano	Chihuahua Durango
				Tepocano **(†)**	Jalisco
		Taracahitan	**Tarahumarano**	Tarahumara	Chihuahua
				Guarijío	Sierra Madre Occidental
			Cahita	Yaqui	Sonora
				May	Sonora Sinaloa
			Opata	Opata **(†)**	Sonora
				Eudeve **(†)**	Sonora
		Corachol-	Corachol	Cora	Nayarit

Fig. 20.2 Languages of Mexico, 2009

Ethnic Indian knowledge was not being taught by schools before the Zapatista Movement; instead, the idea of being part of the mestizo culture was being taught to the students at school. Thus, the Indians felt they were being made inferior to the mestizos and that they were being discriminated against and excluded from the nation as a whole, which was an injustice to the Indians (Gutiérrez, 1998). The Indians in one study agreed that "when Indian knowledge is usurped, uprooted from its original context, and transformed into an item of consumerism acceptable for the non-Indian society that is what is called mestizo. According to this opinion, the Indian per se is not accepted in the social fabric, and the manifestation of indigenous cultural contributions, without the dominant participation of a mestizo's point of view, is discouraged" (p. 297).

A study of the Mayo Indians showed that integration of Mayo Indians and the mestizo societies does not exist. Social integration means that informational exchanges take place at all societal levels, and the subordinate group (Mayo Indians) will accept innovation because they are respected. The traditional Mayo culture is more valuable to the Mayo people than the innovations that the mestizos have to offer. On the individual level, Mayos who have integrated with the mestizos, particularly in terms of religious traditions, are held in low esteem. While a few of the Mayo choose the way of the mestizos, the larger group continues as strong traditionalists of the Mayo way of life, and prefer to maintain their ethnic identity as Mayos and their national identity as Mexicans (Crumrine & Crumrine, 1969). When any of the Indians choose assimilation with

		Aztecan		Huichol	Nayarit
				Pochutec (†)	Oaxaca
			Nahuatl	Nahuatl	Valley of Mexico, Sierra Madre Oriental, Veracruz
Hokan Although this family is still disputed by many linguists, it includes numerous languages spoken in the arid zones of Mexico and the United States. Some theories include the language Seri But in the most recent analysis this language appears as a language isolate. Most of the Hokan languages are extinct and others are about to disappear.	Yuman-Cochimies	**Yuman**		Paipai	Baja Peninsula
				Cocopah	
				Cochimí (Mti'pai)	
				Kumiai	
				Nak'ipa (†)	
				'Ipa huim (†)	
				Kiliwa	
		Cochimies		Cochimí (†)	
				Ignacieño (†)	
				Borjeño (†)	
	Tequistlatecan			Chontal Oaxaca	Oaxaca
				Tequistlatec (†)	
Languages of southern Baja California This is a set of languages spoken in southern Baja California peninsula. Currently they are all extinct. The scant documentation on the languages makes for doubtful classification. It has even questioned the possibility that all these languages have been part of the same family. Some linguists suggest that it may have had some tenuous link to the Cochimí, and therefore form part of the Hokan family.				Guaycura (†)	Baja California Sur
				Laimonas (†)	
				Aripo (†)	
				Huichití (†)	
				Cadégomeño (†)	

Fig. 20.2 (continued)

				Didiu **(†)**	
				Pericúes **(†)**	
				Islander **(†)**	
				Monguí **(†)**	
Languages Algicides The only language spoken in Mexico algicide is the Kickapoo. The Kickapoo tribe settled in Coahuila in the nineteenth century, due to the invasion of their original territory (Oklahoma) By other tribes and whites.	Algonquian languages	**Hostels**		Kickapoo	Coahuila
Languages Manguean	**Western Otomanguean**	**Oto-Pame-chinantecano**	Oto-Pame	Otomi	Central Mexico
				Mazahua	
				Matlatzinca	State of Mexico
				Tlahuica	
				Pame	
				Jonaz	Guanajuato, San Luis Potosi
			Chinantecano	Chinanteco	Oaxaca and Veracruz
		Tlapaneco - mangueano	**Tlapaneco**	Tlapaneco	Guerrero
			Mangueano	Chiapas **(†)**	Chiapas
	Eastern Otomanguean	**Popoloca-Zapotecan**	**Popolocan**	Mazatec	Oaxaca and Veracruz
				Ixcatec	Oaxaca
				Chocho	Oaxaca
				Popoloca	Puebla
			Zapotecan	Rug	Oaxaca

Fig. 20.2 (continued)

				Chatino	Oaxaca
				Papabuco	Oaxaca
				Soltec	Oaxaca
			Amuzgo	Amuzgo	Oaxaca and Guerrero
		Amuzgo - mixtecano		Mixteco	Sierra Mixteca
			Mixtecano	Cuicateco	Cañada Cuicatlan
				Marqui	Oaxaca
		Mixe de Oaxaca		Variety mixes of the Sierra de Juarez	Sierra de Juarez (Oaxaca)
	Mixeano			Popoluca Sayula	Veracruz
		Gulf Mixe		Popoluca Oluta	Veracruz
Mixe-Zoquean The first languages, such as Orozco y Berra, suggested an affinity between Mixe-Manguean Zoquean and languages. However, it has been shown to form an independent family. It is also proposed that some ancestor of this family must have been the language spoken by the Olmec.				Popoluca Texistepec	Veracruz
		Gulf Zoque		Popoluca Soteapan	Veracruz
	Zoquean	Zoque Chimalapas		San Miguel Zoque Chimalapa St. Mary Zoque Chimalapa	The Chimalapas (Oaxaca)
		Zoque de Chiapas		Variety Zoque of Chiapas	West of Chiapas
Totonac-Tepehuas Languages	Totonacan			Totonac Tepehua	Sierra Madre Oriental (Veracruz and Puebla)
Mayan languages	Huasteco			Huasteco	La Huasteca

Fig. 20.2 (continued)

Mayan languages (or mayances) are spoken in southern Mexico and northern Central America. Isolated from this nucleus is the Huasteca language, spoken in northern Veracruz and eastern San Luis Potosi. Some proposals have included in Mayan languages Macro-Penutian group. In other scenarios have suggested that there might be some relationship between families Totonacan, Mixe-Zoquean and Mayan, but the proposal has not gained much traction. Many of the Mayan languages spoken in Mexico have a small number of speakers. This is because several of these languages belong to groups of Guatemalans who fled to Mexico during the civil war. They are currently considered as national languages, like other indigenous languages.				Chicomulteco **(†)**	
	Yucatecan	**Yucatan - Lacandon**		Yucatec Maya	Yucatan
				Lacandon	Chiapas
	Western Mayense	**Ch'olan - Tzeltalan**	**Ch'olan**	Chol	Chiapas
				Chontal de Tabasco	Tabasco
			Tzeltalan	Tzeltal	
				Tzotzil	
		Q'anjobalan - Chuj	**Q'anjobalan**	Kanjobal	
				Jacalteco	Chiapas
				Motozintleco	
			Chujano	Chuj	
				Tojolabal	
	Eastern Mayan	**Quichean**	**Kekchi**	Kekchi	Chiapas
			Pokom - Quichean	Quiche	Chiapas and Guatemala
				Cakchiquel	Chiapas and Guatemala
		Mame	**Teco-Mame**	Mam	Chiapas
			Awakatek-Ixil	Awakatek	Chiapas and Veracruz
				Ixil	Chiapas, Quintana Roo and Campeche
Languages isolated An attempt to group these languages in larger families, but without success.				Purépecha	Michoacán

Fig. 20.2 (continued)

South American origins have been attributed unsuccessfully to the Purépecha and the Huave. Huave has also been linked with Penutian by Swadesh. Although there is very little information, attempts have been made to relate to the late Coahuilteco with Hokan and comecrudanas languages. The Seri has been included for a long time without hard evidence, the large hypothetical Hokan family. The Cuitlatec appears in some classifications as part of the Uto-Aztecan family. Del Pericue is so little known and so were their differences with the other languages of the peninsula of Baja California, which not even the seventeenth-century missionaries dared to establish relationships between this language and the rest of the peninsular. Currently it is proposed that Pericue due to be descendants of the earliest settlers of the region.	Huave	Oaxaca
	Cuitlatec (†)	Guerrero
	Coahuilteco (†)	Coahuila
	Seri	Sonora

Fig. 20.2 (continued)

mestizos, they tended to leave their Indianness behind them and begin to identify as mestizo. (Schryer, 1990).

In a study of the Paracho community in Mexico, when asked about ethnicity, the participants did not distinguish between each other by ethnicity per se, but by where they were born or where their parents were born. With few outsiders moving into the community, over 85% of the people were interrelated through marriage. They basically saw those individuals who lived in the country as Indians and those in the town as mestizo. Ethnicity was determined more by how much the person participated in the mestizo way of life or the Indian way of life (Kaplan, 1953).

3.5 Ethnicity and Religion in the Tierra Caliente Region

The ethnogeny of Mexico has varied across the country. In some areas of Mexico, the indigenous Indians were not as impinged upon by the Castilians as they were in other parts of the country. In the state of Guerrero, also known as the mid-Balsas River Depression of the Tierra Caliente, because the Indians were initially left alone by the Castilians, ethnogeny developed somewhat differently from the other areas of Mexico. Although they were ravaged by disease and their numbers declined, the Indians from Guerrero maintained their Indian culture and grew; however, they integrated outsiders into their way of life (Fisher, 2002). Therefore, it was not only the Spanish that integrated others to the Spanish way of life; the Indians also accepted outsiders and integrated them into the Indian way of life.

Indians initially welcomed Spaniards with food as a gesture of peace. Indian populations did suffer from new epidemics that killed a large number of Indians and many groups became almost extinct. By 1600, the Spanish colonial state systematically moved Indians who survived into communities so that the Catholic Church could instruct them in faith (Acuña, 1985). Many of the original Indian settlements were no longer occupied at this time. Because the number of Indians had declined, there was not sufficient labor for the Spanish in many areas of Mexico. In the Tierra Caliente area, the decline of the local Indians was not followed by repopulating of the region by the Spanish or Afromestizos as had happened in other coastal areas of Mexico. In many areas within Mexico, the emptying of Indians from the rural areas allowed for new Spanish ranches, farms, and plantations. Mines were worked by Indian and African slaves; however, African slaves were more expensive than Indian slaves because there were more Indians than Africans. Indians had to pay tributes to Spanish rulers, which normally took the form of providing food, clothing, and shelter for African slaves (Fisher, 2002).

While converting the Indians to Catholicism worked well in Mexico City and the port areas of Mexico, it was not as easy to convert Indians in the Tierra Caliente because of the inhospitable living conditions. Very few priests were sent into the area, and they were not very effective at converting the Indians in this loaction (Fisher, 2002). As one account states about the Tierra Caliente,

> because the land is the worst that New Spain has, for it is uneven, very hot, full of mosquitoes and evil insects, where the Devil does not find himself uncomfortable, but rather better off, because with the poor qualities of the place he lived more at his ease being adored and respected by those miserable Indians there, who by their disgrace, lived content in such bad lands, and serving a lord so inhumane as the devil (Fisher, 2002, 124).

Even though the friars wee ordered to stay by the Spanish government, those who remained were few compared to the number of Indians they were to convert. So the Indians in the Tierra Caliente were not converted to the degree that other Indian villages in Mexico were. The people held on to their way of life in spite of the Spanish government. It would not be until the eighteenth century that the Spanish again had an interest in the Tierra Caliente for land on which to raise livestock and plant agricultural crops. So for almost 100 years (late sixteenth to the eighteenth centuries), the Tierra Caliente and the Indians were not bothered by the Spanish or their culture. However, Indian society across Mexico including the Tierra Caliente had been changed due to disease and population reduction, sporadic interference by the Spanish colonial rule, and demand for labor for the area mines. Thus, the Tierra Caliente was spared from the land tenure and commercial agriculture development that happened in central Mexico. The Indians in general had very little interaction with the Spanish beyond the parish priest and local crown magistrate. The the situation of the Indians had changed from the fighting between two hereditarily elite Indian groups, to a mining operation with a smaller population and an overthrow of the Indian group's elite members. This time of isolation after mining allowed Indians to make changes. The demographic crisis impacted their survival since there were no elderly Indians. This led to an abrupt break with their social and cultural past and had an impact on their redevelopment as a community (Fisher, 2002).

However, when priests were able to convert Indians, there were problems. The elite Indians had practiced polygamy and drinking. Priests instructed them that they could not have multiple wives and a society developed that included adultery, incest, spells, and drunkenness (Acuña, 1985). An Indian Catholicism developed around the village hospital, brotherhood groups, patron saints, and religious holidays. As there were not many priests, the lay community enacted the Catholic religion with an Indian identity. The priests who were there had to learn native languages in order to administer to their congregations as the Indians chose not to learn Spanish (Fisher, 2002).

Indigenous Indians had a tradition of incorporating outside elements into their religious worship, particularly if it was seen as stronger than their own religion. Given that Indians were a conquered people, they might have seen strength in their conqueror's religion. However, Indians were not ready to accept either only one god or the religious bans imposed by the friars. They had a need for sacrifices both as a nourishment for the gods and as a transformation of human flesh to maintain balance. Indians saw sacrifice as a way of protecting the community at large from suffering. When the sacrifices were discontinued and there was in fact an increase in suffering and mortality of Indians, it was difficult for the indigenous to accept Christianity as the only religion. Friars tying sacrifices to devil worship was confusing for Indians as well. Since sacrifice was good, how could the devil be evil? The devil was simply another god that had to be appeased. Friars would also actually encourage the Indians when they identified Christian saints with Indian gods. Examples of this are the Virgins of Guadalupe and Ocotlán on the sites of the goddesses Tonantzin and Xochiquetzalli. Indian religions and Christianity became intertwined rather than mutually exclusive alternatives (Cervantes, 1994).

In the beginning, the Church controlled not only the ecclesiastical matters but also the social and educational life of the pueblos. During the eighteenth and nineteenth centuries, there were many disagreements between the secular and nonsecular priests over the inclusion of native religious practices into Catholic practices. Many of the liberal priests at the time had been educated and influenced by the revolutionary writings of France. More than 90 priests participated as leaders of the revolution. In 1857, the laws of Reform nationalized the Church's property and adopted civil registration of births, marriages, adoptions, and basic suppression of religion in general. There was complete separation of church and state, and Catholicism was no longer the official religion of Mexico. The revolution of 1910–1918 included many anticlericals. During this time period, many churches and images were destroyed and priests were killed. Although the Catholic Church declined, most Mexicans including Indians remained Catholics. In 1992, the articles in the Constitution dealing with the restrictions of the Church were changed and diplomatic relations with the Vatican were re-established (Torres, 2000).

Religious difficulties ranged from the relations between Indians and the Catholic priests, to the Mexican Catholic clergy schism from Rome, to the 1992 law reinstating religion in Mexico. Many churches in the 1920s were considered radical because they were hostile toward the fact that churches could not own land, that there were sacramental taxes, and that they were being forced to give the liturgy in Latin. Many of the clergy felt this threatened the church in Mexico both spiritually and economically. The Mexican Catholic Church during the 1920s had an antagonistic relationship with Rome because of having accepted pagan rites into many of the church's practices. Church schisms happened with the agrarian revolution. Many revolutionary Catholics gave up their confessional identity, and Catholic intransigents were outcasts from the political process. In many areas of Mexico, Catholicism and politics mixed with the revolution. Many Roman churches suspended public worship, and the schismatics simply came in and occupied these empty churches in order to support the peasants, many of whom were Indians. When there was a critical mass of villagers and former priests, they were powerful enough to continue their own style of worship. Some of these congregations exist today. The religious revolution began when the Roman Catholics violently attacked the schism churches. The more schism churches were suppressed and attacked, the more the followers felt they were righteous (Butler, 2009).

3.6 Political Struggles

The last half of the seventeenth century saw strife between village nobles and their subjects. The commoners were not happy with what they saw as inequality. Many village leaders were exiled from their communities and had to seek protection from the Spanish. These leaders were seen by commoners as corrupt tyrants (Acuña, 1985). The leaders had populations that were decreasing due to disease and to people leaving the community to escape having to pay tributes and work in the mines.

In sparsely populated areas, it was not unusual for Indians and creoles (African and Spanish) to have a higher population than the Spanish. The main colonial economic and political structures also tended to integrate or marginalize these less populated areas over time. Contact with outsiders varied greatly for these regions of Mexico (Fisher, 2002).

As Borah (1954, p. 342) has shown in his research, the term "indio" (Indian) lost its original cultural and racial meanings, and took on an economic meaning of "the most poverty-stricken and retarded dwellers of the countryside [rural areas]." While outside groups may have changed the meaning of Indian, Indians themselves had not changed their sense of who was Indian

The period of 1700–1750 was a period of reintegration with the Spanish colony after having been left alone for a long time. The eighteenth century saw unchecked growth of both the Indian and the non-Indian population. Births were outnumbering deaths. All ethnic groups grew during the first half of the eighteenth century. While Indians' growth rate was very good proportionally, increases in the Spanish, mestizo, and mulatto groups were even higher. The mulatto population would continue to grow, shrinking the percentage of Indians in the Tierra Caliente. While Indians continued their basic subsistence culture, the non-natives were expanding the commercial economy of the area (Fisher, 2002). During this time, the mining industry was reestablished and then discontinued because of a lack of slaves and the difficulty of getting ore out of the area. The mining was done by all of the ethnic groups – mestizos, Indians, and Afromestizos.—hence, there was ethnic mingling between the groups. When the industry died, many of the workers reverted to a subsistence lifestyle in the Indian villages, some worked on cattle ranches, and some became farmers. The farmers gradually developed husbandry that included livestock. During the eighteenth century, the number of Indian families identified in the census decreased and in some communities, the number of nonnative Indians surpassed the number of Indians living in the community (Fisher, 2002).

Depending upon the features a person had, there was some racial passing. The ethnicity of someone was more important than his or her perceived race. Generally, the strategy was to move upward in the social strata; however, there was also movement into the Euromestizo group and the Indian society (Beltrán, 1989). Studies differ as to what was actually happening during the sixteenth and seventeenth centuries. One study emphasized social networks as defining the social/racial identities (Cope, 1994). Another study of Afro-Mexican society says that a folk culture emerged at this time period that united the mixed ethnicity people except for the AfroMexican ethnic group (Bennett, 1993). Ethnicity evolved differently in the urban areas and in the country. Country lifestyle did not afford the opportunity for occupational and class strata that grew in the urban areas. While place of residence and occupation were used by the colonial officials for categorizing individuals, individuals in the rural areas did not pay attention to such categorizations. Residents of indigenous communities were generally classified as Indians, but permanent hacienda workers would be classified as mestizos. Therefore, where one lived determined the standards of ethnic ascription rather than actual race (Jackson, 1999). Many indigenous groups and country areas were alternately integrated and marginalized from the colonial economic and political networks. So the Indians' contact with outsiders fluctuated from migration into their areas, to periods of neglect from the colonial power structure. If these patterns are charted onto the decline and recovery of the Indian population, a cross-temporal comparison of Indian attitudes toward outsiders can show the impact of outside concepts on Indian identity (Fisher, 2002).

During the 1700 s, the Indians integrated outsiders into their community, developed an Indian "folk" Catholicism, and maintained the Indian languages. Although many of the Indian languages did disappear by the 1680 s, and it became more difficult to differentiate the people as direct descendants of particular Indian groups, people still considered themselves Indian. Some of the groups probably died out entirely and others were assimilated into one of the stronger dominant groups at the time. Some of the communities that were reduced to a few families were not reconstituted until the eighteenth century as separate Indian groups (Fisher, 2002). In a 1780's census, the Indians were by far the majority of the population in the Tierra Caliente, and both mestizos and Afromestizos were double the size of the Spanish population. In the census data, 75% of the Afromestizos were identified as mulattos rather than negros, and only four people were identified as slaves. At this time, only 18 Indians out of 2,288 did not reside in Indian communities. This means that the mines, cattle haciendas, and ranchos were non-Indian settlements. Two-thirds of the mulattos, negros, and mestizos lived on the cattle haciendas or mining camps. The cattle haciendas and ranchos were where people of different ethnic backgrounds merged together to work; the Indians during this period continued to live in the Indian pueblos. A small number of the Spanish population resided in the pueblos with mestizos and lived culturally as Spanish. The number of Afromestizos who resided in the pueblos with the Indians was higher than the other two groups. Of the Africans, 45 lived in haciendas and mines, and 152 of 163 mulattos lived in the Indian pueblos. Also important at this time is that of the 23 Indian communities identified, 16 contained a completely Indian population. At the same period of time, the cabeceras (towns) of the Spanish were four settlements that were homogenous and four settlements that were heterogeneous (Fisher, 2002).

During the eighteenth century, Indians of the Tierra Caliente experienced painful integration into the larger Spanish colony. While Indians in the middle of the country had more contact with the Spanish, Indians in the Tierra Caliente and other areas of Mexico had only sporadic contact; this allowed them to keep many of their cultural practices. The main reasons for the integration were economic changes in the Tierra Caliente, especially in the areas of mining, ranching, and farming. Other reasons were changes made by the Spanish government during the last part of the eighteenth century regarding Indian governments and resource allocations to the Indians. Many of the government's rules were not consistent with the Indians' values and economic practices. Indians defined themselves through interactions within their pueblo, with other Indian villages, local Spanish elite and poorer Spanish, and through the genealogical lineage. The interactions that were important to the Indians as far as the ethnicity was concerned, were interactions within their hierarchy and the Spanish elite. The social conflict caused ethnic resurgence in the Indians' view of their ethnicity. As the conflict progressed, Indians began to differentiate an outsider from a community member, and to allow less porosity of ethnic boundaries. Some of the stressors were peasant communities wanting village land and factional fighting within the pueblos. Often the factional fighting was done with outside assistance (Fisher, 2002).

In1857, the law framed by liberals as the Ley Lerdo, divested the Catholic Church of its landholdings and made it impossible for indigenous communities to hold land communally. The Mexican Revolution of 1910–1920 was a direct result of this law. The laws that prevailed from the revolution did not recognize indigenous communities. In fact, constitutional designers thought that the indigenous languages and customs would disappear. The government also passed laws prohibiting religious or racebased parties. President Cardenas organized Regional Indigenous Congresses and created a Department of Indigenous Affairs and the First Inter-American Indigenous Congress at Patzcuaro in 1940. However, even with these organizations, the indigenous movement had little representation in government. Then in the 1970s, there were state funds available and indigenous groups came to the forefront as the First Indigenous Congress of Chiapas in 1974, organized by Bishop Samuel Ruiz. This resulted in the formation of a new organization called the National Coordinator for Indigenous Peoples; however, when they began to make demands, they were pushed away. However, at this point, the indigenous groups had formed an allegiance that was independent of the National Peasant Confederation, leading to Indians acting more with one voice than as individual tribes (Foley, 1997).

Being Indian in eighteenth century Mexico was being attached to a pueblo from which the Mexican government required tribute to be paid, and allowed for exclusion from the Inquisition, and the right to 600 rods of land. Outsiders, of course, used legal mechanisms to obtain land. Indians used corporate landownership, mythic descent, and colonial legal precedent as arguments to retain their land; however, they had no legal title (Gibson, 1964). But given that many Indian groups had disappeared and others had joined together in order to survive, proving continual occupation of a given piece of land was difficult (Amith, 2000).

During the eighteenth century, Indians were attempting to reconstruct what it meant to be Indian. They attempted to do this by reconstructing their local past, by using reciprocity and mutual obligation, kinship, religious faith, land claims, and village identity. Spanish law recognized Indian land ownership; however, it viewed lands that the Indians did not use or occupy as reverting to the Crown of Spain (Amith, 2000). The Spanish Crown promulgated land ownership and the titling of land. However, this meant that land that had been used by many neighboring communities as free range was no longer open, and this set the stage for future conflict among groups of owners. These fights destroyed good infrastructure, since the victors destroyed existing structures and built new ones as a symbol of rejection of the titling of lands. Border battles continued for over 75 years. The different castas (family groups) that lived along the borders and that were neither Indian nor Spanish, were often caught in the fights (Fisher, 2002).

When the colonial era ended, Indian settlements (pueblos) were separated from towns (cabeceras) and were recognized as separate entities. This helped to increase the Indian corporate consciousness. Many times separation of the pueblos from their cabeceras was not easy because Spanish elites needed tax money and services from the subjects of the pueblos. While this was particularly true for the middle of Mexico, it was less so in the Tierra Caliente because few Indian pueblos survived disease and the religious campaigns of the early colonial period. Communities differed in their desire to separate or remain united depending on how the paternal and filial duties were carried out. Beyond legal arguments of living on the land and community relationships, arguments were made based on kinship and descent from Indians of the areas. Many of the Indians in the late eighteenth century were not pure, because the Indians had incorporated outsiders into the community as a means of rebuilding the villages after disease had ravaged their villages. Since many Indian pueblos had been abandoned for a period and then resettled, the role of continuous habitation would come up, followed by the problem of ancestry because of the intermarriage of Indians and outsiders. Corporate kinship, and how local people of different ethnic backgrounds understood their relationships, were important in terms of who were the descendants in the new barrio. It was also important because the two communities had mutual responsibilities such as the church (Fisher, 2002).

Of course, over the course of all the legal battles, decisions favored the Spanish elite and not the Indians. Besides buying land from the Crown, the elite would also negotiate to rent village lands from Indians. Problems, of course, developed as the Indian community grew and needed the lands for cultivation and no longer wanted to rent lands to the Spanish elite (Gibson, 1964). It was not a cordial time. Hostility was growing between the ethnic groups, as illustrated by the following note posted in Tlamatlan in 1777 (Taylor, 1979, p. 123):

> The monkey, even dressed in silk, is still a monkey. Whoever speaks of Indians speaks of shit because the Indian is like the monkey. It is as simple as that, because the Indian, like the monkey, utters a thousand stupidities which have neither beginning nor end. This is the truth and no lie. They are also very malicious and devilish.

The Indians also used such rhetoric to advance in the land game: "the alcalde mayor living in the secure confidence that he will maintain the absolute power to enslave the Indians, due to the distance between this court [in Mexico City] and that cabecera..." (Amith, 2000, p. 359). The last part of the eighteenth century saw a web of economic and political alliances that pitted Indians against the Spanish elite. Corrupt local officials often circumvented the authority of the distant and benevolent Crown and Church. The Bourbon state, in exerting control over village resources, exacerbated the problem between the Indians and outsiders. This contributed to the emergence of the Indian identity in the struggle for village resources (Fisher, 2002).

Bourbon colonial officials moved to align Indian fiscal practices with fiscal interests of the state. The result was that during the last two decades of the colonial period, the Indians' corporate resources were taken by outsiders. Although Indians protested by emphasizing their collective rights as Indians, they were not successful in defending their pueblos from non-Indian society. What the Bourbons wanted to alter was the Indian pueblo's treasuries, lay brotherhoods, and landholdings (Fisher, 2002). The Spanish Monarchy's interest emerged because of serious economic and international problems in Spain. The Bourbons replaced the colonial consensus that had existed, and the regal authority of the Catholic Church (Farriss, 1968). First, the Bourbons were to increase the bullion and commodities to Spain; and second, bolster the royal control by reducing the Mexican Church's powers and increasing tax revenues through better tax-collecting methods. The Bourbon officials transferred traditional church roles to secular officials, resulting in church–state conflict. The main issue was the jurisdiction of the confradias (lay brotherhoods) and their assets, which were a source of income to the Church (Lynch, 1989; Taylor 1996). This change was particularly difficult for the Indian pueblos. To the Indians, there were no differences between sanctioned and constituted confradias, and the informal organizations. For the Indians, the community and the confradia were indistinguishable (Brading, 1994). The change was to control spending on fiestas associated with the church, so that there would be more monies available for secular activities. Since Indians had been in charge of these fiestas, this was a radical change in the religious process (Taylor, 1996). Farriss (1968) calls this period the "second conquest" of the Indian village society. The end of the eighteenth century brought about a loss of autonomy for the Indians and began direct colonial rule of the pueblos. At the beginning of the nineteenth century, the census shows only three groups: Spanish, Indians, and mulattos. The mestizos and Africans were probably then put in the mulatto category (Fisher, 2002).

Currently in Mexico, there is a movement to embrace a theory put forth by José Vascolncelos in 1925 that ethnicities are becoming one in Mexico, and that the mestizos will actually be a stronger race due to the mixture of races within mestizos. Politically in Mexico, the idea of everyone being a mestizo is being put forward to attenuate the tension that has existed in the past between the ethnicities in Mexico.

4 Causes

Ethnic ascription, whether of self-origin or imposed from outside, can make a community feel stronger ties to their ethnic roots, or can make them want to change and join what they consider the ethnic base in power. The strength of ethnic ascription is determined both by what the community feels and how the outsiders classify the community in question. In the present case, both the Indians and the Mexican government must recognize the identity and ethnicity of the group if it is to survive as it has historically developed (Paine, 2000). Ethnic boundaries are a Western idea growing out of land ownership, of which early indigenous people did not partake in or understand (Barth, 2000). How a community accepts or rejects changes forced upon it by an outside group keeps a society fragmented, or helps to assimilate the community into the larger society. A society can be marginalized and still hold on to its own rituals. Some ethnic communities are better able to hold on to their rituals than others (Cohen, 1985).

During the Mexican Revolution, many Indians fought with the revolutionaries. After the war, many of the ideals of the Indians were reinstituted. One was the distrust of the church. The church was no longer allowed to be involved in primary education, to own property beyond church buildings, or to be involved in political actions; neither was the clergy allowed to criticize the Mexican government. Second, the revolution changed the idea of the land, by redistributing the land using the Indian communal ownership model. People had a right to use of the land without personal ownership of the land (Camp, 2007).

In some areas of Mexico, communal lands were surveyed and divided among the Indian heads of households, each receiving 16 hectares of land; however, the government also legalized lands that were owned by the mestizo ranchers and wealthy Indians. Unfortunately, many Indians who were poor sold their titles. It is interesting that many of these Indians were allowed to continue to use the land for nominal rent. However, some Indians kept their titles in trust collectively to maintain the communal land arrangement (Schryer, 1990).

Indian villages were having their own class struggles between the wealthier Indians and the poorer Indians, as well as struggles with Spanishspeaking landlords. Although prosperous Indians saw themselves as authentic Indians, indigenous groups in villages did not always see them that way. Indian self-identity emerged (Schryer, 1990) during the colonial period.

After the Mexican Revolution (1910–1920), the study of the indigenous Indians became very important in Mexico. However, the studies were based particularly on the Aztec past, rather than on other indigenous groups, and emphasized mestizo descendancy for all modern Mexicans. In the end, it further marginalized the contemporary Indian groups and descendants from African slaves who did not choose to live within the mainstream of Mexican society (Frye, 1996; Gutiérrez, 1999). Borah (1954) claimed that there were no indigenous Indian populations in Mexico and that Mexico was dominated by the "new mestizo colonial culture" beginning in the mideighteenth century. Barth (2000) disagreed with this and has taken the stance that biology and cultural differences without allowing for cultural change and adaptation within a group, cannot erase a distinct identity. One has to look at how the indigenous group chose to incorporate changes. As Gibson (1964) and others have shown, many Indian groups survived in spite of the colonial institutions of the Spanish. Many indigenous societies, when pressured by the colonial political structure, were able to negotiate ethnic differences, and either resisted or accepted the differences. The existence of languages from colonial periods bears this out, as reported by many scholars (i.e., Haskett, 1991; Horn, 1997).

Although the Mexican Revolution brought about changes in the status system, it did not achieve change for the lower classes of peasants, many of whom where Indians. What it did do was mobilize the peasants and Indians. Violent conflicts often happened for over two-and-a-half decades following the revolution. Although all of these conflicts were more socially based, they were seen as ethnic conflicts (Gabbert, 2004).

In many areas of Mexico, Indian land was once again taken away during the 1980s and 1990s. Rossell de la Lama in Huejutla, is one example of restructuring the land tenure system so that former landowners could again control the land and the peasants. Land was expropriated for government needs. Many large landowners were paid; however, many small landowners were simply evicted from their land (Schryer, 1990).

The history of having their lands taken away, won back during the Mexican Revolution, and taken away again in the 1990s, has made the Indians, as a group, a people who have not been treated like the rest of the Mexicans.

5 Consequences

For generations Mexico has tried to use the modern ethical practice of finding a way everyone can agree to live, and then legislating code so that it is the law (Bauman & Tester, 2001). However, this causes differences to be "swept under the rug" and not discussed, resulting in passivity or rebellion. This creates the illusion of objectivity but obscures the social identity of groups (Popke, 2004). In Mexico, the consequences of calling everyone a mestizo follows the thinking processes of Levinas (2001, p. 106):

> The other is not other because he would have other attributes, or would have been born elsewhere or at another moment, or because he would be of a different race. The other is other because of me: unique and in some manner different than the individual belonging to a genus. It is not difference which makes alterity: alterity makes difference (p. 106).

In trying to resolve the differences, the Mexican political structure tried to make everyone the same; however, this did not address groups in society who wanted to be different from the whole. As Wingenbach (1999) says:

> The systematic and legal reduction of the other to the same for political purposes helps to create conditions under which the face of the other can be obscured, transcendence hidden, and ethics ignored. It reduces the human to the object, opening space for human beings to be treated as objects rather than as unique subjects (p. 223).

How Mexico has handled the Indian issues has been to make this a political and legal matter, rather than an relational, ethical responsibility issue. The consequences of the mestizo movement have been to disengender the Indians to the mestizo movement. Given that the mestizo movement has not gotten rid of ethnicities, the government has to find a way to work with the Indians as a separate cultural group.

Another interesting change is that many church members are now working with Indian groups and campaigning for Indian rights. Michel Chanteau, a French priest, was expelled from the country after 32 years of working with Indians. The church has also recruited Indians to become clergy, even allowing those who are married to join. Mexican churchmen have allowed Indian rituals to infiltrate the Catholic service, and many Mexican Catholics disapprove of the inclusion of Indian rituals (The right..., 1998).

While land usage was what started the Zapatista rebellion, the campaign became one of speaking about repression and international human rights. Since this happened at a time when the government was very concerned about how it appeared to the outside world, the Zapatista Movement was not repressed as much as such a movement would have been in the past. However, the fact that the Zapatista Movement gained significance with indigenous rights, the movement continued to fail when it came to bargaining for political and economic issues. Ethnic bargaining has limits in Mexico. While the Zapatistas won the right to have indigenous customs respected, they did not obtain indigenous autonomy, particularly land autonomy. In addition, many of the agreements did not reach beyond Chiapas. However, the movement did give other indigenous groups a basis to fight for their own autonomy (Foley, 1997).

6 Suggestions

The government must include Indians as a separate group of people who are Mexican due to their residency in the nation-state of Mexico, but also Indian in terms of their culture. Universal national identities generally do not work for indigenous people who live within a country. Multiculturalism as signified by the amendment to the 1991 Article 4 of the Mexican Constitution will help Mexico look past the mestizo movement to embrace the multiculturalism that exists in Mexico. However, while the Article gives indigenous peoples the right to develop their languages, customs, and specific forms of social organization, it does not give them the political rights given to all Mexican citizens. ILO 169 guarantees all Mexicans the right to self-determination. So while it appears that there are changes through Article 4 and ILO 169, in fact, politically, nothing has changed for the Indians (Levi, 2002).

In February 16, 1996, the San Andres Accords on Indigenous Rights and Culture did include political participation, land reform, and cultural autonomy, and it was predicated on indigenous rights. However, ratification of this legislation was held up due to the Accords' use of the words *pueblos indígenas* rather than *pueblo.* On November 30, 2000, the EZLN presented President Fox with conditions to continue the dialogue. Finally, in April 2001, the Accord was signed into law. Because the document was changed, basically disempowering the Indians, the National Indigenous Congress and the EZLN severed communication with the Fox government (Levi, 2002). Although there has been a lot of talk, so far Indians have not won the struggle to have a complete say about their own destiny. However, the government has embraced the Indian cause and in the end, this may help Indians move forward.

The Indians need to stop blaming the government for all of their economic problems. They need schools for their children and need to increase their literacy rate so that they can obtain positions that are economically satisfying. The government needs to supply schools that teach Mexican history, including the history of the Indian people. Children should be encouraged to learn in their native language as well as the Spanish language. The government's actions in building schools and supplying teachers has taken away some of the impetuous for the Movement (Reygadas, Ramos, & Montoya, 2009).

There are a lot of challenges in the Zapatista social movement. Probably the main one is a lack of money to carry out programs. The government has chosen to go directly to the people and not through the Movement. So while the government is helping the indigenous peoples, the organization that brought everything to the attention of the world is losing ground and members. Once members received answers to some of their immediate concerns, their rebellious spirit was quieted (Reygadas et al., 2009).

7 Summary

The Zapatista Movement's negotiations with the Mexican government have continually been shifting as the Movement and the Government struggle with image and power. The game was constantly changing as supporters, national, and international contexts changed. What is particularly important from the Movement's point of view is how it overcame constraints and enlarged its opportunities to shape politics in Mexico: Its transformation from a guerrilla group to a focused movement for the democratic rights for all Mexicans. The Zapatistas were able to grab power at a certain moment and had the ability to mobilize a constituency beyond their own immediate group. Yet there were limits to what they were able to obtain when the government began supplying economic aid to the Indians (Foley, 1997).

Education became one of the crucial elements that the Zapatistas could not provide as well as the government. This caused many families to end their relationship with the EZLN when the government came in and began building schools (Reygadas et al., 2009).

While the use of mestizo by the Mexican political machine was a way to unify the people and do away with a racial hierarchy within the country, they forgot the Indians who already had an identity that they wished to preserve. Mestizo applies well for immigrants who came to Mexico, and those who do not know their racil background, but it does not work for Indians who have a very rich, long history within Mexico, their native land. In an effort to integrate, politics has repressed and marginalized the native habitants of Mexico, the Indians.

With the passage of new laws in Mexico to protect the Indians, the asymmetrical power within the political structure has the possibility of becoming somewhat balanced. However, with the political/governmental history of Mexico, trust, must be an issue for the Indians. The government will have to prove that the Indians can trust them with favorable laws.

Because there is a great deal of diversity between Indian communities, the government will have to consider these differences when passing laws to help Indians. Some communities are so mixed that although the poor peasants consider themselves Indians for government officials, when they have been offered native education, they have not taken advantage of it. Because the situation is confounded and not the same for all communities throughout Mexico, the class and ethnicity problem will be difficult to rectify in the short run. However, as a whole, Indians have gone from being discriminated against and marginalized to having some political status (Reygadas et al., 2009).

Social movements that promote development of indigenous peoples in a nonviolent way have been limited. Although the Zapatista Movement started with armed struggled, it quickly moved to a rhetoric basis. The Movement did not want to change the government, but instead wanted a voice in that government. This is different from many other ethnic movements. While many different indigenous groups came together during the early days of the Movement, the groups had not only common problems, but also different problems. International media attention forced the government to move from military force to rhetoric. The government may still be trying in its own way to "normalize" indigenous peoples, but it is allowing these peoples to have a say in how this is being done. Media attention draws outsider interest to the area: whether this is good or bad, only time will tell. Whether this proves to help the indigenous people economically and at the same time maintain their social differences from the mainline Mexican people in the long run, remains to be seen; hence, this is a "Pandora's Box." Results of the Movement have left the indigenous groups with three possibilities: the first is selling out to the government; the second, is EZLN autonomy from the government, and the third is a democratic autonomy of knowing how to negotiate with the government and having the knowledge to develop their resources. The Zapatista uprising created favorable growth conditions and helped Indians to develop social skills and political networks to manage resources. The Zapatistas did develop a strong indigenous identity within a national culture. While the social movement was the catalyst for improving the Indians' position, not all Indians are benefiting from prosperity. Problems still remain in agriculture and in subdividing the communal lands (Reygadas et al., 2009). The ethnic struggle of the Indians in Mexico will probably continue for the foreseeable future.

References

Acuña, R. (1985). *Relaciones geográficas del siglo XVI: México* (Vol. 9). Mexico: UNAM.

Aguirre, B. G. (1979). *Regions of refuge*. New York: The Society for Applied Anthropology.

Amith, J. D. (2000). *The Mobius strip. A spatial history of a colonial society: Central Guerrero, Mexico, from the Sixteenth to the Nineteenth Centuries*. Unpublished Doctoral Dissertation, Yale University.

Armstrong, J. A. (1982). *Nations before nationalism*. Chapel Hill, CA: University of California Press.

Badiou, A. (2002). *Ethics: An essay on the understanding of evil*. London: Verso.

Barmeyer, N. (2008). Taking on the state: Resistance, education, and other challenges facing the Zapatista autonomy project. *Identities: Global Studies in Culture and Power, 15*, 506–527.

Barth, F. (2000). Boundaries and connections. In: A. P. Cohen (Ed.), *Signifying identities: Anthropological perspectives on boundaries and contested values*. London: Routledge.

Bauman, Z., & Tester, K. (2001). *Conversations with Zygmunt Bauman*. Malden, MA: Blackwell.

Beltrán, G. A. (1989). *La población negra de Mèxico*. Estudio ethnohistórico. Mexico: INI. Gobierno del Estado de Veracruz, FCE.

Bennett, H. L. (1993). *Lovers, family and friends: The formation of Afro-Mexico, 1580–1810*. Unpublished Doctoral Dissertation, Duke University.

Borah, W. (1954). Race and class in Mexico. *Pacific Historical Review, 23*, 331–342.

Brading, D. A. (1994). *Church and state in Bourbon Mexico: The diocese of Michoacan 1749–1810*. Cambridge: Cambridge University Press.

Butler, M. (2009). God's Campesinos? Mexico's revolutionary church in the countryside. *Bulletin of Latin American Research, 28*(2), 165–184.

Camp, R. A. (2007). *Politics in Mexico: The democratic consolidation* (5th ed.). New York: Oxford University Press.

Carrigan, W. D. (2001). Review voices of Wounded Knee. *Western Historical Quarterly, 32*(3), 375–379.

Cervantes, F. (1994). The devil and the saints in the conquest of Mexico. *History Today*, 38–44.

Chance, J. K. (1979). On the Mexican mestizo. *Latin American Research Review, 14*(3), 153–168.

Chiapas church renews peace efforts after massacre. (1998). *U.S. Catholic, 63*(3), 9.

CIEPAC. (2001, August 16). Retrieved www.ciepac.org/bullentins/ingles/ing.337.htm.

CIEPAC. (2003, March 27). *The World Bank in Chiapas*. Retrieved www.ciepac.org/bullentins/ingles/ing.337.htm.

Historia y Civismo, (1982). In: Gutiérrez, N. (1998). What Indians say about mestizo: A critical view of a cultural archetype of Mexican nationalism. *Bulletin of Latin American Research, 17* (3), 285–301.

Cohen, R. D. (1985). Education for racial and ethnic communities. *Journal of American Ethnic History, 5*(1), 73–79.

Comité de Planeación de Desarrollo (COPLADE). (1997). Chiapas, gobierno del Estado. *Programa de Desarrollo de la Región Selva (1995–2000) Chiapas*, Primera Edición. Tuxtla Guiterrez: Talleres Graficos del Estado.

Cope, D. (1994). *The limits of racial domination: Plebian society in Colonial Mexico City, 1660–1720*. Madison, WS: University of Wisconsin Press.

Couch, J. (2001). Imagining Zapatismo: the antiglobalization movement and the Zapatistas. *Communal Plural, 9*, 243–260.

Country Studies: Mexico, (2008). Retrieved http://countrystudies.us/mexico/54.htm.

Crumrine, N. R., & Crumrine, L. S. (1969). Where Mayos meet Mestizos: A model for the social structure of culture contact. *Human Organization, 28*(1), 50–57.

Deleuze, G., & Guattari, F. (1994). *What is philosophy?* London: Verso.

Esteva, G., & Prakash, M. S. (1998). *Grassroots postmodernism*. New York: Zed Books.

Evans, B. (2008). The Zapatista insurgency: Bringing the political back into conflict analysis. *New Political Science, 30*(4), 498–520.

EZLN. (2001, April 29). *The constitutional reform in no way answers the demands of the Indian people of Mexico*. Zapatista Communique. Retrieved flag.blackened.net/revolt/mexico/marcos_index.html.

EZLN. (2005, July 1). *Sixth declaration from the Lacandon jungle*. Zapatista Communique. Retrieved flag.blackened.net/revolt/mexico/marcos_index.html.

Farriss, N. M. (1968). *Crown and clergy in colonial Mexico, 1759–1821: The crisis of ecclesiastical privilege*. London: The Athlone Press, University of London.

Fehrenbach, T. R. (1973). *Fire and blood*. New York: Da Capo Press.

Fisher, A. B. (2002). *Worlds in flux, identities in motion: A history of the Tierra Caliente of Guerrero, Mexico, 1521–1821*. Unpublished doctoral dissertation, University of California, San Diego.
Foley, M. W. (1997). Forcing the political agenda: The Zapatista rebellion and the limits of ethnic bargaining in Mexico. *International Negotiation, 2*, 123–146.
Friedlander, J. (1975). *Being Indian in Hueyapan; A study of forced identity in contemporary Mexico*. New York: St. Martin's Press.
Frye, D. (1996). *Indians into Mexicans: History and identity in a Mexican town*. Austin, TX: University of Texas Press.
Gabbert, W. (2004). *Becoming maya: Ethnicity and social inequality in Yucatan since 1500*. Tucson, AZ: The University of Arizona Press.
Gellner, E. (1983). *Nations and nationalism*. Ithaca, NY: Cornell University Press.
Gibson, C. (1964). *The Aztecs under Spanish rule: A history of the Indians of the Valley of Mexico, 1519–1810*. Stanford, CA: Stanford University Press.
Gutiérrez, N. (1995). *The culture of the nation: The ethnic past and official nationalism in 20th century Mexico*. Unpublished doctoral dissertation, The London School of Economics of London.
Gutiérrez, N. (1998). What Indians say about mestizo: A critical view of a cultural archetype of Mexican Nationalism. *Bulletin of Latin American Research, 17*(3), 285–301.
Gutiérrez, N. (1999). *Nationalist myths and ethnic identities: Indigenous intellectuals and the Mexican state*. Lincoln, NE: University of Nebraska Press.
Haskett, R. S. (1991). *Indigenous rulers: An ethnohistory of town government in colonial Cuernavaca*. Albuquerque, NM: University of New Mexico Press.
Hayden, T. (Ed.). (2002). *The Zapatista reader*. New York: Nation.
Horn, R. (1997). *Postconquest Coyoacan: Nahua-Spanish relations in Central Mexico, 1519–1650*. Stanford, CA: Stanford University Press.
Indigenous Indian Regions Map (2002). Retrieved http://www.cdi.gob.mx/regiones/regiones_indigenas_cdi.pdf.
Instituto Nacional Indigenista. (1993). *Indicadores economicos de los pueblos indigenas de Mexico*. Mexico City: INI.
Jackson, R. H. (1999). *Race, caste, and status: Indians in colonial Spanish America*. Lincoln, NM: University of New Mexico Press.
Jarque, C. (2000). *La política social del Gobierno de México: resultados 1995–2000 y retos futures*. México: Sedosol. www.sedosol.gob.mx.
Kaplan, B. A. (1953). Ethnic identification in an Indian Mestizo community: I socio-cultural factors. *Phylon(1940–1956), 14*(2), 179–186.
King, A. D. (1991). *Culture, globalization and the world-system*. London: Macmillan.
Knight, A. (1986). *The Mexican revolution, 2 vol*. Cambridge: Cambridge University Press.
Lafaye, J. (1985). *Quetzalcoatl and Guadalupe; la formacion de la conciencia nacional en Mexico* (2nd ed.). Mexico City: Fondo de Cultura Economica.
Languages of Mexico. (2009, December 2). Retrieved http:;//es.wikipedia.org/wiki/Idiomas_de_M%C3%A9xico.
Levi, J. M. (2002). A new dawn or a cycle restored? Regional dynamics and cultural politics in indigenous Mexico, 1978–2001. In: D. Maybury-Lewis (Ed.), *The politics of ethnicity: Indigenous peoples in Latin American states*. Cambridge, MA: Harvard University Press.
Levinas, E. (2001). Is it righteous to be? In: J. Robbins (Ed.), *Interviews with Emmanuel Levinas*. Stanford, CA: Stanford University Press.
Lynch, J. (1989). *Bourbon Spain, 1700–1808*. Oxford: Basil Blackwell.
Marcos, S. (2001). The exceptional interview: interview by Carlos Monsvais and Hermann Bellinhausen. *La Jornada*. Retrieved http://flag.blackened.net/revolt/mexico/ezln/2001/marcos_interview_jan.html.
Nash, J. (1997). The fiesta of the world: The Zapatista uprising and radical democracy in Mexico. *American Anthropologist, 99*(2), 261–275.
Nolasco, M. (1988). Los indios de Mexico. In: R. Stavenhagen & M. Nolasco (Eds.), *Politica cultural para un pas multietnico*. SEP: Mexico City.
Olsen, T. (2004). Globalising the Zapatistas: from third world solidarity to global solidarity. *Third World Quarterly, 25*(1), 255.
Paine, R. (2000). Aboriginality, authenticity and the settler world. In: A. P. Cohen (Ed.), *Signifying identities: anthropological perspectives on boundaries and contested values*. London: Routledge.
Popke, E. J. (2004). The face of the other: Zapatismo, responsibility and the ethics of deconstruction. *Social and Cultural Geography, 5*(2), 301–317.
Reygadas, L., Ramos, T., & Montoya, G. (2009). Pandora's box: The implications of social movements on development. Lessons from the Lacandona Jungle in Chiapas. *Social Movement Studies, 8*(3), 225–241.
Ross, J. (2003). The Zapatistas at ten. *NACLA Report on the, Americas, 37*(3), 11–15.
Ross, J. (2005). Celebrating the Caracoles: Step by step, the Zapatistas advance on the horizon. *Humboldt Journal of Social Relations, 29*(1), 39–46.
Ross, J. (2006). *Zapatistas: Making another world is possible*. New York: Nation.
Rus, J. (1994). The "Comunidad revolucionaria institucional": The subversion of native government in highland Chiapas, 1936–1968. In: J. Gilbert & D. Nugent (Eds.), *Everyday forms of state formation: Revolution and the negotiation of rule in modern Mexico*. London: Duke University Press.
Schmidt-Diaz de Leon, I. (2001). Ethnicity and nationhood. *Hemisphere, 9*(3), 24–28.
Schryer, F. J. (1990). *Ethnicity and class conflict in rural Mexico*. Princeton, NJ: Princeton University Press.
Smith, A. D. (1986). *The ethnic origins of nations*. Oxford: Blackwell.
Speed, S. (2005). Dangerous discourses: Human rights and multi-culturalism in neo-liberal Mexico. *Political and Legal Anthropology, 28*(1), 29–51.

Stahler-Sholk, R. (2001). Globalization and social movement resistance: the Zapatista rebellion in Chiapas, Mexico. *New Political Science, 23*, 493–516.
Stahler-Sholk, R. (2007). Resisting neoliberal homogenization.The Zapatista autonomy movement. *Latin American Perspectives, 34*(2).
Subcomandante Marcos (1994, March). In our dreams we have seen another world. Communique.
Subcomandante Marcos (1999, October). From the underground culture to the culture of resistance. Communique. Subcomandante Marcos (1999, August). Under siege. Communique.
Subcomandante Marcos (2003, January 12). I shit on all the revolutionary vanguards of this planet. Communique.
Taussig, M. (1999). *Defacement: Public secrecy and the labor of the negative*. Stanford, CA: Stanford University Press.
Taylor, W. B. (1979). *Drinking, homicide, and rebellion in colonial Mexican villages*. Stanford, CA: Stanford University Press.
Taylor, W. B. (1996). *Magistrates of the sacred: Priests and parishioners in eighteenth-century Mexico*. Stanford, CA: Stanford University Press. 1996.
The right not to be Hispanic. (1998, March 7). *Economist, 346*(8058), 88–89.
Torres, Y. G. (2000). The history of religion and the study of religion in Mexico. *Method and Theory in the Study of Religion, 12*(1/2), 38–48.
U.S. Department of State. (2001). Country reports on human rights practices: Mexico.
Vasconcelos, J. (1925). *The cosmic race*. Baltimore, MA: The Johns Hopkins University Press.
Vodovnik, Z. (2004). *Ya Basta: Ten years of the Zapatista uprising*. Oakland, CA: AK Press.
Warren, K., & Jackson, J. (2002). *Indigenous movements, self-representation & the state in Latin America*. Austin, TX: University of Texas Press.
Watanabe, J. M. (1995). Unimagining the Maya: Anthropologists, others, and the inescapable hubris of authorship. *Bulletin of Latin American Research, 14*(1), 25–45.
Weinberg, B. (2000). *Homage to Chiapas: The new indigenous struggles in Mexico*. London: Verso.
Weissert, W. (2005). *Mexico's Fox calls guerrilla movement a thing of the past*. Mexico City: Associated Press.
Wingenbach, E. (1999). Refusing the temptation of innocence: Levinasian ethics as political theory. *Strategies, 12*, 219–238.
Zapatista Commission for Information (2005, December 31). Interview in LaGarrucha,Chiapas. In: Evans, B. (2008). The Zapatista Insurgency: Bringing the Political Back into Conflict Analysis. *New Political Science, 30*(4), 498–520.
Zapatistas, T. (1998). *Zapatista Encuentro: Documents from the 1996 encounter for humanity and against neoliberalism*. New York: Seven Stories Press.

Sendero Luminoso (Shining Path) and the Conflict in Peru

21

Marisa Mealy and Carol Shaw Austad

Peru Chapter Summary

In this chapter, Mealy and Austad detail the origins and evolution of the ethnocultural conflict in Peru which continues today. Identification of the involved groups is traced to the caste system formed following Spanish conquest that is based on quantity of European versus indigenous heritage. Values unique to the indigenous culture are discussed as they were manipulated by both sides of the conflict and eventually played a role in uprising against the guerilla movements. Recognition of the current volatility in Peru provides an impetus for the solutions offered.

Exploration of escalating conflict emphasizes the role of revolutionary movements which focused on class distinction rather than ethnicity while duplicating prejudice against those with darker skin who were seen as in need of protection. The authors describe the wide use of propaganda to attract both the educated and peasant groups of mixed and indigenous lineage to the movement, as well as forced recruitment of children by both sides of the conflict.

Existent values of the Quechua indigenous culture are examined as they explain the shift in perception of the guerilla movement from savior to oppressor. The ensuing conflicts and eventual support of the state military are given credit for many victories. New leadership in Peru with a focus on counterterrorism is recognized as reducing conflict further; however, mention of two remaining revolutionary groups acknowledge continuing tension.

Mealy and Austad recount the consequences of conflict for the indigenous people, particularly women and children, which remain largely unaddressed. Formation of a commission to resolve both the causes and effects of war is viewed as a positive step; however, the authors note a lack of execution on the

M. Mealy (✉) • C.S. Austad
Department of Psychology at Central Connecticut State University, New Britain, CT, USA
e-mail: mealymar@ccsu.edu

D. Landis and R.D. Albert (eds.), *Handbook of Ethnic Conflict: International Perspectives*, International and Cultural Psychology, DOI 10.1007/978-1-4614-0448-4_21,

part of the state. Through examining indigenous values of reconciliation and justice, the authors reveal a promising avenue for restoring peace. Lessons learned from the conflicts in Peru are discussed and specific suggestions for changes at the government level are offered.

Cheryl Jorgensen

1 Current Status

During the latter part of the twentieth century, the Peruvian highlands gave rise to one of the most brutal guerrilla organizations in the world *El Partido Comunista de Peru por el Sendero Luminoso de Mariátegui* (PCP-SL), or the Communist Party of Peru on the Shining Path of Mariátegui (Pike, 2003; Starn, 1992). This Maoist revolutionary movement promoted the idea that insurgency would benefit the primarily indigenous peasantry. Thus, many indigenous Peruvians initially found the PCP-SL's discourse of social justice to be highly appealing. However, as the movement progressed, many peasants dramatically altered their opinion and actively resisted the PCP-SL. By 2000, many observers believed the movement to be defunct. Nonetheless, deep ethnocultural and regional divisions, accompanied by social injustice and the discrimination of indigenous persons, remained deeply entrenched in the Peruvian society.

At the turn of the millennium, even as truth and reconciliation efforts in Lima called national awareness to the atrocities that occurred in the highlands, recurrent reports of PCP-SL resurgence spread from isolated, primarily indigenous, coca-producing regions – where guerrilla activity had never ended. Many among Peru's urban and coastal elite have reacted with indifference to the continuous reports of violent incidents, associated human rights abuses, narcotrafficking, and the pervasive fear and bitterness associated with continued guerrilla activity in indigenous highland regions. Thus, while it is currently unlikely that the PCP-SL will attain the same stature it held in the early 1990s (see Table 21.1), the preconditions of the conflict remain in place, awaiting the appropriate spark to set the country afire once again.

2 Demographic Characteristics

From the time the Spanish conquistadors arrived in Peru during the sixteenth century, ethnocultural conflict has resulted in sustained antagonism. People of European descent composed the ruling classes and justified their preferential treatment with perceptions of the indigenous peoples as inferior, even subhuman. To cope with the offspring of Spanish-indigenous unions, a complicated caste system evolved. At the top of the hierarchy were whites and *criollos* (of mostly European descent), followed by *mestizos* (1/2 indigenous), *cholos* (3/4 indigenous), and the indigenous. People who spoke Spanish and adopted European norms tended to be categorized as *mestizo*. Accordingly, to avoid paying tributes to the Spanish and to obtain opportunities not otherwise available, many of the indigenous chose to leave their traditional communities and disguise their ancestry (Langer & Stearns, 2001). To preserve their higher rank, *mestizos* scorned those who retained an indigenous lifestyle (Strong, 1992).

Within this context, success and social climbing required a rejection of everything indigenous, especially uncomfortable reminders of ethnic roots, such as darker skin tones or an appreciation for Andean handicrafts (Strong, 1992). Discrimination was inherent in the interconnected dualisms of indigenous/nonindigenous, highland/

coastal, rural/urban, traditional/modern, impoverished/affluent, and illiterate/educated (Palmer, 1992). Even today many indigenous citizens have lower levels of education (and higher levels of illiteracy) than other Peruvians, are impoverished, wear "folkloric" clothing, and live in the rural highlands. The ruling classes consist of people who are light-skinned, live in coastal areas, and adopt a culture that is both Western and Spanish in origin. As a result, it is common in Peru, as in much of Latin America, for ethnocultural, socioeconomic, and even geographic categories to overlap substantially (Muñoz, Paredes, & Thorpe, 2006).

At present, 45% of Peru's 29 million inhabitants are indigenous, 37% are *mestizo,* 15% are white (*criollo* or of European descent), and 3% are of other descent (African, Japanese, etc.) (CIA, 2009). Spanish is spoken fluently by approximately 80% of the people, while an estimated 4.5 million people speak Quechua as their primary language (Minority Rights Group, 2007). Economically, 44.5% of Peruvians are below the poverty line (CIA, 2009). The top 10% of the population controls 41% of the wealth and the bottom 10% controls 1% of the wealth (World Bank, 2007). For Peruvians, the coast represents an economic and politically powerful Hispanic and *mestizo* population, whereas the highlands represent an impoverished and oppressed indigenous culture (Comas-Diaz, Lykes, & Alarcon, 1998). These ethnocultural divisions contributed directly to the brutality of the violence that occurred during the latter part of the twentieth century.

3 History

In the 1960s, amid oppression, social injustice, and unfulfilled promises of land reform, several short-lived, violent, communist, revolutionary movements arose in the Peruvian highlands. The first of these was brought to a halt in 1963, when its leader, Hugo Blanco, was arrested (Becker, 2006). Two other violent revolutionary movements inspired by the Cuban revolution (the *Ejército de Liberación Nacíonal*, or ELN, headed by Héctor Béjar, and the armed revolutionary group headed by Luis de la Puente Uceda), splintered from the political wing of the Peruvian Communist Party. Both of these guerrilla groups were defeated by the Peruvian military in 1965 (Loveman & Davies, 1997).

Meanwhile, in 1961, Manuel Abimael Guzmán Reynoso ("Comrade Gonzalo" or "Chairman Gonzalo"), the founder of the PCP-SL, completed dissertations in both philosophy and law at *Universidad Nacíonal de San Agustín* in Arequipa (see Fig. 21.1). Shortly thereafter, he took a position as head of the philosophy department at the newly reopened *Universidad de San Cristóbal de Huamanga* in Ayacucho (see Fig. 21.1). This university was centered in one of the most impoverished, remote, and heavily indigenous regions of the country (Becker, 2006). It was here, in the classes of the charismatic Abimael Guzmán, that a core group of PCP-SL supporters emerged as early as 1964 (Becker, 2006).

Beginning in 1965, Abimael Guzmán made a number of extended trips to the People's Republic of China, met Mao Tse Tung, received training, and became familiar with the radical ideology of the Gang of Four, as well as the Chinese Cultural Revolution (Gorriti, 1991). These firsthand experiences intensified his ideological extremism and inspired him to become the leader of a intended to benefit the oppressed peoples of Peru (Gorriti, 1991; Time, 1992). Accordingly, in the 1970s, after a split with the Peruvian Communist Party, Guzmán founded the *PCP-Sendero Luminoso* (Strong, 1992). For the next 10 years, Guzmán proceeded in a slow, thoughtful, and disciplined fashion to build a revolutionary movement (Manwaring, 2004). Then, in 1979, after laying a sufficiently strong foundation for his organization, Abimael Guzmán retired from his position at the university and went underground.

3.1 Ideology and Structure

What was known about the ideology of *Sendero Luminoso* appeared simplistic and erroneous to outsiders, but liberating and inspiring to many who lived within the ethnocultural, economic,

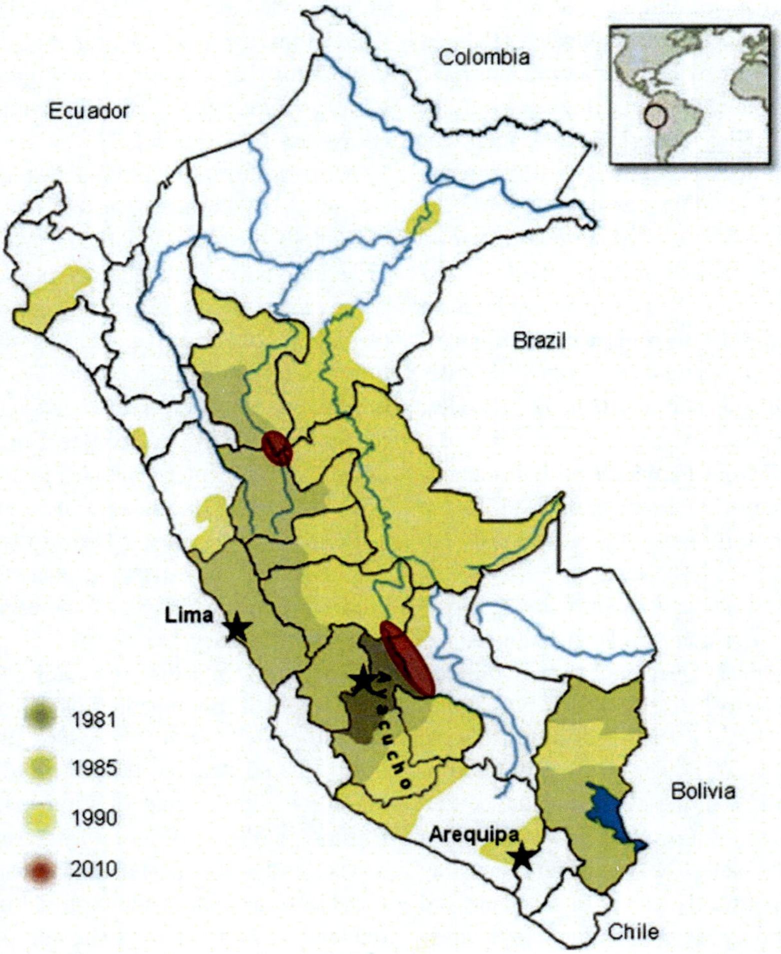

Fig. 21.1 Ethnopolitical violence in Peru 1980–2010

and regional complexities that defined Peruvian social classes (Palmer, 1992). The movement's leadership, or the *Comité Central* (Central Committee), framed their mission solely within international and class terms, largely neglecting the ethnocultural issues that beleaguered the highland peasantry (Strong, 1992). Ideological writings did not mention Peru's ethnic divisions, and direct references to ethnicity were omitted from posters and other publications (McClintock, 2005). In fact, *Sendero*'s central creed, referred to as "Gonzalo Thought", was conspicuously indifferent to indigenous cultures, traditions, and issues (Degregori, 1990; Starn, 1995). These omissions may have been a function of blind faith in the primacy of class struggle or a strategic decision to avoid alienating the majority of *mestizos*. In practice, however, it was nearly impossible to separate ethnicity and economic class in the Peruvian highlands. As explained by an early PCP-SL website, the indigenous peoples "(Quechua, Aymara, etc.) voluntarily join the ranks of the revolution, keeping their class interests in mind. After centuries of exploitation, most of them are now peasants (mainly poor)…" (Quispe, 1998). The result was a movement that has been described as "a strange mix of Gang of Four Maoism and deeply rooted Incan nationalism" (Barton, 1983, pp. 38).

At the core of the revolutionary ideology was a paternalistic prejudice, consisting of superficially charitable emotions that masked a stereotype of the indigenous peasant as innately incompetent, helpless, passive, and generally inferior. Members of the Comité Central (1988) considered themselves representatives of the "leading class of all revolutions" and the "most conscious and best organized section of the masses". Essentially, they saw themselves as the protectors of a primitive and uncivilized indigenous peasantry. Key documents clearly state that "it is incumbent upon Communists to organize and lead [the indigenous peasantry]. [The indigenous peasants] have concrete problems everywhere and we must worry about them and attend to them" (Comité Central, 1988). In other words, the top echelons of the PCP-SL believed the indigenous peasantry was incapable of mobilizing without the aid of the *mestizo* middle class. Accordingly, the internal structure of *Sendero* replicated the ethnic stratification of Peru, with lighter-skinned elites leading dark-skinned youths (Starn, 1992). Furthermore, in line with findings from Ramasubramanian and Oliver (2007), the guerillas treated indigenous peasants who passively accepted the imposed hierarchical power structure of the PCP-SL better than those who opposed it. Overt resistance was met with high levels of brutality. In consequence, as suggested by Gaertner and Dovidio (1986), similar to more hostile forms of prejudice, this seeming benevolence and its associated feelings of protectiveness and pity denied indigenous Peruvians both power and respect.

The PCP-SL guerrilla movement operated under a secretive cell structure with thus, little information was available to the general public (Becker, 2006). As with any small tight-knit group, PCP-SL units would have developed their own internal cultures. In turn, these cultures indoctrinated newer members with the organization's norms of benevolence and hostility.

As the organization grew in power, it built a messianic cult of personality around its charismatic founder, Abimael Guzmán ("Presidente Gonzalo"). For supporters of the PCP-SL, Guzmán was considered the fourth sword of communism after Marx, Lenin, and Mao (Arena & Arrigo, 2006). They believed that only he could offer the necessary interpretations of the complex interrelationships between humanity, history, politics, and destiny (Gorriti, 2006). Thus, Guzmán's mythical status enhanced the insurgents' willingness to demand loyalty to the revolution over affective ties, traditional family relations, and daily life (Stern, 1998).

3.2 PCP-SL Recruitment

To lay the foundations for a successful struggle, the revolutionary movement had to recruit a critical mass of supporters. Accordingly, PCP-SL leaders used highly evolved propaganda campaigns to target specific segments of the population. These efforts focused primarily on educated *mestizo*s, who often felt disenfranchized by the higher echelons of the *criollo* (white) elite (Kirk, 1991). Other propaganda was directed at indigenous peasants, who were viewed as the principal combatants and the people most in need of protection and guidance from *mestizo* leaders. Finally, many recruitment efforts specifically targeted the indigenous youth (Comité Central, 1988).

Educated *Mestizos*. Rural indigenous parents appreciated the benefits of an education. They held it in high regard and often sacrificed both emotionally and financially in order to educate their children. In turn, the children valued their education: Schools and state universities were filled day and night (Strong, 1992). Yet, on a personal level, residents of indigenous communities were often ambivalent toward the *mestizo* teachers, viewing them as both a blessing and a curse. The educators provided access to knowledge that had previously been available almost exclusively to the privileged classes (Primov, 1980). Nonetheless, their close association with the knowledge of the ruling class prompted indigenous communities to view them as "white" – even when a teacher had been raised in an indigenous community (Primov, 1980; Wilson, 2007). Thus, school teachers were not accepted by either the rural communities or urban-*mestizo* society, which harshly discriminated against them for their involvement with the indigenous peasantry (Degregori, 1991; Zavala, 2002).

Many teachers' paternalistic and stereotypical views of their indigenous students added to the complexity. They disdained the Andean cultural values of obedience, mysticism, and fatalism. They condemned these values as culprits for the ruling classes exploitation of the indigenous communities (Wilson, 2007). In contrast, these educated *mestizos* perceived themselves as enlightened individuals, whose responsibility was to tend to the poor, stand up for the mistreated peasants, and simultaneously civilize them (Wilson, 2007). They encouraged indigenous children to discard their own cultural values and to embrace the cultural norms of the dominant White society (Wilson, 2007).

These culturally alienated teachers, longing for respect and companionship, found a like-minded community of other well-educated people living between two cultures in the PCP-SL (McClintock, 2005; Wilson, 2007). They were attracted to Guzmán's argument that the revolutionary movement should alter not only the system, but also the traditional worldview of the indigenous people (Gorriti, 2006). This logic offered a way to "protect" indigenous students, while encouraging them to discard "backward" indigenous superstitions and beliefs. In consequence, educators formed the primary base from which *Sendero* drew support and recruits.

At one point, an estimated 15% (30,000) of all Peruvian teachers were supporters of the PCP-SL (McClintock, 1998; Wilson, 2007). With such a strong appeal among those representative of the urban, educated, and *mestizo* middle class, it is not surprising that the PCP-SL adopted external and paternalistic attitudes similar to those of the urban-*mestizo* teacher. In fact, the followers of the PCP-SL were regarded as students from the rural highlands (Becker, 2006). Even in iconography, Abimael Guzmán was depicted in the role of the teacher wearing glasses and carrying a book (Wilson, 2007). By teaching their indigenous students the ideology of the PCP-SL, militant teachers felt they could rouse the indigenous people, shape their interpretation of past exploitation, channel their future aspirations, and protect their communities from exploitation.

The Indigenous Peasantry. The PCP-SL needed to recruit heavily among indigenous peasants to achieve its political ends. As such, members of the *Comité Central* seemed to take advice from the writings of Héctor Béjar (Ash, 1985; Loveman & Davies, 1997). Béjar argued that, in Peru, a successful guerrilla insurgency depended upon how well the movement related to the indigenous peasant's fundamental cultural values and native language (Loveman & Davies, 1997). He believed that the Peruvian peasantry associated the Spanish language with the image of a feudal *patrón* (boss), making language a significant barrier between the rebels and the local residents. "For the guerrillas to gain the trust of the peasantry they must be able to speak Quechua, and not just any Quechua, but the Quechua of the zone where they are operating…" (Loveman & Davies, 1997, p. 289).

Accordingly, Abimael Guzmán, encouraged by Efraín Morote, the rector of the University, studied Quechua in an effort to recruit from Ayacucho's half million peasants (Gelles, 2002). Guzmán further fostered trust among indigenous families and students by frequently visiting homes in the poorer districts of Ayacucho (Strong, 1992). He urged top leaders, as well as PCP-SL recruits, to fan out into the countryside to study Quechua and learn highland customs (Ash, 1985; Marks, 1996). Furthermore, Quechua-speaking leaders were strategically placed among the principal units of the PCP-SL.

Indigenous cultural beliefs helped frame the revolutionary movement and to evoke deep-rooted ethnocultural and regional tensions (DeQuine, 1984). In Andean lore, evil is embodied by the *pishtaco*, a bogeyman who travels through rural areas raping, mutilating, and disemboweling his human prey as he steals the fat from their bodies (Stimpson, 2001). At the core of this representation is a white male invader (often a businessman, government representative, or landowner) who destroys and profits from his indigenous victims (Stimpson, 2001; Strong, 1992). Each generation has reinterpreted the *pishtaco* as a symbol of its fears and sufferings (Fumerton, 2002), and during the early 1980s, indigenous communities in Ayacucho perceived members of the Peruvian security forces as *pishtacos* (Strong, 1992). This association generated confidence that the PCP-SL was engaged in efforts to eradicate evil.

The PCP-SL's brutal killing and savage ritualistic treatment of early victims (police officers, soldiers, and other government officials) were also strongly influenced by traditional Andean beliefs (DeQuine, 1984). Indigenous customs held that gouged out eyes prevented recognition of the killers, a severed tongue could avert verbal betrayal, and broken ankles would stop a victim's spirit from pursuing the perpetrators (Strong, 1992). Accordingly, guerillas often mutilated bodies to prevent a victim's spirit from leaving the grave and seeking retaliation (DeQuine, 1984).

Other highland beliefs bolstered the image of the PCP-SL leader, Abimael Guzmán, and encouraged the loyalty of the indigenous peasants. According to Quechua tradition, time is composed of a series of epochs. At the heart of this cycle is an Inka (divine king or a messiah), whose location in the temporal and spatial pattern enables him to transcend the otherwise inevitable death (Ossio, 2002). During each epoch, the Inka emerges from the cyclic patterns of time to reorder the cosmos (Loveman & Davies, 1997). To foster the impression that he was this messianic figure, Guzmán carefully cultivated a mysterious persona, one in which he seemed both invisible and omnipresent (Time, 1992; Ross, 2009). Several narrow escapes from government forces further reinforced the attribution of a mythical, quasi-supernatural, status to Abimael Guzmán: "In jungle areas the Indians reportedly say he escapes by transforming himself into a bird and flying out of harm's way, or into a snake, which vanished into the bush. In the southern Andes he is said to fool his hunters by turning himself into a stone" (Strong, 1992, pp. 127). As a result, many indigenous supporters referred to Guzmán as *Puka Inti* (Quechua for "Red Sun"), an appellation that directly associated him with a Quechua deity (DeQuine, 1984; McClintock, 2005).

Youth and Children. Many indigenous youths found themselves caught between the traditional and semifeudal environments of their parents and the semi-modern status of the Peruvian coast (Mancilla, 1999). Living in this indeterminate state produced high levels of psychological discomfort. *Sendero*'s ideology offered some reassurance in a world of insecurity and normalized violence. As a result, many rural youths found the simple explanations and rigid structure of the PCP-SL highly attractive (Mancilla, 1999).

PCP-SL leaders valued younger recruits because they were more idealistic, malleable, and open to absorbing new ideology (Crenshaw, 1995; Granados, 1987). The youths represented the hope and future of the party. Teenage insurgents, who survived the ongoing armed conflict, were likely to become tomorrow's commanders (Crenshaw, 1995). In a protracted war, children were also viewed as human reserve to replace dead combatants (Del Pino, 1999). Accordingly, the leadership of the PCP-SL made the strategic decision to recruit an overwhelmingly young population of supporters and militants, often from targeted indigenous communities. Once they occupied a village, *Sendero* militants established a school to spread PCP-SL propaganda, selectively recruit new militants, and inculcate the indigenous peasantry in their own *mestizo* views (Smith, 1995).

Recruitment was aimed not only at students in rural communities, but also at the more fair-skinned youth who had been chosen to study in towns or cities. These youths quickly discovered that their urban peers and teachers viewed them with contempt because of their indigenous background (Wilson, 2007). As a result, these students felt hurt, resentful, marginalized, and socially isolated. The PCP-SL won their loyalty by framing participation as a prestigious accomplishment and using imagery which depicted members as heroes and proprietors of a mystic revolution. The insurgents also labeled their recruits as the best sons and daughters of the town (Aprodeh, 2004). In short, the PCP-SL offered the youths the possibility of another reality where, regardless of ethnic background, they could gain acceptance, authority, respect, a chance for change, and even an opportunity for ethnic revenge (Wilson, 2007). Some youths, often more educated than their parents, also saw membership in the PCP-SL as an opportunity to challenge their own elders, despite the traditional hierarchy of the indigenous community (Aprodeh, 2004).

While the first generation of young *Senderistas* was motivated by feelings of disenfranchisement, discrimination, and oppression, those recruited later often participated in response to intimidation (Fumerton, 2002). The majority of the indigenous child recruits from the southern highlands joined because they were deceived, coerced, or threatened with violence (Aprodeh, 2004). Insurgents entered schools to recruit the tallest, strongest, and most studious children, with the oldest being between the ages of 10 and 12 years. Teachers who opposed these kidnappings were assassinated (Aprodeh, 2004). Furthermore, when indigenous communities or families did not voluntarily deliver their children to fulfill *Sendero's* quota, the children were drafted against their will through threats of reprisal or actual assassinations. Family members who protested were given the choice to either give up their child or have the entire family killed (Aprodeh, 2004).

At one time, more than a tenth of the armed *Sendero* militants, or approximately 1,000 guerrillas, were under the age of 18 years (Comas-Diaz et al., 1998). Members of the PCP-SL gained the trust of these captured children by caring for them and educating them. Consequently, *Sendero* militants became the reference group for these children, as well as the only reality they knew (Aprodeh, 2004). The youngest of these recruits, often between the ages of 5 and 10 years, formed the "Red Pioneers." The Red Pioneers performed a variety of tasks including surveillance, message delivery, spying, cleaning, and provision of food and other necessities. Other children were used as porters, transporting flags or ammunition. Upon reaching age 12, the children were taught to use guns, spears, and slings, as well as how to make bombs. They were also required to participate in armed conflict (Aprodeh, 2004). Without any outside commitments or influences, these children were fully indoctrinated into party philosophy and became completely committed to the PCP-SL (Crenshaw, 1995).

3.2.1 Government Recruitment

During the 1980s, the Peruvian constitution required universal military service. Less than a quarter of those who enlisted were volunteers, but they comprised the bulk of both the naval and air forces (Huston, 1988). Members of the upper and middle classes avoided conscription by paying bribes or using influential connections (WRI, 1998). Soldiers were drafted from indigenous villages, the rural coast, or urban shanty towns (Huston, 1998; WRI, 1998). Thus, the army was filled with disenfranchised indigenous and *mestizo* conscripts who worked almost exclusively for food and barracks (with little to no pay), lived in appalling conditions, suffered through short and brutal trainings, and endured forced labor and mistreatment at the hands of their officers (Fumerton, 2002; Strong, 1992).

The PCP-SL was not the only party to the conflict to use young boys as combatants. With parental consent, youths were permitted to join the Peruvian armed forces at age 16. In addition, the army forcibly recruited indigenous children as young as age 11 (Aprodeh, 2004; WRI, 1998). After being abducted from their highland communities, these boys were taken to the local military base and posted far from their home region. Months would elapse before families learned what had happened to their sons (Fumerton, 2002). One consequence of these practices was that, at times, members of the same family would fight on opposite sides of the conflict (Personal Communication, 2010).

3.2.2 Drug Trafficking

To the indigenous communities of Peru, coca leaves have spiritual, economic, medicinal, and social value. They dull physical pain, produce energy, and alleviate altitude sickness. Furthermore, the leaves symbolize time and space, as well as the identity and status of the carrier (Ossio, 2002; Strong, 1992). Chewing coca creates a social bond at rituals such as community-building projects, meetings, and marriages (Ossio, 2002; Strong, 1992). The leaves are also commonly used in rituals of a religious nature, where it is an offering to native spirits or Christian deities, or used as a part of a Shamanic curing session (Ossio, 2002). Yet, cocaine is the key alkaloid in coca leaves and the leaves are critical to the manufacture of the drug.

With the growth of the Colombian drug cartels in the 1980s, the coca leaf became a valuable agricultural commodity because the quality of the leaf was higher in Peru than in Colombia (Strong, 1992). Remote valleys that had produced the coca plant for centuries became centers of the illegal activities associated with cocaine trafficking. These coca-growing regions also became a focus of United States' antidrug policies. Military aid helped destroy coca crops through manual eradication, application of herbicides, and crop substitution (Gootenburg, 2008). These attacks were often directed at the primarily indigenous minor employees and coca growers (Taylor, 1998).

Many of the estimated 580,000 indigenous coca farmers had difficulty comprehending how such a useful and beloved plant could also be a destructive drug (Gagnon, Hoffer, & Hoffer, 1993; McClintock, 2005). In addition, many peasants perceived the prohibitions on the sale of the legally grown leaf to be the result of discriminatory state practices (McClintock, 2005; Strong, 1992). Thus, the clash of cultures was again evident. To the indigenous, coca represented sacred aspects of cultural identity. To the government, coca represented drug trafficking and illegal activity. To the PCP-SL, coca represented support and profit.

During the early 1980s, the PCP-SL became established in the coca-growing regions of Peru, including the Upper Huallaga Valley (which at the time was the largest coca-growing area in the world) and the Apurimac and Ene River Valleys (VRAE) (Gagnon et al., 1993; McClintock, 2005). The guerillas gained control over significant portions of the countryside, a continued base of operations, and significant funding (Fitz-Simmons, 1993). The guerillas profited from both sides of the cocaine trade by charging traffickers for protection and shipment rights and charging indigenous peasants for protection (Fitz-Simmons, 1993). By the late 1980s, the cocaine-related activities of the PCP-SL yielded \$20 to \$40 million (McClintock, 2005). Approximately one-third of these funds provided material support and salaries for an estimated 60% of active insurgents. Salaries averaged between \$250 and \$500 in the highlands and Lima (more than 5 times the salary of a Peruvian teacher) and up to \$1,000 a month in coca-producing areas (McClintock, 2005). Furthermore, about 35% of PCP-SL guerillas received material support in the form of rations, accommodations, or stipends for expenses associated with guerrilla activities (McClintock, 2005).

In coca-growing areas, the guerillas protected the indigenous peasants from both the drug traffickers and Peru's antidrug police. They also dispersed effective justice in the face of an expensive, slow, and corrupt judicial system (Fitz-Simmons, 1993; Strong, 1992). *Senderistas* further used the ties built from working with traffickers to obtain higher prices for the indigenous coca growers (Fitz-Simmons, 1993). When peasants failed to cooperate with the PCP-SL, the guerrillas coerced and blackmailed them into complying (Comas-Diaz et al. 1998). Thus, the PCP-SL was able to gain the loyalty, or at least cooperation, of hundreds of thousands of people in coca-growing regions (Fitz-Simmons, 1993).

3.2.3 Armed Conflict and Destabilizing Terror

Like many of the educators in the PCP-SL movement, Abimael Guzmán was an urban-*mestizo* who had lived for many years in indigenous zones. He had seen the rise and fall of revolutionary movements and had gone to great lengths to become familiar with indigenous culture. In addition, Guzmán had travelled to China to be trained by Mao Tse Tung. In keeping with this Maoist instruction, Guzmán viewed the initial stages of the insurrection in terms of strategic defense (Manwaring, 1995). Accordingly, he intended the revolution to have the initial appearance of being both disorganized and embryonic, and hence of little consequence to urban-*mestizos* (Gorriti, 2006). The danger of this tactic was that of appearing weak to potential supporters. Thus, the success of the movement depended upon its being perceived by urban-*mestizos* as destined to fail, but simultaneously strong to the indigenous peasantry, and well-thought out to its intellectual support base.

In 1980, on the night before Peru's first presidential election in 17 years, a unit of young insurgents launched the armed portion of the revolution by burning ballot boxes in the rural town of Chuschi (Becker, 2006). Just a few months later, the PCP-SL left mysterious messages, such as "Teng Hsiao-ping, son of a bitch," on shrouds wrapped around several dogs that had been maimed, killed, and hung from streetlamps. These tactics confused most urban-*mestizos* (Getgen, 2008; Gorriti, 1991). Literal interpretations from cities saw the dogs as representing Chinese political figures that the PCP-SL considered revisionist dogs (DeQuine, 1984). However, the revolutionary movement had been strategically organized for over a decade in a primarily indigenous region, had acquired numerous indigenous supporters, and had educated *mestizo* leaders with international training. Thus, it is unlikely that the "People's War" would have been launched with only a hurried expression of annoyance with "revisionism." In fact, to those familiar with highland culture, the hanging dogs would have been viewed as an expression of disrespect (DeQuine, 1984). Furthermore, the prophetic symbolism of these acts was related to aspects of Quechua lore that associate dogs with ethnic distrust and death. For the Quechua, a black dog helps souls to cross a river on its way to the last judgment, while a white dog is considered unhelpful. The color white represents people "who are unhelpful and who do not want to get dirty in the unclean waters of that river" (Ossio, 2002, p. 210). For the Quechua, the hanging may also have been interpreted as an omen that someone would die or be put to death (Ash, 1985; Bennett, 1984). Thus, Guzmán used the cultural divide between the urban coastal centers and the rural indigenous highlands to offer a different perspective of the PCP-SL to each segment of the population.

Peruvian Security Forces. The activities of the security forces also contributed directly to the escalation of the conflict. For nearly 2 years after the PCP-SL initiated their armed insurgency, the government treated the violence in indigenous communities as if it were little more than criminal activity. Then, in 1983, faced with a quickly deteriorating situation, the Belaúnde administration declared Ayacucho an emergency zone and sent in over 2,000 regular army soldiers to combat the PCP-SL (Loveman & Davies, 1997; McClintock, 2005). Many of these conscripts were ill prepared both physically and culturally for the highland environment. By the late 1980s, nearly 30–40% of the troops stationed in the guerilla areas had deserted the armed forces, many of whom were enjoined to do so by *Senderistas* (Strong, 1992). Those who remained often seemed unwilling or unable to distinguish between the enemy and the rest of the indigenous population (Crabtree, 1992). Members of the poorly trained and unmotivated security forces searched the homes of the indigenous peasantry and were responsible for arbitrary arrests, abductions, and disappearances, as well as summary executions (Fumerton, 2002). Soldiers frequently accused innocent indigenous civilians of collaborating with the PCP-SL. In one incident that illustrates the high levels of prejudice and fear associated with the indigenous peasant, 60 community members were indiscriminately massacred in Accomarca in 1985 (Strong, 1992). When asked to explain the rationale for these killings, Sublieutenant Hurtado responded that "one cannot trust an [indigenous] woman, old man, or a child" (Strong, 1992, p. 133). As a result of the widespread nature of similar attitudes within the military ranks, the Peruvian military was implicated in the death, disappearance, and torture of thousands of innocent peasants within just a few years of their deployment (Aprodeh, 2004; McClintock, 2005).

Escalation of Violence. As the PCP-SL expanded its influence, its violence and brutality intensified. The insurgents imposed an authoritarian and dogmatic ideology on the indigenous communities under their control, along with rudimentary forms of labor that allowed for little exchange of goods (Becker, 2006). Militants denounced innocent peasants as bourgeois for owning a few extra livestock, or for hiring an occasional laborer (Fitz-Simmons, 1993; Wheat, 1990). They destroyed crops and farm equipment, closed regional markets, and tortured and killed community members who resisted (Fitz-Simmons, 1993). As the armed insurgency continued, the *Comité Central* spent less time blending core Maoist doctrine with indigenous appeals and would explicitly target resistant indigenous communities for destruction (Corntassel & Holder, 2008).

Asháninka. Within "liberated zones" it became evident that the PCP-SL intended to eradicate all ethnocultural differences (Corntassel & Holder, 2008). This distaste for diversity was unmistakable in the extermination campaign waged against the Asháninka. The Asháninka populated a forested region of the Peruvian Amazonas, near the VRAE. They were closed to outsiders, spoke no Spanish, and violently resisted all efforts by the PCP-SL to control them (Fitz-Simmons, 1993). Their very existence contradicted the paternalistic ideology of the *mestizo*-educated insurgents, triggering an especially hostile and brutal backlash.

Inter-indigenous hostilities between the Quechua and Asháninka communities had originated years before when Quechua settlers, in attempts to gain the land they had been denied in their own regions, encroached on Asháninka land (Gagnon et al., 1993; Norholt, 2008). In consequence, the guerilla activity in the VRAE sparked intense violence against an estimated 44 Asháninka communities (10,000 people) through assassinations, slavery, and kidnapping (Strong, 1992). Approximately 5,000 members of the tribe were forced to live in inhuman living conditions in internment camps, where they often died of hunger and disease. Pregnant women were massacred or forced to abort, girls were used as sex-slaves, people were forced to kill their own family members or friends under the penalty of death, and many Asháninka children were forcibly recruited to be soldiers in armed *Sendero* operations (Strong, 1992; TRC, 2003).

3.3 A Shift in Quechua Understanding

Although the *Comité Central* had acquired a fundamental knowledge of Quechua culture, they underestimated its patterns of simultaneous resistance and adaptation, skepticism and hope, and rejection and acceptance (Allen, 1981; Ossio, 2002). Over time, *Senderistas* failed to follow the Maoist doctrine of winning hearts and minds. They systematically attacked the indigenous communal government, religion, and culture. As a result, by the end of the 1980s. PCP-SL leaders overestimated the power of their *mestizo* worldview and remained unaware of the profound adaptability and resilience of the contemporary Quechua worldview (Izaguirre, 1996). Many insurgents did not comprehend the Quechua traditions of reciprocal exchange, time-space orientation, and mutability (Folke, Frabricius, Cundill, & Schultz, 2005). In consequence, the guerrillas alienated a significant portion of their support base and contributed to the eventual decline of their own movement (Fitz-Simmons, 1993; Loveman & Davies, 1997).

By most indigenous communities perceived the guerillas as nothing more than new oppressors. Any remaining support for the guerillas was often superficial and based mostly on a fear achieved through the use of terror tactics (Fitz-Simmons, 1993; Getgen, 2008).

Reciprocal Exchange. The ethos of Quechua culture is best embodied by the ideal of *Ayni*, or delayed reciprocity and symmetrical exchange among equals. Through *Ayni*, if a neighbor requests assistance, it is readily given, thereby obligating the giver to an appropriate future exchange. *Ayni* is also inherent in the Quechua sense of justice. Punishments are intended to restore equilibrium and reincorporate an offender into the community (Albo, 1976; Drzewieniecki, 1995). In rare cases, the harshest penalties that a Quechua community might judge appropriate are those of exile and death. Accordingly, in some cases, the initial PCP-SL assassinations garnered support and acceptance as a culturally normative application of a penalty. However, in traditional communal justice, the death penalty was reserved almost exclusively for cattle rustlers who refused to stop stealing and declined to be banished from the village (Theidon, 2000). In these cases, significant discussion was required in a community assembly (Drzewieniecki, 1995).

The PCP-SL's failure to understand this aspect of *Ayni* was among their most grievous errors. For the Quechua, legitimacy is defined by trust in the fair application of justice (Drzewieniecki, 1995). Penalties are not intended to be punitive, but rather remedial, educational, or in the interest of symmetry (Theidon, 2000). Thus, the insurgents' use of disproportionate and unpredictable methods of social control undermined any perception of their legitimacy among the indigenous peasants.

Time-Space Orientation. The most well-known Andean deity is *Pachamama*, or Mother Earth. She is the source of life and symbolizes a blend of nature, humanity, and spirituality. Characteristic of highland tradition, her image is the spiritual integration of the supernatural, the sacred, and the natural (Smith, 1997). *Pacha* refers to both space and time, two elements that are perceived as inseparable and divided into a dualism of proximal and distal (Allen, 1981; Ossio, 2002). When the Quechua become oriented to a location, they also enter into a personal relationship with that space. Moreover, the Quechua define community, or *ayllu*, in terms of space: Closeness implies community, while distance implies foreignness. For the Quechua, that which is familiar and safe is considered part of the community, whereas the unfamiliar or dangerous is viewed as alien (Allen, 1981). By terrorizing indigenous communities and disrespecting traditional values, the PCP-SL grew to be perceived as an invading force and, thus "foreign". The *Senderistas* who lived in the same community were viewed as having "fallen out of humanity" and were no longer perceived as a part of the *ayllu* (Theidon, 2000). This critical shift may be further understood in terms of the mutability of Quechua beliefs.

Mutability. In contrast to the *mestizo* view of time as linear, rational, and absolute, the Quechua perceive it as cyclic and, thus, fluid, changeable, and even ambiguous (Folke et al., 2005; Ossio, 2002). This fluidity and adaptability of Quechua beliefs facilitated the dramatic shift in the indigenous understanding of the PCP-SL. Similarly, understandings of the *Pishtaco*, the tradition that had once dehumanized Peruvian security forces, came to be associated with the PCP-SL. For the Quechua, this marked the transition to a perception of the guerrillas as dangerous outsiders, with white skin and light eyes (Santos-Granero, 1998; Stimpson, 2001). On the contrary for urban-*mestizos* and Western scholars, habituated to a more linear and rational worldview, there remained a lasting perception of the PCP-SL as a movement that was rooted among the highland indigenous.

3.4 Resistance and Counter-Rebellion

Peasants grew infuriated by the PCP-SL's executions of legitimate and highly respected local leaders, people's trials, abstract justice, and other direct violations of *Ayni*. Moreover, they resented the guerrillas' tendency to steal local resources and to confiscate indigenous lands, harvests, and livestock herds (Fumerton, 2002). Such actions rapidly delegitimized guerrilla movement in the "liberated areas." Yet, military actions also took a heavy toll on highland communities (Fitz-Simmons, 1993; Loveman & Davies, 1997). Within the context of this untenable situation, the first self-defense militia surfaced. In January of 1983, when a column of eight PCP-SL guerrillas returned to an indigenous highland community, the villagers surrounded and slaughtered them (Fumerton, 2001). Urban-*mestizos* were stunned by this violent counter-rebellion, which contradicted their conviction that the PCP-SL was an indigenous movement with nearly unanimous support in the highlands. The government immediately praised the bravery and heroism of the small group of indigenous who had defied the insurgents (Fumerton, 2002). Then, less than a week later, a group of *mestizo* journalists from Lima and their guide were mistaken for guerrillas and killed by an indigenous militia just a few miles from the site of the earlier counter-rebellion. This tragedy quickly overshadowed the launch of an indigenous armed counter-rebellion and detracted from images of indigenous heroism (Fumerton, 2001).

In 1983, the Peruvian military became more active in the highlands and began requiring indigenous communities to establish community-based civil-defense militias. This government pressure, combined with waning support for the PCP-SL, motivated many indigenous communities to rescue their image by forming a reluctant and often conflicted alliance with security forces (Theidon,

2000). The result was the creation of numerous indigenous militias, which collectively became known as *rondas campesinas* (Fumerton, 2001; Nuñez-Palomino, 1996). One of the first tasks of these *rondas* was to kill the PCP-SL sympathizers within the community (Theidon, 2000). Thus, through this tenuous partnership with the Peruvian state, the communities not only resisted militant authority, but also eliminated guerrilla support systems within their own communities.

The guerillas responded with savage reprisals that the peasants were ill-prepared to handle. Rural communities experienced periodic violence such as armed incursions, brutal retaliation, regular levies of supplies and recruits (including children), and increased deaths resulting from an execution of "traitors" (Fumerton, 2002; Getgen, 2008). Simultaneously, the Peruvian state used the indigenous peasantry as a weapon to suppress guerilla activity and shield the "less expendable" military forces (Corntassel and Holder, 2008). Yet, in the cities, the *mestizo* elite were profoundly fearful of the prospect of armed bands of indigenous peasants. Consequently, for years, the *rondas* were left to arm themselves with only what they had at hand, often nothing more than farm equipment (Taylor, 1998). Indigenous communities continued to be the primary target of hostility from both military forces. Entire villages vanished, either through massacre or flight. For the Peruvian military, these ghost villages were viewed as beneficial because they left *Sendero* militants exposed, with nowhere to hide and no one to feed them (Strong, 1992).

At the end of the 1980s, the Peruvian government realized that it needed the support of the local population to defeat the PCP-SL. The state policy changed, and *rondas* were provided with training and low-grade armament (Fumerton, 2001; Mancilla, 1999; Taylor, 1998). The increased military support strengthened the peasant counter-rebellion, helping to expand it throughout Ayacucho and into nearby regions. Yet, despite the government's efforts to control the *rondas*, they maintained a clearly rural-indigenous character and autonomy of action (Mancilla, 1999). In fact, in the face of a perceived PCP-SL threat, indigenous communities put aside personal grudges and cooperated in the counter-rebellion (Fumerton, 2002). The number of *rondas* rapidly multiplied from 700 in 1989 to 1,200 in 1991, and finally to 2,400 in 1997 (Fumerton, 2001). Their efforts stalled the highland terror and defeated the PCP-SL in many rural areas (TRC, 2003).

3.5 Calming the Violence

During the 1980s, the Peruvian government had minimal success in fighting the insurgents. The secretive structure of the PCP-SL, its controlled recruiting strategies, and a pervasive lack of trust from indigenous sectors made it difficult for the Peruvian state to obtain good intelligence. Moreover, the counterinsurgency tactics of the security forces were poorly formulated, their intelligence operations unorganized, and their activity permeated by stereotypes and prejudice (Manwaring, 1995).The USA-influenced drug raids exacerbated these problems in coca-growing regions. Instead of deterring the indigenous farmers from growing coca, the attacks increased hostility to and distrust for the armed forces and facilitated an increase of support for the PCP-SL (Taylor, 1998).

In 1990, after running on a platform which targeted Peruvians of indigenous heritage, Alberto Fujimori won the presidential election. He improved military intelligence by implementing an independent counterterrorism unit (GEIN). This unit was better trained and had better resources than the police and military (Fitz-Simmons, 1993). Unlike his predecessors, the leader did not view the indigenous peasants as "backward," but instead saw them as a potential resource to be exploited – once the communities were more amenable to state control (Crabtree, 2001). He aggressively pursued a policy of compulsory mobilization and arming of the indigenous *rondas*. Then, in 1992, Fujimori suspended the constitution. Under these conditions, the counterinsurgency forces were permitted to carry out numerous human rights abuses, including holding anonymous military tribunals with a 97%

conviction rate (Becker, 2006; CDI, 2002). These tribunals not only helped the support structures of the PCP-SL to collapse, but also imprisoned numerous innocent civilians (Becker, 2006). Finally, on September 12, 1992, following a three-month intelligence campaign, the newly founded counterterrorism unit captured Abimael Guzmán and 19 other leaders of the PCP-SL movement and seized key organizational records (Becker, 2006; Fitz-Simmons, 1993). Guzmán was tried by hooded judges on October 7, 1992, and sentenced to life in prison (Strong, 1992). For many, his arrest was considered to be the beginning of the end for *Sendero Luminoso* (Becker, 2006).

In 1992, psychological operations also directly impacted many of the remaining supporters of the PCP-SL, regardless of whether their support had been based on fear, financial considerations, or ideological conviction. One tactic was to portray the legendary "Chairman Gonzalo" as a buffoon. Guzmán was dressed in a striped convict suit, brought to his initial sentencing in an iron cage, and publically ridiculed. Unflattering pictures of him were widely distributed (Taylor, 1998). These actions severely tarnished his legendary image as the Inka in a predestined movement. Guzmán's messianic image was further damaged, in 1993, when the Peruvian state announced that he and several other imprisoned leaders had called for an end to the armed struggle and attempted to negotiate a peace agreement with the government (Becker, 2006). Concurrently, Fujimori's amnesty program encouraged the guerrillas to surrender their weapons and become informants, providing the less ideologically inclined an opportunity to safely lay down their arms and cease the active insurgency (Becker, 2006).

3.5.1 Lingering Violence

After Guzmán's call for peace, the PCP-SL movement split into two factions, both of which have continued to operate in remote and lucrative coca-growing areas (Arnson, 2005). One faction was led by "Feliciano" (Oscar Ramírez Durand) until his arrest in 1999. After his capture, "José" (Victor Quispe Palmino) and "Alipio" (Orlando Borda Casablanca, alias Ronaldo Huamán Zúñiga) assumed leadership (Allmendinger, 2009; Arnson, 2005). This division has operated primarily in the VRAE and professes no loyalty to Guzmán. However, the band has marshaled significant resources through illegal logging and the cocaine trade (Arnson, 2005). Estimates of armed militants operating in the VRAE have risen from 100–150 in 2004 (Arnson, 2005) to as many as 600 in 2009 (Cruz, 2009; Husté, 2009). By 2007, the Peruvian government had instructed police and military forces to begin offensive maneuvers against the PCP-SL, particularly in this region.

"Artemio" (Florindo Eleuterio Flores Hala, alias José Flores Léon), who is believed to be the last free member of Guzmán's inner circle and the highest ranking leader of the PCP-SL at large, leads the other faction. It operates primarily in the Upper Huallaga Valley, with an estimated 150–300 active militants, and maintains ties with ideological factions in Lima and other areas of the country (Allmendinger, 2009; Arnson, 2005; Husté, 2009; MPP, 2009). "Artemio" recognizes Abimael Guzmán as the leader of Sendero Luminoso (Zapata 2010), and materials obtained in 2008 suggest that contact between them continues (Allmendinger, 2009). In March of 2002, members of the well-known Colombian guerrilla organization, the *Fuerzas Armadas Revolutionarias de Colombia* (FARC), or the Armed Revolutionary Forces of Colombia, met with members of the Huallaga Valley faction of the PCP-SL and provided them with weaponry (Semana, 2009). More recent evidence suggests that the contact between the PCP-SL and the FARC has been sustained, and an alliance between them existed as recently as 2008 (AFP, 2008). "Artemio" has also expressed a willingness to engage in political dialog, if Abimael Guzmán is permitted to serve as an interlocutor (24horas, 2010; Zapata, 2010).

Regular reports of PCP-SL activity, both large- and small-scale insurgent attacks, have continued unabated since 2000. One example of a larger-scale attack occurred in 2003 when PCP-SL militants attacked a gas pipeline and kidnapped 71 employees (Becker, 2006; Pike, 2003). In late 2008, the PCP-SL launched raids that resulted in 33 deaths and 43 injuries to soldiers over the course of a few months. In response, the Peruvian state launched a full-scale military offensive with the intent of eradicating the PCP-SL (Keating & Dickinson, 2009; Taft-Morales, 2009). To date, this offensive has failed to make significant headway or even to eliminate any of the group's new generation of leaders (Keating & Dickinson, 2009). Furthermore, the movement may be gaining support among indigenous peasants who continue to feel neglected by the government (Gregory, 2009).

Possible Resurgence. At the time of his initial sentencing in 1992, Abimael Guzmán declared: "Some think this [arrest] is a great defeat for the party, but it is only a bend in the road. The road is long, but the people will win!" (Times News Service, 1992). Guzmán further proclaimed that the PCP-SL would continue to follow its plan of strategic development and would generate a sixth military plan for the "conquest of power" (Guzmán, 1992). The finalized plan instructed PCP-SL militants to surmount the peace accord "hoax" and to reorganize the party (MPP, 1998). Thus, the conviction that the "People's War" continues in accordance with the wishes of its leader ("Chairman Gonzalo") is ingrained in the ideology of the guerrilla organization (MPP, 2003).

While PCP-SL bands are generally considered too weak to launch an offensive against the Peruvian government, some indicators support "Artemio's" 2006 declaration that "we are rising again, we are growing anew, we work in secrecy and we work for the future" (Gregory, 2009). The PCP-SL's continued ties with many of Peru's estimated 600,000 indigenous peasants who reside in coca-growing regions have provided a strong base of power and financial support for continued resistance (McClintock, 2005). Furthermore, military strategists and informants estimate that the number of rebels may have increased to nearly 900 armed militants, from both factions, in recent years (Allmendinger, 2009; Husté, 2009; Romero, 2009). Graffiti in the town of Pisco (2010), signed *Proseguir*, supports this sentiment by stating "Soon we will be in Lima to knock down businesspeople, take the place of the government of Alan García, and his guardian dogs."

Political Activity. At the end of 2009, Abimael Guzmán struck fear into the heart of Peruvian authorities when lawyers smuggled his memoirs out of prison (Ross, 2009; Wade & Velez, 2009). In the published text, *De Puño y Letra*, Guzmán defends the Maoist insurgency, calls for amnesty for both the rebels and soldiers involved in the conflict, and urges current supporters of the PCP-SL to participate in future elections (Wade & Velez, 2009). President Alan García, who headed one of the two administrations that confronted the guerilla movement during the 1980s, quickly moved to prohibit sales of the book and to prosecute Guzmán's lawyers for their part in its publication (Wade & Velez, 2009). Yet, reports suggest that the first edition of the book sold out almost immediately and, only a short while later, a second edition was considered (Guerra, 2009). Currently, the book is also available for download from various internet sites, including mediafire, freelibros, and 4shared. Senior members of the movement confirmed that PCP-SL supporters intend to heed Guzman's call and run for office in the 2010 local and regional elections (LAHT, 2009). Several members of the guerilla organization, who have been released from prison, are slated to run on the ticket of the Communist Party of Peru in the national election in 2011. Peru's justice minister has confirmed that the law does not prohibit the political wing of the guerilla organization from participating in these elections (LAHT, 2009).

Of even greater concern than the armed insurgents is the re-emergence of ideological and political activity by unarmed *Sendero* activists and the spread of PCP-SL's ideology within universities (McClintock, 2005). A striking example of ideological support occurred in 2010, when an organized pro-*Sendero* demonstration took place at the *Universidad Nacíonal Mayor de San Marcos* in Lima. The 30-80 protestors, including faculty and students, carried red flags and chanted PCP-SL slogans (Manrique, 2010; Peruservis, 2010). In addition, propaganda, in the form of flyers, was distributed at the university that day (Morales, 2010) and, among friends, other students expressed opinions supportive of the movement (Personal Communication, 2010).

4 Causes

While the PCP-SL served as the catalyst for the explosion of brutality at the end of the twentieth century, the roots of the violence lay in a more complex framework of both structural and psychological causes. Structural causes included the stratification of different societal sectors and a centralized authoritarian power structure. Typically, the fundamental structural cause of ethnic conflict occurs when leaders of a dominant ethnic group (i.e., Peruvians of European descent) hold power and use societal institutions to distribute benefits inequitably across ethnicities (Richardson & Sen, 1996). The Peruvian ruling class not only awarded themselves a privileged status, but also treated the indigenous inhabitants as inferior, even subhuman. Many of the impoverished *mestizos* and indigenous Peruvians involved in this conflict grew up in a strict and hierarchical military culture, surrounded by a normalized violence resulting from high levels of oppression, poverty, and frustration (Mancilla, 1999). The fundamental stratification and authoritarianism were further exacerbated by a pervasive sense of *machismo* (a "cult of masculinity" which presupposes male aggressiveness, power, and superiority and attaches a strong significance to preserving honor) (Bolton, 1979; Mansilla, 1999).

Social Alienation. Psychologically, social alienation can be a key characteristic of people who perpetrate brutal acts of terror (Hudson, 1999), and the PCP-SL militants and Peruvian security forces were no exception. Many of the PCP-SL's primary recruits were urban-*mestizos* who had relocated to the highlands and, consequently, were culturally estranged (Primov, 1980). Similarly, Peruvian military practices often drafted the most impoverished and disenfranchised segments of the urban-*mestizo* population and sent them to remote geographic and cultural regions. In turn, feelings of social alienation may have increased the tendency of recruits to seek affiliation and approval from their respective organizations, and the tendency to displace their negative emotions into brutal acts of violence.

In spite of poverty and marginalization, the close-knit status of indigenous communities prevented feelings of social isolation for many peasants. Yet, the indigenous youth were particularly susceptible to experiencing communal estrangement. Migrant youths, who had relocated to the city to escape the violence of the highlands, were isolated from their communities. In addition, local youths were often caught between their cultural upbringing and Western education. To exacerbate this problem, both the Peruvian security forces and the PCP-SL were involved in the kidnapping and use of highland children as soldiers. These children were separated from their communities at a young age and had only soldiers or guerillas as role models (Hudson, 1999).

Enemy Image. When the political unrest in the highlands escalated, the government quelled turbulence with force, while favoring Western cultural values. Soldiers often continued to risk their lives far from home, despite minimal reimbursement and maximal hardship. In addition, they were likely to experience a discrepancy between their own moral beliefs and the inhumanity of the atrocities in which they participated. This incongruence of attitudes and behavior may have generated feelings of cognitive dissonance (Festinger, Riecken, & Schachter, 1956; Festinger, 1957). To cope with this psychological discomfort, members of the security forces could justify their individual actions by envisioning themselves as a part of a cause greater than themselves. For example, in 1984, the Commander in Chief of the army publically provided such a justification when he announced that the Peruvian troops were fighting to protect their ethnocultural group: "[The] demented action of a group of [indigenous] subversives will never separate us from the Western and Christian culture in which we have been trained" (as cited in Strong, 1992, p. 134). These words identified the PCP-SL guerillas as alien and culturally threatening. They also justified the brutal efforts of the Peruvian armed forces in the name of a Western and Christian ethos, while explicitly denying the legitimacy of indigenous customs and beliefs (Strong, 1992). In this way, soldiers' attitudes of disdain or apathy toward the local residents may have evolved into self-righteous and unforgiving hatred of the indigenous people.

Dehumanization was another core psychological process that fostered the perpetration of atrocities by both sides. The Peruvian armed forces saw themselves as victims, defending themselves on the frontlines of an ethnocultural conflict. By stereotyping the indigenous peasant as innately violent and immoral, the soldiers justified their brutal actions as a means to preserve a more advanced culture from subhuman forces (Strong, 1992; TRC, 2003). Simultaneously, the PCP-SL promoted an enemy image of indigenous peasants as ignorant creatures, who were easily manipulated by the armed forces into impeding progress toward a Maoist state. As a result, militants considered rural inhabitants to be lower than animals and would kill them with methods considered too brutal for the slaughter of livestock (Theidon, 2000).

To dehumanize the guerrillas, the military used a common counterinsurgency tactic. This approach taps into the framing effect by encouraging different conclusions based on how information is presented (Kahneman & Tversky, 1986). The Peruvian military distributed pamphlets throughout the countryside, warning of the dangers of the subversives. Some pamphlets portrayed members of the PCP-SL as foreign criminals who were intent on destroying the indigenous peasants (Theidon, 2000). These publications played to traditional beliefs about space and time and reinforced the associated perception of outsiders as dangerous. As a result, perceived ethnocultural differences persist in the minds of many indigenous peasants, with the image of the guerillas being conflated with that of foreigners (Theidon, 2000).

However, because many initial supporters of the PCP-SL were indigenous peasants, it was often inadequate for the armed forces to portray *Senderistas* as inferior due to racial or national difference (Theidon, 2000). In consequence, other pamphlets depicted the PCP-SL as an evil and otherworldly monster. In one illustration, indigenous peasants were cowering and running from an enormous creature with sharp claws flying overhead. Behind the beast, a Peruvian soldier, hurried to rescue the peasants (Caretas #7373, 1983, as cited by Theidon, 2000). In the process of purging their communities of PCP-SL supporters, many residents used similar techniques to frame *Senderistas* as having "fallen out of humanity" (Theidon, 2000). Villagers described the guerillas as not fully human, associating them with images of the *pishtaco* (Strong, 1992; Stimpson, 2001) or as being physiologically different (i.e., possessing three belly-buttons, and genitals in an unusual place on the body) (Theidon, 2000). Some communities believed it was possible to distinguish between *Senderistas* and humans through a mark on the arms of those who supported the PCP-SL. These methods of dehumanization helped peasants slaughter members of their own communities.

5 Consequences

In addition to the nearly 70,000 deaths and 4,000 disappearances, countless people were tortured, raped, or forced into combat. More than 600,000 people left their communities and migrated from rural to urban areas as a direct result of the armed conflict (Fumerton, 2002). In fact, during the 1980s and 1990s, approximately 52% of the population of the region of Ayacucho emigrated. Of the estimated 156,575 internal refugees from this region, only 20% returned home after the violence ended (TRC, 2003). This taxed the psychological and physical well-being of the people, as well as cities' resources. The decades of strife also weakened the structures of civil society in the poorest and most indigenous regions of the country (Huancavelica, Ayacucho, Apurímac, and Huánuco), where inclusion and expansion of citizenship were needed most (TRC, 2003). The effects of violence still permeate both rural and urban society, creating pervasive hostility, distrust, and hopelessness (Alarcón & Trujillo, 1997; A. Espinoza, Personal Communication, 2010).

The immediate victims and their families are haunted by the brutality. In 2003, an estimated 4,644 burial sites remained across the country, and less than half have been investigated in any way (TRC, 2003). Thus, even decades after the violence declined, families have not yet had the chance to bury their dead. Exhumations of mass graves continue. For example, it was not until the summer of 2008 that the remains of more than 100 men, women, and children, who died at the hands of the Peruvian military in 1984, were disinterred (US DOS 2009).

Victims of torture and terror continue to suffer from the physical and psychological health effects of their ordeals. Among these victims are many women who were deeply affected by the violence. Coastal military recruits, deployed to combat the PCP-SL, commonly abused local indigenous women (Goolsby, 2004). Some estimates indicate that during the conflict, thousands of indigenous women were raped on military and police bases (LAHT, 2008). Sexual violence was also a common method of torture, and more than 80% of the rapes associated with the conflict were committed by government forces (Becker, 2006). In the 1990s, in association with counterinsurgency efforts and support from the USA, Alberto Fujimori spearheaded a birth control program that sterilized over 200,000 impoverished and indigenous women – often through enticements, pressure, threats, or deceit (Getgen, 2008; Johnson, 2000). Related accounts of state-sponsored violence against indigenous women have remained almost completely unaddressed, even by the the *Comisión de la Verdad y la Reconciliación*, or Truth and Reconciliation Commission (TRC) (Getgen, 2008).

Untreated physical and psychological trauma has also had a severe impact on highland youth. During the conflict, few children under the age of 18 years escaped the impact of violence (TRC, 2003). Estimates suggest that the PCP-SL forced over 1,000 children into combat service, while the Peruvian armed forces recruited an untold number of children (Comas-Diaz et al., 1998). As many as 1,000 children were assassinated, another 250 "disappeared" and at least 7% of all torture victims were under the age of 18 years (Aprodeh, 2004; Comas-Diaz et al., 1998). The 200,000–500,000 youths who fled to Lima or other coastal cities often suffered from malnutrition, chronic disease, and severe psychological traumas (Comas-Diaz et al. 1998; Herrera Abad, 1994). In addition, the parents of roughly 50,000 children were assassinated or disappeared. Economic marginalization, racism, and ongoing random violence further threaten the normal development of children affected by the violence (Comas-Diaz et al. 1998). Today, in many indigenous communities, there is a widespread belief that trauma associated with the conflict can be passed from mother to child (Venturoli, 2009).

6 Possible Resolutions

Finding a way to reject violence and to promote peaceful coexistence is essential to the successful resolution of a conflict (Bickford, 2004). To date, the TRC has been the principal tool used to rebuild peace and resolve past conflicts in Peru. The Commission investigated the root causes of the conflict, as well as its manifestations, in an attempt to make informed recommendations to the Peruvian government to aid in facilitating an enduring reconciliation. Among the primary facets of the conflict noted by the commission was the economic and social marginalization of indigenous peasants (TRC, 2003). The commission increased awareness of interethnic social and economic inequalities, social injustice, and the slaughter of indigenous peoples. Some members of the elite admitted that the tools used to address past and ongoing human rights abuses against the indigenous had been inadequate and uninformed (Corntassel & Holder, 2008). Most people who testified for the TRC experienced a temporary catharsis by telling their stories in an official forum, while being treated with both interest and respect (LaPlante & Theidon, 2007). Accordingly, the TRC accomplished the first step in the process of conflict resolution by raising consciousness and providing official recognition of the events that occurred during the conflict (F. Huilca, Personal Communication, 2010; Kaminer, 2001). The commission also made a number of potentially helpful recommendations. However, while the TRC initially raised expectations for restorative justice, the Peruvian state has left them largely unmet (Laplante & Theidon, 2007). In consequence, the efforts of the TRC are generally considered insufficient to promote full healing (LaPlante & Theidon, 2007; Personal Communication, 2010).

Between 2006 and 2009, of the 700 cases of human rights abuses under initial investigation, only 10 went to court (Peru Support Group, 2009). Many survivors have been further disappointed by repeated delays in dispensing reparatory measures (Laplante and Theidon, 2007). In 2010, President Alan García announced that reparations to the 76,000 documented relatives of counterinsurgency war victims would only begin after the government registry was closed and only if public funds were available for that purpose (Paez, 2010). As a result of these continued postponements, there is concern that many of the 10,000 future beneficiaries who are over the age of 60 years may never directly benefit from any form of restorative justice (Paez, 2010). The Peruvian state has also failed to provide closure for many relatives of PCP-SL victims. In one case, although the burial locations of 72 of 99 people have been reported, prosecutors have not obtained the testimony of survivors or ordered the disinterment of the bodies (Salazar, 2010).

6.1 Indigenous Peace Building

In spite of the harsh violence, discrimination, and overwhelming lack of a governmental support structure, many indigenous peasants have tried to establish peace in their communities. These efforts included voluntary creation of self-defense committees, compliance with military orders to create civil-defense committees, efforts to resist association with any armed actors (Langdon & Rodriguez, 2007), migration, political mobilization of women (to find their family members and raise awareness of the ongoing atrocities) (TRC, 2003), and micro-reconciliation processes with PCP-SL deserters who requested reintegration into the community (Theidon, 2000).

The emergence of the *rondas campesinas* in the southern highlands is the most well-known indigenous peace-building effort. In fact, the active resistance to the PCP-SL played a significant role in the decrease of the intensity of the highland conflict. However, the *rondas* also used violent methods, often killing PCP-SL supporters or occasionally even residents of neighboring communities. The deaths of PCP-SL supporters attracted reprisals from the guerillas and modeled violent solutions to village children.

Subjugation by the Peruvian ruling classes had isolated the impoverished indigenous peasantry from access to any infrastructure that could offer assistance. Moreover, networks linking the rural-indigenous and the urban-*mestizo* were fragile or nonexistent (TRC, 2003). Migration established a certain peace for family members, but was often accompanied by isolation, discontent, and other hardships associated with relocation. Efforts by victim groups to heighten awareness of the conflict in the coastal power centers were met with apathy from an unaffected *mestizo* population (Yates, 2006). As a result, many of the perpetrators of brutal atrocities were often left unpunished (TRC, 2003).

In spite of these difficulties, numerous civic and social organizations advocated for human or victims' rights. One of the most notable victims' rights organizations is the *Asociación Nacíonal de Familiares de Secuestrados, Detenidos y Desaparecidos del Perú* (ANFASEP), or Peruvian National Association of Families of the Abducted, Detained, and Disappeared. Members of ANFASEP are primarily impoverished, Quechua-speaking women, who resolutely worked to locate disappeared family members and to ensure that the perpetrators of crimes were brought to justice (TRC, 2003). Groups such as ANFASEP have chastized the Peruvian government for its behavior and encouraged monitoring of the Peruvian security forces (TRC, 2003). As the conflict progressed, some organizations encouraged human rights advocates to include not only government forces, but also subversive groups, in their analyses (TRC, 2003). Human rights groups also refused to provide legal assistance to militants or leaders of the PCP-SL (TRC, 2003). Many of the victims' rights groups continue to be actively involved in advocating for justice (Paez, 2010; Salazar, 2010).

6.2 Micro-Reconciliation Processes

Indigenous peasants were involved in the conflict not only as victims, but also as perpetrators of the violence. Many (whether they volunteered, were "duped", or coerced) served as low-ranking guerillas in the PCP-SL. Others peasants were military draftees, forcibly recruited child soldiers, or members of the *rondas campesinas* (either voluntarily or compulsorily). The result was an intricate and complex web of fratricidal violence and a landscape where former guerrillas, current sympathizers, and those who fought in *rondas* lived alongside others who were tortured, relocated, or lost family members (Theidon, 2000). At times, members of the same family fought for opposing forces (Personal Communication, 2010). Thus, the micro-reconciliation processes that took place within the Quechua communities may be the most successful, noteworthy, and revealing of the various peace-building strategies.

In Quechua, reconciliation is best translated as coexistence (Theidon, 2000). Accordingly, the goal of these micro-reconciliation processes was not to forgive, or to forget, but to live together. This successful coexistence required a process that would restore sufficient trust and sociability to permit cooperation within the context of daily community life (Theidon, 2000). While these micro-reconciliation processes took place at different times for different communities, they most likely began in the early 1980s. Thus, indigenous reconciliation practices often co-occurred with the conflict.

This process of micro-reconciliation is best understood within a cultural framework of mutability, equilibrium, and sacred spaces. For the Quechua, identity is relational: When time and social relations change, so does the definition of the person (Theidon, 2000). In other words, a person who had been identified as a guerrilla might be viewed as having "fallen out of humanity' due to his or her primary social relationship with the PCP-SL. The same person's could later be identified as a community member because of the preeminence of the person's social relations with the community. However, for this reintegration into the community to occur, former guerrillas had to be re-accepted as human (Theidon, 2000). To accomplish this, the peasants re-framed and revised terminology. For example, the Peruvian elite used the term "*enganado*" (or "fooled") as a derogative reference to the indigenous peasants, implying that they are ignorant and foolish. Community members adopted this phrase to explain how former guerrillas, who were reabsorbed into communities, had been duped into supporting the activities of the PCP-SL (Fitz-Simmons, 1993). Thus, the mutability of the Quechua worldview greatly facilitated the process of reintegrating former guerillas into rural communities.

Consistent with Quechua norms of justice, for a former guerrilla to be reintegrated into a community, a sense of symmetry was necessary. As such, a former PCP-SL militant would appear to community leaders, explain his or her transgressions, offer a heartfelt apology, and declare a peaceful intent. At that point, he or she would request to return to a normal community life (Theidon, 2000). In making the final decision, community leaders weighed the emotions of the former guerilla more heavily than the words. If the decision was to accept him or her back into the community, an appropriate sanction would then be established and administered (Theidon, 2000). Often this punishment would involve a public whipping and an admonition of the treatment they would receive if they offered any support to the PCP-SL. These sanctions were not meant to be purely symmetrical, but rather remedial methods that would allow for communal reintegration (Theidon, 2000).

The Quechua view social relations in terms of collaboration and cooperation to benefit the community. Thus, working communal land alongside community members was a form of reparation and a component of the process of becoming human. Former guerillas showed loyalty to the community by working alongside one another and establishing interdependence (Theidon, 2000). The converted militants further established their value to their community by providing intelligence to the *rondas campesinas* on the operating strategies and weaknesses of *Sendero* cadres (Theidon, 2000). During some stages of the conflict, these individuals were so valuable to communities that members would actively go out into the hills to try to find Quechua guerillas, "rescue" them, and convert them back to human beings (Theidon, 2000).

In Quechua communities, reparation occurs through awareness and a reconsideration of prior events, not by blind forgiveness (Comas-Diaz et al. 1998; González Holguín, 1989). By being fully integrated into the village rather than ostracized or isolated, former guerrillas would be watched night and day in order to see if they made any attempt to return to the guerrillas or to contact them. If they had truly repented and it became evident that their loyalties were now to the community in which they lived, then their acceptance within the community would increase. Thus, on a practical level, emplacement strategies of land distribution and communal work provided opportunities for community vigilance of the former guerillas (Theidon, 2000). On a cultural level, the former guerrillas also became rooted in a local context and associated with sacred spaces and, consequently, grew to be perceived as a part of the community itself. It was then that the "mark of evil" believed to be evident on the guerrillas was believed to disappear and that they were considered human again (Theidon, 2000).

7 Implications for Other Ethnopolitical Conflicts

There are a number of cautionary lessons that the Peruvian conflict can teach the international community. First, it is essential to recognize the destructive power of structural violence associated with prejudice and social segregation. Strong cultural divisions within a country can cause it to rupture along its fault lines. Inequality is a force that can be exploited for subversive purposes. In Peru, the social divide along ethnocultural lines bred discontent among the indigenous who occupied the lower social strata. Moreover, both the urban-*mestizo* and rural-indigenous incorporated the ethnocultural divide into their own identities, solidifying an "us" versus "them" mentality. Different political ideologies may have driven the initial conflict among urban-*mestizos* intellectuals, but the strategies that evolved from both sides directly tapped into perceived threats and real injustices. Harsh ethnocultural divisions facilitated the process of dehumanization and perpetration of carnage on both sides.

Second, education is an important tool for both building and relieving conflict. In Peru, the gap between the goals of the state and the experiences of educators fostered the spread of discontent throughout the educational system. The dissatisfied and socially alienated educators not only discussed government failings, but also propagated dissent among their students. In this academic environment, the PCP-SL was founded and intellectuals disseminated its ideology. Teachers acted as a primary force in the recruitment and the spread of support for the PCP-SL. Conversely, educators are a powerful force that could be similarly mobilized to lessen or prevent the exacerbation of conflict.

Third, global support systems are accessible not only to state governments, but also to subversive organizations. In spite of *Sendero's* apparent self-sufficiency, its primary leaders were trained overseas and the international drug trade supplied the movement's most lucrative financing. The PCP-SL also maintained associations with global Maoist revolutionary movements through participation in the Revolutionary Internationalist Movement (RIM). Other efforts to increase international support have included participation in international conferences, the translation of material into different languages, and the launch of websites such as redsun.org or newperu.org. Finally, if the degree of collaboration between two Latin American guerrilla movements (the PCP-SL and FARC) should strengthen, it could signal a potential increase in the ongoing armed conflict with *Sendero* militants.

Fourth, repressive tactics may subdue immediate violence, but they cannot provide a sustained peace. On the contrary, such tactics are often a root cause of ethnocultural conflict. The early tactics of intimidation and coercive interrogation employed by the Peruvian security forces alienated the local population and, in combination with the apparent momentum of the insurgency, worked to increase support for the PCP-SL (Gorriti, 1999). Furthermore, Fujimori's harsh and repressive tactics may have suppressed the rebellion in the 1990s, but they left strong ethnocultural and regional tensions intact. To date, violent conflicts continue to occur in key regions, and the threat of a possible resurgence creates an enduring sense of national anxiety. In fact, the use of oppressive tactics to regain control may have increased the likelihood of long-term hostilities.

8 Suggestions for Policymakers

To create a lasting peace in Peru, the deep cultural gap between the indigenous and nonindigenous must be bridged. The psychological construction of an internal enemy in the minds of the Peruvian populace is rife with stereotyping and discrimination. Indigenous peasants, especially in the coca-growing regions where the activity of the PCP-SL remains the strongest, live in constant fear of losing their livelihood, being displaced, or being a casualty of the PCP-SL, drug traffickers, the Peruvian security forces, or even foreign military forces waging a war on drugs. Secrecy surrounds the operations of the Peruvian security forces in the affected regions as they continue to violate human rights regularly. Animosity persists between the indigenous peasantry located in the emergency zones and the armed security forces that operate there (Personal Communication, 2010). Moreover, individuals who are taught to hate, from generation to generation, carry out brutal acts of terrorism (Hudson, 1999). The lessons of the past have not altered Peru's pervasive culture of war, and brutal violence may erupt once again. However, without an enemy, blind obedience, violent acts, or an ignorance of critical information, there can be no war (Adams, 2005).

One solution is for the Peruvian government to set an unambiguous goal to replace the culture of war with a culture of peace. This culture of peace should be characterized by a "set of values, attitudes, modes of behavior and ways of life that reject violence and prevent conflicts by tackling their root causes to solve problems through dialogue and negotiation among individuals, groups and nations" (UNSESCO, 2009). To achieve such a cultural change, the Peruvian state must make clear and consistent efforts to address the recommendations of the TRC. In addition, the government should collaborate with indigenous communities in a resolute effort to (1) provide sanctuary from human rights abuses, (2) achieve reconciliation, (3) establish a superordinate identity, and (4) educate the citizenry and the world.

8.1 Sanctuary from Human Rights Abuses

In the aftermath of the violence, and particularly in conflict-ridden emergency zones, human rights abuses abound. An estimated 20,000–40,000 persons continue to work as forced laborers as a consequence of either slavery or debt bondage. Of those, approximately 160 Asháninka families in remote areas are compelled to grow crops (CDI, 2005; TRC, 2003). Furthermore, roughly 5,000 children are thought to work as forced laborers in these same coca-growing regions (USDOS, 2009). Many indigenous persons who lack identity documents, especially those displaced during the height of the armed conflict, cannot exercise basic rights, including claiming their rightful eligibility for reparations (USDOS, 2009; White; 2009). In 2008 alone, government forces were implicated in at least six unlawful killings, the disappearance of 2 minors, 17 cases of aggravated torture, and the use of "excessive force" on other occasions (USDOS, 2009). The victims of these abuses are hesitant to press charges due to a fear that the perpetrators of these acts will not be adequately prosecuted (USDOS, 2009). Thus, a culture of war remains strong in many regions of Peru. To bring about a culture of peace, a feeling of safety within these regions must be nurtured.

One way to tackle this critical issue is for the government to sanction and support zones of peace. These zones should be physical locations of sacred or cultural importance that are protected by the local community and are free of violence and retribution (ZOPIF, 2009). Zones of peace are communal, conflict-free sanctuaries in which weaponry, violence, and injustice are prohibited and peace is supported (Monteil, 2008). The spaces would permit victims of human rights abuses and forced laborers to safely receive necessary services from trained intermediaries, such as assistance in navigating government bureaucracy or accessing systems of social justice.

Peru may be amenable to this type of peacebuilding effort for a number of reasons. A structure for peasant mobilization in the creation of a zone of peace already exists in the *rondas campesinas* (Monteil, 2008). Many *rondas* developed in response to external pressures, but operated in accordance with community norms and maintained autonomy from the primary parties of the conflict (Mancella, 1998). Although many *rondas* engaged in violent acts, these were efforts to protect the communities, and many later dedicated themselves to more development-oriented projects (Monteil, 2008). Furthermore, in accordance with indigenous worldviews, space is naturally imbued with a sacred nature. Thus, once established, a zone of peace is likely to be respected by the local indigenous populations due to its sacred nature. Security forces are also likely to respect this zone if it is upheld by governmental authority.

8.1.1 Reconciliation

The work of the TRC revealed that social and economic inequalities, racism, and contemptuous attitudes toward indigenous Peruvians, and cultural misunderstandings allowed the tragic deaths of thousands of indigenous peasants to go unnoticed (TRC, 2003). The TRC attempted to develop an adequate reparation plan that linked the damage to these causes, but the state has failed to provide adequate reparations (LaPlante & Spears, 2008). Peru continues to face ethnocultural conditions similar to those that led to the growth of the PCP-SL guerrilla movement (Becker, 2006) Racism is omnipresent, with little empathy and solidarity among groups (Portocarrero Maisch, Valentin, & Irigoyen, 1991). Quechua speakers remain marginalized and powerless (Hornberger & Coronel-Molina, 2004). Moreover, through the TRC the victims of the armed conflict told their stories, but the perpetrators did not. Members of the security forces who were responsible for the atrocities were neither punished nor forgiven by the state. Victim testimony may have been cathartic, but did not result in concrete solutions (Theidon, 2000). The commission's recognition that discriminatory state practices led to the death of large portions of the indigenous population was groundbreaking. However, this acknowledgment was insufficient to compel the government to reconsider its relationship with the indigenous communities (Corntassel & Holder, 2008).

The most promising roadmap for conflict resolution between the Peruvian state and the indigenous communities lies in the micro-reconciliation processes that occurred among the Quechua. These processes addressed the Quechua cultural value of symmetrical justice. Many perpetrators are likely to feel guilt or regret for their actions (Stephan, 2008). Thus, reconciliation might be more successful if low-ranking perpetrators were encouraged to tell their story and express repentance for their atrocities. This process would create symmetry for indigenous victims and an opportunity for confession, atonement, and healing for the perpetrator. As suggested by the guidelines of the 2003 Truth and Reconciliation process, amnesty should not be offered. However, justice could be administered through hours of community service and collaboration with the indigenous communities (including *ronderos* and even former guerrillas), perhaps in the creation or maintenance of zones of peace. The general sentiment among many Quechua peasants is "If the soldiers want to reconcile with us, then let them come here and apologize and repent for what they did" (Theidon, 2000).

Such collaborative acts of reconciliation could promote a feeling of closure and reduce prejudice. Intergroup contact reduces prejudice when four preconditions are met: Equal status, cooperative activity, personal interaction, and social norms (Allport, 1954). Teams with individuals from diverse ethnocultural backgrounds could engage in programs of cooperative tasks in addition to activities that encourage personal communication. The Peruvian state could also train project leaders to carry out their responsibility to foster norms that support positive interactions among participants. These efforts are apt to be more beneficial to the construction of a lasting peace in Peru than fiscal reparations alone.

8.1.2 Superordinate Identity

Creating a superordinate identity that encompasses both Western and indigenous cultures is an essential precondition of sustained peace. When disparate groups categorize themselves in terms of a common superordinate identity, stereotyping, prejudice, and discrimination are decreased (Gomez et al., 2008). Care should be taken to not diminish or defeat subgroup identity. In fact, one of the most critical errors made by the PCP-SL was its imposition of a superordinate identity (class), which subsumed subgroup (cultural) identity. In effect, a subgroup identity is compatible with a superordinate identity. It is the combination of the two, rather than a privileging of one of these identities, which decreases hostilities (Eggins, Haslam, & Reynolds, 2002). Accordingly, the TRC recommended that Peruvians be taught to value the ethnic, linguistic, cultural, and religious diversity of their nation, and to create simultaneously a shared historical memory (TRC, 2003).

8.1.3 Education

This culture of war is broader and deeper than war itself. Overt force is not the only ingredient that perpetuates a cycle of violence. Violence is instilled in human thought patterns through secrecy, propaganda, and education (Adams, 2005). A culture of peace is also fashioned through ongoing educational practices that provide insight into ethnocultural issues. While some multicultural initiatives have been implemented in Peru, little has been done to include them in educational curricula (A. Espinoza, Personal Communication, 2010). In ethnically diverse democracies, practices related to multicultural education and cross-cultural understanding have successfully reduced intergroup conflict (Stephan, 2008). Multicultural education provides the learner with a historical perspective on other ethnocultural groups and an awareness of the skills necessary for intergroup interactions. Practices related to cross-cultural understanding evoke the belief that conflict is a result of group differences. Accordingly, educational programs such as these endeavor to increase the learners' understanding of and identification with their own and other ethnocultural groups (Stephan, 2008). In the case of Peru, urban-*mestizos* could learn about key aspects of Quechua culture such as mutability and the time-space relationship. Simultaneously, members of indigenous communities could learn about the contrasting *mestizo* norms of linear thinking and the separation of time and space. Exchanging ideas in a nonjudgmental and accepting environment might facilitate empathic understanding and improve ethnocultural relations. Furthermore, empathy decreases the tendency to perpetrate acts of brutality, such as those performed during the height of the conflict (Mealy & Stephan, 2009). Thus, educational programs should include activities that encourage intergroup empathy.

9 Summary

The Peruvian conflict arose out of ethnocultural, geographic, and socioeconomic divisions that shaped a national atmosphere of hatred, distrust, and stereotyping of the "other". The PCP-SL capitalized on societal problems, fractures, and disagreements among socially alienated *mestizos* and indigenous youths. It gripped underdeveloped and highly conflicted areas by preying on and organizing populations that had been alienated from the process of social and political democratization. Simultaneously, the top echelons of the PCP-SL targeted the indigenous peasantry to obtain material support and bodies to augment the ranks of military combatants (Becker, 2006). Indigenous peasants and communities who did not support the PCP-SL faced ruthless retaliation.

As indigenous persons struggled for survival (both personal and cultural) and autonomy in the face of this harsh physical and psychological brutality, the urban elite reacted with indifference, ignorance, confusion, and political and economic exploitation. Furthermore, the police, armed forces, legislature, judicial system, media, and others were as much a part of the problem as a part of the solution. At their worst, government institutions acted with racial hatred, perpetrating violence in the name of government order. At their best, they acted out of ignorance, neglecting their duties and standing by in the face of atrocities committed against indigenous citizens. Thus, the conflict demonstrated the horrifying effects of unchecked prejudice, discrimination, dehumanization, and implicit biases.

Repercussions include disappeared family members, unexamined mass graves, population shifts, disruptions in family structure and education, untreated psychological and physical trauma, and unfulfilled promises of reparation. The continued corruption and seeming impunity of members of the Peruvian security forces, maintenance of narcotrafficking activity, and the continuation of a culture of violence and ethnic hostility have further compounded the problems. The TRC of Peru documented the violations of civil, political, economic, social, and cultural rights, but fell short of creating a lasting resolution. Unfortunately, recent increases in PCP-SL activity may reflect support from other guerilla organizations, as well as the indigenous peasantry. To prevent future atrocities, the state presence in the highlands must be strong enough to promote citizen participation and prevent subversion while maintaining respect for local identities, social organizations, and cultural diversity. Furthermore, the state must act as a benefactor for these persecuted groups, and support both national and community institutions that provide a sanctuary from human rights abuses and promote superordinate identity, multicultural education, and, most importantly, culturally sensitive reconciliation processes. These processes must be effective not only in healing the wounds of the past, but in laying the groundwork for prevention of future conflict.

Appendices

Table 21.1 Conflict statistics

Violence facts		1980–2000	2000±
Conflict	State of conflict	Active	Active
	Index of conflict	High (1980–1995) Low (1995–2000)	Low
Armed Militants	Shining path	10,000 (estimated)	900 (estimated)
Victims	Displaced	>600,000	Unknown
	Fatalities	61,007–77,552	Unknown
	Disappeared	>4,000	Unknown
	Demography	75% Indigenous Peasants	Unknown
Perpetrator	Shining Path	46–54%	Unknown
	The State	30–44.5%	Unknown
	Indigenous Self-Defense Committees (*Rondas Campesinas*)	<23%	Unknown
Resolution		Decline in Violence	Medium

Table 21.2 Timeline of major events

Year	Event
1930	José Carlos Mariátegui dies; the Peruvian Socialist Party becomes the Peruvian Communist Party.
1934	Abimael Guzmán is born.
1959	The Cuban Revolution takes place.
1959	Hugo Blanco begins to organize a revolutionary peasant movement in La Convención Valley.
1962	Guzmán begins to teach philosophy at the University of Huamanga.
1963	Fernando Belaúnde Terry is elected president of Peru; police capture and imprison Hugo Blanco.
1964	The Peruvian Communist Party splits into pro-Moscow and pro-Chinese factions.
1965	**Guzmán travels to the People's Republic of China for the** first time; Luis de la Puente Uceda's armed ` revolutionary group fails.
1968	A coup d'état led by General Juan Velasco Alvarado succeeds.
1969	Proliferation of Agrarian Reform Law.
1970	Guzmán forms the Communist Party of Peru-Shining Path.
1975	A coup d'état led by Francisco Morales Bermudez succeeds.
1980	**Fernando Belaúnde Terry wins Peru's** first presidential elections in seventeen years;
1980	The PCP-SL launches the armed phase of its "People's War."
1981	**The PCP-SL begins profi**ting from the cocaine trade.
1983	Belaúnde coins the term narcoterrorism to refer to the drug-related activities of The PCP-SL **(and other Peruvian guerrilla movements); the Peruvian government establishes the** first *rondas campesinas* (rural patrols) to combat the PCP-SL.
1985	Alan García Pérez is elected president of Peru.
1990	Alberto Fujimori is elected president of Peru.
1992	Guzmán is captured and sentenced to life imprisonment; Fujimori assumes dictatorial rule.
1993	Guzmán calls for an end to armed struggle and offers to negotiate with the Peruvian government; the PCP-SL splits into two factions.
1995	Peru grants amnesty to members of the police and military who were implicated in human rights abuses since 1980.
1999	The government captures Oscar Ramírez Durand, alias Feliciano, the highest-ranking PCP-SL leader still at large after Guzmán's capture
2000	Fujimori falls from power and goes into exile in Japan.
2001	Alejandro Toledo is elected president of Peru.
2003	**The** final report of the Truth and Reconciliation Commission is released.
2006	Alán García Pérez is elected president of Peru; Guzmán is sentenced to life in prison for terrorism.
2008	The PCP-SL participates in its most deadly attack in 10 years.
2009	The PCP-SL announces plans to re-launch itself as a political movement; Guzmán publishes his book "De Puño y Letra"; Peruvian leaders discuss the possibility of declaring the Apurimac and Ene River Valleys (VRAE) a war zone.
2010	Due to narcoterrorism concerns, Peru declares a 60-day state of emergency in Huánco, Ucayali, and San Martín; in Lima, at the Universidad Nacíonal Mayor de San Marcos, 40 students and faculty members participated in a pro-*Sendero* march.

References

Adams, D. (2005). *Definition of culture of peace*. http://www.culture-of-peace.info. Accessed December 2009.

AFP. (2008). Colombia informed Peru of Contacts of FARC with Sendero Luminoso and MRTA. *El Nuevo Diario*. http://www.elnuevodiario.com.ni/internacionales/17506. Accessed December 2009.

Alarcón, R. D., & Trujillo, J. (1997). La contemporaneidad de la violencia y su afronte multidimensional [Violence's contemporaneity and its multidimensional confrontation]. *Alcmeon 23, 6*(3), 223–240. http://www.alcmeon.com.ar/6/23/a23_02.htm. Accessed November 2009.

Albo, X. (1976). La Paradoja Aymara: Solidaridad y Faccionalismo. *Estudios Andinos, 4*(11), 67–109.

Allen, C. J. (1981). To be Quechua: The symbolism of coca chewing in Highland Peru. *American Ethnologist, 8*(1), 157–171. Blackwell Publishing.

Allmendinger, K. (2009). Dynamic profile of the shining path. Intelligence Analyst. *INT 502: Terrorism*. http://www.krisallmendinger.com/wp-content/uploads/2009/06/Dynamic-Profile-of-The-Shining-Path.pdf. Accessed November 2009.

Allport, G. W. (1954). *The nature of prejudice*. Cambridge, MA: Addison-Wesley.

APRODEH. (2004). Violencia Contra Niños y Niñas: Hasta sus Menorcitos ahora Lloran. In Asociación Pro Derechos Humanos (Ed.), Selección de textos del Informe Final de la Comisión de la Verdad y Reconciliación. http://www.aprodeh.org.pe. Accessed November 2009. Lima

Arena, M. P., & Arrigo, B. A. (2006). *The terrorist identity: Explaining the terrorist threat*. New York: New York University Press.

Arnson, C. (2005). The evolution of internal war in Peru: The conjunction of need, creed, and organizational finance. In C. Arnson (Ed.), *Rethinking the economics of war: The intersection of need, creed, and greed*. Washington, DC: Woodrow Wilson Center Press.

Ash, R. B. (1985). The rural struggle in Latin America: The case of Peru and Sendero. *The RUSI Journal, 130*(2), 39–42. doi:10.1080/03071848508522701.

Barton, C. (1983). Peru-"Dirty War" in Ayacucho. In NACLA Report on the Americas. *17*(3).

Becker, M. (2006). Peruvian shining path. In J. Defronzo (Ed.), *Revolutionary movements in world history from 1750 to the Present*. Santa Barbara, CA: ABC-CLIO.

Bennett, P. (1984). Peru: Corner of the Dead. *Atlantic*, pp. 28–33.

Bickford, L. (2004). Transitional Justice. In Macmillan (Ed.), *Encyclopedia of genocide and crimes against humanity* (Vol. 3). New York: MacMillan Reference USA.

Bolton, R. (1979). Machismo in motion: The ethos of Peruvian truckers. *Ethos, 7*(4), 312–342.

Brouneus, K. (2008). Truth-telling as a talking cure? Insecurity and read trauma to station in the Rwandan Gacaca court. *Security Dialogue, 39*(1), 55–76.

CDI. (2002). *Terrorism project: In the Spotlight: Sendero Luminoso. Center for Defense Intervention (CDI)*. http://www.cdi.org/terrorism/sendero.cfm. Accessed November 20, 2009.

CDI. (2005). *State Department Reports on the Use of Child Soldiers. Center for Defense Intervention (CDI)* http://www.cdi.org. Accessed November 2009.

CIA. (2009). *CIA Peru Factbook*. https://www.cia.gov/library/publications/the-world-factbook/. Accessed 11/09/09.

Comas-Diaz, L., Lykes, M. B., & Alarcon, R. D. (1998). Ethnic conflict and the psychology of liberation in Guatemala, Peru, and Puerto Rico. *American Psychologist, 53*(7), 778–792. doi:10.1037/0003-066X.53.7.778.

Comité Central. (1988). *The Mass Line*. http://www.blythe.org/peru-pcp/docs_en/massline.htm & http://www.massline.info/Peru/ML_PCP.htm. Accessed December 9, 2009.

Corntassel, J., & Holder, C. (2008). Who's sorry now? Government apologies, truth commissions, and indigenous self-determination in Australia, Canada, Guatemala, and Peru. Human Rights Review. doi:10.1007/s12142-008-0065-3.

Crabtree, J. (1992). *Peru under Garcia: An opportunity lost*. Pittsburgh, PA: University of Pittsburgh Press.

Crabtree, J. (2001). The collapse of Fujimorismo: Authoritarianism and its limits. *Bulletin of Latin American Research, 20*(3), 287–303.

Crenshaw, M. (1995). *Terrorism in context*. University Park, PA: Pennsylvania State University Press.

Cruz, E. (2009). El solapado cambio de piel de Sendero Luminoso en el VRAE. La Republica. http://www.larepublica.pe/politica/19/04/2009/el-solapado-cambio-de-piel-de-sendero-luminoso-en-el-vrae-0. Retrieved September 19 2010.

Degregori, C. I. (1990). El Surgimiento de Sendero Luminoso: Del Movimiento por la Gratitud de la Ensenanza al Incio de la Lucha Armada. Lima Instituto de Estudios Peruanos.

Degregori, C. I. (1991a). Return to the Past. In D. S. Palmer (Ed.), *Shining path of Peru* (pp. 33–44). New York: St. Martin's Press.

Degregori, C. I. (1991b). How difficult it is to be God: Ideology and political violence in Sendero Luminoso. *Critique of Anthropology, 11*, 233–250.

Del Pino, Ponciano. (1999). Familia, cultura y revolución. Vida cotidiana en Sendero Luminoso. In S. Stern (Ed.), *Los Senderos Insólitos en el Perú. Guerra y sociedad, 1980–1995*. IEP, pp. 176–177.

DeQuine, J. (1984). The challenge of the shining path: Peru's enigmatic killers. *The Nation, 239*(19), 610–613.

Drzewieniecki, J. (1995). *Indigenous people, law, and politics in Peru*. Washington DC: Latin American Studies Association. http://lanic.utexas.edu/project/lasa95/drz.html. Accessed December 2009.

Eggins, R. A., Haslam, S. A., & Reynolds, K. J. (2002). Social identity and negotiation: Subgroup representation and superordinate consensus. *Personality and Social Psychology Bulletin, 28*, 887. doi:10.1177/014616720202800703.

Festinger, L. (1957). *A theory of cognitive dissonance*. Stanford, CA: Stanford University Press.

Festinger, L., Riecken, H., & Schachter, S. (1956). *When prophecy fails: A social and psychological study of a modern group that predicted the destruction of the world*. New York: Harper-Torchbooks. ISBN 0061311324.

Fitz-Simmons, D. W. (1993). Sendero luminoso: Case study in insurgency. *Parameters*, pp. 64–73.

Folke, C., Frabricius, C., Cundill, G., & Schultz, L. (2005). Communities, ecosystems, and livelihoods. *Millennium Ecosystem Assessment: Synthesis Report*. http://www.millenniumassessment.org/ Accessed November 2009.

Fumerton, M. (2001). Rondas campesinas in the Peruvian civil war: Peasant self defense organizations in Ayacucho. *Bulletin of Latin American Research, 20*(4), 481.

Fumerton, M. (2002). *From victims to heroes: Peasant counter-rebellion and civil war in Ayacucho, Peru, 1980–2000*. Amsterdam: Thela Publishers.

Gaertner, S. L., & Dovidio, J. F. (1986). The aversive form of racism. In J. F. Dovidio & S. L. Gaertner (Eds.), *Prejudice, discrimination, and racism* (pp. 61–89). Orlando, FL: Academic Press.

Gagnon, M., Hoffer, W., & Hoffer, M. (1993). *Warriors in Eden*. New York: William and Morrow and Company.

Gelles, P. H. (2002). Andean culture, indigenous identity, and the state in Peru. In D. Marybury-Lewis (Ed.), *The politics of ethnicity: indigenous peoples in Latin American states*. Cambridge, MA: Harvard University Press.

Getgen, J. E. (2008). *Untold truths: The exclusion of enforced sterilizations from the Peruvian truth commission's final report*. Working Paper. Cornell Law Library.

Gomez, A., Dovidio, J. F., Huici, C., Gaertner, S. L., & Cuadrado, I. (2008). The other side of we: When outgroup members express common identity. *Personality and Social Psychology Bulletin, 34*, 1613. doi:10.1177/0146167208323600.

González Holguín, D. (1989). Vocabulario de la lengua general de todo el Peru llamada Quichua o del Inca [General language vocabulary of the Quechua and Inca of Peru]. Lima, Peru.

Goolsby, R. (2004). The sexual exploitation of Latin American immigrant women in montgomery county, MD. *Libertad Latina*. http://www.libertadlatina.org/the%20sexual%20exploitation%20of%20latin%20american%20immigrant%20women.htm. Accessed December 2009.

Gorriti, G. (1991). Latin America's internal wars. *Journal of Democracy,* (2)1, 85–98. doi: 10.1353/jod.1991.0002.

Gorriti Ellenbogen, G. (1999). *The shining path: A history of the millenarian war in Peru*. Chapel Hill: University of North Carolina Press.

Gorriti, G. (2006). The fog of forgetting: Thirteen years and two trials after first sentencing, the leader of Peru's shining path is back in court. *The Big Chill*, 35(3), 6–13. doi: 10.1080/03064220600922224.

Gootenburg, P. (2008). *Andean cocaine: The making of a global drug*. Chapel Hill, NC: University of North Carolina Press.

Granados, M. (1987). El PCP Sendero Luminoso: aproximaciones a su ideologia. Socialismo y Participacion *37*, 15–35.

Gregory, K. (2009). Shining path, Tupac Amaru (Peru, Leftists). *Council on Foreign Relations*. http://www.cfr.org/publication/9276/. Accessed December 2009.

Guerra, I. (2009). Peru: Publisher of Abimael Guzman's book had been sentenced on terrorism charges. LivinginPeru.com. http://www.livinginperu.com/news/10106. Accessed November 21 2009.

Guzmán, A. (1992). Speech from the Cage. Transcript reported by the Communist Party of Peru (1998) via NY Transfer/Blythe. NY Transfer Archive of Historical Documents by the PCP-SL in the 1990's. Last Updated in November 1998. http://www.blythe.org/peru-pcp/docs_en/speech.htm. Accessed November 2009.

Herrera Abad, L. (1994). Acerca de la guerra, la violencia y la desilusión [About war, violence and disillusion]. In C. Aldana, M. J. Oyague, & C. Torres Llosa (Eds.), *Infancia y violencia 2: Experiencias y reflexiones sobre los niños y la violencia política en el Peru* (pp. 65–80). Lima, Peru: Cedapp-Centro de desarrollo y asesoría psicosocial.

Hornberger, N. H., & Coronel-Molina, S. M. (2004). Quechua language shift, maintenance and revitalization in the Andes: The case for language planning. In N. H. Hornberger & K. A. King (Eds) *International Journal of the Sociology of Language Special issue 67*, 9–67.

Hudson, R. A. (1999). *The sociology and psychology of terrorism: Who becomes a terrorist and why? A Report Prepared under an Interagency Agreement by the Federal Research Division*. Library of Congress. Washington DC. http://www.fas.org/irp/threat/frd.html. Accessed January 2010.

Husté, J. P. (2009). *Peru: Causes for concern. European strategic intelligence and security center analysis*. http://www.esisc.org/documents/pdf/en/peru-causes-for-concern-445.pdf. Accessed November 2009.

Huston, J. V. (1988). Insurgency in Peru: The shining path. A study by the United States marine core. *Civil Service Commission*. http://www.globalsecurity.org/military/library/report/1988/HJV.htm. Accessed December 12 2009.

Izaguirre, C. R. (1996). Shining path in the 21st Century: Actors in search of a new script. *NACLA Report on the Americas*. V. 30. http://www.hartford-hwp.com/archives/42a/016.html. Accessed November 2009.

Johnson, B. E. (2000). Stolen wombs: Imndigenous women most at risk. Native Americas, pp. 38–42.

Kahneman, D., & Tversky, A. (1986). Choices, values, and frames. In H. R. Arkes & K. R. Hammond (Eds.), *Judgement and decision making*. New York: Cambridge University Press.

Kaminer, D. (2001). The truth and reconciliation commission in South Africa: Relationship to psychiatric status and forgiveness among survivors of human rights abuses. *The British Journal of Psychiatry, 178*, 373–377.

Keating, J., & Dickinson, E. (2009). The list: Insurgencies that refuse to die. *Foreign Policy*. http://www.foreign-policy.com/story/cms.php?story_id=4691. Accessed November 2009.

Kirk, R. (1991). Crossing a river of blood: Shining path is gaining in Peru. *The Nation, 252*(16).

LAHT. (2008). 200 women in Peru protest sexual violence. *Latin American Herald Tribune*. http://laht.com/article.asp?CategoryId=14095&ArticleId=321435. Accessed December 2009.

LAHT. (2009). Peruvian says shining path can take part in elections. *Latin American Herald Tribune*. http://laht.com/article.asp?ArticleId=346250&CategoryId=14095. Accessed December 2009.

Langdon, J. & Rodriguez, M. (2007). The rondas campesinas of Peru. In L.E. Hancock & C. Mitchell (Eds.), *Zones of Peace*. Bloomfield, CT: Kumarian Press.

Langer, W. L., & Stearns, P. N. (2001). *The encyclopedia of world history: Ancient, medieval, and modern chronologically arranged* (6th ed.). Boston, MA: Houghton Mifflin.

LaPlante and Theidon Living in Peru. (2006). Law and Order. Peru's Shining Path leader Abimael Guzman sentenced to life. October 13, (20:24) Accessed on line October 2010. http://www.livinginperu.com/news/2589

Laplante, L., & Spears, S. A. (2008). Out of the conflict zone: the case for community consent the case for community consent processes in the extractive sector. *Yale Human Rights and Development Law Journal,* pp. 69.

Loveman, B., & Davies, T. M. (1997). *Che Guevara on Guerilla warfare, with introduction and case studies (3rd edition, revised and expanded)*. Lanham, MD: University of Nebraska Press, Rowman and Littlefield.

Mansilla, H. C. F. (1999). La violencia política en el Perú: un esbozo interdisciplinario de interpretación. *Historia y Sociedad, 8*, 149–177.

Manrique, N. (2010). Sendero en San Marcos. La Republica. http://www.larepublica.pe/22-06-2010/sendero-en-san-marcos. Accessed September 10 2010.

Manwaring, M. (1995). *Peru's Sendero Luminoso: The shining path beckons. Annals of the American Academy of Political and Social Science* (Small Wars, Vol. 541, pp. 157–166). Thousand Oaks, CA: Sage Publications, Inc. in association with the American Academy of Political and Social Science.

Manwaring, M. (2004). Shadows of things past: Lessons for the insurgencies in our midst. Strategic Studies Institute of the U.S. Army.

Marks, T. A. (1996). *Maoist Insurgency since Vietnam*. London: Routledge.

McClintock, C. (1998) Revolutionary movements in Latin America: El Salvador's FMLN and Peru's Shining Path. U.S. Institute of Peace Press. Washington, DC, http://www.cholonautas.edu.pe/modulo/upload/lasaclintock.pdf. Accessed November 2009.

McClintock, C. (1998). Sendero Luminoso in Comparative Perspective. George Washington University. http://www.cholonautas.edu.pe/modulo/upload/lasaclintock.pdf. Accessed December 2009.

McClintock, C. (2005). The evolution of internal war in Peru: the conjunction of need, creed, and organizational finance. In C. J. Arnson & I. W. Zartman (Eds.), *Rethinking the economics of war: The intersection of need, creed, and greed*. Washington, DC: Woodrow Wilson Center Press.

Mealy, M., & Stephan, W. (2009). Empathy in Intergroup Relations. In J. M. Levine & M. A. Hoff (Eds.), *Encyclopedia of group processes and intergroup relations*. Thousand Oakes, CA: Sage.

Minority Rights Group International. (2007). World Directory of Minorities and Indigenous Peoples - Peru: Overview, available at: http://www.unhcr.org/refworld/docid/4954ce0b2.html. Accessed 13 September 2010.

Monteil. (2008). Building peace spaces in protracted conflicts. *Peace and Conflict, 14*, 229–232.

Morales, R. (2010). Sendero Luminoso en San Marcos: L Pasado y presente. Noticias SER: A publication of Association SER. http://www.noticiasser.pe/23/06/2010/opinion-libre/sendero-luminoso-en-san-marcos-pasado-y-presente. Accessed September 10, 2010.

MPP. (1998). Long live the 18th Anniversary of the Revolution. *New Flag Magazine*. Movimiento Popular de Peru. http://www.blythe.org/peru-pcp/newflag/nf9801/mpp98.htm. Accessed December 2009.

MPP. (2003). Close ranks around our great leadership with people's wars toward the conquest of power! http://www.redsun.org/mpp_doc/mpp_0308_en.htm. Accessed December 2009.

MPP. (2009). Ante La Opinion Publica Nacional e Internacional Denunciamos El Mayor Genocidio Contra El Pueblo Para Aplicar El TLC con el Imperialismo Yanqui y Aniquilar La Guerra Popular. Movimiento Popular de Peru. http://www.solrojo.org/mpp_doc/mpp_20091111.htm. Accessed December 2009.

Muñoz, I., Paredes, M., & Thorp, R. (2006). *Collective action, conflict and ethnicity in Peru*. CRISE Working Paper No. 24. Oxford: Centre for Research on Inequality, Human Security and Ethnicity, University of Oxford. http://www.crise.ox.ac.uk/pubs.shtml. Accessed November 2009.

Notholt, S. (2008). *Fields of fire – An atlas of ethnic conflict*. London, England: Stuart Notholt Communications.

Nuñez-Palomino, G. (1996). The rise of rondas campesinas in Peru. *Journal of Legal Pluralism, 36*. http://www.jlp.bham.ac.uk/volumes/36/nunez-art.pdf. Accessed December 2009.

Oliver-Smith, A. (1969). The pishtaco: Institutionalized fear in Highland Peru. *The Journal of American Folklore, 82*(326), 363–328.

Ossio, J. M. (2002). Contemporary indigenous religious life in Peru. In L. E. Sullivan (Ed.), *Native religions and cultures of Central and South America*. New York: Continuum International Publishing Group.

Palmer, D. S. (1992). *Shining path of Peru*. New York: St. Martin's Press.

Paez, A. (2010). No reparations yet for families of civil war victims. Inter Press Service (IPS). http://ipsnews.net/news.asp?idnews=52284. Accessed September 10, 2010.

Peruservis. (2010). Identifican a unos 40 alumnos y docentes de San Marcos que participaron en marcha pro-senderista. Peruservis. http://www.peruservis.com/identifican-a-unos-40-alumnos-y-docentes-de-san-marcos-que-participaron-en-marcha-pro-senderista/. Accessed September 10, 2010.

Pike, J. (2003). Sendero Luminoso (SL) – Shining path. Federation of American Scientists. http://www.fas.org/. Accessed December 2009.

Portocarrero Maisch, G., Valentin, I., & Irigoyen, S. (1991). *Sacaojos: Crisis social y fantasmas coloniales [Putting out eyes: Social crisis and colonial phantoms]*. Lima, Peru: TAREA Asociación de Publicaciones Educativas.

Primov, G. (1980). The political role of mestizo schoolteachers in Indian communities. In B. S. Orlove & G. Custred (Eds.), *Land and power in Latin America*. New York: Holmes & Meier.

Quispe, L. (1998). People's war frequently asked questions. Developed by the Peru People's Movement (MPP) and The New Flag Magazine. PCP Home Page at http://www.blythe.org/peru-pcp. Accessed November 2009. Note: An archive of historical files uploaded by the PCP in the 1990s and maintained by NY Transfer. Last Updated in November of 1998.

Ramasubramanian, S., & Oliver, M. B. (2007). Activating and suppressing hostile and benevolent racism: Evidence for comparative media stereotyping. *Media Psychology, 9*, 623–646.

Richardson, J. M., & Sen, S. (1996). *Ethnic conflict and economic development: a policy oriented analysis*. School of International Service, American University. http://www1.american.edu/jrich/Richardson.ethnic.confl.html. Accessed December 8, 2009.

Romero, S. (2009) Cocaine trade helps rebels reignite war in Peru. *New York Times*. http://www.nytimes.com/2009/03/18/world/americas/18peru.html. Accessed December 2009.

Ross, O. (2009). A New Outrage from Shining Path Leader: Peruvian Terrorist Pens Memoirs from Jail. *The Star.* http://www.thestar.com/news/world/article/698285. Accessed December 2009.

Santos-Granero, F. (1998). Writing history into the landscape: Space, myth, and ritual in rural Amazonia. *American Ethnologist, 25*(2), 128–148.

Semana. (2009). The World of the FARC (Part II: America). *La Semana*. http://www.semana.com/noticias-print-edition/the-world-of-the-farc-part-europe/noticias-print-edition/the-world-of-the-farc-part-ii-america/119362.aspx. Accessed December 2009.

Salazar, M. (2010). Families of victims of biggest shining path massacre seek justice. Inter Press Service. http://ipsnews.net/news.asp?idnews=52335. Accessed November 22, 2010.

Smith, D. E. (1995). The training of terrorist organizations: Executive summary. *Global Security*. http://www.globalsecurity.org/military/library/report/1995/SDE.htm. Accessed December 2009.

Smith, T.P. (1997). Coca and the Mountain: Observations into the worldview of the Quechua of Panao. SIL International. http://www.sil.org/anthro/articles/cocamtn.asp?item=9. Accessed November 2009.

Starn, O. (1992). New literature on Peru's Sendero Luminoso. *Latin American Research Review, 27*(2), 212–226.

Starn, O. (1995). Maoism in the Andes: The communist party of Peru-Shining path and the refusal of history. *Journal of Latin American Studies, 27*(2), 399–421.

Stephan, W. G. (2008). The road to reconciliation. In A. Nadler, T. E. Malloy, & J. D. Fisher (Eds.), *The social psychology of intergroup reconciliation* (pp. 369–394). New York: Oxford University Press.

Stern, S. (1998). *Shining and other paths, war and society in Peru 1980–1995*. Durham: Duke University Press.

Stimpson, C. R. (2001). Foreward. In M. J. Weismantel (Ed.), *Cholas and Pishtacos: Stories of race and sex in the Andes*. Chicago, IL: University of Chicago Press.

Strong, S. (1992). *Shining path: Terror and revolution in Peru*. New York: Random House.

Taft-Morales, M. (2009). Peru: Current conditions and U.S. relations. *Congressional Research Service Report for Congress*. http://www.fas.org/sgp/crs/row/R40716.pdf. Accessed December 2009.

Taylor, L. (1998). Counter-insurgency strategy, the PCP-Sendero Luminoso and the civil war in Peru, 1980–1996. *Bulletin of Latin American Research, 17*(1), 35–58. PII: S0261-3050(97)00059-4.

Theidon, K. (2000). How we learned to kill our brother: Memory, Morality, and reconciliation in Peru. *Bulletin of the French Institute of Andean Studies., 29*(3), 539–554. http://www.ifeanet.org/publicaciones/boletines/29%283%29/539.pdf. Accessed December 2009.

Time (1992). The Myth of Guzmán. *TIME Magazine*. http://www.time.com/time/magazine/article/0,9171,976603,00.html. Accessed November 2009.

Times News Services (1992). Shining Path Leader Has His Say on Peruvian TV- Abimael Guzman Speaks to Journalists From Cage. *Times News Services*. http://community.seattletimes.nwsource.com/archive/?date=19920925&slug=1514986. Accessed December 2009.

TRC. (2003). Perú. Comisión de la Verdad y Reconciliación (TRC) [Perú. Truth and Reconciliation Commission]. *Informe final* [Final report] (Lima, TRC). http://www.cverdad.org.pe.

UNESCO (2009). Culture of Peace. United Nations Education, Cultural, and Scientific Organization, Resolutions A/RES/52/13 http://portal.unesco.org. Accessed December 2009.

USDOS (2009). 2008 Human Rights Report: Peru. Bureau of Democracy, Human Rights, and Labor. http://www.state.gov/g/drl/rls/hrrpt/2008/wha/119170.htm. Accessed December 2009.

Venturoli, S. (2009). Huir de La Violencia y Construir. Mujeres y desplazamientos por violencia politica en Peru. *DEP*, 11, pp. 46–63. ISSN 1824–4483. http://www.unive.it/media/allegato/dep/n_1speciale/04_Venturoli.pdf. Accessed February 2010.

Wade, T. & Velez, P. (2009). Shining Path Leader stirs Peru with Jailhouse Book. *Reuters*. http://uk.reuters.com/article/idUKTRE58F5N820090916. Accessed December 2009.

Wheat, A. (1990). Shining Path's Ideology. *Journal of Political and Military Sociology, 18*(Summer), 41–55.

White, G. D. (2009). *Displacement, Decentralization, and Reparation in Post-Conflict Peru* (pp. 43–36). September: Forced Migration Review.

Wilson, F. (2007). Transcending Race? Schoolteachers and Political Militancy in Andean Peru, 1970–2000 *Journal of Latin American Studies,* 39, 719–746. *Cambridge University Press.* doi:10.1017/S0022216X07003203.

WRI (1998). Country report and updates: Peru. War Resisters International. http://www.wri-irg.org/programmes/world_survey/country_report/en/Peru. Accessed September 10, 2010.

World Bank (2007). Distribution of Income or Consumption. http://siteresources.worldbank.org/DATASTATISTICS/Resources/table2_7.pdf.

Yates, P. (2006). *State of Fear*. New York, New York: Documentary Film. Skylight Pictures.

Zapata, A. (2010). Debate politico con Sendero. *La Republica.* http:\\www.larepublica.pe/sucedio/23/06/2010/debate-politico-con-sendero. Accessed September 2010.

Zavala, V. (2002). *(Des)encuentros con la escritura: Escuela y comunidad en los Andes peruanos.* Lima: Red para el Desarrollo de las siencias sociales en el Peru. Instituto de Estudios Peruanos.

ZOPIF (2009). Definition of a zone of peace. Zones of peace International Foundation. http://zopif.org/. Accessed December 2009.

Part IX

Conclusion

Ethnic Conflict from an Interdisciplinary Perspective: Lessons Learned, Policy Implications, and Recommendations for Conflict Amelioration and Peace Building

22

Rosita D. Albert, Susanne Gabrielsen, and Dan Landis

In 2005 there were 11.5 million internationally recognized refugees and an estimated 21.3 others who were internally displaced. Most of these people were fleeing from civil wars, interethnic rivalries, and campaigns of mass murder and ethnic cleansing.

(World Refugee Survey, cited in Gurr, 2007)

The 286 groups tracked in the Minorities at Risk project include slightly more than one billion people, or one-sixth of the global population...And more than half of these 286 peoples are minorities who seek recognition and rights within existing societies, not a redrawing of international boundaries.

(Gurr, 2007)

For purposes of global survival we must move toward the construction of cultures of peace that seek to reduce conflict and to promote peace and harmony through increased emphasis on consciousness, conscience, and conciliation.

(Marsella, 2005)

This concluding chapter will capture the important lessons from the preceding 20 case studies. We will focus on the nature and characteristics of ethnic conflicts, and on both successful and unsuccessful attempts at conflict resolution. We will consider both common and unique features of such conflicts. We will end on a hopeful note by recommending broad approaches and specific strategies that have the potential to lead not only to conflict amelioration and prevention, but also to sustainable peace.

In Chapter 1, we covered theories and models of ethnic conflict. We will refer to some of these theories in the current chapter. We will also expand well beyond these theories by proposing new research initiatives that utilize the richness of the information present in the case studies and some outside sources. Our aim is to contribute to the understanding, predictability, amelioration, and prevention of these enduring conflicts.

As we enter the second decade of the twenty first century, it is tragic that we live in a world wrought with large-scale violent conflicts. The most noteworthy change that has occurred in violent conflicts in recent decades has been the diminution of wars between nation-states, and the increase of violent confrontations between ethnic groups within nation-states (Gurr, 2007; Marshall & Cole, 2009).

In this volume, we have presented 20 case studies of ethnic conflict. These case studies

R.D. Albert (✉)
Department of Communication Studies, University of Minnesota, Minneapolis, MN, USA
e-mail: alber001@umn.edu

S. Gabrielsen
Department of Psychology, University of Minnesota, Minneapolis, MN, USA

D. Landis
Department of Psychology, University of Hawaii, Hilo, HI, USA
e-mail: dan1@hawaii.edu

D. Landis and R.D. Albert (eds.), *Handbook of Ethnic Conflict: International Perspectives*, International and Cultural Psychology, DOI 10.1007/978-1-4614-0448-4_22,

come from most major regions of the world and depict a variety of conflicts. They were written at our request by authors from different countries and from different social science fields. These authors are deeply familiar with the conflicts they describe. We asked all authors to follow a common outline to improve the coherence of the volume, to facilitate comparisons between various ethnic conflicts, and to allow us to draw important lessons about ethnic conflict as well as suggestions for policy makers in ameliorating or eliminating such conflicts.

Although the selection of conflicts is not comprehensive,[1] the conflicts included represent historical, regional, and cultural diversity, and include many different actors (e.g., government, rebels, military, other ethnic groups). The variety of conflicts presented gives us a general sense of the kinds of issues involved in such conflicts and the kind of approaches to conflict management that have been tried. They also provide suggestions for actions that might prove successful in current and future ethnic conflicts.

The present chapter is divided into seven parts. In part I, we begin by considering the nature of ethnic conflicts and examining the complex, interrelated factors involved in such conflicts. In part II, we examine some important characteristics that are relatively common in ethnic conflicts, while cautioning against overgeneralization. In part III, we consider the relative uniqueness of some conflicts. In part IV, we explore unsuccessful attempts at conflict resolution. In part V, we consider broad approaches to conflict resolution and moving toward peace. In part VI, we present some strategies for conflict management and for building a secure peace. Finally, in part VII, we address the countries' and the world's capacity for building peace and suggest research that would augment this capacity.

Some disclaimers are necessary here: the first four parts of the present chapter are based primarily on the chapters in this volume rather than on outside contributions.[2] We have been truly humbled by the difficulty of the task of highlighting important contributions to understanding, ameliorating, and preventing conflict. While there are many ideas that deserve to be mentioned, we will provide select observations that we believe are particularly helpful to understanding and managing ethnic conflicts.

We never imagined this task would be so difficult! Each conflict is to some extent unique and depends on a confluence of many interrelated factors. Given the complexity of the issues, context is necessary to understand any particular conflict fully. Therefore, we encourage readers to examine the individual chapters to gain a fuller understanding of the factors that we will highlight below.

1 Part I: The Nature of Ethnic Conflicts

Ethnic conflicts are complex, multifaceted, and multilayered; this makes them difficult to resolve. There are interrelated causes and factors that need to be addressed either simultaneously or sequentially. In this section, we will highlight the complexity of ethnic conflicts, discuss ethnic identities and intergroup relations, underscore the violence and suffering inherent in ethnic conflicts, point out the fragility of peace within multicultural societies, and emphasize the enduring nature of ethnic conflicts.

1.1 The Complexity of Ethnic Conflicts

Previous chapters have richly demonstrated the complexity and multifaceted nature of long-term ethnic conflicts. Many of them (in Turkey, Cyprus, Kosovo, Mexico, China, Israel/Palestine, the

[1] Indeed, as we write this chapter, the protests across the Arab world (and previously in Iran) have exploded and are still occurring. The end of the story has yet to be written. Although we realize that some of these conflicts are not based on ethnicity, the conflict in Bahrain is somewhat different: there the conflict is between a majority Shiite and a ruling minority Sunni class. The Bahraini government has employed force to put down the peaceful protests. Perhaps by the time this book is published, we will know how these various protests have ended. We sincerely hope that the rulers and others involved use some of the suggestions in this book.

[2] Many of the ideas proposed by outside contributors are summarized in Chapter 1.

Philippines, and India) have been going on for decades, and some, for centuries. Ethnic conflicts tend to be multilayered, involving political, economic, cultural, and social aspects of society. Underscoring the complexity of these conflicts, these layers tend to be interconnected (see Bhawuk, 2012; Çelik, 2012; Karbo & Mutisi, 2012; Moore & Guy, 2012 as examples). In the Democratic Republic of the Congo, the Philippines, Israel/Palestine, Mexico, Peru, and other countries, issues such as "poverty, social injustice, underdevelopment and corruption" (Montiel, Rodil, & de Guzman, 2012, p. 72), along with conflicts over material resources and group identities, tend to be significant contributing factors.

Feelings of threat and insecurity further complicate ethnic conflicts and are common both among minorities (e.g., Armenians in Turkey, native Hawaiians in Hawai'i, and Serbs in Croatia) and, in some conflicts, among majority groups (Israelis in Israel, Turks in Turkey). At times, ethnic conflicts represent an attempt to deal with real or imagined threat (see Salzman, 2012). Shapiro (2010) notes the importance of emotions in conflicts, and posits that the neglect by policy makers of the emotional and identity-based factors that fuel ethnic conflict, is a major impediment to conflict resolution.

The multifaceted nature of long-term conflict is often underestimated. In the chapter on the Israeli/Palestinian conflict, Moore and Guy (2012) note that presenting the conflict "as a territorial dispute is a misleading oversimplification. The conflict includes economic, social, cultural, and power/dominance aspects that reach far beyond the borders of the disputed land" (p. 200).

Conflicts that tend to endure through the years are not stagnant and may change. Bhawuk (2012) notes that "all conflicts in India have a long history, and what may be religious conflict today could be traced to caste or class conflict of the past" (p. 589).

1.2 Ethnic Identities and Intergroup Relations

Ethnicity and ethnic identity heavily influence and interact with political and religious issues in conflicts. Many conflicts involve ethnic minorities in a country or region where the majority possesses a different ethnicity and, often, different religious beliefs (see Aneas, Garreta, Molina, 2012; Bhawuk, 2012; Broome & Anastasiou, 2012; Martin, 2012; Montiel et al., 2012; Moore & Guy, 2012; Schwegler & Smith, 2012; van Oudenhoven, 2012). Conflicts may also involve several ethnic groups (see De Mel, Samuel, & Soysa, 2012; Karbo & Mutisi, 2012; Kibanja, Mayanja & Johnson, 2012; Montiel et al., 2012; Zeytinoğlu, Bonnabeau, & Eşkinat, 2012).

The overlay of ethnic identity on other issues may lead to more entrenched positions and dangerous and hostile environments. Ethnic enmity among the Sinhalese, Tamil, and Muslim communities was a significant catalyst in the conflict in Sri Lanka, underpinning the struggle for political representation and entitlements (De Mel et al., 2012). The conflict in the Philippines is difficult to resolve because claims over ancestral lands by the Lumad, the Muslims, and the Christians are difficult to untangle from current-day biases. In addition, outside players who have geopolitical aims beyond the Philippines often act to keep the conflicts unresolved.

Socioeconomic disparities along ethnic lines can cause deep-seated anger and resentment that often fuel conflict. Ethnic minorities in most, if not all, conflicts feel that their needs are at best ignored and at worst exploited for the benefit of the majority.

Ethnic identity can become more salient as conflicts intensify (Corkalo Biruski, 2012; Karbo & Mutisi, 2012). For instance, in 1994, as the Rwandan civil war spread to Eastern Zaire (currently the DRC), the government of Zaire attempted to strip the Tutsi of their citizenship. Then, the Alliance of Democratic Forces for the Liberation of the Congo attempted a coup d'état (Karbo & Mutisi, 2012). Thus, as the conflict in Rwanda escalated, ethnic identity became more significant in the DRC.

In Israel, up until the mid-1960s, the creation of an Arab-Israeli ethnic identity was largely successful. However, as a result of three laws that discriminate against Arab-Israeli citizens (The Law of Return, The Law defining the status of the Zionist Jewish Agency, and The Fundamental Law: The State's Land), the first Intifada (the uprising by the

Palestinians against the Israeli occupation in 1987), and the rapidly deteriorating relationships between Israel and surrounding Arab countries, the proportion of people who consider themselves both "Arab" and "Israeli" seems to have changed. Now, most Arabs in Israel see themselves as part of the Palestinian people (Moore & Guy, 2012).

In many conflict areas, indigenous groups continue to struggle for balance between autonomy and peaceful unity with former colonizers in light of a difficult past. The most significant issue in Mexico, for example, is the integration of the indigenous peoples (Martin, 2012). The Mexican government attempted to create unity by prescribing the identity of "mestizo" (originally of mixed European and indigenous ethnicity) to all the inhabitants of Mexico. The government reasoned that one identity would unify the people in the country. However, the indigenous populations have felt that they differ from other groups and believe that they have been cheated by both the European colonizers and the current government.

Ethnic identity is important, as the conflicts in the DRC, Israel/Palestine, and Mexico demonstrate, but the problems mentioned above and in several chapters also reveal that strict ethnic identification can be divisive. Mealy and Austad (2012) discuss the need for an identity apart from ethnic identity, a superordinate identity. We will address this in a later part of the chapter.

1.3 Violence and Suffering

Some ethnic conflicts can be horrifically violent. Violence often includes atrocities, like those perpetrated in the DRC, Sri Lanka, and Kosovo. It has resulted in mortality, sexual violations, human displacement (see Karbo & Mutisi, 2012), physical abuse, and emotional damage inflicted on millions of individuals. The cruelty inflicted on "the other" (used in these chapters to denote those of another ethnic or religious group) can include rape, torture, and murder, and often includes denigration and humiliation (see Lindner, 2006). This cruelty often occurs in tandem with tremendous economic costs and the destruction of cities, lands, and entire regions.

But even when physical violence is limited, ethnic conflicts can cause severe suffering for ethnic minorities. As aptly stated in the China chapter, "on the one hand ethnic minorities are economically and politically disadvantaged, on the other hand, they are culturally vulnerable and fragile" (Jia, Lee, & Zhang, 2012, p. 194). This quote succinctly describes the situation for ethnic minorities in most ethnic conflicts.

In France, Spain, Hawai'i, New Zealand, China, and Mexico, there is deep-rooted prejudice and discrimination, but little open, violent conflict. However, the absence of violent conflict does not mean there is peace and harmony. These conflicts remind us that we must do more than simply react to ethnic conflicts worldwide. Where tensions exist, we need to monitor the treatment of ethnic minorities more closely and encourage efforts to improve their wellbeing and enhance their dignity in order to prevent the escalation of ethnic conflict into violence. Devastating ethnic conflicts are not inevitable, but vigilance and preventive action are needed to ameliorate ongoing conflicts and prevent new ones.

1.4 The Fragility of Peace Within Multicultural Societies

The previous chapters, as well as other historical events, teach us a frightening and important lesson: harmonious multicultural societies can quickly disintegrate. In this volume, we have the example of Vukovar, in Croatia, a prosperous and highly integrated community where Serbs and Croats lived peacefully until the 1991 war. When ethnic identity became a strong political agenda before the war that would ravage the Yugoslavian federation, the community disintegrated. The political elites shaped their politics around ethnic identities, reviving old languages (such as Cyrillic among Serbs), symbols, and traditions. As a result, former classmates in Vukovar now go to separate schools, Serb and Croat colleagues do not socialize, and "Croats visit Croats in their homes, and Serbs visit Serbs" (Corkalo Biruski et al., 2004, cited in Corkalo Biruski, 2012, p. 341).

A similar breakdown occurred in Turkey. Before the collapse of the Ottoman Empire, Muslim Turks, Christian Armenians, and Jews lived together in relative harmony for hundreds of years, largely due to the Ottoman Empire's policy of ethnic tolerance. However, according to Zeytinoğlu, Bonnabeau, & Eşkinat, 2012, the rise of Armenian nationalism and the creation of revolutionary parties led to the expulsion of a very large number of Armenians beginning in 1915. Estimates are that from several hundred thousand to two million Armenians perished, many of them massacred. Many historians consider this to have been a genocide. The Turkish government does not. This tragedy, and the controversy surrounding it, has continued to create a wedge to this day between Armenians and Turks not only in Turkey, but also in the diaspora.

Thus, we must seriously investigate the conditions under which such rapid deterioration of peaceful coexistence occurs. Doing so, we hope, will allow us to provide guidelines and training in the management and prevention of ethnic conflicts to policy makers at all levels, as well as to personnel from international bodies, the media, and civil societies.

1.5 The Enduring Nature of Ethnic Conflicts

It is shocking to note that despite cries of "NEVER AGAIN" after the 1933–1945 Holocaust, and efforts by the international community and local groups to ameliorate and prevent violence in ethnic conflicts, we still have horrific conflicts, ethnic cleansing, and genocides based on ethnic differences.

As previously explained, there are often multiple, interrelated causes, and as we have seen in the DRC and the Philippines, solving only one or a few problems, is clearly insufficient. There are no easy fixes. In some conflicts, the state is weak (Karbo & Mutisi, 2012), "failed," or "stagnant" (Kibanja et al., 2012), while in others, an overly centralized government can have difficulties dealing with conflicts in a distant region (Montiel et al., 2012).

The social and political climates of the regions described in this handbook may have changed over time, yet many of the conflicts have persisted. For example, in Hawai'i, due to the immigration of diverse populations, different ethnic groups besides the native Hawaiians and the white *haoles* (literally "foreigners," but used by the indigenous inhabitants for whites, and more specifically, for people from the continental USA) have been involved in ethnic conflict in the Islands. The stratification of the plantation system, for example, subjected Japanese and Filipino groups to different types of racism, leading to conflicts with the white *haoles* who almost exclusively held managerial positions. Even today Chinese, Japanese,[3] and white Americans maintain economic dominance over Filipino, Polynesian, and native Hawaiian groups.

In Sri Lanka, a number of interrelated factors have made conflict resolution challenging. The lack of economic development and of access to higher education, the animosity between religious groups, and the nature of political representation in the post-colonial era, are some of the factors that led to the continuation of the Sri Lankan wars (De Mel et al., 2012).

Common to ethnic conflicts are deeply ingrained prejudices and mistrust, as well as the devastating possibility that a conflict may become intractable. Even after the violence ends, the possibility of recurrence exists. "As the rate of violence recurrence in war-torn societies suggests, deep-seated conflicts remain long after the ceasefire is negotiated" (Schwegler & Smith, 2012, p. 359).

[3] The Japanese ascendancy is a result of Japanese Americans returning from service in World War II and organizing themselves politically into an organization known as the "442" club, referring to the 442nd Regimental Combat Team, composed of Asian–Americans. This was the most decorated unit in the European theater of operations during the war.

The dominance of these nonnative Hawaiian groups varies from island to island in the Hawaiian chain.

2 Part II: Relatively Common Characteristics of Ethnic Conflicts

As we have seen, many of the conflicts discussed in this book entail a wide array of complicated issues and interactions going far beyond the seven "causes" outlined in Chapter 1. Here, we will highlight some of the major characteristics of these types of conflict; they include historical, social, educational, economic, political, and international factors.

2.1 Historical Characteristics

Historical factors contribute greatly to the perpetuation of many ethnic conflicts. For example, attempts to reconcile with the past have not been successful in Sri Lanka because peace negotiators have simply asked parties to suspend their hostilities toward one another, but have failed to address the root causes of the conflict (De Mel et al., 2012).

Among the most important historical factors are colonization, persistence despite changing environments, divergent framing of ethnic conflicts, and recent historical events.

Colonization. A significant factor in many conflicts is a history of colonization, during which the colonizers entered lands where they were outsiders and laid claim to local resources. These colonizers often favored some ethnic groups over others. After the colonizers departed, the competition between the ethnic groups fueled interethnic animosity, and in some cases, war (Montiel et al., 2012; Karbo & Mutisi, 2012). Thus, in most instances, colonial rule contributed to ethnic division and planted the seeds for future ethnic conflict. Below we provide a few examples.

As the colonizing powers pulled out of the DRC, Cyprus, Malaysia, and other countries, the new governments were too weak to maintain effective control over their countries in the face of conflict. For example, the new state created when Belgium left the Congo was fragile, and its first African President was overthrown after only a few months. Borders were created that artificially divided different ethnic groups, leading to continuing conflict in the eastern DRC and in the whole Great Lakes region. This was also true for Uganda, where political parties that are largely tribal and religion based are in a constant battle for power; they feel no allegiance to the country of Uganda.

As Cyprus was freed from British colonial rule, extreme nationalism, intolerance of cultural differences, and the abuse of minorities led to the separation of the island into two areas (the north under Turkish-Cypriot administration and the south under Greek-Cypriot administration). Broome and Anastasiou (2012) observe that this led to the displacement of approximately one-third of the population from their homes, adding tremendously to the loss of life and property and to the list of missing persons.

Historically, Malaysia has had a diverse population due to its bustling port city, Melaka. European colonization brought a change in the demographic landscape, as Chinese laborers worked in the mines and Indian laborers worked on the rubber plantations. Malaysia was heavily affected by immigrants who, when the British regained rule in 1945 (after the Japanese defeat), were given equal rights as citizens, against the wishes of the native Malay. "The establishment of political parties along ethnic lines that followed has been attributed to the 'divide and rule' policy implemented by the British" (Munusamy, 2012, p. 124). This British strategy "not only changed Malaysia's demographic landscape but also contributed to shaping the political, economical and social landscape of Malaysia today" (Munusamy, 2012, p. 123).

As Salzman (2012) noted, "seeds of anger are embedded in the colonization process through trauma, loss, tragedy, and grief" (p. 31). Hawai'i's colonial situation can be characterized by the deeply embedded notion of the inferiority of the natives and the superiority of the *haole*. This has fueled ethnic conflict over the ability to govern and the right to self-rule. Hawai'i, in contrast to the DRC and Cyprus, has not had violent conflict as a result of the end of colonial rule, but deep-rooted prejudices and mistrust between the ethnic groups still linger. Similarly, in New Zealand, there is no overt violent conflict, but the native Maori find themselves disadvantaged economically and socially, and resent the more privileged New Zealanders of European descent.

In the Philippines, colonization by the USA (which occurred subsequent to Spanish colonization) severely affected ethnic group relations and contributed to ongoing ethnic conflict. Colonization resulted in substantial changes in land laws. As stated by Montiel et al. (2012), the

> US colonial government not only refused to acknowledge the legitimacy of the traditional communal systems of landownership, land use and distribution, it also introduced and institutionalized the Torrens system of private land ownership, including land classification, registration and titling to private entities. (p. 76)

This change in the rules of land ownership and use disrupted the relatively stable economic, cultural, and political balance of power that existed prior to the US' influence.[4] The effect of this change is still felt today as the Muslims and the Lumad demand recognition of their right to ancestral lands, and regularly fight for their right to self-determination.

In summary, the lasting negative consequences of colonialism cannot be ignored. The DRC, Uganda, Cyprus, Malaysia, Hawai'i, New Zealand, and Philippines chapters demonstrate that a number of conflicts originated or were exacerbated by colonization. Countries emerged from arbitrarily drawn borders that did not correspond to existing ethnic groups,[5] and some ethnic groups favored by colonizers emerged with more power than others. Such arbitrary boundaries created multiethnic countries and often led to intergroup conflict within a country or region and, at times, to war and genocide. These multicultural states have struggled to create a lasting peace.

Divergent framing of the conflict. Ethnic conflicts usually have deep roots in historical narratives and events that are remembered and framed differently, sometimes radically differently, by the conflicting parties. Focusing solely on the current status of ethnic conflicts is dangerous because it ignores the implications of past events (see Kibanja et al., 2012). History is rewritten by each group to reflect the current conflict from its own viewpoint, which often focuses on the injustices perpetrated by the other group. In Vukovar, exclusive social structures limit intergroup contact and isolate the ingroups. This lack of contact facilitates the development of abstract, stereotypical images of the other. The "imagined communities" of self and other are used to justify intergroup violence (Corkalo Biruski, 2012).

With the passage of time, the positions of each side often become highly polarized and rigid (Broome & Anastasiou, 2012). Each side uses language that has the potential to increase hostility and polarization between groups. For example, the Turkish government calls the Kurdish Partiya Karkerên Kurdistan (PKK, Kurdistan Workers' Party) "terrorists," while soldiers who die fighting the PKK are referred to as "martyrs." In contrast, the Kurds use the term "martyr" to refer to deceased PKK militants (Çelik, 2012). Mistrust is frequently, if not always, present in the ethnic conflicts (Çelik, 2012; Kelman, 2005a, 2005b; Schwegler & Smith, 2012).

Protracted conflicts over historical narratives can continuously fuel divisions. In Turkey, "cultural boundaries between Armenians and Muslims [are] becoming more pronounced" (Zeytinoğlu, et al., 2012, p. 267). An especially important issue in this conflict is resolving the issue of whether there was an Armenian genocide: "Clearly, improving the situation of Armenians in Turkey will rest to a large extent on first normalizing diplomatic and bilateral relations between the two republics and then working out a resolution on the issue of genocide" (Zeytinoğlu et al., p. 284). Disagreement over

[4] Another lingering sore spot has to do with the treatment of Filipinos who fought the Japanese occupiers on the side of the Allies during World War II. These veterans were promised medical and other benefits similar to those obtained by American citizens after the war. Successive American governments failed to honor those promises, particularly after independence was granted to the Philippines. Recently, some progress has been made to redress this failure, but this is cold comfort to the many brave soldiers and their families who have not lived to see this progress.

[5] Such a division occurred when the Middle East was apportioned between England and France by the Sykes–Picot Agreement of 1916 without any regard for the ethnic affiliation of the populations.

the nature of past events continues to pit each side against the other.

In Cyprus, narratives of blame strengthen the enduring conflict between Turkish-Cypriots and Greek-Cypriots. Cyprus has experienced constant, but failed, political attempts to resolve the conflict between these groups. The result has been a long-lived conflict that has led to distrust.

In Kosovo, while the roots of the conflict are perceived to lie in the struggle for power between the Albanians and the Serbs, the continuation of this struggle is fueled by centuries' old mythologies and ethnic identities. Two ethnic groups with different identities and different constructions of their own mythologized histories must now live with each other after centuries of mistrust and of viewing themselves as victims. Historical frames through which conflicting groups view past events, their societies, and themselves, can become very difficult to change. This provides a serious challenge for efforts aimed at reconciliation and lasting peace.

Historical disagreements and grievances. Both disagreements and grievances must be addressed for conflict resolution to be successful. As previously mentioned, the contested Armenian "genocide" of the early twentieth century and the brutal tactics used against the Turks by Armenians are events that have never been reconciled, and that continue to affect the lives of both groups today.

The conflict in the Philippines has lasted for over 400 years, and as mentioned previously, is difficult to resolve because of claims over ancestral lands by the Lumad and the Muslims.

In Uganda, certain tribes have identified themselves solely as victims and believe that other groups are guilty of all the harms that have befallen them. This unwillingness to let go of the past and forgive other groups for crimes committed against one's people stunts conflict resolution. Some individuals have even criticized Jews in Israel for being unwilling to "let go" of the Holocaust.

Recent historical events. Recent events have served as a catalyst for exacerbating the growing ethnic tensions in Europe. For example, in the Netherlands, the dramatic murder of the Dutch filmmaker Theo van Gogh by a Moroccan Muslim fundamentalist, has fueled ethnic tensions. "Researchers have suggested that attitudes toward Muslims in Europe have become more negative (Gonzales-Castro, Ubillos, & Ibanez, 2009)" (Kamiejski et al., 2012, p. 486). This is due particularly to the various terrorist attacks that have occurred in Europe by religious fundamentalists, such as those "in Madrid in 2004, in London in 2005, and in the Netherlands in 2004" (Kamiejski et al., p. 486).

2.2 Social and Cultural Characteristics

There are a number of social and cultural characteristics that contribute to the persistence of ethnic conflicts and the difficulty of resolving them. Among these we will highlight social and ethnic identities, prejudice, discrimination, marginalization, social inequality, cultural and religious identities, and lack of trust.

Social and ethnic identities. Social identity theory (Tajfel, 1974; see also Landis & Albert, 2012) helps explain how intergroup hostilities develop and are maintained. The theory was developed to increase our understanding of the social–psychological basis of intergroup discrimination. Among others, it was employed in this Handbook to analyze the Hawai'i conflict (Salzman, 2012) and the Israel/Palestine conflict (Moore & Guy, 2012). Individuals have strong tendencies to divide their social worlds into ingroups ("us") and outgroups ("them"), often resulting in discrimination and prejudice against members of the outgroup. This is especially true when individuals feel that the superiority of their own group or culture is threatened by the presence of another group.

When these intergroup relations become based on hatred and mistrust, as in the case of Albanians and Serbs in Kosovo, and Israelis and Palestinians, the seeds of violent ethnic conflict have been planted. In some conflicts, interethnic hatreds have been taken to the extreme, with dehumanization of the outgroup leading to devastating violence. One example of this dehumanization is the written notice at a border post in the DRC: "…we know the Tutsi, that race of vipers, drinkers of untrue blood. We will never allow them to fulfill their dreams in Kivuland" (Karbo & Mutisi, 2012, p. 395). Since dehumanization is one of the crucial steps that leads to genocide (Stanton, 1998), it is critical to combat it.

In the Philippines, the Spanish colonizers characterized the Muslim population as "Moros piratas" – meaning "Muslim pirates." This was due to the "retaliatory attacks on Christian communities in Spanish-controlled territories" (Montiel et al., 2012, p. 73) waged by the Mindanao Muslim population. This label was originally resented, but "in the early 1970s... the name Moro became a badge of honor among Mindanao Muslims" (Montiel et al., 2012, p. 73). The USA also used its own set of labels for the people of the Philippines: "In the census of 1903, the peoples of the Philippine islands were classified into two broad categories – Christian and non-Christian, which were used interchangeably with civilized and uncivilized, respectively" (Rodil, 1994, cited in Montiel et al., 2012, p. 76). Thus, a notion of superiority and inferiority was introduced to the islands by the colonizing powers, leaving the people not only with resentment toward each other, but also with resentment toward their colonizers. "The fighting between Christian and Muslim Filipinos thus resulted in deep-seated mutual animosities, distrust and dislike, which have since been carried over from generation to generation and are still felt to this day" (Montiel et al., 2012, p. 75).

A different type of social identity issue exists for Arab citizens of Israel: Arab-Israelis, although citizens of the state of Israel, have less than full citizenship. Government practices, such as allowing only Jewish-Israeli[6] citizens into the Israeli army, and the struggle between having a national identity (as an Israeli citizen) and a collective or ethnic identity (as an Arab-Palestinian) add to the psychological burden of being an Arab-Israeli in Israel.

Yet another example comes from the conflict in Mexico, which continues to endure because the indigenous population continue to be marginalized. They have been marginalized in the Mexican society since colonial times, and despite the progress made by the Zapatista movement, the Mexican government has undermined many of the indigenous peoples' goals. The government tried to integrate diverse populations under a common "mestizo" identity; however, the indigenous population did not wish to be considered mestizo. While the Zapatista movement has increased the voices of indigenous groups, making their concerns known, and the government has integrated indigenous elements into education (e.g., textbooks in indigenous languages), indigenous peoples have still not received equal treatment in the political system and thus, continue to have a subordinate political identity.

Prejudice, discrimination, marginalization, and social inequality. Ethnocentrism, or the belief that one's own group is superior to others, is prevalent in all the conflicts presented in this handbook. An ethnocentric view leads people to measure all outgroups in relation to their own ingroup, and often results in prejudice and discrimination against outsiders (LeVine & Campbell, 1972). Mistrust and hatred arise as racial and ethnic differences between groups are manipulated, and minority groups are mistreated. Karbo and Mutisi (2012) note that ethnic conflict in the DRC has taken place throughout the country's history, from colonialism to the present day: "the DRC conflict is a replica of decades of interethnic rivalry and marginalization" (p. 388).

In some places, ethnic differences correspond rigidly to difference in class. Although census classifications in Mexico have slowly eliminated the classes of whites and mulattoes, there are still clear distinctions between the mestizos and indigenous peoples.

In New Zealand, Ward and Liu (2012) report that "objective socio-economic indicators reveal relative disadvantage for Maori, Pacific and non-European immigrant and refugee groups. These inequalities have the potential to exert a negative influence on ethnic relations in New Zealand" (p. 56). The Maori population is consistently the most disadvantaged, a situation which spurs resentment toward the more advantaged, ethnically European groups.

[6] The Druze (who opted out of Arab nationalism) are also allowed into the Army, but all other Arabs are excluded, presumably on national security grounds.

It is important to note that prejudice and discrimination occur even in countries with little or only sporadic violent conflict. For example, Muslims suffer discrimination in job applications, apartment renting, club entrance, and racial profiling in France (Kamiejski et al., 2012). Prejudice and discrimination often arise from feelings of threat and can lead to the marginalization of ethnic minorities.

The experience of threat. Integrated Threat Theory (Stephan & Stephan, 1996; Ybarra & Stephan, 1994; see also Landis & Albert, 2012) posits that four basic threats lead groups to be prejudiced toward one another: realistic threat, symbolic threat, intergroup anxiety, and negative stereotypes. The concept of realistic threat has its origin in realistic conflict theory (Sherif, Harvey, White, Hood, & Sherif, 1954). Realistic conflict theory asserts that a real or imagined threat to one's group interests often leads to conflict. Limited access to or limited prevalence of needed resources, an example of a realistic threat, will lead to intergroup competition that generates the perception that the outgroup is a threat (Sherif et al. 1954; Sherif, 1966; see Landis & Albert, 2012).

In the Philippines, realistic threat and intergroup anxiety due to resettlement programs have resulted in hatred and prejudice against Christians who migrated to certain regions of the Philippines and "took" the sacred/traditional land from the original inhabitants. The Christians eventually became the majority in that region of the Philippines, creating anxiety for the minority Muslims and Lumad. The resettlement process was "government-initiated, largely legal and in accordance with law and state policy" (Montiel et al., 2012, p. 77). This process has made it increasingly difficult to overturn the status quo.

Negative stereotypes coupled with realistic threat can also lead to devastating conflict. In Uganda, in 1968, Bakiga group members resettled in the Kibale district, which had historically been occupied by the Banyoro group. In a recent election, Banyoro members were outraged when it was announced that a Bakiga member would be representing the district. Violent and destructive conflict ensued, resulting in the displacement of over 200 Bakiga families from the region (Green, 2009).

Integrated Threat Theory (Stephan & Stephan, 1996; Ybarra & Stephan, 1994) also helps explain the reaction of the French inhabitants to Muslim immigrants in France. The immigrants were seen as an outgroup coming into the French territory. The French majority soon started asserting that "immigrants are stealing our jobs" (Kamiejski et al., 2012, p. 491), which resulted in negative attitudes toward immigrants. Unfortunately, this kind of reaction to immigrants is common throughout the world, particularly during times of economic austerity.[7]

Marginalization of ethnic minorities. In practically all conflicts covered in the handbook, ethnic minorities have been marginalized and disadvantaged.[8] More severe problems arise when the majority culture becomes the only acceptable culture in a society, suggesting that minority groups (ethnic groups in China, Muslim immigrants in the Netherlands, Moroccans in Spain, and Croatians in greater Serbia) must assimilate to be successful. The conflict between the indigenous and the mestizos in Mexico, which we have previously discussed, is an example of an ethnic conflict that arose from marginalization.

Cultural and religious differences. Cultural and religious identities can increase tensions both within and between groups. Differences may be real or perceived, but their effects can compound generational, political, and institutional divides. Van Oudenhoven (2012) states that in the Netherlands, "many young Muslims suffer from an identity crisis as a consequence of strong discrepancies between the culture of the current Dutch society and the culture of their parents" (p. 508).

Discrimination and lack of trust are often seen between religious groups, and religion is often

[7] The fight over restrictive immigration policies, such as the one recently enacted by the American state of Arizona, certainly has its origin in fears of the loss of jobs on the part of nonimmigrants, despite the fact that the state government couches its concern in terms of increased violence due to drug traffic across the border with Mexico. The latter is a claim that seems dubious to many.

[8] In some cases not covered in this book, majorities have been that oppressed by a minority (e.g., Shiites in Bahrain, Africans in South Africa, and, historically, African–Americans in the American South).

used for political ends. Israel, a state founded by Jews, is situated in a Muslim-dominated part of the world, and has had its legitimacy and right to exist denied by most Muslim countries.

In China, distrust over past incidents lingers as a result of religious differences between the ethnic minority groups, which tend to be religious, and the atheist Han Chinese government. This has impacted China's ability to maintain interethnic peace and cooperation.

In India, there is conflict between Muslims and Hindus as well as between Christians and Hindus. One source of the conflicts is the different views of how cows are to be treated: in the Hindu tradition, cows are to be treated with the same respect as one's mother, while this belief is not held by Christians or Muslims. Politicians sometimes take advantage of these differences. Bhawuk (2012) notes "Politicians are known to cultivate vote banks based on caste, religion, and other group identities" (p. 163).[9]

Often, perceived differences have a greater effect in creating conflict than do actual differences. For example, many native Spaniards perceive a great disparity between themselves and Moroccans regarding traditions and values, but according to Aneas et al. (2012), the disparity is overestimated. Moroccans and native Spaniards share the majority of values:

> If we come to look in more detail at the above-mentioned cultural traits we should be able to appreciate that there are in fact few substantial differences between the two cultures under examination. Both groups share similar values concerning the family, the value of social networks, and the importance of reputation and honor. (Aneas et al., 2012, p. 455)

This is likely to be true in many other conflicts; making parties aware of the many values they share could provide an important basis for greater understanding between the conflicting parties.

Buttressing the point made by Aneas et al. (2012), van Oudenhoven (2012) provides empirical evidence that Muslims and non-Muslims view virtues similarly:

> [o]n the whole, Muslims do not differ from the other groups in their interpretation of the virtues. They do, however, attach greater importance to faith, and to some extent, to wisdom... There seems to be more convergence than polarization in the appreciation of virtues in the Dutch community. (van Oudenhoven, 2012, p. 517)

Despite centuries of coexistence and great similarities, religious groups in India see important differences between themselves. Bhawuk (2012) states that "[t]he Muslim population in India constantly faces a two pronged discrimination from other communities resulting from their prejudice that Muslims are 'anti-national' and 'appeased' by the government machinery" (p. 155).

It is not clear whether religious differences between Armenians (generally Christian) and Turks (Muslim) play a role in the conflict between these groups: Zeytinoğlu et al. (2012) reported that some Armenians interviewed think that religion plays a central role in the Armenian community in Turkey, while others note that Armenians are not religious.

In China, the religious beliefs of minorities do not seem to be respected by the government and practitioners feel alienated by some government actions. One example is that the Chinese government appoints Catholic religious leaders without approval from the Vatican.

Symbolic elements. In some situations, history and religious symbols become imbued with symbolic meaning for one of the sides in a conflict. This can be seen in the utilization of nationalistic history and symbols in Serbia, Kosovo, and Croatia during the fall of Yugoslavia, and in the use of Buddhist symbols to represent the military in Sri Lanka.

2.3 Educational Characteristics

Education is an excellent means both to address conflict amelioration and to increase group cohesiveness in areas ridden by conflict. However, it can also play a large role in perpetuating conflict and in creating barriers between ethnic groups. Indigenous children in Mexico are taught in school that they are "mestizo" and not indigenous,

[9] This phenomenon is certainly not restricted to areas of ethnic conflict. It is a common practice among politicians in democratic countries.

which makes it difficult for the indigenous peoples to pass their culture and history on to the next generation.

Educational policies have also been used to isolate certain ethnic groups and prevent their mobility within a nation. For example, the Sri Lankan government instituted policies to confine Tamils; they had to live, work, and attend school in the northeast region of Sri Lanka. This resulted in a concentration of Tamil youth in the region, which paradoxically, caused political radicalization in the 1970s (De Mel et al., 2012). Thus, educational policies can inadvertently affect the political and demographic distribution of ethnic groups within a country.

In India, Muslims lack equal access to education, which leaves them with fewer employment opportunities than their Hindu or Christian counterparts. Unequal educational opportunities create unequal life chances, which, in turn, can lead to, or exacerbate, conflict between ethnic groups.

2.4 Economic Characteristics

In this section, we will consider disputes over the distribution or ownership of land and over the distribution of other resources. In addition we will discuss conflicts as a means to promote strategic interests, and economic disparities.

Economic policies often result in deeply disparate arrangements for one (or more) of the groups involved. In China, national interests take priority over ethnic interests, resulting in policies that benefit the majority Han Chinese and those living in the coastal regions.

In Hawai'i, recent development policies have been designed to attract the affluent, exacerbating homelessness in several communities. Given the lack of affordable rentals, Native Hawaiian communities (such as those in the predominantly Hawaiian Waianae [West] coast of the island of Oahu) are being displaced from their homes and their land.[10]

Decisions about economic allocation can also stand in the way of conflict resolution. In Sri Lanka, the government allocated an extremely large amount of money for military purposes during the war. The expenditures for defense and public security took precedence over all other sectors of the Sri Lankan society. This resulted in spiking the public debt and left little money for education, health, and needed infrastructure development (De Mel et al., 2012).

Ethnic divisions may result in economic hierarchies. In Malaysia, the ethnic populations were split up based on economic tasks. Munusamy (2012) argues that division of ethnic groups into separate occupations was a result of British colonialism. This division prevented cohesion and the acceptance of others.

> For the most part, laborers from China were recruited to work in tin mines and laborers from India (mainly Tamil speakers) to work on rubber plantations. The recruitment and placement strategy of laborers by British not only changed Malaysia's demographic landscape but it also contributed to shaping the political, economical [sic] and social landscape of Malaysia today. (Munusamy, 2012, p. 123)

Distribution or ownership of land. The right to the land is a common source of conflict, especially in situations where the two parties see each other as mutually exclusive inhabitants of an area of land, such as in Israel and Palestine, and in Mindanao, the Philippines. Realistic conflict theory (Sherif et al., 1954; see also Landis & Albert, 2012) helps explain this as a source of conflict. Indeed, several of the conflicts depicted in this handbook include some disagreement over the distribution or ownership of land (De Mel et al., 2012; Karbo & Mutisi, 2012; Montiel et al., 2012; Moore & Guy, 2012).

[10] In an attempt to mitigate these effects, some islands have mandated that developers designate a certain proportion of residences in each new development to be priced at an "affordable" level based on the median income of the area. This has met with limited success as developers try to find other ways to avoid having to build such residences. In a case not involving housing, Native Hawaiians on the island of Hawai'i are insisting on free access to a shoreland beach that was historically open to them via a trail that existed prior to annexation by the USA in 1898. This trail now goes through private property and the current owners have closed off such access.

In the Philippines, the colonizers organized "a land distribution scheme that was patently discriminatory against the local inhabitants" (Montiel et al., 2012, p. 76). Christian homesteaders were allowed to own up to 24 hectares of land, while non-Christians could only have 10 hectares at most. Conflict over land ownership, an extremely scarce resource, has also occurred between the State of Hawai'i and the Native Hawaiian people (Salzman, 2012).[11]

In some conflicts, it is particularly difficult to determine who is "native" to the land in question (Israel, Sri Lanka, the Philippines) because most, if not all, groups in conflict have inhabited the country for so long that they may claim "native" status and because, in some cases (e.g., Hawai'i), inter-marriage between groups has changed the ethnic composition of the population.

Conflict over the distribution of resources. Realistic conflict theory discussed in Chapter 1 by Landis & Albert, 2012, also specifies that different social groups will engage in hostilities if there is a shortage of resources. These resources could be directly needed, such as water and food in Sri Lanka, or could be economically rewarding, such as coltan (a mineral used in the manufacture of cell phones) and gold in the DRC. Areas rich in resources often become battlegrounds between different ethnic groups and different countries.

The DRC is endowed with valuable natural resources that have been exploited by colonizers and by other countries. Internal turmoil has resulted as ethnicity has been manipulated by opportunistic individuals, groups, and countries seeking to benefit from the abundance of resources. External powers supported dictatorships and toppled regimes as a way of securing their own interests in the region.

In the words of Karbo and Mutisi (2012), in the DRC "the prolonged violence and tensions seem to be spreading along areas rich in mineral resources; hence the human rights violations in these regions are directly linked with the extraction of these commodities" (p. 390).

In the DRC, the

> wealth of natural resources was a pull factor for the French, the Arabs, the British, the Germans, as well as the Americans, such that by the nineteenth century, all these external powers had interfered with the Congo in one way or the other. (Karbo & Mutisi, 2012, p. 383)

Poverty among ordinary citizens in the DRC has tended to create a situation of relative deprivation, a phenomenon that lures these populations into engaging in violent conflict (Karbo & Mutisi, 2012).

In Uganda, conflicts occur near regions rich in valuable resources, even though, as is often the case, the economic gains from conflict only go to an elite few.

In China, "natural resources in the ethnic areas have been opened up vigorously to serve national interest with little care of the local interest and ecological losses or stakes" (Jia et al., 2012, p. 189). The authors argue that this is the largest contributing factor to the tensions in China.

Ethnic conflict as a means to promote strategic interests. It could be argued that some of the initiators of suppression of another ethnic group are guilty of manipulating ethnic tensions to promote their true goals, whether these goals are political, social, or economic. According to Zeytinoğlu et al. (2012), in the original conflict between Turks and Armenians, treaties enacted by European powers specifically made the welfare of Armenians a priority. "It gave them a ready excuse to intervene in the internal affairs of the Empire to promote their own strategic interest" (p. 269).

In China, continued emphasis on economic goals comes at the expense of ethnic minorities. There is also growing pressure from globalization, which further undermines meeting the needs of ethnic minorities.

In the DRC the ethnic conflict has been exacerbated by competition over control of natural resources, and the conflict "is not only an ethnic problem but also a political matter fuelled by economic interests" (Karbo & Mutisi, 2012, p. 390).

[11]This debate owes its origin, as Salzman (2012) points out, to the very concept of ownership. Private ownership of land was a concept introduced to Hawai'i in the early nineteenth century by Caucasians, particularly missionaries, from the mainland.

Economic disparities. Differences in economic status between ethnic groups have characterized many conflicts. In some cases, these differences are very large, while in others (van Oudenhoven, 2012) it is not. In China, Jia et al. (2012), state that "the ethnic minority population in absolute poverty by the end of 2004 was 47.7% of the total national population of absolute poverty" (p. 185).

2.5 Political Characteristics

Political characteristics found in some ethnic conflicts include weak governments, discriminatory government policies, and political parties based on ethnicity.

Weak governments. Violence is one of the defining features of a failed state (Karbo & Mutisi, 2012). The DRC as a failed state cannot provide its citizens with basic security. It also cannot provide infrastructure that would meet basic needs. A failed state cannot help its neighbors deal with their conflicts, or prevent them from spilling over into its own borders. In addition, it lacks the power to bring natural resources under government control and keep them out of the hands of combatants.

> Rotberg (2002) posits that failed states prey on their own citizens by oppressing, extorting, and harassing the majority of their citizens while favoring a political and military elite. Ultimately, the exploitation of citizens by rulers will invoke sentiments of resentment, hence the emergence of rebellion and insurgency. (Karbo & Mutisi, 2012, p. 392)

Failed states also lead individuals to seek security in rebel groups, which generally form along ethnic lines.

Discriminatory government policies. Official policies can also prolong conflict. In Sri Lanka, the government adopted Sinhala as its only official language, outlawing the use of Tamil in administrative offices. This discriminatory policy segregated the Sinhala and Tamil-speaking groups and inspired resentment toward the state by the Tamil. The state also sponsored discriminatory education policies that disadvantaged Tamil students (De Mel et al., 2012). These policies were not only discriminatory, but also conflict prolonging, in that the policies distanced groups, discouraging communication and encouraging mistrust.

Political parties based on ethnicity. In a number of ethnic conflicts we have examined, political parties are based on ethnicity, and the government is controlled by the major ethnic group. One example is Cyprus, where "the conflict…was driven originally by extreme nationalist rhetoric, intolerance of cultural differences, abuse of minorities, and use of violence to subvert the political process (Anastasiou, 2002; Anderson, 1995)" (cited in Broome & Anastasiou, 2012, p. 306).

In Sri Lanka, political groups based on ethnicity have not been treated equally at the national level. For instance, Muslim groups have felt that their perspective has been underrepresented at peace talks despite the fact that Muslims comprise 7% of the population and constitute one of the major ethnic groups in the country (De Mel et al., 2012). It seems obvious that in order for effective peace talks to occur, there must be a forum in which all affected groups participate in the discussion.

Political tensions are magnified when tied to ethnic differences. In China, Han Chinese leadership is preeminent in the government, even in areas where ethnic minorities constitute the majority of the population. This practice leaves little room for the voices of the many ethnic minorities in China and creates resentment toward the Han Chinese.

In Turkey, local discrimination and government policies fill the Kurdish population with suspicion and anxiety. And in Uganda, political "parties are still tribal, regional, religious-based, and centralized" (Mukyala-Makiika, 2000, cited in Kibanja et al., 2012, p. 417), thus fueling ethnic tensions. Kibanja et al. (2012) elaborate:

> The formation of political parties in the country was from the start organized along tribal, religious, and regional lines. The idea of a political party being a body of organized opinion along rationalistic, ideological lines does not have a convincing history in Uganda. Yet in-group favoritism based on ethnicity is undoubtedly a motivating force for conflicts in modern Uganda. (p. 416)

2.6 International Impact on Ethnic Conflicts

The international community has been involved in various conflicts, particularly in the conflicts in the DRC, Cyprus, the former Yugoslavia, and Israel, with varying levels of success. In the DRC, for example, despite a number of UN peacekeeping efforts, the superpowers seem to remain relatively unconcerned with the conflict, and the conflict remains unresolved.

As is well known, the Israeli/Palestinian conflict has involved and divided the globe. After World War II and the creation of the State of Israel, the former Soviet Union threw its weight on the side of the Arab states, while the West generally supported the nascent state.

The involvement and impact of neighboring states are important features of several conflicts (Karbo & Mutisi, 2012; Kibanja et al., 2012; Montiel et al., 2012).

International recognition was an important precursor to the Mexican government's acceptance of indigenous peoples as separate ethnic entities (Martin, 2012).

However, there seems to have been a lack of international efforts aimed at ameliorating many ethnic conflicts, even when early intervention might have prevented further bloodshed, mitigated the conflict, or ended it a lot sooner. This was clearly the case in Rwanda in 1994. Part of the reason for the lack of international involvement may be dissention within countries about the role they should play in a given conflict.[12]

The impact of neighboring states. The existence of neighboring regions and countries with their own internal problems has contributed to ethnic conflicts within the DRC. "Events in neighboring countries such as Rwanda and Burundi, have, during key historical moments, impacted on the crises" (Karbo & Mutisi, 2012, p. 389). Additionally, the central government of the DRC has never been able to project authority into its periphery and to control its entire territory fully.

Armed conflict between Pakistan and India (e.g., over Kashmir) has resulted in discrimination and distrust of Indian Muslims within India. There was great fear that the Mumbai massacre, carried out in India by militants based in Pakistan, would result in a precipitous upswing in communal violence against Muslims.

The inadequacy of international involvement. Karbo and Mutisi (2012) state:

> One major reason why the DRC conflict has continued to become protracted is that it has not received noteworthy attention from the important stakeholders in the international community. This is reflected in the level of commitment of the international community towards supporting peacekeeping and peacemaking processes in the DRC, including support of the Mission of the United Nations in the Congo (MONUC). (p. 395)

Thus, although the conflict in the DRC has received some international attention, the level of attention has been insufficient to resolve it.

In Kosovo, Schwegler and Smith (2012) state: "A series of peace accords over the last fifteen years sponsored by the UN, NATO, and the US have attempted to address some of the core issues in the Kosovo conflict with minimal effect" (p. 357). International involvement in the conflict did not yield satisfactory results. Despite an end of outright violence, there is still conflict, and reconciliation has not been achieved.

One important issue that needs to be addressed is what needs to be done to increase the successful involvement of international organizations and the international community in conflict management, prevention, and peace building.

2.7 Summary of Relatively Common Characteristics

Our discussion in Chapter 1 suggested that some commonalities might exist among ethnic conflicts. When we started analyzing conflicts for the current chapter, we began by looking at individual

[12] For example, during the recent uprising in Egypt, certain elements in the American conservative movement demanded that the government intervene to support the Egyptian president against the protesters, rather than throwing its weight on the side of the people in the street.

chapters and identifying the characteristics that emerged from each conflict. We then looked for elements that seemed to occur in a number of conflicts. Despite the diversity of ethnic groups, populations, political systems, geographies, and other features, we found commonalities in historical, social, educational, economic, and political characteristics. We were genuinely surprised, yet rather pleased, that so many commonalities emerged. This finding is instructive, in that it tells us that certain conditions seem to either generate or exacerbate ethnic conflicts. It indicates that if we can learn to deal with these conflict situations effectively and equitably, then we might be able to ameliorate and even prevent such conflicts in the future.

3 Part III: Relatively Unique Circumstances

Often, particularities in the histories, contexts, populations, and other circumstances, make conflicts difficult to compare. In order for us to learn from the past and present, is imperative that we consider not only the commonalities between conflicts, but also the relatively unique features of some conflicts. Here, we highlight aspects of ethnic conflict that occurred in some, but not most, of the case studies covered in this Handbook.

3.1 Historical Circumstances

In this section, we note the influence of neighboring countries in conflicts across national borders, and consider a multiethnic state that experienced rapid disintegration into violence.

Conflict across national borders. The extent to which the conflict in the DRC has spread to and from bordering countries is relatively unique among the conflicts covered in this Handbook. In the Great Lakes region of Africa, conflicts in the DRC, Burundi, Rwanda, and Uganda have mutually reinforced each other.

A state with rapid disintegration of ethnic relations. The rapid disintegration of a "peaceful" federation,[13] which existed successfully for years, is a somewhat unique aspect of the conflict in former Yugoslavia. Why was the violence not anticipated? If it was, why was little or nothing done to prevent it? Perhaps one answer is that some parties (Serbia, Kosovo) stood to gain from the violence and the conflict. The pace at which the disintegration happened and the violence that ensued were surprising, and a frightening reminder of how easily the flames of ethnic conflict can be stoked.

3.2 Societal Circumstances

In this section we highlight the following: a state in "constant repair," a state that is simultaneously democratic and religion-based, a country with many ethnic minorities in an enormous geographic area, a country where propaganda was used in education to spur conflict, and a country with a peaceful opposition movement.

A state in "constant repair." The conflict in Malaysia is not openly violent, perhaps because all prime ministers in Malaysia have been of the opinion that they needed to emphasize "constant repair."

> Malaysia today proudly stands as one of the most successful decolonized countries in the world… It has enjoyed political stability, representative government, economic progress, rural modernization, increased literacy and rapid growth of middle class (Cheng Teik, 1994). However, Malaysia's measure of success in managing ethnic relations has to large extent been limited by the relative absence of violent racial conflict since the violent racial riot in 1969 (Poh Ping, 1999). (cited in Munusamy, 2012, p. 128)

A state that is simultaneously democratic and religion based. Israel is the only Jewish state in the Middle East and the world. It is surrounded by hostile Arab countries and by Iran. The role of

[13] Some might argue that the alignment of some ethnic groups with Germany during World War II reawakened old ethnic animosities that had originated with the incursions by the Ottoman Empire over centuries. These animosities were dampened by the agency of a strongman, Marshal Tito, after the war, and it was upon his death that the fissures that were always present cracked, resulting in the dissolution and ethnic conflict.

Israel as both a democracy and a religion-based state poses some unique challenges for Israeli/Palestinian relations. Although democracy is the core ideology for the secular Jews (the vast majority in Israel), Orthodox Jews consider democracy "less relevant" because the core tenets of democracy fail to replace their religious values.

> For secular Jews, however, democracy is the core ideology. The democratic value system used to be the core ideology for the Arab citizens of Israel. However, shifting their views and becoming more 'Palestinian' than 'Israeli' has led to a decline in their support of democracy as it fails to provide them with legitimation for their socio-political actions (which are, at times, against their state). (Moore & Guy, 2012, p. 220)

Israel must manage these challenges, rooted in politics and religion, in ways that do not marginalize its non-Jewish population. The seeming contradictions that arise from being both religious and democratic must be addressed. Such a political–religious combination may arise in other countries in the future, particularly if a trend toward ethnically based nation-states becomes accepted as a desirable state of affairs.

A geographically extensive country with multiple ethnicities. One of the things that make the conflicts in China unique is the sheer size of the parties involved. The PRC has close to 1.5 billion inhabitants, with 55 recognized ethnic minorities comprising over 9% of the population (equivalent to the population of Japan, and to more than a third of the population of the US). Any recommendations aimed at resolving the ethnic conflicts in China must take into account the vastness of the country in addition to its immense population (Jia et al., 2012).

A conflict where education was used as propaganda. Despite the fact that many actors in conflict situations utilize propaganda to achieve their goals, the role of education in directly spurring the conflict in Peru is somewhat unique. Indigenous Peruvians generally have lower levels of education than other Peruvians. The Shining Path felt that by educating the indigenous population, it would be able to recruit the students to join in the fighting. Efforts to equalize access to education quickly became an exercise in propaganda. Education was used to encourage support for one side and disdain for the other. However, it was also used to reduce inequalities found across ethnic groups. This significant dual role of education is unique among the case studies we covered.

A relatively peaceful opposition movement. In Mexico, although the Zapatista movement started with weapons and violence, it eventually gained more ground when it switched to the use of rhetoric. Over the long term, their nonviolent approach garnered positive, worldwide media attention, helping to advance the movement's cause and attract new supporters. This relatively quick change from militarism to rhetoric is unusual, and provides hope for future nonviolent opposition movements.

3.3 Summary of Relatively Unique Circumstances

As we have seen, relatively unique circumstances covered in the handbook include the influence of neighboring countries in conflict across national borders; a multiethnic state experiencing rapid disintegration into violence; the existence of a state of "constant repair" in Malaysia, a state that is simultaneously democratic and religion based; the large geographic scale of the ethnic conflict in China; the use of propaganda in education in Peru; and the peaceful opposition movement in Mexico.

Additional factors that were mentioned in one or two conflicts and that may apply to other ethnic conflicts are (a) the severe lack of trust between ethnic groups in the same region (Corkalo Biruski, 2012; Schwegler & Smith, 2012), (b) the colonial imposition of religion on indigenous populations (Mexico), and (c) strong nationalist politics on both sides of the conflict (Cyprus).

4 Part IV: Unsuccessful Attempts at Conflict Resolution

Despite over 300 peace and cease-fire agreements over the last 20 years, the war in Sri Lanka, which officially ended in 2010, lasted for more than 25 years. The failure of many agreements in

Sri Lanka was not unique: unfortunately, unsuccessful attempts to resolve conflicts occur far more frequently than successful attempts. Therefore, despite the fact that the conflict resolution strategies described in most chapters in this handbook, regrettably, have failed to create lasting peace, we will consider them in order to learn what factors seem to prevent the conflicting parties from achieving peace.

The unsuccessful attempts we will consider have been shaped by unresolved historical issues, attempts to create unified identities, political issues, and discrepancies in conflict resolution goals. In later sections of the chapter, we will consider general approaches and then specific strategies that hold some promise for ameliorating conflict and leading to peace.

4.1 Unresolved Historical Issues

Past events often haunt conflict-ridden societies long after they have occurred. For a variety of reasons, historical issues constitute a major barrier to conflict resolution.

Winston Churchill is thought to have said, "History is written by the victors," and in conflict situations, different constructions of historical events often create important impediments to conflict resolution. This can be clearly seen in the controversy regarding the Armenian genocide, which has been discussed previously: there has been a long battle over how to describe past grievances and whether or not "genocide" is an appropriate descriptor. The importance of this topic is reflected in current diplomatic efforts, and it remains at the forefront of dialogue between Turkey and Armenia. The approval of protocols to establish diplomatic and bilateral relations between the two republics in 2009 has been stalled. Turkish representatives feel that demands in Armenia's constitution regarding the conflict serve to directly violate the protocols, and block forward progress and agreement. Murat Mercan, the Turkish Parliamentary Foreign Affairs Committee Chairman, stated that Armenia's Constitutional Court "ruled out three vital articles [of the protocols] since the country's constitution demands land from eastern Anatolia and Turkish recognition of its genocide claims" (Sariisik, 2010, cited in Zeytinoğlu et al., 2012, p. 285).

With respect to the Turkish/Kurdish conflict, the Turks have put great effort into the Kurdish Initiative. This initiative was designed "to include greater cultural rights for Kurds… some form of local autonomy, and incentives to demobilize and reintegrate PKK [Kurdish] fighters into the society" (Çelik, 2012, p. 284). Initially, it appeared that the program was well supported by the Kurdish community, including most Kurdish politicians. However, some PKK and Kurdish members of parliament held different ideas about how the initiative should be carried out. As addressed by Çelik (2012), the initiative has come short of any real progress because of the complexity of the issue; renaming the initiative "Democratic Initiative" and then "National Union and Brotherhood Project" demonstrates the government's confusion and lack of a coherent policy to address the Kurdish question.

In New Zealand, efforts have been made to address the issue of past historical injustice, but the efforts have remained insufficient:

> Although Maori are symbolically included in the New Zealand national identity, their claims for redress of historical injustice and their calls for a greater share of national resources are either denied or accepted with great reluctance by negating the relevance of history to the present. (Ward & Liu, 2012, p. 59)

Disagreements that reach very far back into history can create self-sustaining tension and are very difficult to overcome. In Israel, the recent right-wing government is not as ready to make concessions regarding historical contentions as past governments were. In this case, failed conflict resolution attempts in the past make it more difficult for successful conflict resolution in the present. An excellent example concerns the Saudi Initiative, a dramatic proposal put forth by Saudi Crown Prince Abdullah in 2002. He proposed to end the long-standing Arab war against Israel "in return for Israeli withdrawal from Palestinian territories, withdrawal in the Golan and appropriate arrangements regarding Jerusalem and the refugees" (Moore & Guy, 2012, p. 205). At a meeting of the Arab League, most Arab states adopted the Saudi Initiative, which was referred to in UN Security Council Resolution 1397, calling for an end to violence on both sides of the conflict. Sadly, as Moore and Guy (2012) point out, "the resolution was not heeded, and the cycle of Palestinian terrorism and Israeli reprisals continued" (p. 205).

4.2 Attempts to Create Unified Identities

The needs of ethnic minorities tend to receive less attention than those of the majority population. In Turkey, Armenians "are equal to [other] Turkish citizens according to the laws, but this is not always the case in practice" (Zeytinoğlu et al., 2012, p. 286). In China, despite the ability of ethnic minorities to elect some minority officials, the top provincial-level Chinese Communist Party positions in ethnic autonomous regions are held by the Han (majority) Chinese officials.

Conflict resolution strategies that have attempted to address minority/majority conflicts include assimilation to a dominant identity, rigid or forced integration, and managing interethnic relations through community building. These approaches are discussed below.

Assimilation to a dominant identity. Assimilation refers to the absorption and incorporation of a cultural group into the more dominant group. Assimilation policies mandate that all immigrant, ethnic, or racial groups should shed their unique group traditions and practices as quickly as possible and, through acculturation, adopt government-approved characteristics. This has not worked in France or Turkey. As noted by Kamiejski et al. (2012)

> Much like the proposals made within the Common In-group Identity Model, the idea of a "melting pot" implies that immigrants in France should all adopt the French way of life and become "French" as quickly as possible. This is the policy that seems to underlie he actions of the French government in recent years. (p. 500)

This policy, however, is one that according to recent research is prone to violent reaction. "According to Thomsen, Green and Sidanius (2008), assimilation may be threatening to members of the dominant group because it blurs existing status boundaries between groups and thus, raises serious question about the viability of the existing hierarchical system" (cited in Kamiejski et al., 2012, p. 497). Thus, the dominant group may react violently to the destruction of their hierarchical institutions by an assimilationist policy. "As we have seen, the results [particularly the 2005 riots in France] are not pleasing" (Kamiejski et al., 2012, 2012, p. 500). The hundreds of millions of dollars in damage wrought in the 20 days of chaos during the 2005 riots were not the result of Islamic militancy or juvenile delinquents (Kamiejski et al., 2012, p. 488). Instead the riots were "…an instance of collective action, a relatively spontaneous social movement seeking to protest against a state of affairs" (Kamiejski et al., 2012, p. 488), presumably the assimilationist discrimination against immigrants. Kamiejski et al. (2012) conclude that

> …it appears that in France, as in other countries, violence on the part of the dominant group against ethnic minorities and immigrants may be more likely to occur, not less, if immigrants appear to lose completely their culture of origin. (p 497)

Attempting to make Kurds adhere to a Turkish identity rather than to just Turkish citizenship constituted a failed attempt to close the gap between the two groups. Eliminating Kurdish political parties and banning the Kurdish language were considered conflict resolution strategies at one time (prior to the Kurdish Initiative described above), as the country attempted to unify the nation under a Turkish identity. However, these strategies were clearly unsuccessful.

The Mexican government has continuously tried to integrate the indigenous peoples into a common Mexican ethnicity centered on the "mestizo." One could argue that an overarching, common identity such as Mexican might have worked, and later we will discuss the partial success of some attempts at superordinate identity building. However, in this case, the overarching seminational/ethnic identity of mestizo did not work.

> While mestizo has integrated the ethnic diversity that exists in Mexico, it has not successfully included the Indians in the integration. Instead the mestizo movement has left the Indians feeling

> culturally and racially inferior with feelings of having their culture appropriated. (Gutiérrez, 1998, cited in Martin, 2012, p. 532)

In fact, this movement toward a national identity has created a backlash for many indigenous Mexicans, who now wish to maintain their indigenous ethnicity and culture.

Rigid integration. Some countries have tried to create a unified identity by forcing different groups to shed their ethnic identity and be forcibly integrated. Integration involves mixing very different ethnic groups and their customs in an attempt to create a new mixed identity. "Integration strategies were anchored in promoting national identity: one national language, one national culture and one Malaysian race, while pluralistic strategies were anchored in maintaining the cultural freedom of the various ethnic groups" (Munusamy, 2012, p. 126). These rigid integration policies did not work in Malaysia.

In Uganda, the current president, Yoweri Museveni, has advocated an extreme integration approach, "suggesting that Uganda will be fully evolved when only national, not tribal, identities exist" (Kibanja et al., 2012, p. 426). Tribal identities would no longer be the most important identity in Uganda. Museveni has even urged the minority Bakiga group in the Kibale region to shed their traditional language and begin conversing in Runyoro, the language of the majority. Kibanja et al. (2012) have a different view:

> To deny tribal identity (or other types of social and cultural identity) is to deny people of their cultural heritage, social support and positive health and psychosocial benefits that go along with that sense of identity. This view is consistent with theory and research from developmental and multicultural psychology indicating that healthy attitudes towards diverse cultures and identification with one's ethnic heritage can function to promote mental health, protect against behavioral or emotional problems, and prompt civic engagement. (Benson, Scales, & Mannes, 2003; Flanagan & Faison, 2001; Phinney, 1992; Scales, Benson, & Leffert, 2000) (cited in Kibanja et al., 2012, p. 427)

Assimilation and rigid integration have a great deal of overlap. Often, more than one strategy is used in trying to bring groups together. We must also note that the failures documented above do not mean that a single national identity can never be effective in bringing different groups together. Rather, it appears that forcing ethnic groups into one identity that is not authentic to them, and not addressing underlying inequalities between various groups, stand in the way of establishing a common identity.

Community-building policy. "Although many initiatives have been undertaken to advance community building, the reality is that managing diversity has become more complex and challenging" (Munusamy, 2012, p. 128). Thus, due to the complexity of Malaysian society, a society with a growing population and diversity in religion, culture, and ethnicity, these initiatives were unsuccessful. The government has come a long way and now recognizes that "many of the policies and strategies used to achieve the current state of development are now inadequate to take [Malaysia] to the next stage" (NEM report, cited in Munusamy, 2012, p. 129). For example, the New Economic Policy was designed to achieve national unity, specifically to reduce poverty for all Malaysians and to correct economic imbalances between groups. Although framed as a community-building policy, its implementation came closer to an affirmative action program for native Malaysians. This proved to be a divisive force in communities because other groups resented the preferential treatment given to native Malaysians.

4.3 Political Issues

The central government is often regarded as a necessary participant in conflict resolution, but in some countries, such as Uganda, the government is unwilling to play that role and consistently refuses to cede any power.

> The central government, being in a high status position, is key to the resolution of this conflict. This is expected because in a conflict, the highest intergroup bias is displayed by the high status group (Teichman, Bar-Tal, & Abdolrazeq, 2007), and therefore the same can be applied in the resolution of the conflict. Unfortunately, the central government has consistently used state machinery to suppress Uganda's request for a federal system instead of using amicable ways. (Kibanja et al., 2012, p. 422)

Instead of seeking to negotiate this dispute peacefully, the central government attempted to discourage the Buganda, an ethnic group in Uganda, by approving an amendment to a land bill that significantly disadvantaged them. It has also been reported that the NRM government has fueled ethnic conflicts both between and within kingdoms in order to maintain its power. This strategy has been used with the intention of undermining various calls for federalism.

The DRC has seen more international intervention than most conflicts in this handbook. Yet, for various reasons, conflict resolution has consistently failed at all levels. In November 1999, the UN Mission in the Democratic Republic of Congo (MONUC) oversaw the cease-fire within the DRC. Despite their presence, violent conflict continued, culminating in the assassination of President Kabila in May 2001 (Karbo & Mutisi, 2012).

> Efforts to end the DRC crises began to bear fruit in 2003 with the signing of the Lusaka Peace Agreement which led to the formation of a transitional government. Although this was the case, the crimes against humanity continued unabated leading the Southern African Development Community (SADC) to take a leading role in trying to avert further catastrophes that would further escalate what others have dubbed 'Africa's First World War.' (Karbo & Mutisi, 2012, p. 396)

Conflict in the DRC has continued under the peacekeepers sent there to protect civilians. Unlike Uganda, the DRC is a weak, failed state that is unable to assist the UN mission, much less stop the violence on its own.

4.4 Discrepancy in Conflict Resolution Goals

Because a conflict often arises when different parties have different goals, conflict resolution attempts should focus on the goals to which each party aspires. In conflict resolution, discrepancies in these goals can halt progress. For example, numerous peace settlement talks have taken place in Kosovo, but all have failed to address the entrenched, persistent, identity narratives that divide the Serbians and the Albanians. Because these peace settlements have failed to address the discrepancy in identity narratives and goals between the Serbians and the Albanians, the peace process has been stunted.

We will consider discrepancy in conflict resolution goals in terms of failed cease-fires, failed compromises, and failed negotiations and treaties.

Failed cease-fires. Several peace initiatives in the late 1990s attempted to defuse escalating tensions in the former Yugoslavia: the Peace Implementation Council at Bonn in 1997; the Kosovo Diplomatic Observer Mission (the Yeltsin Agreement) in May 1998; the Kosovo Verification Agreement on October 12, 1998, which called for a cease-fire from Yugoslavia and called to allow time for the Christopher Hill Peace Process; and perhaps the most notable failure, the Rambouillet Accords in February 1999. The Rambouillet Accords were signed on March 18, 1999, by the Albanian, British, and American delegations. This accord was designed to grant Kosovo substantial autonomy and reinstitute many of the pre-1989 structures and freedoms. However, it was not signed by either the Serbian or the Russian delegations. "Characteristic of the post-conflict tension in the relationship, the two delegations never even met face to face, staying on separate floors of the same hotel" (Rogel, 2003, cited in Schwegler & Smith 2012, p. 357). Less than a week later NATO inserted itself into the conflict, followed by the adoption of the UN Security Council Resolution 1244 of June 10, 1999, which authorized a civil and military UN presence in Kosovo (UNMIK) and in parts of the Federal Republic of Yugoslavia. Both sides of the conflict eventually agreed to a cease-fire in the Kumanovo Treaty.

Failed compromises. A compromise is a settlement between two conflicting parties where both parties must make concessions. If both parties are satisfied, a compromise can go a long way toward building a tentative bridge between them. However, it is often difficult to get the parties to agree to a compromise. One example of this was The Annan Plan of 2002 for Cyprus (named for the then Secretary General of the United Nations, Kofi Annan). This plan allowed an internationally respected third party to attempt to forge a compromise between the Turkish and Greek-Cypriot sides. The Annan Plan was a detailed and complex plan involving the creation of the United Cyprus Republic, which the nationalist Turkish-Cypriot administration viewed unfavorably. When the Greek-Cypriots also elected a hard line nationalist, then neither side was pleased with the Plan. Invariably, both sides backed out (see Broome & Anastasiou, 2012 for more details).

Failed negotiations and treaties. We have mentioned before that the absence of conflict is not equivalent to the presence of peace. In fact, several authors suggest that in conflict, one must attain negative peace (the end of outright violence) before attempting to achieve positive peace, for "the question remains of how to motivate groups to engage in cooperative contact without focusing on the features of negative peace" (Schwegler & Smith, 2012, p. 364). There is an example of this in the DRC. In spite of three previous peace agreements, 2002 and 2003 were the bloodiest years of the war. In some locations, such as Ituri, civilians are still being murdered and displaced by the thousands (Karbo & Mutisi, 2012). The DRC cannot achieve the positive peace it is striving for while the violence continues.

In Sri Lanka, peace negotiations collapsed because certain stakeholders were not allowed to participate in discussions, and because significant organizations walked out during negotiations. Women's initiatives for peace were excluded from formal peace negotiations. This was partially due to patriarchal stereotypes that caused women to be viewed as victims of war who required protection from sexual violence, rather than as autonomous agents who can effect meaningful change (De Mel et al., 2012). Additionally, the Liberation Tigers of Tamil Eelam, a Sri Lankan separatist group, had walked out on the peace talks, an action that demonstrated the difficulty of resolving issues.

In the Philippines, the government (of the Republic of the Philippines) and the Moro National Liberation Front reached an agreement in 2008 after years of hostilities and negotiations. However, prior to the date on which it was to be signed, opposing politicians brought the document to the Supreme Court of the Philippines, which in turn declared it unconstitutional. As a result of the government's refusal to sign the peace treaty, the Moro Islamic Liberation Front (MILF) initiated attacks on civilian populations. This in turn caused the government to launch a military campaign that lasted ten months. While the government and the MILF have established a joint cease-fire mechanism, they have failed to come to an overall agreement and resolve the conflict.

4.5 Summary Comments on Unsuccessful Attempts

In this section, we have considered various unsuccessful attempts at conflict resolution. We have learned that unresolved historical issues, attempts to create unified identities, political issues, and discrepancies in conflict resolution goals pose real challenges that must be addressed for conflict resolution to be successful. We have learned that peace means more than the absence of violence, that different groups have competing historical narratives and goals, and that the state plays an integral role in resolving conflict. We have discovered that conflict resolution is difficult and that numerous attempts to resolve conflicts have failed.

In order to move toward resolution, we need to encourage parties to reconcile with each other, to learn to reframe their histories, to understand the positions of various ethnic groups, and to create a peace plan that goes beyond cease-fire to positive peace and full cooperation. Without this kind of effort on the part of all parties involved, from countries to ethnic groups, and from the international community to civic groups, these types of conflicts will continue to affect the lives of people around the globe.

In the next section, we focus on some general approaches to promote movement toward resolution and peace.

5 Part V: Moving Toward Peace: Broad Approaches to Conflict Resolution and Peace Building

Addressing ethnic conflicts is as complex and multidimensional as the conflicts themselves. Ethnic conflicts present great challenges, and therefore, require bold, broad, and inclusive approaches. One of our goals for this handbook is to contribute current knowledge and analysis that might provide useful ideas to policy makers in tackling this difficulty. In this section, we illuminate different approaches through which the resolution process might be addressed, beginning to conceptualize the path to peace. This is followed by sections devoted to examples and suggestions of concrete strategies to accomplish resolution goals, and an exploration of what future research can contribute to peace building.

Coleman (2006) offers a number of guidelines for intervening in intractable conflicts: carefully analyzing the conflict system, embedding the analysis and intervention within a multidisciplinary framework, addressing the parties' willingness to de-escalate, working toward finding a resolution process that is both fair and effective, being more respectful toward the diversity of disputants, coordinating short-term interventions with long-term objectives, establishing and sustaining change, and integrating issues from the past, present, and future.

Bhawuk (2012) declares that

> If we start with conflict, we will only find disagreement, clash, divergence, difference, argument, variance, quarrel, inconsistency, discord, contradiction, dispute, tension, controversy, fracas, competition, or aggression, battle, fight, war, struggle, encounter, skirmish, and weapons of mass destruction (WMD); not concord, convergence, cooperation or peace. (p. 142)

Thus, he argues that how we approach a subject may influence the strategies we undertake. While we agree that how we frame a situation is important, we content that we must deal with BOTH conflict resolution AND peace building.

A useful definition of peace building, based on Abiew and Keating (1999), is provided in Schwegler and Smith (2012):

> Peace-building is a time intensive process that involves 'transforming hostile and violent relationships into a peace system characterized by just and interdependent relationships...it is grounded on the premise that societies affected by violence are still comprised of individuals, groups, attitudes, and processes that promote peace. (pp. 81–82, cited in Schwegler & Smith, 2012, p. 350)

In this section, we address the following approaches to conflict resolution and peace building: stopping the violence and beyond, dealing with the past, fostering good communication and dialogue, developing trust and empathy, embracing multiculturalism, addressing the role of the state, and employing the policy of "Muhibbah." These topics will further illuminate the nature of the changes societies must make, for as we will see, making peace entails a lot more than silencing guns.

5.1 Stopping the Violence and Beyond

At the most basic level, we must aim to stop the violence. Protracted, violent conflicts lead to death and destruction, and so the first aim of peace building must be to stop violent warfare or hostile confrontation. However, while the halting of hostilities is commonly referred to as "peace," the absence of conflict does not equal peace, as we have noted above. We must instead recognize a more sophisticated definition of the term that includes both *negative peace* and *positive peace* (Galtung, 1996). *Negative peace* may entail the recognition of a mutual agreement to end the physical violence, while *positive peace* may entail reconciling current social identities and changing negative portrayals in history books.

As Boulding (2000) writes, "a static image of peace, as reflecting human inactivity, is dramatically opposed to the characterization of peace as a process, of peace building as an adventure, exploration, and willingness to venture into the unknown" (p. 1).

As we begin to work with a more nuanced definition of peace, the importance of addressing relationships in peace building becomes evident. Rather than simply stopping violence, the process involves "transforming hostile and violent relationships into a peace system characterized by just and interdependent relationships" (Abiew & Keating, 1999, pp. 81–82).

Below we address some of the key conceptual issues in moving toward peace.

5.2 Dealing with the Past

As we have seen throughout this handbook, a great deal of ethnic conflict is rooted in historical events and their interpretations. Even in a time of relative calm, competing identity narratives and a history of mutually perpetrated violence can still dominate inter-group relations. It is difficult to move forward when there is no reconciliation with the other party, and with the past. The question of the Armenian genocide is indicative of this imperative.

Historical barriers to understanding may range from (relatively) recent political or violent events, to deeply ingrained stories of cultural foundation. For example, myths comprise an important part in the conflicting identity narratives of Serbs and Albanians in Kosovo. Each group's respective story places a special claim on the land, pitting one group against the other. The strength of such identity narratives and ingroup–outgroup distinctions create significant barriers to trust and to crosscommunity respect.

Long troubled histories create circular patterns: "the parties in ethnic conflict usually become involved in an escalation of mutual aggression, and often a circular pattern ensues where it is impossible to know whether a given act is a cause or an effect" (Albert, 2009, p. 133). Thus, addressing only current disagreements will not likely create lasting peace. Strategies to enable communities to reconcile their respective histories will be important to foster the development of positive relationships needed for a peaceful society.

5.3 Fostering Good Communication and Dialogue

Communication is vital to the repair of relationships in conflicted societies. Ellis (2006) has argued that it is a myth that ethnic conflicts cannot be solved, and contends that communication and interaction are central to conflict prevention. Albert (2009) agrees: "conflict resolution and prevention is a process that relies at its very core on communication" (p. 138). Communication is a vital process to foster the repair and reconciliation of relationships on many levels, to deal with history, and to enhance understanding in multicultural societies.

Ellis contends that a focus on communication is less concerned with rational analyses, judgments, or solutions, but more concerned with building relationships, mutual understanding, and constructing new realities. He proposes that what is needed is deep change – a type of change that entails transformation of the system of interaction itself.

Communication interacts with trust and empathy in complex ways. Interaction is necessary to develop relationships and build trust, and yet trust is needed to communicate openly. It is, therefore, vital to address the nature of communication and contact in reconciliation efforts.

When groups in conflict are brought into contact with one another, empathic listening that enables more realistic discussions is difficult, but helpful. "Mutual recognition of one another's suffering creates a favorable atmosphere for progress in negotiation because underneath there is mutual verification of each other's group identity" (Volkan 1999, cited in Draguns, 2007, pp. 6–7).

However, increasing contact among parties engaged in deeply divisive ethnic conflict requires careful thought and consideration. Making contact possible and available between conflicting groups is an important first step. Zeytinoğlu et al. (2012) cite an interviewee who stated: "The opening of the border between the two countries [Turkey and Armenia] will be an important first step to improve the relationship between the two governments" (p.286). As we know from many studies of the contact hypothesis (Allport, 1954; Pettigrew, 1998, 2008), contact is effective only when certain conditions occur (see Landis & Albert, 2012).

Contributions from authors in this book and from outside researchers have provided multiple examples of strategies for creating dialogue between conflicting ethnic groups. As a result of the lack of trust between the MILF and the

Philippines government, Montiel et al. (2012) have advocated local level discussions between government units and the Lumad, Christian, and Moro settler populations. These discussions could "create a climate of mutual recognition of each other's concerns" which would increase the likelihood of them living together in peace (p. 87).

Munusamy (2012) suggests that in Malaysia, the "formulation of good policies and effective implementation of those policies require authentic conversations, open dialogue and respectful debates" (p. 30). And in Cyprus, the divide between Greek-Cypriots and Turkish-Cypriots

> began to be bridged in the early part of the 1990s when international diplomatic missions and individual third-party facilitators responded to requests of individuals from both communities to help them find ways to meet across the buffer zone. Workshops, training programs, and seminars promoted inter-communal dialogue. By the mid-1990s several bi-communal groups had formed and began to meet regularly. The number of people involved in these bi-communal groups grew steadily, and in spite of difficulties securing all the relevant permissions, by late 1997 bi-communal groups were meeting almost every day of the week. (Broome & Anastasiou, p. 307)

Bhawuk (2012) describes a similar use of dialogue to promote peace in India:

> Dialogue is the Indian way of creating peace. This is reflected in the spiritual tradition in which two scholars would have a public *zAstrArtha* (zAstra means scriptures, and artha means meaning; zAstrArtha means interpreting the meaning of the scriptures), and it was customary for the one who was convinced by the other to become a disciple of that scholar. In other words, the two reach harmony and agree to one meaning or interpretation of the scripture. It is in this tradition that Buddha was able to convert all or most of India to his views, and nine centuries later Shankaracarya was able to re-establish the Vedantic view by having dialogues with the Buddhist monks. (p. 146)

Dialogue can become an explicit source of empowerment for minority groups. Jia et al. (2012) advise creating "interethnic town-hall style dialogues to explore how such conflicts developed and what could be done to ameliorate them and prevent them in the future" (p. 192). In a nation in which ethnic groups are not equally represented in the political arena, this can be especially beneficial in giving voice to those who feel powerless.

Cautions about contact. The Volkan quote in the beginning of this section outlines an argument for pursuing contact and dialogue in conflict situations. However, there is significant evidence that the nature of contact between conflicting groups can determine whether or not the experience does indeed elicit positive effects. If not done carefully, intergroup contact can create negative outcomes. And in "intractable conflicts, establishing contact conditions that permit a decrease in conflict presents a major challenge" (Albert, 2009, p. 130).

Ellis (2006) describes an Israeli/Palestinian dialogue regarding attachment to land as wrought with tension. The two parties stood their ground, positing that their respective assumptions were uncontroversial, and accusing each other of "irrationality" and "bias." In light of this, Ellis (2006) has forcefully advocated for a transformation from "oppositional discourse" to "invitational discourse" that is more open to communication, one that views conflicts not as problems, but as opportunities.

5.4 Developing Trust and Empathy

Shapiro (2010) maintains that understanding and respect for the emotional dimension of ethnic conflict is "critical to agreement and long-term positive relations" (p. 643). Shapiro's Relational Identity Theory suggests that there are factors beyond social categorization and realistic conflict over resources that motivate conflict. These factors include concerns for affiliation and autonomy, and produce what Shapiro calls the emotional dimension of ethnic conflict. Conflict resolution must address this emotional dimension.

Many scholars and practitioners note the importance of trust and empathy in ethnic relationships wrought with tension. (See, for example, Draguns, 2007; Kelman, 2008; Pettigrew, 2008).

Schwegler and Smith (2012) describe a cross-cultural trust-building model developed by Schwegler (2008). This model posits four stages through which individuals develop trust in "the other": a) *confrontation*-- a new culture is experienced and insecurity develops; b) *construction*-- the individual begins to react; c) *constitution* –the person develops either negative trust or functional trust; and d) *consolidation*-- beliefs are consolidated. (See Schwegler and Smith for further information about these stages.) Through this process, individuals create and derive meaning and beliefs about the trustworthiness of those around them (Schwegler & Smith, 2012).

A better understanding and implementation of trust-building processes would increase the likelihood of successful conflict resolution. The model proposed in the Kosovo chapter bears some similarity to Milton Bennett's Developmental Model of Intercultural Sensitivity (Bennett, 1993).

In the Philippines, lack of trust between the MILF and the Philippines government has paralyzed efforts to resolve disputes over political representation and land disputes. In Kosovo, a lack of trust and compromise has severely hindered the negotiation process, for both parties must accept the role of both perpetrator and victim, which neither is willing to do (Schwegler & Smith, 2012).

Albert (2009) notes: "Recent research has shown that empathy for another group and the ability to understand the other group's perspective are two of the most important aspects of reducing prejudice and aiding in the de-escalation of conflict (Pettigrew, 2008)" (p. 130). According to Lederach (1997), establishing and fostering relationships across conflict lines and building trust between key players have significant roles in creating "space for the acknowledging of the past and envisioning of the future" (p. 27), which, as we have seen previously, are essential to true resolution. Repairing interethnic trust and empathy, therefore, must remain a priority in peace building. Without addressing relationships in this way, other issues may be insurmountable. Çelik (2012) suggests the need for programs that can heal trauma, support victims, and reconcile the gap between the Kurdish citizens and the state. "However, peaceful coexistence of people requires addressing social polarization and mistrust" (Çelik, 2012, p. 257).

Society-wide relationships, not only those between specific parties perceived to be in conflict, must be addressed as well. Ward and Liu (2012) note that "A major challenge to harmonious ethnic relations in New Zealand... is to ensure mutual acceptance and respect amongst all ethnic groups" and not merely between each minority or indigenous group and the majority (p. 62).

Deutsch (2008) emphasizes forgiveness in repairing relationships. He contends there are two ways to develop forgiveness: "One centers on the victim and the other on the relationship between the victim and the harm doers" (Deutsch, 2008, p. 479).

5.5 Embracing Multiculturalism[14]

In repairing relationships and reducing divisions in ethnic conflict, states must work toward overarching goals of equity, respect, and diversity. As groups come together, there exists the potential for the development of richly collaborative multicultural societies. Many chapters in this book suggest the necessity for embracing multiculturalism, an approach that encourages inclusion.

In the former Yugoslavia, the words used for this were "brotherhood and unity" of nations and nationalities (Corkalo Biruski, 2012, p. 330) and were invoked to advocate "peaceful and harmonious living" (p. 334). Corkalo Biruski (2012) indicates that a typical response of community members about relationships in pre-Balkan war Croatia was "We live normally; we did not even know who was of what ethnic background" (p. 334). In addition, "ethnic promotion was condemned as a sign of nationalism and strongly discouraged." Also important was the fact that political elites in Yugoslavia "did not care about identities and diversity" (Corkalo Biruski, 2012, p. 334).

As noted by Kamiejski et al. (2012), multiculturalism is a policy that accepts cultural diversity as a positive feature of national identity. This implies that categorizing individuals into distinct ethnic groups, based on their self-identity, is an acceptable and beneficial practice. A policy of

[14] This assumes, of course, that the partitioning of states into ethnically homogeneous entities (and the attendant transfer of populations, sometimes called "ethnic cleansing") does not become the normative method of solving conflicts, as some have advocated (see Chapter 1).

multiculturalism has been successfully implemented in Canada and has been tried in Australia and Sweden (Kamiejski et al., 2012). In France, recent research by Er-rafiy and Brauer (2010), (cited by Kamiejski et al., 2012) shows that emphasizing the diversity within the Maghrebians (North African immigrants) was highly effective in reducing prejudice and discrimination against them. (These results are consistent with research by Hewstone and Brown (1986) on the Mutual Intergroup Differentiation Model, which demonstrates the effectiveness of emphasizing diversity within a group.) Kamiejski et al. (2012) proceed to suggest that both multiculturalism and the Mutual Intergroup Differentiation Model offer a good basis for policy development.

One of the strongest policy recommendations made by Ward and Liu (2012) is for the government of New Zealand to bring various ethnic groups together in a shared understanding of both biculturalism and multiculturalism. Historically, New Zealand emphasized biculturalism focused on the Maori and European settlers. But the immigration of other groups, specifically Asian/Pacific Islanders, has resulted in a multicultural society with a bicultural narrative. An understanding of the multicultural present would seem to help reduce intercultural discrimination.

Based on many elements outlined by Cabrera et al. (2008), Aneas et al. (2012) indicate that the goal would be to build a society that overcomes passivity, encourages the development of a participatory democratic culture, combats exclusion and fundamentalist positions, promotes social cohesion, facilitates coexistence, and prevents conflict and violence. To achieve this goal, it is necessary to promote civic participation, social responsibility, diversity, and dialogue; overcome traditional prejudices and stereotypes; and promote sustainable development and civic values. Among many other elements, this will require the acceptance of a more open society that accepts multiple identities, interactions and sharing of values and norms, the promotion of a collective identity and of civic participation, in addition to legislative initiatives, respect for laws, and full recognition by the state of practices, social organization, and traditions of various cultures.

For Malaysia, Munusamy (2012) suggests that the government acknowledge the existence of multicultural issues, accept that multicultural issues can be complex, and aim to take appropriate, proactive action to address them. He also suggests that policy makers shift from "narrow community approaches" toward policies emphasizing national unity. He suggests that implementation, evaluation, and revision of multicultural policies are very important for successful outcomes, and that the government should use the perspective of the community and of all actors involved in developing and implementing these policies.

In examining the contributions above, we may draw the conclusion that building a truly multicultural society is an immense task, and one that most countries have not come close to achieving. Yet, these objectives remain vital for multiethnic societies.

5.6 Addressing the Role of the State

In many places, state failure or inefficiency stands in the way of conflict resolution. The roles and responsibilities of states in peace building are extremely important; thus, creating a state that is able to carry them out is imperative. States must be able to protect and represent those who suffer violence and discrimination. In areas such as the central sub-Saharan region of Africa and the DRC, state-building efforts are needed to enable the prevention and amelioration of rampant insecurity. Mealy and Austad (2012) propose that

> furthermore, the state must act as a benefactor for these persecuted groups, and support both national and community institutions that provide a sanctuary from human rights abuses, promote superordinate identity, multicultural education, and, most importantly, culturally sensitive reconciliation processes. (p. 577)

States that protect their inhabitants lessen the potential of insurgencies and of military repression.

On a policy level, Kibanja et al. (2012) suggest that President Museveni, along with ethnic leaders and NGOs, should work toward accomplishing United Nations Millennium

Development Goals: ending poverty and hunger; making education universally available; realizing gender equality, environmental sustainability, and global partnership; bettering child health and maternal health; and combating HIV/AIDS. While these goals are laudable, we also recognize that they are truly daunting.

Landis (2008) suggested that for multiculturalism to be successful, three important actions need to be taken by a state. First, meaningful jobs and wages should be made available to all members of the working population. Second, safe and affordable housing needs to be made available. And lastly, affordable and effective health care is critical. Whether these goals are to be accomplished preliminary to other social goals or concurrent with them needs to be investigated. What is important is that they occur and be consistent over extended periods of time.

5.7 A Policy of "Muhibbah"

A policy of "Muhibbah" (loosely translated as "the spirit of tolerance and harmony") was popular in Malaysia in the 1970s and provided a "safety net for authentic interactions, conflict resolution, difficult conversations and intercultural dialogue" (Munusamy, p. 134). Munusamy (2012) believes that this spirit has been lost, and that it needs to be rekindled if the recently instituted multicultural policies, legislation, slogans, and campaigns that have been substituted for it are to succeed. Rather than conflict resolution, Malaysian leaders use the term "constant repair": "national unity must always be kept in constant repair" (Shafie, 1993, p. 1, cited in Munusamy, p. 120).

In the next section, we will discuss some strategies that might move societies in the direction of peace building.

6 Part VI: Specific Peace-building Strategies

The important issues outlined in the previous section provide a framework for considering the development of a peace process. In this section, we seek to provide some concrete suggestions to policy makers for engaging in this process. We will offer brief discussions, drawn from various chapters, of programs, policies, and practices used in peace building. These include peace zones; interactive management for peacebuilding, state-building, and interstate relations; legal approaches; educational strategies; use of the media; culturally derived approaches; institutional and organizational linkages; and creating superordinate goals and identities.

Peace building is a process that may require different strategies and follow different trajectories in different conflicts. There is no quick fix, and conflict resolution can take a long time. "Indeed," says Lederach (1997), "it is likely to take more or less as long to get out of a conflict as it took to get into it" (p. 136).

The DRC chapter illuminates just how complicated the peace process can be in violent conflicts. The amount of cooperation that needs to occur and the many policies that must be implemented to address the multitude of interrelated factors in the conflict can seem overwhelming. The states directly involved, civil society, international organizations, and the media may need to be included for a successful resolution. Karbo and Mutisi (2012) break down the causes of the conflict and specify what each level of society (from the individual to the UN) needs to do in order to make peace possible, and ultimately successful, in the region.

It is important to note, as well, that the conflict strategies that are effective at one time can change if the circumstances change. In Israel, identity concerns are becoming more important to the Arab-Israelis, and what is required for successful conflict resolution now is likely to be rather different than what might have worked in the 1960s or the 1980s.

Therefore, those seeking to select any of the approaches discussed here need to consider the particular context, history, previously employed strategies, and a number of other features of the specific region in which the approach would be implemented. In addition, the degree of conflict is important: if there is widespread violence and bloodshed, as in the DRC, safeguarding lives must be the priority. If there is little or no violence, but widespread stereotyping and discrimination, policies and strategies that address these problems should be employed. Often, because of the multiple factors involved in the conflicts, several different strategies need to be employed, either simultaneously or sequentially.

6.1 Encourage and Enlarge Peace Zones

The largely successful implementation of "peace zones" in the Philippines suggests a way of dealing with conflict that could be attempted elsewhere.

> A peace zone is a community that was previously affected by armed conflict, but is now designated by its residents as an area where illegal and violent acts are not allowed and where conflict is resolved in a peaceful manner. (Montiel et al., 2012, p. 81)

Working with local and government officials, a Council of Leaders outlines the rules and conditions for peace zone communities. The rights, traditions, and customs of each ethnic group within the zone are protected and respected, while the Council of Leaders simultaneously aims to prevent conflict outbreaks and resolve conflict in a peaceful manner. In some conflicts, peace zones were established through negotiations between the government and the armed groups. This was done in parts of Mindanao where there are fifty successful peace zones.

6.2 Create Departments or Ministries of Peace

Marsella (2005) argues eloquently for departments of peace:

> All nations should create a department or ministry of peace and conflict resolution and this should be integrated with the justice systems and should be considered to be equal in power and influence to departments of defense, and other military offices. In all instances of national or international conflict, this department should play an active role in decision-making. It should also fund peace research and be a resource for peace through the nation. (p. 670)

6.3 Develop Peace Building and a Peace Constituency

Broome and Anastasiou (2012) describe an Interactive Management (IM) process that helped a bi-communal group to develop a strategy for peace-building efforts through three stages of planning: (1) analysis of the current situation, (2) goal setting for the future, and (3) development of a collaborative action agenda. There were also receptions, concerts, exhibitions, and visits to religious sites that brought together a large number of people from both communities. Broome and Anastasiou (2012) note that despite the fact that these were social events, they allowed people to see that the two communities had similar everyday concerns. In addition, there was professional contact between artists, religious pilgrims, business leaders, and even sewage system workers from both sides, and the economic and collegial ties that ensued provided a stable basis for future cooperation. Thus, a peace constituency evolved. Broome and Anastasiou (2012) noted:

> Especially in divided societies, a peace constituency is an imperative dimension of the overall effort of resolving conflict, in both attaining and subsequently sustaining a final political settlement. The positive impact of a peace constituency was evident in the transformation of the Turkish-Cypriot political reality in 2003 and the negative impact of an insufficiently developed peace constituency was demonstrated in the failed referendum in the Greek-Cypriot side in 2004. (p. 319)

These meetings helped to foster trust between the conflicting groups. From the Cyprus chapter, we learned that dialogue in civil society can help advance the process of peace even during periods when the diplomatic efforts have failed.

6.4 Enhance State-Building and Interstate Relations

New, struggling, and/or failing states prove to be difficult obstacles to conflict resolution. Creating integrated support structures made up of internal agencies, surrounding countries, and the international community may prove to be essential for the legitimacy and maintenance of new states.

By examining examples from the chapters, we will draw out possible strategies for state building.

Because state failure is one of the most pressing concerns in both the DRC and the central sub-Saharan region of Africa, state-building efforts are a top priority. In addition to local, meso- and macro-level organizations, successful state-building efforts need to involve international efforts:

> To address the plethora of post-conflict reconstruction challenges facing the DRC, it is important for the African Union, SADC (Southern African Development Community) and the international community to assist the country to design a coherent state building strategy so that a functioning state will be better able to support and promote any conflict resolution and peace building efforts. (Karbo & Mutisi, 2012, p. 398)

Such a strategy would entail an aid package from the international community that would significantly increase the funding of United Nations agencies, such as the MONUC, so that these agencies can deliver on their mandate to keep peace.

Corruption has been so widespread in the DRC conflict that there has to be some form of vetting or accountability for state officials and military officers. Widespread corruption prevents the DRC from effectively collecting tax revenue and putting it toward much needed social services. Embezzlement in the military has also occurred, causing insecurity and more conflict:

> Corruption in the armed forces has been particularly detrimental. It has been relatively easy for higher authorities to embezzle their troops' salaries. The troops, who live in terrible conditions, in turn harass the local population. The army is itself a threat to civilians in the country, while the police are seen as a menace in many areas. (Karbo & Mutisi, p. 398)

Because an internal review has failed to curb corruption, external NGOs and third parties should regularly conduct evaluations in order to create a disincentive for further corruption and to foster a culture of accountability.

More legitimate and stable states may also require strategies for conflict prevention and the maintenance of equitable and peaceful relationships. De Mel et al. (2012) advocate that the government of Sri Lanka be restructured to become more decentralized in order to achieve lasting peace. They write that the transition of power to less centralized structures, such as the local governments and provincial councils, has not been seen as enough change and that post-tsunami relief has not been effective under the current system of government. In contrast, Montiel, Rodil, and de Guzman (2012) argue that the government in the Philippines should move toward democratization of their Unitary State, and possibly to a Federal System. As these examples show, there is little consensus on the "best" structure for the state in conflict areas. The best organization may depend heavily on the particular geographic, historical, political, and social context.

Following through with diplomatic efforts and other conflict prevention measures must also occur in order to build lasting, trustworthy relationships between conflicting groups, both within and between states. Zeytinoğlu et al. (2012) argue that the government of Turkey should enact measures aimed at promoting ethnic tolerance and should ensure the fair treatment of Turkish Armenians. They also state that "achieving normalization of relations between Armenia and Turkey, though currently mired in discord, would have a positive outcome for Turkish Armenians" (Zeytinoğlu et al., p. 286).

6.5 Utilize Legal Strategies

Legal strategies may help to prevent discrimination and violent conflict. "The Netherlands has a good constitution, which guarantees freedom of religion, equality of men and women, and freedom of expression. These principles offer precious conditions for constructive relations between Muslims and non-Muslims in the Netherlands" (van Oudenhoven, 2012, p. 508).

The French employ a specifically Republican/Color-Blind approach: "Built on elements of the ideology introduced during the French Revolution, French citizenship is perceived as refusing any form of distinction on ethno-racial lines in the public sphere" (cited by Kamiejski et al, 2012, p. 501).

Similarly, Felouzis (2006) states that "The French State, currently, does not recognize any group membership whatsoever based on religious, cultural or other grounds, it only sees "free and equal citizens" (translated and cited by Kamiejski et al., 2012, p. 501). Kamiejski et al. (2012) write that the principle of "republican citizenship," which supports a policy of neutrality in matters of ethnicity and race, is strongly endorsed by both the French and the Maghrebians, and that the Republican/Color-Blind Model has greatly reduced prejudice and improved intergroup relations. Thus, this color-blind approach has deep roots in national policies in France, and has been successfully employed in French society until recently (see Kamiejski et al., 2012).[15]

What is interesting about the Color-Blind Model is the deliberate effort not to emphasize ethnicity. This would support the idea that ethnic classifications are not set in stone, but that they can be changed and manipulated to further conflict, or can be used in beneficial ways to bring about peace.

Peace treaties are another form of legal approach that can be successful in sustaining or bringing about peace. In Malaysia, a small number of Malaysia National Liberation Army members continued to operate in the Malaysia–Thailand border until they and the Thai and Malaysian government in 1986 signed a peace treaty.

6.6 Consider Truth and Reconciliation Commissions

The use of a Truth and Reconciliation Commission (TRC) similar to the one established in South Africa has been proposed for managing conflicts and post-conflict peace building in Kosovo and Peru. TRCs were created with the intention to engage the issue of "dealing with the past," as discussed above, by establishing a shared history and constructing a public narrative of grievances and abuses. A shared history in this regard was intended to help reconcile the differences between ethnic groups, allowing the multiethnic state to be more stable and successful. However, it is not clear that such reconciliation commissions accomplish the goal of peace building (Abiew & Keating, 1999). In fact, as we have seen, the one in Peru was not as successful as was hoped. Before moving to a TRC, one would need to establish the conditions under which such commissions can be successful and then make sure that those conditions are present.

6.7 Hold Interactive Problem Solving Workshops

These workshops, developed by Kelman (1972, 2005a, 2005b; Kelman & Fisher, 2003) and based on Burton's (1969) earlier work, are defined as "an unofficial, academically based, third-party approach to the resolution of international and intercommunal conflicts, especially suited to protracted conflicts between identity groups" (Kelman, 2005a, p. 641). They allow participants to examine their perceptions and misperceptions of the conflict and of each other, while jointly exploring paths for resolving the conflict in a non-threatening atmosphere (Fisher, 1997a, 1997b, 2006). They are employed with politically influential members of the groups in conflict, and a skilled intermediary to facilitate communication. Fisher (2006) found that these workshops have notable "prenegotiation" and "paranegotiation contributions" within the larger peace process (p. 65). Similar workshops have been used in organizations that have experienced conflict over cultural diversity issues in the USA.

6.8 Institute and Vastly Expand Education Programs

Education serves as a powerful tool of conflict resolution and has been mentioned in many chapters. Aneas et al. (2012) contend that education is a major vehicle for creating a respectful and open society with mutual acceptance. One suggestion includes reconciling history books for a more

[15] If this sounds familiar to American ears, it is because it is also the basis of the famous phrase in the Declaration of Independence that "all men are created equal..."

balanced and de-ethnicized view. Educational programs could, and should, focus on combating stereotypes, which are often widespread in societies with ethnic conflict. For this and related goals, many authors have specifically proposed intercultural education programs.

Require intercultural education. In China, the author recommends making education on the history and cultures of minorities a part of the mandatory general education curriculum in all Chinese universities (Jia et al., 2012, p. 193). In the Netherlands chapter, van Oudenhoven (2012) mentions that the Turkish and Moroccan immigrants particularly recognize that "…education is the path to social mobility" (p. 516). The cultural distance between native Dutch and Muslim immigrants can be lessened through education.

Aneas et al. (2012) highlight that intercultural education is particularly important: "Such education in and for citizenship has to be an education for all, an education which is intercultural and anti-racist, one which singles out the values of solidarity, mutual tolerance, equality, and social inclusion" (p. 572).

In the DRC, ethnic stereotypes need to be combated at a variety of levels since there are misconceptions that encourage intergroup conflict. Scholars, academics, journalists, media personnel, the international community, and the development community need to demystify, challenge, and combat these stereotypes (Karbo & Mutisi, 2012).

Mealy and Austad (2012) suggest an important step: to provide multicultural education with an emphasis on the development of empathy. In this regard, Draguns' (2007) work on the importance of empathy in resolving ethnic conflicts should be noted. He argues that cultural empathy training "has the potential for humanizing members of previously conflicted groups, for dispelling negative preconceptions, and for setting the stage for constructive and collaborative interaction" (Draguns, 2007, pp. 7–8). Part of this training involves identifying the prevalent stereotypes of ethnic groups, analyzing their harmful consequences, and then striving to overcome these stereotypes. However, in order for empathic understanding to fully develop, there must be "intensive contact between members of ethnic groups" so that stereotypes and prejudice no longer obstruct conflict resolution attempts (Draguns, 2007, p. 10). Draguns (2007) cites studies by Batson and Ahmed (2001) and Batson and Moran (1999) that have shown that "empathy induction promotes cooperation, even in situations that are designed to foster competition, even when the partner continues to be competitive" (p. 8). Thus, empathy-driven strategies appear to be incredibly helpful in both quelling ethnic tensions and maximizing the chances of conflict resolution.

Moreover, instituting empathy-driven conflict resolution strategies could have increased the prospects of success and speed up the peace process. In writing about increased contact between members of conflicting groups, Draguns (2007) shows that when conflicting groups show empathy for one another, they can much more easily talk through negative preconceptions and have constructive dialogue. Draguns' research on empathic understanding has found that increased contact can increase the chances of success for conflict resolution. He argues that external dialogue facilitators should engage members of conflicting ethnic groups after they

> are immersed into intensive experiential training on site in order to familiarize them not with the academic and abstract aspects of local history, but to confront them with the monuments, artifacts and witnesses that have a bearing on the conflict that is being experienced. (Draguns, 2007, p. 7)

When members of groups learn about each other through facilitators, empathic understanding occurs which "reduces social distance, replaces group stereotypes with more differentiated and individualized social percepts, brings about attitude change, and promotes new patterns of social interaction" (Draguns, 2007, p. 7).

As noted by Landis and Albert (2012), there are methods for increasing intercultural understanding and sensitivity, and thus, creating greater empathy. Among these methods, the Intercultural Sensitizer (Albert, 1983, 1986, 1995; Bhawuk, 2001, Cushner & Landis, 1996) has received the greatest empirical validation for its effectiveness. The Intercultural Sensitizer

(ICS) is an instrument designed to sensitize individuals from one culture to the perspectives, norms, values, and behaviors of "the other." It can focus on behaviors, perceptions, ideas, and attitudes of members of the other culture, and can increase the understanding of social factors and context. The ICS consists of incidents based on actual or reconstructed experiences of persons from the two cultures. They are obtained from interviews, observations, literature reviews, and other methods. The incidents are carefully constructed to focus on "critical problems" or "key differences" between the cultures, and are followed by four alternative interpretations of the situation. In the best ICSs, the alternative interpretations consist of responses obtained from research with each cultural group. The task of the user is to select the interpretation(s) given by persons from the other culture. The reader is then given feedback on his/her choice and is told additional information about the culture and why that interpretation makes sense. This instrument has a number of advantages, including the fact that it actively engages the learner, it provides immediate feedback, it allows learners to progress at their own rate, and it can be used repeatedly either singly or in conjunction with other sensitization approaches. We believe that the ICS can be adapted to increase the understanding of the perspectives of the "other" in a conflict situation, as well as to convey the other's views about specific avenues for conflict amelioration and peace building.

In this world of increasing communication and connection between persons from different ethnicities, cultures, and countries, intercultural education should be required of everyone, and especially of those dealing with policy or programs involving culturally different people, whether domestically or internationally.

We do recognize that the use of education to reduce ethnic conflict may be easier to propose than to accomplish. Even in economically developed societies such as the USA, such efforts meet with extensive resistance, particularly when the economy weakens and unemployment increases. Thus, we have seen the state of Arizona legislation enact rules that discourage the teaching of ethnic differences. In the state of Texas, the organization that controls the approval of textbooks for pre-collegiate use has mandated a view of history that eliminates, or severely reduces, the role of discrimination in the history of the country. Education does not occur in a political vacuum, but is subject to the whims of whichever groups control the levers of power in a society.

Make peace education mandatory. In the Philippines, Montiel et al. (2012) report that peace education has recently become more prevalent and has been integrated into courses at several educational institutions across the country. One of such institutions, Mindanao State University, established a specialized institute specifically designed for peace education, the Institute of Peace and Development in Mindanao. NGOs have also launched peace education initiatives for military officers. Although these educational programs are relatively new, the enthusiasm and support for this policy are promising. Peace education should be mandatory for government officials, policy makers, international agencies, not-for-profit organizations, business persons, the media, and civil society.

Utilize reliable educational resources. There are many resources to increase the understanding of the conflict and the parties involved in them. One example is the online Conflict Information Consortium (University of Colorado), which lists new versions of CRInfo: The Conflict Resolution Information Source (www.CRInfo.org) and Beyond Intractability, the website of the Intractable Conflict Knowledge Base Project (http://www.BeyondIntractability.org). There are databases, online courses, and instructional resources. Documentaries constitute another valuable resource. They can offer material that is vivid and helpful to understand issues. One example is Encounter Point (Avni, Makhlouf, & Rous, 2006), a documentary about "a former Israeli settler, a Palestinian ex-prisoner, a bereaved Israeli mother, and a wounded Palestinian bereaved brother, who risk their lives and public standing to promote a nonviolent end to the conflict" in Israel and Palestine (citation from http://www.justvision. org/encounterpoint/about).

6.9 Utilize Old and New Media for Peace Building

The media can play an important role in education and peace building, as they can strongly influence and inform people's perceptions and understandings of each other. The media have the potential to be very effective in promoting a culture of tolerance. Albert (2009) describes a relevant study carried out by Schiappa, Gregg, and Hewes (2005) that shows "that after watching a television series that portrayed gay men and a male transvestite, college students demonstrated an increase in positive attitudes toward these outgroups. Schiappa, Gregg, and Hewes attributed this increase to the parasocial contact hypothesis. Parasocial contact refers to mediated contact" (p. 137). The authors of the study confirmed "that such contact can provide the sort of experience that can reduce prejudice, particularly if a majority group member has limited opportunity for interpersonal contact with minority group members" (Schiappa, Gregg, & Hewes, 2005, p. 97). This study clearly demonstrates the potential impact of the media on perceptions of the outgroup.

Jia et al. (2012) propose media programs to teach about interethnic communication and help develop skills in interethnic harmony in China. They also suggest that the government needs a long-term strategy to ameliorate ethnic relations through multiethnic understanding among all Chinese ethnic groups. Montiel, Rodil, and de Guzman (2012), authors of the Philippines chapter, argue that the media should work to broadcast a more positive message of peace to people in that country.

In Mexico, world media coverage was able to aid the indigenous population. The media helped on two fronts – drawing attention to the Zapatista movement and moderating the intensity of the violence. With this coverage, the Zapatista movement, which began as a militaristic movement, shifted to become a movement that used rhetoric instead of arms.

It is important to note that the media may have a positive, a negative, or a neutral effect on ethnic conflicts. Thus, the lack of media attention to what has been happening in the DRC may have unwittingly contributed to the prolongation and exacerbation of that conflict.

Marsella (2005) has noted that the media as an institution has a significant influence on individuals, and that its power should be harnessed for positive goals. He writes that the media is one of the most influential means of transmitting knowledge and moral patterns, which makes it "essential that the media consider its impact upon promoting violence" (Marsella, 2005, p. 670). In light of this, Marsella (2005) advocates that the media initiate a PR campaign for peace in which government, business, and media outlets can "unite to promote a PR campaign for peace and non-violence" (p. 670).

6.10 Study Nonviolent Strategies

As the recent demonstrations in several countries have shown, nonviolent strategies that are carefully planned and creative can be very effective. Ackerman and DuVall (2000) cover nonviolent movements throughout the last century and present a powerful argument for the effectiveness of nonviolence. While so far they have been formulated to protest against the state, a strong civil society is necessary to create vibrant multicultural societies. Ackerman and DuVall state:

> If assuring democracy is always the answer, what should have greater priority, freezing in place the parties to a conflict or promoting ways to engage in conflict so that it is more likely to yield democratic outcome? …In a world in which vital human interests are in constant competition, conflicts will occur, and violence will be used in conflicts as long as people believe it will help them win. If another, more effective way to succeed, without the costs of violence, were more widely appreciated, violence would begin to seem less sensible as the way to fight for a cause. (pp. 7–8)

6.11 Employ Cultural Sensitivity

We have often discussed culture as a source of difference and tension in this volume, but integrating culturally unique ways of dealing with conflict offers potential avenues for successful conflict resolution.

An excellent example of how cultural sensitivity can be used as a means of conflict resolution is presented in the Hawai'i chapter, where a potentially explosive situation was avoided in the aftermath of the murder of a Samoan youth by a Micronesian youth. As Salzman (2012) explains, the potential for revenge attacks was high, but these attacks were averted because the Micronesian community offered their apologies employing an indigenous Samoan ritual of apology.

Similarly, Bhawuk (2012) suggests that "we should take an active role in this process of peace creation through dialogue, tentativeness in our worldview about what truth is, and connecting to our spiritual foundation as human beings" (p. 169). Elsewhere he describes how the use of dialogue, tentativeness about absolutes, and a connection to spirituality are attributes of Indian culture. It is clear, however, that they exist in other cultures as well and that these qualities can be cultivated by persons and groups everywhere.

A unique policy in India promotes multiculturalism. India is one of the few countries that celebrates religious diversity by granting national holidays to celebrate important festivals.

> Unlike most countries that only celebrate Christian, Muslim, or Buddhist holidays, India celebrates all of them. India has seventeen national holidays. It includes [sic] 5 Hindu, 4 Muslim, 3 national days, 2 Christian (Christmas and Good Friday), 1 Buddhist, 1 Jain, and 1 Sikha holiday. The three national holidays (Republic Day January 26th; Independence Day, August 15th; and Gandhi Jayanti, October 2nd) are non-religious in nature. The other 14 holidays are chosen by the states depending on which festival people in that state popularly celebrate, and vary across them. (Bhawuk, 2012, p. 151)

As we have seen, the presence of different ethnic/cultural groups in the same country can pose challenges to coexistence and peace building.

> Interethnic relations are affected by the culture in profound and multi-faceted ways. In fact, interethnic conflict constitutes the most challenging kind of intercultural relationship. Therefore, the relationship between culture and ethnic conflict deserves serious attention from scholars and practitioners who want to have a large-scale impact in the world. (Albert, 2009, p. 134)

In terms of reconciliation methods, Albert (2009) notes further that "cultures differ in how they prefer to deal with conflict" (p. 136).

Taking into account culturally specific strategies of conflict resolution can make an important contribution to the successful resolution of ethnic conflicts. Future research on cultural similarities and differences in preferences for certain strategies, and for their sequencing, could make an important contribution to the amelioration and prevention of ethnic conflicts.

Utilize the influence of culturally relevant leaders. One interesting suggestion proposed by van Oudenhoven (2012) is to utilize the influence of spiritual leaders and parents. This brings to mind the important role that religious leaders could play in ameliorating conflict and preventing future genocides. In the Philippines, various religious leaders have contributed to the peacebuilding process. The Bishops–Ulamas Conference (BUC) is a group comprised of Catholic bishops, Protestant bishops, and Muslim *ulamas* from around the Philippines. This assembly of religious leaders emphasizes faith in the search for peace and conflict resolution. In particular, the BUC has promoted positive relations between Christians, Muslims, and Lumad through various types of interactions in organized activities (Montiel et al., 2012). Additionally, the BUC's dedicated work has resulted in the establishment of several interfaith organizations in various provincial districts.

In India, Bhawuk (2012) writes,

> [t]he spiritual saints create a unique bond among people of various religions, which is akin to having a superordinate goal of visiting the holy place that is equally shared by all. When visiting these places people lose their intra religious identities and become part of an intergroup community. (p. 150)

Thus, religious leaders can help unite people rather than dividing them.

As well documented by Bartoli (2006), the settling of the conflict in Mozambique was immeasurably helped by the Community of Sant'Egidio, a Catholic group. The community identified problems in the local society and created successful interventions to help resolve those problems. The strategy used

> was relational. It was an attempt to respond to positive openings by including them into a larger, more creative interpretative framework. The constant presence brought the two parties to speak with members of the Community, and only later between themselves directly. This was done through an incremental process of exploration of possibilities that gradually bridged the gap between the two. (p. 89)

Bartoli (2006) writes that the work of the Community of Sant'Egidio "…contributed to the creation of a setting that was operative during the pre-negotiation, negotiation, and post-negotiation phases of dealing with conflict in Mozambique" (p. 85).

6.12 Build Civil Society: Linking Institutions and Organizations

Civil society can wield great power in conflict resolution, even while strategies falter on a political level.

The Cyprus conflict, which has divided Greek and Turkish Cypriots for nearly half a century, has eluded resolution despite repeated attempts by the international community to broker a viable solution. In contrast to the lack of progress at the political level, peace builders from civil society in the two communities have been able to work together successfully on dozens of projects since the mid-1990s (Broome & Anastasiou, 2012).

Bhawuk (2012) explains that peace-building efforts in India cannot rely solely on new legislation. He states that the ethnic conflicts

> can be handled by the existing administrative system, and the situation could be further improved by having social organizations mediate the peace building process in the daily interactions of people. Resource sharing in the community is likely to be more effective through a social process rather than through legislation, especially since all the necessary laws of equality among people of different castes are already in place. (p. 160)

For the Turkish/Armenian conflict, Zeytinoğlu, Bonnabeau, and Eşkinat (2012) suggest establishing linkages through academic institutions, businesses, the media, and civic society organizations. This has been shown to be a powerful force for peace building in Cyprus. Civil movements for peace have had great significance in preparing Cyprus for reunification, and for changing the attitudes of one ethnic group toward the other. Citizen efforts coupled with international assistance have brought about significantly positive changes in the country. The involvement of civil society also ensures that conflict resolution arises from several parts and levels of society, not just from top-level political structures. Considering the multilayered nature of ethnic conflicts (as discussed earlier in the chapter), this may contribute significantly to the sustainability of resolution.

6.13 Develop Superordinate Goals and Identities

Superordinate goals. Bringing people from two different groups into direct contact can be an effective way to reduce the prejudice and stereotypes held by members of each group toward members of the other group (see our mention of the contact hypothesis above). Working toward a common superordinate goal is especially effective in fostering cooperation and bringing group members together (Gaertner, Dovidio, Banker, Houlette, Johnson, & McGlynn, 2000; Gaertner, Mann, Dovidio, Murrell, & Pomare, 1990). Superordinate goals "elicit intergroup cooperative activity among the conflicting groups" (Gaertner et al. 2000, p. 105).

In Malaysia, the British informed various ethnic groups that independence would only be granted to the country once its ethnic groups were united. Independence, the superordinate goal, strengthened the "alliance" between the United Malays National Organization and the Malayan Chinese Association and ultimately led to the negotiation of Malaysia's independence in 1957. Other superordinate goals were also employed in Malaysia by the first premier: to use English on pragmatic grounds (which defused fights over issues of language), to provide opportunities for Malaysians regardless of race to pursue higher education (which defused the issue of quotas for different groups), and the corporatization of public universities.

In New Zealand, we learned that the lack of superordinate goals contributed to ethnic inequality. The indigenous Maori, who might have found allies among non-European immigrant groups, have viewed these groups as deflecting attention from their own hard efforts to attain equality.

Superordinate identity. While superordinate goals foster cooperation, Gaertner, Dovidio, & Bachman (1996) found that intergroup cooperation tends to foster the development of a superordinate identity. Across a diverse sample of people experiencing intergroup contact, Gaertner and colleagues found that greater superordinate identity predicted lower levels of prejudice toward original outgroup members. Multiple authors in this book discuss the creation or use of a superordinate, inclusive identity in order to unite conflicting groups and foster a sense of cohesion and reduce divisions. Some proponents of a superordinate identity see the benefit of a national identity over separate ethnic identities. Thus, Jia et al. (2012) suggest the creation of an identity in China in which everyone would be a hyphenated Chinese, such as Tibetan-Chinese, Han-Chinese, etc., just as Americans are designated African–American, Asian-American, and so on. This does not remove each ethnic group's unique identity, but emphasizes the fact that all are Chinese citizens. Jia, et al. believe that this would help to counteract the resentment and mistrust that the Chinese espouse against people of different ethnicities.

Kibanja et al. (2012) indicate that having a common work identity, especially among the young, can alleviate ingroup/outgroup bias and help develop healthy intercultural attitudes and behaviors. They cite evidence from a study of intercultural attitudes and ethnic identity among youth members of Wildlife Clubs of Uganda (a government-funded youth conservation education program). Participants reported that as a result of the program, they had a new awareness of diverse groups (Johnson-Pynn & Johnson, 2005, 2010). For example, participants stated, "I learned how to associate with people of different ethnicities," and, "I have got new friends who made me learn about ethnicity and backgrounds" (cited in Kibanja et al., 2012, p. 428). Since 45% of the population of Uganda is under 25 years old, this is a useful and relevant experiment.

Quoting Gomez et al. (2008), Mealy and Austad (2012) write:

> Creating a superordinate identity that encompasses both Western and indigenous cultures is an essential precondition of a sustained peace. When disparate groups categorize themselves in terms of a common superordinate identity, stereotyping, prejudice, and discrimination are decreased. (Gomez et al., 2008, cited in Mealy & Austad, 2012, p. 576)

A superordinate identity need not focus only on national identity. An example is the development of "local culture" in Hawai'i. In the 1940s, a superordinate "interracial" labor movement brought together native Hawaiians and migrant workers from China, Portugal, Japan, and the Philippines, and overcame entrenched racial divisions. Salzman (2012) argues that by connecting plantation workers to a progressive working class movement, the organizers offered a superordinate identity that did not deny race or ethnicity, "but subsumed it under a larger identity and common purpose" (p. 35). A "local" culture that supplemented, but did not supplant, the original ethnic identities emerged. This is exemplified by the statement on the wall at the Japanese Cultural Center of Hawai'i:

> We are no longer only Japanese American, we are local. We have learned from others. We have absorbed their values and traditions while we have preserved our own. We are proud of our mixed heritage-our local Hawaiian way of life. (Okumura, 2008, p. 134, cited in Salzman, 2012, p. 36)

Salzman (2012) concludes that "the appreciation of and familiarity with the different peoples and cultures of Hawai'i is a major dimension of "local" identity" (p. 36).

These recommendations, however, must be implemented carefully. Forcing a superordinate identity can backfire, as it did in Mexico where native groups felt that their indigenous identity was overrun by the mestizo identity. Adopting a collective identity where historical tensions and traditional cultural affiliations remain strong can be difficult. Given deeply rooted ethnic differences in the populations, a number of countries (Malaysia, Uganda, Mexico, France, Peru, and Cyprus) struggle with the creation of a national identity.

In Uganda, attempts to suppress ethnic identification are likely to backfire. Tribal and religious identities remain important to many Ugandans, so important that those identities are worth fighting for. In fact, Kibanja et al. (2012) argue that in Uganda, "a firm and well-developed cultural identity, based on tribe and other affiliations, may be seen as a protective factor or mental health asset that could be cultivated with traditional cultural education" (p. 429).

Research conducted with Latinos and Asian-Americans in the USA has found that those who were the most firmly rooted in their own culture were also better adjusted into the majority culture and had more positive views of other cultural groups (Phinney, Jacoby, & Silva, 2007).

Shapiro (2010) defined any group in which members see themselves as kin-like and emotionally invested as a "tribe." His Relational Identity Theory posits that two motives define relationships between individuals and between groups: affiliation and autonomy. When a tribe's relational identity concerns over affiliation and autonomy are frustrated, and when the focus is only on tribal identity, the stage is set for conflict (see Shapiro, 2010).

It seems clear that an identity based solely on citizenship, or one based solely on ethnicity, can be problematic. Rather, it appears that a policy that champions union and diversity at the same time might be the best for multicultural societies.

Beyond that, for the sake of our planet and to foster worldwide peace, we must emphasize our common humanity. This would not require that people deny their ethnicity or national citizenship, but, rather, that they recognize the dignity and worth of every human being. Salzman (2012) points out that with these steps, a

> person's individuality, culture, and universal humanity are acknowledged and the full humanity of the person is acknowledged so no dehumanization occurs and dehumanization is a prerequisite for discrimination, demonization, and atrocity. This formulation does not 'deracialize' but acknowledges differences while including them in a larger formulation. (p. 39)

This superordinate identity as a "human being" is critical for fostering understanding and empathy across ethnicities, cultures, and countries. Policy makers, citizens, and researchers, in short, everyone, should be engaged in working on how to best foster this crucial superordinate identity.

7 Part VII: Recommendations for Research to Improve Our Peace-Building Capacity

Forbes (2004) indicates that a great majority of reconciliation attempts are carried out in an atmosphere detrimental to positive change. As we have learned, the resolution of ethnic conflict is no small endeavor and may involve micro-level factors such as psychological processes, meso-level organizational and community processes, and macro-level political, economic, and social processes (Montiel & Christie, 2008, cited in Montiel et al., 2012). As Albert (2009) suggests, "The problems are so formidable that bold new approaches and ideas need to be added and existing approaches greatly expanded" (p. 138). There is still much to be discovered and understood about ethnic conflicts and their management. Countless reconciliation efforts have failed, new ethnic conflicts break out, conflicts continue to escalate, and our response is insufficient. We must continuously consider the questions that need to be addressed – questions of practice and of theory and research – that have not yet received the attention they warrant.

Albert (2009) delineated a number of ideas for research "at different levels of analyses and at cross-cutting levels: interpersonal, group, intracultural, intercultural, national, and international" (p. 136) that ought to be carried out. While these suggestions were originally aimed at communication researchers, many of these ideas would be appropriate for researchers in related social science disciplines. They include first, how communicative behaviors, both intended and unintended, are perceived by each party in the conflict; second, the investigation of cultural differences in ethnic conflict management, including how these differences may influence the dynamics of prenegotiation, negotiation, resolution, and post conflict relations; third, how ethnic conflict is attenuated or perpetuated in diasporic communities formed by refugees from the conflict. Albert provided the example of a recent election in the Liberian community in Minnesota in which the armed conflict in Liberia became a point of contention; yet in Minnesota, the groups used the ballot box, not violence, to deal with the conflict. She raised the issue of whether democratic processes in diasporic ethnic communities foster new knowledge that could help deal with the conflict at its place of origin.

Fourth, Albert (2009) suggested that studies focusing on the role of the local, national, and international media (i.e., the Internet, newspapers, and television) in ameliorating or exacerbating conflicts, or in changing the perceptions regarding outgroups, can make important contributions to conflict amelioration and peace building. The recent peaceful protests in Egypt, broadcasted live by media throughout the world, remind us of the important role the media can play in mediating perceptions of events, and at times, in influencing them.

Rigorous research is necessary to determine when media coverage serves to ameliorate conflict and when such coverage contributes to the deterioration of existing interethnic relations. Paluck (2010) investigated the effects of a radio soap opera about groups in conflict, aired either with or without a talk show designed to foster discussions around intergroup conflict and cooperation in the eastern DRC. Surprisingly, Paluck found that listeners who both heard the soap opera and participated in the talk show, were found to be less tolerant of the outgroup than those who only heard the soap opera. These listeners were more mindful of past grievances and were less likely to want to help members of a disliked outgroup. Paluck notes that although the media can help increase discussions about sensitive topics, the negative impact she observed highlights the need for further theory-driven research. This study also demonstrated that simple discussion, without adequate guidance from a skilled intercultural relations facilitator, can be counter-productive, and even harmful.

Fifth, Albert (2009) indicated that it is especially important that researchers investigate the use of social media in the escalation and deescalation of conflict. One can envision the study of tweets, Facebook postings, blogs, etc., as instruments for conflict management. Last year's demonstrations in Iran, and the recent events in Tunisia, Egypt, and other Arab countries remind us of the increasing importance of these new media. Experimental uses of new media might help conflict resolution efforts. In a study by Albert, Godet, & Coggio (2007), French and U.S. students engaged in weekly online communication. This was carried out at a time when the two countries' attitudes toward one another were at a significant low. Email communication led to an increase in positive attitudes toward the other culture.

Sixth, Albert (2009) suggested that when warring parties cannot or will not meet face to face, perhaps members of groups could be coaxed to enter into online exchanges. If properly mediated and managed, such exchanges may help create changes that would lead to de-escalation (p. 137). Bruneau & Saxe (2012) showed promising results of an online intervention designed to reverse the distrust and tolerance of harm toward an outgroup. In an asymmetric conflict situation, members of each group may respond systematically differently to intervention attempts (Bruneau & Saxe, 2012). Using online Skype chat and video (but no audio) communication between Israeli and Palestinian youth, they investigated the benefits of perspective-taking (actively listening to the thoughts and feelings of the outgroup) versus perspective-giving (feeling that the outgroup is listening and hearing). When Palestinians were asked to give their perspectives to their Israeli communication partner and Israelis were asked to take the perspective of Palestinians, Bruneau and Saxe found significant decreases in Palestinians' and Israelis' negative attitudes toward each other. However, when Israelis were asked to give their perspectives to their Palestinian communication partner and Palestinians were asked to take the perspective of Israelis, no effects were found. Bruneau and Saxe noted that Israelis and Palestinians responded asymmetrically to this online intervention as a result of asymmetric histories and asymmetries in power and social dominance. Bruneau and Saxe's findings have important implications for future research and practice.

Seventh, Albert (2009) proposed that

> communication scholars should be involved in developing strategies and approaches that contribute to the training and education of conflict mediators, negotiators, governmental and intergovernmental institutions, nongovernmental organizations, community groups, peace-making groups, educational institutions, and other parties involved in and/or concerned with ethnic conflicts, which, in the final analysis, should be everyone. (p. 138)

We would like to point out that there are vast resources available for educators, policymakers, and government officials. At the same time, by now we hope the reader, like us, is aware of how much there is still to know about ethnic conflicts. The current media offer great possibilities for education. The documentary Encounter Point is one example. Encounter Point documents Israelis and Palestinians who risk their lives and reputations to promote a nonviolent end to the conflict between the two groups. Documentaries are a powerful tool of education for a number of reasons: they can be informative, may be easily accessible and administered, and offer vivid context.

Eighth, Albert (2009) and Ellis (2005) proposed that intercultural and intergroup communication research and practice be expanded to the management of ethnic conflicts. This research should not focus only on interpersonal sensitivity, adaptation to another culture, or intercultural competence (Ellis, 2005).

Worchel (2005) makes an important point: "the perfect storm for intercultural and interethnic conflict is brewing throughout the world" (p. 756). He noted that rapid changes in technology, immigration, and developments in communication are bringing more contact between cultural groups; at the same time, there is a heightened level of fear. He concluded that "these are conditions that demand greater study and wider intervention to ensure the peaceful co-existence between cultural and ethnic groups" (Worchel, p. 756).

Albert (2009) strongly agrees:

> I believe that effective intercultural communication can contribute to conflict amelioration and conflict prevention. It is critical that intercultural and intergroup researchers engage the area of ethnic conflict. We need to develop theories, research, and practices that enhance human possibilities for peace and for the diminution of ethnic conflicts, genocide, and other disastrous consequences. Above all, what can we do to prevent ethnic conflicts and to create a culture of peace (Marsella, 2005) As Marsella so eloquently pointed out, there is a need to greatly expand the involvement of all institutions to create a culture of peace in the world. (Albert, p. 138)

7.1 Concluding Comments

Throughout this chapter we have tried to illuminate important lessons derived from the different conflicts in this handbook; there are many valuable contributions to the understanding of ethnic conflict in these chapters. If we understand the factors that contribute to the onset and build up of ethnic conflicts, we may be able to suggest ways to prevent escalation and find innovative and peaceful means of managing and resolving the conflict. Once deep-seated prejudices, discrimination, and open violence occur, a conflict can become extremely difficult to resolve. We have to be proactive and prevent escalation from the very first sign of a conflict's existence. Deadly ethnic conflicts are *not* inevitable.

As human beings have evolved, they have come to think that slavery is no longer acceptable. Our fervent hope is that soon the day will come when violence against an ethnic group will be condemned as strongly as slavery, and will be eliminated from the face of the earth.

As Gandhi wisely said, "You must be the change you wish to see in the world." Therefore, we must work to make a world without violent ethnic conflicts a reality; to treat "the other" with dignity and respect (Albert, 2006) regardless of ethnicity, race, religion, nationality, or culture; and to foster a genuine superordinate "human" identity. Then "NEVER AGAIN" will truly mean what it says: there will no longer be ethnic cleansing or genocide on our planet, because we worked together to find ways to resolve ethnic conflicts and to build peace.

Acknowledgements The authors gratefully acknowledge the many helpful suggestions made by Claire Stienecker, Jaturong Napadol, and Kelly Ramer, who participated in the first author's seminar on Ethnopolitical Conflicts Worldwide. They wish to also deeply thank the wonderful assistance, often beyond the call of duty, provided by Linnea Trandem, Julian Switala, Keegan Freiburger, Josh Kiley, Sadie Luetmer, Whitney Taylor, Alex Meyers, Eric DeVoe, Keith Philippe, Jessica Fremland, Jessica Lieb, and Erin Wigg. This chapter would not be as comprehensive without their help.

References

Abiew, F. K., & Keating, T. (1999). Outside agents and the politics of peacebuilding and reconciliation. *International Journal, 55*(1), 80–106.

Ackerman, P., & DuVall, J. (2000). *A force more powerful. A century of nonviolent conflict.* New York, NY: Palgrave.

Albert, R. D. (1983). The intercultural sensitizer or culture assimilator: A cognitive approach. In D. Landis & R. W. Brislin (Eds.), *Handbook of intercultural training* (Issues in training methodology, Vol. II, pp. 186–217). New York, NY: Pergamon Press.

Albert, R. D. (1986). Conceptual framework for the development and evaluation of cross-cultural orientation programs. *International Journal of Intercultural Relations, 10*(2), 197–213.

Albert, R. D. (1995). The Intercultural Sensitizer (ICS) or culture assimilator as a cross-cultural training method. In S. M. Fowler & M. Mumford (Eds.), *Intercultural Sourcebook* (Cross-cultural training methodologies, Vol. 1, pp. 157–167). Yarmouth, ME: Intercultural Press.

Albert, R. D. (2006, December). *Violent interethnic conflict and human dignity: Major issues in intercultural research and knowledge utilization.* Contribution to the 2006 Workshop on Humiliation and Violent Conflict Conference at Columbia University, New York.

Albert, R. (2009). What communication scholars and practitioners can contribute to the prevention and resolution of ethnic conflicts worldwide. In L. M. Harter, M. J. Dutta, & C. E. Cole (Eds.), *Communicating for social impact* (International communication association the theme book series). CressKill, NJ: Hampton Press.

Albert, R. D., Godet, C., & Coggio, G. (2007, July). *Can online interactions lead to changes in attitude towards those of another culture? An exploratory study with French and American university students.* Paper presented at the meetings of the International Academy for Intercultural Research, Groningen, the Netherlands, July, 2007.

Allport, G. W. (1954). *The nature of prejudice*. New York: Macmillan.

Anastasiou, H. (2002). Communication across conflict lines: The case of ethnically divided Cyprus. *Journal of Peace Research, 39*(5), 581–596.

Anderson, B. (1995). *Imagined communities. Reflection on the origin and spread of nationalism.* London: Verso.

Aneas, A., Garreta, J., & Molina F. (2012). Moroccans in Spain – So near, yet so far. A long history of meeting while not meeting. In D. Landis & R. D. Albert (Eds.), *Handbook of ethnic conflict.* New York: Springer.

Avni, R., Makhlouf, J., & Rous, N., (Producers) & Avni, R. (Director). (2006). Encounter point [Motion Picture]. Israel: Second Act Studio, Upton Recording, Futura Productions.

Bartoli, A. (2006). Learning from the Mozambique Peace Process: The role of the community of Sant'Egidio. In R. Fisher (Ed.), *Paving the way: Contributions of interactive conflict resolution to peacemaking*. Lanham, MD: Lexington Books.

Bhawuk, D. P. S. (2001). Evolution of culture assimilators. Toward theory-based assimilators. *International Journal of Intercultural Relations, 25*(2), 141–163.

Bhawuk, D. P. S. (2012). India and the culture of peace: Beyond ethnic, religious and other conflicts. In D. Landis & R. D. Albert (Eds.), *Handbook of ethnic conflict.* New York: Springer.

Bennett, M. J. (1993). Toward ethnorelativism: A developmental model of intercultural sensistivity. In R. M. Paige (Ed.), *Education for the intercultural experience* (2nd ed., pp. 21–71). Yarmouth, ME: Intercultural Press.

Benson, P. L., Scales, P. C., & Mannes, M. (2003). Developmental strengths and their sources: Implications for the study and practice of community building. In R. M. Lerner, F. Jacobs, & D. Wertlieb (Eds.), *Handbook of applied developmental science* (pp. 369–406). Thousand Oaks, CA: Sage.

Boulding, E. (2000). Cultures of peace: The hidden side of history. Syracuse, NY: Syracuse University Press.

Broome, B. J., & Anastasiou, H. (2012). Communication across the divide in the Cyprus conflict. In D. Landis & R. D. Albert (Eds.), *Handbook of ethnic conflict.* New York: Springer.

Bruneau, E., & Saxe, R. (2012). *Reducing the negativity resulting from intergroup competition in the context of the Israeli-Palestinian conflict.* Paper presented at the meetings of Society for Personality and Social Psychology in San Antonio, TX, January 29, 2011.

Burton, J. W. (1969). *Conflict and communication: The use of controlled communication in international relations.* London: Macmillan.

Cabrera, F., Donoso, T., Aneas, A., De Santos, J., Mas, J., & Curós, P. (2008). *Diagnòstic de competències interculturals en l'administració pública. En Generalitat de Catalunya Recerca i Immigració.* Barcelona: Publicacions de la Generalitat de Catalunya.

Çelik, B. (2012). Ethnic conflict in Turkey: From the denial of Kurds to peaceful co-existence? In D. Landis & R. D. Albert (Eds.), *Handbook of ethnic conflict.* New York: Springer.

Coleman, P. T. (2006). Intractable conflict. In M. Deutch, P. T. Coleman, & E. C. Marcus (Eds.), *The handbook of conflict resolution: Theory and practice* (2nd ed., pp. 533–559). San Francisco, CA: Jossey-Bass.

Corkalo Biruski, D. (2012). Lessons learned from the former Yugoslavia: The case of Croatia. In D. Landis & R. D. Albert (Eds.), *Handbook of ethnic conflict*. New York: Springer.

Cushner, K., & Landis, D. (1996). The intercultural sensitizer. In D. Landis & R. Bhagat (Eds.), *Handbook of intercultural training* (2nd ed., pp. 185–202). Thousand Oaks, CA: Sage.

De Mel, N., Samuel, K., & Soysa, C. K. (2012). Ethnopolitical conflict in Sri Lanka: Trajectories and transformations. In D. Landis & R. D. Albert (Eds.), *Handbook of ethnic conflict*. New York: Springer.

Deutsch, M. (2008). Reconciliation after destructive intergroup conflict. In A. Nadler, T. Malloy, & J. Fisher (Eds.), *The social psychology of intergroup reconciliation* (pp. 471–485). New York, NY: Oxford University Press.

Draguns, J. (2007). Empathy across national, cultural, and social Barriers. *Baltic Journal of Psychology, 8*, 5–20.

Er-rafiy, A., & Brauer, M. (2010). L'effet bénéfique de l'augmentation de la variabilité perçue sur le niveau de préjugés et la discrimination [The positive effect of increasing perceived variability on prejudice and discrimination]. *L'Année Psychologique, 110*, 103–125.

Felouzis, G. (2006). Ethnicité et ségrégation dans les écoles françaises. [Ethnicity and segregation in French schools]. In J. Polard, A.-G. Gagnon, & B. Gagnon (Eds.), *Diversité et identités au Québec et dans les régions d'Europe* (pp. 305–318). Québec: Presses de l'Université Laval.

Fisher, R. J. (1997a). *Interactive conflict resolution*. Syracuse, NY: Syracuse University Press.

Fisher, R. J. (1997b). Interactive conflict resolution: A social-psychological approach to resolving to violent ethnic conflict. In I. W. Zartman & J. L. Rasmussen (Eds.), *Peacemaking in international conflict: Methods and techniques* (pp. 239–272). Washington, DC: United States Institute for Peace.

Fisher, R. J. (2006). Interactive conflict resolution: A social-psychological approach to resolving violent ethnic conflict. In M. Fitzduff & C. Stout (Eds.), *The psychology of resolving global conflict* (Intervention, Vol. 3, pp. 41–68). New York: Praeger.

Forbes, H. D. (2004). Ethnic conflict and the contact hypothesis. In Y-T. Lee, C. McCauley, F. Moghaddam, & S. Worchel (Eds.), *The psychology of ethnic and cultural conflict* (pp. 69–88). Westport, CT: Praeger.

Flanagan, C., & Faison, N. (2001). Youth civic development: Implications of research for social policy and programs. *Social Policy Report: A Publication of the Society for Research in Child Development, 15*, 3–15.

Galtung, J. (1996). Peace by peaceful means: *Peace and conflict, development and civilisation*. Oslo: International Peace Research Institute.

Gaertner, S. L., Dovidio, J. F., & Bachman, B. A. (1996). Revisiting the contact hypothesis: The induction of a common ingroup identity. *International Journal of Intercultural Relations, 20*(3/4), 271–290.

Gaertner, S. L., Dovidio, J. F., Banker, B. S., Houlette, M., Johnson, K. M., & McGlynn, E. A. (2000). Reducing intergroup conflict: From superordinate goals to decategorization, recategorization, and mutual differentiation. *Group Dynamics: Theory, Research and Practice, 4*(1), 98–114.

Gaertner, S. L., Mann, J. A., Dovidio, J. F., Murrell, A. J., & Pomare, M. (1990). How does cooperation reduce intergroup bias? *Journal of Personality and Social Psychology, 59*, 692–704.

Gomez, A., Dovidio, J. F., Huici, C., Gaertner, S. L., & Cuadrado, I. (2008). The other side of we: When outgroup members express common identity. *Personality and Social Psychology Bulletin, 34*, 1613.

Gonzales-Castro, J. L., Ubillos, S., & Ibanez, J. (2009). Predictive factors of ethnic prejudice toward immigrants in a representative subsample of Spanish young people. *Journal of Applied Social Psychology, 39*(7), 1690–1717.

Green, E. D. (2009). *Demographic change and conflict in contemporary Africa*. Paper presented at a conference on demography and security: The politics of popular change, Weatherhead Centre for International Affairs, Harvard University.

Gurr, T. (2007). Minorities, nationalists and Islamists: Managing communal conflict in the twenty-first century. In C. A. Crocker, F. O. Hampson, & P. Aall (Eds.), *Leashing the dogs of war. Conflict management in a divided world*. Washington, DC: United States Institute of Peace Press.

Gutiérrez, N. (1998). What Indians say about mestizo: A critical view of a cultural archetype of Mexican nationalism. *Bulletin of Latin American Research, 17*(3), 285–301.

Hewstone, M., & Brown, R. J. (Eds.). (1986). *Contact and conflict in intergroup encounters*. Oxford: Basil Blackwell.

Jia, W., Lee, Y., & Zhang, H. (2012). Ethno-Political conflicts in China: Towards building interethnic harmony. In D. Landis & R. D. Albert (Eds.), *Handbook of ethnic conflict*. New York: Springer.

Johnson-Pynn, J. S., & Johnson, L. R. (2005). Successes and challenges in East African conservation education. *Journal of Environmental Education, 36*, 25–39.

Johnson-Pynn, J. S., & Johnson, L. R. (2010). Exploring environmental education for East African youth: Do program contexts matter? *Children, Youth and Environments, 20*(1), 123–151. Retrieved March 1, 2010 from http://www.colorado.edu/journals/cye/.

Kamiejski, R., De Oliveira, P., & Guimond, S. (2012). Ethnic and religious conflicts in France. In D. Landis & R. D. Albert (Eds.), *Handbook of ethnic conflict*. New York: Springer.

Karbo, T., & Mutisi, M. (2012). *Ethnic conflict in the Democratic Republic of Congo (DRC)*. In D. Landis & R. D. Albert (Eds.), *Handbook of ethnic conflict*. New York: Springer.

Kelman, H. C. (1972). The problem-solving workshop in conflict resolution. In R. L. Merritt (Ed.), *Communication in international politics* (pp. 168–204). Urbana, IL: University of Illinois Press.

Kelman, H. C. (2005a). Building trust among enemies: The central challenge for international conflict resolution. *International Journal of Intercultural Relations, 29*(6), 639–650.

Kelman, H. C. (2005b). Interactive problem solving in the Israeli-Palestinian case: Past contributions and present challenges. In R. Fisher (Ed.), *Paving the way: Contributions of interactive conflict resolution to peacemaking* (pp. 41–63). Lanham, MD: Lexington Books.

Kelman, H. C. (2008). Reconciliation from a social-psychological perspective. In A. Nadler, T. E. Malloy, & J. D. Fisher (Eds.), *The social psychology of intergroup reconciliation* (pp. 15–32). New York: Oxford University Press.

Kelman, H. C., & Fisher, R. J. (2003). Conflict analysis and resolution. In D. O. Sears, L. Juddy, & R. Jervis (Eds.), *Oxford handbook of political psychology*. Oxford, England: Oxford University Press.

Kibanja, G. M., Mayanja, K. M., & Johnson, L. R. (2012). Ethnocultural conflict in Uganda: Politics based on ethnic divisions inflame tensions across the country. In D. Landis & R. D. Albert (Eds.), *Handbook of ethnic conflict*. New York: Springer.

Landis, D. (2008). Globalization, migration into urban centers, and cross-cultural training. *International Journal of Intercultural Relations, 32*, 337–348.

Landis, D., & Albert, R. (2012). Models and theories of ethnic conflict. In D. Landis & R. D. Albert (Eds.), *Handbook of ethnic conflict*. New York: Springer.

Lederach, J. P. (1997). *Building peace: Sustainable reconciliation in divided societies*. Washington, DC: United States Institute of Peace Press.

LeVine, R. A., & Campbell, D. T. (1972). *Ethnocentrism: Theories of conflict, ethnic attitudes and group behavior*. New York: Wiley.

Lindner, E. (2006). Making enemies: *Humiliation and international conflict*. Westport, CT: Praeger Security Intl.

Marsella, A. J. (2005). Culture and conflict: Understanding, negotiating, and reconciling conflicting constructions of reality. *International Journal of Intercultural Relations, 29*, 651–673.

Marshall, M. G., & Cole, B. R. (2009). *Global Report 2009: Conflict, governance and state fragility.* Center for Systemic Peace & Center for Global Policy. Retrieved from http://www.systemicpeace.org/Global%20Report%202009.pdf on 12/10/10.

Martin, J. (2012). Mexico's ethnic conflict. In D. Landis & R. D. Albert (Eds.), *Handbook of ethnic conflict*. New York: Springer.

Mealy, M., & Austad, C. S. (2012). Sendero Luminoso (Shining path) and the conflict in Peru. In D. Landis & R. D. Albert (Eds.), *Handbook of ethnic conflict*. New York: Springer.

Montiel, C. J., Rodil, R. B., & de Guzman, J. M. (2012). The Moro struggle and the challenge to peace-building in Mindanao, Southern Philippines. In D. Landis & R. D. Albert (Eds.), *Handbook of ethnic conflict*. New York: Springer.

Moore, D., & Guy, A. (2012). The Israeli-Palestinian conflict: The socio-historical context and the identities it creates. In D. Landis & R. D. Albert (Eds.), *Handbook of ethnic conflict*. New York: Springer.

Mukyala-Makiika, R. (2000). Traditional leaders in the decentralization process civil society, indigenous populist institutions and implications for political reforms in Uganda. In K. K. Prah & A. G. M. Ahmed's (Eds.), *Africa in Transformation: Political and economic transformation and socio-political responses in Africa* (pp. 63–82). Addis Ababa: OSSREA.

Munusamy, V. (2012). Ethnic Relations in Malaysia: The need for "constant repair" in the spirit of Muhibbah. In D. Landis & R. D. Albert (Eds.), *Handbook of ethnic conflict*. New York: Springer.

Paluck, E. L. (2010). Is it better not to talk? Group polarization, extended contact, and perspective taking in eastern Democratic Republic of Congo. *Personality and Social Psychology Bulletin, 36*(9), 1170–1185.

Pettigrew, T. (1998). Intergroup contact theory. *Annual Review of Psychology, 49*, 65–85.

Pettigrew, T. (2008). Future directions for intergroup contact theory and research. *International Journal of Intercultural Relations, 32*(3), 187–199.

Phinney, J. S., & Chavira, V. (1992). Ethnic identity and self-esteem: An exploratory longitudinal study. *Journal of Adolescence, 15*(3), 271–281.

Phinney, J. S., Jacoby, B., & Silva, C. (2007). Positive intergroup attitudes: The role of ethnic identity. *International Journal of Behavior Development, 31*(5), 478–490.

Poh Ping, L. (1999). Stability in racially divided societies: The Malaysian Case. In C. Young (Ed.), *The accommodation of cultural diversity: case-studies* (pp. 19–36). Basingstoke: Macmillan.

Salzman, M. (2012). Ethno-cultural conflict and cooperation in Hawai'i. In D. Landis & R. D. Albert (Eds.), *Handbook of ethnic conflict*. New York: Springer.

Sariisik, D. (2010). Armenia at political deadlock on protocols. *Hürryiet Daily News & Economic Review*. Retrieved from http://hurriyetdailynews.com on 10/10/10.

Scales, P. C., Benson, P. L., & Leffert, N. (2000). Contribution of developmental assets to the prediction of thriving among adolescents. *Applied Developmental Science, 4*, 27–46.

Schiappa, E., Gregg, P. B., & Hewes, D. E. (2005). The parasocial contact hypothesis. *Communication Monographs, 72*(1), 92–115.

Schwegler, U., & Smith, R. (2012). *Reconciliation in Kosovo: The role of trust in post-conflict peace-building*. In D. Landis & R. D. Albert (Eds.), *Handbook of ethnic conflict*. New York: Springer.

Shapiro, D. L. (2010). Relational identity theory: A systematic approach for transforming the emotional dimension of conflict. *American Psychologist, 65*, 634–645.

bin Shafie, M. G., & Institute of Strategic and International Studies (Malaysia). (1993). *National unity: Key to the ultimate Malaysian society*. Kuala Lumpur: ISIS.

Sherif, M., Harvey, O. J., White, B. J., Hood, W. R., & Sherif, C. W. (1954). *Intergroup conflict and cooperation: The Robbers Cave experiment*. Wesleyan: Wesleyan University Press.

Sherif, M. (1966). *In common predicament: Social psychology of intergroup conflict and cooperation*. Boston,MA: Houghton-Mifflin.

Stanton, G. H. (1998). *The 8 stages of genocide*. Paper presented at the Yale Program in Genocide Studies, New Haven, New England, 1998.

Stephan, W. G., & Stephan, C. W. (1996). *Intergroup relations*. Boulder, CO: Westview Press.

Tajfel, H. (1974). Social identity and intergroup behavior. *Social Science Information, 13*, 65–93.

Teichman, Y., Bar-Tal, D., & Abdolrazeq, Y. (2007). Intergroup biases in conflict: Reexamination with Arab pre-adolescents and adolescents. *International Journal of Behavioral Development, 31*(5), 423–432.

van Oudenhoven, J. (2012). Frictions between Muslims and non-Muslims in the Netherlands. In D. Landis & R. D. Albert (Eds.), *Handbook of ethnic conflict*. New York: Springer.

Ward, C., & Liu, J. H. (2012). Ethno-cultural conflict in Aotearoa/New Zealand: Balancing indigenous rights and multicultural responsibilities. In D. Landis & R. D. Albert (Eds.), *Handbook of ethnic conflict*. New York: Springer.

Worchel, S. (2005). Culture's role in conflict and conflict management: Some suggestions, many questions. *International journal of intercultural relations*, 29(6), 739–757.

Ybarra, O. J., & Stephan, W. G. (1994). Perceived threat as a predictor of stereotypes and prejudice: Americans' reactions to Mexican immigrants. *Boletin de Psicologia, 42*, 39–54.

Zeytinoğlu, G. N., Bonnabeau, R. F., & Eşkinat, R. (2012). Armenians in Turkey: From nationalism to diaspora. In D. Landis & R. D. Albert (Eds.), *Handbook of ethnic conflict*. New York: Springer.

Index

D. Landis and R.D. Albert (eds.), *Handbook of Ethnic Conflict: International Perspectives*, International and Cultural Psychology, DOI 10.1007/978-1-4614-0448-4,

J

K

L

M

N

O

P

Q

R